ALSO BY RICHARD M. KETCHUM

AUTHOR

Second Cutting: Letters from the Country

The World of George Washington

Will Rogers: His Life and Times

The Winter Soldiers

Decisive Day

The Battle for Bunker Hill

The Secret Life of the Forest

Faces from the Past

The American Heritage Book of Great Historic Places

Male Husbandry

What Is Communism?

EDITOR

American Testament: Fifty Great Documents of American History

*The Original Water Color Paintings by John James Audubon
for the Birds of America*

Four Days

The Horizon Book of the Renaissance

The American Heritage Picture History of the Civil War

The American Heritage Book of the Pioneer Spirit

The American Heritage Book of the Revolution

What Is Democracy?

THE BORROWED YEARS

THE
BORROWED
YEARS
1938-1941

America on the Way to War

RICHARD M. KETCHUM

RANDOM HOUSE NEW YORK

Grateful acknowledgment is made to the following for permission to reprint previously published material: AMERICAN INSTITUTE OF PHYSICS: Excerpts from "How It All Began" by Otto Frisch from *Physics Today*, November 1967. Reprinted by permission. IRVING BERLIN MUSIC CORPORATION: Excerpts from the song lyrics "Let's Have Another Cup of Coffee" by Irving Berlin at page 20. Copyright 1931, 1932 by Irving Berlin. Copyright renewed 1958, 1959 by Irving Berlin. Reprinted by permission of Irving Berlin Music Corporation. CBS NEWS, A DIVISION OF CBS, INC.: Excerpt from an Edward R. Murrow radio broadcast. Copyright © CBS, Inc. All rights reserved. Used by permission. DES MOINES REGISTER: Speech by Charles Lindbergh from the *Des Moines Register*, September 12, 1941. Copyright © 1989 by Des Moines Register and Tribune Company. Reprinted by permission. E. P. DUTTON: Excerpts from *Bound for Glory* by Woody Guthrie. Copyright 1943 by Woody Guthrie. Copyright renewed 1971 by Marjorie M. Guthrie. Reprinted by permission of the publisher, E. P. Dutton, a division of Penguin Books USA Inc. FARRAR, STRAUS & GIROUX, INC: Excerpt from *Five Gentlemen of Japan* by Frank Gibney. Copyright 1953 by Frank Gibney. Copyright renewed 1981 by Frank Gibney. Reprinted by permission of Farrar, Straus & Giroux, Inc. HARCOURT BRACE JOVANO-VICH, INC: Excerpts from *Wartime Journals of Charles Lindbergh*. Copyright © 1970 by Charles A. Lindbergh. Reprinted by permission of Harcourt Brace Jovanovich, Inc. HOUGH-TON MIFFLIN COMPANY: Excerpts from *The Private Papers of Senator Vandenberg* by Arthur H. Vandenberg, Jr. Copyright 1952 by Arthur Vandenberg, Jr. Copyright renewed 1980 by Mrs. Myron Sands and Joe Alex Morris. Reprinted by permission of Houghton Mifflin Company. THE NEW YORK TIMES: Four lines from the poem "Poet Laureate in Verse Hails Chamberlain Trip" by John Masefield from *The New York Times*, September 16, 1938. Copyright 1938 by The New York Times Company. Reprinted by permission. YALE DAILY NEWS PUBLISHING CO., INC.: Excerpts from a speech by Charles Lindbergh from the *Yale Daily News*, October 31, 1940. Reprinted by permission of the Yale Daily News Publishing Co., Inc.

Library of Congress Cataloging-in-Publication Data
Ketchum, Richard M.
The borrowed years / by Richard Ketchum.
p.   cm.
Bibliography: p. 845   Includes index.
1. United States—Foreign relations—1938–1945. 2. World War,
1938–1945—United States. I. Title.
E806.K5   1989   327.73—dc19   89-3770
ISBN 0-394-56011-6

Manufactured in the United States of America
Picture Research: Laurie Platt Winfrey, Carousel Research, Inc.
Typography and binding design by J.K. Lambert
2 4 6 8 9 7 5 3
First Edition

I have been privileged to know members
of six generations in my own and my wife's immediate
family, each of whom has enriched my life.

This book is about some of them.
It is for all of them.

JOHN LEBO

CARRIE LEBO PATTON WILSON

LUNA BEARD KETCHUM HILL

GEORGE KETCHUM

THELMA PATTON KETCHUM

JANET KETCHUM GRAYSON WHITEHOUSE

THOMAS JOSEPH BRAY, JR.

LOUISE MCKELVEY BRAY ARMSTRONG

BARBARA BRAY KETCHUM

LIZA KETCHUM MURROW

CASEY MURROW

DEREK KETCHUM MURROW

ETHAN KETCHUM MURROW

THOMAS BRAY KETCHUM

PAULINE DENT KETCHUM

DYLAN DENT KETCHUM

DIANA DENT KETCHUM

BENJAMIN DENT KETCHUM

BRAY DENT KETCHUM

The bow of God's wrath is bent,
and the arrow made ready on the string. . . .

JONATHAN EDWARDS,
Sinners in the Hands of an Angry God, *1741*

CONTENTS

ILLUSTRATIONS

PREFACE

This is the story of a prolonged moment in America's recent past, a moment bracketed at one end by the Munich Pact, that negative symbol of appeasement and diplomatic naïveté, and at the other by Pearl Harbor, emblem of the sneak attack which haunts those living in a nuclear age.

It is also about America's lost innocence—the last time we believed in all seriousness that we could remain aloof from the problems of the world. The time we are talking about happens to coincide with my own youth, which means it was not so long ago as history is reckoned, and means as well that a certain element of the personal is included here. Not a lot, but some.

History does not take place in a vacuum. It is an amalgam of personalities and prejudices, ideologies, forces that have been building up for years (even centuries), accidents and miscalculations that destroy the most carefully laid plans, and more. Textbooks tell us that history follows a time line, and of course it does. Yet history is infinitely more complex than a chronology of events suggests. Better to describe it as a global tapestry, the product of many separate strands, coming together sometimes by happenstance, sometimes by design, intertwining according to some strange and random pattern.

Most of us do not think of ourselves as part of history happening. In my case, certainly, in the autumn of 1939 I was thinking more about Saturday's football game and when my date would arrive than about what was happening outside Warsaw. Looking back on it half a century later, it is much easier to see that the headlines I read, the news broadcasts I heard, echoed the cadenced tramp of approaching doom. The reason I wasn't more aware of this at the time is that, like most Americans, I didn't want to be aware of it.

From 1938 until the United States entered the war on December 7, 1941, I was a bystander—an unsophisticated, unaware teenager, representative, I suspect, of millions of other Americans. My mother lovingly stored away all the letters I began writing home from college in September of 1939, and as I went through them I found no mention of the war in Europe—only a monotonous recital of apologies for not being a more faithful correspondent, requests for money, clothing, cookies, and clean laundry, excuses for mediocre grades, reports on sports and other extracurricular activities. Only once during those years before the Japanese struck Pearl Harbor—when I informed my parents that I had refused to sign a peace petition then making the rounds of the university—was there a hint of a world beyond college.

Not until I joined the U.S. Navy would I be even a bit player in what was happening. Yet since history is made up of bystanders and bit players as well as captains and prime ministers, it seemed in the telling of this story that I should include something of that side as well.

What you see here is a selective look at what was once the present—what I have called "the borrowed years," when most of my friends and I were singing and dancing and laughing away the last hours of youth while the lights, as they used to say, were going out all over the world.

We had grown up wearing our fathers' tin helmets and puttees from the Great War in our backyard games, yet we knew with certainty that this country had turned its back on war, that we were not going over there again. America had done it before, had gained little but disillusionment for her pains, and that must be the end of it. We had troubles enough at home and did not need to borrow more from abroad.

No one could know it at the time, but the Munich conference marked the high-water mark of isolationism in the United States, when fully 59 percent of the people surveyed approved of the bargain that abandoned Czechoslovakia to Hitler. From that moment on, this nation was driven relentlessly toward a destiny it had no wish to be part of, compelled to look beyond its own social and economic problems to a present and future infinitely troubling and perilous.

Between 1938 and 1941, Americans were confronted with the challenge of assuming a position of true leadership in the world, with the daunting responsibilities such a role entailed, and a great many of them had no wish to take up that challenge. Behind their reluctance lay a powerful, long-standing isolationist impulse, to which the continuation of the Great Depression only added validity. After all, when the war began in Europe in 1939, one out of six in the U.S. work force was still unemployed, and among those who remained idle and useless the feeling was widespread that the republic itself was in deep trouble and must be mended before we embarked on any foreign adventures. So even though a posture of isolationism had ceased to be plausible, its adherents clung to the illusion that it was, refusing to recognize that the nation could not opt out of the international lifestream and go its own way.

Like America's Civil War, World War II was a watershed, but with a significant difference. Our own century's major conflict cuts between two eras as an unbridgeable chasm—separating the twilight of nineteenth-century imperialism and Victorian splendor, when life was full of certainties, from the nuclear age, when the survival of humankind is no sure bet.

During these borrowed years, scientists found the secret that would unleash the nuclear genie. The U.S. Army was transformed from a puny force smaller than the army of Portugal into a mighty host eight million strong (accompanied by the growth of a military-industrial complex, as President Eisenhower would call it). The northeastern United States was devastated by a hurricane; a president sought and won reelection to office for an unprecedented third term; the Republican Party, in spite of itself, staged the most exciting nominating convention of modern times; New York City put on a memorable World's Fair; network news came into its own; peacetime conscription took place for the first time in America; the U.S. Navy fought an undeclared war in the Atlantic.

But a recitation of events does not call up the central issue of the day. Again and again in the diaries and letters of the time, writers speak of how the war against Nazi barbarism was a war to save western civilization, and in the long, excruciatingly anxious months when Britain held out alone, that is how it was perceived.

Hitler wanted no world war—only "short and local" ones, quick strikes which his military forces were superbly equipped and trained to execute. A year after Munich, on September 1, 1939, he crushed Poland in what Germans disdainfully called the Campaign of the Eighteen Days. It was no eighteen-day affair that Hitler had begun, however, but total war—a catastrophe ultimately involving more than fifty nations and some seventy to eighty million men under arms. Of the military participants, as many as 23 million may have lost their lives, while an estimated 28 to 38 million civilians perished from bombs and gunfire, disease, or starvation or in the concentration camps.

Neville Chamberlain had returned from the Munich conference holding in his hand what he called "peace for our time." But as realists knew, Mr. Chamberlain's peace was a piece of paper, a poor bargain of a truce.

This raised the question of what part the United States would play when that truce ended, and how—should its role demand military action—this unprepared nation could possibly be ready, emotionally or physically. The answer to that was only partly in the hands of political leaders in Washington. In the final reckoning, the response had to come from millions of citizens who hold the real power in a democracy.

Time has a way of blurring the edges of details that once were sharp and fresh, yet it also affords a view from the mountaintop, so to speak, an opportunity to visualize what was by no means so evident long ago.

Looking back, it is plain that my generation of Americans had an appointment with the future, that a clock had begun to tick, telling off the minutes until it came due. What form the rendezvous might take none of us could know. The one certainty was that when the hour struck we would look fate directly in the eye.

THE BORROWED YEARS

PART I

1938

NEW YORK: STUDIO NINE

*The shy smile, the familiar stiff collar,
and the umbrella that came to symbolize Munich
and appeasement were unmistakable
trademarks of Britain's Prime Minister
Neville Chamberlain.*

CHAPTER 1

———◆———

"... *we stopped trying to understand the big issues and kind of lost touch with them.*"

The season of innocence was over. Monday, September 12, 1938—the first full week of school and work after Labor Day, and New York's morning newspapers dealt in reality.

For seven American League baseball clubs the dreams of spring were gone: the Yankees, in first place by fifteen games, were about to clinch their third straight pennant. In my hometown, the Pirates clung to a narrowing lead in the National League; the St. Louis Cardinals, reduced to planning for next year, announced that they were firing their manager, Frank Frisch, the onetime Fordham Flash. In Manhattan, classified ads told of an experienced bookkeeper-stenographer who would work for $12 a week, an elderly lady seeking a part-time companion for $6 a week, and rooms with bath available at the Hotel Brevoort on lower Fifth Avenue for $2 a day. (You wouldn't find it listed among the classifieds, but at the more fashionable Marguery, on Forty-seventh and Park, you could rent a suite for $10.) Farther uptown, on East Fifty-ninth Street, a five-room apartment with three exposures and a wood-burning fireplace was offered for $135 a month.[1]

[1]Such comparisons can be deceptive, but one means of relating the dollar of 1938 to its counterpart half a century later is to use the Consumer Price Index (CPI), which includes the cost of food, housing, energy, and clothing. In CPI terms, $1 in 1988 equals $8.30 in 1938. Thus

Politics—domestic and foreign—consumed the front page. In several state primaries President Roosevelt was attempting to rid the Democratic Party of dissidents who had opposed his effort to pack the Supreme Court in 1937. (A case in point was Maryland, where Senator Millard Tydings was running against FDR's anointed choice, Representative David Lewis.) A bulletin from the Mayo Clinic indicated that the president's son James was resting comfortably after an operation for gastric ulcer (anything having to do with the Roosevelt family was political news—even an ulcer). The Justice Department denied that its investigation of charges against Jersey City's Democratic boss Frank Hague were being dropped; and there was a hint that Justice Ferdinand Pecora might declare a mistrial in the case of Jimmy Hines, the Tammany leader whom District Attorney Thomas E. Dewey was trying to convict of running the numbers racket in New York.

On any other day one of these domestic political stories might have been the lead article in the *Times,* but not on this particular Monday. Dominating page one was the headline "Hitler to Tell Aims Today," followed by a report that Germany's dictator would deliver a major address to the Nazi Party rally in Nuremberg. The speech would be carried by CBS and NBC that afternoon, and the world would have to wait until then to see "whether he decrees peace or war." It was reported that nervous Britons were converting stocks to cash in anticipation of the latter eventuality; in New York the bond market had fallen sharply the previous week, despite one financial analyst's assertion that U.S. investors viewed events in Europe as "a gigantic game of bluff, in which nobody wishes for war, but everybody is maneuvering to attain his objective without war."

What the noninvesting public knew of Europe's problems no one bothered to suggest, but there were hints, amid the ominous tidings from abroad, that America's collective thoughts were elsewhere. Some had already turned toward April 1939 and the opening of the New York World's Fair—a wondrous World of Tomorrow where the woes of today could be forgotten—and the *New York Times* reproduced an artist's sketch of the Turkish pavilion, an Oriental bazaar where costumed native craftsmen would be seen at work, where perfumes, tobacco, and fruits from the Levant would be offered to passersby in quest of the exotic. In movie theaters across the land, Americans were flocking in record numbers to see Walt Disney's first feature-length film, eighty animated minutes of the fairy tale *Snow White and the Seven Dwarfs.* The toast of Broadway this autumn proved to be a lissome Texas girl named Mary Martin, who arrived in the big town on

in 1988 dollars the bookkeeper-stenographer was paid $99.60 per week, the elderly lady's companion might expect to receive less than $50 a week, and the room with bath at the Brevoort could be had for $16.60 a day.

September 13, was hired for a new musical called *Leave It to Me*, and stopped the show on opening night—and every night thereafter—with her singing of Cole Porter's naughty "My Heart Belongs to Daddy." That was for those seeking only diversion; for those longing for a less sophisticated day of homespun innocence, Thornton Wilder's deceptively ordinary *Our Town*—which won a Pulitzer Prize and went on to become the most performed American play ever written—captured a slice of the small-town life that seemed so threatened by events here and abroad.

The reading public's overwhelming preference was for *The Yearling*, Marjorie Kinnan Rawlings's gentle tale of a boy and his pet deer, of which 210,000 copies were already in print. For $16.50 it was possible to own the boxed six-volume life of Marlborough, written by his descendant Winston S. Churchill, a former first lord of the Admiralty and, more recently, member of Parliament. For a lot less—$2.75, to be exact—you could buy Daphne du Maurier's popular new novel *Rebecca*.

If radio was any guide to popular yearnings, one had only to examine the numbing array of folksy daytime serials (occasionally interrupted by programs of light, soothing music) to guess that not all of America was in touch with reality. A relentless procession of *Vic and Sade, Myrt and Marge, The Goldbergs, John's Other Wife, Just Plain Bill, Ma Perkins, David Harum, Mary Marlin, Big Sister,* and *The Road of Life* constituted the fifteen-minute daytime serials. In the afternoon, before supper, younger folk could hear *Don Winslow of the Navy, Jack Armstrong—All-American Boy, Little Orphan Annie, Tom Mix,* and *Uncle Don,* among others. Between 7:00 and 7:15, when thirty million people tuned in to *Amos 'n' Andy,* the use of telephones regularly fell off by 50 percent. According to one survey, the average listener heard 6.6 of these serials every weekday; during the same period New York's principal radio stations offered a total of ten minutes of capsulated news: five minutes of headlines in the morning, five at night.

America had no wish to take on Europe's jitters; domestic catastrophe was all too much in mind. As the novelist Marcia Davenport remarked, "Nobody in the 1930s existed without appalled awareness of the times." The country, after all, was still suffering from what many regarded as the worst disaster ever to befall it—the economic collapse and depression that ended the bright dream of a bountiful, well-ordered society in which every man (save, to be sure, just about all who had the misfortune to be born with colored skins) could, through hard work or luck or a combination of the two, improve his station in life and see that his children were better off by far than his parents had been. The Depression had shocked Americans in a manner unmatched since the 1860s, giving them for the first time in memory a sense of insecurity and foreboding, convincing many that the world they had known was coming apart in some unfathomable way. Ruinous economic conditions symbolized by silent, boarded-up factories had reduced proud men to begging and panhandling, had produced the spectacle of Americans standing in block-long queues for handouts of soup and sandwiches, had uprooted thousands from jobs and homes and sent them roaming aimlessly about the land in desperate search of work for whatever wage someone was willing to give them. "All over America," Loren Eiseley remembered, "men [and he might have added women and children] were drifting like Sargasso weed in a vast sea of ruined industry."

After campaigning for election in 1932, Franklin Roosevelt told a friend that he had looked into the faces of thousands of Americans and seen "the frightened look of lost children," who seemed to be saying, "We're caught in something we don't understand; perhaps this fellow can help us out."

The fellow who was supposed to help them out had promised the people a new deal, and by 1938, when he had been in office for six years, there had been signs of economic improvement, yet the paralysis that had gripped the nation in 1932—the cruelest year of all—was by no means cured, nor was an end in sight. The president was like a doctor brought in to cure a cancer who finds—after trying every remedy he can think of—that the patient's symptoms persist. How much remained to be done was suggested on a rain-soaked day in January 1937, when Mr. Roosevelt delivered his second inaugural address.

"I see one-third of a nation ill-housed, ill-clad, ill-nourished," he said. Tens of millions of Americans were denied the bare necessities of life and were "trying to live on incomes so meager that the pall of family disaster hangs over them day by day." Deprived of education, recreation, and an opportunity to improve their lot, these wretched poor endured conditions "labeled indecent by a so-called polite society half a century ago," while their inability to buy the products of farm and factory meant that millions of others were also out of work.

At the time the president spoke, between 14 and 15 percent of the civilian labor force were unemployed (down, happily, from an appalling 25 percent in 1933), and the average wage in manufacturing plants was less than $1,400 a year. (Anyone who thought that was bad should have spoken to a farmer; the per capita annual personal income from farming for each man, woman, or child over the age of fourteen was exactly $199 in 1937—up, it must be said, from $99 in 1934.) And conditions were going to get worse again before they got better. Newspapers were calling it a recession instead of depression, but whatever it was, by the spring of 1938 some five million people who had found employment since 1933 were out of work again. Some ten million Americans were without jobs.

A nightmare, in short, had taken the place of a dream and, like the residue of some hideous medieval plague, was still evident wherever one looked. Taken by itself, it was more than the average person was capable of absorbing, but now, to top it off, came the rumblings from abroad, the telltale signals that the Europeans were at it again, that the slaughter that had ended in 1918 had accomplished nothing and would almost surely begin anew.

America's first intimation of this unhappy situation had come with Adolf Hitler's unopposed seizure of the demilitarized Rhineland in 1936,[2] followed by the League of Nations' pathetic inability to stop the invasion of Abyssinia by the Italian dictator, Benito Mussolini. Then came the Spanish Civil War—a hopelessly baffling affair to the average American, who liked his problems served up neat, in black and white, and who found himself incapable of distinguishing good guys from bad when both sides were supported by equally distasteful dictatorships. The conflict produced shocking reports of bombers attacking defenseless cities, of civilian slaughter, and it slowly began to dawn on people that this was the shape of war to come. On the other side of the world—far too remote for Americans to consider very seriously but indicative, nonetheless, of how things were going to hell everywhere these days—the Japanese invasion of mainland China, which appeared to be a continuation of the 1931 conquest of Manchuria, went on methodically, and from Russia came rumblings of the purges by which Joseph Stalin was eliminating all real or imagined threats to his power.

In October 1937, a year after Hitler marched into the Rhineland, Franklin Roosevelt went to Chicago to dedicate a bridge built by his Public Works Administration and seized the occasion to voice concern about the worsening situation abroad. "War is a contagion whether it be declared or not," he explained, likening it to an outbreak of disease in a local community, and to him the remedy seemed clear: just as responsible citizens react to an epidemic by quarantining the patients, so the community of nations must act to prevent the spread of lawlessness from undermining the health of the world. What Mr. Roosevelt seemed to be suggesting was that the United States join in common cause with other friendly nations to oppose Germany, Italy, and Japan,[3] but if there was one thing the American public did not care to hear about in 1938 it was the possibility that the nation might embark on a course that could lead to war. If the aggressors in Europe and Asia refused to be quarantined, what then? Would we have to fight to halt the contagion?

The "quarantine speech" was something of a trial balloon as far as Roosevelt was concerned, and it never got off the ground, for the simple

---

[2]Under terms of the Versailles Treaty in 1919, Germany's Rhineland was to be occupied by the Allies for fifteen years and a thirty-mile belt on the right bank was demilitarized.

[3]The chief spokesman for one of those friendly powers had little enthusiasm for the president's suggestion. Britain's prime minister, Neville Chamberlain, remarked, "I read Roosevelt's speech with mixed feelings. . . . seeing that patients suffering from epidemic diseases do not usually go about fully armed . . . [there is] something lacking in his analogy."

reason that the people were in no mood for medicine of this sort, and the president—who usually read the signals as well as any man alive, but had badly misjudged them in this instance—suddenly saw that he was out on a limb and backed off. It was easy to see why. The public was dead against him on this issue; from the press came charges of warmongering; from the political opposition came calls for impeachment; and even from his cabinet officers and Democratic leaders in Congress (none of whom he had consulted in advance of the speech) he heard only a frosty and exasperating silence. In Tokyo, U.S. ambassador Joseph Grew considered the speech's "moral thunderbolts" futile: that kind of talk would only undermine relations between the two countries and destroy his efforts to build goodwill, he complained, and his assessment of the situation appeared accurate when the young up-and-coming Japanese diplomat Yosuke Matsuoka responded to the president in a fiery speech, stating flatly that "Japan is expanding," and asking rhetorically what was wrong in that when her goals were so positive—to throw off white domination in Asia and rid China of communism.

The specter of war, hovering unwanted beyond the horizon, threw into sharp relief a contradictory American attitude on the question of international involvement. Anyone who read a newspaper knew that certain things were happening, realized that the threat of another war was growing and must be stifled before violence erupted; yet in a curious way people did not *want* to know that these things were happening and, what's more, were opposed even to preparing for war for fear that a nation that was ready to fight was very likely to do just that.

As a businessman in Muncie, Indiana, put it, "A lot of us tried to keep up and informed on these big issues early in the Depression and even when the 'bank holiday' and New Deal came. Big things were happening that were upsetting us, our businesses, and a lot of our ideas, and we wanted to try to understand them. But then we all began to get scared. I waked up to the fact that my business was in immediate danger. We small businessmen began to see that we had to save our own necks. And so we stopped trying to understand the big issues and kind of lost touch with them. They're too big for us anyway."

Once the mind was set to shut out the big issues and the possibility of personal or national involvement, it was unlikely that events (especially those an ocean away from home) would register with any degree of clarity. Unfamiliar names and faces and issues blurred and refused to come into focus; isolated reports of incidents in the remote reaches of central Europe tended to bewilder rather than edify; and to millions of people living cocoonlike on this side of the Atlantic, what was taking place on the continent was cause for uneasiness, but, like any other threat of great danger, was something to be avoided. As time passed, few could point to a single day or month and say that what occurred then was a watershed, that from this moment on they had seen the shape of what was to come. It was as if the fragments of news they saw in their morning papers were loose, unsorted tiles from which a mosaic was to be made, but no one was certain—or even wished to know—what the designer had in mind.

CHAPTER 2

"Just around the corner . . ."

I f you wanted to see what the Depression had done to industrial America, my hometown was as good a place as any to look. It was important to realize that Pittsburgh's role, from the very beginning, had been determined by geography, that its destiny, even as late as the 1930s, was still controlled by location. When the first white men came to the Forks of the Ohio early in the eighteenth century, they found an Indian fur-trading post there, a scruffy Delaware village known as Shannopin's Town, and the Europeans quickly decided it was too important to remain in Indian hands.

That decision was the source of occasional regret to an impressionable boy with a love of history who could see in his mind's eye the French and Indians gliding silently down the Allegheny toward the Forks of the Ohio; but no matter—those rivers with their countless bridges possessed a magic that could outlast change and romance you into past or future, wherever you chose to travel, back two centuries to the young George Washington and the frontiersman Christopher Gist locating the site of the fort, or into the unknown, by way of the great Mississippi River to New Orleans, out into the Gulf, and beyond, wherever your fancy took you.

No city worth the name is without water, and the first Europeans to come here realized that whoever possessed the pie-shaped piece of real estate

where the Allegheny and Monongahela rivers come together to form the
Ohio was in a position to dominate the interior of the huge continent, and
the tiny outpost was a prize fought over by French and British as the tides
of empire lapped at North America. After the Revolution the settlement
was a raw village of sixty wooden houses; then it became a town of sorts,
and in 1816 was sufficiently large and brash to call itself a city. Like most
riverfront communities, it was crude, tough, and rowdy, peopled for the
most part by Scotch and Irish who lived, according to a German physician
who visited the place in 1783, "in paltry log-houses, and are as dirty as in
the north of Ireland, or even Scotland."

The site soon came to be regarded as significant for other reasons. As the
Indians had known, it was ideally situated for trade; its waterways were
highways for goods from the East and for local manufactures, which included utensils and implements at first, articles of clothing, and then glass,
leather, and tin and iron ware. A military man passing through in 1791 noted
how widespread the use of coal was: because the town was "a great manufacturing place [it] kept in so much smoke and dust as to effect the skin of
the inhabitants." Twenty-five years later a traveler named David Thomas
told how the "dark dense smoke was rising from many parts, and a hovering
cloud of this vapour" completely obscured the view. Worse was in store:
in the nineteenth century the insatiable demand for iron and steel, much of
it for the proliferating railroads, turned Pittsburgh into the nation's hearth.
It was a city of uncounted hills, of winding, poorly paved streets, layered
with smoke and grime and filth, but for all that a place where the industrial
might of the nation was tangible and alive.

Long before I was born there, it had become the greatest workshop in
the world. Pittsburgh was more than iron and steel, of course; it was also
aluminum and glass, coal and coke, food, turbines, generators, and a host
of other products. But steel was the nub of it, steel was what the city was
all about, and here again, the city's location was everything. Pittsburgh lay
in the heart of soft coal country, where outcroppings fifteen feet thick
gleamed on hillsides, and it was cheaper to bring the iron ore from the
shores of Lake Superior—by freighter through the Great Lakes and by
short-line railroad to Pittsburgh—than to take the coking coal to the ore.
To a Pittsburgher, a sure sign that the ice had broken up on the lakes and
that spring was here was the sight of endless lines of open freight cars,
loaded with red ore from the Mesabi, winding slowly into the city to
replenish stockpiles that had been depleted during the winter.

Between the tangled ribbons of freight tracks and the broad, lead-colored
rivers were the steel mills, a maze of corrugated-iron sheds and smokestacks, everything black, smoke everywhere—smoke and steam and ear-
shattering noise from the switch engines, the clanging rolling mills, the
thundering blast furnaces. The formula for success was simple enough: iron
ore, coke, and limestone came downriver to the mills by barge and rail;

finished pigs, bars, and rods were shipped away; but in the process soot darkened the sky, covered the landscape, killed the vegetation. In our home the curtains were taken down once a month and washed. As long as detachable collars were still in vogue, my father wore at least two of them every day. In the morning, I would look in the mirror and see black smudges below each nostril, where I had inhaled and exhaled soot all night. Every spring, housecleaning meant removing a year's layer of grime from the walls with wallpaper cleaner, and Mother used to buy the stuff by the case. Sometimes my father took me downtown to his office on a Saturday morning, and I remember that the automobiles and trolley cars had their headlights on, the streetlights were illuminated, and lights burned in every office building. The price you paid for prosperity was darkness when there should have been light, and because this was from the beginning a workingman's town—a town where money was to be made and where everyone, rich or poor, worked hard for it—Pittsburgh rejoiced in the name Smoky City: clear blue skies meant that the mills were idle. But hard work exacted more than one price. In a statement written when she got her divorce from A. W. Mellon, his once-gay young Irish wife, Nora, said bitterly: "My husband, locked in his study, nursed his dollars, millions of dollars, maddening dollars, nursed larger and bigger at the cost of priceless sleep, irretrievable health and happiness. Always new plans, bigger plans for new dollars, bigger dollars."

H. L. Mencken was appalled by what he saw in Pittsburgh. "Here was the very heart of industrial America," he wrote, "the center of its most lucrative and characteristic activity, the boast and pride of the richest and grandest nation ever seen on earth—and here was a scene so dreadfully hideous, so intolerably bleak and forlorn that it reduced the whole aspiration of man to a macabre and depressing joke. Here was wealth beyond computation, almost beyond imagination—and here were human habitations so abominable that they would have disgraced a race of alley cats.

"I am not speaking of mere filth. One expects steel towns to be dirty. What I allude to is the unbroken and agonizing ugliness, the sheer revolting monstrousness, of every house in sight."

What he said was true, of course, all of it. And perhaps it was a blessing that smog hung over the place like a scrim, blurring the view, hiding the ugliness. Though when those dark, satanic mills were operating at full blast, the night skies were lit up by the thrilling spectacle of Bessemer converters showering streams of fire into the heavens. If you were within earshot, you heard a terrifying roar that drowned out all other sounds from the mill. When oxygen and carbon combined inside the belly of the converter, the flame at the mouth changed from scarlet to blue, to orange, yellow, and finally to white, as steel was created inside the immense egg-shaped vessel. Then the converter was tilted, ever so slowly, until liquid fire began cascading into an enormous vat below, a vivid, salmon-red stream throwing off light of incredible intensity, hurling an immense shower of sparks into the sky.[1]

But the night skies over Pittsburgh had been lit up less and less during the twenties and thirties. For five or six years before the Depression, unemployment and underemployment had been chronic in the steel mills, and the economic collapse made a bad situation much worse. Between 1923 and 1929 some 27,000 iron and steel workers had been laid off; in the latter year employment in Pennsylvania's blast furnaces was 40 percent below the 1923 level, and during the five-year period ending in 1930 one-fourth of the capacity of the steel mills was unused all the time. By January of 1931 one steelworker in three was totally without work. Two years later, while 223,000 still remained on the payrolls, 280,000—or 56 percent—were unemployed, and the industry was operating at a mere 14 percent of capacity. How hard the steel companies tried to ameliorate their workers' plight may be judged by a few examples. One scheme that was devised was the "stagger plan," which called for a man to work one or two days a week and then yield his place to another, but the worst of that was that it prevented the worker from drawing any unemployment checks from the company. Republic Steel in Youngstown, Ohio, tried an arrangement whereby two full crews spelled each other and the company paid each for half a shift's work, but the workers complained so much that the company abandoned the idea.

Speaking to a meeting of the American Iron and Steel Institute in 1930, the chairman of U.S. Steel's finance committee (later its chief executive officer, and President Roosevelt's personal representative to the Vatican), Myron C. Taylor, urged piously, "Let it be said of the steel industry that none of its men was forced to call upon the public for help." Where else the hapless workers might turn for aid, Mr. Taylor failed to make clear, since the steel companies were providing next to nothing in the way of unemployment relief. Jones & Laughlin, for instance, was giving $2.10 a week to families of workers it laid off; Carnegie-Illinois was providing $3. Then the companies concluded that the payments were too high, and by November of 1932 Carnegie had reduced payments to $1.90 in the form of relief tickets—ranging from one ticket a month to a single man or a married man with no children, to one ticket every two weeks to a man with more than three children. In Gary, Indiana, steelworkers' families were getting $1.75 a week during the summer of 1932; the worker himself was given one day's work every two weeks but was not permitted to apply for relief

---

[1]One evening a group of young people at a dance at the Pittsburgh Golf Club went outside to cool off during an intermission. From the hillside they could see lights above the mills across the Monongahela River, and when the flames from a converter suddenly flared into the black sky a visitor from Virginia, great-granddaughter of a Confederate general, asked a young man: "What in the world is that?" "Oh," he replied casually, "those are the Bessemers." "Really?" she responded, equally casually. "I didn't even know they were having a party."

elsewhere. One of the many ironies in this tragic business was that workers who were fired often received more money in relief checks from public agencies than the wages they had earned when they were working in the mills.

Even before the awful winter of 1932–33 entire towns in the valleys around Pittsburgh were completely dependent on public agencies for their survival (and no wonder: in Donora, for instance, only 277 workers out of 13,900 still had jobs); at the same time local charities in the city were providing destitute families with a food allowance of 90 cents per person per week, supplemented by some flour and milk. According to the state's assistant welfare commissioner, this was a "starvation diet," and in many instances where work had been found for men, they were too weak to perform it.

The reason the Depression hit Pittsburgh's factory workers so hard was that production in the mills—which was already spotty—was cut back as soon as orders were canceled. And every cut in production meant layoffs for thousands or substantial reductions in pay—up to 60 percent—for those lucky enough to keep their jobs. In the worst days of the Depression, U.S. Steel announced that it had no full-time workers whatever on the payroll, and the reason wasn't hard to find. People weren't buying. When men started sharpening their old razor blades and using them again, sales went down and companies like Gillette canceled orders for steel. It didn't much matter what the product was—locomotives or roller skates, automobiles or filing cabinets—as long as it was made of steel and as long as people weren't buying, the mills were idle. And the steelworkers and their families went hungry.

———

Most men in the mills and mines of western Pennsylvania were immigrants (in fact, some 20 percent of Pittsburgh's population was foreign-born)—Poles, Hungarians, Estonians, Latvians, Serbs, Croats, Slovaks, Russians, Ukrainians, Rumanians, Lithuanians, all of them indiscriminately called Hunkies by the blacks, the second-generation Italians, and the descendants of English, Irish, Scotch, Welsh, and Germans who had been earlier arrivals. Few spoke English when they arrived in this country, many never learned it before they died, and their willingness to work for cheap wages and under dreadful conditions was a trial to the proud ironworkers—the skilled puddlers and rollers and their helpers—they replaced. An English immigrant from an earlier day observed that these newcomers were "men that really don't know the difference . . . between light work and heavy work, or between good wages and bad wages. . . . I have been disgusted to find that those people can live where I think decent men would die." And a local craftsman complained, "These fellows have no pride. . . . When the foreman demands it they will throw down the saw and hammer and take the wheelbarrow." While the day of the most abusive working conditions had passed by the late thirties, the steelmaker's life was still a hard one, and to survive he had to be tough. (You could glance at the rosters of the top football teams in the land and see how many of the boys who played hard-nosed ball came from the coalfields and mill towns around Pittsburgh.) It was not merely the job that was difficult to endure; it was the appalling living conditions. Blacks, as might be expected, had the worst of it; most were forced to live in wretched areas like Skunk Hollow, whose horrors were said to rival those of any slum in the industrial world; but well into the thirties, more than three-quarters of the houses on Pittsburgh's North Side had no bathroom, no hot water, no furnace. In the city as a whole, one-fourth of all rental properties were in need of major repairs, one-third had no bathtubs or showers, and 33,000 homes were without indoor toilets. In poor districts working families were jammed into tenements or houses all but unfit for habitation. Traditionally, what made life tolerable for the mill hand was the saloon. The unbearable heat in the mills raised prodigious thirsts, and the city was known for having more bars than any other place in America of comparable size. Prohibition had done little to change the picture: in 1928 alone, almost 38,000 Pittsburghers were arrested for drunkenness.

―――

That was life at the bottom of the financial scale. At the opposite pole, before the turn of the century, as the city's social elite strove to become a leisure class as well as a ruling class, the phrase "Pittsburgh millionaire" had acquired a connotation all its own—a term of derision for those recently rich whose taste, someone said, was all in their mouths. The social commentator Lucius Beebe claimed that these new plutocrats, who were capable of purchasing Locomobiles in half-dozen lots, had given the silk hat industry a new lease on life, turned Scotch whisky into a major import, and made "bathrooms, porte cocheres, and coats of arms a sort of legal tender." Certainly they built some of the ugliest, most ornate houses imaginable, spending millions on the mansions and more on furnishings, paintings, sculpture, tapestries, and paneling imported by the carload from Europe. These were homes on a palatial scale: at least one had its own chapel; most had billiard rooms, many had bowling alleys; R. B. Mellon's residence, built on a hillside overlooking Fifth Avenue, had sixty-five rooms and eleven baths.

Many of these men were self-made and as tough in their own way as the employees in their factories and mines. Even after they became millionaires, Stewart Holbrook wrote, "some of them still smelled a bit of burning coke, and a Penn Avenue barber . . . reported that the first shampoo one of these newly rich men ever had brought out two ounces of fine Mesabi ore and a scattering of slag and cinders." Understandably, Andrew Carnegie was a model for many of them: a sharp-eyed immigrant from Scotland whose starting salary as a bobbin boy in a Pittsburgh cotton mill was $1.20 a week, he became the ablest steel manufacturer of his age, with a personal *income* in 1900 of $23 million (and no income tax to pay). At the time, the average annual wage of all American workers was $500 or less. When Carnegie and his partners sold out in 1901 for $492 million to a consortium put together by J. P. Morgan, the banker shook the little Scot's hand and remarked, "I want to congratulate you on being the richest man in the world." Carnegie—who owned 58½ percent of his steel company—got the lion's share of the booty, but the transaction also made millionaires overnight of some thirty of his associates. Harry W. Oliver, an Irish immigrant and former Western Union messenger, collected $13 million and placed an order for a private railroad car, presumably on grounds that how you traveled showed the world who you were. Alexander Rollin Peacock, a salesman who had fortuitously switched from dry goods into steel plate, took his windfall and erected a palace called Rowanlea on Highland Avenue. It had several acres of formal gardens and greenhouses, a nine-foot-high iron fence, wrought-iron gates so ponderous they had to be rolled on motorized wheels, and four gold pianos in the music salon (a rival had two such musical instruments in *his* salon and Peacock was no man to be outpointed).

Carnegie and many others, once they had made their pile, fled the smoke-choked valleys of Pittsburgh,[2] but some did not, and the wealthiest and most prominent of those who remained were the Mellons—notably Andrew W. and his brother Richard B. The Mellons were bankers, and their formula for business success was really quite simple, when you thought about it: lend money to a bright young man with an idea, and take as security a share in the business—control, if possible. Andrew, or A.W. as he was referred to reverentially by Pittsburgh's business community, was a wisp of a man and shy (one writer suggested that he looked "like a tired double-entry book-keeper afraid of losing his job; worn, and tired, tired, tired"), who had been so successful in avoiding publicity that when his name was suggested to Warren Harding as a likely secretary of the Treasury, Harding replied, "I never heard of him." Neither had many other Americans beyond Pittsburgh, even though someone calculated in the early thirties that the Mellon industrial interests were worth nearly $2 billion and their financial interests more than half a billion. Indeed, when A.W. left the bank to take the Treasury job in Washington, someone noticed that he was not even listed in *Who's Who*.

As secretary under Harding, Coolidge, and Hoover (a contemporary remarked, not entirely facetiously, that Mellon was the only cabinet member in American history to have had three presidents serve under him) he worked unstintingly to reduce the national debt through the practice of

---

[2] A number of these refugees nevertheless contributed handsomely to cultural and other causes in the city where they had made their fortunes. One outstanding example is the immense complex that bears Andrew Carnegie's name—a concert hall, library, museum, art institute, and university.

what would one day be called supply-side economics. He succeeded in this as he did in most financial dealings: between 1921 and 1929 the debt fell from $24 billion to $16 billion. Equally determined to do away with the tax "burden" on the rich, he pushed through the Revenue Act of 1926, one effect of which, Senator George Norris observed, was that "Mr. Mellon himself gets a larger personal reduction than the aggregate of practically all the taxpayers in the state of Nebraska." However one judged his achievements—and there were those who called him the greatest secretary of the Treasury since Alexander Hamilton—Andrew Mellon, along with Herbert Hoover, would be widely blamed for having brought on the Great Depression. As one bitter rhyme went:

> *Oh, Mellon pulled the whistle, boys,*
> *And Hoover rang the bell.*
> *Wall Street gave the signal,*
> *And the country went to hell.*

In 1928, Secretary Mellon assured doubters and nervous Nellies that he saw no cause for worry in the nation's financial future. "The high tide of prosperity will continue," he promised. Then, when the bottom fell out of the market and the economy, he told President Hoover that "a panic was not altogether a bad thing." It would "purge the rottenness out of the system," with the result that "people will work harder, live a more moral life. Values will be adjusted, and enterprising people will pick up the wrecks from less competent people." It was extraordinary how that statement echoed one made many years earlier by his father, Judge Thomas Mellon, founder of the family bank: "Poverty," the judge had written, "may be a misfortune to the weaklings who are without courage or ability to overcome it, but it is a blessing to young men of ordinary force of character: it protects them from excesses, withholds unwise pleasures and indulgences, teaches the value of time and of wealth, and the necessity of well doing to better their condition." One could hardly improve on that as an axiom for Pittsburgh's Scotch Presbyterians.

A.W.'s particular genius as a capitalist was to sniff out, in advance, the future direction of industry. Using T. Mellon & Sons as a financial base, he and his brother Richard invested in coke, then shifted to iron, then to steel, from steel into oil, and from oil to aluminum, always managing to leave the starting gate before the rest of the horses had arrived at the track. By the time Andrew died in 1937 at the age of eighty-two (a few months after John D. Rockefeller's demise) he had given away enormous sums to charity, to his children, and to the people of the United States (in the form of the National Gallery of Art and the core of its art collection), and even so, a personal fortune of $37 million remained.

Although there were few rivals to Mellon on the scene, you did not have to look far in most American towns in the thirties to find extremes of wealth and poverty resembling those in Pittsburgh. And somewhere between those two poles, you would see the majority of people hanging on, doing their best to wait things out, hoping, ever hoping, that the words of the popular song would prove to be right:

> *Just around the corner*
> *There's a rainbow in the sky*
> *So let's have another cup of coffee*
> *And let's have another piece of pie.*

CHAPTER 3

"I still believe that one can learn to play the piano by mail ..."

For nearly a decade the Depression had dragged on, victimizing millions of Americans who were bewildered as to why and how it had occurred. During the twenties, most of them had worked hard, living according to the values that had made the country great, and they had every reason to suppose that the land of opportunity was still exactly that. So for those who had been swept along on the exhilarating wave of postwar prosperity, the impact of the Depression was devastating—a personal blow to many, who supposed that they were somehow to blame for the appalling misfortune that had befallen them.

America had had its share of major economic declines—a regular cycle of them, in fact, at intervals of roughly twenty years—but there had been nothing to equal this. What began as the stock-market "crash" in the autumn of 1929 became a downward slide that continued for almost three months. It was followed by a heartening but brief bull market, which turned into an uninterrupted two-year decline in stock prices and business generally—a depression more profound than any of its predecessors, a collapse of terrifying proportions and duration. As is often the case, the major victims of this particular calamity had had virtually no part in creating the disaster that was their undoing. Herbert Hoover—a good man with the best of intentions and the worst of luck, a man many Americans came to see as the archvillain of the piece—put his finger on one of the principal causes. "The only trouble with capitalism," he once observed, "is capitalists. They're too damned greedy," and the greed was most evident in the shocking maldistribution of wealth in the nation. In 1929 some two hundred corporations controlled almost half of U.S. industry. That same year the top one-tenth of 1 percent of American families had a total income equal to that of the bottom 42 percent; or, to put it another way, the combined income of 24,000 wealthy families was equal to that of 11.5 million poor and lower-middle-class Americans. Those 24,000 rich had incomes of more than $100,000 a year; the vast majority of their countrymen received less than $2,500 annually. (Then, as now, athletes seemed to get a disproportionate share of the rewards: in 1932, when the irrepressible Babe Ruth was asked why he earned $5,000 more than President Hoover, he replied with his usual candor, "I had a better year than him.") It was not only income that was grotesquely skewed in favor of a privileged few: it was also wealth. Some 80 percent of American families—or 21.5 million households—had no savings whatever, while the half of 1 percent at the apex of the pyramid possessed one-third of the net wealth of all U.S. individuals.[1]

Other factors were at work here, among them war debts and reparations, which further weakened Europe's postwar economies; America's virtual withdrawal from its obligations as a member of the family of nations; and a massive agricultural depression in the nation's heartland (the average annual earnings of an agricultural employee in 1929 were $401 and ten years later had sunk to $385). In the twenties, moreover, the United States had suddenly found itself in the unaccustomed position of being the world's banker and chief supplier of food and manufactures, while at the same time it embarked on a policy of purchasing as little as possible from its fellow nations. When the Depression struck down the world's dominant economy, global collapse followed.

The awful irony of poverty and malnutrition in the midst of plenty was nowhere more apparent than in the United States. As Will Rogers told a nationwide radio audience, "We got more wheat, more corn, more food, more cotton, more money in the banks, more everything in the world than any nation that ever lived ever had, yet we are starving to death, we are the first nation in the history of the world to go to the poorhouse in an automobile."

Take Peggy Terry, who lived in the uptown section of Chicago. A child of the Depression, she was sent to the soup line by her mother every afternoon after school, and learned to ask the man ladling the thin, greasy stuff off the top to dip deeper, to give them some meat and potatoes from

[1]Your perception of the situation depended on where you sat. In 1936 the financier J. P. Morgan warned the press that "if you destroy the leisure class, you destroy civilization." By way of explanation, he added, "By the leisure class, I mean the families who employ one servant—twenty-five to thirty million families." Mr. Morgan's facts were as faulty as his opinion was out of step with the times: according to the 1930 census, there were fewer than thirty million families in the United States, and fewer than two million servants.

the bottom. Across the street was a store where stale bread was sometimes available for nothing; that was the next stop she and her sister made. Then down the road to a shed where they might scrounge a pail or two of milk. Some days they had nothing in the house to eat but mustard—mustard and biscuits. At fifteen Peggy married a boy one year older, and for three years they hitchhiked, barely skirting the clutches of the law, always moving on, sometimes picking oranges in the Rio Grande Valley for a nickel a bushel, sometimes gaping at the Hoovervilles where people "really had it rough"— Americans living in shacks made from orange crates, entire families holed up in piano boxes.

For proud men who were suddenly without work and without much likelihood of finding any, it was easy to believe that it was they who had failed, that there must be something wrong with *them,* and the feeling deepened as they arose in the morning, dressed as usual for work, and went off to look for a job, only to find at every door the chilling message NO HELP WANTED. For employers it was a buyer's market, and who could blame them if they chose the best of the lot, settling for the young up-and-comer, instead of the man who had passed into middle age? It didn't take much to convince a rejected fifty-year-old that he was over the hill, in more ways than one. An Oklahoman wrote to Eleanor Roosevelt in 1934, "The unemployed have been so long with out food—clothes—shoes—medical care— dental care etc—we look pretty bad—so when we ask for a job we don't get it. And we look and feel a little worse each day—when we ask for food they call us bums—it isent our fault . . . no we are not bums."

What was so daunting about all this was that no one knew who would be next; yesterday it was the fellow who lived a few blocks away, today it was your close friend, tomorrow it could be you. In our part of town the object lesson was the former banker who could be seen pumping gas in a filling station.

—

My family's world lay somewhere between that of the Mellons and the unemployed mill workers—about equidistant, I suppose, since we were at such a remove from both. During the worst years of the Depression, along with the great majority of people whose lives touched ours, my parents were living one day at a time, hoping the wolf would stay away from the door and that normal times would return. We were a long way from being in Peggy Terry's fix, but in the leanest years I was often sent down the Reynolds Street hill to ask Ray, the fat, rosy-faced manager of the A&P, for day-old bread, because it cost only 8 cents a loaf. Meantime we listened to the radio a lot—or at least my sister Janet and I did—and laughed until our sides ached at Will Rogers and Fanny Brice, at Eddie Cantor,[2] Fred

---

[2]One of Cantor's trademarks in those days was the hit song "Now's the Time to Fall in Love," one of many of its type known in the trade as "silver linings." Tin Pan Alley apparently

Allen, Jack Benny, and Groucho and Chico Marx, playing the world's most inept detective team. When I wasn't listening to radio, I was mailing coupons to the Union Pacific, Southern Pacific, or CB&Q railroads for free literature on Glacier National Park, or Zion or Bryce Canyon; sending for a mouthpiece guaranteed to make me a ventriloquist; dispatching box tops and a dime for my Tom Mix secret code ring; ordering a fragment of a Roman soldier's spear from Bannerman. But mostly I was reading, devouring everything I could get my hands on—the Hardy Boys, Sherlock Holmes, a set of seven volumes on the Great War which everyone's father seemed to have purchased, even the Waverley Novels, when all else failed.

On long July evenings after school was out all the children in the neighborhood gathered to play Release, Prisoner's Base, or Kick the Can until the last glimmer of daylight was spent and flashes from a thousand lightning bugs punctuated the dusk, when from each house came its special family whistle, calling team members to bed. We played hockey on roller skates, rode bikes, built clubhouses, played softball, hardball, and football on the last vacant lot around—all within a neighborhood no more than two blocks wide in either direction that contained the joys that are supposedly wasted on the young, but are not. On Saturday mornings in summer my friend Jack Chesley and I packed lunches and walked to Frick Woods, where we climbed to a huge boulder high on a wooded hill and took aim on unsuspecting settlers walking below (we were Indians). In the winter he and I went to the Enright Theater, home of a mighty, glistening Wurlitzer pipe organ that had accompanied the singer Dick Powell before he went to Hollywood, and sat through an endless procession of serials, mostly westerns. (If any of them ever ended, I was not aware of it.) On Sundays our family went to church together, ate our big meal in the middle of the day, and went for a drive in the country in the afternoon.[3] When dusk began to fall, Mother and Dad would start to harmonize, Janet and I would join in from the backseat, and the four of us would sing for miles on end—songs, for the most part, that my father had learned as a lonely young bachelor through repeated attendance at vaudeville shows. He had an encyclopedic memory and could recall every word of such classics as "There lay Brown, upside down, lapping up the whiskey off the floor . . ." and every verse describing the Zulu Maiden's fateful voyage down the Nile (". . . at the finish of the ride, the Zulu maiden was inside—the smile on the crocodile"), to which my sister and I listened, enthralled.

had the idea that one way to end the Depression was to convince Americans that things weren't as bad as they seemed, and the result was a string of cheerful, upbeat songs like "Happy Days Are Here Again," "Beer Barrel Polka," and "Life Is Just a Bowl of Cherries."

[3]Now and then we rode in a brand-new automobile which an enterprising salesman had dropped off at the house on Friday, saying, "Keep it for the weekend. Take it for a drive and see if you don't think it's got that old Packard beat a mile." On one occasion the stratagem worked: my father liked the ride (and especially the price) of a new Nash well enough to trade.

No one my age wants to admit publicly that he had a wonderful time during the Depression, but the fact is that I did, and I look back on those years as a happy and largely trouble-free time. I was seven when the stock market crashed and nineteen when the attack on Pearl Harbor simultaneously ended America's peace and its economic catastrophe. And in between, as I say, I was all but oblivious to the nation's agony, partly because I was an adolescent, absorbed with myself, my friends, athletics, and school, in that order, and partly because my father never let on that he was having problems, and was not the sort to share with his family (or anyone else) information about private financial matters. In fact, he didn't complain about much of anything except Roosevelt. As far as I could tell, we had enough money, we had plenty to eat, we had an automobile, a cook, and a comfortable, newly built house in a congenial neighborhood, and my parents seemed to enjoy thoroughly the life they had made for themselves, with numerous friends, bridge games, Saturday-night dances, Mother's garden club, Dad's business, summer vacations at the beach[4]—from my vantage point, life simply went on, unclouded and serene. Yet every now and then a ray of reality pierced the comfortable cocoon I inhabited, suggesting that things were not as they should be.

What year it was I could not say, but I remember one particular Sunday when my father and mother, my sister Janet, and I went to Grandmother Wilson's house for a family dinner. The afternoon dragged on interminably, as it always did when you had to stay indoors in your Sunday-school clothes, while Mother and Grandma did the dishes and Mother's stepfather, brother, and husband—three men who had nothing but Mother in common—sat around smoking and talking uncomfortably. On this occasion, Janet and I were reading or playing in the front parlor when we became aware that the decibel level of the conversation had changed in the dining room, behind the big sliding doors. Suddenly we could hear distinctly the voice of Uncle John, the quietest, gentlest man imaginable, spilling out an anguished tale of failure—his own shattering failure. The only job he had found after months of searching was selling Hoover vacuum cleaners on commission, and if ever a man was miscast in a role, it was he in that one. Since the few customers he found bought their machines on time—a couple of dollars a week for weeks on end—when one of them failed to make a

[4]For some reason, the big public fads of the thirties made little impression at our house. We never played miniature golf. We didn't go to Bank Night at the movies, where—if you had registered the previous week—your name might be the lucky one drawn from a revolving drum and you would win a cash prize. Nor did we play bingo, which became a national pastime for a while, and a durable method for churches and other charitable organizations to raise money. Bingo was invented by a man named Edwin S. Lowe, who saw a game called beano at a carnival in Georgia in 1929, a year after he emigrated to this country from Poland. Lowe tried out the game on friends when he returned to his home in Brooklyn, and one of them became so excited at winning that she yelled, "Bingo!" Bingo it was from then on, and one hopes that Mr. Lowe shouted the magic word when he sold his company in 1973 to Milton Bradley for $26 million.

payment (which was often), Uncle John lost his commission. And those pathetically small commissions were his sole source of income. Worse yet, if he could collect no more from the customer, he was expected to repossess the vacuum cleaner or reimburse his employer for its loss. He was then in his middle thirties, and like so many others of his generation, he was truly desperate. Although it occurred more than half a century ago, whenever I think of that Sunday afternoon I am a frightened, embarrassed child again, hearing a grown man's cries of humiliation and rage, wondering what had gone so wrong for Uncle John.

———

When Cyrus Sulzberger came to Pittsburgh in 1934 he was twenty-one years old, just out of Harvard, and he had a job as a cub reporter on the Scripps-Howard paper. His room in a boardinghouse cost $3.50 a week; breakfast was 11 cents, trolley-car fare to his job 5 cents; and for a dime he could splurge on Saturday nights for what was known locally as a Heater and Cooler—two separate glasses, one containing two ounces of whiskey, the other four ounces of beer. That was the bright side. The dark side, as Sulzberger discovered when he outfitted himself as a bum and lived the part in order to write a series of articles on the town's poor, was another matter altogether. There was an ordinance against begging on the streets, but with hordes of unemployed roaming the city, those in authority had neither the muscle nor the heart to enforce it. Instead, bums were directed to one of four principal flophouses, where they stripped and put their clothing into the delousing chamber. (This was a very hot room in which clothes on hangers rotated slowly; the heat was so intense, in fact, that a red-hot metal coathanger burned one leg off Sulzberger's trousers.) While their clothes were being purified the vagrants were given dirty-looking flannel nightshirts which they wore to the evening meal—bread and soup served at long wooden tables. Each flophouse had enormous sleeping barracks, "reeking of humanity," containing three hundred to five hundred double-decker metal beds in rows, so close together they almost touched, where Sulzberger learned through bitter experience that you slept with your shoes under your head if you didn't want to lose them.

When the federal government cut off financial support for the Helping Hand Shelter and similar refuges, saying that men should find work through the Works Progress Administration, the unemployables—as so many of those unfortunates with stricken faces and shapeless clothes were—suddenly became the problem of the community. In Allegheny County, one out of every four citizens was on relief in those days, yet Andrew Mellon still saw the depression as a hiccup in the nation's economic life. "America is going through a bad quarter of an hour," he observed. Four thousand children in the city were unable to go to school in bad weather because they had insufficient clothing. (Families on the dole were buying food with the portion of their relief check that was supposed to be used for clothes, and since relief checks in the county averaged $8 a week, it was not difficult to see why.)

One reporter spoke with a twelve-year-old girl who was ashamed to attend classes because her bare toes stuck out of her worn, broken shoes. She had tried curling them back, she told him, but this made her walk stiff-legged, and the ragged ends of her shoes flopped on the floor. Her father had lost his job in the steel mill, and the entire support for the family of five was $13 a week in relief money, which went for food, rent, coal for the stove, electricity, and medicine, with nothing left over for clothing. The girl had decided she would rather be embarrassed than miss school; it was "the only place where you see or hear about anything except being poor." That same year one could read the story about four men—a twenty-three-year-old white and three Negroes—who had been given ten lashes each by the warden of the Newcastle County workhouse in Wilmington, Delaware, while spectators looked on. (James Welsh, the white man, had pleaded guilty to stealing an overcoat; the unnamed blacks had been convicted of stealing chickens.)[5]

When I was ten, eleven, twelve—growing up in Pittsburgh in what turned out to be the blackest years of the Depression—not a week passed but what one or more men knocked at our kitchen door and asked for food or an odd job to perform. We lived at the corner of Linden Avenue and Reynolds Street, in the city's East End, and from an upstairs window of the house, overlooking the intersection, my sister Janet and I could always tell when we were about to have a caller. At the foot of our steep driveway a man in a frayed suit, collarless shirt, and oversize felt hat would look up at our house, pause for a moment as if to make up his mind, and then start to climb the hill. By the time he reached the door we would be crouching out of sight at the top of the back stairs, listening while he talked to Mary Walsh, the big, bluff Irish woman who was our live-in cook-laundress-cleaning woman-sitter (at $5 a week). If Mary liked the look of him, and if his story rang true, she would ask him in and give him something to eat at the kitchen table. Otherwise, she would tell him we had nothing to spare and suggest that he try the Masten house—"Just over there," she would say in her rich brogue, pointing. "Go along with you, through the hedge and down the next driveway." The picture I retain of all these broken men as they tramped off after an encounter with Mary Walsh is their shoes—shapeless shoes that were brittle and broken, faded almost white from repeated soakings, shoes with newspapers or rags for soles, shoes that were tied to their owner's feet with lengths of clothesline or bits of faded cloth.

Across the land, a million Americans in broken shoes were on the move, 200,000 of them children. Someone took the trouble to count the vagrants

[5]Not until 1972 was the cat-o'-nine-tails legislated out of existence in Delaware. For three centuries the whipping post had been known to black victims as "Red Hannah," and when a man was handcuffed to the post it was said he was "hugging ol' Red Hannah."

who passed through Kansas City and discovered that the daily average was fifteen hundred—many of them young boys or girls dressed in boy's clothing. Wandering from town to town, from state to state, they went from door to door, seeking a meal, shelter for the night, a day's—even an hour's—work. While he was still an undergraduate, Eric Sevareid left home in Minneapolis during the Depression to ride the rails around the country. He found a "great underground world, peopled by tens of thousands of American men, women, and children, white, black, brown, and yellow, who inhabit the 'jungle,' eat from blackened tin cans, find warmth at night in the box cars, take the sun by day on the flatcars, steal one day, beg with cap in hand the next, fight with fists and often razors, hold sexual intercourse under a blanket in a dark corner of the crowded car, coagulate into pairs and gangs, then disintegrate again, wander from town to town . . . happy only when the wheels are clicking under them. . . ." Some of these people, he discovered, were in search of work, others were not. The latter had worked at one time or another, but the job didn't last, the pay was miserable, and they had finally given up trying to find anything else. It was easier just to keep moving.

Not until 1939 did I or many of my friends awaken to what had been happening in that immense, unfamiliar area where the Dust Bowl had claimed so much land and so many of the families that tilled it. It took John Steinbeck's powerful novel *The Grapes of Wrath* to make us see that the Joads, who had lost their tenant farm in Oklahoma and set out for California in hope of finding work as itinerant farm laborers, were not the shiftless, faceless people of our imagination, but honest-to-God human beings. The book sold 300,000 copies within several months of publication, remained on the best-seller list in 1940, and probably did as much as anything to arouse middle-class Americans to the plight of the dispossessed.

To the ragged unfortunates who had neither job nor hope, our neighborhood must have seemed a never-never land. It was a recently developed enclave of about three dozen houses—built during the mid-to-late twenties by businessmen on the way up, plus a scattering of established professional men—each house alive with children and family dogs of the same general age, most with a live-in servant, all with neat lawns and hedges, flower gardens, and an air of settled, genteel prosperity, all within walking distance of Linden School, which our parents firmly believed was the best in the city of Pittsburgh. Our family and the folks who lived nearby, on Edgerton Place and Glen Arden Drive, were infinitely better off than the tramps who came to our door, and yet there cannot have been many men in those well-tended homes who did not feel threatened by what was happening in the country, who did not wake in the middle of the night and wonder if their turn might be next.

Two blocks from our house lived a couple who had been friends of my parents for some years. The man had been successful in real estate, but his particular bubble had burst in '29, and despite a natural charm he had been unable to turn things around, and had taken to drink. His wife, a pretty, frail woman with a look of permanent grief on her face, had gone to work at a job her friends clearly considered beneath her, and eked out some sort of living for the family. Their sons were friends of mine, but I never liked to go inside the huge old house where they lived; the shades were always drawn, and I was afraid of what I might see there. Now and then I would overhear my parents talking guardedly about whether those boys got enough to eat.

My father, George Ketchum, was no stranger to adversity. His own father—a nomadic newspaperman (as most were in the late nineteenth-century West)—had died at the age of twenty-eight, leaving an impoverished widow with four little boys to support on what she could earn as a school-teacher by day and seamstress at night. George, the second son, went to work at seven selling newspapers and *The Saturday Evening Post.* His mother remarried when he was ten and sent him and his older brother, Carlton, to live with her parents in Tennessee, where the two youngsters, both in short pants, were promptly enrolled in a business "college" by their doting grandfather, a Presbyterian minister with a crippled wife, who was determined that they get an education, knew that they would have to make their own way in the world, and realized that stenographic skills would serve them well. As indeed they did. George was so good he was offered employment by the Underwood Company to travel around the country giving demonstrations of typing speed and accuracy (on Underwood machines, naturally) in department-store windows. When he was eleven, his mother found him a job as secretary and bookkeeper for a combination real estate, street railway, water, and cemetery company in the mill town of Monessen, Pennsylvania. The hours were 7:45 A.M. to 6:00 P.M. on weekdays (with thirty minutes for lunch) and 7:45 to 4:00 on Saturdays. Men who worked longer hours drew overtime pay, but since George was a salaried employee ($25 a month), he received nothing extra for what was often a sixty- or sixty-five-hour week. It may have been fortunate for his health that he and Carlton were soon back in Tennessee, working as stenographers in a law firm (the partners were former soldiers—one a Union officer, the other a Confederate—who spent much of their time refighting the war), and then as court reporters while they were still young enough to be in short trousers. George subsequently served as secretary to the presidents of two teachers colleges and to the chancellor of the University of Pittsburgh, as a clerk with a steel fabricating company, and as assistant to a New Yorker who organized and directed money-raising campaigns for schools and hospitals. Somehow, during these years, he also managed to acquire a remarkably full education, though he never attended school continuously for more than three years.

During the World War he was a pilot in France (probably one of the most enjoyable episodes of his life, since he saw no combat, had an educational and generally pleasant tour, and made a number of enduring friendships). On August 1, 1919, back in civilian clothes, he opened an office in downtown Pittsburgh. He had $500 in working capital and an idea. The idea was to offer a publicity service to clients in the area, and soon after his brother Carlton and a college classmate joined him in the endeavor—which turned out to be more fund-raising than publicity—the firm was doing business as Ketchum, Inc. In 1922, the year his son was born, George launched an advertising agency that was later called Ketchum, MacLeod & Grove.

Since an advertising agency—a business totally dependent upon its clients' willingness and ability to spend money—mirrors the economy that supports it, it was something of a minor miracle that George Ketchum's fledgling company survived the worst economic depression in the nation's history. Advertising agencies (about which my father knew exactly nothing when he founded one) had come into being in response to an economic stimulus. During the nineteenth century the nation's burgeoning industries appeared to have conquered the problems of production, and economists of that day were confident that all-out production would lead to all-out consumption. Only it did not work out that way. It turned out that you had to stimulate consumption by some means, and in the second decade of the twentieth century America concluded that the most effective way of doing so was through the relatively new techniques of advertising. Speaking for her generation, F. Scott Fitzgerald's wife, Zelda, once remarked, "We grew up founding our dreams on the infinite promises of American advertising. I still believe that one can learn to play the piano by mail and that mud will give you a perfect complexion."

The lessons of thrift and sacrifice learned by generations of hardworking Americans had to be unlearned, apparently, and the New England gospel— "Use it up, wear it out, make it do, or do without"—was on its way to the ash heap along with the celluloid collar. The remarkable boom times of the twenties were fueled in the first instance by an extraordinary increase in productivity (more than 60 percent per hour per person in nine years' time), and in the second by advertising, since there was no use producing the goods if you couldn't sell them. Thanks largely to Detroit's assembly lines, which were turning out an automobile every ten seconds, and to the magazine ads that made them appear infinitely desirable, this was the decade in which every American family discovered that an automobile was a necessity, not a luxury. (George Ketchum bought his first car—a used black Packard sedan with fitted luggage in the trunk—in 1926.) So, it seemed, were radios and refrigerators, washing machines and electric irons, vacuum cleaners and toasters—all obtainable through the magic of installment buying, another device designed to keep the consumer consuming. Buy now, pay later was the theme, and in five years' time installment credit rose from $1.38 billion to $3 billion, with four of every five radios bought on time, and three of every five automobiles.

By 1929, advertising agencies were a permanent fixture on the American business scene, and that year George Ketchum drew a salary of $12,000 from an enterprise that was clearly on its way. That was big money in those days: it meant that he had joined the elite 2 percent of the population earning between $10,000 and $20,000 annually, at a time when 65 percent of America's families had incomes lower than $2,000. As an indication of the dollar's value in 1929, one of the agency's employees—a valued copywriter and account executive named Chauncey Morley—was paid $5,200, out of which he saved $100 a month. His total income tax that year was $4.50.

Although few people were aware of it at the time, the Depression had not begun with the stock-market crash in October 1929; the economic decline was well under way by then—had, in fact, been going on for two years or more in such industries as construction, and ever since the World War in agriculture. What the stock-market catastrophe did was to eliminate some $30 billion—twice the amount of the national debt—from the American economy; and in the wake of the collapse, business declined slowly but steadily, orders for goods began to fall off, and corporate officers began to wonder how much belt-tightening would be needed, while everyone kept hoping that prosperity was just around the corner, that President Hoover was right when he said that conditions were "fundamentally sound," and that there might be some truth to the hit song people began singing in November 1929: "Happy Days Are Here Again!"

Conditions quickly turned sour for a lot of factory workers, but most executive and white-collar jobs seemed to be secure, most companies went on paying dividends, and most people believed that the downturn would be short-lived. In July 1930, the year my parents' new house was completed, the staff of the Ketchum fund-raising office was booked solid well into 1931. Then the bad news began to come in. By October 1, every contract for a campaign had been postponed or canceled; soon there were prolonged periods when the firm received not one cent of income. The advertising agency was not hit quite as fast—or so it seemed. The first indication that change was in the wind came when clients announced plans to reduce their advertising budgets, eliminating smaller publications from the schedule. Then the budgets were pared again, and again—then canceled entirely. And one by one clients simply disappeared—some into the maw of bankruptcy, some to be absorbed by another company.

The effect of this at Ketchum, MacLeod & Grove was sobering, to say the least. As Chauncey Morley described his own situation at the agency, his $5,200 salary in 1929 had meant that he was "on his way, as the first plateau in earnings at that time was $5,000 a year. The second plateau was $10,000, which represented the ultimate aim of men below the top management level. It meant a fine home, one or even two cars, membership in a country club, and the companionship and respect of other successful citizens." At the end of 1930 all salaries at the agency were cut, and Morley's pay dropped to $5,015. In 1931—about the time Andrew Mellon, secretary of the Treasury, announced, "During the coming year the country will make steady progress"—it was reduced to $4,500. At the beginning of February 1932, George Ketchum announced another reduction in salaries; before the middle of the month an additional slice in pay was necessary; for four months that year the principals had no income whatever. Morley's 1932 earnings amounted to $3,613.75; in 1933 and 1934 they were down to $3,300, just $300 more than he had received as a beginner, ten years earlier. But as he and others at the agency perceived, they were fortunate: "better men were walking the streets, begging for any kind of work." It was a near thing for the principals, though, when their bank failed in 1931 and closed its doors for good; three other lending institutions turned them down before they finally got a $5,000 loan to meet the payroll. In 1934 one client company, unable to pay its bill, gave the agency its own debentures, which were selling at such a low price that Ketchum, MacLeod & Grove received three or four times the face amount of the debt. The understanding was that the agency could not sell the securities but must return them when the bill was finally paid. What the agency could do—and did, to stay alive—was use the bonds for collateral to float a loan.

In 1936 the fund-raising firm was able to pay a modest dividend and George Ketchum's salary from the agency finally surpassed his 1929 pay. Then, in August 1937, the stock market suddenly collapsed again; by March 1938 unemployment nationally was once more hovering near 20 percent. After the market took another sharp drop that month, President Roosevelt, finding himself in a situation not unlike the one Hoover had faced in the early thirties, succumbed to advisers who were urging an increase in deficit spending, and asked Congress to revive or expand several of the New Deal's public works programs. Once again, the nation's economic collapse had an immediate, direct effect on Ketchum, MacLeod & Grove's business, and my father cut his own salary by 40 percent.

Now, as if he and most other Americans did not have all the trouble they could handle, the news from Europe was about as bad as it could possibly be.

CHAPTER 4

"War . . . is not a prospect which the Defence Ministers would view with great confidence."

On a November evening in 1937, in Berlin, Chancellor Adolf Hitler revealed his intentions to a group of six men—his chief military advisers and the foreign minister of the Third Reich. To their utter astonishment, he announced that it was time to "settle the Czech and Austrian questions" and that he planned within months to move against Austria and to descend upon the Czechs "with lightning speed." And to their protests that this would surely bring on a European war for which Germany was in no way prepared, he stated flatly that neither France nor Britain would intervene in Austria and that both countries had already written off the Czechs.

Three months later Hitler summoned Austria's Chancellor Kurt von Schuschnigg to his Berchtesgaden retreat and gave him an ultimatum: either Schuschnigg would appoint several Nazis to his cabinet and restore the rights of Austria's Nazi Party, which had been forced to go underground, or the German army would invade his country. "I shall be suddenly overnight in Vienna," Hitler promised, "like a spring storm." When Schuschnigg referred vaguely to allies and to the fact that Austria was not alone in the world, Germany's Führer replied that no one would stand in his way: "England? England will not lift a finger for Austria. . . . And France?" For an answer, Hitler reminded Schuschnigg of the Rhineland

and of France's failure to oppose him there. (When word of this meeting reached John Wiley, the U.S. chargé d'affaires in Vienna, he observed sadly, "It's the end of Austria," but Great Britain's permanent under secretary of state reacted differently, noting in his diary: "Personally, I almost wish Germany would swallow Austria and get it over with. She is probably going to do so anyhow . . . anyhow we can't stop her. What's all the fuss about?")

Hoping to buy time and a little running room, Schuschnigg did the unexpected and ordered a plebiscite to determine whether the Austrian people wanted "reunification" with Germany. But he underestimated his opponent. On the evening of March 11, 1938, the Führer gave the invasion order to his troops, and all the next day the gray legions streamed across the border—coming on, as he had threatened, like a spring storm, seizing Austria over the weekend without a shot being fired. Three days later Hitler returned in triumph to the old imperial capital where he had once lived as a vagrant, listening in what a German diplomat called "a state of ecstasy" to the deep-throated chant of Nazi mobs: *Sieg Heil! Sieg Heil! Heil Hitler! Heil Hitler! Ein Volk, ein Reich, ein Führer!*" "God protect Austria" was Kurt Schuschnigg's final prayer in a radio address to his countrymen, and it was apparent that if Austria was to receive protection no one but the Almighty was going to provide it.

On the streets of Vienna, German storm troopers stood guard and crowds jeered while groups of Jews crawled on their hands and knees in the gutters, scrubbing pro-Schuschnigg signs from the sidewalks; Jewish men and women were rounded up to clean, with their sacred praying bands, the toilets in barracks where SA and SS squads were quartered; reports of suicides came from all over the city; thousands of Jews were thrown into jail while black-uniformed Germans carried off their possessions by the truckload; those who could afford it bought their freedom by handing over all they owned to a special organization called the Office for Jewish Emigration, set up by Reinhard Heydrich and administered by an Austrian named Karl Adolf Eichmann.

A particular brand of justice was reserved for Schuschnigg, the mild-mannered former lawyer who had thought to defy Hitler. For two weeks he was held by the Gestapo and prevented from sleeping; then, for seventeen months, he was locked up in a tiny hotel room and allowed to emerge only long enough to clean the washbasins and latrines of SS guards with the towel issued for his personal use. (A year later, having lost sixty pounds, he was declared "in excellent health" by an SS physician; then he was sent to the first of a succession of German concentration camps, where he remained for seven years and miraculously survived.)

The head of the Gestapo, Heinrich Himmler, joined his lieutenants in Austria, and he and Heydrich concluded that it would be too much trouble to transport thousands of Austrians to concentration camps in Germany— much easier, they decided, to establish one at Mauthausen on the bank of the Danube, where, during the six and a half years of its existence, more prisoners would be executed than at any other camp.

One American who witnessed the Austrian Anschluss, or "union," with Germany was a lean, handsome man named Edward R. Murrow, European director for CBS Radio, who chartered a plane in Warsaw and flew to Vienna, where he made on shortwave radio his first news report to American listeners. Back in London, he broadcast again to the United States, telling his countrymen how Austria had ceased to exist:

It was called a bloodless conquest and in some ways it was, but I'd like to be able to forget the haunted look on the faces of those long lines of people outside the banks and travel offices. People trying to get away. I'd like to forget the tired futile look of the Austrian army officers, and the thud of hobnail boots and the crash of light tanks in the early hours of the morning on the Ringstrasse, and the pitiful uncertainty and bewilderment of those forced to lift the right hand and shout "Heil Hitler!" for the first time. I'd like to forget the sound of the smashing glass as the Jewish shop streets were raided; the hoots and jeers aimed at those forced to scrub the sidewalk.

On Palm Sunday, 1938, the people of Austria went to the polls for a "plebiscite" supervised by German troops and voted, according to results published by Hitler's minister of propaganda, Joseph Paul Goebbels, 99 percent *ja*—in favor of reunification with Germany. As Hitler had predicted, neither England nor France moved to oppose him, and Austria went the way of the Rhineland.

———

Czechoslovakia was next on the agenda.

Not that this should have come as a surprise to anyone. In a speech to the Reichstag on February 20, Hitler had warned that his next objective was the "redemption" of Sudeten Germans. It was the responsibility of the Third Reich, he proclaimed, to protect the millions of "Germans" living outside the Reich's borders. Those Germans not only had a right to "racial self-determination" but to protection by the fatherland of their "political and spiritual freedom." And it required very little imagination to realize that he had been referring to certain citizens of Czechoslovakia as well as those in Austria.

Czechoslovakia, created in the aftermath of world war by the Versailles Treaty, consisted of remnants of the Austro-Hungarian Empire, and the opening words of the national anthem—*Kde domov muj*, "Where is my home?"—suggest that the country possessed a sense of fate more than a sense of nationhood. While the bulk of its ten million people were Czechs and Slovaks, there were within its borders a million Poles, Ruthenians, and Magyars, and about two and a half million souls known as Sudeten Germans. These German-speaking people had been settled in Bohemia for centuries, and it was an arguable question whether a majority would prefer citizenship in Nazi Germany to that of Czechoslovakia. But as in so many matters of international politics, the wishes of the people involved were not necessarily paramount.

What interested Hitler far more than the Sudeten Germans was Czechoslovakia itself, and for a variety of reasons. In military terms, it could be likened to an aircraft carrier in his rear that might be sent into action by its allies, France and Britain. Czechoslovakia was, after all, the keystone of the French alliance system and, in a sense, of Russia's, since it had a long-standing mutual assistance pact with France and a more recent one with Russia. (Amid all the verbiage, the only clause that counted was one stating that Russia would come to the aid of Czechoslovakia in the event of an enemy invasion, but *only* if France first intervened in the Czechs' behalf.) Beyond all this, of course, Britain and France were allies, and it was generally assumed that England would fight at France's side in the event of war. So to Hitler, the presence of the small, polyglot country on Germany's northeast and southeast borders was not only galling but a constant reminder of the ancient enemies, Britain and France. From the vantage point of the German dictator, moreover, an immensely beguiling aspect of Czechoslovakia was the territory in which the Sudeten Germans lived—an area that contained numerous industrial plants (notably the huge Skoda armaments works) and the fortifications erected by the Czechs to prevent a German invasion of their country.

The implications of the Austrian Anschluss had not been lost on the Czechs. They had, to be sure, an efficient, well-trained army equipped with the latest guns, armor, and airplanes, and they possessed—in the Sudetenland—a well-fortified border. But when Hitler seized Austria, Czechoslovakia was immediately isolated from its principal allies in the west, and its one hope of survival now lay in the willingness of France (and presumably Russia and Britain) to come to its defense in the event of trouble. The Czech government was understandably nervous about French intentions.

Several developments in 1938 heightened the Czechs' anxiety. First was the relentlessly rising propaganda and pressure on the government by Konrad Henlein, leader of the Nazi Party in the Sudetenland, who was obviously erecting a Trojan horse within the country on orders from Berlin and was presenting officials in Prague with increasingly unacceptable demands, all having to do with the return of the Sudetenland to Germany. Then there were the continuing threats, denunciations, and ugly rumors emanating from Nazi Germany, aimed at undermining the authority of the Prague government over the large Sudeten minority. What revealed to the Czechs the direction in which the wind was blowing was a high-level mission from London that arrived in Prague early in August. Headed by Lord Runciman, a small, thin-lipped man, bald as an egg, who checked into the Alcron Hotel with his wife, staff, and a mountain of luggage, its purpose was to mediate between the Czech government and the Nazi Henlein. Startling as this may have been to President Eduard Beneš, who was apparently expected by the British to treat with one of his own citizens as if he were the chief of some foreign principality, it indicated very clearly that Prime Minister Neville Chamberlain had concluded for reasons of his own that Czechoslovakia should give in to Hitler's demands. (Runciman seems to have been keenly aware of the odds against his success: "You are setting me adrift in a small boat in mid-Atlantic," he complained to Lord Halifax, the foreign minister.) Even so, when the *New York Herald Tribune*'s political columnist Walter Lippmann interviewed Beneš that month, he found him "disconcertingly optimistic." Beneš, it seemed, was counting on help from the Russians.

———

The prime minister of Great Britain possessed a sense of his own mission and an utter certainty that men and events could be made to move in the right direction if only they would heed the logic and reason to which the leader of His Majesty's Government could open their eyes. Looking like an awkward, dowdy bird in a homburg, morning suit, and high wing collar that accentuated his prominent Adam's apple, he would have passed for a British statesman anywhere in the world. His hair was graying nicely about the temples, his face was the image of an upper-class Anglo-Saxon—clean-cut and a trifle angular, punctuated with heavy black eyebrows, salt-and-pepper mustache, and poor teeth. There was a familiar, old-shoe look about him: an infrequent smile that was shy, reserved, but somehow winning; a public manner that suggested modesty, duty, good sportsmanship, and fair play. And if there was in all this a strong suggestion that Neville Chamberlain would be incapable of comprehending the mind, manners, and methods of an Adolf Hitler, that was putting it as kindly as possible.

Sixty-nine years old and suffering from gout, Chamberlain was a product of nineteenth-century Birmingham, which had given him faith in sound business practices, prosperity, self-discipline, and work (he was the sort to weed his garden rather than sit in it, someone said). His family meant everything to him; indeed, he had almost no close friends beyond that small circle. During most of his career in politics and government, Chamberlain had labored, as his fellow MP Winston Churchill remarked, like a packhorse—rising finally to leadership of the Tory Party through patience, plodding, and efficiency rather than brilliance. (Lunching with the Walter Lippmanns one day in 1939, the prime minister turned to her and remarked, "I hope you won't think I'm a socialist, but I'm in favor of housing.") There was some resentment that a man with so few apparent gifts should have fallen heir to leadership of the nation at a time so patently requiring imagination and determination and the ability to make Englishmen perceive the perils around them, and one of Chamberlain's political opponents observed sourly that he had only the qualities to be "a good town clerk of Birmingham in a lean year."

Although the times cried out for preparedness and the arms to make it possible, Chamberlain—who considered the World War, which had killed or wounded more than two million British soldiers, the worst calamity in history and was determined that it would not be repeated—had been personally responsible for much of the cheese-paring that whittled away the military budget; his proud achievement as chancellor of the exchequer and later as prime minister was the tight, rigid control placed on military spending. As a cabinet minister he had tended quietly to his own affairs, listening to the advice of acknowledged authorities, keeping his nose out of other departments. But soon after he succeeded Stanley Baldwin as prime minister in 1937 his colleagues became aware of a marked change in his personality. When he took over the leadership of the government, it was apparent that he not only intended to have a personal hand in the running of the Foreign Office, but fancied himself as an international peacemaker.

In order to come to friendly, or at least workable, terms with Hitler and Mussolini, Chamberlain believed he must compromise, giving a bit here and there on what he construed to be minor issues in order to gain on the major ones. While systematically removing or silencing those members of his government who dared oppose him, he began to bypass the Foreign Office, which he considered excessively pro-French and anti-German, and in 1937 sent a personal emissary, Lord Halifax, to talk with Hitler. Concurrently he was dealing with Mussolini through the Italian ambassador in London or through amateur emissaries to Rome—the widow of his half brother being one of them.

In response to a secret cablegram from the president of the United States, proposing an international conference to discuss the principles to be observed in the relations between nations, as a step toward lessening tensions in Europe, Chamberlain rebuffed Roosevelt, telling him bluntly that Great Britain was on top of the situation and could fry its own fish. The prime minister's attitude toward Americans, it must be said, was one of distrust mingled with contempt: you could depend on them for little more than rhetoric, he liked to say, and he was irritated by Roosevelt's seeming effort to move in on what he considered his personal leadership in Europe's affairs. Winston Churchill, the leader of a growing opposition to Chamberlain's policies within the prime minister's own party, described this snub of FDR as "the loss of the last frail chance to save the world from tyranny otherwise than by war." Sumner Welles, the U.S. under secretary of state, put it more baldly: it was "a douche of cold water."

Unhappily, the Sudeten situation could neither be ignored nor brushed aside, and as it approached crisis proportions—the Nazi demands ever more shrill and menacing, Czech obstinacy increasing—a continent that had seen a worldwide catastrophe begin in 1914 over the assassination of a minor Balkan nobleman began holding its collective breath lest a similarly unforeseen incident touch off the fuse again. A major scare occurred in May, when the Czechs, rightly or wrongly, were led to believe that a German invasion was imminent and mobilized their army. When no attack was forthcoming, the western press played the affair as a victory for Czech determination and strength and made crowing noises to the effect that Hitler had "backed down"—the result of which was to infuriate Hitler, who despised the Czechs, and stiffen his resolve to teach them a lesson at the first opportunity.

What it really came down to, of course, was not what the Czechs were going to do, but what British and French intentions were—and that was something not even the governments of Britain and France knew until the late spring of 1938. Readers of the *New York Times* got a clue to France's official posture in a column written by the foreign observer Pertinax, in Paris. Military leaders there were confident, the informant said, knowing that the "French army exceeds by far the German army in quality both as regards men and matériel." Then a note of doubt crept into the account. "The present condition of the air forces, of course, is a cause of alarm," Pertinax suggested, "but if it means that hard blows would be struck at the French nation, it does not mean that the French nation would be brought to its knees." This echoed the gloomy opinion of the commander of the French air force, General Joseph Vuillemin, who had recently gone to Germany as the guest of his opposite number, Hermann Göring, to inspect the Luftwaffe, to tour factories and assembly lines, and to witness tactical maneuvers performed by fighter planes and dive-bombers. That eye-opening visit—so carefully staged by Göring—was all that was needed to send Vuillemin back to France in an acute state of nerves, and he reported to his colleagues and to Premier Edouard Daladier that in the event of war the French air force would be wiped out in two weeks' time.

That seemed to put it up to the British, and at the end of April a delegation from Paris, led by Daladier and Georges Bonnet, the foreign minister, went to London for a round of serious talks. Once the niceties were over, the British made it clear to their allies that they lacked the military strength to back up any brave words that might be spoken to Hitler. Not only did Chamberlain refuse to commit Britain to sending an army to the continent in the event of hostilities; he was also forced to admit that any force that *might* be sent would not be fully mechanized. Lord Halifax, the foreign secretary, iced the cake by informing the visitors from across the Channel that Britain's state of unpreparedness was such that it would be impossible to aid the Czechs if Germany attacked. To which Daladier, being a realist, could only remark that if the common policy of France and Britain was inspired by weakness, the result would surely be violence and aggression and threats of more of the same. And on that note the French departed.

On August 30 the British cabinet met for a long, disquieting discussion of the Czech problem. Viscount Halifax reported that Germany had partially mobilized and gave his opinion that even if Hitler had not made up his mind to attack, his army was poised to do so, and that from now on he could be expected to employ a combination of bluff and force to get his way.

There were those in Britain—among them Winston Churchill and young Anthony Eden—who felt that Hitler's bluff must be called, and soon, but Chamberlain had decided otherwise. England was in no position to do so, as he had recently learned from the men in Britain's military establishment. They reported to him, in a masterpiece of understatement, that "war in present conditions is not a prospect which the Defence Ministers would view with great confidence." (Thinking back on that summer's events, Permanent Under Secretary of State Alexander Cadogan recalled that "of our top military, naval and air people whom I questioned on the subject, I don't think I found one who did not think that 'appeasement' was right.")

To all of which must be added that Neville Chamberlain regarded the crisis as a great deal of bother over an insignificant country. His opinion of the Czechs, when it came down to it, was not very different from Hitler's: as he once remarked, they were "not out of the top drawer—or even the middle."

To many an American there was a baffling unreality to all that had occurred these past months, when it seemed plain enough to anyone who thought about it that Hitler was going to get his way whatever he chose to do. The alliance between Britain and France was floundering, not because the two powers lacked knowledge of the common danger but because they lacked—or thought they lacked—the strength to combat it. It was as though the people of England and France—like those in America—wanted to shove the whole nasty business under the rug, or at least to look the other way if averting danger meant avoiding war. And to anyone who comprehended what they had suffered twenty years earlier, when both nations had lost an entire generation of young men, that was entirely understandable. To those who remembered 1914—and so many did—a disaster of such magnitude could not be permitted to happen again. It was simply unthinkable. So people took refuge in such thoughts as those of Lord Lothian, who had remarked at the time the Germans marched into the Rhineland, "After all, they are only going into their own back-garden." Was not Austria, like the Rhineland, Germany's own back-garden? For that matter, was not Czechoslovakia? Only a small minority pointed out the fallacy in this line of reasoning by asking, what was *not* Germany's own back-garden?

A self-inflicted blindness to Hitler's real intentions disabled Europe in 1938—an unwillingness to believe that the man would actually risk the horrors of world war. Let us take him at his word, men said again and again; he has told us that Germany has no territorial ambitions. Surely, the Sudetenland will be the end of it.

CHAPTER 5

———◆———

"... I've been preparing for this all my life."

W hat was happening in Germany was largely incomprehensible to most people in the world beyond, and the relatively few foreigners who had any knowledge of it were convinced that one had to observe at first hand the orgiastic behavior of a huge German crowd responding to Adolf Hitler in order to understand the dynamism of the Nazi movement. *Nothing,* they said, could equal what went on in the medieval town of Nuremberg during the week in September when the party rally was held.

These annual rites were held in an atmosphere of frenzied excitement and pageantry, calculated to regenerate enthusiasm and a sense of mission among the party faithful. Every one of Hitler's speeches, every appearance, was a meticulously planned performance, designed to bring fervor and an aura of mysticism into the lives of the German people, millions of whom had begun to see him as something of a messiah.

William L. Shirer, the thirty-year-old Berlin correspondent for Universal Service, witnessed the party rally for the first time in 1934, and as he watched Hitler ride like a Roman emperor through the narrow streets of Nuremberg past phalanxes of cheering Nazis, he realized to his surprise that little could be seen of the city—the Gothic houses and gabled roofs were almost obscured by tens of thousands of black-and-red swastika flags, and the streets teemed with brown and black uniforms. As he looked at the faces of these madly cheering masses he was reminded of the crazed expressions he had once seen in the backwoods of Louisiana on a group of Holy Rollers being exhorted by a revivalist preacher.

The climax of the ritual was a pageant for the *Amtswalter*—an assemblage of party functionaries at the Zeppelin Field, which Hitler's young protégé, the architect Albert Speer, had redesigned especially for the purpose. In September 1937, the British ambassador, Nevile Henderson, had attended a Nuremberg rally for the first time, and the spectacle was almost too much for that proper Anglo-Saxon diplomat. He was not given to hyperbole, but his description of the scene was that of a man awestruck by what he beheld. At 8:00 in the evening, 140,000 workers in brown shirts paraded the vast arena. (Henderson was not aware that Speer had suggested that the ceremony be held at night, the better to conceal the ragged, unmilitary ranks of these civilian functionaries, or that darkness suited Hitler's purpose, too; the Führer was certain that "in the evening the people's willpower more easily succumbs to the dominating force of a stronger will.")

First, thousands of flag bearers marched into the arena, peeling off into ten columns and forming lanes into which the party members trooped. Bright spotlights flooded the sea of banners, massed bands blared out the familiar marching songs, and rank upon rank of Nazis poured onto the field. When all was in readiness the bands suddenly stopped, a hush came over the enormous crowd, and Adolf Hitler made his entrance. At that moment, 130 antiaircraft searchlights were turned on, sending long, radiant shafts twenty thousand feet into the sky to form a kind of square roof in the clouds. To Henderson it "was like being in a cathedral of ice." Then the standard-bearers began to move, carrying batons with varicolored electric bulbs attached on top, and the total effect, the Briton wrote, was of "rivers of red and gold rippling forward under the dome of blue light, in complete silence, through the massed formations of brownshirts." The eerie silence prevailed until Hitler reached the podium, when, at a signal, the roar of *"Sieg Heil! Sieg Heil! Sieg Heil!"* thundered from 140,000 throats.

Now, in 1938, the eyes not only of Germany but of the entire western world were on the Nuremberg party rally, with the spectators wondering if what they discerned in the medieval town could be the wave of the future. The curtain rose on the superbly staged theatrical production, and as the spellbound audience waited, the pagan rites built steadily toward their climax—the Führer's speech on September 12. An almost unbelievable tension pervaded the capitals of Europe—all, it was reported, save Prague, which appeared outwardly calm except for the urgent, unceasing activity at railroad station and airport, where families of Jews were arranging passage or departing for some promised sanctuary.

Between September 6 and September 12, 1938, on a railroad siding in Nuremberg stood a private car, in a compartment of which Sir Nevile

Henderson, His Majesty's ambassador, was uncomfortably lodged. Henderson had just received a cable from Halifax, instructing him to warn Hitler of the gravity with which the British government would view any move against Czechoslovakia. Perhaps such a message, Halifax thought, delivered before the Führer made his speech, would deter him from any rash statement that might plunge Europe into war. Henderson, who had been exposed to Hitler's emotional outbursts and rages before (he was always in the position of seeing him on "official and invariably disagreeable business," he complained), was appalled. He had neglected to bring his code book and writing materials to Nuremberg; he had no secretary; and besides, he was ill—already suffering the first pains of the cancer that would kill him. So, in order to answer Halifax, he tore blank pages from the mystery novels he was reading, scribbled an anguished reply on them, and sent the sheets off to London by chartered plane. The burden of his message was that any public warning would almost certainly send Hitler off the deep end, and he begged Halifax not to insist on such a drastic measure.

The effect of Henderson's entreaty—which Alfred Duff Cooper, first lord of the Admiralty, described disgustedly as "hysterical, imploring the government not to insist upon his carrying out these instructions, which he was sure would have the opposite effect to that desired"—was that the British cabinet reneged, abandoning its tentative gesture at firmness.[1] The initiative remained in Hitler's hands.

Nothing like the same degree of concern Europe felt had surfaced in America (three thousand miles of ocean made a great deal of difference in the level of danger one sensed), yet uneasiness and a certain amount of fear were unmistakably present here, too. Newspapers were filled with dire predictions of what Hitler might say and do; tourists returning from the continent told of seeing jackbooted Nazi soldiers everywhere they went in Germany and described the fear and pessimism evident in each country they visited. Europe, they said, had all the earmarks of a volcano ready to blow, and Monday, September 12, began to look like the day it might go up.

A premonition that the worst was to come was heightened by accounts of Saturday's speech to the Nazi Party rally by Hermann Göring, the number-two man in Germany, who cursed the Czechs as "a chit of a race devoid of culture" and, to repeated roars from the crowd, proclaimed the invincibility of the Third Reich. It was taken for granted that this indicated the tenor of Hitler's own address. Still another portent was the unusual announcement that seventy NBC stations and 114 CBS stations would carry the Führer's speech over the air on Monday afternoon; as Americans were

[1] Duff Cooper was not alone in his opinion of Henderson. Hugh Greene, a Berlin correspondent for the *Daily Telegraph,* was convinced that the ambassador was "an absolutely disastrous" choice for the job, and was genuinely unbalanced, perhaps because he was so ill. "He did his level best to suppress the views of other members of the embassy," Greene said, and if they sent dispatches that ran contrary to the Chamberlain-Henderson policy, he accused them of disloyalty.

Hitler's massed followers pack the vast Zeppelin Field in Nuremberg, which 130 antiaircraft searchlights, throwing beams 20,000 feet overhead, transformed into a "cathedral of ice."

aware, no such attention had been paid to a talk by the head of a European government since the dramatic abdication of Edward VIII in December of 1936.

According to the morning *Times,* the broadcast would be heard in New York on station WABC at 3:00 P.M., following a half-hour organ recital; but at 2:15, to the surprise of those listening to a program of dance music, an announcer broke in to say, "We interrupt the program of Enoch Light in order to bring our listeners the world-awaited talk on Germany's foreign policy to be delivered by Adolf Hitler to the Nazi Congress at Nuremberg."

Over the crackle of static came the clear, harsh voice of the German dictator, calm at first, then rising in an explosive burst of anger that was drowned out by cheers.[2] In a tongue and tone entirely foreign to most American ears, he alternately talked and shouted for an hour and a quarter, while a translator in the studio quietly paraphrased his remarks. Just after 3:30 listeners heard the mighty, swelling chant from thousands of German throats, *"Sieg Heil! Sieg Heil! Sieg Heil!"* It was deafening and somehow terribly threatening, because of the nature of the event and because the shortwave reception ebbed and flowed like an ocean tide, surging over the ears like the thunder of waves until it was impossible to tell whether the roaring came from the crowd or from interference across the Atlantic.

If people felt somewhat awestruck by the whole experience, there was in all truth something wondrous about it. Despite the static, the occasional fading of sound, and the barrier of language, what people were hearing possessed an uncanny magic of its own. Americans staring at their Philco and Atwater Kent radios suddenly realized that they were eavesdropping on a major occurrence taking place thousands of miles distant; by what seemed a miracle they were present while the future was being determined. As a writer for *The Nation* described the occasion, "For the first time, history has been made in the hearing of its pawns."

Listening to the actual voices of Hitler and the multitude in the Nuremberg Zeppelin Field cheering on cue to the Führer's speech, the American radio audience became aware, as never before, of the threat Nazi Germany represented. Into the living rooms of the New World had come the old cry for blood raised in the Colosseum centuries before, and those who heard could recognize it for what it was.

The sound of the Nuremberg rally was a novel and altogether sobering experience for those who heard it, yet it was only the beginning of a remarkable eighteen-day episode that saw increasing numbers of Americans glued to their radio sets as if hypnotized, half dreading what might come next, half thrilled by the newness and excitement of it. During those days radio came into its own, replacing the drama of the soap opera with that of real life, providing an audience with the immediacy and suspense of a

[2]Hitler's voice was graphically described by a German contemporary as having "a little of the odor of dirty underwear."

historic event, involving them totally in what was going on in the lands beyond the sea.

———

At 3:36, immediately following Hitler's address, another voice came on the air—a familiar one to those in the New York area who had heard H. V. Kaltenborn before—and in brisk, confident tones the speaker began to analyze the address they had just heard.

Hitler's words, Kaltenborn said, "may mean war, but not immediate war." Nothing in the speech, he explained, could be considered as an ultimatum—rather, it was a declaration that Germany would no longer tolerate what Hitler called the oppression of Sudeten Germans in Czechoslovakia; and it was a promise that if the Czechs did not reach agreement on the matter, Germany would stand firmly behind the Sudetens and insist upon a settlement. Hitler had described the Third Reich's massive military preparations—in particular, the powerful maze of fortifications in the Rhineland known as the Siegfried Line;[3] he had made a direct personal attack on President Beneš, calling him a liar and maker of empty phrases; and he had reminded the world of the contributions that he, Hitler, had made to peace. In conclusion, the Führer had told his ecstatic audience that there was a new Germany now—a Germany that would not hesitate to use its armed might despite what England and France might do.

In a few words, Kaltenborn summed it up: "In substance . . . the speech was very belligerent. It was a threatening speech, hurling defiance to all the world—a speech that emphasized Germany's growing military might. But it was not a speech that creates an immediate crisis. For that we must look to action rather than to words. Good afternoon." With that, he was off the air, and in place of his clipped words and the awesome sounds from Nuremberg's "cathedral of ice," there came again the soothing big-band sound of Enoch Light and his Light Brigade.

No one realized it that afternoon when H. V. Kaltenborn signed off, but for the next two and a half weeks—day and night—he and the midtown Manhattan room from which he was broadcasting would be the focus of attention of tens of millions of Americans. The room itself was unpretentious enough; known as Studio Nine, it was located on the seventeenth floor of a building at the corner of Madison Avenue and Fifty-second Street in New York, and was about the size of an average family living room, furnished with wooden chairs and three desks, on each of which stood a microphone. The walls were hung with sound-absorbent curtains, broken by two doors and a window that opened not on the outside world, but on a control room where an engineer sat behind a panel of instruments. One

[3]The Siegfried Line, or West Wall, along Germany's western frontier, was a bulwark against possible French attack. A deep zone of concrete fortifications and tank traps, it was a long way from completion in September 1938, when Hitler spoke.

door led to the control room, the other to a small anteroom filled with teletype machines, beyond which was an office occupied by Paul White, who was in charge of news for the Columbia Broadcasting System.

The modesty of the room was not matched by that of its lonely occupant, the big man, wearing earphones, who would be sitting at one of the desks in Studio Nine continuously for the next eighteen days, except when he took time out to nap on a cot set up in White's office across the hall. During that time his voice would become as familiar to most Americans as that of their own fathers, and for good reason. As H. V. Kaltenborn described the moment that had thrust him into the limelight to his colleague Robert Trout, "Without knowing it, I've been preparing for this all my life."

Hans von Kaltenborn was already something of a personage in radio and was regarded as a bit of an odd duck even in a business that had more than its share of them. He was a good deal older than most of the men he worked with and was, they agreed, "something of a trial." Born in Milwaukee in 1878, he began working at the age of fifteen in a building materials company owned by his father, a former Prussian soldier, and then spent a year on a small-town newspaper before the wanderlust took him to France, where he earned his keep as a traveling salesman for two years at the turn of the century. In 1902 he was back in the States, reporting for the *Brooklyn Eagle;* then he returned to Europe for two years in Berlin; afterward took a job as private tutor to John Jacob Astor's children; and somehow found time to acquire a B.A. at Harvard in 1909. The following year he married a titled young lady named Baroness Olga von Nordenflycht, and from then until 1925 Kaltenborn worked at the *Eagle* as reporter, drama critic, editor, and high-level tour guide, conducting groups to various national parks and foreign countries.

Insatiably curious, multilingual, widely read and traveled, Kaltenborn was a natural lecturer, and his tours had made him fairly well known by the time he went into radio—first for a series of weekly broadcasts over WEAF, then for WOR. When the *Eagle,* in an economy move, decided it could dispense with Kaltenborn's relatively high-priced services, he moved over to the CBS-owned New York station, WABC, where he was paid $50 apiece for two weekly broadcasts. It was characteristic of the man that he brought the mannerisms of the lecture platform into the studio: although there was no one but the engineer to see him, he would sit at the microphone with his right hand supporting his chin and cheek, as though posing for a portrait, while he gestured with the left hand to his unseen audience.

An imposing figure with a fringe of white hair surrounding his bald head, he dressed in striped trousers, black coat, and a vest trimmed with white piping. All in all, he was an impressive individual, and his broad knowledge of world affairs and his undeflatable confidence got him interviews with the world's great—including Hitler and Mussolini—not often granted to radio men. Kaltenborn was also something of a health nut at a time when there weren't many around, and his regimen of exercise would have worn out an ordinary mortal—daily swimming and workouts at the New York Athletic Club, followed by a brisk rubdown; long and invigorating walks; constant rounds of tennis (he never traveled anywhere without racket and sneakers). Friends who were invited for a weekend at Hans and Olga's country place knew what to expect; the occasions were referred to as "gymkhanas."

Kaltenborn's continuing presence in Studio Nine during September 1938 was a reflection, in part, of the intense rivalry that existed between the only existing networks of the day—NBC's Red and Blue systems, and CBS. The latter was both underdog and challenger, since NBC had most of the powerful stations, two networks in operation, the leading stars, and a gold-studded list of sponsors before CBS even existed. As late as 1933, in fact, when Franklin Roosevelt was being wheeled into the White House studio to deliver a "fireside chat," he noticed a microphone with three unfamiliar letters on it and inquired, "What's the CBS for?" But largely because of the temperament and interests of the chief of its news department, Paul White, change was in the air, and the people at CBS had begun to realize that radio was a medium that could handle news in ways that newspapers never could, by bringing events—as they were happening—into the homes of America. (It was on White's insistence that Kaltenborn, covering the 1932 political conventions, first used a lapel microphone for interviewing delegates on the floor of the hall.)

In the words of a colleague who worked closely with him, Paul White had "the greatest news sense of anyone I ever knew, but he was absolutely without morals. Why, he got kicked out of his college fraternity for cheating at cards." A heavyset, rumpled man with straight, sandy hair, White was erratic, brilliant, a heavy drinker, and driven by a desire to become a vice president at CBS—a title he was denied because the company executives considered him too unpolished ("roughneck" was the phrase used by his boss, Edward Klauber). A card game was usually in progress at the studio during slack periods, and White's associates, like his former fraternity brothers, were certain that he was cheating them; but they wrote it down to his fierce competitiveness and utter determination to win at whatever he did—which were the same qualities that were making NBC nervous about this time. Morals or no, White had the reporter's instinct, and when a story broke he had the thing pegged from beginning to end, knowing uncannily where and how NBC would cover it, sensing where and how CBS could position men to handle the story better. And in the mid-thirties he was already thinking about how CBS should deal with Europe's increasingly turbulent political scene.

Handling news was a tricky business for radio stations in those days. A good many of them were owned by local newspaper publishers, who thought, naturally enough—the profit motive being notably strong in them—that the stations ought to provide entertainment while the papers furnished news. Radio's inevitable inroads into the newspapers' circulation and advertising produced a series of skirmishes between the two media, and for a time the wire services—AP, UP, and INS—refused to provide radio stations with news bulletins. Then a compromise of sorts was reached, and by 1938 something called the Radio-Press Bureau was supplying broadcasters with news items, but hardly on advantageous terms. In the first place, the stations had to agree that no more than thirty words would be devoted to any one story on the air; in the second, they were limited to two five-minute news programs a day—one in the morning and one in the evening, both scheduled to come on the air after late editions of the papers were on the streets.

With the exception of a few commentators like Kaltenborn, Boake Carter, Lowell Thomas, and Raymond Gram Swing, who injected their own views and personalities into their analyses, radio news was thus pretty well confined to a recitation of headlines, the assumption being that people could find the details in their local papers. But more ambitious thoughts were percolating in the back of Paul White's mind. Early in the thirties CBS had established a London office as a base for a skeletal European organization, and it got a test of sorts in 1936, when the Spanish Civil War broke out. Kaltenborn, who was vacationing in Europe, hustled off to Spain to deal with the story; paying his own travel and living expenses, he arranged for a shortwave circuit via Paris and London to New York, and succeeded in making the first live broadcast of a battle, complete with the rattle of gunfire in the background. Hans had located a spot alongside a haystack from which he could see and hear the fighting near Irun, and when everything was in readiness he made contact with New York—only to be told that he (and the battle, presumably) would have to wait until two sponsored programs were broadcast. Since everything that went on the air was live, Kaltenborn had to wait patiently beside his haystack until some unsold air time came up, and only then began broadcasting. After this experience he got into Madrid, where the Republican forces were besieged by Franco, and reported from the cellar of a house from which the bombs could be heard exploding. He was then fifty-eight years old.

At the end of the summer of 1937, White put Kaltenborn on a Sunday-evening show called *Headlines and By-lines,* on which Robert Trout dealt with the news and H.V. handled the bylines, or interpretations, and between them they made an effective team—Trout relaxed and easygoing, using the microphone conversationally, as if it were a telephone; Kaltenborn all business, crisp and precise, issuing Jovian pronouncements. (At about this time an announcer had introduced H.V. with the statement that he would now give his "keen analysis of the news." The phrase stuck, and eventually got to be a joke around the studio, where Kaltenborn was known, behind his back, as "Keenan.") As the winter wore on, however, the suspicion grew among old hands in the newsroom that White wasn't certain how he was going to use Hans; there didn't appear to be a real place for him in the organization, and a rumor circulated that Kaltenborn might not be around much longer. Adolf Hitler put an end to that speculation.

In a sense, the Austrian crisis of 1938 gave White and his staff their first opportunity to show what they could do. The year before, White had sent twenty-nine-year-old Edward R. Murrow to London as European director (a prospect, Trout recalled, about which Murrow was gloomy, since he saw himself as an up-and-coming executive at CBS and felt that he would be out of things in London). Murrow, who had worked summers in a logging camp before graduating Phi Beta Kappa from Washington State College, had been president of the National Student Federation and assistant director of the Institute of International Education before coming to CBS in 1935 as Director of Talks. Part of his job in London was to arrange radio coverage of special events like the coronation of George VI, speeches by members of Parliament and other public figures, and performances by children's choirs—all in the name of "international understanding"—and before long he was giving Americans the true flavor of English thinking with such programs as "Experiences of a London Cabby and Impressions of Americans by Herbert Hodge," or a talk to the English-Speaking Union by Anthony Eden which the BBC had declined to broadcast. In 1938, after discussing with William Paley, the head of CBS, the unfortunate dearth of radio news, Murrow was authorized to recruit a staff to cover European events, and his first acquisition was a down-on-his-luck American correspondent named William L. Shirer, who had learned to his dismay that the news service for which he worked had collapsed just when his wife found out that she was to have her first baby. It was Murrow's notion—a novelty for radio in those days—to hire reporters, not announcers, and the Austrian Anschluss gave him a chance to put the theory into practice.

After witnessing the takeover of Austria, Shirer was thrown out of Vienna by the Nazis, but Murrow—who was in Warsaw arranging concerts to be broadcast on *The School of the Air*—managed to get into the city a few days later and was there when Paul White phoned Shirer in London, telling him to arrange an overseas "news roundup." He wanted reports from London, Paris, Rome, Berlin, and Vienna, and he wanted the program on the air at 8:00 P.M. Sunday, which was only eight hours away. Between them, Murrow and Shirer corralled the *Chicago Daily News* correspondent Edgar Ansel Mowrer in Paris, Shirer's journalist friend Pierre Huss in Berlin, an MP named Ellen Wilkinson in London, and the INS's Frank Gervasi in Rome; hired engineers; somehow leased five separate shortwave transmitters and had them hooked up; timed the individual broadcasts so that they would be received consecutively in New York; and miraculously, by 1:00 A.M. on Monday—8:00 in the evening, New York time—they were ready. That Sunday night, March 13, 1938, the first roundup of news from Europe's capitals was heard in America. Radio had become a genuine news medium.

During the summer the two young men from CBS scurried from one European city to another lining up journalists in order to be ready for the denouement, and when the New York office turned down Murrow's suggestion of regular broadcasts from Prague after the Anschluss, Shirer began shuttling back and forth between the Czech capital and Berlin. For reasons of its own, NBC decided to play down the story, and not until Hitler's September 12 speech did that network expand its coverage as CBS had done.

When the Czech crisis broke six months later, CBS was better prepared and planned to cover the story in an entirely new manner. Network executives had decided that no other scheduled broadcast would be permitted to interfere with coverage of this important event; everything, as Kaltenborn said, "was swept out of the way and kept out of the way." Programs were to be interrupted with bulletins at any hour of day or night; no commercials would intrude on the coverage. And to the format of the previous news roundups, another ingredient had been added in the person of H. V. Kaltenborn, who would interpret the flow of news as it came into the studio.

What gave Kaltenborn an edge over everyone else just then was his knowledge of the world, his familiarity with Europe's political scene, his personal acquaintance with men like Hitler, Mussolini, and Daladier, and his fluency in languages, which enabled him to translate and interject comments while a foreign spokesman was talking in his own tongue. Kaltenborn began speaking one minute after Hitler's speech of September 12 ended and—except for those times when no news was being received from Europe—never stopped until the crisis was over on October 2, by which time he had made 102 separate broadcasts, some lasting as long as two hours. Quite apart from the endurance it required, what made the performance so remarkable was that it was entirely extemporaneous; never during that time did he have a prepared script, rarely did he consult a note other than the news bulletin that was shoved in front of him. As Abe Schechter, the head of NBC News, claimed ruefully, you could wake H.V. out of a sound sleep at 4:00 A.M., say one word—"Czechoslovakia"—and he would talk for thirty minutes on the subject.

CHAPTER 6

———◆———

"I propose to come over at once to see you ..."

In the wake of Hitler's speech—which Russian transmitters "jammed" to prevent its being heard in the USSR—the crisis deepened. Duff Cooper, recognizing that the address was "calculated to give trouble," believed the time for messages and words was past and proposed that the fleet be mobilized, but Chamberlain put off a decision for fear of the adverse publicity that might result. Each new day brought the sensation of a further slide toward the abyss, and woven into the texture of the deadly tale were threads of other stories—side effects of the main event on which attention was riveted.

Only a sensitive ear could detect, in the accounts of European refugees, the extent of human woe and terror and helplessness that lay behind their plight. For instance, it was announced on September 13 that the American consulate in Berlin was swamped with requests for visas by Jews and "other dissidents." Almost as an afterthought came word that the U.S. quota for German and Austrian immigrants was filled for the next two or three years and that no more would be admitted, even though the National Coordinating Committee alone was receiving five hundred letters a day from desperate people begging for sanctuary. The State Department was preoccupied with the presence of tens of thousands of Americans in Europe—most of them residents of foreign countries—and warned all tourists to head for home.

This despite the fact that Europe's ports were jammed with frantic people seeking passage on ships that were booked solid. A few prominent individuals were interviewed by reporters when they landed—including a number of congressmen and senators who prudently avoided comment on Europe's affairs until they checked with Washington. Pennsylvania's Senator Joseph Guffey, who had his mind on matters closer to home, felt obliged to urge a third term for Franklin Roosevelt, so that the president could complete what Guffey called "the salvage of the wreckage of the Coolidge-Hoover regime." A group of 325 British steelmen who had planned to visit industrial plants in this country decided that it would be inadvisable to leave England because of the international situation, and canceled their trip. And Lotte Lehmann, the Metropolitan Opera singer, filed papers for U.S. citizenship, saying she was eager to forget everything she knew about Germany and the rest of Europe. "I'd like to take the American flag and wave it," she shouted fervently.

From London it was reported that U.S. ambassador Joseph Kennedy and his wife had sent their youngest children to southern Ireland "in order to be away from any possible bombings in England," and bald Lord Runciman, returning to England from his unhappy mission in Czechoslovakia, admitted that the situation was extremely delicate; "Everything is on the knees of the gods," he declared. If the gods were angry, few political or spiritual leaders seemed to know how to propitiate them, and in Rome, His Holiness Pope Pius XII was content merely to catechize himself. Gas masks were being distributed in Prague, Europe's Jews were running for shelter, queues of frantic people lined the street in front of foreign consulates in Berlin, women and children were being evacuated from Paris by train, while Pius mused about totalitarianism. "No," he observed solemnly, "the church is not for such a doctrine. But neither is it for the exact reverse."

By midafternoon on September 13 the New York stock market was behaving badly enough to warrant a special bulletin of its own: a huge volume of sell orders had driven prices down as much as six points (this when the *New York Times* average of fifty stocks was only 100), and the tape ran five minutes late. The smart money was rushing into wheat, the flow of gold from England was up sharply, there was gloom in London and "near-panic" in Swiss exchanges, bond prices tumbled, and marine insurance rates were suspended by American underwriters. Within a day or two, Secretary of the Treasury Henry Morgenthau found it necessary to comment on the unprecedented volume of foreign money coming into the United States—mostly in the form of gold shipments, in a "rush to the dollar"—and for the next two weeks the securities and commodities markets behaved like yo-yos, up with one piece of news, down with the next.

By telephone from the Mayo Clinic, where he remained at his son's bedside, Franklin Roosevelt conferred with Secretary of State Cordell Hull, but no comment was forthcoming about the situation—nor would there be for a week to come. The president and his confidant Harry Hopkins had listened to Hitler's speech in FDR's private railroad car on a siding in Rochester, Minnesota; concluding that Hitler meant to go to war, Roosevelt told Hopkins to go out to the West Coast and have a look at the aircraft industry there. He wanted to know what its potential for war production might be. Hopkins made a secret survey and reported to his chief, and soon afterward the president startled everyone by stating that the armed forces ought to have eight thousand airplanes. The upshot, Hopkins wrote, was that "everybody in the Army and Navy and all the newspapers in the country jumped on him." Not quite everybody, as a matter of fact; a few army officers recognized that the WPA administrator had the commander in chief's ear as no one else did, and shortly after Hopkins returned to Washington the deputy chief of staff, a brigadier general named George C. Marshall, called on him to talk about the needs of the army, which he believed was being starved to death. Since no money was forthcoming from Congress for national defense, Marshall wanted to know if Hopkins—as chief of the Works Progress Administration—could find a way to transfer secretly any of his agency's relief funds into machine tools for making small-arms ammunition. Hopkins could and did, and this one move, according to a colonel attached to Marshall's staff, "put the production of small arms ammunition at least a year ahead. . . ."

On September 14, fighting broke out between Czech soldiers and Sudeten Germans near the town of Eger, and subsequent reports indicated that as many as forty people had been killed in a bloody skirmish near Schwaderbach. Hitler met with his military and political advisers in Berchtesgaden; France prepared to call up two million reservists—bringing its armed strength up to four million; and Tokyo and Rome warned that they would stand beside Germany in the event of war.

Much reliance was placed by Americans on the opinions of putative military experts, who claimed to have special knowledge of the situation. Pertinax (the pseudonym used by French journalist André Geraud) had an inside story on Germany's Rhineland fortifications: they were so inadequate, he said, that when Hitler inspected them two weeks earlier "so keen was his disappointment he was unable to control himself and he burst into a hysterical fit, insulting the officers around him." A retired French army general named Brissaud-Desmaillet, interviewed at the Hotel Waldorf-Astoria in New York, stated that Germany's tanks were worthless, as the Spanish Civil War had shown; Hitler's strength lay in his air force. What was coming, he declared, was not a conflict between large armies, navies, and air forces, but an "industrial war" in which the United States clearly had the real potential strength. Noting that an estimated two million soldiers were under arms in Germany, France, and Czechoslovakia, another authority ventured to suggest that France would attack Germany first in the event of an emergency, striking through the Black Forest toward the headwaters of the Danube in order to isolate Munich, cut off Austria, and bring aid to the Czechs.

Writing in the *Times,* Colonel Frederick Palmer, who was described as a "Famous War Correspondent" (his fame dating back to the Greco-Turkish War of the 1890s), observed that even if the Czechs were forced to fight alone, Hitler was in "for a staggering surprise." Officers at the U.S. War College had told him that "a host of dead" Germans would pile up in the mountain passes before they ever reached the Czech heartland, and Palmer confirmed the French view that the performance of German tanks in Spain had been a complete failure. The Luftwaffe's planes, he added, were inferior to Russian and U.S. models; German artillery was still largely horse-drawn; the German army itself was untried and "immensely inferior in numbers, arms, and training to that of 1914"; and, as if that were not enough, the German nation itself was under severe economic strain.

Publicly, at least, the Czechs were optimistic about their chances. They assured newsmen that their defenses were stronger even than the Maginot Line: machine-gun nests were artfully concealed in haystacks, antitank traps lay in wait for the invader, all important bridges were mined, supplies and munitions were concealed in the forests, and the Czech air force was poised to launch attacks from secret airstrips.

When Charles Edison, the assistant secretary of the navy, was interviewed by reporters, he told them that the naval expansion program begun in 1933 had put the United States in an excellent position to meet any foreseeable emergency. Describing the "magnificent armada" in being and on the way, he announced that some $750 million worth of ships were under construction (if foreign governments were interested, Edison thoughtfully provided a list of the shipyards where each capital ship was being built), and he noted that during the past year six light cruisers, two aircraft carriers, five submarines, and twenty-one destroyers had been commissioned. (In case any future enemy wondered about the whereabouts of *these* vessels, their movements were regularly reported with the shipping news in the *New York Times.*)

From what one could discern, the United States Army was in no such state of readiness as Edison's navy. Out at Fort Knox, Kentucky, Major General Hugh Drum's Second Army was holding maneuvers, and the "Blue" Army, defending the industrial Midwest, had counterattacked the "Black" Army and thrown it back after a terrific assault by planes, tanks, and mortars. The catch to all this was that almost no real troops or weapons were being used. As Drum explained, it was merely a "command-post exercise," executed by five hundred regular army and National Guard officers, under the supervision of men experienced in high command in the World War ("General Drum is one of the few of these left," an army press release added helpfully). Drum, who had endured two decades of pinch-penny peacetime budgets, called attention to the economies achieved by this type of exercise. Just to assemble enough troops for war games of this sort, he estimated, would cost $400,000; but by employing only five hundred officers and two thousand troops ("to help in the details"), the cost to the taxpayer would be held down to $50,000. It was further reported that after a full, trying day in the field, General Drum had been induced by a group of "war correspondents" to take time off from the fighting for an evening's celebration of his fifty-ninth birthday.

———

Other voices filtered through the talk of war from time to time. Grover Whalen, president of the New York World's Fair Corporation, was plunging ahead with plans for a lavish exposition in 1939, announcing, among other attractions, a huge style show focusing on American *haute couture* that would be held in an igloo seventy feet high; a Japanese pavilion that would be a replica of a 300 B.C. Shinto shrine, its white stucco walls ornamented with red lacquer and gold, and surrounded by a peaceful veranda harboring Japanese gardens, pools, a waterfall, trees, and ornamental shrubs. But even where ebullience was the watchword, the inevitable somber note intruded. Whalen made public the texts of letters from such luminaries as Albert Einstein, Thomas Mann, and Robert Millikan that would be sealed in a five-thousand-year "time capsule" buried at the Fair. Einstein, reflecting on what he ought to tell someone reading his message fifty centuries hence, observed that "anyone who thinks about the future must live in fear and terror."

Other citizens—less philosophical than the brilliant Jewish scientist who had left Germany in 1933—were pondering the future and what role the United States should play in it, and had arrived at more practicable conclusions. A Texas congressman named Martin Dies, chairman of the House Committee for the Investigation of Un-American Activities, had a vision of tomorrow that was frequently obscured by a red haze. He had already made up his mind to drive out of the federal government such subversive characters as Secretary of Interior Harold Ickes, Secretary of Labor Frances Perkins, and the president's right-hand man Harry Hopkins, as well as other "communists and fellow travelers," and to this end he was conducting an investigation into the New Deal's Works Progress Administration. Among the witnesses to appear before his committee was one Edwin P. Banta, described as an "elderly man of Colonial ancestry, who was a communist until fifteen days ago." Mr. Banta had many a lurid tale to tell of Hopkins's WPA, including the fact that the Communist Party had a grip on 40 percent of the workers in the Federal Writers' Project. Some, he said, were *agents provocateurs* in various civil liberties fights (including one in Jersey City which had recently resulted in the arrest of Socialist Norman Thomas); others were recruiters for the Spanish Loyalists, and Banta predicted that when American volunteers returned from service in Spain they planned to form cadres on which to build a "Red army" in the United States.

Another scheme was fermenting in Dies's mind, and he planned to announce in a few days' time a "league for peace and Americanism." According to him, the idea had its genesis in thousands of letters he had received from patriotic Americans supporting such a program, and he predicted that five million citizens would enroll in the organization, pledged to combating subversion wherever it might be found. Nazism, fascism, and communism were high on his list of priorities, and Dies had thrown in a good many other targets, to keep the pot boiling. The organization would support strict neutrality, adequate national defense, and stronger immigration and deportation laws, while defending the independence of Congress, the judicial system, and the executive department. As for how all this was to be accomplished, Dies did not specify.

Predictably, Europe's seething caldron had unleashed the voices of isolationism in the land, and Senator Gerald P. Nye of North Dakota, who had made a name for himself as head of another Senate investigating committee, concluded that it was time to issue a warning to the nation. Nye's particular committee had probed, in 1934, the machinations of munitions makers in this country and, to the accompaniment of considerable publicity, revealed that America's entry into the World War had been the result of a plot between arms manufacturers and the bankers who financed their operations. Now, seizing upon the prediction of one of Roosevelt's cabinet members that the United States would remain "aloof" from foreign entanglement, Nye proceeded to cite a number of factors that he considered dangerous in the present circumstances. First was that "quarantine" speech of the president's in 1937, which had raised the hackles and blood pressure of every isolationist in the country; another was what he termed "undue military preparedness"—a remark inspired by Secretary Edison's recent statement about the U.S. Navy; still another was the extent of foreign holdings in domestic security markets; and finally he made reference to the sinister cooperation between the government in Washington and "certain European powers" (all unnamed) and their current diplomatic maneuvering.

New York's Representative Hamilton Fish, speaking on the radio, appealed to Americans to oppose the administration's "war commitments" and secret agreements "for concerted action, or parallel action, to police and quarantine foreign nations" which Roosevelt had advocated in his "hysterical and inflammatory Chicago speech"—an address Fish also characterized as "a fire bell in the night." On September 18, Constitution Day was observed in New York City in a drizzling rain, and the keynote speaker called on the nation not to shed the blood of its youth again, even though war might erupt in Europe. (In her newspaper column, "My Day," Eleanor Roosevelt described how she opened each morning's paper with a feeling of dread and turned on the radio for the final news broadcast of the night "half afraid to hear that the catastrophe of war has again fallen on Europe. . . . It seems insanity to me to try to settle the difficult problems of today by the unsatisfactory method of going to war. If you kill half the youth of a continent, the problem will be no nearer a solution, but the human race will be that much poorer." By "continent," the president's wife meant Europe: she was no isolationist, but she was not contemplating American involvement.)

The activities of Nye and Fish were not the only signs of restiveness among the amorphous group that had come to be called isolationists. Several organizations—including Keep America Out of War, the Labor Anti-War Council, and the National Council for Prevention of War—were petitioning Roosevelt to make known his position on the trouble in Europe, but FDR was not only keeping his own counsel, he had gone so far as to request that reporters not ask him questions about the foreign crisis, in order to help "keep the ship on an even keel." That sort of appeal might go down with members of the working press, but as Roosevelt knew, it was not going to keep the isolationists quiet.

There were signs that other factions in the country were thinking about taking sides, although as yet the most positive stand had been taken by a group claiming to represent the million and a half Czechs in the United States, who pledged their aid and support to the homeland. Out in Los Angeles, New York's peppery little mayor, Fiorello La Guardia, addressed the American Legion convention, and, in a seven-minute speech interrupted frequently by cheers and applause, asked the veterans to stand behind the national government no matter what policy it adopted toward Germany, France, and Great Britain. On the face of it, that seemed neutral enough, but the Legionnaires already knew La Guardia's sentiments on the matter; the day after Hitler's speech in Munich, he had made a much-publicized pronouncement to the effect that the German dictator had gone berserk, "lost all sense of proportion and reason," and should be taken into custody.

———

Whatever they might portend, these expressions of opinion were no more than variations on the central, overpowering theme of approaching doom that was being played continuously by the nation's press and radio. No sooner had the public begun to absorb the implications of Hitler's speech than another electrifying piece of news broke. At 4:16 P.M. on September 14, CBS interrupted a program with a special bulletin: "Prime Minister Chamberlain," the announcer stated, "has announced that he will fly to Germany tomorrow to meet Chancellor Hitler at Berchtesgaden in a final effort to head off European war."

The initial reaction—echoed in the *New York Times'* description of the plan as a "magnificent gamble for the highest stake in the world"—was one of astonishment and euphoria. As might have been expected, Britain's poet laureate, John Masefield, produced a solemn verse, complete with classical references, in homage to the occasion:

As Priam to Achilles for his son,
So you, into the night, divinely led,
To ask that young men's bodies, not yet dead,
Be given from the battle not begun.

After the initial rejoicing came second thoughts, and with them reasonable doubts. In the words of the British general Sir Hastings Ismay, "For the next fortnight . . . the whole world held its breath." After all, this latter-day Priam was in his seventieth year, he was none too well, and he had never made an airplane flight before (in the excitement over departure, he had left his umbrella at No. 10 Downing Street and a special car had to deliver it to him at the airport). Yet here he was, risking his nervous system, his position, and his nation's prestige to go, hat in hand, a petitioner, into the lion's den, making a dramatic gesture that might already be too late. (There were those, like Kaltenborn, who were reminded of an unhappy analogy—that ill-starred visit to Berchtesgaden by little Chancellor Schuschnigg, which had proved to be the end of both Schuschnigg and his country.) For all the doubts, however, one had to admire Chamberlain's courage, and for the first time people felt a warmth and affection for the aloof, frosty man who was such an unlikely popular hero. "Good old Neville!" they were saying in the pubs and clubs of London, wondering what in the world had ever given the fellow the idea.

In fact, what lay behind the decision was the prime minister's vision of himself as savior of the peace. He had concluded that he was the one man capable of preserving it at this particular moment in history. There was nothing wrong with that, intrinsically—certainly no leader of a government had tried to have private conversations with the leader of another country in order to prevent the World War. The trouble with this sort of self-indulgence was the unfortunate effect it had on the ego, especially when the man had a naive contempt for his adversary. "Is it not positively horrible," he wrote, "to think that the fate of hundreds of millions depends on one man, and he is half mad?"

Certainly Chamberlain was under no illusions as to Britain's ability to salvage the situation by military means. "You only have to look at the map," he wrote his sister, "to see that nothing France or we could do, could possibly save Czechoslovakia from being overrun by the Germans." Lacking the power to "beat [Germany] to her knees in a reasonable time," he had abandoned any idea of giving guarantees to Czechoslovakia or to France in connection with her obligations to that unhappy land. If Czechoslovakia was to be saved, in short, it required a fresh, innovative approach, and he believed he had one. During the weeks of gathering crisis, racking his brain for a solution, Chamberlain had conceived of a plan "so unconventional and daring that it rather took Halifax's breath away" when he first mentioned it to his colleague. It just might "save the situation at the 11th hour," the prime minister thought; besides which, it possessed the elements of high drama and personal glory that were bound to appeal to a man who had never experienced either. Sometime about the first of September, Neville Chamberlain had decided to meet personally with Adolf Hitler, and then stored the idea away, waiting for the right moment to spring it.

In the back of his mind was a belief that all that was needed to resolve this highly charged situation was a voice of common sense, above-average intelligence, and reasonableness—that is, his own. Surely he could make it clear to the German chancellor what he risked by bulling ahead with his plans. Surely, he thought, British decency and plain-speaking, backed by a long tradition of superior diplomatic skill, would triumph and this whole nasty business would simmer down. One might have thought that the king's first minister was dealing with a rather powerful, rude, and not very bright Hottentot chieftain.

So the plan was hatched and a telegram went off to the Führer: "I propose to come over at once to see you with a view to trying to find a peaceful solution." Hitler read the message, exclaimed, *"Ich bin vom Himmel gefallen!"* (which translated roughly as "Good heavens!"), and Chamberlain, "aloof, reserved, imperturbable, unshakably self-reliant," as one of his fellow travelers portrayed him, umbrella in hand, accompanied by two advisers—Sir Horace Wilson and William Strang[1]—a Scotland Yard detective, a secretary, ham sandwiches, whisky, beer, and a thermos of tea, boarded a little eight-seater British Airways plane at Heston airport and departed, as one Englishman described it, with the bright faith of a curate entering a pub for the first time. Only a handful of Britons knew that the first leg of the PM's four-hour flight to Germany was being tracked by a secret scanning device invented by Robert Watson-Watt. He had begun work on it during the World War, as an instrument for studying weather, and so successful was he that now—as Chamberlain departed—a chain of the devices, which would become known as radar, was being installed along the coast to warn the RAF of approaching enemy aircraft.

Ambassador Henderson and Germany's foreign minister, Joachim von Ribbentrop, met the British party at the Munich airport, and they drove up the long, winding road toward Hitler's aerie, past solid ranks of black-uniformed SS troops, with Wilson wondering to himself whether they would ever come out of this thing alive. Hitler met them on the steps of the Berghof, his mountain residence, and as Wilson glanced at the Führer's plain brown military tunic it occurred to him that he looked "like a draper's assistant."[2] The first order of business was tea before the fireplace, and

[1]Writing years later, Strang observed: "It can fairly be said of Neville Chamberlain that he was not well versed in foreign affairs, that he had no touch for a diplomatic situation, that he did not fully realize what it was he was doing, and that his naive confidence in his own judgment and powers of persuasion and achievement was misplaced."

[2]It was a not uncommon reaction by upper-class Britons. At a reception in 1937, Lord Halifax had mistaken Hitler for a footman and was on the verge of handing him his hat when the German foreign minister whispered frantically, *"Der Führer! Der Führer!"*

Wilson stole further glances at the German chancellor. "I didn't like his eyes," he said. "I didn't like his mouth; in fact, there wasn't very much I did like about him." After twenty minutes of chitchat, Chamberlain suggested to Hitler (who as yet had not the vaguest idea what the Englishman had in mind) that the two of them talk privately, and they disappeared with an interpreter into the Führer's study. For three hours after the "somewhat macabre tea party," their aides sat in the reception room, talking "the small-talk of statesmen whose only point of contact is an international emergency cynically created by one and stoically grappled with by the other," in William Strang's words, getting up now and then to stand by the window and peer into the wet mist that had closed off the view.

In the study, the conversation went badly for the British prime minister. He found the dictator mercurial—calm one moment, emotional the next, enraged whenever the despised Czechs and Beneš were mentioned; and at such moments Chamberlain tried to calm him by interjecting, "This business of the Sudeten Germans isn't really our affair, you know," or "But look here, I am a practical man," or "I have often found that when the events were subjected to closer scrutiny it often turned out that things weren't as bad as they seemed." When the one-sided discussion ended, Chamberlain had made almost none of the points he and his advisers had concocted so carefully for the occasion. He agreed to the Sudeten Germans' right to self-determination and acquiesced—pending consultation with his cabinet and the French—in the cession of the Sudetenland to Germany.

Back in London, a smiling prime minister told reporters at the airport of his "frank but friendly talk" with the German chancellor, added that they were going to meet again, and beyond that gave no details of what had been decided. Huge crowds lined the streets between Heston airport and London, waving hats and handkerchiefs and cheering as he drove past. Closeted with his cabinet ministers at last, he revealed that he had found Hitler "the commonest little dog" (Winston Churchill preferred the term "guttersnipe"), but was nevertheless pleased with the way he had been received. To the dismay of several ministers, he had "got the impression that here was a man who could be relied upon when he had given his word." That night American listeners heard Ed Murrow describe the excitement and sense of relief that had greeted the prime minister's return; from a vantage point overlooking No. 10 Downing Street he interviewed Sir Frederick Whyte, a British journalist, who summed up the reaction of Londoners. "Well," they seemed to be saying, "if the Czechs don't like the plebiscite, Czechoslovakia is perhaps really not worth the worrying over. If the Czechs have got to swallow something they don't like, maybe that's the necessary price to pay for preserving peace." Some outspoken critics said bluntly that Chamberlain and Britain had been had; supporters of the government refused to acknowledge that the prime minister had been given an ultimatum, saying that he had merely accepted the realities of the situation and put off trouble until a later day. As one of them remarked, "It is better to have smallpox three years from now than at once." After all, if the French could not support Czechoslovakia, Britain could hardly be expected to do so, and surely the country could not be asked to go to war merely to prevent a few Germans from joining their fellow citizens.

The Chamberlain cabinet was divided, Halifax arguing that it was indefensible to hand over to Hitler—along with the Sudeten Germans—several hundred thousand Czechs, Jews, and other anti-Nazis who lived in the territory to be ceded. Duff Cooper pointed out that the keystone of British policy was, and had been for generations, to prevent any single power from dominating Europe. Now that they faced a most formidable foe, resistance was more than ever essential, and it was not a question of fighting for Czechoslovakia any more than Britain had gone to war over Serbia in 1914. Another faction demanded that Britain make no binding commitment beyond the Rhine—an action that would be inimical to British tradition, instinct, and self-interest. Underlying all the arguments, of course, was a relatively simple set of premises. Either Britain could fight or it could not. If it could not, then the Chamberlain government should admit that it had neglected the nation's defenses and had never had any business even intimating that it would stand up to Hitler. But that far no official was willing to go. Meanwhile, Daladier and Bonnet were coming to London, and a slim hope persisted that somehow the French might suggest a way out.

All in vain. That meeting between British and French was the beginning of the end of the Munich crisis; and the Munich crisis, as someone observed at the time, was "when the end of our world began." Daladier—who was described by the correspondent Vincent Sheean as "a dirty man with a cigarette stuck to his lower lip, stinking of absinthe, talking with a rough Marseillais accent"—began by speaking in a trembling voice of honor and obligations and finished by admitting that France was powerless; his country had exactly twenty-one airplanes that were roughly equal to late models in Germany's huge Luftwaffe. Chamberlain confessed that Britain had no army that could march to Czechoslovakia—had, in fact, only two divisions that could be sent to France in the event of war. It was agreed by all those present that any aid that might be forthcoming from Russia would be doubtful in quantity and quality, and from the United States would come only "impotent emotionalism." (Chamberlain had concluded, "It is always best and safest to count on nothing from the Americans but words.") The Czechs, it was supposed, might hold out alone for a month, but then what aid could be given them? At the last, Chamberlain put the ultimate question to Daladier and Bonnet. Would France be willing to go it alone? In the words of an eyewitness who described the scene as tactfully as possible, the French premier was "unable to answer boldly in the affirmative."

So there it was. On September 19 a joint British-French communiqué announced that a "way out" had been found: the two nations would accept Hitler's demands and ask President Beneš to surrender the Sudetenland to Germany. The public response to this news, according to the *Times* of

London, which had been the staunchest supporter of appeasement all along, was "instant and universal welcome," and the decision was hailed as an "equitable and honorable settlement by consent."

What consent the Czechs may have given came as a surprise to the president of that unfortunate country, who immediately labeled the British-French accord a betrayal. Czechoslovakia was reduced to the elementary position of a man confronted by an armed burglar, Beneš said, and the choice was to fight or be robbed. His nation would fight.

Meanwhile, the French cabinet approved the plan, Parisians rejoiced at the news, and Bonnet met with the Czech minister, Dr. Stefan Osusky, to tell him the hard facts of life. An hour and a half later Osusky emerged from the Quai d'Orsay looking drawn and haggard, and would say only to reporters, "My country has been condemned without a hearing."

In London, thousands of people filed past the black stone slab in Westminster Abbey that marked the resting place of Britain's Unknown Soldier. Middle-aged women knelt by the grave to give thanks for peace, and a special day of prayer was held in churches throughout Great Britain. But Downing Street knew no tranquillity. Mounted police were summoned to keep anti-Nazi demonstrators from moving closer to the prime minister's residence, inside which the leader of the British government was contemplating a note just received from Jan Masaryk, the Czech minister to Britain, who informed Chamberlain that his country would not be a party to any arrangement negotiated in its absence. Instead of a solution, it appeared, the dramatic flight to Berchtesgaden had succeeded only in producing a new crisis, and in some quarters there was a rising cry of "Shame!"

The Soviet Union charged Britain with using Czechoslovakia "as small change in striking a bargain with Hitler," and called the Berchtesgaden meeting "a betrothal to fascist Germany." In Washington, Harold Ickes recorded in his diary Franklin Roosevelt's reaction: "The President," he wrote, "thinks that Chamberlain is for peace at any price. Britain and France, in the President's graphic language, 'will wash the blood from their Judas Iscariot hands.' " Yet, as H. V. Kaltenborn noted, "Mighty America refuses to speak. We are primarily concerned in keeping out of war." What neither Ickes nor Kaltenborn knew was that Mr. Roosevelt was doing his level best to stiffen Chamberlain's resolve, through an offer of personal assistance. While the British and French awaited the Czechs' decision, the president met secretly with the British ambassador, Sir Ronald Lindsay, to tell him what he thought of what was going on and to volunteer some suggestions. What the Allies were asking of Czechoslovakia, FDR said, was the most terrible of sacrifices—one that would provoke a highly unfavorable reaction in the States. Yet he thought it unwise to condemn Germany's actions publicly for fear of encouraging Czech resistance, which could only result in the sacrifice of thousands of lives.

What he proposed—and here he impressed upon Lindsay that he would be impeached if word of it leaked—was that if the Allies called a conference of heads of states in order to discuss a settlement of the Czech crisis, he, Roosevelt, would attend—*provided* that the meeting was not held in Europe, but in the Azores or another Atlantic island. Obviously, the president hoped to encourage Chamberlain to stand up to Hitler, but when Lindsay received no reply to what he considered a momentously important cable describing Roosevelt's offer, he sent another message to the Foreign Office suggesting how "useful" it would be to have "a friendly expression of appreciation." No reply of any kind was forthcoming.

Neville Chamberlain, stubbornly proud and pleased with what he considered his single-handed accomplishment of finding a solution to the Sudeten problem, began to fret and fume as the Czechs dragged their feet, doubtless hoping that public opinion in the west might alter the situation in their favor. Pressure from the Germans was mounting hourly; Hungary and Poland were clamoring for the return of *their* minority groups in Czechoslovakia; Mussolini, smelling opportunity, said he would not accept the plan for the Sudetenland unless the Hungarian demands were met; and Russian troops were said to be massing along the Rumanian and Polish borders. Chamberlain had already put off his second meeting with Hitler; he could wait no longer. He decided that pressure must be put on the Czechs, and in the early hours of September 21 the French and British envoys in Prague called upon President Beneš and presented him with what could only be described as an ultimatum from his allies. The terms accepted by their governments, the diplomats said, were the only possible means of avoiding war and a German invasion of Czechoslovakia. If Czechoslovakia refused them, she would bear sole responsibility for the consequences, and Beneš should know that if it came to war neither France nor Britain would come to Czechoslovakia's assistance. At that, all the fight went out of the proud old man. He would accept, he said. There was no longer any hope.

So Chamberlain was able to depart on his second journey to Germany, this time bearing a gift of Czechoslovakian territory in his outstretched hands. On September 22 he arrived in Godesberg, in the land of the Lorelei, to be met by a guard of honor and a band playing "God Save the King," and was ferried like an arthritic Rhine maiden across the river from his hotel to the Hotel Dreesen, to meet the German chancellor and tidy up the loose ends.

CHAPTER 7

———————◆———————

"Rain and cool today."

On September 15, while Neville Chamberlain and Adolf Hitler were conferring in Berchtesgaden, the barometer in Atlantic City was falling, and the southerly winds shifted to northerly, with a drop in temperature. The next day rain fell steadily, washing out the tennis matches at Forest Hills on Long Island. On the 17th the tennis was canceled again, and gloom spread in the locker room when three young men on the French team were called home for military service.

Rain fell on September 18 and 19, and the *New York Times,* predicting more of the same for the following day, noted that a "tropical disturbance" 240 miles in width was veering away from the Florida coast, heading northwest. This disturbance was actually a massive hurricane that had formed on September 4 west of the Cape Verde Islands and had rolled across the Atlantic, heading straight for Miami. Hurricanes characteristically become bigger and stronger the longer they travel over water, and this one had been gathering momentum over thousands of miles. On the evening of September 18 it was 900 miles at sea off the Florida coast; the next morning it was only 650 miles away; then the Weather Bureau in Jacksonville reported that it was moving north and would not hit Florida.

Near Cape Hatteras, the Cunard liner *Carinthia* with six hundred cruise passengers aboard was brushed by the storm and the captain reported that the ship's barometer fell one inch in an hour's time—hitting 27.85, one of the lowest readings ever recorded in Atlantic waters, which indicated the incredible power of the gale. Even an average hurricane releases in one day a quantity of energy equivalent to the electrical power used by the entire United States in six months, but this was no average storm.

On September 21, the New York weatherman predicted, "Rain and cool today. Tomorrow cloudy, probably rain." The tropical disturbance was expected to move in a northerly direction, "fairly well off the Atlantic seaboard," although strong winds could be anticipated between North Carolina and Massachusetts. As it turned out, the forecasters were tragically mistaken. In fairness, of course, the United States Weather Bureau of 1938 had no sophisticated tracking devices—basically, it relied on the barometer, thermometer, and weather vane, plus occasional voluntary reports from ships, airplanes, and isolated weather stations. Dr. James H. Kimball, the man in charge of the New York office of the Weather Bureau, said later that he had received only two reports on the storm after its sighting by the *Carinthia,* and that between 9:00 A.M. on September 21 and 3:00 that afternoon, when it was approaching Long Island, he got no reports at all. During these hours, the hurricane was racing from Cape Hatteras toward Long Island at a speed over the water of sixty-one miles per hour—three times the pace of the usual hurricane. What made this possible was the presence of two high-pressure areas, one on either side of the storm, which confined its path to a broad, inviting avenue of low pressure and warm humidity leading directly toward Long Island and New England. Surging along this path, sucking up heat and moisture and gathering even more strength, it approached the south shore of Long Island just at the time of the autumnal equinox, when the moon and sun were exerting maximum pull on the tides, making the level of the sea much higher than normal.

When it struck the coastline, the force of the impact registered on a seismograph in Alaska, and salt spray from the raging surf was carried as far north as Vermont, some two hundred miles away. Trees, chimneys, and church steeples in Long Island towns were the first to go; the walls of buildings collapsed; then whole buildings were carried away. At 3:40 P.M. the eye of the storm was over Great South Bay and for a few minutes the sun broke through the clouds; then the sky darkened again, and the rain and wind shifted from east to south (Long Islanders had assumed at first that the buffeting winds were those of a northeaster, so common at this time of year). Then the wild gale came on again and something thirty or forty feet high rolled in off the ocean "like a thick and high bank of fog," according to one survivor. "When it came closer we saw that it wasn't fog. It was water."

For an hour—until about 5:00 P.M.—the storm pummeled Long Island, sweeping everything in its path, leaving behind a trail of destruction such as no living man had seen. In the darkness huge seas piled over the tops of beach houses and highways, uprooting enormous trees, tossing automobiles and boats about like matchsticks. In Westhampton, 153 of the 179 houses on the ocean beach—including some thirty-room mansions—were swept away, and those that remained were left unfit to live in. Twenty-nine people died in the town, and some of the bodies were found miles from their homes.

On Fire Island, where they had spent the summer to avoid Washington's heat, Katherine Marshall, her daughter, her sister, and her husband's orderly, Sergeant Jones, were packing to leave for home when the front door blew open with a crash. That was the only warning they had that a storm was approaching. Their cottage was on a high ridge inland from the shoreline, and from the upstairs windows they watched those enormous black walls of water destroy the dunes along the beach and pour across the narrow island into Great South Bay, while the crushed wreckage of houses was sucked into the wild seas. In the evening the storm abated, and Jones somehow made his way to the local fire station for help and led the women from the cottage in water up to their waists. They were taken to an undamaged concrete cottage nearby, where they spent the night—the three women in one bed, Jones in another room—and in the morning Jones knocked on the door and called out, "Mrs. Marshall, I think the General is coming. I hear a plane."

Some time later the exhausted woman turned to see "a weird apparition" enter the room—a figure wearing a helmet, goggles, and what she took to be "some kind of deep-sea outfit." All she could do was stare; then she heard her husband's voice, saying, "Can't you speak? Say something!"

"Is it you?" she cried. "You are the most beautiful thing I ever saw in my life!"

At that the apparition turned and shouted, "Sergeant, order another hurricane."

On the way to his office that morning General George Marshall had seen a headline, "Fire Island Wiped Out"; he flew to Mitchell Field on Long Island, hired a small plane, and as the pilot circled over Fire Island saw to his immense relief that his wife's cottage was intact, though the nearby village of Saltaire had all but vanished—only six cottages remained and the surrounding area was a snarled mass of wreckage. They spotted a place to land on the beach, and the newly appointed war plans director of the United States Army ran off to try to find his wife.

———

Much of Manhattan and the Bronx was without power, subways were halted, the Hudson and Manhattan tubes were flooded, and in Westchester County it was estimated that at least ten thousand trees had been torn up by the roots. In the city, winds were clocked at seventy-five to one hundred miles an hour at the height of the storm; in passing, they tore to shreds the U.S. flag on top of the building where the Weather Bureau was located. That day 4.87 inches of rain fell on Manhattan, bringing the total for the past nine days to 8.54 inches.

Had New Englanders been warned by the Weather Bureau that a hurricane was coming they probably would not have believed it; the last one to strike that area had passed through in 1815. As luck would have it now, the summer of 1938 had been unusually wet, and the Connecticut River was already at flood stage because of that and September's heavy rains. Passing through the middle of Long Island, the center of the storm headed across the Sound and struck the Connecticut shore between Bridgeport and New Haven, went through Waterbury and Torrington, hit west of Hartford, and roared into the Berkshires beyond Springfield. Then the path led into central Vermont, across Lake Champlain, and on to Canada.

The great lyric soprano Alma Gluck was seriously ill at her Connecticut home, and when her daughter, the novelist Marcia Davenport, was unable to reach her by telephone, she was frantic, and decided to drive the ninety miles from Manhattan—a trip that ordinarily took about three hours. Nine hours later she arrived, after passing through unimaginable devastation: giant trees snapped in two, long sections of road entirely gone, bridges vanished or under water, houses completely destroyed, barns and crops ruined, the whole landscape a sodden mass of tree limbs, mud, water, and the wreckage of men's dreams. Each time she came to a barricade or a dead end in the highway she had to turn around and seek another route. She finally arrived to find her mother safe, but without electricity or telephone, and the two of them camped out in the house for several days, their only connection to the outside world a battery radio on which they tried to follow the news from Europe.

The *Hartford Courant* called September 21 the "most calamitous day" in Connecticut's history. New Haven was battered and dark, the elms of Yale torn up; the heart of New London was in smoking ruins; and along the shore it seemed that nothing remained but shattered houses and boats and broken trees. In New London a three-hundred-foot lighthouse tender lay on the railroad tracks, deposited there by the storm. An entire downtown block was in flames; a barkentine in the harbor had been blown ashore by the wind and the fire in the galley stove set ablaze the sailing vessel and all the nearby buildings. In the streets of Norwich, the waters of Long Island Sound and the Thames River lay eleven feet deep, and for days the isolated city had to be supplied with food and medicine by air. All but two of Stonington's fifty-five-vessel fishing fleet were destroyed. Just outside the town a New York, New Haven & Hartford passenger train had been stopped by a warning signal ahead, and while it was stalled one man looked out the window and watched a three-story house lift slowly from its foundation and float smoothly before the wind for fifty yards. The train's engineer decided to walk up the tracks to see why he was being held up, got out of the cab, and found himself in water up to his chest. Ahead, the track was blocked by the remains of a house and a cabin cruiser, but when he boarded the engine again the last six cars on the train had begun to sink, so the passengers were herded into the first car, one of the crewmen uncoupled the others, and the engineer opened the throttle, pushing the house and the cruiser ahead of him while he moved to higher ground.

Farther to the east, the hurricane struck Watch Hill, Rhode Island, and on Napatree Point, where thirty-nine cottages, a beach club, a yacht club, and an old stone fort had stood a few hours before, nothing was left but the fort, and forty-two people were carried away with the buildings. In Providence, waves six feet high careened through the center of the city, and a group of men looking out the third-floor window of a building watched in horror as an old man walking through the water threw up his hands and drowned. At the Blue Hill Observatory outside Boston the winds were clocked at 186 miles per hour—the same reading recorded atop Mount Washington in New Hampshire. While the storm roared north through the center of Vermont, fires raged all night in Peterboro, New Hampshire, casting a yellow glow on the flooded streets. At ten o'clock that night the storm center passed over Lake Champlain, went on to batter the city of Montreal, and whirled off toward northern Ontario, where it finally died.

Damage to crops and trees was incalculable. In the Connecticut River Valley, all the broadleaf tobacco harvest, hanging in the barns to dry, was ruined. Vermont lost its entire apple crop and two-thirds of its sugar maple trees; half of New Hampshire's white pine forest was destroyed; and the city of Springfield, Massachusetts, reported that sixteen thousand shade trees were down.

For days, most of New England was entirely cut off from the rest of the country, and the only way urgent messages could be dispatched to the Boston area was by radio from New York to London or Paris and then back to Cape Cod, which had fortunately escaped the worst of the storm. Because of the communications blackout, however, the enormity of the catastrophe did not begin to emerge until days after the storm was over; not until September 23 did the New York Times devote banner headlines to the story. Altogether, on Long Island and in New England, some thirteen million people lived in the path the storm had taken; off to the west, in New York and New Jersey, were six million others sufficiently removed to have escaped the same kind of destruction, but near enough to have felt the lashing winds and severe flood damage. Men and women were killed by falling trees, they were drowned, or they simply vanished, and on the morning after the storm, when only a fraction of the damage and loss of life could be calculated, the Associated Press reported that there were one hundred known dead and more than that number missing.

When the carnage was finally added up, it was believed that seven hundred people had died, 1,754 were injured, and 63,000 were homeless. The property damage, even at Depression prices, was said to be $382 million, but it did not end there. Many manufacturing concerns teetering on the edge of financial collapse simply closed their doors permanently rather than pay to rebuild their shattered plants.

———

All in all, September 21 had been a day of unmitigated disaster. Three thousand miles west of New York, Oscar Westover, the commanding general of the Army Air Corps, was killed when an attack plane in which he and a sergeant were flying crashed in flames in Burbank, California, yet H. V. Kaltenborn, sealed within the windowless Studio Nine, intent upon the biggest story of his life, was as unaware of that as of the havoc swirling about Manhattan. Only once did he allude to the hurricane that was devastating the countryside for hundreds of miles around him: conversing with the journalist Maurice Hindus in Prague, he mentioned that a "severe windstorm" had blown down the antennae on Long Island and prevented CBS from receiving Hindus's report on developments in Czechoslovakia. Kaltenborn's eye was on a different hurricane.

CHAPTER 8

———————◆———————

". . . it is peace for our time."

A s if to emulate nature, the once orderly society of Europe had gone all topsy-turvy, and the unimaginable was actually happening. Leaders of the great British and French empires, Kaltenborn reported, had decided to plead with the German dictator for concessions, triggering a tide of indignation in their own countries. France was having a cabinet crisis, with three ministers threatening to resign because of Daladier's policies (as FDR's ambassador in Paris, William Bullitt, wrote, a good many honorable men had concluded that the French and British governments were acting "like little boys doing dirty things behind the barn"). In England, on the eve of Neville Chamberlain's second flight to Germany, opposition was gathering force. That day both Anthony Eden and Winston Churchill gave the British public their opinions of appeasement, which could be, said Eden, "neither long nor lasting at such a price. . . . There must always be a point at which we as a nation must make a stand." Churchill, described in some U.S. newspapers as an "elder statesman," put it more bluntly: "The idea that safety can be purchased by throwing a small state to the wolves is a fatal delusion." Churchill, it was said, had canceled a forthcoming lecture tour in the United States in order to remain in England and lead the opposition, and even within the government itself men were wondering how much humiliation the country could tolerate. "How much courage is needed to be a coward!" Alexander Cadogan wrote. "We must go on being cowards up to our limit, but *not beyond.* . . . But what of the future?" Ed Murrow, interviewing a London cabbie, heard the voice of the man in the street: this situation in Czechoslovakia was "just like Spain and China," the fellow said. "Most people's sympathies are with the Spanish government, but they don't feel strongly enough about it to want to go to war. At least those of military age don't. The older people are much more warlike. But then they won't have to do the fighting." People were swinging around toward Eden's point of view, the taxi driver thought, but they were disappointed by the attitude of the United States.

It was a time of anguish in Czechoslovakia. The Czech people, after waiting calmly and grimly for weeks, expecting war at any moment, could not believe what they suddenly heard from loudspeakers in the city streets, when the government announced that it had capitulated. "It cannot be true!" was the reaction. "It's another of those German broadcasts!" Men bought copies of newspapers, tore them up in a rage, and stormed through the city shouting threats: "Away with the government! Down with Beneš!" At the mention of Chamberlain and Daladier, people booed, and men and women stood on the sidewalks, sobbing. Then, just as suddenly, the mood changed; Premier Hodža's cabinet resigned and was replaced by a government headed by General Syrový, the tough, one-eyed hero of the World War, who had led the Czechs in Russia against the Germans. At long last, there was total mobilization in Czechoslovakia—a summons, Maurice Hindus reported, that could be likened to the tolling of the Liberty Bell in America, and the procession of men answering the call to arms was endless.

Meanwhile, things were not going well in Godesberg. As the morning news report described it on September 23, "Mysterious events are under way. . . ." A few hours before Hitler and Chamberlain were to meet, William L. Shirer got a curious insight into the German dictator's state of mind. Shirer was eating breakfast at the Hotel Dreesen, where Hitler was staying, and suddenly the Führer strode past and walked toward a door that overlooked the Rhine. A German editor seated at the table with Shirer nudged him and whispered, "Look at his walk!" and the American correspondent turned to see what he meant. He noticed the dainty, almost ladylike steps, and then saw something else—a sudden, nervous cocking of the right shoulder and a quick, upward jerk of the left leg. A few minutes later Hitler returned, Shirer looked again, observed the same spastic twitch and, noting the gray patches under the Führer's eyes, decided that the man was on the verge of a nervous breakdown. He was reminded of the talk at the hotel bar the night before, when he overheard a German describing Hitler as the *Teppichfresser,* or carpet-eater. Shirer didn't get the point. He asked the man what he meant, and was told that Hitler had been suffering one of his frequent bouts of nerves recently and that it took an unusual form. Whenever he went into a rage over the Czechs or Beneš, people had seen him throw himself to the floor and chew the edge of the carpet. To an uneasy world, Hitler seemed to be getting his way on everything, and the image of the strong man was carefully cultivated. In fact, however, since the Austrian Anschluss he was beset with recurring fears that France and England—and possibly Russia—would resist his attempt to take over Czechoslovakia. He suffered from such severe gastrointestinal pains and was so concerned about his health that he wrote a new will on the train to Rome in May, when he sought (and obtained) Mussolini's blessing to look the other way in the event Germany had to resort to force.

Neville Chamberlain, blithely innocent, totally unaware of Hitler's fits of anger and nerves, arrived at the Dreesen looking, Shirer said, the image of a smiling owl. His host led him to an upstairs room, where the two sat at opposite ends of a long, baize-covered table, and Chamberlain began the discussion by describing at length the laborious negotiations by which he had persuaded the British and French cabinets and the Beneš government to accept the German chancellor's demands. What remained, he stated, was to determine how these steps should be implemented, and he had come prepared with positive suggestions. Britain would accept the return of the Sudetenland to Germany without a plebiscite; a three-member commission would oversee the exchange; and Czechoslovakia's treaties with France and the Soviet Union would be replaced by an international guarantee of Czech neutrality.

This little speech was delivered with considerable satisfaction, for Chamberlain was pleased with how rational and simple the solution had proved to be, and he paused to hear the Führer's reaction.

Was he to understand, Hitler inquired, that the British, French, and Czech governments had agreed to the transfer of Sudeten territory to Germany?

"Yes," Chamberlain replied with a smile.

There was a pause, almost as if Hitler were making up his mind. Then he said, abruptly, *"Es tut mir furchtbar leid, aber das geht nicht mehr."* ("I am exceedingly sorry, but that is no longer of any use.")

There was a stunned silence. Chamberlain sat up with a start, his face flushed with anger and indignation. Surely, he declared, he could not be expected, after all he had done, to return to London with fresh proposals. Profoundly shocked, he suddenly realized that all his efforts had been for naught, that the peace that seemed so close was more than ever a will-o'-the-wisp. The remainder of their three-hour meeting was rancorous and difficult, and at the end Chamberlain departed for his hotel across the river, "full of foreboding," as he later told the House of Commons, to consider what he should do in the face of Hitler's new demand that Hungarian and Polish claims to Czech territory must now be dealt with, and that German troops must occupy the Sudetenland at once.

As the British ambassador in Berlin, Nevile Henderson, described it, "Godesberg was the real turning point in Anglo-German relations." At the very least, it was the moment of truth for the British prime minister, who left the meeting to sulk in his tent, while a waiting world learned that the conference scheduled for the afternoon of September 23 had been canceled.

France, Kaltenborn announced, was placing troops in the Maginot Line on a war footing; the German army was moving into various positions along the frontier; severe fighting had broken out in the Sudetenland between Czech police and Nazis; and from London and Paris came word that the attitude of both governments was stiffening. "The situation is very grave," Daladier stated. "France has gone to the limit in the matter of concessions." Shirer, broadcasting from Godesberg, described how Henderson and Sir Horace Wilson had met for several hours with Hitler's foreign minister, Joachim von Ribbentrop, after which Wilson told reporters that Chamberlain planned to fly to London the following morning. There was, it appeared, a complete breakdown in the discussions, and a CBS evening news bulletin noted, "All Europe is preparing for a threatened invasion of Czechoslovakia."

Late that same night, Ed Murrow called Kaltenborn to tell him that he had Jan Masaryk, the Czech ambassador to London, in the studio with him, and the American radio audience was treated to an eloquent and persuasive message from the man who, as an immigrant to America, had worked in a Bridgeport brass factory, and whose father had founded Czechoslovakia. Telling listeners that his nation would defend the principles of democracy for which his father had struggled, he said, "I tell you, Americans, our powder is dry. As one who has spent many years in America, who knows and loves it, who earned his first dollar in New York City when he was nineteen years old; as one whose mother was an American; and as a citizen of a small country . . . I greet you, brother democrats, and may God give us peace." And for those hundreds of thousands of Czech-Americans, he spoke a few words in their native tongue: "Truth must triumph and will triumph. I salute you, brother democrats."

While Neville Chamberlain was still in the air, homeward bound, a sense of almost certain calamity descended on Europe, and the morning news reports on Saturday, September 24, sounded like the drumbeats for Armageddon. Heavy troop movements throughout Germany . . . Belgium and Rumania mobilizing . . . partial activation of the French navy . . . Great Britain calling up its armed forces, air force leaves canceled, bombs and weapons being distributed to all units . . . forty-two ships of the home fleet putting to sea. And in Rome, Mussolini sounded what appeared to be the death knell: speaking in behalf of his Axis partner, he declared that October I was the ultimate deadline for compliance with Hitler's demands. "The Prague government," he announced, "has six days in which to find its way to wisdom." Kaltenborn, ever mindful of the reasons behind events, informed his audience that the call-up of German reservists expired on that date, which meant that Hitler had to act by then or allow his army to be demobilized.

The strange thing, considering this intensifying crisis, was that the people of Germany seemed so inapprehensive; as Shirer reported, nothing resembling a war spirit existed there. He attended a rally in Berlin's Sportpalast on the 26th and listened to Hitler "shouting and shrieking in the worst state of excitement I've ever seen him in," cursing Beneš, promising to go to war unless the Sudetenland was turned over to Germany by October 1. Fifteen thousand of the party faithful were in the hall, cheering the Führer, yet Shirer noticed that the crowd was "good-natured, as if it didn't realize what his words meant." From his seat in the balcony, he could see that Hitler still had his nervous spasm—one shoulder would suddenly cock and the opposite leg from the knee down would bounce up, uncontrollably; he had a wild, fanatical expression in his eyes; and for the first time Shirer was certain that the man had lost control of himself.

On Tuesday, September 27, Sir Horace Wilson called on the German chancellor with another message from Chamberlain, only to be told that Hitler's determination to go to war was inflexible unless the Czechs accepted his terms. If they did not, Hitler shouted savagely, *"Ich werde die Tschechen zerschlagen,"* which the interpreter Paul Schmidt translated as "I will *smash-sh-sh* the Czechs." The Führer added that he was completely indifferent as to whether France and England decided to join in hostilities. He was prepared for any eventuality. "It is Tuesday today," he stated, "and by next Monday we shall all be at war."

That afternoon Ambassador Henderson witnessed a singular event which seemed to him to have altered Hitler's intentions. A German mechanized division, on its way to the frontier, rolled through the streets of Berlin past the Wilhelmstrasse, and for three hours Hitler stood on the balcony outside his window and watched it pass. None of the Germans in the streets applauded or cheered as the tanks and armored cars rumbled by, and Hitler, who knew as well as any man the German love of a military parade, may have sensed then that the people were not behind him. The strange scene, in Henderson's phrase, "was almost that of a hostile army passing through a conquered city," and it was to have a profound effect as the day of decision approached.

Hitler also heard, for the first time, from the president of the United States (this was soon after Eleanor Roosevelt received a cablegram from a former schoolmate in England saying, "One word from America will save Europe"). On September 26, Franklin Roosevelt cabled a request to the governments of Europe urging them to continue negotiations, to which Hitler replied that peace depended solely on the attitude of the Czechs. Then, on the 27th, came another message from Washington, proposing an immediate conference of all nations directly concerned and implying that if war began on the continent the world would hold Hitler responsible. Although Roosevelt's appeal was framed within the constraints of domestic politics, the German ambassador in Washington could see which way the wind was blowing, and warned Hitler that if he invaded Czechoslovakia and forced Britain to intercede, "the whole weight of the United States [would] be thrown into the scale on the side of Britain."

———

What confronted the Führer at that moment was a combination of circumstances that began to eat away at his resolve. He had sensed the apathy of the German people; Admiral Raeder, chief of the German navy, had appealed to him not to go to war; his army staff opposed a move against Czechoslovakia; resistance was evidently stiffening in Paris and in London (Horace Wilson had informed the chancellor, in fact, that if France became involved in hostilities in fulfillment of her treaty obligations, the United Kingdom "would feel obliged to support France"); from the United States had come an implied warning that that country would at least observe a benevolent neutrality in favor of the nations that had tried to preserve the peace; and Prague remained defiant. To cap it all, his ultimatum was due to expire within a matter of hours. On the evening of September 27, he summoned Dr. Paul Schmidt, the interpreter who had been present at his meetings with Chamberlain, and dictated a letter to the British prime minister. As Schmidt listened and wrote, he became aware that the Führer was retreating "from the extreme step."

By the time his relatively moderate letter reached Neville Chamberlain, the Englishman had undergone some very bad moments himself. Upon his return from Godesberg he had held a meeting of his "inner cabinet" and informed them, to their utter astonishment and dismay, that he had "established some degree of personal influence over Herr Hitler"—a statement that "completely horrified" Alexander Cadogan, who realized that the prime minister "was quite calmly for total surrender." Cadogan could only conclude that Hitler had hypnotized Chamberlain. A telegram from Sir Eric Phipps, Britain's ambassador in Paris, indicated that France was unalterably opposed to war, almost at any price, and on the heels of that message came Daladier and General Maurice Gamelin, chief of the French general staff, to discuss the realities of any Franco-British involvement in active hostilities. What that meeting revealed was the intention of France to launch a minor offensive, then to retire into the Maginot Line until a British expeditionary force arrived.

On the afternoon of September 27, Americans heard what H. V. Kaltenborn called "a great speech, great for its moderation," by the British prime minister. Speaking to his countrymen, the tired old man remarked in his public-school accent, "How horrible, fantastic, incredible it is that we should be digging trenches and trying on gas masks here because of a quarrel in a faraway country between people of whom we know nothing." However much we may sympathize with a small nation that is being bullied about by a larger neighbor, he went on, the people of the Empire should not become involved in such a wrangle. "If we have to fight," he said, "it must be on larger issues than that."

If the Czechs did not know where they stood by this time, that message should have made it unmistakably clear. Chamberlain, in fact, had that evening warned President Beneš that unless he accepted a limited German occupation of his country on October 1 the result would certainly be full-scale invasion of his country. Whatever else he may have intended, Chamberlain's broadcast convinced a good many Britons, as they retired for the night, that their country would be at war with Germany within twenty-four hours.

Two hours after the broadcast, Chamberlain received the letter Hitler had dictated to Dr. Schmidt, and it was like a straw to a drowning man. Immediately he cabled the Führer, stating his readiness to come at once to Berlin for a conference that would include representatives from Czechoslovakia, France, and Italy, as well as Germany and Britain; and to Mussolini he telegraphed an appeal to urge Hitler's acceptance of a big-power meeting.

The next day, while many of London's underground stations were closed for what were termed "urgent constructional repairs" and schoolchildren were sent away from the city, members of Parliament walked toward the House, where Neville Chamberlain was to speak that afternoon. The pigeons were clustered around the fountains in Trafalgar Square, where some young people were feeding them, and Harold Nicolson's companion remarked, "Those children ought to be evacuated at once, and so should the pigeons." Near the House of Commons a large crowd was placing flowers at the base of the Cenotaph—people anxious and silent, staring at the MPs with "dumb, inquisitive eyes," Nicolson recalled.

A microphone had been placed in front of the prime minister's chair, and members realized that for the first time in history a speech was to be broadcast from the floor of the House (in fact, it was relayed only as far as a room in the House of Lords, and reporters broadcasting to the United States received stenographic copies of the prime minister's address as it was brought to them, page by page). In the ladies' gallery, making an unprecedented visit for the solemn occasion, was the king's mother, Queen Mary, dressed in black. The House was packed, every seat filled, and American listeners were told that Lloyd George had walked to his seat with the jaunty step of a youngster, while Winston Churchill had entered with an "air of historic tragedy about him."[1] Feeling the tension mount, those in the chamber could only wonder if the horror of 1914 was about to repeat itself, as Neville Chamberlain rose from his seat to the slow, time-honored chant of "Hear, Hear, Hear," arranged the pages of his speech, and began to recount the inexorable chronology of events that had led the nation to this pass. The House was dead silent as he related his repeated efforts to stave off disaster;

[1]Among those in the galleries was John F. Kennedy, the ambassador's twenty-one-year-old son, who would subsequently write a book about the Munich crisis, called *Why England Slept.* More than two decades later, as president of the United States, he would face up to a Soviet dictator and demand—at the risk of war—that he remove the nuclear missiles he had installed in Cuba.

when he reached the point in his narrative about which they knew little or nothing as yet, members leaned forward expectantly.

At twelve minutes past four the prime minister had been speaking for more than an hour, and just as he informed his listeners of the telegrams he had sent to Hitler and Mussolini the previous night, a sheet of Foreign Office paper which had been rushed to the House by Cadogan was passed rapidly along the government bench and handed to him. He adjusted his pince-nez and for a full five minutes stood there, silently reading, while a thousand people held their breath, waiting to hear what the message contained. Watching Chamberlain read, Nicolson saw that "his whole face, his whole body, seemed to change. He raised his face so that the light from the ceiling fell full upon it. All the lines of anxiety and weariness seemed suddenly to have been smoothed out; he appeared ten years younger and triumphant." At last he cleared his throat and spoke.

"Herr Hitler," the prime minister announced in a dramatic voice, "has just agreed to postpone his mobilization for twenty-four hours and to meet me in conference with Signor Mussolini and Monsieur Daladier at Munich. I need not say what my answer will be," he continued. "I will go to see what I can do as a last resort."

It was one of the most dramatic pieces of timing ever witnessed in that or any other legislative hall. For a moment there was absolute silence, then the members rose almost as a man and cheered; against all the rules, visitors in the galleries stood and shouted; Queen Mary, who had burst into tears, was so touched she was unable to speak to the women seated near her, many of whom reached out to touch her hand; Chamberlain's predecessor in office, Stanley Baldwin, was in the peers' gallery, thumping his stick on the floor in time to the applause, while the archbishop of Canterbury slapped the rail with his hands again and again. In the diplomats' gallery there was pandemonium, the Brazilian ambassador shouting at the top of his voice, the Italian ambassador waving his arms wildly and roaring, *"Viva! Viva! Viva!"* Finally the House adjourned while Chamberlain's supporters crowded around him to offer congratulations. Only a few, like Nicolson, refused to stand in tribute when he left the floor, and Winston Churchill, stomping out, was heard to remark sourly, "The government had to choose between shame and war. They chose shame and they will get war." Jan Masaryk, who was in the diplomatic gallery, later confronted Chamberlain and Halifax to say, "If you have sacrificed my nation to save the peace of the world, I will be the first to applaud you. But if not, gentlemen, God help your souls."

It seemed, however, to a welcoming world, that the crisis was over. Never since it had begun, Kaltenborn observed in the wake of Chamberlain's dramatic announcement, "have I approached my task of news analysis as cheerfully as I do at this particular moment." The conference itself was almost an anticlimax, so great was the rejoicing that the opposing powers had agreed to talk instead of fight, but not for some time would the French or British know that it had not been Neville Chamberlain's last-minute appeal to Hitler and Mussolini that produced the meeting. Hitler himself, looking for a way to save face, had arranged for Mussolini to suggest the conference, and the German dictator had immediately "accepted" his henchman's invitation. "At the request of my great friend and ally, Mussolini," Hitler informed Ambassador Henderson, "I have postponed mobilizing my troops for twenty-four hours."

———

Only the Czechs did not rejoice. Jan Masaryk, summoned to the Foreign Office in London to be told of the forthcoming meeting, replied, "But this is a conference to discuss the fate of my country. Are we not being invited to take part?" No, he was informed, it was to be a meeting of "the Great Powers only"—a meeting in which four governments would make decisions involving the cession of territory of a fifth state without even giving that state a hearing, and then, when the matter was settled, would communicate the information in the dead of night to the nation most concerned.

The British pound rallied from $4.62 to $4.75 and there was a wave of buying on the London Exchange as Chamberlain, for the third time in two weeks, took off by air for Germany. The Munich conference at which he was joined by Edouard Daladier, Adolf Hitler, and Benito Mussolini was "a hugger-mugger affair," according to William Strang, a chaotic discussion in which the negotiations were conducted according to no agenda or plan. Outside the room in which the British delegation sat waiting for the principals to come to terms, Strang could see the lower echelons of Nazis coming and going, "flocks of spruce young SS subalterns in their black uniforms, haughty and punctilious, as though life were a drill, acting as ADCs and orderly officers, one or other of whom would from time to time come to us, click his heels, and ask if we required anything." The presence of Hitler's entourage reminded Strang of some great barbarian chieftain of Germanic heroic legend attended by his companions, retainers, and house-carles; at Godesberg he had seen the Führer emerge from the conference room, advance toward his retinue, halt, and fix them with his eye to assert his authority. They sprang to their feet and "froze to immobility and silence. The Führer then turned on his heel without a sign and moved away."

The meetings began on the morning of September 29, 1938, and business was concluded at 2:30 A.M. the following day. During those hours two of Prague's emissaries, Vojtech Mastny and Hubert Masarik, waited anxiously in an anteroom to learn the fate of their nation. When the meeting broke up, Hitler and Mussolini swept out with their dozens of uniformed aides, and the Czechs were admitted to the nearly empty conference room. As Daladier poured himself a drink and Chamberlain yawned uncontrollably, a French diplomat handed the Czechs the text of the accord. Did the parties to the agreement, the Czechs inquired, desire an answer from their government in Prague? No, the Frenchman replied, no answer was required. The pact had been accepted by the four powers.

As the French diplomat spoke, Mastny began to weep, and Masarik's eyes filled with tears. "They don't know what they are doing to us or to themselves," he said to Mastny.

At that Horace Wilson glanced over at Chamberlain, saw that he was yawning again, and announced, "Come, gentlemen. It is very late. I am sure we all must be very tired." There was silence. Then Chamberlain and Daladier left, leaving the two Czechs alone in the empty room.

"It's all settled. It's just a matter of minor details," H. V. Kaltenborn reported, pointing out, "The terms which you have just heard represent a complete victory for Adolf Hitler," but that was hardly a judgment with which Neville Chamberlain would have agreed. After a few hours' sleep on the morning of September 30, the prime minister wakened Strang, told him he had arranged to meet Hitler privately—without the French—before departing, and asked the Foreign Office man to draft a memorandum covering future Anglo-German relations. The session which then took place between the two leaders was as cordial as its antecedents had been stormy, with Hitler in good form, almost jovial, replying "*Ja! Ja!*" to each of Chamberlain's proposals, covering the entire range of disputes between Britain and Germany, while Chamberlain, convinced that he had caught the Nazi leader in a rare conciliatory mood, seized the moment to settle the problems that had divided Europe since the World War. "*Ja! Ja!*" Hitler repeated when asked if he would sign the memorandum Strang and Chamberlain had prepared. When did the prime minister wish to do so? he asked, and when Chamberlain replied, "Immediately," the Führer said, "Then let us sign." Without another word they moved to a writing table and affixed their signatures to the document which proclaimed "the desire of our two peoples never to go to war with one another again." Back at his hotel, Neville Chamberlain sat down for lunch with his aides, complacently patted the breast pocket in which he had placed the memorandum, and announced triumphantly, "I've got it!"

From Paris next morning came reports that huge crowds had met Daladier's plane at Le Bourget field, that half a million Frenchmen had lined the route between the airport and the city, many of them breaking through police cordons and running up to the premier's car to shout, "Peace! Peace!" Daladier himself, acutely conscious that the agreement he had signed in Munich was a tragic defeat for France, kept his counsel and wished only that those around him might offer solace, instead of rejoicing. Cardinal Verdier, a thoughtful cleric, understood: he refused to allow the great bells of Notre Dame Cathedral to be rung in celebration. They would remain silent, he said, in mourning for what had occurred.

George F. Kennan, a young American career diplomat en route to his new post as secretary of legation in Prague, flew out of Paris the day the

Munich conference was to begin, and as he took off he saw Daladier's special plane warming up on the apron. As it turned out, Kennan's aircraft was the last to leave Paris for Prague for seven years. The following day, in the Czech capital, he stood on the Vaclavske Namsti and watched the people weep as news of the Munich calamity came over the loudspeakers. General Syrový, the prime minister, explained why the government had accepted the terms handed to them: they had been informed that if they did not do so, they could expect no assistance from Great Britain or France. Under the settlement, Czech troops would withdraw from the defense installations on which the nation had spent so many millions, he said, leaving them intact for the Germans who would march into Czechoslovakia the next day.

On September 30, Ed Murrow was on the air. "This is London," he began solemnly, using the phrase that was to become so familiar to American listeners, and he told of throngs waiting at Heston airport and at Downing Street to greet the prime minister. Englishmen were speculating that Chamberlain might be knighted while still in office; some believed he would receive the Nobel Peace Prize. Prices soared on the London stock market, and when Chamberlain arrived the bells of Westminster Abbey pealed a joyous welcome. City councils in Britain renamed streets in his honor; Versailles declared him an honorary citizen; elsewhere in France a subscription was raised to present him with a country home and a trout stream, where he could pursue his favorite sport; Lisbon announced plans to erect his statue, paid for by "grateful mothers of Portugal"; letters and poems, telegrams, flowers, and gifts by the truckload poured in on 10 Downing Street. A craftsman requested a piece of the much-traveled umbrella to fashion into an icon. From Holland, where he had lived quietly in exile for two decades, the man who had led Germany into the World War wrote a letter to Queen Mary. "I have not the slightest doubt," former Kaiser Wilhelm informed her, "that Mr. N. Chamberlain was inspired by Heaven & guided by God who took pity on his children on Earth by crowning his mission with such relieving success. God bless him. I kiss your hand in respectful devotion as ever." The old queen forwarded the letter to her son Bertie, the king, with a covering note. "Poor William," she clucked, "he must have been horrified at the thought of another war between our 2 countries."

At such an hour few wished to hear or heed the chronic Cassandra, Winston Churchill, who chose this moment to stand alone in the House of Commons and, ignoring the hoots of protest that greeted his words, to declare: "We have sustained a total and unmitigated defeat. . . . Do not blind ourselves to that. . . . And do not suppose that this is the end. This is only the beginning of the reckoning. This is only the first sip, the first foretaste of a bitter cup which will be proffered to us year by year unless, by a supreme recovery of moral health and martial vigor, we arise again and take our stand for freedom as in the olden time."

This was not the olden time nor a time for doubts, however, but a time for joy and thanksgiving. The true mood of Britain could be seen in the deliriously happy faces of people surging out onto the landing field singing "For he's a jolly good fellow" to their returning hero (who had once again forgotten his umbrella, leaving it behind in Munich to be flown in on the next plane), and in the gesture of Chamberlain himself—as excited as a child by their wild enthusiasm—who reached into his pocket, pulled out a piece of paper, and waved it in the air for the roaring throng. It took an hour and a half to drive the nine miles into London, so thick were the crowds around his car, and before he reached Downing Street he was summoned to the palace to receive the king's congratulations. Back at his residence at last, he leaned from a window, flourished the paper Hitler had signed, and announced triumphantly, in words that would haunt him for the rest of his life, "It is peace with honor. I believe it is peace for our time."[2]

[2]The phrase was unfortunate, but it is only fair to note that the piece of paper he waved was not the agreement on Czechoslovakia, but the memorandum he and Hitler signed privately— the personal accord in which he placed such faith, believing that it would prove the foundation for an enduring peace in Europe.

CHAPTER 9

———————◆———————

"Isn't there anyone?"

Throughout that agonizing fortnight, while the British leader shuttled
back and forth to Europe, Cordell Hull and his principal advisers at
the State Department maintained a "death watch" and a low profile,
not knowing what might happen, realizing that there was "nothing for us
to do except to steer clear and keep quiet." None of them had any illusions
about the meaning of the agreement, however Mr. Chamberlain might
choose to characterize it; Hull's blunt opinion was that France and Britain
had been humiliated, their prestige badly damaged, with Germany now
supreme in Europe.

Beyond the State Department, America wanted desperately to take
Chamberlain at his word, but in some quarters there was a queasy feeling,
as an editorial writer for the *Norfolk Virginian-Pilot* put it, that Europe's
statesmen had cobbled together "an ill-smelling peace." Public opinion
polls showed that 43 percent of the people believed that the United States
could not stay out of a European war. A recent émigré from Hungary, the
physicist Leo Szilard, wrote to an English scientist, "I believe that this last
breach of faith which led to the Munich agreement has definitely settled the
fate of Europe for a long time to come. It will not be possible for either
England or France to make international agreements and get anybody to
believe that they will keep these agreements if keeping them means risking

war." A similarly bleak view of the future was brought to President Roosevelt by the financier Bernard Baruch, who had been in London during the Munich crisis and was told by his friend Winston Churchill, "War is coming very soon. We will be in it and you will be in it."

Baruch, who had made his way from office boy to Wall Street millionaire by the time he was thirty and had then amassed a great deal more money as an industrialist, had emerged unscathed from the 1929 crash, and the combination of his financial acuity and his commonsense advice to presidents since Woodrow Wilson lent him a peculiar aura in middle America, the mantle of park-bench statesman whose words carried a great deal of weight in Washington. In 1937 he had returned from his annual trip to the spa in Vichy, France, convinced that Hitler would go to war, and had warned reporters who met his ship that the continent was a tinderbox. In the summer of 1938, before leaving for Europe, he called on Roosevelt at the White House. Baruch had been chairman of the War Industries Board under Woodrow Wilson and knew the enormous difficulty of converting American industry from peace to war. For some time now he had been sending up smoke signals, urging the president to appoint a group to draft mobilization legislation—as much to give Germany cause for concern as to organize the U.S. home front—but to date neither the White House nor anyone else had paid much attention.

After their chat, FDR asked him to look into the military situation abroad and then scrawled a note which he handed to Baruch:

DEFENSE COORDINATION BOARD
To start Sept 1 and study
& report to Pres. by Dec. 1st
Chairman—B. M. Baruch

Baruch's weeks in Europe did nothing to assuage his fears of Germany, but they opened his eyes concerning that country's potential opposition. Stopping off in Paris, he spoke with businessmen, politicians, and military leaders and discovered how unprepared France was for war. The great French army was no more than a shell, and France's air force was hopelessly inadequate. In London he learned that England's defenses were, if anything, in worse shape, and when he asked the British minister for the coordination of defense where he planned to get shells, ammunition, guns, and other weapons, the reply was "From France." "You won't get anything," Baruch told him.

If neither France nor Britain had the capacity even to produce artillery shells with which to fight a war that threatened to begin at almost any moment, how much security did the European Allies really afford the United States? How realistic was it to think that America was sheltered from Hitler by the Allies' armies and the Atlantic Ocean?

Alarmed, Baruch telephoned Roosevelt from Scotland on August 19 to say that the democracies had absolutely nothing with which to stop Hitler. He volunteered to come home immediately and convene the Defense Coordination Board, but the president was noncommittal. Before sailing for New York, Baruch had his talk with Winston Churchill, who had not had a cabinet post since 1929 and was in general disrepute because of his repeated warnings about Hitler, and heard him speak almost wistfully about the big show that was coming soon. The Englishman's reason for regret was clear: "I'll be on the sidelines here."

After his return Baruch had dinner with the president and summarized his conclusions. Western Europe's unpreparedness meant that America was running out of time. That made it imperative to increase taxes immediately and begin building a modernized, mechanized army, a two-ocean navy, and "airplanes and more airplanes"; but as he spoke, the financier realized that Roosevelt had lost interest in the Defense Coordination Board and that even though he subscribed to Baruch's views, he was not going to enunciate them himself. The people, Roosevelt said, would not accept an approach that smacked of preparations for war. He suggested that Baruch hold a press conference and report on his findings, after which the president would back him up. It was late at night when Baruch left the White House, and as he walked across Lafayette Park he was "troubled and unhappy at what I thought was the president's excessive caution." (Along with his other worries, Baruch was a Jew and still had relatives in Germany whom he had been unable to help flee.)

The upshot of their meeting was a press conference the following morning, at which Baruch told reporters the United States could not even defend its own borders, that it should increase its army to 400,000 men equipped with modern weapons, build a two-ocean navy, vastly increase its air force, and place industry on a mobilized basis immediately. He concluded with his usual plea that the only way to pay for these huge expenses was to increase taxes. Despite the president's promise to support him, FDR failed to declare for all-out mobilization and remained silent on the need for higher taxes, so Baruch found himself in the unpopular role of the prophet—attacked from all sides. Headlines in Germany read, "The Jew Baruch Smells Business Profits," and the "bellicose clique of Churchillians" was denounced; in the United States, Father Charles Coughlin's *Social Justice* echoed those remarks; and almost no support for the idea was forthcoming from politicians or editorial writers.

While the Germans, Poles, and Hungarians were carving up Czechoslovakia in the wake of the Munich Pact, Ambassador William Bullitt returned to Washington from his post in Paris and reported at the White House on October 13. No record was made of his talk with the president—a conversation that lasted late into the night—but significantly, the following day Roosevelt announced that he was ordering a thorough study of defense preparations, and a War Department report noted, "President Roosevelt became convinced for the first time that American airplane production should be greatly stimulated with all possible speed." Apparently Bullitt made clear that the awesome strength of Germany's air force had been a determining factor in enabling Hitler to call the tune at Munich, and Roosevelt seems to have made up his mind then and there that no time should be lost in increasing U.S. aircraft production to furnish planes for the European Allies as well as for the nation's own Army Air Corps. This was another factor in his decision to have Harry Hopkins investigate the productive capacity of West Coast aircraft factories, after which the president astonished his top civilian and military advisers by proposing a program to build eight thousand planes.

It was probably just as well for the president that the American people knew nothing of all this. In general, the public's sense of relief after Munich was almost palpable, and while it was mixed with dismay over the cynical dismemberment of hapless little Czechoslovakia, there were few signs of guilt over the ugly business. That was "a problem for the Europeans to solve," the *Baton Rouge State-Times* observed, and Americans could be "thankful our own country has no direct part in it." Just beneath the surface ran the somber undercurrent of apprehension that had persisted since 1929, when the nation's solidity and sense of security had collapsed along with prosperity. To appreciate how raw the nerve ends were, one had only to consider the events of Sunday evening, October 30—a month after Munich, the night before Halloween.

———

Perhaps had there been no Munich, it would not have happened the way it did; but people were jumpy and ill at ease, while fascinated by the way radio was serving up events as they occurred. Radio had brought them the gripping drama of Edward VIII's abdication, not to mention play-by-play descriptions of more mundane occurrences. On a soft June evening in 1938, for instance, Dodger fans had tuned in to a broadcast of the first night baseball game ever played at Ebbets Field in Brooklyn and listened in disbelief while young Johnny Vander Meer of the Cincinnati Reds pitched his second consecutive no-hit, no-run game. A week later a substantial segment of America's male population turned the dial to a broadcast from Yankee Stadium and—if they were lucky enough to tune in on time—heard a breathless ringside account of Joe Louis knocking out the German challenger, Max Schmeling, in two minutes and four seconds of the first round. Then came Munich and the marathon reporting of Europe's convulsive hours. By now, in short, there was every reason for the average American to accept as gospel what he heard on a live news broadcast.

Between 8:00 and 9:00 on this final Sunday night in October, most of the listening public was happily removed from the world's troubles: nearly 35 percent of them were tuned to NBC and *The Chase & Sanborn Radio Hour,* a variety show featuring Edgar Bergen, the ventriloquist, and his dummy, Charlie McCarthy. To listen to this vastly popular program was, as Frederick Lewis Allen wrote, to be taken into "a safe little world of small boys' pranks, a world in which nothing more distressing happened than that Edgar Bergen grew bald, a world in which there were no unemployed men, no budget deficits, no marching dictators." And Americans loved it.

For upwards of a year, CBS had been casting about for a show that could compete with Bergen and McCarthy, and the one currently offered was no more successful commercially than its predecessors. Since June *The Mercury Theatre on the Air* had been heard on the network, and still no sponsor was in sight. The impresario—director, producer, master of ceremonies, and star—of this sustaining program was a brilliant *enfant terrible,* a twenty-three-year-old Kenosha, Wisconsin, native named Orson Welles, who had become familiar to millions of radio listeners as the sepulchral voice of "the Shadow" and had excited theatrical circles with his work in WPA-sponsored plays, including a black *Macbeth.* After founding the Mercury Theatre with John Houseman he put on a startling, innovative production of Shakespeare's *Julius Caesar* in modern dress, with overtones of fascist Italy. Welles had already presented a variety of dramatizations on *The Mercury Theatre on the Air,* and on October 30 the program opened with an announcement—unheard or unheeded by many listeners—that the evening's entertainment would be an adaptation of H. G. Wells's twenty-year-old novel *The War of the Worlds.*

Curiously, nothing resembling a dramatization followed. The show started with a routine report of weather conditions; then the program switched to a hotel ballroom in New York, where Ramon Raquello's orchestra was heard playing "La Cumparsita." In the middle of the song an announcer interrupted to bring listeners a "flash": an astronomer at Mount Jennings Observatory in Chicago, he stated, had observed a series of explosions on the planet Mars. Robert Saudek, an editor at Pittsburgh's radio station KDKA, and his wife, Betty, were listening to *Mercury Theatre,* as they always did, and when the dance music came on, followed by a news break, Betty told him he had the wrong station—this wasn't Orson Welles. He fiddled with the dial and then came back to the program. This must be it, he said, and they settled back to hear the rest. What they heard was more music—a few bars of "Star Dust"—before a voice broke in with a succession of news bulletins: a meteorite, it was said, had fallen not far from Princeton, New Jersey, killing an estimated fifteen hundred people. On the heels of this came another startling report: police rushing to the scene of the catastrophe had discovered that the object was not a meteor but a huge metal cylinder that suddenly disgorged creatures from Mars—loathsome things with leathery tentacles and terrible, pale-eyed faces—armed with death rays. As they began to emerge from their spacecraft, the announcer froze, unable to describe what he was seeing, spoke a few faltering words, retched, and then continued. A few moments later he was dead—one of the first victims of the Martian ray guns—and this was followed by a moment of total silence. It was broken after what seemed an eternity by a few bars of "Clair de Lune," superseded by the voice of the commanding officer of the New Jersey state militia, placing most of Mercer and Middlesex counties under martial law. Then an eyewitness, describing a battle in the Watchung Hills; then that eerie tinkle of "Clair de Lune" on the piano. At 8:31 the secretary of the interior came on the air urging Americans to remain calm; whereupon the broadcast switched to further reports of the Martian invasion. The cabinet officer's voice—remarkably like President Franklin Roosevelt's—was heard again, advising citizens to leave the cities, and someone shouted into a microphone, "Get gas masks!"

By now, all hell was breaking loose in the nation's living rooms. In addition to the program's regular listeners, as luck would have it, a substantial number of Edgar Bergen's fans had twisted their dials to avoid a not very popular singer and had come in on the middle of the Welles broadcast. They assumed at once that they were hearing a news report. Understandably, people were calling friends and neighbors to tell them to turn on CBS and find out what was going on, and things were beginning to get out of hand.

At the first announcement that a meteor had fallen in the vicinity, Professor Arthur F. Buddington, chairman of Princeton's geology department, and his colleague Professor Harry Hess grabbed some instruments and drove off through the night to Grovers Mills, where the object was supposed to have fallen. They arrived to find an excited crowd of folk wandering about, trying to find the meteor. Those who were still listening to details from the broadcast were in a less objective state of mind. Terrified New Yorkers began leaving their apartments, some heading for city parks, others in automobiles jamming Riverside Drive in an effort to get out of town, still others crowding rail and bus terminals. San Franciscans got the impression that New York City was being destroyed. In the state of Washington one town had a power failure during the broadcast, and shaken residents were certain that the day of judgment was at hand. A woman called the *Boston Globe* to report that she "could see the fire."

Meantime, further bulletins from CBS brought word that Martians had routed the New Jersey militia; it was reported that the city of New York was being evacuated; the attack was said to be spreading across the entire United States, with Martian ray guns and flame throwers leaving a trail of havoc. Hearing this, more than twenty families living on one city block in Newark dashed from their homes into the street holding wet handkerchiefs and towels to their faces to ward off poison gas; a monumental traffic jam ensued, stopping all movement of vehicles. A Newark housewife decided that she wanted to be with her husband and nephew "so we could all die together," so she ran to the nearest bus stop. In her panic she thought that every oncoming car was a bus and tried to flag it down, meantime shouting to everyone and to no one in particular, "New Jersey is destroyed by the

Germans—it's on the radio!" In Caldwell, evening services at the First Baptist Church were interrupted by a near-hysterical parishioner who charged in yelling that a meteor had fallen and that north Jersey was about to be demolished. At that, the Reverend Thomas Thomas led the congregation in a prayer for deliverance. Much the same scene was repeated in Indianapolis, where a woman rushed into a church, screaming, "New York destroyed . . . It's the end of the world! You might as well go home to die—I just heard it on the radio." And the service broke up in chaos, with people scattering in all directions.

A man in Mount Vernon, New York, telephoned local police to say that his invalid brother had driven off in an automobile and "disappeared" after hearing the broadcast. A Pittsburgher returned home to find his wife in the bathroom, preparing to swallow poison. "I'd rather die this way than like that!" she screamed. In another Pennsylvania town, three high school girls clung to each other hysterically. "We felt it was terrible we should die so young," one of them remembered thinking. Police stations in Harlem were besieged with people, many with their worldly goods packed for a journey, asking where they could go. The *New York Times* switchboard logged 875 frightened requests for information; newspapers elsewhere were flooded with frantic calls; the Associated Press put out an explanatory bulletin over its wires to member papers.

The reaction to Welles's broadcast was, all things considered, about like the response to Henny Penny's message that the sky was falling down.

———

Blissfully unaware of the panic they had created, the Mercury players were enjoying the show immensely. As Welles's partner John Houseman recalled, "a strange fever" was present in the studio—"part childish mischief, part professional zeal"; but at about 8:32 the supervisor of the broadcast, a thin, long-faced man named Davidson Taylor, was summoned from the control room and told that the CBS switchboard was besieged, that there were rumors from across the land of deaths, suicides, and injuries caused by the broadcast. Meanwhile, the dramatization continued: over the air came reports of heavy smoke clouds rising from Newark, of Martians wading the Hudson River and blanketing New York City with their poison gas. Listeners heard New York's "last announcer" choking to death, the ghostly whistles of boats carrying refugees out of the harbor, and—just before the station break—the plaintive words of a lone amateur shortwave operator, calling into the night. . . .

> 2X2L calling CQ
> 2X2L calling CQ
> 2X2L calling CQ
> Isn't there anyone on the air?
> Isn't there anyone?

Five seconds of deathly silence were broken by the voice of a genuine announcer: "You are listening to the CBS presentation of Orson Welles and *The Mercury Theatre on the Air* in an original dramatization of *The War of the Worlds,* by H. G. Wells. The performance will continue after a brief intermission."

The script for the second part of the show described a lone survivor, the eventual extermination of the Martians by disease, the rebuilding of a new world, and finally Welles, playing himself, giving an informal little talk about Halloween. As Houseman said later, this concluding half of the program was "extremely well written and most sensitively played—but nobody heard it."

The control-room telephone rang and the voice of an infuriated Midwestern mayor was heard, screaming for Welles, shouting about mobs, violence, and looting in his city, threatening to come to New York and personally assault the perpetrator of the hoax. The building was suddenly filled with platoons of blue-uniformed policemen; the actors were hustled out of the studio and into an empty office downstairs while network employees destroyed or locked up the scripts and recordings of the broadcast, and hours later the stunned Mercury players were let out of the building through a back door.

Although CBS officials could console themselves with the knowledge that announcements had been made—before and during the program—advising listeners that what they were hearing was only a play, they realized before the hour was half over that they had a panic of major proportions on their hands, and from then until midnight they broadcast another announcement at regular intervals:

For those listeners who tuned in to Orson Welles's *Mercury Theatre on the Air* broadcast from 8:00 to 9:00 P.M. EST tonight and did not realize that the program was merely a modernized adaptation of H. G. Wells's famous novel *The War of the Worlds,* we are repeating the fact which was made clear four times on the program that, while the names of some American cities were used, as in all novels of dramatization, the entire story and all of its incidents were fictitious.

By then it was too late. The damage had been done. Listeners who had never heard the initial announcement had fled their homes before this reassuring message came over the air. After leaving the studio, Welles and several companions passed Times Square and looked out the taxi window to see a large crowd peering at the moving electric sign on the Times Building. When they realized that the news flash was describing the extraordinary effects of their broadcast, the actor Joseph Cotten turned and told Welles he was through in show business.

The next day a somewhat equivocal apology, over the impresario's signature, appeared in the daily papers:

Orson Welles, in behalf of *The Mercury Theatre on the Air,* is deeply regretful to learn that the H. G. Wells fantasy, *War of the Worlds,* which was designed as entertainment, has caused some apprehension among Columbia's network listeners. Far from expecting the radio audience to take the program as fact rather than as a fictional presentation, we feared that the classic H. G. Wells story, which has served as inspiration for so many moving pictures, radio serials, and even comic strips, might appear too old-fashioned for modern consumption. We can only suppose that the special nature of radio, which is often heard in fragments, or in parts disconnected from the whole, has led to this misunderstanding.

That was precisely it, of course. The "special nature of radio" was indeed at the heart of what had happened, and CBS officials—mindful of potential ramifications in Washington, D.C.—apologized for the incident and announced that the technique of simulated news broadcasts would not be used again. That seemed to mollify members of the Federal Communications Commission, who decided not to take action against the network since "there appeared to be no likelihood of a repetition of the incident." A few days after the broadcast, William S. Paley, the man who controlled CBS and who was not about to allow anything of the sort to happen again, received an envelope containing a note and a $2 bill. The writer said he was a man of limited means but wanted to express his gratitude to CBS: his mother-in-law had been seized with a heart attack during the Welles program and died on the spot.

In the aftermath of the broadcast, suits for damages, injuries, and distress of various kinds were inevitably filed against Welles and *Mercury Theatre,* but none was legally proved and only one was settled—out of court, and against the advice of Welles's attorneys. It involved a Massachusetts worker who had heard the program. "I thought the best thing to do was to go away," he wrote. "So I took three dollars twenty-five cents out of my savings and bought a ticket. After I had gone sixty miles I knew it was a play. Now I don't have money left for the shoes I was saving up for. Will you please have someone send me a pair of black shoes size 9B?" Welles did.

All in all, when you stopped to think that of an estimated six million people who heard the program, at least one-fifth of them had taken it literally, it was a sobering glimpse into the troubled American psyche.

PART II

1938

WASHINGTON: VOICES FROM THE HEARTLAND

*Charles Lindbergh's personal magnetism
is evident in this photograph,
taken at an America First rally at New York's
Madison Square Garden in 1941.*

CHAPTER 10

"... they can't realize the change aviation has made."

On the same September day that Neville Chamberlain returned in triumph to London, waving a scrap of paper before his countrymen, Charles A. Lindbergh arrived at the U.S. embassy in Paris. Ambassador William Bullitt had invited him to a conference and thoughtfully offered him the same room in which he had stayed on the momentous night of May 21, 1927. It seemed strange, Lindbergh thought, to see again the familiar surroundings of the embassy—the court, the staircase, the corner parlor he remembered—and he noticed that there was now a brass plate on the bed he had slept in eleven years before.

Surely other memories flooded back—of 100,000 deliriously happy Frenchmen swarming onto the field at Le Bourget to greet him when he landed after the thirty-three-hour flight, some of them ripping pieces of fabric off the *Spirit of St. Louis,* others dragging him from the cockpit and carrying him away on their shoulders until he escaped to the pilots' quarters, identified himself self-consciously—"I am Charles A. Lindbergh"—and handed letters of introduction to Ambassador Myron Herrick. The medals, the speeches, the crowds—always the crowds—and the trip home to the States aboard the cruiser *Memphis,* to be greeted with half a million letters, 75,000 telegrams, two railroad cars filled with press clippings, and the engulfing admiration of his countrymen. President Coolidge, awarding

him the Congressional Medal of Honor and the nation's first Distinguished
Flying Cross, told throngs in Washington that the transatlantic flight was
"the same story of valor and victory by a son of the people that shines
through every page of American history." Then New York, a city gone
berserk, with some four million ecstatic people cheering their hearts out
during the incredible ticker-tape parade up Broadway.

Of all the public figures who had captivated America in that decade of
noise and hero worship, only Lindbergh retained his almost magical hold
on the public into the thirties, perhaps because he embodied the youthful,
unquenchable spirit Americans felt they had left behind, the national belief
that the unattainable was somehow within reach. His achievement alone
would have caught the imagination of the entire world—and did—but the
fact that he was a boyish Galahad out of the West, a guileless, modern-day
knight in aviator's helmet and goggles, with tousled blond hair and a smile
that melted the heart, brought him such adoration as few men in history
have known. And it proved to be more than he had bargained for.

Harold Nicolson, the English writer and statesman who became his
friend while writing a biography of Lindbergh's father-in-law, said some
years later that there was almost a ferocity to Lindbergh's efforts to remain
himself. "And in the process of that arduous struggle his simplicity became
muscle-bound," Nicolson concluded, "his self-control thickened into arrogance, and his convictions hardened into granite." It was a harsh judgment,
yet even before the end of 1927, that wondrous year, Lindbergh admitted
to being "so filled up with this hero guff that I was ready to shout murder."

He was discovering that he could not write checks because people kept
them for his autograph instead of cashing them; he could not send out his
laundry because it would not be returned. Once he learned that a woman
attempted to rent the hotel room he had just vacated so she could bathe in
the same tub. He maintained that he had no wish to be a celebrity, but
America would not allow him *not* to be one, and in a perverse sort of way
he abetted the process. He flew the *Spirit of St. Louis* to all forty-eight states
after his transatlantic flight; he went to Mexico and South America; he
wrote a book, *We,* about his famous adventure, and this and a series of
newspaper and magazine articles brought him wealth along with additional
fame; he flew from coast to coast, setting a new speed record; he had a
whirlwind romance with Anne, the lovely daughter of Dwight Morrow, a
prominent lawyer, Morgan partner, and ambassador to Mexico; and he and
his bride flew off the next year to Canada, to Alaska, and to Siberia, Japan,
and China—a journey chronicled in Anne Morrow Lindbergh's best-selling
North to the Orient. It seemed that he was never out of the news, was
constitutionally unable to avoid being the public figure, all the while insisting that he wanted only privacy and to be let alone. But the paradox was
that he appeared to be sustained in a curious way by these frequent forays
into the public eye, even as he denied that it was so and raged at newspaper-

men and photographers who considered it their job to document the doings of the famous man.

Then came the cruelest time, the hour of lead, as Anne Lindbergh would call it. On March 1, 1932, their firstborn child, Charles Augustus II, was kidnapped from his nursery crib in their Hopewell, New Jersey, home. A $50,000 ransom payment was delivered to a designated cemetery in the Bronx, but the baby was not returned; on May 12 his body was found in a shallow grave not far from their house. To the Lindberghs it seemed that the newspaper and radio publicity, the reporters' morbid curiosity about every personal facet of the tragedy, would never end, and when Bruno Richard Hauptmann, a Bronx carpenter, was arrested and tried in 1934, their nightmare had to be relived in agonizing detail, imposing an almost unendurable strain on the family. They had to leave their home, which was overrun with curiosity-seekers, one of whom dug up and carried off the dirt from where the child's body had been buried. From cranks came letters threatening to kidnap their second son, Jon. Incident after incident created a revulsion in Lindbergh's mind, eventually against Americans in general and the press in particular, so that years later, when photographers told him they would give their word of honor to let him alone if he would permit them to take just one picture, he could only burst out, "Imagine a press photographer talking about his word of honor! The type of men who broke through the window of the Trenton morgue to open my baby's casket and photograph its body—they talk to me of honor!"

Believing that the only escape from the "tremendous public hysteria" surrounding him in the United States was to leave the land of his birth, Lindbergh took his family to England in December 1935 to seek sanctuary and peace. He found both, and during this self-imposed exile he probably had a better opportunity to see what was going on behind the scenes in Europe than any other American private citizen. The British and French treated him with respect, allowing him the privacy he so much desired, and because he was a distinguished aviator he was sought out by Europe's public figures and invited by government officials to inspect the aircraft, the factories, and the aviation facilities of the major nations on the continent.

In early May 1938 he and Anne dined with Lord and Lady Astor in London and met the new U.S. ambassador to the Court of St. James's for the first time. Joseph P. Kennedy interested him greatly: "He is not the usual type of politician or diplomat," Lindbergh noted. "His views on the European situation seem intelligent and interesting. I hope to see more of him." As, indeed, he did; later deciding, "I cannot help liking Kennedy. He is an unusual combination of politician and businessman." A quality that appealed particularly to the aviator was the importance Kennedy attached to his children, and not surprisingly, Lindbergh was curious about the ambassador's attitude toward the press. While Kennedy did not seem to want publicity, he appeared to be attracted to it—whether because he enjoyed being in the spotlight, or whether he simply considered it necessary in his present position, Lindbergh could not decide. All in all, the colonel was impressed with him: "I place him among the men who are a constructive influence in this so-called modern world."

In mid-September of 1938, Lindbergh—who was on the French island of Illiec with his family—received an urgent request from Kennedy to come to London. It was the eve of the Munich crisis, and after the ambassador had introduced Charles and Anne to six of his children, he discussed the grave situation with them. At any moment, he said, fighting might break out; Hitler's divisions were massed on the Czech border. Chamberlain had informed Kennedy that the Nazi dictator was prepared to risk a world war in order to get what he wanted and that England, although unready, would fight to stop him.

Lindbergh knew as well as the prime minister that the British were in no condition to go to war. Always before, they had been able to keep the fleet between themselves and an enemy, but as he said, "they can't realize the change aviation has made. I am afraid this is the beginning of the end of England as a great power." From what he could tell, the British government seemed blissfully unaware that Germany's preponderance of air power would permit Hitler to bomb any city in Europe with impunity, and not only was Germany's strength underestimated—Russia's was almost as much overestimated. Kennedy asked his guest to put his opinions in writing, so he could pass them on to Neville Chamberlain and the State Department.

On this same visit to London the Lindberghs were entertained by Colonel and Mrs. Raymond Lee, who told them that the British diplomatic delegation was returning from Germany and that negotiations had broken off. Lee was the military attaché for air at the embassy in London, and no admirer of the newly appointed ambassador, whom he considered "crude, blatant, and ignorant in everything he did or said." Joseph Kennedy, Lee felt, had the acumen that might be expected in a speculator, along with an "insensibility to the great forces which are now playing like heat lightning over the map of the world."

On the night of September 27, Lindbergh slept fitfully, thinking of the prospect of England being bombed, and the next day, approaching the U.S. embassy, he observed a long line of people waiting for visas. Inside, he was informed that a shipment of gas masks had just arrived from the States, and he asked if he might have two of them. Just then Kennedy walked in and remarked, "You may not need them. There's some good news coming in."

The following day the ambassador observed, "Everything is looking better," and Lindbergh received the strong impression that Kennedy had played an important role in bringing about the conference between Hitler, Chamberlain, Daladier, and Mussolini.

═══

It was his visit to Paris on September 30 that convinced Lindbergh to make a personal study of the general situation on the continent during the approaching winter. "I don't know how much I can do here," he wrote, "but I feel that if anything can be done to avoid European war, it must be based upon an intimate understanding of conditions in Europe."

He had already visited the Soviet Union, where he found the state of aeronautical development far behind that in the United States, Germany, or Great Britain. The Russians' skill at towing gliders and landing paratroops impressed him favorably, but their planes—although "good enough to be used effectively in a modern war"—were not up to those of other countries. En route back to England he stopped off in Czechoslovakia, spending half an hour with a tense President Beneš before touring the country's aviation establishment. This visit occurred just before the Munich agreement, and it convinced Lindbergh that "Czechoslovakia is not well equipped in the air"—her pursuit planes were too slow, and there were too few fast bombers to mount any kind of counterattack.

Before going to France that same month, Lindbergh had heard from Ambassador Bullitt about the parlous state of that nation's air force. France did not possess enough modern military planes even to "put up a show in case of war," Bullitt told him, and in a conflict between France, England, and Russia on one side and Germany on the other, the Germans would have immediate air supremacy. As Lindbergh had suspected, "Germany has developed a huge air force while England has slept and France has deluded herself with a Russian alliance." From Guy la Chambre, the French minister of air himself, he learned how desperate the situation was. France was producing about forty-five or fifty warplanes a month compared with Germany's five or six hundred.

When Lindbergh arrived in Paris on September 30, Bullitt said he hoped he would take part in a discussion with la Chambre and Jean Monnet, the French banker and economist, to consider the possibility of establishing factories in Canada to manufacture planes for France. The idea, of course, was to circumvent the terms of the U.S. Neutrality Act, and Monnet was talking about a production potential of 10,000 planes a year. (Bullitt's opinion was that it should be 50,000.) In the course of that day and the next, Lindbergh discovered that French intelligence put the existing German air fleet at 6,000 modern planes, plus 2,000 to 3,000 older models, and estimated that the Reich had the capability of building 24,000 planes a year—versus France's existing potential of 540 and a predicted capacity of 5,000 a year. It was believed further that Britain—which had 2,000 aircraft (only 700 of them modern types)—might be producing 10,000 planes annually in a year's time; but this left an immense gap of 10,000 aircraft a year between Germany's output and the combined expectations of Great Britain and France.

Lindbergh was glum. His private reaction to what he was hearing was that far more than military might was needed to overcome the German advantage. What was required in France, he believed, was "a different spirit among the people" and "the absolute necessity of a changed attitude toward

Germany." Might could not be purchased with gold, except temporarily; "Strength is an inherent quality in a people," he wrote, and nothing he had seen in France persuaded him that democracy could last much longer there. Far better, he believed, to invest money in the effort "to bring back life to a corrupt and demoralized nation" than to use it for purchasing aircraft. The latter course seemed to him like hiring mercenaries—"the last act of a dying nation."

Pondering France's seemingly insurmountable problems—the appalling lack of preparedness (he was told that not a single modern pursuit plane was available for the defense of Paris, that France had no aircraft of any type as fast as the new German bombers), and the impossibility of obtaining planes from the United States (quite apart from the restrictions of the Neutrality Act, the U.S. Army and Navy and commercial airlines were absorbing virtually all of America's productive capacity)—Lindbergh ventured an astonishing suggestion to the group. Why not, he asked, purchase bombers from Germany?

At first the Frenchmen laughed, assuming that he was joking, but he argued that such an arrangement might quickly smoke out Germany's military intentions and could, indeed, be to the interest of both parties. While giving France the aircraft she needed, opening up some trade between the two countries, possibly decreasing tension, and reducing the arms disparity, it would also afford Germany a measure of relief from the staggering cost of constructing warplanes. The meeting broke up without a decision, but in the months to come the French began taking Lindbergh's proposal ever more seriously. In December, la Chambre asked him to ascertain whether or not the Germans would sell planes or aircraft engines to France, and he undertook this mission on a visit he made to Berlin that month. At the same time he learned that the Italians had actually offered the French some engines, prompting him to observe "how little the public knows about what is really taking place! Back of the curtains they offer to exchange airplane engines for phosphate." Finally, in mid-January of 1939, a surprised Lindbergh was informed by General Erhard Milch, inspector general of the German Luftwaffe, that Germany *would* be willing to sell 1,250-horsepower Daimler-Benz engines to France, provided absolute secrecy was observed while the negotiations were taking place and provided further that France paid in cash, not goods.

Meanwhile, what of England? His stay in that country persuaded Lindbergh that it, like France, had neither the spirit nor the capabilities required for a modern war. The factories were amateurish and inefficient operations at best; he was told that as many as 30 percent more workmen were required in a British factory to equal American production of the same item. The nation's military strength could not even be compared to Germany's: the empire was disintegrating at the same time England's importance as a world power was declining. Although the average Englishman knew nothing of his country's unpreparedness, on the streets that autumn all the talk was of war; people were having gas masks fitted in the center of London; and during the Munich talks trenches were being dug in most of the parks and open areas of the city. As Lindbergh saw it, the English possessed confidence rather than ability, tenacity rather than strength, and determination rather than intelligence; yet he had to admit that "any conclusion one reaches in regard to the English is constantly shaken by the exceptions which arise." He was appalled, however, to see how "the spirit of the Light Brigade" suddenly took hold of the country during the Munich crisis. The British were up to their old tricks—ready to fight for their principles, casting judgment to the winds, and as usual moving too late—which, in the long run, could only mean "the destruction of European civilization."

Now there was Germany to consider, and on October 10, Charles and Anne took off from Le Bourget in Paris and flew to Berlin's Tempelhof airport. It was their third trip to Nazi Germany in as many years and the first of two they made in the fall of 1938. Thanks to Major Truman Smith, the American military attaché in Berlin, the couple had been invited there in 1936 and 1937 by Hermann Göring, Reichsminister for air and, after Hitler, the most powerful man in the nation. Smith, who was an infantryman by trade, was responsible for reporting to Washington on developments in aviation as well as those in land warfare, and he was not satisfied with the quality of intelligence he was receiving. At the breakfast table one morning his wife read him a news story about Colonel Lindbergh inspecting an airplane factory in France, and it occurred to Smith that an official visit by the famous aviator to Germany might uncover information the United States wanted. So the trips were arranged, resulting eventually in more than Smith ever dreamed of obtaining—a full and detailed "general estimate" of German air strength. Sent to Washington over Smith's signature, it was based entirely on Lindbergh's firsthand inspection, expert analysis, and experience of the factories, airplanes, personnel, research, and command structure that constituted Germany's air establishment. That nation, the report declared, had outdistanced France in all respects and was generally superior to Great Britain, except for aircraft engines. By 1941 or 1942, it was estimated, Germany's technical development would equal that of the United States—a "phenomenon of the first diplomatic importance." Lindbergh himself put the case even more strongly, writing to a family friend: "The growth of German military aviation is, I believe, without parallel in history. . . ."

On October 8, 1938, a week after the Munich conference, General Henry H. Arnold (known universally as Hap) wrote to Lindbergh in Illiec, telling him the United States badly needed information on the present and potential air strength of other nations, particularly Germany, adding that he would consider it a great personal favor and an act of patriotism if Lindbergh would send whatever information he could assemble. Two years earlier, when the Lindberghs first visited Berlin, correspondent William Shirer grumbled that "the Nazis, led by Göring, are making a great play for them," but that was nothing compared to the reception that greeted them on their return in 1938. During the course of a month the American flier was given an opportunity to talk with all the principals of the aviation establishment—General Erhard Milch, head of the Air Ministry; General Ernst Udet, a World War ace who had developed the dive-bombing technique first employed in Spain; Heinrich Focke, the aeronautical engineer; and Marshal Hermann Göring—not to mention scores of pilots and technicians. He met members of the diplomatic circle in the capital, visited aircraft factories, inspected bomb shelters and antiaircraft batteries, and then was permitted to see—and to fly—many of the latest German planes, including the Ju-90 transport and the Messerschmitt 108 and 109 fighters, and he was the first non-German to see the secret new Ju-88 bomber. (As Anne Lindbergh remarked later, almost all of their conversations were with aviation people; neither she nor her husband spoke or read German; most talks went through an interpreter; and they felt they learned little about what the ordinary people of the country thought, beyond an almost pathological fear of the Russians. And the French, she concluded, felt about the Germans the way Germans felt about Russians.)

Neither Lindbergh nor the Americans to whom he was supplying information seem to have given the possibility much thought, but his seeming freedom of access to Germany's secrets was very carefully planned. Like Lindbergh, high-level visitors from other countries were also taken on conducted tours to see the impressive Messerschmitt assembly lines, the performance of the latest model planes, the exhibitions of precision bombing. Understandably, this thoroughly memorable experience was guaranteed to make the visitor return home and speak with awe of what he had beheld. Since it was state policy in Germany to magnify the strength of the nation's military might by any means, numbers were exaggerated—numbers of aircraft in being, numbers of aircraft German factories were capable of producing; and by repeating often and loudly that the Third Reich was all-powerful, completely mobilized for war, equipped with the most and the best aircraft, tanks, or whatever, Hitler's propaganda machine ensured that the story would be believed.

Now, for Charles Lindbergh, more was in store. On the night of Tuesday, October 18, Ambassador Hugh Wilson gave a stag dinner at the embassy, and the occasion was the scene of an incident that was to plague Lindbergh for years to come. In addition to German officers and members of the U.S. embassy staff, Wilson's guests included the Belgian and Italian ambassadors, Generals Milch and Udet, Heinkel and Messerschmitt, and Göring. As an aviator, Hermann Göring ranked at the top of Germany's pantheon: a World War ace, he had succeeded to the command of Baron Manfred von Richthofen's "Flying Circus" after the Red Baron was killed. Under his leadership, the Luftwaffe had become the most fearsome weapon of the Third Reich. Vain, arrogant, and complex, Göring was a diplomat, economic planner, art connoisseur, gourmand, dandy, morphine addict, and

Hitler's most powerful associate in the high command.[1] Given the nature of the ulterior motive Ambassador Wilson had in mind, he could be forgiven for using Charles Lindbergh as bait to lure Göring to this dinner. Wilson was eager to establish friendly relations with the number-two Nazi in hopes that he would do something to ameliorate the financial plight of Jews who were being forced to emigrate from Germany in a penniless state. Göring was no humanitarian and he lacked the courage to stand up to Hitler, but at least his attitude toward the Jews was ambivalent, which was more than could be said of other top Nazis, and it was known that he opposed the use of indiscriminate violence and had helped his actress wife get her Jewish friends away from the Gestapo on a number of occasions.

Lindbergh was standing at the back of the room when Göring arrived, and he noticed that the marshal was carrying a red box and some papers in his hand. Göring chatted briefly with several other guests and gradually made his way over to Lindbergh, handed him the box and the papers, and spoke a few sentences in German, which Lindbergh did not understand. Afterward, the American said, "I found that he had presented me with the German Eagle, one of the highest German decorations, 'by order of *der Führer.*'"

Perhaps a man accustomed to receiving medals does not give much thought to their political significance, but Lindbergh's wife did when he spoke to her about it later that night. She called it the Albatross, and albatross it would be, as he learned to his lasting discomfort.

After the embassy dinner, the group split up into small groups; Göring came over to Lindbergh and suggested that they move into the next room. Most of his questions to the American had to do with the latter's impressions of Russia, after which Göring turned the conversation to the subject of Germany's plans and accomplishments—mainly in the field of aviation, about which he was surprisingly candid. In the journal he kept, Lindbergh described the encounter rather casually, as one might speak of any pleasant social occasion, but one gets the impression that he considered it an event of more than usual significance, which indeed it was. For when he and Anne left Germany at the end of October he could say that he had a fairly clear picture of the overall situation in Europe. "I had seen the strength of Germany," he wrote, "and I knew the weakness of England and France."

[1] In 1935, William Bullitt had sent President Roosevelt a delightful description of Göring's appearance at Marshal Joseph Pilsudski's funeral in Warsaw, saying that he swept into the cathedral like "a German tenor playing Siegfried. . . . He is at least a yard across the bottom as the crow flies [and] nearly a yard from rear to umbilicus and as he is not even as tall as I am and encases himself in a glove-tight uniform, the effect is novel. He must carry with him a personal beauty attendant as his fingers, which are almost as thick as they are short, carry long, pointed, carefully enameled nails and his pink complexion shows every sign of daily attention. His eyes pop wildly as if he were either suffering from a glandular derangement or still taking cocaine. His lips are as thin as those of an infant. When he was 250 pounds lighter he must have been a blond beauty of the most unpleasant sort. He is really the most appalling representative of a nation that I have ever laid eyes on."

In his opinion the Germans were a great people, whose welfare was inseparable from the rest of Europe, and he was certain that the only hope of avoiding war and preserving western civilization was to establish a rapport between Britain and Germany. If that failed, and if war should come, America must stay out of it.

Charles Lindbergh had the type of mind that absorbed immediately every detail of the airplanes he saw, that took in all the fine points of design and performance, and what he had learned during this crucial moment in history was to be of inestimable value to the authorities in Washington, because he could give it to them straight, in factual and unemotional terms, the way a superb technician might describe a piece of machinery. But certain political and social implications of what was going on in Germany seem to have escaped him, not because he was indifferent or callous but because such matters were largely beyond the focus of his interests. Not until he returned to England, for example, did he pay much attention to what was happening to Germany's Jews—and then it was to wonder why the Germans, with their sense of order, could tolerate the anti-Semitic demonstrations he had seen. Undoubtedly they had a Jewish problem, he thought, but why handle it so unreasonably?

CHAPTER 11

—————◆—————

". . . much of the soul has gone out of America."

C harles Lindbergh was by no means the only American who was oblivious to or unconcerned about the plight of Germany's Jews, and the reasons were at once simple and complex.

Start with the simple. When I was attending Linden School, probably around the time I was in fourth grade, I had one of those brief youthful attachments to a boy named Sylvan Jubelirer. I thought he was the funniest kid I had ever seen; I'm sure he had a number of other accomplishments (being very bright, for one), but all I now remember is his talent for rolling his prominent eyes. They didn't rotate in slow, lazy circles, but incredibly fast, like pinwheels, and he only had to begin this extraordinary perform-ance before he had me, and most of the class, in hysterics, enraging the uncomprehending teacher, who had seen nothing. One day Sylvan invited me to his house for Saturday lunch, and we spent the afternoon playing with his toys, wandering around a neighborhood that was unfamiliar to me, doing not much of anything but having a relaxed time in the manner of boys who have little on their minds.

The next week I asked if I could invite Sylvan to our house for lunch, and Mother said no, she was busy. That happened several times before I realized that for some reason I didn't understand she wasn't enthusiastic about having Sylvan to visit. This never became an issue, because he told me he was moving away—to Milwaukee, as I recall—and within a few weeks he had gone out of my life, briefly mourned but never entirely forgotten, and to this day I wince at the thought of why he may not have been welcome at our house.

So much of America in the thirties was a narrow world, and the Jew was only one victim of prejudice. On September 26, 1938, the great blues singer Bessie Smith was in an automobile accident near Memphis. One of her arms was nearly severed, and she was rushed to the nearest hospital, bleeding profusely. But because she was black, she was turned away at the door and died on the way to another hospital. Jim Crow's pervasion of society extended even to the manner in which stories about Negroes appeared in a newspaper like the *Pittsburgh Press*. It happened that Barbara Hutton, heiress to a $40 million Woolworth fortune, had been divorced from Prince Alexis Mdivani, and the next day married Count Kurt Haugwitz-Reventlow. The train carrying the newlyweds stopped in Pittsburgh en route to New York and a ship bound for Europe, and when the couple failed to emerge from their bedroom, the reporter, desperate for a story to take back to his managing editor, questioned the Pullman porter attending their car. It was not what the man said but the manner in which he was quoted that reflected those times: " 'She done retired afore we all got into Beaver Falls,' one of the dark and stalwart said, 'Man alive, yuh think Ah's gwan call her?' "

Our neighborhood was determinedly white, Anglo-Saxon, and Protestant, an enclave in which upwardly mobile people behaved according to their conception of what was best for them, their children, and their hardwon success. Yet beneath the generally serene surface of life on those quiet streets, I feel certain, was a layer of insecurity, a fear of the unknown and the unacceptable, an instinctive shying away from the alien, that were all part of the emotional baggage passed along from one generation to the next. A kind of thoughtless prejudice was the way of our carefully structured world in the mid-1930s, and if anyone there sensed that this small island of security might someday succumb to outside forces of change, or that our world might expand, that was not a topic of discussion that reached children's ears.

Yet America's disregard for what was happening inside Nazi Germany was caused by more than unthinking prejudice. The easiest, most charitable explanation lay in America's preoccupation with itself. Adolf Hitler's appointment as chancellor of Germany on January 30, 1933, virtually coincided with Franklin Roosevelt's swearing in as the thirty-second president of the United States, and the chaos that confronted Roosevelt as he took office dwarfed consideration of what was occurring elsewhere in the world. America was paralyzed financially: nearly thirteen million people—onefourth of the labor force—were unemployed; national income was half what it had been in 1928; every bank in the country had closed its doors; and the republic was at or near the nadir of the gravest economic depression in its history. With good reason, many thoughtful citizens believed that revolution was at hand.

Americans were understandably obsessed with the woes that afflicted themselves and their families. Would their savings be intact when the bank reopened—if, indeed, the bank reopened? Would they have a job? Would their children have enough to eat? Would they be able to keep their home or farm? In the face of preoccupation with questions like these, it was little wonder if the average American was largely unaware, initially at least, of the terrifying brutality that had been unloosed in Germany. And only a handful could have known that Hitler had signaled his ultimate intentions more than a decade before: "None but those of German blood, whatever their creed, may be members of the nation," he had written. "No Jew, therefore, may be a member of the nation."

In the years between 1933 and 1938, however, it would have been almost impossible for a literate American to be insensible to events in Germany. Increasingly, newspapers carried stories and editorials about the Nazis' violent anti-Semitism, the acts of individual and group savagery, the book burnings, even the concentration camps (as early as April 22, 1933, a *New York Times* correspondent wrote a firsthand description of conditions at Dachau, where four thousand new inmates had just been incarcerated). Nor was this information confined to newspapers. In 1938, in their September-October issue, the editors of *Story* magazine printed a short piece of fiction by Kressmann Taylor entitled "Address Unknown," and never in that publication's seven-year history, they said, had anything created so much comment. The issue was sold out in ten days, and the story was then reprinted in the January 1939 *Reader's Digest* and published in book form by Simon & Schuster. As a result, a great many readers were exposed to the haunting exchange of letters between a German Jew named Max, living in San Francisco, and his Gentile friend Martin Shulse, a former suitor of Max's sister, who had taken the money he made in the United States and returned to Germany to participate in the rebirth of a new Germany under Hitler. After Martin ignores Max's pleas to help his actress sister to get out of Germany, and turns her away from his door when she arrives there begging for sanctuary, pursued by storm troopers, Max begins sending Martin a series of letters and cablegrams that convince the Nazi authorities that he too is Jewish. The final letter is returned to Max, stamped ADRESSAT UNBEKANNT.

On January 21, 1939, Hitler informed Czechoslovakia's foreign minister, "We are going to destroy the Jews," and ten days later, speaking before laughing, wildly applauding members of the Reichstag, he warned that if Jewish financiers plunged the world into war the result would be "the annihilation of the Jewish race in Europe." Alas for Hitler's intended victims, outside Germany's borders an inertia or catalepsy in high places produced what might be described charitably as a policy of inaction.

In America, some of this had to do with domestic politics. By 1938, Roosevelt's bold New Deal had gone sour. Instead of improving, economic conditions deteriorated steadily that year, and when a public opinion poll was taken during the summer barely half of the people interviewed indicated that they would vote for Roosevelt if he were running for office then. Hatred of the president in conservative circles had never been more intense. Senators and representatives on the Hill were balking after years of behaving like rubber stamps; conservatives still had their backs up over Roosevelt's attempt to pack the Supreme Court in 1937; and the plain truth was that the New Deal program for the general welfare had slowed almost to a halt because of congressional resistance or foot-dragging. Roosevelt decided to act, and action took the form of trying to purge the Democratic Party of men he regarded as mossbacks, especially Senators Walter George of Georgia, Cotton Ed Smith of South Carolina, and Millard Tydings of Maryland. The results of the off-year election were a shattering defeat for the president: in the House the Republicans picked up eighty-two seats, in the Senate, eight. The GOP won a dozen governorships, and Ohio's Robert Alphonso Taft took over a Senate seat that he would fashion into a national rostrum.

Compounding the political problems fueled by unemployment and depression were two other factors: flagrant anti-Semitism and a nativism no less virulent than the anti-Catholic, anti-immigrant forces that had produced the Native American and Know-Nothing parties of the 1840s and '50s. What this meant to the beleaguered Jews in Germany was that the leader of the world's most powerful democracy—the man they counted on to offer them support and relief—was in a very touchy position vis-à-vis many of this country's political conservatives, who were the last people likely to do much to assist the Jews. The searing realization that little help would be forthcoming from America came in the wake of a devastating pogrom known as Kristallnacht, the Night of Broken Glass.

On October 28, 1938, the Nazis—confident after Munich that no European nation was prepared to interfere with anything they did—swept up thousands of Polish Jews living in Germany, herded them into trucks and trains, and dumped them, without clothes, food, or money, in the no-man's-land between the German and Polish frontiers. One of the families deported was named Grynszpan. Seventeen-year-old Herschel Grynszpan had previously fled to France, and when the already distraught young man received a letter from his father describing the family's suffering, he bought a pistol and went to the German embassy in Paris, intending to kill Ambassador Johannes von Welczeck. Wearing a khaki raincoat and looking like a worried schoolboy, he was ushered into the office of Ernst Vom Rath, third secretary of the embassy, and in reply to Vom Rath's question of why he had come Grynszpan pulled out the revolver and shot the diplomat five times. Afterward he told police, "It is not a crime to be a Jew. I am not a dog. I have a right to live. The Jewish people have a right to some part of the earth. Wherever I have been, I have been treated like an animal."

The popular columnist Dorothy Thompson, back in the United States after several years as a foreign correspondent in Europe, had a gift for dramatizing events that still seemed so remote to Americans, and in her regular Monday-evening radio broadcast on *The General Electric Hour,* which reached an estimated five million households, she spoke of the unfortunate Herschel Grynszpan: "I feel as though I know that boy, for in the past five years I have met so many whose story is the same—the same except for this unique desperate act. . . . They say he will go to the guillotine, without a trial by jury." Then she asked, "Who is on trial in this case? I say the Christian world is on trial [and] we who are not Jews must speak, speak our sorrow and indignation and disgust in so many voices that they will be heard." Within a month her readers and listeners had contributed $40,000 to Grynszpan's legal defense fund, but the Nazis had gone beyond listening to voices of protest or worrying what a French court might decide.

As fate would have it, Grynszpan's victim, Vom Rath, was under investigation by the Gestapo, or secret police, because of his opposition to the Nazis' anti-Semitism, but that made little difference to Joseph Goebbels, minister of propaganda, who addressed Hitler's Old Guard on the night of Vom Rath's death, which happened to coincide with the anniversary of the Munich Beer Hall Putsch of 1923, when Hitler first attempted to seize power. Goebbels told the brownshirts what to do, and on the evening of November 9 the pogrom commenced.

Teletyped instructions went out from the Gestapo to every police headquarters in Germany, and the night of terror began, wild mobs swarming through the streets, smashing the plate-glass windows of Jewish-owned stores and looting the contents, storming the homes and apartments of Jews, beating the men, raping women, destroying or stealing all the possessions they could lay hands on. Nearly two hundred synagogues were burned, more than eight hundred shops destroyed and 7,500 looted, thousands of homes ransacked, littering the streets of Germany with tons of shattered glass and the ruined hopes of its Jewry. While flames leaped from the domes and windows of the great temple in Fasanenstrasse, the Nazis ordered a jazz band in a nearby café to play louder, so the music could be enjoyed by the crowd watching the fire. Trucks filled with Jews began rumbling toward concentration camps—to a point where the state police in Berlin had to inform all branch offices, "The Buchenwald concentration camp is filled to capacity with current deliveries." Walking along the Kurfürstendamm, the British reporter Hugh Greene saw gangs, often in uniform, breaking into shops and beating people up. He ran into a German journalist who asked what he was doing there and Greene replied, "I am observing German culture."

Some twenty thousand German Jews disappeared on the Night of Broken

Glass; in Austria, where the devastating pattern was repeated, all of Vienna's twenty-one synagogues were burned. In Stuttgart, almost every male Jew between the ages of eighteen and sixty-five was arrested, and a horrified American consul telegraphed Ambassador Hugh Wilson in Berlin that the Jews of southwest Germany "have suffered vicissitudes during the last three days which would seem unreal to one living in an enlightened country during the twentieth century if one had not actually been a witness of their dreadful experiences."

Kristallnacht did not end there. The Nazis imposed a fine of a billion marks (about $400 million in 1939 dollars) on the Jews as "money atonement" for Vom Rath's death; decreed that the Jews were responsible for repairing all the damage done to their property, and that work must commence at once; and ruled that owners would receive no insurance on their ruined buildings.

In the wake of the pogroms, Secretary of State Cordell Hull announced that Hugh Wilson was being recalled for consultations, and on November 15, President Roosevelt followed up with a statement: "The news of the past few days from Germany has deeply shocked public opinion in the United States. . . . I myself could scarcely believe that such things could occur in a twentieth-century civilization." He went on to say that he had asked the State Department to order Wilson home for good.[1] The White House statement and the recall of an ambassador were the extent of U.S. protest, and when no move was made to alter the nation's business-as-usual relations with Hitler Germany, a group of prominent writers—including Dorothy Thompson, Thornton Wilder, Robert Sherwood, Eugene O'Neill, John Steinbeck, Lillian Hellman, and others—sent a telegram to the president calling for an end to silence on the persecution of the Jews and condemning the continuation of economic relations "with a country that avowedly uses mass murder to solve its economic problems." By now, as Anthony Drexel Biddle, Jr., the U.S. ambassador in Warsaw, informed the secretary of state, Nazi officialdom considered world public opinion bankrupt. They had known all along that people would throw up their hands in horror, but they also knew that nothing would be done.

For an American who cared deeply about the sufferings of Germany's Jews—and thousands did—the question was how to instigate effective action. Justine Polier, a children's court judge in New York, decided that the place to start was with Eleanor Roosevelt, the wife of the president, and late in December, Mrs. Polier, the daughter of Rabbi Stephen Wise, proposed to Mrs. Roosevelt a child refugee bill that would permit the admission of ten thousand children a year in addition to the existing immigration quota for Germany.

---

[1] Hitler countered by recalling Ambassador Hans Dieckhoff from Washington. That left two chargés d'affaires to deal with relations between the two countries: Alexander C. Kirk in Berlin, Hans Thomsen in Washington.

By 1939 the immigration policy of the United States could only be described as a tangled thicket that was better at keeping people out than allowing them in. Between 1820, when immigration statistics were first recorded, and 1933, more than 37 million foreign-born had entered the country, but late in the nineteenth century and early in the twentieth a variety of xenophobes had begun lobbying to close the doors on newcomers, and as the movement gathered momentum the image of America as a haven for the victims of poverty, exploitation, and persecution began to pale. In 1921 the Quota Act placed numerical restrictions on European immigration for the first time, establishing a maximum of 335,000; in 1924 the Immigration Act reduced the maximum allowable number of aliens to 153,774 annually, with quotas to be based on the ethnic composition of the U.S. population in 1920. If anyone wanted a summary of how hard-line opponents of immigration felt about the subject, it was laid out for them by Congressman Martin Dies, in a 1934 magazine article: "We must ignore the tears of sobbing sentimentalists and internationalists, and we must permanently close, lock, and bar the gates of our country to new immigration waves and then throw the keys away." And should anyone doubt the effectiveness of Dies and the lobby he represented, statistics revealed that during the five-year period from 1926 to 1930, nearly 1.5 million people were admitted to the United States; in the five years that followed, the number had been reduced to 220,000.

With the massive unemployment of the 1930s, a new wrinkle was added to existing laws: admission to the United States would be permitted only if the immigrant could convince consular officials that he or she would not become a public charge. Because the Nazis, by 1934, had limited the amount of money Jews could take out of Germany to 10 reichsmarks, or about $4, the effect was to amalgamate U.S. and German policies, making it all but impossible for a German Jew to emigrate to the United States. And Hitler could gloat that America—through restrictive immigration laws—"has inhibited the unwelcome influx of such races as it has been unable to tolerate in its midst. Nor is America now ready to open its doors to Jews fleeing from Germany."

James G. McDonald, the League of Nations' appointee as high commissioner for refugees coming from Germany, called upon Roosevelt to relax these stringent requirements, thereby making it possible for more Germans to enter the United States, but for reasons that have never been altogether clear, the president refused. Even after the Kristallnacht horror, when a reporter asked if he would recommend relaxing immigration restrictions to admit more Jewish refugees, Roosevelt stated flatly, "That is not in contemplation. We have the quota system."[2]

---

[2] When Sir Ronald Lindsay, Britain's ambassador to the United States, generously offered to relinquish some of the 65,000 places from his nation's quota, a State Department official informed him that immigration quotas were established by law and were not subject to change (even though a mere four thousand Britons had come to the United States in 1938).

Yet it appears that what Roosevelt did not dare do publicly for fear of arousing anti-Jewish opposition he was willing to have handled *sub rosa,* and when his wife broached Justine Polier's proposal, he suggested that Mrs. Polier go ahead with the plan, making sure to get two people from the Republican side in both the House and Senate to sponsor the legislation. As Eleanor Roosevelt explained matters to Justine Polier, "The State Department is only afraid of what Congress will say to them, and therefore if you remove that fear the State Department will have no objection." The president also advised Mrs. Polier to select the bill's sponsors with great care, and "if possible," he urged, "get all the Catholic support you can."

Early in February of 1939 the child refugee bill was introduced by Democrat Robert Wagner of New York in the Senate, and by Edith Nourse Rogers, a Massachusetts Republican, in the House, and it was supported by a blue-ribbon committee including Cardinal Mundelein of Chicago; Herbert Hoover, the former president; Alfred Landon, the GOP candidate in 1936; and Frank Knox, publisher of the *Chicago Daily News,* who had been Landon's running mate. The bill called for admission of ten thousand children under the age of fourteen in 1939 and 1940, whose entry would be *in addition to* the regular German quota. Each child would be adopted temporarily by an American family, none would be permitted to work, and they would be reunited with their own parents as soon as it was safe and practicable to do so. The American Friends Service Committee had agreed to supervise the program, and the Quakers would be aided by a committee of distinguished American businessmen, clergymen, and educators. A day after the bill was introduced, some four thousand families volunteered to adopt the children. To the compassionate, it seemed a most reasonable and logical plan.

But the compassionate were not representative of the forces that dominated the Congress of the United States. There were, at the time, sixty anti-alien bills before the nation's lawmakers, and when opponents of the Wagner-Rogers bill wheeled their guns into position it was plain to see what the source of that anti-alien legislation was. Francis H. Kinnicutt, president of the Allied Patriotic Societies, speaking for the American Legion, the United Daughters of the Confederacy, the Society of Mayflower Descendants, the Sons of the American Revolution, the Daughters of the American Revolution, and a score of other groups, informed congressmen that the bill was "just part of a drive to break down the whole quota system—to go back to the condition when we were flooded with foreigners who tried to run the country on different lines from those laid down by the old stock."

Colonel John Thomas Taylor, representing the American Legion (which had already announced support for North Carolina Senator Robert H. Reynolds's bill abolishing *all* immigration to the United States for the next ten years), warned that if Congress passed the Wagner-Rogers bill the United States might as well admit "twenty thousand Chinese children. Certainly they are being persecuted too."

A speaker for Young Americans, Inc., said, "If we are going to keep this country as it is and not lose our liberty in the future, we have got to keep not only these children out of it, but the whole damned Europe." And Mrs. Agnes Waters, claiming to represent the widows of World War veterans, announced, "The refugees have a heritage of hate. They could never become loyal Americans." Why, she asked, "should we give preference to these potential Communists? Already we have too many of their kind in our country now trying to overthrow our government."

John B. Trevor, in behalf of more than one hundred patriotic societies of the American Coalition, reminded committee members of a poll taken by *Fortune* magazine, in which Americans were asked, "If you were a member of Congress, would you vote 'yes' or 'no' on a bill to open the doors of the United States to a larger number of European refugees than now admitted under our immigration quotas?" The results had been overwhelmingly negative: a resounding 83 percent of the respondents had voted no, 8.7 per had voted yes, and 8.3 percent had replied, "Don't know." At the same time the poll was taken, Under Secretary of State Sumner Welles told Eleanor Roosevelt that his desk was flooded with angry protests against admitting more Jews than the quotas allowed.

Clarence Pickett, the Quaker who had agreed to supervise the children's program, said at the Congressional hearing that the bill involved an issue far more serious than rescuing German children. The question, he said, was "whether the American people have lost their ability to respond to such tragic situations as this one. If it turns out that we have lost that ability, it will mean that much of the soul has gone out of America."

And so it seemed. President Roosevelt, having sampled the political wind, had been as accurate as ever in his assessment, and when the hearings on the bill closed on June 1, 1939, one of his aides handed him a memorandum stating that New York Representative Caroline O'Day was requesting an expression of FDR's views on the Wagner-Rogers bill. Roosevelt reached for a pencil and scribbled his comment on the memorandum: "File No Action FDR."

A month later the bill was reported out of committee with an amendment that appalled its sponsor, Senator Wagner: visas for twenty thousand children would be issued against, not in excess of, the regular German quota. The plan born of compassion was dead, and Wagner withdrew his legislation.

——

No American knew the names of those children for whom the senator had sought sanctuary, and perhaps that anonymity explained why the nation, which had so many nameless victims of the depression in its midst, failed to welcome them to the land of the free. Perhaps. But one might also reflect upon the tragic odyssey of the Hamburg-American Line's ship *St. Louis,* which sailed from Germany on May 13, 1939, with 936 passengers aboard.

All but six were Jewish refugees carrying a passport stamped with a red J. (Dorothy Thompson wrote that year, "It is a fantastic commentary on the inhumanity of our times that for thousands and thousands of people a piece of paper with a stamp on it is the difference between life and death.") They had paid for their passage; they had landing certificates signed by Cuba's director general of immigration; and 734 of them had also been assigned quota numbers by the U.S. Immigration Service, which meant that they could enter this country between three months and three years after their arrival in Cuba. Or so it appeared.

If ever a ship carried a cargo of memories—better call them nightmares—mixed with hope, it was the *St. Louis.* Rabbi Gelder, who was sixty-seven years old, was planning a reunion with two sons who had already emigrated. A twenty-three-year-old dressmaker's assistant named Gerda Weiss would be met on the dock in Havana by her fiancé—he was bringing the marriage license and ring, he promised. The wife and children of Bruno Glade, a pianist from Berlin, would be waiting when the ship landed; so would the wife and daughter of Moritz Schoenberger, an artist. A woman from Breslau named Feilchenfeld was taking her four small children to meet their father in New York. Elisabeth Broder, known as Liesl, would be joined in Havana by her fiancé, Hellmut Lewin. The two of them had become acquainted in Prague, where both were students, and where Hellmut was already a refugee from his native Berlin. Alarmed by what was happening there, he had gone to Prague, where university courses were taught in German as well as Czech and Slovak, and there he and Liesl had fallen in love.

After Munich, he decided he would be wise to get out of Czechoslovakia and join his parents in America, since he had a U.S. visa. Unfortunately, Liesl had none, so after he arrived in New York and found work (he was a trained engineer, but the only job that turned up was assembling radios, joining the mechanism and cabinet with two screws, for which he was paid $12 for a fifty-hour week), he sent her money for passage on the *St. Louis* and the price of a visa for Cuba. His idea was that if she could get to Havana, they would be married and he could bring her into the United States on his own papers. Until then, he was counting the minutes until they were reunited.

Only weeks, days, hours before, the *St. Louis* passengers who were so buoyed by hope had been bereft of it. Stigmatized as something less than human, they had lived through the terror, the summons by night, the brutality, and the continuous fear, and somehow, miraculously, because they had had enough money left to buy a Cuban landing certificate from the Hamburg-American Line, they found themselves aboard a floating pleasure palace, bound for the New World. The flight from reality began like a festive cruise, with dances, deck games, entertainment, delicious food, and superb service. Captain Gustav Schroeder was a compassionate man, determined somehow to make up to his passengers for what they had endured at the hands of the Nazis, so now, men and women who a few months before had been sweeping the streets of debris from the Kristallnacht were sitting back in upholstered chairs in the lounge, serenaded by a string quartet.

How to imagine what passed through the minds of those men and women and children? How to conceive the relief they felt? No more to lie awake in the dark, awaiting the footsteps on the stairs and the knock on the door while the cold sweat and the smell of fear enveloped them. They had lived in what an American reporter in Germany called "the terror of expectancy," which is worse than actual persecution, and now every turn of the propellers, every tick of the watch, took them farther from the horror, blunting the memory of what lay behind the ship's wake, beyond the vanishing eastern horizon.

Some, with the pessimism born of all that had befallen their people, said it was too good to last, and they were right. Before the *St. Louis* reached Havana a telegram to Captain Schroeder from officials in Cuba indicated that serious doubt existed about the validity of his passengers' landing certificates. Unbeknownst to anyone on the ship, President Federico Laredo Bru of Cuba had signed a decree eight days before the *St. Louis* left Hamburg, invalidating the travelers' immigration documents. Those original papers had been purchased in wholesale lots from the Cuban director of immigration by the Hamburg-American Line for resale to refugees; the Cuban government now declared that they had been sold illegally and that the refugees must obtain visas approved by the State, Labor, and Treasury departments of Cuba.

A few optimists on board knew in their hearts that things would work out, since they held a quota number for the United States. But there cannot have been many who had such hopes. No Jew who got out of Germany in 1939 was likely to be an optimist. These people could smell danger and death, knew the unutterable cruelty of fate, the grisly twists of chance, and if they were fatalists, they had every reason to be. Almost as an omen, an elderly professor named Moritz Weiler died. Captain Schroeder had seen this coming, realizing that the old man had lost the will to live when he left his homeland behind, and had him buried at sea so as not to give the Cuban authorities an added excuse to turn the *St. Louis* away.

It was the 27th day of May when the *St. Louis* slid into Havana harbor, and among those on hand to greet her were the families of Bruno Glade and Moritz Schoenberger, and Hellmut Lewin. A sizable welcoming party had hired little boats that bobbed up and down in the bay, circling the incoming ship, while the greeters waved and shouted, "*¡Mañana! ¡Mañana!*" But *mañana* came and went and nothing happened. None of the passengers on the *St. Louis* was permitted to go ashore and Cuban guards allowed no relative or friend to board the ship. As night fell, the waterfront became a scene out of purgatory, with guards patrolling the piers, searchlights sweeping the waters around the ship to reveal anyone attempting to swim ashore (but no one did—they had seen the sharks). By day, passengers called and waved futilely from the decks to their loved ones on shore. One woman held her two babies up to the porthole of her stateroom so that her husband, paddling a canoe in the water below, might catch a glimpse of his children. Hellmut Lewin never did get close enough to see Liesl: at such a distance it was impossible to pick her out from the hundreds of people lining the ship's rails.

The intransigence of Cuba's government was beyond all comprehension. The official position was that the landing certificates had been illegally sold and were therefore invalid; but what lay at the heart of the matter was too many recent immigrants, a wave of anti-Semitism in Cuba, and an outbreak of greed among government officials, from the president on down. Rival groups on the island were actually contending for money that might be extorted from these desperate people or from their friends and relatives. And for the jackals waiting for booty, things were looking up. The Jewish Joint Distribution Committee had sent two representatives to Cuba—Cecilia Razovsky and Lawrence Berenson—who were authorized to post a bond up to $125,000 to guarantee that no passenger would become a ward of the Cuban government, plus additional assurance that none of the Jewish refugees would seek employment in Cuba. Berenson was promised an interview with the Cuban president on June 1, but on May 31 Captain Schroeder was ordered to sail from Havana on the following day. When this news spread among the passengers, a Breslau lawyer named Max Loewe slashed his wrists and leaped overboard, leaving his wife and two children behind. Those standing nearby suddenly saw blood all over the deck; a woman screamed; a seaman leaped into the water and rescued Loewe; and a police launch picked up the two men and took them ashore; but rescue was the last thing Loewe wanted. He had been in Buchenwald and knew what faced him if he was returned to Germany.

Berenson met with President Bru and Colonel Fulgencio Batista, the Cuban chief of staff, but the only concession offered was to delay the ship's departure by one day, and on June 2, while sobbing passengers lined the rails and called *"Auf Wiedersehen"* to their relatives standing on the seawall, the *St. Louis* hove to and left port. Captain Schroeder, hoping that negotiations would result in permission to return to Cuba, headed for the Florida straits with 907 passengers. (Twenty-nine had finally been allowed to leave the ship in Havana: two were Cubans, five were visiting Spaniards, and twenty-two were refugees who had been skeptical of their landing certificates and, before leaving Europe, had hired lawyers to make certain their documents were valid. After paying legal fees plus $500, they were given visas that enabled them to land. The thirtieth person to remain on shore was Max Loewe, hospitalized in grave condition, whose wife and children were not permitted to leave the ship.) Rabbi Gelder never even got to shake the hands of his sons on the pier, nor had Liesl Broder exchanged a word with Hellmut Lewin. For Gerda Weiss it was the same; her fiancé had arrived with the marriage license and the ring, as he had promised he would, but the only messages the two could exchange were what could be conveyed by means of a pathetic pantomime between the ship and the shore.

After a fashion, one could at least understand the Cubans: they were greedy and the smell of money was in the offing. But what motivated American officialdom was unfathomable. From Washington came only an ominous silence—not a whisper of encouragement even for the *St. Louis* passengers who possessed U.S. quota numbers. On June 5, alongside a *New York Times* front-page story that appeared under the headline "Refugee Ship Idles off Florida Coast," it was reported that President Roosevelt had sent a message to the national meeting of Moral Rearmament, stating, "The underlying strength of the world must consist in the moral fiber of her citizens," yet no arrangements could be made for the *St. Louis* passengers to land in a United States port, it was learned; the State Department was quoted as saying immigration quotas must be upheld. How could it be? people on the ship asked one another: America is so big, it has a long tradition of freedom, yet the government won't intervene for only nine hundred people? And back in Havana the whole ugly blood-money scheme was finally out in the open, with the president of Cuba dickering with Lawrence Berenson, informing him that for a payment of $500 for each man, woman, and child aboard the *St. Louis* the ship might be recalled. Berenson said it would take time to raise that kind of money—nearly half a million dollars. "We have to have a cash deposit," insisted the president of Cuba. "The post that I occupy has painful duties, which oblige me to disregard the impulses of my heart and follow the stern dictates of duty."

By then the *St. Louis* was off Miami, close enough for passengers to see the glow of lights from the promised land and catch a glimpse of the official welcoming party—U.S. Coast Guard Cutter 244, which had been assigned to prevent refugees from jumping overboard and swimming ashore. "I grew up with the idea that America was something wonderful," one woman said. "My father always promised us we would go there one day, and the lights of Miami seemed to hold out hope that we would be permitted to land. But from the Coast Guard vessel came orders to move on." Berenson's negotiations with the Cubans ground to a halt, and by June 7, Captain Schroeder had no choice but to head for Europe. A group of frantic passengers cabled President Roosevelt, imploring him to help, but no reply ever came. Neither the United States nor any Latin American country offered sanctuary, despite urgent appeals from the Joint Distribution Committee, while every passing hour took the *St. Louis* closer to Hamburg. On board the ship a committee of the more stable passengers, most of them young adults, took turns patrolling the decks to prevent suicides, while the little children played a game Captain Schroeder would not forget.

Two boys formed a barricade out of chairs and stood guard behind it while the other children formed a queue. Then the first one in line requested permission to enter.

"Are you a Jew?" he was asked.

"Yes," the child said, he was.

"Jews are not admitted!" came the response.

"Please let me in," the child asked. "I'm only a little Jew."

Meantime, Morris Troper, the European chairman of the Joint Distribution Committee, and others were in continuous touch with officials on the continent, and word finally came that Belgium would accept 250 of the passengers, Holland 194. A day later, when the French and British agreed to take in the remaining refugees, Troper received a cable from those on board the ship:

THE 907 PASSENGERS OF ST. LOUIS DANGLING FOR LAST THIRTEEN DAYS BETWEEN HOPE AND DESPAIR RECEIVED TODAY YOUR LIBERATING MESSAGE. . . . OUR GRATITUDE IS AS IMMENSE AS THE OCEAN ON WHICH WE ARE NOW FLOATING SINCE MAY 13 FIRST FULL OF HOPE FOR A GOOD FUTURE AND AFTERWARDS IN THE DEEPEST DESPAIR. . . . ACCEPT THE DEEPEST AND ETERNAL THANKS OF MEN AND WOMEN AND CHILDREN UNITED BY THE SAME FATE ON BOARD THE ST. LOUIS.

Hellmut Lewin had returned to New York after the ship sailed for Europe, and when he learned that several nations—England, among them—would accept the passengers, he cabled close friends there, who said they would take Liesl. As it turned out, she was one of the fortunate survivors; after spending two years in England she secured passage on a Greek freighter bound for the United States. Several ships in the convoy were torpedoed and sunk; her vessel was separated from the others and landed in Sydney, Nova Scotia; and at last, after one more nerve-wracking voyage, she was able to take a train to New York, where she and Hellmut were married. Her parents and two married sisters died in Dachau.

———

At 4:00 A.M. on June 17, Morris Troper went out to greet the *St. Louis* as she lay off Flushing, near Antwerp, where the passengers were to disembark. No words, he said later, could possibly describe his feelings when he looked up at the ship from the tug and saw the *St. Louis*'s human cargo, "all standing as one man along the rails. . . ." It must have been an equally poignant moment for the heroic Captain Schroeder, who had, in an anguished hour, considered running his ship aground on the coast of Britain if the efforts of the JDC came to naught. Of his 907 passengers, the largest number—287—went to England, 224 were sent to France, 214 remained in Belgium, and 181 were taken in by the Dutch. Presumably those fortunate enough to reach the British Isles actually found the sanctuary they had sought for so long, but for all the others, respite from the Nazi terror could only have been temporary. Only two and a half months after the *St. Louis* docked in Antwerp the Germans invaded Poland and the Second World

War began. When the Nazis swallowed Belgium, Holland, and France, many of the *St. Louis* refugees were swept up by the conquerors, to die in the gas chambers. Those who escaped that fate had another sort of horror to reckon with: their journey of sorrow had revealed, one young man said, that "nobody wants us. Nobody wants the Jews."

There was, it should be noted, a 907th passenger aboard the *St. Louis*—a man not included among the refugees taken in by Belgium, Holland, France, and Britain. For good reason: he was not a Jew. He was a traveling salesman from Hungary named I. Winkler, who had boarded the vessel in Hamburg by mistake and had presumably been regretting his error ever since. As soon as the *St. Louis* docked in Antwerp, Mr. Winkler hurried ashore and disappeared as rapidly as possible.

CHAPTER 12

"I'll teach 'em how to hate."

A share of blame for the tragic episode of the *St. Louis* could be laid at the door of the United States Congress, but Congress is not a mirror of the American people by accident, and its members were affected as their constituents were by the shrill, divisive voices abroad in the land. One did not have to look far to see the ugly evidences of anti-Semitism. Except in a few major cities and in the upper echelons of business and finance, science and the arts, Jews were an alien minority, still the butt of vaudeville and radio jokes, often physically segregated into certain neighborhoods, excluded from hotels, resorts, and clubs ("Restricted Clientele," read the advertisements or the sign at the gate), admitted to most colleges on a quota system, and as often as not the object of suspicion or disdain by their Gentile neighbors. And during the 1930s this ugly theme of intolerance was being orchestrated by a rum bunch of homegrown demagogues.

One was Father Charles E. Coughlin, a sleek, pink, bespectacled Roman Catholic priest of the Shrine of the Little Flower in Royal Oak, Michigan, who had become a man beloved or hated, respected or feared, as a consequence of his Sunday-afternoon radio broadcasts that reached an estimated thirty to fifty million listeners. According to *Fortune*, Coughlin was "just about the biggest thing that ever happened to radio"; he outdrew such favorites as Ed Wynn and *Amos 'n' Andy*, giving him the largest regular audience in the world. Social Justice was what he called the message he preached over the air and in the pages of his weekly newspaper, but what he served up was essentially isolationism, heavily larded with anti-Semitism—an appeal to the narrow-minded, who regarded Coughlin as a heaven-sent champion against Jews, atheists, and Communists. The gospel was powerful enough that when he denounced a U.S. move to join the World Court in 1935, condemning it as a "fraudulent tribunal" and a "den of international thieves," and called on his flock to urge their senators to vote no, the Senate was deluged with telegrams from his followers (200,000 of them, Coughlin claimed). Millions of Americans were hypnotized by the resonant, impassioned voice, with its trace of Irish brogue, that exuded trust and a sense of purpose; audiences applauded his angry denunciation of the New Deal as the "Jew Deal"; they listened with rapt attention to his violent anticommunism; they heard him castigate the "modern Shylocks" of banking—the Mellons and Morgans and Rothschilds; and they were stunned by his revelation of a purported centuries-old Jewish conspiracy to dominate the world. When Father Coughlin described the violence inside Nazi Germany as a "defense mechanism" against Jewish-sponsored communism, his radio listeners nodded their heads in agreement and went to work Monday morning a little more certain that their suspicions of Jews were accurate after all.

Another man of the cloth who sensed the advantages to be gained from combining racial prejudice with attacks on America's growing international involvement was the Reverend Gerald Lyman Kenneth Smith. A penniless fundamentalist preacher from Arkansas, he had received the call at the age of nineteen, had become such a popular orator at the Seventh Christian Church in Indianapolis that several parishes vied for his talents, and had finally accepted an offer from the King's Highway Church of Shreveport, Louisiana, where he met an upwardly mobile lawyer named Huey P. Long. In those days, Smith was a left-winger concerned with "grave social injustices," a social reformer and union organizer. That was before he tied his fortunes to those of Long, the self-styled Kingfish, who became the governor of Louisiana and a United States senator, and who came as close to creating a totalitarian state in America as any man in politics. Huey was capable of spellbinding, but Smith outdid him. As H. L. Mencken said of Smith, all you had to do was mix "a flashing eye, a hairy chest, a rubescent complexion, large fists, a voice both loud and mellow, terrifying and reassuring, *sforzando* and *pizzicato,* and finally, an unearthly capacity for distending the superficial blood vessels of his temples and neck, as if they were biceps—and you have the makings of a boob-bumper worth going miles to see."

After Long was assassinated in 1935 (to die in Smith's arms), Smith snatched up the banner of Huey's Share Our Wealth program, declared himself the Kingfish's successor, and in 1936 joined forces with the radio priest, Charles Coughlin, and a somewhat mystified Dr. Francis E. Townsend, who had been promising the nation's old folks a $200-a-month pension. Although Coughlin viewed his new partners with contempt, he was accepting all the support he could muster, and the ill-assorted trio formed the Union Party to challenge Roosevelt and his Republican opponent, Alfred M. Landon. ("One is a promise breaker. The other is dumb," Coughlin announced.)

There were almost no limits to what Smith, whom Mencken called "the greatest rabble-rouser since Peter the Hermit," could do with a partisan crowd. "Religion and politics" was the way to get people "het up," said Smith. Once he had an audience with him, he promised, "I'll teach 'em how to hate." And hate they did. Even Coughlin admitted he was afraid of Smith, but the two worked together after a fashion, doing their level best to stir up animosity against the Jews until the press forced Coughlin to state that he was not really anti-Semitic ("Jew-baiting won't work here," he announced condescendingly). Smith went from villainy to worse, at last proclaiming that he planned to lead a new movement that would seize control of the government of the United States, and on election eve of 1936 someone with some sense put him in a New Orleans jail for using obscene language and disturbing the peace. During the campaign Coughlin told a reporter, "Democracy is doomed, this is our last election. . . . It is fascism or communism. We are at the crossroads." And when the reporter inquired, "What road do you take, Father Coughlin?" the reply came back at once: "I take the road of fascism."

Their ill-conceived Union Party was, of course, buried in the Roosevelt landslide of 1936 (as was the GOP), but Coughlin remained undaunted. The next year he founded the Christian Front Against Communism; his radio broadcasts became increasingly anti-Semitic—on the one hand accusing the Jews of originating communism, on the other defending the Nazis for preventing a Jewish-Communist subjugation of Germany. He was a speaker at German-American Bund rallies, pledging, "When we get through with the Jews in America, they'll think the treatment they received in Germany was nothing." And when war finally erupted in Europe he endorsed Hitler's "sacred war . . . against the Jews." As the noninterventionist movement spread in the late thirties, Father Charles Coughlin was a force to be reckoned with. His voice was particularly effective among rabid Irish-Americans, whose natural inclination was to cheer anyone opposed to England, and because the radio priest's activities were so highly visible, the Catholic Church became associated in many Americans' minds with the cause of extreme isolationism. Yet it is worth remembering that while the isolationist movement at times seemed heavily populated with racists, the idea of Fortress America was in no sense the franchise of extremists: it was a powerful and pervasive current in American life—a habit of thought that came naturally to millions of people, and the reasons were not difficult to trace.

Not until the twentieth century did isolationism come into its own as a political force, and even then it was more a feeling in the gut than an organized faction. Geography, of course, was a big factor. Life had gone on on the prairies pretty much unaltered since the red man had been pushed aside. In the heartland of America, the rhythm of people's days was governed by the whistle of the eastbound express, the shrill toot of a steamboat nosing alongside the town dock, or the tolling of a church bell. Except for violent extremes of weather, there was no outside threat, east or west, north or south. Word from the East came with a peddler, selling millinery supplies, notions, and household goods, and that word did not, in the usual circumstances, include news of Europe. The peddler brought tidings of Cincinnati or Pittsburgh, not of Munich or Vienna. Middle America turned its eyes inward, and for good reason: there was nothing visible beyond the eastern or western horizons. "East were the dead kings and the remembered sepulchres," wrote the poet Archibald MacLeish, "West was the grass."

It was a long, long way from Blair, Nebraska, or Yankton, South Dakota, to New York—let alone London. In 1938 it took a day and a night to fly across the continental United States, and only a tiny number of people had done it. Beyond the West Coast the distances were incomprehensible to an inlander: with luck, you might travel from San Francisco to Japan in fifteen days—by ship, of course. Pan American Airways' famous China Clipper flew mail only, and took nearly sixty hours, including stops, for the trip between San Francisco and Manila. Between the East Coast and Europe no regular transatlantic flight schedule existed until 1939, and even then, almost all travelers went by ship. Although the *Queen Mary* had made a crossing in 3 days, 21 hours, and 48 minutes, most of the good liners took five days for the passage between the United States and England or France, and it was a ten-day voyage from New York to Genoa.

So geography was part of the explanation, but not all. Behind the intensity of the isolationist outlook was the hard fact that, for generations, the Midwestern farmer had seen his enemy as the Eastern banker and industrialist—the money man. In 1887 the Right Reverend William D. Walker, Episcopal bishop of North Dakota, pointed a finger at the "Shylock money-loaners who, by a pleasing fiction, are called bankers," but his flock scarcely needed the reminder; the economic disadvantage at which the farmer found himself in relation to Eastern industrial and shipping interests was as much a fact of life as the never-ceasing winds off the Rockies. Charles Lindbergh's father, a successful lawyer, land speculator, and freethinker in Little Falls, Minnesota, was positively obsessed with the power of Eastern banks and insurance companies; he had stumped the state in a car driven by his son, advocating farmers' cooperatives, preaching what amounted to socialism, condemning "the money trusts," founding the Farmer-Labor Party, and finally winning election to Congress.

The relationship of Midwesterner to Easterner was curiously like the eighteenth-century Virginia planter's dependence upon London merchants and agents, his source of manufactured goods and credit, and the Midwestern farmer's attitude was about what might be expected in the circumstance. The Eastern money man was believed to be rich, overeducated, in league with the hated English, the internationalists, the munitions makers, and the politicians who wanted Midwestern boys for cannon fodder. This frame of mind had been given an enormous boost by the collapse of the stock market in October 1929 and by the ensuing Depression. Abroad, nations raised their tariffs at the expense of neighbors; the have nations began calling their loans while the have-nots repudiated theirs; and Americans, seeing their creditors (except for little Finland, which achieved universal popularity for meeting its interest payments) renege on their debts, reacted angrily. President Coolidge, insisting that the European governments meet their obligations, was supposed to have said tartly, "They hired the money, didn't they?" Even the Depression was attributed to America's 1917 intervention in Europe's war; war production, it was argued, had created a phony prosperity that had evaporated. Joblessness and hunger, debts private and public, bank failures and bankruptcies—all were blamed on the war and the debtor nations that had welched on their payments. As successive waves of aggression—apparently unstoppable—swept Asia and Europe, the temptation to sit tight within the continental fortress was all but irresistible to millions of Americans. "Keep out of war" had a far more compelling ring than the battle cry of the twenties, "Keep out of the League"—but both protests stemmed from the same root.

Franklin Roosevelt, determined to push his New Deal program of social welfare, took pains to appease the powerful Midwestern progressives in Congress—principally Idaho's William E. Borah, Gerald P. Nye of North Dakota, and Burton K. Wheeler of Montana—whose support would be forthcoming only so long as the president did nothing that smacked of involvement in Europe. In his first term he left largely undisturbed the isolationist policies of his Republican predecessors, who had been responsible for the Kellogg-Briand Pact, which "outlawed war," and the Hawley-Smoot Act, with its punitive protective tariffs—both blindly nationalistic measures, effectively isolating the country from reality as well as from the community of nations. During this period Roosevelt's messages to Congress stressed the nation's economic welfare, not its international obligations, and if he had qualms about the way the United States had shunned the League of Nations or failed to participate in collective action against the dictators, he kept them largely to himself. But through no fault of FDR's, from 1935 on the isolationists' power in Congress mounted steadily.

Echoing the prevalent attitude about U.S. involvement in international affairs, the beloved humorist Will Rogers remarked how Europeans had taken to calling us "Uncle Shylock" and "Uncle Sham," saying how terrible it was that the greedy Americans wanted their wartime loans repaid. On his Sunday-night broadcast for Gulf Oil, a few months before his death in a plane crash in Alaska, Will observed: "They blame us for everything, I don't care what it is that's wrong with the world; we done it. Whether it's famine or pestilence, acne, or tight underwear.

"When I was in Europe they had a little jail break over there, and the newspapers blamed it on us. It's the truth. They said that American motion pictures gave the prisoners the unusual idea of breaking out of jail.

"And when I was in Paris, some American tourists were hissed and stoned. But not until they'd finished buying.

"If we get linked up with this World Court," he went on, "I guess it won't be long before they'll be calling us 'Uncle Sucker,' and we'd deserve it. . . ."

America listened—to Will Rogers as well as to Father Coughlin—and in 1935 the Senate turned down adherence to the World Court, prompting Senator Borah to exult, "Thank God! This will end forever any thought of the entry of the United States into entangling alliances." That year, too, Congress passed the first Neutrality Law; six months later it passed the Second; and in May 1937, the Third Neutrality Law.

Some highly charged emotional factors lay behind this legislative desire to remain aloof from further foreign involvement. Not least among them was the legacy of George Washington, whose farewell address was as much a part of the national mystique as Plymouth Rock and the Minute Man, and was the keystone of public policy. (Contrary to common supposition, the "address" was never delivered as a speech but had been published inconspicuously on the second page of Philadelphia's *American Daily Advertiser* on September 17, 1796.) The Father of His Country had warned against making permanent alliances which could "entangle our peace and prosperity in the toils of European ambition, rivalship, interest, humor, or caprice," and if ever events had proved a man right, it had been the nation's enlistment in what was called the war to end wars. The festering bitterness and disillusion that followed the 1918 Armistice had been given expression in such films as *All Quiet on the Western Front* and *The Big Parade* and in such publications as Engelbrecht and Hanighen's indictment of the munitions makers, *Merchants of Death,* Walter Millis's *The Road to War,* and Laurence Stallings's collection of stark, horrifying battlefield photographs, *The First World War.* In a series of books and articles, the influential historian Charles A. Beard spun his thesis that America must till its own economic and social gardens, becoming so strong internally that there would be neither necessity nor temptation to become involved in Europe's conflicts. "War," editor William Allen White wrote, "is the devil's joke on humanity."

The First Neutrality Law required the president to proclaim the existence of any foreign war and prohibit American vessels from carrying arms to or for the belligerents. That seemed sensible and harmless enough, but there was a sequel to it, inspired by Mussolini's invasion of Ethiopia—an event that was still in progress when the First Neutrality Law expired (FDR duly called Italy's war a war even though the Roman dictator had neglected to do so). The provisions of the First were renewed in the Second Neutrality Law on February 29, 1936, the latter act further forbidding the granting of loans to belligerents—either directly or through the purchase of their securities. This piece of legislation meant that the United States would hold itself aloof from any collective security efforts and would even be unwilling to halt out-and-out aggression where aggression might occur. It also meant that this country was not going to come to the aid of its friends, no matter what kind of trouble they were in.

In the 1937 act, the Third Neutrality Law, Congress took still another step, extending previous arms embargoes and the strictures against loans to belligerents and then, because Spain was still torn apart by its internal struggle, empowering the U.S. president to apply these terms to foreign civil wars if appropriate. The chief executive could, moreover, prohibit the shipment of nonmilitary goods to belligerents unless (and the conjunction was important) this material was paid for in advance and unless it was carried in foreign vessels, which was a neat way of enabling enterprising Americans to make a profit while risking no American ships. Roosevelt had apparently hoped to persuade Congress to let him distinguish between aggressor nations and those whose peaceful intentions were clear, but Congress had the bit in its teeth, and when the president saw the overwhelming majorities by which the Third Neutrality Law passed both bodies (376 to 16 in the House, 63 to 6 in the Senate), he accepted the inevitable, raised no objection, and signed the bill.

What this cumulative neutrality legislation signaled to the Axis powers, naturally enough, was that the United States, in its almost pathological desire to stay uninvolved in Europe's quarrels, would sit back while any aggressor gobbled up whatever territory it coveted. Indeed, how far along the road to isolationism the nation had traveled might be judged by a piece of legislation introduced on Capitol Hill as the year 1937 drew to a close. On the bright Sunday afternoon of December 12, 1937, ten months before Munich, two flights of Japanese Mitsubishi planes had dive-bombed and strafed the U.S. gunboat *Panay* in China's Yangtze River, killing three Americans and wounding eleven others and prompting America's ambassador to Japan, Joseph C. Grew, to assume that the United States would declare war immediately. Not at all. Mr. Roosevelt fired off an indignant message, expressing dismay at the indiscriminate attack on a ship clearly flying the American flag, after which Washington docilely accepted the Japanese government's apology, the State Department solemnly announced that the unhappy episode had been a "mistake" (which it was not), and the leaders of Japan no longer found it difficult to believe that the United States was a paper tiger.

Yet what else could have been done? Before the Japanese apology was received, the president conferred with his cabinet officers, asked Secretary of the Treasury Henry Morgenthau by what authority he might seize Japanese assets in this country as surety against damage claims, considered imposing economic sanctions, and discussed with the British ambassador the possibility of an Anglo-American commercial blockade of Japan, extending from the Aleutian Islands to Singapore.[1] Note, however, that military action or even the threat of it was not contemplated, as it surely would have been if his cousin Theodore had been confronted with the same circumstances, and for two very simple reasons. One was that U.S. military power was all but nonexistent; the other was that peace sentiment in the country had never been greater—with the result that the president was obliged to cast about for other solutions to his problem.

"After all," he observed to the members of his cabinet, "if Italy and Japan have developed a technique of fighting without declaring war, why can't we develop a similar one?" If the totalitarian nations managed to achieve their territorial ambitions and diplomatic triumphs through such devices as "incidents" or "undeclared wars," why couldn't we employ economic sanctions or—harking back to his speech a few months earlier—quarantines? Roosevelt wanted results, in other words, but he did not dare risk war to get them, and in the days and weeks that followed he quickly backed away from any notions of blockades or sanctions.

As if to prove to Mr. Roosevelt that he had no chance whatever of talking tough to Japan or anyone else, in the aftermath of the *Panay* affair, Indiana congressman Louis Leon Ludlow prepared to bring to the floor of the House of Representatives a resolution he had first introduced there three years earlier. At that time, his bill had been quietly tabled by the Judiciary Committee, whose members had promptly forgotten its existence. But Ludlow had not, and now—sensing that the moment was ripe—he dusted off his resolution and began collecting the signatures needed to get it onto the floor of the House.

Simply put, Ludlow's proposed amendment to the Constitution would make it illegal for Congress to declare war except in the event of an armed invasion. At other times, the amiable Hoosier's bill stipulated, "the authority of Congress to declare war shall not become effective until confirmed by a majority of votes cast in a national referendum." In other words, unless the continental United States was physically invaded by a hostile foreign power, the Congress could declare war only after taking the issue to the people in the form of a nationwide vote and getting their approval. How long this referendum might take was anyone's guess, but as 1938 rolled

[1]To pursue the blockade idea further, Roosevelt sent Captain Royal Ingersoll, chief of the navy's War Plans Division, to London in December for "purely exploratory" conversations with the British Admiralty. Ingersoll was to make no commitments, but the idea was to make tentative arrangements for joint communications, liaison, and intelligence, so if war came, as Ingersoll put it, "we would not be floundering around for months until we got together." One result was a nonbinding agreement assuring that the waters of the British Commonwealth would be available to U.S. vessels (and vice versa) in the event the two fleets were involved in a war with Japan. That was the first step in a process formalized in 1941 with the "American-British Conversations."

around it began to look as though the nation might be forced to reckon with that very problem. Ludlow had gathered the signatures of 218 representatives in support of his amendment, and the bill was scheduled for debate on January 10.

Arthur Krock, writing in the *New York Times,* suggested that this "dream-born" foolishness of Ludlow's would make it possible for any foreign country to peacefully occupy any part of the United States and sit tight until a national election could be held. Secretary of State Hull announced acerbically that he could not perceive the "wisdom or the practicality" of Congressman Ludlow's proposal. Rules Committee chairman John J. O'Connor called the bill "monstrous," and majority leader Sam Rayburn said he would exert all his influence to prevent its acceptance.

In retrospect it is easy to pass off the episode as an aberrant piece of nonsense, but the gravity with which it was viewed by the White House may be judged by the weight of the opposition that was mustered against it. No less a figure than Alfred M. Landon—Roosevelt's Republican opponent in the 1936 election—sent the president a telegram pledging his support and criticizing the members of Congress ("of both parties," Landon was careful to say) who were trying to "hamstring your conduct of extremely delicate foreign situations." And from Henry L. Stimson, Hull's Republican predecessor as secretary of state, came a masterly four-thousand-word letter to the *New York Times,* calling the Ludlow amendment a device that would dangerously divide American public opinion in the event of war while hobbling U.S. diplomacy. As Stimson saw it, "no more effective engine for the disruption of national unity on the threshold of a national crisis could ingeniously have been devised."

All things considered, that first week of January 1938 had been eventful in more ways than one. Don Marquis, creator of the much-loved archy and mehitabel stories, died. So did Maurice Ravel, the French composer whose *Bolero* was so well known to Americans. At Radio City's Center Theater, 3,650 customers (350 of them standees) turned out to see Ruth St. Denis, Martha Graham, Charles Weidmann, Doris Humphrey, Helen Tamiris, and Hanya Holm put modern dance on the map in New York. Across the nation, members of the Communist-dominated American Student Union were demonstrating—the women throwing silk stockings and underwear and the men neckties onto bonfires in protest against Japan's attack on the *Panay.* "Make lisle the style, wear lisle for a while," they chanted. "If you wear cotton, Japan gets nottin'." And at Vassar College, 652 happy ASU delegates marched out into the snow singing "Solidarity Forever," no doubt satisfied that they had made a start on boycotting the importation of raw silk from Japan. (Silk was big business: it made up half of Japan's total exports to the United States, and 92 percent of America's silk came from that country.) During the same week a book titled *Red Star over China,* by Edgar Snow, was published amid general agreement that it was a historic document—the first real report on China's Communist leaders, on their "long march," and on Chinese life, Soviet-style.

Franklin Roosevelt was distracted by none of these events; deeply troubled by the threat posed by the Indiana representative, he dictated a letter to the speaker of the House, Alabama's William Bankhead, lest there be any doubt concerning his views. Bankhead knew what to do with the letter; just before the House voted on Ludlow's proposal, he read FDR's words to the members. "I must frankly state," the president had written, "that I consider . . . the proposed amendment . . . impracticable in its application and incompatible with our representative form of government.

"Such an amendment to the Constitution as that proposed would cripple any president in his conduct of our foreign relations, and it would encourage other nations to believe that they could violate American rights with impunity."

Roosevelt carried the day, but only just. The Ludlow resolution fell nine votes short of the total necessary to bring it to the floor, and it was sent back to committee to die. But those 209 votes—against 188—meant that an actual majority of the United States House of Representatives believed that the power to declare war should be removed from the hands of Congress and turned over to the American people.

CHAPTER 13

———— ◆ ————

"... it's a hell of a long way from East Boston."

Not long after the *Panay* incident, George Gallup took a poll of voters and concluded that nearly three-quarters of them favored the complete withdrawal of all U.S. citizens—including missionaries—from the Far East. A significant segment of the American public also believed that the nation should remain aloof from Europe's imbroglios, Gallup reported, but whether these people were the leaders or the led was a moot question.

A year after that poll was taken, it seemed quite clear that a handful of United States senators held the whip hand in foreign affairs. Indeed, in the sense that they were capable of preventing the president from doing what he thought best for the nation, it might be said that they were the most powerful individuals in the land. Because of them, Congress was getting its own way in the spring and early summer of 1939, and the executive branch—even led by so dominant a personality as Franklin D. Roosevelt— was doing well to stay even in the field of foreign affairs.

These senators were not part of the lunatic fringe; they were not the likes of Gerald L. K. Smith. On the contrary, they were solid, respectable, in some respects heroic figures, who had risen from humble beginnings to positions of considerable political strength and influence. They were Westerners, liberals by their own lights and after their own fashion, and populists. The political deputies of America's last frontier, they were as quirky and colorful a band of mavericks as ever rode out of the sunset, and whatever one thought of their views on foreign policy, one had to accord them respect. Which was exactly what the president of the United States was doing.

The public's attitude toward a U.S. commitment in Europe was becoming polarized, and the heightening drama was reminiscent of the years before the Civil War, when the voices that echoed across the land had also emanated from the well of the Senate. But now Fortress America, not slavery or abolition, was the rallying cry, and its chief exponents on Capitol Hill were, by and large, men who believed and spoke as they did on grounds of principle, not because they expected to gain politically from their acts. Foremost among them was shaggy, unpredictable William E. Borah of Idaho. Born in the year Robert E. Lee surrendered at Appomattox, Borah began reading law during Grover Cleveland's first term, ran unsuccessfully for Congress the year McKinley beat Bryan, and took a seat in the U.S. Senate in 1907, Teddy Roosevelt's next-to-last year in office. He had been there ever since, presiding since 1924 over the Committee on Foreign Relations, which made him one of the most powerful figures in the nation on international affairs.

As a boy, Borah had longed to be an actor, and for a brief moment he ran away and had his fling with a touring Shakespearean company before he was dragged home by his outraged, tyrannical father, who was determined that he should become a minister. Something of the actor and the man of God had remained with Borah ever since, and when he rose to speak in the Senate, shaking his great mane, his colleagues and visitors in the galleries knew they were in for a rare show; with his rich voice and his genuine gift for language, Borah sounded for all the world like a Presbyterian minister thundering to his flock about predestination. And like many a minister of the 1930s, Borah still wore the blinders of a nineteenth-century man, perceiving the world in terms of the simpler society in which he had grown up. He took pride in never having left the continental United States, as though that somehow enhanced his standing on the Foreign Relations Committee; ironically, because of his key role on that committee, he was probably the one senator whose name was known in every foreign capital, whose speeches every foreign diplomat studied with care.

"I follow issues, not men," Borah once proclaimed, and that was plain enough to see. He also liked to say, "I will travel with the devil, if he is going in my direction," and that commitment to principle had earned him the grudging respect of more than one president. It was said that Calvin Coolidge, seeing him riding along a Washington bridle path, had turned to a companion to remark, in mock astonishment, "There goes Senator Borah riding horseback and both he and the horse are going the same way." From Woodrow Wilson had come what may have been the ultimate compliment, considering what Borah had done to defeat the League of Nations: just before his death, the normally unforgiving Wilson said of the Idaho senator, "There is one irreconcilable whom I can respect."

Borah's voting record in the Senate followed an erratic pattern, thanks in part to his devotion to issues. He had introduced in 1922 a resolution for the recognition of Soviet Russia and initiated the Washington disarmament conference the year before; yet he fought tooth and nail against America's joining the League and worked with equal fervor against the World Court. It was characteristic of him that he should support Herbert Hoover for president in 1928 and then oppose him on virtually all important measures throughout his term in office.

The independent, prickly Borah had been mentioned as a possible presidential candidate in every national election from 1912 to 1936 and in 1924 had turned down the Republican vice-presidential nomination. But what made him anathema to many Republican conservatives in the thirties, despite his outlook on foreign affairs, was that he had supported more New Deal legislation than he opposed and once warned that unless the GOP rid itself of its reactionary leadership it would die "of sheer political cowardice." He stated flatly that there was no room in this country for "an old conservative party," and to his own rhetorical question of what the Republican Party had to offer voters he replied scathingly, "The Constitution." Although Borah revered that document, he knew that "the people can't eat the Constitution."

Known to colleagues on the Hill as "the Big Potato," he was not an especially effective leader in the Senate, having no interest in detail or committee work,[1] but few contemporaries possessed his ability to arouse people on public issues. For three decades Americans had listened to what the senator from Idaho had to say, and Borah, looking back on his career toward the end of his life, said he was proudest "of doing what little I have been able to do to keep us out of Europe." The question now, however, was whether Borah—who represented the old center of America, the America that had gone its way, largely unchanged and unquestioning—could really comprehend or adjust to a world that was increasingly dominated by the Nazi dictator, Adolf Hitler.

Borah's counterpart from Montana was Burton Kendall Wheeler, a freewheeling, independent character who was as much of a high-principled loner as the senator from Idaho. The tenth son of a poverty-stricken shoemaker, Wheeler was born in Massachusetts and eventually made his way west, arriving in the raw, rough town of Butte with a law degree and not much more. He was his own man from the beginning: battling giant Anaconda Copper, which ran Butte and just about everything else in the state; fighting for better working conditions in the mines; supporting pacifists and

[1] At the time of Borah's death, Harold Ickes, secretary of the interior, noted in his diary that the nation had lost a great senator, but remarked that although Borah had been in the upper chamber for thirty-three years, his name was attached to no piece of legislation.

Wobblies (the revolutionary Industrial Workers of the World) during the World War, a stand for which he was labeled a radical and driven out of one Montana town; and in 1920 doing the unthinkable—running for governor on a Non-Partisan League ticket that included a Negro and a Blackfoot Indian. (He lost.) Still, in 1922 Wheeler was elected to the United States Senate, thanks to the miners, farmers, and railroad men who supported him (and despite his opponent's charge that he would introduce free love to Montana). In the nation's capital he was as unpredictable as ever: for a time he led a group of "New Democrats"; then, sickening of the party regulars' lack of leadership, he became a Progressive; tiring of that, he returned to the Democratic fold in 1928. For a while he supported Roosevelt's legislative program, but, along with Borah and other Western progressives, he fell out with the president over his plan to pack the Supreme Court, seeing it as an effort by FDR to acquire "dictatorial power."

Unlike Borah, Wheeler had been around the world twice and was a gregarious, jovial joiner. One reporter described him as "a lanky, rumpled man who walks with a rapid shamble, smiling quizzically, his glance a friendly, direct glare through octagonal spectacles, smoking a cigar with the superb nonchalance of Groucho Marx." Wheeler had a quick mind and a ready sense of humor: in 1924, when he campaigned for vice president on the ticket with La Follette, he placed an empty chair on the platform beside him to represent the taciturn incumbent, Calvin Coolidge, and asked questions of the chair. And, tenacious as he was in a good legislative fight, he knew how to relax. "Nearly everything except dinner," he liked to say, "seems less important after a nap." It was a measure of Wheeler's ability and intelligence that he had the respect of two of the most powerful men in the Senate, Borah and old George Norris of Nebraska—both of whom had concluded, by 1939, that the Montanan was the only thinkable Democratic alternative to FDR as president.

Another anti-involvement senator who had made his political reputation fighting big business (in his case, the Southern Pacific Railroad) was Hiram Johnson of California. A year younger than Borah, Johnson had more in common with him than advancing age. Both had dedicated their active political careers to keeping the United States free of foreign alliances, entanglements, or commitments, and Johnson's constituents seemed to think that he had followed exactly the right course. (In 1940, when he ran for a fifth term on the Republican, Democratic, and Progressive tickets—he was "as happy as a clam at high tide" to get all three nominations, he said—he was returned to the Senate after receiving the votes of 483,000 Democrats and 582,000 Republicans.) Beginning in 1917, his long record of dissent in the Senate had seen him oppose the League and the Four-Power Treaty, the London Naval Treaty, and membership in the World Court. He admitted, "A man must be a crank to do this sort of thing. I guess that's what I am. It always seems that the unpleasant jobs fall to me."

Conservatives took Johnson for a liberal; liberals considered him a reactionary; and in fact he was a curious combination of revolutionary and stand-patter. His first brush with politics was as a prosecuting attorney investigating the bribery of city officials in San Francisco. He ran for governor in 1910, campaigning in a little red automobile, riding from town to town with two sons—one of whom drove while the other rang a cow bell to let people know his father was about to speak. Johnson's principal target was the Southern Pacific, which he vowed to chase out of politics, and when he was elected he kept all his campaign pledges, bringing California the direct primary, a shorter ballot, prison reform, workmen's compensation, and shorter working hours for women, and in general making the state a bellwether of reform.

By 1912 Johnson was well enough known to run as vice-presidential candidate on the Bull Moose ticket with Theodore Roosevelt, and five years after that he arrived in the U.S. Senate. He turned down a request from Warren Harding to be his running mate (thus missing out on the presidency) because he was totally antipathetic to Harding's political philosophy; cordially hating Herbert Hoover, he opposed almost every major proposal his fellow Californian made while in the White House. For a time, Johnson managed to get along with FDR, but only until foreign policy became a substantive issue; then they were bound to split. Indeed, Johnson believed that the appropriate posture for America to take toward the rest of the world was one of complete isolationism.

When it pleased Johnson to be genial and cooperative, few men could be more winning, but as someone remarked, "When he is pleased to be cantankerous, he steps out of competition." He was the only senator to have an office in the Capitol; when the Senate Office Building opened for occupancy, Johnson characteristically refused to move to it. A hard worker, he was also a poor mixer; he had a reputation of being the best domino player around, but what really suited him was to walk home and spend the evening with his wife. As Borah once observed, "The difference between me and Johnson is that I regard questions from the point of view of principles while he regards them from the point of view of personalities. When a man opposes me I do not become angry with him. On the next issue he may agree with me. When a man opposes Johnson, he hates him." And as the thirties drew to a close, hatred was certainly the best word to describe Hiram Johnson's attitude toward Franklin Roosevelt.

Of the Senate's powerful advocates of Fortress America, the most pugnacious and controversial was an undefinable North Dakotan who had arrived in Washington, D.C., in 1925 wearing yellow shoes and hair that looked as if it had been cut with a bowl for a pattern. But Gerald P. Nye was not the rube he appeared to be.

Cast by newspapermen as "the village Greeley"—a reference to his career as a small-town editor—Nye had been appointed to fill a senatorial vacancy and was forced to cool his heels outside the Capitol for a month while the Senate debated the legitimacy of his claim and while Nye's daughter asked plaintively when they would "give Papa a place to sit down." (Friends sent him a milking stool.) Seated at last by a two-vote margin (prompting the *New York Times* to cluck, "a bad day's work"), Nye was soon reelected in his own right and was rewarded, by his senior colleagues in the Senate, with a dubious prize—chairmanship of one of the lowliest committees, Public Lands.

What no one could have foreseen was that the chairman of that obscure committee would preside over the investigation of one of the juiciest scandals of the scandalous twenties—an inquiry into the Continental Trading Company that produced a series of revelations concerning Secretary of the Treasury Andrew Mellon, the Republican National Committee, and oilman Harry Sinclair, to whom Harding's secretary of interior, Albert B. Fall, had generously and secretly leased the U.S. Navy's oil reserves at Teapot Dome, Wyoming.

Nye was sharp-nosed and contentious, willing to tangle with just about everyone from the president on down. He was against industrialists and bankers in particular, along with monopolies, chain stores, the rich, the New Deal—whatever outraged his old-fashioned, agrarian rebel soul. "Gerald, the Giant-Killer," the *Baltimore Sun* called him, and that was precisely how he appeared to a growing number of Americans when, in 1934, he began presiding over the Senate's investigation of armaments manufacturers. Nye was in his element, and the public soon learned about the "merchants of death" and the "economic royalists" who had apparently duped the nation into entering Europe's war as a means of lining their own pockets. The outlandish profits made by the munitions makers and financiers were emphasized again and again at the hearings, bolstering Nye's claim that the men who stood to benefit handsomely from war had—through their international cartel and their lobbyists in Congress—maneuvered the country into intervening on the side of the Allies. Nye was in great demand as a speaker, and he hit the circuit with relish, playing on the national mood, exploiting the widespread prejudice against the rich. Because of the forum his committee gave him, Nye more than any other senator was responsible for the neutrality legislation enacted between 1935 and 1937. As long as that legislation remained on the books, it meant that U.S. policy, like that pursued by Neville Chamberlain, would be peace at almost any price.

Borah, Wheeler, Johnson, Nye—those were four formidable opponents Roosevelt had to reckon with on the question of American involvement in Europe's deepening crisis; yet not all of the outspoken noninterventionists came from west of the Allegheny Mountains or sat in the Senate. One highly placed individual who did not was the man who had so impressed Lindbergh in London—Joseph Patrick Kennedy, ambassador to the Court of St. James's.

The son of Patrick Joseph Kennedy, a bartender and hard-fisted Boston ward boss, Joe Kennedy had married the daughter of John "Honey Fitz" Fitzgerald, another Boston politician, of whom it was said, "When Fitzgerald was mayor everybody in City Hall had to pay, from the scrubwomen to the elevator man." (Kennedy once remarked plaintively to Franklin Roosevelt, "I can't help it that I married into a son-of-a-bitch of a family!")

From the time he sold newspapers and candy and ran errands for a bank, Joe Kennedy had his eye on the main chance and a nose for money, but neither won him the recognition he sought from Old Boston—a longing that echoed in his admonition to his children, "Always be first!" When he graduated from Harvard in 1912 he set himself a goal of making $1 million before he was thirty-six. As one of his classmates remarked, "Joe was born mature," and he became, in quick succession, a bank examiner, the youngest bank president in the United States, assistant manager of a shipbuilding plant during the World War, manager of a Boston brokerage office, and partner in a group that was buying up small motion-picture theaters in New England. By his tenth college reunion he had achieved his goal of making a million, and soon afterward opened an office with the words "Joseph P. Kennedy, Banker" lettered on the door. He became a stock-market speculator, a Wall Street mystery man, a trader who manipulated low-priced stocks by means of well-placed rumors and sold at a large profit when the public rushed to buy. He bought a small company called Film Booking Offices which distributed and produced cheap movies, moved to Hollywood and took the glamorous Gloria Swanson as his mistress, and eventually combined Film Booking Offices with RCA and Keith-Albee-Orpheum. The company became known as RKO; Joe Kennedy became known as "the financial wizard of Hollywood."

His investment motto was "Never go for the top dollar," and in the summer of 1929 he sensed it was time to get out of the great bull market. What decided him, he said, was a boy shining his shoes who told him what would happen in the market that day. "When the time comes that a shoe-shine boy knows as much as I do about the stock market, tells me so, and is entirely correct," Kennedy said, "there's something wrong either with me or with the market, and it's time for me to get out." Which is exactly what he did—just before the crash—with a profit on his securities estimated at $15 million.

As sensitive to political as to financial winds, he concluded that Franklin Delano Roosevelt would be the Democrats' nominee in 1932 and possibly the only man who could save the country. "I was really worried," Kennedy recalled. "I knew that big drastic changes had to be made in our economic system and I felt that Roosevelt was the one who could make those changes. I wanted him in the White House for my own security and the security of our kids—and I was willing to do anything to help elect him." At the convention Kennedy played kingmaker by helping to persuade publisher William Randolph Hearst—who controlled the California and Texas delegates committed to Texan John Nance Garner—to release them on the fourth ballot to Roosevelt. Kennedy, who knew his man, kept warning Hearst that if Roosevelt's strength evaporated, an internationalist like Newton D. Baker would be certain to get the nomination. If there was anything Hearst did not want in the White House it was an internationalist, so he advised Garner to throw in his hand, and Garner released his delegates to Roosevelt after receiving assurance that he would get the vice-presidential nomination. When California switched to Roosevelt, it was all over save the shouting.

Kennedy always said it was he who "brought Hearst around for Roosevelt," and while this was not altogether accurate, since other forces had been at work too, there was enough substance to it to make him suppose that he would be favored with an important political appointment once FDR moved into the White House. But despite all he had done—and that included a contribution of $25,000 to Roosevelt's campaign, a loan of $50,000 to the Democratic National Committee, and arrangements for another $100,000 in anonymous donations—he waited in vain for the phone call summoning him to Washington. Finally, in 1934, the president named Kennedy to the recently formed Securities and Exchange Commission, of which he became chairman, prompting Wall Street wags to observe sourly that it takes a thief to catch one. (While waiting impatiently for a federal appointment, Kennedy had managed to run up the stock of Libby-Owens-Ford and Owens Illinois, two glass-bottle manufacturers that would presumably profit when Prohibition ended, and—with Roosevelt's son James—cornered the American franchises for Gordon's gin and John Dewar, Haig & Haig, and King William whiskies, which rewarded them handsomely after December 5, 1933, when Prohibition was repealed.)

Joe Kennedy's real goal, now that he had all the money he needed, was prestige and acceptance, and he worked prodigiously at the SEC, changing the financial community's doubts to praise and cooperation and making the SEC a first-class regulatory agency. His fondest hope was to be made secretary of the Treasury, but the president stuck with Henry Morgenthau, realizing that Kennedy would run the Treasury his own way, and not FDR's. Soon Joe was angling to be ambassador to England, dropping the word to congressmen, newspapermen, members of the White House staff, and to the president's son James. James passed along the request and recalled that his father "laughed so hard he almost toppled from his wheelchair," thinking what a good joke it would be on the British. But in the months that followed, Roosevelt seriously weighed the possibility. On the positive side were Kennedy's wealth, which would permit him to entertain in grand style, his toughness, his shrewd business ability, his candor and friendship with the president, and—best of all, in Roosevelt's eyes—the irony of having an Irishman at the Court of St. James's. At a dinner party at his home in Hyde Park, FDR burst out laughing and called it "the greatest joke in the world."

Roosevelt had second thoughts when Kennedy leaked the story of his appointment to Arthur Krock of the *New York Times;* the president told Morgenthau that he considered the Bostonian "a very dangerous man." He was sending him to England, he said, with the understanding that the appointment was for only six months and that any political obligation he owed Kennedy was thereby discharged. In response to Morgenthau's suggestion that his outspoken appointee might prove a liability in London, Roosevelt replied, "I have made arrangements to have Joe Kennedy watched hourly—and the first time he opens his mouth and criticizes me, I will fire him."

"Very dangerous man" or not, on February 18, 1938, Joseph Patrick Kennedy took the oath of office for the most prestigious, glittering diplomatic plum there was, ambassador to the Court of St. James's—the one post that might make an Irish-American son of a bartender acceptable to Old Boston. In the spring Kennedy arrived in London with his wife, Rose, and their nine children, aged six to twenty-two (each with a $1 million trust fund, it was said), and before the year was out the new ambassador was aglow with triumph. His daughters had been presented at court, and he and his wife had been entertained by the king and queen. ("Well, Rose," he said as they dressed for dinner with Britain's royal family, "it's a hell of a long way from East Boston.") What was equally important, he had been befriended and consulted by the prime minister ("I'm just like *that* with Chamberlain," he confided to an acquaintance). As Chamberlain's occasional confidant, the American ambassador soon became his ally, fully supporting the prime minister's policy of appeasement in hopes that Hitler would eventually destroy himself in an attack on Russia. Kennedy had four sons, and the thought of their going to war was more than he could bear to contemplate.

While the English welcomed the Kennedys with unexpected cordiality, there were those at home who regarded the appointment as a disaster. Harold Ickes fumed: "At the time when we should be sending the best that we have to Great Britain we have . . . sent a rich man, untrained in diplomacy, unlearned in history and politics, who is a great publicity seeker and who is apparently ambitious to be the first Catholic President of the United States." Nor was Ickes alone in suspecting that Kennedy had an eye on the White House. In the wake of Kristallnacht, when the new diplomat announced his plan for resettling Germany's Jews in empty areas of South America and Africa, *Life* magazine commented: "Kennedy is rated the most influential ambassador to England in many years. If . . . the Kennedy plan [for resettlement] succeeds, it will add new luster to a reputation that may well carry Joseph Patrick Kennedy into the White House." Whatever Roosevelt may have thought about Ickes's concerns, he was no man to encourage a potential rival's presidential yearnings, and he was soon to recognize that his ambassador in London would prove a personal pain in the neck and a first-class political liability—as much a thorn in his side as those unyielding isolationists in the Senate, or the towering leader of an insurgent working class, the man frequently mentioned as labor's first presidential candidate.

CHAPTER 14

———◆———

"Labor in America wants no war nor any part of war."

A fortnight after Orson Welles's broadcast terrorized the citizenry, four days after Germany's barbaric Night of Broken Glass, a man stepped from a railroad car in Pittsburgh's Union Station who was probably more alarming to my father and his business friends than any Martian or Nazi storm trooper. Neither of the latter had caused them to lose much sleep, but this giant in a tentlike overcoat and broad-brimmed fedora they regarded as the most villainous man of the day, a sinister figure who threatened to shred the very fabric of American business. And here he was in Pittsburgh, in November 1938, attending the constitutional convention of the three-year-old Committee for Industrial Organization, or CIO, for short.

John Llewellyn Lewis had emerged during the 1930s as the individual who was challenging the nation's business community, the man who declared war on the capitalist system and the sacred right of management to hire, to fire, to pay whatever wages it could get away with, and above all to keep the workers in its factories under the strictest possible control. "A man's right to his job transcends the right of private property," John L. Lewis had dared to declare, and it was clear to those who owned that property that they had a genuine revolution on their hands, led by a man who had every intention of winning it.

Part preacher, part rascal, part crusader, he was a looming bear of a man, six feet tall and well over two hundred pounds, massive in the chest and shoulders. His physical presence was intimidating enough, but when he chose to play the ogre, as he often did, the huge head with its shock of unruly hair and flashing blue eyes beneath the implausibly shaggy eyebrows were awesome to behold, the big voice and the majestic rhetoric wondrous to hear. In private, he was charm and wit personified, a quiet man of intense personal conviction and great dignity, with a highly refined sense of honor; but in public he had the presence and timing of an actor, his manner and mien changing according to his mood and circumstance, and no one appreciated the superb act more than the performer himself.

Whenever he turned up at big, public rallies—and that was often enough, since he was in demand as a speaker—he was cheered wildly, as befitted the leader of a massive popular uprising that had carried an organization of ordinary workingmen to a position of national power. Partly because he had channeled into constructive action the festering discontent that was so prevalent among working Americans in the thirties, he was constantly written about in newspapers and magazines, he was cultivated by prominent public officials, consulted by the mighty, mentioned seriously as a presidential candidate. At his favorite dining spot in Washington's Carlton Hotel, he could be seen with the rich and powerful; at his Alexandria home he entertained cabinet officers and ambassadors, congressmen and military chieftains, business and social leaders; at his office he staged press conferences as skillfully as the man in the White House, which was saying a lot. In the United Mine Workers' splendid headquarters building in the capital, his photograph glowered from just about every available wall; one newspaper columnist compared his cavernous office to Mussolini's; another observed that he was the most visible sight in the capital, next to the Washington Monument.

Lewis had long ago learned the uses to which an imposing physiognomy could be put. His stock in trade, he remarked to a friend, was playing the villain; he told Frances Perkins, Roosevelt's secretary of labor, that his scowl was worth a million dollars, and it was all of that, considering how it had made capitalists quake in their shoes.

John L. Lewis was more than the apotheosis of labor on the march; he was also, somewhat ironically, the very personification of the Horatio Alger stories, those rags-to-riches tales of plucky young men destined to become capitalists, thanks to their initiative and enterprise. On the other hand, if you were a businessman struggling to stay afloat during the Great Depression (or, for that matter, a rival labor leader), the thought of John L. Lewis, wearing custom-made clothes, being driven to his sumptuous office in a twelve-cylinder Lincoln limousine by a uniformed chauffeur (who was also his valet) from his antique-filled colonial home in Alexandria, Virginia—all of it paid for by a union that was anathema to the businessman—was the stuff of which apoplexy is made. Yet certainly if anyone had triumphed over the humblest, most obscure origins it was that very man, the eldest of a coal miner's seven children, who had grown up in a succession of company towns in Iowa and gone on to become the most powerful figure in the American labor movement.

Not much is known with certainty about Lewis's early years, so successfully did the man shield himself, his family, and his past from close scrutiny, but as a child he was never far from the Iowa coal mines where his father labored. He started digging coal as a teenager, building up a lifelong hatred of the operators, who held miners in such bondage that they might have been medieval serfs[1]—men whose past, present, and future were as black as the hazardous pits in which they labored for ten and eleven hours a day, nearly suffocated by dust and fumes.

In the Lewis household they sang the old Welsh folk songs and quoted the Bible and Shakespeare familiarly, and Thomas Lewis's six sons learned from their father's example that arguments were as often as not settled with fists. With a wavy mane of luxuriant auburn hair, John was taller than most boys his age and a lot broader in the chest and shoulders. As a born ham, he spent enough time on the stage of the Lucas, Iowa, Opera House to pick up an acquaintance with some of the classics, enlarging his vocabulary with images that rolled richly off his Welsh tongue, so that for the rest of his life he would delight in such phrases as "high wassail will prevail at the banquet tables of the mighty." (The dining habits of the privileged provided him with many a purple passage: once he accused a union foe of sitting "at luxury-laden tables with the dissolute sons and the butterfly daughters of the idle and vicious rich, with captains of industry and malefactors of great wealth. Royally was he entertained. . . . Merrily he tripped through Folly's halls.")

At the age of twenty-one, Lewis left home, a pugnacious character of prodigious physical strength, energy, and courage, to begin five years of wandering through the West, living from hand to mouth, mining coal in Colorado, copper in Montana, gold in Arizona, silver in Utah, and acquiring, in the process, an oversize, Bunyanesque reputation.

Returning to Iowa, he married, ran unsuccessfully for mayor, started a feed business that failed, and in 1908 decided that his future lay in trade unionism. He and his wife moved to Panama, a company town in the Illinois coalfields, where they were soon followed by John's parents, five brothers, and sister, and within a year John was president of the United Mine Workers local. A decade later, thanks in part to support from Samuel Gompers, the first great spokesman of America's trade unionism, control of the

[1]In the words of "Harlan County Blues,"
> "You didn't have to be drunk," they said,
> "To get throwed in the can;
> The only thing you needed to be
> Was just a union man."

United Mine Workers Union, the biggest single bloc within the American Federation of Labor, was in Lewis's hands.

Ironically, Lewis's ideas about unionism were the opposite of those advocated by Gompers, and more than anyone, Lewis was to be responsible for promoting the very program Gompers abhorred. The difference in their ideologies was a reflection of the same attitudes that had divided Pittsburgh's iron craftsmen from the common laborers, the skilled from the unskilled. Whereas Gompers's American Federation of Labor pursued the ideal of an association of craft unions, each one based upon specific skills within a particular occupation, Lewis believed that the only way organized labor could ever bargain successfully in a world in which mass production prevailed was to recruit a huge number of unskilled workers. Recognizing that the coal miners' union, for example, could not survive—much less prosper—unless it joined with workers from other industries to form an effective organization, he perceived that one of his missions within the trade union movement was to overturn the craft unions, upending the entrenched and the privileged. To continue as before, he argued, was elitist and protectionist, detrimental to the masses of unskilled workers and to unionism itself. The next step beyond that premise was that the industrialized workers, fully unionized, represented a base for organizational strength, provided the economic muscle for power, and offered the machinery for political action. Involvement in politics, in other words, was inevitable.

By 1938, John L. Lewis was at the pinnacle of success. He had arrived there by being hugely egotistical, brutal, and ruthless when occasion warranted, and utterly single-minded in his pursuit of power. The best place to see this remarkable man in action was at a union convention, the arena in which he had battled his way to the top, the milieu from which he derived his immense strength and influence.

On November 14, 1938, as the five-day convention got under way at the Islam Grotto on Pittsburgh's North Side, the growing might of the CIO was immediately evident, as was the widening rift between that organization and the American Federation of Labor, from which Lewis and his allies had seceded three years earlier. Convention delegates were in no mood to compromise with the parent body, despite a letter from the president of the United States reminding them, "Continued dissension can only lead to loss of influence and prestige to all labor." What was needed to encourage collective bargaining, the president urged, was "a united labor movement making for co-operation and labor peace." Another chief executive in Washington—President William Green of the AFL—after denouncing as "a fraud" the CIO's claim that it had some four million members, expressed hope that the Pittsburgh convention would "make its contribution toward [labor] peace." Messrs. Roosevelt and Green were not alone in their desire for harmony; the country had had a bellyful of plant shutdowns and violence and strife during the past two years, and the feeling was widespread that John L. Lewis and the CIO were behind it.

But labor amity was not what the 513 boisterous delegates in the Grotto had in mind, and they roared approval every time Lewis or a lesser figure called on the AFL to "recognize established facts and deal with the CIO on a basis of equality and justice. . . ." As James Carey, the youthful president of the United Electrical, Radio, and Machine Workers Union, put it, there could be "no compromise with the fundamental purpose and aim of organizing workers into powerful industrial unions," and that was the crux of the CIO position.

During the convention, the CIO changed its name (but not its initials) from Committee for Industrial Organization to Congress for Industrial Organizations; initiated a "per capita tax" of 5 cents per member per month which would produce a whopping $3 million a year for organizing purposes; advocated a program of sweeping social reform, including what sounded suspiciously like socialized medicine, along with increased unemployment compensation and workmen's compensation; carefully avoided taking a position on whether or not Mr. Roosevelt should be nominated for a third term as president; saw its own president, Mr. Lewis, squelch a threatened outbreak of opposition with the customary iron fist and lofty phrase ("It will profit no man to rail against the convention's rules," he informed delegates who had the temerity to request delay in approving the new CIO constitution long enough to see if it conflicted with that of their own union); and finally voted for officers of the newly named organization. When the name of John L. Lewis (whom the *Pittsburgh Press* called "the messiah of industrial unionism") was placed in nomination for president, the Westinghouse High School band, led by kilted bagpipers and drummers, marched into the hall as clappers, whistles, horns, and tons of confetti were being distributed, whereupon an all but unendurable twenty-eight-minute din began, with the entire assembly on its feet whooping and hollering and the United Auto Workers hoisting chairs over their heads and pounding them on tables. To the surprise of no one, Mr. Lewis was elected and in his acceptance speech said humbly, "My strength is only the strength of a multitude, and only when the multitude grants me its authority." (So much for charges that the CIO was run by a dictator.)

While half a thousand delegates inside the Grotto roared approval of the union's elected leaders—Lewis as president, Philip Murray and Sidney Hillman as vice presidents, and James Carey as secretary—a cold front swept through town, bringing wind, rain, snow flurries, and a 31-degree drop in temperature. Pittsburghers hurrying from the office along drab, cheerless streets bought a copy of the *Press* or *Sun-Telegraph* before boarding a trolley car bound for home, and after glancing at the banner headlines about the CIO convention, were sorry to see that R. B. Mellon's widow, Jennie King Mellon, a generous, civic-minded woman, had died after a brief illness. A few may have noticed that a Los Angeles judge had declared a woman teacher in contempt of court for appearing in the courtroom dressed in slacks.

What no one could possibly ignore on that wintry evening was the news from Europe on the front pages: Hitler expelling all Jews from Germany's public schools, prices on the Berlin stock market tumbling as panic-stricken Jews sold securities in order to repair business premises looted by rioters and pay off the $400 million penalty demanded by the Nazis for Vom Rath's murder. "Aryans," the story noted, "were seeking quick funds to take over businesses of prominent Jews." In Düsseldorf Hitler's car drove past tens of thousands of Nazis paying tribute to Ernst Vom Rath, and the Führer entered the hall where the diplomat's body lay in state, stood silently before the coffin, took a seat, and listened as Foreign Minister von Ribbentrop condemned the "lies, slander, blood, and terrorism of international Jewry." A spokesman for the elite SS guards, hinting darkly at "mismanagement and immorality in monasteries," threatened to expropriate Catholic Church property in Germany. From Italy came news that Mussolini had just banned all Rotary Clubs as "unfascist." A United Press dispatch reported that General Francisco Franco, after four months of savage fighting that cost him twenty thousand casualties, had finally cleared the west bank of the Ebro River of Loyalists and was renewing his drive on Valencia. All in all, it had been a big week for fascism.

So, perhaps as important as any union business that was accomplished within the Grotto were the positions taken by the delegates—thanks to John L. Lewis's insistence—on several matters affecting international affairs. Long before many other public figures, Lewis realized what was happening in Nazi Germany and took his stand. Early in 1937, speaking before a mass meeting in New York City, he had warned, "Fear is king in Germany. By day and by night each man's hand is against his brother. The days and nights of the swastika terror have swept one hundred thousand men and women into concentration camps where the torture of defenseless prisoners seems to be the choice pastime of Nazi heroes." Meantime, he continued, "The horrors which have been visited upon the Jewish people in Germany and . . . upon the representatives of free organization of labor" should leave no doubt in American minds about the threat to human liberty in Nazi Germany. Significantly, he warned Americans then and later that "Europe is on the brink of disaster and it must be our care that she does not drag us into the abyss after her."

Lewis opened the CIO convention with an attack on "bloodthirsty Germany," demanding that the United States government protest that country's "aggression against Jews." Many of these delegates had ties to central Europe and were acutely conscious of what was going on in Czechoslovakia, and to them he predicted that there would be other attacks on other democracies, asking, "Who is going to protect the institutions of this country? Who, its wealth?" And to thunderous applause, he roared, "Labor!"

"The workers of this country will never make a profit out of war," he pledged, making implicit the difference between labor and the nation's industrialists. Then he reminded his audience, in the hall and beyond, that the United States and the nations of Europe were going to need the cooperation of the CIO's millions of workers, should war come—cooperation that would command a price. "We're going to ask that those who are the beneficiaries of that service and loyalty give proper treatment to ourselves," he said, laying his cards face up on the table. And John L. Lewis by now had played so many winning hands that no one could have the slightest doubt about his ability to make good on that promise.

In 1933, Lewis had tried to persuade William Green, who was by then head of the AFL, that the time was right to put on a tremendous drive to "organize steel, autos, shipbuilding, rubber—everything." But "Sitting Bill," as Lewis called him, was against it: it would cost too much and Green had no intention of organizing the mass-production industries.

Through the United Mine Workers Union, Lewis gave money to David Dubinsky's struggling International Ladies Garment Workers Union (ILGWU) and got their support; he lined up Sidney Hillman and his Amalgamated Clothing Workers, Charles Howard's Typographical Union, Max Zaritsky's Hat, Cap, and Millinery Workers, and Thomas McMahon of the Textile Workers; and he then took the most dramatic manner possible to walk out of the AFL convention in 1935. As anticipated, that convention turned down a proposal to embrace industrial unionism, and Bill Hutcheson, the three-hundred-pound boss of the Carpenters Union, declared all further discussion of the subject out of order. Lewis objected, he and Hutcheson exchanged heated words, and when Hutcheson made the mistake of calling him a "big bastard," Lewis floored him with a punch. Lewis had almost certainly decided to pull out of the AFL, but his attack on Hutcheson got the attention of every unorganized worker in the nation. Hutcheson, Lewis knew, symbolized the type of leadership in the American Federation of Labor that most industrial workers detested, and that blow to his jaw was a signal that a significant segment of organized labor was going to move in an entirely different direction. For months, Lewis had had dozens of organizers at work, the UMW membership was back up to 400,000 (after falling to 100,000 or less in 1930), its treasury was bulging, and Lewis was elated to be free of the AFL and the way it hobbled his plans. ("They smote me hip and thigh," was his comment, "and right merrily did I return their blows.") On November 9, 1935, shortly after his "excommunication" from the AFL, John L. Lewis and his supporters formed the Committee for Industrial Organization and went on the attack.

The method they chose was the sit-down strike—in which workers suddenly put down their tools, stopped work, refused to leave the plant, and barricaded the gates. In a day when private property was sacred, this was the supreme outrage, and it was assumed by most business executives (in some instances, quite rightly) that the perpetrators were Communists. With his factory and machinery in the hands of the strikers, the owner could not operate his plant even with strikebreakers; nor did he dare risk using force to get his property back, since that could lead to its destruction. From the time of the first major sit-down at a Firestone tire plant in Akron in 1936, throughout the violent months of 1937, some seven thousand strikes involving nearly two million workers brought chaos to industrial America and fear to the hearts of those who had little sense of what was behind this upheaval. Strikes broke out in shipyards, prisons, rubber and steel plants, textile and paper mills, newspapers, shoe factories, aluminum and glass works, hosiery mills, hotels, power plants; there was a national coal strike, a strike by the seamen's union—everywhere, and all at once, America seemed to be shut down, idle. At first the sit-down strike was the source of innumerable jokes for radio comedians and newspaper cartoonists; then violence erupted, with hundreds of workers beaten, gassed, or shot by city police or company detectives, and by 1938, when the CIO was claiming some four million members, thoughtful Americans might be forgiven for wondering if the riots and strikes, the broken heads and burning crosses, the picket lines and bloody fighting, would ever end—or worse, if the convulsion spearheaded by John L. Lewis might produce a dictatorship as real and as terrifying as the one in Germany. Like America's other revolutions, past and future, this one was born of injustice and won in the face of violence and suffering, and when that terrible year ended, Frances Perkins, Roosevelt's secretary of labor, observed that 1937 had been the most savage twelve months in the twentieth-century story of labor.

Indeed Lewis, saying, "We are the workers—they are the enemy," had declared war on American business, proclaiming that the hour of labor's redemption was at hand, and before he was done the CIO had humbled many of the great corporations in the land—U.S. Steel and Jones & Laughlin, General Motors and Chrysler, General Electric, Caterpillar Tractor, Firestone, Goodrich, and Goodyear among them.

In the notable instance of Little Steel, he failed, and that, it turned out, was the turning point in his relationship with the president of the United States, a relationship that had served both Roosevelt and Lewis well. Little Steel, as the group of independent producers that included Republic, Inland, National, Bethlehem, and Youngstown Sheet and Tube was called, refused to deal with the CIO's organizers and had picked a man as tough and as ruthless as John L. Lewis to lead their fight against the union. Thomas M. Girdler, who ran Republic, had announced that he would go back to hoeing potatoes rather than meet the strikers' demands, and had promised, "I won't have a contract, verbal or written, with an irresponsible, racketeering, violent, communistic body like the CIO, and until they pass a law making me, I am not going to do it." Girdler conveniently ignored the fact that exactly such a law—the Wagner Act—had been passed and signed by the president, but he was prepared to do battle and was unlikely to let a piece of legislation stand in the way.

On Memorial Day 1937, near Sam's Place on South Green Bay Avenue, not far from Republic Steel's South Chicago plant, a crowd of striking mill hands and their families had collected to protest police interference with their picketing. Chicago's Mayor Edward Kelly had given them permission to hold a peaceful demonstration, and as the marchers—some of them dressed up for the holiday, many carrying small children on their shoulders—sang, "Solidarity forever! The union makes us strong," and approached the gate to the mill, they saw hundreds of armed Chicago cops, heard a captain shout, "You dirty sons of bitches, this is as far as you go!" and suddenly a number of the bluecoats closed in on some of the mill workers' wives, jabbing them in the breasts and groin with nightsticks. Strikers began yelling, "Stand fast! Stand fast! We got our rights!" Police shouted, "You Red bastards, you got no rights!" And while a Paramount newsreel camera turned, recording the scene, all hell suddenly broke loose: policemen swinging billies and clubs, lobbing tear-gas grenades, shooting pistols into the air and into the crowd. While children screamed in terror, men and women gasped for breath and panicked, began to run, and the police fired volleys, charged up to those who had fallen and shot them in the back, held men and women down and beat them insensible. When the carnage finally ended, ten people were dead and more than ninety wounded. "There can be no pity for a mob," Tom Girdler announced the next day.[3]

Wherever Little Steel workers were on strike, Lewis appealed to state governors (most of whom had been elected with CIO support) to protect them, but the only action taken was to send troops to guard corporate property and disperse pickets. By June 21, twelve victims of the Memorial Day massacre were dead and another ten were "gasping for their lives in hospital beds," according to Lewis, and he put his case before President Roosevelt: "Labor," he wrote, "will await the position of the authorities on whether our people will be protected or butchered." When Mr. Roosevelt responded at a press conference a week later, it was to remark that "the majority of the people are saying just one thing, 'A plague on both your houses.' " He explained later that he was referring to the extremists on both sides, but Lewis never forgot, never forgave, and on Labor Day 1937, in a speech broadcast over the CBS network, he delivered his scathing reply.

"Labor, like Israel, has many sorrows," he said. "Its women weep for

[3]Paramount News refused to distribute its film of the Memorial Day Massacre, claiming that theater audiences might stage "riotous demonstrations" if they were allowed to see it. Although Colonel Robert McCormick's *Chicago Tribune* insisted that the mill workers and their families had been "lusting for blood," the *St. Louis Post-Dispatch* revealed the story of the film and its suppression. In the wake of the tragedy, a Senate committee headed by Wisconsin's Robert M. La Follette, Jr., held an investigation and concluded that "the force employed by the police was far in excess of what the occasion required."

their fallen, and they lament for the future of the children of the race. It ill behooves one who has supped at labor's table and who has been sheltered in labor's house to curse with equal fervor and fine impartiality both labor and its adversaries when they become locked in deadly embrace."[4]

That same year the CIO had faltered on other fronts, including abortive efforts to organize Southern textile workers, federal employees, and those on the WPA rolls. During and after the "Roosevelt depression"—which cost two million workers their jobs—the union lost thousands of members and much of the momentum it had built up. As 1939 began, it became evident that the unity so apparent at the Pittsburgh convention had been a surface impression, that real differences existed between Lewis, on the one hand, and Hillman and Murray on the other. These differences, moreover, were essentially the same ones that were widening the gap between Lewis and Roosevelt, dividing the nation itself into two bitterly opposed camps.

In the wake of the 1938 congressional elections, when President Roosevelt saw his political strength slip seriously for the first time, he was diverted both by external events and the new conservatism in Congress from pressing forward with domestic reforms,[5] and turned his primary attention to foreign affairs. Here he ran head-on into the formidable opposition of John L. Lewis. It soon became clear, if it had not already been so, that Roosevelt's vision of world affairs demanded a vigorous, active, at times risky foreign policy. Lewis, on the other hand, saw the international role of the United States much as Senator Borah and many noninterventionists did—and in his traditional Labor Day radio speech in 1939, three days after Germany invaded Poland, he elaborated on the message he had delivered two years earlier, condemning war as "the device of the politically despairing and intellectually sterile statesmen." Then he added: "Labor in America wants no war nor any part of war. Labor wants the right to work and live—not the privilege of dying by gunshot or poison gas to sustain the mental errors of current statesmen."

Looking ahead, he predicted: "In the march of years 1940 will be one of the crossroads of destiny for the people of the United States. . . . Let those who will seek the votes of the workers of America be prepared to guarantee jobs for all Americans and freedom from foreign wars."

Any way you considered it, the presidential election campaign of 1940 promised to be significant, and in no respect more so than in the coming showdown between Franklin D. Roosevelt and John L. Lewis. As Lewis

[4]No one had any doubts about what Lewis meant by that reference to supping at labor's table. In 1936 the CIO had contributed $500,000 to FDR's reelection campaign fund.

[5]Unlike the president, Lewis was still defending the New Deal's legislative reforms in 1939, and when Vice President John Nance Garner attempted to swing congressional conservatives into line against his own administration's wages and hours law, Lewis appeared before the House Committee on Labor and delivered his unforgettable characterization of the Texan as a "labor-baiting, poker-playing, whiskey-drinking, evil old man"—an image Garner never lived down.

foresaw on that September day a few hours after the storm broke over Europe, America was approaching a fateful fork in the road, where the signposts pointing to the future would be dim and confusing. At that junction a choice would have to be made, willy-nilly, but what he could not know was that the direction the nation would take might hinge as much on what happened across the Atlantic as on anything said or done here, while the "foreign wars" he abhorred would somehow prove to be our wars, with inescapable domestic consequences.

CHAPTER 15

"All the luck in the world!"

Ever since the coronation of George VI in 1937, Canada's prime minister, Mackenzie King, had been trying to persuade the British sovereign to make a tour of North America, and Franklin Roosevelt had been an ardent seconder of the proposal. The president's representative at the coronation had broached the idea of a royal visit to Washington, and late in the summer of 1938, Mackenzie King received word that a trip to Canada was in fact taking shape. He passed the information on to Roosevelt, who sent a letter to King George at the height of the Munich crisis. Writing informally, as if to an old family friend, the president extended an invitation to the royal family, saying, "It would be an excellent thing for Anglo-American relations if you could visit the United States." If the king should think well of the plan, he went on, and "if you bring either or both of the children with you they will be very welcome. . . . I shall try to have one or two Roosevelts of approximately the same age to play with them!" (Since the two princesses—Elizabeth and Margaret—were twelve and eight years old, respectively, FDR was thinking of his own grandchildren as playmates, since his youngest child, John, was twenty-two.) What he had in mind for the visit, Roosevelt continued, was a relatively casual affair, with "three or four days of very simple country life" at Hyde Park and "no formal entertainments" in the schedule, giving the king and queen "an opportunity to get a bit of rest and relaxation."

The last thing Roosevelt needed was for isolationists in Congress to get wind of this invitation prematurely, so he asked his man in London, Joe Kennedy, to deliver the message personally to Britain's sovereign. Having taken care of that errand, Kennedy naturally assumed that he would be in on the arrangements for the trip and would surely accompany the royal party, but he was mistaken. FDR intended to keep negotiations private, and in his own hands. Piqued, feeling more and more like a glorified messenger boy, the ambassador wrote Hull, saying, "I suppose nothing can be done about this and that I can continue being a dummy and carry on the best I can."

In October, after the Czech crisis was settled, the king announced his plans to visit North America and informed Roosevelt that he and the queen looked forward to the trip, but that the children were "much too young for such a strenuous tour." How strenuous he would soon discover.

As they boarded the ship that was to carry them across the Atlantic, the king and queen waved farewell to his mother, Queen Mary, the stern, ramrod-straight dowager who personified the past, the continuity of royalty, and the imperial glory of Victoria's day, which so many looked back to with longing. Flanking her on the dock stood the future—the two little princesses so beloved in England, Elizabeth, known as Lilibet, and Margaret Rose.

Whatever may have gone through the king's mind at that moment, the trip was bound to be something of a trial for him. He was heading for a land that had opened its arms to his older and wildly popular brother, David, when he visited as the dashing Prince of Wales—a land whose newspapers and radio had supplied an enthralled public with every juicy detail (Britain's press had been sworn to secrecy) of that brother's romance with the handsome American divorcée, Wallis Simpson, the ensuing constitutional crisis, and Edward VIII's abdication. The prince who had been christened Albert Frederick Arthur George, and was known to his family as Bertie, never expected to become king, never wanted any part of it, in fact, and only when it was thrust upon him had he shouldered the unwanted burden because it was his duty to do so. As a child he had shared with David the nursery and the abuse of a psychopathic nurse named Mary Peters. As a three-year-old, David was covered with bruises where Nurse Peters, before handing him to his mother, pinched him or twisted his arm so that he would always cry and be returned at once to his nanny. Worse, Bertie was ignored by the nurse, who underfed and neglected him, and by the time he began to speak he had developed a bad stammer that proved to be permanent. To him, the crown meant the humiliating agony of giving speeches in public.

George VI had never achieved the popularity of his older brother (the *New York Times* uncharitably called him "dry and not very human"), but if he lacked Edward VIII's charm and modern outlook, he had inherited his mother's attitude toward responsibility, duty, and work, and somehow the stammer he found so galling *did* make him more human to his subjects. A man who knew him well said he had "no wit, no learning, no humor, except of a rather schoolboy brand," and added that he was "nervous, ill-at-ease, though slightly better after some champagne." In fact, the king, as his family knew, had a drinking problem, which his mother always explained away as the result of his nervous nature. (One of the arguments employed by Queen Mary, who did her utmost to prevent her oldest son's marriage and abdication, was that the responsibilities of monarchy would kill "poor Bertie.") Fortunately for Bertie, he had married a woman he worshiped, who was clearly an enormous asset to him and to the throne.

Queen Elizabeth, the former Elizabeth Angela Marguerite Bowes-Lyon—whom Anne Lindbergh once compared to "an old-fashioned rose"—was a dark-haired, attractive woman with a spellbinding smile and lilting voice. She was perfectly cast for the lawn parties and fêtes and formal occasions she had to attend in numbing succession. She dressed in feminine but rather uninteresting clothes that made her look almost Victorian, short, and just a little plump, which seemed to endear her the more to her subjects. Although she and her husband had been on the throne for only two years, the British public had taken the quiet, unassuming pair to their hearts, which was exactly what thousands of Canadians and Americans were about to do.

On May 15, 1939, officials of the Canadian Pacific Railroad announced with considerable chagrin that their liner *Empress of Australia* had been so delayed by fog and ice that the king and queen would be unable to attend the reception planned in Quebec. In fact, at the same moment French-speaking schoolchildren were practicing singing "God Save the King" in English, that gentleman was taking part in a lifeboat drill. Two days later, just before midnight, the ship finally dropped anchor twelve miles downstream from Quebec and the first visit of a reigning British monarch to North America was about to begin.

On June 7, after the Canadian tour ended, the blue-and-silver train bearing the royal party steamed across the suspension bridge at Niagara Falls and into the brick station where the smell of fresh paint, a niggardly length of red carpet, and a delegation headed by Cordell Hull awaited the visitors. The door of the observation car opened and out stepped the slight, self-effacing man known to his subjects as His Most Excellent Majesty George VI, by the Grace of God, of Great Britain, Ireland, and of the British Dominions Beyond the Seas, King, Defender of the Faith, Emperor of India. (The empire, it must be remembered, then extended over one-fourth of the earth's surface.)

When the party arrived in Washington, to be greeted by President and Mrs. Roosevelt and a small army of notables at Union Station, the temperature was a humid 94 degrees Fahrenheit, the king was perspiring heavily

in the braided full-dress uniform and fore-and-aft hat of an admiral of the
fleet, and his host was near suffocation in cutaway coat, striped trousers,
and top hat. Two days, a few twenty-one-gun salutes, and countless changes
of clothes later, after a triumphant motorcade through the streets of the
capital, where they were cheered by hundreds of thousands of Washingtoni-
ans gaga for a glimpse of royalty, after luncheons, dinners, and soirées at
the White House and the British embassy, the visitors were driven to
Capitol Hill, where a delegation of fidgety congressmen awaited. Weeks
earlier, when it first had learned that Britain's king and queen were coming
to the United States, Representative Ham Fish had predicted that America
would revert to its status as a colony, and Senator Borah had suggested slyly
that whenever a lull in the conversation permitted, the president might ask
when it would be convenient for Their Britannic Majesties to repay the $5
billion outstanding on the 1914–18 war debt. Vice President John Nance
Garner seemed determined to outdo the Idaho senator at ineptitude: at a
lawn party at the British embassy he clowned outrageously and gave the
king a solid Texas slap on the back; now he was regaling his fellow legislators with stories, not all of them appropriate to the occasion, and when the
royal party appeared at the foot of the Capitol steps, he hurried to the
rotunda and announced in a rasping stage whisper, "The British are coming!"

Whatever suspicion or animosity may have existed vanished at once.
Congressmen positively melted before the queen's lovely smile and charm;
they broke up in delight when they heard the king greet South Carolina's
Senator Ellison D. Smith as "Cotton Ed." Even old Borah was on his good
behavior; in honor of the occasion he had dusted off a morning suit he
hadn't worn for thirty-five years. A Texas congressman greeted the king as
"Cousin George," saying he brought greetings "from the far-flung regions
of the Empire State of Texas," then turned to a colleague and added, "If
America can keep Queen Elizabeth, Congress will regard Britain's war debt
as canceled."

Late that evening, after a cruise down the Potomac to Mount Vernon on
the presidential yacht and a visit to a Civilian Conservation Corps camp,
the royal party and fourteen hundred "carefully chosen guests," as the
newspapers put it, attended a formal dinner at the British embassy. Katherine Marshall, whose husband, the army's newly named chief of staff, was
on a mission to Brazil, was one of the lucky invitees and remarked that she
had "never known such bitterness, such recriminations, nor such an extraordinary display of ill-breeding" as Washington society displayed over
who was or was not on the invitation list. (She was nevertheless mightily
impressed by the guests of honor: the queen had the bluest eyes and the
sweetest smile imaginable and looked "exquisite"—very slender and very
young in an embroidered white muslin gown, matching picture hat, and
parasol; and the king seemed much younger than his pictures.)

The following day, when the exhausted couple boarded a train for Red Bank, New Jersey, was, if possible, more rigorous than those that preceded it, and—at 84 degrees—almost as hot. Leaving the train at Red Bank, they were joined by a welcoming party that included New York's Governor Herbert Lehman and New York City's Mayor Fiorello La Guardia, and drove to Sandy Hook along a route lined with 200,000 cheering people, a high school bagpipe band, and an Episcopal choir singing "God Save the King." Overhead roared ten bombers from the Army Air Force; and when they boarded the U.S. destroyer *Warrington,* which was to take them to the Battery in downtown New York, they were treated to another deafening twenty-one-gun salute.

According to the *New York Times,* 3.5 million Americans (a number exceeded only by those welcoming Charles Lindbergh home from his transatlantic flight) turned out to watch the royal couple's motorcade speed past, as they were whisked to the New York World's Fair in Flushing Meadows. There they were welcomed by Grover Whalen, New York's official greeter, contingents of marines and national guardsmen, bands, assorted dignitaries, the Meyer Davis orchestra, and countless thousands of gawking fair-goers. If the royal visitors were bewildered by all this, the man who chauffeured them to various exhibits on the fairgrounds in a special lounge car was unfazed. "It didn't shake me," George Michael Blonigan remarked stolidly. "When I was a sergeant in France, I stood close to Clemenceau, Lloyd George, and President Wilson. I'm kind of used to it now." Through it all, the queen smiled and waved while the king looked progressively more tired and cranky. Apparently it had occurred to no one to accommodate the physiological needs of the royal visitors. The king, being a king, was not accustomed to informing total strangers that he had to relieve himself, and the result was that he became increasingly testy as the hours wore on, until he finally refused to take another step along the planned route unless someone told him where "it" was—"it" being the men's room. When his errand was accomplished, the program continued, but it had been a difficult and strained couple of hours for the monarch. (At the British Pavilion, His Majesty encountered two Scottish women and asked, "It's still the tenth of June, isn't it? We've been up so long I feel it must be another day.") At last, while films of their trip to the Fair were rushed to a waiting Pan American Clipper to be flown to London, the royal couple left on the penultimate leg of their American journey: the drive up the Hudson River to Franklin Roosevelt's ancestral home at Hyde Park.

The Roosevelts had been warned by telephone that their visitors would be late, and when they finally drove in the president had a pitcher of martinis waiting on a tray. As soon as the king had changed his clothes and reappeared, FDR remarked, "My mother thinks you should have a cup of tea—she doesn't approve of cocktails." "Neither does mine," replied the king, reaching for a martini.

While they were in Washington, an awesome list of protocol had been observed. Not so at Hyde Park, where informality and intimacy afforded an opportunity for the president and the young king to exchange views candidly. Remarkably, considering the harrowing day the king had endured, after everyone else retired for the night, he, Roosevelt, and Prime Minister Mackenzie King—who accompanied the British monarch—stayed up and discussed the alarming developments in Europe. After FDR went to bed the king continued his conversation with the Canadian, asking at one point, "Why don't my ministers talk to me as the president did tonight?" Roosevelt, he felt, had spoken as frankly as a father to a son, giving him considered and wise advice.

As Eleanor Roosevelt was to write, her husband and the king were both awaiting the blow that was certain to fall in Europe before long, knowing that "we all might soon be engaged in a life and death struggle, in which Great Britain would be our first line of defense. . . ." After their conversations, George VI made notes (he carried them in a dispatch box that never left his side during the war), and among them he listed Roosevelt's extraordinarily candid "ideas in case of War," which first called for the president to inform the American public what it would cost them financially if Hitler conquered Europe. FDR also disclosed his plans for defending the Atlantic approaches to the western hemisphere, in order to remove some of the pressure from the British fleet, and told the king of sea and air patrols ("about which he is terribly keen") which would fan out across a thousand-mile radius from Trinidad and Bermuda. In that connection he mentioned his hope that Britain, when war came, would grant the United States rights to certain naval bases in Newfoundland, Bermuda, and the Caribbean, and the king could not help wondering how the president could possibly consider such a move without a declaration of war. Touching on the subject of Nazi intruders, the president said, according to the king's notes, that "if he saw a U boat he would sink her at once & wait for the consequences." And finally he made a promise the king must have wanted above all to hear: "If London was bombed U.S. would come in."

Undoubtedly the most important outcome of the king's visit was intangible—the confidence he gained that the president of the United States was a friend to be trusted, to be regarded as one of the family. This was the assurance he passed on to the chiefs of British intelligence, who had ceased confiding their most important secrets to Prime Minister Neville Chamberlain, in the belief that his judgment was not to be relied upon.

By the time the king and queen were to depart, they had experienced an American-style picnic with beer, hot dogs (the king ate two), smoked ham, and strawberry shortcake; they had worshiped with their hosts at the local church; they had been urged to swim in the Roosevelt pool (the king accepted and wore a one-piece suit that James Roosevelt pronounced an antique; the queen refused—"I discovered that if you are a queen you

cannot run the risk of looking disheveled," observed Mrs. Roosevelt tactfully); and had been driven around the neighborhood by the crippled president in his hand-operated convertible Ford. What was considerably more
important, they had been symbolically embraced by the American people,
who were forcibly reminded by the royal visit that when all was said and
done, their ties were strongest to the great English-speaking empire of
which these two people were then the most eminent human symbols.

After the final dinner given them by President Roosevelt's mother, Sara,
the king and queen—still in evening dress—boarded their special train at
the little Hyde Park station. The king was in black tie, the queen in a deep
rose chiffon evening gown, a white-ermine-and-fox cape, and diamond ear-
rings, and as they stood on the observation platform, looking for all the
world like a fairy-tale prince and princess, waving to their hosts, the president called out, "Good luck to you! All the luck in the world!"

The train began to move, and suddenly, out of the dusk, came the
haunting strains of "Auld Lang Syne," sung by hundreds of voices. While
the Roosevelts and the royal couple had been saying their goodbyes, local
people by the scores had silently made their way onto the rocks above the
banks of the Hudson and were unable to resist adding their own farewell
to that of the president and his family. Eleanor Roosevelt remembered,
"There was something incredibly moving about this scene—the river in the
evening light, the voices of many people singing this old song, and the train
slowly pulling out with the young couple waving good-bye. One thought of
the clouds that hung over them and the worries they were going to face,
and turned away and left the scene with a heavy heart."

CHAPTER 16

"He's from Baltimore, and that's not his wife."

In suggesting that Great Britain's royal couple include the New York World's Fair on their itinerary, Franklin Roosevelt was only echoing the absolute certainty of millions of Americans that the extravaganza on Long Island's Flushing Meadow was far and away the best show in town in 1939.

The idea to hold a world's fair at this particular time and in this place had come about in a curious, characteristically American manner.

The year was 1934, the scene the Jackson Heights home of a civil engineer named Joseph Shadgen, where little Jacqueline was telling her father what she had learned in school that day. According to her teacher, the United States of America was 158 years old because the Declaration of Independence had been signed in 1776. Mr. Shadgen digested that piece of information and then informed Jacqueline that her teacher was wrong: since George Washington had not been inaugurated until 1789 (at the corner of Nassau and Wall streets in downtown New York, he reminded her), the nation wouldn't really have its 150th birthday—let alone a 158th—until 1939. That was what gave Joseph Shadgen the idea that New York should hold a world's fair to celebrate the country's sesquicentennial year.

He spoke to his business partner, who introduced him to a man who introduced him to George McAneny, a banker and booster. McAneny knew a good commercial idea when he heard one, and before long he had spread the word to a number of New York merchants, to Mayor La Guardia, to Governor Lehman, and even to President Roosevelt. In October of 1935 the New York World's Fair Corporation was formed, with McAneny as chairman of the board and Grover Whalen—a mustachioed Wanamaker department store executive turned police commissioner who had made the greeting of notable visitors and returning heroes into a New York art form—as president. The corporation borrowed some money to pay expenses (Whalen had been put on salary at $100,000 a year, for starters; Shadgen was also hired, at a more modest $625 per month) and sold $27 million in bonds, and the city of New York coughed up $48 million to put Flushing Meadow in shape for the big event. It cost $2 million to rent the site, a fortune to drain it (the sewers alone came to $7.5 million), $1.2 million to build a special subway spur, and $2.2 million for the amphitheater (where Billy Rose would turn a profit of $1.4 million from his Aquacade). By the time the Fair opened, the corporation had laid out $42 million—which included $29 million for construction and a whopping $13 million for "organization, promotion, and other expenses." Mr. Whalen was unperturbed. The Fair, he promised stockholders, would attract at least fifteen million out-of-town visitors who would spend $1 billion—$230 million of it for food and drink alone. As time passed and opening day drew closer, those estimates rose considerably, but even Whalen's original projections were heady ones for a city that still had Hoovervilles on the outskirts of town—squalid communities where the homeless built shanties out of packing crates and scrap metal—and whose merchants had not known a really good year for a decade. The show would go on.

By the spring of 1939, a combination of twelve thousand workers and some $150 million had transformed the former Queens dump into what promoters were calling "The World of Tomorrow." In the process, ten thousand trees, a million Dutch bulbs, and tons of bluegrass were planted on the 1,211-acre site; more than two hundred buildings were erected and sixty-five miles of streets and walkways paved; some fifteen hundred exhibitors, including fifty-eight foreign nations, thirty-three states, and Puerto Rico, along with a host of business concerns, signed up to display their wares; and if you could believe the official guidebook, the result was a "magnificent spectacle of a luminous world, apparently suspended in space." Hyperbole aside, it was difficult to see how any visitor could go away disappointed.

Grouped around the Fair's Theme Centre—a seven-hundred-foot, needlelike obelisk known as the Trylon, and a two-hundred-foot, 4.2-million-pound globe called the Perisphere—was a mind-boggling array of technological wonders, promotional gimmicks, educational displays, and amusements calculated to suit just about every taste. (On instructions from Fair officials, the midway was never to be referred to as a midway; it was the "amusement loop.")

On April 30, when President Roosevelt opened the fair "to all mankind," he proclaimed to an audience of sixty thousand that "our wagon is hitched to a star of peace." During a day of parades, concerts, and fireworks, 206,000 people paid a 75-cent admission charge before the counting mechanism—which kept a running tally on a giant business machine revolving atop the National Cash Register building—broke down; an eight-year-old Wisconsin cow gave birth to a fifty-three pound bull calf; and Albert Einstein, the renowned German physicist who was now a refugee in America, threw a switch that lit up a myriad of fountains and floodlights "with cosmic ray impulses."

For only $7, it was said, the average family could have a dandy time at the Fair, and who could not, when the free exhibits included such marvels as General Electric's ten-million-volt man-made lightning; a twenty-two-foot transparent man; Westinghouse's robot named Elektro that had twenty-six different tricks, including walking, talking, and smoking a cigarette; a Children's World; a City of Tomorrow; a miniature rocket voyage to the moon; and, best of all, according to a poll of fairgoers taken by the Gallup organization a few weeks after opening day, General Motors' Futurama. This stunning glimpse of a vast cross section of the United States, all of it in miniature, for which GM had coughed up $7.5 million, was designer Norman Bel Geddes's vision of what the country was going to be like two decades hence. To behold what lay in store for 1960 America, you sat for fifteen minutes in an armchair on a moving conveyor belt, peering out over a gigantic scale model that contained 500,000 individually designed buildings, more than a million tiny trees, and fifty thousand scale-model automobiles scooting across an intricate network of superhighways and multideck bridges. As you progressed along this wondrous panorama, a sound device explained that happy-go-lucky Americans of the coming generation would spend a great deal of their time roving thither and yon about the countryside, thanks to express highways with separate fifty-, seventy-five-, and hundred-mile-per-hour lanes, in which speeds, lane changes, and periodic stops would be controlled by radio towers, facilitating accident-free trips from coast to coast in little more than a day's time. Raindrop-shaped, air-conditioned, diesel-powered cars, with a sticker price of only $200, would be the favorite mode of transportation for these mobile, fun-loving folk, who would be blessed with two-month vacations and a mere handful of possessions to tie them down. Interestingly, the most contented people in 1960, according to an article on the Futurama in *Life* magazine, would "live in one-factory farm villages producing one small industrial item and their own produce."

After making a five-year study of the highways of tomorrow, Bel Geddes and his engineers had reached a number of conclusions, including the notion that vehicular and pedestrian traffic should be completely segregated, as should the flow of traffic in opposite directions. Traffic lanes would be separated by barriers, and safe means of entering and leaving highways would be provided. Alas, what these visionary designers neither foresaw nor saw the need to solve was the parking problem that would be generated by so many cars entering so many cities. And in the designers' recommendation that a national highway planning authority be appointed to develop a fifty-year plan for traffic growth, one visitor to the Fair perceived the ultimate irony. Walter Lippmann, the distinguished political commentator for the *New York Herald Tribune,* called the General Motors building "as proud an exhibit as one can find of what men can achieve by private initiative, individual leadership, and the personal genius of scientists and inventors," but paradoxically, the creation of a future motorist's paradise was to be in the hands of a public works administration. GM had spent a fortune, in other words, to convince the public that Detroit's bounty could be enjoyed only at the cost of enormous government expenditures. (GM could afford the promotion expense: in 1937 it was one of six companies that together rang up one-fourth of all corporate profits in the United States.)

Lippmann spent less than a full day at the Fair and came away exhilarated but somehow saddened by what he had seen. The displays ranged from precision instruments to "a regiment of perfectly formed human creatures"—a strange mix suggesting man's "preposterous incapacity to enjoy the fruits of his genius, to be as wise as he is intelligent, to be as good as he is great." After inspecting exhibits of America's remarkable industrial technology he wondered why it was that we could "calculate the fineness of a machine to a millionth of an inch and cannot calculate a government budget within four billion dollars." The unintentional message of the Fair, he decided, "is that the human race is a collection of the most marvelous, ingenious, and engaging idiots that ever got possession of a noble planet."

If the Fair was not precisely the world of tomorrow it was certainly the hope of a better day ahead, an extension of the old American dream that if things didn't work out where you were, you could always move on to the next frontier. Implicit in the wonders of Flushing Meadow was the assurance that science and technology would provide that next frontier, and thousands of Americans who were deathly tired of the world of today, sporting GM Futurama buttons that read "I have seen the future," wandered hot and footsore through the fairgrounds, gawking with a sense of awe and excitement at the miracles of a promised land. They saw a rich amalgam of dreams—a streamlined General Motors car in every garage, an airport in every village, a world where cancer and infantile paralysis were diseases of the past, where agriculture was infinitely bountiful, where the nations of the world lived side by side in harmony. To show the folks of a distant future—fifty centuries hence—what the world of 1939 was really like, Westinghouse Electric's president and Grover Whalen lowered into the ground a gleaming metal time capsule, containing such items as an alarm clock, a can opener, a Mickey Mouse plastic cup, some of the latest fabrics, coins, the Lord's Prayer in three hundred languages, the alphabet, photographs, magazines, films, books, a speech by Franklin D. Roosevelt, and a gloomy message from the great Albert Einstein for anyone who might be lucky enough to find and disinter the time capsule in the year 6939.[1]

There was, of course, a less earnest side to this exhibition. "As an attraction for crowds, science does not seem to compete with an undressed woman," Charles Lindbergh commented wryly after touring the World of Tomorrow, and by the time the Fair closed in November, six months after opening day, it was a safe bet that the 26 million visitors had spent considerably more time on the "amusement loop" than at the more serious exhibits, uplifting though the latter might be. There were girlie shows and freaks, live monsters and a Laff in the Dark, a tank where you could watch Oscar the Obscene Octopus wrestle with an almost-naked maiden in "Twenty Thousand Legs Under the Sea," and the crowds' particular favorite, Billy Rose's Aquacade, starring the shapely Olympic medalist Eleanor Holm and several score "Aquafemmes"—precision swimmers who splashed around the pool in time to waltz music.

Equally successful was the 250-foot parachute jump from the Life Savers tower. Strapped in your seat, you were hoisted slowly into the air, up and up, to get a bird's-eye view of the restaurants and rides, the huge exhibition halls, the fountains playing in the Lagoon of Nations, the Japanese pavilion modeled after an ancient Shinto shrine, and beyond it the Soviet Union's monolithic marble tower, topped by a statue of a worker holding the red star and Lenin's uncompromising dictum: "The Russian Revolution must in its final result lead to the victory of Socialism." Off to one side, beyond the roller skating, beyond Gay New Orleans and the Aquacade, was the Lake of Liberty. Far in the distance, visible from the very top of the tower, you could see the United States building and the Court of Peace, surrounded by the pavilions of various nations. Farther to the north were the British pavilion with its gleaming gold imperial lion and the Coldstream Guards band, Italy's determinedly modernistic structure, the League of Nations building, and Poland's graceful tower, rising above a restaurant that served Polish vodka and forty different hors d'oeuvres, and that nation's pavilion, where officials urged visitors to enter an essay contest that began, "I would like to visit Poland because . . ." Then suddenly you had reached the top, the parachute was released, and your stomach dropped out from under you in that breathtaking instant before the chute filled with air and floated slowly to earth.

On one memorable evening things did not go according to plan. Alvin Josephy, an assistant director of news and special features for New York's radio station WOR, had been dispatched to the fairgrounds to interview Mrs. Rushmore Patterson of the Daughters of the American Revolution

[1]After E. L. Doctorow completed his novel on the 1939 New York World's Fair he visited the site of the great event, but no one seemed to know where the time capsule was. Finally the chief of security at the Queens Museum located it in a grove of trees about three hundred yards south of the museum—a small cement disk covered with graffiti.

A needle and a sphere, known as the Trylon and the Perishere, dominated New York's "World of Tomorrow"—the 1,200-acre fairgrounds built on what had been the Queens city dump.

and Howard Fast, whose book *Conceived in Liberty* was published that year. The interview, which was on the air live from 11:15 to 11:30 P.M., took place inside the DAR building, a replica of George Washington's Mount Vernon, and toward the close of the program an engineer handed Josephy a note, saying that a couple were stuck on the parachute jump. As soon as he could finish his chat with Mrs. Patterson and Fast, Josephy and the crew hurried through the amusement area and the backstage disarray of a girlie show, arrived at the Life Savers tower, and started to broadcast. He was the first reporter on the scene, and as soon as his news hit the air hundreds of motorists began turning off Grand Central Parkway onto World's Fair Boulevard, where they stopped to watch the impromptu show.

While Josephy was describing the scene over the air, the society photographer Jerome Zerbe came up to him and asked him not to reveal the name of the man who was stranded.

"Why not?" Josephy asked. "What's the matter with telling his name?"

Just this, Zerbe indicated—it could cause the fellow a lot of trouble.

"He's already in a lot of trouble," Josephy replied.

"Not like he's going to be," Zerbe said, shaking his head. "He's from Baltimore, and that's not his wife."

====

By the time the Fair closed for the year on November 1, 1939, many of the international exhibitors that had assembled here a few months earlier as peaceful competitors had become mortal enemies of their neighbors across the Lagoon of Nations. By then, war had shattered the hopeful tomorrow that brought a community of nations and commercial enterprises together in Flushing Meadow. The Poles, whose homeland was overrun by the Germans and the Russians, continued in a daze to go through the motions of summer, urging those who visited the pavilion to enter the contest and write an essay about why they wanted to visit Poland. Before winter was out, the Soviet building would be torn down and the site landscaped, so that when the Fair reopened in 1940, groups in foreign costumes could perform folk dances and native songs on what would be called the "American common." Of the amusement concessions, only Billy Rose's Aquacade, the parachute jump, and Frank Buck's Jungleland made money the first season. New York's merchants and hotelkeepers were calling the Fair a flop, since their revenues for the year were below those of the non-Fair years 1937 and 1938. The New York World's Fair Corporation was broke, with an operating loss of $10 million and its bonds in default. Grover Whalen's projected fifty to sixty million paying customers proved to be exactly 25,817,625, and Whalen himself, in an effort to drum up business for 1940, was tiptoeing around the edges of Europe's battlefields looking for prospects. An embittered Joseph Shadgen, whose idea it had been in the first place, never went near the fairgrounds, lost his job with the corporation, sued for $1 million, and settled for $45,000. His daughter Jacqueline, however, whose offhand remark about what she had learned in school had started the whole thing, visited the Fair any number of times and loved it, as did almost everyone else who was fortunate enough to see the fantastic paradise in Flushing Meadow during that final summer of peace.

Maybe the Fair was merely an illusion or a conjurer's trick, but it enabled nearly 26 million visitors, mostly Americans, to broaden their painfully cramped horizons by exposure—never mind how superficially—to the cultures of scores of foreign nations, letting them see in the flesh who their true allies were, reassuring them with the physical presence and the rich accents of English and French, Canadians, Australians, and New Zealanders, Finns, Belgians, and Brazilians, even Czechs and Poles, as if to say that war was only a temporary aberration and that one day soon we friends would get together again. For four happy, shining months, the World of Tomorrow provided a bright vision of a world without poverty or war or hatred, a world of dreams where everyone had plenty to eat and a General Motors automobile, where nations lived side by side in peace, where bands played and strangers smiled at each other because they had nothing more important in mind than having a good time.

PART III

1939

MOSCOW: DEATH OF AN ILLUSION

*A speech by Adolf Hitler was a performance,
designed to manipulate an audience. More persuasive
than his words was the intensity of his passion,
hatred, and sensitivity to a crowd's mood.*

CHAPTER 17

———————— ◆ ————————

"You haven't got the votes, and that's all there is to it."

Spring had burst upon Europe but its coming brought no hope. Already the dictators were on the move—Franco's Nationalists triumphantly entering Madrid on March 27, 1939; Hitler seizing what remained of Czechoslovakia on the Ides of March and gobbling up the Lithuanian seaport of Memel a week later; Mussolini invading Albania on Good Friday. Beyond the fascist world there was general dismay over these latest outrages, but as before, no one did much.

The British response to Italy's attack on Albania was farcical: when Sir Percy Loraine, the new ambassador to Rome, presented his credentials to Victor Emmanuel, king of Italy and (more recently) emperor of Ethiopia, the documents pointedly omitted the king's latest title, king of Albania. That was the extent of England's protest, and as the episode suggests, British and French diplomacy had reached a dead end. The policy of appeasement, in case anyone was still wondering, was not working. Each time President Roosevelt telephoned Joe Kennedy, telling him to put some iron up Chamberlain's backside, the ambassador replied that putting iron up his backside did no good unless Britain had some iron with which to fight, and they did not. Hitler's seizure of the remainder of Czechoslovakia made it clear that his ambitions were Napoleonic in scope, and though there was no certainty yet when or where the next crisis would occur, it began to appear that if Great Britain and France did not meet it when it came, the entire continent might soon be in Germany's grasp, with Britain isolated across the Channel.

It sometimes seems that the tale of humankind is determined by the whims and moods of the men who hold power. Because of Poland, it is said, the Second World War began. But Poland was not so much the cause as the spark that set off the explosion. As time ran out for that unhappy country, you had three or four megalomaniacs, each a powerful man, each imagining or claiming that he and his nation had been insulted, injured, traduced. And who knows how these calumnies, real or fancied, contributed to all that followed—to the deaths of an estimated fifty or sixty million men, women, and children? Who knows, for that matter, what actually precipitates the catastrophic events of human history? Perhaps, as some people believed in 1939, it all had to do with the movement of Mars, the red planet, god of war, which dipped as close to the earth during August as the two planets' orbits permit. It did not seem to matter, as Winston Churchill was to write years later, that "there never was a war more easy to stop than that which has wrecked what was left of the world from the previous struggle." In 1939 no one was heeding the voices that might have halted the rush toward disaster.

Long before fall arrived, spring had revealed itself once again as a time of foolishness—silly season for statesmen who should have known better, should have realized what a deadly game was being played. Take what came of a message from Roosevelt to the two dictators, Hitler and Mussolini. The president was worried. On the strength of cables to the State Department from the capitals of Europe, he concluded—as he told Charles Edison, assistant secretary of the navy—that "we won't get through the summer without seeing the world in a hell of a mess," and when Edison asked when he figured war was coming, Roosevelt said he thought it might happen by the end of June or the beginning of July. (Edison went back to his office and carefully put a red mark on his calendar, in the third week of June.)

Word reached the White House that the British planned to send their Mediterranean fleet to Singapore, and this was further cause for concern: the way the president figured it, if Britain lost the Far East they could take it back, but if they lost the Mediterranean they would have nothing; and as a way of sending a message to London and to the Berlin-Rome-Tokyo axis, he canceled a scheduled visit of the U.S. Fleet to the New York World's Fair and ordered it back to San Diego. Now Mr. Roosevelt decided to go farther than he had gone before, hoping to persuade the German and Italian leaders to behave like reasonable men in order to avert disaster. On April 14 he sent personal messages to both men, appealing to them to give their neighbors "a minimum period of assured nonaggression" for ten years—or even twenty, "if we dare to look that far ahead." Enumerating some thirty nations in Europe, the Near East, and the Middle East, he asked the dictators not to invade them and offered—if Hitler and Mussolini agreed—to convey their assurances to the governments concerned.

"Keep your fingers crossed!" Roosevelt remarked to his secretary of the Treasury, Henry Morgenthau, Jr., after telling him about the message. "There is one chance in five."

"And if they turn you down," Morgenthau replied, "you will know where you are at."

Harold Ickes, the secretary of the Interior, thought it a brilliant move on Roosevelt's part—"an act of striking statesmanship" that would "put both Hitler and Mussolini in a hole."

The trouble was that Roosevelt and his cabinet officers were operating as if they were dealing with decent, rational men,[1] and Roosevelt had no inkling that his message would play directly into Hitler's hands, affording the Führer an opportunity that was made to order for a man of his talents. In what William L. Shirer described as the most brilliant oration Hitler ever gave—and the longest—he spoke to the Reichstag deputies in Berlin's Kroll Opera House on April 28, recounting his efforts to achieve a peaceful settlement of Europe's problems, then describing how England and France, through alliances with Poland and others, were attempting to encircle Germany, to strangle her. With that, he denounced the Anglo-German naval agreement of 1935 and the 1935 German-Polish treaty of friendship, and turned to the message he had received from Roosevelt. In a voice dripping with sarcasm, he referred to Yankee imperialism in South and Central America and to the British and French occupation of Palestine and Syria, and said that although he had approached all the states Roosevelt had mentioned, to ask if they felt threatened by Germany, "not all of them have been able to reply." Shirer reported that "the sausage-necked deputies . . . rocked with raucous laughter" at this and roared again when Hitler solemnly promised not to invade the United States. The Führer seemed to speak directly to America's isolationists when he stated, "Mr. Roosevelt! I fully understand that the vastness of your nation and the immense wealth of your country allow you to feel responsible for the history of the whole world and for the history of all nations. I, sir, am placed in a much smaller and more modest sphere." And he went on to remind his audience, there in Kroll Opera House and elsewhere in the world, that he had been called upon by Providence to do nothing more than "look after my people alone"—people who had been "deserted by the rest of the world." He recalled that he and Roosevelt had come to power at the same time, since when he, Hitler, had restored order in his country, increased production, found work for the unemployed, united Germany politically, rearmed it, retrieved the provinces taken from it by the Versailles Treaty, and "reestab-

[1]Secretary of Agriculture Henry Wallace knew better: he regarded an appeal to the dictators as "in the same category as delivering a sermon to a mad dog."

lished the historic unity of German living space." All this, he claimed, without spilling blood or resorting to war. Unlike Germany, however, the United States was blessed with unlimited resources—and fifteen times as much lebensraum for only one third again as many people. Still addressing Roosevelt, Hitler said, "So you have time. Conditions are such with you that you have time to bother about universal problems. . . . But my world is much smaller, although for me it is more precious than all else, for it is limited to my people. I believe that this is the way in which I can be of service to that with which we are all concerned—the justice, the well-being, progress, and peace of the whole human community."

It was a speech by a master orator who had an uncanny sense of timing and drama, and as he sat down there were cheers of approval from the brown-shirted deputies and even some shouts from diplomats in the gallery, who had been notified that this would be a major speech. Although none of them knew it, what they had heard was also the last important public address Hitler would deliver in peacetime.

America's ambassador in Paris, William C. Bullitt, harbored no illusions about the effect of Roosevelt's message to the dictators: ". . . words no matter how wise have small effect on Hitler and Mussolini," he had warned the secretary of state. "They are still sensitive to acts." Even so, he knew the psychological effect the president's letter might have on other countries, and he cabled Hull urging that "the usual routine communication of felicitations will not be sent to Hitler on the occasion of his 50th birthday [on April 20, 1939]. Such a communication at the present time would diminish greatly the effect of the president's magnificent appeal."

In Washington, Roosevelt's isolationist foes on Capitol Hill reacted to Hitler's response as might have been expected. Gerald Nye was heard to say that the president had "asked for it"; William Borah remarked, with what sounded like satisfaction, that the man in the White House had met his match; and Hiram Johnson clucked happily that "Hitler had all the better of the argument," since "Roosevelt put his chin out and got a resounding whack." The California senator was sure Roosevelt was itching for an excuse to go to war: "He wants," said Johnson, "to knock down two dictators in Europe, so that one may be firmly implanted in America."

Even in the best of circumstances, Roosevelt could count on opposition to his foreign policy from the likes of Nye, Borah, and Johnson, but isolationists on the Hill were more suspicious of him now than ever, because of something that had come to light in January, revealing his secret dealings with the French on arms purchases. As an indication of the contest between president and Congress—mainly the Senate—one could hardly find a better example than the story that began with an insignificant news item and within a week commanded front-page headlines everywhere. On January 24, 1939, a brief Associated Press account appeared on page five of the *New*

York Times, describing the crash of "America's most modern light bomber" in a parking lot near the Los Angeles Municipal Airport. The test pilot, John Cable, had been killed when his parachute failed to open. Ten people in the parking lot were injured, and nine cars demolished. Another test pilot—a fellow who worked for a New York aircraft company— watched what he described as an "unfamiliar twin-motored ship with tricycle landing gear" warm up, and heard engines that sounded "as powerful as any I've ever heard." As this eyewitness described the incident to a *Los Angeles Times* reporter, Cable put the plane through two semi-power dives, pulling out each time at a hundred feet or more over the runway, and at about three thousand feet, had switched off one engine to climb at half power when the plane suddenly went into a horizontal spin and began "the wildest gyrations I ever saw." At about five hundred feet, Cable jumped out and pulled his ripcord, but the chute merely trailed behind him like a long white string. Miraculously, a passenger in the rear cabin of the bomber survived the crash, and was dragged from the wreckage before it burst into flames. And that's where the trouble began.

According to the airport physician, the passenger's name was Paul Chemidlin and he came from Paris, France—a statement quickly denied by Douglas Aircraft officials, who identified him tersely as "Smithin—a mechanic." On this mysterious note the story ended. Then, three days later— again on page five of the *New York Times,* under the headline "600 War Planes French Goal Here"—government officials were quoted as saying that France had an aviation mission in the United States seeking hundreds of American-made planes, but that "no secret parts or devices would be sold to any foreign power." Even Germans could buy here, it was noted; the only nation proscribed from purchasing planes in this country was Japan, which was "bombing civilians." Donald Douglas, head of the California aircraft company, surprised everyone by saying that the U.S. War Department was aware that representatives of the French government were looking at the experimental airplane that crashed, and that the presence of Paul Chemidlin (who was in a closely guarded room in the Santa Monica hospital recovering from a fractured leg and severe lacerations) was "not in violation of any law, rules and regulations, or policies of the United States government." The next day, January 28, the story hit the front page of the *Times,* with a headline reading: "Roosevelt Lets France Buy Planes; Senate Inquiry on Policies Is Likely."

Predictably, the president's acknowledgment that he had approved the purchase of an undesignated quantity of modern "battle planes" by France sent a number of senators and representatives into orbit—not only because he had acted without consulting Congress, but also because he had done so against the advice of U.S. military officials. The president's policies, one representative observed, appeared to be "directed toward active participation on the side of France in any European crisis," and Congress would investigate to see if the French mission had "access to military aviation secrets over the heads of the army and the navy." The Senate Military Affairs Committee immediately summoned Secretary of War Harry Woodring, Chief of Staff General Malin Craig, and the head of the Army Air Corps, Major General Henry H. Arnold, to a closed hearing, and after listening to their testimony, Senator Nye told reporters that the "airplane deal with France constitutes, in my opinion, a military alliance," while Senators Clark and Sheppard declared that they would study the need for legislation to restrict the sale of planes abroad.

It didn't require an intimate knowledge of Washington to know that the military chiefs, who had subsisted on starvation budgets for years and had only recently been cheered by the prospect of finally obtaining a respectable number of new aircraft, were enraged by what had happened—the more so because their protests had been ignored and they had been bypassed by the White House. Indirectly, this flap could be traced to Charles Lindbergh's conversations with the French about how they might remedy the appalling shortcomings of their air force, since Ambassador William Bullitt, following Lindbergh's advice, had encouraged the French financier Jean Monnet to go to Washington in the fall of 1938 and make confidential inquiries about purchasing aircraft from American manufacturers. One thing led to another: U.S. military men dug in their heels against parting with any planes that would delay their own deliveries and opposed the acquisition of the latest models by foreign governments; President Roosevelt was equally determined to let the French buy the planes it needed, and in order to circumvent army objections, turned the problem over to Secretary of the Treasury Henry Morgenthau, Jr., who wisely asked the president to put his orders in writing before he would give the French permission to negotiate for Douglas's new plane. Finally, after objections by Woodring, Assistant Secretary Louis Johnson, and the military failed to change Roosevelt's mind, Hap Arnold was ordered by the White House to instruct his subordinates in California to demonstrate the Douglas attack bomber to the French purchasing mission. When the plane crashed, there was not the slightest possibility that this can of worms would remain unopened.

The tale revealed Mr. Roosevelt at his most devious, and nothing was more infuriating to the isolationists than the explanation he gave reporters when it was no longer possible to deny or cover up the plain facts. After Monnet's visit, he said, Ambassador Bullitt had come to Washington in January and appealed to the army and navy to deliver late-model planes to France. The French need for aircraft was both obvious and urgent, since America's neutrality laws would prohibit the purchase of these planes should France go to war. Roosevelt said he had discussed the matter with his cabinet, reminding them that many aircraft companies in the United States were idle or operating at much-reduced capacity. That being so, it "seemed very desirable to facilitate new orders to start the plants going" in order to accommodate our own expansion plans, and what could be more opportune than having another country finance the gearing-up of those factories with orders for airplanes? Furthermore, the plane that crashed was a "manufacturer's plane" flying from a municipal airport, and it had not yet been accepted by the U.S. government. This, of course, was the most disingenuous statement of all, since the plane had been described in *Time* magazine as "bright with red, white, and blue Air Corps paint."

It was no accident that while this controversy raged, the president sent Speaker Bankhead a letter asking Congress to appropriate $50 million for immediate expenditure on 565 planes for the Army Air Corps, nor could congressmen be blamed for suspecting that the Air Corps would be ordered to turn over the planes to France at a later date, when the argument of an emergency could be used. To allay congressional fears, Roosevelt invited doubting members of the Senate Military Affairs Committee to the White House for a discussion, and this meeting produced a story even more lurid than the crash of the Douglas bomber.

The president began by warning his guests that war was imminent, that it would soon engulf all the small nations of Europe, not to mention Britain, France, the Netherlands, and their colonies, and that war would directly threaten the peace and safety of the United States. Although America was theoretically protected from this worldwide convulsion by the Atlantic and Pacific oceans, the economic consequences were certain to endanger us. And that, he went on, is why the Rhine frontier necessarily interests us.

"Rhine frontier? Do you mean that our frontier is on the Rhine?" asked one of the senators.

"No," Roosevelt replied quickly, "not that. But practically speaking, if the Rhine frontiers are threatened the rest of the world is, too. Once they have fallen before Hitler, the German sphere of action will be unlimited."

All of which was probably true, but it was too much for the visitors from Capitol Hill—especially the irreconcilables among them—and as they left the meeting, shaking their heads, the word got out very quickly that the man in the White House had taken leave of his senses and was saying that America's frontier was on the Rhine. It would take a long while for the dust from this episode to settle, but the congressional mood improved in April, when General Marshall issued orders aimed at preventing French weapons procurement from interfering with U.S. rearmament. Gradually, the military came around to Mr. Roosevelt's way of thinking, once they discovered that there was a real virtue to having foreign governments place orders that stimulated industrial output, enlarged plant capacity, and produced a trained work force.

All that spring, FDR had been trying yet again to persuade Congress that the arms embargo must be repealed if Europe was to be saved. At first he had used a backstairs approach, meeting with wavering senators and representatives, cautioning that war was increasingly likely, warning of the consequences of a possible British-French defeat. Secretary of State Hull was making the rounds, too, telling legislators that they were making "the mistake of their lives" if they thought this was "another goddam piddling dispute over a boundary line." Anyone who failed to understand that the existing neutrality legislation was a "wretched little bobtailed, sawed-off domestic statute," the Tennesseean went on, was "just plain chuckleheaded." But despite their efforts, the message wasn't working, as Hull discovered in a talk with an old friend, the Senate minority leader, Charles L. McNary of Oregon. Years in the upper chamber had softened McNary's partisanship, and Hull respected his judgment, so he invited the senator to his hotel suite one evening and asked for a frank opinion on the chances of repeal.

"Well, Cordell," was the reply, "I don't just exactly know how the boys stand, but I guess you will be in for considerable trouble if you press repeal. Some people feel pretty strongly, and most of the rest don't want to do anything now."

As McNary predicted, neither the president's honeyed words nor Hull's salty talk had the slightest effect on isolationists in the Senate. And the House was proving equally intractable—so much so that Hull, asked to predict how neutrality revision might fare in the lower chamber, told a folksy tale about a teacher who was demonstrating to the school board how bright her pupils were. She called on one lad to respond to a question in arithmetic.

"Tommy," asked a member of the school board, "if there are sixteen sheep in a field and one jumps the fence, how many are left?"

"None," Tommy replied.

"Well," said the board member, "I'm afraid you don't know anything about arithmetic."

"The trouble is," said Tommy, "you don't know anything about sheep."

In July, the president tried again in the Senate, only to have the Foreign Relations Committee, by a vote of 12 to 11, postpone consideration of the neutrality legislation. (Some of FDR's chickens were coming home to roost: the majority on that vote included Walter George of Georgia and Guy Gillette of Iowa, two of the Democrats he had attempted unsuccessfully to "purge" in 1938.)

On July 18, the president decided to make an all-out effort to deal with the recalcitrant congressmen. FDR was a great believer in the strength of public opinion, and he sensed that it was beginning to run in his favor on this question just now. In a recent Gallup poll, it had been reported that 65 percent of Americans favored a boycott of Germany, while 57 percent wanted the neutrality laws changed. (At the same time, it might be noted, only 10 percent of those polled said they would be willing to fight unless the United States were invaded.) So it seemed possible, the president may have reasoned, that the gentlemen of the Senate might be persuaded by figures where all else had failed. What could be more sensible than doing away with a mandatory arms embargo that only injured friendly powers and aided potential foes? Why not do so now, before the fighting began, while there was still time for arms to be of use to our friends? And why not use the repeal of the law as a warning to Hitler—the only kind of warning he seemed capable of heeding—that the United States would not stand idly by while the western democracies were defeated?

It had become clear that Hitler might move against Poland at almost any moment, and probably without warning. By July 1939, in fact, the German army was on a war footing—in such a state of readiness that it could attack without resorting to a general mobilization that would give away its plans. From Paris, on June 28, Bullitt cabled Hull, reporting that the Polish government viewed the chances of war by mid-August as eighty out of one hundred. (Presumably the Poles didn't know it, but Hitler had given secret orders to his generals on April 1, setting September 1 as the invasion date.)

Alben Barkley, the majority leader, rounded up five of his Senate colleagues and at 9:00 P.M. on July 18 they were mixing drinks for themselves in a corner of the president's upstairs study while Mr. Roosevelt joked with Vice President Garner on the couch, telling him the proper method of making an old-fashioned. They were all in shirt sleeves, relaxed and genial, until FDR called them to order on a serious note: "It might be the proper thing to open this meeting with prayer," he began; "our decision may well affect not only the people of our own country, but also the peoples of the world."

Then he and Hull pulled out the stops in an attempt to convince the legislators that war might be averted if the Neutrality Act was amended or repealed. Roosevelt and Hull knew how pitifully short of men and matériel the western Allies were and realized that the only way to get supplies to them before it was too late was to repeal the embargo. If the nations of Europe were overrun by the Germans, Roosevelt told the senators, the balance of power was going to shift dramatically away from the United States. Hitler had warned that the world was his oyster, *die ganze Welt* his goal. But the United States was not prepared to fight anyone just now, much less the mighty German army, navy, and air force. As *Time* magazine commented, compared to the armed strength of Europe's nations, "the U.S. Army looked like a few nice boys with BB guns."

The president discussed what he knew of Hitler's plans and then gave his opinion that the Allies had no better than a fifty-fifty chance of survival in the event the Nazis attacked. He reminded his visitors that what seemed to impress Hitler about the United States was its vast size and enormous wealth (if anyone remembered this, it would have been Roosevelt, after reading Hitler's speech). Why not take advantage of those very elements to intimidate Germany? Otherwise, Roosevelt admitted, "I've fired my last shot. I think I ought to have another round in my belt."

When Roosevelt had said his piece, Hull took up the argument, concluding with the prediction that there would be war in Europe by summer unless the United States did something to head it off.

Then the man to whom the president and the secretary of state had really addressed their arguments, William E. Borah, spoke up. Shaking his head, he said, "There is not going to be any war in Europe. At least not soon. Germany is not ready for it. All this hysteria is manufactured and artificial."

"I wish Senator Borah would come to my office and look over the cables coming in," said Hull testily. "I feel sure he would modify his views."

The senator from Idaho was unimpressed. "I've listened to what the secretary of state has to say about the information he has," he said to Roosevelt, ignoring Hull, "but I have my own sources of information that I regard as more reliable than those of the State Department, and I can say to you that there is not going to be any war."

At this criticism of his beloved department, the proud old Tennesseean was reduced almost to tears, but before he could argue the point, Vice President John Nance Garner ended the meeting. Turning to Roosevelt with a smile, Cactus Jack remarked cheerily, "Well, Captain, we may as well face the facts. You haven't got the votes, and that's all there is to it."

Indeed, the president did not, and as Robert Sherwood wrote, he "did not forget that experience and neither did Hull, who had more respect than Roosevelt did for the dignity and authority of the Congress. Before Roosevelt asked for anything else in the next two years, he was extremely careful to make sure that he had 'the votes.'" More defeats of the kind he had suffered at Borah's hands, FDR knew, could only give aid and comfort to the Germans, Italians, and Japanese, while discouraging those who opposed them. So, as Congress left the capital for the summer recess, the Neutrality Acts remained the law of the land, leaving the president's hands tied as tightly as ever when it came to supplying war matériel to the Allies.

That summer Sir Percy Bate, chairman of the Cunard Lines, was assuring friends that there would be no war. And one of Sir Percy's passengers, the banker J. P. Morgan, sailed for Scotland to shoot grouse after commenting gruffly, "If they start war, my shooting will be interrupted." As it turned out, a great many people's plans were interrupted by the end of the summer of 1939, and what triggered it all was an alliance that should never have happened.

CHAPTER 18

———— ◆ ————

"What about Russia?"

B efore, during, and after the Munich settlement, the leaders of Britain and France had dealt with the Russians as they might have cozied up to a long-dead mackerel—very, very gingerly. The British prime minister, in particular, feared that Stalin might prove more intransigent than Hitler. "I must confess to the most profound distrust of Russia," Chamberlain confided to one of his sisters. "I have no belief whatever in her ability to maintain an effective offensive, even if she wanted to. I distrust her motives." So Soviet interests in Europe's deepening crisis had simply been ignored.

The feeling among many members of Parliament, however, including most notably the outspoken Winston Churchill, was that Britain was going to need all the aid and comfort she could assemble in the months to come, and Neville Chamberlain was at last prevailed upon to offer Moscow something more than the back of his hand. Talks accordingly began in the Soviet capital between the British ambassador and Foreign Minister Maxim Litvinov, the idea being that Britain, France, and the USSR might profitably combine in a mutual assistance pact, ultimately drawing into their orbit the smaller states of central and eastern Europe that lay directly under the Nazi menace. But the difficulty, as Churchill had foreseen, was that "Poland, Rumania, Finland, and the three Baltic States did not know whether it was

German aggression or Russian rescue that they dreaded more." (Years before, the Polish hero Marshal Pilsudski had described bluntly his nation's eternal dilemma: "With the Germans we risk the loss of our liberty, but with the Russians we lose our souls.") Before any such Hobson's choice could be put up to the border countries, however, the Poles managed to maneuver Great Britain into the position of choosing between Russia and Poland.

Meantime, while Litvinov and the British talked, Stalin was approaching the German Foreign Office via the Soviet ambassador in Berlin, hinting at the possibility of "normalizing" relations between their two countries. If France and Britain chose not to join him in a league against Hitler, the Russian dictator decided, he would see if Germany might ally itself with him against the western powers. Joseph Stalin was nothing if not a realist. Knowing that Russia was the ultimate target of Hitler's drive for lebensraum, he was behaving as the French and British had at Munich—buying time and breathing room in which to build up his army, and if those two necessities had to be purchased at the price of Poland, so be it. Whether he knew it or not, his timing was impeccable, for on May 23, 1939, Hitler summoned the chiefs of his armed forces and treated them to a harangue on the theme "There will be war." Germany could not expect a repetition of the Czech affair, he said. There was no possibility of a peaceful settlement with England (and France, of course, which would follow where England led). Since the British were "proud, courageous, tenacious, firm in resistance, and gifted as organizers," it would be a life-and-death struggle in the west, and Holland and Belgium would have to be occupied with lightning speed to prevent them from joining their two allies. Meantime, first things first: the western nations must be kept out while he secured Germany's rear. "Our task is to isolate Poland, for the Polish problem is inseparable from conflict with the west. There is no question of sparing Poland." And as for the likelihood of Soviet interference, "It is not impossible that Russia will show herself disinterested in the destruction of Poland." Which was exactly what Stalin had concluded.

Had the stakes not been so deadly, the ensuing dance of the diplomats had all the earmarks of a Marx Brothers comedy set in Ruritania. There was Stalin, wooing the British and Germans simultaneously; Chamberlain talking with the Russians and secretly sidling up to the Poles—chiefly to Colonel Jozef Beck, one of three military men who ran that country; and Beck negotiating with Britain, doing his utmost to face down the Nazis while letting the British know that Hitler was demanding the free city of Danzig and the so-called Polish Corridor. The Führer wanted the corridor—a strip of land twenty to seventy miles wide that was Poland's sole connection to the Baltic Sea—because it cut Germany in two, separating East Prussia from the rest of the country, requiring Germans to cross Polish terrain ignominiously in sealed trains whenever they traveled from one section to the other. All Hitler asked, Beck was told, was the return of Danzig, whose population was almost wholly German (the Poles, it was said, would continue to have access to and from the city), and permission to build a six-lane autobahn and a railway line connecting East Prussia with the fatherland. Beck was under the impression that he held the face cards, and he was playing them very close to the chest, buying time; so confident was he that he had flatly rejected an offer from Hitler that would have allied Poland and Germany. Somehow or other, the colonel and his fellow officers and a great many of their countrymen had gotten it into their heads that Poland's armed forces were capable of taking on either the Germans or the Russians and coming out on top. It was a fatal enough delusion for the Poles to have, but in the process Beck had also succeeded in deluding the prime minister of Great Britain.

Thanks in part to what he had heard from Joseph Kennedy and Charles Lindbergh, Chamberlain was convinced that the Polish army and air force were superior to the Russians'; he was worried, moreover, that the Germans would soon move against Rumania; and what he wanted was Beck's assurance that Poland would guarantee Rumania's security in return for an alliance with Britain and France. Beck was an unsavory character who, some years earlier, in France, had stolen documents and sold military secrets to the Germans before being expelled from that country. He was vain, a braggart, and a bore; now he had cancer, and was seeking relief in alcohol—and the combination of these assorted flaws should have suggested that he was a highly unstable ally for the British to pin their hopes on. Yet for reasons that are difficult to comprehend even now, Beck succeeded in persuading the British to do almost exactly what he wanted them to do. By the time Beck had done with Chamberlain, the Englishman had lost all interest in an alliance with Russia and was trying to think of ways to *compel* the Poles to join Britain and France. Which was precisely what Beck had had in mind all the time.

Beck studiously avoided any mention of the pressure Hitler was putting on him, never hinting that relations between Poland and Germany had deteriorated to such an extent that Ribbentrop, the Nazi foreign minister, was threatening the use of force if the Poles did not return Danzig to the Reich. Almost blithely, Chamberlain and Halifax, his foreign secretary, proposed to guarantee Poland's frontiers, and without even seeking his French ally's acquiescence, Chamberlain announced to the House of Commons that Poland was now under British protection and that if "any action were taken which clearly threatened [Polish] independence, His Majesty's Government and the French Government would at once lend them all support in their power." Beck came to London, and, after flimflamming the British leaders yet again, returned to Warsaw with a "permanent and reciprocal agreement" by which Great Britain guaranteed Poland's security.

"What about Russia?" astonished MPs shouted at Chamberlain, while Lloyd George expressed the fears of many Britons when he said, "If we are going into this without the help of Russia we are walking into a trap."

"Never before in our history," wrote Alfred Duff Cooper, who had angrily resigned as first lord of the Admiralty when he learned the news of Munich, "have we left in the hands of one of the smaller powers the decision whether or not Great Britain goes to war."

What every British official knew, of course, as Alexander Cadogan pointed out later, was that their own "military capabilities were deplorably inadequate. We were being swept along on a rapid series of surprises sprung upon us by Hitler with a speed that took one's breath away. He was pursuing his tactic of 'one by one.' And it was that in the end that drove Chamberlain to take a sudden and surprising decision to guarantee Poland. Of course our guarantee could give no possible protection to Poland in any imminent attack upon her." What Chamberlain and his colleagues had completely ignored was what the Soviet Union might do. And that, as it turned out, was what precipitated the Second World War.

———

For more than a year, the American embassy in Moscow had been picking up hints—nothing very tangible, no more than straws in the wind—that Stalin might be considering a deal of some kind with Hitler. Charles E. Bohlen, the thirty-five-year-old second secretary, had it from an American correspondent, who had it from a reporter in Prague, that Germany would soon approach the Soviets with a proposal to improve diplomatic relations between the two countries, but when Bohlen asked a friend at the German embassy what he knew of this, he was told that such a move was inconceivable because of Hitler's implacable hatred and distrust of the Communists. And so it seemed to everyone. Yet the rumors persisted, and the diplomatic people continued assembling bits and pieces of the puzzle, hoping to catch a glimpse of the future.

The spring of 1939 produced a definite sign that Stalin was taking steps to placate Hitler. He ousted the sixty-three-year-old Maxim Litvinov (and subsequently his entire staff) from the Foreign Ministry, replacing him with Vyacheslav Molotov, a tough, unsmiling Old Bolshevik (his surname, which was an alias, meant "Hammer") who was chairman of the Council of People's Commissars and a member of the Politburo. Litvinov had been commissar for foreign affairs since 1930, but once you put together the fact that he was a Jew and therefore anathema to Hitler, and that he was also an advocate of collective security against the German menace and had tried in vain to align France and Great Britain with the USSR, then you might guess that Stalin was using the ouster of Litvinov to tell the Germans something.

Hitler got the message immediately: as he told his military chiefs at a meeting in August, Litvinov's dismissal "came to me like a cannonball as a sign of change toward the Western powers."

Observers at the American embassy also detected, about this time, a marked slackening of Russian propaganda attacks on Germany. In March, Stalin, speaking to the Party faithful who had escaped his enormous purges of the previous three years, told them that their task was to prevent Russia's being drawn into a war as another nation's cat's-paw. The USSR, he said, would not become involved in war "to pull somebody else's chestnuts out of the fire." Which might refer to Poland. Or to Britain and France.

Another item noted by American diplomats was that when Hitler's troops moved into what remained of Czechoslovakia, completing the destruction of that unhappy country, Soviet denunciation of the action had been merely perfunctory—as if, Bohlen thought, the Russians didn't have their hearts in it.

What Stalin knew, and what a majority of the Russian people may only have suspected, was that the political bloodbath he had unloosed in 1936 had not only demoralized many of the surviving political leaders and intellectuals, but had decimated the leadership of the Red Army.[1] Stalin had neither the intention nor the capability to fight Hitler now, and he worried—the old Communist paranoia about capitalist encirclement being strong—that France, England, and Germany might jointly find cause to attack the USSR. So, as long as Germany and Poland were at swords' points, Stalin had no fear that either would march against Russia. And once Great Britain made its unilateral guarantee to Poland, he had no need to commit himself to fight at Britain's side in the event that Poland was invaded.

At the U.S. embassy in Brussels, Ambassador Joseph Davies received what he considered reliable information about Hitler's intention to wean Stalin away from Britain and France. As Davies observed, "It is vital to [Hitler's] military success that he closes his Eastern door before he makes his attack on the Western front."

But the most reliable source of information on a possible rapprochement between the Third Reich and the Soviet Union proved to be the young second secretary in the German embassy in Moscow, one Hans Heinrich Herwarth von Bittenfeld, known to the diplomatic corps as Johnny Herwarth, who began in May to talk with astonishing candor to his friend Chip

---

[1]Starting as a quiet political "cleanup" in 1935, the liquidation of Stalin's real and supposed opposition swelled into a full-scale purge that lasted until 1939. The number of arrests, exiles, and executions—many of them secret—eventually reached a total of nine or ten million people from all levels of society. By the eve of World War II, the Soviet army, navy, and air force had been dangerously crippled: three of five marshals, eleven vice commissars of defense, seventy-five of the eighty generals and admirals who formed the supreme military council, possibly 90 percent of all generals and 80 percent of the colonels—some ten thousand officers above the rank of lieutenant colonel—had been killed or jailed. Usually the charge was treason; Marshal Tukhachevsky, for example, who was responsible for mechanizing the Red Army, was convicted of espionage and "betrayal." Later, six of the eight judges who had served at his court-martial were shot without trial.

Bohlen. The Russians and the Germans were meeting more and more frequently, Johnny Herwarth told Bohlen, and as the summer wore on the conversations between the two governments became ever more specific—on both economic and political matters. In July the Soviets placed a large order with the Germans for turbines, and there were rumors around Moscow that orders for antiaircraft guns and other machinery were forthcoming. At a ball at the German embassy on August 15, Herwarth informed Bohlen that the Nazis and Soviets had agreed in principle to settle outstanding differences between the two countries, and he promised to give the American diplomat full details the following day. Bohlen met him again and listened intently as Herwarth told of a pending nonaggression pact between Germany and the USSR, a promise from Germany not to encourage Japanese aggression in the Far East, and discussions between Germany and Russia concerning mutual interests in the Baltic. All this was promptly relayed to Secretary Hull in Washington, as a result of which neither the State Department nor President Roosevelt was as stunned as the rest of the world when, on August 21, 1939, it was announced on the German radio that Foreign Minister Joachim von Ribbentrop would journey to Moscow to sign a mutual nonaggression pact with the Soviet dictator.

What Bohlen had also learned from his anti-Nazi informant—and what the world at large did not know—was that a secret protocol to the ten-year pact provided that western Poland was to be in the German sphere of influence and eastern Poland, Estonia, Latvia, and Bessarabia in the Soviet. The two powers agreed not to join any group of nations allied against the other (thus denying the USSR an Anglo-French alliance and Germany a Japanese pact). When the treaty was signed, Stalin drank a toast to Ribbentrop's absent boss, calling Hitler *molodets,* a slang term for "fine fellow." The Nazi leader had already voiced his feelings about the arrangement. Two days earlier, when he learned that Stalin had agreed to meet with Ribbentrop, he exclaimed, "We've done it! Now we can spit in everybody's face!" Later, describing his plans to the general staff, the Führer confided: "Stalin and I are the only ones to see the future. . . . So I shall shake hands with Stalin within a few weeks on the common German-Russian border and undertake with him a new distribution of the world." Then, he added, at the appropriate time, "we shall crush the Soviet Union."

Heinrich Hoffmann, Hitler's friend and personal photographer, accompanied Ribbentrop to Moscow and took pictures of the historic event; when he returned to Berlin, Hitler examined the photographs closely—he wanted to see if the Soviet leader's earlobes were "ingrown and Jewish, or separate and Aryan." Although he satisfied himself that his new comrade in arms passed the test he had devised and was therefore not Semitic, he was disgusted to see that all the pictures showed Stalin with a cigarette. "The signing of the pact is a solemn act which one does not approach with a cigarette dangling from one's lips," he commented disdainfully, and ordered that the cigarette be retouched out of the prints before they were released to the press.

The agreement, of course, was utterly cynical, with the two dictators achieving their immediate objectives. Stalin got his breathing room and could concentrate on rebuilding Russia's defenses; Hitler got Russia's pledge not to intervene in Poland and secured Germany's rear should war come unexpectedly in the west. Although there were those who might have agreed with William Allen White, proprietor and editor of the *Emporia* (Kansas) *Gazette,* who said, "It's much simpler now that the dictatorships are arranged in one neat pile," news of the Nazi-Soviet alliance hit most of the world like a thunderbolt, and none more so than the Communist Party faithful. In Paris, the physicists Frédéric Joliot and his wife, Irène Curie, along with other French intellectuals, signed a statement denouncing Stalin's about-face and expressing their "stupefaction" at his betrayal. Earlier in the summer, Earl Browder—leader of America's ninety thousand Communist Party members—had been asked if he thought Stalin and Hitler might sign a treaty of alliance, and his reply was about what might have been expected: "I could easier imagine myself being elected president of the U.S. Chamber of Commerce." Now the best face he could put on the situation was that the announcement of the agreement "has done no injury whatsoever to the Communist Party here," that it "is a distinct contribution to world peace." Fritz Kuhn, the brownshirt leader of the German-American Bund—a Nazi-style organization which he used as a means of embezzling money, chasing women, and attacking "Franklin D. Rosenfeld of the international Jewish conspiracy"—took the same line as Browder: what happened in Europe made no difference to Nazis in the United States. Heywood Broun, columnist and member of the Popular Front, voiced his anguish: "The masquerade is over," he wrote sadly. "The dominoes are dropped and it now becomes possible to look at the faces of [those] who pretend to be devoted to the maintenance of democracy."

To other Americans of the left, word of the treaty came as a shocking disillusionment. Malcolm Cowley, then an editor of *The New Republic,* was to write of his fellow liberals, "They had learned over the years to regard Hitler as an embodiment of active and positive evil, almost the Devil of Protestant theology. His new German empire was Satan's realm and the obstacle that had to be surmounted before one could dream of achieving a better tomorrow." And since by 1939 a good many radicals of the early Depression years had turned conservative, they were no longer so interested in attacking the status quo, for fear that it might be followed by something worse. Above all else they hoped for peace in the world, and in this longing they had seen Russia as their "surest ally." The Soviet Union, after all, supported the League of Nations, called for sanctions against aggressors, and advocated collective security on the basis of treaties that would protect every country against invasion, and for these reasons a good many liberals considered an alliance between the western nations and Russia to be the best defense against Hitler. Or did, until that fateful day in August when their hopes evaporated. After the pact, Cowley said, everything was different; he suddenly realized that he was "a survivor, emotionally scarred and lonely, from a simpler, friendlier, and more confident world."

Arthur Koestler, a spokesman for the left who had recently turned his back on the Party, was in the south of France with his young English mistress when he heard the news. A gifted journalist and novelist, Koestler had experienced in Berlin the never-never world of the Weimar Republic before Hitler came to power; subsequently he roamed about Europe on a Hungarian passport, and went to Spain as a correspondent with the Loyalists only to be captured by Franco's men and condemned to death. Just recently he had been released, thanks to the intercession of friends in England. Now thirty-five, he had been a Communist for seven of those years and "had paid dearly for it." A year and a half earlier he had left the Party in disgust, and while some of his friends had done the same, "some were still hesitating; many of them had been shot or imprisoned in Russia. We had realized that Stalinism had soiled and compromised the Socialist Utopia just as the Medieval Church had soiled and compromised Christianity.

"We had realized all this and had turned our backs to Russia, yet wherever we turned our eyes for comfort we found none; and so, in the back of our minds there remained a faint hope that perhaps and after all it was we who were in the wrong and that in the long run it was the Russians who were in the right. Our feelings toward Russia," Koestler explained, "were rather like those of a man who had divorced a much-loved wife; he hates her and yet it is a sort of consolation for him to know that she is still there, on the same planet, still young and alive.

"But now she was dead. No death is so sad and final as the death of an illusion. . . ."

A decade later, Koestler would fill in some of the grim details of that dying illusion in his autobiography: "At a conservative estimate, three out of every four people I knew before I was thirty were subsequently killed in Spain or hounded to death at Dachau, or gassed at Belsen, or deported to Russia; some jumped from windows in Vienna or Budapest; others were wrecked by the misery and aimlessness of permanent exile."

When William Shirer and his journalist friends in Berlin heard the news they concluded that the Nazi-Soviet pact would "kill world communism." How could a French Communist, who had been taught for six years to hate Nazism above all else, stomach Moscow's embrace of Hitler? Shirer found it hard to believe that Stalin "would play such crude power politics and also play into the hands of the Nazis." He could only account for it by supposing that Stalin's aim was to bring on a war between Germany and the west which would result in chaos, after which the Communists would move in and take over. But what if Stalin had misjudged Hitler? As Shirer knew, "Hitler has broken every international agreement he ever made."

Not even members of the Soviet Politburo had known what was coming; Stalin and Molotov had handled the negotiations alone, keeping them secret. Until the official Nazi newspaper, *Völkischer Beobachter*—printed for the first time in red ink—trumpeted the news in headlines seven inches high, probably no more than a dozen high-level Germans were aware that discussions were being held between their government and the Russians. Their Italian allies, with whom Hitler had recently signed a "Pact of Steel" in order to protect his southern flank and neutralize France, had no prior knowledge whatever of the agreement with Moscow; in fact, Mussolini was doing what he could to promote a political solution in Europe—war being the last thing he wanted just now. During the weeks before the pact was signed, Il Duce's son-in-law and minister of foreign affairs, Count Galeazzo Ciano, began to sense a cooling in the Germans' attitude toward him; then from Ribbentrop he learned the Nazis' real goal.

Ciano was visiting the German foreign minister in Salzburg, and one evening before dinner they walked together in the garden. The Italian suddenly turned to his host and asked, "Well, Ribbentrop, what do you want? The Corridor or Danzig?"

"Not that any more," Ribbentrop replied, and Ciano remembered how cold and metallic the German's eyes were. "We want war!"

That was on August 11, 1939, and in the days that followed Ciano was profoundly disturbed by his conversations with Ribbentrop and Hitler. "Nothing," he wrote later, "could have prevented the execution of this criminal project long meditated and fondly discussed in those somber meetings the Führer had every evening with his intimates. The madness of the Chief had become the religion of his followers." So confident was one of those followers—Ribbentrop—that everything would go according to plan that he bet Ciano that Britain and France would remain aloof: if the western Allies remained neutral, Ciano would give the German diplomat an Italian painting; if not, Ribbentrop would owe the Italian a collection of old armor. "But von Ribbentrop," Ciano observed sadly in the final hours before his execution by the Gestapo in 1944, "has preferred to forget the bet and has never paid up—unless he believes that he is discharging his debt by having me shot. . . ."[2]

While the world wondered what was happening and what this latest development meant, Germany's controlled press was orchestrating the Polish crisis. In Germany, Shirer reported, the newspapers printed the exact opposite of what was published as news elsewhere. If you believed what you read in Berlin, it was Poland that was disturbing the peace of Europe, Poland that was threatening Germany with invasion, Poland that was running amok, Poland that was warning of aerial attacks. On August 20, Shirer was in Warsaw, broadcasting to America at 4:00 A.M., telling his

---

[2]An opponent of the war and of the Nazis, Ciano turned against Mussolini, was seized by the Gestapo, and was executed in January 1944.

countrymen that the Poles were calm and confident. The American military attaché believed that the Polish army could hold out alone against Germany for six months, but Shirer considered the Poles "too romantic, too confident." Four days later he was back in Berlin, thinking, "It looks like war tonight." He saw antiaircraft guns being moved into position, heard German bombers in the sky overhead, and observed the profound relief Berliners revealed when they heard the news of the treaty with Russia. For them, it meant that there would be no two-front war, as in 1914, no long Russian front to hold, no more nightmare of encirclement.

Twice more, Roosevelt appealed to Hitler, urging him to settle the differences between Germany and Poland without resort to arms. ("These messages," observed the State Department's Adolf Berle gloomily, "will have about the same effect as a valentine sent to somebody's mother-in-law out of season, and they have all that quality of naïveté which is the prerogative of the United States. Nevertheless, they ought to be sent. The one certain thing in this business is that no one will be blamed for making any attempt, however desperate, at preserving peace.") The king of the Belgians, speaking for his own country, the Netherlands, Luxembourg, Finland, and the three Scandinavian nations, broadcast a moving plea for peace, calling on "the men who are responsible for the course of events to submit their disputes and their claims to open negotiation." The pope broadcast his own peace message, following it with notes to the governments of Germany, Poland, Italy, France, and Great Britain, "beseeching [them] in the name of God . . . to avoid any incident." In London, where it was suffocatingly hot, citizens were told to black out their windows at night until further notice. The RAF and the fleet were on alert, and an embargo had been placed on the export of essential materials. Those who saw Neville Chamberlain were shocked by the change in the man. He had aged visibly and his face was drawn, as though every ounce of vitality had been drained from him. When he spoke in public, there was neither hope nor inspiration in his words; as Harold Nicolson put it, he was "exactly like a coroner summing up a case for murder."

Meantime, all English journalists had been ordered out of Germany and some of Berlin's telephone and telegraph lines had been closed down. At 1:00 on the morning of August 25, when Shirer broadcast to America, it was New York's first word from Berlin that day, and he was told that there was relief "when I reported all calm here and no war yet." It was hot and sultry in Berlin, too, heightening the strain everyone felt; Hermann Göring told an acquaintance that "war might break out at any moment," and on the 26th, Shirer informed his American radio listeners that there would be war "unless Germany's demands against Poland are fulfilled." Two days later Ed Murrow telephoned from London to say that the British weren't going to back down this time.

Murrow and Shirer were bone-tired; they were broadcasting every day from noon until 4:00 in the morning, doing their utmost to size things up for the American people, talking to everyone, listening intently, tracking the rush of events. An old German reading about an exchange of letters between Hitler and Daladier looked up in disgust from his newspaper and said to Shirer, "*Ja,* they forget what war is like. But I don't. I remember." And the moving vans and grocery trucks loaded with troops rumbled through the streets of Berlin, heading east. (What depressed Berliners more than anything else was the issuing of ration cards, a sure sign of war.) On August 30, Shirer reported, "The sands are running fast tonight," and the next day he wondered, "How can a country go into a major war with a population so dead against it?" Every German he spoke to opposed war, everyone talked openly against it, everyone complained that he was being kept in the dark.

CHAPTER 19

"...it's come at last.
God help us all."

The man who was keeping them in the dark was "exceptionally irritated, bitter, and sharp" these days, according to a high-ranking German officer. Now that he had passed his fiftieth birthday, the onrush of time was increasingly on Hitler's mind, and he informed the British envoy that he preferred to fight a war while he was fifty rather than wait until he was fifty-five or sixty. (Ciano confided the same information to his diary that month after an audience with Hitler, noting that the Führer was "implacable in his decision. . . . He has decided to strike and strike he will. . . . the great war must be fought while he and the Duce are still young.")

A year earlier, at the time of the Munich crisis, Britain's ambassador to Germany was the man in the middle, and he was still there, coping not at all successfully with the demands of Adolf Hitler and London's efforts to resolve the Polish stalemate by diplomatic means. For the past twelve months Henderson had been obsessed with the idea "that we were moving remorselessly through the pages of a Greek tragedy to its inevitably disastrous and sinister ends," and it was apparent that unless some unlikely *deus ex machina* appeared, and soon, Sir Nevile's gloomy prediction would prove accurate. The Englishman came across as a dedicated, if fusty and not very discerning, diplomat, always concerned with punctilio, with face;

yet he could read the signs as well as the next man, and he knew that the barometer was falling fast. There was the Nazi-Soviet Pact, about which Hitler spoke to him gleefully on August 23, describing it as "definite and permanent." The ambassador knew that the German army was within three or four days of being on a full war footing, and assumed that Hitler was waiting only for the most favorable moment to strike. More, he saw the same atrocity stories that had been told about the Czechs a year before appearing in the press now about the Poles, and observed an anti-Polish propaganda campaign in full swing.

Starting on August 23, Henderson found himself at dead center of what became an almost continuous round of conversations and notes between Hitler, Ribbentrop, and Ernst von Weizsäcker, the German undersecretary of state, on the one hand, and Chamberlain and Halifax on the other. That day Hitler greeted him in a mood of "extreme excitability," ranting about 100,000 German refugees from Poland, about British responsibility for Poland's behavior, about his distrust of Chamberlain.

On August 26 all German airports were closed without warning; the next afternoon telephone communication between Berlin and London and Paris was cut off for several hours; the Nazi Party rally at Nuremberg was canceled; all naval, air, and military attachés were forbidden to leave the city without permission; and Berlin began a week of trial blackouts—all of which convinced Sir Nevile that Hitler had planned to invade Poland on August 26 and had, for some unknown reason, changed his timetable. Perhaps, Henderson speculated, the German dictator hoped he might detach Britain from her allies. He had warned the ambassador that the war in Poland would be over in two months and after that, if England opposed him, he would hurl 160 divisions onto the western front.

When the two met on August 25, Hitler had been calm and reasonable, suggesting that Henderson fly to London in a plane provided by the German government, carrying the Führer's proposals for a settlement with Poland and an offer of friendship or alliance with Great Britain. Henderson had taken him up on it and was back in Berlin on the 28th with His Majesty's Government's reply, which urged direct discussions between Germany and Poland, with Great Britain to use its good offices wherever possible. Failure to solve the Polish problem, the note continued somberly, might well plunge the entire world into war.

Not that it made much difference at this late hour, but the British Foreign Office could scarcely have been more maladroit in its timing. After months of negotiations with the Poles, the British-Polish Alliance was signed on August 25 in London, and news of this preceded Henderson's return to Berlin, persuading Hitler—not illogically—that this was Britain's reply to his message.

The tension in Berlin was palpable; an American diplomat described the atmosphere as "being in a house where you know someone upstairs is dying. There is relatively little to do and yet the suspense continues unabated." As

Henderson got into his car for the three- or-four-hundred-yard drive to the Reichschancellery, he caught sight of the expressionless faces watching him silently from the square—nameless delegates of the German people, hoping to divine their future from the movements of His Majesty's ambassador. Otto Meissner, chief of protocol, greeted him at the chancellery door and remarked that he was glad to see Henderson wearing a boutonnière. Except for the three critical days preceding the Munich crisis, the Englishman had always worn a dark red carnation in his lapel, and Meissner and others remembered, and took the boutonnière as a barometer of the official British attitude. On Tuesday, August 29, Henderson had his final interview with Hitler; he was handed what amounted to an ultimatum to the Polish government, and as he left the chancellery he told Meissner he feared he would never again wear a carnation in Germany.

"My soldiers," Hitler had told him, "are asking me to say 'Yes' or 'No' "—as if to say that the matter was no longer in the Führer's hands. (The military men were indeed complaining that they had lost a week of good weather, that they could not afford further delay lest the rainy season interfere with the movement of troops and armor.) Then Hitler spoke heatedly about the alleged Polish atrocities: "You do not care how many Germans are being killed and tortured in Poland!" he shouted, and Henderson shouted right back at him—"at the top of my voice," he reported to Halifax. When the Nazi leader said he had no intention of sacrificing "vital German interests," Henderson calmed down enough to ask what those interests were. To which Hitler replied that he would provide the British with a list of proposals acceptable to Germany and that he would expect a Polish negotiator to come to Berlin within twenty-four hours to discuss terms.

"That sounds like an ultimatum!" Henderson exclaimed.

As the ambassador informed Halifax later, Hitler was clearly determined to achieve his goals by a show of strength or, failing that, by the use of force. And if no one called his hand he would "pursue the same course again next year or the year after." Between that gloomy prediction and Henderson's report of the angry meeting he had had with the Führer, analysts in Britain's Foreign Office assumed that this was one more bellicose outburst from the intemperate German chancellor and not a genuine overture.

The notes were flying thick and fast now, back and forth between Whitehall, its embassy in Berlin, and the Reichschancellery, and finally at midnight on August 30—the German deadline for a Polish plenipotentiary to appear in Berlin—Henderson called on Ribbentrop to remind him that the British had not yet received the list of proposals Hitler had promised him. (If Henderson assumed that Britain's position was a surprise to the German, he was mistaken; the Nazis had a tap on the embassy telephone and knew the details of everything the ambassador had been indiscreet enough to discuss with London on an open line.) Listening to the foreign minister's reply and watching his movements, it dawned on the Englishman that he had never seen him so edgy and that he probably mirrored precisely the Führer's state of mind: he was intensely hostile and kept leaping to his feet in great agitation, folding his arms, pacing back and forth while asking Henderson if he had anything further to say. In fact, Ribbentrop's self-control was gone, Henderson's own hands were trembling as he read him Great Britain's answer to Hitler's last note, and it quickly became clear that this meeting was going nowhere, that it was not to be a give-and-take between diplomats but a confrontation of two fighting cocks—both fighting mad, glaring at the other, their faces angry and red. Paul Schmidt, the hapless interpreter who was supposed to be translating their conversation, had no idea what to do or how to behave. He was certain the meeting was going to progress "from words to deeds," as he put it, and he pretended to be writing furiously in his notebook while the two diplomats sputtered and glowered at each other. For a moment, Schmidt said, he thought Ribbentrop might try to throw the Englishman out the door.

When the foreign minister finally produced a document, he read it in German, Henderson said, "or rather gabbled through to me as fast as he could, in a tone of the utmost scorn and annoyance." It contained sixteen articles, of which Henderson was able to get the gist of only half a dozen, and when he asked Ribbentrop if he could read the text himself, the German refused, slammed the papers on the table, and announced that the proposal was already "out of date" since no Polish representative had arrived in Berlin. Schmidt realized that Ribbentrop's reason for rattling off the list of articles was that Henderson might accept them if he was allowed to read them, and it seemed to the Englishman, too, that Ribbentrop and his master had deliberately thrown to the winds the one remaining opportunity to settle the problem peacefully. "I returned to His Majesty's Embassy that night," he wrote, "convinced that the last hope for peace had vanished."

The next afternoon Henderson had a most curious experience. Hermann Göring invited him to come see him at 5:00 P.M., and for two hours the field marshal talked of Poland's iniquities and of Germany's desire for friendship with England and the rest of the world. "It was a conversation which led nowhere," Henderson remarked, and he was stunned by the realization that Göring, who had just been made president of Germany's war cabinet, could afford the time for such nonsense. Obviously it meant that "everything, down to the last detail, was now ready for action." As indeed it was.

At the same time Henderson had his audience with Göring, Joseph Lipski, the Polish ambassador, met with Ribbentrop to tell him that his government was weighing favorably the British proposal for direct discussions with Germany. It proved a brief, unsatisfactory interview, and when Lipski returned to the embassy to telephone his superiors in Warsaw, he found that the line was dead. The next morning he received a call from Henderson, who told him that there would be war within two or three hours unless the Poles did something quickly; then Henderson called London to give his own government the same message. As before, his words were taken down verbatim by the wiretappers who were monitoring the line.

In Washington, D.C., during that steamy final fortnight of August 1939, the seventy-sixth Congress adjourned after hacking away at a number of Roosevelt's budget requests. A so-called economy Congress, it had nevertheless appropriated $13 billion—the most in history—and its perspiring, weary members hurried to Union Station, where their wives and luggage awaited them, to board trains for home. The president was also bound for a much-needed vacation—his first stop the family estate at Hyde Park, in New York's Hudson Valley, to be followed by a fishing trip off Newfoundland. By the time the general exodus from the capital was over, the senior U.S. official present in Washington was the acting secretary of the navy, Charles Edison.[1] Everyone who outranked him was out of town.

Elsewhere, despite the frightening rush of events in Europe, life in America went on about as usual. A Chicago grand jury indicted Moses Annenberg, publisher of the *Philadelphia Inquirer* and various magazines, on ten counts of income-tax evasion. The popular humorist Irvin S. Cobb, suffering from a stomach ailment, sat up in his hospital bed ("like a bullfrog in a pan of milk," he said) and told reporters, "I can't say the X-ray pictures flatter me." The doctor told him he was going to have to "quit eating anything fit to eat, smoke nothing, drink nothing, and go to bed at 7:00 P.M. This is calculated to make me live at least five years longer, but what the hell for I don't know."

A new movie, *The Wizard of Oz,* starring old-timers Ray Bolger, Bert Lahr, Jack Haley, and Frank Morgan, and a young newcomer named Judy Garland, opened to enthusiastic reviews and large crowds. The book everybody seemed to be reading was John Steinbeck's *The Grapes of Wrath;* 205,000 copies were already in print—619 pages, nicely bound, for $2.75. Next year's model cars were making their debut earlier than usual: new Packards were selling for $867 and up, with prices $120 to $400 lower than the '39 models; Hudson was offering a cheaper six-cylinder and a more powerful eight-cylinder car; and the latest Nash was available for $770. Anyone who had money to invest could consider an attractive $30 million issue of 3 percent debentures, due in 1959, from the Union Oil Company of California. And anyone concerned about his health could ponder an announcement by Dr. Clarence Alonzo Mills of the University of Cincinnati, who concluded that the biggest cause of disease in the United States was "cold polar waves traveling down the central trough of the continent," resulting in tuberculosis, diabetes, mental instability, and suicide. Dr. Mills

[1] A scientist as well as a politician, Edison was the son of the famous inventor Thomas A. Edison. He left the government in 1940 to campaign for the governorship of New Jersey, was elected, and served for four years.

cautioned that too much air conditioning in summer was unhealthy (not that many Americans had to worry, since air conditioners were all but unavailable): "Body and mind seem to need this annual period of biologic rest" from the accelerated pace of winter, he said.

Anticipating what was almost certain to occur any day now in Europe, *Time*'s editors published a lengthy article in the magazine's August 28 issue entitled "Background for War," with a two-page map showing the historic battlegrounds on that continent. A good many other editorial writers were prophesying war, but without suggesting that the United States might have a substantial stake in the European crisis. The general theme was that there could be no compromising by England, France, and Poland; that Hitler's outrageous demands and intransigence were to blame, as everyone knew. The *Providence Evening Bulletin* declared, ". . . the Poles cannot surrender to Herr Hitler without inviting a far more serious crisis later. For Hitler will not stop with Poland. Poland is but a means to the larger end of his policy: the domination of Europe by force.

"Let's have the showdown now," the editorial concluded. Let's you and him fight, in other words. Most Americans felt, as did many Europeans, that the potential belligerents were about evenly matched: that France's huge defensive complex known as the Maginot Line would prove a standoff for Germany's Siegfried Line; that the armed forces of France, Britain, and Poland—bolstered by the mighty British navy—would be a match for Hitler's Wehrmacht.

One American journalist who opposed appeasement but who felt that there must surely be an alternative to war was a woman whose warnings about the threat from the Third Reich had been heard increasingly in recent years. Dorothy Thompson, the columnist and commentator who was inevitably introduced on speaker's platforms as "the first lady of American journalism," was a big, handsome, mannish-looking woman, highly intelligent and extremely well informed, who tended to monopolize a conversation as though no one else were in the room. She had definite views on every political subject, and in her writing favored the moralistic essay, swayed no doubt by the teachings of a father who was a Methodist minister in the Genesee Valley of New York. ("God was everywhere," his daughter wrote in a reminiscence. "Jesus was father's personal friend . . . and the Thompson family was under special protection.")

After arriving in central Europe in the early twenties, Dorothy Thompson had become Berlin correspondent for the *Philadelphia Public Ledger* and the *New York Evening Post,* and had moved, as John Gunther said, "like a blue-eyed tornado" to the center of an unusually able group of foreign correspondents that included Gunther, Shirer, Vincent Sheean, Floyd Gibbons, and Edgar Mowrer. In 1934 she was expelled from Germany "for journalistic activities inimical" to that country—among them being her description of Adolf Hitler as a man of "startling insignificance" who was "formless, almost faceless, a man whose countenance is a caricature. . . . He is inconsequential and voluble, ill-poised, insecure. He is the very prototype of the Little Man." (In her book *I Saw Hitler!* she made the mistake of saying that when she was first introduced to the little man she was certain that "I was meeting the future dictator of Germany. In something less than fifty seconds I was quite sure that I was not." Her fellow journalists did not let her forget those last words.)

By 1938 her column for the *New York Herald Tribune* was syndicated in 130 papers; she wrote a popular column for *The Ladies' Home Journal;* she was heard every Monday night at 9:00 P.M. on *The General Electric Hour,* to which an estimated five million radio sets were tuned. She had, in fact, an audience matched by only one other woman, Eleanor Roosevelt, whose newspaper column, "My Day," first appeared in January 1936. In a cover story on Thompson, *Time* described this disparate pair as "the most influential women in the U.S.," and indeed they probably were. Dorothy Thompson's devoted, partisan public was unaware that her stormy marriage to America's first Nobel laureate in literature, Sinclair Lewis, was virtually at an end, or that she was involved in a succession of attachments to lovers of both sexes. What her followers were certain of was that she was right about Hitler and fascism, and that she perceived the struggle against the Nazi dictator as one in which victory would be achieved only through the equivalent of a religious revival. In late August of 1939 she sent a long cable to Harold Nicolson urging him to use his influence as a member of Parliament to arrange a worldwide day of prayer and meditation, broadcast by shortwave radio and featuring readings from the Sermon on the Mount and appropriate chapters of the Bible, along with selections from Germany's great religious music. "England's strength," she informed the Englishman, "is not appeasement with the enemy of peace nor war but a glorious Christian resistance. I mean this with all seriousness. I am not at all crazy. Love from Red [i.e., Sinclair Lewis] who thinks I am."

On August 29, the same day Ambassador Henderson had his final interview with Hitler in Berlin, Nicolson responded to Thompson, saying that he agreed with her. "The conflict, if it comes, will be a moral conflict," he wrote, "and it is for that reason I have minded so terribly in the last few years that we have soiled our moral case by trying to appease the dictators."

By then it was too late for the day of prayer. On August 28, Ed Murrow reported in a broadcast from London that the English were proud that their government was finally talking tough, proud that Britain was not backing down as she had a year earlier. But if Hitler moved against Poland, a terrible decision would have to be made in London and in Paris. As a British politician asked Murrow: "Are we to be the first to bomb women and children?" Word had come through during the day that luggage was piled in the hall at the British embassy in Berlin, with a folded umbrella the most prominent item in view.

Three days later England was preparing for the worst. The Royal Navy had been fully mobilized, army and air reservists had been called up, and women and children were helping the men dig trenches. In front of a London church someone put up a sign: IF YOUR KNEES KNOCK, KNEEL ON THEM. In the city's parks the purple autumn crocuses were in bloom, but thousands of Londoners would not be there to enjoy them. "Tomorrow we shall see the children, the halt, the lame, and the blind going out of Britain's cities," Murrow told Americans. "Six hundred fifty thousand will leave London tomorrow. The exodus will start at 5:30 in the morning. In all, there are three million people to be evacuated . . . one million three hundred thousand from London alone. Nine roads out of London and only one-way traffic. It's not going to be a very pleasant sight."

The plan was to house all those children with rural families in what was the greatest mass evacuation in English history, and on Friday, September 1, when the children arrived at school, each one—who brought from home a gas mask, a knapsack with clothing and toilet articles, plus rations for forty-eight hours—was handed a postcard to be mailed home upon arrival at his or her assigned billet in the country. Some children wept, some danced and sang the popular "Lambeth Walk" on station platforms, and thousands of desperately anxious, heartsick parents were left to wonder what would become of their little ones and when or if they would see them again. In Paris, much the same scene was being enacted, with children carrying dolls, toys, knapsacks, and gas masks, crowding the railroad stations before being sent off to "safety zones" in the countryside. Berlin's young people were told to remain in the city, where their days began with a gas-mask drill and dummy runs to the closest bomb shelter. Warsaw's children, unprepared, helped their parents dig earthworks; not until the bombs began falling on Friday morning would some take trains to the country.

Thousands of Americans who had spent the summer in Europe were scrambling to get aboard westbound ships, and before long twenty-two luxury liners were on the high seas, jammed with returning tourists. In Europe, every U.S. consulate was aswarm with Americans desperate to get home, and at Villefranche, in France, the light cruiser *Trenton* and the ancient destroyers *Badger* and *Paul Jones* were standing by to transport stranded American nationals to various embarkation ports. Young Bruce Baldwin, a June Princeton graduate who had sailed to Europe for a vacation, observed something in London that made him appreciate the seriousness of the situation. "One day," he said, "we saw a Mercedes showroom complete with cars, salesmen, and photo posters showing Mercedes drivers winning races; the next day the door was locked and the salesmen were gone; the next day the cars were gone too, and only the posters remained."

Franklin Roosevelt's eighty-four-year-old mother, Sara Delano Roosevelt, was sure her son would be worrying about her, so she cut short her European trip and, after packing her luggage with the help of her nonagenarian sister, Dora Delano Forbes (who elected to remain in her Paris home—she had had a full life, she said, and wouldn't be sorry if a

German bomb ended it), was driven to Le Havre, where she boarded the U.S. liner *Washington.* Her grandson John Roosevelt and his wife, Anne, with their friends the Edward G. Robinsons of Hollywood, were anxiously waiting for her. A reporter who spoke with John was told, "Nobody ever knows what grandmother will do next."

Every departing vessel was filled to capacity. Chesley Robert Palmer, president of Cluett, Peabody, the makers of Arrow shirts, had taken his family to Europe in grand style—in a deluxe suite on the *Nieuw Amsterdam.* The best accommodations they could get for their unscheduled return were three mattresses on the deck of a ship.

J. P. Morgan's shooting *was* spoiled, after all. The banker managed to book a small stateroom with a single bed on the *Queen Mary,* along with 2,330 other passengers and $44 million in gold bullion that was being removed from England for safekeeping in the States. One of his fellow passengers was a balding gentleman carrying an album of rare stamps given him by France's minister of posts and telegraphs. He described himself as a "postage-stamp merchant," which indeed he was in a manner of speaking; he was U.S. Postmaster General James A. Farley, returning from a European holiday. Another cabinet officer, Secretary of the Treasury Henry Morgenthau, was rushed from Bergen, Norway, aboard the Coast Guard cutter *Campbell* to St. John's, Newfoundland, where a Coast Guard plane flew him to Washington. Morgan, Farley, and Morgenthau were among the lucky ones: some three thousand less fortunate Americans were still in Paris, with a thousand in Berlin, and two thousand in London. For them a harried State Department set up a special unit to provide protection, advanced money on the strength of promissory notes, and began booking passage on merchant vessels wherever space could be located.

Franklin Roosevelt, his cruise to Newfoundland ruined by fog and un-cooperative fish, was heading south on board the USS *Tuscaloosa,* and he passed the hours drafting a peace message to Hitler, Poland's President Ignacy Móscicki, and Italy's King Vittorio Emmanuele III, who was trout fishing in the Alps. In Washington, which was normally a nine-o'clock town, lights burned late on either flank of the White House. At State, while Cordell Hull vacationed at White Sulphur Springs, unflappable Sumner Welles was in charge, monitoring the avalanche of incoming telegrams, arranging to protect and repatriate stranded American citizens. At the Treasury, Under Secretary John Wesley Hanes was awaiting Morgenthau's return, brooding over the effect of the falling British pound, worrying about what might happen on the New York Stock Exchange. He and his associates were prepared to close the Big Board for ninety days in case foreign interests began liquidating their $9.5 billion in U.S. holdings—almost half of it in stocks and bonds. George L. Harrison, president of the Federal Reserve Bank of New York, had the unenviable task of protecting U.S. money markets: if inflation-minded investors started to unload their holdings of government bonds, it was his job to see that the market didn't slide too far.

Each passing hour brought Europe closer to the brink, yet a great many Americans refused to believe that there would be war, could not conceive that another horror like the one a quarter-century earlier was possible. So removed from reality were some CBS executives in New York that they had asked Ed Murrow and Bill Shirer to arrange a program called "Europe Dances"—snatches of dance music to be broadcast from nightclubs in London, Paris, and Berlin. This request came at a time when English schoolchildren were participating in a test evacuation, and Murrow and Shirer refused to have anything to do with it. What Americans did hear on their radio sets, along with peace appeals to Hitler from the world's leaders, was increasingly grave reports from correspondents in the capitals of Europe. On the night of August 31, after Ed Murrow said that "war is being regarded as inevitable" in London, he and Shirer—who was in Berlin— discussed the situation by means of a radio hookup with New York, since communications from Germany's capital to the rest of Europe had been cut off.

In Lloyd Neck, Long Island, Anne Lindbergh called the news from across the Atlantic "clear and cold and metallic." The long, terrible week just past, she wrote in her diary, had been one "of piling up hopes and then fears, a week of listening at the radio, trying to sort out truth from lies, of terrible clinging to one straw and then another, of seesawing with each new word, up and down, of telegrams from Washington and phone calls, and not sleeping, and talking, passionately arguing, first this way, then another, but all this against war—war which is now upon us." She found herself comparing the meetings, the negotiations, the diplomatic missions, with all the comings and goings of police at their home in Hopewell, New Jersey, after their firstborn son was kidnapped, and she couldn't help asking, "For what use, for what purpose? The child is dead. The child is dead in Europe."

Faced at last with the reality of war, Chamberlain and his colleagues, having striven for so long to appease the madman in Berlin and avoid a showdown, suddenly seemed incapable of action. Someone remarked that the prime minister's internal clock had stopped running; as Joseph Kennedy described the situation in a cable to the State Department, Chamberlain "says the futility of it all is the thing that is frightful. . . . After all, they cannot save the Poles." Whether they could or could not was now beside the point. There were a few last-minute efforts, consciously without hope, too little and too late, on the part of Chamberlain, Halifax, and Henderson, but what touched off the event they all dreaded was a telegram from the Polish government in Warsaw to Ambassador Lipski in Berlin—a message that was deciphered immediately by the Germans and delivered to Hitler.

"Do not under any circumstances enter into any factual discussions," it read. "If the German government makes any verbal or written proposals, you are to reply that you have no authority whatever to receive or discuss such proposals and that you . . . must await further instructions."

That made it plain to Hitler that the Poles were not going to follow the timetable he had set for them. And so, on the last day of August 1939, shortly after noon, he issued the order for the invasion of Poland—justifying his action by the intercepted telegram and by a published report that German nationals had been killed by Polish soldiers advancing into German territory. "They'll pay for this!" he shouted. "Now no one will stop me from teaching those fellows a lesson they'll never forget! I will not have my Germans butchered like cattle!" And with that he went to the telephone and ordered General Wilhelm Keitel to issue "Directive Number 1 for the Conduct of the War." Probably the Führer did not bother to inform Keitel that the handful of Polish troops whose bodies had been found on German soil were not Poles but Germans, inmates of the Oranienburg concentration camp, whom Heinrich Himmler's SS had clothed in Polish uniforms, injected with a lethal drug, and then shot inside the German border. After their corpses had been arranged to make it appear that they had been killed while advancing into Germany, foreign journalists and other witnesses were taken to see the evidence.

That same evening, while bombers warmed up on German airstrips, while truckloads of gray-uniformed troops raced through the gloom toward the Polish frontier, H. V. Kaltenborn sat before a microphone in CBS's New York studios. He had just returned from a visit to Europe, he said, and the message he broadcast confidently to his American listeners was that Britain would not fight. There would be no war.

━━

At 4:45 on the morning of September 1, the 11-inch guns of the old German battleship *Schleswig-Holstein* opened fire on the Polish garrison in Danzig. At the same moment, Junkers 87 dive-bombers—Stukas—screamed across the Polish border, followed by the motorcycles, tanks, and armored infantry and artillery of General Heinz Guderian's panzer divisions. Before Poland's planes could get off the ground the air bases at Kraków and Katowice were bombed; then the Luftwaffe hit Gdynia, Lwow, Krosno, and Warsaw. There was no declaration of war by Germany, nor would there be—only a proclamation from Hitler to his armed forces, stating that the time had come to put an end to the "mad acts" of the Polish government, to "meet force with force and fire with fire." To cheering members of the Reichstag, summoned into emergency session, he announced: "I have put on my old soldier's coat, and I will not take it off until we win victory for the Fatherland!" And his listeners thundered the answering chorus: "*Sieg heil! Sieg heil!*"

At 2:40 A.M. on Friday, September 1, Washington time, the telephone rang at Franklin Roosevelt's bedside. The call was from Paris.

"This is Bill Bullitt, Mr. President."

"Yes, Bill."

"Tony Biddle has just got through from Warsaw, Mr. President. Several German divisions are deep in Polish territory, and fighting is heavy. Tony said there were reports of bombers over the city. Then he was cut off. . . ."

"Well, Bill," said Roosevelt. "It's come at last. God help us all."

A few minutes later the president called Hull.

"Cordell," he said, "Bullitt has just been on the phone. The Germans have invaded Poland."

Hull was prepared for the news. He told his wife what had happened, dressed, drove to the State Department, and walked through the deserted corridors to his office. It was about 3:30. Soon Sumner Welles came in, then others, "their faces alert and anxious," and Hull got on the phone to Paris and London, to ask Bullitt and Kennedy for their appraisals of the situation.

After calling Hull and Welles and notifying Secretary of War Harry Woodring and Acting Secretary of the Navy Charles Edison, the president went back to sleep until 6:30, when he took a second call from Bullitt. The ambassador had spoken with Daladier, who stated flatly that France and Britain would go to Poland's aid lest they lose entirely their moral standing before the world. Roosevelt rested for another three-quarters of an hour, when Kennedy telephoned from London in a mood of black despair; then he summoned his valet, ate his breakfast from a tray, and lay in bed for another hour, thinking. When Sumner Welles arrived to discuss a special Pan-American conference to be held in the event of war, he found Roosevelt lying relaxed against the pillows, a blue bed cape around his shoulders, a cigarette glowing in the holder clenched between his teeth. Welles departed, and the chief executive sent for Edison to talk over what he called a "neutrality patrol" off the U.S. coastline; then he dressed and was wheeled to his office for a press conference; after that, Hull arrived and the White House switchboard started placing calls to London, Paris, Berlin, and Warsaw. The presidential day had begun.

The telephone by George Marshall's bedside rang at 3:00 that morning, and fifty minutes later a message went out from the office of the chief of staff to all army commanders: "Fighting has developed on Polish border and Warsaw is being bombed. Precautions will be taken accordingly." Several hours later, Marshall, who had been acting chief of staff since April, was scheduled to be sworn in as successor to Malin Craig, who was retiring, but with the news from Europe, he decided to dispense with ceremony and took one oath as a permanent major general and another as chief of staff and temporary four-star general, promising to "support and defend the Constitution of the United States against all enemies, both foreign and domestic." In a letter to a friend, the new head of the United States Army admitted,

"My day of induction was momentous, with the start of what appears to be a world war."

So Europe was at it again, and *The New Yorker* magazine expressed the feelings of most Americans when it observed that "it is still hard to understand what the headlines mean. Unless there is a miracle, ten million more young men will die (very few of them especially heroically or quickly); millions of children will die (very few of whom had had time to form very strong or dangerous political opinions); cities that rose proudly and slowly over the centuries will be ugly ruins between a morning and a night. . . .

"The best minds in the world will now think continuously and cleverly of death. . . ."

CHAPTER 20

"This nation will remain
a neutral nation ..."

While Poles died by the thousands and the rest of the world waited to see what Britain and France would do, the leaders of those two nations were trying to wriggle out of the mess they had done so much to create. There were conversations with the Italians, talk of a possible armistice, plans for a conference at which Mussolini might mediate between Germany and Poland. In London, on Saturday afternoon, August 26, the cabinet met in emergency session against a background of rising anger, public and political. "Why are we waiting?" people wanted to know; why, in the face of Poland's agony, was the government procrastinating? Why were France and Britain not fulfilling their pledges? Chamberlain told members of the cabinet that the French did not wish to press an ultimatum until noon on the following day, at which time they would give the Germans forty-eight hours in which to respond, and it would be "unfortunate," the prime minister said, if the Allies did not synchronize their actions. But in the House of Commons the same message produced open rebellion. When Chamberlain appeared the members expected another of his dramatic surprises, Harold Nicolson said. "But none came. It was evident when he sat down that no decision had been arrived at. The House gasped for one moment in astonishment. Was there to be another Munich after all?" The entire chamber oozed hostility, and the pent-up emotion suddenly crystallized when Arthur Greenwood of the Labour Party rose from his seat. Among members, Greenwood was not considered a figure of particular consequence,[1] but during the past week, speaking for the ailing Clement Attlee, he had begun to come into his own as a deputy for all Englishmen who felt betrayed by Munich and who were confronted now with the possibility of another humiliating surrender. Tall, lanky, with dank hair hanging on either side of his forehead, Greenwood swayed a little unsteadily as he clutched at the box in front of him and peered through his glasses at Chamberlain, who was sitting directly opposite. For a moment the chamber was silent, then something astonishing happened. A Conservative member, unable to contain any longer his rage at the policy of the party leader, stood up and shouted across to Greenwood, "Speak for England, Arthur! Speak for England!" and at this cry of defiance and rebellion the House erupted in cheers. Greenwood was no orator; he spoke with a homely accent in a rather muffled, slow voice; but what he said, simply and sincerely, against further delay or sacrifice of the nation's honor, was the speech of a lifetime, and before the applause and shouting finally died away Nicolson felt certain that "the PM must know by now that the whole House is against him." That night Chamberlain learned as well that five members of his cabinet had deserted and were taking a stand in opposition to his do-nothing position; they sent word that they were in the Chancellor's Room in the House of Commons and there they planned to stay until Britain declared war. Confronted with mutiny, Chamberlain summoned the entire cabinet to No. 10 Downing Street, where they met about midnight, deciding at last that the British would act alone if necessary, giving the Germans until 11:00 A.M. on Sunday, September 3, to respond to an ultimatum to withdraw from Poland. Evidently the god of war was listening: as the meeting broke up, the heavens over London suddenly reverberated to the crash of thunder and lightning.

Next morning, Englishmen watched the minute hands of their watches creep toward 11:00, and at fifteen minutes after the hour the prime minister was speaking on the radio from Downing Street. The BBC announcer who introduced him noticed that Chamberlain's "shoulders were hunched and he was very, very serious. . . . He looked crumpled, despondent, and old." (Ten days later Daladier saw Chamberlain and found him a broken man— one who had passed "from middle age into decrepitude.") Millions of Americans sat silently by their radios, listening to the crackling and distortions of the shortwave broadcast. They had no way of knowing how the British statesman looked, but there was no missing the ineffable sadness in his voice as he said, "This morning the British ambassador to Berlin handed the German government the final note stating that unless we heard from them by eleven o'clock that they were prepared to withdraw their troops from Poland, a state of war would exist between us.

[1]His "value was impaired by his addiction to the bottle," a contemporary wrote.

"I have to tell you now that no such understanding was received and consequently this country is at war with Germany."

Later, Chamberlain admitted to colleagues in Parliament, "Everything I have worked for, everything I have hoped for, everything I have believed in, has crashed in ruins." His friend the U.S. ambassador was equally stricken. After the prime minister informed Joseph Kennedy what he would tell members of Parliament on that fateful September morning, Kennedy returned to the embassy from No. 10 Downing Street, called the White House, and, in a voice choked with emotion, attempted to convey his impressions of Chamberlain's speech to the president. Roosevelt could scarcely recognize the voice of his old friend, predicting the Dark Age that would descend over Europe, the chaos that would ensue no matter which side won the war. Over and over Kennedy cried, "It's the end of the world . . . the end of everything."

That same day Americans heard another broadcast from England and another equally sad voice—this one the somewhat halting speech of a man who had been unable to overcome a stammer. King George VI was speaking to his people and to their friends around the world. "For the second time in the lives of most of us," he said, "we are at war."

Nicolson and a group of friends, having listened to Chamberlain's broadcast, walked to the House of Commons and on the way heard a siren wailing. It was 11:32, just seventeen minutes after the prime minister had begun his radio address. One man in the party remarked, "They ought not to do that after what we have heard. . . . People will think it is an air-raid warning." At which another siren began to blow. "My God!" Nicolson cried. "It *is* an air-raid warning!" Bobbies began waving at them, the crowd around Parliament Square broke up "like a flock of pigeons" and ran toward Westminster Hospital, and before long Nicolson and his group were in an air-raid shelter, occupied "by all manner of people from Cabinet Ministers to cooks. It is very hot. People chat to each other with forced geniality." (Winston Churchill and his wife repaired to a shelter armed, he said, "with a bottle of brandy and other appropriate medical comforts.") When the all-clear signal sounded (it had, in fact, been a false alarm), Nicolson and the others proceeded to the House, joined in prayers, and then listened to Chamberlain's speech to Parliament. "He looks very ill," Nicolson observed. Throughout the session sirens continued to wail, and afterward Nicolson drove down to his country place with a friend; they passed a succession of lorries evacuating people from London's East End, in one of which they saw an old woman who shook her fist at them and shouted that the war was the fault of the rich. In the week that followed Hitler's attack on Poland, those three million children, invalids, and elderly about whom Ed Murrow had spoken were removed from London and twenty-eight other cities in Great Britain. One of the least enthusiastic refugees was the venerable Queen Mary, but she acquiesced to the request of the government and her son, the king, and moved to Gloucestershire, to spend the war years at Badminton House, the noble mansion of the Duke and Duchess of Beaufort. They had invited her to stay with them, perhaps without calculating that the war might be a long one. Little did they know that they would be left with only two bedrooms and a small sitting room for their own use: the Queen arrived with fifty-five servants and more than seventy pieces of personal luggage, and at once commandeered a group to begin cutting down trees and removing ivy—which she detested—from the walls and trees of her hosts' house and grounds.

"Very hot and sunny," Alexander Cadogan wrote of Sunday, September 3, 1939. "In a sense, there is relief; doubts resolved." That afternoon Neville Chamberlain chose expedience in order to retain his job and offered posts in a war cabinet to two of his ablest political enemies. One was a man the prime minister cordially disliked—his former foreign secretary, Anthony Eden, whom he had forced to resign a year and a half earlier by means of a devious and unworthy scheme. The other was Winston Churchill, who had long been a lone voice in the wilderness, calling for Britain to beware the dictators and rearm, who accepted the position of first lord of the Admiralty as well as a seat in the cabinet. Churchill had been in charge of the Admiralty a quarter of a century earlier, in what would be known from now on as the First World War, and as he returned to his old office (where he found the same chair and the same wooden map case he had had installed in 1911) a signal went off to the fleet: "Winston is back."

From Finland came word that preparations for the 1940 Olympic Games, scheduled to be held in Helsingfors in the summer, had been halted, and the world took it for granted, though nothing had been heard from Germany, that the Winter Games in Garmisch-Partenkirchen were off. In Japan, Admiral Isoroku Yamamoto, who had just been appointed commander in chief of the Combined Fleet by Emperor Hirohito, learned that Germany had invaded Poland and confided to a friend his profound misgivings: "The great upheaval now occurring in Europe makes me feel terrified when I think of our relationship with Germany and Italy."

In Washington on September 11—the same day Charles Lindbergh was writing his first radio speech—President Roosevelt dictated several important letters, one of them to the British prime minister, holding out hope that the U.S. embargo on arms shipments would soon be repealed; another—most unusual in the circumstances—addressed to the new first lord of the Admiralty. After welcoming Churchill back to the navy post, Roosevelt asked that he "keep me in touch personally with anything you want me to know about." It was an odd request, and what was out of the ordinary was that a head of state should invite correspondence from a man who was not the head of the government or even in charge of its foreign relations. The letter indicated that Roosevelt had not forgiven Chamberlain for rebuffing his suggestion for an international peace conference, while it clearly revealed his support for a man who had struggled for years to awaken Britain to the danger of Hitler and had been an insistent foe of Chamberlain's appeasement policy. (At the time Chamberlain spurned Roosevelt's request, Churchill characterized his response as "chilling," and afterward brilliantly described his country's plight: "Poor England!" he wrote, "Leading her free, careless life from day to day, amid endless good-tempered parliamentary babble, she followed, wondering, along the downward path which led to all she wanted to avoid.")

Churchill had been something of a political pariah since World War I, thanks to his unwelcome prophecies about Hitler's ambitions and his calls for Britain to rearm, which were ridiculed as much as ignored. One American correspondent in London was advised by his editor "not to bother to make an appointment with Churchill," since he was "a maverick or a crackpot." Yet intuitively, Roosevelt sensed that the Englishman was unlikely to remain first lord for long, and a letter he wrote to Joseph Kennedy in December 1939 indicates that he had a practical as well as a philosophical motive for taking action: "I'm giving him attention now because there is a strong possibility that he will become the prime minister and I want to get my hand in now," he said. It was typical of Churchill's remarkable sense of timing that his most recent book—*Step by Step: 1936–1939,* in which the man "who knew too much, saw too clearly, and spoke too plainly," as someone described him, recounted the inevitable coming of war—should be reviewed in the *New York Times* on Sunday, September 3, 1939, the very day Britain and France declared war on Germany.

More than anything else, Roosevelt's gesture opened the door to a relationship that became far more than a friendship: it launched a remarkable partnership that would alter the course of history. Even though the two men were complete opposites in many ways, with what Isaiah Berlin called an "incompatibility of outlook," overriding all their differences was an iron determination that Hitler must and would be defeated at all costs. Arthur Schlesinger, recalling how Churchill was run down by an automobile and very nearly killed in New York City in 1931 when he looked the wrong way before crossing the street, and how Roosevelt missed by a hair being assassinated in Florida in 1933, suggested, "One might invite those who believe that individuals make no difference to history to tell us what would have happened to the world a decade later had the automobile killed Winston Churchill on Fifth Avenue and the bullet killed Franklin Roosevelt in Miami. Fortunately, the two men survived to find each other and to save us all."

━━

And meantime, what of Poland? Even as the air-raid sirens keened across London, Poland's crack cavalry brigade, the Pomorska, took up position to prevent the closing of the Polish Corridor. Partially hidden by trees, the horsemen awaited the German advance, and as a line of patrol cars and infantry came into view the sound of bugles split the air, the elite corps trotted out, formed into line, unsheathed their sabers, and spurred their mounts to a gallop. Following orders, the German troops quickly turned and ran, and suddenly General Heinz Guderian's tanks and armored vehicles appeared as if from nowhere. In what was surely one of history's most futile gestures, the cavalry rode headlong at them, the riders beating at the sides of the steel machines with lances and sabers, firing pistols, but it took only forty minutes for the panzers to destroy the Pomorska brigade and leave behind a field of dead and dying men and animals. As only the Germans seemed to understand, twentieth-century warfare had a brand-new face.

The German general staff had estimated that it might take a month to conquer Poland (British military intelligence gave the Poles at least four months), but by September 17 that nation's armies were in flight or surrounded, its cities captured or under siege. The secret of Hitler's military successes, readers of *Time* learned, was something called *Blitzkrieg,* "lightning war," which was described as "a war of quick penetration and obliteration." It was, more particularly, high-level bombers that destroyed much of Poland's air force on the ground, thwarted troop movement by smashing railroad tracks and highways, and set fires raging in the cities. It was Stuka dive-bombers peeling out of formation to plummet from the sky, sirens screaming, carrying terror along with death to helpless civilians and soldiers on the ground. It was, more than any other single element, armored panzer divisions—wave upon wave of cars, tanks, artillery, and infantry. These self-contained units—each division a team of all arms—were the creation of Heinz Guderian, who had fought for them for years as a young officer. Simply stated, the role of the panzer division was to concentrate its awesome power at the enemy's weakest point, to break through on a narrow front (followed by other army units which widened the gap), and then to penetrate as deeply as possible to his rear. Speed, flexibility of attack, unpredictability, and momentum were the key ingredients, and when the young Major Guderian was first given the opportunity to explain his theories to Hitler in 1933, the new chancellor, captivated, bought them lock, stock, and barrel, saying, "This is what I need! This is what I must have!" For a nation with few natural resources, supply lines threatened by France's army and Britain's navy, and potential enemies on all sides, short, lightning-like warfare was essential, and six years later Guderian's theories were being put into deadly practice for the first time. They were Germany's answer to the hideous bloodletting that characterized the trench warfare of 1914–18 and cost the nations of Europe an entire generation of young men.

When Hitler visited Guderian at the front on September 5 and asked about casualties, the general replied that his four divisions had lost only 150 killed and seven hundred wounded. Hitler was astonished: on the first day of battle in the Great War, he said, his regiment alone had lost more than two thousand soldiers. The difference, Guderian assured him, was the effectiveness of the German tanks, which he called "a life-saving weapon." And to the infantrymen in the ranks the massed armor seemed exactly what Guderian said it was. As one soldier wrote in his diary, "It is a wonderful feeling, now, to be a German. . . . The row of tanks has no end. A quarter of an hour, tanks, tanks, tanks."

In Norris, Tennessee, on the morning of September 3, a forty-year-old man who was as much of an innovator as Guderian tuned in his radio just in time to catch a fragmentary remark by a commentator. David Lilienthal, whose field was peace, not war, was in charge of what many considered the crowning achievement of Franklin Roosevelt's New Deal—the immense Tennessee Valley Authority, the comprehensive development of a great river basin which had altered the landscape of an area the size of England and Scotland combined, while reshaping the lives and futures of millions of Americans. What he heard this morning was an announcer saying something about "the action taken by England," and he knew at once what that meant. The son of immigrants from Austria-Hungary, Lilienthal had grown up in Indiana, the heart of isolationism, but he remembered how stirred he had been as a boy by Woodrow Wilson's war message to Congress.

Until this day he had been certain that all the talk about the European crisis simply meant that there would be a repetition of Munich, that Hitler would get substantially what he wanted, and without war. But there seemed no blinking the facts now: he turned to his wife, Helen, and saw how forlorn she looked as she said, "I don't want war." The two of them were torn by dread, on the one hand, that England and France would back down again and let Hitler get away with his threats, and by horror, on the other, of what it would undoubtedly take to destroy what Winston Churchill called the "pestilence" of Nazism.

The two Lilienthal children were uninterested in what was happening, their father could see, although young David complained constantly about the way radio broadcasts were interrupted with war reports: "He says the papers are bad enough, crowding out his beloved baseball news, but to stick it into the radio all the time is too much." David, soon to be twelve years old, was also groaning that his teacher would "make us work like anything at current events now."

So, less than a year after the Munich crisis began, war news interrupted America's Labor Day weekend. From Washington on Sunday night, in one of his famous radio "fireside chats," Franklin Roosevelt hinted at what might lie ahead. "Passionately though we may desire detachment," he said, "we are forced to realize that every word that comes through the air, every ship that sails the sea, every battle that is fought does affect the American future.

"This nation will remain a neutral nation," he assured his countrymen, "but I cannot ask that every American remain neutral in thought as well [which was what Woodrow Wilson had asked of them in 1917]. Even a neutral has a right to take account of facts. Even a neutral cannot be asked to close his mind or his conscience. . . .

"I hope the United States will keep out of this war. I believe that it will. And I give you assurance and reassurance that every effort of your government will be directed to that end."

Whether the president was indulging in wishful thinking or whether he was being disingenuous is hard to say, but he undoubtedly felt the need to stress his determination to remain aloof from any type of involvement in Europe if he was to influence congressional action in the weeks ahead. The tenor of the times was such that the head of the American Legion demanded "absolute neutrality," while Senator Henry Cabot Lodge, Jr., told the Veterans of Foreign Wars convention in Virginia that the first duty of every American was to keep his country out of war. Senator Borah delivered a radio address asserting that revision of the Neutrality Act at this time would be tantamount to entering the war in Europe. Senator Hiram Johnson, interviewed by reporters in San Francisco, literally shouted his reply: "Beware the words 'We cannot keep out,' 'Our entry in the war is inevitable,' 'We must fight to preserve democracy,' and all the Devil's messages we heard twenty years ago!" New York's feisty little Mayor Fiorello La Guardia announced that he would permit no protest rallies at foreign consulates. "The battles will be fought on the fields of Europe," he declared. "They cannot be fought or settled on the streets of New York."

Meantime, the State Department banned all foreign travel, and the American Psychological Association, convening in Palo Alto, discussed the question of Adolf Hitler's sanity. The New York Stock Exchange began trading on Friday, September 1, with the Dow Jones average at 134; with the news from Europe it closed at 138, up four points—a reminder, if one was needed, that Gerald Nye's "merchants of death" might once again profit from war. Clifford De Roode, a former pilot in World War I's Lafayette Escadrille, enlisted in the French army—the first American to do so after the outbreak of hostilities. And in New Castle, Pennsylvania, forty-five miles north of Pittsburgh, where the tinplate mills had stood idle for years, a man stood in the street shouting "Hallelujah!" at the news.

━━━

The great debate that was beginning to cut across all levels of American society was now to be governed by an entirely different set of premises. The question was no longer "What do we do if war comes?" War *had* come. It was here. The chessmen were on the board and the first move had been made. And this meant that the arguments about intervention or nonintervention were no longer theoretical. On the outcome of the debate would hinge the nation's peace and security and the lives of all those who might be sent into battle, in what still seemed to just about everyone to be Europe's, not America's, war.

Charles Lindbergh was acutely aware of this. On April 14, 1939, he had arrived in New York aboard the liner *Aquitania,* one of a passenger list that included numerous refugees. (As usual, he had to deal with the small army of reporters and photographers that swarmed around him—more than he ever recalled seeing—shoving, asking questions, giving him "a barbaric entry to a civilized country.") Because of his incisive knowledge of Europe's air fleets, he was immediately sought after by government officials, among them Congressman Sol Bloom, chairman of the House Committee on Foreign Affairs, who hoped Lindbergh would testify on the neutrality legislation then under consideration. Lindbergh declined that invitation, but accepted one to attend a meeting of the National Advisory Committee for Aeronautics, and another to meet with General Henry H. Arnold, chief of the U.S. Army Air Corps, with whom he had been corresponding for six months. Arnold was eager to learn more about the Luftwaffe, in particular, and the two aviators arranged to get together at the Thayer Hotel at West Point, in the dining room, which was closed to the public to ensure their privacy. For several hours they talked before strolling out to the military academy's baseball diamond, where the Army team was playing Syracuse, and where they continued their discussion while the game went on. What he obtained from Lindbergh, Arnold said later, was "the most accurate picture of the Luftwaffe, its equipment, leaders, apparent plans, training methods, and present defects" he had yet received.

It is of more than passing interest that Arnold and another man—both destined to play significant roles in the war to come—heard Lindbergh's reports on the Luftwaffe and reacted exactly the opposite from Joseph Kennedy and others to whom the statistics and frightening conclusions spelled German victory. The effect on Hap Arnold was to heighten his determination that the American air force should surpass and be capable of overpowering the Nazis; to Vannevar Bush, the message was that American science must be mobilized to defeat Hitler. Bush was known to colleagues in the scientific community for his work in applied mathematics and electrical engineering, notably with a forerunner of the modern computer; he had been vice president and dean of the Massachusetts Institute of Technology before going to Washington as head of the Carnegie Institution; and he was associated with Charles Lindbergh on the National Advisory Committee for Aeronautics (NACA). Recognizing the need for close collaboration between the scientific community and the military—a partnership whose cordiality would be assured by having a scientific organization that reported directly to the president and had its own funds—he drafted a congressional bill that was the basis for establishing the National Defense Research Committee in 1940.

Arnold asked Lindbergh to meet him again in Washington, to see if he would be willing to make a study of American aeronautical research and manufacturing operations with an eye to improving their efficiency. Lindbergh accepted, and went on active duty as a colonel almost immediately. On April 20 he met with Harry Woodring, the secretary of war, and—after pushing his way through a crowd of press photographers and "screeching women" at the door—entered the White House to meet Franklin Roosevelt for the first time. Lindbergh found both interviews disquieting: the one with Woodring because the secretary asked him not to testify before any congressional committees; the one with Roosevelt because he thought the president "a little too suave, too pleasant, too easy." He was predisposed to like Roosevelt, who was an accomplished, interesting conversationalist, but he believed that since the president was "mostly politician," the two of them "would never get along on many fundamentals." He also got the impression that the chief executive was a very tired man, who seemed unaware of how fatigued he was. The young, vigorous colonel detected "the gray look of an overworked businessman" and noticed the flat, even tone of voice that comes from "a mind dulled by too much and too frequent conversation. It has that dull quality that comes to any one of the senses when it is overused: taste, with too much of the same food day after day; hearing, when the music never changes; touch, when one's hand is never lifted."

In the months that followed, Lindbergh talked with the men who constituted the U.S. aviation establishment, visited the drafting rooms and factories where aircraft were being designed and built, and reported to Arnold and other Air Corps chiefs his conviction that only by instituting a significant research and development program could the nation catch up with the European countries, even in five years. As August wore on, his thoughts were continuously on Europe and the imminent likelihood of war: he was reminded of the tense hours before Munich, except that now, in the United States, he did not sense the same atmosphere of apprehension and depression he had felt in England a year earlier.

On August 28 he received a telegram from his friend Truman Smith, who was now in Washington after four years as military attaché for air with the U.S. embassy in Berlin. The message read simply, "Yes, 80," which was Smith's estimate of the percentage probability of war. It started Lindbergh to wondering if anything he might say in a radio broadcast would be constructive, perhaps helping in some way to halt Europe's rush to battle, but then came Friday, September 1, and the huge headlines: GERMAN TROOPS ENTER POLAND. "The future of the human world hangs in the balance today," the flier wrote in his journal. "This war will change all of our lives." Along with millions of people everywhere, he speculated about what Britain and France would do and concluded that if they tried to break through Germany's West Wall in an effort to support Poland they would surely lose the war before America entered the fight. What in the world were the two allies thinking of? he wondered. Why, if they wanted to prevent the Germans from moving eastward, had they chosen this particular set of circumstances as an excuse to go to war? He had heard that Chamberlain had not even consulted his general staff before making the Polish alliance, and now people everywhere were asking why the governments of Britain and France had not yet declared war. Lindbergh spoke about that to his wife, Anne, who replied, "Maybe they've talked to a general."

What stand should the United States take? Lindbergh kept asking himself. He and Anne listened to Roosevelt's radio talk on Sunday evening, September 3, and the next morning read in the paper that the Cunard liner *Athenia,* carrying fourteen hundred passengers, had been torpedoed off the Hebrides and that German troops were overrunning Poland. On September 7, Lindbergh made up his mind. "I do not intend to stand by and see this country pushed into war if it is not absolutely essential to the future welfare of the nation," he decided. "Much as I dislike taking part in politics and public life, I intend to do so if necessary to stop the trend which is now going on in this country." On September 10 he made a brief entry in his journal: "Phoned Bill Castle and Fulton Lewis. Decided to go on the radio next week."

William R. Castle was a conservative Republican who had served in the State Department during the Harding and Coolidge administrations, to become under secretary of state under Hoover. At Castle's home Lindbergh had met Fulton Lewis, Jr., a conservative (some thought reactionary) commentator who appeared nightly on the Mutual Broadcasting System, and had heard him describe an instance in which "Jewish advertising firms" threatened to remove their sponsorship if a certain program was carried by Mutual. The network, Lewis added, had decided to drop the feature. "I do not blame the Jews so much for their attitude," Lindbergh observed, "although I think it unwise from their own standpoint." When Castle suggested that Lindbergh speak out against U.S. involvement in the European war, Lewis said he could make arrangements for a network broadcast, and it was later agreed that the address would be carried on Friday evening, September 15, by Mutual. When this news was released, NBC and CBS also decided to carry the speech.

The day before the broadcast, Lindbergh informed Hap Arnold of his plans, and the Air Corps chief suggested that he go on inactive duty while he was actively involved in politics. Arnold read the speech Lindbergh was going to deliver, agreed that it contained nothing that could be considered unethical, and asked if he planned to show it to Woodring. The colonel replied that he had no confidence in the secretary of war, and as he said so he "could tell from Arnold's eyes that he was on my side." He decided not to let Woodring read the talk. The following day Arnold reported this conversation to Woodring and let Lindbergh know that the secretary was "very much displeased." Woodring's reaction had been to state sourly that he "had hoped to make use of" Lindbergh in the future, whatever that might mean, but that any such plans were out of the question now. The next day Truman Smith told him that the administration was deeply troubled by his intention to take an active role in this touchy political matter, and Smith had been authorized to inform him that if he did not make the broadcast a cabinet post of secretary of air would be created and he would be appointed to the job.

Having sized up Roosevelt as a political animal, Lindbergh was not surprised that he would resort to such a ploy; what astonished him was that the president would think that he, Lindbergh, might be influenced. Since the offer had come from Woodring to Arnold to Smith, it was evident that word of it would get around, and the colonel thought it a great mistake for the president "to let the Army know he deals in such a way." (When Smith was told by Arnold to take the offer to Lindbergh, he asked the general if he thought the flier would accept it. "Of course not," was Arnold's immediate reply.)

And so, at 9:45 on Friday evening, September 15, the only man in the United States who could rival Franklin Roosevelt for the public's attention stood before six microphones in the Carlton Hotel and made the first broadcast in what would become his crusade against American intervention in the war.

In a clipped, slightly nasal tone he declared that the war just begun was a continuation of "an age-old struggle between the nations of Europe." His voice sounded unnatural to Anne, even though it was "strong and even and clear." She was sitting in the hotel room with a group of friends and network technicians, praying that the American people might understand, that they might realize how difficult it was for her husband to give this speech, turning his back on the France and England that had given their family sanctuary.

"Our safety does not lie in fighting European wars," he was saying. "It lies in our own internal strength, in the character of the American people and of American institutions." Western civilization itself was at risk, he went on, and if Europe was prostrated by war, then the only hope for the survival of those rich traditions and culture lay in America's hands. "By staying out of war," he said, "we may even bring peace to Europe more quickly. Let us look to our own defenses and our own character. . . ." Behind this view lay his certainty that Germany was far more powerful militarily than either France or Great Britain, and that the only way Hitler could possibly be defeated would be in a long, exhausting war. Lindbergh was by nature a questioner and a seeker, and when he asked himself whether the consequences of such a terrible struggle could be measured in terms of winning or losing, he was sure that victory could not possibly be worth what it would cost the United States.

Elaborating again and again on this basic theme, during the course of the next year Lindbergh would make a dozen major addresses—four of them on network radio—speak at major public rallies, write several magazine articles, testify before congressional committees, and devote countless hours to discussions with leaders of the noninterventionist movement. (He considered most of the latter hopelessly conservative, incapable of assuming positions of national leadership, and though he was with them on this particular issue, he was not one of them.) Almost as important as the dedication he brought to his self-appointed task, according to a man who shared speakers' platforms with him, was the way he "evokes a fervor, a tension, such as an ambitious politician would give anything to arouse. Hitler has the same thing; Roosevelt has it sometimes; Huey Long used to get it, and Coughlin, occasionally. I know Lindbergh doesn't seek it, especially, and does nothing to stir it, but it's there."

As a result of his increasing involvement in the debate, he suddenly became one of the most controversial figures in American politics, feared and reviled by the administration, which perceived him—quite accurately—as the most forceful opponent of the president's foreign policy and the man most likely to appeal to and influence the public. Indeed, the immediate reaction to Lindbergh's first speech was overwhelmingly favorable: it was front-page news in the New York and Washington papers; telegrams and letters from all over the country greeted the colonel and his wife when they returned home from Washington, including one from Herbert Hoover congratulating him on "a really great address" and a polite note from General Arnold saying that he and Secretary Woodring thought the speech "very well worded and very well delivered." Several days later, when Lindbergh called on Hoover in New York City, the former president suggested that a nonpolitical organization should be formed to keep the country out of war, and he hoped that Lindbergh would play a significant role in it.

There were brickbats as well as roses: it was only a matter of days before the opposition was in full cry. Dorothy Thompson lashed out at Lindbergh in her column, calling him the "pro-Nazi recipient of a German medal." ("I expected this," Anne Lindbergh said, "but not from her.") And that was but a beginning. As the great debate over America's neutrality grew ever more passionate and strident, Lindbergh and his wife would discover that old friends dropped them, that streets honoring the hero of the first solo transatlantic flight had been renamed. Harold Ickes, who was known for good reason as "the old curmudgeon" (privately, it seems, FDR referred to his secretary of interior as "Donald Duck"), was to say publicly what many of Lindbergh's political enemies were thinking: "How can any American accept a decoration at the hand of a brutal dictator who, with that same hand, is robbing and torturing thousands of fellow human beings? Perhaps Henry Ford [who had also been decorated by the Nazis] and Colonel Charles A. Lindbergh will be willing to answer." To cap it all, the president of the United States would insult him publicly by likening him to Clement Vallandigham, the Ohio congressman who spoke, during the Civil War, for a group called the Copperheads and predicted the North would never win.

CHAPTER 21

"... you will send your boys back to the slaughter pens of Europe."

I n Poland, autumn blessed the German invaders with what they called "Hitler weather": day after day dawned sunny and hot, baking meadows and grain fields to the consistency of concrete, enabling Guderian's motorized columns to travel crosslots whenever highways were blocked. The day before Charles Lindbergh's broadcast, the Germans surrounded the city of Warsaw and demanded its unconditional surrender.

The answer was defiance: civilians and soldiers dug in for a siege. Then, suddenly, the Russians struck: on September 17, Stalin, having let his new allies do all the fighting, sent his own troops streaming across the undefended eastern frontier of Poland, and a dismayed world saw photographs of Russian and German troops—until a month before the most unreconcilable of enemies—laughing and shaking hands on the bank of the Bug River, which delineated their respective occupation zones. The Soviet excuse for the attack, incorporated in a note from Foreign Minister Vyacheslav Molotov, was cabled to Washington by Laurence Steinhardt, the U.S. ambassador in Moscow. Russian soldiers, Molotov declared loftily, had "entered East Poland to protect the lives and property of the populations of the western Ukraine and western White Russia." Poland's capital, swollen with refugees, was being hit by round-the-clock air assaults, artillery bombardment, and gunfire from approaching tanks and infantry, but every thirty seconds Radio Warsaw broadcast a few bars of Chopin's "Polonaise Militaire" as evidence that the ancient city was still free and in Polish hands.

On September 25, from the roof of a sports stadium, Adolf Hitler watched through binoculars while his artillery pounded the capital. Millions of leaflets urging surrender were dropped from planes, but there was no sign of submission from the Polish commander. On the 26th, under cover of an artillery barrage, German infantry units moved forward, and on the 28th, instead of the polonaise, a funeral dirge was heard over the air, followed shortly by a triumphant "Deutschland über Alles." For seven days Warsaw had had no water, no food, no electricity; the mayor of the prostrate city estimated the dead at forty thousand—most of them lying unburied in the ruins. Within hours of the city's surrender, Heinrich Himmler's dreaded Schutzstaffel (SS) began rounding up Jews and other "enemies of the Reich"—clergy, intellectuals, nobility, members of any group that might constitute a core of resistance. The operation was known in SS and Gestapo parlance as a "housecleaning," a euphemism for what General Wilhelm Keitel called "demographic extermination."

———

While men and women desperate for food hacked chunks of flesh from dead horses in the streets of Warsaw, members of the U.S. Congress returned grudgingly to the heat of Washington. The president had summoned them to the capital for a special session, two days after writing Neville Chamberlain, "I hope and believe that we shall repeal the embargo next month. . . ." Now that Europe was actually at war he thought he could count on the legislators to repeal the arms embargo provisions of the nation's neutrality laws and restore the system of cash-and-carry that had expired several months before the fighting erupted. "I regret that the Congress passed that Act [of 1935]," Roosevelt told them. "I regret equally that I signed that Act."

It took very little imagination to understand why. Since Germany had no merchant fleet worthy of the name and—for the present—had adequate manufacturing facilities and raw materials, the terms of the law were of little moment to that country. Britain and France were the nations that stood to benefit from repeal, since they were in a position to purchase American munitions and carry them across the Atlantic (though Great Britain, it would become clear before long, with her cargo vessels increasingly under attack by German submarines and aircraft and her supply of gold steadily diminishing, would find the cash-and-carry terms impossible to honor). There was yet another factor that had to be confronted by any congressman whose constituents were out of work: when Roosevelt on September 5 proclaimed the Neutrality Act to be in effect, the large armaments orders placed with American industries by Britain and France had automatically been frozen. Lifting the embargo would permit them to be filled.

One of the oddities about this struggle to change the neutrality law was that the two staunchest apostles of change, two individuals charged with formulating and executing the foreign policy of the republic, each a widely popular, respected man, were currently viewed with deep suspicion, if not actual distrust, by members of the Congress and public alike, who believed that the president and his secretary of state were secretly conniving to involve the nation in what should remain Europe's quarrel. A chief cause of that mistrust was that most Americans wanted at all costs to steer clear of the problems brought on by aggressor nations and international lawlessness and couldn't understand why any sensible person would feel otherwise. Unlike their critics on Capitol Hill and among the public, however, Roosevelt and Hull had far greater access to privileged information than any representative or senator (William E. Borah's claims to the contrary notwithstanding), and both men, moreover, were obliged to think in broad-gauge terms, considering the national interest within an international framework, unlike the average congressman, who viewed the world with a parochial eye.

Roosevelt had been in the hot seat of the presidency long enough to have grown accustomed to attacks both personal and political, but Cordell Hull was still smarting from the slur on his beloved department by Senator Borah, and Hull was no man to forget or forgive. Now sixty-eight years old, the secretary was a lean, soft-spoken six-footer who had entered this life in a rented log cabin in the Cumberland Mountains of Tennessee. According to his father, an energetic country trader named William Hull, as a young man "Cord wasn't set enough to be a school teacher, wasn't rough enough to be a lumberman, wasn't sociable enough to be a doctor, and couldn't holler loud enough to be a preacher. But Cord was a right thorough thinker." And right thorough thinking had led Cordell, by the time he was eighteen, into Tennessee politics, where he was elected to the legislature a year after he was old enough to vote. Afterward he served in the Spanish-American War, became a circuit court judge, and in 1906 was elected to the United States Congress. First as a representative, then as a senator, and later as FDR's secretary of state, Hull relentlessly pursued two particular goals: passage of an income tax (he drafted the Underwood Tariff Act, the federal income tax legislation of 1913) and free trade.

By 1939 the income tax had been a fact of life for many years, but the protective tariff remained "the king of evils" in Hull's book, because it taxed consumers to subsidize manufacturers, thereby abetting monopoly and fostering hostility among nations. As a man truly dedicated to the cause of world peace, Hull was a tireless foe of protectionism, and his labors on behalf of the administration's Good Neighbor policy toward the nations of Latin America earned him several nominations for the Nobel Prize—an honor that would finally come his way in 1945.

Beneath a statesmanlike exterior that suggested old-fashioned Southern courtliness and courtesy, Hull was suspicious by nature, alert for hint of

A group of Jews is herded from the burning Warsaw ghetto by Nazi SS squads. Notice the little girl, walking between an older man and woman at right in the front row.

grievance or slight. He possessed the convictions of a fundamentalist who knows beyond the shadow of a doubt that he is right, and when his temper got the better of him he could string together some rich frontier expletives in a high-pitched voice, often starting with an angry "Jesus Cwist!" (he had a slight lisp, and his r's tended to become w's when he was agitated). As a man reared in an area where blood feuds were not uncommon (after the Civil War, Hull's father hunted down a Kentuckian who had severely wounded him in a guerrilla raid and shot him dead on the main street of his hometown), Hull was a good hater. People who knew him liked to say that he carried a long knife.

Most of the time, Roosevelt and the Tennesseean worked well together, the president's resourcefulness and ability to roll with a punch complementing the secretary's caution and rigidity. Now, while Roosevelt worked his side of the street to line up support for repeal of the neutrality legislation, Hull helped Judge Samuel Rosenman draft the chief executive's speech to Congress (avoiding any mention of the possibility that lifting the embargo might benefit Great Britain or France—which would have been "the peak of folly," in Hull's opinion). And when he wasn't lobbying members of the Senate Foreign Relations Committee, he was soothing the ministers of friendly foreign countries, assuring them that terms of the revised bill would not adversely affect their commerce with the United States.

The focus of this maneuvering was the coming confrontation with noninterventionists in Congress, of course, but beyond that it had to do with the constituency those members represented—a matter of continuous and considerable concern to the occupant of the White House. In that very month of September 1939, in the wake of the brutal attack on Poland, a Roper public opinion poll revealed that Colonel Lindbergh was not alone in his beliefs—indeed, that 30 percent of all Americans wanted nothing whatever to do with any warring nation, not even trade on a cash-and-carry basis. Another 37 percent wished to "take no sides and stay out of the war entirely," though they would agree to sell arms to belligerents on cash-and-carry terms. Between them, then, those two groups represented two thirds of the American public. Only 2.5 percent of those polled expressed a willingness to enter the war at once on the side of England, France, and Poland.

Within that 67 percent of the populace was an astonishing range of political opinion and religious and racial prejudice—folk of just about every persuasion imaginable, all of them feeling intensely about an issue that might so easily alter the lives of their families and the future of their country. There was, to repeat, the long-standing disillusionment over the military slaughter and political consequences of the First World War, plus resentment that America's only reward for its role in saving the world for democracy was to be stigmatized as "Uncle Shylock"; but there was also an ingrained suspicion of "foreigners" (although every American family had come originally from somewhere else). Besides which, it was an almost universal article of faith that this country was big enough and powerful enough to go it alone; that the United States, secure behind two oceans, had no business bailing out the French and English, whose stupidity at Munich had brought about the mess they were in. (Herbert Hoover and Ohio's Senator Robert A. Taft were among the many believers in the security of geography; what was more, Roosevelt's predecessor declared confidently, the Allies would win without any help from us.)

Composing the hard-core 30 percent who would "have nothing to do with any warring country" was a real Mulligan stew of conflicting passions, loyalties, and affiliations. There were clergymen and liberals with the most sincere pacifist convictions. There were the native fascist (and essentially anti-Semitic and subversive) organizations—Fritz Kuhn's German-American Bund, William Dudley Pelley's Silver Shirt Legion, George Deathrage's Knights of the White Camellia, Joseph E. McWilliams's Christian Mobilizers, the Christian Front, which boasted 200,000 members loyal to Father Coughlin, and the Lord only knew how many others. Now that Hitler and Stalin were allies, the brew also included former Communist Party members and fellow travelers. There were the hyphenated Americans—Irish-Americans, German-Americans, Italian-Americans, first- and second-generation Americans from the Scandinavian countries. There were disciples of Roosevelt-hating bigots like Father Coughlin and Gerald L. K. Smith, and workers who belonged to Communist-dominated unions, and those under the powerful spell of John L. Lewis, president of the United Mine Workers and its parent organization, the CIO, who had had a change of heart about the man in the White House and had become the most outspoken Roosevelt-hater of them all. Isolationism had the rabid, daily support of the Hearst papers and the McCormick-Patterson press—notably Colonel Robert R. McCormick's *Chicago Tribune*. In Congress its chief spear carriers, in addition to Borah, Johnson, Wheeler, and Nye, included Joseph W. Martin, Jr., of Massachusetts, Arthur Vandenberg of Michigan, Robert M. La Follette, Jr., of Wisconsin, Hamilton Fish of New York, and John E. Rankin of Mississippi. There were, in addition, businessmen, educators, writers and editors, liberals and conservatives, Democrats and Republicans of every stripe, not to mention millions of ordinary, middle-of-the-road citizens without labels whose response to world events was more emotional than reasoned, and who simply didn't want their sons sent off to be killed in a European war.

Although interventionists and noninterventionists alike tended to support the modest amount of rearming that had begun belatedly in the United States, on grounds that we had to be able to defend our own country against hostile attack, dyed-in-the-wool isolationists could see secret alliances and plots behind every door—most particularly the porticoed door to 1600 Pennsylvania Avenue in Washington, D.C. George Holden Tinkham, a vain, unreconstructed conservative with a high, bald head and a huge hooked nose that appeared on the verge of spearing his heavy, spade-shaped beard, had represented the 11th District of Massachusetts in Congress since

1915, and he knew exactly what Roosevelt was up to: "A sinister secret diplomacy is now directing American foreign policy [with] collusive political engagements between the United States and Great Britain," he announced darkly.

No less a Republican, no less suspicious of what Roosevelt had up his sleeve, was Arthur Vandenberg, a level-headed, responsible senator from Michigan, who believed firmly that it was the responsibility of the United States to safeguard the western hemisphere. Period. Honest, conscientious, and an indefatigable doer, Vandenberg had had a successful career as a newspaper editor in Grand Rapids before being appointed to serve out the unexpired term of a senator who had died in office. After he was reelected on his own he became a leader of the "young Turks" rebelling against the Republican Old Guard (to be denounced as "the sons of the wild jackasses" by crusty Senator George Moses of New Hampshire). In the congressional elections of 1934, Vandenberg survived the New Deal landslide, and in his second full term he played a prominent role on Gerald Nye's committee investigating the munitions industry and helped to frame the neutrality legislation of 1937. By 1939 he was a national figure, widely regarded as the most respectable spokesman for the noninterventionists, and as the battle for repeal of the arms embargo heated up, he wrote, "The story of 1917–18 is already repeating itself. Pressure and propaganda are at work to drive us into the new World War." He predicted, "The same emotions which demand the repeal of the embargo will subsequently demand still more effective aid for Britain, France, and Poland. . . ."

What troubled Vandenberg above all was what he termed Roosevelt's "treacherous idea that we can help these countries by 'methods short of war.' My quarrel is with this notion that America can be half in and half out of this war . . . which—if we are really in earnest about this business of 'helping the democracies'—is utterly cowardly as a public policy for a great country like ours." Vandenberg was as much opposed to Nazism and communism as the next man, but he could not swallow the argument that you could stop what was happening in Europe without going to war.

He was also a realist about the protection afforded the United States by its ocean barriers. "It is probably impossible," he remarked, "that there should be such a thing as old-fashioned isolation in this present foreshortened world when one can cross the Atlantic Ocean in 36 hours." Probably the best we could hope for, he concluded, "is 'insulation' rather than isolation. I should say that an 'insulationist' is one who wants to preserve all of the isolation which modern circumstances will permit."

The president was under no illusions that he might win over the likes of Congressman Tinkham or Senator Vandenberg, but he was certainly going after everyone whose vote might be susceptible to change, meanwhile performing one of the most exquisite balancing acts ever seen on the White House stage, leaning first this way, then that, going out of his way not to affront, not to ruffle any feathers, taking every conceivable care to avoid offending a potential ally. He once remarked to his close friend and adviser Judge Rosenman, "It is a terrible thing to look over your shoulder when you are trying to lead—and find no one there." As matters stood just now, he held three cards and was drawing to an inside straight and he needed all the luck he could get. When the governor-general of Canada, Lord Tweedsmuir,[1] asked if he might "slip down inconspicuously" to Roosevelt's Hyde Park home, the president urged him to put off a visit until the repeal fight was over. "I am almost literally walking on eggs," he wrote; "I am at the moment saying nothing, seeing nothing, and hearing nothing." At a press conference on September 8, after issuing a Proclamation of Limited Emergency, he blandly told reporters, "There is no thought in any shape, manner, or form, of putting the nation, either in its defenses or in its internal economy, on a war basis. That is one thing we want to avoid. We are going to keep the nation on a peace basis, in accordance with peacetime authorizations." When he pleaded with Congress on September 21 to repeal the Neutrality Act, his message might have been mistaken for Lindbergh's: he stressed that his goal was peace through noninvolvement, that repeal offered "far greater safeguards than we now possess or have ever possessed to protect American lives and property from danger." And all the while he was calling in every marker at his disposal. Friendly mayors, governors, congressmen, and businessmen were asked to help; cabinet officers were sent off in search of votes; the loyal opposition was enlisted. The president arranged for such leading Republicans as Alfred M. Landon, Henry L. Stimson, who had served as Taft's secretary of war and Hoover's secretary of state, and Colonel Frank Knox, a Rough Rider with Teddy Roosevelt and publisher of the *Chicago Daily News,* to reply to radio addresses by Borah, Nye, Vandenberg, Father Coughlin, Lindbergh, and others, which had produced such a deluge of mail that some senators were receiving four thousand impassioned messages a day. Landon and Knox were invited to a conference at the White House with congressional leaders of both parties. William Allen White, editor of the *Emporia Gazette* and a respected Republican, was persuaded to launch an organization with the jawbreaking title Non-Partisan Committee for Peace Through Revision of the Neutrality Law, which vigorously supported the presidential efforts.

Two considerations were paramount in Roosevelt's mind. In the first place, he could hardly avoid the thought that his success—or failure—in this campaign for repeal was bound to have an effect on the future of Britain and France, on the course of history, in fact. Of secondary concern, but important nonetheless to one who was by temperament and practice an intensely political man, was the impact his actions in the fall of 1939 might have on the campaign and election of 1940. He was in the final year of his second term and there was a sanctified tradition going back to George

[1]The first Baron Tweedsmuir was better known to Americans as Sir John Buchan, author of *The Thirty-nine Steps* and some thirty-seven other works of fiction and nonfiction.

Washington that that would be that—there *were* no third terms for American presidents. Even so, if he announced now that he did not intend to seek reelection, he would be a lame duck with little influence on the direction of foreign policy and diminished authority and prestige abroad. And Roosevelt was no man to yield authority or prestige willingly. Contrariwise, if he *did* announce that he would seek another term he would certainly be regarded less as a president than as a highly controversial candidate, thereby subjecting his party and the nation to violent political schisms in the year ahead.

Roosevelt's solution was entirely in character: to do nothing and say nothing that might even suggest what he had in mind. And while he remained sphinxlike about his plans, the neutrality debate raged in Congress for six weeks, with the president and his supporters on one side, isolationists on the other. Senator Borah, warning that revision of the act would signal to the whole world that America had taken sides, predicted in a speech that went on all afternoon, "You will send munitions without pay, and you will send your boys back to the slaughter pens of Europe." It was the old man's swan song, and the visitors who packed the Senate gallery knew it when they heard his voice, so thin it was difficult to make out what he said. The fire had gone out, and one reporter was reminded of an aged actor whose reputation outlasts the ability to speak his lines.[2]

In the end, in the manner of most American political solutions before and since, a compromise resulted, and the United States entered a twilit zone that lay somewhere between peace and involvement in the war. The onset of fighting had a lot to do with that solution, obviously, but so did skillful lobbying tactics by the White House and Democratic legislative leaders, who succeeded in changing the minds and votes of many congressmen. In the House, for instance, the administration picked up support from twenty-eight Democrats and nine Republicans who had not voted on the issue the last time it was put before them, and changed the votes of twenty-four Democrats and eight Republicans who previously had opposed any change in the neutrality law. At that, how the principal protagonists perceived the outcome depended on the point of view. When an elated president signed the Neutrality Act of 1939 on November 4, Cordell Hull felt that "we had won a great battle," but regretted that victory had not come sooner—in the spring or summer, when it would have been more beneficial to the Allies. From the opposition came Arthur Vandenberg's observation "We were beaten 63 to 30 [in the Senate]. But we won a great moral victory. . . . It is going to be much more difficult for FDR to lead the country into war." The senator's feeling of elation was qualified, though: "In the name of 'democracy' we have taken the first step, once more, into Europe's power politics," he wrote. "What suckers our emotions make of us!" He and his

---

[2]Somewhat surprisingly, Borah confessed privately that he favored cash-and-carry, but said he had to put up a fight "so as to keep the president from leading us into war."

fellow isolationists were as certain as they were about anything in life that repeal would lead inevitably to America's involvement in the fighting, and two years later, when they were proved right, Vandenberg recorded in his diary that we had "openly embraced" and "*nominated ourselves* as active participants" in the belligerent cause "when we repealed the arms embargo."

The president got his way, for the most part. The arms embargo was repealed, permitting weapons of war to be purchased by all belligerents (meaning, for all practical purposes, the British and the French) on a cash-and-carry basis. But for fear that the isolationists might carry the day against repeal, Secretary Hull had been obliged to suggest a compromise by which a number of "combat zones" were forbidden to American ships and travelers. What this meant was the closing off of certain Atlantic and Baltic sea routes to more than ninety U.S. ships earning some $52 million annually. As one observer noted sourly, it "aided the German blockade of Britain as effectively as if all our ships had been torpedoed."

Never mind Cordell Hull's brave talk of a victory won. For the next two years the administration would almost never make a move in the field of foreign policy without an uneasy backward glance to see if the opposition might be gaining.

CHAPTER 22

"When people fight like that, personal enmity is lost."

Summer turned to autumn and autumn toward winter, and Europe's war became a daily presence in America's households, asserting itself in somber black headlines and a mounting tide of news broadcasts. On September 3, 1939, two days after the Germans invaded Poland, and even before Britain and France had fumbled their way to a declaration of war, a Nazi submarine torpedoed the British liner *Athenia* off the Hebrides, killing 112 people, including twenty-eight Americans. Two weeks later, five hundred British seamen were lost when HMS *Courageous,* an aging aircraft carrier, was sunk in the Bristol Channel, off the west coast of England. On the moonless night of October 14, the same day the Russians came swarming across the frontier into Poland, German U-boat 47, commanded by Lieutenant Gunther Prien, picked its way through the intricate channels, swirling tides, and man-made hazards protecting the main anchorage of the British fleet at Scapa Flow, in the Orkney Islands north of Scotland, and sank the battleship *Royal Oak,* killing 786 officers and men.

Then, as an object lesson in how difficult it was going to be for even a determinedly neutral nation to remain isolated from Europe's conflict, Americans read with mounting indignation and dismay the saga of the *City of Flint.* In the third week of September, the little black-hulled American freighter, commanded by a lean, hard-bitten Yankee named Joseph Gainard,[1] had steamed into the harbor at Halifax, Nova Scotia, carrying 223 survivors from the *Athenia*. After returning to the States, she picked up a cargo in New York, cleared the Narrows on October 3, and headed off into the Atlantic's rolling swells, bound for Liverpool, England. Her estimated time of arrival came and went without a sign of the ship; then a passenger, James G. McConnochie, turned up in Bergen, Norway, with a story that the *City of Flint* had been overhauled in midocean on October 9 by the German pocket battleship *Deutschland*. What evidently saved the American freighter from being sunk was its large cargo of oil, which was useful to the Germans; the captain of the warship transferred thirty-eight survivors from the British ship *Stonegate,* which had been torpedoed by the *Deutschland,* put a prize crew aboard, and slipped off in search of other prey.

The prize crew, bristling with pistols and daggers, set a course north by northeast, heading for the icebergs and cruel winter seas of the North Atlantic. After putting a time bomb in the engine room in case the British caught them, they removed evidence of the *Flint*'s American registry by painting out the U.S. flags on the sides of the vessel, changed her name to *Alf,* and hoisted a homemade Danish flag. Eleven days later, now flying German colors, they made port in Tromsö, on the west coast of Norway above the Arctic Circle, where the authorities let them take on water after they released the British prisoners (with whom McConnochie escaped), but insisted that the American flags be repainted before the ship cleared for Murmansk, in Russia. When last seen by McConnochie, the *Flint* was hugging the coast, heading toward the North Cape, the Barents Sea, and Murmansk.

[1]Two years earlier, Gainard had been at the center of another drama on the high seas. President Roosevelt, in September of 1937, had just finished warning members of the National Federation of Federal Employees that "militant tactics have no place in the function of an organization of government employees" when the crew of the SS *Algic* went on strike in the Río de la Plata off Montevideo. Uruguayan longshoremen had walked off the job, and the crew of the *Algic* refused to help unload cargo onto a lighter in midstream—swore, in fact, that they would not work with scab longshoremen until the river froze solid (which it never does, even in midwinter). Now, going on strike when a ship is docked in a home port is bad enough, but to do so when the vessel is outside U.S. waters is considered mutiny.

Captain Gainard reported the situation to the U.S. vice consul in Montevideo, who went aboard and tried to talk sense to the mutineers, but they stuck to their guns. Gainard then cabled the owner of the the the 5,496-ton freighter—the owner in this case being the National Maritime Commission, whose boss was Joseph Patrick Kennedy—and the reply was immediate and unequivocal: "Instruct crew to proceed with your lawful orders. If they refuse, place ringleaders in irons. . . ." If that didn't change their minds, the message continued, Gainard was to remove striking crew members from the ship and give their jobs to other Americans, if available, and if not, to foreign seamen.

The crew returned to duty, and Kennedy, summing up the official government attitude, declared: "The Maritime Commission takes the position that the action of the crew is unlawful . . . that such an act constitutes a strike against the government. Neither situation can be tolerated."

To the British, those freed prisoners carried the worst possible news: that the *Deutschland,* and possibly her sister ships *Admiral Scheer* and *Admiral Graf Spee,* were at large as raiders. Those warships were ingenious by-products of naval restrictions placed on Germany by the Versailles Treaty: forbidden to build vessels larger than ten thousand tons, German designers had produced "pocket battleships" that were faster, lighter, and more heavily gunned than any ships of similar tonnage in the world, and a match for anything the British might send after them, save the battle cruisers *Hood, Repulse,* and *Renown.*

To the Soviet Union, and to Laurence Steinhardt, the United States ambassador in Moscow, the arrival of the *Flint* in Kola Bay, north of Murmansk harbor, created a real test of diplomacy. Here was a U.S. ship, flying a German flag, with a German prize crew holding twoscore American seamen captive, and it was clear to Steinhardt that the runaround he was getting from the foreign office meant that the Russians were caught in a real bind. If the captured vessel were permitted to remain in port, the USSR would be violating international law. If the Soviet Union chose to release the ship to the American owner, the action would certainly antagonize Stalin's prickly ally, Adolf Hitler. The compromise solution was a form of Russian roulette for the forty-one Americans on board; the *Flint* was finally permitted to sail from Murmansk flying the Nazi swastika—on the one hand risking capture or sinking by British warships, on the other facing a thirteen-hundred-mile winter voyage through blockaded waters and fifty miles of known minefields, in order to reach a German port.

In the first week of November the *Flint* put into Tromsö again, seeking supplies. The German consul boarded the ship, held whispered conversations with the prize chief, and went ashore, whereupon the uneasy Norwegians, having furnished no supplies, escorted the *Flint* to sea. Sixty miles south of Bergen the *Flint* dropped anchor in Haugesund. The German prize chief went ashore and informed the local officials that he was under orders to put in there, after which the Norwegians promptly interned the German crew and turned the ship over to Captain Gainard. Berlin had decided not to risk a North Sea crossing or the loss of face resulting from giving the ship back to the Americans, and as a way out, deliberately sought internment of the prize crew, knowing it was only a matter of time before the men would be released. Hitler had plans for Norway.

As for the *City of Flint,* on January 27, 1940, the rusty, ice-flecked freighter finally docked at Baltimore, having been out for 116 days.[2]

---

[2]Captain Gainard had skirted disaster throughout his career, having been torpedoed aboard a transport vessel in World War I while serving as an ensign in the naval reserve. For his distinguished service, skill, judgment, and devotion to duty aboard the *City of Flint* he received the first Navy Cross to be awarded in the Second World War, but in 1943 his luck ran out: he was killed while commanding a naval transport.

Less than two weeks before the *Flint* first vanished in the Atlantic mists, to be seized by the *Deutschland,* an inter-American conference initiated by President Roosevelt had met in Panama, its purpose to devise hemispheric neutrality plans and some means of dealing with financial and trade problems the European war was bound to create. The administration's fear was that economic instability in Latin America would inevitably invite inroads by the Nazis, and that commercial and financial footholds would be followed by the establishment of military bases from which submarines could prey on Allied shipping.

In the meeting that began on September 23, twenty-one remarkably united American republics endorsed the proposals presented by Under Secretary of State Sumner Welles, the U.S. delegate; established an Inter-American Neutrality Committee and a Financial and Economic Advisory Committee; and—in what was called the Declaration of Panama—designated an area beginning south of Canada and extending from three hundred to a thousand miles off the Atlantic coast, which was to be "free from the commission of any hostile act by any non-American belligerent."

How the war at sea was to be prevented from spilling over into this "maritime security zone" was unclear, for even though the signers of the Declaration of Panama undertook to maintain patrols, the U.S. Navy informed President Roosevelt that effective reconnaissance of this enormous area was out of the question, and the European belligerents immediately condemned the neutral zone as a violation of freedom of the seas. (The British understandably refused to accept the concept unless the United States assured them that the Germans would not use it as a privileged sanctuary.) As passionately as the American republics might avow their faith in a world "not based on violence but on justice and law," the impossibility of keeping Europe's war from intruding on the western hemisphere would be demonstrated in spectacular fashion before the year was out.

Much as Americans fumed over the Nazis' highhanded treatment of a U.S. merchantman, horrified as they were by graphic evidence in newsreels and magazines of yet another sinking of Allied and neutral ships (*Life*'s issue of December 4 noted that in the first eleven weeks of war, 113 vessels were sunk by mines and U-boats; in the week of November 18 alone, twenty-seven ships were lost—eighteen of them to the new mines the Germans were employing), what dramatized the struggle at sea as nothing else could have done (while revealing the naïveté of that "maritime security zone" notion) was the first real naval engagement of the war, a thriller of a battle that occurred on the western shore of the Atlantic.

At dawn on December 13 the *Admiral Graf Spee,* another of Hitler's pocket battleships, was running down the coast of Brazil when she sighted the French freighter *Formose* plodding along, apparently unescorted. The

Graf Spee was about to fire a warning shot across the Frenchman's bow when the lookout spotted a British cruiser, moving up fast to throw a protective smokescreen around the *Formose.* That proved to be the 6,985-ton *Ajax,* and she was joined in short order by the 7,030-ton *Achilles* and the 8,390-ton *Exeter.* Commodore Henry Harwood, who was responsible for protecting British shipping off the River Plate and Rio de Janeiro, was convinced that the *Graf Spee,* sooner or later, would be tempted by the possibility of prizes in the area, and he had concentrated his available forces to meet her.

The German raider was commanded by Captain Hans Langsdorff, a navy veteran of twenty-seven years who had encountered the British at Jutland in 1916 on the battleship *Grosse Kurfürst* (hit eight times in that battle and then torpedoed, she was scuttled by her crew), and Harwood, aboard the *Ajax,* knew he had a fight on his hands. His two light cruisers carried 6-inch guns, the *Exeter* 8-inchers, but the *Graf Spee* had two turrets of 11-inch guns, six of them all told, plus eight 5.9-inchers, giving her a three-to-one advantage in firepower over Harwood's little squadron. In the circumstances, the Briton's only advantages lay in numbers and speed; his three ships, clean after a recent overhaul at their Falkland Islands base, could make thirty-two knots, while the German battleship, her hull barnacle-covered from weeks at sea, was capable of about twenty-five.

Harwood headed out to sea, trying to flank the *Graf Spee* in order to put the rising sun in the Germans' eyes, hoping at the same time to keep the big ship in shallow water between the British and the coast, and the engagement at once became a running dogfight, the cruisers running out from behind smokescreens long enough to get off a salvo, then ducking back under cover, the *Graf Spee* altering course frequently, firing whenever she could catch a glimpse of the enemy. One lucky hit cost the *Graf Spee* her eyes: a reconnaissance plane on the catapult was smashed and the launching mechanism was so badly jammed that the other plane could not be used. A big shell from the *Exeter* tore a gaping hole in the German's port quarter, and another knocked out her control tower, cutting off lights, telephones, and the central fire control, killing or wounding some of Langsdorff's best plotters and gunnery officers. Every time the German battleship was hit, cheers could be heard belowdecks, where sixty-two British seamen, one of them only fifteen years old, one seventy-two, all of them captives from the *Graf Spee*'s nine earlier victims, listened to the roar of battle.

Meantime, the *Graf Spee*'s big guns had crippled the *Exeter,* virtually demolishing her superstructure, blowing one gun turret to bits, killing five officers and fifty-six men, and wounding twenty-three others, and at 10:00, with the fight already four hours old, *Exeter* limped off toward the Falklands, some fourteen hundred miles to the south. *Ajax* and *Achilles* kept up the attack, working together superbly, each taking its turn driving in toward the wounded *Graf Spee* to fire a salvo, screened by smoke laid down by the other, until several of the German ship's guns were silenced and one 5.9-

inch turret was badly tilted, out of action for good. Langsdorff's only chance was to head into port for repairs, and he set a course for Montevideo. But the British stayed with him, nipping at his heels, and within full view of the headland called Punta del Este, where throngs of Uruguayans had gathered to watch the battle, *Ajax* and *Achilles* managed to slip around and inshore of the *Graf Spee,* so that her starboard side was illuminated by the setting sun while they were camouflaged by the gathering darkness onshore. The fight had been going on for more than fourteen hours without a break, and just before night fell there were two sharp little actions, one of which left the *Graf Spee* with a deadly wound—a hole in the bow, at the waterline, so that she shipped water as she moved through the sea.

Saved by the cover of night, the German raider turned around, backed into the harbor at Montevideo, and dropped anchor. Captain Langsdorff summoned his sixty-two captives and set them free, after giving them a stiff but heartfelt little speech: "The cruisers made a gallant fight. When people fight like that, personal enmity is lost."

Now, as with the *City of Flint,* the diplomats took over, the British maneuvering to have the Uruguayans send the raider back to sea, the Germans trying to prevent it. According to the Hague Convention of 1907, a belligerent ship might remain in a neutral port for only twenty-four hours, unless obliged to repair damage affecting its seaworthiness, so Uruguayan officials went aboard, concluded that the *Graf Spee*'s seaworthiness was indeed impaired, and granted her a seventy-two-hour stay. While the welders went to work, thirty-six swastika-draped bodies were taken ashore for burial, and some sixty wounded were treated.

Outside the Río de la Plata the *Ajax* and *Achilles* patrolled the estuary, searchlights sweeping back and forth across the exit channels all through the night; between them the two ships had eleven dead and eight wounded, comparatively light casualties considering the ferocity of the day's action, and they were spoiling for another crack at the Germans. Meantime rumor fed on rumor as the world waited for news. The carrier *Ark Royal* and the battle cruiser *Renown* were known to have put in to Rio de Janeiro to refuel; the battleship *Barham,* the cruiser *Cumberland,* and the French battleship *Dunkerque* were reportedly waiting over the horizon; the *Graf Spee*'s sister ship, *Admiral Scheer,* and an undisclosed number of German submarines were supposedly on their way; the *Graf Spee* was going to slip across the river mouth to Buenos Aires, to be interned.

At 6:15 on a clear Sunday evening—more than two hours ahead of his deadline—Captain Langsdorff gave orders to weigh anchor and the big ship slipped downstream toward the harbor mouth. The sun was setting, a half-moon had climbed into the sky, clouds drifted slowly overhead, and crowds of curious Uruguayans again lined the harbor and the roofs of buildings to see the excitement. Out in the river the ship slowed and dropped anchor, and men scrambled down the sides into launches. The last to leave the ship was Captain Langsdorff, who stepped into a boat that trailed a long cable. Just as the rim of the sun disappeared, Langsdorff and his officers stood at attention, saluting; the captain pressed a button on the end of the cable, there was an explosion, and flames shot up from below-decks. In three minutes the *Graf Spee,* shrouded by billowing smoke and steam, settled slowly into the mud of the shallow river.

Three days later, after attending the funeral for his dead, Captain Langs-dorff had a long conversation with his officers, then went to his room and put a bullet in his head. Commodore Harwood, who was to be rewarded with a knighthood and promotion to rear admiral, may or may not have known that twenty-five years earlier, to the very month, in a naval battle off the Falkland Islands' Port Stanley, Admiral Graf Spee—namesake of the pocket battleship Harwood had helped destroy—had lost his ship, his battle, and his life.

Photographs of the spectacular naval engagement and its denouement were slow to arrive in the United States, and *Life,* making the best of the situation, published an artist's rendering of the action, showing the track of the British and German warships during the action. The magazine also printed a set of stark photographs showing the last of the German liner *Columbus,* whose captain had orders to scuttle her rather than allow her to be captured by the British. When a British destroyer came in sight off Cape May, New Jersey, 450 miles at sea, Captain William Daehne ordered his crew into lifeboats, opened the sea cocks, and set fire to the big passenger vessel.

═══

Spectacular as they were, it is doubtful if these naval engagements had anything like the impact on *Life*'s readers as the account, in the same issue, of an event the moviegoing public had been anticipating for three years—the world premiere of the motion picture *Gone With the Wind.* In 1936, producer David O. Selznick had purchased the screen rights to Margaret Mitchell's best-selling novel about the Civil War[3] for $50,000, a huge sum for that time, and in an inspired moment of press agentry, announced that

[3]The book—which its author "didn't think worth retyping and trying to sell"—was, of course, one of the great publishing successes of that or any other day. Miss Mitchell, who was Mrs. John R. Marsh, the wife of an advertising executive, began writing it in 1926 when she was twenty-six years old, and she told a friend, "It stinks and I don't know why I bother with it, but I've got to have something to do with my time." She wrote the last chapter first and worked backward from there, and nine years later she had almost finished her gripping tale of a world irredeemably lost when H. L. Latham, an editor at Macmillan who had heard about her manuscript, sought her out. Meeting her in a hotel lobby, he found "a tiny woman sitting on a divan, and beside her the biggest manuscript I have ever seen, towering in two stacks almost up to her shoulders." On June 30, 1936, the novel was published, and eleven people, including Miss Mitchell's father, showed up at the autograph party at Davison's department store in Atlanta; for twenty-one consecutive months thereafter the book was on the best-seller list, with two million copies sold. When the fiftieth anniversary of the novel's publication came around, someone calculated that more than 25 million copies of *Gone With the Wind* had been purchased.

he would conduct a nationwide hunt for a "new face" to play the heroine, Scarlett O'Hara, thereby convincing every aspiring actress that she had a chance at the role. The premiere came to pass, appropriately, in Atlanta, where thousands of cheering fans jammed the streets outside Loew's Grand Theatre to ogle the stars of the film—among them Clark Gable, Leslie Howard, Olivia de Havilland, Hattie McDaniel, and the actress whose selection as Scarlett had set off storms of protest because she was English—Vivien Leigh.

When the show was over, the president-general of the United Daughters of the Confederacy effectively put an end to the carping by declaring that Miss Leigh was "Scarlett to the life." Miss Mitchell seemed genuinely pleased to be introduced to Clark Gable, who played her hero, Rhett Butler, and when asked for her reaction to the premiere, replied, "It was a great thing for Georgia to see the Confederates come back."

Inside the theater, where Georgians had paid $10 and more for admission, at the moment an actor on the screen announced that war between North and South had begun, the audience of two thousand rose as a man and gave the blood-chilling rebel yell. Outside, bands played "Dixie," four ancient Confederate veterans who had probably forgotten what their long-ago war was really like were helped into waiting automobiles, and the president of the Georgia Trust Company, emerging from the theater, said, "I've been crying and, by God, I'm not afraid to say so." When the picture opened in Boston, which had once been the center of opposition to the Old South, seventeen thousand people bought tickets the first day.

If the real war seemed as remote to Americans as the conflict that had swirled about Tara in 1864, it must be remembered that the real war was still young enough for the ideals of another era to linger on, as Captain Langsdorff's final forlorn act had indicated. (The press was careful to point out that the captain was no Nazi, that he would have chosen to fight against odds but had scuttled his ship on orders from Hitler, that he was a product of the imperial German navy and had given the old salute, not the Nazis' outstretched arm, when the *Graf Spee* went down.) Somehow reality and romance had blended in his deed, as they often did in Hollywood: outnumbered, he had fought his crippled ship bravely and skillfully, and when he was beaten fairly had taken the honorable way out, sacrificing his life for an ideal in a gesture that reminded the world of a more chivalrous past when warfare was a contest between champions, or at least between gentlemen.[4]

But the twentieth century's second global war—like the first—would see the death of many such illusions, and those who saw what was coming and

----

[4]Following the captain's funeral, which was attended by an estimated 300,000 Argentineans, many of the *Graf Spee*'s crew members returned to Germany, but at war's end more than half of them came back to Argentina to live, citing their admiration for Langsdorff as a reason for doing so. Into the 1970s, members of the Buenos Aires *Graf Spee* veterans' association still met once a month to drink beer and reminisce.

were determined to be ready for it were not the likes of Margaret Mitchell's Ashley Wilkes, who preferred to watch life go by, who "did not like the outlines of things to be too sharp," but those like tough, realistic Rhett Butler, who had learned that life must be seen for what it is, and dealt with accordingly.

CHAPTER 23

"The democracies are again too late."

One of the genuine oddities of that hazy, mixed-up time was that so many of the young Americans who were most susceptible of being sent to "the slaughter pens of Europe" seemed so unconcerned about the prospect. On college campuses across the nation students entered in September an environment that seemed unchanged, as if unaffected by the turbulent events across the ocean. Years later, a man who began his junior year at Yale in the autumn of 1939 recalled the prewar period as "pleasantly fat and essentially untroubled," with few undergraduates aware that they had an attitude or position on issues.

Yet for others the thirties was a time, as the playwright Arthur Miller wrote of his own undergraduate days at the University of Michigan, when "the spirit of the nation, like its soil, was being blown by crazy winds." As a result of the ferment of ideas generated by the Depression and by the First World War, some of the privileged young who were in college "saw a new world coming every third morning," and years afterward, whenever Miller's thoughts turned to the university library, he could recall the sound of a speaker's voice outside the window and think of how he would look up from what he was reading "to try to hear what issue they were debating now. The place was full of speeches, meetings, and leaflets. It was jumping with Issues." Somehow those Issues—for most young men, at any rate—did not yet translate into the possibility of being called on to fight and perhaps be maimed or killed in a war. Students who took the so-called Oxford Oath, pledging not to bear arms for flag or country, could not imagine that they were helping America remain unprepared any more than they could imagine anyone really wanting war. They were certain that war was the creation of a capitalist society, through its munitions makers and international bankers, and what had to be done was to change society.

———

Saturday, September 23, 1939, was unusually warm for the season in New Haven, Connecticut, but inside the reddish-brown tunnel of Phelps Gateway it was shady and cool, with a breeze blowing, and there a regular stream of pink-faced, perspiring young men paused to enjoy the sensation before emerging onto the sun-dappled lawn of Yale's Old Campus. The moment an incoming freshman, laden with suitcases, a reversible raincoat slung over one shoulder, asked directions to his room—"How do I find Vanderbilt Hall?"—he was greeted by several smilingly aggressive young men who turned out to be classmates and who somehow knew the ropes well enough to have arrived two or three days early in order to sign up latecomers to try out for (it was called "heeling") the *Yale Daily News,* the *Record,* the *Lit,* the *Banner,* the glee club, the football or soccer team, the debating club, the student laundry—there was no limit, apparently, to extracurricular life.

Although averages can be misleading, Professor George Pierson calculated that the 836 individuals who registered with the class of 1943 were eighteen years, four months, and twenty-four days old; five feet ten inches tall (168 of them, including me, stood six feet or more); and weighed 151 pounds. For almost none of them, however, could college be reckoned an average experience, save perhaps for the droves of boys from Andover and Exeter, who seemed to travel in packs and gave the impression of having done just about everything before. For many, this would be the first real time away from home, and to a young man who grew up in the 1930s in Pittsburgh, Pennsylvania, or Parkersburg, West Virginia, or Ponca City, Oklahoma, and found himself entering Yale University thanks to a scholarship or the good luck that his father had enough money,[1] the sensation was a mixture of anticipation and excitement and anxiety unlike anything he had known before.

[1] In that day, with no financial assistance from the university, it was possible to cover all expenses—tuition ($450), room ($200 to $325 a year, depending on size and location), board, books, clothing, travel to and from all but the most distant homes, entertainment, dates, everything—for $2,000 or less. That was my experience, in any case: my father gave me $200 a month for ten months of the year and expected me to take care of all my bills. Of course, if the Consumer Price Index (see the first footnote in Chapter 1) can be applied to such items, and the 1938 dollar was worth 8.3 times that of 1988, my $2,000 expenditure translates to $16,600 today.

To begin with, there was no escaping the awesome, pervasive presence of a great university; wherever you went in New Haven you were never really out of sight of it. An extraordinary collection of turreted, ivy-laden, and generally ugly buildings formed the outer walls of the Old Campus, where the freshmen roomed. Beyond were nine magnificent residential colleges (a tenth, to be known as Silliman, was being completed), each an enclave of tranquillity, its walls enclosing hidden green courtyards, baffling the noise and bustle of a medium-sized city—blocking out the world itself, in fact, creating both the illusion and reality of sanctuary and serenity, but most of all suggesting that here lay the opportunity for learning. Indeed, opportunity was what it was all about—such an opportunity, one suspected, as might not come again in a lifetime.

Some of the awe those 836 young men felt could be laid to the sheer wonder of seeing for the first time the catalogue of courses offered at such an institution—page after page describing what appeared to be the sum total of man's learning, all of it here for the taking. Another aspect of the experience could only be called a sense of liberation, the realization that they were for the first time in life truly on their own, free to go to a double feature at Loew's Poli or drink too much beer at the Knick, to play bridge most of the night with friends or play the piano or read or talk until three in the morning, and what an exhilarating feeling it was! They could play tennis on the university courts or play golf on the university course or swim or play squash at the university gymnasium—and the gym was twelve stories high, for God's sake; and the library—have you seen it?—there must be a million books in the place! They could sneak off in the afternoon to a pizza parlor or the tawdry Lincoln Theatre to catch *Reefer Madness*—a "first-run" film that played for years, recounting the baleful tale of young people forever doomed as a result of taking a puff of marijuana and going berserk ("She took a moment of ecstasy that killed her soul," read the newspaper teaser). They walked through New Haven's interminable rain, singing, joking, hailing new friends on the way to evening meals in Freshman Commons, and occasionally one of them would glance upward and notice the somber names incised in the pediment of the Renaissance-style dining hall: CAMBRAI, ARGONNE, SOMME, CHÂTEAU-THIERRY, YPRES . . . where Yale men just about their age had fallen in the war to end wars only two decades before. Then the student returned to a suite of rooms shared with one other classmate, and before hitting the books some of them would turn on the radio at 7:00 P.M. to listen to the fifteen-minute broadcast by Fred Waring's Pennsylvanians, hoping to hear the great new arrangement of Jerome Kern's haunting hit song, "All the Things You Are."

Everyone on the campus wore jacket and tie—would, indeed, wear jacket and tie to meals, to classes, even to football games, as long as they were undergraduates, and somehow this was part of being an adult and being treated like one, even to being called "Mister" by the professors. All in all, it was a moment to savor, and some young men took immediate and lasting advantage of it, reaching out to grasp and absorb everything in sight; others did not—possibly because they were too young, too naïve, too insecure or undisciplined. Whatever the reason, years later they would regret more than almost anything else their failure to make the most of that golden, bygone opportunity.

It was all beyond knowing, of course, in those radiant September days of 1939, but of the 836 incoming freshmen in Yale's class of 1943, only 518 would graduate three and a half years later, the first group to be "accelerated" on account of the war. And of those 518 graduates, forty-three—8 percent—would lose their lives in that war. "For God, for country, and for Yale," went the final line in the anthem "Bright College Years," and many of those young men had total faith in that sequence as the proper order of loyalties.

The war was going to touch these Yale underclassmen in a way they could not have conceived in that autumn of freshman year, but a few of them, at least, had developed more than a passing interest in what was happening in Europe and had begun to wonder how it might affect them. There was John Tabor, for instance, my close friend and prep-school classmate from Pittsburgh, a thin, black-haired boy whose family had retained its close ties to the Old World. His father, a second-generation Czech, had been decorated twice by the Republic of Czechoslovakia for raising funds for the new nation in the formative years after the World War. A photograph of Tomáš Masaryk, the first president of Czechoslovakia, hung in the Tabor home on Bartlett Street, and each year the birthdays of Masaryk and the republic were celebrated by the family. (It had not been forgotten that Masaryk, as chairman of the Czecho-Slovak Nation Council in exile, addressed a cheering, capacity crowd in Pittsburgh's Exhibition Hall in May 1918, demanding formation of an independent Czechoslovakian nation.) When that nation mobilized in the face of Hitler's ultimatum in 1938, John felt so much a part of his patrimony that he seriously considered enlisting in the Czech army. For two weeks in the summer of 1938 the Tabors shared a beach cottage with the family of Dr. Karl Breska, who had been the Czech consul in Pittsburgh and was now at the embassy in Washington, and the days were spent talking endlessly of Czechoslovakia, her allies, and what course events might take. Then came Munich, ending the dream of a free Republic of Czechoslovakia; a year later, when it became Poland's turn, the talk at the Tabor dinner table was of how England and France, this time, must honor their commitments. By the time John reached New Haven the fighting had begun at last, but with Czechoslovakia swallowed up by Hitler he was no longer so certain that it was his war. He threw himself into his new life at Yale.

Another member of the class was a slight, impish native of Sewickley, Pennsylvania, the quiet suburban community downriver from Pittsburgh.

John M. Thornton, known as Jake, was just back from Europe and could vastly amuse Tabor and me and our friends by putting on a swastika armband he had picked up in Germany, holding a pocket comb to his upper lip, and, shouting in fluent German (no one knew it, but the words were from *Die Lorelei* and other poems), give an imitation of Hitler that was irresistibly funny. Although he had not seen *der Führer* in the flesh, Jake Thornton was certainly Yale's most recent eyewitness to what was going on in Europe.

As an enthusiast of the German language, he had hoped to go to that country as an exchange student in 1938, but since the Hitler regime permitted no one to take money out of Germany, no exchanges were available and Jake chose instead a fellowship in England. Early in September 1938— shortly before the great hurricane lashed the Atlantic coast and before Neville Chamberlain flew to Munich—he and seventeen other American boys sailed for Southampton on the German liner *Bremen*. His school was Rossall, in Lancashire on the Irish Sea, and the first realities he faced were poor food, no central heating, a cold bath every morning, a two-mile run in the afternoon if the weather was too foul for other sports (plus a caning if you didn't keep up), and toilet facilities protected from the elements only by a roof; but "it was a great experience," he recalled, "and their games appealed to me—rugby, fives, field hockey on the beach at low tide, boxing. The only one I didn't like was cricket."

That first autumn there was a war scare before the Munich Pact was signed, and the Rossall boys were issued gas masks and dug three-foot trenches in the cricket fields. The consensus at the school was that Hitler was dangerous but there was not much Britain could do, being so poorly prepared. Everyone Jake talked to, though, was confident that France's superb army, behind its Maginot Line, would prove a match for the Germans.

One of the boys in Jake's dormitory was a Polish Jew named Theodor Czeczowicza, whose family owned some textile mills in Poland. Nazi sympathizers, someone at the school said, "were starting to give Jews there a bad time," Theodor's relatives in Germany were also "being pushed around," and whenever the Polish lad received a letter from home, Jake noticed, he would take it to his room and return later with his eyes swollen from weeping.

Spring came, and early summer, bringing a succession of lovely, carefree days when the boys' thoughts were on whether they would beat Stonyhurst at cricket, not on the state of the world. When school was over, toward the end of July, Thornton said goodbye to his friends and favorite masters, promised to keep in touch, and with his mother and twenty-year-old sister, Jean, who had just arrived from the States, traveled to Holland, Belgium, and Germany. They were impressed immediately by how clean Germany was, and how remarkably prosperous, and although they saw military men everywhere, "they all looked like Americans—nice, friendly young guys, happy and courteous," who would come over to the Thorntons' table of an evening and ask if they might dance with Jean. Since Jake spoke fluent German, he would translate ("Tell your sister I think she is very pretty"), and before long they would all be dancing.

What troubled the Thorntons was that all the Germans they met "were crazy about Hitler"; they spoke proudly of how he had pulled them out of the Depression with his construction projects—the public buildings and the autobahns, and in Cologne the three Americans were taken to see a new recreation hall Hitler had purportedly built for Jews, which showed that "he had the Jews' interest at heart."

Once, when some German soldiers asked what Americans thought of Hitler, Jake replied that they hated him because he seemed determined to plunge the world into war. The Germans retorted that that was ridiculous: surely if Hitler was planning a war, so many soldiers would not be on leave, having a good time, would they? Of course not—they would be with their units. Then one of the soldiers told a joke about a man who went to the railroad station and asked for a ticket to eastern Germany. The clerk asked, "What city?" "Warsaw," was the reply. "But Warsaw is in Poland," the clerk protested. "I know," said the man, "but I don't plan to go until late September." And at that all the men in uniform laughed.

On August 24, when the Thornton family left Cologne for Paris, they found it impossible to believe that war was imminent, despite the chilling news about the Nazi-Soviet Pact. Paris was filled with vacationing Americans, many of them students, and the Thorntons—remembering the holiday atmosphere in Germany—assured everyone they met that surely there would be no war. Then, with shocking suddenness, the Germans invaded Poland, Britain and France declared war, and the rumor raced through the city that Paris would be bombed. A blackout one night added to the general fear—that, and the number of drunken French soldiers who were seen on the streets.

On September 10, Jake and Jean Thornton and their mother managed to get aboard an overcrowded train, occupied the only vacant space, which was the toilet, and were lucky in Le Havre to book three passages on the SS *America*. As soon as they landed in New York, Jake telephoned the Yale admissions office and learned that he had been accepted. The next day he took a train to New Haven.

From some four thousand miles east of New Haven, Connecticut, came reports that autumn that Russian troops were moving into three republics on the rim of the Baltic Sea, but those tiny countries were so remote geographically and culturally that few people on this side of the Atlantic could get worked up over their plight. The Soviets, having seen how effortlessly Hitler had absorbed Austria and Czechoslovakia, were doing some territorial expanding of their own. During September and October, the foreign ministers of Estonia, Lithuania, and Latvia were invited, one by one, to Moscow under the guise of discussing trade relations, only to be summoned to the Kremlin and informed by Stalin and Molotov that large numbers of Red Army troops would henceforth be stationed in their nations. Since the unfortunate Baltic states were small and virtually helpless, that was that.

President Roosevelt was aware that his influence in Moscow, as in Berlin, was "just about zero," but he could guess what country would be next on the Russians' list of acquisitions, and in response to pleas from the crown prince of Sweden and the president of Finland he sent a cable to President Mikhail Kalinin of the USSR, expressing hope that the Soviets would "make no demands on Finland which are inconsistent with the maintenance and development of amicable and peaceful relations between the two countries, and the independence of each."

In western Europe, to the surprise of nearly everyone, including the soldiers involved, the fall of Warsaw appeared to mark an end of hostilities. Although the British and French had declared war in behalf of Poland, neither was doing much fighting. The French sent a few token patrols across the border into Germany, but not to stay; British bombers dropped leaflets by night over German cities, denouncing Hitler and his henchmen and vowing that the Royal Navy would cut off the Reich's supplies; sporadic antiaircraft fire around the French capital alerted Parisians to the presence of German planes overhead, either on reconnaissance or showering dirty pictures on the city, showing British Tommies making love to naked French women while French soldiers lay dead on the battlefield, draped over tangles of barbed wire. Construction continued on Hitler's uncompleted West Wall, or Siegfried Line—a deep zone of antitank barriers and concrete fortifications. Facing it was France's vaunted Maginot Line—a monument to a nation's defensive mentality if ever there was one, eighty-seven continuous miles of underground forts bristling with barbed wire, pillboxes, tank traps, and guns protected by concrete ten feet thick, where thousands of troops hibernated in cement caverns, living with sunlamps and deadly boredom for three months at a stretch. Between their two defensive complexes, French and German soldiers hung out their washing, exchanged greetings and polite notes, and sat watching and waiting in what the French called *drôle de guerre*, or "funny war," the Germans called *Sitzkrieg*, and Senator Borah derisively labeled "the phony war." His colleague Arthur Vandenberg observed, "This so-called war is nothing but about twenty-five people, and propaganda." Rumors persisted of secret peace negotiations between Britain and Germany, and an American correspondent writing from Paris explained the general unwillingness to take the war seriously by saying, "You cannot keep your mind indefinitely on a war that does not begin." During the winter, Winston Churchill visited several European countries that were determined to remain neutral, hoping to buy immunity through appeasement of Germany, and remarked, "Each one hopes that if he feeds the crocodile enough, the crocodile will eat him last."

———

Troops of the British Expeditionary Force had begun debarking from transports onto French soil a few days after the outbreak of war in September 1939, and since then huge quantities of stores, ammunition, and equipment of all kinds had crossed the Channel to pile up in depots from the Seine River well beyond the Somme. Even so, the French, ever suspicious of *les Anglais,* were certain that they would limit their military operations to air and sea, leaving the land battles to French *poilus* who would bear the brunt of the fighting and the casualties. A Quai d'Orsay man ruefully told Ambassador William Bullitt, "The game is lost. France stands alone. . . . The democracies are again too late."

Since the two allies had been unable even to synchronize their declarations of war on Germany, it was hardly surprising that when the BEF began arriving in France, all ranks were treated with condescension: at the first joint staff meeting held by General Maurice Gamelin, who had been named supreme commander, he did not bother to include an interpreter and spoke French so fast that few British officers had any idea what he was saying. The British were appalled by the lack of spirit and discipline they observed among their ally's forces. As General Alan Brooke, chief of the British II Corps, wrote, "Seldom have I seen anything more slovenly and badly turned out. Men unshaven, horses ungroomed, clothes and saddlery that did not fit, vehicles dirty, and complete lack of pride in themselves and their units. What shook me most . . . was the look in the men's faces, disgruntled and insubordinate looks, and although ordered to give 'Eyes left,' hardly a man bothered to do so."

General Gamelin's problems went far beyond the soldiers he commanded. One was the Maginot Line, the mighty shield on which France depended for her defense. Since the line covered less than one hundred miles of France's five-hundred-mile frontier, and since a large gap existed between the northernmost end of the Maginot Line and Belgium's fortifications, Gamelin's task was to plug that gap with Allied troops and whatever defensive works they had time to construct before the Germans struck.

The general's plan was to form a south-to-north position extending from the Maginot Line as far as Antwerp, with the Belgians manning the left, taking advantage of their own heavily fortified defensive positions, the British in the center, and the French First, Ninth, and part of the Second Army on the right. The idea was that British and French units would move swiftly into place inside Belgium (with another French army advancing into Holland to bridge the gap between Antwerp and the Channel); a small French force would defend against an unlikely enemy movement from the direction of the Ardennes Forest;[2] and the main body of France's army—some forty-three divisions—would remain inside the Maginot Line to repel what was expected to be the heaviest German assault.

Unfortunately, the plan was fatally flawed. Since the British and French armies could not enter Belgium without the permission of that government, and since the Belgians had no wish to provoke Hitler by allowing Allied troops on their soil, no such permission would be forthcoming until and unless a German invasion was under way. Given the speed with which the Wehrmacht had overrun Poland, it was entirely possible that such a delay would give the Germans an insurmountable advantage, since the British and French would probably need between five and ten days to move into line and assume their fighting positions.

Neville Chamberlain had made the mistake of saying that Hitler missed the bus; now General Sir Edmund Ironside, his chief of the imperial general staff, was actually inviting Hitler to attack, giving the British public the impression that the enemy would be foolhardy to strike the best-equipped force ever to leave England's shores. Posters in London read, "We will win because we are strongest," and BBC broadcasts jeered at the Germans, but the men in the ranks, awaiting the assault that was bound to come, knew they possessed not a gun or tank that was the equal of the Germans'.

Phony this war might be, but President Roosevelt's ambassadors in Paris and London were convinced that calamity lay ahead. In October, Bullitt informed his chief of the "enormous danger that the German air force will be able to win this war for Germany before the planes can begin to come out of our plants in quantity." Unless ten thousand aircraft from the United States reached the Allies in 1940, Bullitt warned, the two countries were as good as done. From London came new predictions that serious fighting would mean the defeat of Britain and "the complete collapse of everything we hope and live for," prompting Roosevelt to grumble that Kennedy "always has been an appeaser and always will be an appeaser. . . . If Germany or Italy made a good peace offer tomorrow . . . Joe would start working on the King and his friend, the Queen, and from there on down, to get everybody to accept it." Roosevelt was increasingly exasperated by the ambassador's pessimism: "He's just a pain in the neck to me," he told Henry Morgenthau. "Although everybody hates Hitler," Kennedy assured the president in another communiqué, the English "don't want to be finished economically, financially, politically, and socially, which they are beginning to suspect will be their fate if the war goes on very long." Germany, he maintained, could outlast Britain and France economically as well as militarily, and a year of war would leave Europe in such chaos that

[2]According to France's former premier, Léon Blum, "By one of those strange aberrations of the military mind the generals quite definitely decided that the Germans would not attack through the Ardennes." Faithful to their logic, they placed the worst French troops there.

it would be "ready for communism or some other radical change in social order."

Raymond Geist, the American consul general in Berlin, returned to Washington saying that a German-Russian victory was a distinct possibility. If true, the State Department's Adolf Berle commented to FDR, such an eventuality would pose a terrible threat. "If this nightmare proves real (and it seems too damnably logical)," he said, "you will have two men able to rule from Manchuria to the Rhine, much as Genghis Khan once ruled and nothing to stop the combined Russian-German force. . . ."

From just about every quarter, it seemed, the president was receiving warnings, counsel, and privileged information, but in retrospect it is clear that no tidings reaching him that autumn would produce such profound and lasting consequences for the world as the message delivered by an unscheduled visitor on October 11, 1939.

PART IV

1940

PECONIC:
A VISIT TO THE
PROFESSOR

*One of the most illustrious refugees from
Nazi Germany was the physicist Albert Einstein,
who accepted an appointment at Princeton's
Institute for Advanced Study.*

CHAPTER 24

———◆———

"... the collaboration
of scores of scientists from
many different lands."

T he President's guest that autumn day was an acquaintance named
      Alexander Sachs, who had done economic research for some of
      FDR's speeches in the 1932 campaign and had been a self-appointed
adviser off and on since then. A man of varied talents and strong opinions
who considered himself something of a prophet (a "Jeremiahesque observer," as he put it) and an expediter, Sachs had come to this country from
Lithuania at the age of eleven, had received a scientific degree from Columbia at nineteen, and had gone to work for the Wall Street firm of Lee
Higginson. Before long he was back at Columbia doing postgraduate work
in philosophy, then he was appointed a fellow in jurisprudence and sociol-
ogy at Harvard, and from time to time acted as an economic adviser to a
number of private investors.

   Sachs was a tall, heavyset fellow with curly hair who bore a striking
resemblance to the popular comedian Ed Wynn. In 1933, when he was
working for the NRA in Washington, his colleagues got a kick out of telling
visitors that Ed Wynn worked there, and to prove it they would open the
door to Sachs's office so the outsiders could have a peek at the famous
comic. The economist had a habit of carrying research around with him,
presumably so he could get at it whenever the need arose, and some wags
at Lehman Brothers, where he worked after 1936, had presented him with

some forty-odd secondhand briefcases for this purpose. Briefcase or no, Sachs always had his pockets stuffed with memoranda, and when he was looking for something he would empty the contents of his pockets and deposit them in piles on the floor until he found what he wanted. With both the spoken and the written word he employed a style so florid it almost qualified as circumlocution, and he seemed to delight in rolling such phrases as "if only we could overcome the scleroticism of the right and the infantilism of the left" into long, frequently impenetrable sentences. (His letters offering economic counsel to one of his clients in the early thirties typically included single sentences of more than 150 words.) It was said that he supplied the columnists Dorothy Thompson and Major George Fielding Eliot with numerous ideas, and they, in turn, translated Sachs's baroque prose for the general public.

Sachs was confident that he knew how to deal with a busy man—particularly the chief executive of the United States. He had a theory that it was simply a waste of time to give an important person something to read. "Any public figure is punchdrunk with printer's ink," he liked to say, adding that an idea presented on paper inevitably got the brushoff. And what Sachs had for the president on this October morning was so important that he wanted it to reach him "by way of the ear, and not as a soft mascara on the eye." Which was why Franklin Roosevelt found himself in the unaccustomed and doubtless unwelcome position of being catechized by his visitor.

What emerged from Sachs's overstuffed pockets to be read to the president were three letters, none of them even remotely financial. One was a letter from Sachs himself. Another had been written by a Hungarian scientist named Leo Szilard. The third was a message whose antecedents went back to 1905, when an obscure German working in the Swiss Patent Office by day and pondering the laws of nature in his rented room at night published in the *Annalen der Physik* a paper entitled "On the Electrodynamics of Moving Bodies." In that nine-thousand-word paper and in another, shorter essay published in the autumn of the same year, the twenty-six-year-old author, Albert Einstein, stated that the energy contained in matter is equal to its mass multiplied by the square of the velocity of light. What he was suggesting is that there exists in all matter, even in the tiniest particles, an almost unimaginable quantity of energy if some means of releasing it could ever be found.

The most important document Alexander Sachs read to Roosevelt before handing it to him was a letter from that same Einstein, who in the intervening three and a half decades had come to be known to laymen the world over as the most eminent scientist of his day or perhaps any other day, as well as the archetype of the untidy, absentminded professor, the genius with his head in the clouds, his feet sockless, his baggy trousers suspenderless.

Roosevelt did not know it, of course, but the letter had not originated with Einstein; he had been put up to it by fellow scientists, and behind their use of the great man as go-between lay a tale of the numerous twists and turns taken by the arcane world of physics during the twentieth century.

═══

At the end of the World War a few great centers of learning dominated the discipline of physics, and it was assumed almost as a matter of course that any truly serious scholar would make his way, sooner or later, to one (perhaps to all) of them. There was Copenhagen, where the brilliant theoretician Niels Bohr, a Nobel laureate, presided over the red-roofed Institute of Theoretical Physics; there was the Cavendish Laboratory in Cambridge, England, headed by an outspoken New Zealander named Ernest Rutherford, the world's leading authority on radioactivity; there was Berlin, where as many as seven Nobel Prize winners might be seen at a single academic seminar; and there was Göttingen, on the edge of Germany's Harz Mountains, a medieval town with ancient ramparts, half-timbered houses, a splendid botanical garden, and the Georgia Augusta University, where Max Born, David Hilbert, and James Franck were the guiding spirits. During the decade that followed the World War at least fifty promising young American physicists went to Europe on fellowships for postdoctoral study, spent time at these intensely exciting centers of advanced studies, and formed friendships that dramatically affected the course of physics in their native land. In the late 1920s, American science—physics in particular—was held in contempt in Europe. Ten years later, thanks to the small but influential group that had returned to the United States determined to make American physics respectable, there was a depth of scientific talent in this country virtually unimagined in European nations.

Thanks to the relatively small number of people involved, there existed in those days what amounted to an extended international family of physicists—small in number but great in enthusiasm, all of them caught up in a true voyage of discovery, traveling hither and yon to conferences, corresponding with one another, exchanging information and ideas, offering advice and assistance and criticism, rushing to publication the news of interesting experiments and the results they had achieved. As I. I. Rabi recalled that intoxicating time, he and his colleagues at Columbia were teaching sixteen hours a week and working another fifty hours in the laboratory. "It was the happiest period of our lives. . . . we worked every day of the week. During the year we would take something like three or four days off. . . . people worked very hard and very joyfully." Physics, he went on to say, "requires a taste for things unseen, even unheard of"—demanding the sort of insatiable curiosity children have, which is why he considered physicists "the Peter Pans of the human race. They never grow up, and they keep their curiosity."

As another scientist described it, the physics field resembled a community of ants, in which an individual would hurry excitedly to the surface of the anthill, bearing a tiny fragment of knowledge he had just acquired, and the moment he turned his back, the fragment would have been removed and put to use by others. James Chadwick called the work he was involved in at the Cavendish Laboratory "a kind of sport. It was contending with nature." (It was also, of course, contending with other scientists in friendly but intense competition.) "It was a heroic time," wrote the young American Robert Oppenheimer, who was gaining a reputation as one of the brightest of these brilliant people. "It was not the doing of any one man. It involved the collaboration of scores of scientists from many different lands. . . . It was a period of patient work in the laboratory, of crucial experiments and daring action, of many false starts and untenable conjectures. It was a time of earnest correspondence and hurried conferences, of debate, criticism, and brilliant mathematical improvisation. For those who participated it was a time of creation. There was terror as well as exaltation in their new insight."

Their new insight, as he put it, was based upon certain radical departures from what had been regarded as the immutable laws of physics. From the work of Max Planck, Einstein, and Bohr, in particular, had emerged the so-called quantum theory, which explained the emission and absorption of energy by matter and described the motion of particles of matter. From Einstein's immensely difficult theory of relativity came a number of propositions, including the ideas that the maximum velocity attainable is the velocity of light in a vacuum, that mass increases with velocity, and that matter and energy are equivalent and interchangeable—matter being essentially "frozen energy." From the Joliot-Curies in Paris, from Rutherford, Bohr, and other seekers after the truth, came discoveries suggesting that nothing was what it seemed, that the indivisible was in fact divisible, that the stable was not only unstable but in a state of constant motion and change.

Until the late thirties these revolutionary ideas, which rattled the foundations of man's image of the physical world, were by and large the currency of a handful of scientists, and, since they appeared to hold no promise of practical application, they seemed likely to remain so as far as the average person was concerned. But the physicists were beginning to worry that what had been entirely theoretical might, in the not too distant future, be put to some practical and perhaps even dangerous use. As early as 1903, Ernest Rutherford had sensed the possibility that, if a proper detonator could be found, a "wave of atomic disintegration might be started through matter, which would indeed make this old world vanish in smoke," as one of his correspondents wrote. And in 1921 the German Nobel laureate Walter Nernst worried that "we are living on an island of guncotton"—to which he added, "But, thank God, we have not yet found a match that will ignite it." Another German physicist, Pascual Jordan, recalling those heady years after the World War, said: "Everyone was filled with such tension that it almost took their breath away. . . . It became more and more clear that . . . we had stumbled upon a quite unexpected and deeply embedded layer of the secrets of Nature."

What had set this train of thought in motion was the Frenchman Henri Becquerel's discovery, in 1896, that substances containing uranium spontaneously gave off radiation. When salts of uranium were placed near an unexposed photographic plate, he found, the plate became exposed even though it was carefully protected from light. Two other Parisians, Pierre Curie and his Polish-born wife, Marie, discovered that certain other elements (thorium was the first one they found) also emitted radiation in the same manner. They determined, for example, that pitchblende—a heavy rock that looks like tar and has a high concentration of uranium oxide— contains polonium (which she named for her native land) and the highly radioactive radium, which was so difficult to isolate that after four years of treating tons of pitchblende they succeeded in separating out a minuscule one-tenth of a gram of pure radium salt.

———

Meantime the British were active. In Cambridge, Joseph John Thomson— after studying charged particles in a cathode tube—concluded that those particles, eventually known as electrons, were "matter in a new state" and were one of the fundamental building blocks of the atom. Ernest Rutherford discovered that radiation from radioactive atoms was more than it seemed—that it consisted, in fact, of several different types of rays. It was made up of very fast particles charged with positive electricity, called alpha particles, each of which carried two positive electrical charges. And there were very fast rays charged with negative electricity, known as beta rays. Later a French physicist discovered a third type of ray—the highly energetic gamma ray—which is similar to light rays and x-rays, but more penetrating. Since these alpha, beta, and gamma rays all came from atoms, and since atoms gave off fast particles and gamma rays, it followed that atoms are not only divisible, but that they must contain large amounts of energy. Rutherford suggested that the atom of a radioactive element can break down, and when it did, he believed, it gave off either an alpha particle or a beta particle, and sometimes gamma rays as well. Further, when a radioactive atom broke down, he said, it changed into a different atom. In other words, certain elements are capable of changing spontaneously into other elements. A good example is the radium atom: when it breaks down, it gives off an alpha particle and gamma rays and changes into the atom of radon. Clearly, radon differs from radium: the former is a gas, the latter a solid.

Bohr and Rutherford achieved a significant breakthrough when they formulated the theory of the nuclear atom—a theory that helped to explain radioactivity. They concluded that the atom consisted of a tiny central nucleus containing positively charged particles called protons. Circling this nucleus, but at a relatively great distance from it, was an equal number of negatively charged particles called electrons. In each atom, it was thought, the number of protons in the nucleus was equal to the number of electrons circling it. Since each proton carried one positive charge and each electron one negative charge, the atom was neutral. In any element, all the nuclei contained the same number of protons, and this number was that element's atomic number. What gave each element its distinctive personality was that each had a different number of protons and electrons.

Rutherford and Bohr were dealing with a concept of something so small as to be all but unimaginable: the diameter of the nucleus of a radium atom, for instance, was one millionth of one millionth of a centimeter. Yet while the space between the nucleus and its encircling electrons was infinitesimally small, it was actually large by comparison with the nucleus. And that meant, in turn, that the atom was not—as had been supposed for so long—a solid object, but something that consisted largely of empty space.

As early as 1920, Rutherford had speculated that the atom must consist of something more than protons and electrons—something, in fact, that would likely be a combination of the two, with a zero electrical charge. Again and again he would speak about this particle, and the staff in his Cavendish Laboratory eventually gave it a name—they began calling it the neutron. In 1932 one of Rutherford's protégés, James Chadwick, while irradiating beryllium with alpha particles, found that it gave off particles with the same mass as hydrogen and *no* electrical charge. These, he decided, must be the neutrons they had been seeking. Chadwick's discovery, for which he received a Nobel Prize, meant that the nucleus of an atom had to contain only enough protons to make up its nuclear charge; the rest of its nuclear weight could be accounted for by neutrons, instead of protons and electrons in balance.

At the two ends of the atomic scale are hydrogen, the simplest element, and uranium, the most complex. Hydrogen is made up of a single proton around which a single electron moves. Its atomic number is 1 and its atomic mass is 1. Uranium, at the other extreme of the naturally occurring elements, has ninety-two electrons circling a nucleus that contains ninety-two protons, so its atomic number is 92. But there are, to complicate matters, three slightly different varieties of uranium, with different atomic mass. The first, and most common, is uranium 238, or U-238, whose nucleus contains 146 neutrons as well as the ninety-two protons, which add up to 238. The second is U-235, which contains 143 neutrons; and the third is U-234, with 142 neutrons. These three are known as the isotopes of uranium.

In Italy, at the University of Rome, a young physicist named Enrico Fermi, equally brilliant at experiment, theory, and teaching, had been experimenting since 1934 with a method of bombarding atoms quite different from the one Rutherford had pioneered. As the physicist Otto Frisch said of this work, "Only Fermi had the intelligence to strike out in a different and tremendously fruitful direction." Instead of using alpha particles as "bullets," Fermi was using neutrons. His reasoning was that neutrons— unlike alpha particles, which were slowed rapidly by the electrons circling the nuclei and repelled by the positive charges of the protons within the nucleus—were not attracted or slowed by electrons, nor were they repelled by protons, since they had no electric charge. So Fermi and several colleagues, including Emilio Segré, began irradiating numerous elements with neutrons, with results that were very confusing indeed. They discovered that they were producing, as by-products of their experiments, a variety of radioactive isotopes not found in nature, and the amounts of each were so tiny the scientists weren't certain what they were. And then, as Frisch went on to say, "Fermi got on the wrong track: he felt that uranium, like other heavy nuclei, would obediently swallow any slow neutron that fell on it." But it did not, and the Italians, not realizing what was happening, believed they had produced element number 93. In fact, quite unknowingly, they had achieved what every physicist knew to be impossible—they had split the atom. Not for years would anyone be aware of what they had done.[1]

News of their work reached physicists in other countries almost immediately. A young American, John Wheeler, who was putting in an apprenticeship at Bohr's institute in Copenhagen, recalled years later that "nothing was more impressive in nuclear physics than the message that Moller brought back during the spring of 1935 from a short Easter visit to Rome. It told of Fermi's slow-neutron experiments and the astonishing resonances that he had discovered."

At the ancient University of Freiburg, on the edge of Germany's Black Forest, a young couple named Walter and Ida Noddack, who were regarded as leading authorities on the chemical analysis of the so-called rare earths, repeated the Fermi-Segré experiment and proved by means of chemical tests that the Italians' assumption that they had produced a transuranic element was incorrect. Writing in *Zeitschrift für angewandte Chemie,* Ida Noddack advanced the bold premise that "when heavy nuclei are bombarded with neutrons the nuclei in question might break into a number of larger pieces which would no doubt be isotopes of known elements but not neighbors of the elements subjected to radiation." Ironically, no one paid any attention.

Instead, other scientists who learned about the Fermi-Segré experiment concluded that what they had observed might be an isotope of protoactinium, which is element 91. This possibility was of considerable interest to two scientists at Berlin's Kaiser Wilhelm Institute—Otto Hahn and his close associate Lise Meitner. Having discovered the element protoactinium almost twenty years earlier, they believed they would be able to recognize it easily.

In experiment after experiment over the next several years, Hahn and Meitner bombarded uranium with slow neutrons and found a large number of substances, but no element 91. As a result, they surmised that what they were recovering each time was a transuranic element—that is, an element

---

[1]One reason for their failure to recognize what had occurred was the size of the experiment. Splitting atoms one or a few at a time has trivial observable consequences: as a physicist remarked, on that scale "it is something like burning a couple molecules of coal."

with a higher atomic number than uranium. But before these two experienced collaborators could solve the puzzle that had engaged their energies and attention for so long, politics intervened.

In 1938, in the wake of the Anschluss in Austria, the anti-Semitic laws of Germany were applied to Austrian citizens, and that included Lise Meitner, who was a Viennese-born Jew. There were rumors that she might lose her position at the institute and then be prevented from leaving Germany because of her knowledge. So in July, when friends offered to smuggle her into Holland without a visa, she crossed the border into that country with the assistance of a Dutch physicist, and then made her way to Stockholm, where she continued her work in the laboratory of Manne Siegbahn, a Swedish scientist.

Before Meitner fled from Berlin, however, she and Hahn had been engaged in duplicating an experiment first performed by Irène Joliot-Curie and a Yugoslav colleague named Pavel Savitch, who were convinced that they had discovered a new transuranic element. The substance did not correspond with what Hahn and Meitner had been finding, but their plan to repeat the Paris experiments was halted by Meitner's precipitate departure for Holland. Picking up where he and Meitner had left off, Hahn and another colleague, Fritz Strassmann, repeated the Curie-Savitch experiment, checked and rechecked their results, and found in each instance that what was produced when neutrons were used to bombard uranium had all the chemical characteristics of barium, and not a new element. This simply was not plausible, since barium contains only fifty-six protons in its nucleus—only a little more than half as many as uranium—and their initial assumption, understandably, was that an error had been made.

Hahn was a chemist, and before long he was as certain that he had produced barium as he could be certain of anything. He decided to send a report of the findings to the scientific journal *Die Naturwissenschaften*. On December 21, in his laboratory, he described the experiments he and Strassmann had been conducting. "We publish these results rather hesitantly," he wrote, noting that they were at variance with "all previous experience in nuclear physics." His dilemma, of course, was that he was a chemist stepping across the line into another discipline, and he was reluctant to announce a discovery that went against all the rules of physics.

At the same time that he sent off his report to *Die Naturwissenschaften*, Hahn wrote a letter to Lise Meitner, describing the conclusion of the experiments on which they had worked together. As a chemist, he was satisfied that he had produced barium when he bombarded uranium with neutrons, but he was hoping that she, a physicist, would be able to explain the apparently inexplicable process by which this had occurred. And suddenly the great puzzle was about to be solved.

CHAPTER 25

———◆———

"... the uranium nucleus has only small stability ..."

In November 1938, Lise Meitner had just turned sixty. A shy, handsome, independent woman who never married, she had devoted her life to nuclear physics. When she was thirty-one and a student of Max Planck she sat in the audience in Salzburg and heard young Albert Einstein deliver his first "invited paper," and she never forgot it. At the time she did not fully realize the implications of his theory of relativity, but when, in the lecture, he took that theory and from it derived the equation energy equals mass times the square of the velocity of light, showing that "to every radiation must be attributed an inertial mass," she found the facts "so overwhelmingly new and surprising" that fifty years later she remembered the lecture as though she had just heard it. During her thirty years in Germany, she and mild, kindly little Otto Hahn had achieved worldwide renown for their work in radioactivity. Like so many other scientists, she found the Kaiser Wilhelm Institute a congenial and stimulating environment, where she worked on equal terms with some of the great figures of science—von Laue, Planck, Einstein, Born, Hahn, and others—becoming recognized, in the process, as one of the two outstanding women scientists in the world. The other, of course, was her well-known rival Irène Joliot-Curie, daughter of Pierre and Marie Curie and the discoverer, with her husband, of artificial radioactivity, who seemed, in Meitner's words, "afraid of being regarded rather as the daughter of her mother than as a scientist on her own account."

Now those heady days were behind her and she was alone and lonely, a refugee who, for fear of the concentration camp, could not go back to Germany or her beloved laboratory, and whose first holiday season in exile was to be spent in an almost-deserted, snow-covered resort near Göteborg, Sweden. Here in the little village of Kungalv she was to be joined by her young nephew, Otto Frisch, also a physicist and a refugee, who was then working with Niels Bohr in Copenhagen. When he arrived he found her at breakfast at her small hotel, brooding over the letter she had received from Hahn. She handed it to Frisch, who read it and immediately told his aunt that Hahn could not be right in suggesting that barium had been formed from uranium by means of neutrons. Meitner did not agree. She argued that if fifty-six of the uranium atom's protons had formed the nucleus of a barium atom, it was likely that the remaining thirty-six (ninety-two minus fifty-six) had formed the nucleus of an atom of krypton, an inert gas with an atomic number of 36.

During that day and the next, Frisch recalled, "We walked up and down in the snow, I on skis and she on foot (she said and proved that she could get along just as fast that way)," and although it took her awhile to get him to listen, "eventually we got to arguing about the meaning of Hahn's result, and very gradually we realized that the breaking-up of a uranium nucleus into two almost equal parts was a process so different . . . that it had to be pictured in quite a different way. The picture is not that of a 'particle' breaking through a potential barrier, but rather the gradual deformation of the original uranium nucleus, its elongation, formation of a waist, and finally separation of the two halves." It was Bohr who had first conceived the image of the nucleus as a drop of liquid which might elongate and divide itself, and Meitner and Frisch realized that that was almost certainly what had occurred in Hahn's laboratory. They also realized that the separation of those two halves—the splitting of the nucleus—was something inexpressibly violent, "two fairly large nuclei flying apart with an energy of nearly two hundred million electron volts, more than ten times the energy involved in any other nuclear reaction."

What started as a brief holiday had proved an overwhelming experience, as Frisch wrote his mother. "I feel as if I had caught an elephant by its tail, without meaning to, while walking through a jungle," he told her, "and now I don't know what to do with it."

By the time he left his aunt, however, they had agreed that he would inform Niels Bohr of Hahn's discovery and their interpretation of it, and Frisch arrived in Copenhagen just in time to catch Bohr before he sailed for the United States. When he heard what Frisch had to say, the Dane hit himself on the head and cried, "Oh, what fools we have been! We ought to have seen that before." And he was so excited by the news that he very nearly missed his ship. Meantime, over the long-distance phone between

Copenhagen and Stockholm, Frisch and his aunt began composing a paper describing their theory. Before it was finished, Frisch ran into the physicist George Placzek, told him about the momentous events of recent weeks, and got a highly skeptical reaction. Placzek could not believe that the uranium nuclei were so unstable and suggested that Frisch test the theory in a cloud chamber. Frisch didn't have a cloud chamber at hand, but he decided he could use an ionization chamber instead.

With a small amount of uranium in the chamber, some radium and beryllium as a source of neutrons, an electron tube for amplification, and a set of headphones, he was able to observe on a screen that the bombardment of uranium with neutrons produced the largest electrical impulses from an ionization chamber ever recorded—an energy 100 million times that produced by the burning of a hydrogen atom in oxygen. It was, in fact, precisely the amount of energy that he and Lise Meitner had predicted if a uranium atom was split into two parts. For the first time ever, the fission of uranium had been demonstrated as a fact, and it may have been an omen that the successful experiment occurred on Friday, January 13, 1939. On that day in Niels Bohr's laboratory in Copenhagen, it may be said, the atomic age began.

Before that moment the great scientists of the twentieth century had made enormous strides toward understanding the mysteries of the physical world. From pure theory had come astonishingly practical results that were changing entire industries, making virtually instantaneous global communication possible, giving new direction to medical diagnosis and treatment. But until Meitner and Frisch interpreted Hahn's experiments, throwing a thin ray of light for the first time into a room that had heretofore been dark, no physicist had come close to revealing the ultimate secret of the atom— which was the awesome prospect of using the energy that lay hidden inside its nucleus.

Although the report he and his aunt had written was nearly finished, Frisch held off mailing it for three days, giving him time to complete a second paper describing the experiment that proved their case. Having observed that what occurred in his experiment bore "a striking similarity . . . with the process by which bacteria multiply," he asked an American biologist, William A. Arnold, what term was used to describe the phenomenon of cell division, and was told that it was "fission." On January 16, Frisch mailed the two papers to the British scientific journal *Nature*, and they were published in successive weeks. The first, entitled "Disintegration of Uranium by Neutrons: A New Type of Nuclear Reaction," appeared in the issue of February 11 and included the first use of the word "fission" to describe the splitting of an atomic nucleus. It also included a statement that was to have the most profound implications for humanity: "It seems therefore possible," Meitner and Frisch had written, "that the uranium nucleus has only small stability of form, and may, after neutron capture, divide itself into two nuclei of roughly equal size. . . . These two nuclei will repel each other [since they both carry large positive charges] and should gain a total of kinetic energy of about 200,000,000 electron volts, as calculated from nuclear radius and charge."

Behind that statement lay the realization that transforming matter into energy follows Einstein's formula—$E = mc^2$. Although the amount of matter thus transformed might be small, the energy released would be immense, and could be determined by multiplying the mass by the square of the speed of light, which is 186,000 miles per second.

Put in other terms, it was estimated to be an amount of energy twenty million times that produced by a comparable amount of TNT.

CHAPTER 26

"Hitler is my best friend."

Had it not been for Hitler seizing power in Germany, the tight little coterie of physicists might have continued along the same path, theoreticians and experimenters in half a dozen countries each contributing his or her particular piece to the great puzzle they were so eager to solve. But in the late spring of 1933 the academic community in Germany had received a devastating blow as a result of the Nazis' brutal insistence on conformity. Along with the burning of all books regarded as subversive, the nazification of the universities commenced. What this meant was that all professors and instructors who were, or were said to be, antipathetic to the regime were dismissed. In April a law for the "cleansing of the civil service" was announced, and in short order the purge of educational institutions was on. The flow of refugees from Europe's tyrannies that began in 1933—principally from Germany, and from Italy, Russia, and countries overrun by the Nazis—was to bring to the United States by 1941 at least 25,000 immigrants whose work had been professional in nature.

Fortunately for those few individuals who were at or near the top of their profession, the higher levels of American universities were not overcrowded, and in certain fields there was an actual shortage of teachers. Yet available positions were the exception, especially at the middle and lower levels: according to an article in the *Yale Review,* some five thousand Ph.D.s were unemployed in June 1933. An American with a doctoral degree who had tried for a year or two to land a teaching job at a college could consider himself fortunate to be offered a lecturer's position paying $1,500 a year; as in all other levels of the work force, jobs were few, and as a consequence, xenophobia worked against the new immigrants. In 1932, when it was learned that Einstein (whose property in Germany had been confiscated) planned to emigrate to the United States, a women's "Patriotic Corporation" tried to prevent his admission on grounds that he was a Communist, and the National Patriotic Council, labeling him a German Bolshevist, announced that his theory of relativity "was of no scientific value or purpose, not understandable because there was nothing there to understand."

Among Germany's intelligentsia, a high percentage was vulnerable to oppression because many were Jews. In that nation as a whole, Jews constituted only .009 percent of the population, but in the universities some 12 percent of the professors were Jewish. What was incomprehensible was that a nation so culturally advanced, so proud of its many intellectual achievements, could virtually ignore the destruction of its culture. There simply was no outburst of public indignation when, on May 10, 1933, thousands of students in university towns burned those books that represented what was called the "un-German spirit," including the works of such national figures as Thomas Mann, Erich Maria Remarque, and Albert Einstein, and such foreign authors as Upton Sinclair, Helen Keller, H. G. Wells, Freud, Gide, Zola, and Proust. In Berlin, five thousand youths wearing swastika armbands paraded through the streets singing Nazi songs, following trucks loaded with books—books by Jew and non-Jew alike—and while forty thousand Berliners looked on, threw the volumes onto a flaming pyre in front of the Opera House.

American colleges and universities perceived the dismissal of academics in Germany as a rare opportunity to attract some of the world's outstanding scholars, and approaches were made, inevitably, to wealthy individuals and foundations for financial aid for this purpose. One haven for the intellectual refugees was the Institute for Advanced Study in Princeton, New Jersey, an organization founded and directed by the educator Abraham Flexner as a place where "everyone—faculty and members—in their individual ways endeavored to advance the frontiers of knowledge." An institution of general knowledge and science, it would be "afraid of no issue," according to Flexner, "under no pressure from any side which might tend its scholars to be prejudiced either for or against any particular solution of the problems under study. . . . Its scholars should enjoy complete intellectual liberty, and be absolutely free from administrative responsibilities and concerns." Happily, the opening of the institute in the early thirties coincided with the beginning exodus of scholars from Germany (on a recruiting trip to Europe, Flexner had offered Albert Einstein a position even before Hitler came to power), and for a long period the institute was a way station for homeless

Europeans, who were passed along to "infuse new life into struggling institutions" elsewhere in America, as Flexner put it.

Another institution that came to the aid of scholarly refugees was the
New School for Social Research in New York City, founded in 1921 by the
editor of the Encyclopedia of the Social Sciences, Alvin Johnson. Because
of his position, Johnson knew or had corresponded with most of the political and social scientists ousted by Hitler, and after reading in the spring of
1933 the first lists of dismissed professors he realized that here were "nearly
all the social scientists who had any creative spirit in them." To assist them,
he came up with the idea of a University in Exile, which would function
as a graduate faculty for the New School, an undergraduate institution. His
plan was to hire fifteen scholars for a two-year period, pay them $4,000 a
year, and in this way "make what return I can for liberties I have enjoyed."
When his plan was announced on May 13, 1933, in the *New York Times* he
received a telephone call from a man named Hiram Halle, whom Johnson
did not know, offering to guarantee the necessary $60,000 for two years. By
summer, thanks to Halle's funding, refugee scholars were "arriving ship by
ship," and Johnson was meeting them at the foot of the gangplank.

Yet another such organization was the Emergency Committee in Aid of
Displaced German (later Foreign) Scholars, founded in the same month as
Johnson's University in Exile by a group that included Robert Hutchins,
president of the University of Chicago. The director was Stephen Duggan,
founder and president of the Institute of International Education, whose
assistant director—until he left to take a position at CBS—was Edward R.
Murrow. The aim of the Emergency Committee was to scatter refugee
scholars across the United States so they would be assimilated, and to
accomplish this the displaced academics were given temporary appointments of one to three years, with jobs going only to truly eminent figures
in an effort to cause the least possible disruption in American academic
circles. During the two years he worked with the committee, Murrow
sometimes received as many as fifty letters a day from dismissed professors
in Germany, and helped about a hundred of them to relocate in the United
States. One beneficiary of the program was the Institute of Fine Arts in New
York, whose grateful director, Walter W. S. Cook, once wrote, "Hitler is
my best friend. He shakes the tree and I collect the apples."

If ever a man had seen the refugees' plight from both sides of the fence it
was Leo Szilard. Born in 1898, Szilard was a short, stout, owlish-looking
Hungarian who was customarily bursting with irrepressible ideas and
schemes, as often as not designed to prod his associates into action of some
sort. As Enrico Fermi put it, "He seems to enjoy startling people." The
scientist and writer C. P. Snow once described him as "a man of the left,
so far as he could be classified at all. He had a temperament uncommon
anywhere, maybe a little less uncommon among major scientists. He had

a powerful ego and invulnerable egocentricity: but he projected the force of that personality outwards, with beneficent intention toward his fellow creatures. In that sense, he had a family resemblance toward Einstein on a reduced scale. He also had an unusually daring scientific imagination."

Szilard's scientific imagination was matched by an extraordinary intuitiveness. As a teacher in Berlin he had been one of the first to smell danger: hearing Dr. Hjalmar Schacht, president of the Reichsbank and later Hitler's minister of the economy, state that Germany could pay no reparations from the World War until her former colonies were returned to her, he transferred every pfennig of his savings from a German bank to one in Switzerland. When Hitler came to power in January of 1933, Szilard had no doubt whatever that there was trouble ahead—big trouble; he was living at the faculty club of the Kaiser Wilhelm Institute and he immediately packed his suitcases. "By this," he said, "I mean that I literally had two suitcases which were packed standing in my room; the key was in them, and all I had to do was turn the key and leave when things got too bad." At the end of February 1933, fire broke out in the Reichstag, home of Germany's parliament, and the old building was gutted. Although rumor and subsequent evidence strongly suggested that Hermann Göring had planned the blaze, the Nazis used the fire as an excuse to round up thousands of Communists, real and imagined, who were said to be responsible for the outrage. A few days afterward, Szilard turned the key in his bags and left Berlin for good. To succeed in this world, he remarked later, "you don't have to be much cleverer than other people, you just have to be one day earlier than most people."

His next stop was Vienna, where Szilard sought out Sir William Beveridge of the London School of Economics, who was said to be interested in the plight of academics dismissed from Germany's universities. Beveridge told Szilard to come to London and "occasionally prod him on this," and soon afterward the Hungarian did exactly that. Before long Beveridge launched the Academic Assistance Council, which served as a specialized employment agency, keeping files on scholars who had been fired, paying them small living allowances until work could be found for them, and in general serving as a clearinghouse for refugees from Germany, and later from Austria, Hungary, Czechoslovakia, Italy, Poland, and Spain.

Another of Szilard's projects was to persuade British scientists to start a rescue program for their German-Jewish counterparts. Perhaps a hundred or more of these people were brought to England and given work before someone thought to ask about Szilard himself. As a Briton remarked later, "We thought that Szilard was a rich Hungarian aristocrat, but he turned out to be as much in need of assistance as all those he had helped to leave Germany—only he did not mention it."

While he was in England, Szilard gave a lot of thought to what he would do next, and was tempted, he recalled later, to go into biology (a switch he eventually did make in 1946, at the age of forty-eight). What decided him on physics in the thirties was reading a book by that novelist of ideas and science fiction H. G. Wells, called *The World Set Free,* written in 1913, a year before the World War. In it, the farseeing Englishman prophesied the discovery of artificial radioactivity in 1933 (the year before it in fact occurred), the release of energy from one atom to another in a chain reaction and the use of atomic power for industrial purposes, and a future in which nuclear weapons leveled cities with fire and radiation. At about the same time he read Wells's book, Szilard had a memorable conversation with an Austrian acquaintance who suggested that man's need for heroism and adventure should be channeled into something other than wars—possibly an enterprise aimed at leaving the earth. And as Szilard pondered this, he concluded that if he wanted to do something to aid mankind he should go into nuclear physics, "because only through the liberation of atomic energy could we obtain the means which would enable man not only to leave the earth but to leave the solar system."

Yet another significant moment in Szilard's progress toward nuclear physics occurred in London. He had just read a newspaper account of a speech by Lord Rutherford, quoting the eminent physicist as saying that anyone who thought atomic energy could be used on an industrial scale was talking "the merest moonshine." Szilard was walking alone through the city, turning this over in his mind, and as he paused to wait for a traffic light to change it suddenly came to him that "if we could find an element which is split by neutrons and which would emit *two* neutrons when it absorbed *one* neutron, such an element, if assembled in sufficiently large scale, could sustain a nuclear chain reaction. I didn't see at the moment just how one would go about finding such an element, or what experiments would be needed, but the idea never left me." And not long after that, when the Joliot-Curies announced their discovery of artificial radiation, Szilard realized that the tools were at hand to produce a chain reaction. In the spring of 1934—the year of the Fermi-Segré experiment and of Ida Noddack's unheeded paper—he applied for a patent which described the laws governing a chain reaction and assigned it to the British Admiralty without financial compensation. The reason for secrecy, he wrote later, "was my conviction that if a nuclear reaction can be made to work it can be used to set up violent explosions."

On January 2, 1938, Szilard arrived in America. One year later, to the day, Enrico Fermi, his wife, Laura, and their two small children stood on the deck of the *Franconia* as she steamed past the Statue of Liberty toward a berth in the Hudson River. "We have founded the American branch of the Fermi family," the Italian announced proudly. Less than a month earlier he had received the Nobel Prize in physics for his "disclosure of new radioactive elements produced by neutron irradiation and for his related discovery of nuclear reactions brought about by slow neutrons." Laura Fermi was Jewish, the Nazis' influence was being felt increasingly in Italy, and when Fermi went to Stockholm to accept his award he took his family along and then, as a friend put it, "just kept traveling west." As a distinguished scientist, he had received offers from several American universities and decided to join the staff at Columbia, which was by this time an important center for research in nuclear physics. (When the American physicist Norman Ramsey returned from a two-year fellowship at Cambridge and took his Ph.D. at Columbia, he appeared before a six-man committee of whom all but one had received or would receive a Nobel Prize.)

Meantime, Niels Bohr—having almost missed his ship's sailing because of the extraordinary news Otto Frisch had brought him—arrived in New York two weeks later aboard the Swedish-American liner *Drottningholm* and was greeted at the dock by a group that included Enrico and Laura Fermi and John A. Wheeler, Bohr's former student, who was now an assistant professor at Princeton. The Fermis had last seen the Danish scientist when they stopped off in Copenhagen en route to Stockholm early in December, and both were struck by the way he had aged even in that short time, because of his anguish over events in Europe.

Bohr told his friends something of what he had learned from Frisch just before sailing, but he was reluctant to say too much: he felt an obligation to wait until Hahn, Meitner, and Frisch made public their findings before he released information about their work. After visiting with Wheeler and the Fermis, Bohr left for Princeton, where he was to spend several months at the Institute for Advanced Study. Inevitably, though, the news spread, and the physics department at Columbia, as elsewhere, Laura Fermi recalled, "was astir with talk of fission." Fermi, like Szilard, realized at once that if neutrons were emitted in the fission process it might be possible to achieve a chain reaction, and he was already planning an experiment to prove that hypothesis. One afternoon, Willis Lamb, a young physicist who had been visiting at Princeton, burst into Fermi's lab, wildly excited, to announce that Bohr "had leaked out great news"—news, of course, of the discovery of fission and "at least an outline of its interpretation."

On the following day, January 26, 1939, the Fifth Conference on Theoretical Physics opened at George Washington University in the nation's capital, and Bohr and Fermi—both Nobel laureates—spoke to a crowd hushed with suppressed excitement, telling them of the Hahn-Strassmann experiment and the thesis developed by Meitner and Frisch. It was an audience that appreciated fully the irony of Fermi's position—Fermi, the brilliant Italian who had missed by a hair's breadth arriving at the full concept of fission five years earlier.

On the very day of the conference someone handed Bohr the issue of *Die Naturwissenschaften* containing the report by Hahn and Strassmann, which meant that he could talk more openly, and even before he and Fermi finished speaking, some of the young physicists began to leave the room, hurrying to their laboratories in hopes of being the first to perform the fission experiment, or telephoning colleagues to tell them the news. As

Fermi recalled, experimentation "started feverishly in many laboratories, including Pupin [at Columbia]," and before he left Washington he received a telegram from his associate John Dunning announcing a successful experiment. Within forty-eight hours the key experiment had been repeated in several laboratories, and in the wake of the conference Edward Teller wrote to his fellow Hungarian Leo Szilard to tell him that "there is a chain-reaction mood in Washington. I only had to say 'uranium,' and then could listen for two hours to their thoughts." Predictably, news of fission struck each physicist like a hammer blow. On the campus of the University of California in Berkeley, twenty-seven-year-old Luis Alvarez was getting a haircut when he saw a headline in the paper—"Uranium Atom Split in Two Halves." Leaping from the barber's chair with his hair only partly cut, he ran from the shop with a white sheet trailing behind him and arrived breathless at the Radiation Laboratory, where he gasped out the story to his astonished colleagues. The February 6 issue of *Time* carried the story of Hahn's experiment under the heading "Great Accident"; when the German scientist's report reached the United States, it was said, "physicists sprang to their laboratories to see if they could confirm it," and already researchers at Columbia, Johns Hopkins, and the Carnegie Institution in Washington had done so. Two weeks later the magazine ran a follow-up story, describing how news of Hahn's "atomic explosion" had "streaked over the physical world like a meteor," adding that "atomic physicists are off on the biggest big-game hunt since the discovery of artificial radiation was announced. . . ." The *Physical Review* of February 15 carried not only Bohr's authoritative account of the Hahn, Meitner, and Frisch findings, but reports of three corroborating experiments in the United States. The next issue reported other successful experiments, and by the end of 1939 almost one hundred articles on fission had been published in America and abroad.

By one of those extraordinary coincidences, Frédéric Joliot-Curie had also confirmed the uranium fission experiment on January 26—two weeks after Frisch proved it, and on the very day Bohr made his electrifying announcement at the Washington Conference. A copy of the Hahn-Strassmann paper had arrived at Joliot's office about ten days earlier. He read it at once, realized it meant that uranium atoms could be split, and was so upset not to have seen this himself that he locked himself into his room and would speak to no one for several days. His wife, Irène, equally frustrated to learn how close she and Savitch had come to the truth, exclaimed, in the manner of Bohr, "What fools we have been!" Joliot dropped everything else in order to put his mind to the problem and soon reached two significant conclusions: each splitting of an atom would release a large amount of energy; and since the products of that splitting would have fewer neutrons than the original uranium atom, some extra neutrons might be released each time fission occurred.

It suggests the brilliance and dedication of Joliot and his team, which included the Russian Lew Kowarski (like Szilard, Kowarski had been led into nuclear physics by reading H. G. Wells's utopian novel *The World Set Free* at the age of ten) and the Austrian Hans von Halban, that before the year was out they had discovered that the fission of the uranium nucleus not only released immense energy but unloosed neutrons that had been locked inside the nucleus. They learned, moreover, how many neutrons were released and concluded that under the right conditions further fissions would occur, creating even more, until within a fraction of a second so much energy would be released that it would be infinitely more damaging than any chemically produced explosion. During that same year of extraordinary achievement they also applied for five patents for the use of nuclear energy including one for a uranium bomb, designed a workable nuclear reactor, and managed to enlist the support of industry and the French government for their work. It was, all in all, a remarkable performance, and to one of Joliot's colleagues the highly charged atmosphere in their Collège de France laboratory, where they frequently worked ten or twelve hours a day, was reminiscent of a Jules Verne novel. The pressure they felt was not entirely self-imposed: they were reasonably certain that only they and the Columbia University group, which by then included Fermi and Szilard, were making serious progress toward achieving a chain reaction. In the spring of 1939 both teams were progressing at about the same rate, and Joliot and his colleagues had every intention of being first at the finish line. By the end of March, Halban wrote, "We were absolutely bent on creating a nuclear chain reaction which could be used for industrial power." And by this time there was an additional incentive to succeed: in the middle of that same month, Germany, following up its bloodless victory at Munich, had marched into what remained of democratic Czechoslovakia, thereby gaining possession of Europe's richest uranium mines.

There was a certain irony to Hahn and Strassmann's having started all this, for the mere fact that they were Germans led physicists elsewhere to suppose that if a nuclear weapon was within the realm of possibility, the Nazis might well be first to develop it, and to prevent that from happening was of paramount importance. Indeed, the vision of the German dictator with an atomic bomb in his hands was to affect the decisions of the democratic nations for the next six years. On the same day that Hitler's troops occupied Czechoslovakia, Dean George Pegram of Columbia University, goaded by Szilard and Fermi, got in touch with Admiral Stanford C. Hooper, the technical assistant to the chief of naval operations, warning him of "the possibility that uranium might be used as an explosive that would liberate a million times as much energy as any known explosive." Pegram ventured his personal opinion that the likelihood of this occurring was slim, but even so he and his colleagues thought the matter should not be disregarded. One of those colleagues who felt very strongly indeed about the matter was Enrico Fermi, who visited the Navy Department the next day, spoke with a group of navy and army officers and civilian scientists, and told them in his cautious, low-key manner that what was going on at Columbia might eventually lead to the construction of bombs capable of blasting craters several miles in diameter, as well as making possible the use of uranium to power submarines.[1] The navy promised to keep in touch, and three days later Admiral Harold G. Bowen, director of the Naval Research Laboratory, recommended that funds be allotted for investigating the potential of uranium as an explosive.

In Holland, after a leading physicist notified the government of uranium's potential, the Ministry of Finance ordered fifty tons of the ore from Belgium's Union Minière de Haut Katanga, which controlled the world's largest supply in the Belgian Congo (and was, as yet, happily unaware of the sinister uses to which it might be put). In Britain, the Committee of Imperial Defence urged the Treasury and the Foreign Office to obtain uranium for research and to do what they could to keep the ore out of German hands. On May 10, Sir Henry Tizard, chairman of the Royal Air Force's research program and a pioneer in the development of operational radar, met with the president of Union Minière and received assurances that Britain would receive the uranium it needed. Meantime, in Germany, the threat Szilard and Fermi had dreaded was beginning to materialize. Dr. Siegfried Frugge, an associate of Otto Hahn, submitted a paper to *Die Naturwissenschaften* in which he discussed in depth the current state of research into uranium fission. Published on June 9, 1939, it contained such detail that scientists in Britain wondered if Frugge was trying to warn colleagues abroad that Germany was seriously contemplating the exploitation of nuclear energy, using uranium. Another disturbing clue was a conference held in Berlin at the end of April, attended by a number of prominent physicists who reportedly agreed to step up research in nuclear physics. And yet another Berlin conference was called by the head of the research division of Germany's Army Weapons Department, largely in response to a letter from two Hamburg physicists named Paul Harteck and Wilhelm Groth. They summarized the latest research in support of their belief that it would be feasible to produce an atomic device whose explosive power would dwarf that of conventional weapons. When the physics community in the United States and Britain got wind of these developments, their worst fears were confirmed.

Suddenly it seemed that Frisch's fission experiment was being duplicated just about everywhere: in addition to the work at various institutions in America and France, Joseph Rotblat had conducted similar experiments in Poland; and results similar to those achieved at Columbia were reported at

---

[1] The diesel-powered submarine had to operate on batteries while submerged. The nuclear-powered sub, on the other hand, with an atomic reactor driving a high-speed engine, could achieve much higher underwater speeds and could remain submerged for almost unlimited periods of time.

the Leningrad Physico-Technical Institute. What was significant, of course, was that once they were aware of the Hahn-Strassmann report and its significance, physicists anywhere could do what Otto Frisch had done. And it did not take the imaginative Leo Szilard long to project what the consequences of this might be. As something of a permanent refugee who had neither position nor prospects, he had become an unheeded oracle in his own and his adopted countries—the latest of which was the United States. He had attempted without success to persuade Britain's scientific establishment to restrict significant information about nuclear physics to a select group; he had tried unavailingly to raise money for his own research in England and America; he had told Niels Bohr in 1936 that uranium might hold the key to what all physicists were looking for, but could never get the financing to prove his thesis. Now, in January 1939, he had no home, no job, and no money, and the news of the discovery of fission revived all of his old nightmares. But Szilard never lacked initiative or audacity. He had a pretty good idea what was going on in the laboratories at Columbia, and as a means of involving himself in that activity he cabled Professor Frederick Lindemann at Oxford, asking him to return a cylinder of beryllium he had purchased in 1934 when he began looking for chain reactions. Then he borrowed $2,000 from an inventor friend, took the check and rented a gram of radium for $120 a month, and with beryllium and radium in hand persuaded George Pegram to give him guest status and a three-month appointment at the university so he could perform some experiments.

At the time of the Washington conference, Szilard was laid up with a bad cold and fever, and in his room at the Hotel King's Crown opposite the university he took advantage of the enforced inactivity to write to Lewis L. Strauss, a financier with the investment banking firm of Kuhn, Loeb, calling his attention to "a very sensational new development in nuclear physics."[2] During a visit to Princeton the previous week, Szilard wrote, he found the physics department there "like a stirred-up ant heap." What Strauss should know was that there was an aspect of the matter that might reach far beyond mere scientific interest—"possibilities in another direction," as the Hungarian put it. "These might lead to a large-scale production of energy and radioactive elements, unfortunately also perhaps to atomic bombs."

So there it was at last, out in the open. While there would be many a wide and turbulent river to cross before it would be possible even to contemplate construction of a nuclear device that could be used in warfare, the findings of Hahn and Strassmann, as interpreted by Meitner and Frisch, had provided scientists everywhere with the vital clue, meaning that the possibility of the ultimate weapon existed, no matter how remote it might be. Its creation was probably inevitable in the challenge suggested by the physicist Freeman Dyson when he wrote, "To command nature to release in a

[2]Years later, Strauss was to become chairman of the Atomic Energy Commission.

pintpot the energy that fuels the stars, to lift by pure thought a million tons of rock into the sky—these are exercises of the human will which produce an illusion of illimitable power."

On March 3, 1939, on the seventh floor of Pupin Hall at Columbia, Szilard and Walter Zinn—employing the same methods that the Joliot team was using in Paris—performed an experiment to determine whether "neutrons were emitted in the fission process of uranium." That, in turn, "would mean that the large-scale liberation of atomic energy was just around the corner." Once their equipment was set up the two men sat back to watch a screen and, as Szilard wrote later, "we saw the flashes. We watched them for a little while and then we switched everything off and went home. That night there was little doubt in my mind the world was headed for grief."

CHAPTER 27

—————◆—————

"Certain aspects of the situation ...
call for watchfulness and,
if necessary, quick action ..."

A month before he saw those telltale flashes of light on the screen, Szilard had written to Frédéric Joliot-Curie. Knowing that the Frenchman and his team were working on fission, he urged him to maintain secrecy about their experiments. It was Szilard's belief that "these things should be discussed privately among the physicists of England, France, and America," and while his letter to Joliot made that clear enough, it also revealed another horn of the dilemma as he perceived it: "We all hope," he observed, "that there will be no or at least not sufficient neutron emission and therefore nothing to worry about." In other words, while he wanted in the worst way to see a chain reaction demonstrated experimentally, he hoped even more that a bomb might prove impossible to produce.

Joliot was not about to go along with this request from a man he knew only by reputation: the French team was on the verge of achieving an experimental chain reaction, and he was aware, moreover, that he and his colleagues were running neck and neck with the Columbia physicists in a race each group wanted desperately to win. And there was more to it than that. Understandably, Joliot felt that Fermi would not hesitate to publish first if he reached the finish line first, so he decided to ignore Szilard's appeal. His position, backed by long tradition, was that the goal of all science is discovery, and the only way a scientist gets credit for achieving that goal is to publish.

Meantime, Szilard was learning that he was in a minority of one at Columbia on this business of secrecy. Enrico Fermi and Herbert L. Anderson, who had done a successful fission experiment shortly after Szilard and Zinn completed theirs, believed they should make known their findings; so did the experimental physicist I. I. Rabi; so did Dean Pegram; so did everyone else. At the heart of Szilard's problems, of course, was that he was not part of the university establishment; he was merely a guest, invited for a short stay, and his period of grace was running out. But the impetuous Hungarian was by no means the only scientist who was concerned about keeping vital information out of Hitler's hands.

In December 1938, more than twelve hundred scientists and other scholars had issued a manifesto attacking the Nazis' racial policies and suppression of science, stating, "Any attack upon freedom of thought in one sphere, even as nonpolitical a sphere as theoretical physics, is an attack upon democracy itself." In February 1939, a more forceful stand was taken by a professor at Harvard.

No one who knew Percy W. Bridgman could have been surprised to learn that he had taken a position on this matter. When it came to his particular branch of physics, and his total immersion in it as scholar, teacher, experimenter, and philosopher, Bridgman was a man without peripheral vision: he simply had no patience with activities such as faculty meetings or social engagements that diverted attention from the far more important business at hand. It wasn't that Bridgman didn't have other interests: he did, and they included music, chess, handball, gardening, mountain climbing, and photography—all of which he pursued with the intense concentration of a perfectionist. But neither those pastimes nor much of anything else was permitted to interfere with the single-minded pursuit of the truth which took place in his laboratory. He had been Hollis Professor of Mathematics and Natural Philosophy since 1926, which meant quite simply that he held the highest position in Harvard's scientific faculty.

Bridgman's specialty—which was to win him a Nobel Prize—was high-pressure physics, and because he was a pioneer in the field it meant that he had to design and construct much of the equipment used for his experiments and for his elaborate and painstaking measurements. The man was something of a mechanical genius, and in his laboratory, a colleague said, "every adjustment and every measurement [was] dictated by his own mind and controlled by his own muscles." William A. Shurcliff, who was a student of Bridgman's, recalls that air under terrific pressure was piped through the laboratory for use in the professor's experiments with various metals, and every time Bridgman came into the room he would do a little leap when he walked past a certain point. It seems that there was a weak spot in the pressure line just there at floor level, and the professor suspected it might blow out sometime. Since the air would emerge at the speed of a bullet he was simply being prudent, but it made for a highly unusual entrance.

Bridgman—a Harvard classmate of Franklin Roosevelt's—was a good-looking man in his late fifties with a full head of hair and bushy eyebrows. The rather commanding appearance didn't prepare you for the fact, as Shurcliff said, that he was "a terrible lecturer": he had a squeaky voice and he spoke rapidly and in spurts, without regard for enunciation, so listening to him was difficult, to say the least. But the clarity of his thinking and his way of going to the heart of a subject, no matter how obscure, had a profound effect on students.[1] Early in his teaching career, Bridgman had been obliged to make a critical examination of the logical structure of physics, and as he observed later, "I was able to think the situation through to my own satisfaction." Which was precisely what he had done before sending a letter off to *Science*.

In the February 24, 1939, issue of that publication, under the heading " 'Manifesto' by a Scientist," Bridgman announced his position. He began with brief prefatory remarks acknowledging that many scientists were profoundly disturbed by the implications of totalitarianism. While others might well have found a satisfactory means of dealing with the moral dilemma, Bridgman said, in his own case "this urge to find something to do has resulted in the decision to close my laboratory to visits from citizens of totalitarian states." He had had a statement printed, which he intended to hand to every visitor to his lab, and the words were those of a man who knew his own mind.

"I have decided from now on," the manifesto read, "not to show my apparatus or discuss my experiments with the citizens of any totalitarian state. A citizen of such a state is no longer a free individual, but he may be compelled to engage in any activity whatever to advance the purposes of that state. The purposes of the totalitarian states have shown themselves to be in irreconcilable conflict with the purposes of free states"—in particular, the "free cultivation of scientific knowledge for its own sake." What he was doing would serve two purposes, Bridgman predicted: it would stifle scientific intercourse with the dictatorships, depriving them of useful knowledge; and it would give the scientist an opportunity to stand up for his beliefs. "This statement," he concluded, "is made entirely in my individual capacity and has no connection whatever with any policy of the university."

In an afterword, Bridgman reminded readers that science was probably the one human activity "which knows no nationalisms," which was why it had been such an important factor in the development of civilization. All the more reason, he went on, why he deplored the action he was taking and

---

[1]When Robert Oppenheimer went off to Harvard, his father urged him to concentrate on anything he wanted to do, but Bridgman persuaded the brilliant young man to "do physics," and evidently treated him as an intellectual equal. Under the professor's tutelage, Oppenheimer flowered, mastering some of the most abstruse concepts; as he recalled fondly years later, "I was Bridgman's caddy."

did so only after the "gravest consideration." What was at issue, Bridgman believed, was survival, and once the totalitarian governments had destroyed science as an ideal, it was up to the individual scientist to take on the burden of social responsibility.

It was such a remarkable position for an American scientist to take in those early months of 1939 that the *New York Times* published it as front-page news and endorsed Bridgman's action in the lead editorial. Princeton's Dean Christian Gauss was one of several prominent educators to back Bridgman—which was no surprise, since Gauss had delivered a speech a few days earlier declaring "intellectual war" on the totalitarian nations, stating that humanity had suffered too much at their hands to tolerate appeasement.

A month later, William Shurcliff mailed questionnaires to a 10 percent sampling of the American Physical Society's membership, asking what action they believed individual scientists should take. By a modest majority the physicists agreed that it was a good idea to express disapproval of what was going on in Germany, but rather surprisingly they voted overwhelmingly against withholding the usual courtesies from visiting German, Japanese, or Italian scientists, as Bridgman had done, and recommended that scientific journals continue to be sent to scholars in Axis countries. A curious business, this: as Americans in many professions were beginning to discover, these were far from ordinary times, and before long a great many of the rules and assumptions people had lived by for years were going to come increasingly under question.

═══

At this stage, despite the fears of a few scientists that the Germans might find a way to produce an atomic bomb, the problems of doing so looked to be just about insurmountable. Niels Bohr had suggested that it was the rare uranium 235 isotope which was subject to fission—not the slightly heavier, far more plentiful U-238—and no one knew how much 235 would be required. What they did know was that uranium as found in nature is a mixture of 140 parts of U-238 to one of U-235, which meant that it would take immense, possibly unobtainable, quantities of U-238 to create an explosive chain reaction. (One of Joliot's colleagues calculated that the mass required would be forty tons, and a refugee from Berlin named Rudolf Peierls, who was now in England, refined the estimate and produced a mathematical equation showing that the critical mass of pure uranium necessary to make a bomb meant that "there was . . . no chance of getting such a thing into an aeroplane." Peierls's paper was published in the *Proceedings of the Cambridge Philosophical Society* several weeks after the war began; he had not hesitated to submit it, since he could not see how it would have any practical use.)

Szilard, meanwhile, continued to fret about the Nazis and what might happen if they got their hands on large quantities of the uranium ore the

Belgians were mining in the Congo. In June his three-month stay at Columbia ended, and he was discussing with a fellow refugee from Hungary, Eugene Wigner, what was to be done. The two had known each other as students in Germany; Wigner was now a professor of physics at Princeton, where he had a half-time position paying $550 annually (for the balance of the year he returned to the Institute of Technology in Berlin, where he had taught since 1926), and he was as alarmed as Szilard was by the possibility that the Germans might develop an atomic weapon. Suddenly Szilard had an idea. Einstein, he reminded Wigner, knew the queen of the Belgians; Einstein could warn the queen, and through her the Belgian government and the Union Minière de Haut Katanga, against selling any uranium to Germany. What made this plan seem feasible was that both men had known Einstein in Europe, and Wigner was particularly close to him now; the great scientist was ill at ease conversing in English, so he and Wigner spent long hours walking in the woods, speaking German while they discussed politics and physics. And so it was agreed that the two of them would ask the famous man to convey the vital message to the Belgians.

It was July, it was hot, it was a good time to be at the shore, and a telephone call to Einstein's Princeton office produced the information that the professor, who loved to sail, was staying at the cottage of a Dr. Moore, in Peconic, on Long Island. Wigner had a car, and he and Szilard set off on a beautiful day. They drove mistakenly to Patchogue, on the south shore, where they learned that Peconic was near Cutchogue, toward the northeast tip of the island. When they arrived in Peconic, no one could tell them where the Moore house was. After driving around for an hour they were about to give up when Szilard saw a small boy standing on the curb. Leaning out the car window, he asked, "Say, do you by any chance know where Professor Einstein lives?" The eight-year-old promptly led them to the famous man's door on Old Grove Road.

Einstein, dressed in an undershirt with his trousers rolled up, greeted them, and as soon as they were seated on the screened porch the two Hungarians voiced their fears and their hope for assistance. "This," Szilard wrote later, "was the first Einstein heard about the possibility of a chain reaction. He was very quick to see the implications and perfectly willing to do anything that needed to be done." For some time, when obliged to answer questions from inquiring reporters, Einstein had said, "I feel absolutely sure—well, nearly sure—that it will not be possible to convert matter into energy for practical purposes." And why not? He would go on to explain the difficulties of bombarding atoms with subatomic particles—atoms so small that direct hits are few—and with his gift for the picturesque phrase, add, "It is like shooting birds in the dark in a country where there are only a few birds." While it seems implausible that a man of Einstein's erudition would be unaware of the recent momentous progress in the field of nuclear physics, it appears that that was the case, so preoccupied was he with his own reflections, and so isolated from current developments. Moreover, even if he did recognize the theoretical possibility of a nuclear weapon, he may have been extremely skeptical about its practicability. (Shortly after the neutron—the "magic bullet" used in smashing atoms—was discovered in 1932, Einstein observed, "There is not the slightest indication that energy will ever be obtainable. It would mean that the atom would have to be shattered at will.") He had, moreover, talked with Bohr during the Dane's stay in Princeton and probably was aware of Bohr's conclusion that the problem of separating U-235 from U-238 seemed all but insoluble. Whatever the case, Einstein wrote later, "I did not, in fact, foresee that [nuclear energy] would be released in my time. I only believed that it was theoretically possible." What meant much more to Szilard and Wigner than whether he subscribed to their scientific views was that he shared their fears about the Nazis and the importance of keeping essential materials and information out of their hands.

He was somewhat reluctant to write to the queen, Einstein told them, but he would send a letter to a Belgian cabinet minister he knew. Then Wigner interposed a suggestion that no letter should go to a foreign government without initial clearance from the U.S. State Department; after all, they should remember that two of them were Hungarians and the other a German-born Swiss. Before Szilard and Wigner left to drive back to the city, Einstein dictated in German while Wigner wrote down a draft of a letter to the ambassador of Belgium, calling his attention to certain discoveries that might affect the welfare of his nation and others. (Wigner recalled later his amazement at how Einstein's "words just flowed out.") It was agreed that Szilard would write to the secretary of state, enclosing the Einstein letter, inquiring if the secretary cared to hear more about the subject so that he could approach the Belgian government, or if Einstein should go ahead and inform the Belgian ambassador on his own.

Back in New York City, Szilard typed a draft letter, mailed it to Einstein, and then had second thoughts. Reflecting on the plan they had devised, he concluded that it was clumsy and probably unworkable, and decided to seek advice from friends who had "more experience in things practical." He took his problem to Gustav Stolper, an economist, publisher, and former member of the German Reichstag who had come as a refugee to America in 1933, and was told that he should pay a call on Alexander Sachs. Surely, since Dr. Sachs, an economic adviser to the Lehman Corporation, had worked for Roosevelt in the early days of the New Deal, he would know how to approach the government—whether to go directly to the State Department, to another agency, or perhaps even to the White House. Stolper called Sachs and arranged for Szilard to see him.

Alexander Sachs had been increasingly interested in what was going on in nuclear physics since 1936, when he heard Lord Rutherford lecture, and in February 1939, on a visit to Princeton, he saw a copy of a letter Niels Bohr had written to the editor of *Nature* concerning recent developments. Sachs was sufficiently excited about what he learned to have informed President

Roosevelt about the significance of these recent experiments. He had also composed a memorandum for his files, with the extraordinary title "Notes on Imminence World War in Perspective Accrued Errors and Cultural Crisis of the Inter-War Decades," in which he observed: "There is still time for Western Civilization, and especially for the exceptionally and fortunately situated United States, to use the time-drafts that can still be made on the Bank of History, for the preparedness that has and will become more and more urgent and inevitable for all members of Western Civilization as a result of the past errors committed and in the course of the prospective unfolding aggressions of Nazi Germany." Sachs, in short, was in a receptive mood to see Szilard. Like Szilard, he was a gadfly who liked to get things done, and he wanted to get things moving while the Bank of History was still open for business.

His immediate reaction to Szilard's request for advice was to say there was no use whatever in going to any of the agencies or departments of government, that this was a matter for the White House. Sachs then revealed a piece of disquieting news: he had heard that the U.S. Navy, turned off by what was perceived as the negative attitude of Fermi and Pegram, had decided not to push uranium research after all. If that was true, it would probably be necessary to get a letter from Einstein directly before the president, and Sachs was confident that he could accomplish that. So Sachs came up with a draft of a new letter, Szilard worked it over, and in the end Szilard and Edward Teller, another Hungarian physicist who owned a car (Wigner having gone to the West Coast), paid a call on Einstein in Peconic to see if he would be willing to sign a letter addressed not to the Belgian ambassador but to the President of the United States. Einstein required no persuasion, they discussed the draft, and several days later Szilard sent Einstein two versions of the letter—one short, one long, both dated August 2, 1939. With them he included a covering note saying that Sachs was now proposing either the financier Bernard Baruch or Karl Compton, president of MIT, as the most effective courier for their message, but that both Szilard and Teller had vetoed them. The compromise on whom all three men agreed was Charles Lindbergh, and Szilard asked Einstein for a letter of introduction which he could enclose with a message he was writing himself to the famous aviator.

Since Lindbergh's name was anathema at the White House it was fortunate for Szilard and his colleagues that the flier apparently never saw the letters from Einstein or Szilard; he was receiving enormous quantities of mail that year and it is understandable, though curious, that these particular communications should have gone astray. In any event, by September 27—by which time Lindbergh was enmeshed in his campaign to keep the United States out of the war that had just begun in Europe—Szilard wrote Einstein once again, saying, "I am afraid [Lindbergh] is in fact not our man." Germany's victory over Poland was by that date virtually complete, and Szilard supposed gloomily that it would be Belgium's turn before long;

before that occurred, he told Einstein, "I want to . . . see that at least 50 tons of uranium oxide is purchased" by the U.S. government.

Given Szilard's temperament, it can't have been easy for Alexander Sachs to keep him at bay all this time. In mid-August, Szilard sent Sachs the longer version of the Einstein letter, asking if he would bring it to the attention of the president. But the financier knew how preoccupied FDR was with the European crisis and the battle over the arms embargo, and realized that any effort to interest the chief executive just then in Szilard's cause would be counterproductive. Moreover, he believed the manner of presentation was critical: he didn't want a piece of paper to float unescorted across the president's desk, and he saw himself as the messenger who would both deliver it and make certain that it was heeded and digested. By early October Sachs felt the time was ripe, and he arranged to see Roosevelt on the 11th.

===

When Sachs arrived at the White House he found two ordnance specialists—Colonel Keith Adamson of the army and Commander Gilbert Hoover of the navy—waiting to see him, and after explaining his mission he was ushered into the Oval Office. The two old friends exchanged greetings, and Sachs eased into the discussion with a smile, saying that since he had paid for his trip to Washington and couldn't deduct it from his income tax, he hoped the president would pay close attention. He produced three items— an August 15 note from Szilard mentioning the vast destructive potential of an atomic bomb and urging the purchase of pitchblende from the Belgian Congo before the Germans invaded Belgium; a letter from Sachs urging government support for the expansion and acceleration of experimental work which could no longer be carried on within the limited budgets of universities; and the pièce de résistance, the letter addressed to F. D. Roosevelt from A. Einstein, which read:

"Some recent work by E. Fermi and L. Szilard, which has been communicated to me in manuscript, leads me to expect that the element uranium may be turned into a new and important source of energy in the immediate future. Certain aspects of the situation which has arisen seem to call for watchfulness and, if necessary, quick action on the part of the Administration. I believe therefore that it is my duty to bring to your attention the following facts and recommendations:

"In the course of the last four months it has been made probable— through the work of Joliot in France as well as Fermi and Szilard in America—that it may become possible to set up a nuclear chain reaction in a large mass of uranium by which vast amounts of power and large quantities of new radium-like elements would be generated. Now it appears almost certain that this could be achieved in the immediate future.

"This new phenomenon would also lead to the construction of bombs, and it is conceivable—though less certain—that extremely powerful bombs of a new type may thus be constructed. A single bomb of this type, carried by boat and exploded in a port, might very well destroy the whole port together with some of the surrounding territory. However, such bombs might very well prove to be too heavy for transportation by air."

From there the letter went on to warn the president that the Germans were known to be working toward the same goal, to remind him that the United States possessed "only very poor ores of uranium in moderate quantities," and to urge him to appoint a permanent liaison between the administration and the physicists who were working on chain reaction.

Franklin Roosevelt had no more knowledge of physics than the next educated American, to whom the notion of a device that would explode as a result of atoms splitting would have seemed like a bizarre idea out of the Buck Rogers or Flash Gordon comic strips. Rather surprisingly, though, since Great Britain was by then at war, an article about just such a weapon had appeared in the September issue of a reputable English publication, *Discovery,* whose editor, C. P. Snow, had written: "Some leading physicists think that within a few months science will have produced for military use an explosive a million times more violent than dynamite. It is no secret; laboratories in the United States, Germany, France, and England have been working on it feverishly since the spring. It may not come off. The most competent opinion is divided upon whether the idea is practicable. If it is, science for the first time will at one bound have altered the scope of warfare. The power of most scientific weapons has been consistently exaggerated; but it would be difficult to exaggerate this."

Unfortunately, the message Sachs was laboring to get across was neither so clear nor to the point, and it was small wonder if the president's interest flagged at times during the verbal barrage. At one point, sensing that he was losing his audience, Sachs told the story of the young American inventor who had called on Napoleon and offered to construct a fleet of ships without sails, enabling Napoleon to ferry his troops to England no matter what the weather. The French emperor had found the proposal preposterous and had sent the American away. And what a pity that was, said Sachs, since the young man's name was Robert Fulton and his steamships might have made Napoleon's dream of invasion come true. Then he read a prediction from F. W. Aston, a British physicist who observed that one day man would learn to "release and control [the atom's] almost infinite power. We cannot prevent him from doing so," Aston added, "and can only hope he will not use it exclusively in blowing up his next-door neighbor."

FDR reacted favorably. ("He was a man of quick apperception," Sachs recalled. "He seemed to share the sense of urgency.")

"Alex," Roosevelt remarked, "what you are after is to see that the Nazis don't blow us up."

"Precisely," Sachs replied.

At that the president summoned General Edwin Watson, the genial

Southerner who was his appointments secretary, and told him, "Pa, this requires action."

A triumphant Sachs left the Oval Office with Watson, and by that evening an Advisory Committee on Uranium, headed by Dr. Lyman J. Briggs, director of the National Bureau of Standards, with Colonel Adamson and Commander Hoover, had been appointed to consider the novel ideas carried to the White House by the New York economist.

CHAPTER 28

"... *things were not moving at all.*"

At the time Alexander Sachs paid his call on President Roosevelt, relations between America's scientific community and the government were tenuous, at best. A few attempts had been made during the early days of the New Deal to establish some lines of communication between the two groups, but nothing much had come of those efforts, and there existed neither an atmosphere of mutual confidence nor the machinery for effective liaison.

The Advisory Committee on Uranium met for the first time on October 21, ten days after Sachs's appearance at the White House, and it was clear from the outset that there was going to be a certain amount of friction between the old-line bureaucrats and the foreigners responsible for creating this fuss about nuclear fission. Lyman Briggs, director of the Bureau of Standards, an amiable, tweedy fellow who liked to fiddle with an empty tobacco pipe, was the committee's chairman. He had entered government service in 1896 as a soil scientist, and after more than four decades of playing it safe it was unlikely that he would go out on a limb with some half-cocked scheme to create a secret weapon. The same was true of the two service ordnance men, Commander Hoover and Colonel Adamson. It was going to take some fancy persuading to convince Adamson, in particular, of the potency of this bomb they were talking about; his position was made clear when he remarked that he had once been outside an ordnance depot when it blew up and "it didn't even knock me down." In addition to these three, two Washington physicists were present—Richard Roberts of the Carnegie Institution and Fred Mohler of the Bureau of Standards—and since Lyman Briggs had appointed them, they probably could be counted on to be cautious.

Feeling very much like outsiders and supplicants were the foreign-born visitors—Sachs, Szilard, Wigner, and Teller, of whom only Sachs was a member of the committee. (Einstein had been invited but had begged off, pleading poor health.) It was not the intention of Szilard and his colleagues to ask for funds at this meeting, even though money was a pressing necessity; what they wanted was the official blessing of the government, to gain the credibility they needed in seeking funding from foundations. But, as Szilard said, "these things never go the way you have planned them." Inevitably, the subject of money did come up, and when Colonel Adamson asked how much they were talking about, Szilard replied that they would need about $2,000 for graphite (which they planned to use as a moderator to slow down neutrons) and perhaps another $4,000 for materials for further experiments. At that, Adamson launched into a tirade, saying it was naïve to suppose they could make a contribution to the military by creating a new explosive, that it required two wars to determine whether a new weapon was any good, and that in any case, it was not weapons that won wars, but the morale of the troops. On and on he went, until the mild-mannered Wigner finally interrupted: it was interesting to hear the colonel's theory, Wigner said, because he had always supposed that weapons were important to the military. But since they were not, the army probably did not need such a large appropriation; perhaps its budget could be cut.

"All right," the colonel snapped, "you'll get your money."

In their first report, the members of the Advisory Committee on Uranium summarized the situation as best they could, given the number of unknowns in this elusive equation. A chain reaction was possible, they stated, though it remained to be seen if one could be brought off; if a chain reaction *could* be achieved and controlled, it might power submarines; and if the reaction proved to be explosive, it might be the source of bombs whose destructiveness would far exceed anything known. That was a lot of ifs, and in hopes of resolving some of the open questions the committee recommended the purchase of four tons of pure graphite and fifty tons of uranium oxide. Beyond that there wasn't much to be said.

"The Washington meeting," Szilard wrote, "was followed by the most curious period in my life. We heard nothing from Washington at all. By the first of February [1940] there was still no word. . . ." On February 8, Pa Watson informed Briggs that he intended to put the matter before the president again. Then silence. As time wore on, Szilard and the others grew more anxious than ever, alarmed by fresh reports that the Germans were intensifying their research into uranium. Szilard had assumed, with the innocence of a scientist consumed by his work, that once it had been demonstrated that neutrons are emitted in the fission of uranium, the world would sit up and take notice and there would be no difficulty interesting influential people in the project. He was wrong, he discovered, and to make matters worse, not even Fermi seemed troubled by Washington's inactivity; the Italian was philosophical about their failure to get the money to buy graphite and had turned his attention to cosmic rays.

It was an incredible fact, Szilard observed, "that between the end of June 1939 and the spring of 1940, not a single experiment was under way in the United States which was aimed at exploring the possibilities of a chain reaction in natural uranium." He read, doubtless with some envy, a paper by Joliot describing the possibilities of a chain reaction in a uranium-and-water system and concluded that Joliot had come very close indeed to achieving a chain reaction. He fretted and fumed, he pestered Fermi and others at Columbia, and finally he went to Princeton to tell Einstein that "things were not moving at all." It goes almost without saying that Szilard had a scheme for getting the project back on the rails. He was convinced that a system employing graphite would be chain-reacting, and he suggested to Einstein that they warn the government that he would publish this theory in *Physical Review* unless someone in authority asked him not to do so and unless Washington evidenced interest by taking action on the uranium program.

Once again Sachs agreed to act as go-between. On March 15 the financier wrote to Roosevelt, enclosing another letter from Einstein which called attention to the intensification of atomic work in Germany and stated further: "Dr. Szilard has shown me the manuscript which he is sending to *Physical Review* in which he describes in detail a method for setting up a chain reaction in uranium. The papers will appear in print unless they are held up, and the question arises whether something ought to be done to withhold publication." To this somewhat bewildering threat the president responded as a man under a great deal of pressure from all directions might be expected to respond: he sent for Pa Watson and told him to have the Advisory Committee on Uranium hold another meeting.

Accordingly, Sachs phoned Lyman Briggs and urged him to assemble his committee. Briggs replied that he was in fact about to do just that, and he wondered if Sachs and Dean Pegram of Columbia would be willing to attend.

"What about Szilard and Fermi?" Sachs asked.

"Well," Briggs responded somewhat hesitantly, "you know, these matters are secret and we do not think that they should be included."

At that, Sachs blew up. He reminded Briggs that he was the one who had written to the president, he who had been asked to schedule another meeting, and he—with his colleagues Szilard and Fermi—who had brought this business to the attention of the government in the first place, and why in the name of all that was holy would the people who were doing the work be excluded on grounds of secrecy? When Briggs finally got Sachs calmed down, it turned out that they had been talking about different meetings, and Fermi and Szilard were duly included. But there was something significant about this brief exchange, a suggestion that before long the government boys were going to be imposing certain strictures on this project that were not likely to sit well with scientists whose careers had been built upon the open exchange of information. Szilard had experienced at first hand the outrage of his colleagues when he urged them to keep their findings secret, and in the spring of 1940, when the munificent sum of $6,000 voted by the Uranium Committee at last became available and Columbia's physics department was able to purchase some graphite, the question came up once more. Fermi had just completed an experiment that measured the absorption of neutrons by graphite, and Szilard said to him, "Now that we have this value, perhaps the value ought not to be made public." Fermi lost his temper and told Szilard that it was absurd to keep the results of their work under wraps, and that might have been the end of the matter had not Dean Pegram dropped in to see Fermi and told him that the data he had collected should not be published. "From that point on," Szilard wrote, "secrecy was on."

Secrecy might be on, but it began to look as if the uranium project itself might be off. Late in May of 1940, an associate professor of physics at Princeton named Louis Turner wrote to Szilard, pointing out that in a chain reaction a new element would be formed as a by-product, and this element would also be capable of undergoing fission.[1] It was a possibility that had not occurred to Szilard or Fermi, and since it was clearly of great importance, Szilard asked I. I. Rabi for advice, and Rabi suggested that he discuss it with Harold Urey.

An authentic homegrown genius, Urey had come up through the academic ranks, teaching school in Indiana, getting a zoology degree at Montana State, working for a chemical company, earning a Ph.D. at Berkeley, and studying with Niels Bohr in Copenhagen before joining the faculty at Johns Hopkins and then Columbia. By 1940 he was one of America's renowned scientists, having shared a Nobel Prize for the discovery of deuterium (a heavy isotope of hydrogen) and heavy water. What was important for Szilard's purposes, he had the credentials to be named a member, along with five other American scientists, of the reconstituted Uranium Committee and enough clout to persuade Chairman Briggs that Szilard and others "who were actively interested in this problem" should function as a team of technical advisers. With high hopes that they were going to get some

---

[1] Had Fermi published the results of his work with graphite, it might well have set the Germans—who had abandoned the use of carbon as a moderator—back on the track. And had Turner published his paper, predicting the element known later as plutonium—which proved to be the easiest way to build the bomb—that information would have provided the Germans with an essential clue. So Szilard's determined efforts to keep progress secret paid off handsomely.

action at last, Szilard, Fermi, and Wigner were present on June 15, 1940, when the Uranium Committee met once again in Washington, and their dismay at the sudden dashing of those hopes echoes in Szilard's description of what occurred the moment Briggs opened the meeting. They were stunned when the chairman began by announcing that the committee would be dissolved at the close of the current session, because, in Szilard's words, "if the government were to spend a substantial amount of money (we were discussing sums of the order of a half million dollars) and subsequently it would turn out that it is not possible to set up a chain reaction based on uranium, there might be a congressional investigation. If this were the case, in such a situation it would be awkward if the government had made available funds on the recommendation of a committee whose membership comprised men other than American citizens of long standing." There was the nub of it. In this as in so many other matters, the fear of what Congress might say or do was affecting decisions that in turn determined high policy.

"Fermi and I were not American citizens," Szilard continued ruefully, and the words have the sound of a death knell. "Though Wigner was an American citizen, he was not one of long standing. Thus the work on uranium in the United States was brought to a standstill for the next six months."

Even the irrepressible Sachs was depressed—he was as ever conscious that those time drafts on the Bank of History were being exhausted, and he knew why. The trouble was that the government officials who were now involved in this affair were not only fearful of the Congress, they were incapable of thinking big; they could not adjust their sights to the grand scale, to envision the immense program the making of the bomb would inevitably entail. For too long their outlook had been colored by the parsimony demanded by the Depression, and Sachs could see that they were going to insist on "bit-a-bit procedures."

Fortunately for Szilard and Sachs, events—not bureaucrats—were going to dictate the direction of their project from now on. The situation in Europe had changed suddenly and dramatically, and more than ever, America's hand was being forced by what was occurring across the Atlantic Ocean.

PART V

1940

DUNKIRK: THE DELIVERANCE

Prime Minister Winston Churchill
leaves No. 10 Downing Street to inform Parliament
of the fall of France while exhorting his countrymen
to prove that "this was their finest hour."

CHAPTER 29

———————◆———————

"...he missed the bus."

I t was to be a year of defeat, a year of panic and disbelief, a year of
bitterly contested campaigns, military and political. Yet afterward,
when people looked back upon it, it was perceived to have been a year
of miracles, which had meant survival for the British, and yet another
breathing spell for their partisans in the western hemisphere.

Before 1940 began, King George VI broadcast a touching Christmas
message to his subjects around the world, telling them: "I said to the man
who stood at the Gate of the Year, 'Give me a light that I may tread safely
into the unknown.' And he replied, 'Go out into the darkness, and put your
hand into the Hand of God.'"

If anyone doubted that the unknown was closing in or that the Hand of
God would be welcome, he needed only to look to Finland, where the
Russians had launched a full-scale attack on November 30, 1939, with half
a million troops crashing into the shadowy forests on four fronts. Like
Churchill in England, Finland's military commander, Baron Carl Gustav
Emil Mannerheim, had unavailingly warned a succession of Finnish gov-
ernments to prepare for the worst, and had done the best he could on his
own by mobilizing the army under the pretext of practicing war games, after
which he sent a caustic message to the civilian chiefs on November 27:
"While everything has pointed to a gigantic conflict approaching, the indis-

pensable demands of our defense have been treated with parsimony." Worse, even now, "questions regarding the most urgent necessities of the armed forces are treated in as leisurely a manner as if we lived in normal times." The only normal aspect to the times was that the Russians emulated the Nazis, arranged a border "incident," and at the end of the month, as Red Army tanks clanked across the border, the Winter War began.

Americans—in part out of sentimental attachment to the Finns, in part because of a long tradition of rooting for the underdog—were at first outraged by the bombing of undefended cities and then buoyed by the unexpected show of strength by the Finns, the staggering Russian losses. On December 14 the USSR was expelled from the League of Nations—not that action by the League counted for much, but it was, after all, the only forum in which beleaguered nations could appeal to world opinion. A week later Joseph Stalin observed his sixtieth birthday—a state occasion with the obligatory factory parties, prizes established in his honor, a biography, *A Book About the Leader*, written by President Mikhail Kalinin (with a first printing of one million copies), adulatory songs, countless portraits, and all the other paraphernalia of celebrations in a dictatorship. But one important figure was absent from the festivities. Andrei Zhdanov, political boss of Leningrad and the leading advocate of the subjugation of Finland, was in disgrace: he had made the mistake of promising Helsinki to Stalin as a birthday gift, and the Red Army was a long way from taking the Finnish capital.

Behind the Russian attack lay the accident of geography—Finland being Russia's immediate neighbor. Added to that was Stalin's certainty that Hitler would one day invade the Soviet Union, driving in on its second city, Leningrad, in a pincer movement—the right claw slicing through Latvia and Estonia, the left down through Finland. Leery of Finland's traditional friendship for Germany, Stalin tried unsuccessfully to negotiate joint defense arrangements with Finland against Germany, and when that failed, made it a condition of the Nazi-Soviet Pact that he would have a free hand in Finland.

Russia's armored divisions were operating virtually blindfolded in blizzards where the visibility was nine feet, the cold unbelievable. Donald Day, correspondent for the *Chicago Tribune*, reported seeing two thousand Russian bodies strewn about in a small, scraggly, forested area of stunted Arctic pines, where the thermometer read 22 below zero and men "froze into rigid, icy blocks after they were shot down." Major George Fielding Eliot, commenting on the war in *Life*, suggested that the Soviet forces might not be so mighty after all, but he cautioned readers that the "difficulties of Arctic weather and Finnish terrain are enormously greater than those faced by the Germans in Poland." Enormously greater, indeed—on top of which the Red Army was running up against all but insuperable problems of supply, and a tough little army that was everything it was not: superbly trained, well equipped, and excellently led. Dressed in warm white clothes, traveling swiftly and silently on skis, transporting supplies and equipment on sleds drawn by reindeer, the Finns were lightly armed with submachine guns and German automatic pistols and could move so much faster than the enemy that the Russians were often surrounded before they knew what was happening.

Near Suomussalmi, the Finns mustered eight hundred regular troops, a few reservists, and men from nearby villages to combat a force of seventeen thousand Russians. They set up a defensive position south of town, across a body of water which had not yet frozen hard enough for the Russian tanks to cross, and when some reinforcements showed up, had the audacity to attack, with ski troops outflanking the invaders; the Russian armor, strung out over ten miles of narrow forest track, stalled and froze, and the Finns cut it to pieces. They pumped water from the lakes onto the tanks at night, so the machines and the men inside turned into blocks of ice, or they varied the treatment by pouring gasoline over the vehicles and igniting it. After three weeks, the Russians who were lucky enough to survive finally broke out of the trap under heavy aircraft cover.

Life's photographer Carl Mydans sent his editors pictures and text describing an action along the Kemi River, where Red Army supply trucks were hit so suddenly that they had no time even to turn around. The Russians leaped out, and several thousand of them died in the pine forests. Through Mydans's camera lens, Americans were exposed to the somber face of war once again, to heaps of dead men lying like fallen leaves, their arms, legs, and facial expressions grotesquely frozen. A Finnish official told Mydans that wolves had been seen in Finland the previous winter for the first time in many years. "This year," he predicted, "the wolves will find much food." The Finns prayed for snow and more cold (in January, on the northern front, temperatures ranged from minus 20 to minus 50 Fahrenheit), but without material aid, neither snow nor cold nor skill would be enough to hold off the hordes of attacking Russians. The parlous state of the little nation's arsenal was revealed when Finnish planes appeared over Leningrad and dropped leaflets that read, "This might have been a bomb."

Sympathy for the plight of the Finns took the form mainly of financial aid or promises: Herbert Hoover, back in harness in his World War I role of relief administrator, collected donations of $200,000. President Roosevelt refused to proclaim the existence of a state of war, since that would have prevented Finland from borrowing from the United States, meanwhile asking Congress to return the Finns' most recent payment of interest on its World War I debt and to grant a $10 million loan to help that country purchase weapons. Alas, military equipment was in pitifully short supply. George C. Marshall, the new chief of staff of the U.S. Army, had informed members of a congressional committee in November that the nation's armed forces were not building up so much as they were trying to *catch* up to the level of preparedness authorized in 1920. What the Finns received was a promise of forty-four Brewster fighters from the navy. In mid-December the president unburdened himself to William Allen White of the *Emporia Gazette*. It worried him, he wrote, that the American public was content to pat itself on the back every morning and thank God for the Atlantic and Pacific oceans, underestimating the seriousness of what was happening in Europe and in the Far East. "Therefore, my sage old friend," he went on, "my problem is to get the American people to think of conceivable consequences without scaring [them] into thinking that they are going to be dragged into this war." In another letter he complained, "The country as a whole does not yet have any deep sense of world crisis," and at a cabinet meeting he called the parsimonious senators who resisted sending aid to Finland "a bunch of Uriah Heeps" who were blind to the way events in Europe would affect this nation. As usual, Mr. Roosevelt was having a tough time with the people and their representatives on this unpopular topic.

He had company in his frustration. In England, David Lloyd George told the House of Commons, "It is the old trouble—too late. Too late with Czechoslovakia, too late with Poland, certainly too late with Finland. It is always too late or too little or both, and that is the road to disaster." In the same chamber, Winston Churchill, first lord of the Admiralty, rose to speak of "Finland, superb, nay, sublime in the jaws of peril, Finland shows what free men can do. . . ." But neither words nor good wishes were of any avail to the Finns, who could be saved now only by the intervention of an Allied expeditionary force. That highly unlikely event was made more so when Sweden, warned by the Nazis that they would attack if Allied troops were permitted to transit Swedish soil, arranged for peace talks between the Russians and Finns, and a denouement to this tragic, faraway war was in sight.

At the last, the Finns—who had no more than a handful of tanks and some obsolete biplanes—were pounded into submission by aerial bombardment, artillery fire (300,000 shells a day fell on some forts in the Mannerheim Line, commanding the Karelian Isthmus), and overwhelming numbers. For what consolation it may have been, of nearly a million men finally engaged, the invaders lost a quarter of a million killed and a like number wounded, along with seventeen hundred tanks and seven hundred planes, while the Finns, according to tough old General Mannerheim, who had spent two decades building his nation's army and three and a half months leading it in a death struggle, lost fifteen thousand dead. After the Finnish peace delegation was humiliated in Moscow and forced to yield more territory than Stalin had initially demanded, Mannerheim bade farewell to his troops. He reminded them proudly that they had been outnumbered fifty to one but had outfought the enemy thirteen to one and were still unconquered. To the rest of the world, he added bitterly, "We have paid to the very last penny any debt we may have owed to the West."

Mortifying as the campaign had been for the Russians, it spared them from a fate infinitely worse. By revealing the weaknesses of their equipment, training, officer corps, and strategic planning, in the long run the Finnish experience helped to save them from disaster when Hitler turned on them in 1941.

———

In January of 1940 the plaza outside the Capitol in Washington was white with snow when one of the senators who had resisted sending aid to Finland walked slowly down the steps and headed toward home.

William Borah of Idaho was seventy-four years old, and a little girl who saw him noticed how he shuffled, leaving a trail of slurred footprints. The next morning the newspapers reported that he was ill, and when a child phoned his office to find out how he was, the secretary asked who was calling. "Oh, I'm just a little girl that talks to him in the park," was the reply. After he died, a weekly magazine observed that Borah had no close friends in the Senate, only illustrious official mourners who bowed at the passing of a towering figure. It was noted that among those attending the service for him in the Senate chamber were President and Mrs. Roosevelt, members of the cabinet, Chief Justice Charles Evans Hughes, members of both houses of Congress, 150 Idahoans, and a little girl in blue overalls and a bright red sweater, whose name nobody knew and who was his friend.

So old Borah was gone, and within three months the phrase he had coined, "phony war," would follow him to the grave. In the meantime, the man who had done his level best to make a convert out of Borah was still out in front of the parade, beating the drum, trying to persuade Congress and the people to get in step behind him before time ran out. In his January 3 State of the Union message, President Roosevelt had tried once again to suggest what lay ahead. After assuring listeners that the United States was going to stay out of war, he reminded them that "there is a vast difference between keeping out of war and pretending that war is none of our business." The nation's leaders would continue to work tirelessly for peace, he promised, but he hoped to see "fewer American ostriches" now that the intentions of Europe's aggressor nations were so clear. "It is not good for the ultimate health of ostriches," he observed, "to bury their heads in the sand." FDR was nothing if not a realist in such matters, but after calculating that he would need the combined strengths of "the Holy Ghost and Jack Dempsey" to pull off a one-nation peace effort, he determined to give it a try, and within a month's time dispatched Under Secretary of State Sumner Welles to the warring capitals of western Europe—Rome, Berlin, Paris, and London—in the belief that "no possibility, however remote and however improbable, should be overlooked."

In handing this mission to Welles, the president demonstrated once again his penchant for an administrative technique that could only be described as quixotic. He liked to see sparks fly, in the belief that they often kindled fresh ideas, and he had a peculiar knack—abhorrent to old-line bureaucrats and political appointees alike—for selecting top lieutenants whose temperaments clashed, a process that frequently encouraged friction, bickering, and backbiting. Washington hands had seen how Roosevelt seemed to take perverse delight in the discomfiture his choices produced; what was less apparent was that he disliked being committed to a particular individual and, as a master of manipulation, was careful to prevent the establishment of a power center in any government agency. By avoiding concentrations of opposition, he reduced the likelihood that efforts might be made to gang up on him, and the effect was to make each government agency more dependent on the White House than might otherwise have been the case.

Sumner Welles, a remote, frosty, self-assured man who was, like FDR, an alumnus of Groton, had been chosen by the president as under secretary of state in 1937 despite Cordell Hull's preference for another man, and Roosevelt's habit of dealing directly with Welles understandably infuriated the secretary. According to Dean Acheson, Hull was "slow, circuitous, cautious"; Welles "grasped ideas quickly and got things done," and the more the latter appropriated to himself the responsibility for liaison with the White House on international political affairs, the more Hull resented him, and the more the State Department was divided into two camps. In his admirable account of the Roosevelt administration, Robert Sherwood observed that "the most lasting and most deplorable element in the distant relations between the White House and its next-door neighbor to the west [i.e., the State Department] was the president's close association with Sumner Welles—an association based on long friendship and genuine admiration." Sherwood was reluctant to speculate on the animosity that existed between the secretary and under secretary, but said that "there is no question of doubt that their conflict became so ugly and so extremely dangerous that it eventually compelled the resignation of Welles, which was a serious loss to Roosevelt, for he placed great dependence on Welles' judgment. . . ."[1]

Harold Ickes, who was no fan of Welles, called him ambitious and arrogant ("glacially toplofty" was his phrase) and regarded him as a typical member of Hull's department, which the interior secretary characterized in his diary as "a conglomeration of ambitious men consisting mainly of careerists who, because they are career men, feel no obligation to follow administration policy." What was worse, Ickes added, the department was "shot through with fascism."

Although Ambassadors Bullitt and Kennedy opposed sending Welles into their territory on what they regarded as a fool's errand, and isolationists were outraged at this evidence of meddling in Europe's affairs, Roose-

---

[1]While Welles's resignation from the State Department was three years into the future, it came about in thoroughly unpleasant circumstances. There is no question that Welles frequently overreached his authority and made embarrassing comments to the press about his feud with Hull, but what ended his usefulness to the president and, indeed, his government service was the talk about his "criminal" homosexual activities—rumors that were apparently spread by William Bullitt. FDR angrily told Bullitt that he never wanted to see him again, but the damage was done and Welles made his exit.

velt had good reasons for selecting him. He had a quick mind and superior intelligence and knowledge, and he had had considerable experience as a diplomat, having served in Japan, Argentina, and Cuba. He had also been a principal architect of the president's popular Good Neighbor Policy in Latin America and had participated in several peace conferences, even though he was late to realize the scope of Hitler's ambitions and had welcomed the Munich Pact as a step toward peace.

Roosevelt, who was certain that the "phony war" would last only until good weather enabled Hitler to launch an offensive against the western Allies, directed Welles to talk with the heads of government in Italy, Germany, France, and Great Britain in order to assess the "possibilities of concluding any just and permanent peace"—not a "temporary or tentative armed truce." The odds, as Roosevelt well knew, were a thousand to one against altering the course of events, but on February 25, Welles arrived in Rome on the first stop of his journey.

Count Galeazzo Ciano, Mussolini's son-in-law, who was also Italy's foreign minister, spoke candidly to Welles of his annoyance at the way Italy was treated by her German partners. As an instance of their dealings, he said that Hitler had not called him on the telephone until August 21 to inform him of the Nazi-Soviet Pact, and before Ciano had time to relay these tidings to Mussolini, the news was on the radio. Ciano detested Ribbentrop, disliked Hitler, and was convinced that the latter made no foreign policy decisions without consulting the former.

Welles was profoundly astonished during his initial encounter with Mussolini; his prior impression of the Italian dictator, based on photographs and newsreel footage, was of an active, quick-moving, animated personality, but here was a man with close-cropped, snow-white hair, looking fifteen years older than his fifty-six years, moving "with an elephantine motion" as if every step were an effort. He was ponderous, heavy for his height, with rolls of flesh hanging from his face, and since he kept his eyes shut during much of the conversation, Welles had the feeling that he was laboring under a terrible strain. Nevertheless, when the American asked whether negotiations for peace might be undertaken between Germany and the western Allies, Mussolini's response was an encouraging and emphatic yes.

The hand of fascism lay heavy over Italy, with normally light-hearted Italians restive under the strict controls, yet Welles described that atmosphere as carefree compared with what he found in Berlin. There the feeling of oppression was palpable, and his first glimpse of a newspaper made him realize the extent of Goebbels's propaganda: the only three items he saw that related to England and the United States were "fantastically untrue."

His meeting with Ribbentrop set the pattern for what was to follow in Berlin: the wine salesman-turned-foreign minister refused to acknowledge Welles's greeting, and, although he spoke excellent English, stared at the American icily and ordered the translator to interpret. Whereupon Ribbentrop, without looking at his visitor, proceeded to talk for two hours without stopping, giving Welles a fanciful version of German history since Hitler had become chancellor on January 30, 1933. Delivered pompously and contemptuously, the message was a packet of misinformation and deliberate lies and a vicious attack on England, and Welles concluded that he was dealing with a man who had no background in foreign affairs and a stupid and completely closed mind.

Hitler was next on the envoy's list, and as Welles entered the chancellery, a "monstrous edifice" with a facade like a modern factory, his immediate impression was of a prison courtyard, with soldiers and storm troopers everywhere. Hitler, who greeted him cordially, was taller than he had supposed and gave the impression of being in excellent physical shape, with good color, clear eyes, and a low, well-modulated voice.

With a gesture of his hand, Hitler indicated that the American should begin, and Welles explained that he had come to see if a way was open for a stable, just, and lasting peace. Surely, he went on, there could be no real victor in a war of annihilation that exhausted Europe's human and economic resources; even neutrals like the United States would lose, which was why his country was determined to go to any lengths to achieve a peaceful settlement now. To Welles's astonishment, Hitler's reply was the same as Ribbentrop's, including the long, distorted historical summary, and the statement that war had been forced on Germany by England. "I did not want this war," said Hitler, his voice rising, becoming suddenly strident, as his features lost their composure. "It has been forced upon me against my will. It is a waste of my time. My life should have been spent in constructing and not destroying." Germany's goal, he assured his visitor, "whether it comes through war or not, is lasting peace," and Welles departed from the interview with the awful realization that "all decisions had already been made," that the best anyone could hope for was delay.

On the following morning, a Sunday, he called on Hitler's close friend and Nazi Party deputy Rudolf Hess, who sat in an office barren of anything but desk and chairs. Behind him stood a handful of young party functionaries, who had apparently rehearsed with Hess everything he was to say. Hess—who "had only the lowest order of intelligence"—spoke entirely from typewritten file cards and delivered the same line Welles had already heard from Ribbentrop and Hitler.

From Hess's spartan office, Welles was driven north through swirling snow to Karinhall, Field Marshal Hermann Göring's vast palace in the National Game Reserve. ("It would be difficult," Welles noted sourly, "to find an uglier building or one more intrinsically vulgar in its ostentatious display.") Göring's huge bulk was squeezed into a white tunic covered with various emblems, jeweled insignia, and the Iron Cross he had won in World War I, and on his hands—which were "shaped like the digging paws of a badger"—were enormous rings, one set with diamonds, another with an inch-square emerald. He was more cordial and candid than the other Nazi leaders Welles had met, but once again the American was exposed to the rote he had first heard from Ribbentrop, repeated almost word for word as though these men had been catechized. The only difference, as far as Welles could see, was that while Göring was as ruthless as the others, he at least had some conception of the world outside Germany and some notion about the psychology of other peoples.

So there he had the Axis point of view. Now it was time to talk with the leaders of France and Great Britain, and as he left Berlin, having driven for miles through the city, he realized that he had not seen a single smiling face. In Paris the mood was different, but no more encouraging: the feeling there seemed to be one of sullen apathy, and Welles had a sense of people waiting—waiting with the expectation of calamity. He talked with President Albert Lebrun, who said that unless at least one generation of Frenchmen could live a normal life span without their country being devastated by German aggression, France could not survive; and that set the tone for his visits with the top figures in France—among them Edouard Daladier, Edouard Herriot, Georges Bonnet, Paul Reynaud, and Léon Blum, the former premier—most of whom argued that disarmament, enforced by a European police force, was the only answer to the current dilemma. Reynaud, who had been a lonely advocate of fighting in 1938 to save Czechoslovakia, told him that Munich had been "the cardinal error of French and British policy"; Blum observed sadly that for France the hours were numbered. No sooner had Welles reached England than he learned from the embassy in Paris that some three thousand violent, insulting letters of protest had been received from Frenchmen, protesting that he had dared to call on Blum, who was a Jew. It suggested to him that Goebbels's anti-Semitic propaganda was very effective in France.

In London, which was totally blacked out at night, with most of the private houses closed, he saw the Earl of Halifax, who commented that peace was impossible without confidence, and asked how anyone could possibly have confidence in a German nation that pursued a policy of aggression and repeatedly broke its agreements. Welles made a courtesy call on the king and queen, who recalled wistfully their visit to the United States; it seemed a long time ago, they said, in a world that had passed.

He found Neville Chamberlain a spare man who looked younger than his seventy-one years, with large, piercing eyes and a low, incisive voice. The prime minister was frank to admit his own mistakes, but spoke with "white-hot anger" when he described the Nazis' policies. He had been deceived and lied to by Hitler, and England had been forced to go to war as a last resort to preserve freedom and democracy.

Later, Welles would write of Winston Churchill's "fierce energy and . . . amazingly comprehensive executive ability, his grasp of facts and his initiative," but when he met the first lord of the Admiralty he found him seated in front of the fire, "smoking a 24-inch cigar and drinking a whiskey and soda. It was quite evident that he had consumed a good many whiskeys before I arrived." Churchill began to speak and never stopped for an hour and fifty minutes, and while Welles enjoyed this "cascade of oratory, brilliant and always effective, interlarded with considerable wit," he would have been more impressed had he not already read Churchill's book *Step by Step,* of which this talk was essentially a reprise. Churchill informed him that he was sitting in the same office he had occupied twenty-five years earlier, confronted by exactly the same situation—all because British governments had refused to follow a realistic policy toward Germany, a nation whose goals of world supremacy and conquest would not change. Churchill had foreseen the present crisis, he continued, he had spoken out again and again, but no one had listened, and now the only solution was "outright and complete defeat of Germany, the destruction of National Socialism," along with provisions in the ultimate peace treaty that would give Europe and the world peace for one hundred years or more.

Before returning to the United States, Welles had a final round of calls to make in Rome, and on the trip to Italy he reflected on the difference he had noted between the people of France and England. Where there was apathy and a foreknowledge of defeat in Paris, he sensed that Londoners, while bitterly resenting their involvement in the war and loathing the prospects of what they would have to endure, had a "relentless determination" to see it through, no matter how far down the road the end might be.

When he arrived in Rome, Ciano told him that Ribbentrop had visited after Welles was in Berlin, to tell Mussolini and Pope Pius XII that Germany was determined to launch an all-out offensive soon, that she would consider no peace solutions other than those dictated by Germany when victory had been achieved—and victory, the Nazi foreign minister promised, would come within five months. Welles again saw Mussolini (looking much better than he had two weeks earlier, as if a great load had fallen from his shoulders), and Il Duce told him to tell Mr. Roosevelt that "the minute hand is pointing to one minute before midnight," that he would try to persuade Hitler to delay his attack, but only if France and England were willing to cooperate, and allow Germany the lebensraum—the living space—it required. Welles's final impression from his trip was that the Italians—in spite of the pleas he received from all sides, including the pope, for President Roosevelt to use his influence to prevent Italy from entering the war—would soon be involved. In a nation of forty million people, Mussolini was a majority of one and would certainly support Hitler.

By the time Welles returned to Washington it was clear that the assessment he and Roosevelt had made of his trip before it began was accurate: the dictators had been hostile and unyielding, the Allies suspicious. It had been a forlorn hope from the start, since the only possible way to change Hitler's plans was to let him know that the power of the United States would be used against him. And that was not a suggestion that Roosevelt or any other U.S. official could make. What it came down to was that the president had tried and failed, and in the wake of Welles's mission came a flood of rumors—a letter from Bullitt in Paris, with a malicious version of the official French reaction, plus a report that Welles had "eulogized" Mussolini and conveyed the impression that Germany was invincible. In Britain fears arose that Roosevelt was seeking a negotiated peace that would ratify Hitler's territorial gains, and to set these to rest the president stated on March 16 that no settlement could possibly endure "if small nations must live in fear of powerful neighbors."

On April 5, 1940, the prime minister of Great Britain, speaking to the Central Council of the National Union of Conservative and Unionist Associations, was unusually optimistic for a man at the head of a nation that was as unprepared for war as his critics claimed. He felt "ten times as confident of victory" as he had in September, Neville Chamberlain said, because the country had grown so much stronger in relation to Germany. If it was recalled that Germany had been preparing for war for years, becoming an armed camp while Britain was carrying on peaceably, minding its own affairs, was it not curious that the enemy had made no effort to overwhelm the Allies before they had time to make good their deficiencies? Whatever the reason for Hitler's failure to strike, Chamberlain continued, employing a phrase that would ruin him a month hence, "one thing is certain: he missed the bus."

Four days later there began a lesson the prime minister would not forget. On April 8, the Germans invaded and overran Denmark before the Danes knew what was happening, and simultaneously—in a bold, brilliant operation that combined carefully synchronized troop landings by air and sea— seized the chief ports and every major airfield in Norway. (That nation's only relatively modern aircraft were nineteen Curtiss pursuit planes, still unassembled in crates that had arrived from the United States.) As the president of the Norwegian Parliament was to write, "the Germans under the mask of friendship tried to extinguish the nation in one dark night, silently, murderously, without any declaration of war, without any warning given," and indeed, within the space of twelve hours, by April 9 the country was firmly in Hitler's grasp. Transport planes and paratroopers seemed to be everywhere, and the cities fell almost simultaneously: Oslo, with a population of 300,000, surrendered to a handful of combat troops and a military band that marched boldly into the capital, entirely unopposed; then Bergen and Trondheim, the second and third largest cities; Kristiansand, Arendal, Egersund; Stavanger in the south, Narvik far to the north, above the Arctic Circle. King Haakon VII and his family, with members of the government and twenty-three tons of gold bullion from the Bank of Norway, barely escaped from Oslo by train, to be pursued relentlessly before the haggard monarch finally reached temporary sanctuary in Tromsö, eventually to board the British cruiser *Devonshire* and sail for England to form a government-in-exile. "All civilization seems to have come to an end," he remarked sadly before leaving his homeland. "I cannot understand how such terrible things can happen."

No more could the rest of the world. Americans who had retired for the night untroubled and unconcerned awoke on April 8 to discover that the phony war was now a real war, that even as they slept, Denmark and Norway had fallen to the Nazis. It was simply incredible: friendly little Denmark and remote Norway, which had for generations been neutral, beyond the strife of world politics, gobbled up by Hitler despite the protective shield of British seapower, which had seemed virtually helpless to stop him.

What prompted this unexpected attack, oddly enough, was the loss of the *Graf Spee* in December, which taught Hitler that pocket battleships, formidable though they were, had no place to hide from the ubiquitous British fleet. Submarines, on the other hand, could prey all but unseen on enemy shipping, exacting a terrible toll. But there was a catch: if they were to have unlimited access to the Atlantic, his U-boats had to break free of the heavily mined and patrolled North Sea and operate from bases in Norwegian territorial waters. Furthermore, Germany's vital supply of iron ore from Sweden depended, in winter, on the shipment of ore from the Norwegian port of Narvik through those very same waters. Taken together, these two requirements were behind the directive issued by Hitler on March 1, 1940, calling for simultaneous landings in Denmark and Norway and emphasizing the need for complete surprise and maximum speed.

Naval battles suddenly erupted all over the North Sea—battles as savage as the stormy waters in which they were fought. On April 7 the British Admiralty received an air reconnaissance report that a German battle cruiser, two light cruisers, fourteen destroyers, and another ship were heading toward the Naze, across the mouth of the Skagerrak, between Denmark and Norway, but the Admiralty—certain that the Germans were attempting to break out into the Atlantic—completely misjudged the situation and dispatched the home fleet to intercept them. Meanwhile, the battle cruiser *Renown* and her accompanying destroyers were covering a minelaying operation off Narvik when one of the destroyers, the *Glowworm,* strayed off station in the towering seas while searching for a man overboard and stumbled onto two German destroyers and the cruiser *Hipper.* A ferocious, one-sided engagement ended when the badly crippled *Glowworm* rammed the cruiser and then blew up, but not before she had radioed a contact report, alerting *Renown* to the enemy's presence.

The *Renown,* steaming into a furious gale with snow and wild winds, spotted two darkened ships, which turned out to be the battle cruisers *Scharnhorst* and *Gneisenau,* cruising at quarter speed because of the storm. At eighteen thousand yards the *Renown* opened fire on the enemy ships, which were bobbing around in the gigantic waves, and almost miraculously hit the *Gneisenau,* destroying her main gun-control equipment. Although the *Renown* was hit twice, she was not badly damaged and managed to wound the *Gneisenau* twice more before the Germans vanished in the storm.

On April 8 a Polish submarine sank the German transport *Rio de Janeiro* in the Skagerrak; a Norwegian minelayer, two minesweepers, and a whaler with a single gun took on a German force that included two cruisers and several destroyers; ten miles from Oslo three 1905-vintage guns and some torpedo tubes at old Fort Oscarsborg blasted Hitler's newest cruiser, the *Blücher,* sinking her with one thousand men and damaging the *Lützow,* which was sunk the following day by a British submarine. Another sub sank the light cruiser *Karlsruhe;* shore batteries damaged the *Königsberg,* which was polished off the next day by a British plane from the Orkneys—the first major ship to be sunk in World War II by an aircraft. A German destroyer was beached at Trondheim. Then German destroyers sank two coastal defense ships near Narvik.

At dawn on the following day one of the wildest battles of all took place in the harbor at Narvik, when a squadron of five British destroyers commanded by Captain B.A.W. Warburton-Lee, screened by snow and mist, completely surprised five much larger German destroyers, sinking two, disabling the others, and sending eight German merchantmen to the bottom. Then five more enemy destroyers showed up. Warburton-Lee and every officer but one on the *Hardy* were mortally wounded and the ship beached; another British destroyer went down; and the three surviving vessels—two of them badly damaged—headed for open sea. On the way out of West Fjord they met a big ship coming in—a German ammunition vessel—and blew her up.

When the losses were tallied, it was evident to the British public that their navy, pride of the empire, had somehow been surprised and outwitted, and in the House of Commons the first lord of the Admiralty rose to explain how it had happened and to remind a shocked audience that "command of the seas . . . does not mean command of every part of the sea at the same moment, or at every moment." Members listened intently, with grudging acceptance, as he predicted that "these costly operations may be only the prelude to far larger events which impend on land. We have probably arrived now at the first main clinch of the war."

Three days later, Winston Churchill had better news to report. On April 13, the *Warspite,* with nine destroyers and dive-bombers from the *Furious,* entered the fjord that led to Narvik and sank eight German destroyers without the loss of a British vessel. But what he had termed a "clinch" might better have been described as brutal, no-holds-barred fighting that in four days had crippled the opposing fleets.

Now began what Churchill called a "ramshackle campaign" that the British were as badly equipped to fight as they were ill prepared. Starting on April 15, a collection of British, French, and Polish troops landed on the coast near Narvik, Namsos, and Andalsnes—the latter two towns to the north and south of Trondheim—the idea being to support the badly scattered but determined Norwegian resistance, while capturing Trondheim and Narvik from the Nazis and establishing a land base for future operations in the country. At best, it was an improvisation, and it fared no better than might have been expected, since the Germans were in possession of all the key cities and airfields and were strengthening their positions with every passing hour. Leland Stowe of the *Chicago Daily News* wrote of a British unit, "They were dumped into Norway's deep snows and quagmires of April without a single antiaircraft gun, without one squadron of supporting airplanes, without a single piece of field artillery," and he quoted British officers as saying, "We have simply been massacred. . . . We were completely at the mercy of the Jerries."

In Washington, D.C., a former secretary of the navy who was now commander in chief of America's armed forces was following with intense interest the events in Norway, discovering in the process the new meaning of air power. Roosevelt was highly impressed with the dispatches from Captain Alan G. Kirk, the U.S. naval attaché in London, analyzing the reasons for Britain's failure in Norway, which made it clear that the British had not yet learned to coordinate their sea and air power with their military operations, and had not recognized the vulnerability of warships to air attack. The Admiralty, Kirk was told by a high-ranking British officer, was still fighting the last war, pursuing the ghost of a German "grand fleet" that did not exist, ignoring the fact that "naval units cannot be maintained in sea areas close to shore-based enemy aircraft unless, and until, control of the air has been wrested from the enemy."

These were gloomy days at the White House: the president cut short a vacation at Warm Springs because he had the "jitters about the European situation" and was deeply troubled that "the English were going to get licked"; he was worried by reports that the Italians would enter the war soon; and he fretted continuously about his inability to get the sort of vigorous action "short of war" that he considered imperative. "If you ever sit here [in the White House]," he told a group of young people, "you will learn that you cannot, just by shouting from the housetops, get what you want all the time."

Before April was out, some eleven thousand British troops around Trondheim were evacuated under heavy fire, but they lost all their heavy equipment, and two destroyers escorting them home were sunk by German planes. Meanwhile, the fight for Narvik went on, with the British hampered by all sorts of bad luck: an army and a navy commander who possessed exactly different temperaments (General P. J. Mackesy could think of a dozen reasons not to attack, while his opposite number, Admiral of the Fleet Lord Cork and Orrery, could barely be restrained) and, what was worse, conflicting orders; a week-long blizzard that gave way to the spring thaw, clear skies, and the return of the Luftwaffe; an unyielding opponent who was steadily reinforced; and catastrophic events on the continent which made the star-crossed Norwegian campaign an impossibly expensive sideshow. Before pulling out of Norway on May 28 the British at last fought their way into the burning town of Narvik while the German defenders, who had held out against four times their number, retreated to the mountains. It was a hollow victory at best, and before the ill-fated campaign ended one final act remained to be played out.

To cover the embarkation, a squadron of shore-based Hurricane fighters and naval aircraft held off the Luftwaffe, and when the convoy left for England the fighter pilots all landed on the carrier *Glorious,* to be transported home. With the *Ark Royal,* two cruisers, sixteen destroyers, and a number of smaller vessels, the troop transports got under way, but the *Glorious* was short of fuel and and was detached, with the destroyers *Acasta* and *Ardent* to proceed independently. At 4:00 P.M. on the afternoon of June 7, *Glorious* was sighted by the enemy battle cruisers *Scharnhorst* and *Gneisenau,* was hit before any planes could get into the air, and by 5:45 she went to the bottom. The *Ardent* was destroyed at about the same time, and the *Acasta,* after making two torpedo attacks on the *Scharnhorst,* blew up and the captain ordered all hands to abandon ship. The sole survivor saw the skipper, standing on the bridge, take a cigarette from his case and light it while calling out, "Goodbye and good luck." In this calamity 1,474 officers and seamen of the Royal Navy perished, plus forty-one irreplaceable pilots from the Royal Air Force; only forty-five men were picked up.

All told, it had been a horror story for both navies. Germany had lost at least twenty-eight ships, including three cruisers, ten destroyers, and four submarines, plus numerous others damaged and out of action for months to come. The British and French lost a carrier, two cruisers and eight destroyers, some smaller craft, and—like the Germans—a number of vessels severely damaged which they could ill afford to have idled. As it turned out, however, the effective surface fleet of the German navy by the end of June 1940 consisted of no more than three cruisers and four destroyers—a fact that was to have a crucial effect on Hitler's plans.[2]

[2]On the strength of the Führer's promise that there would be no war until 1944 or 1945 (so certain was he that the French and British would not fight over Poland), the German navy in 1939 had begun an ambitious, long-range building program that was to include a fleet of thirteen battleships, thirty-three cruisers, four aircraft carriers, and 250 U-boats. Only the first two keels had been laid when Hitler surprised everyone—including his own navy—by attacking Poland, prompting Admiral Erich Raeder to comment glumly: "The surface forces are so inferior in number and strength to the British fleet that, even at full strength, they can do no more than show that they know how to die gallantly. . . ." As a consequence of the Norwegian campaign, any future invasion of Britain would have to be undertaken without the protection of an effective surface escort; and in fact, during the course of the war, no warship larger than a destroyer was ever launched by Germany.

CHAPTER 30

———————✦———————

"We are on our way at last."

In that first spring of the Second World War, after the longest and coldest winter in living memory, the big workhorses, lathered with sweat in the warm sun, moved steadily back and forth across the rich soil of Picardy, Champagne, and Lorraine, drawing plow and harrow, preparing the ground for seeding, commanded by the ancient rhythm of the seasons as though politics and war did not exist. April came in delicate and golden, and as the days lengthened French *poilus* emerged from their concrete bunkers in the Maginot Line long enough to spade up little plots of ground and plant potatoes. Then began the softest, most beautiful spring Europe had known in years—crystal-clear days and nights, without a cloud, without a sign of rain. East of the Rhine, German soldiers looked at each other, nodded knowingly, and called it *Hitlerwetter.*

For eight months the French and British governments had behaved as though they were in a trance, lulled by the self-induced illusion that they had plenty of time and impregnable defenses at their disposal—two nations hanging back, holding on to the past, not daring to open the door that might let them glimpse what the future held. Even years afterward, it is almost impossible to imagine how the Allies—two nations with a long tradition of detesting each other's philosophy and manners, each dubious and misinformed about the other—hoodwinked themselves into believing they had the slightest chance of waging a successful war against Hitler's Wehrmacht.

The British were deeply disturbed by what they perceived as French halfheartedness for the business at hand. In November, General Sir Edward Spears, back from a mission to Paris on behalf of Winston Churchill, urged His Majesty's Government to bind the French with an agreement not to sign a separate peace, since they were "uncertain starters and their hearts were certainly not as yet in the war." In the wake of the Nazi-Soviet Pact, France's Communist Party had denounced the war as "an imperialist and capitalist crime against democracy," and had succeeded in undermining morale in the factories and the military, which by now included five million conscripts, many of them very reluctant soldiers. Meantime, nightly German radio broadcasts assured Frenchmen that the Reich had no quarrel with them, that they had been dragged into war by the British, and the result—as Spears had observed—was that the average citizen now had less stomach for the war than when it had begun.

Had the French known the truth about Great Britain's lack of preparedness, they would have had even less heart for what lay ahead. The British navy was one of the world's finest, of course, and its air force was superbly equipped, but the army was so small and so widely scattered along the outposts of empire as to be virtually discounted in the coming conflict. Winston Churchill wrote to the first sea lord, Sir Dudley Pound, in January 1940, "Our army is puny as far as the fighting front is concerned; our air force is hopelessly inferior to the Germans. . . . Do you realize that perhaps we are heading for *defeat?*" While the French were counting on Britain's army for support, the English were relying on the French army to carry the burden of the fighting. The British did not begin conscription until six weeks before the outbreak of war, and by the spring of 1940 only one man in forty-eight had been called up, compared with one in eight in France. (Between September 1939 and May 1940, Great Britain equipped six new divisions; during the same period the Germans—already at full strength—raised forty more.)

The public knew little of this; what it did know, and found most disturbing, was that the Allies were undergoing a dramatic change of leadership at this crucial moment. In mid-March, following the military collapse of Finland, the French Senate made clear that it had no faith whatever in the way the Daladier administration was handling the war effort, and a few days later, after a vote of confidence was called in the Chamber of Deputies on a motion to conduct the war with increased vigor, with the government to operate at last under wartime conditions, Daladier resigned. President Lebrun called on Paul Reynaud to form a new government, and on March 23, Reynaud presented a cabinet (the 107th in the seventy-year history of the Third Republic), with a promise of "rousing, uniting, and directing the nation's energies so as to fight and win. . . ." France's Assembly was skeptical about his ability to make good on the promise: the vote on Reynaud's program was 156 against, 111 abstentions, and 268 for, giving him a majority of one.

The small, dapper Reynaud was persuasive and energetic, with a lively, brilliant mind, but he was a man with a defect of character that was likely to prove fatal as time ran out for France: he was extremely slow to make decisions. And the reason he could not make up his mind, as everyone in Paris seems to have known, was the woman he had lived with for many years, a former friend of his wife's named Countess Hélène de Portes, who meddled endlessly and maliciously in the premier's affairs—to the extent of preparing his state papers, dismissing generals and diplomats, breaking into cabinet meetings, and behaving generally like a modern-day Madame de Pompadour, though without that remarkable woman's intelligence or patriotism. Worse, she was almost hysterically anti-British, persistently urged Reynaud and his ministers to negotiate peace with Germany, and—at the last—would persuade her lover not to take the government to Morocco, where he might have carried on the fight against Hitler. Indeed, the story of France after 1940 might have been very different had it not been for the influence of Madame la Comtesse de Portes on Paul Reynaud. Paris was awash in rumor and gossip, much of it centered luridly on Reynaud and his mistress, but the American correspondent Vincent Sheean saw at first hand the extent of Madame de Portes's influence. He had an appointment with William Bullitt at the embassy on May 7 and had been with the ambassador for approximately two minutes when Madame de Portes telephoned. She wanted Bullitt to join her at her apartment for some hot chocolate and a chat, and Bullitt left immediately, clearly pleased to be on such good terms with the premier's mistress, and returned some time later to resume the conversation with Sheean.

When the editor of *Paris-Soir* called at Reynaud's apartment-office and discovered that the premier was in bed with flu, he could not help noticing that Madame de Portes was seated at her lover's desk, surrounded by generals, members of the assembly, and other high government officials, and that she was presiding authoritatively over the meeting and doing most of the talking. Now and then she would open a door to another room and call out, "How are you feeling, Paul? Keep resting. We are carrying on." Once, when she disappeared into Reynaud's room, the assembled officials began whispering about the dangerous rift between the premier and Daladier, his minister of defense, caused by the animosity between the two men's mistresses.[1]

The mystery was that no one, other than Reynaud himself, seems to have

---

[1] French wags referred to the Comtesse de Portes as "La Porte à Côté," meaning the side door; while Daladier's mistress, Marquise de Crussol—whose family fortune came from the sardine business—was known as "La Sardine qui s'est crue Sole," the sardine which takes itself for a sole.

found Hélène de Portes even slightly attractive: Sheean complained of her "clamorous, demanding manner," quick temper, and incessant chatter; General Spears thought her a homely, untidy woman whose "voice even in an undertone made one think of a corncrake [a European rail bird], a corncrake muffled under an eiderdown."

If these boudoir politics revealed France at its worst, a moribund society that was very near collapse, across the Channel what Winston Churchill termed the "sedate, sincere, but routine character" of the Chamberlain government had utterly failed to rally public opinion or the energies of the people, and opposition to the administration reached a critical stage on May 7, after the disastrous campaign in Norway[2]—a campaign for which the first lord of the Admiralty bore a heavy responsibility. By now, Neville Chamberlain recognized his own inadequacy as a war leader, yet he continued to believe himself indispensable and was convinced that no one else could handle the job (although Churchill was taking on more and more of it, as Norway had shown). Just as bad, he refused to credit the numerous rumors of a coming German offensive and was more certain than ever that economic warfare and a shortage of oil would frustrate any German plan to attack and eventually do them in. So it came as a shock when he addressed the House of Commons on the war situation and was interrupted repeatedly with jeers and reminded of his statement that Hitler had "missed the bus." Speaker after speaker rose to attack him, and finally Leopold Amery, an aging Conservative who was the prime minister's longtime friend and colleague, made his own damning indictment of the government's blundering and then, to cheers from the House, repeated Oliver Cromwell's famous command to the Long Parliament: "You have sat too long here for any good you have been doing. Depart, I say, and let us have done with you. In the name of God, go!"

The *coup de grâce* was delivered next day by seventy-seven-year-old David Lloyd George. As Edward R. Murrow described the scene, absent members rushed back into the House of Commons as the cry "L.G. is up!" went through the lounges, for the appearance of the little gray-haired man at this critical moment had an electrifying effect. "He traced the history of Czechoslovakia, Spain, Poland, and Norway," Murrow reported, "and he whipped off his gold-rimmed spectacles to pour scorn and condemnation upon the government front bench facing him ten feet away." Concluding his indictment, the bold, eloquent Welshman who had been prime minister for the final two years of World War I said: "The nation is prepared for every sacrifice, so long as it has leadership. . . . I say solemnly that the prime minister should give an example of sacrifice, because there is nothing which

---

[2]It says much about the Anglo-French alliance that the French derived a certain pleasure from the British failure in Norway that was only partly concealed. In the salons and cafés of Paris, the journalist Vincent Sheean observed, the talk was of how France would have managed things better, and there were "echoes of a sinister cackling," the glee of "a bad ally who compensated for his own inadequacies by dwelling upon those of his friend."

can contribute more to victory in this war than that he should sacrifice the seals of office."

Chamberlain realized by now that there was no going on as before, and after trying unsuccessfully to form a coalition government, he invited Lord Halifax and Winston Churchill to 10 Downing Street, calmly looked at them across the table, and indicated that he would advise the king to choose one of them as his successor. A very long pause followed, a pause that may have determined the fate of the western world. Churchill—who said he kept silent for once in his life—was aware that Chamberlain preferred Halifax, but Halifax declined, saying it would be impossible for him as a peer and a member of the House of Lords to lead the House of Commons. It was clear, as Churchill wrote later, "that the duty would fall upon me—had in fact fallen upon me," and that evening when King George summoned him to the palace and asked him to form a new government, Churchill accepted at once, saying he would confer with the leaders of the Labour and Liberal parties, form a coalition war cabinet, and give the king the ministers' names before midnight. When he finally retired at 3:00 A.M., the new prime minister experienced a profound sense of relief. "I felt," he recalled, "as if I were walking with Destiny, and that all my past life had been but a preparation for this hour and for this trial. . . . I was sure I should not fail."

The times belonged to the strong and audacious: Roosevelt in the United States, Hitler in Germany, Stalin in Russia, Mussolini in Italy. Yet as late as the spring of 1940 the man who would come to personify the struggle against tyranny and the hope of democracy and freedom was barely on the scene, and his own countrymen regarded him as finished, a has-been.

Winston Leonard Spencer Churchill was sixty-six years old, and his early, meteoric career seemed far behind him. Born into an upper-class English family—descendant of the great Duke of Marlborough, and son of Lord Randolph Churchill, who as a young member of Parliament seemed destined to become prime minister, and of a beautiful, vivacious American woman, Jennie Jerome—it might seem that he was blessed with advantages, yet the reverse was true. His father, a syphilitic who went mad and died at the age of forty-six, actively disliked his only child; his mother neglected him (she ignored Winston, she told friends, until he reached an age when he could be interesting to her) and devoted her attention instead to a succession of lovers. Despite her behavior, he would say that "she shone for me like the Evening Star. I loved her dearly—but at a distance." His only real childhood friend was his nurse, and he was wrenched from her devoted care to attend a boarding school, where a brutal headmaster caned him until his back was covered with welts, where the boys mocked his speech impediment (he had a tendency to lisp, and to pronounce "s" as "sh"), and picked on him unmercifully because of his lack of coordination, his puny body, his small, delicate hands that were so much like his mother's. By ordinary lights, he was no student: at Harrow he was a failure at mathematics and classics, but he remarked later, taking the long view of that momentary setback, "By being so long in the lowest form I gained an immense advantage over the cleverer boys. They all went on to learn Latin and Greek and splendid things like that. But I was taught English. . . . Thus I got into my bones the essential structure of the ordinary British sentence, which is a noble thing."

Equally happily for the world, Winston Churchill possessed a sense of his own destiny, an indomitable will to succeed, an unwillingness to succumb to his frailties, and the recognition that his photographic memory and ability to write could be put to profitable use. Haunted in his early days by the ghost of his father's sudden, early decline and the fear that he might not have time for all he wanted to achieve ("We Churchills damp off after the age of forty," he told a friend), he found himself famous in his twenties, thanks to his skill with a pen and a questing spirit that made life an adventure. From Harrow he had gone to the Royal Military College at Sandhurst, at twenty he was a second lieutenant of cavalry in the Queen's Own Hussars, and the career that followed, part military, part journalism— taking him to the Cuban insurrection, to Kipling's India, to the Sudan with Kitchener, and to the Boer War (where his dramatic escape after being captured by the enemy made him a hero at home)—was not only colorful in its own right, it supplied his publishers with some of the liveliest copy imaginable, and Winston with a respectable income, which he never failed to spend. During the long, stifling afternoons in India, while his fellow officers slept, Churchill devoured and filed away in his prodigious memory the works he had neglected in school—Malthus, Darwin, Schopenhauer, Adam Smith, and especially Macauley, whom he found "crisp and forcible," and Gibbon, "stately and impressive." And all the while he was continually writing, developing his own incomparable prose style. History was his great love, and he was steeped in it; for him the glory and grandeur of Britain's past was a palpable thing.

Back in England, the public career began in 1900 when he was elected to Parliament as a Tory and urged, in his maiden speech, reinforcement of the army in South Africa and civil, rather than military, governance of conquered territory. This, he said, would "make it easy and honorable for the Boers to surrender, and painful and perilous for them to continue in the field." It was a credo he held to for the rest of his life: that no hostile foe should be appeased, that no revenge should be taken on a beaten enemy, and that the military should not encroach on civilian responsibility. He was a parliamentarian to the bone, a House of Commons man to whom the institutions of government meant everything, and his intense dislike for dictatorship was at heart an expression of his reverence for representative constitutional democracy as the only suitable form under which man could live in relative freedom.

In 1904 he stunned his party by switching allegiance to the Liberals, because they stood for free trade (not until 1925 did he return to the Tories); in 1911 he was appointed first lord of the Admiralty; and during the Great War, with France and Britain bogged down interminably in the war of the trenches, he advocated forcing the Dardanelles, to knock Turkey out of the war. Through no fault of his, the campaign was bungled at Gallipoli. Churchill was forced out of the Admiralty and the cabinet, but, instead of sulking in his tent, went as a lieutenant colonel to France with the army. From 1924 to 1929 he served as chancellor of the exchequer; then came the fallow time of the 1930s, his years in the wilderness, someone termed them, when he was out of favor and out of office, after having been in public life almost continuously for two decades. Now he devoted his immense energies to painting, laying bricks, traveling, and writing, always writing, averaging something like a million words annually, to support his style of living and his growing family—turning out among other works what was by all odds the best account of World War I, and the superb biography of his ancestor Marlborough, which was as much a portrait of an age as the study of an individual. But he never strayed far from the political arena, and he made use of his knowledge of history and his intuitive sense to prophesy the future. Before most Britons he recognized Hitler as the archenemy and foresaw that Germany's mounting strength in the air represented England's greatest peril; yet Tory, Liberal, and Labourite alike ignored his warnings, as did the public at large. Only a few friends, who risked their careers by slipping him inside information about the nation's appalling military unpreparedness, stayed with him. To the others, he was a rogue elephant, too impetuous and foolhardy by far: "Before all things," H. G. Wells declared, "he desires a dramatic world with villains and one hero."

It has been said that the English public distrusts brilliance, that what it wants in a leader is good, solid common sense, and surely between the wars a public that desired peace and safety at all costs did *not* want a Churchill rocking the boat, preaching the futility of appeasement. Certainly no other politician of stature dared say that fascism was not appeasable—that it was, in fact, insatiable, and must be destroyed, like a dragon. Churchill believed that Hitler could—and should—be stopped before he went into the Rhineland, since that coup would leave him free to turn on Austria, Czechoslovakia, and Poland, and it was the failure of Britain and France to act in that crisis that led him to call World War II the "unnecessary war."

The American physicist Norman Ramsey was at Cambridge in the midthirties and recalled how everyone was down on Winston because of his unpopular predictions and his bleak view of the world situation. Yet as Ramsey points out, Churchill was nothing if not consistent, and what he said a few years later that America found so bold and inspiring was very much what he had been saying five years earlier. His eloquence was old hat to those who had sat with him in the House of Commons: they had been hearing what one man called his "rhodomontades" for years and were weary of them; but to a threatened British public and a world desperately eager for a message of hope and a promise of victory, his voice came through like a bugle call, bold and clear and inspiring. Alexander Cadogan, who was to work loyally and tirelessly for Churchill (and, not incidentally, completely revise his opinion of him), believed at the time of the cabinet crisis that Chamberlain was still the best prime minister in sight, Halifax the only alternative, and Churchill "useless."[3] John Colville, who was to become Churchill's private secretary and one of his warmest admirers, felt the same way at first: he understood that the king was reluctant to send for Winston, and Colville and his colleagues thought Churchill would be "a terrible risk" as prime minister, involving "the danger of rash and spectacular exploits." One of them spoke condescendingly of "Winston and his rabble," calling him the "half-breed American," and Colville was certain that "everybody here is in despair at the prospect" of Churchill leading the government. A week later, Colville discovered that his new boss "is full of fight and thrives on crisis and adversity"; a day later he was saying that whatever Churchill's shortcomings, "he seems to be the man for the occasion. His spirit is indomitable and even if France and England should be lost, I feel he would carry on the crusade himself with a band of privateers." As well he might have.

Cadogan and Colville and the others around the new prime minister quickly discovered that his leadership produced a sense of invincibility and urgency, changing the entire pace of government during the early weeks of his administration. In his first appearance in the House as prime minister, on the day the Germans crossed the Meuse, the day before the Dutch surrendered, he looked out over the crowded benches and, speaking slowly, told the members, "I have nothing to offer but blood, toil, tears, and sweat."

Then he asked, "What is our policy?" and replied, "It is to wage war, by sea, land and air, with all our might and with all the strength that God can give us; to wage war against a monstrous tyranny, never surpassed in the dark, lamentable catalogue of human crime. That is our policy."

As the House roared approval, he issued the ultimate challenge: "What is our aim? I can answer in one word," he said. "Victory."

In earlier days, as a young MP, Churchill had imitated his father's dress and manner; wearing a long frock coat, wing collar, and tie, he would address the House leaning forward, neck thrust out, hands on hips, the tails of his coat parted; but as the years passed he preferred to stand erect at the table, referring to the prepared text he placed on the box before him, his arms hanging almost limp at his sides unless he made a gesture. If his manner of delivery changed, the substance and the method of preparation did not. He was a natural writer, but he had to make himself into a great

[3]Seven generations earlier, the first Earl Cadogan had been the Duke of Marlborough's chief of staff and intelligence officer during ten campaigns, and General Spears was reminded of that when he saw Churchill and Cadogan together in France on June 13, 1940. "Here were the descendants of the two great leaders," he wrote, "brought together as their forebears had been by virtue of the services their Houses have rendered, generation after generation, to the country."

parliamentarian, and he did so by first dictating a speech (he calculated that it took six or eight hours to prepare a forty-minute address), memorizing it word-for-word, including even the gestures and pauses for applause, and then practicing constantly in front of the mirror until he had it right. Even the dictation was a performance: while a secretary sat at her typewriter, taking down everything he said, he would pace up and down, head bent, hands behind his back, trying out phrases, acting out his points as though an audience sat before him. Harold Nicolson said that Churchill gave even ordinary conversation the force of oratory by his peculiar way of handling emphasis and pauses, creating the impression that each sentence was carefully punctuated; but what may have seemed impromptu and extemporaneous in the House of Commons was far from that. Lord Moran, Churchill's doctor, observed that "his assurance evaporated" when he got up to speak; his heart raced, and only through a great exercise of willpower could he calm his nerves. Yet he wanted a speech to appear effortless, spontaneous, and to that end took special care to see that certain words were underlined, or capitalized for emphasis, and that the text included keys for pauses or slow delivery. When the speech was finally typed in what his staff called "psalm form," it looked a good deal like blank verse, a single phrase on a line, one after another down the page.

In the only novel Winston Churchill wrote, his description of how his hero drafted a speech was certainly based on personal experience. First "his ideas began to take the form of words" and the words grouped themselves into sentences; then "he murmured to himself; the rhythm of his own language swayed him; instinctively he alliterated. Ideas succeeded one another. . . . He seized a piece of paper and began hurriedly to pencil notes." And when he had finished? He spoke to the crowd, feigning nervousness, pausing as if searching for a word, and at last "he raised his voice, and in a resonant, powerful penetrating tone which thrilled the listeners, began the peroration of his speech."

Churchill's remarkable power of concentration was a great boon to him. Although he was capable of jumping like a grasshopper from one subject to another, General Spears admired the way he could "pull out one drawer of his mind and then another with great rapidity, yet nothing can deflect him from the subject in the drawer he is dealing with at any given moment. Every question appertaining to it is carefully sorted out and catalogued, nothing is forgotten or mislaid and everything flashes back to his memory in orderly array when required."

He knew he had become the king's first minister because England's survival was at stake, but he also had a keen, highly objective sense of the drama of that particular hour in the world's history, and he became a man with a mission, with a crucial role to play. To Lord Moran he remarked, "It's when I am Joan of Arc that I get excited."

The mood of his countrymen had changed by May of 1940; the yearning for peace was gone, replaced by a powerful will to resist, and the people of

Britain wanted to hear the truth, to learn the worst if need be, and he gave it to them straight from the shoulder, along with a powerful dose of faith and hope. If he was made for this hour in history, it was in part because of his unswerving independence of thought—the very unpredictability and the strange intuitive power that had made men chary of his judgment in the thirties. Now, when another man would have known that all was lost, he refused to accept it; when by all logic the British had no chance in a hopelessly unequal contest, he told his countrymen to believe in him and where he would lead them. Indeed, one of his incalculable services to his nation was in keeping the government from coming to terms with Hitler. The chief of the air staff remarked, "They say there was no danger that we should have made peace with Hitler. I am not so sure. Without Winston we might have." And as a friend of Churchill's put it, once Winston was in power, "bargaining with Hitler was out of the question, a separate peace unthinkable."

Before long, he became a legend, but above all he was human, and the British man in the street knew he was one of them—knew, in fact, that he *was* them. On one of the blackest days of 1940, when the French were about to quit the war, the novelist J. B. Priestley watched Churchill enter the House of Commons, his face set, grave, and unsmiling, so immersed in his thoughts that without looking where he was going he took a seat next to Ernest Bevin, the Labour leader—"a fine lump of that England which we all love; one of those men who stand up among the cowardices and treacheries and corruption of this recent world like an oak tree in a swamp." Alongside him, Churchill, "representing the other half of the English people and English history," was lost in meditation on what he had to say, when suddenly he came out of his revery, noticed who was next to him, and "gave his colleague a sharp little punch of greeting—a little dig in the ribs." As he did so, Priestley said, "there flashed across his face a sudden boyish, mischievous, devil-may-care grin. And I said to myself, 'these are the men for me.' " For just a moment, the man on whose shoulders rested the fate of Europe let slip a glimpse of the inner man who was still a boy at heart, still full of devilment, and somehow it seemed to Priestley that that was what the English, Scots, Welsh, and even the Irish wanted at this hour, rather than "weary gentlemanly muddling and mumbling of platitudes."

The transfer of power from Neville Chamberlain to Winston Churchill, which was to have such profound significance for Britain and her allies, could not possibly have come at a more fortuitous moment, for in the early-morning hours of May 10, 1940, before Chamberlain began talking to Halifax and Churchill about his successor, the Germans had struck. The battle that was to decide the destiny of the west had begun.

———

Three quarters of a century earlier, not far from Frederick, Maryland, a corporal and a sergeant in General George B. McClellan's Army of the

Potomac discovered, half hidden in the tall grass, an envelope containing three cigars wrapped in a piece of paper. The cigars were a rare find for the two soldiers, but the paper around them, which they delivered to their captain, was like a gift from the gods: on it were written the complete battle plans for General Robert E. Lee's army, giving the disposition of every Confederate division. For an opposing general it was the opportunity of a lifetime, and it was a measure of McClellan's incompetence that he failed to capitalize on what fell into his lap. A similar, heaven-sent accident put Hitler's plans into the hands of the Allies just before the German invasion of the Low Countries was scheduled to begin, but fate, which has a way of helping those who make the most of opportunities, was no kinder to the French, British, and Belgian commanders than it had been to George McClellan.

It happened on the morning of January 10, 1940. Thick fog smothered the valley of the Meuse, in Belgium, and near the little town of Mechelen farmers could hear the sound of an airplane circling, the sputter of an engine dying, then silence, followed by rumbling, tearing noises as a plane suddenly appeared out of the fog, landed on a frozen field, and sheared off its wings before tilting onto its nose in a hedgerow. Out of the little Messerschmitt scout plane climbed two Luftwaffe majors, shaken up but not badly hurt, and one of them scurried into the bushes and put a match to some papers. Just then a Belgian border patrol came up, seized the Germans, and put out the flames before the papers were badly burned.

What lay behind this bizarre episode was a chance meeting the previous night in Munster, Germany, between Major Hellmuth Reinberger, a staff officer in the 7th Airborne Division, and Major Erich Hoenmanns, a World War I veteran, at the local officers' club. After a couple rounds of beer, Reinberger mentioned that he had an important meeting in Cologne the following morning and was dreading the all-night trip on a crowded train. Hoenmanns, who was eager to log some extra hours of flying time, said he'd be delighted to take him—they would leave at dawn. When they took off the sky was clear, but they ran into traces of fog that soon built up into thick cover, and between that and an unfamiliar airplane and a stiff tailwind, Hoenmanns lost his way. Wherever he looked he saw dense fog or the white, frost-covered ground, and he was circling, hoping for a glimpse of a familiar landmark, when he ran out of gas.

What Reinberger had not bothered to tell Hoenmanns was that he was carrying in his briefcase certain top-secret plans for Germany's offensive on the western front, an attack scheduled for January 17 along a broad front between the North Sea and the Moselle River in eastern France. When the Belgians brought the two officers to headquarters for interrogation, Reinberger again tried to destroy the papers by shoving them into a woodstove; a Belgian captain rescued them, and Reinberger began banging his head against the wall, moaning that his career would be ruined for betraying his country. (He was right about that. When the news reached Berlin, "the

Führer was possessed," General Wilhelm Keitel said, "foaming at the mouth, pounding the wall with his fist and hurling the lowest insults at the 'incompetents and traitors of the General Staff,' whom he threatened with the death penalty. Even Göring came in for a terrible scene," and Reinberger's commanding officer, General Hellmuth Felmy, was summarily fired.)

The information gained from the secret documents might have united the Allies in common purpose at last, but it did nothing of the sort. It merely compounded their confusion, lack of coordination, and mutual distrust, revealing how deplorably unprepared they were to meet the demands of all-out war. Once the Belgians assured themselves of the authenticity of the plans and informed the British and French what they had in their hands (they would not reveal the documents themselves, only a précis of the contents), King Leopold demanded formal guarantees of aid, present and future, before he would permit the Allied armies to cross into Belgium. He feared, naturally enough, that the Germans would use any Allied troop movement as an excuse to attack. The king's conditions touched off an angry exchange, with the British arguing that they exceeded those of Britain's commitment to France, a full ally. Both British and French military commanders were itching to get their troops into position in Belgium, since they were certain that the German assault would come in the Low Countries, north of Liège, following the route of the Schlieffen Plan of 1914. General Maurice Gamelin went so far as to assemble his troops on the Belgian frontier on the night of January 14, and while the government in Paris appealed to the Belgians, saying that every minute counted, Gamelin's men and horses huddled in the cold, unprotected from the falling snow. When the attack did not come on the 14th as the Belgians had anticipated, they relaxed, for their attaché in Berlin advised them that Hitler had called it off because of adverse weather conditions.

What had begun with a few beers and an unscheduled plane flight might easily have proved disastrous for the Germans; instead, it was only a footnote to a much bigger story—something that might have happened but did not. What was worth noting was the way the Allies reacted to the episode—French and British blaming the Belgians as well as each other for what had gone wrong; each of the three parties certain that the other two were lying, or concealing the truth; the Belgians convinced that the overzealous French and British were all too willing to risk Belgium's neck in order to save their own, making the Belgians more determined than ever to maintain a policy of strict neutrality. The captured documents should have indicated to each of them that Hitler meant business and that the attack was actually coming—if not today, then tomorrow, or one day soon; but instead, for the Allied command the episode served only to obscure, rather than reveal, German intentions, creating mystery where none should have existed, while weakening the resolve and effectiveness of the alliance.

From Germany's standpoint, the temporary setback caused by the chance revelation of the plans proved, in the long term, the best possible thing that could have happened. Unbeknown to the West, what was called the phony war was in reality a period during which Hitler canceled one scheduled attack after another, while continuously updating and modifying the plan itself. The previous autumn, while the Wehrmacht was busy mopping up resistance in Poland, the German high command had been appalled to learn that Hitler intended to strike in the west as soon as the troops could be moved. Some generals were so dismayed that there were secret talks of eliminating the Führer, and it is interesting to speculate on what might have happened if the French had chosen that particular moment to emerge from the Maginot Line, cross the Rhine, and move against the uncompleted Siegfried Line. But risk-taking was not being contemplated by France's high command then or later—not after the bloodbath of World War I, when a million and a half young Frenchmen had lost their lives attacking fortified positions—and the result was that Germany gained a breathing spell in which to consolidate its gains and refine its strategy. Even so, the German high command, like the French, came close to doing nothing: according to General Erich von Manstein, the leaders of the Wehrmacht rejected the idea of an offensive in the west because "they did not think the German army capable of striking a decisive blow . . . or of gaining a swift victory over the French forces."

Until Reinberger's mishap gave away the game, the only plan that existed was a straightforward thrust through Holland and northern Belgium toward the English Channel. That particular offensive had already been scheduled and then called off on eight occasions, beginning on November 19, before the documents captured in Mechelen disclosed what would have been the ninth attempt. Had the movement taken place according to plan, the Allied generals would have been exactly right in supposing that they would have to make their stand in Holland and Belgium, but what neither they nor their German counterparts reckoned with was Adolf Hitler's strangely intuitive feel for military tactics. Sometime in October he had conceived the idea of directing the main weight of the attack through the Ardennes Forest in southern Belgium toward Sedan in France. No, his generals told him; that was impossible—the terrain was absolutely unsuitable for the movement of armor. (No one on either side seemed to remember that the French army had conducted maneuvers in this area in 1938, and had successfully demonstrated the possibility of attack by moving a number of "German" divisions, supported by tanks, through the Ardennes to reach Sedan.) Several general officers, including Gerd von Rundstedt and his chief of staff, Erich von Manstein, who had the best strategic brain in the army, supported Hitler, arguing persuasively at supreme headquarters that the existing plan would simply end in stalemate, as it had in the First World War, and that what was needed was a decisive stroke that would trap and destroy the greater part of the Allied armies. The attack they envisioned, as subsequently refined by the Führer, was an advance into the Low Countries, to draw French and British forces northward where the Germans were expected to strike, while the big surprise would be sprung in the south, with seven panzer divisions exploding across the border toward Sedan—a town above the northern terminus of the Maginot Line—and slicing like a gigantic scythe across France until they reached the Atlantic coast, cutting off all French and British forces north of them. Early in March the decision was made: the offensive would begin on May 10.

The one thing everyone in Europe could agree on was the weather: it was the most hauntingly beautiful springtime in memory—soft, radiant, dazzling days stretching on one after another as if to blind people to what was to come. In Paris, during that first week of May 1940, chestnut trees burst into extravagant leaf after the long, savage winter, blooming as though this might be their last chance, and while the government and the military marked time, waiting to see what would happen, everyone talked and talked. Some were deeply pessimistic, saying the English possessed no military skill and would arrange for the French to fight the war for them; they were certain that the government in Paris was lying, had lied about everything since Munich—false figures about the Maginot Line, about conditions in the defense factories, about aircraft production and the number of armored divisions, about the state of the army. Others had perfectly logical reasons for the Allies' ultimate victory—France's army and defensive network, England's navy and ability to enforce a blockade against Germany, America's productive might, which Ambassador Bullitt would persuade President Roosevelt to put at the Allies' disposal. The phrase on the optimists' lips was a remark attributed to the recently ousted prime minister of Great Britain—*Il faut en finir,* "This time we must put an end to it"—and tidbits of inside information were cast about by all those supposedly in the know. For an attack to be successful, people were saying, a three-to-one superiority in men and matériel was essential: Hitler had not attacked in September; therefore, Hitler had no such superiority. Everywhere the talk was conjectural: Hitler would sit out the war until the following spring; the German invasion, if it came, would dash itself to pieces against the Maginot Line; General Weygand, a hero of the first war, would be called back if the going got rough. Someone even recalled that Nostradamus, in the sixteenth century, had predicted victory by England and France over Germany, and they nodded knowledgeably over the quotation "The betrayed lion will unite itself with the cock, and then the barbarian will be absorbed." (One of the beauties of employing Nostradamus was that he was subject to such a variety of interpretations. In Berlin, Joseph Goebbels was broadcasting the seer's "prediction" that London would be bombed in 1940.)

Meanwhile, Paris remained Paris. Schiaparelli, Molyneux, Balenciaga, Lelong, and the other couturiers were showing their spring collections and setting dates for the fall openings; dressmakers were swamped with orders from clients. Maurice Chevalier, entertaining nightly at the Casino de Paris, delighted the customers with "Paris sera toujours Paris" and a hilarious new song about France's democratic army, whose one desire was to be left in peace; his act was followed by a chorus of beautiful, half-naked women singing "We'll Hang Our Washing on the Siegfried Line." Old men and women sat in the sidewalk cafés sipping apéritifs and reading bullish headlines in the newspapers, shops were doing a steady business, French and American films played to full houses (signs in theater lobbies read: "In the event of an air raid, customers not retaining their seat stubs will not be reseated when it is over"), and there was no noticeable letup in city traffic. Cartier, Van Cleef and Arpels, and other jewelers reported a boom in diamond sales, a sign that some people were converting their wealth into what they could carry with them. Young women in Red Cross outfits were everywhere; the Duchess of Windsor, who was democratically dispensing food to soldiers in a canteen, was seen wearing a chic navy-blue uniform with a cap cocked over her sleek hairdo.

Someone heard Jean Giraudoux discussing the recent visit of Sumner Welles to Europe. How very odd, said the poet and playwright, who had not troubled to learn which Welles was which—how odd that America would "send on a *peace* mission the man who terrified the whole world by broadcasting a Martian invasion." As the minute hand of Europe's clock moved closer to midnight, a learned discussion was in process at the Académie Française: scholars compiling a new dictionary could not agree whether the wing of a chicken was a muscle or a limb.

In Germany the pace of life was altogether different, and the Wehrmacht generals, most of them veterans of the First World War with old scores to settle, were ready. Erwin Rommel, commander of the 7th Panzer Division, took a moment from his duties to send a note to his wife at the end of the first week in May: "We are on our way at last. . . . You will get all the news from the papers in the days ahead. Don't worry. Everything will be all right."

CHAPTER 31

"We are beaten; we have lost the battle."

Despite the mounting violence on the high seas and the bitter fighting in Scandinavia, this war still had a Wonderland quality to it, partly because the situation in Europe appeared to have stagnated since the defeat of Poland, but also because the Allied nations that were supposed to be doing the fighting appeared to have no plan or wish to do so. The French had the army but not the heart to carry the war to the Reich. The British had no army to speak of, which pretty well eliminated them from any major offensive role on the continent, while the Royal Navy was under intense pressure to patrol the Atlantic, defend the homeland, protect merchant shipping, and cover actions like the recent failed offensive in Norway.

The surreal nature of the war made for some bizarre sidelights. Take the strange offer of a reward for kidnapping Adolf Hitler that appeared in the letters column of the *New York Times* on May 1, 1940. Signed by Dr. Samuel Harden Church of Pittsburgh, it read:

In order to prevent further bloodshed and outrage in this war of the German aggression, I am authorized by competent Americans to offer a reward of $1,000,000 to be paid in cash to the person or persons who will deliver Adolf Hitler, alive, unwounded and unhurt, into the custody of the League of Nations, for trial before a high court of justice for his crimes against the peace and dignity of the world. This proposal will stand good through the month of May, 1940.

The *Times* did more than print the letter; because Dr. Church was president of the Carnegie Institute and a respected citizen of Pittsburgh, the editors felt obliged to interview him and find out what was behind this curious business. Dr. Church assured a reporter that he was not joking, that he had discussed his plan seriously with fellow members of the exclusive Duquesne Club in Pittsburgh, that the offer was backed by fifty or so citizens who were ready to put up the cash, that his idea could work, and that it "chimes perfectly with the ideals of Andrew Carnegie. After all, he founded a peace organization." What had triggered the offer, Dr. Church added, was information from sources in Europe indicating that Hitler would shortly mount an attack on the western front, and was determined to go ahead even if it cost half a million German lives.

Now, although a good many people who saw the letter thought otherwise, Samuel Church was no nut. He was a self-made man who was born in a log cabin and started work at the age of eleven for $1.50 a week, gradually making his way as a telegrapher, stenographer, and clerk to become a vice president of the Pennsylvania Railroad, a power in Pennsylvania politics, and a senior officer of the Carnegie educational interests in Pittsburgh, as well as a poet, novelist, playwright, and historian. As a critic of Prohibition (it encouraged intemperance, vice, and crime, he complained) he launched a "wet third party" to secure repeal of the Eighteenth Amendment; as a Republican who supported Roosevelt in 1932 and broke with him four years later, he regularly attacked government policies he regarded as socially and economically risky departures from American ideals. In 1933, before other Americans were doing anything about it, he led a protest meeting condemning Germany's treatment of the Jews; later he spoke out against Father Coughlin, capital punishment, Pennsylvania's blue laws, communism, and Charles Lindbergh's "sophomoric" views on war. Above all he was an idealist who believed passionately in peace: in the early days of World War I he was the first American to disregard Woodrow Wilson's naïve admonition on neutrality by giving an interview in which he charged Germany with the murder of civilization. Now, twenty-six years later, his oddball notion of how peace might be attained was giving the State Department fits: Cordell Hull's agency warned that anyone attempting to carry out Church's plan would be in violation of the neutrality laws designed to prevent U.S. citizens from becoming involved in a foreign war.

From all sides came hoots of laughter and derision. The syndicated columnist Hugh Johnson declared Church's offer "an index of war hysteria" and likened it to "tactics of gangsterism condemned by federal statutes and those of every state." The *New York Herald Tribune* labeled it "incredible stupidity"; the dean of Columbia's journalism school claimed it would involve the United States in Europe's conflict by stampeding public sentiment, forcing Congress to declare war; a newspaper in Britain dryly inquired why on earth Church would want Hitler unharmed. Seven students at a Mennonite school in Ohio offered $3.23 for the capture of Dr. Church, someone else said he would pay $10,000 for Chamberlain and Reynaud, dead or alive, and so it went—a lot of tomfoolery, as far as anyone could tell, including letters from at least two volunteers who knew exactly how they would capture Hitler (one wanted $25,000 in advance for expenses, the other a $100,000 drawing account). And from outraged members of the Duquesne Club came indignant sputters that the club should be implicated in this embarrassing nonsense. What no one seemed to have noticed was how accurately Dr. Church's European sources predicted an attack on the western front.

Predictably, the whole thing came to naught, and years later one of Church's sons reminded a questioner that his father was eighty-two at the time he made the offer—intimating that senility may have been to blame. Whatever the truth of the matter, Church's letter to the *Times* and the flood of supportive mail he received before the offer was withdrawn a month later were indications of an almost childish faith Americans had that there must be a way to settle the trouble in Europe before the war got out of hand. At quite a different level, President Roosevelt had acted on the same impulse when he sent Sumner Welles on what everyone regarded as a hopeless mission, and vaguely similar motives, combined with insatiable curiosity and a desire to keep America from repeating Europe's follies, had led Clare Boothe, the playwright, to travel to the continent this fateful spring.

Even with the advantage of hindsight, it seems unlikely that any woman, even one as determined as Miss Boothe, would board a ship in midwinter, cross the ocean in which sinkings had become common, and journey to Italy, France, England, Holland, and Belgium in wartime unless she was at least reasonably certain she would be safe from harm. All of which is to say that even well-informed people were not yet sure this war was serious, and that it was going to take an outbreak of real fighting to convince them it was for keeps.

Clare Boothe had sailed on February 24 for Naples, one of only seventy-five cabin-class passengers. She was purportedly on assignment for *Life,* but she seems to have used her credentials as a correspondent—and, possibly, the fact that she was the wife of Henry R. Luce, editor of *Time* and *Life*—to gain admittance to people and places no ordinary tourist would have seen. She had a long conversation with Count Ciano in Italy, visited the Maginot Line, listened to endless rounds of sophisticated talk in Paris, and—after cabling Luce that "the curtain is about to go up on the greatest show the world has ever seen"—arrived in London on April 25, when spring was "lovely beyond even an Englishman's belief," with bright azaleas in the window boxes, tulips in the court of Buckingham Palace, sheep grazing in the parks, ducks in the ponds, and the cuckoos, nightingales, and swallows home from their winter wanderings.

What made this scene different from the London she knew was barrage balloons floating high overhead, sandbags piled at street corners and entrances to buildings (some of the bags had sprouted greenery, indicating that the contents were dirt, not sand, and that profiteers were already at work), and military and government personnel carrying gas masks. Despite the blackout, London at night was gayer than Paris, gayer by far, with couples in evening clothes dining at Claridge's and going to see John Gielgud's *King Lear* as though nothing had really changed. Miss Boothe was annoyed to hear Ambassador Kennedy—whom she admired—criticized as a defeatist, a publicity hound, and a gauche parvenu. Chamberlain was still in office when she was there, and she found it shocking that he was permitted to remain when the bankruptcy of his policy was so evident (the English seemed only to be amused about the matter: they quoted an appropriate line from Gracie Fields's music-hall song—" 'E's dead, but 'e won't lie down"). She was disturbed to see that nothing had altered the pride of the rich and the humility of the poor and that "nearly everybody in England was sleeping on his ancestors' laurels." And her blood boiled when she heard the one-liner making the rounds in London: "If this war spreads," it went, "the two yellow races, Japan and America, will be fighting each other."

On the same sunny May day that Neville Chamberlain was stubbornly defending his policy in Norway before the House of Commons, Clare Boothe flew to Amsterdam, where the U.S. minister to The Hague, George Gordon, greeted her with the words "You've picked a bad hour for a visit." During her three days there she discovered how scrupulously neutral the Dutch were trying to be, hoping the danger might pass and that they might somehow be spared, even though German troop movements made invasion appear an imminent certainty. (Someone said that Hitler was only trying to scare the Dutch and the Belgians in order to see where they would concentrate their troops, and that the real attack would come in the Balkans.) The Netherlands' foreign minister was still saying that peace was possible, and so convinced of this were Boothe's hosts that as she took the train for Brussels on the afternoon of May 9 she was persuaded that the "flat, pretty, flower-painted dinner plate of a country, the land of ditches and dikes and dimpled babies," was safe—at least until spring a year hence.

When her train pulled into Brussels at 11:00 P.M., North Station was full of smoke and steam, with soldiers and the families that had come to see them off to the front milling about on the platforms, the young men and women embracing, only their eyes daring to say farewell, parents and grandparents standing slightly aloof, arms about one another's shoulders, too shocked to speak, wondering how it could all be happening again, so soon. Despite what she could see, the American was told that the crisis was over; it was just that the mobilization was still going on. A taxi dropped her at the U.S. embassy, where she found the exhausted ambassador, John Cudahy, waiting up for her, and during their abbreviated conversation he and the second secretary suggested, as though this were just another tourist season, that she might enjoy a visit to the battlefield of Waterloo the next morning. But the next morning at 5:20 a maid shook her by the shoulder, shouting, "The Germans are coming again!"

Clare Boothe got out of bed, stood in her nightgown by a tall window overlooking the park, and saw a formation of about twenty airplanes overhead, their bellies gleaming in the gold-and-red sunrise, and moments later heard "a thin, long, long whistle and a terrible round *bam!*" as a bomb pierced the roof of the house across the square, showering glass and wood and stone into the little green park. Antiaircraft guns opened fire, and for an hour or more, bombs fell on the city.

In the basement kitchen of the embassy the frightened staff was getting breakfast, "because not eating will not keep the Germans away," and Cudahy told her, while he gulped down a cup of coffee, that he had not been to bed the previous night: at 12:30 A.M. the foreign office in Luxembourg[1] had informed him that the Germans were on the march, and at one o'clock he had phoned the White House, giving President Roosevelt his first knowledge that the attack everyone dreaded had come at last.

In some extraordinary fashion life went on in Brussels as though this terrible thing that was happening were only a temporary aberration in the city's normal rhythm; Boothe walked to the public square and found people waiting for trains, buying newspapers, going to their offices or shops, gathering in sidewalk cafés for rolls and coffee. An American journalist at the next table told her that the Dutch had opened the dikes, flooding the countryside to foil the German attack, that King Leopold was at the front with the Belgian troops, holding off the invaders, and that the English and French were coming to the rescue.

A number of Americans appeared at the embassy to ask how they could get out of Belgium and were advised to come back the next day, when the roads and trains would not be so crowded with troops. Behind the scenes in this outpost of America the impression was one of business as usual: maids dusting and sweeping, the butler in frock coat and silk stock, the ambassador serving his best wine with the eggs Mornay, all of this domestic bustle accompanied by reassuring words about how strong the Dutch army was, how many tanks and antitank guns the Allies had, how impregnable Belgium's defensive positions were. Local radio stations, on the other hand, were beginning to echo a growing confusion: that morning German announcers mysteriously broke in on every program, and the Belgian government issued brief, uninformative bulletins; in the afternoon, performances of American jazz and Tchaikovsky's *1812 Overture* were interrupted by a message from the pope, who said he was "profoundly moved" by Belgium's

[1]The Duchess of Luxembourg later told Clare Boothe that her countrymen had been alerted to an imminent invasion when they discovered extraordinary numbers of German "tourists"—fifth columnists, in reality—suddenly swarming across the borders that night, coming by car and bicycle and on foot.

plight and would pray for Leopold and his people. That night ten of the eighteen people who had been invited to dinner to meet Miss Boothe arrived at the embassy, dressed in evening gowns and dinner jackets; there were jokes and laughter, punctuated by an occasional silence when planes droned overhead, but the high point of the evening was a Belgian count's story of his near-fatal experience that morning at dawn, when he was shooting woodcock and was greeted with a burst of machine-gun fire from a German patrol. Ambassador Cudahy reported that twenty German planes had been shot down during the day, that the French and English were moving into position in Belgium, that the Dutch were holding the Germans on the Ijssel and Maas (or Meuse) rivers, and as the guests departed and faded into the blacked-out streets, the voices called gaily into the shadows of the soft spring night, *Bon soir, Bonne chance, Au revoir,* with everyone "feeling very brave and very confident that tomorrow's news would be good news."

But the news next morning was not good; it was awful. While a servant pasted strips of paper across the big glass window in his office, Cudahy told Boothe she had to get out of Brussels while it was still possible. Until that moment she had believed "that as an American, a woman staying in the embassy of a great neutral country, by all the laws of other wars I should be safe." But as she and millions of innocents were about to learn, the war Hitler had unleashed was going to be waged without rules or codes of honor or limitations of any kind, and it would be a struggle for survival in which civilians were often as much at risk as those who wore a uniform.

Luckily, the Belgian wife of Hugh Gibson, the former U.S. ambassador in Brussels, was driving to Paris that afternoon; she offered a ride to Clare Boothe and to three Royal Air Force men whose plane had been forced down in Belgium—one a Virginian, another a Canadian—and off they set for Paris, with the lovely, gray-haired Mrs. Gibson at the wheel, driving "like an inspired taxi-driver." En route they saw one little bombed-out town after another, where old people stood in the doorways and watched with blank faces as they drove by; they passed streams of refugees on foot, on bicycles, in old carts, hay wagons, and broken-down cars; they were stopped at every town by military police who examined their papers and waved them on; they paused for tea in a candy shop still filled, unaccountably, with delicious pastries; they watched jaunty soldiers of the Scots Guards and the Queen's Own Westminsters marching toward the front—heading for the positions they were to take in line along the River Dyle—grinning and laughing, giving them a confident, thumbs-up gesture, while they sang "Tipperary" and "So Long, Sally" and the catchy new tune with the chorus "Roll out the barrel, we'll have a barrel of fun!" Through the smiling countryside of Flanders, down long lanes of poplars they drove, past a sign pointing to Armentières, home of the Mademoiselle of World War I, past Vimy Ridge and the monument to thousands of young men who had sung "Tipperary" as they swung into battle only two decades before, past Lille, and finally to Paris. On the afternoon they reached the French capital (it was "like arriving at a summer resort"), Miss Boothe checked in at the Ritz, changed for the evening, and left for a dinner party in Versailles.

———

A. J. Liebling had come to Paris the previous fall, toward the end of 1939, and he liked to cite what he called "an old proverb" to explain how he managed to get there. "A girl may sleep with one man without being a trollop," the saying went, "but let a man cover one little war and he is a war correspondent." Liebling had slipped into the latter category by first persuading the management of *The New Yorker* that his profound knowledge of France made him the man to replace the magazine's Paris reporter, Janet Flanner, who was coming home to be with her ailing mother. During the winter, while Liebling and millions of others waited for something to happen in the war, the captain of an Algerian regiment provided him with an explanation of what the Maginot Line meant to the French. "It means the high wall topped with broken bottles that the provincial bourgeois puts around his garden," the captain said. "Behind it he is secure with his cabbages. He can wear his slippers, live the good life without bothering to button all the buttons of his trousers."

When the attack finally came on May 10, 1940, Liebling's neighbors in the Second Arrondissement (whose representative in the Chamber of Deputies was Paul Reynaud) called to one another with a smile and a wink, *"Finie la drôle de guerre"*—"That's the end of the funny war"—knowing that the real roughhouse was about to begin. They were confident, these Frenchmen. "The Boches have business with somebody their own size now!" they would say belligerently. "They will see we are not Poles or Norwegians!" And while the men of France waited knowingly for the familiar pattern of 1918 to be repeated—prolonged artillery barrages and short advances, followed by enemy barrages and counterattacks—the women clung to the hope of a miracle, of a war without hard fighting, refusing to believe that their sons and husbands might be killed, never imagining that those soldiers had before them "the bitterest destiny an army ever had."

Meantime, Parisians went on talking and shopping and walking the boulevards, queuing up for movies and crowding into sidewalk cafés, not yet comprehending that France was losing the war even as it began. It was, in all truth, impossible for anyone in Paris to get an accurate picture of what was happening, so chaotic was the front and so swiftly had the Germans overrun Holland and poured into Belgium. The first inkling of what might be in store came with the arrival of a trainload of refugees at the Gare de l'Est on the evening of May 10. As it slowly pulled to a stop, people on the station platform were astonished to see that no one got out. The passengers were so shocked and exhausted by their sudden uprooting, by the danger and the journey, an eyewitness wrote, that "the children's drawn faces made them look like old men and women, and their grandparents, jolted into their dotage, gave way like children."

Not even the Germans had any idea of the speed with which the Low Countries would be overcome. As the hours flew by it was clear at Hitler's headquarters that Plan Yellow, as the offensive was called, was proceeding exactly as conceived but at a pace beyond anyone's expectations. By glider and parachute, airborne divisions moved swiftly into Holland and seized bridges intact, enabling armored units to avoid flooded areas. When the invasion stalled in Rotterdam, Hitler ordered a massive bombing attack, and within hours the heart of the city was destroyed—business district, railway stations, municipal buildings, and 25,000 homes gutted by explosions and fire. The Dutch fell back, exposing the Belgian left flank; that forced the Belgians to pull back, allowing the Germans to cross the Albert Canal. On May 10, the first day of fighting, the Belgians' supposedly impregnable fort, Eben Emael, fell to a superbly trained airborne unit of eighty Germans, led by a sergeant, who landed on the roof, jammed explosives into gun and ventilator openings, and blew gaping holes in the steel and concrete works. Flamethrowers followed, and by noon on May 11 the twelve-hundred-man garrison surrendered.

French and British troops arriving to take their appointed positions in the line found themselves in an open plain, with no antitank barriers, no trenches, no prepared defensive structures of any kind, and by May 12 the Germans had broken the Belgian front in several places. Throughout that night the Wehrmacht kept coming, the long motorized columns plunging toward the battle line with their headlights ablaze, contemptuous of the enemy. In England, General Spears read a communiqué from British Expeditionary Force headquarters stating that the Luftwaffe had not interfered with Allied troops rushing into Belgium, and found himself wondering if the French and British were doing exactly what the Germans wanted them to do. Certainly the German air force had the strength and the opportunity to harass those units. Why weren't they doing so?

Spears was right to wonder. The Allied commanders were following to the letter the script Hitler had written for them: as they rushed their armies northward into Belgium to block what they believed to be the main attack by Fedor von Bock's Army Group B, the mightiest armored force ever assembled struck through the Ardennes Forest. Spearheaded by some eighteen hundred tanks and more than three hundred Stuka dive-bombers, Gerd von Rundstedt's Army Group A crossed the River Meuse, broke through the weakly held French position at Sedan, and roared west toward Abbeville and the Atlantic coast. Hitler, watching the movement of Allied forces toward the Dyle River line, knew his gamble was about to pay off. "I could have wept for joy," he gloated later. "They had fallen into the trap. It was vital that they believe we were sticking to the old plan, and they *had* believed it!"

Within five days the Allies' defenses had been irreparably shattered, and their forces north of the Somme, cut off from the French army south of that river, were about to be swallowed up in a giant pincers movement.

No one could have been more baffled by all this than the Allied field commanders, whose prior experience was of no use whatever in the present situation. They were being initiated brutally to the *Blitzkrieg,* an innovative combat technique that was precisely what the German word meant: lightning war, in which massed tanks—supported by relays of dive-bombers and artillery battalions followed by motorized infantry—smashed and broke through the enemy's front lines and kept on going without pausing even to establish communications, appearing suddenly miles behind the front to spread terror among the civilians. It was a battle of continuous, unstoppable movement that bypassed entrenched positions and troop concentrations when necessary, and it was simply beyond the capacity of the defensive-minded French to comprehend.

In one tiny hamlet in the heart of France villagers had heard rumors of approaching Germans, but nothing definite was learned until the morning when there came "a great noise as of an approaching cataract, the sound vibrating through the early morning mist. The little village shook and trembled as the noise became a great metallic roar, out of which suddenly loomed the German tanks. . . . On and on went the tanks, none stopped." And behind the good-looking, tanned young Germans in the armored divisions came the black Gestapo and the terror.

That this was bewildering beyond even the capacity of trained soldiers— let alone villagers—to absorb is suggested by eyewitness accounts involving the top levels of command. On May 14 two French officers arrived at the headquarters of General Alphonse Georges, who was Gamelin's commander for the northeast front, and found the general pale, verging on hysteria, as he told them, "Our front has been broken at Sedan! There has been a collapse. . . ." Then Georges threw himself into a chair and burst into tears. A British liaison officer met General René Billotte, group commander of the French, British, and Belgians in the north, and watched him break down completely as he pored over a map, counting, "One panzer, two panzers, three panzers . . ." up to eight panzer divisions. "And against them all I can do nothing. I am dead tired, I am dead tired. And against them all I can do nothing," he repeated. A few days later Billotte, the only French field commander who was fully informed about Gamelin's plans and the arrangements that had been made with the Belgians and with General Lord Gort, leader of the British Expeditionary Force, was killed in an automobile accident, and the resulting change in command created further confusion. Billotte's replacement, General J.M.G. Blanchard, was as demoralized as his predecessor: after his troops attempted to reinforce Arras and were driven off with huge losses by General Erwin Rommel's 7th Panzer Division, a junior staff officer found Blanchard sitting "in tragic immobility, saying nothing, doing nothing, but just gazing at the map spread on the table, as though hoping to find on it the decision that he was incapable of taking." General Spears encountered a staff officer from Blanchard's command and described the man as "deliquescent, that is, in a state where he was fit only to be scraped up with a spoon—an embodiment of catastrophe."

In France's capital, the end to confidence and the beginning of real fear came with news of the breakthrough at Sedan, shocking Paris with the realization that the high wall topped with broken bottles had not been sufficient, that the enemy was in among the cabbages. Because of censorship, news of disaster usually arrived unofficially and twenty-four hours late, Liebling noticed, but it did not take long for people to understand that the war had been lost when the Germans split the French army in two, isolating one half, with the British, in the north.

The panic began in Paris on May 15, the day food suddenly became scarce, the day it began to dawn on the rest of the world that they were witnessing the death agony of a great nation. The next day the government declared the capital to be in *la zone des armées,* all young men had been called up, and a relentless flood of refugees from Holland, Belgium, and northeastern France streamed into the city—thousands of homeless people with bewildered white faces, faces swollen from weeping, carrying bundles and battered suitcases, bird cages, babies—the hale and the halt, the young and the old, mostly the old, driven like dry leaves before the storm from the east. Boy Scouts helped them off the trains, stacked their belongings for them; Red Cross nurses tended their wounds and their blistered feet, gave the children oranges and chocolates; and the refugees boarded green Paris buses to be driven to military barracks, to wait in the hot sun to be sent somewhere else in France, no one knew quite where. Within a matter of days there was not enough food, not enough shelter, not enough beds for these pitiful victims, and the Germans were reported to be seventy miles away.

Only a few months before, A. J. Liebling had interviewed the supreme commander of the Allied armies in France and found him as optimistic as "a somnambulist jauntily strolling off a roof"; General Gamelin's idea at the time had been to remain on the defensive until the Allies accumulated a superiority of weapons, when he would attack. The scheme, unfortunately, was based unwisely on the very shaky premise that French and British factories would one day outproduce the Germans. Now Gamelin no longer had the luxury of options. With his back to the wall, he ordered his troops, "Conquer or die," but it was no battle cry that swept across France but a wail of despair and anger: *"Trahi, trahi"*—"Betrayed, betrayed." Who was to blame for the catastrophe? people wanted to know. Who was responsible?

To a thoughtful man like the writer Antoine de Saint-Exupéry, who was now a captain in the air force, it was no good blaming individuals: the problem went much deeper. "If the civilization to which I belong was brought low by the incapacity of individuals," he reasoned, "then my question must be, why did my civilization not create a different type of individual?" But that was the sort of question for another time and place, not for this desperate hour. What the Parisians knew in their bones was that the war was nearing an end for the Allies. It was a knowledge that came not from newspapers, which carried mostly wishful thinking, or from refugees, whose news was a week old, but from sheer intuition, a deep inner awareness, because Paris was France and Paris could smell what was happening, could feel beyond the slightest doubt that things were terribly and irretrievably wrong.

Not that anyone in Paris or anywhere else in France had much solid information, even a week after the fighting began; no more could those in charge at the front make sense of the carnage and confusion enveloping them.[2] All that could be said was that a whirlwind of fire and smoke and death was sweeping across the land, destroying logic and reason along with whatever else lay in its path, and what it was doing to France and to an army that had been considered invincible was simply beyond the ability of anyone to grasp. No one, moreover, could possibly foresee that the thundering waves of battle would bring in their wake a revolution as sweeping as those of 1776 and 1789 and 1917, altering the political, social, and economic complexion of France and the western world in such a way that it would never again be the same.

Saint-Exupéry sensed correctly that profound changes were in the making, and he compared France's futile efforts in those final days to dashing glassfuls of water into a forest fire in the hope of putting it out, knowing all the while that the nation would descend into the long night of defeat and a future no one could foretell. Antoine de Saint-Exupéry was the leader of a reconnaissance crew, of which there were only fifty for the entire French army. There had been twenty-three crews in his outfit, and in three weeks seventeen of them had vanished, yet every morning the survivors were sent out again on missions they were extremely unlikely to survive, even though everyone knew the information they collected would not reach headquarters in time to be of any use.

France had gone to war knowing she could not win, sending one man into the field against three, pitting a nation of forty million against eighty million, and within a fortnight 150,000 Frenchmen were dead. Now an image came to Saint-Exupéry's mind of a nation's clocks all out of order, of a land where nothing went according to pattern or design, where there was nothing but futility. "Ineffectualness weighed us down, all of us in the uniform of France, like a sort of doom," he said. "It hung over the infantry that stood

---

[2]Beyond the physical and psychological havoc the German offensive created, it caused the Allied command and communications systems virtually to cease functioning. Those systems might have been suitable in a stalemate like the one World War I produced, but in the face of Hitler's Wehrmacht they were as outdated as the crossbow. The British and French communications network alike consisted almost exclusively of motorcycle couriers. No teletypes had been installed; telephones—unreliable even in peacetime—were all but useless; telegrams were impossibly slow. Gamelin's headquarters did not even have a radio (or a carrier pigeon, as one aide complained wistfully).

with fixed bayonets in the face of German tanks. It lay upon the air crews that fought one against ten."

———

On May 15, Winston Churchill was awakened in London at 7:30 A.M. by a call from Paul Reynaud, who was clearly overwhelmed by what was happening. Speaking in English, the French premier said, "We have been defeated. We are beaten; we have lost the battle." Surely, Churchill replied, it could not have happened so soon; surely the German attack would run out of steam and there would be opportunity for a counterattack. But Reynaud insisted, "We are defeated; we have lost the battle." And so it went, this collapse of France's leaders who were overcome by the magnitude of the disaster and were powerless to stop it.

The next day Churchill flew to Paris with General Ismay, his chief of staff, and General Dill, chief of the imperial general staff, and what he found there exceeded his worst fears. Gamelin reviewed the situation for them, explaining what had occurred, and when he had finished Churchill asked, "Where is the strategic reserve?" Gamelin shook his head. *"Aucune"*— there is none. Churchill walked to a window to digest this appalling information and saw wreaths of smoke rising from bonfires where government clerks were burning official documents to prevent their falling into German hands. By now it was clear to English and French alike that Gamelin was not the man to salvage the situation, and Reynaud replaced him with seventy-three-year-old General Maxime Weygand, a cold, efficient technician who had been Foch's chief of staff in the first war. In hopes of restoring morale in the army and the nation, the premier also summoned Marshal Henri Pétain, the eighty-four-year-old hero of Verdun, making him deputy premier, and the return of these old ones brought a sense of relief to the French public.[3] As one optimist pointed out, if you put the ages of these two and Winston Churchill end to end, you had enough years of experience to go back to Louis XIV.

But whatever feeling of security these changes brought about was short-lived: by now, unfortunately, the situation in France was beyond remedy by leaders young or old. To make matters worse, at the very moment when coordination and understanding between the Allies were imperative, Weygand's and Pétain's dislike of the English was only slightly less than their hatred of the Germans. The new commanding general, impeccable in riding breeches and brass-spurred boots, was a wizened little yellow-skinned man with sparse mustache, pointed chin, and high cheekbones that gave him an Oriental look. In contrast to his weary predecessor, he was all motion and

---

[3]Pétain was serving as ambassador in Madrid when he was called home by Reynaud. Before leaving he paid a courtesy call on Spain's dictator, General Francisco Franco, and told him, "My country has been beaten and I am being called upon to make peace and sign the armistice. . . . This is the result of thirty years of Marxism. I am being called to take the nation in hand." These were hardly the words of a man who might inspire the populace to victory.

bustle, darting about like a minnow. A Briton who saw Weygand at this time described him as "a jack-in-the-box, a very ancient toy whose vivacity still startled, though he had but one trick to play." The army now commanded by this man was beaten when he arrived to lead it; he was contemptuous of his British allies; he hated the politicians who, he supposed, had ruined France; and he detested Pétain (the feeling was mutual). Perhaps all that bile could somehow have been accommodated had he been the leader young Charles de Gaulle proved to be (Weygand despised him, too), but he was not: regrettably, as General Sir Edward Spears said, Weygand was "a backroom boy" who had never commanded in the field. His fault lay in trying to imagine what Foch would have done and remembering only that Foch had cursed the government, and that is just what France's supreme commander did.

In too many respects, Weygand reflected France itself at this agonizing moment in its history, a France filled with hatred—hatred of politicians, of other Frenchmen, of the English and the Belgians, of the old ways of doing things that had not worked out (accompanied by fear of the future), and most of all, of course, hatred of the Germans. France was crumpled and broken, feeling itself finished, and it was going to take someone other than this man to galvanize the army, arouse public opinion, and resurrect the nation's feeling of pride and honor and accomplishment. For that job, Reynaud seems to have been counting upon the man known as "the Marshal."

Pétain was regarded reverently, the kindly grandfather of the nation. There was an immense, almost mystical, bond of affection between him and the French people, for he was, after all, the leader who had stood fast at Verdun, the general officer who had dealt so humanely with the mutinies of 1917, the personification of victory in the Great War. He was also, to the nation's misfortune, more responsible for the French strategy in 1940 than anyone, for he had opposed the upstart Charles de Gaulle's advocacy of mechanized warfare and rapid movement (tanks and aircraft do not alter the basic aspects of war, Pétain had written), and had been a leading apologist of the theory of the defensive line, arguing that the key to France's security was the continuous front, bolstered by permanent fortifications.

Pétain became deeply disillusioned after 1918 as he observed the moral disintegration of the nation he believed he had saved. He was at heart a cautious, pessimistic peasant who believed in no miracles, and in June of 1940, with France confronted by a choice from which there would be no turning back, he accepted defeat as inevitable, rejecting Reynaud's proposal (in which the premier was firmly supported by de Gaulle and Admiral Darlan) of fighting on with Britain. (Such an alliance, Pétain remarked icily, was "fusion with a corpse.") Now, moreover, he was frequently off in a world of his own, partly a product of advancing senility, partly of deafness, and what remained of the hero of Verdun was the white, expressionless face, the long white mustache, the memories, and an incredible vanity that was the legacy of all the adulation he had known.

If France was to survive the next few weeks—perhaps even the next few days, the way things were going—it would be because these haughty old men did in fact pull off some major miracle, a modern equivalent of Joan of Arc's achievement, turning a badly beaten and thoroughly bewildered army around, and Reynaud appears to have thought such a thing was possible. Whatever the premier's failings, there was fire in the man, a burning wish to save his country; but the odds against him were hopelessly long, and the people at his side seemed as determined to lose as he was to win. As he described his attitude, if someone told him only a miracle could save France, he would say, "I believe in the miracle, because I believe in France." Unfortunately, neither of the old men thought another miracle of the Marne could be conjured up; and certainly the army knew better. Its appalling deficiencies in leadership, training, matériel, communications, armor, airplanes—everything a military organization requires—were all too evident to the French soldiers by now and the reality of defeat had penetrated all ranks.

On May 20 the first panzer units reached Abbeville and turned north toward the Channel ports of Boulogne, Calais, and Dunkirk. Three days later Boulogne fell; three more days and Calais surrendered; then the Germans headed for Dunkirk, closing in on that town from the east and southeast.

CHAPTER 32

———◆———

"... until, in God's good time, the New World, with all its power and might, steps forth to the rescue and liberation of the old."

Britain's expeditionary force had arrived in France equipped, physically and mentally, to fight the previous war, and exactly two weeks after the Germans launched their all-out attack through Holland, Belgium, and Luxembourg, these hopelessly outmatched soldiers—the carefree Tommies Clare Boothe had seen swinging along a road in Flanders—were in just about the worst predicament an army can face. Guderian's daring vision had yielded results far beyond anyone's expectations, and by May 24 the British and French—a huge force, some 400,000 men, all told—were surrounded, trapped with their backs to the sea near the French port of Dunkirk, with the hard-pressing Germans only ten miles away. They were confined within a giant noose which the enemy was drawing tighter by the hour, savaging the retreating Allies with overwhelming firepower on the ground and in the air, closing in from all sides with vastly superior numbers. In the process, France's strategy of the "continuous line," which left half a million fresh troops impotent inside fortifications that had been bypassed, was revealed as a tragic piece of foolishness.

Millions upon millions of francs, countless tons of concrete and steel purchased with the tax money of a generation of Frenchmen, availed the nation exactly nothing, for during and after the German breakthrough at Sedan, almost two thirds of all the French forces available on the northeast front were idle inside their concrete bunkers, while the fate of France was being decided outside and beyond the Maginot Line, where the remainder of the nation's forces were so badly outnumbered and outgunned. It had happened time and again in the history of warfare, this belated discovery that the measures taken for defense were obsolete against a novel weapon or tactic, and the sudden realization that the Maginot Line was not only outmoded but virtually useless was as agonizing and decisive as the French knights' brutal introduction to the English longbow at Agincourt.

The great military lesson of World War II, with its plethora of new weapons—a lesson that would be learned the hard way by the British in the desert and by the Russians in their homeland—was that offense prevailed at first against defense. That being the case, a defense must be at least as mobile and flexible as the offense it is supposed to overcome. So it is not quite fair to blame France's failure on the failure of the Maginot Line. It was a Maginot *mentality* that made it impossible for them to understand the need for fluidity, with the result that in forty days the Germans succeeded in accomplishing what they had been unable to do in four years in World War I.[1]

For the British who were successfully holding a line with the Belgians along the River Dyle, what happened came as a cruel surprise. To take one example: General Montgomery's 3rd Division had struck hard the moment fighting broke out on May 10, moving at once into Belgium; but they soon had to retreat, their weapons pathetically inadequate against the overwhelming enemy firepower and the ferocious attacks from the air. One day they were facing Germans to the east, then they were suddenly attacked on the flank and ordered to face south and southwest in order to defend a totally different front. What they were up against, of course, was panzer divisions that had demonstrated an ability to travel as much as forty miles in fourteen hours through enemy territory; having cut France in half, the German armor turned north to deal with the Allies isolated there, and for the victims, it was bewildering, to say the least. For twenty days, Montgomery's troops did nothing but retreat continuously. On May 17, General Gort, the burly, unflappable commander of the BEF, had no direct communications with the Belgians on his left or with his immediate superior, General Georges, who was somewhere to the rear. A few days later, what he knew, communications or no, was that things were going to hell in a hurry, that London had no conception of how bad the situation was (just now London, with the enthusiastic concurrence of the French high command, was ordering him to fight his way south to the Somme), and that if anything was to be salvaged from this chaos it had better be done immediately.

[1]Ironically, one of the Germans most often associated with the new tactics forgot the lesson his Afrika Korps taught the British in the desert. As Alan Moorhead points out in his biography of Montgomery, in 1944 Field Marshal Erwin Rommel rushed all his forces to the coast to defend the Atlantic Wall against the Allied landing; in vain, von Rundstedt argued that he must let the Allies land and then, when they had shown their hand, attack.

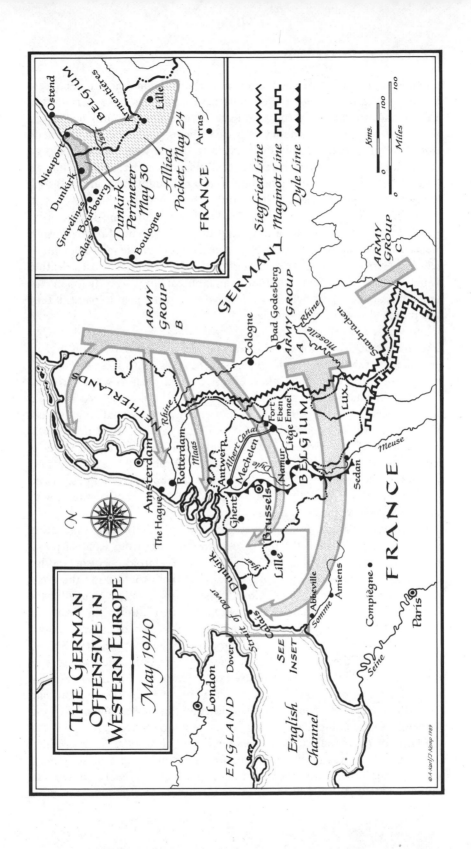

THE GERMAN
OFFENSIVE IN
WESTERN EUROPE
May 1940

Siegfried Line
Maginot Line
Dyle Line

Kms. 100
0
Miles 100
0

ARMY GROUP B
GERMAN
ARMY GROUP A
ARMY GROUP C

NETHERLANDS
Amsterdam
The Hague
Rotterdam
Maas
Rhine
Cologne
Bad Godesberg
Rhine
Moselle
Saarbrücken

Antwerp
Ghent
Brussels
Mechelen
Albert Canal
Dyle
Namur
BELGIUM
Fort Eben Emael
Liège
LUX.

Dunkirk
Yser
Lille
Abbeville
Somme
Amiens
Sedan
Meuse

Calais
Strait of Dover
SEE INSET

Compiègne
Paris
FRANCE
Seine

Dover
London
ENGLAND

English Channel

N

© A. Karl / J. Kemp 1989

BELGIUM
Ostend
Armentières
Lille
Arras
FRANCE
Nieuport
Dunkirk
Gravelines
Bourbourg
Calais
Yser
Dunkirk Perimeter May 30
Boulogne
Allied Pocket, May 24

On May 25, word reached Gort that the Belgian line was about to collapse; if that happened, it was a sure bet that Bock's Army Group B in the east and Rundstedt's Army Group A in the west would link up and cut off the British from the sea and all hope of being rescued. That afternoon Gort sat alone, searching his soul, trying to decide whether he should go against all the precepts of his career and disobey orders. After telling an aide, "You know, the day I joined up, I never thought I'd lead the British Army to the biggest defeat in its history," he concluded that duty lay in saving his army to fight another day, and at 6:00 P.M. he canceled the order for an advance to the south and ordered the troops to head north, toward the coast. By happy coincidence, just after Gort made his momentous decision General Alan Brooke brought into the command post a leather wallet that had been found in a German staff car; in it were the plans for a major attack at Ypres, which would have cut Gort's men to pieces if they had marched toward the Somme.

On May 26, Anthony Eden, secretary of state for war, conceded what Gort had been urging for days; the army's safety was paramount and he should withdraw to the north, "where all beaches east of Gravelines will be used for embarkation," but how effective a rescue effort would prove at this critical juncture was anyone's guess. Alan Brooke believed it would take a miracle to save the BEF. Gort himself wired Eden that "a great part of the BEF and its equipment will inevitably be lost even in the best circumstances," and General Sir Edmund Ironside, chief of the imperial general staff, concurred: "We shall have lost practically all our trained soldiers by the next few days—unless a miracle appears to help us." Even as determined an optimist as Winston Churchill thought they might, with luck, save twenty or thirty thousand troops.

Across the Channel, England was preparing for the worst—evacuating old people, cripples, and the few remaining children from Kentish ports, girding for the invasion that was certain to come. Harold Nicolson and his wife, Vita Sackville-West, were planning what they would do in the event of a German landing near their beloved Sissinghurst Castle: "You will have to get the Buick in a fit state to start with a full petrol-tank," he wrote her from London. "You should put inside it some food for 24 hours . . . your jewels and my diaries . . . clothes and anything else very precious." Should the worst occur, they had decided on suicide ("a bodkin which will give us our quietus quickly") to avoid capture by the Germans. From Ambassador Kennedy and from Colonel Frank Knox (whose *Chicago Daily News* had a London bureau) President Roosevelt learned that politicians in England were quietly discussing the possibility of a negotiated peace. But no thought of appeasement was entertained at Buckingham Palace, where a determined Queen Elizabeth was receiving instructions each morning in how to fire a revolver. Her Majesty was also ignoring the pleas she received from Dominion governments to send her two young daughters to a safe place, saying,

"The Princesses could not leave without me—and I could not leave without the King—and, of course, the King will never leave."

By May 28, the day Leopold, king of the Belgians, surrendered, more than a third of a million men had collected on the Flanders beaches within the steadily constricting perimeter, and this jumbled mass of humanity was hopelessly disorganized, most of the troops having lost touch with their units and their officers. Around this sea of castaways lay the flotsam of defeat: every conceivable article of equipment, clothing, weapons, personal belongings, had been discarded in fright or had come loose at the moment of death—abandoned overcoats, helmets, shoes, wrecked vehicles of every description (some 63,000 of them), more than 20,000 motorcycles, a vast tonnage of military stores, ammunition, and gasoline, nearly 2,500 guns, and everywhere the dead, the bodies sprawled where they had been machine-gunned or bombed by the relentless waves of Stukas that dove screaming at the crowded beaches, by the squadrons of Heinkels that flew high overhead. The horde of beaten Allied soldiers had lost all sense of time and place, and at times some of them threatened to behave like packs of angry hoodlums, poised on the edge of violence, ready to take out their rage and frustration on anyone who happened to get in their way. Thousands were hurt or wounded, dazed, exhausted in mind and body, and while the fighting went on continuously along the perimeter and in the air overhead, some men took shelter in what was left of the town, others wandered aimlessly around the beaches. Those fortunate enough to have picked up some champagne or wine during the retreat quietly got drunk; others played games and bathed in the surf; some sat in deserted cafés and sipped drinks; little knots of men prayed and sang hymns; here and there a soldier could be seen calmly shaving or getting a haircut from a buddy.

The town of Dunkirk, where a thousand civilians had been killed by the bombing, was a ruin—the railhead smashed, huge overhead cranes twisted wrecks, the docks and quays a mess of rubble. One obstacle to potential rescue efforts was that the beaches sloped off so gradually that nothing but a tiny boat could get close to shore; the alternative means of embarking were the East and West Moles, long wooden structures set in concrete that stuck out into the harbor almost three fourths of a mile—but beneath them swirled three-knot tides, making it difficult to bring a vessel alongside, and both moles and the beaches were exposed to steady, driving winds out of the north. All in all, it was not a place one would have chosen from which to extricate hundreds of thousands of men.

———

A miracle—or several of them—was what the British had asked for, and that, in the end, was what they got—that, and a full measure of good luck.

The first real break to come the Allies' way was that Hitler and some of his top generals lost their nerve, or, to put it another way, were so determined to follow their plan, moving south to destroy French military power in the field and bottle up the Maginot Line defenders, that they failed to kill off the Allied force marooned in Flanders. This thing had all happened so fast, victory had come so unexpectedly, that they had not had time to absorb the extent of the Allied catastrophe or to recognize fully that the French army was smashed beyond repair. On May 24, Guderian's panzers were in Bourbourg, ten miles southwest of Dunkirk, and nothing—no Allied force whatever—stood between them and the town. Most of the British army was still forty miles to the south, near Lille, but at German group and army headquarters concern was growing that the tanks had gone too far, outrunning their support troops, leaving the attacking army's southern flank dangerously exposed. General Franz Halder, chief of staff, had observed on May 17 that Hitler was already worried: "A very disagreeable day!" he noted. "The Führer is excessively nervous. He mistrusts his own success; he's afraid to take risks; he'd really like us to stop now. His excuse is anxiety about our left flank." And the following day was worse, with Hitler raving and shouting, saying that the generals "were well on the way to spoiling the whole operation and even risking the danger of defeat."

Meantime, the strategy that had been responsible for their early successes was beginning to work against them: to enable Rundstedt to exploit his dash to the Channel, all the reserves had been sent to him and none to Bock's Army Group B; in addition, Bock's armored and motorized units were added to Army Group A. As a result, Bock now had only twenty-one infantry divisions, some of them reduced to using horse transport, while Rundstedt had more than seventy divisions, and all of the panzer units. Army Group A was preparing to throw everything at the Allies when Hitler flew to Rundstedt's headquarters, where the two of them agreed that the tanks should be spared for future operations against Paris while Bock's infantry continued attacking the shrinking Allied perimeter from the east.

In this crucial decision the massive ego of Hermann Göring had played a part: he had been following the westward movement of the armored divisions with mounting annoyance, craving a share in the victory for his Luftwaffe, and on May 23 he put through a call to the Führer, urging him to let the air force destroy the enemy. Göring knew how to play on Hitler's mood: the air force was the creation of the Third Reich, not, like the army, of Prussian aristocrats; and allowing it to administer the *coup de grâce* offered an easy way out, conserving the tanks for the advance on Paris, which Hitler regarded as the real target. And so it was decided. The air force was ordered to "break all enemy resistance on the part of the surrounded forces [and] prevent the escape of the English forces across the Channel," and at 12:41 P.M. on May 24, orders went out to the panzer commanders, spelling out precisely where they were to halt. "We were utterly speechless," Guderian said later, describing the effect the order had on his eager armored crews, but until the hours before dawn on May 27, by which time it became clear that a substantial segment of the British Expeditionary Force was going to elude the Germans entirely, the halt order was in effect and the

Allies managed to set up an escape corridor from the south, enabling tens of thousands of troops to pour into Dunkirk. Even then, Bock's chief of staff sensed the long-range significance of Hitler's decision: ". . . in the discussions between the Führer and von Rundstedt on the 24th were born these decisions that cost us an assured victory in Flanders," he wrote in his diary, "and which perhaps have lost us the whole war."

Those three days made the difference between life and death for the British Expeditionary Force—sixty-four precious hours during which the weather in the Channel was as calm as a millpond and the skies cloudy, heavy with rain and mist, limiting the Luftwaffe to three major assaults on the beaches. And while the German high command and the weather were cooperating, one of the most extraordinary armadas ever assembled had sailed to carry off troops from the beaches.

From a command post cut into the chalk cliffs of Dover by French prisoners during the Napoleonic Wars, a superb organizer named Bertram Ramsay, who had been called back from the navy's retired list, was in charge of Operation Dynamo, as the rescue effort was named. The call had gone out across Britain for any small craft, and Vice Admiral Ramsay and a staff that began working around the clock soon cobbled together a fleet of just about every known type of vessel to join the destroyers, minesweepers, and other naval craft already at work. These coasters, dredges, pleasure boats, ferries, barges, "skoots" (some fifty of the broad, self-propelled barges known as *Schuitjes* that worked the canals of Holland had escaped with their crews and were now heading back to the continent manned by Englishmen), a float from the London fire brigade, even T.O.M. Sopwith's America's Cup challenger *Endeavour,* all with civilian volunteer crews, were brought together at Ramsgate for supplies and fuel and a final message—"Every man for himself. Make for Dunkirk, and good luck"—before taking off for the coast of Flanders. Among them, as J. B. Priestley told his radio audience, were the little steamers that once carried day-trippers on holiday to seaside resorts, with "the gents full of high spirits and bottled beer, the ladies eating pork pies, the children sticky with peppermint," and these *Brighton Belle*s and *Brighton Queen*s, summoned to rescue the troops, were creating an English epic by making excursion trips into hell and coming back glorious. By no means all of them returned: the good ship *Gracie Fields,* which used to ply the ferry run to the Isle of Wight, was one that "paddled and churned away—forever." Of something like 850 vessels involved, at least 235 were lost.

On May 31, Gort was ordered to return to England, but he stayed on the beach until the last possible moment, dreading to abandon his army; at midnight he boarded a little antisubmarine vessel, took a seat in the wheelhouse, and in the middle of a sentence fell into an exhausted sleep. Among the last to leave the beaches were two major generals whose names would become household words before the war had grown much older—Harold Alexander and Bernard Montgomery. Alexander, calm, capable, and at forty-eight the youngest general in the British army, had made a name for himself leading a cavalry charge against the Bolsheviks as a twenty-two-year-old colonel, and just now he had the unenviable task of staying in Dunkirk until the last British soldier had been evacuated.

The crews aboard the little ships were done in from fatigue and continuous exposure to air and sea attack: those who were still able to stand on their feet often found themselves trembling uncontrollably from exhaustion; some civilians absolutely refused to make one more trip. When the minesweeper *Sutton* approached the dock at Harwich, not a man had enough strength to throw a line ashore. At 10:00 P.M. on June 2, looking as fresh as if he were dressed for parade, General Alexander, accompanied by the remnants of his command, boarded a destroyer loaded with so many troops she almost rolled over, and an hour later Captain William Tennant, the senior naval officer at Dunkirk, who had been in charge of onshore arrangements for the evacuation, sent Admiral Ramsay a final radio message: "BEF evacuated."

Even so, it was not yet over. Until the final hours, Ramsay's flotilla kept coming, and as late as June 5 the boats were still taking Frenchmen off the beaches. A young lieutenant commanding a motor torpedo boat took a last look at the harbor before turning for home. "The whole scene," he remembered, "was filled with a sense of finality and death; the curtain was ringing down on a great tragedy." David Divine, a free-lance writer who took a little motor sailor to Dunkirk, had been stranded on a sandbar and in the final hours of the evacuation had picked up a ride home on the *White Wing*, a thirty-foot launch, when he saw what must have been a thousand French soldiers silhouetted by the flash of exploding shells. They were waiting patiently to board a ship when it suddenly exploded and vanished from sight. With their last hope of rescue gone, the Frenchmen turned around and headed through the gunfire toward the shattered town. It was, Divine said, "quite the most tragic thing I have ever seen in my life."

During nine frantic and heroic days, between May 26 and June 4, some 338,000 Allied troops were rescued from almost certain disaster in what Winston Churchill properly called "the deliverance." But the cost to Britain had been awesome. As Churchill's chief of staff, General Sir Hastings Ismay, described it, "Our men left Dunkirk as naked individuals, in no semblance of formation, and without any equipment except their rifles." All told, Gort lost 68,000 men killed, wounded, or taken prisoner during the campaign. (Montgomery's command alone suffered two thousand casualties on the way out of Dunkirk to the boats.) The army left behind most of its heavy equipment. The thirty-two RAF squadrons that took part in the action lost 177 planes in nine days, 106 of them fighters, and by May 30 there remained in southern England only 283 operative aircraft and 362 pilots to fly them. Within two weeks, the British would be left to fight on alone, and they now had at most twenty divisions, virtually without equipment, to send against two hundred victorious, superbly armed Wehrmacht divisions. Anthony Eden subsequently admitted that only one division in the entire British Isles, the 2nd Canadian Infantry, was up to strength and fully equipped. Of the navy's two hundred destroyers, only seventy-four were fit for duty (thanks to the Norway campaign as well as to Dunkirk), and for the defense of the coast, as Churchill revealed much later, Britain had no more than five hundred cannon, many of which were borrowed from museums. Not since Napoleon held Europe in his grasp had the British Isles been so isolated or in such peril.

For the immediate future, it was the end of any effective political or military alliance against Germany. The Dutch were out of the war, and so were the Belgians, none of whose fighting units had been rescued. The French perceived the Dunkirk evacuation as the beginning of the end, a further step down a road that led to ultimate catastrophe, and to make matters worse, they believed they had been abandoned by the British, even though 139,000 French troops had been taken off by Ramsay's makeshift fleet. In accordance with Churchill's promise to Reynaud, the BEF and the French were brought away in equal numbers—*bras dessus, bras dessous,* as the Englishman phrased it, arm in arm—but no matter; Dunkirk marked a new low in relations between the two countries.[2] On the night of June 4, General Spears, who had gone to Paris as Churchill's liaison with the French, dined with some of his closest French friends; for years they had known the same people, liked the same things, spoken the same language, and nothing had ever come between them. "But that night there was a rift between us," he realized, "a slight crack in the crystal cup sufficient to change its sound when touched. I had my password and they did not have theirs. We no longer belonged to one society bounded by the same horizon. A lifetime steeped in French feeling, sentiment and affection was falling from me. England alone counted now."

Understandably, most Germans regarded the evacuation as an unparalleled triumph. As one magazine put it, " 'Dunkirchen' will stand for all time for victory in the greatest battle of annihilation in history." The BEF had been pushed into the sea, disposed of, and would be a threat no more.

While the world waited in an agony of suspense, never knowing until the last how many British would be saved, a miracle had actually taken place, and General Ismay's wife saw the results with her own eyes. She was waiting for a connection at Oxford Station after a long day of Red Cross work, and the crowd on the platform was hot and tired, already resigned to the vagaries of wartime travel. A train rumbled in, filled with dirty,

---

[2]Despite Churchill's promises to the French, the British on the scene inevitably did their best to get their own men safely home, and not entirely for selfish reasons. They were certain they would soon have to defend the British Isles; for this reason RAF strength was husbanded insofar as possible, and orders were even given for unwounded soldiers to take precedence over the wounded since more of them could be carried on the evacuation ships. At the outset of the evacuation, moreover, the French were dead set against the operation, for they intended to hold the Dunkirk harbor as they would a beleaguered fort.

On the beach at Dunkirk, some soldiers dug foxholes in the sand while others queued up in long lines and waited patiently for the boats that would pick them up and take them to England.

unshaven troops in ragged uniforms, many of the men bandaged and in shock, all of them exhausted, and when the civilians on the platform suddenly realized who these soldiers were and why they were here they made a rush for the refreshment stand. Everything available to eat or drink was thrust through the windows of the train to the men, almost without a word being spoken, and as the train pulled out of the station, Lady Ismay and the others, the tears streaming down their faces, never took their eyes off it until it faded from sight in the distance.

Across the countryside, railway cars filled with evacuees rolled day after day, and on one hospital train that had traveled all night a wounded man awoke in the morning to find his car filled with a brilliant, pale green light. Glancing around, he noticed that the other men in his compartment were crying, and he looked out the window to see "what the poets have been writing about for so many centuries"—the fields and rolling hills of England in all the glory of a magnificent June morning. For those who had seen the ghastly face of war, the dying and the destruction, the ruination of a once-lovely countryside, this sight of their native land's undisturbed beauty was almost too much.

———

And so the epic of Dunkirk might have ended, but in the tradition of British politics it fell to the prime minister to give an accounting of the Allied armies' collapse in France. As Edward R. Murrow explained the background to his American listeners, Churchill's predecessors were responsible for the shocking lack of training and equipment that had handicapped the British Expeditionary Force; at Munich, Chamberlain had "purchased a few months of normal living and normal working, while assuring the country that . . . time was on the side of the allies. But they bought that quiet and complacency in an expensive market." Fortunately for Britain and those who stood beside her in these hours of borrowed time, a new leader had taken charge, and the meaning of Dunkirk was about to be perpetuated by one of the great orators of that or any other day.

Winston Churchill rose in a House of Commons packed with members and visitors. He reminded them in detail of what had happened in the wake of the German breakthrough at Sedan, when Hitler's armies "swept like a sharp scythe around the right and rear of the armies of the north," until all that prevented the enemy's armor from overrunning the port of Dunkirk was four thousand Tommies and French *poilus* defending Calais, heroic men who held out through four days of street fighting until only thirty unwounded survivors remained to be taken off by the navy. A week earlier, Churchill had feared that no more than twenty or thirty thousand men might be saved at Dunkirk, that "the whole root and core and brain of the British Army" would have to surrender; yet despite all the enemy had hurled against them, the worst had not happened, thanks to the untiring efforts of the navy and air force. The losses in matériel, however, had been enormous—a thousand guns, all the army's transport, all the armored vehicles that had been in the north of France. The nation's thankfulness at the escape of the army, he cautioned, "must not blind us to the fact that what has happened in France and Belgium is a colossal military disaster," and he warned, "We must be very careful not to assign to this deliverance the attributes of a victory. Wars are not won by evacuations." Nor should anyone forget that another blow could be expected almost immediately.

Two days earlier the prime minister had prepared this speech, and his secretary Mary Shearburn told the historian Richard Collier how he worked on it in his accustomed manner in the Cabinet Room at 10 Downing Street—Churchill pacing the floor, collecting his thoughts, trying the words aloud, dictating, she sitting at her typewriter at one side of the room, taking it all down as he spoke.

It was past midnight when he neared the end, and his voice was so tired she could barely hear what he was saying. The words were coming harder now, for he was nearly overcome by emotion, and tears ran down his cheeks as he contemplated what lay ahead for the country he loved. Yet whatever might come, he was saying, "We shall not flag or fail. We shall go on to the end, we shall fight in France, we shall fight on the seas and oceans, we shall fight with growing confidence and growing strength in the air, we shall defend our Island, whatever the cost may be, we shall fight on the beaches, we shall fight on the landing grounds, we shall fight in the fields and in the streets, we shall fight in the hills. . . ."

Here he stopped, choked with grief, unable to go on, while Mary Shearburn waited silently; then suddenly he stood erect and all the sorrow was gone from his voice as he almost shouted the next phrase, a great roar of defiance—"we shall *never* surrender"—and his voice and the tempo picked up, driven now by the man's unquenchable determination—"even if, which I do not for a moment believe, this Island or a large part of it were subjugated and starving, then our Empire beyond the seas, armed and guarded by the British Fleet, would carry on the struggle, until, in God's good time, the New World, with all its power and might, steps forth to the rescue and the liberation of the old."[3]

---

[3]It is tempting to suppose that Churchill, with his extraordinary memory and his love of history, may have had in mind Clemenceau's pledge in 1918, when France's chances of survival in World War I looked to be virtually hopeless. "I will fight in front of Paris," the Old Tiger had said, "in Paris, and behind Paris." Indeed, Churchill had reminded Pétain of that promise when the French spoke of making the capital an open city rather than defending it, but when Reynaud sent a message to Roosevelt, just before fleeing the city, he wrote, "We shall fight before Paris, we shall fight behind Paris," omitting the keystone of Clemenceau's line.

CHAPTER 33

"The most productive nation in the world has thrown its productive capacity into the scales."

Americans who could remember the deadly trench stalemate of World War I, when progress was measured in yards (and for millions the memory of that horror two decades earlier was still very much alive), were stunned as much by the speed of the Allies' collapse as by the disaster itself, but Churchill's magnificent cry of defiance after Dunkirk—which Harold Nicolson called "the finest speech I have ever heard"—sent shivers down the spine. Nicolson's wife, writing to say how she wished she could have heard Churchill address the House, observed that "one of the reasons why one is stirred by his Elizabethan phrases is that one feels the whole massive backing of power and resolve behind them, like a great fortress: they are never words for words' sake."

The rescue of Britain's army began to be perceived as a triumph, and a miraculous one at that, and a *New York Times* editorial spoke for a host of Americans in observing, "So long as the English tongue survives, the word Dunkirk will be spoken with reverence." By all odds the most hopeful sign in all of this was that the British people themselves chose to regard Dunkirk as a victory, yet for at least one British soldier, the real sign of hope was less the speech than the man who gave it. After Dunkirk, General Bernard Montgomery admitted, "I could not for the life of me see how we are going to win this war." Then the prime minister visited his headquarters in southern England on an inspection tour and they had a talk, after which Montgomery realized, "I still didn't know *how,* but I knew that we *would*— we had found the man."

Whereas most of the English-speaking world was appalled by the plight of the British standing alone against the Nazi juggernaut, it was becoming apparent that the average Londoner was going to take the matter in stride, as if he had known all along that the fight would eventually come down to him against the Boche. Something Eric Sevareid discovered was that "since the Londoner had never thought of London as anything but the world's center, it did not surprise him that the world's attention was now fixed upon London. . . ." Now, more than ever, it was more than a city, it was Britain—"a city-state in the old Greek sense, and [its] peaceable people had gone to war in their aprons and bowlers, with their old fowling pieces, with ketchup bottles filled with gasoline and standing ready on the pantry shelves." The American reporter was reminded of something William Pitt had said during a long-ago crisis involving these same bold and stubborn people: "England will save herself by her exertions and Europe by her example."

As much as Americans esteemed the British and their dogged determination to fight on, there remained a deep-seated reluctance to be involved more than tangentially in what was still regarded as someone else's war, yet it was evident from the tenor of editorial comment around the nation that people were groping their way toward a position that lay somewhere beyond goodwill gestures, yet short of open hostilities. "Winston Churchill's voice . . . resounded around the world," a New Orleans paper observed, when he "held out hope that with the help of France the democracies would win." (How much more help the French were capable of providing was by no means clear.) After reminding readers how American strength "probably decided" the First World War, the editorial writer put his finger on how millions of Americans felt: "Let us hope that this country will never have to go into another war. Let us see to it that it doesn't. But you can't stop Americans from admiring bravery wherever it may be found."

Significantly, an increasing number of editorials went substantially beyond admiring bravery: Omaha's *Morning World-Herald* observed that the status of this nation had already changed from neutrality to nonbelligerency, and asked if anyone could doubt that Ambassadors Bullitt and Kennedy would soon be "asking for men as well as supplies." In such an event, America might have to choose between war and peace. According to the *Youngstown Vindicator,* "The United States will not only get into the war but is already in it, because it cannot afford to do anything else"; while the *Dallas Journal* observed, "We're in the army now. . . . And our own defenses must be made quickly so formidable that no power will dare to threaten with armed force our way of life or the democratic unity of the Americas." The *Syracuse Herald-Journal* was blunt: if Germany, Italy, and Japan should win the war, how could the United States possibly survive in a world under their domination? Furthermore, if we knew now that the Axis nations would be victorious, would Americans be willing to fight today—while the French and the British were still in the war—or would they prefer to wait until tomorrow, when they might have to fight alone? Whatever Americans should decide, they had better face up to the fact that they were doing it out of self-interest—"not for the purpose of saving France or Britain, but to save themselves."

Until now, an unbroken string of defeats had made it less and less likely that the Allies had any chance of winning, and the New Yorker or the Californian or the Georgian who was still struggling with the actuality of the Great Depression was in no mood to donate scarce weapons to sure losers. But the epic of Dunkirk and the eloquence of Mr. Churchill produced a dramatic change of attitude—an upsurge of hope throughout the United States. On May 29, when the evacuation from the Flanders beaches was less than half complete, when it seemed that the men still trapped within the defensive perimeter might be destroyed at any moment, a public opinion poll revealed that only 47 percent of Americans favored selling airplanes to England and France. Twelve days later, after the rescue and the speech, the poll showed that the number in favor had soared to 80 percent.

Slowly, but ever so surely, certain realities were emerging from the smoke of Europe's battlegrounds and penetrating America's collective consciousness. One of those realities had to do with loyalties, or with self-interest, and what it came down to was this: when push came to shove, this nation's heart *was,* after all, with the Allies, and particularly with Britain, for many the ancestral motherland, which—thanks to Dunkirk—plainly had a better chance of survival than France. Another sobering fact to be absorbed was that there was no isolating or even insulating the United States against the threat of an aggressive dictator who seemed capable of destroying the Allied armies as well as the civilization they were defending. When all was said and done, the only way this country could possibly avoid going to war on the one hand, while doing its best to help Britain on the other (whether the motivation is idealism or pure self-interest does not make a lot of difference to the recipient at critical moments), was to supply that beleaguered nation with the weapons of war, and to do so as quickly as possible. So Dunkirk and Churchill's speech marked a definite turning point in the way Americans perceived the war, and no one was more alert to this change of heart than Mr. Roosevelt.

The eyes of Europe had been focused achingly on the battle for France, but they were turning now toward America, to see what the somnolent giant beyond the Atlantic would do. While the evacuation of the BEF was going on, a memorandum from a member of the British Foreign Office expressed what was in the minds of many Englishmen: "It seems to me that the way the retreat to Dunkirk is being managed should convince the Americans that we are worth saving and that Germans are not invincible supermen." Harold Nicolson thought it "practically certain that the Americans will enter the war in November [after the presidential election], and if we can last till then, all is well."

Whether the British could hold out until November 1940 and when or if the United States would enter the war were questions subject to a bewildering number of factors, yet there was no denying that American attitudes toward the conflict in Europe were shifting, thanks to Dunkirk, Churchill's inspired speech, and a growing awareness that Britain would soon be left to fight alone. In Washington, Harold Ickes noted with satisfaction how Churchill had "served notice that England would go on fighting to the very end," ensuring that the British fleet would not be surrendered to Hitler. The speech convinced Hull and Roosevelt that there was no longer any danger that London might sue for peace, and from Chicago the publisher Frank Knox wired the president, "Moves designed to aid the Allies now command overwhelming support in the Middle West"; he assured FDR that the country was behind him, now that the "fate of civilization hangs in balance." The British ambassador in Washington, Lord Lothian, was skeptical about that support for aid to the Allies; as he wrote Lady Astor, "The president is afraid that if he goes too fast you will get another 'battalion of death' in the Senate like Wilson did over the League of Nations—a group which will exploit the natural human reluctance to war, excite the women (saying they are going to keep their boys out of the war), and get the Senate so balled up as to produce complete paralysis of action in any direction."

Lothian,[1] who was now fifty-seven years old, had been Lloyd George's wartime secretary and was reputed to have written much of the Versailles Treaty. Surprisingly, considering the importance of the task before him, he had never held a diplomatic post before, and had frequently differed with Churchill (until Munich, Lothian had favored appeasement; then he saw the light and advised Chamberlain to adopt a stiffer policy). Even so, the prime minister considered him a "singularly gifted and influential envoy," which indeed he was. He had not been long in the job, having taken the post in Washington late the previous summer, but he had a sure sense of how to present his nation's case in America and a sharp eye for how the wind was blowing on this side of the Atlantic, and he was the first envoy of a major power to be received informally by President Roosevelt. A rosy-cheeked six-footer with the look of a slightly paunchy Roman tribune, Lothian was a bachelor and a Christian Scientist. He knew the United States

[1]Philip Henry Kerr bore the formidable titles of Marquess of Lothian, Lord Newbattle, Earl of Lothian, Baron Jedburgh, Earl of Ancrum, Baron Kerr of Nisbet, Baron Long-Newton and Dolphingston, Viscount of Brien, Baron Kerr of Newbattle, and Baron Ker. His principal seat, Blickling Hall, in Norfolk, is a seventeenth-century mansion, said to be the place where Anne Boleyn's ghost walks about "with 'er 'ead tucked underneath 'er arm." (Anne's childhood was spent in a house that once occupied the same site.)

well, having visited frequently and having served as secretary of the Rhodes Trust, which sent thirty-two American scholars to Oxford each year; and now, recognizing that every move he made would be scrutinized for signs of British propaganda, he was also acutely aware that his country stood an excellent chance of losing the war unless U.S. assistance was forthcoming quickly. All of which meant that he must walk a very slender line, even though he was convinced of America's "present unwritten and unnamed naval alliance with Britain." So in the aftermath of Dunkirk, with France on the verge of collapse, he journeyed to New Haven, Connecticut, to speak to a group of Yale alumni. The message was one he would be delivering as frequently as possible during the coming weeks—a clear statement of the case for a firm, continuing partnership between the United States and Britain.

Since the First World War, he reminded his audience, command of the seas had been exercised jointly by Great Britain and the United States, and until the European dictators began abusing the system, it had worked well enough to prevent another outbreak of fighting. Because of the development of air power, however, the security that British and American sea power had given the world no longer existed—particularly now, when Hitler's objective was to capture the British and French fleets and destroy the capacity of those two countries to maintain sea and air bases. Once Hitler was the master of Europe, he could control the world, and if he gained control of the British fleet, America would "then have only one navy to protect a two-ocean front."

It was time to speak bluntly, Lothian added. The only way the United States could possibly have the luxury of time in which to prepare its military defenses was if the armaments and factories of the British Commonwealth, and above all the British fleet, were kept out of Hitler's hands. And if Americans were under the illusion that the Royal Navy was going to cross the Atlantic and make itself available as a subordinate part of the U.S. defense system, they had better think again.

He did not want to leave them with a pessimistic impression: his nation's fleet, its air force, and its people would give a good account of themselves in the desperate hours ahead, for he and his countrymen believed, quite literally, that Britain was the last bastion of freedom in the world and that "if Britain goes it will be very difficult to preserve it for long . . . anywhere else." Whatever material assistance America could send should be dispatched as quickly as possible, since it might mean the difference between survival and defeat. For "if we can hold out till Christmas, if we can prove that Hitler . . . cannot break our spirit or conquer our island, we shall, I believe, have turned the tide."

===

By the time Lothian spoke, the question of when Italy would enter the war had been decided. A number of efforts—all of them futile—were made to see that it did not happen. Roosevelt had done what he could through diplomatic channels and personal messages to Il Duce, only to receive a reply described by Count Ciano as "cutting and hostile." Churchill did the same, and was similarly rebuffed. Hélène de Portes urged Reynaud to reach an accommodation with Italy, but nothing came of her maneuvering. Ambassador Bullitt suggested that Roosevelt invite Pope Pius to take refuge in the United States, since nothing, Bullitt believed, "could have a greater restraining influence on Mussolini than a genuine fear that the pope might leave Rome." But all was in vain.

For Italy's dictator, the matter of timing was crucial: as surprised as anyone else by the rapidity of the German advance into France, he knew he could not delay entering the war much longer if he was to share in the spoils. As Ciano phrased the dilemma, "Italy cannot remain absent from the terrible struggle which will forge the destinies of the world," which was high-flown language for what Mussolini himself put so brutally to Marshal Badoglio: "I need a few thousand dead to be able to sit down at the peace table as a belligerent." With that cynical justification, Il Duce strutted onto his balcony in Rome's Piazza Venezia late in the hot afternoon of June 10 to announce that Italy was taking up arms in "the conflict of poor, numerous peoples who labor against [those] who ferociously cling to a monopoly of all riches and all gold on earth. . . ." He called on the Italian people to "rush to arms and show your tenacity, your courage, your valor," thereby adding a million-man army, nearly three thousand first-line aircraft, and a good-sized navy to Hitler's war machine.

In a broadcast to the French people, a weary, resigned Paul Reynaud said, "Signor Mussolini has chosen this moment to declare war on us," and to President Roosevelt he cabled a sardonic message that included a phrase the recipient would use to advantage: "What really distinguished, noble and admirable persons the Italians are, to stab us in the back at this time."

Roosevelt received the cable and the news of Italy's entry into the war an hour before he left for the University of Virginia in Charlottesville, where his son Franklin Jr. was graduating from the law school and where the president was to deliver the commencement address. Working on the speech with his advisers, he decided to use the "stab in the back" phrase, but the State Department people—notably Sumner Welles—objected, saying it would jeopardize U.S. relations with Italy, and Roosevelt reluctantly deleted it. But on the train to Charlottesville with his wife and son he reinstated it and immediately felt a sense of satisfaction: a reporter noticed that the president, who had appeared grave and pale when he boarded the train, seemed visibly stronger and more relaxed as he waved and smiled at the crowd standing in the rain to greet him.

The line by which the speech would be remembered came from Reynaud, but the more important message was pure FDR—one he had been longing to proclaim, a promise dating back to his quarantine speech in Chicago three years earlier.

"On this tenth day of June, 1940," the president said, speaking slowly, his voice heavy with contempt, "the hand that held the dagger has struck it into the back of its neighbor."

The tone changed. "On this tenth day of June, 1940," he continued, "in this university founded by the first great American teacher of democracy, we send forth our prayers and our hopes to those beyond the seas who are maintaining with magnificent valor their battle for freedom."

Then came a statement that went beyond prayers and hopes—a pledge that Winston Churchill and Lord Lothian had been longing to hear, committing the United States to a sharply different course of action. America was ready, he said, to provide those who were fighting the Axis powers with "the material resources of this nation," while at the same time it would "harness and speed up the uses of these resources" so that this country would be armed and trained for any emergency that might lie ahead. Furthermore, "All roads leading to the accomplishment of those objectives must be kept clear of obstructions. We will not slow down or detour. Signs and signals call for speed—full speed ahead."

With this speech, *Time* happily reported, "The U.S. had taken sides. Ended was the myth of U.S. neutrality. . . . Ended was the utopian hope that the U.S. could remain an island of democracy in a totalitarian world." If the weekly news magazine could be believed, "The President spoke for the nation," although powerful voices in the Congress and elsewhere in the land were determined to prove otherwise.

Ordinarily, Franklin Roosevelt was too canny to take a position much beyond the shadowy zone where intuition told him public sentiment lay, but in his Charlottesville speech he was as angry as he had ever been in public, and because of that, and because he knew the tide of public sentiment was running in favor of the Allies, and because he realized he had to shout from the housetops yet another time, he took the nation around a bend in the road into new and unexplored territory. The *New York Post* recognized his speech for what it was: "He rose to the occasion and gave to the country the pronouncement for which it has waited. . . . The most productive nation in the world has thrown its productive capacity into the scales. . . ." If Franklin Roosevelt had anything to say about it, from this moment on, that awesome industrial might would be dedicated to the war against Hitler.

CHAPTER 34

———◆———

"...in a few days French resistance may have crumbled and we shall be left alone."

Square in the middle of France's nightmare, Eric Sevareid was frantically trying to get his wife and three-week-old babies to a safe haven, while carrying on what was to become an inhumanly demanding job. Late in April, Lois Sevareid had given birth to twins, and on May 9 she was still in a Paris hospital when Eric left the city, bound for Algiers and Tunis, to line up correspondents in case the Italians attacked there. The next morning he was in the little Provençal town of Valence, watching a shopkeeper painstakingly chalk a series of words in block letters on a blackboard: THE GERMANS—THIS MORNING—HAVE INVADED—HOLLAND—LUXEMBOURG—BELGIUM—THEY BOMBED—THE LYON AIRPORT. He raced back to Paris, arriving at the hospital to find his wife, who was still unable to walk, wondering if she had been left alone in the deserted building. Somehow he arranged to get her and the twins out of the city. He hired a Danish nurse to look after them and left for press headquarters near the Belgian border, where "the terrible pressure began, the pressure of crisis which was never to relent for many weeks."

When the Germans broke through at Sedan and Nazi tanks poured onto French soil, flanking the Allied army that had moved toward Belgium and Holland, Sevareid found it impossible to get his story past the censors and finally resorted to a one-line telegram, a code message he had devised months before. Fortunately, someone at CBS in New York remembered it, and the commentator Elmer Davis went on the air with the announcement that "according to a usually well-informed source" the Germans had breached the French frontier defenses. Day after day the German "pocket" expanded (French military spokesmen kept talking of huge German losses), and the French and British were steadily pushed back in the direction of the Channel ports. A French attempt to cut the German salient failed, and each night the jeering voice of "Lord Haw-Haw," a renegade Englishman who broadcast Nazi propaganda, mocked the weary, discouraged allies, telling them their days were numbered. As indeed they were.

Sevareid, returning to Paris, was stunned to learn that the government had no intention of defending the capital[1] and was in fact telling Frenchmen to remain *tranquille,* and he sent Lois and the twins with friends to Genoa, where they caught the *Manhattan,* bound for the States. A few days later came the first serious bombing of Paris. At noon on June 4 the minister for air was throwing a party for a group of dignitaries—military officers, politicians, and foreign diplomats, including Ambassador Bullitt—and the guests were standing around, drinking cocktails and chatting, when a bomb crashed through the roof, plummeted through each successive floor, and landed at the feet of the assembled guests. "The discipline of social poise has its advantages in warfare," Sevareid commented; "nobody so much as dropped his glass, and the bomb did not go off." With that first aerial attack on the French capital, the people of Paris were exposed for the first time to what their countrymen in the north had endured for three weeks—the experience of crouching in a cellar with the children crying in fear at the look in their parents' eyes, "while droning like that of a million bees fills the sky" and the house shuddered from the concussions and dust filled the rooms. Parisians learned "how it is to walk over powdered glass on the sidewalks, thick as drifted sand . . . to see an old woman on her hands and knees at the doorstep, mopping up the blood of her husband with the parlor curtain."

From CBS came orders for Sevareid to leave the dying city: if the French government evacuated the capital, arrangements had been made for William Shirer to come in with the Germans and take over the news coverage. On June 10, Sevareid got word that Paris Radio would be abandoned that night, but he was informed that the studio would remain open until he made his midnight broadcast to the States. When he arrived with a colleague, another CBS man in Paris, officials informed them they had received no authorization for the Americans to use the facilities, so the two men cooled their heels while a young woman played recorded dance music. All over France, all over the world, people waited desperately for news of Paris, and what they got was a crooner. The *poilus* at the front at least had an outlet for their rage and frustration; civilians could only wait anxiously for govern-

[1]Paris was declared an open city on June 11, 1940.

ment officials to tell them what was happening, and they were told nothing that was of any help.

Earlier that day, Parisians hoping for words of assurance and strength, for advice about what they should do, for word about what would happen to the capital—whether or not it would be defended, whether they should leave the city or stay—heard instead the gloomy voice of Paul Reynaud, telling them that Mussolini had broken his word and declared war on France. In the meantime Sevareid waited at Radio Paris for permission to broadcast the news to America. Before midnight someone finally reached the station manager, who gave the okay, and Sevareid went on the air on schedule; but that was the end of it—the staff from the station drifted into the night, climbed into cars and trucks, and joined the thousands of other vehicles, loaded to the rooftops with belongings, jamming the roads that led from Paris.

In a little Citroën, Eric Sevareid and his associate Edmond Taylor, a newspaperman who had been commandeered by CBS, became part of the ghostly train of automobiles and people on foot that inched through the darkness, abandoning the City of Light. Through Chartres, Tours (where they miraculously ran into Taylor's wife), and on toward Bordeaux they traveled, typing their broadcasts on the fender of the car, at a crossroad, in a town square, wherever the growing river of refugees (five million of them, someone reckoned) paused for a halt. In the silent villages the houses were shuttered, the shops stripped of everything that could be eaten; gas pumps were empty, water was scarce, food unobtainable; along the road-sides lay the casualties of the exodus, with cars overturned, wrecked, or simply abandoned, dead horses that had been dragged off the road, families sleeping in ditches where they had fallen exhausted, "sprawled in careless heaps like bundles of rags tied with strings."

Thirty-three thousand feet overhead, Captain Antoine de Saint-Exupéry could see the patches of motionless smoke that lay across the entire land-scape where villages were burning, and, like syrup flowing toward the horizon, highways swarming with refugees. It looked as if "somewhere in the north of France a boot had scattered an ant-hill, and the ants were on the march." In the towns where he had been billeted he had witnessed this crazy contagion of exodus—homes, shops, hospitals abandoned on the say-so of a figure in authority. Because the mayor told people to leave, here they were, heading south as though the south had room for them or food with which to feed them or friends to welcome them. How many of those ancient vehicles would break down, how many people would be stranded to wait in vain by the side of the road for a shepherd? How were they to be fed, these millions of migrants traveling two to ten miles a day, fleeing (or so they thought) before tanks that moved at fifty miles a day, airplanes that flew four hundred miles an hour? Even if there were food aplenty, there was no way it could be moved along highways strangled with refugees and vehicles—the gigantic traffic jam the Germans had done everything possible to create, knowing it would prevent the French from moving troops from one front to another.

Few of those refugees knew it when they left Paris, but the French premier and his cabinet had also fled the capital and what remained of the nation's army was on the brink of collapse. In their retreat, the nation's military chiefs were not obliged to struggle with the monstrous traffic tie-ups: they traveled by train. As General André Beaufre of the headquarters staff remarked, "We carried our misery away in sumptuous drawing-room cars." Before leaving Paris for Tours, Reynaud beseeched Roosevelt to send "new and even larger assistance"—including "clouds of war planes"—before it was too late, reminding him that the world owed a debt to France for fighting the Germans and that France was calling in her markers. What almost no one knew was that not even a small cloud of aircraft existed in the United States: the nation had at that moment the grand total of 160 fighter planes (a five-day supply for the Allies, at their current loss rate) and fifty-two heavy bombers, which meant that the president, when he spoke at Charlottesville, had been dealing in extremely long-range futures. The French premier told Bullitt he wanted Roosevelt to ask Congress for a declaration of war against Germany or, failing that, to proclaim that the United States "could not permit the defeat of France and England," whereupon the ambassador assured the president of "Reynaud's determination and the determination of the French army to make the end of France as noble as her past." Bullitt was vain, egotistic, and an idealist, and he had a romantic notion that if he remained in Paris he would become a symbol of freedom and a rallying point in the occupied capital. To the dismay of his nominal boss, Cordell Hull, who abhorred the special relationship Bullitt enjoyed with the White House, he tried to persuade Roosevelt that that was what he should do. The secretary of state believed that Bullitt's place was with the French government, wherever it might go, and was furious when FDR caved in, allowing the ambassador to stay in Paris, to the detriment of the Allied cause. "If Bullitt had maintained contact with the French Government," Hull wrote later, "it is possible, if not probable, that the Government would have taken the fleet, gone to North Africa, and continued the fight from there."

Churchill, who was less sanguine than Bullitt about French determination, flew once again to the continent to try to bolster Britain's ally, and cabled Roosevelt that anything he could say or do to help the French might influence them to continue fighting. Soon both he and Reynaud were pressing Washington for assurance that the United States "will come into the war within a very short time."[2] Unless Roosevelt made such a statement, Rey-

[2]At the same time, Reynaud and Weygand were imploring Churchill to furnish more air support. "Now is the decisive moment," Weygand insisted. "The British ought not to keep a single fighter in England." Churchill, who had been warned by Air Chief Marshal Dowding that if any more fighter squadroms were sent to France he could not guarantee the defense of the British Isles, resisted despite his strong emotional attachment to France. In what was

naud said, "the fate of the world will change. Then you will see France go under like a drowning man and disappear, after having cast a last long look toward the land of liberty from which she awaited salvation." Back in London, the British prime minister predicted gloomily that without a promise of American intervention, "in a few days French resistance may have crumbled and we shall be left alone."

Reynaud and his fugitive government settled temporarily in Tours, adrift in a void without telephones, dependent upon news that traveled ten miles a day, exposed to the wildest rumors; ministers searched in vain for their ministries while their indignant mistresses blamed their protectors for the inconvenience, for the inadequate rooming facilities, for the state of the world in general. Here *The New Yorker*'s Liebling encountered Anthony J. Drexel Biddle, Jr., the former U.S. ambassador in Warsaw, who had followed the Polish government to Paris and was serving as envoy *extraordinaire* to the government of France now that Bullitt had chosen to remain in the capital. Biddle was "making a career of pursuit diplomacy," Liebling wrote, keeping Washington informed about France's collapse in cables that "must have read like a play-by-play account of a man falling downstairs." Reynaud, fearing that his mistress would be recognized and attacked if she was seen in a French vehicle, asked Biddle to drive Hélène de Portes to Bordeaux, where the government was moving next, and the American—knowing that without her Reynaud "couldn't have carried on at all"—did so, listening to her rail against General de Gaulle during the entire trip.

Bordeaux had "a climate of death, heavy and unhealthy like the smell of tuberoses," and Liebling watched, fascinated, as Biddle arranged to be seen in Reynaud's company as frequently as possible, giving outsiders the illusion that he bore important tidings from Washington, when in fact he could do no more than offer good wishes.

On June 14 the Germans entered Paris. Across the world, wirephotos of Nazi troops parading in the Place de la Concorde appeared on the front pages of newspapers; Le Havre was gone, so was Verdun, the Germans were about to take the Maginot Line from the rear. An impenetrable pall of gray smoke descended over the capital, obscuring the Arc de Triomphe, prompting rumors of a secret German weapon, a smokescreen blown in from the front. Some thought it the work of Paris's own Sainte Geneviève; others believed it an act of God. In the City of Light the postman continued to make his rounds, buses and the Métro ran, the cafés remained open, and *You Can't Take It with You* played in a Champs-Elysées theater, but Nazi officers had taken over the civic departments, a 9:00 P.M.-to-5:00 A.M.

surely one of the most agonizing choices he ever faced, he replied to Weygand, "This is not the decisive moment. The decisive moment will come when Hitler hurls his Luftwaffe against Britain." Then he added, "Whatever happens here, we are resolved to fight on and on for ever and ever and ever." When told of Weygand's prediction that "in three weeks England will have her neck wrung like a chicken," Churchill filed the remark in his archival memory, and in a speech eighteen months later growled, "Some chicken! Some neck!"

curfew was in effect, and local radio stations were broadcasting official German news bulletins, "Deutschland über Alles," and the Horst Wessel song. "Our successes are extraordinary," General Rommel wrote to his wife. "We had never imagined the war in the west would turn out like this." Thanks to Ambassador Bullitt's misplaced determination, the Stars and Stripes still flew over the American embassy, just off the Place de la Concorde, but now the building was surrounded by German infantrymen.

To be on the scene at France's tragic moment was the opportunity of a lifetime for a reporter, as Eric Sevareid knew, but there was nothing easy about the job—either in the ordinary sense of finding a place (not to mention the time) to sleep and something to eat, or in locating the facilities that would enable him to carry on with his work. All the French overseas cable communications were out of commission, casualties of the war; one channel, and only one, existed by which the reporters from all the news agencies, newspapers, and broadcasting companies could file their stories. That was Press Wireless's transmitter, an hour's drive from Bordeaux, and to make life more difficult for those using the facility, copy could not be phoned to the operators there—it had to be delivered by courier car.

When Sevareid learned that Reynaud had resigned and saw the list of new cabinet members appointed by Pétain, he recognized them at once as henchmen of Pierre Laval, the sinister political opportunist known to be an apologist for Mussolini, an advocate of collaboration with Hitler, and an adviser to Pétain.[3] Somehow Sevareid had to get word to New York about the new government, but the courier had already left for Press Wireless. By a happy accident, he had discovered that a shortwave radio in the vicinity was still operating, and he and a friend from United Press got there in time to scoop the world on the story of France's capitulation; while Sevareid spoke without a script, the UP man called his New York office and spelled the names of the new cabinet members. From this moment on, Sevareid and his associate Edmond Taylor found themselves broadcasting night and day, for long stretches every hour on the hour, and they were on the scene when Pétain, the aged marshal of France, vain and doddering, dressed in a belted raincoat, went on the radio to inform his countrymen that *il faut cesser la guerre,* telling them that he had "made France the gift of his person" as if that were a fair exchange for surrender and humiliation. Nature itself protested at these words, Sevareid recalled; as the old man finished speaking, "the sky exploded in a violent thunderstorm, sheets of water lashed the windows, and sparks crackled out of the radio control panels." With Pétain's announcement that he had sent a message to Hitler requesting "a way

---

[3]Liebling observed that Laval "had been lurking on the fringe of the battle like one of those naked peasants armed with a knife who waited on medieval battlefields until an armored knight was unhorsed and helpless, when they cut his throat. When France was down, Laval's knife flashed."

to put an end to hostilities," the balance of power on the continent suddenly shifted in a moment as decisive as the defeat of the Spanish Armada.

When it became clear that the fighting was over in France, Sevareid and other correspondents, along with hundreds of refugees and quantities of war matériel that had been intended for use by the French army, were taken aboard the *Ville de Liège,* a Belgian-registered ship bound for England. They were the fortunate ones, and as the ship moved slowly out of the Bordeaux estuary they saw along both banks "a thick black line on the sands, which extended for miles toward the sea"—a reminder that Europe, from the Bay of Biscay to the Baltic, was in Hitler's hands. The long queue was composed of "living human beings, thousands upon thousands of them—Poles, Czechs, Austrians for the most part, men and women who had reached the end, the place where French sanctuary came to a stop. They were the people who could not live under Nazi occupation. They were the hunted, who would be as wise to walk into the water, leading their children by the hand until they perished, as wait until the Germans found them."

German troops were almost in Bordeaux by now, and as the *Ville de Liège* cleared the estuary, someone had a radio going and the correspondents found themselves listening to a familiar voice. It was Friday, June 21, 1940, at 3:15 P.M., William Shirer was saying, and an open touring car had just pulled into a clearing in the Forest of Compiègne. When Adolf Hitler, dressed in a gray field uniform with the Iron Cross dangling from his left breast pocket, stepped from the car and paused to look disdainfully at a monument commemorating France's victory over the Germans two decades earlier, it was so still that correspondents could hear the beat of a thrush's wings and the sound of a woodpecker tapping.

Shirer noted that Hitler's face "is afire with scorn, anger, hate, revenge, triumph. He steps off the monument and contrives to make even this gesture a masterpiece of contempt. . . . Suddenly, as though his face were not giving quite complete expression to his feelings, he throws his whole body into harmony with his mood. He swiftly snaps his hands on his hips, arches his shoulders, plants his feet wide apart. It is a magnificent gesture of defiance, of burning contempt for this place and all that it has stood for in the twenty-two years since it witnessed the humbling of the German Empire."

Followed by Göring, Hess, Ribbentrop, Generals Keitel and von Brauchitsch, and Admiral Raeder, the Führer walked toward an old railway dining car bearing the number 2419D, seated himself in the chair from which Marshal Ferdinand Foch had dictated surrender terms to the Germans on a bleak November day in 1918, and listened as General Keitel began reading the armistice conditions to the French delegation.

Of paramount importance to Great Britain and the United States was the disposition of the French fleet, and the armistice dealt with that matter in what the British ambassador in France called "diabolically clever" terms, declaring that the ships would be demobilized and disarmed under German and Italian supervision. While the German government coyly disclaimed any interest in the ships, saying it had no intention of using the fleet for its own purposes, those in the railway car and the anxious onlookers in London and Washington knew exactly what Hitler's word would mean in that regard.

When the grim performance was over, the railway carriage was hauled off to Berlin, France's World War I victory monument was blown up, and four days and endless discussions later, the humiliated and exhausted French representatives flew to Munich and Rome, to sign the final surrender documents. At 1:35 A.M. on June 25—only forty-seven days after Clare Boothe had seen the bombs fall on Brussels—the shroud of captivity descended upon France.

Among the thousands of refugees who turned up in Bordeaux were Hans Halban and Lew Kowarski, the Austrian and the Russian physicists who had been working with Frédéric Joliot-Curie in Paris, and who had come so close to creating a nuclear chain reaction. The reason they were in Bordeaux involved as unlikely a tale of intrigue as can be imagined, which began just before the Germans invaded the Scandinavian countries.

Heavy water—a mixture of oxygen and the heavy isotope of hydrogen, which reduces the speed of neutrons—had been discovered by the American Harold Urey, and a number of physicists, including Joliot-Curie, thought it might prove the ideal substance for a moderator, since it would slow neutrons at the same time it would not absorb them. Joliot needed heavy water, and the Norsk Hydro Company in central Norway was the only place in the world producing it on an industrial scale, so Lieutenant Jacques Allier, a young French businessman who had been called up as a reserve officer in the Deuxième Bureau, was assigned to obtain it. He left Paris in March 1940 in great secrecy, arranged to acquire Norsk Hydro's entire stock of 185 kilograms, had special containers built, and through some extraordinary sleight of hand managed to have his precious booty put aboard a plane for Edinburgh, and from there to Paris, where he delivered it to Joliot.

On April 10, only hours after the Germans marched into Denmark and Norway, Lieutenant Allier was in London, attending the first meeting of a curiously named group—the Maud Committee[4]—eaded by George Thom-

---

[4]The name "Maud" supposedly derived from a cable sent to Otto Frisch by Niels Bohr on April 9, as the Germans were overrunning Denmark. The last words in the message were "MAUD RAY KENT," which someone with a vivid imagination took to be a code message from the Danish physicist—an anagram (if the "y" was changed to "i") of the words "radium taken." According to this theory, the secret Bohr was attempting to reveal was that the Germans had captured his supply of radium, which meant that they wanted it for purposes of making a nuclear device. The theory, however, was wrong. Maud Ray was in fact the name of the Bohrs' former governess, she was living in Kent, and Bohr wanted to get a message to her.

son, a professor of physics at London's Imperial College, who was working on atomic fission with a number of refugee scientists not cleared by security for work on radar. Allier gave Thomson's committee a list of German scientists capable of engaging in nuclear research and suggested that British intelligence try to find out what these people were doing and whether they were working together. Two months later, when it became clear that France might collapse, the British decided that they had better do something about that heavy water Allier had liberated before it fell into German hands.

A similar thought occurred to Joliot. With amazing prescience, he told Halban and Kowarski there would be an armistice, followed by the occupation and subjugation of France for as long as Hitler and Stalin were allies. After that, he predicted, the resistance in France would commence under new leadership. He intended to keep his laboratory going and help organize the resistance, but he urged his colleagues to carry on their research abroad. Halban took the heavy water, along with what radium they had, plus certain documents, and, as he told it, "I put my wife and one-year-old daughter in the front of the car, the one gram of radium at the back, and, in order to minimize any possible danger from radiation, the cans of heavy water in between."

After a series of misadventures, Halban, Kowarski, and other colleagues from the Collège de France arrived with their families and the heavy water at Bordeaux,[5] where they boarded the little British coaler *Broompark* and encountered a crew that might have emerged from Central Casting. The man in charge—who knew exactly who the scientists were and what they had brought with them—was the twentieth Earl of Suffolk, a swashbuckling character with a thick mustache and tattoos on both arms, wearing hunting boots and swinging a loaded hunting crop. At his side, lighting his cigarettes, was his secretary, Miss Morden; hovering nearby was his chauffeur, Fred Hards. The tattoos, it turned out, had been acquired in the earl's youth, when he had run away to sea; his present assignment had been given him by Britain's minister of supply, who very badly wanted certain objects and certain people salvaged from the chaotic wreckage of France and brought intact to England. Among the objects on Suffolk's shopping list were the heavy water, certain rare machine tools, and some £2.5 million worth of industrial diamonds, and he had succeeded in collecting all of

[5]After seeing Halban and Kowarski and the heavy water safely evacuated from Bordeaux, Joliot returned to Paris and informed German interrogators that his supply of uranium had disappeared, he knew not where, and that the heavy water had been put aboard a ship that sank. In return for a promise of cooperation, he was permitted to remain as director of his laboratory and perform fundamental research, not war work. Fortunately, German physicists decided that his cyclotron could not be dismantled and moved to Germany before the war in the west ended, which they expected to occur soon. Joliot did indeed work actively in the resistance—a perilous business where, as Georges Bidault was to write, "the front was nowhere and the enemy everywhere."

them. He had been less fortunate in rounding up the people—some fifty scientists and engineers considered to be too valuable to fall into German hands; but he had twenty-five of these important folk in hand, including Halban and Kowarski.

The earl, who was handy with tools, had constructed a large wooden raft to carry the diamonds and the heavy water, the idea being that the coaler would tow this rig and, if the ship was sunk, the raft and its contents might still reach England. (A vessel that left Bordeaux at the same time as the *Broompark* was indeed sunk, and it was that loss that lent verisimilitude to Joliot's story of the loss of the heavy water.) Thus Europe's entire stock of heavy water arrived in England, to become part of Britain's nuclear effort, while Halban and Kowarski were installed at the Cavendish Laboratory in Cambridge. There, before the year was out, the two of them would prove that uranium oxide, used with heavy water as a moderator, was capable of producing a self-sustaining chain reaction. It was to be the first successful demonstration that a nuclear reactor would actually work.

The Earl of Suffolk was less fortunate than the men he rescued. He and his colleagues Miss Morden and Fred Hards—known collectively as the Holy Trinity—went off together the following year to investigate new techniques of defusing German mines and were blown to bits.

———

France had slipped into the abyss. Ambassador Bullitt, after talking with Marshal Pétain, Admiral Darlan, and other officials of the new regime, informed President Roosevelt that "their physical and moral defeat has been so absolute that they have accepted completely for France the fate of becoming a province of Nazi Germany. Moreover, in order that they may have as many companions in misery as possible they hope that England will be rapidly and completely defeated by Germany."

The British had other ideas: left to fight on alone, they breathed a rather astonishing sigh of relief. King George, reflecting the mood of a surprising number of his subjects, wrote his mother, "Personally I feel happier now that we have no allies to be polite to and pamper." Air Chief Marshal Hugh Dowding, who had seen the planes that were Britain's only salvation slowly drained away in the Battle for France, remarked, "I don't mind telling you that when I heard of the French collapse, I went on my knees and thanked God." And Alexander Cadogan, writing in his diary, predicted, "We'll all fight like cats—or die rather than submit to Hitler." Then he added disgustedly, "U.S. look pretty useless. Well, we must die without them."

In the United States, the first shock gave way to a terrible sense of foreboding. Military planners in Washington, contemplating the nation's defenses, its need for weapons of all kinds, and its woefully unprepared army and navy, suddenly began to argue against any further commitments of aid to Britain. The chief of the War Plans Division, having concluded that the only sensible posture was a defensive one, recommended to General George Marshall that we admit "our inability to furnish arms in quantities to affect the situation and . . . recognize the probability that we are next on the list of victims of the Axis powers and must devote every means to prepare to meet that threat."

President Roosevelt, characteristically, was saying one thing and doing another. Before the French collapse he wrote to the banker Lewis Douglas, who was urging him to send aid immediately to Britain, saying, "Actually, I am adopting the thought that the more effective useable material we can get to the other side will mean the destruction of an equivalent amount of German matériel—thereby aiding American defense in the long run. So you see I am doing everything possible—though I am not talking very much about it. . . ." Roosevelt blamed this need for secrecy on "a certain element" in the press that would distort the meaning of his actions, and that was logical enough; but there were other, more potent reasons. Even as he neared the end of his second term the gulf between liberals and conservatives was as wide as it had been when he took office, while the chasm separating interventionists and isolationists had never been deeper. Although no connection existed between the latter division and the former— liberals, after all, were as likely to be isolationists as conservatives might be interventionists, and vice versa—the president ran the risk that if he moved too far ahead of public opinion, sending quantities of aid to Britain in her hour of need might look like a Democratic program and opinion might begin to coalesce along party lines. Paradoxically, what he needed for the long pull ahead was the support of the very individuals who were most violently opposed to him and the New Deal—the men who owned and operated the steel mills, the automobile and airplane factories, the oil refineries, and the myriad industries that would have to be enlisted in the war effort.

In short, the president was going to have to walk the most tenuous tightrope, and his best chance of reaching safety on the other side was to impress upon the public—friend and foe alike—the threat to democracy, to national security, and to the American way of life. He was going to have to do so, moreover, in such a way that the conservatives whose help he needed were not thrown into the isolationist camp. America possessed— could have at its disposal, if it could figure out what they were and how to use them—a thousand sources of strength, but someone was going to have to discover and unlock these sources of power and utilize them in such a way that the matchless energy of a free society could be unleashed. Not many people had thought things through just then, of course, but what lay ahead was not simply another war. It was a global revolution, and when it was over—no matter how it turned out—the possibility existed that there would be no turning back to the tried and true, to the good old days we had known before the Depression.

It was apparent to many Americans that their strongest asset at this point in time was the nation's productive might. The French had known this when they pleaded for weapons; the British knew it; Hitler feared it. What none of those nations realized, however, was how badly crippled the industrial giant was.

PART VI

1940

PHILADELPHIA: WE WANT WILLKIE

Elwood, Indiana, was the "political capital of the world" when native son Wendell Willkie arrived to deliver his acceptance speech to an estimated 200,000 people in 102-degree heat.

CHAPTER 35

"... the Battle of Britain is about to begin."

If ever there was a time when external forces conspired to push Americans down a road most of them had no intention of traveling, it was during the summer of 1940, when at last it began to penetrate the national consciousness that we were living on borrowed time. It was as if a train were pulling into the station, hissing steam, bell clanging, brakes squealing, while the passengers stood in line at the ticket counter, trying to decide what their destination would be. Until June, Americans had viewed the European calamity with a kind of detached sympathy; now whatever hope may have existed for a settlement in Europe had vanished, with the German juggernaut apparently unstoppable, France gone, Britain seemingly on the verge of defeat, and the familiar world turned upside down. If you could have asked millions of Americans what single moment made the war real to them, finally bringing it home, many would have answered that it was the day the Germans marched into Paris. And on the morning the news of surrender came crackling over the radio from Compiègne Forest, people on the street wore a worried look and walked a little faster.

A few days before I packed up to go home at the end of my freshman year at Yale, I received a letter from Demass Ellsworth Barnes, a rumpled teacher with a true gift for conveying his love of history to the boys at Shady Side Academy (and the curious habit of beginning each class with the words

"Sufficient unto the day is the evil thereof . . ."). Europe was on his mind as June began, as it was on everyone's, and the future he foresaw was not bright. "Things of the spirit are taking a terrific beating these days," he observed. "If Germany wins the war we shall be isolated in an unfriendly and hostile world. We shall have to fight to keep our heritage [and] in America there must be a rededication of our people to the ideals of democracy and a moral rearmament. . . . You young men in college," he went on, "must gird yourselves for that great struggle."

Mr. Barnes was troubled, as were we who were expected to gird for the struggle, by the sensation of too many voices singing different tunes. Walter Millis, the isolationist author of *The Road to War,* personally declared war on the Third Reich in the *New York World-Telegram;* Charles Lindbergh advised his countrymen not to make idle gestures with an empty gun; young McGeorge Bundy, delivering the Class Day oration at Yale, urged his classmates to think carefully before they went off to die for an ideal: "It is advisable for you to make sure that your death will be of some use." President Roosevelt, who had been alternately praised and branded as a warmonger for his Charlottesville speech condemning Italy, was roundly denounced for predicting a form of universal conscription that would include young women as well as men. Meanwhile, the city fathers of Rome, Georgia, voted to remove the statue of a wolf suckling Romulus and Remus, donated by Benito Mussolini; and the little town of Italy, Texas, informed President Roosevelt by letter that the Italy which had declared war on France was the one in Europe.

In the June 24 issue of *Time,* under the heading "Five Years of Dates," appeared a listing of significant international events, all of which had occurred during Franklin Roosevelt's presidency. Beginning with the signing of an Anglo-German naval treaty in 1935, the ledger revealed the steady, downhill procession toward all-out war—Italy's invasion of Ethiopia, Germany's remilitarization of the Rhineland, Spain's agony, Japan's invasion of China, the Munich Pact, Hitler's seizure of the Sudetenland, Czechoslovakia, and Austria—on through the stark roll call of catastrophe that had engulfed Europe within the space of three horrifying months:

March 13:	Finland surrenders to Russia.
April 9:	Germany invades Denmark and Norway.
May 10:	Germany overruns the Netherlands and Belgium.
May 14:	The Netherlands capitulates.
May 27:	King Leopold of the Belgians surrenders.
June 10:	Norway capitulates.
June 11:	Italy enters the war.
June 14:	Paris falls.
June 15:	Russia invades Lithuania. Spanish troops take over Tangier.

June 16:   Russia invades Latvia and Estonia.

June 17:   France surrenders.

Not since Napoleon had Europe been dominated by a single man, nor had Great Britain faced such mortal peril. Seventy-five million non-Germans were now under Nazi rule.

The day after France capitulated, the prime minister volunteered a characteristically Churchillian answer to the question of Britain's survival in a speech to the House of Commons. After casting up "the dread balance sheet" and outlining the dangers that lay ahead, he calmly informed his countrymen that there were "great reasons for vigilance and exertion, but none whatever for panic or fear." Lest anyone had forgotten, he reminded them how all had seemed lost in the last war, and how many disasters and disappointments the Allies endured before Germany finally collapsed.

Now, he went on, "What General Weygand called the Battle of France is over," and "the Battle of Britain is about to begin. . . . The whole fury and might of the enemy must very soon be turned on us. Hitler knows that he will have to break us in this island or lose the war. If we can stand up to him, all Europe may be free and the life of the world may move forward into broad, sunlit uplands. But if we fail, then the whole world, including the United States, including all that we have known and cared for, will sink into the abyss of a new Dark Age, made more sinister, and perhaps more protracted, by the lights of perverted science." Then he threw down the gage: "Let us therefore brace ourselves to our duties, and so bear ourselves that, if the British Empire and its Commonwealth last for a thousand years, men will say, 'This was their finest hour.' "

The American correspondent Drew Middleton was there, and wrote that the members were deadly quiet, mesmerized by Churchill's words. He sensed that the moment could be compared with Pitt at the Guildhall or Lincoln at Gettysburg and that he had been privileged to witness one of England's great moments, for surely the words spoken here would endure far beyond the lives of anyone in the chamber. When Churchill sat down the House rose as one man and roared its approval; they had heard the call to arms, they saw their duty, and as the American watched them walk out into the street he had the feeling that the sunshine seemed brighter than he had seen it for a long while.

Yet inspiring as Churchill's words were, and for all that the world might yearn for those broad, sunlit uplands, one had to wonder if the prime minister was whistling in the wind, or if the skeptics in Britain might not be right—those who were saying that poor old Winston's blind optimism was misguided, that he needed to realize how military tactics and weaponry had changed since World War I.

The same doubts applied to another rare gesture of defiance made in London on July 14, the 151st anniversary of Bastille Day. In Whitehall, within sight of most of Great Britain's government buildings, a pathetic little attempt at a parade took place—a parade made up of a few files of French soldiers, airmen, and sailors who had survived the debacle in their homeland and, more recently, the shock of seeing their British allies seize or destroy much of the French navy.[1] They could have remained in France, these fellows, but they had chosen instead to continue the fight, driven by some inner belief that their country would be freed from the conqueror, no matter how long or how painful the process might be, and now they were being reviewed by a towering, gawky man whose determination not to surrender equaled Churchill's, whose name had become a banner to which Frenchmen were flocking.[2] For his uncompromising views, Charles de Gaulle had been as unpopular with the leaders of his country as Winston Churchill had been in England, for if there is anything men who have been proved wrong do not care to hear, it is the prophet reminding them, "I told you so"—especially when the message is delivered by an outsize man with an ego to match. De Gaulle's long, chinless face, dour expression, hooded eyes, and huge nose gave him the appearance, one Englishman said, of "a secret face at Catherine de' Medici's council chamber," and on this particular day in July he was about as communicative as that description suggests. Eric Sevareid watched the proud, stubborn commander stride along the thin ranks of survivors, "never opening his tightly compressed lips, glaring, almost, into every pair of rigid eyes," and had the sense that General Charles de Gaulle might have been surveying a great army. "Somehow, you could not feel sentimental, nor could you smile. You had the impulse to remove your hat and stand rigidly at attention yourself."

Perhaps these summonses to duty by two imperious men *did* amount to no more than bravado, even in their own minds. What mattered just then— although the odds on their chances of ultimate success were incalculable— was that their message of hope and defiance was being heard around the world, by the conquered as well as the free.

———

Meantime, although it was by no means apparent to the British in their lonely hour of preparation, Germany's Supreme Command of the Armed

[1]A specter that haunted both Churchill and Roosevelt—that the French fleet might fall into German or Italian hands—had been laid to rest early in July. After the cabinet made what Churchill called "a hateful decision, the most unnatural and painful in which I have ever been concerned," more than two hundred French ships in British ports were seized. The real prizes, including several of the most powerful ships in the fleet, were at Oran and Mers-el-Kebir in Algeria; there, after negotiations with the French admiral failed, the British sank or crippled several of the most important vessels, while others fled to Toulon. For the time being, at least, the action removed the French fleet from Axis calculations.

[2]At the time de Gaulle proclaimed the existence of the Free French, which became the rallying point for his countrymen determined to fight on against the Nazis, he was still a figure of mystery to most Britons. "I can't tell you anything about de Gaulle," Alexander Cadogan confided to colleagues in the Foreign Office, "except that he's got a head like a pineapple and hips like a woman."

If ever a photograph told the story of what happened, it was this picture of German occupation troops parading past the Arc de Triomphe in Paris in the summer of 1940.

Forces—the Oberkommando der Wehrmacht (OKW)—had a first-class strategic problem on its hands. The principal weapon at its disposal was the most powerful army in the world, victorious, confident, virtually unhurt by the recent campaign. Yet it happened to be the wrong sort of army for what lay ahead just now. The OKW had expected to eliminate the British Expeditionary Force in France, but after Dunkirk, they had no way of getting at it. What was more, the German army was geared to ground warfare, and while it had accomplished river crossings with considerable success, it was certainly not equal to an amphibious operation on the scale or with the hazards of a cross-Channel movement. Still another question was whether this huge fighting force might in fact be *too* large for the particular task at hand, and whether thousands of these young German soldiers might better serve their country in the fatherland, on farms and in factories.

Germany's navy, which would bear the burden of transporting and escorting an invasion force, lacked the means to do so. It had no fleet of landing craft, other than the assorted barges it had been able to scrounge from the Rhine and the canals of Holland and Belgium. Because of the crippling losses suffered in the Norwegian campaign, the only surface vessels available to safeguard a landing force against the mighty British fleet were three cruisers, a handful of destroyers, and a few torpedo boats. Nor would a solution be forthcoming for months. In 1939, having been assured by Hitler that no war with Britain would take place before 1944, Admiral Erich Raeder had launched an ambitious capital-ship construction program, but to Raeder's dismay, the keels of two huge battleships had just been laid when Hitler unexpectedly ordered the assault on Poland. Now, at the very moment when big ships were urgently needed if England was to be invaded, the mighty pocket battleships *Bismarck* and *Tirpitz* were not ready for battle; *Admiral Graf Spee* was gone; *Admiral Scheer* was being overhauled; the new heavy cruiser *Prinz Eugen* was not yet available; and *Scharnhorst* and *Gneisenau* were badly crippled.

Granted the OKW had a major dilemma on its hands, even so, the army's lack of experience in amphibious warfare and the navy's shortage of transport vessels might somehow be rectified in the days ahead if the order to invade was issued in time for preparations to be made. Given the weakness of Britain's army after Dunkirk and the confidence of the Luftwaffe that it could control the air over the Channel, the risks might be worth taking. What was lacking was a clear indication of Adolf Hitler's intentions, without which the OKW was not about to proceed on its own. It was the Führer's ambivalence, his backing and filling on this question of invasion, that was to have such a profound effect on events in the months to come.

Two weeks after the French signed the armistice at Compiègne, Hitler was still euphoric over the triumph of his armed forces, but he was listening to Raeder's words of caution (the admiral was trying to persuade him to drop the invasion plans in favor of economic blockade) and he was temporizing, hoping to avoid a frontal assault if there was any chance the British might sue for peace. Always, in the back of the Führer's mind, lay the matter of Russia and his timetable for dealing with the festering problem that obsessed him. As George Orwell had surmised in the wake of the Nazi-Soviet Pact, it was inevitable that Hitler would turn on the hated Bolsheviks; the only question was when. It was the French surrender that suddenly caused him to scent opportunity, provided he could achieve an accommodation with Britain. Peace in the west would give him a free hand in the east, and the terms of the armistice with France were drawn with just such a possibility in mind. German troops occupied the area north of Tours to the Channel and Atlantic coasts, plus a strip down the seaboard to the Spanish border. South of that neutralized zone was Vichy France, a puppet government under the senile Marshal Pétain and the collaborator Laval. By dividing the country in two and occupying the northern half, Hitler created two Frances, and in all likelihood they would be at loggerheads with each other and no threat to his rear, while Britain would be insulated from the rest of Europe by the Channel and the buffer of Occupied France.

He had no wish to conquer England, Hitler told an adjutant, "I want to come to terms with her." But while he vacillated between negotiation and the use of force, he informed Italy's foreign minister, Count Ciano (who had come to Berlin to say that Mussolini wanted to participate in any attack on England), that he had not yet reached a decision, that he was putting off a speech to the Reichstag in which he would make "a gesture" to the British, because he wanted to weigh every word carefully. According to Ribbentrop, who saw an advance text of the speech, it contained "a very magnanimous peace offer to England"—so generous, in fact, that the parties might soon be "seated at a peace conference."

Meantime, talk would continue in Germany's armed services about the probability of an invasion, but until Hitler made up his mind, until he picked up the reins of command and issued the order, it was little more than talk, and the Wehrmacht drifted, lacking the leadership or sense of urgency the situation demanded. For nearly six weeks after Dunkirk, the Germans did nothing—six precious weeks during which the British worked around the clock to prepare for what was coming.

Inevitably, reports of Hitler's indecision reached London, persuading Harold Nicolson that the Führer seemed "to be funking the great attack upon England"—in which event, he concluded, "we really shall have won the war." By no means all of his countrymen possessed Nicolson's sang-froid: if asked, a good many may have had feelings akin to those of Herbert Morrison, leader of London's County Council, who admitted that he was "a frightened man. Frightened by what's going to happen if we aren't ready." The Imperial Defense Committee predicted that 600,000 deaths and a million wounded would result from massive German air attacks; heaven only knew how many casualties would follow an invasion. For months, preparations for both contingencies had been under way: primitive (and wholly inadequate) metal bomb shelters were distributed; ambulances, first-aid stations, hospital beds were readied; a Home Guard was organized and air-raid wardens appointed; women enrolled in factory jobs and non-combat military duty to relieve men for active service; vehicles and city streets were readied for blackouts; and in these and dozens of other ways the civilian population found itself getting ready for what now seemed certain. Meanwhile, under the watchful eye of General Sir Alan Brooke, who had carried out the evacuation from Dunkirk so skillfully, the last great democratic state of Europe was being transformed into an island fortress, with Canadians, Australians, New Zealanders, Poles, Czechs, and French troops added to the British army. The Dover beaches were rimmed with barbed wire and machine-gun nests (some inside flimsy wheeled bathhouses filled with stones). For twenty miles behind the beaches were tank traps, roadblocks, and concealed artillery positions. In London, a small contingent of Americans who called themselves "the Gangsters"—sixty expatriates led by a retired brigadier general named Wade Hampton Hayes, a former member of General Pershing's staff in the First World War—were training with the Scots Guards as a mobile defense unit. Heartening as this was, it was not without a price. Late in May, Ed Murrow reported that Parliament, in two hours and half, "swept away the freedom acquired in the last thousand years" when Clement Attlee, speaking in his new role as lord privy seal, announced that the government was taking over control of all persons and all property—becoming, in effect, a totalitarian state as it finally geared up for total war. On June 19, Murrow announced that millions of pamphlets, entitled "If the Invader Comes," had just arrived in Britons' homes, providing specific instructions: remain where you are; don't believe rumors and don't spread them; report anything suspicious to authorities; don't give a German anything (least of all food, gasoline, maps, or a bicycle) and don't tell him anything; help the British military in any way possible; and "think always of your country before you think of yourself." That afternoon, Murrow continued, the House of Commons would hear a plan to send 200,000 children to the Dominions and perhaps to the United States, and the worst of it was that "parents will not be able to go with their children. . . ." Of all the preparations, none was more poignant, more dreaded, than the continuing evacuation of city children to safer areas.

Since the previous autumn, mounting numbers of children, some looking forward to the adventure, some bewildered and terrified, each carrying toothbrush, towel, a change of clothing, an identification card, and a gas mask, had given their parents a last tearful hug before being herded onto buses or trains by schoolteachers and social workers, bound for foster homes in the U.K. During the first months of the war more than three quarters of a million young people had been evacuated to small towns and farms in the British Isles. When France fell and an invasion of England seemed ever more likely, the rush began to send children abroad—especially to Canada and the United States. With seven thousand applications coming in every day from anxious parents, the government temporarily suspended evacuation plans for lack of ships and because of alarm about the number who wished to leave.[3] What finally put a halt to the evacuation was the sinking of several ships carrying children to "safety," among them the *Arandora Star,* the *Volendam,* and the *City of Benares,* the last of which was carrying 406 passengers—ninety-eight of them children—when she was torpedoed on a stormy night, six hundred miles from England. Even so, by October, when the government stopped sending children abroad under its aegis, more than sixteen thousand had sailed away from home.

Lady Margaret Barry was one who left, taking with her thirteen children—six of her own, five belonging to one of her brothers, two to another—and sailing on an old tub called *Duchess of Bedford.* They took the northernmost route to avoid submarines, and as luck would have it, the ship was hideously overcrowded, the crossing extremely rough, and all but Lady Margaret and one child were seasick for the entire trip. After arriving in Montreal they went to Westbury, Long Island, where descendants of the Pittsburgh industrialist Henry Phipps turned over their house to them. Because of stringent wartime restrictions, Lady Margaret had not been permitted to take any money out of England and was dependent on her hosts even for groceries and toilet articles until she succeeded in getting a job with the British consulate in New York helping to expedite the eastward passage of those Britons who were needed at home for the war effort. Not until 1943 did she and her charges finally return to England.

Young Anthony Bailey, who spent his final evening in London with his father in a hotel basement during a bombing attack, sailed from Liverpool on the last vessel to include children as passengers. What he remembered most vividly about those terrible days when he was sent away by his family was shaking hands—with his father (who chose to hug him instead), with the woman who was escorting him and the other children to America, with various celebrities in New York who appeared to cheer up the little refugees, and with a small, somewhat wary-looking boy in short pants on the station platform in Dayton, Ohio, who was introduced as his new foster brother. (Four years later—just after entering junior high school—Tony Bailey learned that he was to go home, said goodbye to his American family and his new friends in Dayton, promised to write, and after a long sea voyage sailed up the Firth of Clyde to a port in Scotland. "Finally," he wrote, "I put out my hand to shake that of the woman, with premature streaks of gray hair . . . who I thought might be my aunt, but who, as she put her arms around me, I realized was my mother.")

As one would expect, the plight of these children had touched America's heart, and a Committee for the Care of European Children was organized

[3]Regrettably, the program inspired criticism; it was widely believed that children of wealthy families had been sent away first, thanks to the publicity those children got when they arrived in the United States. In fact, greater numbers of poor children, "with less news value but equally vulnerable bodies," as *The New Yorker*'s Mollie Panter-Downes put it, reached safe havens.

with Mrs. Roosevelt as honorary chairman. Back in July, when it was revealed that the parents of at least 100,000 young people hoped to send them to North America, a Gallup poll indicated that some five to seven million U.S. families were willing to take in French and British children for the duration of the war. The State Department, moving swiftly, cut through the red tape of immigration laws, and late in August the first shipload of evacuees from England arrived in Manhattan. That so few eventually came was the fault not of the would-be foster parents, but of the lack of ships in which to carry them. America's desire to welcome these youngsters may well have indicated, as *Time* commented, that people who could not resist an appeal for aid involving children had finally found an outlet for their emotional reaction to the war. What few seemed to recall was that only a year had passed since the Congress of the United States had found it impossible to admit ten thousand Jewish children to the land of the free.

On July 2, an OKW order, signed by Generaloberst Wilhelm von Keitel, revealed Adolf Hitler's rather ambiguous decision that "a landing in England is possible, provided that air superiority can be attained and certain other necessary conditions fulfilled." The tentative tone—that the landing would be "possible," but only if air superiority could be achieved, the vague reference to fulfilling "certain other conditions," plus an admission that "the plan to invade England has not taken any definite shape"—suggested Hitler's wavering state of mind. A few days later he told Ciano that he was "not yet in a position to say in what form the attack against England will develop"; the problem was "very delicate and difficult" and was being studied by the general staff. Keitel confirmed that nothing had been decided about a landing in England, except that it would prove "extremely difficult," and observed that it would be easier, indeed essential, "to make a large-scale attack on the airfields, factories, and principal centers of communication." Since the navy had begged off, leaving the army with no means of crossing the Channel, that put the question of how to attack the British up to Hermann Göring, commander in chief of the Luftwaffe, a man cordially despised by the generals of the OKW for his arrogance, his posturing, and his indifference to the accomplishments and importance of the ground forces. (To make matters worse, Hitler was inclined to leave management of the Luftwaffe entirely in Göring's hands, and the air force commander seldom bothered to clear his plans with the army, much less inform Wehrmacht leaders of his intentions or coordinate strategy with them.)

Göring had been rewarded for his role in the victory over France by having a new rank created for him—Reich Marshal of the Greater German Reich—a glorious new uniform to go with it, and a decoration, Grand Cross of the Iron Cross, which was given to no other German during the war. He was cock-o'-the-walk now, and with good reason. To all appearances, the air force was the spectacularly successful arm of victory, the weapon that made *Blitzkrieg* possible. Anyone who had seen a newsreel had watched the waves of heavy bombers, the fighters, and the vulturelike Stukas thundering ahead of the armored columns, tearing up the enemy's defenses in Poland, in Belgium, Holland, and France, and anyone who gave the matter serious thought recognized that the Luftwaffe had never been successfully challenged. Against it, Poland's air force had held out for less than forty-eight hours, the Dutch and Belgians for less than a full day, the French for twelve days. What remained to be seen was how—and how quickly—that mighty force would deal with the RAF.

———

The day after the last British soldier was evacuated from Dunkirk, Göring's deputy, General Erhard Milch, a tough-minded World War I veteran who was inspector general of the Luftwaffe, had urged his boss—and through him, Hitler—to invade England at once. "If you give the English three or four weeks to recoup, it will be too late," he warned, and the Luftwaffe concocted a plan that would begin with a massive bombing attack on the southeast coast, followed by paratroop drops and an air-transport shuttle of fresh, battle-proven veterans who would spread out across the English countryside, unhindered by the shattered British army. For Göring, the scheme had two particularly attractive features: it would draw the Royal Navy and Air Force into the narrow confines of the English Channel, where the Luftwaffe could destroy them; and it would put the entire operation—land, sea, and air—under his personal command. But Hitler, still convinced that the British had had enough and would be willing to negotiate a peace because they realized the hopelessness of their situation, had said no.

The possibility of a negotiated settlement was more than wishful thinking on the Führer's part. A number of influential Britons, some of them highly placed, patriotic men, were appalled at the prospect of death and destruction that would result from the mass bombing of their country and believed that the way to avoid it was to come to terms with Germany while the opportunity existed. Flying time, after all, was twenty minutes from France to the Dover cliffs, and an hour to London. Their attitude was reinforced by a regular stream of rumors and peace feelers originating in Berlin. Some evidence exists that Churchill was encouraging appeasers in Britain and on the continent—but not in order to reach an accommodation with the Nazis: he was stalling for time, when every minute that Germany delayed was a minute gained in England's preparations to resist.

While the pot simmered, the Luftwaffe attacked convoys, tried to draw the RAF into battle in order to test its planes and pilots, and made sporadic raids on remote targets beyond the well-defended coastline. Until Hitler made his decision, however, it was a waiting game, an anxious one, and not only for the British. Churchill was to write, "Deep alarm spread through the United States. . . . Americans gravely asked themselves whether it was right to cast away any of their own severely limited resources to indulge a generous though hopeless sentiment." Unlike the Germans or the Americans, however, the prime minister was privy to what was going on in Britain's factories, where men and women were working until they fell to the floor exhausted, to be replaced by a fresh shift that came early to the job. The Canadian-born newspaper publisher Lord Beaverbrook, to whom Churchill had given the task of stimulating the aircraft industry, collected scrap aluminum from Britain's kitchens, set up the manufacture of components in garages and small shops, required a seven-day work week in the factories, and succeeded so well that in one month's time—the very respite Milch had feared—British workers produced 446 fighter planes. From then until the end of the war, British aircraft production would exceed Germany's.

What Churchill also knew was that his beleaguered island possessed two extraordinary new weapons—one of them totally unsuspected by the enemy. The Germans were familiar with radar—indeed, they had their own system, which was in some respects superior to Britain's; but it was under the control of the navy, which used it effectively for reconnaissance but failed to recognize its potential either for aerial defense or for combat. During 1939 and 1940, scientists in Britain (among them refugees from the Nazi terror) had been striving to improve the quality and extend the range of the radar network that was the island's first line of defense. By now the installations extended from the North Sea to Land's End, at the westernmost tip of the Channel coast, and reports from coastal radar stations and members of the Observer Corps were being fed regularly to plotters at Bentley Priory, an eighteenth-century mansion that was headquarters for the commander in chief of the RAF Fighter Command, Air Chief Marshal Sir Hugh Dowding, and the heart of Britain's air defense.

The second, and most secret, weapon, was contained within a curious bronze-colored column housed in a hideously ugly red-brick Victorian house called Bletchley Park, about fifty miles north of London. In 1938 a Polish mechanic working in a factory in eastern Germany had memorized and smuggled out of the country—in his head—the rough plans of a curious machine the Germans were making. He got in touch with British intelligence, and they set him up in a workshop in Paris, where he proceeded to construct a large-scale mockup of the machine he had worked on in Germany. The British quickly identified it as some sort of mechanical ciphering device, which was called Enigma by the Germans, and realized that they would have to obtain an actual machine before they could see how it operated and make much sense of it.[4] Thanks to a near miracle that intelligence operatives dream about but seldom pull off, the British—in coopera-

---

[4]The story is reminiscent of Samuel Slater, an apprentice in an English cotton mill, who memorized the details of Richard Arkwright's textile machinery—at a time when its exportation was forbidden by law—and brought to Rhode Island in 1789 the plans that were the basis of the American cotton-spinning industry.

tion with the Polish and French intelligence services and cryptographers—obtained a production model of the Enigma machine just before war broke out in 1939. The secret of the device was a series of rotors, each operating independently of the others, each bearing cryptographic signs representing the letters of the alphabet. When a code clerk typed a plain-language message into a typewriter connected to Enigma, electrical impulses spun the rotors, aligned the letters, and produced an enciphered message that was impossible for a cryptanalyst to solve. Since the rotors moved into a different position each time the operator touched a key, so that a different symbol stood for a particular letter each time it appeared, and since there were five rotors, the number of possibilities was immense.

Before the Battle of Britain began, a team of mathematicians and cryptographers constructed what amounted to a primitive computer capable of unscrambling the Enigma signals. This sophisticated equipment was contained inside the bronze-colored column in Bletchley Hall, and the intelligence system it made possible was known as Ultra, for its ultrasecret classification. Since the Germans were confident that their Enigma ciphers could not be broken, they kept using them. As a result, Ultra was employed throughout the war to read messages flowing back and forth between Germany's top commanders, including Hitler himself. The messages deciphered by Ultra were delivered personally to No. 10 Downing Street by Brigadier Stewart Menzies, the head of MI6, who was known as C. They were not shared with the Free French, who were notorious for leaking information, or with the Americans (until they entered the war), who were regarded by the British as only marginally better at keeping secrets than the French.

Before the attack on the Lowlands and France, few operational signals were employed by the Germans, because they were keeping wireless traffic as near normal as possible, to avoid rousing enemy suspicions. On May 23, however, a deciphered Enigma message from General von Brauchitsch, ordering two army groups "to continue the encircling movement with the utmost vigor," had alerted the British to the BEF's imminent peril, prompting Churchill and Gort to get the army to the Channel ports and out of France before it was too late. Just as Ultra had been partially responsible for the evacuation at Dunkirk, it was now to play an important part in the Battle of Britain. Göring was sending an increasing volume of signals to his commanders by Enigma, and the knowledge they provided concerning the disposition and strength of the Luftwaffe units enabled the outnumbered RAF to assemble its squadrons where they would do the most damage.

On July 10 the British got the first indication of what lay ahead. A German pilot sighted a convoy moving through the Channel, escorted by half a dozen Hurricanes, and Luftwaffe headquarters ordered the commander of the fighter group based at Cap Blanc-Nez to attack. (Those convoys were absolutely vital to Britain: the day before, 250,000 rifles with ammunition and three hundred cannon had arrived by ship.) When the planes took off, a cluster of blips appeared on radar screens twenty miles away, on the cliffs of Dover, and British spotters counted seventy or more enemy fighters. Orders went out from Bentley Priory to four RAF squadrons to assemble in support of the six Hurricanes, and within minutes the first real dogfight of the Battle of Britain had commenced. The Germans lost four planes, the British three, plus one small ship from the convoy. Both sides congratulated themselves on how well their efforts had been coordinated and executed, and the day's work proved to the British the effectiveness of their warning system, and to the Germans that the more RAF fighters they could lure into the air, the more they could destroy, and the sooner the invasion might begin.

By now, Hitler had concluded that England "in spite of her hopeless military situation, shows no signs of being ready to come to an understanding," and on July 16 he issued a directive describing an operation with the code name Sea Lion, whose aim was "to eliminate the English homeland for the prosecution of the war against Germany and, if necessary, to occupy it completely."

Prior to the invasion, the Luftwaffe was to eliminate the British air force, so reducing its numbers that it would be incapable of offering any real resistance to the invading army. The landing was to take the form of a "surprise crossing" of the Channel with units of the Luftwaffe to "act as artillery, and units of the Navy as engineers." How surprise was to be achieved while the RAF was being "reduced morally and physically," while British mines were cleared from the Channel and German mines laid, was not revealed. But the significant point was that Hitler had finally made up his mind.[5]

Even so, before slamming the door on negotiations, he decided to have one more go at the British—the "last appeal" he had told Ciano he was delaying in order to get the wording exactly right. Speaking in public for the first time since the brilliantly successful invasion of the Low Countries, he addressed the Reichstag, the top commanders of the armed forces, and foreign diplomats in the Kroll Opera House on July 19, took personal credit for the strategy that had led to victory in Norway and France, praised his military forces, and condemned the "Anglo-French warmongers"—notably Churchill, whom he called an "unscrupulous politician who wrecks whole nations and states" and who would soon flee to Canada, where the British

[5]After the war, Field Marshal Gerd von Rundstedt said, "The proposed invasion of England was nonsense, because adequate ships were not available. . . . I have a feeling that the Führer never really wanted to invade England." And Raeder, looking back from a similar vantage point, revealed that at the time the German navy was straining to prepare for invasion, Hitler was secretly moving troops to the Russian frontier, assuring Raeder that this was only being done to conceal invasion plans from the British. Earlier, Hitler had confided to Raeder, "On land I am a hero, but at sea I am a coward." An Englishman who had known the Führer in the thirties sensed his fear and speculated that he had no enthusiasm for an invasion because he hated the sea, or possibly because he was afraid of being *seen* seasick.

had sent their money and their children. Then, after threatening the British people with a rain of bombs and "unending suffering and misery," he finally got around to extending an olive branch, if that is what it could be called.

It had never been his intention to wage wars, he said virtuously; his goal was to build a new social order, and war only kept him from that important task. Yet let no one forget, he continued proudly, that "I am not the vanquished, begging favors, but the victor speaking in the name of reason." If the "criminal warmonger" Churchill brushed aside this appeal to reason and common sense, he added, "a great empire will be destroyed, an empire which it was never my intention to destroy or harm. It gives me pain when I realize that I am the man who has been picked by destiny to deliver the final blow. . . ." One of his listeners, seated in the front row of the diplomatic box, was Galeazzo Ciano, who believed that the Führer's "desire for peace is sincere," and considered the speech "unusually humane." Others—including Paul Schmidt, the official translator, who thought it incomprehensible that Hitler could believe that such a "meaningless, purely rhetorical" gesture would have any effect on the British—realized that the Hobson's choice being offered Great Britain was surrender or destruction.

Before anyone in the British government could reply, Hitler received an unofficial response from a journalist named Sefton Delmer, broadcasting in German over the BBC: directing his remarks to the Führer, Delmer said, "Let me tell you what we here in Britain think of this appeal to what you are pleased to call our reason and common sense . . . we hurl it right back at you—right back into your evil-smelling teeth." To the astonishment of Hitler, his Foreign Office, and members of the general staff, the official reaction, delivered in a radio address by Halifax, was little different except for the language.[6] Hitler's "last appeal" was dismissed out of hand, and what happened next would be up to the Germans.

It was late at night in Washington, D.C., more than ten hours after Hitler made his speech to the Reichstag, when the president of the United States delivered a speech of his own, and Germany's former ambassador in Washington, Hans Dieckhoff, was so disturbed by what was said that he promptly wrote a memorandum to colleagues in the foreign office. "Never before," he noted, "has Roosevelt . . . spoken so plainly and undisguisedly about the aims and intentions of his foreign policy," and "Never has Roosevelt's complicity in . . . this war come out so clearly as in the speech of July 19." The president might describe his policy as striving to preserve the peace, Dieckhoff sneered, but what it amounted to was "encouragement of the encirclement of Germany and incitement to opposition, that is, to war. . . ."

---

[6]Quite apart from other considerations, the British were privy to Hitler's invasion plans. The gist of the Führer's directive of July 16, describing Operation Sea Lion, had been put on the air by Göring for his generals' information, and had been duly received and deciphered by Ultra.

Whatever Dieckhoff may have supposed, U.S. foreign policy was not the most pressing topic on Mr. Roosevelt's mind that evening. In fact, his brief references to German aggression caused not a ripple in the American press, since the occasion had larger significance than Europe's war for his countrymen. His reason for giving the speech was to accept the Democratic Party's nomination for president.

CHAPTER 36

"I want to go home to Hyde Park."

While the fate of Britain hung by the slimmest of threads, the people who were potentially capable of providing the assistance so urgently needed were engaged in the quadrennial spasm of a presidential election. This political contest, on which the direction of U.S. foreign policy would likely depend, was going to be played out against the terrible thunder from abroad, but it was going to be carried on nonetheless with all the hoopla and blarney and venom that had characterized such affairs since 1796. In short, America's politicians were going to put on their conventions, their campaigns, their dog-and-pony acts, as though nothing else were happening in the world. Yet whether they realized it or not, the sounds of falling bombs and screaming children would not be stilled, and would profoundly influence the outcome despite anything mere politicians might say or do.

The reason this particular election held the attention of America and the world in the spring of 1940 was the as yet unanswered question whether Franklin Delano Roosevelt would ignore one of the republic's most sacred traditions and seek a third term.

Of all the political hands he had dealt and played, Roosevelt was keeping this one closer to his chest than any—literally not telling another soul what his intentions were, if indeed he knew himself. What made secrecy imperative was a custom unbroken since the end of the eighteenth century. The special nature of his role as president of the United States, as for the twenty-nine men who had preceded him, had been shaped by the austere Virginian who first held the office—the man whose bicentennial had been celebrated the very year Franklin Roosevelt first ran for president, whose long, enduring shadow lay heavy on the generations that followed.

When George Washington's second term drew to a close he was tired— weary of political strife, angry at the factionalism and vicious partisan attacks that were making life miserable for him—and he longed to return to the tranquillity of his Mount Vernon estate and enjoy his declining years. At the age of sixty-four, he was an old man: time and illness had taken their toll, and his memory was failing. Yet one cannot help but wonder how he might have felt if he had been in the prime of life when he completed eight years in the job. Would he have been so willing to yield that great office, that position of power? Unlike virtually everyone who followed him as chief executive, Washington had not initially sought the office, and he was as doubtful of his ability to cope with the task as citizens of the new nation were confident of it. "Integrity and firmness is all I can promise," he had said. It was a foregone conclusion that he, and only he, could be the nation's first president, but he intended to retire at the end of four years, feeling that rotation in office was a requisite of a free society. When he was persuaded to accept a second term there were those, like Thomas Jefferson, who assumed that he would continue to serve until he died, as kings did, since the Constitutional Convention had set no limit on the length of time a president might remain in office.[1]

Alexander Hamilton, whom Washington asked for assistance in writing his farewell address, knew that his chief had decided not to stand for a third term, but urged him to stay publicly uncommitted; that way, "a serious opposition to you will . . . hardly be risked." So Washington had withheld publication of his farewell address until the last moment, and his decision not to run for the office a third time was a tacit declaration of the principle that presidential succession should be determined by the electorate. Until Ulysses Grant, no man who followed Washington in office had had the audacity to seek a third term, and the last to have tried before Franklin Roosevelt appeared on the scene was his cousin Theodore.

In 1940, Franklin Roosevelt was fifty-eight years old. Like George Washington, he came from a moneyed, patrician background; unlike Washington, who was a national hero before he was elected president, Roosevelt's stature became evident to millions largely because of what he did after he reached the White House. At the outset, he appeared to have everything

---

[1]As presiding officer of the Constitutional Convention, Washington said nothing about the presidential term of office, but later he wrote to Lafayette, saying he did not see how a president could continue in office without the consent of the electorate, unless the nation was "in a state of depravity."

going for him: Will Rogers observed the day after his inauguration, "The whole country is with him. Even if what he does is wrong they are with him, just so he does something. If he burned down the capitol we would cheer and say, 'Well, we at least got a fire started, anyhow.' " And no one, not even his detractors, could deny that Mr. Roosevelt had tried to do something.

If you were a voter between 1932 and 1944 you were not neutral on the subject of Franklin Delano Roosevelt. I was never certain why my father and his older brother (both ardent supporters of Theodore Roosevelt from the moment they were taken to hear him speak on July 4, 1902) disliked Teddy's distant cousin Franklin so passionately,[2] but they had plenty of company in the thirties and forties, and their attitude was typical of a particular social and economic group. In their case, I surmise that distaste for Mr. Roosevelt was based on a combination of factors. They had begun their working lives at a very early age, without money or influence of any kind. Blessed with intelligence, a desire to learn and succeed, and a willingness to work hard, they had prospered—up to a point—before their progress was rudely interrupted by the country's economic crisis. Then, out of the blue, appeared that patrician with his inherited money, his Groton and Harvard education, his Eastern-establishment voice that was so phony to their ears, a man who had never worked at anything much but politics, and here he was, raising their taxes and distributing their money to indigents like the bums who came around to our kitchen door looking for handouts. Maybe they didn't put words to their inner thoughts in quite that way, but their outspoken dislike of Roosevelt was heartfelt, it was based in part on a sense of having been victimized, and the feeling was warmly shared by millions of their contemporaries.

Beyond the belief that Roosevelt was playing Robin Hood at their expense, there was the matter of loyalty, something that counted for a lot with George and Carlton Ketchum—and their loyalty was to the party of Abraham Lincoln and Theodore Roosevelt (who was, of course, a Republican until the insurgents broke off from the regulars, formed the Progressive Party, and chose him as their candidate in 1912). My father and uncle had lived with their grandparents in the Republican stronghold of east Tennessee, where "the war" meant only one thing, at a time when the veterans of the GAR, the Grand Army of the Republic, were still very much in evidence. It was, after all, only three decades or so after the Civil War ended, and the graying men who had left their youth behind at such places as Shiloh Church and Antietam and Gettysburg were respected pillars of the community, keepers of the patriotic flame, and regarded with awe by small

---

[2]My cousin David Ketchum writes that his father, Carlton, considered Roosevelt "a consummate liar" and "an unprincipled opportunist." He feared Roosevelt's efforts to grab power, as in his plan to pack the Supreme Court; but most of all he was alarmed by the attempts to "buy voters," believing that this would erode the character of many Americans and lead to a huge group of welfare recipients unwilling to work.

boys. The grandfather George and his brother so admired, who with his crippled wife had taken them in when their father died, was himself a veteran of the Union Army, and to his dying day regarded the Democratic Party as "the hiving place of traitors and rascals."

So it was that in my family "Roosevelt" was a pejorative, and this usage was hardly an isolated phenomenon. Even in an election that was disastrous for the GOP, when Alfred M. Landon carried only Maine and Vermont, seventeen million Americans voted Republican, and those ballots were cast as much against Roosevelt as for Landon. Harold Ickes was struck by the way his boss had polarized politics: "It seems to be a quality of the Roosevelt character," he observed, "either to inspire a mad devotion that can see no flaw or to kindle a hatred of an intensity that will admit of no virtue." Of all the reasons to hate Roosevelt, and they seemed to be legion, none cut deeper than the manner in which he threatened to end the dominance of well-heeled white Anglo-Saxon Protestants, who had been running the country (and just about everything else) for a century and a half. What made it even harder to accept was that Roosevelt had been a member of that very group since birth; hence the charge that he was a "traitor to his class." As Marquis Childs observed in 1936, hatred of FDR permeated an entire level of society, and it went far beyond normal political opposition or animosity: it was visceral, an obsessive fanaticism that inspired wild, ugly rumors of his plan to become a dictator and outdo Hitler and Mussolini and Stalin. His wife, it was said, would succeed him and remain in office until their sons could take over. There were vile canards about the intimate life of the family (they were drunks, with Communist leanings; Roosevelt had gonorrhea, which he'd caught from Eleanor, who'd gotten it from a Negro) and revelations of sinister plots to undermine the Constitution and the church. It was charged that the president had brought to Washington a pack of radical Jews who were running the government. "Documentation" existed (which, it turned out, originated with Goebbels) that the president was himself a Jew. Stories linked him with John L. Lewis and other labor leaders in a conspiracy to overthrow "the American way." To a large and embittered minority, FDR personified the threat of an entirely different kind of society—one that pampered the unemployed, ran roughshod over tradition, and, worst of all, challenged the rights and privileges of a ruling clique.

═══

As difficult as it was for that minority to comprehend, another, much larger group—the great majority of America's households—was crying out for what this man had to offer them. When he delivered his first inaugural address on March 4, 1933, a cheerless Saturday in a cheerless land, Franklin Roosevelt stood in the cold wind, looked out over the huge crowd, and to those thousands and to millions listening to their radios spoke words that radiated hope and reassurance.

". . . the only thing we have to fear is fear itself," he told them, "nameless, unreasoning, unjustified terror which paralyzes needed efforts to convert retreat into advance."³ Calmly, firmly, in a voice that exuded confidence, he said how important it was to realize that the problem confronting America was material, not spiritual, that it had been brought on by discredited money changers who had "fled from their high seats in the temple. . . ." The nation's confidence must be restored, and that required a change in ethics, a change in social values, and, above all, action: "We must act and act quickly." After pledging to wage a war against the emergency, he closed his speech with a prayer for divine guidance, waved to the audience, smiled radiantly, and rode off to a series of conferences at the White House. "It was very, very solemn, and a little terrifying," Eleanor Roosevelt said of the inaugural. "The crowds were so tremendous, and you felt that they would do anything—if only someone would tell them what to do." Intuitively, her husband had sensed precisely the black mood of despair and the terrible needs of America, and the extent of the support he received was revealed during the "Hundred Days," the period from March 9 to June 16, when he proposed, and Congress accepted, one of the most remarkable and sweeping legislative programs ever undertaken. After declaring a bank "holiday"⁴ to stop the run on banks and give the Treasury Department a breathing spell while it devised measures to shore up the financial system, he forbade the export of gold, silver, and currency, summoned Congress into special session, pushed through an emergency banking act that very day, obtained the legislators' consent for special powers to effect economies in the budget, and got them to legalize the production and sale of beer and wines, ending Prohibition.

During those first three extraordinary months the president never once dropped the initiative, and by the time an exhausted but exhilarated Congress went home, the new administration had in its hands a dramatically new agricultural bill, a civilian conservation program that would put a quarter of a million young men to work almost at once, the biggest relief program in history, new securities regulations and a banking bill, legislation based on a plan by Senator George Norris creating a Tennessee Valley Authority, provisions protecting small home mortgages from foreclosures, an emergency bill streamlining the railroads, and a National Industrial Recovery Act to encourage reemployment, shorten the work week, increase wages, and put people to work in public construction. A public bewildered by the alphabetical shorthand for the proliferating federal agencies—AAA,

---

³As the historian Richard Hofstadter pointed out, the message was the same one Herbert Hoover had tried unavailingly to get across to the people when he called for a "restoration of confidence." The difference was that Hoover was discredited and few believed that he knew what to do. They thought Roosevelt did, and they were eager for a change.

⁴In fact, many banks in the country had already shut their doors; Roosevelt's order simply kept them closed.

NRA, PWA, TVA, CCC, and the others—could take comfort in Will Rogers's depiction of 1933 as "the year of the big switch—from worse to better."

Recalling those exciting days, Harry Hopkins said, "Whatever we thought was the matter with the world, whatever we thought ought to be done about it, we could take our ideas to him, and if he thought there was any merit in them, or if anything we said got him started on a train of thought of his own, then we'd see him go ahead and do it, and no matter how tremendous it might be or how idealistic, he wasn't scared of it."

Reveling personally in the excitement of what he was doing, Roosevelt showed Americans who had been battered by economic reverses what confident, upbeat leadership could achieve. During that crisis of 1933, Congress supported him on virtually every measure he proposed, recognizing that action was essential if the nation were to be pulled out of the pit into which it had fallen; only later, when the crisis abated and conditions slowly began to improve, did relations between the White House and Capitol Hill begin to deteriorate. By then the president had seen the truth of a remark Woodrow Wilson once made to him: "It is only once in a generation that a people can be lifted above material things. That is why conservative government is in the saddle two-thirds of the time."

Eleanor Roosevelt once observed, "The so-called New Deal was . . . nothing more than an effort to preserve our economic system," and that was true enough. But the Roosevelt revolution—which is what it seemed at the time—penetrated every level of society, and before it was over the man in charge had succeeded in restoring some of the confidence and self-esteem Americans had lost, while making it possible for many who had been excluded from the mainstream of that society—blacks, Jews, Catholics, foreign-born—to become part of it. To those—and to others who had shuffled along the streets with hand outstretched, asking, "Buddy, can you spare a dime?"—he stood for hope, the hope of salvation.

William Allen White, the editor of the *Emporia* (Kansas) *Gazette,* who had written Hoover's epitaph as "the greatest innocent bystander in history," was trying very hard to figure out Franklin Roosevelt. He could not help admiring the man's "vast impudent courage" and his "vivid but constructive imagination," but it was difficult to avoid the conclusion that he was a wizard working "a weird spell upon a changing world." White worried about the way "we are getting our revolution through the administrative arm of the government, without legislation." He could see that Roosevelt would make mistakes, loads of them, and that he had his weaknesses; but what was reassuring was that he didn't hesitate in a crisis, that he appeared to be brave, honest, and strong, so that people would forgive him when he erred. As for the charge that Roosevelt might become a dictator, White couldn't get excited about that: "He laughs too easily. He is too soft-hearted in many ways."

How this infinitely complex man should have come to be so much maligned and feared, on the one hand, and praised and revered, on the other, was a function of his own upbringing, personality, and experience, and their interplay with the tumultuous political, social, and economic forces that were on the loose in twentieth-century America.

The thirty-second president of the United States was the antithesis of the familiar log-cabin-to-White House tradition that began with Andrew Jackson. "All the good that is in me goes back to the Hudson," he once said, by which he meant Springwood, the Hyde Park estate in New York's Dutchess County that was the fixed star in his universe. From the day of his birth in 1882, as the only child of James and Sara Delano Roosevelt, he was the focus of their household. It was an intimate, leisurely, privileged world of serenity and wealth, and the estate was young Franklin's domain, where, as he grew up, he shot birds, swam and skated and sailed his own boat on the Hudson, rode his pony through the forest, was taught by governesses and tutors, and spent his time in the company of adults—most of them Roosevelts, Delanos, and others from equally privileged Hudson River families. Years later, Franklin would remember the "peacefulness and regularity" of Springwood, and recall that "Hyde Park was the center of the world." Certainly he was the center of his parents' world, and his upbringing—like Winston Churchill's—was that of another era.

For all his subsequent immersion in the rough-and-tumble of twentieth-century politics and his keen knowledge of the contemporary scene, his roots in a particular place and a particular class made him at heart a nineteenth-century man. He was raised in a gentler day in the tradition of stability, raised to believe that man (upper-class man, at any rate) was perfectible, and his world subject to improvement; at Springwood and at the Groton School he was taught that the old standards of rectitude were the proper guides to conduct, no matter how the world might change.

Believing that the world had to alter certain of its ways, he turned to a form of evangelism. His political speeches, often enough, were sermons, and his election to the nation's highest office provided the pulpit from which they could be delivered most effectively to the largest number of people, as his Uncle Ted had discovered years earlier. Even his fireside chats—so called because he sat in front of a fireplace in the White House when he spoke into the microphone—had the quality of sermons, though they were softened by his genius of seeming to enter the living rooms of America and engage in a very personal, quiet conversation in language every man and woman in the audience could follow. Roosevelt was not the first president to speak on the radio (a number of his predecessors' speeches had been broadcast), but he was the first to see it as a distinctive medium of communication and to use it with striking effect.

He was a born actor-producer, with the talent to play the impresario's and the leading man's roles simultaneously, and even the costumes and props he employed—the cape, the pince-nez, the long cigarette holder—delighted his fans, infuriated his foes, and were meat and drink to cartoonists. His confident grasp of what people wanted was based on a voracious consumption of newspapers—between eleven and sixteen a day—plus a digest of articles and editorial comment culled from five hundred U.S. journals. (He was not, incidentally, an equally dedicated reader of books; what idle time he had was spent with his stamp collection or playing solitaire.) The familiarity with newspapers extended to the reporters who filled their pages, and no president was his master at the press conference. The first time the writer John Gunther was exposed to this particular phenomenon was in 1934, and he couldn't get over the president's gaiety and ease, the friendly give-and-take on the wide range of questions, that sent reporters away in such good humor. Yet, Gunther noticed, ". . . he *said* almost nothing. Questions were deflected, diverted, diluted. . . . I never met anyone who showed greater capacity for avoiding a direct answer while giving the questioner the feeling he had been answered."

———

The politician's ultimate goal is power, and Roosevelt probably desired it as much as Mussolini or Hitler did, though for entirely different reasons. Power, to FDR, meant an opportunity to lead people along a path toward ideals he had chosen for them—which was precisely the way he had been directed throughout his young life.

His father, James Roosevelt, was a fifty-two-year-old widower when he married Sara Delano, who was just half his age. Born in the last year of John Quincy Adams's presidency, James was an old-fashioned man with enough inherited capital to live very comfortably as a country squire. (The Roosevelt money came from real estate, sugar refining, and marrying well; the Delano fortune had been made in the China trade, principally in tea and—something Franklin may never have suspected—opium.) When the Roosevelts traveled, which was often, they went first-class, whether in a steamship or private railway car; pilgrimages to the important cities and watering spots of Europe were the norm; they had a summer place on Campobello Island, off the coast of Maine; they visited relatives and friends in Boston, New York, and Oyster Bay; they called on President Cleveland in the White House; and wherever they went, until Franklin finally went to school at the age of fourteen, he was almost never out of his mother's sight or out from under her autocratic presence.

Sara Delano Roosevelt idolized her father—"There was no one like my father," she said proudly when she was in her seventies—but after she was married her life focused just as determinedly on her husband and their son (who, she pronounced, was more Delano than Roosevelt). No hour of Franklin's day was unsupervised, no moment unplanned. He was expected to be obedient, to exhibit the proper manners, to ignore unpleasantness,⁵ to behave like an adult, to keep his mind "on nice things, at a high level," above all, to be a gentleman. As an only child of wealthy parents, it might be said that Franklin had just about everything he desired except the companionship of young people and the freedom to do what he wanted.

Photographs show him as a tall, very thin, good-looking young man, with eyes set a trifle too close, hair parted precisely in the middle, and something stiff and reserved about his appearance, an impassive look that suggests something going on inside his head that no one else is to know. Even in photographs where his companions stare and smile at the camera, he is withdrawn, inward-looking, part of—but not part of—the group. At Groton and later at Harvard he struggled to excel at athletics and other extracurricular activities, to be one of the boys, but his academic record was undistinguished, he was, as the Groton headmaster put it, "rather too slight for success" in athletics, he tried too hard, his close friends were not numerous, and at college he failed to be elected to membership in Porcellian—the exclusive social club to which his father and Theodore Roosevelt had belonged, which meant more to him than any other prize. According to his wife, that rebuff left him with "an inferiority complex," and FDR admitted long afterward that it was the worst disappointment of his youth. The political columnist Joseph Alsop, who was related to both Franklin and Eleanor Roosevelt, was convinced that the resulting sense of failure or inadequacy, the feeling that he had somehow not measured up, was a significant factor in FDR's ultimate decision to go into politics. In an arena that was *terra incognita* to others in his social milieu, he could "stake out his own territory, where he would not be in competition with other young men of his own sort."

The man who would begin his radio fireside chats by calling millions of listeners "my friends" had few, if any, intimates who could say they truly knew him, for it was his nature to conceal a part of himself from everyone. Eleanor Roosevelt once remarked that "he had no real confidantes," and revealed the nature of their own relationship when she added, "I don't think I was ever his confidante, either." Henry Morgenthau, his old friend, neighbor, and secretary of the Treasury, said it was all but impossible to describe FDR. Harold Ickes complained, "I cannot come to grips with him," and once told him to his face that he was one of the most difficult men he had ever known.

"Because I get too hard at times?" asked Roosevelt.

"No," said Ickes, because "you won't talk frankly even with people who are loyal to you. . . . You keep your cards close up against your belly. You never put them on the table."

⁵Once learned, the habit stuck. As Eleanor Roosevelt remarked, "If something was unpleasant, and he didn't want to know about it he just ignored it. . . . I think he always thought that if you ignored a thing long enough, it would settle itself."

Robert Sherwood, one of his speechwriters and biographers, spoke of the "thickly forested interior" that kept one from getting a good view of him, and perhaps it was this refusal to give himself completely to friendship that accounted for what Harry Hopkins called the side to his character that was lacking in generosity, a form of jealousy. According to Averell Harriman, "He always enjoyed other people's discomfort. I think it is fair to say that it never bothered him very much when other people were unhappy."

Unlike his cousin Theodore, whose insatiable curiosity led him into ever-widening circles of interest and knowledge, Franklin Roosevelt was seldom drawn to intellectual subjects. Socially as well as intellectually, he was something of a lightweight (girls called him "Feather Duster," for the initials F.D., and because, one of them recalled, "he pranced around and fluttered"), and it is not easy to reconcile the picture of the somewhat superficial young man who had the good looks of an Arrow Collar model, the too-easy smile, and the too-winning ways with the self-assured, commanding personality that would emerge in the White House years.

While he was still at Harvard, to the surprise and dismay of his mother, Franklin announced his intention to marry his fifth cousin, Eleanor Roosevelt. He was twenty-two, she was nineteen, but youth and inexperience troubled neither of them—only Sara Roosevelt, who resented and opposed the match and remained a trial to her daughter-in-law as long as she lived. For a stark reminder of that strained relationship, all one has to do is visit the Roosevelt home in Hyde Park and see Franklin's spacious bedroom, filled with his treasures, his mother's equally commodious room, and—between them—Eleanor's meager quarters. A tiny cell furnished with old wicker castoffs, it has no attached bath, and has the look of a servant's room. She always felt like a guest at Hyde Park, Eleanor wrote, recalling the time a friend telephoned to ask for her. When a servant answered, "Mrs. Roosevelt is not at home," Sara announced to the maid: "*I* am Mrs. Roosevelt!"

When the couple was married in 1905, President Theodore Roosevelt gave Eleanor away (again living up to his reputation of being the bride at every wedding and the corpse at every funeral, as his sharp-tongued daughter Alice remarked). Eleanor was tall—"coltish-looking," according to Alice Roosevelt Longworth's description, with "masses of pale, gold hair rippling to below her waist, and really lovely blue eyes," but painfully shy as a result of a childhood that had been insecure and often traumatic—"one long battle against fear," she called it. Her father, whom she adored, was an alcoholic, in and out of sanitariums, who died when she was ten.[6] Her beautiful but indifferent mother, who had died two years earlier, regarded the plain, gangling girl as an ugly duckling and an inconvenience, and was

[6]Except for her Uncle Theodore and her husband, Eleanor did not have a single male relative of her own or her parents' generation who did not end his days as a drunk. Understandably, she had no use for strong drink as long as she lived.

so annoyed by her awkwardness and "funny, old-fashioned" ways that she called her Granny. After Eleanor's parents died, she was turned over to her grandmother, who was said to have "the greatest knack for making her surroundings gloomy of all the women in New York." All in all, it was a childhood that could blight a life; instead, it left Eleanor deeply compassionate and understanding of the misfortunes of others. It was no accident that she came to regard the elevation of the human condition as her special mission in life, or that she probably did more to broaden her husband's perceptions of social problems than any other individual. Apart from everything else, she became a great asset to him politically: as David Lilienthal wrote, how the two of them "manage that business of meeting you in a crowd as if they had been waiting all afternoon for you to show up is a great mystery, but they do it every time." At the time of their marriage, other, more obvious qualities attracted Franklin. Like him, she had spent much of her youth in the company of adults; she was intelligent and serious, she had a modest income of her own, she was the niece of Theodore, the man he most admired, and as a relative whom he had known for years, she fit admirably into his life.

For ten years after their wedding, Eleanor said, she "was always just getting over having a baby or about to have one"; meanwhile, Franklin went to law school, found that he was bored by law practice, and in 1910 decided to run for the New York state senate. Capitalizing on family connections and money, plus his enormous energy, capacity for hard work, and aptitude for politics, he astonished everyone except himself by winning, and in Albany began his education in practical politics, learning to understand people and how to influence them, delving into what he liked to call "the science of government." He was a young man on the make, with his eye on the main chance, and chances of the right sort soon came his way.

An early supporter of Woodrow Wilson, he was invited to join the administration as assistant secretary of the navy, and leaped at the opportunity.[7] Since childhood he had been a sailor, and as he consciously modeled himself after his hero, Uncle Ted, the more his interest grew in geography and sea power. The job with the navy delighted him. He relished the ceremonies, the seventeen-gun salute and four ruffles to which his position entitled him, the opportunity to make important friends (among them Sir Cecil Spring-Rice, the British ambassador, with whom he agreed absolutely on the necessity of Anglo-American friendship; and the man whose classic *History of Sea Power* he had all but memorized as a boy, Captain Alfred Thayer Mahan), his share of responsibility for preparing the fleet for the day America would enter World War I, and an official mission to Europe to inspect navy bases and meet Allied leaders (including Winston Churchill,

[7]As a matter of courtesy, his appointment was cleared with New York's senators, one of them Republican Elihu Root, whose reaction was, "You know the Roosevelts, don't you? Whenever a Roosevelt rides, he wishes to ride in front."

then a cabinet minister). When the war in Europe ended, he declared, "I have loved every minute of it."

In the process, Roosevelt demonstrated a talent for administration; more important, he gained an experience of people that had been lacking in his upbringing, and from them he soaked up information and ideas. For the first time in his life he was exposed to a variety of individuals—from shipyard workers, sailors, and clerks to justices of the Supreme Court, congressmen, cabinet officers, President Wilson—from whom he began to learn about the real world beyond the constricted circle of Hyde Park society. Secretary of War Newton D. Baker, observing FDR in action, remarked how "he seems to clarify his ideas and teach himself as he goes along by [his] conversational method." It was a trait Eleanor Roosevelt elaborated on years later. Her husband was "particularly susceptible to people," she said, and "took color from whomever he was with, giving to each one something different of himself." He had a way of seeming to agree with them, no matter what they said, when what he was really doing was listening to their ideas, trying them on for size, as it were, to see if he could use them. But when it came to making a decision, she added, "I have never known anyone less influenced by others." He sorted through the ideas, picked and chose what he wanted, and then made up his mind. This gift for drawing out those people whose opinions he valued, paying rapt attention to what they volunteered, enabled him to discover what dissonant groups and individuals really wanted, allowing him to come to terms with them in such a way that nobody's ox was gored. To Herbert Hoover, who observed Roosevelt's methods under the most trying circumstances, the man was an opportunist, pure and simple—a "chameleon on plaid"; but a major reason for Roosevelt's stunning success was his perception that politics demanded the ability to compromise. It was the art of the possible.

After the war, friends in New York urged him to run for governor or senator in 1920, but he decided to wait and see what happened at the Democratic convention in July. What happened, as it turned out, was that Governor James Cox of Ohio won the presidential nomination on the forty-fourth ballot, and the thirty-eight-year-old Franklin Roosevelt (whom Cox had never met) was chosen by acclamation as his running mate. With a broken Woodrow Wilson dying in the White House, the Democratic ticket made U.S. membership in the League of Nations the central issue of their campaign; Roosevelt alone gave more than a thousand speeches; but there was little popular support for the League. America was voting that year not so much *for* Harding and Coolidge as *against* Wilson and his failed crusade to keep the world safe for democracy. He was the scapegoat, Cox and Roosevelt the victims. The Republicans, with Harding staying home and saying nothing much about anything, won a sweeping victory. "We had a chance to gain the leadership of the world," Wilson said bitterly, as he surveyed the wreckage of his dream. "We have lost it, and soon we shall be witnessing the tragedy of it all."

In the education of Franklin Roosevelt, the most brutal and tyrannical tutor was the infantile paralysis that struck him down in the summer of 1921, when he was thirty-nine years old. It cost him the use of both legs and changed his life irredeemably. Suddenly he was at the mercy of crutches or canes, a wheelchair, or someone's arm; he had to be lifted in and out of an automobile, carried up and down stairs; after he became president, he delivered his speeches to Congress in the House chamber, standing and holding onto the Speaker's podium, supported by the steel braces on his legs, which were attached to a wide leather belt around his waist. Infantile paralysis, as poliomyelitis was then called, was the Black Death of my generation's childhood, and President Roosevelt, as its most prominent victim, was a constant reminder of the disease's cruel effects. But it was a mark of his will to survive and conquer that the image people retained of him was that not of a cripple, but of an exuberant, handsome, high-spirited man with an electrifying smile. He could so easily have copped out—his mother offered him whatever money he needed and urged him to return to Hyde Park and never work again—but apparently he gave the possibility no serious consideration. What seems to have occurred physically, thanks to the regimen of exercise he undertook in his determination to recover, was a compensatory strengthening of his upper body and a toughening of his mental outlook, the way metal is tempered in the annealing oven. Ever the optimist, he tended to believe that something could always be done with apparently hopeless enterprises. As Roosevelt once joked, "If you have spent two years in bed trying to wiggle your big toe, everything else seems easy." From then until his death, Eleanor wrote, only once did she hear him make a remark suggesting discouragement or bitterness, and that had to do with a decision to spend money on a certain treatment on the chance that it might alleviate his helplessness; but "he never, never gave up the idea that he was going to walk again," and she "never heard him say that he was afraid of anything."

It was his paralysis that coincidentally gave his wife an opportunity to play an ever-growing role in politics—acting as his eyes and ears, for she could go places and talk to people he could not reach, and over the years she seemed to be going everywhere,[8] visiting breadlines and WPA projects, steel mills and union halls, attending every known variety of political and social function, until she became almost as well known (and as controversial) as her husband.

[8]Alice Roosevelt Longworth reported that after the election returns came in in 1932, Eleanor was found in a corner weeping, saying, "Now I will have no identity. I'll only be the wife of the President." If that really troubled her, she gained an identity soon enough. In 1933 *The New Yorker* published a cartoon by Robert Day, showing two miners shoveling coal deep underground; one of them stops work long enough to say to his buddy, "For gosh sakes, here comes Mrs. Roosevelt!"

If anything, FDR's customary gaiety and native optimism seemed to increase after he was paralyzed, leading those who did not know him to think he was all veneer and no substance, but the smile and the easy joke concealed an absolute refusal to knuckle under to despair and disappointment. Beneath the surface levity and buoyance was a determination—ruthless at times—to get what he wanted.

If contracting polio can possibly be said to have brought Franklin Roosevelt a bit of luck, it was the way the long period of recuperation delayed his emergence as a potential presidential candidate until the day when a Democrat had a chance. One of his first political acts after his illness was to nominate New York's Governor Al Smith for president in 1924. Four years later, after working tirelessly at politics, writing thousands of letters to Democrats all over the country, visiting with them whenever the opportunity presented itself, he became better known within the party. In 1928 he nominated Smith once more, in a speech notable for its suitability for a large radio audience; as one of the first politicians to recognize the extraordinary potential of this new medium, he was quick to master the techniques of using it. Several months after the convention, at the urging of Smith and the party in New York—who believed he would help carry the state—he agreed to run for governor and was nominated by acclamation. To counteract Republican innuendo that a cripple was no man to govern the nation's most populous state, he assembled a staff that included Louis Howe, Steve Early, Samuel Rosenman, Jim Farley, and others who would be at his side in the years to come, and set out on one of the most vigorous campaigns New York had ever witnessed. Roosevelt wanted to reach in person as many voters as possible, and worked tirelessly in his efforts to do so. Frances Perkins, who was to become his secretary of labor, saw him carried up the stairs to a speaking engagement and said, "He came up over that perilous, uncomfortable, and humiliating 'entrance,' and his manner was pleasant, courteous, enthusiastic. He got up on his own braces, adjusted them, straightened himself, smoothed his hair, linked his arm in his son Jim's, and walked out on the platform as if this were nothing unusual."

For all his efforts, Roosevelt failed to swing New York's votes behind its former governor; neither at home nor elsewhere could Al Smith match the prosperity Republicans claimed as their own or overcome the prejudice against a Catholic occupying the White House. Roosevelt ran ahead of Smith in New York, but the election was so close that he did not learn until the next morning that he was the new governor. During his term, he began the tradition of radio fireside chats, made frequent tours of the state with Eleanor gathering intelligence for him, and used the machinery of state government skillfully and vigorously to deal with the growing problems of the Depression. Two years later, in an extraordinary triumph, he was reelected by a 500,000-vote majority in New York City alone, won forty-one of the fifty-seven counties outside Manhattan, and carried upstate New York, which was unprecedented for a Democrat. In a victory statement on election night, his campaign manager James A. Farley told the press, "I do not see how Mr. Roosevelt can escape becoming the next presidential nominee of his party."

By the time of the 1932 primary elections it was apparent that Farley was right—up to a point. Roosevelt was far out in front of the pack, but when the Democratic convention opened in Chicago on June 27, 1932, he did not have enough support to win the two-thirds vote necessary for victory. His relationship with Al Smith had soured, thanks to Roosevelt's popularity in New York and Smith's defeat at the polls, and now the once-happy warrior was resentful and hostile, and in control of some two hundred delegates badly needed by FDR.

On the fourth ballot, when it began to look as though his candidate's lead was beginning to slip, Farley made a deal with Speaker of the House John Nance Garner to release his Texas delegation in return for the promise of the vice presidency, California fell into line, and Franklin Roosevelt had the nomination. In a stunning break with the tradition which had seen presidential candidates accept their party's nomination weeks after the convention adjourned, Roosevelt and his family boarded a trimotored plane in Albany and flew to Chicago, where he spoke to a cheering crowd: "I pledge you, I pledge myself, to a new deal for the American people." Within a few days, editorial writers and cartoonists were using the New Deal label to describe his program. Neither Roosevelt nor his advisers, it seems clear, had attached any particular significance to those two words in his speech.

With farm prices collapsing, retail sales stalled, unemployment and foreclosures mounting by the day, and the stock market moribund, the nation was desperately eager for change, and it heard Roosevelt's call for "bold, persistent experimentation," his pledge to put his faith in "the forgotten man at the bottom of the economic pyramid." Hapless Herbert Hoover, who appeared to be the villain who had done the forgetting, had alienated a huge segment of the electorate and was being booed in the streets. When the votes were in, the challenger had won all but six states, with a vote of almost 23 million to Hoover's 16 million, and carried with him overwhelming majorities in both houses of Congress.

Despite Hoover's pleas for cooperation in the four-month period between election day and the inauguration, Roosevelt sensed that the defeated president was trying to draw him into the vortex of the economic crisis and would have none of it. Tension mounted as the business of government and the country slowly ground to a halt, and press and public speculated on what type of chief executive Roosevelt would be. At the time of the Democratic convention, H. L. Mencken had dismissed him as the weakest candidate of the lot—"one of the most charming of men," but "shallow and futile." Why? ". . . maybe his Christian Science smile is to blame, or the tenor overtones in his voice." The *Herald Tribune*'s political observer Walter Lippmann informed readers that this Roosevelt was no crusader, no enemy of entrenched privilege, merely "a pleasant man who, without any important qualifications for the office, would very much like to be President."

Roosevelt's political family provided few clues to his personality or intentions: it included a staff of loyalists who had served him ably in New York, what reporters termed a "brain trust" of professors and theorists from whom he plucked ideas with what one of them called his "flypaper mind," and a cabinet that was a mixed bag of political philosophies and included the first woman to head a department. What should have been apparent was that no member of this group was likely to loom larger than the man at the top. "There won't be any presidential possibilities in the Roosevelt cabinet," James Farley assured reporters before FDR took office, and indeed, from then until his death twelve years later, no one inside his administration could be considered a serious rival to Franklin Delano Roosevelt.

That fact lay behind the vexing conundrum facing the Democratic Party as the election of 1940 drew nigh. One measure of power is the holding of it, and after eight tempestuous years that valuable commodity was still firmly in Roosevelt's hands, all but excluding anyone but a handpicked successor from carrying on the work he had begun.

From the president's standpoint, there was every reason to remain publicly uncommitted, as George Washington had done so many years before, keeping his own counsel and maintaining silence about his intentions. To announce his candidacy was to split the Democratic Party and unite the Republicans. To announce that he would not run was to become a lame duck, losing authority at home and influence abroad. Like many another occupant of the White House, he was acutely conscious of his place in history, and if there was anything he did not intend to do it was to run for a third term and be defeated. Yet on the strength of the evidence, that was not an unlikely prospect. According to one public opinion poll, more than half the voters opposed a third term. The New Deal was no longer new, no longer the fresh, exciting answer to the nation's problems; it had never come up with a lasting solution to those problems, and everyone knew it. Some 9.5 million Americans remained unemployed—17.2 percent of the total work force—and by any other measure, recovery was still somewhere beyond the horizon. Roosevelt had been badly burned in his efforts to pack the Supreme Court, Congress was increasingly hostile, his strength among farmers, labor unions, and blacks was eroding, and even under normal circumstances he and his New Deal were probably due for a reaction at the polls. In other words, if he had to run purely on his domestic record, he was in for trouble.

Beyond that, personal considerations argued against another term in office. Eleanor Roosevelt opposed it on grounds that he had done his part, that the New Deal—if it was so dependent on him—was in real trouble. Besides, she knew, he was bored with the administrative detail. Franklin's mother, interviewed on the occasion of her eighty-fifth birthday, declared, "I don't think my son has the slightest wish for a third term." And most of his children hoped he would not run again because they had seen him age so visibly in the job. The president was actually bursting with plans for retirement—"I want to go home to Hyde Park," he told a labor leader. "I want to take care of my trees. . . . I want to make the farm pay. I want to finish my little house on the hill. I want to write history." He was eager to set up the presidential library there, work on his papers, play the role of elder statesman. He even discussed with the owners of *Collier's* magazine a position as contributing editor at a salary of $75,000 a year. In March, speaking at a Democratic dinner, he stated that it was his ambition, on January 20, 1941, to turn over to his successor his desk and chair in the White House, and "a nation intact, a nation at peace, a nation prosperous."

On the other hand, he had no intention of allowing the New Deal's social achievements to go down the drain, as they might be permitted to do if Garner or Farley were to follow him in office. (He had drifted away from both men, seeing them as reactionaries and isolationists, and as potential threats to his candidacy, if it should come to that.) What it boiled down to was that a successor had to have a political philosophy acceptable to him, the strength to beat the Republican candidate, and the skill to steer the ship of state through increasingly treacherous international waters. That was a tall order.

With the Democratic convention scheduled to open in July of 1940—after the Republicans chose their standard-bearers—he was too canny a politician to slam the door on the possibility that he might decide to run. Some time remained, during which he would test the wind.

Several years earlier, Harry Hopkins—then WPA relief administrator— had been mentioned as a presidential aspirant, and Roosevelt had in fact encouraged that hope, in private, and publicly by making him secretary of commerce. Then Hopkins's wife died, and he had an operation for cancer followed by deteriorating health, and by 1940 he was clearly out of the running. But in 1938, Roosevelt had discussed the 1940 election candidly with Hopkins, dismissing the list of hopefuls one by one: Hull (too old), Ickes (too contentious), Farley ("the most dangerous" candidate), ticking off the possibilities through Henry Wallace and several Democratic governors. Hopkins could hardly help noticing that FDR did not rule out the possibility of a third term—especially if war should come.

That same year, Harold Ickes returned from a honeymoon trip to Europe, where everyone he met was talking war, and came out in favor of a third term for Roosevelt. He got no encouragement from the president in this, Ickes said, but "he did not tell me to stop." After the Munich crisis, speculation about another term for FDR began in earnest—at a time when "you couldn't throw a brick in any direction without hitting a candidate," as Ickes put it. In June of 1939, Hopkins spoke publicly of a Roosevelt candidacy (perhaps, his biographer Robert Sherwood suggests, with himself as the vice-presidential nominee). In December, during the "phony war," Ickes predicted that FDR would run for a third term because of his interest in foreign affairs and his unwillingness to "surrender command to another" if the war heated up. Well, the war had most assuredly heated up, and while the president dealt with the foreign situation, he was concurrently performing as ringmaster on the political front, diverting attention from his own intentions by building up first one candidate, then another—Hull, Alben Barkley, Robert Jackson, Herbert Lehman, Paul McNutt, and Henry Wallace among them—at the expense of Farley and Garner. And all the while, he kept mum about his own future.

With speculation rampant concerning his plans and the major party conventions drawing closer with each passing day, silence became increasingly difficult. Furthermore, Roosevelt's hand was being forced by events—by the frightening speed of German victory, by France's surrender, by the plight of Britain standing alone, desperately in need of material aid—and there is every reason to suppose that the president was by now convinced that he was the only man capable of dealing with the critical situation. Given that premise, if he were to run it would be on his own terms. He would insist on a mandate: a spontaneous draft by his party, to be followed by a summons to duty from the American people in November. That was the only way the third-term taboo could be exorcised, the only way he could appear not to be seeking office again. But in order to get what he wanted, he first had to deal with the ambitions of the three Democrats most likely to be selected in his stead—Hull, Garner, and Farley.

In the meantime, he would wait to see who the Republicans nominated.

CHAPTER 37

---

*"He could charm
a bird from a tree."*

T he opening shot in the 1940 political campaign—a small, not very
loud one—had been fired in Washington on April 7, when the Socialist Party nominated its perennial candidate, Norman Thomas, for
the fourth time.[1] In May, the economist Roger Babson became the Prohibition candidate; in June, predictably, the Communists nominated Earl
Browder; and at last, two days after France surrendered, one thousand
delegates, one thousand alternates, wives, functionaries, and aficionados of
the Grand Old Party, bursting with energy and determination and money
to spend, smelling victory for the first time in eight years, began assembling
in Philadelphia, and suddenly politics took center stage, collecting some of
the headlines that had been preempted so long by Europe's war.

Republicans had reason to feel they had a fighting chance to win. They
knew that millions of Democrats also opposed a third term for Roosevelt;

---

[1]Thomas, whose courage was matched only by the strength of his convictions, had campaigned for a quarter century against war and injustice and would continue to do so into his
eighties, speaking out against the Vietnam War. Without ever winning a single electoral vote,
he became the conscience of the nation, and by the time age and infirmity forced him to quit
he had seen most of the causes he advocated made into law or custom—low-cost housing, slum
clearance, unemployment insurance, old-age pensions, public works, the minimum wage, the
five-day work week, and the abolition of child labor.

everywhere, moreover, people were angry—angry over labor's insistent demands, over an economy that had worsened badly in 1937–38 and showed little sign of improvement, over the president's highhandedness, which had been seen at its worst in his effort to "pack" the Supreme Court. They were fed up with the way power was concentrated in the hands of political bosses like Frank Hague of Jersey City and Ed Kelly of Chicago, disillusioned by Munich and its aftermath in Europe and by the New Deal and its failures at home. In the '38 congressional elections the Republicans had almost doubled their membership in the House and picked up six Senate seats and eight governorships, and a Gallup poll taken in May 1940 showed that they were continuing to gain strength in thirty-eight states, while the Democrats had picked up in a mere ten (all border states and in the Deep South). So there was hope for the Republicans after their barren years, but everything hinged on finding the right candidate.

On Saturday, June 22, at 2:15 P.M., a man who had decided he was the man the GOP was looking for stepped off the train in central Philadelphia without a cent in his pockets. Two hours earlier, when he had gone to buy a ticket at New York's Penn Station, Wendell Willkie realized he had left his money at home, but fortunately the reporters dogging his steps chipped in and paid his fare. Lack of money—temporary though it was—was not the only un-Republican quality about Willkie, and because of that there was an electricity in the air, a heightened sense of excitement about him and about what might happen during the week ahead because of his presence in town, even though the convention was not scheduled to open for two days. A fair-sized crowd met him at the depot, friendly, curious, eager to get a close look at the man about whom so much talk was circulating. Willkie, a big bear of a man, wearing a straw hat cocked slightly to one side and a suit that looked as if he might have slept in it, grinned and waved at the welcoming party, answered a few questions from reporters, and walked out of the station; whereupon the crowd, swarming around him like bees and joined by more curious onlookers and well-wishers, overflowed onto the sidewalk and began moving en masse around City Hall, onto Broad Street, picking up strength at each block en route to Willkie's hotel, the Benjamin Franklin. As one of the candidate's admirers remarked, Willkie had an instinctive feel for public relations, and knew it was much more effective to walk from the station to the hotel as a means of drawing a crowd and attracting attention. For a fellow who was the longest shot among all the candidates for the nomination, this was not a bad entrance into town.

Until Willkie appeared on the scene, it looked as though one of three men would almost surely get the Republican nomination—Thomas E. Dewey, Robert A. Taft, or Arthur Vandenberg—and according to a Gallup poll in February, their chances of success were in that order, with Dewey holding a commanding lead of 56 percent, the other two tied at 17 percent. There were other possibilities, to be sure—Ohio's Governor John Bricker, Henry Cabot Lodge, even former President Herbert Hoover—but the only way one of them stood a chance was if the convention deadlocked and had to cast about for an outside choice.

Tom Dewey was a little man with a black mustache and a smile that seemed too quick, and there was a patent-leather look about him so that he would be forever remembered in Alice Roosevelt Longworth's epigram as "the bridegroom on the wedding cake." His assets included a smooth baritone voice and, as my father put it, "the big handshake and the smile and the where-have-you-been-all-my-life, but only a very young person could have believed in it." He had come to public attention as the crusading young district attorney of New York County (he was now only thirty-eight years old), with an enviable record of convicting racketeers, big-time and small, and had proved his ability to attract voters when he lost an unexpectedly close race against Herbert Lehman, the incumbent governor, in 1938. During the recent winter and spring he had labored tirelessly in the Midwest and West: by the time he reached Philadelphia he had won primaries in Wisconsin, Nebraska, and Illinois (all considered Vandenberg country) and claimed that he would have 433 delegates in his corner when the first ballot was called. Yet despite his record and his position as front-runner, the suspicion lingered among many party regulars that Dewey was really no more than a big-city DA, with no experience in high elective office to suggest that he was qualified to run the country.

Robert Alphonso Taft, who would become known somewhat later in life as Mr. Republican, had not reached that lofty status yet, but you could see he was headed in the right direction. A shy, private man whose abrupt manner and certitude concealed a sensitive nature, he was a successful corporation lawyer, a solid, civic-minded citizen, and a firm believer in party regularity. He came from a family of comfortable means, bulwarks of the old middle class, and he found himself increasingly at odds with what was wrong with the modern world—and that included especially the New Deal, centralized government, bureaucracy, labor unions, speculators, big business, special interest groups, and communism. In his family it was assumed that a Taft would take an interest in political matters—after all, his father had given most of his career to public life, most notably as president and as chief justice of the United States Supreme Court—for politics was a civic duty, public service an obligation. The Tafts had an abiding respect for education and intellect, and in Ohio they still bore the brand of their New England background, that stern credo that individuals are here to work hard and excel, persevering until success comes by dint of character and integrity. When you put these qualities together—work ethic, sense of duty, intelligence, strong convictions, honesty—you had a man a lot of Republicans would willingly follow right down the line, and even though Taft had been a member of the U.S. Senate only since 1938, he had been a fixture in Ohio politics long enough for people to know where he stood. The trouble was that Taft came across as something of a cold fish, and no matter what the pros thought of him he lacked the magnetism that brings out the voters on election day.

In 1936, after the GOP convention in Cleveland had nominated Alfred Landon, the candidate's campaign manager—John D. M. Hamilton, who was still the national chairman when the delegates convened in Philadelphia four years later—called on Arthur Vandenberg and asked if he would accept the vice-presidential nomination. No, Vandenberg told him, he would not; and later he wrote in his diary, "I think I should die of inaction in the VICE presidency," suggesting that a higher position would be more to his liking. The senator from Michigan had been trying to avoid inaction for almost half a century, since the Panic of 1893 had wiped out his father's business as a harness-maker and he, at the age of nine, had gotten a job hauling freight in a pushcart. After high school and a year in college, he went to work as a reporter, when suddenly a friend made him editor of a nearly bankrupt newspaper. Vandenberg took over, soliciting ads, writing news stories, setting type, composing editorials, making a success of the paper, and he had done little to break his pace since. Of the three leading contenders, he had done least to promote his own cause. He "abhorred" the thought of life in the White House and only reluctantly permitted friends to promote his candidacy, principally because he resented the way the president was keeping the country in the dark concerning his secret arrangements to aid the Allies. He and Mr. Roosevelt had been antagonists on many an issue, domestic and foreign, and Vandenberg was firmly opposed to any break in the third-term tradition.

Three more honorable, intelligent, capable candidates would have been hard to find, but as for being chosen to lead a major political party at this particular moment in 1940, all three suffered from a fatal flaw—a flaw that might not have been recognizable as such just two and a half months earlier. Taft and Vandenberg stood, as a matter of principle, for isolation, the Michigan senator urging what he called "insulation," the Ohioan calling for strict neutrality. At times Dewey gave the appearance of being more sympathetic toward the Allies than either of the others, but he was widely regarded as an isolationist, and one of his most persistent campaign themes was an attack on the administration for leading the nation toward war. No one, least of all Vandenberg himself, would accuse the senator of being anything but an isolationist; as for how Taft and Dewey stood on the question of aid to the Allies, Walter Lippmann described theirs as "a record of having been deaf, dumb, and blind in the presence of every warning and every epoch-making development."

If a man was unwilling or unable to see that the security of the United States would be seriously affected by the outcome of the war in Europe, as a majority of Americans had belatedly come to realize, it stood to reason that such a man might not be an ideal candidate for presidential office. In which case, by all that was logical, not one of these front-runners could be elected even if nominated. But whether the delegates to this convention, the party professionals, if you like, were going to be swayed by logic was open to considerable doubt, and it was precisely that doubt which had given such impetus to the rise of Wendell Willkie. The argument of the amateurs and more liberal-minded Republicans went something like this: if the Old Guard was not willing to nominate someone who was realistic about the world scene, someone who could also take on Franklin Roosevelt (who was almost universally presumed to be the Democratic candidate, despite his refusal to declare) with a chance of success, then they, the amateurs and liberals of the party, were going to find just such a man, because otherwise it was going to be 1932 and 1936 all over again.

Putting a finger on the moment Wendell Willkie emerged as a potential candidate was like trying to locate the separate pieces of a whirlwind, it had all happened so fast. Oren Root, who had experienced the Willkie phenomenon and helped create the whirlwind, said that Willkie "happened" to people, and what was clear was that he had happened to a number of people at about the same time, and each of those people had then decided to take action. Root, the grandnephew of a former secretary of state, a Princeton graduate, and an associate in a Wall Street law firm, heard Willkie speak in January 1939, and came away deeply impressed. Samuel Pryor of Greenwich, a vice president of Pan American Airways and Republican national committeeman from Connecticut, heard Willkie on the radio a year earlier and sized him up as an enlightened businessman and leader who was a presidential prospect. In 1939, Arthur Krock devoted two of his *New York Times* columns to the possibility of Willkie as a candidate. One evening that July, after Willkie was a guest at a Round Table sponsored by *Fortune* magazine, the publication's managing editor, Russell Davenport, came home and announced to his wife, Marcia, "I've met the man who ought to be the next president of the United States."

"Whose idea is it?" she asked. "His or yours?"

"It's spontaneous," her husband replied. "You see him and you know it."

Others had been struck by the same bolt of lightning, and by the time the Republican convention opened in Philadelphia, a genuine grass-roots boom had developed for Willkie, though no one had any idea how big or how effective it might be.

In just about every important respect, Willkie was the antithesis of the Hudson River squire in the White House. He was one of six children born to an Elwood, Indiana, family of modest means, a household where money was often wanting, but intellectual stimulation was not. His four grandparents were political refugees from Germany, both of his parents had been teachers and practiced law, and the children grew up surrounded by six thousand books and a continuous flow of ideas. As an Indiana senator who knew the Willkies described them, they were all "smarter than Christ, but a little queer." From the beginning, Wendell was something of a nonconformist, something of a ham (like all the children, he had read Shakespeare to his father, and could play Hamlet from memory), and by the time he finished at Indiana University and the law school, where he graduated at the head of his class, he had held a score of humble part-time jobs to pay for his education. He compiled quite a record in those years: challenging the Bible, preaching socialism, advocating the abolition of inheritances, teaching a high school history class so vividly that his students could remember his descriptions three decades later. It was no wonder Marcia Davenport's first impression of him was of "an old-fashioned, hell-raising, hard-wrangling liberal, with some of the evangelism of John Brown and the Boston abolitionists," but he was not exactly the type you would expect the Republicans to pick as their candidate in 1940 or any other year.

He had enlisted during World War I, married an Indiana girl named Edith Wilk, and after a short hitch overseas come home to practice law. He was almost immediately successful, thanks to an enormous capacity for work and skill in the courtroom. Another attorney, remembering the conviction and emotion with which Willkie argued his cases, said, "I never saw a lawyer who could make a jury swallow so often." By one of those satisfying coincidences that history has a way of producing, he was present at the 1924 Democratic convention where Franklin Roosevelt made his return to political life after the attack of infantile paralysis and nominated Alfred E. Smith, "the happy warrior." Willkie was for Smith, too; he would have been for almost anyone other than William Gibbs McAdoo, who had the support of the Ku Klux Klan, but his enduring antipathy toward Roosevelt dated from this initial encounter. One of Willkie's idols was Newton D. Baker, the eminent Cleveland lawyer and reform mayor who became Woodrow Wilson's secretary of war. At the convention, Baker was fighting to include a plank in the platform endorsing the League of Nations, but Roosevelt refused to support his effort (despite having campaigned for the League in 1920), and that was enough to turn Willkie against him.

By 1929, Willkie's success as a practicing attorney in Ohio earned him an invitation to become a partner in a New York firm that was general counsel to Commonwealth & Southern, an electric public utility holding company. (Although he and his wife lived in Manhattan, someone observed that Willkie never really left the Midwest—he took Indiana with him to New York. Nor did he lose his passion for books or his love of discussion that would see him so absorbed in ideas that he lost track of his surroundings. His idea of leisure well spent, a friend wrote, was "a rolling boil of ideas thrashed out with other brilliant and challenging minds," but in the world of business he seldom found the stimulation he enjoyed. "You can't imagine what limited intellectual interests businessmen have," he told Irita Van Doren, the book critic.)

Four years after moving to New York, one month before Franklin D. Roosevelt took the oath of office as president of the United States, Willkie became president of Commonwealth & Southern, and within another four years found himself engaged in a life-and-death struggle against the New Deal's proudest achievement, the Tennessee Valley Authority, and against a piece of New Deal legislation—the Public Utility Holding Company Act. Under the terms of the latter, the Securities and Exchange Commission was given the power to decide which holding companies would be permitted to survive, and Willkie—as president of a particularly vulnerable target—described it as a "death sentence." Since the TVA, conceived originally as a huge system of dams and waterways to control floods and erosion, was generating enormous amounts of electricity and, in direct competition with private industry, supplying cheap power to an area of the Tennessee basin already serviced by four Commonwealth & Southern affiliates, Willkie argued that the government was hindering economic recovery and discouraging private enterprise, and when he took his case to the public, people started listening.

"Whenever a householder in Tupelo, Mississippi, switches on a light," he said in a radio broadcast, "everybody in the United States helps to pay for it." In the process of speaking out effectively for C&S against the New Deal and unfair competition by big government, Willkie became something more. He was one of the first executives of a major corporation to appreciate the importance of public relations and endeavor to sell his company's story to the public, and in the course of doing so he became a respected spokesman for American business in general, and a symbol of the business community's opposition to the New Deal. It was Willkie's peculiar gift to combine idealism with realism, and his attacks on the extremes of the New Deal went beyond mere opposition: he had a program to offer, and he did so clearly, eloquently, with conviction and common sense, giving voice to the legitimate complaints of responsible, middle-class business people against a government that had become too big, too stifling of individual enterprise, too shrill and divisive.

In formal and informal speeches, in magazine articles, in radio talks, Wendell Willkie picked away at the New Deal, and, like the Pied Piper, picked up followers along the way. They were attracted to him for a variety of reasons, including the fact that he was a big businessman who sounded like a small businessman, but above all for his candor. He told a crowd in St. Louis, "The curse of democracy today, in America as in Europe, is that everybody has been trying to please the public. Almost nobody ever gets up and says what he thinks." Willkie did, and it seems never to have occurred to him that speaking out would hurt his chances at success in what he wanted to do. He possessed intellect, warmth, humor, and ideas by the dozen, and "He could charm a bird from a tree," in Marcia Davenport's phrase. To many Americans whose view of politics and politicians was jaded or disillusioned, Wendell Willkie was all but irresistible.

His followers, by and large, were Republicans, but they were outside the Republican Party. They were not reactionaries but moderates, open-minded and independent, and many of them objected less to what Roosevelt had done or tried to do than to the way in which he did it. They were small businessmen and entrepreneurs, professionals, white-collar workers, teachers, small-town bankers and insurance agents and attorneys, allied in their opposition to the threats represented by big government, big-city bosses, and big labor unions. In the simplest terms, they were looking for a champion: a candidate who offered a real alternative to the New Deal, on the one hand, and who had the sense to strengthen America's defenses while giving all possible aid to Britain, on the other. That meant a candidate who could beat Roosevelt, and few of these people thought Dewey or Taft or Vandenberg had a ghost of a chance of doing so. To them, Willkie looked like a winner.

In the spring of 1938 the Supreme Court upheld the constitutionality of the Holding Company Act, which meant the ultimate demise of Commonwealth & Southern, and Willkie went on the offensive, asking that the government buy out Tennessee Electric and Power Company, which could not compete against TVA. A year and a half later, after protracted negotiations, the government backed down and gave Willkie a price close to what he wanted. When David Lilienthal, the chairman of TVA, who had been Willkie's chief antagonist in the long struggle, handed him a check for $78.6 million, Willkie grinned and said, "Thanks, Dave. That's a lot of money for a couple of old Indiana boys to be handling." And press and public alike perceived the ceremony as a great personal triumph for Willkie and the cause he had championed. It was on the following day that Arthur Krock devoted his *New York Times* column to the possibility of Wendell Willkie as a candidate for president, commenting, "If he's a Republican—is he?— you can't wholly count out Willkie. . . . I'd watch [him]. He still has his haircuts country style."

At the time Krock wrote, Willkie was, in fact, a Democrat—a technicality he remedied a year and a half later—but that was only one reason the Republican Party regulars had little enthusiasm for him. He may have been an Indiana boy, but as far as they were concerned he was a corporate executive whose office was only a block from Wall Street (not until after the war would the GOP become a coalition of Main Street and Wall Street), and he was in a business—utilities—that had become virtually synonymous with corruption in the twenties. What's more, he sounded too liberal for their liking, and he had never even run for public office. No, Wendell Willkie was no man for the Old Guard.

If he sounded like a liberal, it was because he was one. Talking to undergraduates at Indiana University, he described a liberal as someone who "attempts to do the most difficult thing in the world—namely, to strike a true balance between the rights of the individual and the needs of society." It was a road Wendell Willkie had traveled all his life, and as he knew better than most, "Frequently you find yourself in the minority, and sometimes you will find yourself alone."

This liberal from the heartland of Indiana, a man so lately turned Republican, began in January of 1940 to have serious thoughts about running for the presidency. It was that month, when he heard of the death of Senator William Borah, an isolationist with enough power to prevent the nomination of any internationalist, that he said to Russell Davenport, "This gives me a chance." More and more often now, he was in the public eye. When someone asked if he was running for president, he said he was not, but "if the nomination were given to me without any strings I would have to accept it. No man in middle life and in good health could do otherwise." Yet he continued to be himself, to be his own man, behaving like no presidential aspirant Americans had seen. In one breath he would attack the "personal government" of Franklin Roosevelt and the New Deal's repressive regulation of business (". . . while a strait jacket will keep a man out of trouble, it is not a suitable garment in which to work"); in another he would blame businessmen's greed for what had happened in 1929. The American people "want business to have a chance again," he argued, "but they want to keep the social controls over it." He wrote an article for *The New Republic* supporting equal treatment under the law as the basis of liberty, and had the temerity to defend such victims of political persecution as Eugene Debs, Huey Long, Sacco and Vanzetti, the American Nazi Fritz Kuhn, and the Communist Earl Browder—all of them anathema to conservatives. "Justice," he wrote, "is not something you hand out at one time because it is convenient and withhold at another for the same reason. Nor is it something you accord to one man, but not to another. . . . remember that any man who denies justice to someone he hates prepares the way for a denial of justice to someone he loves."

In April 1940, *Fortune* published a two-page editorial written by Russell Davenport, summarizing Willkie's career and emphasizing his advocacy of progressive, liberal ideas, which sounded suspiciously like an abbreviated campaign biography. In the same issue appeared an article entitled "We, the People," by Willkie himself. In it, he expressed his belief that power resides in the people, not in the government, and that Roosevelt's New Deal had taken that power "out of our hands; power that belongs to us as citizens of a federal democracy." As an attack on the New Deal and an expression of Willkie's own political philosophy, it could pass for a platform. It was also an essentially middle-of-the-road statement—condemning the New Deal's "vested interest in depression" while agreeing that the welfare and health of America's people and its land are the responsibility of government;

accusing business of having caused the Depression, and the Roosevelt administration for prolonging it by its antibusiness attitude; attacking the isolationists for failing to reckon with the aggressor nations, praising the trade reciprocity advocated by Cordell Hull. With the article Willkie included a "petition"—in the manner of the Declaration of Independence—enumerating the people's grievances against the "politicians of both parties," calling on them to "open your eyes to the future [and] help us to build a New World."

The *Fortune* article created something of a sensation, producing more than two thousand requests for speeches by Willkie, but perhaps the most important single result was its effect on young Oren Root. "I had heard so many of my friends say they thought Wendell Willkie would make a good president but that he would never get the nomination," he recalled, "that I thought it might be one of those situations where many people are thinking the same thing but are not in touch with others who feel the same way about it. I decided to test this theory." His method was simplicity itself. He obtained alumni directories for Yale's class of 1924 and Princeton's class of 1925, selected about nine hundred names with good geographical distribution, and on the night of April 9, while Willkie was appearing on the popular *Information Please* radio program, impressing its huge audience with his humor and his breadth of knowledge about English literature and the U.S. Constitution, Root and his friends were stuffing envelopes with what he called "a Declaration." The mailing incorporated Willkie's "petition" and was modeled on a chain letter: it had space for fifteen signatures of people willing to work for Willkie's nomination, and requested that each signer line up fifteen others. Root's reason for choosing those particular college classes was that the men were about fifteen years out of college, old enough to care and to get involved politically. If they had been older, he felt, "the chances were that they were more conservative and would be for Dewey or Taft."[2] Whatever he may have anticipated in response to his mailing, it could not compare with the overwhelming reality. "I felt like a surf rider," he said, "trying to ride this enormous wave I'd started and keep my head above water." That was the beginning of the Willkie-for-president clubs.

With remarkable perception, Root wrote to the organizer of a San Francisco club in April: "The time is so late and Willkie's position with the politicians and delegates is necessarily so questionable that the only way I see of nominating him is to demonstrate to the politicians that he has more public support among ordinary people than anybody now believes." At the time Root sent that letter, Willkie was doing his best to conceal his efforts to capture the nomination, yet his campaign was a going business by now

---

[2] Many of the original Willkie backers were young: Root was only twenty-eight, Stassen thirty-three, Russell Davenport, Samuel Pryor, and Charles Halleck about forty. Willkie himself was forty-eight.

and moving into high gear at just the time Dewey's campaign peaked and started to lose ground. Less than a week after his "Declaration" was mailed, Root had printed and mailed out another twenty thousand of them; he had met with Davenport, who wanted him to stop his activity for the time being lest it reveal Willkie's plans prematurely (Root persuaded him that it might produce the momentum Willkie's candidacy needed); he had met Willkie; he had run an ad in the *Herald Tribune* appealing for help; and he had taken a leave of absence from his law firm because his telephone never stopped ringing and the office was inundated with mail—all giving him the answer he wanted to hear. He was receiving more than two hundred cash contributions a day, and by May 1 had 200,000 signed declarations in hand. By the time the convention opened, the number of Willkie clubs had reached 750, new ones were being formed at the rate of forty a day, fifty thousand volunteers were at work passing out buttons, getting signatures on petitions, and they had mailed out 750,000 pieces of Willkie campaign literature.

The drive that had begun so spontaneously was blessed with more than its share of luck and good timing, and in Philadelphia, on the eve of the convention's opening, an accident provided the Willkie people with another unexpected break. Samuel F. Pryor, Jr., national committeeman from Connecticut, was a member of the committee on arrangements, which was responsible for most of the housekeeping at the convention, including a determination of who was to receive seats in the gallery. Pryor had been a Dewey man until he heard Willkie's performance on *America's Town Meeting of the Air,* read his articles, and arranged for him to speak at a meeting with Connecticut's governor, Ray Baldwin. That was the clincher: Pryor was convinced that a Willkie-Baldwin ticket was unbeatable, and for a year he had been working quietly behind the scenes to advance Willkie's candidacy. On May 16 the arrangements committee had been meeting all day with seventy-year-old Ralph Williams in the chair. Someone suggested that they continue for another hour and a half in order to wind things up, and as Williams stood with his hands on the back of a chair, taking the vote, he suddenly collapsed and was taken to a hospital, where he died. The following day, national chairman John Hamilton announced that Williams's place would be taken by Samuel F. Pryor, Jr., of Greenwich, Connecticut.

Also on May 16 a Gallup poll appeared, revealing that the percentage of those favoring Willkie had risen from 3 to 5 percent in two weeks' time. Momentum was building, just as Oren Root had promised Russell Davenport it would, and now those Willkie clubs he had created were beginning to add an entirely new dimension to the proceedings. Following a suggestion by Harold Talbott, a Dayton businessman and early Willkie supporter, Root sent letters to all the Willkie clubs, urging members to come to Philadelphia to demonstrate support for their champion; he also prodded them to send telegrams and letters to their delegates, to let them know how many Willkie backers they had at home. Talbott himself put on a one-man campaign soliciting wires and letters from fellow businessmen and their employees; other Willkie enthusiasts followed suit; and before long the faithful began arriving in droves, looking for rooms in a city already packed with visitors.

From the very beginning, there was something different about this convention. In addition to the normal maneuvering by candidates and their managers, the jockeying for position within each delegation and between delegations, you had hundreds of delegates trying to shake hands with this fellow Willkie, to see if he was real and to find out what he had to say about their special interest, and to compound the confusion, Willkie club members by the hundreds were milling around hotels and the convention hall, bent on seeing Willkie and determined to pin down their delegates to see that they voted the right way.

The two-room suite on the sixteenth floor of the Benjamin Franklin, where the Willkies had originally planned to sleep, became his headquarters by default; at times a solid line of people stretched from the elevator to his rooms, and with crowds pushing in and out the place resembled a zoo at feeding time, with Willkie sitting on the floor or sprawled with one leg over the arm of a chair, talking, answering questions with a candor unknown in a presidential candidate. (Thanks to Harold Talbott's generosity, the Willkies soon had a quiet place to sleep in his suite at the Warwick Hotel.) Shortly after arriving in Philadelphia, Willkie told reporters he had no campaign manager and no campaign fund, which was somewhat disingenuous, considering the help he was getting from Davenport, Pryor, Root, and many others, and along with financial support that was coming in every day, particularly from the clubs. But his statement that "All the headquarters I have are under my hat" rang true. (In contrast with the makeshift arrangements for Willkie, Taft and his entourage occupied more than a hundred rooms and had confidently obtained a headquarters telephone number of ME-1940; Dewey had seventy-eight rooms, Vandenberg almost fifty. What no one seems to have noticed was that Willkie's people had thousands of feet of space in an office building and an empty store not far from their candidate's hotel.)

In one way or another, the amateurism and lack of organization became evident to just about everyone. *Times* columnist Arthur Krock was dismayed to learn from Willkie that he had no floor manager and didn't seem to know what a floor manager was supposed to do, yet the disorder worked to Willkie's advantage, making entirely plausible his claim that he had not entered into any deals. "If I accidentally am nominated and elected president of the United States," he said, "I shall go in completely free of any obligations of any kind." Oren Root was untroubled by the lack of organization. "Willkie probably wanted it that way," he said later. "He was disorganized himself—which I mean not in a critical sense, but to indicate his approach to problems. Some people go through life following an orderly pattern. Willkie was a trial lawyer, and he approached problems as he would a jury—circling around the issue, trying one tack and then another until he found what would work."

But what Willkie faced now was no courtroom; it was more like a giant crap game in which each player rolled with his own dice; and what those delegates were going to vote for was a sure winner, not an orator.

CHAPTER 38

———————◆———————

"A whirlwind . . .
is wrecking delegations
all around the convention."

O n Thursday, June 20, the clerk of the United States Senate read out
the names of two men whom President Roosevelt was nominating
as members of his cabinet. The isolationist Bennett Champ Clark of
Missouri could not believe his ears; he leaped to his feet and shouted,
"Who?"

If senators of both parties were thunderstruck, their reaction was mild
compared with that of the Republican early birds happily trouping into
Philadelphia for their twenty-second nominating convention, who saw the
headlines the next day. As every one of them knew, the man in the White
House was a conjurer with a bottomless bag of political tricks, but this time
he had gone too far. He had had the unmitigated gall to name two Republicans—Henry L. Stimson and Frank Knox—as secretary of war and secretary of the navy, and had done so with the pious pronouncement that the
appointments "are in line with the overwhelming sentiment of the nation
for national solidarity in a time of world crisis and in behalf of our national
defense—and nothing else." As if there could be the slightest doubt that the
move was planned to embarrass the Republicans and grab the headlines.

Stimson had been active in Republican politics since the 1890s. Now
seventy-three years old, he had been Taft's secretary of war, Hoover's
secretary of state, a distinguished lawyer in Elihu Root's Wall Street firm,

and a friend of Teddy Roosevelt, and the idea that he would take a cabinet post under FDR was simply preposterous.[1] The same was true of Knox, who had been one of Teddy Roosevelt's Rough Riders, a veteran of San Juan Hill, a Bull Mooser in 1912. Always active as a Republican, he had been Landon's running mate in '36, and when he wasn't politicking he was publishing newspapers, Republican newspapers—the *Manchester* (New Hampshire) *Union-Leader,* and most recently the *Chicago Daily News.*

What was particularly infuriating to isolationists on both sides of the aisle was that Roosevelt should have substituted two outspoken interventionists for the two members of his cabinet who were most isolationist. (Secretary of the Navy Charles Edison was a poor administrator and a lukewarm New Dealer, and had removed himself by deciding to run for governor in New Jersey; Harry Woodring, the secretary of war, whose isolationist sentiments and talent for obstructing FDR's policies were major liabilities, was sacked.) This trick, which was typical of the man, was immediately denounced as creating a "war cabinet." John Hamilton, the Republicans' national chairman, read Stimson and Knox out of the party, saying they could not be loyal to both party and president at the same time and were "no longer qualified to speak as Republicans for the Republican organization." Thomas Dewey said the appointments had "the gravest implications," and could only be interpreted as a direct step toward war. Colonel Theodore Roosevelt, Jr., saw overtones of what had happened in Germany, Italy, and Russia; destroy the two-party system, he observed, and you get collectivism, totalitarianism, and then dictatorship.

Harold Ickes was delighted: Hamilton and other leaders of the party, he remarked, "reacted like silly children" and played into the president's hands. Stimson felt the same way: the GOP gained nothing by repudiating him and Knox on grounds that they had been willing to serve the country in a time of crisis. Had party leaders applauded the move, on the other hand (as the convention's keynote speaker had the wit to do), it might have diverted attention from how deeply divided the Republican house was over foreign affairs. Instead, their reaction reminded everyone that Wendell Willkie was the only nonisolationist among the leading candidates. Furthermore, the outburst could only reflect favorably on Roosevelt, indicating that he had risen above politics for the good of the nation.

To some Democrats, the appointments were a sure indication that FDR was going to run for a third term. When Henry Morgenthau told his wife that Roosevelt was considering replacing Secretary of War Harry Woodring with the New York lawyer, her immediate reaction was: "And you tell me the president isn't interested in reelection if he has Stimson in mind?"

---

[1]Stimson's roots went deep into America's past: his forebears came to New England in the seventeenth century and he was fortunate enough to have known four of his great-grandparents, one of whom used to tell him of her conversations with George Washington. Born in New York City two years after Appomattox, he had explored parts of the West when it was still a frontier and had witnessed what he called an "Indian outbreak."

Whatever else the move might mean, the surprise announcement made it abundantly clear that the man in the White House was going to play a dominant role in the Republican convention.

In Paris, another individual whose actions would influence every stage of the deliberations in Philadelphia slid into the front seat of an open car beside his driver and set out as excitedly as any tourist on a sightseeing trip around the city his legions had occupied. Sunday was a bright, hot day, ideal for his purpose, and after seeing the Opéra and declaring it the most beautiful theater in the world, Adolf Hitler visited the Eiffel Tower, removed his cap and silently contemplated Napoleon's tomb,[2] as if communing with his fellow conqueror, toured Montmartre, and rejoiced that he had ordered the Wehrmacht to bypass France's capital and spare that most beautiful of cities.

===

Black rainclouds hung over Philadelphia that Sunday, and afternoon twilight slipped quickly into night. From the new airport and from Broad Street Station, scores of taxicabs ferried thousands of visitors—most of them men—through the gathering darkness to overcrowded hotels and restaurants, where they greeted old friends, talked gloomily about the news from Paris and Washington, and fretted about what they must do in the days ahead. Just in on the train from the west was the Pittsburgh delegation, headed by Allegheny County's chairman, Frank Harris, owner of a string of movie theaters, and bolstered by such business magnates as Ernest T. Weir, boss of Weirton Steel, and Howard J. Heinz, the pickle king. George and Carlton Ketchum were with them—Carlton because he was the paid director of the party's national finance committee, George because he had worked with his brother for years on Republican business even though his duties at the advertising agency prevented him from giving it more than part-time attention.

For Republicans like my father, whose affection for Teddy Roosevelt had never dimmed and whose loyalty to the party had been sorely tested by Harding and Coolidge, Wendell Willkie appeared as a gleaming banner of hope. On the one hand, he represented business, the capitalist system's underpinning; on the other, he was forward-looking on international issues, unwilling to see America bury its collective head in the sand. It was not that people like my father would not vote for a Dewey or a Taft if one of them became the nominee—party loyalty and dislike of Mr. Roosevelt would see to that—but they would take neither man to their hearts. Willkie, however, was more than a candidate they could vote for: he was someone to get excited about, to cheer as rabidly as the Ketchums cheered the Pitt football

[2]He was so moved by his visit to the crypt that he instructed his aide Martin Bormann to collect the remains of young Napoleon from a tomb in Vienna and move them to the emperor's side in Paris.

team. It may be that my father was for Taft before he went to Philadelphia: he admired the Ohioan for his absolute honesty and his determination to stand for what he believed in whether it was popular or not. But he was close to both Harris and Weir, and they were enthusiastically for Willkie. If indeed George Ketchum left Pittsburgh a Taft supporter, he came home a devout Willkie man, and thirty years later he would write: "From meeting him several times, from various forms of exposure, I can assure you that Wendell Willkie had what people only later got to calling charisma. I have voted for a lot of Republicans, but often without a high pulse rate. Wendell was different. The only other presidential candidate who affected me the same way was TR."

What had brought these Pittsburghers and their fellow Republicans together was the quadrennial need to nominate a ticket for the fall elections, but few could have suspected when they left home that they would be meeting in the hour of democracy's greatest defeat and Hitler's greatest victory. It was difficult not to agree with the columnist Raymond Clapper, who observed on the eve of the convention, "Democracy has been a failure in Europe. It has been blind, slow, inefficient, unable to understand its interests and to protect them. . . . Republicans have just one issue in this campaign. It is whether Mr. Roosevelt or a Republican could do a faster, better job of obtaining the industrial production for defense. . . . They must look ahead and offer a man who can make the country believe he would do a better job." According to Clapper, "Mr. Willkie is the only man the Republicans have who stands a chance of making an effective case."

The possibility that the GOP might follow that advice was troubling the inner circle of the Roosevelt administration. At a cabinet meeting in mid-June, Ickes and Farley talked about the coming Republican convention, and the latter said he thought Taft would be nominated, but that Willkie might just surprise everyone. Both men agreed that Willkie would be the strongest candidate the Republicans could field; if he had two or three more weeks' time before the convention he would surely get the nomination. Ickes hoped that would not happen: he was certain Willkie was dangerous. "With him in the White House, the monied interests would be in full control and we could expect an American brand of fascism as soon as he could set it up."

———

Before Willkie or anyone else would be chosen, the convention had certain traditional chores to perform, including writing a platform proclaiming the lofty goals of the Grand Old Party. This task was in the hands of the Resolutions Committee, whose forty-odd members had been meeting for more than a week without notable progress. For two hours they had suffered in silence as John L. Lewis, at the top of his form, reminded them that if the Republican Party wanted to be restored to power it had better produce a platform and a program that had the confidence of the working people. "Labor cannot eat platitudes," he growled. "The greatest menace to America is not the foreign agent or the fanatic," he told them, "not the fascist, the totalitarian, or the communist, [but] the shrunken bellies of one-half of the population who are not getting enough to eat.

"What are you going to do about it?" he roared. If they thought they could blame the present economic conditions on the Democrats, they could think again: "Don't forget that you Republicans left an army of twelve million men out of jobs." Finally he gave them something they could applaud, as he denounced Roosevelt's conscription plan as a "fantastic suggestion from a mind in full intellectual retreat." (Lewis made no bones about his own position on the military draft: any politician who expected that Americans "are going to send their sons to be butchered in another foreign war," he said in a speech in April, "is going to show himself as nothing more or less than a fool.")

Despite Lewis's advice, the committee managed to take a prudently ambiguous stand on most controversial domestic issues, but it came close to foundering on the matter of foreign policy. That thorny subject was in the hands of a subcommittee headed by Alfred M. Landon of Kansas, the titular head of the party, who hoped to produce a foreign-policy plank that would somehow be agreeable both to isolationists and to those who were determined to aid Great Britain. For the better part of a week the subcommittee held day-and-night meetings; discussions were heated, to put it mildly, with members in a lather, divided in their own views and pressured incessantly from outside by the likes of Representative Hamilton Fish, who invited fifty congressmen to Philadelphia to testify in support of a "keep out of war" plank. Variously described in the press as uneasy, confused, perplexed, hesitant, and evasive, the subcommitteemen emerged at last from their marathon sessions with a document that provoked feeble applause and loud complaints from partisans on both sides of the debate. No one could say they had not produced a masterpiece of expediency. "The Republican Party," the plank stated, "stands for Americanism, preparedness, and peace. We accordingly fasten upon the New Deal full responsibility for our unpreparedness and for the consequent danger of involvement in war." Landon had managed to include a passage supporting aid to "all peoples fighting for liberty, or whose liberty is threatened," but to that was added a proviso that "such aid . . . shall not be in violation of international law or inconsistent with the requirements of our own national defense."

It would not be stretching things, the *New York Times* suggested editorially, to brand the foreign policy plank a bald-faced lie, since a majority of the Republican spokesmen in the Senate had been doing their utmost for two years to defeat every effort to increase America's military strength, and since it was difficult moreover to see exactly what the Republican Party had done recently to advance the cause of peace. The foreign policy plank, H. L. Mencken sneered, "is so written that it will fit both the triumph of democracy and the collapse of democracy, and approve both sending arms to England or sending only flowers."

Perhaps it was an omen that the Philadelphia zoo's forty-two-year-old elephant Lizzie suddenly died; but the gloom lifted when Frank Gannett, the New York publisher who fancied himself a candidate for the presidency and was apparently prepared to buy himself the nomination, imported three live elephants and had them marched back and forth through the city's streets, festooned with "Frank Gannett, Our Best Bet" signs. To date eleven other hopefuls were being mentioned in the press: Taft, Dewey, Vandenberg, and Willkie, of course, plus Hoover, Senators McNary, Bridges, and Capper, Hanford MacNider of Iowa (an isolationist and former assistant secretary of war), and two governors—Baldwin of Connecticut and James of Pennsylvania. To that list, a few other names were occasionally added: Governor Bricker of Ohio ("Bricker is an honest Harding," Alice Roosevelt Longworth chortled), Congressman Joseph W. Martin of Massachusetts, advertising executive Bruce Barton, and Congressman Hamilton Fish—the last three of whom would play a memorable role in the final days of the campaign.

As the hour approached for the nominations to begin, downtown Philadelphia wore carnival clothes—two thousand American flags, scores of banners. Brass bands were blaring everywhere, candidates glad-handed delegates and made promises, pretty, smiling volunteers handed out campaign literature and buttons, the Uncle Sam Marching Club in peppermint-striped trousers and top hats paraded through downtown streets for Dewey. Hotel switchboards were overwhelmed, elevators were jammed, and Negro delegates, *Time* reported, "enjoyed their quadrennial privilege of being received at swank hotels." Frank Gannett's headquarters, where fifteen-foot color portraits of the publisher were draped inside and outside the lobby, was the only one serving free liquor (something of an irony, since the Gannett newspapers did not accept beer advertising). The Benjamin Franklin Hotel was headquarters for five candidates, but the management was playing it safe: a sign on the marquee read, "Benjamin Franklin Welcomes Chicago Cubs." Outside the Hotel Walton an enormous blue-and-white banner labeled "Thomas Dewey" hung in the still, humid air. Inside Convention Hall, signifying the seriousness of the occasion, none of the usual red-white-and-blue bunting had been hung. Perspiring visitors in the gallery, waiting for something to happen, moved hot air around with yellow fans labeled "Fan with Van."

Scenes like these had been played at American political conventions as long as anyone could remember; so had the relentlessly boring rituals that preceded the nominations. What made this one different was the enormous outside pressure that was building, hour by hour, for one candidate. It struck many of those present that a kind of madness had set in and was taking over the proceedings. By Tuesday, someone estimated, the delegates had received a million pro-Willkie messages from all over the United States. Each night they returned to their hotels to find fresh piles of mail stacked outside their doors: one man said more than 100,000 letters and telegrams addressed to him had arrived in a twelve-day period. Each day the galleries filled early with fresh-faced, jubilant young men and women wearing Willkie buttons, waving Willkie pennants, waiting eagerly for the important business to begin. Delegates sent their clothes out to be laundered or cleaned and they came back the next day with Willkie literature tucked into the pockets. The Willkie clubs of New Jersey produced a declaration for their candidate with 300,000 signatures and said they would have another 100,000 in a day or so. Willkie had been endorsed by the *Philadelphia Ledger* (which claimed to be first to do so), then by the Scripps-Howard papers, the *New York Herald Tribune*, the Luce and Cowles publications, the *Saturday Evening Post.* A pro-Willkie cab driver, someone said, refused to pick up a fare who was wearing a Taft button. Willkie was so engaging and obliging, so quotable, that reporters followed him everywhere, and in response to their questions, one of them wrote, he "took street-corner positions on anything and everything." While his opponents fumed and worried, he joked about his boom. "I would like to think it means I'm a hell of a fellow," he said with a grin, "but I think it means I represent a trend, or am ahead of a trend." Dr. George Gallup had just published some data confirming that view: his latest poll, conducted before the convention opened, showed Willkie in second place with an astonishing 29 percent, Dewey's lead reduced by 5 percentage points, Taft and Vandenberg tied at 8 percent, and Hoover at 6 percent.

Like Adolf Hitler and Franklin Roosevelt, Wendell Willkie was an uninvited guest at this convention. Like the other two, he was a powerful and unpredictable force, and a lot of the delegates were wishing he were almost anywhere else but in Philadelphia. For a month and a half, in speech after speech, Willkie had been advocating all possible aid, short of war, for the Allies, along with a substantial increase in the armed strength of the United States, and after he arrived in Philadelphia he warned Harold Stassen, Minnesota's thirty-three-year-old governor, who was to be the keynote speaker, that if he tried to suggest that Europe's problems were none of America's business, the Republican Party might just as well fold up its tent and go home. Stassen concurred, and when he delivered his speech to the delegates on Monday night he did not claim, as Taft and Dewey and Vandenberg and the national chairman had done regularly, that Roosevelt was leading the country into war. (That was what you could expect from the "boy-governor," delegates grumbled, making it clear that no flash-in-the-pan represented the views of *this* convention.)

On Monday, before the first session was called to order, forty-eight congressmen issued a statement urging delegates to "nominate a candidate for president whose personal views will present an opportunity for a clear-cut vote on foreign and domestic issues in harmony with the Republican record in Congress." Whoever that candidate might be, it was assuredly not Wendell Willkie. On Tuesday, full-page ads appeared in newspapers in New York and Philadelphia: STOP THE MARCH TO WAR! STOP THE INTERNA-

TIONALISTS AND WAR-MONGERS! They might as well have read, STOP WILLKIE!

That evening, after the permanent chairman, Congressman Joe Martin, called the convention to order, the packed house sang "God Bless America," and, as the band struck up "California, Here I Come," leaped to its feet and roared when John D. M. Hamilton walked down the center aisle escorting former President Herbert Hoover to the speaker's platform. The whistling, the cheering, the foot-stamping were a tonic for the man who had been vilified for eight years by the Democrats. He was here to claim his place in the limelight and, it was widely believed, to remind the party of his availability, and for a few moments it almost seemed as if the delegates might throw their hats in the air, break up the furniture, and turn to Hoover if he gave them the sign.[3] But Hoover was Hoover, after all, and he read his well-prepared speech with the zest of a graduate student lecturing a zoology class, mumbling the words, muffing his punch lines, standing before them stiffly and awkwardly, a "near-great man," as one journal described him, "whose fate has been to cast his mother-of-pearl words before mobs who, whether friendly or bitter, always yell 'Louder!'" His message, though, was what most delegates wanted to hear. "It is nonsense that we cannot defend freedom here even if the Old World fails," he declared. If the United States should enter the war, we would sacrifice "the last sanctuary of liberty."

———

If you were a betting man, you figured that Dewey had to win on the first ballot: if he couldn't make it then, his strength was going to bleed away as delegates pledged to him for a single vote switched to other candidates. At that point, the experts said, the Taft movement would start to roll. Should Taft *and* Dewey lose their momentum, and the convention become deadlocked, a dark horse—either Vandenberg or Willkie—might start to pick up steam. That was the way Vandenberg himself saw it, too. On the Tuesday before the convention opened, Willkie was in Washington, D.C., and asked the senator to have breakfast with him at the Carlton Hotel. As Vandenberg recalled his host's pitch, all he needed to put him over was "the support of some outstanding, recognized Republican leader like me. I thanked him and told him that I thought the final show-down would come between the two of us (in which I was wrong). We parted good friends—but nothing doing." What was to prove so disconcerting to Vandenberg and the old pros who had seen things happen in an orderly, predictable manner in the past was

[3]One man who believed that Hoover might stampede the convention was John L. Lewis, who had been working behind the scenes to create a boom for the former president. Lewis had prepared a statement that was astounding, considering the average American workingman's opinion of Mr. Hoover, saying, "He is the only Republican whom I and my colleagues can support." Because the Hoover boom never got off the ground, the labor leader never had an opportunity to read his remarks.

an entirely new factor in the equation—what Raymond Clapper called "a whirlwind that is wrecking delegations all around the convention." Rumors were flying, delegates who were supposedly in this candidate's or that one's pocket were coming unhitched, and nothing was staying in place the way it should.

The likelihood that this would be a truly open convention was increasing by the hour and was nowhere more evident than in what was happening inside the Pennsylvania and New York delegations. Joseph N. Pew of the Sun Oil family, unchallenged boss of Philadelphia's Republicans, had decided long before the convention that it would be prudent to have a favorite son—a straw man—to whom the state would give its votes on the first few ballots, holding off a commitment to any of the leading candidates until the decisive moment, when Pennsylvania could have the glory and the credit of putting over the winner. Arthur James, governor of Pennsylvania, received the nod as favorite son, and Pew announced that he would stick with him "to the bitter end" or "until it was shown that he had no chance of winning." Perhaps that bit of hyperbole gave James the idea, but it didn't take long for him to fancy himself as a candidate who had a real chance for the nomination, and he was abetted in this delusion by the presence of many delegates who figured they had better not cross him, since he would be governor for two more years and a governor has a lot of favors to pass out. "Candidates," George Ketchum observed, "are sometimes a distillation of all the vanity and pride and self-love in the world," and the longer Arthur James thought about himself as the Republican Party's nominee for president, the more certain he became that he was the man for the job.

Not surprisingly, Wendell Willkie would have nothing to do with Pew. "I don't know Joe Pew," he told reporters, "but I am one hundred percent against his policy of turning the Republican Party back to the days of Harding and Coolidge." Since no love was lost between the delegates from Pittsburgh and Philadelphia and since Ernest Weir of the Pittsburgh group was to be national finance chairman in the coming campaign, his enthusiasm for Willkie was a matter to be reckoned with. To complicate things further, Frank Harris, who controlled the contingent from western Pennsylvania, didn't like Governor James (the feeling was reciprocated) and had been leaning on his colleagues to desert James in favor of Willkie as soon as the first ballot was cast. One of those colleagues was David Aiken Reed, who had served two terms in the United States Senate before his defeat by Joseph Guffey in 1934. Reed, the senior partner in Pittsburgh's biggest and most prestigious law firm, was close to "the Mellon interests," as the power structure was customarily described in the Smoky City, and thanks to that exalted connection was commended to Frank Harris as a delegate. Intelligent, stuffy, and high in self-esteem, Reed couldn't get used to the idea of the owner of a theater chain being county chairman, and had to be persuaded to attend a caucus of delegates and alternates in Harris's house in Crafton, an unfashionable suburb, Reed's idea of a proper meeting place being the boardroom at the Mellon Bank. Harris and Reed were miles apart socially, and right now Reed was distancing himself from the Allegheny County chairman politically, holding out against Harris's blandishments, declining to pledge to anyone but the favorite son.

Just before the balloting was to begin, several businessmen who had some clout with Reed's law firm persuaded the former senator that he should at least consider voting for Wendell Willkie, to which Reed replied that he would have to meet the candidate and "cross-examine him on the issues" before making his decision. At the request of Ernest Weir and Howard Heinz, George Ketchum went to the Benjamin Franklin, picked up Willkie and shepherded him through the mob there, and took him to the Warwick, suggesting as they walked how he might get along with Reed. (Willkie was not aware that Reed had been a U.S. senator, which would have been the unforgivable gaffe.) The meeting was not a success: after the two had talked, Reed allowed as how he would "consider" Willkie, but said he still considered Taft the better man.

New York, the little district attorney's own state, was as divided as Pennsylvania, and the fault was largely Dewey's, for being too greedy. His backers, after seizing control of the state committee, had ousted Kenneth Simpson as national committeeman, replaced him with J. Russel Sprague, and thereby alienated the Simpson and Gannett people. (Simpson, a Manhattan congressman, was the man who said, "You had to know Dewey very well to dislike him.") The result was that the New York delegation arrived in Philadelphia with Dewey controlling only two thirds of the delegates; the balance, it was assumed, would go to Gannett.

One of Dewey's efforts to pick up support before the balloting began took the form of a message to Arthur Vandenberg, delivered by his Senate colleague Styles Bridges of New Hampshire. "He wants you to take the vice presidency with him," Bridges reported; "he says this will sew up the whole thing on the first ballot." Vandenberg replied that while he considered the vice presidency important, he considered his place on the Senate floor more so. On the other hand, if Dewey would agree to be his vice-presidential running mate, "I shall be a pre-pledged one-termer [and] he will be in direct line for the White House in 1944. Also tell him that if this is too much for him to swallow all at once, I'll make him a sporting proposition. I'll meet him at eleven o'clock and flip a coin to see which end of the ticket we each take." Dewey was not that much of a sport, and the negotiations ended: Vandenberg never heard from him until Thursday night, when it was too late. Thinking back on it, the senator remarked wistfully, "Between us we could have controlled the convention if it had been done in the first instance."

Even without Vandenberg's support, Dewey's men were saying he had between 430 and 450 first-ballot votes, not far short of the 501 needed to win, but those who knew better gave him 350 or so. Taft, they said, would get 250 to 275, and Willkie 100. On the second ballot, according to these educated guesses, Dewey would slip a little, Taft would reach 300, and Willkie might get 150. After that, anyone might win, but Taft was the odds-on pick. At most, Willkie could get 190 votes.

The main business of the convention got under way on Wednesday night, when the roll of the states was called and the names of candidates were placed in nomination, each followed by a demonstration with cheering supporters pouring into the aisles, bands playing, confetti and balloons filling the hall—the theory being that the man whose backers generated the most noise must look like a winner. Thomas E. Dewey was first to be nominated; then came Frank Gannett, who was reputed to have spent $500,000 on what everyone but Gannett knew was a hopeless effort. After Taft was nominated and seconded, Indiana's Representative Charles Halleck walked to the platform and stunned everyone by ignoring the time-honored convention of "the man who" speech in which the name of the nominee is never uttered until the final sentence. After a few opening words, Halleck said, "I am here to nominate Wendell Lewis Willkie," immediately provoking two responses from the crowd of twenty thousand in Convention Hall.

From the floor came boos: hundreds of Taft and Dewey delegates wanted no part of the interloper, the renegade Democrat who had come unbidden to their convention. From the gallery came an explosion of noise—"We want Willkie! We want Willkie!"—a steady, rhythmic chant that soon drowned out the catcalls from below, and increased as Halleck concluded his speech and demonstrators burst onto the floor with an enthusiasm that dwarfed all previous parades. Joe Martin pounded the lectern repeatedly with his gavel, calling again and again for order, finally shouting, "The chair must remind the occupants of the galleries that they are the guests of the convention!" at which someone shouted, "Guests, hell! We *are* the convention!" It was an indication of what was to come.

———

The next day Philadelphia was unbearably hot and muggy. There was no air-conditioning, and Convention Hall was a haze of smoke and noise, with a smell compounded of sweat, anger, and tension from thousands of closely packed bodies, with the temperature over 100 degrees and the blazing lights making the two-tiered indoor stadium "a hell of sealed-in heat," as Marcia Davenport described it. Radio broadcasters were present in full force, newsreel crews were setting up their lights, and a few television cameramen from the National Broadcasting Company were at work, feeding pictures by coaxial cable to the fifty thousand or so Americans who owned television sets, plus those who were watching at the RCA exhibit at the World's Fair.[4]

[4] As early as January 1939, NBC had announced plans to transmit the inauguration of the next president of the United States by television. This achievement would be possible, it was said, because of the development of "mobile television stations, operating with the so-called all-electronic system."

It was Thursday, June 27, 1940, at 4:50 P.M. when Chairman Martin called for the first ballot.

During the day Western Union messengers had delivered more than forty thousand telegrams demanding Willkie's nomination, and while many delegates were just plain infuriated by the deluge of unwanted advice, a growing number were edgy, unnerved by the size and strength of the Willkie crowd and by the unbelievable pressure being exerted by constituents back home. "I doubt that most of the pros ever gave their hearts to Willkie, even at the height of the excitement," my father wrote later. "He wasn't their kind of guy, as was demonstrated over and over; he owed nothing to most of them, and they were afraid they never would owe anything to him." But something totally unexpected—beyond their range of experience—was happening in Convention Hall, and the people who had come here knowing how these matters were normally handled, knowing that deals would be struck and that this bloc and that would eventually combine to produce a candidate more or less acceptable to all of them, began to sense that this thing was getting out of hand, going beyond their power to control.[5]

Willkie's strategists wanted to keep his vote low on the first ballot—somewhere around 70—hoping that it would increase steadily from there on, but the tally was 105, which put him ahead of Vandenberg and surprised everyone. Included in his total were all 16 of Connecticut's votes, as expected, plus 12 from New Jersey, 9 from Indiana, with a scattering from twenty other states and the Philippines. Dewey's total of 360 was far fewer than he had predicted but about what the experts thought he would get; his state had given 17 to Gannett, and 8 had gone unexpectedly to Willkie. Taft, at 189, was well below his quota; Vandenberg had 76; Arthur James of Pennsylvania 74; Joe Martin 44; Gannett 35; Hanford MacNider of Iowa 34; and Hoover 17.

John Hollister of Cincinnati, who was working with Taft's floor manager, David Ingalls, recalled that they hadn't paid much attention to the "Willkie blitz." Their primary effort was devoted to stopping Dewey, and they were confident that they had done just that: after the first ballot, the Taft people believed that a number of delegates pledged to Dewey would jump to Taft, but "Willkie came along faster and took away a great many of the people we were counting on." (One Pennsylvanian defected from James to Willkie on the first ballot; four more jumped on the second.) On the second ballot, Dewey lost 22 votes, a sure sign to the pros that he wasn't going to make it;[6] Taft gained only 14; while Willkie soared to 171. Every Willkie vote was

---

[5]It was not known at the time, but a Gallup poll taken between Tuesday and Thursday of that week—that is, during a period that coincided with the nominating speeches and the balloting—indicated that 44 percent of the nation's rank-and-file Republicans were for Willkie. The percentage had risen from less than 1 percent in late March and revealed the enormous impact of the convention proceedings on public opinion.

[6]They knew their history: no candidate who had lost ground on any ballot had ever been nominated by either party.

cheered to the rafters by the galleries, every defection from Dewey to Willkie was followed with a roar, "We want Willkie!" rolling like prairie fire from section to section of the auditorium.

By previous agreement with representatives of the leading candidates, Joe Martin adjourned the session after the second ballot until 8:30 P.M. Willkie wanted to keep going without a break to capitalize on the momentum, and by way of compromise Martin promised Stassen—who was now Willkie's floor manager—that if he could possibly manage it he would not halt the proceedings again that night until a decision was reached.

Following the recess, on the third ballot Martin released his Massachusetts delegates to Willkie and the galleries went crazy; when 27 of New York's 92 followed Simpson into the Willkie camp, a huge roar went up; when 15 of Joe Pew's Pennsylvanians voted for Willkie, there was pandemonium. (Stassen wanted to approach Pew after the second ballot, but Willkie wouldn't permit it. Following the third ballot, when Baldwin spoke with Pew and learned that he did not intend to abandon James, Willkie was disgusted: "Pew be damned!" he snapped.) Dewey had slipped further; to everyone's astonishment Taft had gained only 9; and Willkie was now in second place, having gained 88 votes, for a total of 259. Over and over came the chant, "We want Willkie! *We want Willkie!* WE WANT WILLKIE!" And the thunder from the galleries in Philadelphia was heard in the living rooms and kitchens of America, where men and women put aside whatever they were doing to listen to thousands of ordinary folk just like themselves who were turning politics and the politicians upside down.

Shortly after 10:00, Joe Martin called for the fourth ballot. This was a critical vote for the three leaders—the last time around for Dewey, in all likelihood; the vote that would determine whether Taft really commanded the reserve strength he was supposed to have; the supreme test of Willkie's momentum. The big hall was alternately deafening noise and dead silence as each state announced its tally, and when it was over Willkie had taken the lead with 306 votes, Taft was second with 254, and Dewey had fallen to 250. Willkie's pace had slowed, though, while Taft's support seemed finally to be taking shape, and the big question now was what Dewey's delegates would do. Rumors flew around the hall: the bosses would pool their strength, make deals to keep Willkie from getting the nomination; the pros would all join ranks behind Taft. Only it did not happen that way. The Taft people did not have the delegates everyone else thought they had, and they knew it.

John Hollister telephoned Taft at his hotel after the fourth ballot and said, "If we keep going we're licked, but I think I can get Joe Martin to order an adjournment because it's so late. Maybe we can do something overnight."

"Do you really think we can stop the landslide if we adjourn?" Taft asked.

"No, I don't really think so," Hollister replied.

"Well, it's up to you and Dave Ingalls," the senator said. "You're on the floor and I'm not, but it looks to me as if you had better go ahead and take your chances."

Whoever they had been supporting, the delegates now had to choose between Taft and Willkie if they were going to get aboard a bandwagon, and as the roll was called, favorite sons were dropped in state after state, delegates pledged to Dewey switched to one of the leaders, and with loyalties coming unstitched in the terrible heat and clamor and confusion, men from the same state were shouting and cursing at each other. Kansas had given eleven votes to Dewey, five to Willkie, and two to Taft, and before the fifth ballot Joe Martin and other Willkie people talked with Alf Landon, hoping to persuade him to release all eighteen votes to Willkie. Like many a delegate, Landon found it hard to swallow the idea of giving the nomination to a man who had been a registered Democrat until recently, but Martin said Willkie was on his way to winning, reminded him that they had agreed this would be an open convention, and Landon replied, "All right, let her go the way she's going." When Kansas was called, there was silence . . . until Alfred Landon announced in his flat twang, "Kansas gives all of its eighteen votes to Wendell L. Willkie"—then came a torrent of cheers. The New York delegation all but abandoned Dewey, giving 75 of its 90 votes to Willkie, and the people in the gallery seats shouted until they were hoarse. A North Dakotan announced that his state cast 4 votes for Senator Taft and 4 votes for Vendell Villkie; Martin asked "For who?" and the man repeated "Vendell Villkie," and the crowd roared with laughter. Oklahoma cast 22 for Taft, but when a delegate asked that the group be polled, it turned out that only 18 were for Taft, with 4 for Willkie. At the end, the man who had been scorned as "the barefoot boy from Wall Street" had picked up 123 votes, for a total of 429. Taft had gained the same number, and now had 377, but the real pressure was on the Ohioan now, and Ingalls asked Martin to recess the convention. During the long intermission, delegations were frantically trying to decide whether or not this was the moment to switch to Willkie, and a number of states, including Pennsylvania, went into caucus. Late as it was, and exhausted though the delegates were, Martin kept his promise to Stassen and at 12:20 A.M. pounded his gavel and called for the sixth ballot.

Incredibly, telegrams were *still* being delivered to the delegates, urging them to vote for Willkie, the continuous uproar from the galleries had turned the place into bedlam, and now even people wearing Dewey and Taft buttons had been swept along by the tide and were yelling deliriously, "WE WANT WILLKIE! WE WANT WILLKIE!" The change of a single vote produced a new wave of chanting or groans of despair, and as the roll was called and each man gained a bit here and a little there, the tension built. California gave Willkie 8 new votes, but Taft got 10 more. In Colorado, Willkie gained 1, Taft 2. After Kansas, Willkie was ahead by 35; then Kentucky and Louisiana gave Taft all their votes and Willkie's lead was cut to 1. When Michigan's turn came, a gray-haired man in spectacles came to the platform to a rising crescendo of applause as people recognized Vandenberg's campaign manager, Howard Lawrence. In the galleries, they were holding their breath until he announced that Senator Vandenberg had authorized him to release his delegates, giving Hoover 1, Taft 2, and Willkie 35. Here was the big break Willkie needed, and everybody on the upper tier of the hall was on their feet, knowing the end was in sight, cheering, screaming at the top of their lungs: "WE WANT WILLKIE! WE WANT WILLKIE!"

Martin finally restored some order to the place, and the roll call went on—Minnesota, Mississippi, Missouri, New Jersey, New Mexico, New York, and North Carolina, giving Willkie modest gains. Then came Oklahoma, where 13 Taft votes switched to Willkie. A poll of the Oregon delegation gave 3 votes to Taft, then all 10 decided to go to Willkie. A few more, and it would be over.

Meantime, Pennsylvania was still caucusing, with Arthur James pleading almost tearfully for the delegates to stick with him for one more ballot; if they did, he said, he could win the nomination. That absurd statement split the delegation for good, enraging the growing number of anti-James people. Some of the delegates left the room in disgust, discovered to their dismay what was happening on the floor, and rushed back to tell the group that the roll call was nearly to Pennsylvania, and that Willkie was sure to win on this ballot. On the floor someone—authorized or not—picked up the microphone to say, "Pennsylvania passes." When the delegates in caucus heard this, there was a stampede onto the floor, many of them, including David Reed, realizing what a disaster it would be if Pennsylvania had nothing to do with deciding the nominee. Reed grabbed the microphone and blurted out that Pennsylvania cast its 72 votes for Wendell Willkie. One of James's cronies snatched the mike from his hands and stated that Reed had no business saying what he had, whereupon James himself shouted that Pennsylvania was still voting for him and tried to prevail upon Martin to get a recount from Pennsylvania. By this time Virginia had given Willkie 16 of its 18 votes, the long fight was over, pandemonium had broken loose in the galleries, hats and paper were sailing into the air, and no one except Pennsylvanians cared in the slightest what Pennsylvania did.[7]

All over the hall chairmen were on their feet, shouting to be recognized,

[7]In fact, twenty-nine Pennsylvanians had voted to stick with James, so Reed's assertion was completely erroneous. Newspapers the next day described the sixth ballot as "incomplete" and published an "unofficial" total for each candidate. While the so-called incomplete ballot gave Willkie all 72 of Pennsylvania's votes, the unofficial total for the candidates listed Arthur James with 1 vote—presumably his own. None of this kept the Pennsylvania delegation, collectively, from being the goat of the convention, with James getting individual credit for making a fool of himself and his colleagues. For the balance of his two years as governor he was remembered as the laughingstock of the convention, and he never recovered politically or personally from the stigma.

wanting to change their vote; Governor Bricker of Ohio shouldered his way to the platform to move that the nomination be made unanimous; Dewey's lieutenant, J. Russel Sprague, seconded it, as did other Willkie opponents; and at 1:57 A.M., Joe Martin recessed the convention until later in the day, when nominations for vice president would be in order.

The Republican Party's candidate for president, interviewed at his hotel, had only a few words for reporters: "I am very happy, very humble, and very proud." When the press asked Herbert Hoover for a statement, he replied coolly, in words that should have warned the candidate what he would face in the campaign ahead: "I wouldn't like to make any statement about Mr. Willkie without having time to think it over." Alfred Landon returned to his hotel room, looking "white and scared," and his wife asked what was wrong. "I wonder what I've done to my party and to my country," said the man who had led the Republicans to their worst defeat ever in 1936.

According to Samuel Pryor, it was 5:00 in the morning, barely three hours after the nomination, when Wendell Willkie called to say he was in a bind. The reason was that Pryor's Connecticut delegation was the only one that had given the nominee all of its votes from the first ballot onward, and it had done so in the belief that Willkie was committed to Governor Raymond Baldwin as his running mate; from the beginning, Pryor had pushed for a Willkie-Baldwin ticket. Now, Willkie said, he was getting a lot of pressure to choose a Westerner to balance the ticket geographically. He was surprised to find that he was regarded as an Easterner, not a Hoosier; he was being urged to pick someone other than Baldwin for the vice presidency; and he found himself in an acutely embarrassing dilemma. "What shall I do?" he asked.

"Wendell," Pryor replied, "you're *pledged* to Baldwin. I'm not going to tell him. That's one job you'll have to do yourself." And after that, Pryor recalled, "McNary got the nomination."

Quite a different story of how the vice-presidential nominee was selected was told by my uncle, who heard it from John Hamilton, who was also in a position to know what happened. How much substance there is to the account is difficult to say at this remove, but it bears repeating if for no other reason than to illustrate the confusion, lack of planning, and general disarray of the Willkie people at the moment of victory.

Hamilton, a right-wing Republican who had been national chairman since the Landon-Knox campaign of 1936, was no Willkie man, and probably knew that the nominee would replace him. (He did.) Even so, after he and Ernest Weir and others gathered in a hotel room immediately after Willkie's nomination to discuss the vice-presidential nomination, it fell to him, he said, to remind Willkie that he had to decide quickly on his running mate, since it was then between 2:00 and 3:00 A.M. and the convention would reconvene that very day for the purpose of picking the second man on the ticket. When Hamilton called, Willkie was exhausted, annoyed at being telephoned at that hour, and replied that he hadn't given the matter any thought and who did Hamilton suggest?

Hamilton said it was Willkie's choice to make. Willkie then suggested that Tom Dewey would be an asset to the ticket, and why didn't Hamilton sound him out? Hamilton remonstrated, knowing exactly how the New Yorker would react, but Willkie insisted, Hamilton called Dewey, learned in a few well-chosen words how the district attorney felt about playing second fiddle, and phoned the nominee again.

By now Willkie was sound asleep and angry at being awakened, but before signing off and telling Hamilton under no circumstances to disturb him again, he said he had always admired Bob Taft, and that Hamilton could try him. Again Hamilton tried to beg off, but Willkie insisted, and in the morning the Ohioan was called and reacted exactly as Hamilton had known he would.

An equally abortive attempt was made to line up Hanford MacNider of Iowa, and finally, Charles McNary was proposed to Willkie.

"Who's he?" asked the nominee.

Hamilton reminded Willkie that McNary was a senator from Oregon, highly regarded in the party, and it was thought he would give balance to the ticket. Willkie urged Hamilton to try him.[8]

Whatever the facts about how he was chosen, everyone agreed on the prospective vice president's reaction to the invitation. "Hell no, I wouldn't run with Willkie!" said Charles McNary.

His arm was twisted, he was reminded of his duty to the party, and it required only a single ballot to make the senator from Oregon Wendell Willkie's running mate. "I wish they had imposed this chore on someone else," McNary remarked sourly. "However, I'll be a good soldier and do the best I can."

As it turned out, he did not, and was no special asset to Willkie in the campaign, but no one could foresee that in those heady hours of late June when the Republican convention was winding down. Traditionalists believed that McNary would balance the ticket because he was a Westerner,

---

[8]Although John Hollister's version of the effort to woo Senator Taft differs slightly, it lends credence to the Hamilton account. "Taft," he said, "was approached by a little group headed by Warren Austin [of Vermont]. The Ohio delegation was caucusing the next morning after the Willkie nomination when I was called to the door, and Warren Austin asked me to find out if Taft would take the vice-presidential nomination. The answer was an immediate 'No,' which I transmitted to Austin." It is only fair to say that when the Hamilton story was repeated to Samuel Pryor, he commented that "none of those men [i.e., Dewey, Taft, or MacNider] was ever mentioned as a vice-presidential possibility." Yet Hollister's recollection indicates that Taft was certainly approached. One more piece of the puzzle is Cornelia McNary's reaction when she learned in a Salem, Oregon, grocery store of her husband's nomination: "I couldn't believe it. Charles had wired me this morning that he wouldn't accept the nomination." That suggests further that negotiations with others may have been going on before McNary received the bid.

an advocate of public power, a farmer, an experienced politician, and a lifelong Republican—all that Willkie was not. What they ignored was that he and his senior partner in the coming adventure had never seen each other and had almost nothing in common, politically or otherwise. Before he was elected to the Senate, McNary was known for developing the world's largest prune in his experimental laboratory. In Washington, he was known for the political cunning that made him minority leader, and for being something of a maverick, and if his penchant for going it on his own had led him to support a number of the New Deal's domestic programs, including the TVA that was anathema to Willkie, surely, it was thought, that was something he and Willkie could overlook in the interest of party unity.

It rained hard on the afternoon Charles McNary was given the plum he did not want, and when Wendell and Edith Willkie arrived at Convention Hall they were soaked. The hall was a mass of fluttering banners, handkerchiefs, hats, and flags; only the diehards still wearing Taft and Dewey buttons sat on their hands, complaining as before that the hall was packed with Willkie people. The candidate and his shy, quiet wife received huge ovations, Joe Martin introduced the "next president of the United States," and Wendell Willkie stepped to the microphone to say a few words. It was a brief talk: all gratitude and appreciation, praise for the way Martin had handled the convention, and a promise to wage an aggressive campaign to unify the nation, to bring "all classes to this great cause of the preservation of freedom."

Then, surely without realizing the import of what he was saying, he blundered.

"And so," he concluded, "you Republicans, I call upon you to join me, help me. The cause is great. We must win." It was the *you Republicans* that confirmed what so many delegates had believed all along—that he was not really one of them, that he was an outsider who intended to use their party to satisfy his own ambitions.

Those two words could stand for all the problems Wendell Willkie would have in the grueling campaign ahead, for even as he told the convention he was going home to sleep for a week, the regulars among them turned their backs on him, certain beyond all doubt that he was not a genuine Republican. What they failed to understand, then and later, was that that was precisely the reason he had been nominated. Those thousands of independents in the galleries and in the Willkie clubs across the land did not *want* a real Republican—a Taft or a Vandenberg or a Dewey; which is why they rose up in revolt against the politicians, took the convention away from them, and forced the nomination of a man they perceived as an enlightened leader, who was just incidentally the only candidate who had a chance of winning. Raymond Clapper put it well: "The people have saved the Republican politicians from themselves. . . ."

Already they were calling it the Miracle of Philadelphia, and in many ways it was. Certainly the manner in which Willkie triumphed was beyond all comprehension and revealed to the public and political insiders alike that what had been judged impossible was not. A quarter of a century later, Marcia Davenport could still recall the suspense and tension of those few exhilarating hours, and at the same time feel "the bitterness of the Old Guard, the adamant resistance to the interloper, the hatred against him and against all of us who had worked for this aim which was, after all, visionary and fantastic." The delirious Willkie fans in the galleries, the Willkie clubs, the amateurs so derisively called Boy Scouts by the pros—all deserved a share of credit for the outcome, yet other forces were at work, too. Willkie's nomination was openly supported by businessmen, suggesting that business-men themselves, after their decade-long exile in the desert, were back in favor now that the defense effort was getting under way, and suggesting further that they would play an increasingly important role in political affairs. As for the party's leaders, they were politicians, after all, and they could roll with a punch. But the hatred and bitterness Marcia Davenport sensed there would not die. The pros knew that Willkie had never—until the final ballot, when everyone was obliged to jump aboard his galloping band wagon—had any real strength outside the Northeast and the Middle Atlantic states. He had been put over by the liberal Eastern establishment, and the politicians stored away this knowledge for the future.[9] For now, they figured that the candidate was a typical businessman; if he had unfortu-nate lapses into liberalism, those ideas would change quickly enough if he was elected. And if he was elected, he could be managed.

They also knew that while the amateurs might have taken over the convention, neither they nor their candidate would take over the Republi-can Party.

[9]For twenty-four years the resentment would fester, the schism would be unresolved, until Senator Everett McKinley Dirksen rose on the floor of the 1964 convention, pointed a finger at the New York and Pennsylvania delegations, led by Nelson Rockefeller and William Scranton, and shouted at those reminders of Wendell Willkie: "You led us down the road to defeat. . . ." And at last the Old Guard chose one of its own, Barry Goldwater, only to see him crushed in the worst defeat in any presidential election to that time. (Indeed, those same liberal, largely Eastern, Republicans had prevailed upon Dwight D. Eisenhower to run in 1952, and although he kept the GOP in power for eight years, the Dirksens of the party were unreconcilable.)

CHAPTER 39

———◆———

"... the finest party I ever attended."

Ah, but those were grand times—maybe even the best of times if you were lucky enough to have been born at the right moment, in the right place, in the right circumstances. Europe was ravaged by barbarians, America's underprivileged were jobless and hungry, much of the world was at war, but a Pittsburgh boy whose family had managed to survive the Depression more or less intact could drive through a mill town's silent slums, en route to the country club to play tennis and swim, and scarcely notice the lines of gray figures patiently shuffling toward the soup kitchen, or the shabby houses where women and children sat on rotting doorsteps, staring at an alien world with eyes that knew no hope. I know, because I was one of the lucky few.

My thoughts were not on the tumultuous events in Europe, either. At the time of the Munich Pact I was sixteen, starting my senior year at Shady Side Academy, a private school outside Pittsburgh, and what was of far more concern than the diplomatic maneuvering in Germany was winning the Tri-State Preparatory League's soccer championship. While Neville Chamberlain was shuttling back and forth between London and Munich, I was writing a stream of letters to a girl at the Madeira School in Virginia, trying to sign her up for as many dates as possible during the Christmas holidays. In the spring of 1939, about the time Chamberlain told the House of Commons that Britain and France would go to the aid of Poland if the independence of that nation should be threatened, I was driving east with three classmates—Johnny Atwood, Don Gow, and John Tabor—to look at colleges. All four of us decided we liked Yale, and since admission, in those days, was all but automatic if you passed the college entrance examinations and could pay the tuition, we took the news as a matter of course when we were accepted. For a graduation present my family sent me to South America with two other Pittsburgh boys and their mother—whose watchful eye was on us as much as the sights—plus another young man from Connecticut who was a family friend, and it was on that cruise that I first felt the existence of forces inimical to the United States.

One of our shipboard companions was an American girl traveling with her family to Argentina, where her father was to serve as naval attaché, and from her we learned, even before we arrived in Buenos Aires and decided it for ourselves, that the city was full of Nazis who were up to no good. And on the last morning of the six-week voyage, our ship was moving ever so slowly through thick fog outside New York harbor when the horn that had been sounding a long single warning for hours suddenly blasted repeatedly, the engines shuddered into reverse, and across the liner's bow slid a freighter, so close that we could see men standing on deck, grinning. As the cargo vessel vanished into the mists we saw that she was flying the red-and-white rising-sun ensign of Japan, and anger took the place of fear, for it was almost as if it had been a deliberate act, intended at the very least to humiliate an American ship.

By the time I arrived in New Haven to begin my freshman year, war had started in Europe, but the big, black headlines were pushed into the background by the excitement and diversions of college. That fall I was trying to juggle a demanding academic schedule, the newfound responsibility of being on my own in an adult community, and the experience of being in love, and I was doing my utmost to maneuver classroom schedules, assignments, football weekends, and other extracurricular activities in such a way that I could see the young lady at every possible moment (she was at Sarah Lawrence College, which was less than two hours away). What was complicating matters was the uncertainty of not knowing exactly how she felt about me. Maybe, I thought, we will settle things during Christmas vacation, when we would see a lot of each other at parties in Pittsburgh and Sewickley.

If it hadn't been for Herbie and Marian Herr, my life might have taken a very different course. I didn't call them Herbie and Marian, of course, but they were my parents' friends, and since that's what they called them, that's how I always thought of them. Herbie was the biggest man I had ever seen. He was simply immense: a good six feet tall, and well over three hundred pounds. Every so often my father would regale us with stories about Herbie's gargantuan appetite—of how he had eaten a five-pound box of

Reymer's bonbons on the sleeper from Pittsburgh to New York, or how he had consumed eleven hot dogs at a Pirate baseball game. Marian was a diminutive woman, blond and handsome, with a no-nonsense air about her.

But this is to digress. The point is that the Herrs had a daughter, Betty, and for several years at Christmastime they gave a dance at their house for her friends. I still have a photograph of the first one of these affairs I attended (for all I know, it may have been the first one they gave, since Betty and I were of an age), and there, posing solemnly for the cameraman, is just about everyone who was in our crowd when I was growing up—the girls decoratively costumed, suggesting that the invitations had specified fancy dress, and a majority of the boys in mufti, no one being less daring or more insecure than a fourteen- or-fifteen-year-old male. Half a century later I look at those solemn faces staring into the camera and wonder what became of them, how much joy or sorrow they encountered, how many became heroes or villains, doctors, lawyers, mountebanks, pillars of their community, how many of those lives were cut short, and then I slip back into that moment frozen in time in the Herrs' living room, and the music is about to start, with the rugs and furniture removed so that we graduates of Miss Hubbell's or Mrs. Hess's dancing classes can demonstrate what we learned.

The following year the Herrs put on another dance, and for the first hour or so it was the same crowd, the same gang we always saw. But about 9:30 or so, a small group of sophisticated-looking strangers appeared, and someone whispered that they were from Sewickley, a suburb about twenty miles down the Ohio River from Pittsburgh. What I noticed immediately was the extraordinary beauty of one particular girl—a girl with long brown hair that came to her shoulders, brown eyes so dark they were almost black, who was wearing a mulberry-colored evening dress with spaghetti straps that showed off a beautiful figure, and who was clearly the best dancer I had ever seen. (And I had seen Ginger Rogers.) I didn't know the boy she was dancing with; I just knew that I hated him, because she looked as if she was having the time of her life, and I was sure she gave her partner the same impression.

I turned to Joe Bennett, who was standing beside me watching the dancers, and asked if he knew the dark-haired girl.

"Yes, why?" he asked.

"Because that's the girl I'm going to marry," I said.

He and I pushed our way onto the dance floor, he tapped the girl's partner on the shoulder, and although I have no recollection of anything other than holding her in my arms and discovering that she was a dance partner unlike any I'd ever had, Joe must have told me that her name was Barbara Bray, and she must have told me then or sometime later that she liked to be called Bobs.

———

In a city like Pittsburgh, because most of the young, chosen few were away at boarding school or college, the debutante year had to be planned ever so carefully, with parties shoehorned into a "little season" at the end of June, and *the* Season, which ran its breathless course during the Christmas holidays, from mid-December to New Year's Day.

For a fortnight at the end of June and during three glorious weeks in December, when the daughters and granddaughters of Gulf and Alcoa, Big Steel and Little Steel, the Mellon Bank and Pittsburgh Plate Glass were the cynosure of Pittsburgh's socially prominent, there were so many coming-out parties that it was not unusual to have a luncheon, a tea dance, a dinner dance, and a ball on the same day (not to mention the occasional roller-skating or ice-skating party, and the festivities surrounding the annual visit of the Princeton Triangle Club, which had to be sandwiched in)—all of them attended by much the same people, who would almost certainly see each other in virtually identical circumstances the next day, and the next, until the season finally drew to an exhausted close.

Pittsburgh's debutantes had been emerging since 1888, when twenty young women were presented to local society, but the recent hard times had worked certain changes in the ritual. By 1940, not so many Pittsburgh daughters were "coming out"; the number was well below the banner year of 1930 (before the Depression really hit home), when sixty girls had been introduced to society, though it was an improvement over 1936, when only thirteen debutantes had made their bows. Back in the twenties, a popular girl—or one whose family was especially eminent—might have as many as four or five parties given in her honor,[1] but nowadays even if her family could afford to launch her in proper style, a young lady could hardly avoid a twinge of embarrassment over the number of these affairs she attended in "her year" and how much each of them cost. Of course, Pittsburgh had seen nothing to equal the well-publicized debut of New York's Brenda Diana Duff Frazier, the acclaimed Glamour Girl of 1938, who set the style for every debutante of the day with her pale skin, shoulder-length black hair, startling red lipstick, penciled eyebrows, and face whose perfect features never seemed to move, to judge from her photographs. The seventeen-year-old Brenda had popularized the strapless evening gown, she had danced with Douglas Fairbanks, Jr., her picture had appeared on the cover of *Life,* she was going to inherit $4 million when she was twenty-one, and her debut party, according to the *New York Daily News,* had cost $60,000. (Brenda's mother issued an anguished denial: the correct figure, she said, was less than $16,000.)

Although one seldom read about them, New York doubtless had debutantes who were not as well endowed financially as Brenda was; certainly Pittsburgh did. Indeed, whispered stories made the rounds about parents who had lost everything in the Crash who were stubbornly determined to

[1]During Andrew Mellon's brief tour as ambassador to the Court of St. James's, a number of Pittsburgh's post-debutantes sailed to England to be presented to King George V and Queen Mary, among them A.W.'s daughter, Ailsa, and his niece, Sarah.

present a daughter to society, even if that meant bringing her out at a small luncheon or tea at home, thus publicly owning up to their pecuniary plight. The next-higher option, as expenses went, was a luncheon at one of the good clubs (which meant the Fox Chapel Golf Club, the Pittsburgh Golf Club, the Twentieth Century Club, or Sewickley's Edgeworth Club and the Allegheny Country Club), where a meal for fifty guests, with cigarettes, invitations, flowers, tips, and the services of a social secretary included, might be arranged for as little as $200. An afternoon tea dance was likely to cost $1,500 or more, including $500 for champagne punch and liquor, $125 for the invitations, $400 for food, $300 for a local orchestra, $75 for tips and cigarettes, plus a fee for the club.

The ante for a dinner dance or ball was at least $3,000, and for these occasions the best dates on the calendar had to be reserved a year or two in advance. That carefully guarded calendar, together with an exhaustively screened list of eligible debutantes, post-debutantes, and young men of the proper age, was in the businesslike hands of Mrs. Frank W. Jarvis in Pittsburgh and Mrs. Francis Dunham in Sewickley. These hardworking, genteel women saw to it that the correct number of invitations, on the best vellum stock, were ordered from the firm of J. R. Weldin, to be engraved by hand by their English-born craftsmen, addressed and mailed, with the replies meticulously recorded so an anxious hostess might know exactly how many young people to expect. In a normal year, it was said, the Mesdames Jarvis and Dunham oversaw the processing of twenty thousand such invitations.

If the debutante's parents elected to have a top band from out of town (Harry Marshard from Bar Harbor was the favorite in Pittsburgh, though Meyer Davis was considered very good indeed), and if the dancing (and the open bar, and the hired help, and the rental of the club) extended into the small hours of the morning, as they did in the case of most balls, the cost might exceed $5,000. That was a great deal of money at a time when the annual income of a Pittsburgh steelworker was $1,500 or less, so if some of the young ladies tended to be uncomfortable about the splash their parents wanted to make for them, it was easy to see why. (And was the splash for them or was it really for the parents? a few girls wondered.) My new friend Barbara Bray was one of those who felt that something was wrong in having an expensive coming-out party with a war being fought in Europe, let alone the poverty and misery here at home, but it was an era when young people still did pretty much what was expected of them, and no open rebellion disturbed the smooth progression of the debutante year.

Regrettably, no one asked those who were most directly involved what they thought about such matters. Instead, in November 1940, the *Bulletin-Index,* a local weekly news magazine, published the results of a survey of that year's debutantes' opinions on more trivial subjects, with results that were about what you would have expected from any group of young Americans. The girls' favorite magazines were *Life, Reader's Digest,* and *The New*

Yorker. The radio programs they liked best were *Information Please,* a sophisticated quiz show, and four regular broadcasts featuring popular music—the Fred Waring, Tommy Dorsey, and Horace Heidt shows, and the *Lucky Strike Hit Parade.* The best motion picture of the year, all agreed, was *Gone With the Wind,* followed by *All This and Heaven Too* and *Rebecca.* Their favorite movie actors were Cary Grant, Gary Cooper, Laurence Olivier, and Donald Duck; their favorite actress, unanimously—Bette Davis. To the question "Do you think a couple should get married if the man is only making $150 per month?" most of the young women responded, "Sure." And to the follow-up "Would you?" a majority replied, "No."

Those girls and their contemporaries had had the good fortune to grow up at a time when movies, radio, and record players were coming into their own as major cultural influences. Even in the early thirties, with the Depression at its worst, some 75 million Americans—60 percent of the population—went to the movies every week,[2] and the fact that talking pictures were still something of a novelty was only part of the explanation. Hollywood was an unrivaled purveyor of dreams, and since so little glamour and romance attached to most people's daily lives, America was going to the movies to escape reality.

The addition of sound to the silents had forced filmmaking in new directions—into good writing, for one, dialogue that could stand on its own, with the result that writers like Ben Hecht, Anita Loos, Dorothy Parker, S. N. Behrman, S. J. Perelman, Billy Wilder, Charles Brackett, William Faulkner, and Scott Fitzgerald were turning out scripts that were occasionally brilliant, more often very good indeed. Writing of such caliber made possible a new genre of pictures, some of them elegant and sophisticated, most of them freewheeling and imaginative, known as "screwball" comedies. Many of these films had an underlying gentleness to them, as well, reflecting an unwillingness to dwell on the horror stories coming out of Europe; in the fantasyland of a theater, it was all but impossible to divine that Americans had a care in the world. Since movies no longer depended solely on the sight gag, as the silent comedies of the twenties had, but increasingly on the witty spoken word, such women as Carole Lombard, Myrna Loy, Katharine Hepburn, Jean Arthur, Irene Dunne, and others now had an opportunity to show that they were every bit as clever as Cary Grant or Melvyn Douglas. How could anyone resist those attractive, clever women, or the equally attractive, clever men who were paired with them? Not I, certainly, because I had discovered that for two hours on Saturday afternoons, in the darkness of the Sheridan Square, the Liberty, or the Manor, I could see myself as cosmopolitan as William Powell or Charles

---

[2]There were plenty of films to see: by 1939, Hollywood turned out 466 pictures, many of them excellent—including *Stagecoach, Ninotchka, Goodbye, Mr. Chips, The Wizard of Oz, Gone With the Wind,* and *Mr. Smith Goes to Washington.* Nor did the country lack for motion-picture theaters—there were more than fifteen thousand of them.

Boyer, as debonair as Clark Gable or Cary Grant, as devil-may-care as Gary Cooper or Tyrone Power.

With sound, too, came new dimensions for music and dance, and suddenly we had Fred Astaire and Ginger Rogers and what some consider the greatest musicals in movie history. What made them so was the emphasis on dance—in particular, the way this perfectly matched couple danced together, and the way dancing gave expression to their emotions and the mood of the film. After all, neither Astaire nor Rogers had much of a voice, they had some of the sappiest lines ever written, and plots that were farcical, but no matter. Instead of acting, they danced, totally absorbed in each other, dancing as they did because words were inadequate to express their feelings.

We who were sixteen or seventeen at the time had not the slightest difficulty seeing ourselves as Fred and Ginger dancing the Continental, singing the haunting "Night and Day" or "Never Gonna Dance" to that special partner in our arms. Probably every generation thinks its music is the very best; still, it is difficult to imagine a happier combination of musical talent than that which happened to come together during the thirties. The musical awareness of my generation coincided fortuitously with a flowering of composers and arrangers who were creating music for the Broadway stage, for Hollywood's new musicals, and for the extraordinary group of performers who made these years the Big Band Era. Benny Goodman, Tommy Dorsey, Count Basie, Duke Ellington, Bunny Berrigan, Harry James, Artie Shaw, Glenn Miller, and others were performing live on radio, traveling the country to play in theaters, dance halls, amusement parks, nightclubs—wherever the young or the young at heart congregated. It was not considered unusual for teen-agers to drive a hundred miles to hear their favorite singer or dance to their favorite band, and the aficionado could tell you the name of every musician playing for Goodman or Dorsey, and who had arranged the numbers in their repertoire, as well.

Years later I met Benny Goodman and told him that one of the most memorable nights of my youth was listening—and dancing—to his band when they came to Pittsburgh. "I remember," he said, "that was at Kennywood Park," and his smile told me that he had as fond a recollection of it as I did. In 1935 the Goodman band had started the swing craze that swept the country—the big, swinging band playing music in a new way that was irresistible for dancing.[3] Five brasses, five reeds, four rhythm—those were

[3] The subject never occurred to me at the time, but I was astonished to read years later how young the members of the Goodman band were—like the Beatles when they first appeared in the United States. In 1938—the year they gave the first purely jazz concert in Carnegie Hall—Benny himself was twenty-eight, trumpeter Harry James and singer Martha Tilton twenty-one, Lionel Hampton twenty-four, and Teddy Wilson twenty-five. (The climax of that particular evening was a twelve-minute version of "Sing, Sing, Sing" with the audience on their feet, trucking and shagging at their seats and in the aisles.)

the basic ingredients in Goodman's band, and when they got going on "Don't Be That Way" or "Blue Skies," there simply was no better dance music anywhere. Following a break, the quartet would take over—Goodman on clarinet, Gene Krupa on drums, Teddy Wilson on piano, Lionel Hampton on the vibraphone—playing "Avalon," and "I Got Rhythm," and "Stompin' at the Savoy," the four of them starting off together, playing it straight, then breaking into a succession of solos, each man moving in and taking over, building on what the man before him had done, all of it pure inspiration, improvised on the spot, and as soon as one soloist dropped out and into the background he was followed by another, each one challenging the next to something better, while all around them the electricity built in a crowd mesmerized by the music and the rhythm. The kind of music they made was something you could not believe, and without being conscious of it you and your partner were moving in time to the beat along with hundreds of others, swaying back and forth and from side to side rather than dancing, because this was something you had to watch in order to be part of it. Before the night was gone the band would swing into "Bugle Call Rag" and the obligatory "Sing, Sing, Sing" and the crowd would go wild, cheering them on, inspiring the musicians to heights you would not have thought possible, with the brass taking the melody, throwing it back to the reeds, back and forth, the rhythm section going like madmen, the drums like thunder, everything in perfect balance, with soloists coming in and out on cue while the dancers, ecstatic, intoxicated, striving to equal the performance of the musicians, were lost in the magic of rhythm and a sound so full it was almost physical. And finally it was over, with the ghostly notes of Goodman's clarinet bidding the sad, sweet "Goodbye."

What a time to go dancing it was, what a time for singing, when it seemed that so many of the songs were written and played especially for you and your girl. There were Cole Porter's unforgettable "Night and Day," "You're the Top," "I Get a Kick Out of You," "Anything Goes," "It's Delovely," "I've Got You Under My Skin," and a score of others. From Harold Arlen had come "It's Only a Paper Moon," "Stormy Weather," "Over the Rainbow," "I've Got the World on a String." George and Ira Gershwin had written "Summertime," "The Man I Love," "Let's Call the Whole Thing Off," "But Not for Me," "Embraceable You." There were Jerome Kern's "A Fine Romance" and "The Way You Look Tonight"— both introduced in Astaire and Rogers films, along with so many others, including "All the Things You Are," and "Smoke Gets in Your Eyes." You had the wonderful Rodgers and Hart tunes: "The Lady Is a Tramp," "Where or When," "I Didn't Know What Time It Was," "This Can't Be Love," "My Funny Valentine"; Irving Berlin's "Isn't This a Lovely Day," "Cheek to Cheek"; Duke Ellington's "I Let a Song Go Out of My Heart," and "Sophisticated Lady"—the list went on and on, with scarcely a song among them we could not sing by heart.

As a recipient of invitations to "meet" the girls who were making their debuts (all of whom I already knew or recognized), I was a beneficiary of their families' largess, and was much too busy enjoying what was going on to ask myself whether such parties should be given at this critical time in the world's affairs or to consider how spoiled we young men were. In the first place, we were indulged by the debutantes' parents, who needed us to fill the stag line so that all the girls would have a good time (what the ideal proportion of males to females was, I cannot say, but I suppose the ratio was close to two-to-one). It cost the host a pretty penny to supply food and drink (mostly drink) to these supernumeraries—a flock of hungry, thirsty young blades he might never see again and who might not even have the courtesy to dance with his daughter. In my own house, I know, it required some financial strain to outfit me with both a tuxedo and a suit of tails (one was expected to have both, and that meant two sets of studs and cufflinks and two types of shirts and ties), along with a chesterfield overcoat and a derby. (My parents' closest friend decided that I needed an opera hat, too, so thanks to her generosity I owned one.)

Long after those hedonistic years, a picture occasionally crosses my mind of five carefree young men in white tie and tails piling out of a gleaming, two-toned, custom-made convertible Buick on North Craig Street near Centre Avenue. It is around 3:00 A.M. and all of us feel the need (as we invariably did, at that hour of the morning after a dance) of a hamburger or two, and a milkshake. That automatically meant a stop at the White Tower, a miniature white-brick building with a ridiculously small, crenellated "tower," inside which were seven stools and a stand-up counter accommodating another four or five customers. Here, twenty-four hours a day, seven days a week, they served what we considered the best hamburgers in town for a nickel apiece, and to the five young men—two of them attending the Choate School, one at Lawrenceville, one at St. Paul's, and one at Shady Side Academy—there was nothing the least bit odd about being in that place in evening clothes. Nor was it thought strange by the man behind the counter: having long ago learned to expect just about anything—the drunk, the panhandler, the stick-up man, the predawn visits from prep-school boys in dress suits—he took our appearances in stride.

That was all well and good for a counterman whose only real concern was whether the customers paid before leaving; but I often wondered how in the world my father put up with my social life. Until his health deteriorated when he was in his seventies, he never really stopped working. I can recall the day he came home and told Mother somewhat wistfully that he was yielding to pressure by some of the employees (and the rest of the business community) and closing the office at noon on Saturdays instead of the usual 6:00 P.M. (though for a long time thereafter he and a few of the old-timers continued to work all day Saturday out of habit). His business, in other words, was far more than a job: it was what he loved doing, his avocation as well as his career, for he had no hobbies other than reading. And during the Depression, when he was often working seven days a week in an effort to keep the business afloat, his brief encounters with his son during the social season must have been a real trial.

Not infrequently during the Christmas holidays I arrived home in my evening clothes just when my father was coming downstairs to breakfast. We would exchange a few words, then I would go to bed and he would leave for the office. By late afternoon I was up, having showered, shaved, and dressed again in black tie or tails, and was about to leave the house when he walked in the door, briefcase in hand. How he kept his patience, how he tolerated this, I will never know. Perhaps it was because he had never had anything like my experience in his own youth, and felt that I should take advantage of the opportunity.

I didn't realize it at the time, but my career in the stag line was nearing an end. In January 1940 the *Bulletin-Index* informed its readers that Pittsburgh, "still panting from its 1939–40 holiday deb season," was already setting dates and making reservations at clubs for the parties that would commence in June. No wonder. As it turned out, the "little season" began in earnest on Saturday, June 15, with a tea for Lucia Buchanan, followed by a tea dance and a dinner dance for Elaine Darlington (Elaine's mother, Mrs. George Garrett of Washington, D.C., had brought her daughter "home" to Sewickley for the occasion, and it was noted in the crowded society pages of the Pittsburgh papers that Elaine would also be presented to Long Island society later in the month by David K. E. Bruce and his wife, the former Ailsa Mellon). In quick succession there were parties for Caroline Craig, Dorothea Eddy, Elizabeth Richey, and Nancy Herron, a tea dance for Marion Collin, a dance for the Slocum sisters, Mary Lou and Bets, an open house here, a supper there, more teas and dances, until the final day of the season, when a tea dance for Suzanne Swan was followed by a ball given by Mr. and Mrs. Thomas Bray for their daughter Barbara at the Allegheny Country Club.

It was late on Friday afternoon, June 28, 1940, when a taxi drove up our driveway and deposited my father, hoarse from shouting and cheering, as happy and excited as I had ever seen him, bursting with news of what had happened in Philadelphia at the Republican convention. He would have returned by train with members of the Allegheny County delegation, arriving the next morning, he said, but he was acutely aware of the importance I attached to the timely appearance of my parents at the Bray party that night, and he had taken a plane.

At 10:00 o'clock the first of five hundred guests began making their way through the receiving line, to be greeted by Tom and Louise Bray, Barbara, and her mother's married sisters, Barbara Keeble and Jane Harwell, who had come from Nashville, Tennessee, for the affair. The ballroom, where Harry Marshard's band was playing, had been decorated to resemble a garden. Along the edges of the room was a white brick wall covered with ivy; in the trees above it silk-covered lanterns gleamed in pastel colors; on the tables were salmon-colored geraniums in turquoise vases; and in the center of this setting, carried away by the music of a superb band playing some of the best dance music ever written, swirled scores of happy couples—boys in white jacket and black tie, girls in every hue of silk, satin, taffeta, and chiffon—twirling, dipping, swinging around the floor.

That night, from the time Marshard began playing his theme song, "I'm Just Wild About Harry," until he and his exhausted musicians gave the Brays' indefatigable guests an absolutely final "Good Night Ladies" nine hours later, no one had a better time than the guest of honor (once she could leave the receiving line), for no one enjoyed dancing more—or was a better dancer. It was her evening, and in the blur of motion and color in the ballroom she was the central figure, a strikingly beautiful girl with long brown hair and a radiant smile, her tan skin accentuated by the low-cut bodice and billowing skirt of the white tulle gown that set her off against the other dancers.

Nobody had supposed the dance would go on until daylight, and when the party at last broke up, Bobs's mother invited me to come back to their house and get some sleep before driving to Pittsburgh (my parents had long since returned home). When I awoke it was after noon, and I was eating a leisurely lunch with the Brays when the phone rang. It was for me. My father was on the line, and he was not bothering to conceal his irritation: "Our train for Wyoming leaves in three hours. Are you coming with us? Because if you are, you'd better come home and pack." *Click.* I might be a college undergraduate and a heck of a partygoer, but the parental command was still a command, and I left in a hurry.

Two weeks after the party, Louise Bray received a letter, postmarked Canton, Ohio. In the envelope with it were two extremely fuzzy photographs that appeared to have been taken by someone with a tremorous hand, showing the last of the departing guests outside the Allegheny Country Club—one couple still dancing in the driveway, others with glasses in hand, all of them wreathed in smiles. The writer, a Sewickley boy named Jack Schroeder who had learned his manners, was thanking his hostess "for what was without question the finest party I ever attended," and he had delayed doing so, he said, because he wanted to "enclose proof that you had everyone so enthused that they could not go home. The pictures were taken at about eight [A.M.] . . . and the shaky hand was caused by exhaustion."

PART VII

1940

CHICAGO:
THE THIRD TERM

*Franklin D. Roosevelt at a Jackson Day dinner
in a pose beloved by cartoonists—relaxed, grinning,
with the ever-present cigarette holder
clamped between his teeth.*

CHAPTER 40

"...they want a rest from Roosevelts."

On Saturday, July 13, 1940, the long black touring car known around the White House executive offices as the *Queen Mary* rolled down the gravel drive and out the East Gate. In the backseat, President Roosevelt, wearing a rumpled seersucker suit and a battered Panama hat, waved occasionally to passersby as he was driven to the Washington Naval Yard, where the presidential yacht, USS *Potomac,* awaited his arrival. A twenty-one-gun salute, the trilling of the bos'n's pipe, the four-starred flag of the commander in chief run up the mainmast, the sound of a bugle, and the *Potomac* was under way, down the Potomac River, headed for the open sea.

It had the earmarks of a normal weekend cruise, giving the president an opportunity to escape the city's ferocious heat and humidity and the troubles of the world, to fish, work with his stamp collection, and relax. One difference on this particular weekend was that Mr. Roosevelt's old friend Samuel Rosenman was on board with him—had been summoned, in fact, from a family vacation to spend a week at the White House. Since Judge Rosenman wrote many of Roosevelt's speeches, and since his presence in Washington coincided with the Democratic convention, it could be supposed that a speech was forthcoming which had something to do with what was happening in Chicago, and Rosenman's task was made clear to him on the cruise: he was to prepare a rather subtle message indicating that Roosevelt would not be a party to any contest for the nomination and that the delegates must freely decide who was to be the Democrats' candidate for president. It required very little imagination to see that within the framework of these rather ambiguous guidelines a good deal of flexibility remained for a man who intended to keep his plans to himself until the last possible moment.

Until the end of June it had been dry and cold in the capital—sweater weather; but on the night of July 18, with the president back from his cruise, in residence at the White House, the heat was suffocating. Even old-timers in the District had a hard time remembering worse. Air conditioning was still a novelty, though it was certainly available to the nation's chief executive if he wanted it, but Roosevelt complained that refrigeration irritated his sinuses and refused to have it in any of the rooms he frequented. The result was that he—and those who worked closest with him—suffered mightily at times. He kept as cool as possible by wearing light clothing, opening his collar, and rolling up his sleeves, but he perspired heavily and appeared to be extremely uncomfortable, though he usually denied it. This evening the president sat at a card table, playing solitaire, listening to a broadcast of the Democratic convention, while drops of perspiration rolled down the back of his neck. Every once in a while he would take a handkerchief from his pocket, wipe his balding head, and run the cloth around the inside of his collar. When the telephone rang, as it did frequently, he would pick it up, listen, say a few words, hang up the receiver, and go back to his game and his listening. In the room eight or ten others were paying equally close attention to the radio, talking quietly, but mostly watching the man at the table and wondering what he had in mind.

Franklin Roosevelt had received his party's nomination as president the night before, in circumstances that were trying for him and unusual—some said sordid—for those present in Chicago, and now the question of who would get the nomination for the vice presidency had turned the convention into a nasty free-for-all. At least seventeen men were being boosted for the second spot on the ticket, and a number of them labored under the impression that they had been promised the job, and were busy lining up delegates. The hopefuls included Senators James Byrnes and William Bankhead, Supreme Court Justice William O. Douglas, former Solicitor General Robert Jackson, Assistant Secretary of War Louis Johnson, Speaker of the House Sam Rayburn, Federal Security Administrator Paul McNutt, the banker and former RFC director Jesse Jones, Secretary of Agriculture Henry Wallace, and several others, among them Robert Maynard Hutchins, president of the University of Chicago, who had lately concluded that he was the man for the job and was trying to drum up support. In addition, several men thought the office belonged by rights to them, were acutely aware that they had been promised nothing, and were both hurt and angry—most notably Postmaster General James Aloysius Farley and Secretary of the Interior

Harold Le Claire Ickes. What had shattered the illusions of all but one of these would-be candidates was the word from the presidential nominee himself, passed along by Harry Hopkins, that he wanted Henry Wallace as his running mate and would accept no one else. As bursting a balloon often produces shock and anger and hard feelings in a child, so with vice-presidential hopefuls, and those emotions were in plain view in Chicago Stadium on the night of July 18, 1940. In fact, the place was alive with hostility and frustration, as the pent-up rage against a manipulated convention suddenly burst into open mutiny against the man who sat playing solitaire in the White House.

For the ugly situation in Chicago, Franklin Roosevelt had only himself and his penchant for finagling to blame, and the disappointed and the disaffected were determined to get even, to prove that they were going to have a say in their party's future. As the debates on the convention floor grew more acrimonious, as it became increasingly clear that the delegates might actually nominate the conservative Alabaman, William B. Bankhead, Roosevelt's expression became grimmer and grimmer. He listened and went on dealing and picking up cards. In exasperation, he asked for a pad and pencil and, while those in the room continued to watch, began to write. He completed five pages, handed them to Samuel Rosenman, and asked him to work on them—to "smooth them out, and get them ready for delivery—in a hurry." Rosenman knew him well enough to know that he was in dead earnest, and as he read the president's handwritten notes, he saw that it was a short speech he would give to the convention, declining the nomination.

What was so bizarre about the caldron bubbling in Chicago was that an immensely popular, enormously powerful president, who had been twice elected by overwhelming majorities, should have let matters get so far out of hand in the party he led. How had things gone so wrong? What had brought matters to this pass?

===

The confrontation between FDR and the organization had its basis in opposition to the third term, of course; many Democrats believed as firmly as Republicans in the tradition of two terms, believed that a democratic society has a reservoir of talent capable of throwing up new leadership, believed that one of the chief threats to democracy is the possibility that an overly ambitious president will use the enormous leverage of his office to maintain himself in power. But there were other, equally valid reasons for the party regulars' opposition to another term for the incumbent.

Theodore Roosevelt had put his finger on one of those reasons years before, reacting to the pressure he was getting to run for a third term. The American people "are sick of looking at my grin and they are sick of hearing what Alice had for breakfast," he said; ". . . they want a rest from Roosevelts." Even though most delegates to the 1940 convention supported Franklin Roosevelt, a good many of them wanted a rest from him and his

New Deal—wanted in particular to be rid of the amateurs and professors and Johnny-come-latelies he had brought into his administration. No longer were his progressive measures so much admired: many middle-class Americans were turning conservative, heading for the Republican fold; and Southern Democrats, who resented the New Deal's social reforms, were alienated. More to the point just now, the lives of the men and women attending the convention revolved around what went on in their wards and precincts and local party headquarters, and they wanted no more "purges" of their party, conservative or otherwise; they wanted no more adventures like the Supreme Court disaster; they wanted a fair share of the patronage they felt they had been denied; they wanted politics the way it was meant to be. And since the president was not on hand in Chicago to listen to this catalogue of complaints, the target of all the accumulated rage and frustration was the man correctly presumed by one and all to be Roosevelt's alter ego and political deputy—Harry Hopkins.

The convention fight merely pointed up what a good many Americans felt about Hopkins, who had the dubious distinction of being disliked as cordially by Roosevelt's partisans as by his enemies. This son of an Iowa harness-maker had devoted his working life to the poor—in a New York settlement house, child welfare, the Red Cross, a tuberculosis association; in 1932 he was appointed Federal Emergency Relief administrator, then head of the Works Progress Administration, where he put into practice his theory that relief must be work relief, to use people's energies and skills, giving them a feeling of worth; and in 1938 he became secretary of commerce. Although Hopkins denied it categorically, several well-known columnists quoted him as saying, "We shall tax and tax, and spend and spend, and elect and elect." Canard or not, it was a juicy item for the Roosevelt and Hopkins haters, and it endured for years. From the time he first came to Washington the feeling grew that there was something sinister about the man, suggested in part by his appearance: although he was just shy of his fiftieth birthday, he had the unhealthy, undernourished pallor of a man chronically ill, a stooped, cadaverous look accentuated by the chain-smoking, the yellowed fingers, the laugh that sounded like a cough. His uncombed hair lay in thin strands across his skull, his baggy trousers were a trifle too short, his paunch suggested a desk-bound bureaucrat: all in all, not the image of a fellow you'd like to see running the country. A few weeks after Hopkins's wife died of cancer in 1937, he had much of his stomach removed and learned that he had the same malady, and although the disease never recurred, he was prone to various ailments caused by nutritional problems that brought him close to death on several occasions and would kill him at the age of fifty-five.

He had been so ill during 1939 and early 1940 that when he went to his office in the Commerce Department on May 10, the day the Germans invaded the Low Countries, it was only the second time he had been there in ten months. That evening he was a guest for dinner at the White House

and looked so sick that Roosevelt suggested he spend the night. He did—
and remained for three and a half years, living in a suite of rooms that had
once been Abraham Lincoln's study. This proximity to the seat of power
only increased his detractors' resentment over the way he had insinuated
himself into a position of immense influence, and it was not mitigated by
glimpses White House visitors sometimes had of Hopkins in a worn bath-
robe, shuffling along the upstairs hall to the president's room. Without
doubt he was a political liability, but the president liked him and, above all
else, trusted him. One observer said, "He seems to know precisely when
Roosevelt wants to consider affairs of State and when he wants to escape
from the awful consciousness of the presidency." Hopkins was both tough-
minded and idealistic, he had a relentless drive to get things done, and he
possessed an instinctive feeling for what was in Franklin Roosevelt's mind.
If he had the presidential ear it was undoubtedly because he seemed to know
what was wanted and how the president wanted it done.[1]

Whether or not Roosevelt had told Hopkins what to do in Chicago is
almost beside the point. Hopkins was sure enough of the president's
thoughts to know what he had to do. What was more, he had in his pocket
a sheet of lined yellow paper on which Roosevelt had written four sentences
in pencil. The message was addressed to "Dear Will"—which meant William B. Bankhead, speaker of the House of Representatives and temporary
chairman of the Democratic National Convention—and the message asked
Bankhead to make one thing "utterly clear" to the assembled delegates, to
wit, that "I . . . have not today and have never had any wish or purpose
to remain in the office of President, or indeed anywhere in public office after
next January."

So successfully had Franklin Roosevelt shrouded his intentions that
when the Democratic faithful began arriving in Chicago on the weekend of
July 13-14, not one of them knew what the script called for. Bankhead—who
had not been given the note from FDR because of a change in plans—was
the keynote speaker but had no idea what to say, since he did not know if
the president would be a candidate. Ickes, before leaving Washington, had
asked the president whether "we were to be permitted to go to Chicago
without a program, without a floor leader, without knowing who was to
make the nominating speech—in effect, leaderless and planless." To which
question FDR just grinned and said that he was "trusting to God." Ickes
replied tartly that he could trust to God and still have a vague idea what
ought to be done. Yet by Tuesday morning, the second day of the conven-

---

[1]In January 1941, just before Roosevelt's third inauguration, Wendell Willkie called on the
president at the White House and during their conversation asked why he maintained his close
relationship with Hopkins, when the latter was so resented and distrusted. Roosevelt replied
that if Willkie ever sat in his chair as president of the United States he would learn that
"everybody who walks through [that door] wants something out of you. You'll learn what a
lonely job this is, and you'll discover the need for somebody like Harry Hopkins who asks for
nothing except to serve you."

tion, no one—unless it was Harry Hopkins—knew whether Roosevelt's name would be placed in nomination, and if so, by whom.

The president might be trusting in the Lord, but he was also putting a lot of faith in his advance man, and it was soon obvious to the delegates that the person to see was Hopkins—so obvious that the Democratic convention of 1940 might as well have been held in his suite of rooms at the Blackstone Hotel. Off the red-carpeted hall, in a large sitting room with a fireplace, two of Hopkins's aides carefully screened visitors. Adjoining the sitting room was a room with twin beds where Hopkins—who received in shirtsleeves and suspenders, or in pajamas—could get off his feet occasionally (he had nighttime lodgings at another hotel, but when he found time to use them was a good question). And beyond the bedroom was a bath, distinguished by the presence of a telephone with a direct line to the White House. The location guaranteed that Hopkins's conversations with his boss would be private.

By extraordinary coincidence, Harry Hopkins occupied the very space in which the head of the Republican ticket opposed by Cox and Roosevelt in 1920 had been chosen on a June night two decades earlier—the notorious smoke-filled rooms shared by George Harvey and Will Hays, where boozy party leaders had decided in the small hours of the morning to nominate Warren Gamaliel Harding because he was the most available candidate, with the fewest strikes against him. ("There ain't any first-raters this year," Connecticut Senator Frank Brandegee had stated baldly, ". . . we got a lot of second-raters and Warren Harding is the best of the second-raters.") Apart from party affiliation, the chief difference between the politicians who had drifted into this suite in 1920 and those who stopped by twenty years later was that only those who were 100 percent behind the candidate were welcomed in 1940. And the candidate, as Harry Hopkins's presence made clear, was Franklin Delano Roosevelt.

====

Whether or not he wished to serve another term as president, by now no one doubted that Franklin Roosevelt would be the Democratic candidate— if for no other reason than that the Republicans had nominated Wendell Willkie. Roosevelt himself believed that the opposition had named its strongest possible ticket in Willkie and McNary, and other top Democrats agreed. More important, against the vigorous, dynamic Willkie, they saw Hull and Garner as too old and tired, Ickes and Hopkins as too controversial, Farley as too inexperienced and a Catholic, besides. That left only one man capable of beating the challenger, and that was the champ himself.

By the time the convention was called to order, Roosevelt had managed to squelch his potential opposition. In a talk over luncheon with the secretary of state, who had a shot at the nomination if FDR decided not to run, he had pulled on the Tennesseean's powerful sense of loyalty. Although Hull was sixty-nine years old, a Gallup poll in May indicated that he had a higher vote-getting potential than Roosevelt, based on his ability to carry the Democratic vote of 1936, his greater popularity with Republicans, and the third-term stigma against the president;[2] yet Roosevelt, even while pooh-poohing the idea that he would run for another term, dwelt on Hull's weak points as a candidate. Hull had made no effort whatever to collect delegates, probably because it was his nature to accept the nomination if offered, but not to seek it; so when, in the course of their conversation, the president implied that he, FDR, might have to run for the good of the country and the party, that ended any thoughts the Tennesseean may have had about becoming the nation's chief executive.

As for Garner, he was popular with his fellow legislators, and that was about the extent of it; he was three years older than Hull, for one thing, and between that and the president's success in persuading some of Cactus Jack's delegates (among them Sam Rayburn and the man Rayburn called "that kid Congressman," Lyndon Johnson) not to take part in a stop-Roosevelt movement, FDR had broken the back of the Garner-for-president drive. All that remained for the vice president was to play a spoiler's role and deny Roosevelt the draft he wanted, and Garner had every intention of doing exactly that. With Hull and Garner out of the running, Farley was the only opponent worth mention.

The big Irishman, a brickmaker's son from Grassy Point, New York, had managed Roosevelt's campaigns for governor in 1928 and '30 and his presidential campaigns in '32 and '36, and as chairman of the Democratic National Committee and postmaster general he had been the principal dispenser of patronage, the man to whom office-seekers came in droves. Blessed with a phenomenal memory (it was said he could call fifty thousand party functionaries by their first names), enormous industry, and what Raymond Moley called "inexhaustible geniality," it was Farley to whom the regulars turned for favors and for guidance. You could count on Big Jim: he knew who you were and how many votes you represented, and if he told you he would do something it was as good as done. What delegates in Chicago found bewildering was the way the familiar ground rules had changed so that someone other than Jim—a rank amateur who didn't know what made politics tick—was calling the shots at the convention.

Understandably, Farley had broken with Roosevelt over the third term; he had been bitten by the presidential bug himself, and felt that it was now his turn—even to the extent of informing others in the party that FDR would be the weakest candidate they could name against Willkie. (The president bristled when this was reported to him: "I suppose Jim thinks that *he* is the strongest candidate. . . .") Yet in the best of circumstances, even if FDR had not been running, Farley would have faced an uphill race. As

[2]The public's opinion was not shared by Rexford Tugwell, FDR's loyal friend and adviser, who described Hull as an "elderly gentleman from Tennessee [who] would have suited the professionals in every respect except the vital one that he could not possibly win."

Al Smith had discovered in 1928, the country was not ready to elect a Catholic president. To compound Farley's problem, Roosevelt, with his usual shrewdness and keen sense of timing, had recently broken precedent by appointing a personal representative to the Vatican, thereby enhancing his standing with the Catholic voters to whom Farley looked for support.

The point of no return between the two men was reached in July, just before the convention, when Farley paid a visit to Hyde Park ("He came in looking like a thundercloud," his host said) and was informed by Roosevelt, "I don't want to run and I'm going to tell the convention so." Farley replied curtly, "If you make it specific, the convention will not nominate you."

Then, to Roosevelt's question "What would you do if you were in my place?" the postmaster general responded, "Exactly what General Sherman did many years ago—issue a statement saying I would refuse to run if nominated and would not serve if elected."

The president protested that he could not, in these perilous times, refuse to serve "if nominated and elected," and Farley finally had his answer. He now knew what Roosevelt would do.

After telling FDR that his opposition to a third term would not permit him to manage the 1940 campaign, he left the meeting in a rage—certain that Roosevelt would run for a third term, certain that he would not choose Farley as his running mate.

═══

By Tuesday night, July 16, Harry Hopkins was sure of nine hundred of the eleven hundred delegates, but he wanted a genuine draft—nomination of the president by acclamation. Standing in the way of that goal was Jim Farley, and as long as the man held in such esteem by most delegates chose to hold out, anything resembling a unanimous draft seemed unlikely if not impossible.

What worried Hopkins was that Ed Kelly had been given only 10 percent of the gallery seats, instead of the 20 percent customarily allocated to the local mayor, which lent credence to the rumor that Farley had stolen a leaf from the Willkieites and was planning to pack the galleries with anti-Roosevelt people. Yet, as the president had known when he insisted on Chicago as the site of the convention, Mayor Kelly was nothing if not thorough. This was the same Mayor Kelly who had promised the workers picketing Republic Steel that they could hold a peaceful demonstration on that fateful Memorial Day in 1937, and he was not a man to leave matters to chance. He had made arrangements for hundreds of noisemakers and placards, plus two bands and a pipe organ for a "spontaneous" demonstration, and to ensure that the delegates and the folks in the galleries knew what to do at the appropriate moment, he had stationed a leather-voiced, potbellied gentleman named Thomas D. Garry, Chicago's superintendent of sewers, in a tiny basement room, where the amplifier circuits for the stadium's public address system were located.

That afternoon, President Roosevelt—as sly and evasive as ever—told reporters at his press conference to be sure to listen to the radio that evening, when Kentucky's Senator Alben Barkley would read a message from the White House. It was the first real break in the story that had preoccupied the press for months.

Barkley launched into a typical tub-thumping convention address, but before he was fifteen minutes into it, he made the mistake of mentioning the president's name prematurely, and suddenly the delegates—given their first opportunity in two days to behave like real partisans at a political convention—let loose a genuinely spontaneous outburst which Barkley finally quieted by shouting into the microphone, "A lady has been seriously injured!"

Until this moment the Democratic conclave had never gotten off the ground, and some of the party faithful like Harold Ickes despaired that it ever would. Inevitably, the listening public compared it with the open proceedings that had produced the thrilling cliffhanger in Philadelphia a few weeks earlier. In Chicago, by contrast, the delegates were subdued, almost without hope or expectation, and the affair had the unsavory odor of an assembly rigged by and for one man—Franklin Roosevelt.

On the heels of the demonstration for FDR, waves of Mayor Kelly's friends silently moved into the aisles, carrying signs that read, "Roosevelt and Humanity," as Barkley reached the climax of his speech and began reading the message Roosevelt had originally addressed to Bankhead. When he repeated the statement that the president had not tried to influence the opinion of delegates, and that he had no desire to continue in office or to be nominated, the stadium was dead still.

Barkley went on. "He wishes in all earnestness and sincerity to make it clear that all the delegates to this convention are free to vote for any candidate. That is the message I bear to you from the president of the United States."

For a moment there was utter silence as the thoroughly baffled delegates looked at each other wondering what on earth was happening. Then, suddenly, from all the loudspeakers in the stadium came the roar of a single voice: "WE WANT ROOSEVELT! WE WANT ROOSEVELT!" Kelly's legions started marching through the aisles, Barkley and a few of the delegates began shouting, "We want Roosevelt!" and again, from the loudspeakers came "WE WANT ROOSEVELT!" over and over, "THE PARTY WANTS ROOSEVELT!" and "NEW JERSEY WANTS ROOSEVELT!" and "EVERYBODY WANTS ROOSEVELT!" For forty-five minutes the unseen owner of the voice chanted, at last lifting the stunned delegates to their feet and sending them yelling and cheering into the aisles, waving their banners, pushing and shoving. Six times during the hour-long demonstration Tom Garry ran upstairs from the catacombs to Mayor Kelly's box in order to survey the results of his work. "It was a job right up my alley," he told reporters the next day. "I figured out a lot of my own angles."

What came to be known as the Voice from the Sewer finally subsided, so did the demonstration, and the convention adjourned until the following day, when Franklin Delano Roosevelt's name was put into nomination by Senator Lister Hill of Alabama. Hill was followed to the platform by Carter Glass of Virginia, born before the Civil War, a principled man of Jeffersonian and Jacksonian persuasion who had opposed Roosevelt's deficit financing and heavy spending, who nominated James Aloysius Farley, "a man on whose word every human being can always rely." After the nominations of Millard Tydings of Maryland, John Nance Garner, and Cordell Hull, the roll was called, and an hour and ten minutes later—after Farley had moved that the rules be suspended in order to nominate Franklin Roosevelt by acclamation, and the great hall shook with a roar that was more affection for Big Jim than enthusiasm for FDR—a president became a candidate for a third term for the first time in U.S. history.

It was not the unadulterated draft he had wanted, but it was close enough to one, and Roosevelt could now turn to the question of his running mate. He informed Hopkins in Chicago that Henry Wallace was his man, and when Hopkins replied that the convention might not go along with that choice, the president shouted into the phone, "Well, damn it to hell, they will go for Wallace or I won't run and you can jolly well tell them so." At breakfast the next morning he told Rosenman that he would not make an acceptance speech until he saw who the delegates nominated for vice president.

——

That was the situation on the night of July 18, when the president and the little group of associates sat in the stifling heat and listened to the radio, hearing things go from bad to worse in Chicago. Hopkins had negotiated a deal with the big-city bosses at the convention—Kelly, Pendergast of Kansas City, Hague of Jersey City, Flynn of New York—who agreed to support the nomination of FDR and his vice-presidential choice and get out the votes to elect them. In return, the bosses took over the dispensation of patronage Farley had controlled, and Flynn received Farley's job as national chairman. But Roosevelt, in naming his secretary of agriculture— whom he wanted because he was a good liberal, and because he was expected to attract votes in the normally isolationist farm states—managed to pick a man who was anathema to most Democrats. Henry Wallace's father had been a Republican—secretary of agriculture under Harding and Coolidge, no less; Wallace himself had joined the Democratic Party only recently, and was, in any case, a babe in the woods politically. He might know a lot about hybrid corn and hogs, but a host of Democrats regarded him as a poor administrator, a terrible campaigner, a radical, and a theorist who paid farmers not to grow crops. Not only that: he was a mystic, interested in the occult, and was said to spend hours lying on the ground staring at the stars, to check out a theory about the relation of heavenly bodies to weather cycles.[3] Whatever else he might be, he was definitely not a man the delegates wanted as their vice-presidential nominee, and by the time this had been made plain, Frances Perkins called the White House to see if she could persuade FDR to fly to Chicago to set matters straight.

"Absolutely no," he told her. "I'll have to promise this and that. They'll begin to trade with me. I must not be in a position where I'm going to be traded with."

"The situation is very bad," the labor secretary warned. "Just as sour as it can be."

He was silent for a moment, thinking. Then he said that his wife might go. "Eleanor is pretty good about this kind of thing. You call her. If she says no, tell her to see what I say, but don't tell her that you've talked to me." Whereupon Eleanor Roosevelt, who was at Hyde Park with friends, received a call from Frances Perkins, saying that things were looking black, that the temper of the convention was very ugly, and that if the president wanted Wallace nominated he should come to Chicago. If he wouldn't come, his wife should.

Despite her misgivings, after talking with her husband and Jim Farley, Mrs. Roosevelt flew to Chicago, where the postmaster general met her. She was horrified to discover that "Franklin had not talked to him since the convention opened and had never told him who was his choice for vice president," and she found it difficult to believe that relations between the two men had deteriorated so badly. By the time she reached the convention hall, all the potential candidates except Paul McNutt and William Bankhead had dropped out, angry and disappointed, and the appearance of the president's wife—with her brief, extemporaneous plea that her husband be given the man of his choice to help ease the strains of a third term—restored a certain amount of calm among the delegates, but not much and not for long. While the president sat grimly before the radio, playing solitaire, and finally writing the statement rejecting the nomination, Eleanor Roosevelt endured the agony of sitting with Mrs. Wallace, who asked plaintively, "Why do you suppose they are so opposed to Henry?" after hearing the boos and hisses every time her husband's name was mentioned. Meanwhile, Senator Jimmy Byrnes was rushing up and down the aisles, going from one delegation to another, saying angrily, "For God's sakes, do you want a president or a vice president?" McNutt withdrew from contention, the

---

[3] In her book *Scoundrel Time,* Lillian Hellman tells how the elder Wallace gave his son and daughter-in-law a new Ford for a wedding present. When the newlyweds came out of the church, Henry was so excited to see the automobile that he jumped in and drove off. Hours later he returned, and with the motor still running, called out the window to his bride, "Get in, Ilo, I'd forgotten you."

urban states with their big-city machines swung into line, and at the last, 627 of the 1,100 votes were cast for Henry Wallace. It was enough to win, but it meant that almost half of those present had refused to go along with the president.

Before the tired, embittered delegates could head for their hotels, one last scene remained to be played out. At the White House, the exhausted president, his clothes damp and wrinkled, was wheeled into his bedroom and emerged shortly with his hair freshly brushed, wearing a clean shirt, seemingly as cheerful and carefree as ever. The group that had spent the long evening with him went along to the broadcast room, where he now faced the microphone and began speaking in a clear, strong voice to the delegates in Chicago.

After describing how he was torn between the desire to retire, on one hand, and his conscience, on the other, he stated his reason for accepting their unprecedented nomination.

"Lying awake, as I have, on many nights, I have asked myself whether I have the right, as commander in chief of the army and navy, to call on men and women to serve their country or to train themselves to serve and, at the same time, decline to serve my country in my personal capacity, if I am called upon to do so by the people of my country.

"In times like these—in times of great tension, of great crisis—the compass of the world narrows to a single fact. The fact which dominates our world is the fact of armed aggression, the fact of successful armed aggression, aimed at the form of government, the kind of society that we in the United States have chosen and established for ourselves. It is a fact which no one any longer doubts—which no one is any longer able to ignore."

He had made plans to retire, he went on, but those plans had been made "in a world which now seems as distant as another planet. Today all private plans, all private lives, have been in a sense repealed by an overriding public danger. . . ."

The president's firm, resonant voice came over the loudspeakers, promising that if the people drafted him he would serve to the best of his ability and with all his strength. And as the sound of his words faded away, the delegates in Chicago Stadium were at last united as they rose in a body to cheer the man who would lead them for the third time.

His speech, which Germany's former ambassador to the United States found so menacing, was music to the ear in London. There the mood of the people was cheerful and confident, *The New Yorker*'s correspondent noted. Roosevelt's words—and the knowledge that he would run again—heartened Britons enormously, convincing them that as long as he remained in the White House, help would be forthcoming from America. In the next four years, they were going to need every friend they could get, and in Roosevelt they knew they had one.

CHAPTER 41

———————◆———————

"... the transfer ... may be a vital factor in keeping war from our shores."

O ddly enough, the nominations and the manner in which they came to pass turned out to be more significant than the election campaign that followed. Looking back on what happened, it seemed that the shape of things was frozen at the time the conventions ended, when Roosevelt stated imperiously that he would attend to the nation's needs and stay clear of politics: "I shall not have the time or the inclination," he said in his acceptance speech, "to engage in purely political debate. But I shall never be loath to call the attention of the nation to deliberate or unwitting falsifications of fact." (Which of course left him free to enter the fray whenever he chose to do so.) Although Willkie would soon be barnstorming around the country, shouting himself hoarse, he came across too often as a me-too candidate who appeared to go along with the president on foreign policy and endorse many of the New Deal's domestic achievements, while promising that he could do better in both fields. (As might have been expected, Norman Thomas had a wry comment: Willkie, he said, "agreed with Mr. Roosevelt's entire program of social reform and said it was leading to disaster.")

Just about everything that could go wrong in the Willkie campaign went wrong: he was slow getting started, then, on a sweltering, 102-degree day in his hometown of Elwood, Indiana, before an immense crowd, he delivered an acceptance speech that laid an egg; he put on a whirlwind campaign that took him to every nook and cranny in the United States, in the course of which he was shouted down by hecklers, pelted with eggs and tomatoes, and lost his voice to the extent that it was no more than a croak.

No matter what they may have intended, the two candidates were buffeted this way and that by the unrelenting tide of events. Issues kept intruding, unexpected demands continued to be made on them, and both men found themselves obliged to alter earlier positions in response to the caprice of public opinion or the reality of the situation in Europe.

What had been background noise for so many months was now drowning out just about everything else, as the extreme attitudes on foreign involvement became polarized. Somewhere between those opposing points of view—no one knew exactly where—lay the great body of American public opinion. By the summer of 1940 it was apparent that the Nazi *Blitzkrieg* which had brought France to her knees and left Britain fighting on alone was a milestone, no less than the battle of Hastings or the shelling of Fort Sumter; the relationships that had contained Europe's enmities in fragile equilibrium since 1918 were shattered for good, forcing a change in everyone's perception of the world. Until then that shaky balance of power (which had existed more in people's minds, it proved, than in fact) had provided a sort of intellectual respectability for isolationism in America, but a great many people who had been dodging the question of American involvement had to admit that a watershed had been passed, that true isolation was no longer possible. This realization was being reinforced daily on thirty million radios, Americans having discovered that the broadcast coverage of events in Europe was more immediate, more alive and real, than what they read in their newspapers and magazines, and they relied increasingly on certain voices to give them the truth. Murrow in London was one such authority, certainly; so was Shirer in Berlin; and Elmer Davis in New York was another.

Davis, in fact, could serve as a case history of the changes that had taken place in American thinking. An Indiana boy who went on to Oxford on a Rhodes scholarship and then to the *New York Times* as a reporter, Davis had been a free-lance writer from the early twenties until the day in August 1939, just before war broke out in Europe, when Paul White of CBS hired him to fill in temporarily for H. V. Kaltenborn, who was on vacation. Davis was an idealist who clung to a conviction that America owed its greatness to the many freedoms its people enjoyed, among them access to the truth. From what he had seen of the First World War and its aftermath, he was certain that collective security held the true key to peace; yet even before Munich he realized that collective security, as represented by the weak governments in England and France, was no security at all. He was no isolationist, and had no illusions about Hitler and Mussolini, but he had no faith whatever in Neville Chamberlain and nothing but contempt for British and French imperialism, and had concluded, "The present British government [by which he meant Chamberlain's] is an excellent argument for American isolation." What convinced him that the United States should stay out of the war was a certainty that no fascist power was likely to attack the Americas for some time to come, which meant that this country could limit its commerce in the Atlantic to "open trade, but on a cash-and-carry basis, with belligerents."

Munich changed his mind. Following the betrayal of Czechoslovakia, he wrote sadly, "There is only one great power in Europe," but since this new reality made American security dependent on a British government that was patently unreliable, Davis was more positive than ever that nonintervention was the only course that made sense.

Ten days after Davis joined CBS, Hitler invaded Poland. Sitting in for Kaltenborn, speaking in a no-frills, flat monotone that was unmistakably Indiana, Elmer Davis demonstrated a gift for explaining fast-breaking news so clearly and objectively in the five minutes allotted him that he won the immediate attention of listeners and a permanent job with the network. Before long his prime-time broadcasts had an audience estimated at twelve million; he could be heard in the middle of the morning, as well; occasionally he broadcast a fifteen-minute analysis of the news; and frequently he was the so-called anchorman on news roundups from Columbia's European correspondents.

On the air he was completely impartial,[1] but in magazine articles he began urging economic aid for the Allies. Along with the great majority of his countrymen (including the president) he still believed firmly that no American interest could possibly be served by sending an army to Europe. What provoked the next shift in his thinking was the speed and magnitude of German victory in May and June of 1940. France's surrender ended his preconceived ideas about the war and the probability of Allied victory, and suddenly Davis began wondering if economic aid could possibly be enough to save the British. Within several weeks' time he had joined a loose fellowship of like-minded individuals known as the Century Group, which was seeking a radically different solution to the problem.

———

As Charles Lindbergh was the chief spokesman and point man for the isolationists, William Allen White was widely regarded as his opposite number, and although White claimed to be "only the rooster on the cow-

---

[1]"If I denounce Hitler once," he wrote, "I might do it so forcibly as to impress some of my hearers; but if I denounce him again the next night, and every night thereafter, the customers will say 'We have heard that already' and turn the dial to something else. Meanwhile, when I have occasion to analyze and estimate something that Hitler has done, they will have a little less confidence in my interpretation—even if it is only a recital of a factual record—than if they had never heard me turn loose with unrestrained emotion."

catcher, crowing lustily at the crossroads," he was the man most often associated by the public with the internationalists. White was seventy-two now, and about as close to being a national institution as an elderly newspaperman could be. As he aged he lost some of the round, cherubic look that made him appear, as he put it, like a rear view of Cupid and kept him from being taken as a serious thinker, but he still had the beguiling smile of a mischievous boy and he *was* a serious thinker, particularly when it came to the question of involvement in another European war.

White had been editor of the *Emporia* (Kansas) *Gazette* for almost half a century. He was a popular novelist, the biographer of Calvin Coolidge, the author of countless articles and short stories, a Pulitzer Prize winner, and a tireless foe of the Ku Klux Klan, and what endeared him to so many of his countrymen was the way his writing reflected the values in which they believed. What he wrote came from the heart and the heartland of America. It was homespun and plain-spoken, and as his son remarked, his convictions matched those of the average American more accurately than any Gallup poll could. White believed he knew the values that had made the nation great, and his editorials embodied them: enlightened public opinion; progress that was divinely ordained; the importance of church, school, and small towns in building and preserving democracy; the responsibility of public officials to follow the honest, moral path, to play fair and square. A friend of presidents since Theodore Roosevelt, he had been converted by Teddy from an anti-Populist Republican to a Progressive reformer, and although he returned to the arms of the GOP he never quite lost hope that a truly progressive leader would someday appear on the scene. White was no fan of the New Deal, believing that it relied too heavily on special-interest groups and too little on individual entrepreneurs, yet he liked Franklin Roosevelt, after a fashion. He had known him for two decades, and with acquaintance had come recognition of the other's weaknesses (they "put up with each other," White said), but he missed in Franklin what he had admired in Theodore: "a certain ruggedness, the ability to quarrel bitterly with a man and then take him to his heart and forget the quarrel."

At the president's behest, White had come to Washington in the fall of 1939 to head up a committee working to repeal the arms embargo, and that was the genesis of another group he founded in mid-May of 1940 with Clark Eichelberger, the national director of the League of Nations Association. The two men were alarmed by America's complacency, and that spring they began discussing how they could arouse the public. Immediately after the Germans invaded the Low Countries, White sent a telegram to several hundred prominent citizens, urging them to join him in trying to win public support for increased aid to the allies. On May 20, he announced the formation of a nationwide organization called the Committee to Defend America by Aiding the Allies (CDAAA), which White described as an "engine of publicity and propaganda." The group supported all-out aid for

Britain and France, and within six weeks nearly seven hundred local chapters were functioning in forty-seven states, sending telegrams, letters, and petitions to the White House and Capitol Hill, while sponsoring rallies, radio broadcasts, and newspaper ads.

If "the future of Western civilization is being decided on the battlefield of Europe," as White was certain it was, then it was folly for this nation to be "chained to a neutrality policy determined in the light of last year's facts." America, he said, must "spend every ounce of energy to keep the war away from the Western hemisphere by preparing to defend herself and aiding with our supplies and wealth the nations now fighting to stem the tide of aggression. . . . If they fail, we shall not have time to prepare to face their conqueror alone." By now neither White nor Roosevelt, whose warm blessings the committee had, doubted that a substantial majority in the United States hoped for Allied victory. During the period of the "phony war," most Americans simply assumed that the British and French would ultimately win, and saw no pressing reason to send them aid. (Indeed, as late as May 24, a thin 51 percent of those polled thought we should sell airplanes on credit to the Allies, if they could not pay cash; 49 percent believed we should not.) At the beginning of June, however, according to a Gallup poll, two thirds believed that Germany would triumph and would one day attack the United States. A like number thought that America would ultimately go to war, and three fourths felt that the nation should provide greater assistance to the Allies. So public sentiment was as clear as it could possibly be, favoring Great Britain and France, opposing Germany—except on one absolutely vital point. Only one citizen in fourteen supported a declaration of war on Germany. What it came down to was wishing the French and British well in their struggle, but not caring enough, or not feeling sufficiently threatened, to become deeply involved. Along with William Allen White, Americans believed that Hitler's defeat was a matter of vital concern to the United States, but under no circumstances should we become involved in the war.

Editor White shared President Roosevelt's reluctance to move too far ahead of public opinion, but another group that was becoming active at this time—the organization Elmer Davis had joined—felt that White and his committee did not go far enough. These interventionists, who favored some kind of immediate action by America or, at the very least, a form of action that would eventually lead to war, had been influenced—as had both Theodore and Franklin Roosevelt—by the theories of Alfred Thayer Mahan, the philosopher of sea power, particularly by Mahan's recognition of the British fleet as America's shield in the Atlantic. They believed, moreover, that our failure to join the League of Nations was the cardinal sin of U.S. foreign policy, an egregious mistake that had evaded responsible action and led to Europe's present war. In the years since, adherents of an active international policy had formed organization after organization, pushing for membership in the League[2] and the World Court, advocating disarmament, economic sanctions against aggression, support for Britain and France against Germany, repeal of the neutrality legislation—everything, in short, that the isolationists opposed.

While interventionist sentiment was heaviest in New England and along the Atlantic seaboard, where geographical proximity to Europe, familial and cultural ties to England, and the presence of a large Jewish population all favored active opposition to Nazi Germany, ideas on what form American assistance should take varied widely. The common denominator was that the nation must do *something,* and soon. Now that Britain alone survived, there was the fear of eventual Axis hegemony in Latin America, Africa, and much of the Far East, with the appalling possibility that America would be cut off from its sources of vital raw materials.

———

The results of the latest Gallup poll of American attitudes toward Europe appeared on Sunday, June 2, the same day that seven friends of Mr. and Mrs. Francis Pickens Miller joined them at their home in Fairfax, Virginia, for a discussion of this very topic. The gathering of friends came about at the urging of Richard Cleveland, son of the former president and a leader of the National Policy Committee, and as they discussed the frightening prospects facing the nation—loss of the British fleet, invasion of England, Nazi conquest of Africa and Latin America—the group agreed unanimously that the United States should declare war on Germany at once. One of those present was Whitney Shepardson, author of the annual report published by the Council on Foreign Relations, and as the others began compiling a list of influential people who might be enlisted to help, he retired to another room and drafted a statement to be signed by those influential people. The Miller group called the statement "A Summons to Speak Out," and its message was unmistakable: after summarizing the clear and present threat posed by Germany and the reasons America should be deeply concerned, it stated that U.S. interests could be defended most effectively by General Weygand's troops then fighting along the Somme. Since the Allies were really fighting our battle as well as their own, the United States ought to dispatch "all disposable air, naval, military, and material resources" to the front and declare "that a state of war exists between this country and Germany."

That was strong medicine—too strong for most of the 127 influential

---

[2]Franklin Roosevelt was indisputably an internationalist, but his attitude toward the League of Nations had been colored by the practicalities of politics. He and Cox had been roundly defeated in 1920 on that issue, and in the late twenties and early thirties he could see that Americans generally wanted no part of it. In 1932, rather than risk the opposition of the isolationist press baron William Randolph Hearst to his campaign for the Democratic nomination, he bowed to expediency and came out against membership in the League.

citizens to whom it was sent—yet thirty agreed to sign, and on Monday, June 10, 1940, the "Summons" appeared in a number of leading newspapers throughout the country. What the group could not have foreseen was that the headlines that day would be preempted by Mussolini's invasion of France, the Germans' approach to within thirty-five miles of Paris, and speculation concerning President Roosevelt's speech in Charlottesville that afternoon. The "Summons" also had to compete with a dramatic full-page ad in *The New Yorker* and other magazines entitled "Stop Hitler Now," sponsored by White's committee and written by playwright Robert Sherwood, which called on the public to demand that the U.S. act immediately by sending planes, guns, munitions, and food to the Allies (but by no means declaring war). That was the only way, the Sherwood ad stated, that "we can help to end the fear that American boys will fight and die in another Flanders, closer to home." Given the attitude of most Americans, the White committee's approach stood a far better chance of success than any appeal to declare war. So the "Summons" was ignored or largely forgotten by most who saw it, but it caught the eye of a Protestant clergyman who was annoyed that its sponsors had not asked him to sign the statement. The message said precisely what he had been itching to say publicly, and when he saw his friends Francis and Helen Miller later that month he complained about their failure to include his name on the list.

The name was Henry Pitt Van Dusen, and the man taught at New York's Union Theological Seminary, where he was at odds with some of the faculty members and most of the students over his view that a Christian should be willing to take up arms to defend his faith against the infidel. Van Dusen was a big man with a big voice and a big, expansive manner—so persuasive, one of his students said, that you could imagine him selling snake oil to the Indians; even without the marvelous red robe he wore with such obvious zest in the pulpit, he was a distinct, almost overpowering presence. In the course of his talk with the Millers, it was decided that they would enlist an influential interventionist to play host at a small dinner to rally folk of similar persuasion. In the meantime, Dr. Van Dusen headed for Washington to see the British ambassador, Lord Lothian. Pitt Van Dusen was not one to withhold his opinions, and in his powerful, resonant voice he informed Lothian about the group that was forming and stated that the members would undertake to rally all-out aid for the British on condition that they would not surrender, that the government would move to Canada in the event of a successful German invasion, and that the Royal Navy would fight to the finish. It seems not to have occurred to Van Dusen that this might be more of a commitment than Lothian would make on behalf of His Majesty's Government to a clergyman he had just met for the first time, but he was relieved to hear that the Royal Navy had every intention of fighting to the last man. Having reassured him on that score, the ambassador then suggested that the minister and his colleagues devote their energies to a specific problem that needed urgent attention. How would they like to persuade the United States Navy to release some of its overage destroyers for the defense of the British Isles?

———

A week later, Lewis W. Douglas, an insurance executive who had been Roosevelt's first budget director, gave a dinner in New York City for eleven friends, five of them signers of "A Summons to Speak Out." All agreed that the United States had to become involved in the war, and the question before them was how to convince other Americans. Within a couple of weeks, sixteen others had joined this band of believers, and they began calling themselves the Century Group because they usually met at a private men's club in New York known as the Century Association. It was, by and large, a collection of considerable talent and influence—and unmistakably Eastern establishment. In addition to Miller, Douglas, and Van Dusen, the group included two attorneys who would become secretary of state—Dean Acheson and John Foster Dulles; clergymen Henry Sloane Coffin of Union Seminary and Episcopal bishop Henry W. Hobson; publishers Harold Guinzburg and Henry Luce; playwright Robert Sherwood and the film-maker Walter Wanger; a retired admiral and former chief of naval operations, William H. Standley; businessmen Will Clayton and James Warburg; several college presidents—James Bryant Conant of Harvard, Henry Wriston of Brown, and Ernest Hopkins of Dartmouth; and several eminent journalists, among them Geoffrey Parsons, George Fielding Eliot, Joseph Alsop, and Elmer Davis.

In short order, the Century Group and White's Committee to Defend America by Aiding the Allies were working together (their divergent philosophies would take them on different paths, but that was in the future), and they had agreed that one of the first orders of business was to do something about that transfer of destroyers the British ambassador had suggested to Pitt Van Dusen.

The public was unaware of what was going on behind the scenes, but five days after Winston Churchill became prime minister he had sent Roosevelt a desperate request for fifty or sixty overage destroyers, since which time the president had been seeking a way to circumvent the legal and political stumbling blocks, and had just about despaired of doing so. For all anyone in Washington or London knew, the invasion of England might begin in a week or two, but the president could have been bound hand and foot. His frustration appeared to the columnist Joseph Alsop as lethargy; to William Allen White it seemed excessive caution; as White put it, the man in the White House had "lost his cud." Right or wrong, Roosevelt had decided that he had to look to outside help, and whether or not it would materialize in time to be of use to the British was anybody's guess. The circuitous, often devious, route that was taken says something about how difficult it was to accomplish anything of this nature in 1940, while suggesting at the same time what a small band of determined individuals outside the government can accomplish once they set their minds to it.

No one could doubt the need. Thirty-year-old Joseph Alsop, the youngest member of the Century Group, was given the task of determining the Royal Navy's plight and the availability of U.S. ships, and he learned that after Dunkirk the British had only sixty-eight destroyers fit for service. (That compared with almost 450 in 1917, when the demands on them were far less formidable.) On the other hand, the United States Navy certainly had ships to spare: the fleet boasted more destroyers than the combined navies of the world, including 140 recommissioned World War I "four-pipers" (so called because they had four smokestacks, or pipes). On the face of it, a simple matter, surely, but the destroyer issue quickly became a very hot potato. Secretary of State Hull hemmed and hawed about the legal implications; President Roosevelt feared the political risks at a time when he was running for a third term and trying to fend off the isolationists in Congress; Wendell Willkie suddenly realized that he represented the entire Republican Party and that the party included such unreconstructed noninterventionists as Ham Fish, Gerald Nye, Robert Taft, Arthur Vandenberg, and a lot more; and if that weren't enough to kill the scheme, the so-called Walsh rider to the naval appropriations bill of June 1940 forbade the sale of such "surplus military material" unless the chief of naval operations certified that it was not essential to national defense. (David Walsh, chairman of the Senate Naval Affairs Committee, had written the amendment to avert precisely the kind of monkey business that was now being proposed.)

Faced with what looked to be an unscalable stone wall, Alsop hit on the idea of asking Roosevelt and Willkie to state jointly that the transfer of destroyers to Britain was in the national interest. Hull, Stimson, and Knox, he knew, all favored that approach, Hull in particular welcoming it on the remote chance that it might help to keep divisive foreign policy arguments out of the campaign. Meantime, Henry Luce was insisting that some *quid pro quo* be provided by London—a promise, on the one hand, that the British fleet would not be surrendered, plus an arrangement by which the United States could use British possessions in the western hemisphere for naval and air bases. Earlier, Winston Churchill had had the same idea, but for entirely different reasons: the United States, he observed bitterly, "had given us practically no help in the war, and now that they saw how great was the danger their attitude was that they wanted to keep everything which would help us for their own defense." He was willing to offer the Americans the use of British bases, but only in return for definite assurance of assistance. For their part, American officials were somberly contemplating the likelihood of British defeat and the surrender of the fleet, which could open the door to German intervention in South America and further Japanese expansion in the Pacific, and they wanted guarantees that the Royal Navy would remain a bulwark for the United States. It was all very well for the Americans to engage in such speculation, but Winston Churchill would have none of it, fearing the effect on his people's morale if they learned that the possibility of eventual defeat was even being whispered. In a cable to Roosevelt on July 31, he stated that four British destroyers had been sunk and seven others damaged within the past ten days; he hoped the president could "ensure that 50 or 60 of your oldest destroyers are sent to me at once." Three days later his cabinet approved the concept of exchanging bases for destroyers—but on some kind of lease basis, at Mr. Churchill's insistence.

Three delegates from the Century Group called on Mr. Roosevelt to "talk turkey" and obtain his approval of several ideas, including what they euphemistically called a "radio program of education," and he responded by suggesting that a broadcast by General John J. Pershing would be very helpful indeed. Francis Miller and another man promptly called on a close friend of Pershing's, who persuaded the general's former chief of staff to make an appointment; Herbert Agar of the Century Group and Walter Lippmann drafted a speech, Alsop arranged for radio time, and Agar went to see Pershing to tell him of the president's request.

Steely-eyed, lean, and erect, Black Jack Pershing was the picture of what a General of the Armies ought to be.[3] Now in his eightieth year, he had served in the cavalry during the Indian wars, fought in Cuba and the Philippines, pursued Pancho Villa in Mexico, and commanded the American Expeditionary Force in France, helping to turn the tide against the Germans in 1918. For these and other reasons he was an authentic hero to Americans, and although he was now in poor health, he recognized a call to duty when he heard one, and against the advice of his doctor agreed to give the talk. On Sunday evening, August 4, the old warrior told his countrymen that he was speaking to them because he considered it his duty and because "all the things we hold most dear are threatened." The British are in desperate need of destroyers right now, he said; the next weeks will be crucial; we have "an immense reserve" of those vessels left over from the last war, and if they could be employed to save the Royal Navy, "they may save us from the danger and hardship of another war." As for the argument heard in Congress that we should do nothing lest we risk having to send our boys to Europe again, "it would be absolute folly even to consider sending another expeditionary force. No one is considering it and those who may say that anyone is considering it are deceiving themselves and deceiving you."

As luck would have it, Charles Lindbergh spoke that same night to forty thousand cheering partisans in Chicago's Soldiers Field, urging cooperation with the Germans if they won the war. America's goal is the supremacy of

---

[3]At the coronation of George VI in May of 1937, Pershing was one of three representatives of the United States and appeared in an extraordinary uniform he had designed himself—fore-and-aft hat with ostrich plumes; gold stars and gold oak leaves on his collar, cuffs, and belt; blue trousers with a gold stripe; buff sash draped over his right shoulder. The American press found it incomprehensible that the old boy could wear a uniform he had designed himself, and it caused quite a stir back home, where fancy uniforms were hardly the rage.

western civilization, he argued, and only by offering a plan for peace, staying out of Europe's internal affairs, and strengthening this nation's defenses could that goal be achieved. This coincidental juxtaposition of the aging hero summoning the country to aid a stricken ally and the young one suggesting that we side with the winner was made to order for a *New York Times* editorial writer, who observed that fifty overage destroyers in the British Channel *now* would be a far greater deterrent to the Germans than the same fifty destroyers patrolling the coasts of Brazil and Patagonia long after Hitler had won. In any policy there are risks, the writer continued, but aloofness might be riskiest of all.

Senator Claude Pepper of Florida put the case more bluntly. The American people were going to have to decide whether to follow "the chief of the fifth column in this country, Colonel Lindbergh," or General Pershing. The general, he added somewhat gratuitously, "never had a medal from the head of the German air force." At which his colleague Senator Lee of Oklahoma chimed in to say that "Lindbergh clasped the hand of Hitler which was slithering in blood."

At a cabinet meeting described afterward by Henry Stimson and Harold Ickes as one of the most important they ever attended, it was decided that the release of the destroyers was imperative, that the United States must be granted the right to use British bases in the Atlantic, and that the president should ask William Allen White to approach Willkie to see if he would support a destroyers-for-bases deal. White, who was joined in his mission by Lewis Douglas, found Willkie in favor of the exchange but unwilling to make a public statement to that effect. Congressman Joe Martin, his newly appointed national chairman, had visited him just before White got to him and urged that he leave legislative matters bearing on foreign policy to those on Capitol Hill who had been fighting the administration tooth and nail for some time. Willkie was an internationalist, obviously; the most important Republicans in House and Senate were not; and it would not do to give the public the impression that the candidate and the party were going in opposite directions. Walter Lippmann, who had been urging the GOP nominee to take a hard line, to be "the Churchill rather than the Chamberlain of the crisis" and convince the voters that Roosevelt was neither strong nor competent, by now realized that Willkie was "unable to master the Republican Party." He had been nominated by it but he certainly had no control over it, so when Willkie spoke out on the question on August 9, it was to say that he did not think it appropriate for him to enter into advance commitments. That, he reminded his listeners, was precisely the position Roosevelt had taken when asked for similar assurances by Hoover in November of 1932.

Lest the president think his mission a failure, White telegraphed the White House: "It's not as bad as it seems. . . . I know there is not two bits difference between you on the issue pending." That was cold comfort to a man hard pressed, unsure if his opponent would use the matter for political advantage, but for the time being it was all the assurance he was going to get.

From another quarter came the breakthrough the president had been seeking. On August 11 the *New York Times* published a letter signed by the Century Group's Dean Acheson and several other distinguished lawyers, setting forth the opinion written by Acheson and Benjamin Cohen that "there is no reason for us to put a strained or unnecessary interpretation on our own statutes contrary to our national interests." If it was in the national interest to let the British have fifty overage destroyers (and we had that on no less an authority than General Pershing), then there was no necessity for Congress to pass new legislation to make it happen. An approach to Congress was, of course, exactly what the president wished to avoid; as he informed Lothian, all it would take to kill the destroyer exchange was a filibuster by fifteen or twenty isolationists in the Senate. The lawyers, citing Acts of Congress, rulings by the attorney general, and decisions of the Supreme Court, argued that the intent of all those precedents was to prevent the United States, as a neutral nation, from constructing, fitting out, arming, and delivering ships of war to belligerents. (Indeed, the cash-and-carry terms of the neutrality legislation authorized private concerns to sell arms to belligerents while making it illegal for the government to do so.) However, since none of the destroyers had been built or armed on the orders of a belligerent or with the intention of entering the service of a belligerent, there was no reason they could not be released to a private contractor and sold to the British—particularly when "General Pershing is high authority for the view that the transfer . . . may be a vital factor in keeping war from our shores." It was conceivable, in fact, that as a result of the transfer of destroyers, "arrangements might be made which would increase our defensive power in this hemisphere." And who could argue with that? (Well, Admiral Harold Stark, for one, although it was doubtful if he would choose to do so: this business of the warships put the chief of naval operations on the spot, since he had recently recommended that the nation build a two-ocean navy with all possible speed and would now be faced with the task of telling Congress he didn't really need those fifty men-of-war.)

The legal justification suited President Roosevelt, which was what mattered, and with that in hand the other pieces fell into place. It was reasonably certain that Willkie would at least be cooperative, and Charles McNary, the vice-presidential nominee, let it be known that he would make no objections to the deal (though he would not support it in the Senate). Although Churchill would permit no discussion relating to the future disposition of the fleet, he said he would reiterate what he had said in his speech of June 4—that Great Britain would never surrender, and that even if England was subjugated, the empire, "armed and guarded by the British fleet, would carry on the struggle." Finally, a public opinion poll taken in mid-August indicated that 62 percent of those Americans questioned approved of selling the destroyers.

So success was in sight, but at the last moment the whole carefully concocted scheme threatened to come apart over a question of appearances. From the beginning, Churchill had resisted any effort to portray the exchange of bases for destroyers as a horse trade. On August 20, in another great speech to the House of Commons, when he paid tribute to the small band of RAF fighter pilots who were fighting off the Luftwaffe, saying, "Never in the field of human conflict was so much owed by so many to so few," he spoke of how the British Empire and the United States "will have to be mixed up together in some of their affairs for mutual and general advantage," and went on to say that he viewed the process with no misgivings whatever. On the contrary, he said, "I could not stop it if I wished; no one can stop it. Like the Mississippi, it just keeps rolling along."

That was the kind of allusion that appealed to Americans, and Churchill knew it. Even though the agreement on the bases seemed to many of his own countrymen to be a distinctly one-sided bargain favoring the Americans, he was determined that the relationship between the two countries be perceived as one based on generosity and dedication to a common cause, not money (though he was painfully aware of the parlous state of Britain's finances), and he refused to have it cast as a *quid pro quo*. Roosevelt, of course, was guided by a knowledge of how Congress and a large segment of the American public would react to giving away fifty men-of-war no matter what their age or condition, and he wanted the exchange to be seen as a hardheaded business arrangement. At the last moment, the dilemma was solved by a lawyer in the State Department, who suggested dividing the bases into two groups—some to be given to the United States, some to be leased—thus providing Churchill with his generous gesture and Roosevelt with his shrewd Yankee trade.

What no one involved in the complex negotiations foresaw was the enthusiasm with which most of the American public would view the agreement.

To the delight of the Century Group, William Allen White, and the Roosevelt administration, Wendell Willkie promised not to attack the deal, and the president was able to announce it to the White House press corps on September 3. Comparing it to the Louisiana Purchase, he explained somewhat disingenuously that he—like Thomas Jefferson—had been obliged to proceed without consulting Congress lest the opportunity vanish. That created a predictable stir on Capitol Hill, with old George Tinkham of Massachusetts condemning it as "the first long step toward war" and saying there was no difference between Roosevelt's action and those of Hitler, Stalin, and Mussolini. Yet the furor was surprisingly mild and short-lived. Even the rabidly isolationist *Chicago Tribune* applauded the arrangement as a triumph, since it gave the nation "naval and air bases in regions which must be brought within the American defense zone," and the public appeared to be all for it.[4] Henry Stimson decided that the tide of opinion had swung: people were beginning to think that Britain might survive after all.

The parties most directly affected were on the far rim of the Atlantic, and Winston Churchill was secretly elated, knowing that the gesture—which was the act of a nation that could by no stretch of the imagination be considered a neutral any longer—might prove far more important than the destroyers. He predicted that it would bring the United States "definitely nearer to us and the war." In Germany, Admiral Erich Raeder saw it the same way, recognizing that it moved American air and naval frontiers far into the Atlantic Ocean, from which the United States might occupy Spain, Portugal, and parts of West Africa in the future. Mussolini warned Hitler that U.S. involvement in the war was "a possibility to be faced any day now." On the other hand, it was difficult to see how the British could hold out much longer. They seemed to be "fighting on as bravely as ever," Harold Ickes wrote in his diary, "although I doubt whether any people have ever had to take such terrific punishment."

[4]The seven bases, located between the Caribbean and Newfoundland, included Trinidad and Bermuda, and were leased for ninety-nine years.

CHAPTER 42

"You burned the city of London in our houses ..."

In the pandemonium that followed his broadcast about the Martian invasion of America, Orson Welles was surrounded by a small army of reporters throwing questions, and in that unguarded moment he hit upon the most plausible explanation of a remarkable phenomenon. "Radio is new," he said, "and we are learning about the effect it has on people." One man who was acutely aware of its effect on people was Adolf Hitler; another was Franklin Roosevelt, who well knew how to employ radio on special occasions for special purposes. But neither possessed quite the same mastery of the medium as the man who was describing for Americans, night after night, the real war between the worlds.

What happened, as the British people began their excruciating trial by fire, was that thirty-two-year-old Edward R. Murrow became their ambassador-without-portfolio, their objective advocate before the people of the United States. Murrow had come untutored to his task, but he was a natural—born to the role, it seemed, and no one matched his extraordinary talent for going to the heart of the news, interviewing the most ordinary people, and, in the retelling of their tales, making you realize that you had heard the authentic voice of Britain at war. Radio had truly come into its own by the summer of 1940, and the medium and the men who were spreading the word from London were admirably suited to the moment.

Chief among them were Churchill, of course, inspiring his countrymen and the entire free world; the English novelist and playwright J. B. Priestley, giving three or four talks a week to millions of Englishmen at home and in the outposts of empire, at the same time reaching people in occupied Europe who crouched over radio sets turned down to a whisper lest the Gestapo discover them; and Ed Murrow, broadcasting to his fellow Americans. In England, as the battle wore on, radio came to be the primary source of news. In heavily bombed areas, newspaper deliveries were haphazard at best; the shortage of newsprint limited the coverage of events; and people had little energy left for reading after spending the night in a shelter—it was easier to sit back and listen. In addition to what they got via the BBC, Britons could hear the voice of Irish-born William Joyce, the so-called Lord Haw-Haw, who had moved to England in 1921 and then to Germany in 1939, where he offered his services to the Nazis—his services just now being a nightly broadcast from Hamburg, a mixture of fact and fiction in which he called special attention to such unfavorable aspects of British life as unemployment, malnutrition, and profiteering. You could even hear Lord Haw-Haw in New York at 3:15 and 5:15 on weekday afternoons, and 9:30 P.M. on Sundays, but America's listening public preferred its news from London direct, and there was plenty of it to choose from, with thirteen shortwave broadcasts on weekdays, and eleven on Sundays.

A number of first-rate reporters were on the job in England, and while none had Murrow's particular gift for radio, the unique place he occupied in America's households came about for other reasons as well. He reached millions whose only source of foreign news was a provincial paper; yet whatever paper they read, he beat it by hours, delivering the news first because often he was reporting it as it happened. His voice had become more familiar than those of most other reporters, he was more believable than the politicians people heard on radio, and above all, listeners felt, he could be trusted. At the time of Munich, when he was still new in the job, he had already formed a clear picture of his mission: "We are trying to provide material on which an opinion may be formed," he said, "but we are not trying to suggest what that opinion should be." During that crisis, Americans grew accustomed to hearing someone at CBS in New York: "Calling Ed Murrow in London. Come in, Ed Murrow." And two years later they were listening for Murrow's unmistakable voice to begin his broadcasts with a portentous "This is London."

Murrow came as a guest into America's living rooms each night at an appointed hour and became as much a part of the daily routine as coming home from the office and asking what's for dinner. While style had something to do with it, his remarkable acceptance by the public was more a consequence of his determination to bring them the unvarnished truth, his refusal to stoop to easy emotionalism, even when dealing with the most emotional of subjects—the questions of life and death. It was his particular talent to give an account of the day's news with little or no editorializing (though he knew as well as any skilled actor the value of a brief pause—as in "This . . . is London"—or a slight change of inflection)[1] and to tell it straight enough to pass the British censor yet compellingly enough to keep his audience in America on the edge of their seats. "I'm standing on a rooftop looking out over London," he would say. "You may be able to hear the sound of guns off in the distance very faintly, like someone kicking a tub. . . . you'll hear two bursts a little nearer in a moment. There they are! That hard, stony sound." Eric Sevareid believed that Murrow led a charmed life, because he had that "extra mysterious sense that detects danger without benefit of sight or hearing." Leaving the BBC studio one night, Murrow, Sevareid, and Larry LeSueur were walking along the side of the building and suddenly, although they had heard nothing, Murrow stepped quickly into a doorway, the others following immediately. As they did, a large, jagged casing from an antiaircraft shell landed precisely where they had been.

The Murrows' apartment was in one of the most severely bombed areas of London, he was bombed out of three offices, and as the war drew ever closer to America, having Ed Murrow in your living room was like having a close friend on the scene of a great historical event—a friend who stopped in to see you on his way home each evening to tell you exactly what had happened. In the process of informing Americans how things went in England, assuring them through one homely example after another that the British could take everything the Germans threw at them, he was helping to break down the wall of isolationism while building a feeling of unity between the two countries. In September he mentioned that his Italian barber was still doing business even though the shop had no windows: "Someday we smile again," the man said, "but the food it doesn't taste so good since being bombed." On another occasion Murrow stopped at a store and asked for three flashlight batteries. As he reported the incident, "The clerk said: 'You needn't buy so many. We'll have enough for the whole winter.' But, I said: 'What if you aren't here?' There were buildings down in the street, and he replied: 'Of course we'll be here. We've been in business for a hundred and fifty years.' "

His stories were revealing, and they gained in the telling from his low, resonant voice (someone described it as "sepulchral" and at times it did have that quality)—a voice that occasionally reflected utter exhaustion, sadness or anger or revulsion at what he had seen. It didn't seem to matter if he was broadcasting from the studio deep beneath street level in the BBC building or talking into a microphone from Trafalgar Square, you knew it was real, and he made you see what was happening, thanks in part to that newness of radio Orson Welles had mentioned, and to the peculiar magic

[1]The pause was suggested to him in a letter from Ida Lou Anderson, with whom he had studied drama and speech at the University of Washington. She said she thought it would be more effective if he hesitated ever so slightly after the word "This," as indeed it was.

of radio that allows you to use your imagination. Murrow was not only a gifted man at the microphone; he was a remarkable reporter. As soon as the big bombing raids over London began, he liked to get in his little Sunbeam-Talbot with the top down and drive all over the city, to see what he could find. His friend Vincent Sheean, the writer, was terrified by Ed Murrow's driving but amazed at how "his courage, endurance, and obliviousness to fatigue made it possible for him to survive many months of a cruel schedule. He could go without sleep as long as might be necessary, broadcasting at all sorts of hours and working like a slave between times. His courage was of the kind I most respect; that is, it did not consist in lack of sensitivity to danger, but in a professional determination to ignore it in the interests of his job."[2]

When Murrow returned briefly to the United States late in 1941, CBS put on a dinner in his honor, and Archibald MacLeish, the poet who was Librarian of Congress, rose to pay tribute to the man from London. During the months when the world watched to see if the British would survive, MacLeish said, Murrow succeeded in destroying America's "superstition that what is done beyond three thousand miles of water is not really done at all; the ignorant superstition that violence and lies and murder on another continent are not violence and lies and murder here; the cowardly and brutal superstition that the enslavement of mankind in a country where the sun rises at midnight by our clocks is not enslavement by the time we live by; the black and stifling superstition that what we cannot see and hear and touch can have no meaning for us." How much of that achievement was Murrow's and how much was the medium he used, MacLeish was not prepared to say, but the fact was that Murrow had accomplished some sort of miracle when others using the medium had not. Looking directly at the reporter, the poet said, "You burned the city of London in our houses and we felt the flames that burned it. You laid the dead at our doors and we knew the dead were our dead—were all men's dead—were mankind's dead—and ours."

———

Ed and Janet Murrow had arrived in London three years before the Battle of Britain began, and as it became apparent that things were going to get very rough there, he urged her to return to the States, to get out while she could, but she had no more wish to leave than he did: they had made so many friends, as yet they had no child to consider, and so she stayed. For a while, she had a job with the State Department, helping with the evacuation of young people to America, but that ended when the *City of Benares* and other ships carrying children were torpedoed. Then she was asked to

---

[2]Murrow and his wife, Janet, avoided air-raid shelters—she because she feared being trapped underground more than she feared being blown up, he because "once you start going to shelters, you lose your nerve."

organize a committee to distribute gifts of clothing and food from Bundles for Britain, and for a year, during the worst of the bombing, she worked at that. "Everyone was in the same boat," she said, "living day to day, not thinking about tomorrow, working as hard as possible." Janet's hours were basically 9:00 to 5:00; Ed's were anything but normal, but usually they managed to have dinner together. He broadcast regularly at 1:00 A.M., so he could be heard "live" in America during prime evening listening time, and after signing off he often went out with friends—other correspondents, mostly—stopped in at a pub, or went around the city to see what was happening. Sometimes he didn't return to their Hallam Street flat until 3:00 A.M. or later, and usually slept until 10:00—long after Janet had left for work.

Fortunately, their life in London had its sane, normal moments: some days Ed played golf; they found a place outside the city where they could spend weekends, usually with friends in tow, from which Janet commuted to London to lunch with friends, work at Bundles for Britain, shop, give the occasional dinner at the Savoy, or go to the theater; and she spent a lot of time looking for a house in the country—an improvement on what they had—which they could share with another couple.

Like so many others, Janet Murrow recalled vividly that "glorious, glorious summer" of 1940 and how the business of living became increasingly difficult even before the bombs began falling. A young Welsh girl named Betty, the daughter of an unemployed miner, worked for them, and because the Murrows were so busy, she made the rounds of the shops, getting in food. Rationing was in effect, and since just about everything—meat, produce, fish, baked goods—came from a different store, shopping was a trying, tedious business. Plenty of milk was available, fortunately, and fish was unrationed, but meat could be had only once a week; the weekly quota of eggs was two to a person; to the dismay of Londoners, tea was rationed at the rate of two ounces per person per week; and it was increasingly hard to come by many other foods. But food, it soon became clear, was to be the least of their worries.

———

For a period of six months, between the fall of France and the end of 1940, what was called a world war was waged solely between Germany and Britain, the two powers that had emerged triumphant from the Victorian era, whose rivalry had grown in intensity for half a century. As they faced each other in what appeared to be the final showdown, it was logical to assume that the world's greatest army or the world's greatest navy would decide the outcome, but the battle was in fact taking place not on land or sea but in the sky, fought by the two rival air forces, and on a scale unexpectedly small. The fate of Britain and perhaps of the empire was to be decided in a new kind of conflict in which the worst day's fighting involved a total of 2,800 combatants, of whom 105 lost their lives.

From Hermann Göring's point of view, the task of knocking out the RAF looked easy. The first bombs were dropped on England near Canterbury on the night of May 9, and in short order the collapse of France presented the Luftwaffe with fifty-odd bases in northern France and Holland, putting even short-range planes within a twenty-five-mile striking distance of the English coast. It was not to be so simple.

The Nazis' air assault on Britain, Winston Churchill remarked, proved to be "a tale of divided counsels, conflicting purposes, and never fully accomplished plans," and it was characterized by three distinct phases. Central to German strategy was the destruction of the Royal Air Force, which had to be accomplished before an invasion could be launched, and it was that goal that led to the first phase, known then and ever after as the Battle of Britain, the daylight battle which began during the first week of July and lasted until the climactic 15th of September, commemorated as Battle of Britain Day.[3]

At the beginning came the harassment of convoys and Channel ports from Dover to Plymouth, and the bombing of coastal airfields and radar installations during July 10 and early August, the purpose being to clear the Channel of British shipping, while drawing the Royal Air Force into battle to knock it out of the sky. Next, the Luftwaffe would press inland, seeking out the RAF's airdromes and its entire support system, including the factories in which Britain's planes were made, and this second phase would occur between the end of August and late September. By the time the Luftwaffe had carried out these first two assignments, it was believed, the way would be clear for the grand finale: Sea Lion—the invasion of England.

Phase One of the onslaught was made to order for the press, and seldom have participants in battle been made more of, and for good reason, than the RAF fighter pilots. Because the range of Luftwaffe fighters was limited, most of the fighting occurred within a space about forty miles wide, twice that long, and five or six miles high. Ben Robertson, a South Carolinian reporting for the New York newspaper *PM,* wrote, "No journalist could stay away from Dover after he had sat all day on Shakespeare Cliff and watched those battles. Nowhere in England could the fighting be observed with such detachment and perspective. We could see the raids start, see them fought and ended, and we could get some idea of their general aspect, of how their tactics changed from day to day. The cliff was almost a stage-setting, so perfect was it as an observation point, and as a result the press of the whole democratic world gathered on it."

Dover, chief of the Cinque Ports, only seventeen miles from France, for a thousand years and more has held a magnetic appeal for invaders from

---

[3]In 1945 a Russian officer asked Field Marshal Gerd von Rundstedt what he considered the decisive battle of the war, assuming, no doubt, that he would say Stalingrad. The stiff old Prussian replied, "The Battle of Britain," adding that if the Germans had won in 1940 they would have defeated the Russians the following year.

the continent. The Romans built a fort here, and Dover was the starting point of Watling Street, their great road through Canterbury to London. Brooding over the cliffs east of town is Dover Castle, with walls more than twenty feet thick, constructed by Henry II in the twelfth century to repel enemies; within sight of it, the Spanish Armada received its first crushing blow; and here, in 1909, Englishmen standing on the cliffs witnessed the coming of the future as the Frenchman Louis Blériot piloted a wobbly little monoplane in the first heavier-than-air flight across the Channel's narrowest stretch.

Shakespeare Cliff, just west of Dover, is the traditional setting of that scene in *King Lear* in which Gloucester and his son Edgar walk "the dread summit of this chalky bourn," where "The crows and choughs that wing the midway air/ Show scarce so gross as beetles," and "The fishermen that walk upon the beach/ Appear like mice." For weeks, in that violent and terrible summer of 1940, with the days waxing golden and warm, the owner of the down-at-heels Grand Hotel, beneath Dover Castle, did the kind of business innkeepers dream about, with every room filled to capacity, the bar and dining room jammed every night by the correspondents—many of them Americans—who virtually lived on the cliff, drawn to the drama unfolding high above them, sensing that the destiny, not merely of kings but of Great Britain itself was being decided. Day after day, waves of German bombers, escorted by tiers of fighters, whose job it was to engage as many RAF aircraft as possible, would come over as if on schedule, the Spitfires and Hurricanes would rise to meet them high in the sky, frequently out of sight of watchers on the ground; and in the subzero temperatures the contrails formed a kind of mad skywriting that looked to observers like the squiggly lines skaters make on ice. Now and then a parachute would billow, taking as long as fifteen minutes to descend, while the pilot swung from side to side, often badly wounded, usually violently airsick; if he was British, they would see a Spitfire fly slowly in rings around him to keep him from being machine-gunned by the Germans. Pilots (even the enemy) were more precious by far than planes, and the British went to great lengths to rescue them— capturing Germans to prevent their flying against them another day; retrieving British to get them back in the air as fast as possible.

My father had been a pilot in the First World War, and as a small boy I used to play at fighting in his helmet, goggles, and shiny brown boots, sit by the hour leafing through his photograph album, and nothing was more thrilling than to hear him tell about those days in France, the aces he had met, or the time he crashed in the treetops, climbed to the ground unscathed, only to be marched ignominiously to a village at the points of a pitchfork by a farmer who had never seen an airplane and thought my father was an agent of the devil, if not Old Nick himself. My generation grew up on books and movies about World War flying aces—tales of the Lafayette Escadrille, a squadron of Americans who went to France in 1916; the stories of Elliott White Springs; films like *Wings,* the last of the memorable silent spectaculars, or *Dawn Patrol,* which left us with a lump in our throats when Richard Barthelmess, grimly triumphant, with oil spattering his face and goggles and the white silk scarf that trailed from his neck, saluted the mortal enemy he had just shot down in flames. We were prepared to believe that the man-to-man combat that took place in the skies was the only glorious thing about the Great War, and when a second Great War came along and the same sort of dogfights and aerial pursuits recurred (though on a different scale), we read and listened spellbound, applauding the little band of daring, outnumbered RAF pilots for their exploits against the waves of Nazis sent to crush them.

In August the talk among the Kentish folk turned to earthly matters—to the hop harvest, the wheat crop, the plague of wasps, the swarms of white butterflies that meant a bad winter; but overhead the Germans came on relentlessly, wave after wave of them with no end in sight, their passage punctuated with the rattle of machine-gun fire and the distant rumble of bombs. Those on the ground had the feeling that they were witnessing a clash of modern-day knights, a duel in the air, as Vincent Sheean put it, between "two hawklike youths in armor, brief falcon lives launched one against one in the briefest, purest combat ever known."

A few of the RAF pilots were "old men," like Douglas Bader, who was thirty and flying with two artificial legs, but many were only nineteen or twenty. Every day, they were on alert from dawn until dark, waiting for the bell to ring signaling them to scramble, to dash to their aircraft and get into the sky as fast as possible, climbing up and up, hoping to put the sun at their backs. With a top speed of 362 miles per hour even in level flight, it took a Spitfire about twelve minutes to climb to twenty thousand feet, a Hurricane three minutes longer, and the crucial timing of that ascent—which could mean the difference between life or death—was determined by a ground officer who ordered a particular squadron into the air, to get above and behind the incoming enemy. Everything was action—quick, immediate action, with the dogfights often lasting no longer than fifteen minutes, when the pilot had to return to base for fuel and more ammunition. As the fighters circled the field, coming in for a landing, the ground crews watched and counted, wondering if the missing ones were on the way home or if they had gone down in flames or bailed out over the Channel. By mid-August someone calculated that the life expectancy of these young men was eighty-seven hours of flying. Fighting against planes armed with cannons, they had eight machine guns of the same caliber as an infantryman's rifle. Their aircraft had no radar, no automatic pilot, no armor (even though a ninety-gallon fuel tank sat in front of the pilot's lap), and the flier wore no protective clothing, no crash helmet, only a silk parachute. Increasingly, as the fighting took its toll, the squadrons were made up of Scots and Welshmen, Canadians, Australians, New Zealanders, South Africans, Poles, Czechs, even a few Americans, in addition to the Englishmen. None of these fellows took themselves very seriously, but they were deadly earnest about the job they had to do, and they had an aura of glamour about them, because they were reckless, brave, and so very proficient at killing. Some were old-timers, some were new to the service; most had an irreverent attitude toward the army and the navy, no use for military punctilio, and little regard for the fame they were acquiring. What mattered was flying and fighting, and few military outfits have ever had a higher *esprit de corps*. Below them, every time they took to the air, they could see the lush green countryside of England, and beyond it the sprawl of London—for many, their native land, the homes and families that depended on them for survival.

—————

Given the circumstances of aerial combat, it was hardly surprising that both German and British claims of enemy losses should have been exaggerated. In the wild melee of a dogfight, it was all but impossible for a man flying at five or six miles per minute to be certain of a kill: a Hurricane pilot had three seconds in which to identify his enemy, after which he made a pass at a Messerschmitt 109, opened fire with eight machine guns, saw—or thought he saw—the enemy plane go down, but could not be sure whether he, or a buddy in his squadron, actually hit the Me-109 (and the buddy may have claimed it, too). By that time the pilot was likely so busy trying to avoid an attacking plane coming up on his tail that he couldn't possibly see whether the crippled German plane crashed or limped back to its base. Intelligence officers often debriefed pilots while they were still in a state of nerves, sometimes in shock, fresh from battle, knowing only that they were still miraculously intact, and in the long run no one could sort out fact from fiction until someone on both sides took a count of the airplanes that remained after the day's work.[4]

The British needed no special intelligence to know that the Germans kept coming, day after day; but the reports Göring received convinced him by August 1 that he had won the first phase of the battle, that the RAF was so badly crippled it could no longer be regarded as a factor in the invasion, and that the second stage—the destruction of airfields, aircraft factories, refineries, the entire RAF support network—could begin. Hitler concurred, but only on condition that "bombing with the object of causing a mass panic" be left for last. In particular, he said, there was to be no bombing of London unless he ordered it. Although the reasons behind this policy are unclear, it may be that Hitler was concerned about retaliation against Berlin; he may have thought the bombing of London would increase the Briton's will to resist; or perhaps he wished to spare one of the world's great

[4]In the biggest week of the Battle of Britain—the seven days ending August 17—the RAF claimed to have destroyed 496 enemy planes when, in fact, as postwar figures revealed, the German loss was 261. The British thought they were shooting down Luftwaffe aircraft at a ratio of three for every RAF plane lost. The ratio proved to be two to one, but that was still enough to alter Göring's strategy.

cities, as he had saved Paris. Whatever his reason, London was left un-touched—for a time.

From Spain, from a German agent who was reporting on Ambassador Joseph Kennedy's correspondence with Washington, from Lisbon (where the exiled Duke of Windsor was condemning the war as a crime), and from other sources, Hitler was getting the picture of a Britain shaken and close to collapse, which confirmed his personal hope that an invasion would be unnecessary. That a man to whom so much cruel purposefulness was as-cribed should lack the instinct for the jugular, the ability to be ruthless when it mattered the most, was curious, to say the least; yet the absence of that quality was evident in his refusal to commit his tanks at Dunkirk, his unwillingness to bomb London in the summer of 1940 despite the urging of advisers, his failure to humiliate a nearly prostrate Britain when it lay in his power to do so. It was almost as if he clung still to the notion that Britain could be driven to sue for peace and that he could achieve a bloodless victory without the need for invasion. In mid-August he wrote to Vidkun Quisling, the head of the puppet government in Norway: "After making one proposal after another to the British on the reorganization of Europe, I now find myself forced against my will to fight this war against Britain." He added, curiously, "I find myself in the same position as Martin Luther, who had just as little desire to fight Rome but was left with no alternative." As his deputy Rudolf Hess interpreted his motives, "The Führer never wanted to batter the [British] empire to pieces, nor does he want to now. Is there nobody in Britain willing to make peace?" Once the problem of Britain was out of the way, Hitler told one of his generals in June, "I will begin the final settlement of scores with bolshevism."

While the Battle of Britain was at its height, Hitler and his staff were at the Berghof, his country house above Berchtesgaden on the Obersalzberg, watching newsreel films of the Russian invasion of Finland, running them over and over, studying them to see what they revealed about the Red Army's tactics. He warned Field Marshal Wilhelm Keitel, chief of the OKW, that "our relationship to Russia might undergo a change," and Admiral Canaris, Keitel's chief of intelligence, was informed of his plan to attack Russia in the spring of 1941. The old obsession had Hitler in its grasp; his eyes were fixed on Russia and the Bolshevik menace to the Third Reich.

———

Meantime, what Göring had in mind was a massive assault on England by the largest air armada ever assembled—three fleets consisting of a thousand bombers, three hundred dive-bombers, and almost a thousand fighters. The idea was that one flight of bombers would make a feint toward London to lure RAF Fighter Command into the air, then the Luftwaffe's entire fighter force would attack. The first days of August were not suitable for such a complex operation, the Reich Marshal complained; he needed three days of good weather to make it possible. On the 6th of the month he was still temporizing, a delay that had the army chief of staff muttering sourly about "the peculiar situation in which the navy is tongue-tied with inhibitions, the Luftwaffe is unwilling to tackle the task which they first have to accomplish, and the OKW . . . lies lifeless."

Göring's deputy, Erhard Milch, jokingly described the plan for the massive assault as a "grand slam," but headquarters decreed that it should carry the high-flown code name Adlerangriff, or Eagle Attack, and on August 12 the Reich Marshal announced that Eagle Day would commence within twenty-four hours. Off to the south and east of England, in the coastal towns of Holland and France, preparations for invasion continued: while French peasants sat on their horse-drawn mowing machines, looking back at the swaths of grain, German mechanics were stripping tires from the thousands of abandoned vehicles on the beach at Dunkirk; armored divisions were getting their instructions, practicing loading and unloading exercises; tanks were being waterproofed and fitted out with special air intakes, so they could roll off the ramp of a barge into the water and travel along the bottom onto the beach; the navy was frantically trying to collect and assemble barges, freighters, and tugs; and every German radio station was playing the song "We Sail Against England." The days were growing shorter, summer was more than half gone, and with the time for action at hand, Hitler continued to hesitate. He would postpone the decision, he told an aide, until he saw the results of the Eagle Attack. At a ceremony at the Reichschancellery in which he handed out magnificently jeweled batons to seven newly promoted field marshals, he said he did not intend to carry out the invasion if the risk proved too great: the defeat of England could be accomplished by other means. What was most important, he went on, was that the *threat* of invasion be maintained. Göring, hearing this, was certain that no invasion would take place in the fall of 1940.

Thanks to Ultra, British intelligence knew about the impending Eagle Attack, and on August 8, Air Chief Marshal Sir Hugh Dowding issued an order of the day to Fighter Command, warning RAF pilots that "the fate of generations lies in your hands."

On August 13 the Luftwaffe came with a vengeance, the distant throb of hundreds of bombers audible long before the planes were in sight, with the main attack concentrated on targets in southern England from the Thames estuary to Southampton, and when it was over, Göring's pilots had accounted for seventy Spitfires and Hurricanes and eighteen Blenheims, at a cost of only twelve German planes. Or so they thought. In fact, the Luftwaffe knocked down only thirteen RAF fighters while losing twenty-three bombers and eleven fighters, and the perplexed German pilots reported to debriefing officers that the British always seemed to know where they were and when they would reach the English coast. That was the work of radar, of course, abetted during the next few days by the unpredictable English weather, which kept Göring's three air forces from coming together as planned.

In the first four days of Eagle Attack, the RAF shot down 194 Germans. On August 18 alone, when the Luftwaffe flew 850 sorties and the RAF 927, the price to the Germans was ninety-four airmen killed, twenty-five wounded, and forty taken prisoner (compared with eleven RAF pilots killed and nineteen wounded). That was more than Göring had bargained for; he pulled the Stukas—which had proved vulnerable and ineffective—out of the battle and ordered the fighter squadrons to provide more protection for the bombers. Soon he had big formations of planes flying back and forth along the French coast in order to confuse English spotters, who had no idea when they would make a sudden dash across the Channel. Bombers began to penetrate farther inland, damage to RAF bases mounted, and the last day of August was the worst yet for Fighter Command—thirty-nine planes and fourteen pilots lost, landing fields all over southeast England destroyed, planes blown up on the ground, crews killed, factories shattered.

What troubled Dowding far more than lost or damaged aircraft was the shortage of experienced, seasoned pilots, for in addition to those killed, many had been badly wounded or psychologically scarred beyond remedy, and the survivors, who would stumble exhausted from their planes after engaging in as many as six battles in a day, were nearing the limit of endurance and wore a haunted look about the eyes. Often a fighter would taxi to a stop and the ground crew would find the pilot slumped forward in the cockpit, sound asleep. Some took refuge in drink: "If you weren't in the air, you were plastered," one squadron leader commented. Others couldn't drink at all; they were so tense that even a taste of whisky caused them to throw up. Some squadrons had been fighting continuously since May, and pilots were close to despair, wondering how much longer they could hold out against such odds. Dowding was a deeply religious man who believed the Lord was on the side of England, but he was prepared to admit that it might take divine intervention to pull off a victory. Something like a miracle is exactly what he got.

On the last Sunday of the first year of the war, J. B. Priestley arrived in London from the Isle of Wight, where he had finished work on a book, and found it a different place from the one he had last seen six weeks earlier. It was now "a strange city of sandbags and shelters and first-aid posts." It was also a city "at the end of one chapter of world history [and] at the beginning of another." The streets were deserted, and at Paddington Station he had the eerie sensation that the trains might not be traveling to their old destinations, that they were simply leaving, never to return.

The correspondents in Dover sensed that something was up; word reached them that the sirens were at last sounding in London, which had been off-limits for the Luftwaffe for so long. Quite a few reporters left for the city, to stay, because as Ben Robertson noted, "the Germans had altered their tactics, the main battle had shifted." The saturation bombing of London was beginning, and it seems to have come about as the result of an accident, for as late as August 24, the OKW was still insisting, "Attacks against the London area and terror attacks are reserved for the Führer's decision." What happened to change that decision began with a raid made on the very night of that OKW order, when several German bombers on a mission against oil refineries and storage tanks east of London strayed from their flight pattern, lost their bearings in the intense antiaircraft fire around them, and jettisoned their bombs over the heart of the city, where they destroyed an ancient church and toppled a statue of John Milton, and in the crowded eastern boroughs, where they killed a number of people just leaving the pubs at closing time. What followed quickly changed the Germans' plans, the course of events, and quite possibly the outcome of the war.

Churchill and his war cabinet decided on reprisals, and RAF Bomber Command was ordered to retaliate against Berlin. At that distance, the twin-engined planes available couldn't carry enough of a load to do much damage, but on August 25 they struck the outskirts of Germany's capital. Until that moment, Bill Shirer observed, Berlin had been "utterly spared the slightest inconvenience from the war," but half an hour after midnight the sirens started to wail and it was three hours later before the all-clear sounded. Despite an immense concentration of antiaircraft fire, not a plane was hit, not a plane was even picked up in the searchlights; but the most important result, Shirer thought, was that "Berliners are stunned. They did not think it could happen. When this war began, Göring assured them it couldn't. He boasted that no enemy planes could ever break through the outer and inner rings of the capital's antiaircraft defense." And the Berliners had believed him. On the 28th, Germans were killed by bombs for the first time in the capital, and the next morning's papers carried headlines about the brutality and cowardice of British "pirates." (Shirer complained that censors forbade him from saying anything about a raid while it was on, noting that Ed Murrow not only mentioned raids, but described them in detail.) On September 1 all Berlin could see the bomb craters in the Tiergarten; on the 7th came the biggest and most effective raid to date, and Shirer noted in his diary the widespread disillusionment he had observed, the damage to morale that was far more significant than the damage to any targets.

By then, Hitler had reacted. Enraged by the attacks, he gave a speech on September 4, promising to drop a hundred bombs on London for every one that fell on Berlin, and on the afternoon of Saturday, September 7, Hermann Göring stood at his observation post on Cap Gris-Nez watching more than a thousand planes—372 bombers and 642 fighters—roar overhead, bound for London. Once again, the Germans had altered their plans.

———

Ed Murrow, Ben Robertson, and Jimmy Sheean took advantage of a beautiful day to drive out the East India Dock Road through the East End of

London, heading for the Thames estuary, where the bombs had been falling for weeks, to see how much damage had been done and how the repair work was coming along. In the ruinous streets of Tilbury, beneath barrage balloons floating lazily overhead, children were picking up souvenir bits of shrapnel from the streets, and after lunch the three men took the ferry to Gravesend and, before going on, rented rooms for the night at the inn. For a while they poked around the neighborhood trying to locate a Dornier that was said to have crashed nearby, found a Hurricane instead that was being stripped of all its usable parts by RAF mechanics, and late in the afternoon, after buying three tin-hatfuls of apples from a farmer, drove up to a little plateau, not far from the RAF's Hornchurch airdrome, to eat and sleep in the sun. That was when they heard the first air-raid siren begin its uneven screaming, followed by the far-off hum of hundreds of motors.

Already, little puffs of white showed against the sky where antiaircraft shells were exploding. The fighters from the airfield took off—Hurricanes and Spitfires climbing for altitude. Then, very high, the black shapes of German bombers, the noise of machine guns firing, the sound of shrapnel falling around them, and silence as the planes moved out of sight and earshot. Leaving the car at the side of the road, they took refuge in a ditch, where they were joined by two cyclists and the passengers from a bus that had been abandoned (the conductor sat stolidly, counting up his passengers and fares). They saw the RAF fighters returning to base to refuel and rearm, and as fast as a plane was ready it took to the air again, not waiting for flight leader or formation. Another wave of bombers was coming into view—twenty-four of them, followed by thirty-six more, then others, flying at great height in perfect formation, glistening like steel birds in the sunshine. Off toward London immense clouds of smoke were rising, and the bombers were overhead again, returning down the river, heading for France, pursued by British fighters.

The all clear sounded after two hours, and they headed for a pub in Gravesend to have dinner. Beside the road a cart lay in the bushes and two little boys were sobbing, trying to back a nervous mare between the shafts; inside the pub the proprietress informed them the raids were bad for chickens, dogs, and horses. Along the river, as far as they could see, huge blobs of flame and greasy black smoke marked the site of oil tanks; beyond, where more dense clouds could be seen, they knew the docks were burning.

After deciding that the Germans would come again that night, they went back to their plateau and, looking toward London, saw that flames had turned the moon blood-red while smoke had formed a great canopy over the Thames. Now the Germans were thundering overhead again, two or three planes at a time, flying in at three-minute intervals as though it were a shuttle service; the guns and searchlights followed them, and not long afterward the correspondents could hear the hollow grunt of bombs and see bursts of flame rising into the smoky pall that blanketed the city. Along the riverbanks the fires that had been ignited in the afternoon guided the incoming bombers to the city like runway lights. Sheean, lying in a ditch beside Murrow, was cursing in five languages, talking about the war in Spain; Robertson kept repeating, "London is burning . . . London is burning," in his South Carolina drawl. It was growing cold now, and they walked over to a nearby haystack and burrowed into it to keep warm, thinking how the London that had taken thirty generations to build was being destroyed in a single night. At 3:00 in the morning the bombers were still flying over, but the three men figured they would be in no greater danger at the Gravesend inn than here, close to the fighter base, so they drove off to claim their rooms. Gunfire was rattling the windows, the floors and walls were shaking with the explosions, but they were too exhausted to care. Not until daylight did the all clear sound; a pale, red-eyed chambermaid brought them coffee and said, "I hope you slept well, sirs." Then they headed for the great gray city that had been under continuous attack for twelve hours. "The Battle of London had started," Ben Robertson observed, "and on that first Sunday it seemed to all of us like the end of civilization."

They found entire blocks flattened, streets roped off, houses and shops smashed, factories gutted, the ruined remains still burning or smoldering. Everywhere were signs of injury, suffering, and death, but what stuck in Murrow's mind was the lines of red buses taking away the homeless—"men with white scarfs around their necks instead of collars and ties, leading dull-eyed, empty-faced women across to the buses. Most of them carried little cheap cardboard suitcases and sometimes bulging paper shopping bags. That was all they had left."

While the three men watched the Germans come in again over the Thames estuary, Londoners heard the heaviest antiaircraft fire to date and noticed that the sound was moving closer all the time. Sometime after 5:00 in the afternoon, Janet Murrow could hear firing around the perimeter of the city; then would come a lull; then the noise again, closer than before. At 6:00 she saw twenty bombers overhead, flying in the sun with the AA fire bursting all around them. She saw people standing in the street, looking up into the sky. "Bombs in the east," she noted in her diary. "Poor Ed. I'm really worried. . . . I wish he'd stayed here. . . . Planes whirring and humming overhead. Sky blue." It was becoming hazy, she noticed, from the heat. A few minutes later she heard a new sound and found herself wishing that her vision weren't limited to what she could see from the windows of the apartment. Overhead she caught a glimpse of fighter planes twisting and turning, one falling out of control; on the street corner below, a taxi driver sat calmly in his cab, waiting for a fare.

At 8:15 the Welsh girl, Betty, telephoned to tell her "a brave fire" was burning east of the city and suggested that Janet could see it from her roof. Thinking Ed might be in the midst of it she dreaded to look, but she climbed the stairs leading to a door onto the roof and went outside. The weather was fine, and she stayed until nightfall, when the bombs began dropping closer and she had had her "fill of ugly red flames and smoke." She decided to go back downstairs, turned toward the door, and discovered to her horror that it had locked behind her. She was trapped in the open, on the roof.

First she tried calling to Mr. Smith, the building super, and gave up after deciding that he "was in his inevitable pub." Then she went to the edge of the roof and began calling to people below, but it was six floors to the street, bombs were exploding, and down there it was bedlam—people running to shelters, sirens wailing, antiaircraft guns blasting—and there was no way anyone could hear her. Finally she lay flat on her stomach and leaned out over the edge of the roof, calling, waving her flashlight in hopes of attracting attention. She had about decided she would have to spend the night on the roof and was wondering which side of the chimney would be safest when a lone man walked by on the street below and chanced to look up. A few minutes later he opened the door onto the roof and escorted her to her flat.

During the afternoon and night of September 7, Drew Middleton wrote, a thousand Londoners were killed.[5] On that first night of the bombing, more panic and fear were evident than at any later time; no one was used to the shelters yet, many of them were inadequate, the people were terrified and wanted to get out into the country, beyond the reach of bombs. Those on the outskirts of the city that evening noticed how red the setting sun was; then they realized that it was not the sun they were seeing—it was the reflection in the sky of the flaming East End. At 1:00 P.M. on Sunday, Janet Murrow heard on the radio that eighty-eight German planes had been brought down the day before, that twenty-one RAF squadrons had been engaged in the fighting, but the Germans were over the city again, as numerous as before, and it was clear that London's agony was only beginning. As Middleton reported, between September 7 and November 3 an average of 250 German bombers attacked London each night. Although the attacks would continue for four and a half years, this was the most critical phase—the test of whether the people could take it or not.

That Sunday, Ed Murrow visited the bombed areas and saw men shoveling great mounds of broken glass into trucks, watched the people being evacuated from their shattered homes in the East End, and noticed that for the first time there were queues outside air-raid shelters instead of the theaters, that people were carrying blankets and mattresses to the shelters even before the sirens sounded. Amid all this, a policeman was giving a ticket to a motorist who had driven through a red light.

The terror had begun. Ben Robertson could see that people took courage when daylight came; it was the darkness that was so frightening, and before long no one was without a personal story of woe or near disaster. A chambermaid in Robertson's hotel had been buried for three hours in the

[5] By comparison, the number of American combatants killed in the D-day landing in 1944 was 1,465. During the months of August, September, and October 1941, 12,696 civilians were killed in the London area alone, and 20,000 were seriously injured.

basement of her house, but came to work as usual. The headwaiter's house had been hit, and he arrived at the job in a pair of pajamas and an overcoat—all he had left. After the second night of bombing the damage was appalling, and all over the city crews of civilians were at work, digging in the ruins of homes, repairing gas lines and water mains, filling huge craters in the streets, relaying railroad track, pumping out flooded tubes so underground train service could resume, trying to keep the city functioning, knowing they had to clean up this debris before the next raid began. Ambassador Kennedy said that seventeen time bombs had fallen between his house and his garage; Ed Murrow's office was destroyed (for the first time); Eric Sevareid and Larry LeSueur of CBS were bombed out and took temporary lodgings with the Murrows; six of eight American correspondents to whom Murrow talked had been forced to move; and so it went for everyone else. With the coming of autumn, an estimated 177,000 Londoners were camping underground every night. In the middle of the morning they went down to stake out a claim, leaving newspapers, bundles of bedding, or rugs to mark it; not until 4:30 in the afternoon were they allowed to descend into the dank, blue-lit shelters and tube stations where they spread out their bedding on gritty concrete floors. Life in the shelters meant adjusting to eating, drinking, sleeping, feeding the baby, without a shred of privacy; to lying down for the night like sticks of cordwood, with barely enough room to stretch; to primitive sanitary conditions—buckets placed behind makeshift screens; to emerging the next morning stiff and tired and red-eyed to scenes of appalling desolation, homes opened up like broken doll houses with pictures still hanging on the walls, streets filled with huge mounds of powdered glass, clouds of dust, smoking ruins; and to action—the atmosphere of a frontier town where everyone was working, pitching in, tearing down the remnants of buildings, shoveling the glass into trucks. More and more frequently, people arrived at their places of work to find them gone, or learned that they could not return home because of a bomb that had not exploded. Every dawn found the number of homeless on the rise. As one American correspondent wrote, "For Londoners, there are no longer such things as good nights; there are only bad nights, worse nights, and better nights." Britain was a nation fighting in darkness; Londoners had already noticed that after the blackouts began, the owls returned to Hyde Park and began hooting at night.

There was no way to describe what was happening, there was no predicting an individual's reaction to the shriek of falling bombs. Vera Brittain, a journalist, lecturer, and Londoner by adoption, heard the bombs scream past her windows, saw two houses fifty yards away receive direct hits and collapse with a roar, felt the building above her crack and shudder, and wondered if the mass of steel and concrete would fall on her head. Her house, which had echoed with the laughter of her children, was silent and desolate: dust and plaster blanketed the nursery where her children had played before she sent them away; on the floor of her study lay piles of books and an abandoned vacuum cleaner, covered with rubble. As one of a committee of Quakers trying to help the people in London's poorest districts, she had gone to see the East End, and concluded that the wreckage there was of such magnitude that it was beyond the power of any agency but the government to tackle. The journey back to her own battered home was right out of H. G. Wells—sections where every other house was demolished; processions of forlorn office workers with gray faces and deep circles under their eyes, looking as though they had not slept for weeks—driven from their homes or offices by time bombs, they held everything they owned in a suitcase; streets that were a maze of detours, gaping holes in the ground, piles of brick and stone, glass, always glass, ankle-deep, and over everything the stench of burning wood.

Inevitably, the rhythm of city life began to change: people went to bed at sundown or soon afterward and rose with the first light, keeping farmers' hours. And at the end of the first week of it, Robertson concluded, most people to their surprise were still alive, most of the city still stood, and the survivors had concluded that the battle was not quite as bad as they had thought it would be. Here were the British, he thought to himself, the people who ruled a quarter of the globe, the people on whose empire the sun never set, who had exploited and subjugated others, showing that they could take the same punishment they had handed out. In Paris, the government had run away. In London, Churchill and his government took their stand with the people, and six million of them decided that they could take it, come what might. There was food to eat, water to drink, most mornings the milk miraculously arrived on the doorstep and the paper was delivered, buses and trains continued to run, the Grenadier Guards band still played in Trafalgar Square, and one day Robertson heard an organist playing Handel in St. Giles's Cripplegate, though the church had not a window left.

The RAF provided the British with a new set of heroes; now London produced another lot of them—the brave, tireless men of the Voluntary Fire Service, who were putting out as many as a thousand fires a night. A couple of them told Ed Murrow that the waiting around in fire stations was the hardest part of the job; somehow they didn't mind the danger when there was plenty to do. But within a few weeks after the big raids began, more than a thousand of them had lost their lives.

———

London's anguish—and that of other industrial cities in the British Isles—would go on for four and a half more years, costing untold hardship, destruction, and death.[6] But the message that gripped the average American was not so much the Britons' suffering, but their courage and essential toughness. No small thanks for this went to Winston Churchill, who had

---

[6]The total number of Londoners killed during the war was more than 51,000, with some 61,000 seriously wounded. Most of the casualties occurred during the 1940–41 bombings.

told his countrymen that these were days of greatness, not of sorrow, had made them aware of the opportunity to demonstrate that they were un-afraid, that they would not yield, and then expressed that will with incom-parable eloquence to those beyond his island. When the smoke of battle cleared briefly in January of 1941, the British people were still there, weary beyond measure, heartsick over the loss of life and the destruction of their national treasures, but *there,* as determined as ever that Hitler would not prevail. And it occurred to them and to others like them that a democratic society, with all its faults, its sometimes ponderous deliberations and de-bates, its apparent inefficiency, has an inner strength that is a match for the most powerful dictatorship.

J. B. Priestley wrote of a Londoner who was fined 15 shillings by the police for drunk and disorderly conduct. It seems he had been arrested for standing in the middle of a street after the air-raid warning had sounded, shaking his fist at the sky and shouting, "Rule Britannia! Rule Britannia!" Maybe he had the right idea, Priestley said, for showing that the war had at last become the war of the British people, not only of their government. These people knew they were not doomed and had begun to show the world what stuff they were made of. One night he saw the fires burning so fiercely that half the sky was aglow, with the tall terraces around Portland Place "like pink palaces in the Arabian nights." In the distance he saw the dome and the cross of St. Paul's silhouetted black against the red-and-orange flames, looking like "an enduring symbol of reason and Christian ethics seen against the crimson glare of unreason and savagery."

Ed Murrow had similar thoughts about its becoming a people's war. When Buckingham Palace was bombed for the first time, it was reported in the United States ("by certain editors and commentators who sit in New York," he remarked acidly) that the Germans had blundered, causing a spirit of unity to sweep England. Murrow disagreed: Americans had to realize that this was not the last war—the old values and prejudices, the old bases of power and prestige, were dying, people's reactions were differ-ent—and it did not require a bombing of the royal residence to convince Londoners that they were all in this together. "There is nothing exclusive about being bombed these days," he commented. "When there are houses down in your street, when friends and relatives have been killed, when you've seen that red glow in the sky night after night, when you're tired and sleepy—there just isn't enough energy left to be outraged about the bombing of a palace."

He was right. Queen Elizabeth was quoted as saying, "I'm glad we've been bombed. It makes me feel I can look the East End in the face." At first, the Cockneys in the squalid East End bore the brunt of the bombings; badly nourished, poorly clothed, ill-housed, they were the worst equipped to stand the physical strain of repeated attacks; shelters there were virtually nonexis-tent; the people felt abandoned by their government; and finally an angry crowd marched on the posh Savoy Hotel, demanding food and shelter, "to show you buggers how the other half is living." Fortunately, the bombing of the fashionable West End and the palace—which Churchill insisted on publicizing—took the heat off the government, and by the end of September someone noticed that the East Enders had stuck Union Jacks in the piles of rubble that used to be their homes. By then, despite all that had happened, an entirely new spirit had taken over the city.

Priestley took the long view, seeing the war as a single chapter in the history of a changing world, as the breakdown of one system and the construction of a new and better one. He was no friend of the old order in England, in which he had seen far too many pleasant, able-bodied persons yawning away their lives, wondering what to do between meals, in shocking contrast to all the others who wondered "how to get it all done between meals"; and there was a time before the blitz when he thought he hated London, with its vast colorless suburbs, and the "extremes of wealth and poverty that we found, cheek by jowl in the West End, where at night the great purring motor cars filled with glittering women passed the shadowy rows of the homeless, the destitute, and the down-and-out." Now, suddenly, everybody was in the same boat—an ark that seemed to be sailing to a better world—and his spirits brightened as he reflected that people might stop thinking in terms of property and power and begin considering community and creation. Maybe, he hoped, they would see this war as an opportunity to remodel the old life and create a new one. Along with everything else that was happening, beneath the surface of Britain's fight for life, what Murrow and Priestley sensed was the revolution that was brewing, a social upheaval that would keep the nation from ever returning to the way things were the day before war was declared.

——

On September 12, in Berlin, William Shirer heard a rumor that the invasion of Britain was planned for the night of September 15, to take advantage of a full moon and a favorable tide in the Channel. But in England, rain began falling on September 10 and continued for four days, hampering air operations. The 15th dawned fair, and the greatest concentration of German bombers by far headed for London in what Göring hoped would be the knockout blow. September 15 was little Anthony Bailey's last night in England before boarding ship for America, and he spent it in the basement dining room of a London hotel, with the other guests, on mattresses tucked in among the potted palms and sideboards, while two hundred German bombers thundered overhead and the devastating roar of bombs and the boom of antiaircraft guns alternated with the wail of sirens. The sound, he recalled, was like the crack of doom. He thought the earth must be caving in.

Prime Minister Churchill's favorite post in those perilous weeks was the operations room of Fighter Command's No. 11 Group at Uxbridge, the nerve center from which he could follow the progress of the air battles. On

September 15 he was there with his chief of staff, General Ismay, fifty feet below ground, his eyes glued to the gigantic blackboard that showed which squadrons were standing by at two minutes' notice, which at readiness, meaning ready within five minutes, and which were available in twenty minutes. In another column were lights showing those squadrons that were in action, and those that were returning to base. As he sat watching, it became apparent that an enormous battle was developing, and one after another the RAF squadrons went into the air. Hugh Dowding had anticipated Göring's move, recognizing that it was now or never for Sea Lion, and decided to throw everything he had at the Germans. Ismay felt "sick with fear" as he looked on, and with his mind on the young men in the Spitfires and Hurricanes, a line from the Old Testament came to him: "And they shall be mine, saith the Lord of hosts, in that day when I make up my jewels." Outlying reinforcement squadrons were called to cover London and some of the inland airdromes, the reinforcements were soon involved in the battle, and Churchill turned to Air Vice Marshal Park to ask, "What other reserves have we?"

Park replied: "There are none."

At that moment on September 15, 1940, every single fighter plane Britain possessed was in the air.

Within that cube of air space forty miles broad, eighty miles long, five miles high, as many as two hundred individual dogfights were going on, and the sky was crowded with one plane after another in wild chase, throttle wide open, guns firing until they were empty. One RAF fighter group engaged the incoming bombers on the coast; another hit them near London; and the weight of the attack was too much for the Luftwaffe pilots, who had been told the RAF was finished. Göring ordered a second raid, and his signal was picked up by Ultra and relayed to Dowding by direct line, and the RAF fighters refueled, rearmed, and were ready for the second wave of attackers as they arrived. When it was over at last, Churchill left the operations room, climbed the long stairs to ground level, puffing hard, obviously overwrought, and as he got into the limousine asked Ismay not to speak to him. He closed his eyes, stretched his legs, and was so quiet for five minutes that Ismay thought he had fallen asleep. When he spoke at last, it was to say, half to himself, "Never in the field of human conflict has so much been owed by so many to so few."

For Britain—and for America, too—the bombing of London was a major turning point in the war. The assaults that cost the people of that city such devastation and sorrow proved the salvation of the RAF, for they took the intolerable pressure off the airfields, the factories, the planes, the pilots. Once the nonstop attacks on the city began, the RAF squadrons could hit the Luftwaffe hard, knowing almost certainly where they were headed. So Hitler's irrational decision to bomb the city, made in anger, proved fatal. Because the Royal Air Force survived, the Germans never achieved the mastery of the air that was essential for a successful invasion; and Britain's

Night after night during the London blitz, the wardens and fire fighters of St. Paul's patrolled the cathedral, throwing incendiary bombs off the roof or smothering them with sand.

survival guaranteed that if Hitler should attack Russia he would have a war on two fronts which he very likely could not win.

Hitler's stupidity was one thing; but other factors helped to change the course of the war in Britain. One was the remarkable record of aircraft production and pilot training that was achieved in such a short time. On June 7, 1940, the RAF had nineteen fully operational squadrons of Hurricane fighters. On August 8 there were twenty-eight and a half. On September 15, there were thirty-two—and this during the time when the British were fighting for their lives in France, at Dunkirk, and then meeting the onslaught of the Luftwaffe at home. At the same time, it became evident that Germany's vaunted superiority in the air—in both quantity and quality of aircraft—was not insurmountable after all; and when you added to that the Luftwaffe's lack of heavy, long-range bombers, and the fact that it had been designed not for missions over London but to support advancing ground forces in limited, lightning strikes, you began to see a rather different picture from what had been generally supposed when the Battle of Britain began. Yet for all that, for the RAF and for England it was "a damned nice thing," as Wellington remarked after Waterloo, "the nearest run thing you ever saw in your life."

———

After leaving the command post at Uxbridge, the prime minister returned to Chequers, lay down for his afternoon nap at 4:30, and did not awaken until 8:00 P.M. His private secretary came into his room with gloomy news from around the globe, and finally added, "However, all is redeemed by the air. We have shot down a hundred and eighty-three for a loss of under forty." No matter that the actual German losses later proved to have been only fifty-six; what mattered was that the Germans had lost their nerve and the British had not. On September 17, Admiral Raeder dictated for the War Diary,[7] "The enemy air force is by no means defeated. On the contrary it shows increasing activity. The Führer therefore decides to postpone Sea Lion indefinitely." The Battle of Britain was over, and with it the threat of invasion.

The British learned of Hitler's decision in a roundabout way. On the morning of September 17, 1940, the German officer in charge of air-loading at Dutch and Belgian airfields received an order to dismantle all his equipment at the bases in Holland. Crucial to the invasion plan was the loading of supply planes and troop-carrying aircraft, which were to have an unopposed flight to England, after which they would return, reload, and fly back across the Channel. That signal—which was deciphered by Ultra—meant that the invasion could not take place if the loading equipment was being

[7]After listening to daily reports from his top commanders and discussing the situation, Hitler issued his orders, and a full account of the proceedings was incorporated into what was known as the official War Diary.

dismantled, and Group Captain F. W. Winterbotham sent the message to the prime minister at once.

Underground, in Churchill's war room, the chiefs of staff had collected at 7:30 P.M., and when Winterbotham arrived he noticed that "there were controlled smiles on the faces of all these men" as Churchill read them the signal and the chief of the air staff explained its significance, giving his opinion that it meant the end of Sea Lion, at least during 1940.

Churchill lit one of his great black cigars and suggested that they all take the air, although a raid was at its height. Ignoring the warnings of his military advisers, he walked out into the open, into a wild scene, to see Carlton House Terrace ablaze on the other side of St. James's Park, bombs exploding to the south, fires silhouetting the trees. As Churchill stood there alone in front of the group, "his dark blue boiler suit undone at the neck, a tin hat on his head, his hands folded on his stout stick in front of him, his chin thrust out, the long cigar in his mouth," Winterbotham knew he was witnessing a moment to remember. Above the din of battle he could hear the prime minister's angry growl: "By God, we will get the bastards for this."

CHAPTER 43

"... your boys are not going to be sent into any foreign wars."

One sign that a measure of financial stability had returned to the Ketchum household was the real vacation we took that summer of 1940—three weeks on a ranch in the Big Horn Mountains of Wyoming, which I remember as one of the best times we ever had together. (It was also the last occasion on which the four of us would vacation as a family.) After the interminable train trip from Pittsburgh, Pennsylvania, to Sheridan, Wyoming, my father, mother, sister Janet, and I were outfitted at Rudy Mudra's and other local emporia with stiff new jeans, boots, Stetsons, and work shirts, before being driven into the mountains to the ranch and shown to our cabin as dusk was falling. It was a million miles from the problems of the world, with no decisions more demanding than whether to ride in the morning or the afternoon, or both, and to a Pittsburgher accustomed to middays that might be as dark as night, the incredibly clear air that made it possible to see for thirty miles or perhaps reach out and touch the stars was a revelation. All too soon the slow rhythm of ranch life—a succession of lazy, hot, sunny days, with long rides along the mesa, pack trips to a remote fishing camp, hearty food, and the easy companionship of cowboys and other guests—gave way at last to Pittsburgh, August, and reality.

The young woman who occupied most of my thoughts was at Bennington

College for a summer dance program, working with Martha Graham, Doris Humphrey, Hanya Holm, and other moderns; most of my other friends were away; and when I grumbled about this at the dinner table one night it reminded my father of the time he was running a fund-raising campaign for a large local charity. The centerpiece of the drive was a benefit circus performance, which warranted hiring the Pittsburgh Pirates' Forbes Field. When at last my father had completed the complex arrangements and reported his achievement proudly to the nominal chairman of the fund drive, a socially prominent *grande dame,* telling her that everything was set for the evening of August 15, she looked at him with horror and disbelief and stated flatly: "My dear Mr. Ketchum, *no one* is in Pittsburgh in August!" And at her insistence, the date was changed to September.

In my family we were all out for Willkie and the first real chance to knock the socks off Roosevelt, and I had work to do—Republican work, which meant spending the dog days of August walking the hot streets of unfamiliar neighborhoods, ringing doorbells, giving the lady of the house a big smile and what passed for a political message as I handed her a Willkie button and a campaign leaflet. "Be sure to vote for him!" I would call over my shoulder as I walked away, but more often than not I had the sinking feeling that she would not. I was unaware of the phenomenon, but until the late twenties and early thirties, a mill hand living in or near Pittsburgh knew he had to register as a Republican and vote that way. To admit to being a Democrat was suicidal; it was well known that the steel companies had methods of finding out how a man marked his ballot. If he voted Democratic, he was out of a job. It was that simple. But all that had changed with the coming of unions and the triumph of Franklin Roosevelt in 1932; from then on, most of Allegheny County consistently went Democratic, and the likelihood of my changing any votes in the neighborhoods I visited was slim indeed.

Nowhere were the differences on politics and foreign policy being debated more often or more passionately than on college campuses, and as if to get the fall term off to a lively start, the August 1940 issue of *The Atlantic Monthly* included an "Open Letter to Undergraduates" under the bold headline: "Where Do You Stand?" The author was a Yale professor named Arnold Whitridge, and while I was not acquainted with him as a teacher, I had met him, because he was the master of the residential college into which I would move in September, and I felt a moment's pride to think that someone I actually knew was being published in a national magazine. Whitridge had the tweedy look of an English country squire, and what I took to be an English accent (or was it only Groton?),[1] and his article made it very clear that he was not merely an Anglophile but an out-and-out interventionist.

[1] Mr. Whitridge, I learned later, was the grandson of the English writer Matthew Arnold and had studied at Oxford.

Speaking as one who had fought in the last war, he said frankly that he was baffled and deeply troubled by the attitude of undergraduates at Cornell, Dartmouth, Harvard, Yale, and other colleges who had petitioned the president of the United States not to intervene in Europe, who had warned against granting credits, sending supplies, aircraft, or men to the Allies, who had stated during the Nazi invasion of the Lowlands that "never under any circumstances will they follow in the footsteps of the students of 1917," and who had maintained that "there is no preponderance of good or evil on either side."

"Most of you," Whitridge pointed out, "are not conscientious objectors. Whatever objections you have are economic and political rather than moral. I picture you hovering on the sidelines, some of you inclined to cheer for the Allies, but most of you still contemplating the tragedy of Europe as something interesting but remote." He, too, had hoped that the Chamberlain policy of appeasement would work, had hoped that Hitler would be satisfied once he had Czechoslovakia, had hoped that the Maginot Line would prove impregnable, but his capacity for hope had been exhausted, and the time had come to take a stand.

"If the way of life which we have evolved in America is worth preserving," he concluded, "I believe we shall have to do something besides hope for victory and sell secondhand ships to Great Britain on a strictly cash basis. I believe that, much as we hate war, we shall have to fight, and the sooner we get ready for it, the better." To one in his eighteenth year, who was as confused as most Americans about what we should do, and who was keenly aware that the first peacetime draft in U.S. history had recently been made the law of the land, his message was not altogether welcome.

The following month's *Atlantic* brought a starchy reply, entitled "We Stand Here," by two undergraduates—Kingman Brewster, the chairman of the *Yale Daily News,* and Spencer Klaw, his opposite number at the *Harvard Crimson.* I knew Brewster slightly and regarded him with some awe, since he was two years ahead of me at college and was the chairman of the *News* while I was "heeling" the paper as a freshman. I had discovered that heeling the *News* meant giving up sleep and just about everything else for several months while you worked long into the night or early morning, every day but Saturday, investigating and writing stories, concocting clever headlines, and reading proof at the compositor's before the paper was put to bed. It was exhausting, enervating, and exhilarating, and I loved everything about it until the end, when the time came for the heelers to learn who had made the staff and who had not. Late one afternoon, as dusk was falling, and before the lights had been turned on in the *News* building, I was summoned to the chairman's office. There, seated behind a desk, wearing a somber three-piece suit, with a thick gold watch chain stretched across his vest, was a genuine Big Man on Campus, and not until long afterward did it occur to me that this ordeal may have been almost as difficult for Kingman Brewster as it was for me, for he told me with infinite kindness that while I had earned more editorial points than anyone else in the competition, I had accumulated almost no "business" points (which meant selling ads, which I hated), and since a balance between business and editorial was one of the rules by which the game was played, it meant that I had not made the staff. He went on to say how sorry he was to have to tell me this, after all my hard work, and he hoped that I would try again. (Some months later I was writing a column for the paper with my good friend Dick Drain.) I do not know what it is like to be fired from a job, but I have sometimes thought the world of commerce would be a better place if a man could be discharged as compassionately as Kingman Brewster informed me of my defeat, so that I walked away not humiliated but with a feeling of having achieved something of which I could be proud. Shattering as the news was, the interview left me with a high regard for Brewster, and the appearance of an article in *The Atlantic* bearing his byline reinforced my sense of his maturity.

The argument he and Klaw set forth, cradled in language that revealed their sophistication (they were seniors, remember) and thinly veiled disdain for academic authority (Whitridge's "casuistry and acrimony [were] as unworthy as they were unjust," but since "he has been gracious enough to clothe his indictment in question form, he should be answered"), seemed right on target, since it jibed with my own views. "We will not fight just for the sake of fighting," they declared, "but convince us that war is the best means of serving our American ideals and we will follow you anywhere." Yet how could those ideals possibly be preserved by entering a foreign war, they asked, when we have nothing to fight with? By the time the United States was prepared to take effective action, they argued, it would be necessary to cross the Atlantic and conquer a continent dominated by a nation whose manpower and materials of war had been mobilized for years. And along the way, the very ideals Americans were fighting for—democracy and freedom— would have to be abandoned. Surely if we had learned anything from the last world conflict, it was that devastation and hatred do not produce lasting peace. The course for Americans, they insisted, was "to take our stand on this side of the Atlantic . . . because at least it offers a chance for the maintenance of all the things we care about in America." By keeping out of war, we stood a chance of preserving American democracy, and should Germany someday attempt to attack us here, we would have the advantage of an impregnable defensive position, resources untapped by the demands of total war, and a preparedness ensured by the wonders of American productivity. It was, of course, the Fortress America argument which Charles Lindbergh was advocating, and for millions of Americans it had an almost irresistible appeal, despite all that had occurred in Europe during 1940.

═══

Kingman Brewster had been thinking about Europe's unhappy situation a lot longer than most of his contemporaries. After graduation from prep school in 1936 he spent the summer in Nebraska working for Senator George Norris, who was campaigning for reelection, and after Norris had safely won, Brewster went to Europe to join his family. There he was oppressed by the atmosphere in Germany and by the extent of German remilitarization, and troubled as much by England's economic chaos as by France's inability to form a viable government. In the fall of 1937 he entered Yale and found university life "pleasantly fat and essentially untroubled," with few undergraduates knowing or caring what was happening in Europe. Two years later came the invasion of Poland—a terrible shock; then the baffling phony war, triggering an "aloof and intellectualized discussion about the conflict."

Starting on May 10, 1940, Europe's unfolding agony became a topic for more than the lecture platform; it began to be part of the daily thought and talk at Yale. Few of the undergraduates Brewster knew took kindly to the label "isolationist," which implied indifference. As he saw it, "America was a world promise, not just a promise for Americans," and the promise would be fulfilled far better by an America at peace. It was a premise quite similar to the one advanced by Anne Morrow Lindbergh in her new book, published in October at $1 a copy—*The Wave of the Future.* Like Brewster, she insisted that our first duty was to our own nation; that instead of crusading against what was essentially a revolution in Europe, instead of "climbing down into the maelstrom of war," we should strive for a peaceful reformation at home. Only in this manner would we find a peculiarly American solution to the many ills of the world. Finding that solution was "the creative act demanded of us," and we must not surrender the clear, unobstructed vantage point from which we could see a bright vision of the future.

From the time that young men on campus began to realize how events on another continent might affect their personal futures, they could see the difficulty of reconciling their sympathy for Britain with opposition to American involvement in the war, and Brewster began meeting with a group of Yale law students who were focusing on the need to create a national voice for people who felt as he did.

In the middle of June 1940 the Yale Law School group—which included Potter Stewart and Sargent Shriver, and was led by an energetic Chicagoan named Robert Douglas Stuart, Jr.—mailed a letter outlining its goals and plans to students and alumni of other universities, and shortly afterward Stuart and Brewster attended the Republican convention in Philadelphia. Neither was swept up by the Willkie tidal wave; both found Robert Taft's ideas on foreign policy more compatible with their own; and after talking with the Ohio senator and his staff and finding them sympathetic to the idea of a national noninterventionist organization, Stuart went on to Washington to see if he could drum up further interest. From all sides, he heard the name of General Robert E. Wood, chairman of Sears, Roebuck, as a man who might be willing to help.

Through his father, who was head of the Quaker Oats Company, Stuart already knew Wood slightly and had received a letter from him recently commending him for his noninterventionist activity, and when he returned to Chicago he called on the general to discuss his ideas for a national organization. Stuart wanted action, and Wood—whose favorite expression was said to be "Let's charge!"—was certainly the man for that. A West Pointer who had achieved a certain fame as director of the Panama Railroad Company while the canal was under construction, he had served during World War I as quartermaster general, buying and distributing food, clothing, and matériel for four million Americans, and with that experience under his belt had gone to Montgomery Ward, turning it into a real competitor to Sears, Roebuck, before being hired by Sears. Unlike many other corporate executives, Wood had supported Roosevelt and the New Deal's social programs, but he was bitterly opposed to policies that were taking the United States ever closer to war, and before Stuart left his office he had promised to act as temporary chairman of the organization, helping to line up a sponsoring committee, and providing some financial assistance to get things going. Later, when a friend asked Wood why he had agreed to serve as head of the organization, the general replied that he had promised to be acting chairman until they located a chairman, but they never did find one. His reason for doing so, he explained, was very simple: "How could I turn down that nice young man?"

By the end of August, Bob Stuart had an office in Chicago, a sponsoring committee that included six prominent corporate executives, the master of the National Grange, a bishop of the Methodist Church, the president of the American Olympic Association, a Nobel laureate in medicine, the former editor of *The Nation,* and such other luminaries as Alice Roosevelt Longworth, Edward Rickenbacker, the World War I flying ace, Hanford MacNider, former national commander of the American Legion, and John T. Flynn, who had been an adviser to the Senate committee investigating the munitions industry in 1934 and 1935. The committee's first public announcement listed four guiding principles which were remarkably similar to the ideas set forth in the *Atlantic* article by Brewster and Klaw: (1) the United States must build an invulnerable defense for America; (2) no foreign powers can successfully attack a *prepared* America; (3) American democracy can be preserved only by staying out of war in Europe; (4) "aid short of war" weakens national defense at home and threatens to involve America in war abroad. (It might be noted that the foreign powers everyone had in mind were European, not Asian.)

In pursuit of these principles, the organization planned to rally all Americans, regardless of their differences on other matters, who saw eye to eye on the goals; it would work to see that Americans kept their heads "amid rising hysteria, provide sane leadership for the majority of the American people who want to keep out of the European war," and ensure that the president and members of Congress became aware of these opinions. The group had decided against an earlier, cumbersome name; instead, they opted for the simpler America First Committee.

Back in New Haven, Kingman Brewster was troubled by the rising opposition of Yale alumni to the isolationist point of view on campus, and annoyed because former President Herbert Hoover had delivered a blatantly partisan speech in Woolsey Hall. It was Brewster's impression that the large auditorium, which was one of a complex of buildings erected in 1901 to commemorate the university's bicentennial, was not permitted to be used for political purposes, and he went to see President Charles Seymour to ask if he was correct in this assumption. Seymour, an internationalist who had been a delegate to the Peace Conference in Paris in 1919, managed to maintain a detached, middle-of-the-road point of view on campus, and he told Brewster that the university had no policy against political speeches in Woolsey Hall. What troubled the administration was that it was such a cavernous place, with 2,700 seats, that important speakers and their sponsors were often embarrassed by a relatively small turnout.

Brewster asked, "If I can get the right kind of speaker, can I have Woolsey Hall?"

Seymour said he could.

Brewster telephoned Bob Stuart, Stuart met with Charles Lindbergh and asked if he would be willing to speak to a gathering of Yale students, and on October 24 Lindbergh called Brewster to say he would be in New Haven on October 30.

———

Along with three thousand others—hundreds of them standing along the walls because every seat was filled—I was in Woolsey Hall to hear Lindbergh that night. Despite its size, the auditorium has an unusual intimacy, created by the balcony that runs along three sides of the great buff-gold-and-blue room, so that the seats on the sides face each other and are perpendicular to those in the rear and the main section below. While Kingman Brewster, as head of Yale's America First Committee, delivered his brief introductory remarks, I glanced at the faces of other members of the committee seated behind him on the platform (several were my classmates; two law students, Potter Stewart and John Ecklund, had lived across the hall from me and had been my freshman counselors) and noticed that the group also included two faculty members whose courses I was taking— Samuel Flagg Bemis, the authority on U.S. diplomatic relations, wearing as usual a high, stiff detachable collar and high button shoes, and Whitney Griswold, who taught government and international relations.[2]

When Lindbergh rose and walked to the lectern, and stood there, leaning on it with outstretched arms, smiling, waiting for the great wave of applause

[2] Griswold succeeded Charles Seymour as president of the university in 1950, and was himself succeeded by Kingman Brewster thirteen years later.

to subside, most of us were for the first time in the flesh-and-blood presence of our boyhood hero, the most famous American of our childhood, and you could feel the electricity because of that and because of the sheer magnetism of his presence—a magnetism that was a blend of his almost boyish appearance (he still could have been mistaken for the "Slim" Lindbergh of early barnstorming days), his sheer animal health, his extraordinary smile, his courage and conviction, and our awareness that he probably knew more about the strengths and weaknesses of the air forces now locked in combat in Europe and more about the awesome potential of air power than any man alive. Seeing him on that platform was to imagine Frank Merriwell returning to Yale, except that Charles Lindbergh was no fictional hero but the personification of the air age that was shaping the destiny of our generation. Speaking for most of those who were in Woolsey Hall that night, Kingman Brewster would later tell members of the Senate Foreign Affairs Committee, "We are resentful of the deceit and subterfuge which has characterized the politics of foreign policy. Perhaps that is why we have listened to Colonel Lindbergh whether we agree with him or not, and have admired his courage and straightforwardness."

As an illustration of how recently the air age had come upon us, Lindbergh began by saying that his father had been chased by Indians in Minnesota, and that a mere ten years after the father's death, the son was surveying transoceanic air routes between the hemispheres. (Lindbergh himself, young as he was, had been born one year before the Wright brothers proved that man could fly in a heavier-than-air craft.) What America now faced, he said, was a set of problems infinitely more complex than anything that had confronted man before, and to solve them, we had to reorient our ideas, policies, and ideals. As a starter, we had to realize that war would be a disaster for our country.

Why? Because America's internal problems were severe enough without imposing the burden of war on them. And because America was totally unprepared to fight. Not so many years ago we had gone to war to make the world safe for democracy, and only one generation later the fruits of that crusade were dictatorships and another European war. Like the English and the French, who had vacillated between a policy of backing down at Munich and a policy of intervention with Poland, the United States had behaved with similar lack of purpose. After sending troops abroad to fight in 1917, we had pulled out of Europe, turned our backs on the League and Wilsonian idealism, reduced our navy, neglected our air force, let our army dwindle to skeleton size, and passed strict neutrality laws, all the while Germany and Italy were rearming. And then, to compound the folly, once Germany had reached maximum strength, we began to take an active interest in Europe's affairs, encouraging England and France to declare war, repealing our neutrality legislation, initiating a huge rearmament program—making the moves we should have made five years earlier if we were going to make them at all.

What was lacking was a clear-cut policy, Lindbergh said. "We must decide whether we are going to place our security in the defense of America, or in an attempt to control the affairs of the rest of the world." Once we made that choice (and he had no doubt as to which it should be), we had to prepare calmly and adequately for the action we would take. Our diplomatic naïveté and our military inadequacy left us with "only one safe course of action: that is, defense of America." And Lindbergh then went on to discuss in detail the four air routes by which a European nation or combination of nations might invade the United States. (The threat could only come from Europe, he explained, because "no nation in Asia has developed [its] aviation sufficiently to be a serious menace to the United States. . . .") As he described the northern route over Greenland and Iceland, the southern route over Bermuda, the great circle route, and the South Atlantic route, we were reminded that this was the incomparable aviator and navigator who had flown those very aerial paths, and if he told us that "no country in the world today has a fleet of bombing planes capable of operating nonstop across the Atlantic Ocean," who was to contradict him?

Stressing that we must build our security upon "the bedrock of our own continent and its adjacent islands" and proceed toward "the independent American destiny that Washington outlined in his Farewell Address," he reminded us finally that we were the ones who would be called upon to bear arms and make the sacrifice in the event of war—we who would inherit the burden of shaping the peace that followed.

It was the longest speech Lindbergh had given, and he thought it by far the most successful. He had anticipated opposition and heckling from the Yale audience, but what he got was rapt attention and a prolonged standing ovation before the students filed out of the hall, talking excitedly about what they had heard, and headed back to their rooms to discuss his message, long into the night.

═══

In spite of the weather—cold, dreary, sodden with rain—another distinguished visitor turned up in New Haven on the same day Lindbergh made his speech. By fate or by design, the man whose policies had forced Lindbergh to take the stump pulled into the railroad station, and some two thousand people braved the downpour to hear the president of the United States deliver a short campaign speech from the rear platform of his special train. Smiling broadly, Mr. Roosevelt spoke for less than ten minutes, passing lightly over what was on the minds of a great many people—the Selective Training and Service Act passed by Congress in September, which empowered the president to call up the National Guard for duty in the Americas and had caused sixteen million American men between the ages of twenty-one and thirty-five to register for the draft just two weeks earlier. He deplored the war scare that had been injected into the campaign by his opponent, the president said, referring casually to selective service as though it were the most natural thing in the world: "We have started to train more men not because we expect to use them, but for the same reason your umbrellas are up today—to keep from getting wet."

The crowd may not have sensed it, but by the time Mr. Roosevelt appeared in New Haven it seemed that his fears about the political consequences of the draft legislation had been justified, for within recent days the campaign—which had commenced with the candidates appearing to agree on foreign affairs—had degenerated into what Robert Sherwood called "a national disgrace." According to Sherwood, FDR enjoyed this particular campaign less than any in which he had engaged: Willkie was not an easy target for the old pro; despite the lingering taint of Wall Street, he was in truth a liberal, fighting as much against the reactionaries of his own party as against the New Deal. Nor did the political philosophies of the two men differ that much, with the result, Sherwood said, that they were playing out "a dreadful masquerade, in which the principal contestants felt compelled to wear false faces, and thereby disguised the fact that, in their hearts, they agreed with one another on all the basic issues."

Supremely self-confident, certain that he could win by the sheer force of his personality, Willkie had embarked on his campaign suspicious and disdainful of the professional politicians, determined to talk straight to a public weary of politics and all its trappings, determined to do everything for himself—even to writing his own speeches. Again and again he challenged "the champ" to come out and fight,[3] but the champ had been down this same road many times, he was acutely aware of what he was doing, and he never mentioned Willkie by name, simply ignored his existence for almost three months. Willkie was shouting himself hoarse in the stockyards of Chicago, in downstate Illinois, Missouri, and Kansas, in a huge outdoor stadium in Tulsa, the heat of Amarillo, in Fresno in California's San Joaquin Valley, in San Francisco, Oregon, Montana, North Dakota, Iowa, and back again in Chicago, where he summed up the experience by saying that he had seen the spiritual hunger in thousands of upturned faces, the faces of people puzzled and uncertain. And all the while Roosevelt gave him the silent treatment, behaving as if no election campaign existed.

At the time Willkie gave his acceptance speech to a shirt-sleeved crowd estimated at a quarter million people in Elwood, a friend suggested that he take some lessons in voice placement, to make the campaign ordeal easier, enabling him to spare his vocal cords, but Willkie would have none of it—it smacked of sissy stuff. Even before he left on his Western trip, his voice had become a hoarse, rasping croak. At one point his throat was almost paralyzed, and by the time he reached California he admitted defeat and sought

[3]In Robert Sherwood's opinion, Willkie made a grievous mistake when he shouted, "Bring on the champ!" for the public interpreted this to mean "To hell with the third-term taboo. Let's make this a *real* fight!" Willkie, in other words, dramatized the contest, turning it into a sporting event, not realizing that the more popular enthusiasm it generated, the more to FDR's liking it was.

help. A Hollywood throat specialist named Harold Barnard joined his campaign train and ministered to him from then on, but Barnard was dealing with a nonstop talker; it didn't matter to Willkie if he had an audience of five or five thousand, he would try to get their votes. "My God, I can't make him stop," Dr. Barnard complained. "He goes right on night and day."

Traveling back and forth across the industrial heart of America, Willkie felt the wrath of labor that was a residue of sit-down strikes and so much violence. He and his wife were booed and pelted with eggs in Detroit and Pontiac, but he persisted, reasoning, exhorting, joking, pleading, attacking the New Deal record and the way Roosevelt "played politics with preparedness," speaking about the strength of the land and the people, reminding his audiences that "only the strong can be free, and only the productive can be strong." His hair was more rumpled, his voice more like gravel, but he was drawing big crowds, and his incredible energy never flagged, his determination to win mounted. And somewhere along the way America began to respond, as it frequently does to the underdog fighting against the odds; something of the crusading fervor that had been so evident in Philadelphia was reawakened, and the tide began to turn. When that happened, no one was quicker to sense the shift of mood than the Democratic Party regulars.

On September 27 the nation was stunned by the announcement of a treaty of alliance between Germany, Italy, and Japan. The so-called Tripartite Pact recognized the leadership of Germany and Italy in establishing a "new order" in Europe, and Japanese leadership in "Greater East Asia." That the agreement was aimed directly at the United States was made plain by a pledge of mutual assistance should any of the signatories be attacked "by a power at present not involved in the European war or the Sino-Japanese conflict." Ribbentrop viewed it as putting a brake on Roosevelt's ability to maneuver the United States into war. Hull and the British perceived it as merely formalizing what had long been a fact. And Stimson, while realizing that it was "a very serious proposition," knew that there was little likelihood of Germany or Italy materially assisting the Japanese—or vice versa—and he looked on it as positive, since it would wake up Americans to how isolated the nation was.

Several of Hull's associates at State saw the matter quite differently. Adolf Berle, for one, believed that the United States was moving rapidly toward war and saw little hope of avoiding it. Breckinridge Long felt the same way: "And so we go," he wrote in his diary, "farther and farther along the road to war. But we are not ready to fight any war now—to say nothing of a war on two oceans at once—and that is what the Berlin-Rome-Tokyo agreement means. Nor will we be ready to fight any war for eighteen months in the future."

No matter what the Axis Pact might portend, the long and short of it was that no responsible person in Washington wanted to provoke an incident with Japan. When Roosevelt suggested dispatching a National Guard division to Hawaii, both Stimson and Marshall opposed it (they did give in to the extent of sending an antiaircraft regiment), on grounds that every day of peace meant another day's support for the British.

Suddenly, between reaction to news of the Tripartite Pact and admiration for the way the British were holding out against the blitz, public sentiment in favor of aid to Great Britain—even at the risk of war—increased from 16 percent to 52 percent, according to a Gallup poll. Then, midway into October, the pace of the campaign picked up perceptibly and Roosevelt found himself under fire from all directions. Two days after sixteen million men registered for the first peacetime draft in U.S. history, Senator Hiram Johnson of California announced for Willkie. Five days later, as the War Department announced that more planes were being sent to the Philippines, Al Smith started campaigning for the Republican. Two days after that, in a radio speech heard by an estimated 25 or 30 million Americans, John L. Lewis poured out his hatred for Roosevelt, scoring him for playing "a game that may make cannon fodder of your sons," accusing him of an "overweening, abnormal" lust for power. And whom did Lewis support? Wendell Willkie, of course. For Willkie "has the common touch. . . . He has worked with his hands, and has known the pangs of hunger."

Lewis's attack on Roosevelt, even his endorsement of the Republican candidate, came as no surprise, but his next statement was a bombshell. The only way Roosevelt could win, he asserted, was if labor supported him, and he appealed to CIO members not to give the president their vote. If they did so in spite of his advice, he, John L. Lewis, would resign as president of the union.[4]

Not all the news favored Willkie. The *St. Louis Post-Dispatch* endorsed the president, despite its opposition to the destroyers-for-bases agreement, and a big surprise came when Dorothy Thompson, who had welcomed Willkie's candidacy, explained to readers that FDR's superior knowledge of foreign affairs had persuaded her to support the president. "He has assets on his side that nobody can match," she said. "The president knows the world. He knows it . . . better than any other living democratic head of a state [and] no new president could acquire this knowledge in weeks or in months or in four

[4]A story appeared in the *New York Times* on October 16, suggesting that Lewis would endorse Willkie unless the White House could patch up its differences with the labor leader, and Roosevelt promptly invited Lewis to a meeting. But Lewis was not having any reconciliation: when they met the next day, instead of discussing substantive issues, he accused the president of having the FBI tap his telephone, demanded that it cease, and stalked out of the room. His ugly attack on Roosevelt and his arrogant threat to resign caused great consternation among labor leaders, many of whom repudiated his endorsement of Willkie. In the closing weeks of the campaign, Lewis continued to insist that the workers must choose between him and Roosevelt. He was convinced that labor would decide the election and that his speech had won the presidency for Willkie.

years." When this thunderbolt appeared in the staunchly Republican *New York Herald Tribune,* it produced a storm that did not abate until Miss Thompson's contract expired (by mutual consent) in March 1941.

In spite of themselves, both candidates were ultimately forced to change tactics, take off the gloves, and go at each other with some of the wildest charges imaginable, and when they did the campaign turned very nasty. Democratic Party regulars were not so much worried that Roosevelt would lose as they were concerned that all the candidates who expected to ride his coattails to victory—the congressional hopefuls, the gubernatorial candidates, everyone down to the county and municipal races—might be defeated unless the president climbed off his lofty perch and conducted a normal campaign, by which they meant an attack with no holds barred.

To compound their concerns, Willkie was taking a different tack. Until well into September he had relied on the advice of the "amateurs" who had made possible the great victory in Philadelphia—men like Russell Davenport and Sam Pryor, who had as little use as he had for the Old Guard isolationists and reactionaries—and in the process he picked up substantial public support. Yet for all his talk about unemployment and unpreparedness and the evils of a third term, he failed to hit on an issue compelling enough to undermine Roosevelt's enormous popularity, and the polls showed him losing ground. Even as he spoke, moreover, the war boom had begun, and workers were heading back to good jobs in steel mills and aircraft factories and shipyards. The national chairman of the Republican Party, Congressman Joseph W. Martin, and his colleagues were contemptuous of the amateurs and had come to dislike Willkie almost as vehemently as they hated Roosevelt, but they knew they had to win with this candidate or sit out another four years without patronage, so they badgered Willkie, working on him to give up the bipartisan nonsense. If he wanted to win, they told him, he had to scare the public, convince people that a vote for Roosevelt was a vote for war, and he should strike that note and play it for all it was worth.

As the campaign moved into its final weeks, Willkie's eagerness to win took precedence over everything, including conscience and good sense. He seemed not to have questioned the justness or consequences of calling Roosevelt a warmonger, and he began making statements he would ultimately regret. If the president's "promise to keep our boys out of foreign wars is no better than his promise to balance the budget," he said, "they're already almost on the transports." Roosevelt, he told an audience in Portland, Oregon, "has left us virtually alone in the world and brought us to the brink of war." In Chicago, he promised that "when I am President I shall not send one American boy into the shambles of another war."

To judge from the latest polls, the scare tactics were working in Willkie's favor, and nowhere was this more evident or more alarming than at Democratic headquarters. The party, after all, had not recovered from the trauma of the Chicago convention. Delegates had returned home angry and rebel-

lious, resentful of having Wallace shoved down their throats; the leadership—notably Farley, Garner, and Bankhead—felt betrayed and were still
seething over the role played by Hopkins; and one result of this wrath and
uncertainty was that letters and telegrams flooded the White House, suggesting that a wave of fear might sweep Willkie into office unless the
president answered him, and pulled something dramatic out of the hat
before election day.

With Wendell Willkie attacking Roosevelt as "the man whose trademark
is on the depression, the man whose foreign policies helped disrupt the
democratic world," and charging that he was remaining aloof from the
campaign because "he will not discuss the issues that trouble people," it was
no wonder that Democratic leaders were panicky. Harold Ickes, Jimmy
Byrnes, Ed Flynn, and Justice Black were among the many who put pressure on the president to get out and take the offensive. Even Eleanor
Roosevelt urged her husband to schedule more speeches, to respond to
Willkie's charges.

It was not only Willkie, of course, who was giving the Democrats fits—it
was the anti-Roosevelt extremists, the isolationists, the America Firsters,
the fringe groups traveling in their wake. Father Coughlin railed against
those who supported aid to Britain, calling them sneaks and subversives,
"the most dangerous fifth column." Charles Lindbergh spoke at a rally in
Madison Square Garden in October, calling for the election of "leaders
whose promises we can trust, who know where they are going, and tell us
where we are going." That was a legitimate enough appeal, but a British
journalist who was present was disturbed by what he saw and by what
Lindbergh had failed to say. He felt that the crowd was as "hysterical as
any Hitler mob, but much more unpleasant. . . . Reading the text of
Lindbergh's speech, I realized that—the war having been on for a year,
France and much else of civilization enslaved, London bombed, the march
to the death camps underway—it contained no word of even mild disapproval of Hitler."

━━━

Adding to the president's problems at home was the matter of Joe Kennedy
in London. For a year, the ambassador to the Court of St. James's had
alternated between the sulks, anger, and fear that FDR was going to push
the United States into war. He had sent his family home to America, he was
lonely and depressed without them, his business interests were "shot to
pieces" because of the war, he was bored, and because he had sided with
the appeasers in England and made no bones about his belief that the British
would be defeated, he was increasingly disliked by the British and bypassed
by the White House.[5]

[5]To the hard-pressed British, the U.S. ambassador was anathema. A memorandum in the
Foreign Office files—written by Sir Robert Vansittart, chief diplomatic adviser, and initialed

In December of 1939, Kennedy had taken home leave to spend Christmas in Palm Beach, and he stopped off in Washington to see Roosevelt. His visit came at a time when FDR was doing his level best to camouflage his own intentions by encouraging other candidates to enter the presidential race, and when Kennedy heard him tick off a list of potential nominees, naming McNutt, Hopkins, Frank Murphy, Bob Jackson, and then heard him say, "There's yourself," ambition reared its head. In February the *Boston Post* carried a carefully planted story beneath the headline KENNEDY MAY BE CANDIDATE.

In the end it came to nothing. Kennedy decided not to run, and before returning to London in March he ran into William Bullitt at the State Department. Bullitt was also home on leave, and Kennedy found him being interviewed by Joseph Patterson, publisher of the *New York Daily News,* and the paper's Washington correspondent, Doris Fleeson. According to Harold Ickes, who had the story from Bullitt, Kennedy joined the conversation, and was soon predicting that Germany would win the war and that everything in France and England "would go to hell." He then denounced the president, whereupon Bullitt took issue with him, and the argument became so heated that the embarrassed journalists left the room. Bullitt accused him of disloyalty and said he ought to keep his mouth shut, and "Joe said that he would say what he Goddamned pleased before whom he Goddamned pleased," and after a few more angry words the two parted. Bullitt told Ickes he didn't think he would ever speak to Kennedy again.

Back in London, the British were cooler to Kennedy than ever, and he grumbled that a "fifty-dollar-a-month clerk" could handle his job. By the time France fell, Joseph Alsop wrote, Kennedy was forecasting "the collapse of capitalism, the destruction of democracy, and the onset of the dark ages. He says that only an early peace, at almost any price, can save the world." About that time the ambassador called on the dying Neville Chamberlain and left him to record in his diary that "everyone in the U.S.A. thinks we shall be beaten before the end of the month." July found him fretful, a cast-off kingmaker who believed he had been responsible for Roosevelt's nomination in 1932, listening intently to news of the Democratic convention, where his son Joe Jr. was a delegate pledged to Farley. So removed was he from the diplomatic mainstream that he had to learn of the destroyers-for-bases arrangements from the British, not Washington. "I do not enjoy being a dummy," he complained in a letter to Roosevelt, meanwhile threatening Hull that he was going to resign, which was precisely what the president did not want just then. Kennedy was a troublemaker, "entirely out of hand and out of sympathy," Roosevelt said, and he wanted him out of the way, in London, during the campaign. Soothing letters went

by Lord Halifax, the secretary of state for foreign affairs—had this to say about him: "Mr. Kennedy is a very foul specimen of double crosser and defeatist. He thinks of nothing but his own pocket. I hope that this war will at least see the elimination of this type."

forth from the White House and the State Department, but Kennedy was not fooled by FDR's attempt "to soft-soap me" or by a statement from the White House that he was essential to the nation. However, once the heavy attacks on London began in September he was unwilling to return to the United States unless he was officially recalled, for fear of being labeled a coward.

Meantime, while he kept score of the air raids he survived, Kennedy had the satisfaction of seeing a book by his second son hit the best-seller list in the States. The ambassador had persuaded Jack to turn his Harvard thesis into a book: through the embassy, interviews with British officials were arranged; Arthur Krock of the *New York Times* was enlisted to find a literary agent and rework the manuscript; and Kennedy Senior asked Henry Luce to write a foreword. (Unbeknownst to the editor of *Time,* the Englishman Harold Laski had been approached first and refused on grounds that it was "the book of an immature mind; that if it hadn't been written by the son of a very rich man, he wouldn't have found a publisher.")

What ended the unhappy ambassador's exile was a combination of circumstances that convinced Roosevelt he needed Joe Kennedy at home. At the height of the campaign a rumor reached the White House that Henry Luce was urging Kennedy to leave London in order to campaign for Willkie. This coincided with a heavy-handed threat to Cordell Hull from his man in London that unless he was recalled, he would release for publication on November 1 an article criticizing the administration for "having talked a lot and done very little." Meanwhile, Supreme Court Justice Felix Frankfurter took fright at the number of Catholics he perceived abandoning Roosevelt, and with Frank Murphy and Lewis Douglas went to the White House and urged the president to recall Kennedy so he could speak out in FDR's behalf. And so it came to pass on October 22, 1940, that Joseph Patrick Kennedy, after bidding farewell to the embassy staff and posing for photographs, left his diplomatic post for the last time and headed across the Atlantic, bound for home.

In New York, his arrival on the *Atlantic Clipper* was eagerly awaited by Henry and Clare Boothe Luce. The previous spring Kennedy had informed Mrs. Luce, "I'm going to come back home, get off the plane, and endorse the Republican candidate for president," and when her husband received the same impression in a telephone conversation with the ambassador, plans took shape for Kennedy to deliver a radio address backing Wendell Willkie. What the Luces did not know was that the retiring ambassador received messages from President Roosevelt at every stop on his return trip, cautioning him against making statements to the press until "you and I have had a chance to agree upon what should be said. Come straight to Washington," was the command; the president wanted to be the first to talk with him.

On the final day of the New York World's Fair, Pan American's *Atlantic Clipper* flew in over Flushing Meadow and descended into the bay off La Guardia Field, where Kennedy disembarked with a souvenir of London—

an air-raid siren—in his hand, to be greeted by a battery of officials and a personal note on White House stationery. Before joining his waiting family, Kennedy telephoned Washington. The president was lunching with Speaker Sam Rayburn and the Texan's young protégé Lyndon Johnson, but he took the call. "Ah, Joe," he purred into the phone, "it's so good to hear your voice." He wanted him to come to the White House right away—"tonight, for a little family dinner. I'm dying to see you." And as Rayburn and Johnson looked on in amusement, the president drew a finger dramatically across his throat.

While the Luces waited in vain at their Manhattan home, the ambassador shrugged off the waiting reporters with a grin, saying he would make no statement until he had talked with the president, and he and Rose were whisked aboard a plane for Washington. On the trip, Mrs. Kennedy worked on her husband, calming him down, urging him not to resign lest it damage their sons' political chances. At the White House one of the president's secretaries greeted the Kennedys effusively (her instructions were "Be sure and butter Joe up when you see him"), while the presence of Senator Byrnes and his wife indicated to Kennedy that Roosevelt did not want to be left alone with him.

After they joined Roosevelt upstairs for cocktails, the ambassador answered questions about conditions in London before the talk turned to business and the importance of a speech by Kennedy in support of the president. Kennedy had naturally hoped to discuss his grievances privately with FDR, but when it became clear that that was going to be impossible, he announced that he would have his say in front of everybody—at which, Rose Kennedy noticed, the president looked "rather pale, rather ashen." Her husband reminded the president how loyal and supportive he had been, and how he had come out in favor of a third term a year ago. With what result? That he had been consistently bypassed, ignored, left in the dark. The president nodded sympathetically, saying it had been the fault of the foreign service crowd, and that he had had no idea it was going on. More talk followed, and Kennedy somehow got the impression that he had the presidential blessing for a candidacy of his own in 1944, but the upshot of the conversation was what Franklin Roosevelt had had in mind all along. Joe Kennedy agreed to give a speech endorsing him for a third term.

Kennedy was not the only one to be misled by that meeting. When he left the White House, he told reporters rather mysteriously that he had turned down Roosevelt's request to accompany him on the train to New York, that he was taking a plane instead and would hold a press conference in Manhattan the following morning, giving the journalists—and the Willkie people—the distinct impression that he would announce in favor of the Republican candidate. On Tuesday night, October 29, one week before the election, he spoke on the CBS network, and after confessing that he and the president had had their disagreements, said that this was no time to risk the fate of the nation to untried, inexperienced hands. The Kennedy children—his "nine hostages to fortune"—were more important than anything in the world, and since the kind of America they inherited was of grave concern, he concluded that Franklin D. Roosevelt should be reelected president of the United States. "As a vote-getting speech," *Life* observed, "it was probably the most effective of the campaign."

Democrats loved it and asked for more of the same. Republicans said it merely confirmed their opinion of Joe Kennedy as an opportunist. Henry and Clare Luce were baffled, and Kennedy did nothing to dispel the mystery about his change of heart. But Mrs. Luce always wondered what had occurred that evening at the White House, and years later she asked him. He grinned and told her that he and the president had made a deal. "We agreed that if I endorsed him for president in 1940, then he would support my son Joe for governor of Massachusetts in 1942."[6]

In the meantime, Roosevelt was not idle. The Democrats' pleas that he hit the campaign trail happened to jibe with his own plans: he had intended all along to give over the final two weeks of the campaign to political speeches, and he delivered the first of these in Philadelphia on October 23, saying that he would "answer falsifications with facts. I will not pretend that I find this an unpleasant duty. I am an old campaigner, and I love a good fight." Five days later he was in New York, and had Kennedy joined him on the platform at Madison Square Garden that Monday night, October 28, he would have seen the master politician in top form, devastating his opponent. In an otherwise equivocal address, in which he defended himself against Willkie's charges, Roosevelt hit upon a phrase that was far more effective than anything he said about his record. Citing the voting records of certain congressmen, he named, in order, Joe Martin, Bruce Barton, and Hamilton Fish. The repeal of the embargo act, he said, had gone through despite the opposition of certain Republican leaders—among them "Senators McNary, Vandenberg, Nye, and Johnson; now wait," he said, pausing and smiling, "a perfectly beautiful rhythm—Congressmen Martin, Barton, and Fish." The crowd loved it, especially the way he pronounced the names, "Maahtin, Baahton, and Fish." Twenty-two thousand partisans cheered with delight. And when the president a few minutes later worked in the euphonious names, saying, "Great Britain and a lot of other nations would never have received one ounce of help from us if the decision had been left to"—here a pause—"Martin, Barton, and Fish," the crowd repeated the names along with him, roaring "Maahtin, Baahton, and Fish" until the words echoed from the rafters, somehow linking Willkie in the public mind with the dinosaurs of Old Guard Republicanism.

[6]There was to be no governorship for Joseph Kennedy, Jr. In August 1944, he volunteered for the dangerous job of flying explosives over the coast of Belgium, and his plane exploded in midair. By coincidence, Franklin Roosevelt's son Elliott was flying with the air escort.

Willkie, more than anyone, knew how that simple catchphrase hurt. "When I heard the president hang the isolationist votes of Martin, Barton, and Fish on me, and get away with it, I knew I was licked," he said later.[7]

===

The drawing of the first draft numbers was scheduled for October 29, and Roosevelt briefly considered delaying it until after election day. His advisers were urging him to do just that; but even with hysteria over involvement in the war at a peak (adding to the sense of peril, Italy had just invaded Greece), the president decided to go ahead with the ceremony, to be present himself, and to mark the occasion with a radio broadcast. He knew he had to choose his words with exceptional care, and rather than refer to it as conscription or a draft, he called the process a "muster," evoking memories of the Minute Man, the citizen-soldier who was such a strong tradition in America's past, before reading from a letter written by the Catholic archbishop of New York, Francis Spellman: "It is better to have protection and not need it than to need protection and not have it. . . . We really cannot longer afford to be moles who cannot see, or ostriches who will not see. . . . We Americans want peace and we shall prepare for a peace, but not for a peace whose definition is slavery or death."

With the election a week away, Democrats had the jitters and wanted more from the president than evocations of Minute Men and quotations from the clergy. Fear of war was the one completely unpredictable factor, the great emotional question that might so easily determine the outcome of the voting. Willkie was gaining steadily, the polls said, and it was going to take a special effort to reassure the electorate that Roosevelt was not going to push the nation into war. In short, the politicians were demanding a guarantee, and in Boston, a few hours after his brief pause in New Haven, the president gave it to them. With Rosenman, Sherwood, Harry Hopkins, and his secretary Grace Tully, FDR had worked on his speech all day between whistle stops, at each of which more telegrams were delivered, pleading for a solemn promise to the mothers of America. One came from Ed Flynn, the Bronx boss and Democratic national chairman. Hopkins handed it to Roosevelt.

"How often do they expect me to say that?" the president asked testily. "It's in the Democratic platform and I've repeated it a hundred times."

"I know it, Mr. President," Sherwood replied, "but they don't seem to

---

[7]Robert Sherwood, who quoted this remark by the Republican candidate, added: "I must say that I doubt that statement; it was a virtue of Wendell Willkie's that he never knew when he was licked." No one, however, was more skilled than Roosevelt at planting in people's minds the danger of changing horses: "If our government should pass to other hands, untried hands, inexperienced hands, next January," he said piously, "we can only hope and pray that they will not substitute appeasement and compromise with those who would destroy democracy everywhere, including here."

have heard you the first time. Evidently you've got to say it again—and again—and again."

In the presidential limousine en route to Boston Garden that night sat two tokens of FDR's newfound esteem for Joe Kennedy—Joe's oldest son, and Joe's father-in-law, John "Honey Fitz" Fitzgerald. And in his speech was the promise the Democrats wanted: "And while I am talking to you mothers and fathers, I give you one more assurance," the president declared. "I have said this before, but I shall say it again—and again—and again: your boys are not going to be sent into any foreign wars." A month earlier, Willkie's sense of humor might have saved him; at this late hour in the campaign the tension was too great, his nerves too raw, and his reaction was outrage: "That hypocritical son of a bitch! This is going to beat me!"

The president's pledge was what caught the headlines, but another, less dramatic assurance in the speech was to have profound results. After noting that Great Britain had requested permission to negotiate with American manufacturers for additional airplanes, bringing their current orders for aircraft to more than 26,000—not to mention tanks, artillery, machine guns, rifles, and other arms on order—he declared that the productive capacity of the United States, which had made it the wonder of the world, "is not failing now. It . . . is making us the strongest air power in the world." In essence, he was saying that Britain's survival was the key to America's security and that all aid short of war was the cornerstone of his administration's policy.

Roosevelt gave his final speech of the campaign in Cleveland on the Saturday evening before the election. It was the kind of positive, upbeat message at which he was superb, an almost poetic evocation of America's future—a land of immense educational opportunity, a land whose natural resources were protected "as the rightful heritage of all the people." That same raw, rainy November day, Wendell Willkie's campaign train pulled into New York's Pennsylvania Station, after a journey of almost nineteen thousand miles (he had also traveled another nine thousand miles by air), and in the evening he spoke to 22,000 wildly enthusiastic supporters in Madison Square Garden, who chanted "We want Willkie!" over and over again until they were as hoarse as their candidate. After the rally, and before he fell exhausted into bed, he asked Joe Martin what his chances were. "We've got a chance to win," was the reply. In Martin's opinion, it was just that—a chance; fourteen key states would decide it, and Willkie had to carry them all.

It was over, then—all but the voting, and although Willkie knew intellectually what the outcome was likely to be, he was emotionally incapable of admitting defeat. At one point he asked the reporters traveling with him on the train how they figured the election, and they let him have their opinions. Like Martin, they were seasoned in these matters, they knew what they were talking about, and they were blunt. Willkie heard them out, and said, finally, "To hell with everything. If I can't beat the isolationists in Wisconsin, I would rather not be president." The morning of election day he told a friend that only a miracle could produce victory. As he had observed in the *Fortune* article "We, the People," Americans "do not give their vote to policies; they give their vote to *men.*" And no one knew better than Wendell Willkie how much the enormous personal popularity of Franklin Delano Roosevelt would affect the election's outcome.

Roosevelt would have been opposition enough for any challenger, but it is hard to escape the conclusion that Willkie was beaten by the very factor that made it possible for him to win the Republican nomination in the convention fight in Philadelphia. The war had become the dominant force in American life, as public opinion polls made clear. When asked how they would vote if there were no war, Americans said they favored Willkie by a 5.5 percent margin; however, if America should become involved, they preferred Roosevelt by a striking 18 percent. So, as Wendell Willkie had become the Republican nominee because of events in Europe, he was defeated for the same reason. He had hoped to base his campaign on domestic issues, attacking the New Deal for its shortcomings, but that was a side issue now, not important enough to command people's attention. America's eyes were on the conflagration.

When it comes to accuracy, counting the Xs in a particular box on the ballots has it all over a public opinion poll, and the final tally on November 5, 1940, showed Roosevelt with 27,243,466 votes to Willkie's 22,304,755. (Those fifty million votes cast represented the all-time high in a U.S. election and would remain a record until 1952, when Dwight Eisenhower defeated Adlai Stevenson.) Willkie received 6.6 million more popular votes than Hoover in 1932, 5.6 million more than Landon in 1936. He won ten states, with 82 electoral votes, while Roosevelt carried thirty-eight states with an electoral count of 449.

From London, during that final weekend of the campaign, *The New Yorker*'s correspondent wrote, "As men once watched the East for a portent, millions are now looking to the West with hope and confidence." Apparently a good many Britons had concluded that Roosevelt and Willkie had much the same outlook on foreign policy; but the president's reelection was cheered because it meant a familiar hand on the tiller. "It is the best thing that has happened to us since the outbreak of the war," said a jubilant Harold Nicolson. "I thank God!"

———

On that last evening as the results were being tabulated, when nothing remained to be done but listen to the returns, a little group of family, close friends, and advisers gathered in Hyde Park, as they had in 1932 and 1936. Eleanor Roosevelt served a stand-up supper of creamed chicken, ice cream, and coffee in her cottage near the main house. The president dined with his mother. Afterward, the only man in U.S. history who waited to learn whether or not the voters had accepted him for a third term as president took off his jacket and tie and retired to the dining room with his sons, his uncle, and members of his staff. In a small room off the front hall his mother and several elderly lady friends chatted over their sewing and knitting. In the living room another group listened intently to a big radio. In the pantry, news tickers chattered. Eleanor Roosevelt moved from room to room, smiling, asking guests if they needed anything, never stopping to hear the returns—or so it seemed. Upstairs Harry Hopkins was listening to a little $15 radio in his bedroom.

At 9:40 P.M. the telephone rang and Franklin Roosevelt picked up the receiver. Ed Flynn was calling, to report that the *Cleveland Plain Dealer* had conceded the election to Roosevelt. At 11:00, Elmer Davis announced on CBS that the president had been reelected, and after hearing that, Mr. Roosevelt and the guests walked out on the front porch to greet a parade of local people, carrying red flares and posters, while a band played "The Old Gray Mare." The president was elated to learn that he had carried his solidly Republican home district by a margin of 376 to 302—his best showing ever in Hyde Park. Then he went back inside the house to listen to more returns. He was too keyed-up and restless to sleep, but at 2:30 A.M., finally convinced that victory would not slip away, he went to bed.

At the Commodore Hotel in New York City, Willkie's campaign workers and enthusiasts filled the ballroom, but after Elmer Davis's announcement the crowd of five thousand began to thin out before the candidate came downstairs from his suite at 12:15 to say a few words (though not to concede). The familiar chant "We want Willkie!" was followed by shouts of "Don't give up!" and Willkie smiled, shoved a lock of hair back in place, and replied, "I guess those people don't know me."

Not until late in the morning did he finally send a telegram to the president, congratulating him on his election. Even then, it was not over for the man who had received more votes than any Republican in history, in a campaign that saw him running against both major parties. He had fought the New Deal for setting class against class, and for failing to solve the nation's economic dilemma. He had fought the Republicans for their isolationism, for standing in the way of social reforms, and that was why the Old Guard could not forgive him, during the campaign or afterward, and why one day—four years later—they would refuse to let him play any part whatever in their convention. But Wendell Willkie would have the last word, in spite of them.

At the time, during and after the campaign, he made it clear that no matter how members of his party might vote in Congress, it was essential for the nation to support its allies and oppose the Axis powers. And when the election was history, instead of retiring into silence or sniping at the man who had beaten him, he called upon his supporters to become "a vigorous, public-spirited loyal opposition which would not oppose for the sake of opposition." It was time to set aside partisan politics and domestic differences, he said, and in a series of speeches he summoned all Americans to support Franklin Roosevelt in the awesome task of mobilizing against Hitler.

PART VIII

1941

LOUISIANA:
THE BLACK BOOK

*Public opinion was so antagonistic
that military men like General George Marshall,
the army's chief of staff, here testifying
for the Burke-Wadsworth bill,
wore civilian clothes in Washington.*

CHAPTER 44

"... the Army has about twenty medium tanks."

Ten thousand people were waiting at the airstrip when the plane touched down, many of them miners and workers in the coke ovens, come to pay tribute to Uniontown's most illustrious son. As a boy he had known "about everybody" in the little Pennsylvania town, he had shot grouse with his father in grassy clearings cut by Braddock's men on their doomed march toward Fort Duquesne, he had sat in the moonlight talking to girls on a white board fence ringing the British general's grave, he had hunted and fished where George Washington and a party of Virginians and Indians threw up a little log building called Fort Necessity. He had not been much of a student in those days, but he did love history: so much of it was evident still in the woods and fields around the town, in the National Road that went past his family's house, in the White Swan Hotel that had been a way-stop for the nameless tide heading west in the nineteenth century.

He was seventeen when he went away to college in 1897, having chosen Virginia Military Institute after overhearing his older brother, whom he disliked, try to persuade their mother not to let him go there for fear he would disgrace the family name. After a tour at the army's staff school at Fort Leavenworth, he served with the 1st Division in France in 1917, then on General Pershing's staff, and peace brought him, as it did so many other career officers, a demotion from his temporary wartime rank of colonel, a succession of dreary posts, and waning hopes of advancement as economy-minded Congresses clamped a tightening lid on military expenditures. Duty took him to the Philippines and China, to Fort Douglas, Fort McKinley, Vancouver Barracks, and Fort Benning (where he was assistant commandant of the infantry school and virtually reshaped the training program that turned out officers who would rise to top commands in World War II). He had a tour with the Illinois National Guard; he set up and supervised a score of Civilian Conservation Corps (CCC) camps. For thirty-two years he waited for his colonel's eagles, and he had all but given up hope of a top command when he was summoned to Washington and made deputy chief of staff two weeks after the Munich Pact.

Now he was fifty-nine years old and a four-star general, and a week earlier—on the day Germany invaded Poland—he had taken the oath as chief of staff of the United States Army. Uniontown had declared September 9, 1939, "George Marshall Day," and the general obviously relished the opportunity to return to his roots, as if he might draw strength from these scenes for the trials ahead. After the local dignitaries drove him around town to show him how the place had changed, they laid on a formal reception at the new White Swan, which had replaced the tavern of his youth. In the back of everyone's mind, a local editorial writer noted, was the thought of the enormous burdens Marshall was being asked to shoulder, but all they cared about just now was making this a special day for " 'Flicker,' the snub-nosed, freckle-faced redhead who was a natural-born leader in the '90s, who coasted on Gilmore's Hill, staged shows in Thompson's Stable, and kept things generally astir," and his fellow townspeople urged him for a few hours to lay aside his cares and "make friends with your youth."

In those surroundings it would have been difficult for George Catlett Marshall to do anything else. His mind was very much on the past this evening, and it was as if he could see again "the great life of the nation which flowed through the National Pike and stopped overnight at the inn, just two blocks beyond the house where I lived as a boy." He reminded his audience how close they were to the spot where the young Washington fired a volley that set the world on fire—a conflict that eventually cost France and England their American colonies—and how extraordinary it was that the eighteenth century's global war should "leave the prize of the greatest fame with him who struck the first blow." It was no accident that George Marshall's thoughts turned to George Washington that September evening, and something in his words was reminiscent of the great Revolutionary commander in chief, a man as serious, as self-effacing, and dedicated to duty as the United States Army's new chief of staff. "I will not trouble you with the perplexities, the problems and requirements for the defense of this country," he said in a passage that was classic George Marshall, "except to say that the importance of this matter is so great and the cost, unfortunately, is bound to be so high, that all that we do should be planned and executed in a businesslike manner, without emotional hysteria, demagogic speeches, or other unfortunate methods which will befog the issue and might mislead our efforts. Finally, it comes to me that we should daily thank the good Lord that we live where we do, think as we do, and enjoy blessings that are becoming rare privileges on this earth."

George Marshall had that indefinable aura of command. Dean Acheson, who was to succeed him as secretary of state after the war, described how "the moment [he] entered a room everyone in it felt his presence. It was a striking and communicated force. His figure conveyed intensity, which his voice, low, staccato and incisive, reinforced. It compelled respect. It spread a sense of authority and of calm." He had the look of a commander: even in civilian clothes, which army officers wore in peacetime Washington because of the ingrained prejudice against military men, he was impressive—a six-footer with graying sandy hair, intense blue eyes, and a trim, erect figure from years in the saddle. Better yet, he had the temperament for crisis. As a reporter noticed, "He moves with a quiet steadfastness that inspires confidence in the men around him." Marshall was a private man, quiet and introspective, who tolerated neither fools nor the blunders of those who should have known better. At Dwight Eisenhower's first important meeting with the general, his immediate impression was of "an eye that seemed to me awfully cold," and of a man who knew precisely what he expected. "Eisenhower," Marshall said, "the [War] Department is filled with able men who analyze their problems well but feel compelled always to bring them to me for final solution. I must have assistants who will solve their own problems and tell me later what they have done." What he wanted from his subordinates he generally got, for the chief of staff's temper was famous: it took the form of icy contempt or blistering rage, and either way it could be devastating. "I cannot allow myself to get angry," he once confessed to his wife, but practicing patience was an uphill struggle for a man who had decided that "forbearance and self-restraint are very wearing on the individual and probably do more harm than violent exercise."

His new job would demand every ounce of forbearance Marshall could muster: as chief of staff he was not only the military chief of the War Department, reporting to the civilian secretary of war, who directly represented the president; he was the army's adviser to the president and the secretary of war and congressional committees concerned with military affairs, and the army's spokesman in interagency matters. In practical terms, it was up to him to persuade Congress to appropriate the funds needed to modernize the army, transforming blueprint into reality, and in order to accomplish that objective he had to get along with the members of those important committees on Capitol Hill. Marshall had the ability to do exactly that, thanks to the patience he worked so hard to attain, plus good humor and a superb command of his subject. Of almost equal importance was his popularity with newspapermen, for whom he was currently scheduling one or two press conferences a week despite a natural wariness: "No publicity will do me no harm," he once remarked, "but some publicity will do me no good."

For what was surely his most delicate role—adviser to the president—he set the tone of the relationship just after becoming deputy chief of staff, at a meeting crucial to the rearming of the nation. In the wake of the Munich agreement, Ambassador William Bullitt had given President Roosevelt a chilling picture of the situation in Europe, emphasizing the alarming disparity between German and Allied air forces, and on November 14, 1938, the president summoned to the White House a group that included Henry Morgenthau, Harry Hopkins, Louis Johnson, and Generals Malin Craig, Henry "Hap" Arnold, and Marshall. Roosevelt did most of the talking, making it clear that he wanted a large increase in military appropriations with which to buy airplanes for the British, the French, and the United States Army and Navy. He didn't want to hear about ground forces or rifles or new barracks, he said; what he wanted was airplanes, and lots of them— almost certainly not the twenty thousand he would like to have, but the ten thousand Congress would probably give him. Not much was said, Marshall noticed, about the men who would man and maintain those planes: it was almost as if a host of airplanes by themselves, in American, British, and French hands, would intimidate Hitler; and most of those present nodded agreement "and were very soothing."

Finally FDR turned to Marshall and said pleasantly, "Don't you think so, George?" Now, few people called the mature Marshall by his first name, and apparently Roosevelt caught the frosty look in his eyes, because he never addressed him as George again. But that was only the first sign that Marshall was no yes-man: "I am sorry, Mr. President," he replied stiffly, "but I don't agree with that at all," and there the conference ended. Roosevelt gave the new deputy chief of staff a startled look, but said nothing, and when the door had closed behind them several of those present shook Marshall's hand and said they were sorry his tour in Washington was over.

Two men less alike can scarcely be imagined, and Marshall seems to have recognized and accepted that difference from the moment, some months later, when Roosevelt informed him of his appointment as chief of staff. He warned the president that he intended to speak his mind at all times, even though that would not always be pleasant.

"Is that all right?" he asked, and when Roosevelt replied affirmatively the general told him, "You said *yes* pleasantly but it may be unpleasant." From then on Roosevelt knew that Marshall would give him the unvarnished truth, and it was typical of their relationship that the general—unlike some other presidential advisers—maintained an absolutely correct, distant attitude. "I found informal conversation with the President would get you into trouble," he said. "He would talk over something informally at the dinner table and you had trouble disagreeing without creating embarrassment. So

I never went."[1] It was Henry Morgenthau who suggested to Marshall the best way to deal with Roosevelt. "When you go to see the president," he advised, "stand right up and tell him what you think and stand right there. There are too few people who do it and he likes it." The chief of staff also discovered that proposals to the chief executive should be on one sheet of paper, in clear, simple language, with headings underlined. "You have to intrigue his interest," Marshall found, "and then it knows no limit."

George Marshall had reached the top of the heap in the United States Army, but he would have been less than human if he did not occasionally wonder in the small hours of the night if the job could possibly be worth "the perplexities, the problems, and requirements" that came with it, for they were as numerous as they were alarming. Put simply, he was in charge of the army of one of the great powers, at a time when the world was as unsettled as it could possibly be, yet that army had two civilian bosses who were at each other's throats, it had no definitive operations plan for the immediate future, almost no money, modern weapons, or public support, a commander in chief whose sentiments clearly lay with the navy, an officer corps that was burdened with deadwood at the top, whose enlisted ranks were hopelessly inadequate for much more than garrison duty. And to ice the cake, at a moment in history when air power was suddenly perceived as the offensive weapon that would probably determine the outcome of a war, the Army Air Corps possessed exactly nineteen B-17 bombers, its most important weapon, and had neither the money for nor prospects of obtaining more. Even if the army had the means to buy them, Boeing—the manufacturer—was then capable of producing only thirty-eight a year.

———

The mess George Marshall inherited started at the highest level. Secretary of War Harry Woodring was a glaring example of how politics and politicians can play hob with the system. A banker and a Democrat, Woodring had been governor of Kansas from 1931 to 1933, and when he was defeated by Alf Landon in that normally Republican state he was given what looked in those days to be a sinecure—the assistant secretaryship of war under another political appointee, a former Utah mining executive named George Dern. In 1936, Dern died, and Woodring fell heir to his job (Harold Ickes grumbled that he was appointed with the understanding that the post was temporary, "but now nothing could budge him"). One of several things wrong with having Woodring in the secretary of war's seat was that he was an isolationist. In his opinion, money for the military was to be used strictly

[1]Dean Acheson, too, disliked Roosevelt's habit of calling "everyone from his valet to the secretary of state by his first name." FDR "could charm an individual or a nation," Acheson admitted. "But he condescended. Many reveled in apparent admission to an inner circle. I did not, and General Marshall did not. . . . He objected, as he said, because it gave a false impression of his intimacy with the President."

for the defense of this hemisphere, and when the selective service bill was introduced in Congress he denounced it as unnecessary, unjustified, and a crazy idea that "smacks of totalitarianism." Although the isolationist senator Bennett Champ Clark called Woodring "the biggest man in America," he was no favorite of his fellow cabinet members: Morgenthau considered him a third-rater, Ickes thought him "a small-bore person." Having Woodring at the head of the department was bad enough, but Roosevelt had compounded the folly by naming Louis Johnson assistant secretary. A former national commander of the American Legion who advocated a large air force with long-range bombers capable of carrying war to the enemy, Johnson was temperamentally and philosophically the antithesis of the man who was nominally his boss, he was at odds with him on just about everything, and he made no secret of his ambition to get Woodring's job. The two men cordially detested each other and carried on a running battle in the press, and it was easy for a chief of staff to be caught in the crossfire of their vendetta, as Marshall's predecessor had been. "They have crucified my husband," Mrs. Malin Craig told Katherine Marshall when the latter arrived in Washington.

How difficult this was for Marshall may be judged from his account of the situation before he received his appointment to the army's top job. "Johnson wanted me for Chief of Staff," he wrote, "but I didn't want Woodring to know he was for me. Craig was for me, but I wanted it kept from the President. Woodring was for me, but I didn't want the others to know." Then and later it was suggested that the reason Woodring and Johnson supported Marshall's appointment was that each thought the other opposed it. Whether the president would have opposed Marshall's appointment because Craig recommended him seems unlikely.

Roosevelt was not unaware of the ugly situation: he disliked firing subordinates and usually avoided doing so by hoping the problem would go away. This one would not. Ickes described the feud as a public scandal, and suggested to the president that he get rid of Woodring by offering him the embassy in Dublin, telling him that it was a very important post. FDR doubted that the secretary of war would fall for that, and Ickes replied, "In that event you ought to tell him that he has the choice of Dublin or Kansas." Marguerite ("Missy") LeHand, Roosevelt's private secretary, also disliked and mistrusted Woodring and was eager to see him go, and in May 1940 she informed Ickes that the president had decided to make his move. The news from Europe had forced his hand, and Woodring was summoned to the White House and asked to resign.

The Republicans may have thought that the appointments of Stimson and Knox were made to embarrass them at the time of their convention, but this shift had been a long while in the making—only the timing was suspect. In fact, Stimson was not the president's first choice—William Donovan, Lewis Douglas, and Frank Murphy were among those considered—but Grenville Clark and Justice Felix Frankfurter urged Roosevelt to appoint Stimson, whose outspoken support for universal military training and aid to Britain recommended him, and finally the president agreed, after assuring himself that the seventy-two-year-old Stimson was healthy enough to take on the job. One of Stimson's stipulations was that he be able to pick his own subordinates, and when FDR agreed to that, it meant that Louis Johnson would also have to go.[2] With the leadership of the War Department in the capable hands of Stimson and the team he brought with him—Judge Robert Patterson, Robert Lovett, Harvey Bundy, and John McCloy— George Marshall could devote his undivided attention to a dilemma that looked all but insoluble—the pitiable state of the United States Army.

In the army of 1939, every man was a regular, a volunteer who had chosen to make a career of the military. As might be supposed, many were fugitives from breadlines. A private's base pay was only $21 a month, but that was $21 more than some men had been making before they enlisted, and if the food and lodging left something to be desired, they were better than what was generally available in soup kitchens and flophouses. On the other hand, if the army did not always attract the best men, that was understandable: a first sergeant in a rifle company, absolute czar over one hundred men, made $105 a month after twenty years' service—the same pay a streetcar motorman received, and half what the average plumber made (though it must be remembered that the sergeant also received his living expenses).

Countless hours were spent on the manual of arms, marksmanship exercises (when ammunition was available), spit-and-polish inspections. Russell Reeder, a regular officer in that peacetime army who would lose a leg on a Normandy beach, recalled having participated in "a tent-pitching formation in Panama that involved 5,000 men and lasted about 4 hours. The general stormed about, angry that the 2,500 pup tents were not EXACTLY aligned."

One of the unhappy chores facing George Marshall when he took over as chief of staff was the task of uprooting tradition, seniority, and old friends. If he was going to modernize the army, he had to move younger men into positions of command, he had to take advantage of ingenuity and brains at whatever level he could find them, and in order to make room for the junior officers, he had to let go many colonels in their sixties, who were on the brink of retirement. They were too old physically and mentally to command troops and make split-second decisions under the intense pressures of modern warfare, but as logical as it was to get rid of them, the purge of the senior ranks was an experience that scarred Marshall as well as the

[2]Bernard Baruch was in FDR's office with Johnson when he learned of Stimson's appointment. According to Baruch's account, the assistant secretary "sat in flushed and indignant silence while FDR tried to explain the 'reasons of state' which made it necessary for him to break his promise. After a while Johnson could no longer contain himself. 'But Mr. President, you promised me not once but many times . . .' he began to protest, his face flushed and his voice unsteady. I recognized the danger signs on both sides," Baruch continued. "Reaching over with my foot, I gave Louis a gentle kick to tell him to shut up. He did."

victims. "He was once our dear friend," the wife of one officer lamented, "but he ruined my husband." To replace the top echelons, Marshall turned again and again to his "little black book," in which he recorded the names of men who had impressed him favorably or who had been recommended by someone whose judgment he trusted, and the list would eventually include such young officers as Omar Bradley, Mark Clark, Lawton Collins, Dwight Eisenhower, Courtney Hodges, George Patton, and others who before long made up the leadership cadre of a force that expanded from 187,000 in 1939 to more than eight million six years later under Marshall's aegis. Each was put to the test, given a heavy load of responsibilities, shifted from one assignment to another, made to think the chief of staff was unreasonable, and those who failed were out. It was no accident that Dwight Eisenhower was jumped over 350 senior officers and picked to be U.S. commander in Europe; it was an instance of Marshall's excellent judgment and his determination to have the best possible men in the important jobs.

Nine months before Marshall took charge of the army, *Life*'s editors described it accurately as the smallest, worst-equipped armed force of any major power. Weapons were on hand for only one third of its soldiers— arms that had come home with the troops after the 1918 Armistice, and they were obsolete and the worse for wear. To make matters worse, Congress insisted that surplus equipment be used up before anything new was purchased. When General Hugh Drum tallied his army's strength for maneuvers in the summer of 1939, he calculated that he was short of combat strength by some 3,000 machine guns, 348 howitzers, 180 field guns, and 246,000 men. A current inventory of the army's weapons was a catalogue of embarrassment. Its first-line troops were supposed to carry the Garand semiautomatic rifle, said to be the finest in the world, but only eight thousand soldiers had one; the others had to make do with World War I Springfields, with hand-operated bolt, and one fourth of them were too worn for use in battle. The arsenal contained twenty-four 3-inch guns, fifty 75mm howitzers, two test-model 105mm howitzers, four 155mm field guns, and assorted harbor-defense guns dating back to 1888. Some three thousand 75mm guns (the famous French 75s, developed in 1897) were on hand, but they had the old-style carriage, which necessitated moving the gun by hand in order to shift aim.[3] As for mobility, *Life* noted, "The U.S. Army does not aspire to such masses of mechanized troops as Germany possesses. . . . Even if it could afford it, it would not mechanize itself completely. Mechanized cavalry is valuable for swift, surprise attacks on flanks and rear, but for steady advance and holding ground, infantry and horse cavalry

---

[3]Even in 1940, the habits of frugality died hard. General Marshall testified to the House Appropriations Committee that scrapping the 75mm and replacing it with 105mm howitzers would be "difficult to justify" financially. Replacing the guns would cost $36 million, but new ammunition would run into real money—$192 million. The result was that the army recommended gradual replacement of the 75s.

are still the best. Ground vehicles, like airplanes, are limited in their action by weather and ground conditions. Horses will always be needed for towing artillery over rough terrain. For infantry mass attack the Army has about twenty medium tanks. . . ."

═══

From 1919 on, the nation had been antimilitary, as ignorant as it was apathetic concerning national defense needs, secure in the illusion that the 1922 arms limitation treaties and the 1929 Kellogg-Briand Pact pledged the big powers to defense, not offense. To compound the armed services' woes, when economic catastrophe struck, they had to be content with budgets below the basic maintenance levels. Public hostility to military spending was a great deal more than resistance to unnecessary expense: Americans were against the very principle of rearming, and following the First World War, it became clear that the army had become the government's unwanted stepchild. Fortunately for its sister service, America's trust in its ocean bulwarks was unwavering, and the navy—especially after 1934, when Japan renounced the limitations of the Washington Naval Treaty—fared better than the army, prying loose small budget increases for new construction in the mid-thirties. The navy, most legislators felt, was not only the first line of defense, but the only one that was needed. What was more, in Franklin Roosevelt the navy had an unusually enthusiastic advocate, and it could count on a few congressional supporters to take its side (generally those with shipyards in their districts), but almost no one had a kind word for the army, with the result that its strength declined from four million in November 1918 to 117,000 in 1933—barely enough to post guards and carry on routine maintenance work at army posts. Well before the Depression, Calvin Coolidge asked Congress for even less money than the armed services had requested. And as late as 1939 a West Virginia congressman who was a member of the Military Appropriations Committee said he did not want to give the outside world the impression that the United States was a warlike nation by voting vast sums on rearmament: "It might be an embarrassing situation," he said. That same year the House of Representatives refused to appropriate funds for fortifying the island of Guam: it might appear provocative to the Japanese, opponents argued. When the bill's sponsor, a Kentuckian, waved the flag and proclaimed that a man's vote would indicate whether he was pro-American or pro-Japanese, the response he received from the floor of the chamber was "The Stars and Stripes Forever," hummed by a group of irreverent colleagues. Later still, the supposedly well-informed Walter Lippmann, writing in the *New York Herald Tribune,* made what he called "The Case for a Smaller Army," and criticized efforts to raise a large army in a hurry as unnecessary and undesirable. To cure "the cancer which obstructs national unity" and various other ills, he said, a "surgical operation is indicated—an operation to shrink the army." His remarks appeared in September 1941, less than three months before the Japanese struck.

Some idea of federal budgets and staffs in those lean, budget-conscious days before World War II may be had by recalling that the old State, War, and Navy Building next door to the White House received its name because it housed those three departments of government for half a century, from 1888 until the summer of 1939, when the army transferred its effects to the dilapidated Munitions Building on Constitution Avenue, a shabby wooden structure built as "temporary" quarters during World War I.[4] Making his biennial report to the secretary of war for the period from July 1, 1939, to June 30, 1941, General Marshall noted ruefully that by 1939 the "continuous paring of appropriations had reduced the army to the status of a third-rate power." Specifically, with 174,000 men it ranked nineteenth in the world, between Portugal and Bulgaria, though when considered as a percentage of population under arms, it was forty-fifth. Military appropriations for the 1939 fiscal year totaled $646 million, and almost one third of those funds were for such tangential military purposes as maintaining rivers, harbors, and the Panama Canal. Only 1 percent of the money—slightly more than $5 million—was destined for research and development; so pinched was the army for essential equipment that immediate acquisition had to take precedence over future needs. The inevitable consequence of meager budgets and repeated rebuffs was that the army chiefs, until 1939, rarely asked Congress for what they wanted, but for what they thought they could get, and in some respects President Roosevelt was as gunshy of Congress as the military was—at times, more so.

Between the wars, army spokesmen bravely trooped up to Capitol Hill to sound their warnings, only to be knocked down by a penurious Congress and ignored by a public unwilling to listen. In 1933, when the nation's military forces were at low ebb, the army's authorized strength was 280,000 enlisted men. In fact, funds were available for fewer than half that number, and the complement of many units was so reduced that they had ceased to exist. Referring to the shocking shortages of manpower and matériel, the then chief of staff, Douglas MacArthur, remarked bitterly, "The secrets of our weakness are secrets only to our own people." On one of his frequent

---

[4]The State, War, and Navy Building, an awesome Victorian pile with steep mansard roof and nine hundred exterior columns and pilasters, took seventeen years to build and was promptly scorned by Mark Twain as "the ugliest building in America" (Herbert Hoover called it "an architectural absurdity"). It contained 553 rooms (most with eighteen-foot ceilings), 1,572 windows (each with an awning), and housed twenty-nine cannon captured in battle in addition to the nation's diplomats and desk-bound warriors. The State Department moved in first, in 1875; the navy second, in 1879; and the army last, in 1888. More recently the edifice has been known as the Old Executive Office Building, and shelters such tenants as the vice president, the Office of Management and Budget, and the National Security Council. The Pentagon, so colossal that there was no space for it in the city, was designed to contain all the armed forces. It was begun in September 1941 and completed in 1943, at which time it was found to be too small.

trips to the Hill, General Marshall explained to a congressman that when he commanded a post in the mid-thirties, the garrison consisted of a battalion of infantry, the basic fighting unit of armies the world over. Whereas battalion strength in most other armies was between eight hundred and a thousand men, Marshall could count on barely two hundred, and then only "when every available man, including cooks, clerks, and kitchen police, [was] present for the field training that could be accomplished with available funds."

In 1939 the army's 174,000 enlisted men were scattered among 130 bases— one fourth of them overseas, principally in the Philippines, the Hawaiian Islands, and the Canal Zone. Almost without exception the units were understrength. Nine infantry divisions were authorized, but only three were organized, and those were at less than half complement; the nation's entire tank force consisted of a single mechanized cavalry brigade at half strength, plus a handful of tank companies destined for infantry divisions but not yet attached to them; and so it went in every branch of the service. Motor transport was in such short supply that it was just about impossible to hold maneuvers, as General Drum had discovered. When George Marshall appealed to the Senate Military Affairs Committee in February 1939 for funds, he mentioned that the army lacked ammunition even for target practice: what was available was left over from World War I, and had deteriorated with age. During that war, fifty-three new powder and shell-loading plants had been built between April 1917 and Armistice Day, at a cost of $360 million, making the United States the number-one producer of explosives in the world; with the nation at peace, the factories were abandoned or sold, and the army had to make do with defective ammunition. Marshall informed the senators further that the Ordnance Department had developed a splendid 37mm gun to replace its .50-caliber machine guns: "We consider [it] very fine," he remarked sadly, "but at present we have only one gun."

Even after Hitler invaded Poland and FDR proclaimed a limited national emergency, rearming moved at a glacial pace; the years of isolationism, public antagonism or indifference, and congressional parsimony had left deep scars, and the army was increased by only seventeen thousand men, with a mere $12 million authorized for new mechanized units. As the president cautioned the frustrated chief of staff, this small expansion "was all the public would be ready to accept without undue excitement." Money considerations aside, the military seemed strangely out of touch with reality, averse to change. If the old-timers (with a few exceptions like George Patton) had learned anything from the massacre of Poland's Pomorska cavalry brigade by Guderian's tanks, it was not yet apparent. America's horse-drawn army of 1938 was very much alive, and the notion that the United States might someday be obliged to face Hitler's panzer divisions had barely penetrated the military consciousness. What motor transport was scheduled for purchase was largely intended to move personnel from here to there, and even that was regarded by many an old army hand with deep misgivings, in the belief that "unnecessary" use of trucks would soften the infantry's collective leg muscles as well as its traditional spirit. The movement of foot soldiers was still calculated in terms of the distance men could walk in the course of a day.

During 1940, the army's hand-to-mouth existence would finally begin to improve, echoing events in Europe, yet even in the face of those calamitous events Congress was slow to awake to reality. The president's own caution was evident in his request, in January, for a modest $2 billion increase over the prior year's national defense budget, and the House, characteristically, spent the next three months pecking away at it, trimming here, eliminating there. In those days Congress looked toward Europe and saw a "phony" war. George Marshall looked and saw what was to come. "If Europe blazes in the late spring or summer," he warned in February, "we must put our house in order before the sparks reach the Western Hemisphere." And in May, when his fears were realized, America's house was a long way from being in order; despite Marshall's appeal the House granted the War Department 9.5 percent less for new obligations than he had requested.

On May 10, as Nazi troops were surging into the Lowlands, the War Department reported to the press that it could field five divisions with a total of eighty thousand men. By contrast, Germany had 140 divisions—two million troops—in western Europe alone, prompting a reporter to observe that George Marshall's daunting task of expanding and rebuilding "resembled the reconstruction of a dinosaur around an ulna and three vertebrae." As Marshall himself perceived the situation, even after unprecedented budget increases finally came his way, "A few years ago the army had lots of time and no money. Now we have lots of money and no time."

CHAPTER 45

————◆————

"...the sooner we get in the better."

Until France collapsed, Americans could go to bed secure in the knowledge that the Atlantic Ocean, controlled by the fleets of two friendly nations, stood between them and any military mischief the Nazis might be planning for the western hemisphere. With the moment of truth, it looked as though the worst might indeed be in store—the worst being the currency military planners must deal in—a world in which the United States was truly isolated, standing alone against hostile Axis powers in the Atlantic and Pacific.

That perceptive observer the British ambassador in Washington saw precisely how matters stood: "The USA is at last profoundly moved and frightened," Lord Lothian wrote to a friend. "It had been dreaming . . . that the Allies would keep the tiger away. And now the spectre has suddenly arisen that the British fleet may disappear and then what is to happen to itself? It has only one navy. Is it to keep it in the Atlantic or Pacific? If it keeps it in the Pacific, Germany and Italy will be able to take Brazil . . . and threaten the Canal. If it keeps it in the Atlantic the Japanese will take over the Pacific. If it divides its fleet it will be impotent in both oceans."

Franklin Roosevelt once told his friend Henry Morgenthau, "I like it when something is happening every minute," and in the summer of 1940 he got his wish with a vengeance, what with the deteriorating situation across the Atlantic, growing pressure by Japan on China and Southeast Asia, an oncoming election campaign, and the need to prepare the nation against the increased likelihood of war.

His attitude and response to each of those problems were strongly influenced at a meeting in the White House on May 13, only three days after waves of German paratroops, followed by 135 divisions, poured into Holland, Belgium, and France. The most important item on the agenda was a proposal by General George Marshall for an additional $657 million to expand the United States Army, and those attending, in addition to the president and the chief of staff, were the director of the budget, the Treasury secretary, and the two civilian chiefs of the army. It was a meeting marred by constant bickering by Woodring and Johnson (who did not speak to each other and refused to show each other significant documents) and by a playful sort of bantering on Roosevelt's part. When Secretary Morgenthau spoke up in support of Marshall's request, the president reacted with a "smile and sneer" and an unplayful warning: "I am not asking you, I am telling you." By the time Roosevelt dismissed the group after an unproductive, indecisive hour, Marshall was visibly disturbed, and Morgenthau asked, "Mr. President, will you hear General Marshall?"

Half joking, Roosevelt said, "I know exactly what he would say. There is no necessity for me to hear him at all."

The general walked over to the chief executive's chair, stared down at him with that cold fury his subordinates feared, and asked, "Mr. President, may I have three minutes?"

"Of course, General Marshall," was the reply.

Mincing no words, the chief of staff proceeded to tell the astonished commander in chief in exact detail why the army was in desperate need of these funds, and in conclusion snapped, "If you don't do something . . . and do it right away, I don't know what is going to happen to this country."

Only a month earlier, Marshall had been pleading for the restoration of a paltry $18 million to the army's appropriation. Three days after the May 13 meeting, President Roosevelt delivered a speech to a hastily convened joint session of Congress, and the chief of staff said later that this was the action that broke the logjam that had frustrated army planners for so long. It was one of those cold, rainy days that sometimes make Washingtonians wonder if spring will ever come, and the mood on the House floor was as somber as the weather. The president arrived looking tired and grave, yet while the message he had for the congressmen was deadly serious, there was an inspirational lift to it, something that told them and their constituents back home that this nation would rise to the challenge, would in fact pull off a miracle. At that particular moment, it seemed the wildest imaginable proposition—that the nation could gear up to produce at least fifty thousand airplanes a year, while increasing the size of the army to 255,000 men and constructing new ships for what was to be a "two-ocean navy"; but new weapons of destruction made this program essential, Mr. Roosevelt claimed, and in asking for $1 billion more for the armed services he warned that "no old defense is so strong that it requires no further strengthening, and no attack is so unlikely or impossible that it may be ignored." Rather surprisingly, when you considered that not many senators and representatives were eager to display enthusiasm for a president who had not yet revealed his intentions regarding a third term, cheers and thunderous applause filled the well of the House, especially when he mentioned the fifty thousand planes. By the time news of his speech hit the headlines, the public's first reaction was disbelief or scorn (Charles Lindbergh called the speech "hysterical"); and there were those who thought the president had taken leave of his senses if he thought America could produce aircraft on that scale, as if a magician could wave a wand and say it would be so. His request stunned even the public relations boys at Army Air Corps headquarters. A reporter who went around there to learn what was going on was told that of course we needed a larger air force . . . but fifty thousand planes? Confidentially, he was told, that many aircraft would mean ground crews of more than a million men, and besides, where would we find fifty thousand pilots? So figure it out for yourself.

Implicit in Mr. Roosevelt's message was that he had reached two major decisions—those decisions he would later make crystal-clear in Boston at the end of the political campaign. The first was that America would rearm as rapidly as possible; the second was that as long as Great Britain held out against the Germans, this country would furnish her with weapons. Presidential pronouncements often appear to have been made in a vacuum; more often than not they are the result of intensive planning and deliberation on the part of many people, and this was no exception. Both decisions happened to reflect the president's personal predilections, yet behind them also lay countless meetings of the military planning staffs, drafts and revisions of documents without number, a continuing dialogue about all the alternatives that must be considered in the formulation of policy and plans.

═══

As much as the ordinary citizen in a democratic society might dislike the idea that the military men are secretly plotting a war against one or more nations, plans for all possible contingencies are at the heart of preparedness, even if those plans are unmatched by the state of readiness of the armed forces, as they were in 1940 and 1941. For four decades regular interservice consultation and planning had been conducted through an instrument called the Joint Board, consisting of the army's chief of staff, the chief of naval operations, their deputies, the chiefs of their respective war plans divisions, and representatives from the two air services. Still, when George Marshall became chief of staff in the autumn of 1939, war plans were far from settled. Years of peace and stingy budgets had left the army no real alternative but a posture of "passive defense" whenever and wherever hostilities might erupt. What produced a change of direction was the aggressiveness of the Axis powers, and the realization that in spite of its ocean barriers, the nation's security was at risk. For more than a year, the eyes of America's military planners had focused warily on Latin America and the implications of potential Nazi penetration on hemispheric defense. Observers had been reporting increased activity on the part of Axis agents. Edwin Wilson, U.S. minister in Montevideo, warned of plans for a Nazi uprising there. Claude Bowers, ambassador to Chile, wrote: "It is commonly thought here that the Germans, who are numerous [in Santiago], are thoroughly organized with the view of a coup d'état." So when it was learned that the Nazis were offering the services of military officers to certain South American countries, the Army War College was ordered to conduct secret studies to determine what was required to protect Brazil and Venezuela, in particular, from this and other threats. The fear was that such a coup, carried out by a relatively small group of Nazi fifth columnists, landing without warning from merchant vessels, might easily overthrow a weak government and seize control of a country for the Germans and local Nazi sympathizers.[1] That and other eventualities were in Marshall's mind when he wrote a statement intended to guide the army's War Plans Division: "Dictator governments are arming heavily and penetrating economically and politically in Central and South America. Japan is establishing a 'new order' in China and has been informed that we will have something to say about this 'new order.' These activities emphasize the possibility of this nation becoming involved in war in the Atlantic, in the Pacific, or in both these areas."

Now, there was not the slightest prospect whatever of the United States coping militarily with challenges of that scope at that particular time, but one facet of the planners' job is to substantiate a request for funds, and if Marshall was right, and if there was any risk that the United States would truly be involved militarily in a two-ocean war, then the army was going to need a great many more men than the 174,000 regulars it had in 1939 when he outlined the dangers. Neither then nor much later could anyone know with certainty where a military blow would fall—whether it would come in the form of an attack on the Panama Canal, or in the Philippines, or in the North Atlantic—but it was the responsibility of the Joint Army-Navy Board to consider all the questions and come up with answers. On one point, and one point only, was there some certainty: hemispheric defense and defense of the approaches to the Canal would fly, in budgetary terms, because they were "defensive" operations. Anything else was almost certain to be turned down on the Hill.

Those anxious weeks at the time of the Munich crisis had convinced

---

[1]In May 1940, a report that just such a movement was afoot was sent to President Roosevelt by the British government, prompting him to direct the chief of naval operations to plan on ferrying 10,000 troops by air to Brazil, with 100,000 more to follow by sea. Where he would have found 100,000 troops just then is another question. Fortunately, the report proved false.

nearly everyone that the principal threat to America's security lay in Europe, and in November 1938 the Joint Board's planning chiefs received instructions "to make exploratory studies and estimates as to the various practicable courses of action open to the military and naval forces of the United States in the event of (a) violation of the Monroe Doctrine by one or more of the Fascist powers, and (b) a simultaneous attempt to expand Japanese influence in the Philippines." What resulted was a prophetic document which recognized that the nation's primary interest was in the Atlantic and the Caribbean, and that the United States was incapable of defending the Atlantic and Pacific simultaneously. The syllogism went along these lines: Germany and Italy could attack only if the United States were engaged in the Far East; therefore, even should Japanese aggression occur, the United States must refrain from taking the offensive in the Pacific, and remain in a state of readiness to prevent intrusion by the European dictatorships in South America. As the planners foresaw events unfolding, the Axis powers would force the United States to defend the western hemisphere, thereby leaving Japan a free hand to capture the Philippines and Guam and control the western Pacific. If that occurred, Japan would undoubtedly make an effort to "damage major fleet units without warning, or . . . attempt to block the fleet in Pearl Harbor."

Although the point was not discussed publicly, U.S. strategy had not been to defeat Japan at sea; the idea was to keep the fleet in such a position that it could deter Japan from embarking on new military adventures in Southeast Asia. The Philippines and Indochina, British Malaya and the Netherlands East Indies (from which America obtained virtually all of its crude rubber and almost 80 percent of its tin) were what counted. But what governed in the Pacific was the rule of distance. The only base west of San Diego where the fleet could be sheltered, fueled, and repaired in wartime was Pearl Harbor, and from Pearl Harbor it was between five and six thousand miles to Japanese waters—more than twice the practicable battle radius within which the fleet could go, maneuver, fight, and return to base. In other words, war with Japan was not the type of war the ponderous battle fleet was designed to fight. The navy's planners had come to see that hostilities with the Japanese would mean an increased role for carrier-based aircraft and submarines (which were in short supply) and a diminished likelihood that lines of big battle wagons would slug it out as they had in the First World War. But the point on the graph at which plans and battle-readiness would intersect was a long way off. On June 19, 1940, the day Italy entered the war, FDR signed the "two-ocean navy" bill authorizing the largest expansion in American naval history; as yet those projected 1.3 million tons of new combatant ships existed only on paper.

In the summer of 1939 the U.S. Joint Board, after considering five plans known as Rainbow 1, 2, 3, 4, and 5, was leaning toward the last one, which called, in the event of a two-ocean war, for maintenance of the Monroe Doctrine, protection of the United States and its sea trade, defense of the western hemisphere, and cooperation with Great Britain and France in the Atlantic while maintaining a defensive posture in the Pacific. It was a giant step from this précis to an elaborate operational plan to be used in the event the United States became involved in hostilities. Rainbow 5 was, however, The Plan, and although in the coming months it would be studied and restudied, modified and refined, essentially it would remain the underlying philosophy that governed U.S. actions from the time war began until the final victory.[2]

––––

On May 21, 1940, the day after the Germans reached the English Channel, Marshall received a memorandum from Major Matthew Ridgway in the War Plans Division, citing several of the threatening contingencies that now seemed more likely—all of them calling for "National Strategic Decisions." One was that the Japanese might attack U.S. possessions in the Pacific, another was that German-inspired revolts might erupt in Latin America, a third was that the Nazis might put troops ashore somewhere on that continent; and the memorandum called bluntly for a high-level decision as to which area of the world was considered most important—which one, in short, should receive the army's urgent attention. It was patently impossible to send troops everywhere, and the time to establish priorities was now. According to Ridgway, the *most* the army could hope to do was conduct defensive operations in South America and Mexico, while occupying a few European colonies in the western hemisphere and defending the continental United States and its possessions "east of the 180th meridian." What that geographic reference signified was that the Philippine Islands, Wake, and Guam were considered expendable. (The memo phrased the dilemma more tactfully; their loss was considered "acceptable.")[3] Plans were finally coming in line with reality.

The next day, May 22, Marshall took the Ridgway memorandum to a meeting at the White House with Roosevelt, Chief of Naval Operations Admiral Harold Stark, and the State Department's Sumner Welles, where it was agreed that the United States must avoid a confrontation with Japan,

––––

[2]The five Rainbow plans were the outgrowth of a number of single-color plans devised before and during the first World War. Each color represented a hypothetical enemy—Red for Great Britain, Black for Germany, Green for Mexico, Orange for Japan, and so on—and each plan outlined steps to be taken by the army and navy if the United States should become involved in hostilities with that particular nation. By 1939, the plans were becoming more sophisticated in order to grapple with more complex situations; and when the various colors were combined—to represent, for example, a combination of the United States, France, and Britain against the three Axis powers, in the Atlantic, or in the Atlantic and Pacific simultaneously, they became known as Rainbows.

[3]In fact, navy planners had for decades concluded that in the event of war with Japan the Philippines were doomed—and with them most Americans on the islands. But since no one was willing to tell this to the American or Philippine people, it was shoved under the rug, while it was assumed by higher authority that the planners would work something out in due course.

should not attempt to defend any position beyond the 180th meridian, and, for the foreseeable future, would concentrate on South America. At the same time, discussions were held in the State Department about the advisability of moving the fleet to the Atlantic—one group arguing that its presence in the Pacific was a stabilizing force and a deterrent to Japanese ambitions, another faction contending that in the event Britain was defeated, the navy would be needed in the Atlantic—and in a hurry.

A month later all bets were off. When France capitulated, the question of the hour in Washington was "Who gets the French fleet?"—for whatever the fate of that navy might be, it was no longer a force on which the United States could rely. The dilemma so neatly defined by Lord Lothian now had to be confronted head-on by the planners, and on June 22, Marshall, Stark, and the president met to discuss a list of pressing military questions in the light of this and other rapidly changing circumstances. From the American embassy in Tokyo had come disturbing reports of Japanese troop-training exercises in Formosa and Hainan, suggesting to American, British, and Russian observers alike that the Japanese might soon invade French Indochina.[4]

Five days later, Marshall and Stark were back at the White House with a document they called "Basis for Immediate Decisions Concerning the National Defense." This document assumed that the United States, while maintaining nonbelligerent status, would support Great Britain and China, speed up defense production and manpower training, and enact a peacetime draft to facilitate mobilization, in preparation for the "almost inevitable conflict" with the totalitarian powers. The two commanders also recommended that most of the fleet be transferred to the Atlantic and that arms aid to Great Britain be halted. Considerable sentiment in the armed forces favored the latter step, one advocate being the chief of the War Plans Division, Major General George Strong, who was not sanguine about Britain's hope of survival and cautioned that the United States had to prepare for the worst. Some officers didn't trust Churchill (memories of his advocacy of the disastrous Dardanelles campaign were still green), and, as ever, everyone feared how Congress would react if the military appeared to be giving away the store. As the assistant secretary to the general staff, Major Walter Bedell Smith, remarked, if war came and it was discovered that we were short of weapons because we had given them to the British, "everyone who was a party to the deal might hope to be found hanging from a lamppost."

But Mr. Roosevelt would have none of this. Aid to Britain would con-

[4]In September 1940, the Vichy government was intimidated into permitting the Japanese to establish military bases in the northern area of the country for operations against China. In July of the following year Vichy signed an agreement with the Japanese declaring French "sovereignty" there while allowing fifty thousand Japanese troops to occupy Indochina, which meant establishing naval and air bases within striking range of the Philippines, Malaya, and the Dutch East Indies.

tinue—as much of it as we could possibly send, he declared, while making it abundantly clear that he wanted to hear no more defeatist talk about Britain's will or ability to survive. What was more, he wanted the Pacific fleet to remain at Pearl Harbor, as a warning to the Japanese that there were limits to how far they could go. And that was that.

The individual most affected by the presidential decree concerning the fleet was its commander, Rear Admiral James O. Richardson. As a young midshipman, Richardson (who was known as J.O.) had helped chart the waters around the Philippines, and one reason he had made it to the top in the navy was his thorough knowledge of the Pacific. The U.S. Navy, in case anyone wondered, considered the Pacific its ocean. A good-natured, popular officer with a special fondness for penny-a-point cribbage, the admiral was no stranger to strategic thinking. For a time he had served as the navy's chief planner, and in 1938, with General Stanley Embick, he had worked out a revision of the 1924 Orange Plan for war against Japan, which Embick had characterized as "an act of madness." Their scheme called for assuming a "position of readiness" along a line from Alaska to Oahu to Panama, while the armed forces prepared to seize Japanese mandates in the Pacific, as a prelude to moving in the direction of the Philippines. But the modified Orange Plan, like so many others, was overtaken by the realities of the world situation, and superseded by Rainbow 5.

On January 6, 1940, Richardson was appointed Commander in Chief, United States Fleet (CinCUS), an assignment that was expected to last for two years. His title was somewhat grander than the post he would fill, and it reflected the ambiguity Ambassador Lothian had perceived. Like the British and Japanese, the United States had in reality a single fleet, although in practice those vessels were divided most of the time between the Atlantic and Pacific oceans. So Richardson's *de facto* title was Commander in Chief, U.S. Pacific Fleet (CinCPAC), and in the spring he and his fleet were ordered from the West Coast to the Hawaiian Islands for maneuvers. At the time, the handful of ships based at Pearl Harbor was known as the Hawaiian Detachment, and consisted of one carrier, some heavy cruisers, and destroyers. Richardson expected to complete the fleet exercises off Maui and return in May to San Pedro, California; instead, as Admiral Stark informed him, the Navy Department decided to retain his command in Hawaiian waters for "the deterrent effect which it is thought your presence may have on the Japs going into the East Indies."

In July, Richardson went to Washington, where he conferred with the president and with Stanley Hornbeck, Hull's adviser on political relations, and returned to the fleet a puzzled man. Hornbeck, he concluded, "was exercising a greater influence over the disposition of the fleet than I was." It appeared to the admiral that the State Department official was "the strong man on the Far East" who was behind the fleet's orders to remain in Hawaii, and what troubled Richardson was that Washington was operating under the illusion that Japan could be bluffed, which made no sense whatever. Still fretting, he was back in the capital three months later, lunching with President Roosevelt and Admiral Leahy, his naval aide, warning them that the Pacific Fleet was unprepared for war and, what's more, that the Japanese knew it. The ships under his command could not take the offensive unless they were provided with sufficient auxiliaries; they ought to return to their base on the West Coast, he argued, where they could be maintained and serviced properly, where the men could be better trained, where morale would improve, and where the fleet would be just as much of a deterrent as it would be in Hawaii.

Mr. Roosevelt responded stiffly that Richardson was wrong; he *knew* that the presence of the fleet in Hawaii was having a restraining influence on Tokyo. Not only that: what might appear to the admiral like a sensible move looked to the president like a step in the wrong direction, and he figured the American public and the Japanese would both see it that way.

"I still do not believe it," Richardson retorted, and went on to say that in any case, the fleet in Hawaii was in the wrong place to wage war.

Give the man credit for sticking to his guns: not many officers risk speaking out to their superiors, let alone to the president of the United States, for what they believe to be right. But Richardson didn't stop there. Ignoring the fact that he was already in deep water for arguing with the commander in chief and contradicting him, now, quite deliberately, he took a plunge that would prove to be fatal. "Mr. President, I feel that I must tell you that the senior officers of the Navy do not have the trust and confidence in the civilian leadership of this country that is essential for a successful prosecution of the war in the Pacific." Roosevelt's reaction to that statement may be imagined, but he managed to conceal his anger with a mild, non-committal response, and Richardson departed.

Nor was this the last of the admiral's counterattack. Two days later, he met with Knox, Stark, and others to be told that FDR was considering a trade embargo with Japan, plus a string of naval patrols from Hawaii to the Philippines and from Samoa to the Netherlands Indies. He was dumb-founded, and said so, asking if Roosevelt planned to declare war on the Japanese and protesting again that the fleet was unprepared. The secretary of the navy was no happier than the president to learn that the fleet was not in condition to fight (on top of that, only the previous month, Knox had made an inspection tour and found an astounding lack of awareness of war's imminence), and he snapped, "If you don't like the president's plan, draw up one of your own to accomplish the same purpose." With Stark, Richardson did just that before heading west to join the fleet. But he still carried a full head of steam: en route to Hawaii he wrote a memorandum to Stark, telling him what he thought of the existing war plans against Japan (which was not much), and stating tartly that he needed to be better informed about Navy Department intentions if he was to perform his duties properly.

Sunday, January 5, 1941, was the final day of J.O.'s first year as CinCUS, and just before noon the navy lowered the boom. His flag secretary, George

Dyer, handed him a dispatch from Washington—orders relieving him of command—and Dyer saw that his chief was shocked by the news. Someone asked Richardson what had happened and he responded as if stunned: "I don't know."

At the same hour, Rear Admiral Husband E. Kimmel, Commander of Cruisers, Battle Force, was winding up a game of golf with his chief of staff, Captain Walter DeLany. Afterward they drove to the dock, where Kimmel was handed a message to report at once to the fleet flagship, the *Pennsylvania*. Aboard ship, he read the dispatch informing him that he would become Commander in Chief, United States Fleet, on or about February 1. DeLany, watching him read the message, thought Kimmel was going to faint.

Two days after receiving the bombshell from Washington, Richardson endorsed and sent on to Stark a memorandum from Rear Admiral Claude Bloch, commandant of the Fourteenth Naval District,[5] who had been giving serious thought to the security of the fleet and the ability of local defense forces to deal with a surprise attack. Logically, Bloch assumed that any attack on the base at Pearl Harbor would have to be made by aircraft, launched from carriers, and probably supported by submarines, mines, and sabotage. Against such an attack, Bloch warned Washington, the naval component of the local defense forces had "no planes for distant reconnaissance with which to locate enemy carriers"; the only planes available for the purpose, in fact, were fifty-nine army B-18 bombers, of which "neither numbers nor types are satisfactory." To drive off attacking planes, the army had thirty-six pursuit planes, all classified as obsolete. The army's antiaircraft guns were hopelessly inadequate for the defense of Pearl Harbor. The aircraft warning system consisted of three fixed and five mobile radar stations, and the network would not be operating properly for months. As for defense against submarines, no aircraft were available, only three of Bloch's destroyers were equipped with listening gear, and neither antisubmarine nets nor antitorpedo nets were in place. Bloch believed that the two oil-tank farms on Oahu—where the lifeblood of the fleet was stored—were fairly secure against sabotage, but certainly not against air attacks.

In endorsing this doleful and alarming memorandum, Richardson softpedaled the underlying message. The fleet, he pointed out, would simply have to defend itself, if shore facilities were not up to the job, but as far as he was concerned, "the improbability of such an attack" did not warrant curtailing or interrupting the training of fleet air units. He could not conceive of Japanese aircraft attacking the ships or their base, so he saw no particular need to install torpedo baffles or nets, which would only hamper

[5] As such, Bloch was commander of the Hawaiian Naval Coastal Sea Frontier and commandant of the Pearl Harbor Navy Yard. He also had administrative control over Rear Admiral Bellinger, who commanded the Naval Base Defense Air Force.

the movement of ships in and out of Pearl Harbor. Not only was an attack such as Bloch envisioned extremely doubtful, he repeated, there was "the unlikelihood of an enemy being able to advance carriers sufficiently near in wartime in the face of active Fleet operations." Having said that, Richardson nevertheless recommended that Washington strengthen the Fourteenth Naval District's defense forces so that they could function effectively independently of the fleet, and whether or not the ships were in port. The fleet, in other words, could take care of itself.

The navy had a new chief of war plans named Captain Richmond Kelly Turner,[6] and he and Admiral Stark had been digesting the results of a British attack on the Italian fleet at Taranto on November 11, which had disturbing implications for the U.S. fleet at Pearl Harbor. Shortly after darkness fell on a moonlit night, 170 miles from Taranto, the carrier *Illustrious* had launched twenty-one planes, eleven of them carrying torpedoes, the rest loaded with bombs or flares, and they had flown into the magnificent harbor that was thought to be secure against all forms of attack, and in an hour's time disabled half the Italian fleet for at least six months. Three battleships were torpedoed, one cruiser was reported hit, and the dockyard was badly damaged, at the cost of two aircraft shot down.

So when Turner saw Bloch's memorandum, he had already been doing some homework on the subject of carrier-based attacks and was prepared to read carefully. In fact, after studying the techniques used in the Taranto assault, he drafted a letter from Stark to Richardson, suggesting that the obvious target of an attack in Hawaiian waters would be the fleet at its base, and inquiring about the desirability of placing torpedo nets inside the harbor. No, Richardson replied; the area was too restricted, and besides, ships were not moored within torpedo range of the entrance. (Clearly, he had a submarine attack in mind; after the war he admitted he had not thought it likely that the fleet would be attacked from the air.)

Despite Richardson's lukewarm endorsement of the Bloch memorandum, Turner knew a hot potato when he was handed one and drafted a letter from Navy Secretary Knox to Army Secretary Stimson. On January 24, 1941, it went out, with copies to the Commander in Chief, U.S. Pacific Fleet, and the Fourteenth Naval District. It read:

The security of the U.S. Pacific Fleet while in Pearl Harbor has been under renewed study by the Navy Department. . . . This reexamination has been, in part, prompted by the increased gravity of the situation with respect to Japan, and by reports from abroad of successful bombing by torpedo plane attacks on ships while in bases. If war eventuates with Japan, it is believed easily possible that hostilities would be initiated by a surprise attack upon the Fleet or the Naval Base at Pearl Harbor.

In my opinion, the inherent possibilities of a major disaster to the fleet or naval

[6]Within two weeks, Turner would receive a spot appointment to rear admiral, giving him the rank he needed during the Anglo-British planning discussions.

base warrant taking every step, as rapidly as can be done, that will increase the joint readiness of the Army and Navy to withstand a raid of the character mentioned above.

There was more: a list of the possible dangers, including aerial bombing and torpedo attacks, "carried out successively, simultaneously, or in combination with . . . other operations"; proposed countermeasures, most important being the necessity to locate and engage enemy carriers before an attack could be made; and a recommendation that army and navy forces in Oahu hold weekly exercises to prepare for defense against surprise air attacks. It was almost certainly the most important letter ever to be sent over Frank Knox's signature.

===

Meanwhile, Secretary Knox faced what appeared to be a more urgent problem closer to home. Setting aside the question of what aid America could and would send to the British, what troubled the navy was how to preserve what Secretary Stimson called "the lifeline of Great Britain in the North Atlantic." Shipping losses in recent months had been calamitous, and if supplies did not get through, the islands would starve for lack of food and the goods of war. If the sinking of merchant vessels continued at the present rate, Admiral Stark estimated, the British might hold out for six more months. Since Stark was in charge of the only force then capable of conducting operations outside the United States, it was natural that he should prod Roosevelt on this matter of aiding the British. His relationship with the president was close, and because he had served as a staff officer in London during the First World War he was unusually sympathetic to Britain's dilemma. What Stark had in mind as a first step, and what he figured he had a chance of getting, once the election was over, was the authority to convoy ships in the North Atlantic, but he was angling for more than that.

Harold Stark was a pink-cheeked, white-haired, blue-eyed officer who had survived the indignity of the nickname "Betty"[7] to be appointed by FDR in August 1939 to the navy's top job. In just about everybody's book, he was the very model of a staff officer—a precise thinker and methodical planner who understood better than most military men the political ramifications of a given situation. With his rimless glasses, he looked like a scholar, and he had a gentleness about him that made people think, as Robert Sherwood observed, that he lacked "the quickness and ruthlessness of decision required in wartime." (Dwight Eisenhower once characterized him unfairly as "a nice old lady.") In temperament he was the exact

---

[7]As a plebe at Annapolis, Stark was constantly braced by upperclassmen and ordered to recite the words allegedly spoken by the crusty Revolutionary general John Stark at the battle of Bennington: "We'll beat them before night, or Betty Stark will be a widow." (Although the history books usually have Mrs. Stark as Molly, the records are on the side of the midshipmen: her name was Elizabeth.) And Betty Stark he became, for the rest of his days.

opposite of FDR—restrained, logical, steady, suspicious of grandiose schemes, a believer in the practicable, whereas the impulsive, breezy president loved surprises and improvisations, was unfailingly optimistic, and resented being told that something could not be done—yet the two got on famously. For one thing, Stark was a great asset on the Hill. After working his way up the command ladder from destroyer to cruiser to battleship, he became chief of the Bureau of Ordnance, where the modesty of his demands and his knowledge of his business made him a host of friends in the House and Senate. He and FDR had been friends since World War I, when Assistant Secretary of the Navy Roosevelt had cruised aboard Lieutenant Stark's destroyer, but there was more to it than that. The president was not merely partial to the navy; he felt passionately about it, felt that he was a part of it, and liked nothing better than talking with officers about the days "when I was in the navy." These factors gave Stark an entree to the White House that George Marshall never had, but since Stark did not have the same steel in him that the army's chief of staff possessed, or the willingness to state his convictions freely, they also led to the criticism that he was "unduly responsive" to the president's views. Henry Stimson, for one, considered him too timid and ineffective for the CNO's job, and the weakest adviser Roosevelt had.

Like George Marshall, Betty Stark was a military philosopher, a man who gave thought to where the world and the United States Navy were likely to be one year or five years hence, and for the long haul he wanted a "definite pronouncement" by the president setting forth the navy's responsibilities in the event the United States entered the war. It was not that simple, of course, for those responsibilities naturally involved a multitude of considerations—questions of strategy, tactics, the movement of huge numbers of men, vast quantities of supplies, the flow of matériel from factory to battlefield, and so on. But Stark had thought this thing through and believed he had it pretty well pegged, and his point of view is reflected in a memorandum he later addressed to Secretary Hull:

It has long been my opinion that Germany cannot be defeated unless the United States is wholeheartedly in the war and makes a strong military and naval effort wherever strategy dictates. It would be very desirable to enter the war under circumstances in which Germany were the aggressor and in which case Japan might then be able to remain neutral. However, on the whole it is my opinion that the United States should enter the war against Germany as soon as possible, even if hostilities with Japan must be accepted. . . . I have assumed for the past two years that our country would not let Great Britain fall: that, ultimately, in order to prevent this, we would have to enter the war. . . . I have long felt and often stated that the sooner we get in the better. . . . I do not believe Germany will declare war on us until she is good and ready: that it will be a cold-blooded decision on Hitler's part, if and when he thinks it will pay and not till then.

In trying to persuade the president, Stark had to start somewhere, and one morning, as he worried about the possibility that the navy would be expected to fight a two-ocean war with a one-ocean fleet, he "drew up a paper"—which was his way of clearing his mind. It was a thoughtful appreciation of where matters stood in those troubled times, and after he showed a draft to his assistants, they rolled up their sleeves and went to work, keeping at it day and night, including weekends, until it was finally ready for consideration by Secretary Knox and the president on November 12, 1940, Stark's sixtieth birthday. As Stark saw it, the United States had four strategic options: (A) to defend the western hemisphere without doing much more to influence the war in Europe than supplying material aid to Britain; (B) to take a defensive stance in the Atlantic and concentrate its strength against Japan in the Pacific; (C) to give Great Britain active assistance in both oceans; or (D) to assume a defensive posture in the Pacific while building up its offensive strength in the Atlantic. Stark favored the fourth one, and since each alternative was designated by letter, his choice— labeled D in his twenty-four-page memorandum—was known then and thereafter, in military parlance, as Plan Dog.

At first blush, Plan Dog appeared to be an elaboration of Rainbow 5, calling for defense of the western hemisphere and "prevention of the disruption of the British Empire, with all that such a consummation implies." This meant that the United States would be unable to take meaningful action against Japan, even if the situation demanded it: realistically, Stark observed, the nation could "do little more in the Pacific than remain on the strict defensive." But the admiral was proposing something that went well beyond mere naval assistance to the British. Clearly, Britain's limited manpower and resources were no match for Germany's, and it was absurd to think that American naval assistance by itself would tip the scales and bring about the defeat of Hitler. As he put the case, "If Britain wins decisively against Germany, we could win everywhere; but . . . if she loses, the problems confronting us would be very great; and, while we might not *lose everywhere,* we might possibly not *win anywhere.*" Moreover, since a Nazi victory was unthinkable, the United States "would also need to send large air and land forces to Europe or Africa, or both, and to participate strongly in this land offensive," Stark added. Those words, committed to paper, meant that someone in a position of considerable authority had at last dared to mention the unmentionable—the indisputable fact that before the business with Hitler could be settled, great numbers of American boys were going to have to cross the sea once again to participate in a European war.

The necessity of close cooperation with the British was as obvious as it was urgent, and Stark's memorandum concluded with a recommendation that secret conversations be held in Washington. In October, Lord Lothian urged that "comprehensive" military talks be held, and in London, Admiral Sir Dudley Pound was pressing for the same goal; but these requests came at the height of the U.S. political campaign, and nothing was done until Roosevelt was safely elected. Then Lothian and Pound revived their recommendations, reassuring the Americans that a British delegation consisting of "a small party which would easily pass unnoticed in the stream of missions, observers, and other officials" could come to Washington without causing a stir. So, thanks to the initiative taken by the naval chiefs of the two nations, the far-reaching American-British Conversations were held between January 29 and March 27, 1941. Stark's Plan Dog had been endorsed by the army and expanded and modified by the Joint Board planners for submission to the president, but although it was to be the keystone of American military policy, President Roosevelt was not ready to buy it. He approved the exploratory talks and agreed that Stark's plan should be the basis of the U.S. position, but at his insistence the U.S. military chiefs were to steer clear of any considerations of joint offensives and were to make no commitment whatever regarding the use of U.S. troops. His policy was— and would remain, for the foreseeable future—all-out aid to Britain, short of war. While this was not the sort of grand alliance or even the strategy that Winston Churchill would have preferred, what mattered most to the British was that the United States had settled irrevocably on a policy of Europe first, which meant taking a defensive position in the Pacific, along with a proviso that no hostile action would curtail the supply of matériel to England.

Within the constraints of the presidential guidelines, the talks foreshadowed so long ago by the London visit of Captain (now Rear Admiral) Royal Ingersoll got under way. As promised, the British naval officers arrived in mufti, posing as advisers to their country's purchasing mission to avoid the predictable reaction by the isolationists; and thanks to prodding by Churchill and Lothian, who were determined to win American support at all levels, they came in a spirit of candor and openness. To be sure, it was a two-way street: Roosevelt and Stark were equally determined to avoid a costly mistake of World War I, when Woodrow Wilson stubbornly refused to permit any exchange of information between the United States and Britain until after America had entered the war, with the result that months of precious time were wasted establishing the ground rules of cooperation between the two navies.

At the outset of the talks, Admiral Stark stressed that these were discussions of "tentative agreements . . . should the United States be compelled to engage in war against the Axis powers," but the British, understandably, wanted to know when and how Plan Dog would take effect, when the United States would enter the war. Perhaps equally understandably, both sides were wary of the other, proud of their own service and its traditions, and inevitably there were frayed tempers and egos and a failure to achieve complete harmony. Even so, what the meetings produced was a framework and a basis for future collaboration, and, of more immediate significance for

Americans, the decision to beef up naval strength in the Atlantic. President Roosevelt promoted Ernest J. King to full admiral and put him in charge of the Atlantic Fleet, which by April consisted of 159 vessels, including two carriers, three battleships, eight cruisers, seventy-eight destroyers, twenty-nine submarines, and various auxiliaries. For a neutral nation, that was a formidable force to send cruising in hostile waters, but the author of Plan Dog had no illusions about where his plan might take the nation. Recently Stark had written to his fleet commanders, "The question as to our entry into the war now seems to be *when* and not *whether*. . . . Public opinion, which is now slowly turning in that direction, may or may not be accelerated. My own personal view is that we may be in the war against Germany in about two months [by which he meant April 1], but that there is a reasonable possibility that Japan may remain out altogether."

———

The fluidity of military plans was matched by the changes in budget, and George Marshall suddenly found himself in the unfamiliar position of being offered *more* money than he had requested, and of having the public, the president, and Congress clamoring for more equipment than the service could intelligently use until it had trained personnel to match. G-4, the Supply Division, was so unaccustomed to largess of any kind it was temporarily incapable of coping with all these riches, and quite unexpectedly Congress and the president seized the initiative and began calling for even more planes. Marshall and his ally Henry Morgenthau realized that what was needed in addition to aircraft of all types and the crews to man them was a balanced program of national defense—what Marshall called a Protective Mobilization Plan (PMP)—to include increases in the number of regular troops and National Guardsmen while providing for their weapons, ammunition, rations, clothing, pay, shelter, training—all the items that enable an army to function.

May 17, the day after Roosevelt's call for fifty thousand planes, found Marshall contemplating a troop level of 400,000 men, and before another month was out—in response to a request from production boss William Knudsen—he had revised his estimates to provide for a one-million-man army by October 1, 1941, two million men by January 1, 1942, and four million by April 1, 1942. On top of these astonishing figures for the ground forces, the Army Air Corps came up with requests for 9,000 planes to be produced by October 1, 1941, 18,000 by the following January, and 36,000 by April 1, 1942.

What had been going on during 1940 could only be described as catch-up planning, when what was needed was a far more detailed, long-range program than the harried military staffs had yet had an opportunity to devise. Catching up required more than throwing money at the problem—mostly it demanded time, for it was now evident that the nation's military strategists had to think on a global scale, assessing needs in terms of involvement in Europe and in the Pacific, and in the light of the needs of future allies, wherever in the world they might be found. As Stark had pointed out, without enormous increases in the amounts of food and war matériel reaching Great Britain, it was difficult to see how that nation could outlast the German assaults. More important, without a vastly increased, newly constituted U.S. Army, no long-range plans would amount to more than the paper on which they were written.

=====

When Franklin Roosevelt's campaign special stopped off in New Haven, Connecticut, on that cold, rainy day in October of 1940, the candidate did his level best to gloss over the selective service act recently passed by Congress. Though he knew it was at the heart of the nation's move toward preparedness, he wanted badly to be reelected and was taking no political risks.

Nobody cared much for conscription, least of all the young men who were likely to be conscripted, not to mention their mothers, or clergymen who feared for their morals. *Life* quoted a Methodist minister, testifying before the Senate's Military Affairs Committee, who stated, "Conscription takes boys shortly out of high school—boys who all their lives have been trained to respect women—and places them in situations where the absence of contact with normal girls induces a mass lust which has always characterized army units." When a bewildered senator interrupted, "What?" the man of God replied, "Mass lust. I will clarify that."

"That's not necessary," said the senator quickly. "That's clear enough."

To repeat, the American people might not like conscription (let alone the mass lust to which it might lead), but in this as in some other important matters they were a step ahead of their elected representatives; they acknowledged the need for a draft and were resigned to having one. Even so, the authorities responsible for enacting it dragged their feet, while the opposition—college undergraduates, isolationists, churchmen, parents of draft-age youths, members of the Communist Party—was loud and ubiquitous. Congress wanted no part of it before election day in November, and the lawmakers seemed mesmerized by an otherworldly illusion that the war might suddenly end, leaving the United States with thousands of unhappy and redundant citizen-soldiers on its payroll. As for President Roosevelt, without whose involvement the raising of a two-million-man army was patently impossible, he somehow contrived to inch toward a goal of conscription while appearing to keep his distance, as if he were merely a disinterested spectator. The president knew better than anyone that the U.S. Army was pitifully undermanned, but so long as he was engaged in the political race of his life, he was not about to take a leading role in calling for a peacetime draft.[8] And conscription was the only conceivable way to transform the existing army into a force capable of making a difference in the war against Hitler. The army that had been thought sufficient between the two world wars would form the core of the expanded force, to be sure, providing the commissioned and noncommissioned leadership, the technicians, the know-how, and the framework for what was to come, but when you were talking about two million men and had only 10 percent of that number in uniform, conscription was the only possible answer, distasteful as that course might be to politicians and draftees.

Like the Willkie nomination and the destroyers-for-bases agreement, the movement for compulsory military training began with a small band of patriotic, enthusiastic citizens who, in this instance, brought about what neither Congress nor the president seemed willing or able to accomplish. The group's origins went back a quarter century, to 1915, when a hundred or more young men—most of them Harvard alumni—met after the sinking of the *Lusitania* to consider what they might do to prepare the United States for war. General Leonard Wood had traveled to New York from Washington to talk with them, and in the course of the evening assured them of the War Department's support and cooperation—to the extent, at least, of providing training if the men would pay their own expenses. Out of this came a camp at Plattsburg, New York, which eventually imparted the rudiments of military knowledge and drill to some sixteen thousand men—a number of whom became junior officers—while imbuing them with what became known as the "Plattsburg idea." The program also led to the postwar Citizens' Military Training Camps offering two weeks' annual training to acceptable men between the ages of eighteen and twenty-nine.

Twenty-five years later, two young officers of the Fiduciary Trust Company in New York, Howard Slade II and Peter Jay, both Harvard alumni, decided the idea of the Plattsburg encampments was worth reviving in these increasingly troubled days, and they organized a meeting at the New York Bar Association's headquarters, with General Hugh Drum as guest speaker. Like Wood in 1915, Drum promised the cooperation of the army, and seventy-five men ("from Harvard, Yale, and the *Social Register,*" as one publication described them) signed a resolution urging the government to reopen the camps. With surprising speed it was done, and early in July, five hundred men (all that could be accommodated of the two thousand who had signed up) each paid $43.50 for food and rented equipment, boarded trains in Grand Central Station, and headed north for Plattsburg.

More important by far than the month's training they received was the impetus they provided for a program of civilian preparedness. On May 22,

[8]Even so, he had had the matter under serious consideration for some time. In July 1940 he wrote Norman Thomas, "we ought this autumn to take some kind of action which will better prepare Americans by selection and training for national defense than we have ever done before."

at a dinner attended by Grenville Clark, an old friend of Roosevelt, who had been one of the leading spirits in the 1915 Plattsburg program, Henry L. Stimson, Robert Patterson, William Donovan, and about a hundred others, a resolution was adopted urging the War Department to initiate a civilian draft. One of the dinner guests was a retired brigadier general named John McAuley Palmer, and he went at once to Washington to present the views of the Citizens' Military Training Camps Association to General Marshall.

No one had to tell Marshall how badly needed conscription was, but better than most people, he realized that political considerations were against it, for one thing, and for another, the army was not yet ready for it. The pressure for universal military training happened to come at a time when the chief of staff could finally see an opportunity to bring the army's existing divisions up to strength in other ways, and he was determined that nothing should get in the way of that program. Draftees required instructors—the very men needed to train new platoons of regulars; large numbers of raw recruits would dilute the strength of the regular units, take away equipment needed by National Guard outfits; and he was not going to break up the few trained units he had to provide training cadres. In short, he wanted no part of a draft just then. Neither did he want to be seen by Congress or the public as the military man calling for compulsory service. He wanted that initiative to come from others; once civilian leaders proposed the legislation, he said, "I could take the floor and do all the urging that was required." Unfortunately, word got around that the chief of staff opposed the draft—"There was some difficulty in persuading George Marshall to come out for it," Walter Lippmann said—but that was unfair. Behind the general's caution was a fear that the public would not support conscription unless the nation was at war; after all, civilians had never before been drafted in peacetime, and this was a measure that would eventually affect every community in America. Marshall's understandable sensitivity to the attacks he anticipated from isolationists reflected his reluctance to have the army advocate universal military training before it was politically safe to do so. Above all, he did not want to jeopardize passage of the legislation. Under the circumstances, Marshall had little choice but to do what he did, which was to send three officers[9] to New York to help draft a bill, and to include in the "Basis for Immediate Decisions" which he and Stark presented to the president the recommendation for a peacetime draft.

Meanwhile, Grenville Clark—whom Lippmann described as "the master mind in preparing the material for [a draft] and rushing around and persuading everybody"—and his cohorts approached Representative James W. Wadsworth of New York and Senator Edward R. Burke of Nebraska, who consented to sponsor a bill in Congress. Wadsworth was a Republican in

[9]One of them was Major, later Major General, Lewis B. Hershey, who became the longtime director of the Selective Service System.

a Democratic House, he had been chairman of the Military Affairs Committee years before, and now, he said, the Democrats on the committee "were perfectly willing to see an outsider stick his neck out . . . and I was perfectly willing to do it."

While this was going on in Washington, Henry L. Stimson was doing some missionary work of his own in New Haven, speaking to Yale alumni on the topic of compulsory military training, and the next day he delivered a radio speech setting forth his views on the world crisis, including seven recommendations. What these came down to was repeal of the remaining neutrality legislation, all-out aid to the Allies, and "a system of universal compulsory training and service . . . which is at the moment imperative if we are to have men ready to operate the planes and other munitions . . . which Congress has just authorized by a practically unanimous vote." The following day, at his New York law office, Stimson received a call from President Roosevelt, offering him the position of secretary of war. Before accepting, Stimson asked the president if he had seen his radio speech, and if it would be embarrassing to him, to which FDR responded "that he had already read it and was in full accord with it." Then the lawyer asked: "Do you know that I am in favor of general compulsory military service?" and the president replied that he not only knew but was in sympathy with Stimson's position.

That conversation took place on the same day the Burke-Wadsworth bill was introduced in the House and Senate—a bill extraordinary in that it had no visible support from the White House or the military, only the backing of a handful of farsighted civilians (one of whom was the newly nominated secretary of war). To the surprise of just about everyone, the bill picked up immediate support in Congress and influential newspapers around the country, yet the president hung back, unwilling to commit himself, and even after Stimson and Knox were confirmed to their new posts, they were unable to come before Congress to speak in support of the legislation until Mr. Roosevelt declared himself in favor of it. "Their mouths were closed," Congressman Wadsworth recalled, "and, in turn, the mouth of the chief of staff, the chief of naval operations, and all the subordinates down the military line, were closed, waiting for the tip from the White House. The two committees sat waiting! Obviously, you can scarcely begin hearings on a measure of that importance unless the Secretary of War, the Secretary of the Navy, and others responsible for the conduct of military activities are ready to appear."

Stimson, in particular, was tearing his hair in frustration at the way the bill was languishing. "God, Wadsworth," he cried, "we ought to start it! Look what's going on in this world!"

But not a sign came from the White House, not a word of encouragement—until the Republican convention was history and FDR was the chosen nominee of the Democrats. Then, at a White House press conference, Roosevelt was asked what he thought of a selective service bill, and replied, Wadsworth remembered, "in a curiously cautious sentence" along the lines of "Well, I wouldn't be surprised if, after all, we've got to have it." That was all Stimson and Knox needed: they hurried up to the Hill, and the hearings began in mid-July. Predictably, the isolationist bloc in the Senate was out in full cry, the galleries were packed with angry opponents of the bill, delegates from two organizations said to represent the mothers of America hanged a senator in effigy for his outspoken support of conscription; but the tide was running against them. Unquestionably the ferocity of the blitz in England had much to do with the public's attitude, but whatever the reasons, you could sense the changing mood in ball parks, movie theaters, church outings, and public meetings, where Americans were singing a song Irving Berlin had written in 1918 and set aside because the moment for it had passed. Two decades later he offered it to Kate Smith, the jolly fat lady with the big voice that was as true as a bell, and in 1940 she and everyone else, it seemed, were belting out "God Bless America." However much they might oppose intervention in the war, Americans knew they must prepare, even if preparing meant drafting the nation's young, and on September 16, 1940, the Burke-Wadsworth bill (which was kept deliberately simple, its New York sponsor said, "to include only the single principle or issue involved, Selective Service") became the law of the land.

During the course of the hearings, George Marshall had warned Congress repeatedly against being caught, like the European nations, with preparations that were too little and too late, but he made one major error in his eagerness to get the bill passed. After cautioning skeptical lawmakers that it would take as long as two years to see the fruits of the draft,[10] the chief of staff urged that the legislation provide for a tour of at least eighteen months; then, to placate the opposition, he finally settled for a year's service, unless Congress should declare a national emergency at the end of the twelve-month period, in which case the draftees could be retained. On the theory that half a loaf was better than none, he agreed to the reduced term, but it was a compromise that would come back to haunt him.

October 16, 1940, was the day all male Americans aged twenty-one through thirty-five were required to register for service,[11] and thirteen days later, Secretary Stimson, blindfolded and looking very small and vulnerable, reached into the glass fishbowl that had been used in 1917 for the same purpose and began drawing the numbers that would determine the order in which men would be called up. The capsule containing the first number was handed to President Roosevelt, who opened it solemnly and read, "One-hundred fifty-eight." Each registrant had been given a number between 1 and 7,836, and since he was the only man within a single draft board to hold that particular number, it meant that he would join thousands of

[10]Marshall's candid opinion was that the army would not be ready to fight a war until December of 1941.

[11]More than sixteen million registered; only thirty-six individuals refused publicly to do so.

young men from other parts of the country when he was called. The idea, of course, was to spread the damage thinly, over the widest possible area, giving each community the impression that only a small number of its boys were being taken.

So the administration finally had the authority to raise a respectable army, but on the debit side it was clear that the whole summer had been wasted, with the result that no work was done on the roads, the utilities, or other facilities at camps to which draftees would be sent. Good weather would turn to bad, unhappy recruits would flounder around in the mud and cold of winter without adequate blankets, construction costs would mount, congressmen would hear from outraged parents and caustic newspaper editorial writers, and all these complaints and concerns would have their effect when it came time to renew the legislation a year hence. Yet a beginning had been made. The immediate effect of the Selective Training and Service Act of 1940 was that General Marshall could call up enough men to bring to full numerical strength nine infantry, four armored, and two cavalry divisions, while increasing the strength of eighteen National Guard divisions. For the first time in American history, the army was able to begin training and procurement before hostilities began. Beyond that, by declaring all males between the ages of twenty-one and thirty-six subject to call, selective service would create a manpower pool ultimately reaching 32 million, from which the army, navy, air force, and marines would draw to fill their ranks.

CHAPTER 46

———— ◆ ————

"We must be the great arsenal of democracy."

At the end of November 1939, the Neutrality Acts had been revised, establishing the principle of "cash-and-carry," and three days later a British purchasing commission headed by a charming, immensely energetic Scot named Arthur Purvis began placing orders for U.S.-made machine tools, engines, small arms and ammunition, explosives, and a variety of other war materials. Fortunately for Purvis and the British, they had a tireless American champion in the person of Henry Morgenthau, secretary of the Treasury, who shared President Roosevelt's sense that time was running out, and who, since the Munich crisis, had been prodding the president to mobilize U.S. opinion in support of Great Britain, France, and China.

Morgenthau was not only the chief executive's valued counselor, he was a close personal friend, an intensely loyal partisan on whom FDR could rely to execute certain programs he was unwilling to entrust to others. Aid to the Allies, principally aid to Britain as 1940 began, was probably the most important.

The British, as Purvis remarked, had to act "as if we were on a desert island on short rations which we must stretch as far as we could." By autumn of 1940 their dilemma was far more serious than that suggests. During the summer and fall, while the Luftwaffe pounded England from the air, destroying her industrial plants along with everything else, German U-boats and aircraft were sinking British ships at a rate entirely beyond the possibility of replacement, and every ship lost, moreover, went down with a critically needed cargo. As the war spread to Greece and into North Africa, increasing in violence, British purchases in the United States approached astronomical proportions, and at last the well ran dry. Great Britain was broke.

By November, having paid cash for all goods received, the British had spent nearly £5 billion of its gold and foreign assets and had £2 billion left—most of it in investments that were not readily marketable; besides which, the government had on order far more than it could possibly pay for, with unguessed-at quantities yet to come if Britain was to continue fighting. Lord Lothian had flown home to England in mid-November and urged the prime minister to write a full statement of the British position to FDR, who would be more likely to take action now that the election was behind him. On November 16, the "Former Naval Person," as Churchill signed himself, cabled the president to advise that he was writing "a very long letter on the outlook for 1941 which Lord Lothian will give you in a few days"; but what with other urgent matters and the necessity to have the message approved by the chiefs of staff, Treasury officials, and the war cabinet, the letter was not sent until December 7, 1940, and arrived, as luck would have it, while Mr. Roosevelt was taking an overdue vacation in the Caribbean, aboard the cruiser *Tuscaloosa.*

From all outward appearances, the only serious business to be transacted aboard the *Tuscaloosa* was fishing. The president had seen Lothian when the ambassador returned to the capital and blandly assured reporters that nothing concerning aid to Britain had been discussed during their meeting. From the moment he boarded the cruiser, his mood was that of a carefree man on holiday: the ship put in at Guantanamo Bay to pick up Havana cigars for a smoker laid on for the presidential party by the wardroom officers; he received a message from Ernest Hemingway (whose novel *For Whom the Bell Tolls* was the season's best-seller) promising that big fish awaited the president in the waters between Puerto Rico and the Dominican Republic. Days were spent fishing, chatting in the sun; evenings the president, his personal physician, Admiral Ross McIntire, Harry Hopkins, and the military aides watched movies, attended boxing matches between crew members, played poker. The ship anchored briefly off St. Lucia in the Windward Islands and off Nassau in the Bahamas, where Mr. Roosevelt entertained the Duke and Duchess of Windsor (the former king was now governor of the Bahamas). All very relaxing, and a real tonic for a fifty-eight-year-old polio victim who had just come through an exhausting political campaign; but the pleasure trip was profoundly disturbing to Mr. Churchill, who waited on tenterhooks for an indication that immediate action would be taken to ease Britain's plight, and saw at a distance a man behaving as though he had not a care in the world and no end of time in which to make up his mind. Churchill had felt rebuffed a month earlier when he cabled Roosevelt to congratulate him on his election victory and to say how much he looked forward to exchanging ideas "in all that confidence and good will which has grown up between us." Curiously, the president never replied, and Churchill had to swallow annoyance and injured pride to compose the letter he called "one of the most important I ever wrote."

The prime minister wrote also with the shadow of Coventry across his heart. On the night of November 14, the Luftwaffe struck the ancient city with almost five hundred bombers, lighting fires that were visible for miles even in the brilliant moonlight, destroying the famous cathedral and the entire center of the city, killing four hundred people and wounding thousands. It was, Churchill said later, "the most devastating raid we sustained."

On the morning of December 9, 1940, while the *Tuscaloosa* lay to in the soft swells off Antigua, two U.S. Navy seaplanes landed alongside to deliver mail. In one of the pouches was the expected letter from Winston Churchill, and the president settled into his deck chair to read it. He went through it once, then again, and for two days brooded, saying nothing, according to Hopkins, seemingly unable to reach a conclusion.

The letter was indeed long, as Churchill had predicted, almost four thousand words, and it was masterful, cataloguing in detail the grim situation in which Great Britain found herself after a full year of war, skillfully linking each specific to the big, global picture he described in sweeping terms. Since the future of the United States was bound up with the continued existence and independence of the British Commonwealth of Nations, the prime minister said he felt obliged to lay before the president certain prospects for the coming year. "It is our British duty in the common interest, as also for our own survival," Churchill wrote, "to hold the front and grapple with the Nazi power until the preparations of the United States are complete." He foresaw a two-year lag before America's military and industry were at full strength, and during that time, "even if the United States were our ally, instead of our friend and indispensable partner," he continued, "we should not ask for a large American expeditionary army. Shipping, not men, is the limiting factor. . . ." (Mr. Churchill well knew the sentiments of most Americans.)

The danger that Great Britain would suddenly be overwhelmed had happily receded,[1] but in place of the invasion threat was the less visible but no less deadly menace of strangulation. "The decision for 1941 lies upon the seas," the prime minister warned. His countrymen could and would endure the destruction of their homes and the barbaric slaughter of civilians, but

---

[1] In the same vein, Harold Nicolson wrote his wife at this time: "I think we have managed to avoid losing this war. But when I think how on earth we are going to win it, my imagination quails."

"unless we can establish our ability to feed this island, to import the munitions of all kinds which we need, unless we can move our armies to the various theatres where Hitler and his confederate Mussolini must be met . . . we may fall by the way, and the time needed by the United States to complete her defensive preparations may not be forthcoming." In 1941, "the crunch of the whole war will be found" in the Atlantic, he said, echoing the conclusions of Harold Stark and U.S. military planners.

Shipping losses of British, other Allied, and neutral vessels for the five weeks ending November 3 totaled 420,000 tons, and for a year of war they were 2.5 million tons, of which almost 70 percent were British.[2] In order to maintain the struggle against Germany, the British calculated their need for imports at 43 million tons a year, and in recent months deliveries had fallen 12 percent below that rate. This was not like the last war, Churchill pointed out, when the British had the support of the French, Japanese, Italian, and U.S. navies, plus access to many more ports. Adding to the perils from enemy submarines, surface vessels, and aircraft, the dreaded *Bismarck* and *Tirpitz* would soon be at sea, and the Royal Navy had only two comparable vessels with which to meet them. No one could predict whether the Vichy government would find some excuse to add its undamaged ships to the German navy; and in the Far East, meantime, where the Japanese threatened Singapore and the Dutch East Indies, "we have no forces . . . capable of dealing with this situation. . . ."

Churchill knew the British army was no match in numbers for the Germans; perhaps because he could conceive of no alternative, he hinted that victory would come in the air. "It may well be," he said, "that the application of superior air-power to the German homeland and the rising anger of the German and other Nazi-gripped populations will bring the agony of civilization to a merciful and glorious end." Coming from a leader whose own civilian population was displaying the most extraordinary courage and capacity to endure continuous aerial attack, that was a somewhat illogical conclusion, but at this point faint hopes were virtually all that remained to him.

As he saw it, the paramount need was to build up a supply of weapons that would "lay the foundations of victory," and toward that end the United States could assist in several ways. One was to reassert boldly the doctrine of freedom of the seas, and protect by naval and air escorts trade with those countries that were illegally blockaded. (Great Britain, not surprisingly, was one of the very nations he had in mind.) Failing that, he wondered if it would be possible to provide his country with American warships—more destroyers, especially, while at the same time extending American control in Atlantic waters farther to the east. And would it not be useful for Irish-Americans to pressure Ireland to provide the British with naval and

---

[2]Churchill was indulging in no hyperbole. Postwar figures revealed that actual losses were in fact higher—3,139,190 tons total, of which 2,109,286 were British.

air bases on its southern and western shores? Perhaps, he suggested slyly, if the government of Eire demonstrated "its solidarity with the democracies of the English-speaking world at this crisis," some way might be found after the war to bring unity to that unhappy land.

Meanwhile, his own country needed more merchant ships, more aircraft (would two thousand additional planes a month be feasible?), more small arms, more artillery, tanks, and food—all of which brought him to his ultimate point, which he began with a capital letter: Finance. The moment was nigh when Great Britain could no longer pay cash for its orders. "While we will do our utmost, and shrink from no proper sacrifice to make payments . . . I believe you will agree that it would be wrong in principle and mutually disadvantageous in effect if at the height of this struggle Great Britain were to be divested of all saleable assets, so that after the victory was won with our blood, civilization saved, and the time gained for the United States to be fully armed . . . we should stand stripped to the bone." Strong words, but Mr. Roosevelt should understand that this was no appeal for aid, but "a statement of the minimum action necessary to achieve our common purpose."

———

Mr. Roosevelt was acutely aware of Britain's financial dilemma. He had been pondering the matter for a long while, and from his vantage point, the problem was as much political as practical. More troubling than the mechanics of producing and shipping an infinitude of goods was the ticklish question of how this could be accomplished within the framework of U.S. laws, and how he might persuade a balky Congress that it was essential to America's own, as well as Britain's, security to furnish those goods. He had been saying all along that in accepting orders from the British "we are following . . . hardheaded self-interest," since the purchases created a plant capacity for military hardware that would serve the United States well in any emergency. But when it came to delivering the goods he had a tough fight on his hands—with the military, no less than the legislators on the Hill. In September, for example, when he urged Stimson and Marshall to release a number of B-17 Flying Fortresses to the British, the chief of staff informed him that outside Panama and Hawaii, the nation had just forty-nine bombers fit for service. (At that, Stimson noted, "the president's head went back as if someone had hit him in the chest.") But Franklin Roosevelt was not the man to give in, and immediately after the election he came out publicly with what he called the fifty-fifty rule, under which Britain would receive half of all newly manufactured weapons, including the latest bombers.

Meanwhile, in the back of his mind a plan was stirring that would take the financial onus off Britain's back. During the summer he had suggested, "It should not be necessary for the British to take their own funds and have ships built in the United States, or for us to lend them money for this purpose. There is no reason why we should not take a finished vessel and lease it to them for the duration of the emergency." Before leaving on his cruise he prodded Morgenthau: he wanted the United States to build the facilities needed to manufacture what the English required, and he was not too fussy about how it was done. "All of you use your imaginations," were his parting words to the members of the cabinet. Despite their instructions, and despite what Morgenthau called "one of the most exciting meetings" he ever attended, when Cordell Hull suddenly came to life in favor of aiding Britain ("I don't know what has happened to the man," the Treasury secretary wrote in his diary; "He is red hot"), the cabinet made little headway on the matter beyond obtaining George Marshall's assurance that any war matériel ordered from abroad would certainly be useful to the United States if the British were defeated. All those tanks, planes, and ordnance, he promised, would be vital for America's defense in case of a Nazi victory.

===

On December 11, Lord Lothian was scheduled to address a meeting of the American Farm Bureau in Baltimore, but his speech was read instead by the counselor of the British embassy, who told the audience that the ambassador was indisposed—a "slight illness" regrettably prevented his appearance. The message Lothian had for the farmers of America was that 1941 would be crucial, with mounting attacks on Britain's sea lifeline. That being so, "it is up to you to decide whether it is in your interest to give us whatever assistance may be necessary to make certain that Britain shall not fail."

Alas, Lothian had more than a slight illness, and within hours of the time his speech was delivered for him he was dead of a uremic infection; his faith in Christian Science had prevented an operation that might have saved him. And it was an irreparable loss, for as Walter Lippmann wrote, Lothian was "one of the great figures of the war," the man who worked out the intellectual relationship that formed the basis of Anglo-American cooperation in the destroyers-for-bases deal and in what would be known as Lend-Lease. Thanks to him, Roosevelt had arrived at a *modus operandi* by which the United States could gradually intervene to save Britain.

The manner in which it occurred serves as an almost perfect illustration of how adept the president was at cutting through the bureaucratic thicket when he had something he wanted done, as well as his extraordinary facility for putting across rather complicated programs in homely, almost simplistic terms. He knew, as his friend Sam Rosenman observed, that the test of presidential leadership was an ability to educate and lead the people—in this case, to make them appreciate the imminence of the Nazi and Japanese threats, to rally them behind drastic efforts to prepare, and to gain their support for sending huge quantities of our own military hardware to Great Britain. Speaking with Morgenthau shortly after he returned from his cruise, he said he had been thinking hard about the problem of getting aid to England and had decided that the way to do it was to get away from the dollar sign. That afternoon at his press conference, after telling reporters casually, "I don't think there is any particular news" (thereby immediately setting them on guard), he reverted to the theme of "hardheaded self-interest" and the need for additional manufacturing capacity, explaining that orders from Britain would help the U.S. economy and automatically create additional production facilities. "I am talking selfishly, from the American point of view—nothing else," he said pointedly. Then, repeating what he had told Morgenthau—that he wanted to eliminate the dollar sign—he came up with the charming little fable that was as responsible as any single factor for putting over Lend-Lease with the American public and their representatives in Congress.

"Suppose my neighbor's home catches fire," he began, "and I have got a length of garden hose four or five hundred feet away; but, my heaven, if he can take my garden hose and connect it up with his hydrant, I may help him to put out his fire. . . . I don't say to him before that operation, 'Neighbor, my garden hose cost me $15; you have got to pay me $15 for it.' I don't want $15—I want my garden hose back after the fire is over."

The point of this, he added, was that Britain's best defense was also our best defense, and by leasing certain arms to that country, we would derive more benefit from them than if they remained in storage here. Now, as anyone knew who gave the matter serious thought, there was not the slightest chance that the United States would want or demand the return of a much-used tank or airplane when the war finally ended, but the inspired notion of the garden hose, and the phrase "Lend-Lease" used to describe the program, planted in the public mind the idea that we weren't giving the British money—only lending them some useful tools which they would return when they had no further need for them. (The theme was exploited soon thereafter in a speech by Britain's alert prime minister, who cried, "Give us the tools and we will finish the job!")

Immediately, questions were asked. Did this mean convoys? Would American ships be sent into the war zone to deliver the goods? And the answer to both came quickly—no, of course not. Was congressional approval needed? Yes. What about speeding up defense production? We are not proposing a lengthened workweek, said the president, but the idea is "to keep all the machines that will run seven days a week in operation seven days a week." (Which sounded suspiciously like an increased workweek.)

Whether or not the president realized the historical significance of what he was proposing is hard to say. Taken at face value, it was no less than a new era in Anglo-American affairs—a relationship of exceptional intimacy, whose extent and efficacy only time would reveal. It meant that British and Americans would be obliged to plan and carry out their defense production and the allocation of matériel in the closest imaginable harmony. Already, in fact, though it was known only to a handful of insiders, an agreement existed under which the British would work closely with Americans in developing new weapons and modifying the old, for interchangeable use in both nations' armed forces. Those secret talks between naval officers that were scheduled to begin at the end of January would put one more piece in place.

———

By year's end, public support had swung noticeably in favor of Roosevelt's policy of all-out aid short of war. For one thing, the idea of Lend-Lease appealed to people who were anxious to aid Britain and equally eager to stay out of the fighting. The proposal came at a time when Americans were increasingly shocked by the saturation bombing of London and Coventry and other English cities, and angered by a recent German "warning" of the consequences to the United States should it persist in "insupportable . . . challenges, insults, and moral aggression." They had heard Ed Murrow report from London, moreover, that Britain was in mortal danger, that the English knew now that decisions taken in Washington were going to determine the course of the war.

For the moment, the momentum was going the president's way, and he appeared confident and relaxed as he was wheeled into the White House diplomatic reception room on the evening of December 29, 1940, to face the microphones on the desk. It is difficult to imagine, in an age of instantaneous and continuously accessible electronic communications, what it meant to have the voice of the president of the United States come into your living room, speaking as a friend and neighbor in his informal, chatty manner— but it meant a great deal indeed to millions of people who may not have seen or heard any other leader of the nation and who felt for the first time that the occupant of the White House cared about their opinions and was sharing his thoughts with them. Frances Perkins watched the president delivering one of these fireside chats and noticed how "his head would nod and his hands would move in simple, natural, comfortable gestures. His face would smile and light up as though he were actually sitting on the front porch or in the parlor" with his listeners, and the people listening to their radio sets sensed the very neighborliness of the man. There was nothing eloquent or high-flown about these talks; on the contrary, they tended to be homely, even banal, often rambling discussions, but as far as most Americans were concerned, they had a magic to them.

On this night a small audience was seated around the room—his mother, several cabinet members, and the movie stars Clark Gable and Carole Lombard—and they watched as he received his cue and began speaking: "This is not a fireside chat on war," he said, setting the tone for what was to follow. "It is a talk on national security"—a security that hinged on the survival of Great Britain. Simply, clearly, he spoke of the threat to American civilization, the impossibility of compromise between that and the Axis philosophy of government, the futility of appeasement or of negotiated peace. This government did not intend to send an expeditionary force outside its borders ("You can . . . nail any talk about sending armies to

Europe as a deliberate untruth," he emphasized), but it must do all it could to support those nations fighting the Axis powers—it must produce the weapons of war quickly and without respite. Then another of those inspired phrases: "We must be the great arsenal of democracy. . . . There will be no 'bottlenecks' in our determination to aid Great Britain. No dictator, no combination of dictators, will weaken that determination. . . ."[3]

On the American political scene, Franklin Roosevelt was unrivaled at this kind of upbeat, inspirational message that was half sermon, half pep talk, and as he reached the end and called for a miracle of production—a great national effort—the telegrams began pouring into the White House endorsing his program.

To sorely tried Londoners his words brought hope at a time of special need. As he spoke, they were enduring the heaviest bombing attack they had yet known. The Luftwaffe was concentrating on the City—the old heart of the capital, center of the financial district, which was dotted with historic churches—and on what many fire wardens and spotters had expected to be a quiet Sunday night, 244 bombers caught them off guard and dropped thousands of incendiaries, setting fire to the roofs of buildings all over the district. After the exceptionally dry summer and autumn, the Thames was low, the pumper engines drained the river to the foot of its banks, and with thin muddy streams of water trickling from their hoses anguished firemen watched helplessly as hundreds of ancient buildings burned to the ground. The majestic dome of St. Paul's was aflame when Ed Murrow prepared his broadcast, and the opening words he wrote were: "Tonight the bombers of the German Reich hit London where it hurts most, in her heart. St. Paul's Cathedral, built by Sir Christopher Wren, her great dome towering over the capital of the empire, is burning to the ground as I talk to you now." Thanks to a small army of volunteers—choirboys, clergy, vestrymen, parishioners—who had watched over their beloved cathedral since the raids began, the fire was extinguished, and those sober opening lines were never delivered.

———

In the early weeks of the new year, public opinion polls demonstrated that Americans supported Lend-Lease by two to one and that a majority would even help England win at the risk of entering the war. At the same time it was evident that the president's call for Lend-Lease was provoking a storm of protest louder even than the clamor over the fifty destroyers and selective service. The outraged folks who made up the minority were creating a lot of noise and making a prodigious effort to see that the scheme went

[3]According to Joseph Lash, the "arsenal of democracy" phrase originated with Jean Monnet, the French economist who was working with the British. On a trip to Washington, Monnet used the phrase in conversation with Felix Frankfurter, and the justice recommended it to Roosevelt.

Among the numerous vocal and well-organized opponents of Lend-Lease was this "Mothers' Crusade," praying for the bill's defeat in the shadow of the Capitol.

nowhere in Congress. Those opinion polls were no guide to how the balloting might go on Capitol Hill, and Roosevelt knew it.

Senator Robert Taft saw through Roosevelt's stratagem at once: "Lending arms is like lending chewing gum," he said. "You don't want it back." Senator Burton K. Wheeler of Montana said Lend-Lease reminded him of a "triple-A foreign policy" because "it will plow under every fourth American boy." Furious, Roosevelt retorted that that was the rottenest thing that had been said in public life in his generation. The *Chicago Tribune* called it "a bill for the destruction of the American Republic . . . a brief for an unlimited dictatorship with power over the possessions and lives of the American people, with power to make war and alliances forever." Across the land, ordinary citizens were speaking out for or against the bill wherever they could find a platform; America Firsters fought figuratively and literally with William Allen White's Committee to Defend the Allies; mailboxes were jammed with pamphlets and petitions. Mothers' groups marched, the Paul Revere Sentinels picketed the British embassy, clusters of people representing every conceivable political stripe appeared on the steps and in the halls of the Capitol, buttonholing senators and congressmen.

In the weeks to come, they were all there on the Hill, it seemed, the pantheon of isolationism, including the shade of old man Borah, all the strident voices of America's deeply troubled spirit, for now the future of Lend-Lease lay in the hands of Congress. Opponents of the bill saw this as the last chance for the United States to turn its back on Europe's war: to them, a policy of aiding Britain by all measures short of war was merely a detour on the road to Armageddon, and the isolationist speakers were primed. Charles Lindbergh, looking fit and youthful, spoke confidently before the House Foreign Affairs Committee, telling them that with twenty thousand modern combat planes the United States could keep any enemy at bay for years. HR 1776 was a step away from democracy, a step closer to war, and the only salvation of the American way of life was "to defend it here at home and not attempt to enter a war abroad." In any case, he went on, "it would be better for us and for every nation that the war in Europe end without conclusive victory."

In the Senate, Hiram Johnson, who would have been president if he had agreed to run with Warren Harding in 1920, and who had tangled with every chief executive from Wilson to FDR, was on his feet. He was something of a museum piece now, in his last term in the Senate (his obituary would be published on the same day the newspapers announced the atomic bombing of Hiroshima), and his were the words of an old cynic: "Those in command of us are perfectly mad to be part of the game. When it is propitious, from their point of view, they'll take us in."

The man who had recently seen the Republican nomination torn from his grasp, Ohio's Robert Taft, spoke as though he were arguing a case in court: the bill, he pointed out, "authorizes the president to make war on any nation in the world and to enter the present war if he wishes to do so, as he apparently does." Bennett Champ Clark of Missouri called the proposed legislation "the king's royal tax for the support of the British Empire." A former president and a former would-be president turned up at the Capitol, Herbert Hoover to warn Congress against "the enormous surrender of its responsibilities," Alf Landon to describe the proposal before them as "a slick scheme to fool the taxpayers." In public, Joe Kennedy straddled the issue (Dorothy Thompson accused him of out-Hamleting Hamlet, by adopting a position of "to be *and* not to be"); privately he wrote to Congressman Louis Ludlow (of the national referendum to declare war), and Ludlow read Kennedy's statement on the floor of the House to urge that aid to Britain be limited.[4] Another actor in the wings was the historian Charles A. Beard, intellectual guru of the isolationists, who declared Lend-Lease to be "a bill for waging undeclared war." Chicago University President Robert M. Hutchins predicted that "the American people are about to commit suicide."

At the very last session, a witness who had flown across the Atlantic just in time to testify made a dramatic appearance, and a large crowd gathered outside the Senate Caucus Room to see and hear the popular fellow who had recently taken on the champ and the two major political parties and lost, but in losing had gained the admiration of millions of Americans. Wendell Willkie had returned that very day from London, and he was here to tell the Senators what it was like over there, and to advise them whether the British were entitled to aid on the scale and terms proposed by the administration. Willkie had decided to go on his own to England, and before leaving he came to Washington to talk with Cordell Hull. The secretary naturally informed the president about his visitor, and Roosevelt said he would like to see him. In what could have been an excruciatingly uncomfortable and awkward encounter, they met on January 19, the day before the third-term inaugural, these two powerful and magnetic men who had done their utmost to defeat one another, and FDR to his surprise took an immediate shine to Willkie. (Apparently the feeling was not reciprocated. Roscoe Drummond, the *Christian Science Monitor* reporter, editor, and bureau chief who saw a lot of Willkie during and after the campaign, believed that the Republican candidate just plain did not like Roosevelt, and that his "incalculable services to the government in dissolving what would have been a perilous partisan controversy over the war" were performed out of a high sense of duty rather than any particular esteem for the president.) After their chat, Roosevelt gave his guest a short note to take with him. It read:

⁴After a long session at the White House on the day before Roosevelt left on his cruise, Kennedy had announced his resignation as ambassador to the Court of St. James's. He was needed now, he said, "to help the president keep the United States out of war."

"Dear Churchill, Wendell Willkie is taking this to you. He is being a true help in keeping politics out of things.

"I think this verse applies to you people as well as to us:

> "Sail on, O Ship of State!
> Sail on, O Union, strong and great!
> Humanity with all its fears,
> With all the hopes of future years
> Is hanging breathless on thy fate!"

In London, Willkie was astounded to see that the traffic at midday continued and elderly women went right on feeding pigeons in Trafalgar Square even when the sirens sounded, enemy planes appeared overhead, and AA guns boomed; he talked with Churchill, Eden, Attlee, Beaverbrook, the king and queen, and dozens of others—even with Harry Hopkins, who was there on a mission for FDR; he went to Dublin hoping to persuade Eamon De Valera to change his mind about neutrality; and everywhere he was followed by crowds of smiling Britons, drawn to this warm, friendly Indianan who returned from his trip convinced that Britain *must* be supported.

Now, here he was, a big, rumpled man just off the plane, grinning broadly as he followed a wedge of policemen breaking a path through the crowd, pushing the lock of hair back off his forehead. Inside the hearing room, while photographers' flashbulbs popped, he shook hands with the senators, had a word of greeting for several of them, burst into a laugh, and at last—after someone had dashed to his hotel to retrieve the statement he had left in his room—began to speak in the familiar voice that was still hoarse from the campaign. He supported Lend-Lease, he told them, although he had certain modifications to suggest—among them a proviso that aid should go only to Britain and her empire, China, and Greece, with Congress to decide on other recipients; but "if aid to Britain is what is going to get us into war," they might as well realize that the United States was already in it and the real question was how to make that aid most effective. "The people of Britain are united almost beyond belief. They are a free people. Millions of them will die before they give up that island." And what we should be sending them was *all* of our bombers and as many as five or ten destroyers a month.

The hearing room was designed to hold five hundred people, and three times that many were there, packed shoulder to shoulder in ranks against the marble walls, alternately applauding or groaning as the witness enthusiastically endorsed Lend-Lease, as the senators, one after another, quoted to him his own campaign words in which he had attacked Roosevelt's secrecy and his plans to get us into war. Then Willkie put an end to it. His jaw muscles tightened and his voice was firm: "I struggled as hard as I could to beat Franklin Roosevelt, and I tried to keep from pulling any of my punches. He was elected President. He is my President now." The crowd applauded loudly, the chairman rapped for order, and Gerald Nye made one final attack. He quoted Willkie's October 30 prediction that on the basis of the president's past failure to make good on his pledges, the United States could expect to be at war by April 1 if he was elected.[5]

"Are those still your views?" Nye demanded.

Willkie began to answer, then grinned broadly and said, "It was a bit of campaign oratory." The senators laughed along with the crowd, and that was the last of it.

The next day a spate of newspaper editorials appeared in support of HR 1776 following Willkie's statement, and the day after that the Senate committee reported out the bill favorably by a vote of 15 to 8. Isolationists kept sniping, trying to water it down; Nye spoke for twelve hours against it; and finally, after Jimmie Byrnes, Harry Byrd, and Robert Taft got together on a provision to give Congress the final say over appropriations, Roosevelt agreed to a compromise limiting his authority.

Before the final vote was taken, one of Wendell Willkie's convention opponents rose in the Senate chamber to deliver a brief, emotional speech, stating why HR 1776 should not become law. Michigan's Arthur Vandenberg was afraid that time and events in what he described as a "foreshortened world" were running against the nation, and after he had had his say he slouched back into his seat and crossed his long legs, watching each of his colleagues as the roll was called on the vote. It came to him as he realized what was happening that time was really running out on the cause he had espoused so sincerely and with such dedication. It was 7:10 P.M. on Saturday, March 8, when the Senate voted, 60 to 31, in favor of the bill, and Vandenberg took careful note of it in his diary. "If America 'cracks up,' " he wrote, "you can put your finger on this precise moment as the time when the crime was committed." Vandenberg was nothing if not a real patriot, sincere in his strongly held beliefs about what the republic should and should not do, and the troubled thoughts he recorded that night were as good an indication as might be found of what some principled men found objectionable in the administration's foreign policy.

It was not necessary, he wrote, to give the president the sweeping powers he requested; Taft had offered amendments that provided direct, immediate aid to Britain without turning the White House "into G.H.Q. for all the wars of the world." Sponsors of the bill had said that it was the way to peace, and Vandenberg prayed to God that they were right and he was wrong; yet he had a sinking feeling, as the result of the balloting was announced, "that I was witnessing the suicide of the Republic."

"This is what I believe is the result," he noted. "We have torn up 150 years of traditional American foreign policy. We have tossed Washington's Fare-

---

[5]That statement of Willkie's may have been responsible for a persistent belief in London that Roosevelt would have the United States in the war by spring.

well Address into the discard. We have thrown ourselves squarely into the power politics and the power wars of Europe, Asia, and Africa. We have taken the first step upon a course from which we can never hereafter retreat. We have said to Britain: *'We will see you through to victory'*—and it would be unbelievably dishonorable for us to stop short of full participation in the war if that be necessary. . . ." In passing this bill, it appeared to him that the Senate was telling Britain and all her allies to charge their war bills to the United States; telling Germany and Italy and Japan that we were "at undeclared war" with them; telling President Roosevelt, *"You* pick our allies; *you* pick our enemies. . . *you* lend, lease, or give away what you please . . . out of the reservoir of our resources. . . . I believe we have promised not only Britain but every other nation that joins Britain in this battle that we will see them through. I fear this means that we must actively engage in the war ourselves. I am sure it means billions upon billions added to the American public debt [but] I do not believe we are rich enough to under-write all the wars of the world. I fear it means the ultimate end of our own democracy."

It is a measure of Vandenberg's stature that, having gotten the anger and the worry off his chest, he closed his diary entry vowing cooperation with the administration: "If we stand any show, it will be from pursuing this new, revolutionary foreign policy to the last limit with swiftest speed. I shall vote hereafter accordingly." And to a friend in Michigan, he wrote, "I fought it from start to finish. I think it was wrong. . . . I think it will *not* stop short of war. But it is now the law of the land [and] we have no alternative except to go along. . . ."

Between the lines, one could sense that Arthur Vandenberg's attitude toward foreign affairs was changing ever so slightly, that he was beginning to sense that domestic solidarity was imperative at a time of great crisis. And therein lay the germ, the first vague stirrings, of the bipartisan foreign policy he would be so instrumental in forging.

On March 11, after the bill passed both Senate and House by decisive majorities, the president signed it into law and within hours asked Congress for an appropriation of a staggering $7 billion to fund it. It could now be said, as Walter Lippmann put it, that the country had made the transition "from large promises carried out slyly and partially by clever devices to substantial deeds openly and honestly avowed." Yet it remained to be seen if Henry L. Stimson's judgment on Lend-Lease would prove accurate. "I feel confident," he noted in his diary, "that we cannot permanently be in a position of toolmaker for other nations which fight and sooner or later I feel certain from what I know of young American men that when once they appreciate this issue between right and wrong they will not be satisfied unless they are offering their own bodies to the flames and are willing to fight as well as make munitions."

CHAPTER 47

"...whether the country knows it or not, we are at war."

The president had been hoping to meet with Winston Churchill, to see for himself what sort of man he was dealing with; he also wanted to learn how genuine the need was for the ever-growing shopping list the British were presenting. These goals he achieved initially by proxy, when he sent the ailing Harry Hopkins to London in January 1941. One of the first meetings Roosevelt's emissary had was with Ed Murrow, whose broadcasts he had admired for some time, and during dinner and a five-hour conversation at Claridge's he told the CBS man that the purpose of his trip was "to find a way to be a catalytic agent between two prima donnas." He also urged Murrow to consider returning to the States: the big fight in the next three years (over U.S. entry into war) was going to take place there, and he should be on hand for the fireworks.

Hopkins had gone to England with a chip on his shoulder, supposing that he would not care for Churchill or his imperialist attitude, and was quickly and totally taken in by the prime minister's toughness of mind, his determination to win, his unmatched gift for appraising the war situation, his encyclopedic knowledge, and the impression he gave of being on a battlefront at all times—whether the battle happened to be Dunkirk or Cannae or Omdurman. "Churchill is the gov't in every sense of the word," Hopkins reported to Roosevelt, "he controls the grand strategy and often the details. . . ."[1] Happily, Churchill found a friend and ally in Hopkins, too, sensing that he had finally established "a definite, heart-to-heart contact with the president," while finding a man who shared his hatred of Nazism. Once, in an expansive mood, he remarked to the former social worker that he planned to provide a good life for the cottagers after the war, and Hopkins replied, "I don't give a damn about your cottagers—we're only interested in seeing that goddam sonofabitch gets licked." What endeared the American to so many of his hosts on this trip was his warm, sympathetic nature: as an English editor wrote after hearing him talk off the record at a dinner, "His speech left us with the feeling that although America was not yet in the war, she was marching beside us, and should we stumble she would see we did not fall."

He journeyed with the prime minister and his physician, Lord Moran, to Scapa Flow to see the fleet on a January day when sheets of wind-driven sleet took the breath away, and that evening at a small dinner in Glasgow, Hopkins got to his feet, turned to Churchill, and said, "I suppose you wish to know what I am going to say to President Roosevelt on my return. Well, I'm going to quote you one verse from that Book of Books in the truth of which . . . my own Scottish mother was brought up: 'Whither thou goest, I will go; and where thou lodgest, I will lodge: thy people shall be my people, and thy God my God.' " And before he sat down he spoke very quietly four words that were not to be found in the Book of Ruth: "Even to the end."

To Lord Moran, the words were like a rope thrown to a drowning man, and when he glanced at the prime minister he saw that tears were streaming down his cheeks.

After six weeks in England, the presidential agent returned with what was by far the best and most complete report the United States had of Britain's current situation, her needs, and her prospects. He also discovered that he had a new job.

Roosevelt wanted Hopkins to take charge of Lend-Lease (which meant, of course, that FDR would have his hands firmly on the tiller), and to make it as difficult as possible for critics to attack the program or Hopkins, he gave him no title, did not even put his name on the rolls. Despite the handicaps, Hopkins—operating out of his bedroom in the White House, using a card table for a desk and a four-poster bed to spread out papers and notes—somehow managed to get the program off the ground so that by the spring of 1941 what Robert Sherwood termed a "common-law marriage" between the United States and Britain was beginning to appear workable. Such a relationship was defined in the dictionary, Roosevelt's speech writer said, as an agreement that had not been formalized and was not recognized

---

[1] As an instance of how Hopkins was captivated by the prime minister, Alexander Cadogan described an occasion when the company at Chequers, Churchill's country estate, retired about 2:00 A.M., and one of the British guests "was prevented from sleeping by Mr. Hopkins, who slunk into his room and ensconced himself in a chair in front of the fire, muttering at intervals, 'Jesus Christ! What a man!' "

in certain "jurisdictions" (notably the Congress of the United States). Loose as the arrangement was, it had already produced some promising developments. An exchange of scientific information had begun, as had the pooling of military intelligence—cooperation between J. Edgar Hoover's Federal Bureau of Investigation and British intelligence operations in the United States, under William Stephenson, and an exchange of technical people between the two countries, chiefly to facilitate the improvement of weapons. Steps were being taken to beef up the Atlantic Fleet so that U.S. vessels could take some of the load off the Royal Navy; damaged British ships were being repaired in American shipyards, British pilots and crews were being trained here, those high-level staff talks had begun, and the administration was quietly considering the occupation of Greenland and Iceland, to forestall any attempt by the Germans to do so.

So far, so good, but the best intentions in the world were not going to get Lend-Lease goods to England until and unless the administration solved two enormous problems. The first was how to get business and labor into this thing so that a sufficient flow of vital war materials to the British (*and* to the U.S. armed forces, as Stimson, Knox, Marshall, and Stark never let the president forget) began in earnest. The second was how to get the goods safely from here to there—what, in short, we were willing and able to do to help the crippled, overextended Royal Navy fight off the chief menace to Britain's survival.

Between July 1940 and April 1941 the German U-boat fleet in the Atlantic had expanded from twelve to thirty, and Admiral Dönitz expected to have more than fifty boats on patrol by August. Deployed as wolf packs, attacking at night on the surface for greater accuracy, the submarines were taking a rising toll of merchant ships—sixty-one in June alone. Nor were U-boats the only threat to Britain's lifeline. Luftwaffe planes sank almost ninety ships in the first three months of the year; raiders disguised as cargo vessels accounted for thirty-eight between January and July. Britain's shipyards and repair facilities were bombed repeatedly; her ports were plugged with merchant ships and escorts in need of repair. Worse yet, Admiral Raeder's formidable capital ships were at sea at last. During February and March the *Scharnhorst* and *Gneisenau* sank twenty-one ships in the western Atlantic; the heavy cruiser *Hipper* destroyed seven; the *Admiral Scheer* accounted for sixteen on one voyage to the Indian Ocean. And the *Bismarck* and *Prinz Eugen* were rumored to be ready.

Clearly, the damage was out of hand and had gone beyond the capacity of the Royal Navy to control. Roosevelt wrote to Churchill on May 10 to say he believed "the outcome of this struggle is going to be decided in the Atlantic, and unless Hitler can win there he cannot win anywhere in the world in the end." But with the death toll of ships at three times the rate of construction, it could be asked whether there was any stopping Hitler in the Atlantic.

Thanks to Mr. Roosevelt, the United States Navy had a leg up on the problem—not much of one, but a start. Back in 1938, about the time Neville Chamberlain was proposing to go and see Adolf Hitler in Munich, President Roosevelt had directed the chief of naval operations to expedite the reconditioning of World War I destroyers that had lain idle at Philadelphia for two decades, and to assemble a temporary force to be called the Atlantic Squadron. In the spring of 1939 he informed cabinet members of his plan to inaugurate a naval patrol extending from Newfoundland to South America, adding that "if some submarines are laying there and try to interrupt an American flag and our navy sinks them it's just too bad. . . ." At the outbreak of war he put it into effect—announcing a "neutrality patrol" two hundred to three hundred miles offshore to report the presence of belligerent vessels. (The word "neutrality" was crucial in those innocent days of September 1939, when the nation was dead set against a hint of military activity.)

A year later, while talking with Stark, FDR turned to a chart on his wall, drew a line from Newfoundland south to British Guiana along the 60th meridian, and asked the admiral, "How would the navy like to patrol such a neutrality zone?" Since this was a thousand miles off Charleston and since the navy already had its hands full with a "neutrality patrol" two hundred miles offshore, Stark ducked the question by saying noncommittally that it would require a good many planes and ships. To the dismay of the Navy Department, on September 27, Assistant Secretary of State Adolf Berle requested details of the plans for the new security zone which had been "thoroughly discussed" by the president and Stark, and on October 10 a starchy memorandum from Mr. Roosevelt arrived, expressing displeasure at how long it was taking to get the patrol under way. He wanted operations "rushed to completion"; he wanted submarine sightings reported immediately and in the clear; he wanted suspicious vessels followed day and night; and, just in case the department did not get the gist of his remarks, he added that "loss of contact with surface ships cannot be tolerated."

All this was to be done as quietly as possible, of course; the president did not intend for Americans to learn what the neutrality patrol was doing, lest it become apparent that the operation was decidedly unneutral. By the time navy vessels began shadowing German merchantmen, submarines, and raiders and reporting their positions so the British could take action, the "patrol" began to look perilously like hostile action, as Stimson warned the president.

In its early stages the patrol was strictly a jury-rig operation, with aging ships and green crews—many of whom had never seen a gun fired—coming aboard constantly to replace old hands who were being transferred to new construction. Training and drills, notably gunnery practice and maneuvers, were all but impossible in the rough seas and bitter cold of the North Atlantic. Ships ran aground and collided; guns caked with layers of ice were all but useless; in the towering waves of winter storms, men stood with their feet braced wide apart, trying to compensate with their bodies for the frightening roll of the old four-stackers, to anticipate the frightening ascent, the sudden drop, and the shuddering crash into the trough that sent the bottom falling out of their stomachs, and they learned the meaning of doggerel inspired by these cranky tin cans in World War I:

> *Pitch, pitch, goddam your soul,*
> *The more you pitch the less you roll.*
> *Roll, roll, you mean old bitch,*
> *The more you roll the less you pitch.*

In that cold cruel sea, even the most routine shipboard tasks demanded extraordinary exertion, and when the duty was not difficult it was excruciatingly monotonous and boring. For the sailors who had to endure the psychological and physical stress of what amounted to combat duty, the most frustrating part of all was not to be able to discuss what they were doing, to get no credit for a job that was as tough as they come—fighting alone and unrecognized an undeclared war their countrymen didn't want.

I was in and out of New York City a lot in the winter of 1940–41, traveling to see Bobs at Sarah Lawrence College in Bronxville, and often enough our dates took us into the city, to dance to the big bands at the Hotel Pennsylvania, listen to jazz on Fifty-second Street or in the Village, go uptown to Spivy's Roof,[2] or see a show on Broadway, and every time we went to the theater district we would see increasing numbers of sailors, wandering around looking cold and lost and lonely, an ocean away from home, envious of me having a good time with my girl. For a time most of the servicemen in evidence were British, with their funny beribboned hats; now there were more and more Americans, and we sometimes used to wonder why so many were in port and what they were doing.

However little American citizens might know about what was happening, and whatever the patrols might mean to the officers and crews out there on the Atlantic, they satisfied Franklin Roosevelt's desire to do something. It was not much, to be sure, but it was action of a sort, a showing of the flag to remind Germany that America was on the side of the British and might open fire at any time. Shackled as FDR felt he was by the isolationists, the patrols were also a means by which he could test Hitler's intentions, and bit by bit—as a fencer probes to find his opponent's weakness—he discovered that the Führer was unlikely to respond, was apparently unwilling to

---

[2]Spivy—a big, homely woman with a whiskey voice—had run a successful speakeasy during Prohibition, and now she had a nightclub and was legitimate. We were attracted to the place by an extraordinarily talented quartet—two men and two women—who wrote and performed their own stuff. Their names meant nothing to me then, though they did later; all I knew was that it was some of the most original and entertaining material I'd heard, and probably because of that I remembered the performers when I heard of them later: Adolph Green, Betty Comden, Judy Holliday, and their young pianist—Leonard Bernstein.

take on the United States in the Atlantic. That, to Roosevelt, meant that the path lay open for bolder adventures.

It was a game of chicken in which the stakes were dangerously high, and not the least interesting aspect of it was the remarkably similar way in which two men whose philosophies and goals were poles apart were striking a balance on a knife edge between war and peace, each for his own good and sufficient reasons. Although Roosevelt was the more aggressive under the circumstances, neither wished to provoke an incident that would lead to war. Hitler's strategy was that of the landsman whose traditional enemies are at his borders, threatening, east and west; Roosevelt's was that of a lifelong advocate of sea power whose homeland is safeguarded by water, who sees the oceans as avenues for transporting large forces across great distances, where they can concentrate to strike an enemy whose strength is dispersed to prevent surprise. By the spring of 1941, Hitler and his general staff had concluded that they were not going to invade England—not now, anyway; they would strangle her instead. The use of French ports enlarged the range of Dönitz's submarines dramatically, permitting them to hunt in midocean, well beyond range of British bombers, and to cruise on the surface at higher speeds, without fear of attack. The result—even with a limited number of U-boats operating at any given time—was a continuation of the appalling and unsustainable losses of Allied shipping.

As frustrating as a standoff was to both Hitler and Roosevelt, each, against the advice of his principal advisers, had made the decision that brought it about. The president's hard-liners, the all-outers as someone called them, kept pushing for action. Frank Knox told Morgenthau and others in the fall of 1940, "The English are not going to win this war without our military help. That is what we have got to keep in our minds. We needn't talk it outdoors, but I think it is true." And he had gone on to suggest to some of his fellow cabinet members that "we can't afford to let [England] go down unless we want to fight the rest of the world. . . ." In the eyes of Knox, Stimson, Morgenthau, and the service chiefs, among others, the man in the White House was dragging his feet, failing to take the initiative, and several of them even considered handing the president a "petition for action." Stimson wanted "forcibly to stop the German submarines by our intervention," to which Roosevelt replied with a smile that he hadn't quite reached that stage yet. Ickes thought we should make an open declaration of war. At Morgenthau's instigation, the president did transfer ten Coast Guard cutters to Britain, to be based in Iceland for antisubmarine-warfare work; and he ordered the Treasury Department to seize a number of Axis and Danish ships already interned in U.S. ports. Yet beyond that, Roosevelt was unwilling—because of congressional opposition—and unable—because the nation was unprepared militarily—to make the moves that might lead to open hostilities. On a fishing trip in the Bahamas in March, he told Ickes and Hopkins that things were coming to a head, that Germany would make a blunder soon. In May he remarked to Morgenthau,

"I am waiting to be pushed into this situation." A week later at a cabinet meeting someone voiced the hope that he would declare the country "ready to do something," but he replied, "I am not willing to fire the first shot." To Stimson, that meant he was "waiting for the accidental shot of some irresponsible captain on either side to be the occasion of his going to war." But the incident he was seeking failed to materialize. Until it did, all *but* war was possible, he seemed to be saying. War was not—not yet, anyway.

So perhaps for the last time, a U.S. president was holding back, loath to risk armed conflict—a caution that would seem to support the contention of pacifists that when a nation lacks the weapons and the manpower to wage war, it does not go to war unless attacked. Much as Roosevelt wanted to escort convoys of merchant ships, much as he desired to furnish ships and men to relieve the hard-pressed British, he had to exercise extreme care, moving one step at a time along a road where he could always see around the corner to what lay ahead.

Similarly, Hitler was being pushed by some of his military men and diplomats to take the war to the Americans. If the United States became a belligerent instead of a self-styled neutral, the German navy could move at will in the western Atlantic and destroy more cargoes bound for England; at the same time, the argument went, the United States would be forced to hold on to most of its war production for its own use, instead of shipping huge quantities to the British. But the Führer was determined to avoid a conflict with the United States as long as possible, and his submariners were under orders to avoid incidents that might provoke American intervention. He had a compelling reason to avoid such a confrontation in the Atlantic, for he was about to give substance to the old German nightmare of a two-front war. Final plans and preparations for Operation Barbarossa—the invasion of the Soviet Union—were scheduled to be complete by May 15, 1941. "If the U.S.A. and Russia should enter the war against Germany," he said in January, after a failed attempt to persuade Stalin to join the Tripartite Pact, "the situation would become very complicated. Hence any possibility for such a threat to develop must be eliminated at the very beginning. If the Russian threat were nonexistent, we could wage war on Britain indefinitely. If Russia collapsed, Japan would be greatly relieved; this in turn would mean increased danger to the U.S.A."

He was relying on Japan's eagerness for military adventure to neutralize U.S. efforts to aid Britain, to keep America occupied while he struck a sudden, decisive blow in the east. From the time he invaded Poland, his idea had been to achieve victory through a series of quick, relatively inexpensive wars—"lightning wars" executed by his dominant army and air force— which would not disrupt the civilian population of Germany or what still remained in many respects a peacetime economy. In the late spring of 1941, he had two hundred divisions standing idle. Now they would be put to work in the east, to smash the hated Bolsheviks, seize the oil and grain he needed, and move onto the lands he craved for Germany's future living space.

In February of 1941, as Stark's Plan Dog began to be implemented, Roosevelt directed that the navy's patrol force be greatly expanded, renamed the Atlantic Fleet, and brought to a state of readiness. "This step is, in effect, a war mobilization," Stark told Ernest J. King, who was now in command of that fleet's 159 ships. King had just been promoted to full admiral and, following the president's instructions, issued an order delineating the western hemisphere as extending to 26 degrees west longitude—slightly west of Iceland and east of the Azores. What had once been called a neutrality zone was moving closer and closer to Europe, and there was a peremptory and distinctly aggressive tone to King's order, which read: "Entrance into the Western Hemisphere by naval ships or aircraft of belligerents other than those powers having sovereignty in the Western Hemisphere is to be viewed as possibly actuated by unfriendly interests." This could come as neither a surprise nor a deterrent to Hitler, but it certainly intimated that trouble lay ahead.

If clash there was to be, the Atlantic Fleet was in good hands. Ernest King was grim, resolute, immensely competent, with a range of experience all but unmatched by his fellow officers (he had served in submarines and carriers, had his aviator's wings, had been a staff officer and a salvage man, and had commanded a fleet at sea), and no one ever doubted that he would have his own way when he took command. He was capable of verbally taking the skin off a subordinate who made a mistake, and junior officers throughout the fleet quailed at the prospect that King might notice them, let alone dress them down. "He is the most even-tempered man in the navy," one of his daughters observed. "He is always in a rage." His theory of command was simplicity itself: "I give my men the tools, the assignment, and the authority. The rest is up to them. I will tell a commander to patrol a certain area but I'll never tell him how. He should know how. If he doesn't, we must get a man who does." It is part and parcel of the King legend that when Roosevelt appointed him Commander in Chief, United States Fleet,[3] on December 15, 1941, the admiral is supposed to have commented, "When they get in trouble they send for the sonsofbitches." (He denied having made the remark, but said he would have if he'd thought of it. The point is, *someone* said it, and no one ever suggested it wasn't so.)

After Dwight Eisenhower had seen something of King he decided he was "an arbitrary, stubborn type, with not too much brains and a tendency toward bullying his juniors. But I think he wants to fight." The general was wrong about King's lack of brains, but right on target concerning his combativeness. Stark considered Ernie King the best man for the Atlantic

[3]Characteristically, King informed the president that he refused to accept the abbreviated title CinCUS. Whether you read it or said it, the sound was "sink us." Henceforth, the form of address would be Cominch.

job. "He will lick things into shape," he said, and King was not long in proving that he could.

By the end of March, the joint staff talks in Washington had produced a plan assigning specific roles to British and American ships, and Stark, for one, was raring to go, urging naval assistance immediately. The hitch was that the navy had plans but was still short of ships and men; despite its construction program, the Atlantic Fleet was as yet in no shape to perform what the president and the CNO wanted it to do. New, up-to-date destroyers were in desperately short supply; ships were undermanned, too many of them with inexperienced crews, at that; too few trained sonar operators were available for the antisubmarine warfare that was contemplated; there were shortages of every type of equipment, from splinter shields for gun crews to antiaircraft guns and adequate depth-charge racks. King's people were dealing with these frustrations to the best of their ability, but time seemed to be running out in the last two weeks of May 1941—a period when Secretary Hull kept saying, over and over, "Everything is going hellward." The president was in a foul humor; for most of those two weeks he kept to his bed, supposedly with a bad cold, but when Bob Sherwood commented to Missy LeHand that he seemed to have no signs of an ailment, she smiled and replied that he was suffering from "a case of pure exasperation."

In London that spring, morale reached low ebb. The drab ration book was a daily reminder of growing food shortages and the worst diet the nation had ever known (even the moat around the Tower was now producing cabbages), with unending meatless, eggless days. Work stoppages were alarmingly frequent, absenteeism in the factories growing. Britons felt cut off from the rest of the world, abandoned, and still the bombings went on relentlessly, shattering cities and the whole fabric of life. One evening Ed and Janet Murrow walked home from a late supper during a raid (Janet on tiptoe, worrying because her heels made so much noise). From the roof of their flat they watched incendiaries going off to the south, flares hanging like red lanterns in the starry sky, searchlights sweeping slowly through the dark. Suddenly they heard the angry "whish" of a bomb, and Janet thought they would be hit as they raced for the stairway. She was knocked against the wall. "Are you all right?" she called to her husband. He was, but behind his shoulder she saw "an awful black cloud shot through with sparks."

His first thought was, "It's the office," and he grabbed his tin hat and raced off. Hours later he was back—the helmet on the back of his head, a typewriter under one arm, and a bottle of whiskey under the other. His secretary was safe, he said, but the office was gone—his third to be bombed.

Next morning they learned that nearly five hundred planes had attacked, leaving Piccadilly, Mayfair, the Strand, and Hallam and New Cavendish streets a shambles. "Underfoot was glass, glass, and more glass," Janet wrote in her diary. "Window frames blown out, torn curtains, dust—horrid gray-white dust, and smoke in the air, fires smoldering," and here and there a blazing broken gas main.

In all likelihood, Hitler was never closer to ultimate victory than in May and June of 1941, when his air force pounded London almost at will, his submarines controlled the Atlantic, his armies overran the Balkans and Libya, and he threatened to seize the entire Middle East and Gibraltar and drive the British from the Mediterranean. Seemingly invincible, the Wehrmacht stormed into Yugoslavia and Greece, overwhelming the former in less than a fortnight, the latter in four weeks. In North Africa, Rommel pushed the British back to the Libyan-Egyptian border east of Tobruk, imperiling the Suez Canal. Rumors abounded: the arrival of many German "tourists" in Lisbon, Casablanca, and Tangier, plus evidence that the Vichy government was caving in to German pressure, led to assumptions that the Nazis would move into Spain, Portugal, and Gibraltar. From sources on the continent came reports of a massive buildup of German forces in the east, indicating an impending invasion of Russia. And to cap it off, the Japanese were known to be stirring on the other side of the world—probably planning to drive southward.

The final week of May brought terrible news. In the first large-scale airborne attack the world had seen, the Germans seized the Aegean island of Crete. The British lost some thirteen thousand troops, two thousand naval casualties, and—of vital consequence for the Battle of the Atlantic— three cruisers and six destroyers, with two battleships, a carrier, six cruisers, and seven destroyers damaged by bombs. At the same time, the British suffered a shocking and humiliating defeat when the *Bismarck,* which had put to sea despite Hitler's fears that the dreadnought might be lost, sank the British battle cruiser *Hood* in a fight that lasted only twenty-four minutes. Only three men of a crew of more than fifteen hundred survived, and the battleship *Prince of Wales* was so badly damaged she had to limp away from the action.

The *Bismarck* headed south, trailing oil, pursued by every vessel the Royal Navy had within range, and although hit by a torpedo from a carrier-based plane, somehow managed to escape in the darkness. More than four hundred miles west of the French coast, the great ship was sighted again by a lumbering Catalina PBY piloted by Ensign Leonard B. Smith, an "adviser" from the U.S. Navy, who barely eluded the ship's antiaircraft fire and radioed her position. From all directions British warships closed in, and the following morning, after being hit repeatedly by shellfire and torpedoes, the world's most powerful dreadnought capsized and went to the bottom with two thousand of her crew. In all, during the eight-day hunt for the German warship, four thousand sailors had died, and at best it was a Pyrrhic victory for the Royal Navy.

Against this background, President Roosevelt spoke to the nation by radio to proclaim an unlimited national emergency. For five days and nights, FDR, Rosenman, and Sherwood had labored on the speech, which the president considered one of his most important messages about the war. The cabinet was deeply divided over what he should say—Stimson and

Knox, in particular, urging him to announce that the navy would start escorting convoys at once, and Hull arguing just as hard for restraint. (The secretary of state was engaged in delicate informal discussions with the Japanese ambassador, Admiral Kichisaburo Nomura, aimed at avoiding war with that nation, and was determined that the United States should not appear to be unduly aggressive just now.)

In the final version of the speech, Mr. Roosevelt satisfied few of his advisers completely; as he often did, he skated a thin line somewhere between the ideas they had suggested, adding certain nuances that were truly his own. Adolf Berle thought the message "calculated to scare the daylights out of everyone" (which it did not), and Roosevelt cabled Churchill a few hours before he delivered it, to say that he was going further than he had imagined possible several weeks earlier. Speaking to an audience estimated at eighty-five million—almost two-thirds of the total U.S. population, he began by saying that what had started as a European war had developed, "as the Nazis always intended it should develop, into a war for world domination." So it was only common sense that we should prevent them from establishing a foothold in the Americas, and he intended to defend a line in the Atlantic stretching from Iceland to the Azores and Cape Verde Islands, and would deliver the goods the British needed, no matter how great the risk. As remote and unimportant as Iceland might seem to the average American, it was important in the president's overall scheme for several reasons: it was an obvious way station for convoys, whenever the Atlantic Fleet should begin escorting; it was a potential stopover for planes ferrying matériel to England; and besides, there was the risk that if we did not occupy it the Germans might.

A month after the speech, two marine brigades set sail secretly, escorted by a task force that included two battleships, two light cruisers, thirteen destroyers, and other vessels, and on July 9—taking German intelligence completely by surprise—the troops came ashore in Reykjavik, which immediately became known as "Rinkydink." Until that moment, many Americans had believed with all their hearts that this would remain a European war. Now, before the public knew what was happening, the United States Navy had carried American troops and weapons into the war zone and landed them on foreign soil. What was implicit in this event, when anyone stopped to think about it, was that those troops would have to be supplied with all manner of food and other necessities, perhaps even relieved or reinforced (the plan, in fact, was to send as many as ten thousand soldiers to Iceland when the weather improved, but the public did not know that, either), and American merchant ships were going to have to haul the supplies. What did that mean? Well, quite possibly a repetition of what had happened to the American freighter *Robin Moor,* which had been torpedoed by design or error in the South Atlantic in May. You did not have to possess any military expertise or second sight to see that any ship traveling in the North Atlantic would be sailing in dangerous waters indeed.[4] Should such ships be escorted by the United States Navy? If not, how could we ensure that the troops in Iceland would be supplied?

Again, the president seemed unable to make up his mind: to the despair of Stark, who warned that every day of delay in entering the war increased the risks, FDR ordered, and then canceled, escort plans on two occasions. One reason for the apparent indecisiveness was Roosevelt's concern about the Pacific. No matter how much he wished it to go away, the problem of Japan intruded increasingly on his thoughts. Intercepted messages revealed Japanese plans to move into southern Indochina, and the president was leery of being overcommitted in the Atlantic with crises looming on the other side of the world. So he temporized until it became clear that there was no altering the situation in Indochina short of war; only then did he agree to the navy's plans to escort convoys. Even so, he imposed a condition: U.S. ships would escort only U.S. and Icelandic vessels, and before they did much of that, he would attend to an important piece of business.

———

On Saturday, August 3, the president breezily informed the press that he was going fishing, and on Sunday he boarded the *Potomac* in New London, Connecticut, along with a group that included Crown Princess Martha of Norway and her three children (who, with a governess, a nurse, a maid, a lady-in-waiting, and a gentleman whose position was never made clear, had visited at Hyde Park for two weeks, taxing the facilities of the large house and even the abundant patience of Eleanor Roosevelt). They were seen cruising off Martha's Vineyard; then the visitors came ashore; and the presidential yacht headed toward the open sea for what was described as "serious fishing." After that, silence. Not for ten days did the headlines reveal that the *Potomac* had rendezvoused with the cruiser *Augusta*, Admiral King's flagship, off Cape Cod, where Mr. Roosevelt was hoisted aboard to join General Marshall, Admiral Stark, Under Secretary of State Sumner Welles,[5] and other top advisers on a top-secret mission (though not so secret as to prevent the Japanese ambassador in Washington from learning what the American public did not, and informing his government what was happening).

The *Augusta* steamed north and dropped anchor two nights later in a desolate cove on Newfoundland's southeast coast, near the fishing village of Argentia. As the thick white mist rose off the water the following morn-

---

[4] Many Americans, but not Vermont's perceptive legislators. Knowing a spade for a spade, they passed an act on April 7, 1941, providing for payment of ten dollars per month to any Vermont resident in U.S. military service in the event that the nation should "become actively involved . . . in armed conflict with [the] forces of another nation. . . ."

[5] The president's selection of Welles to accompany him was one more indication of his preference for his old friend over Cordell Hull, and one more bitter pill for the secretary of state to swallow.

ing, the sun broke through, and suddenly the new British battleship *Prince of Wales,* wearing scars from her encounter with the *Bismarck,* slid majestically into Placentia Bay, band playing, a detachment of Royal Marines presenting arms, while seamen lining the decks of U.S. ships at anchorage waved their caps and cheered. A boat carrying a U.S. Navy captain sped across the water to the *Prince of Wales* and returned to the *Augusta* with a man some of the sailors recognized as Harry Hopkins. Shortly afterward, a short, chubby man in a blue uniform and what might have been a naval cap of some sort, accompanied by an array of British military and naval brass, set off in the admiral's barge, arrived at the *Augusta,* and climbed aboard. The cruiser's marine band struck up "God Save the King," and Winston Churchill, His Britannic Majesty's first minister, walked across the deck toward the president of the United States, who, standing beneath an awning, leaning on the arm of his son Elliott, held out his hand and said with a smile, "At last we've gotten together."

President Roosevelt had been longing for this meeting for months, but an event that took place half a world from America made it all but imperative. At 3:30 on the morning of June 22, 1941, without a declaration of war or even the pretext of an "incident," Germany's drive to the east had begun. With the Balkans securely held and the continent seemingly impervious to invasion, Adolf Hitler at the age of fifty-two set out to conquer the USSR. It was the day after the anniversary of Napoleon's assault on Russia in 1812, and in an awesome display of power, his gray legions swept across the immense open spaces along a thousand-mile front, beginning the greatest land war in recorded history. For Germany to win, everything depended on timing: it was crucial for the Wehrmacht to destroy the enemy's armies on the western frontier and reach a line from Leningrad to Moscow to Rostov before the savage Russian winter descended, before the Soviets could bring up reinforcements from the Far East and new levies from their huge manpower reserves. Only time would determine whether General Jodl's confident prediction of victory would hold: "The Russian colossus will be proved to be a pig's bladder," the OKW's chief of operations had promised; "prick it, and it will burst." Jodl was not alone in his estimate of the Soviets' chances: upon hearing of the German invasion, Secretary of War Stimson sent a message to President Roosevelt saying that "Germany will be thoroughly occupied in beating Russia for a minimum of one month and a possible maximum of three months." At that, his expectations were more optimistic than those of British military authorities, who reckoned that Moscow and the Ukraine might be occupied in three to six weeks.

The meeting between President Roosevelt and Prime Minister Churchill first began to take shape on July 11, during a long talk the president had with

Harry Hopkins in his study. As they chatted, Roosevelt tore a map from the *National Geographic* and, before handing it to Hopkins, drew a line around the east and south coasts of Iceland, then due south in the Atlantic along the 26th parallel. Hopkins, he said, should take this map with him to England and show Churchill the area to be policed by the United States Navy. Then he should sound out the prime minister about the possibility of a meeting with Roosevelt, and if the Englishman agreed to come, stipulate that one of the rules was that no questions were to be asked about when the United States would enter the war. Two days later, Hopkins flew to England in one of twenty-one B-24s being delivered to the RAF as part of Lend-Lease, met with Churchill, and obtained his enthusiastic agreement to a meeting. For various reasons, it could not be scheduled immediately, but in the meantime, Hopkins had decided that the conference was going to be held in a vacuum if no one present possessed any firsthand knowledge of what was happening in the Soviet Union, and he decided to fly there and find out.

With Roosevelt's blessing and a message to Stalin requesting the Soviet leader to "treat Mr. Hopkins with the identical confidence you would feel if you were talking directly to me," he left on July 27 aboard a Catalina PBY and flew to Russia on what Robert Sherwood called "one of the most extraordinarily important and valuable missions of the whole war." He spent three days in Moscow—six uninterrupted hours of them with Joseph Stalin—and came away with more information concerning the USSR's strength and prospects for survival than had been divulged to any outsider. Armed with that information, he altered permanently the perception of British and American officials that the Russians were going to collapse, later if not soon. From that moment on, the Russians were viewed as allies, as legitimate, long-term partners in the war against Hitler Germany.

Before leaving for England, Hopkins had been sick and in considerable pain. By the time he returned from the Soviet Union, he was desperately ill. He left his life-sustaining medicines behind in Moscow; he endured an unbelievably rough, twenty-four hour flight from Archangel to Scapa Flow, during which the plane was fired on by an unidentified destroyer; when they landed in rough seas he was thrown about, then hauled aboard the admiral's launch by a sailor with a boathook, while his luggage—including the irreplaceable notes he had taken, detailing the Soviet position and needs—was tossed after him. Taken aboard the *Prince of Wales,* he was so sick at first it was feared he would not survive long enough to report to President Roosevelt on his mission. Meantime, Winston Churchill, who left England "as excited as a schoolboy on the last day of the term," according to his private secretary, boarded the battleship for the trip to Newfoundland, accompanied by Admiral of the Fleet Sir Dudley Pound and General Sir John Dill, chief of the imperial general staff, as well as Sir Alexander Cadogan, permanent under secretary of state for foreign affairs; Lord Cherwell, the prime minister's scientific adviser, whom everyone called "the

Prof"; and various other staff members. As Hopkins slowly regained his strength, he informed Churchill in detail about his conversations with the Soviet dictator, and in the evenings they played backgammon (Hopkins won $32) and watched movies.[6] On the morning of Saturday, August 9, the *Prince of Wales* entered Placentia Bay.

Since the meeting had been arranged at the suggestion of President Roosevelt, it had been assumed from the beginning by Churchill and his colleagues that there was more here than met the eye, that the U.S. president was going to reveal a major new policy direction, surely a more active American role in the war. In this they were largely disappointed, and had it not been for Churchill's determination that nothing would stand between his developing friendship with the American chief executive,[7] the published results of the conference would have been even more frustrating to the British public. The fact of the matter was that Roosevelt had no intention of stepping up American aid because he lacked the resources to do so: he had no real agenda beyond a desire to meet the British prime minister face to face and learn more about him at first hand, and, above all, to produce a joint declaration of broad principles—or war aims—that would "hold out hope for the enslaved peoples of the world."

Hopkins's "two prima donnas" approached the meeting with mixed emotions: both had been savoring the moment for some time, but were understandably edgy, Churchill asking anxiously, "I wonder if he will like me," Roosevelt out of sorts, seemingly jealous in advance of the British leader's reputation and eloquence. Churchill was all too aware of his people's terrible war-weariness, their discouragement after two years of fighting and mostly losing, or at best holding their own, and although he had agreed in advance to leave the big question unspoken, what governed his conversation was naturally the matter of when the United States would come in.

It is tempting to think of the partnership between these fascinating men as a deep friendship that sealed the burgeoning alliance between their two nations, yet one has to wonder if the relationship ever became as warm or intimate as people imagined it. The two had met before, during the First World War, when Roosevelt was Wilson's assistant secretary of the navy and Churchill was Lloyd George's minister of munitions, and at Placentia Bay Roosevelt was irked to find that the prime minister did not recall the occasion. Churchill had been a cabinet member and Roosevelt a rather junior official, which illustrates the point that a generation of political experience—far more than the eight years difference in their ages—divided them. Roosevelt had reason to envy his elder's gift for language, his often

---

[6]On the last night out the film was *Lady Hamilton,* about Lord Nelson (played by Laurence Olivier) and his mistress (acted by Vivien Leigh), which moved Churchill to tears—although he was seeing it for the *fifth* time.

[7]As Joseph Lash points out in his study of the American and British leaders, the two had communicated by letter, transatlantic telephone, and cable and through intermediaries, and Churchill's messages were clearly "acts of courtship as well as expressions of policy."

brilliant ideas and insights, since the American's talent was more for the fireside chat than the set speech and since he relied (as Churchill did not) on others to write his speeches and habitually reached out to advisers for ideas. The balance was redressed, however, when it came to the authority they wielded, for Roosevelt was a head of state, invested with the executive power of the republic; Churchill was not, and in this respect was outranked (a fact he unfailingly acknowledged). In his memoirs, Churchill stated that his regard for the president heightened as time passed, yet one cannot read the words he used without wondering if the relationship was truly so close, or whether the two were real friends. He formed a very strong affection, he wrote, for "this formidable politician who had imposed his will for nearly ten years upon the American scene, and whose heart seemed to respond to many of the impulses that stirred my own." Winston Churchill chose words carefully, and these seem to describe someone whose qualities are not altogether admired. They also suggest, as does the record, that he began the connection with the highest hopes for mutual trust and friendship, only to be disappointed at the end that he had never quite penetrated Franklin Roosevelt's shell.

By the time the meetings began, Hopkins had convinced both men that the Russians would hold out somehow, and FDR felt that if they could survive until October, the winter respite would give them time to make good their losses in matériel and equipment. Although Churchill called the USSR "a welcome guest at a hungry table," he had grave misgivings about Stalin as an ally and was concerned lest the Russians receive a lion's share of arms so badly needed by his own country. He hoped to persuade the president to take a strong stand against Japan, warning that country in "hard language" against further aggressive moves, and to agree to go to war in the Pacific if Britain should be attacked; he was anxious to obtain more Lend-Lease; and he wanted United States naval vessels to escort the convoys bringing him the goods of war.

During the four days the two leaders and their advisers met and talked continuously—mornings, afternoons, evenings, over meals, and at a memorable Sunday church service aboard the *Prince of Wales*. As usual, Churchill best described the scene aboard the British battleship, saying in *The Grand Alliance* that no one who took part in the service would forget the spectacle "that sunlit morning on the crowded quarterdeck—the symbol of the Union Jack and the Stars and Stripes draped side by side on the pulpit," the highest-ranking civilian and military leaders of both nations, "the close-packed ranks of British and American sailors, completely intermingled, sharing the same books and joining fervently in the prayers and hymns familiar to both." No one could know, of course, that almost half of those who sang "For Those in Peril on the Sea," and "Onward, Christian Soldiers," and "O, God, Our Help in Ages Past" were soon to die. The *Prince of Wales* was sunk by Japanese torpedo planes on December 10, 1941.

These sessions clearly drew Churchill and Roosevelt closer—until "the cigarette-in-holder and the long cigar were at last being lit from the same match," as Alexander Cadogan put it—but the benefits did not stop there. Expanding on the talks that had begun in Washington, Dill conferred with Marshall, Pound with Stark, Cadogan with Welles (Welles, Cadogan recorded in his diary, "improves on acquaintance, but it is a pity that he swallowed a ramrod in his youth"), the Americans were assured that the British had no secret agreements affecting postwar control of territory (Roosevelt wanted no repetition of the problems that had plagued the League of Nations), and the British stated confidently that no large bodies of troops would be required for the eventual invasion of Europe. As Dill and others saw it (or perhaps as they sensed the Americans wanted to see it), huge armadas of bombers and fighter planes, plus armored divisions equipped with the most modern weapons, would do the job—overrunning territory on the continent and then turning it over to resistance forces.

With all this a skeptical George Marshall disagreed absolutely: he believed that the superb German army would have to be defeated by ground forces before any victory was won, but just now—at a time when he was having trouble finding enough troops to relieve the marine garrison on Iceland, and when the continuation of selective service was still touch and go—he was not prepared to contemplate landing armies of Americans in Europe. Although at the time it did not seem that way to the participants, the conversations and the resulting plans did ensure that the United States was strategically better prepared for war than at any time in its history.

Roosevelt and Churchill were delighted with the outcome of their meeting in personal terms: it was clear to everyone present that they hit it off extremely well. Indeed, the fact that everything went as smoothly as it did at the conference, and in the years to come, could be attributed to the optimism and confidence of these two men at a time in history when it was just about impossible to see any light at the end of the long, black tunnel. (After the prime minister reported on his trip to George VI, the king told a friend that "Winston was greatly taken" by the president, "and has come back feeling that he knows him." Roosevelt, too, was elated: he told members of his cabinet how much he liked the Englishman and took a certain perverse pleasure in telling his wife that Churchill was "the orator" while he was the realist.) For all the exchange of information and views and the camaraderie, the enduring accomplishment of the Atlantic conference proved to be what President Roosevelt had insisted on all along—a declaration of moral principles that would govern the Allies' future actions and serve as a beacon of hope to those people and nations suffering under the Nazi terror. Ironically, the idea may have been stimulated by a remark made to Harry Hopkins by Joseph Stalin, whose savage treatment of millions of unfortunate people certainly equaled and may have surpassed Hitler's. The Soviet dictator had asked Hopkins to pass along to President Roosevelt the message that "Hitler's greatest weakness was found in the vast numbers of oppressed people who hated Hitler and the immoral ways of his government," and that these people would look to the president of the United States for encouragement and the moral strength needed to resist the Nazis.

A statement embodying this idea was well down on Winston Churchill's priority list, but in the interest of harmony he went along, and had Cadogan prepare a draft which he edited himself, and that formed the basis of the final document. In it, the two leaders—speaking for their respective countries—proclaimed "certain principles which they both accept for guidance in the framing of their policy and on which they base their hopes for a better future for the world." Considering that it was a charter for all mankind, it was a fairly simple statement, consisting of eight points. They sought no territorial or other aggrandizement; wanted no territorial changes that did not accord with the wishes of the people involved; respected the right of all peoples to choose the form of government under which they lived; and wished to see self-government returned to those who had been deprived of it. They supported equal access to trade and raw materials; they expressed their desire to bring about international cooperation in the economic field and to improve labor standards, economic progress, and social security. Turning their attention to the peace that would come "after the final destruction of the Nazi tyranny," they declared that all nations must be secure within their own boundaries, so that people could live in freedom from fear and want. Freedom of the seas was to be ensured. And all nations, they insisted, must abandon the use of force. More than good intentions would be necessary: "the disarmament of . . . nations is essential," to prevent aggression and to remove "the crushing burden of armaments."

The joint declaration, soon to become known as the Atlantic Charter, was not an official state document in the usual sense of the term. In form, it was no more than a press release issued jointly on August 14 by the British and Americans, handed to radio operators aboard their ships for transmission to shore. But in substance, it meant much more than the form suggested. Sumner Welles described it aptly when he said that it was as valid in its binding effect as if it had been officially signed and sealed—"notice to the world by the President of the United States and the Prime Minister of the United Kingdom that . . . the two nations which they represented would adhere to the great principles set forth in the declaration." Without the participants knowing it, their meeting was the forerunner of and a model for other high-level conferences during the war, and the joint statement they put together during those four days in August of 1941 would ultimately serve as the foundation for the United Nations.

Nonetheless, and understandably, the British public was disappointed and depressed when the outcome of the conference was revealed. They had been hoping for a definite American commitment to enter the war, they were waiting for fleets of ships and planes to arrive, and what some saw as the pious platitudes of the Charter were small comfort. Lord Halifax, who—as Lothian's successor in the Washington embassy—was finding dealing with the Roosevelt administration immensely frustrating, compared his task with "a disorderly day's rabbit shooting." As he described it, "Nothing comes out where you expect and you are much discouraged. And then, suddenly, something emerges quite unexpectedly at the far end of the field." Churchill himself, despite his report to the war cabinet that the president "would wage war but not declare it," and despite a commitment from Roosevelt—not revealed to the American public—that the U.S. Navy would take over the America-to-Iceland leg of all convoy runs, was gloomy about the future. "I don't know what will happen if England is fighting alone when 1942 comes," he cabled Hopkins later that month.

In the States, an immediate hue and cry was raised by the isolationists. The *Chicago Tribune,* scorning the "pretentious and meaningless eight points," demanded to know what right the president had to meet with the leader of a belligerent nation and discuss war and peace aims. Was this country at war? Other newspaper editorials compared Roosevelt with Wilson, his eight points with Wilson's ill-starred fourteen. In the Senate they accused FDR of a secret deal, of agreeing to furnish an expeditionary force that would invade Europe. And in one way or another, of course, they were all right. The fact was that in suggesting steps the United States would take to overturn the results of the Nazis' military conquests, and in speaking about "the final destruction of the Nazi tyranny," Mr. Roosevelt was tacitly assuring the world of American intervention. It might not be now, but it was coming, as surely as autumn would follow the summer.

From that moment on August 14, 1941, when the Atlantic Charter was made public, the direction of U.S. policy was set. The uncertainty that had existed was ended, and whether all segments of the American public liked it or not, their president had determined that the nation was going to join hands with Great Britain and bring about the defeat of Nazi Germany. Exactly how and when and where that was to happen was unclear, to say the least, but across the land there was an uneasy feeling that war was suddenly a great deal closer, that time was running out.

Much as Roosevelt tried to cast the Atlantic Charter in a favorable light before the public, emphasizing the religious service on the *Prince of Wales* and the unity between leaders and servicemen of both nations, from his standpoint the response was disappointing. At a news conference the president quoted a letter, without naming the source, he had received from Felix Frankfurter: "We live by symbols," the justice said, "and you two in that ocean . . . in the setting of that Sunday service, gave meaning to the conflict between civilization and arrogant, brute challenge; and gave promise more powerful and binding than any formal treaty could, that civilization has brains and resources that tyranny will not be able to overcome." Winston Churchill left Placentia Bay with the definite impression that the president was determined to bring the United States into the war, but if Roosevelt believed he had the American people behind him in any venture involving open hostilities, he was badly mistaken. They were not ready, would not be made ready by high-flown words about shared values and responsibilities, civilization and tyranny, and an opinion poll taken immediately after the conference revealed that 74 percent of the nation opposed direct involvement.

═══

Suddenly, as had happened so often during the past three years, events took charge once more, and the president took advantage of those events to lead the nation in a direction in which no amount of persuasion could have taken the American people.

On September 4, some 125 miles southwest of Reykjavik, the old four-piper *Greer* was heading for Iceland with mail for the marines, a few army officers, and some supplies when a British bomber flew over and signaled that a German U-boat was submerging ten miles away. The *Greer* located the submarine and began tracking it; the plane ran low on fuel, but before leaving for its base dropped four depth charges in an unsuccessful attack on the German. That left it up to the American destroyer, which maintained contact for several more hours until the submarine suddenly turned and fired a torpedo. The *Greer* responded by firing depth charges; the sub launched one or two more torpedoes, then disappeared. More than two hours passed before the destroyer regained contact and dropped additional depth charges, again without effect; then, after receiving orders to proceed to Iceland, the *Greer* broke off the engagement. Neither U-boat nor destroyer was damaged, no one was hurt. But for the first time, units of the German and American navies had fired at each other.

Two days later an angry President Roosevelt was on the air, speaking to a nationwide audience. A German submarine, he informed his listeners, had "fired first upon this American destroyer without warning, and with deliberate design to sink her." (That was accurate enough, but what he carefully omitted saying—and what isolationists in the Congress soon learned and used against him—was that the *Greer* had determinedly tracked the U-boat for three and a half hours before being attacked.) It was piracy, he said, an act of international lawlessness that demonstrated Hitler's plan to "abolish the freedom of the seas" and create "a permanent world system based on force, on terror, and on murder."

America had sought no shooting war with Hitler, he continued, and did not seek one now. "But when you see a rattlesnake poised to strike, you do not wait until he has struck before you crush him. These Nazi submarines and raiders are the rattlesnakes of the Atlantic. . . . The time for active defense is now." In conclusion, he warned German and Italian warships that if they entered the waters considered necessary for American defense, they would do so at their own peril.

"Active defense," he called it, but to everyone listening it sounded more like "shoot-on-sight." The public he had sought to convince was convinced:

62 percent of those polled approved the policy he had enunciated, confirming his belief that a majority of Americans believed that Hitler must be defeated. Whether they would have responded the same way if Roosevelt had told them the whole truth—that the submarine had fired after being attacked, and that Hitler seemed determined to avoid hostilities with the United States, especially after he invaded Russia—is by no means clear. As the historian Robert Dallek suggests, the president's deviousness was less harmful under the circumstances then existing than it was as a precedent, for his not entirely truthful use of the *Greer* incident to influence public opinion was repeated by later chief executives in circumstances that were less justifiable.[8]

Lord Halifax, after talking with Roosevelt, tried to explain the president's dilemma in a letter to Churchill. "His perpetual problem," he said, is to "steer a course between (1) the wish of 70% of Americans to keep out of war; (2) the wish of 70% of Americans to do everything to break Hitler, even if it means war. He said that if he asked for a declaration of war he wouldn't get it, and opinion would swing against him. He therefore intended to go on doing whatever he best could to help us, and declarations of war were out of fashion."

Ernie King's sailors, frustrated so long by Washington's apparent lack of direction, supported that view. "United States declares war on Axis," read the entry in the log of an aviation tender bound for Iceland. "Declaration not made in the obsolete formal exchange of diplomatic notes, but by the president's declaration of a 'shooting war' in his speech." Despite what had happened, Hitler remained adamant in his refusal to extend operations westward; he would tolerate accidental attacks by U-boats on American warships, he told Admiral Raeder, but he would not strengthen Roosevelt's hand by ordering an expansion of hostilities.

Certainly what was occurring in the North Atlantic had the look of real war even if it had not been legitimized. For a while the business of escorting convoys seemed to be going nowhere: problems of logistics—of assembling the merchant ships and their escorts at the right time and the right place, in particular—were formidable, and the Americans were new to the game. Then, abruptly, in mid-September, after Admiral King had moved his support vessels to Maine and reorganized his destroyer squadrons and training and refitting programs, things began to click and the escort cycle began with American protection covering convoy lanes from the continental United States to 150 miles beyond Iceland, with the fleet operating under battle conditions, ships darkened, and crews on the alert for any sign of the enemy. Between the middle of September and the end of October, U.S. destroyers escorted fourteen convoys, totaling 675 ships, across the North

[8]In 1971, Senator William Fulbright, alluding to Lyndon Johnson's use of the Tonkin Gulf incident to increase American action in Vietnam, observed that "FDR's deviousness in a good cause made it easier for LBJ to practice the same kind of deviousness in a bad cause."

Atlantic. Events were still driving policy, however; by no means all the merchant vessels crossing the Atlantic could be included in convoys, and these unescorted vessels had no better than an even chance of surviving the trip. At the very least they should be permitted to be armed, and the president realized that the time had come to ask Congress once again to revise the neutrality legislation. If arming merchant ships was approved by a strong margin in the House, he planned to beef up the revisions in the Senate so as to permit American ships to enter combat zones and deliver Lend-Lease cargoes to friendly ports. Before the House vote, a public opinion poll showed that almost three-quarters of the people favored arming merchant ships, and the president got the support he needed in the lower chamber after the destroyer *Kearny* was attacked by a submarine with the loss of eleven American lives. But the unreconcilables in the Senate hung on, resisting every step of the way; the more comprehensive revisions squeaked through by the slimmest of margins, and only when Roosevelt warned members of the House that failure to pass the Senate revisions would strengthen the Axis powers and weaken America did they give the measure a bare margin of victory.

You would have thought that the sinking of a United States destroyer would have changed a good many legislators' minds. Ernest King was sure that another attack on an American warship would lead to an "open assumption of war status," but he misjudged both president and Congress, for that very occurrence played little part in the vote. The *Reuben James* was a World War I tin can, an old wreck with twenty-one years of service behind her, ancient 4-inch guns, and leaks that refused to stay plugged. She had a first-rate skipper, a lieutenant commander named Tex Edwards, and a hardworking crew that took pride in mastering the quirks of a cranky ship. The *Rube* was overdue for time in the navy yard, but with orders to make one more run to Iceland, she left Newfoundland on October 23 with four other destroyers, heading for a rendezvous with convoy HX 156, which was being escorted by Canadians on the first leg from Halifax. The first day out, the U.S. ships ran into dirty weather—thick fog and ice—before sighting the forty-three ships of the convoy, seven columns of them carrying a mixed bag of cargoes that included grain, sugar, petroleum products, and steel; the Americans relieved the Canadians and took up station patrolling the perimeter around the merchantmen.

On the 25th one of the destroyers had a contact with what might have been a sub, but nothing came of it. On the 27th the convoy received orders to change course, to elude some U-boats that were reported ahead. That day a real North Atlantic gale blew up, and the ships fought to stay on course and on station, with forty-foot waves breaking over their bows, driven by a sixty-five-knot wind. An officer on the USS *Hilary P. Jones* was swept overboard and drowned despite a heroic effort by two men who jumped into the wild ocean to save him. The storm abated, and on October 29 the escorts made contact with several unidentified objects. The next day they had reports of submarines in their area, a tanker began straggling badly, and throughout the day General Quarters was sounded repeatedly. Cold, exhausted sailors ran to their battle stations; those close enough to hear the steady, steely pinging of the sonar gear stood silently, listening, waiting for the echo that meant a contact, waiting to hear a change in pitch of the echo that meant the object was moving—lower if headed in the opposite direction, higher if coming closer.

At 5:30 A.M. on November 1 it was still black on the North Atlantic. One of the escort ships picked up a radio transmission on its radio direction finder—a signal from the port side of the convoy, close by. The escort commander ordered Tex Edwards to run it down, and the *Reuben James,* about a mile abeam of the last merchant ship in line, was starting to make a turn when a torpedo slammed into the hull below the bridge, forward of number-one stack. The detonation tore open a huge hole, and the water gushed in; another deafening explosion followed—either from a second torpedo or from the forward magazine. A sheet of orange flame lit the night sky, trailed by a surging cloud of oily black smoke, and with a gigantic hiss of steam and smoke, everything forward of number-four funnel vanished beneath the waves. Two men were blown clear of the bridge into the sea, but everyone else in the forward half of the ship died immediately.

Many of those in the after section were luckier, although luck in these circumstances was relative. Some were trapped belowdecks and couldn't get out before the stern section sank; some never made it to the life rafts; everyone in the water was coated with oil, and some drowned, some suffocated, some died of wounds or burns. When the stern sank, the depth charges exploded, blowing men and rafts high into the air. The *Hilary P. Jones* came by to pick up survivors and missed seeing them on the first pass. Then the USS *Niblack* appeared and began rescuing men who were vomiting oil and were so heavily coated it was almost impossible to get hold of them; the *Jones* returned, and the crew started pulling men from the water. Suddenly both destroyers made contact with a submarine dead astern, and both captains knew what they had to do. Engine-room telegraphs signaled full speed ahead, sailors from the *Reuben James* were left bobbing in the ships' wakes, screaming to be saved, and the *Jones* came barreling in among them to drop a pattern of depth charges. An eyewitness reported that the huge plumes of spray from the explosions, in the first light of dawn, were tinted the color of blood.

By some miracle, forty-five men from the *Reuben James* were saved. One hundred perished. And in Washington, in the wake of the disaster, nothing much happened. The president's advisers could not fathom his failure to take action, now that the incident he wanted had occurred. Harold Ickes showed FDR a letter from an old friend, a businessman who pointed out that while the power to declare war rests with the Congress, the power to wage a defensive war is in the hands of the chief executive. That was an interesting point, Roosevelt replied, but what Ickes's friend didn't realize was that "it was simply a question of timing." The discouraged interior secretary noted in his diary, "Apparently the president is going to wait— God knows for how long or what." Betty Stark, more than ever convinced that a real showdown was at hand, lamented to a friend, "The Navy is already in the war of the Atlantic, but the country doesn't seem to realize it." Apathy and even open opposition were evident in a considerable section of the press, yet "whether the country knows it or not, *we are at war.*"

CHAPTER 48

"... the entire program to date must be doubled ..."

Eric Sevareid was back in New York, having survived the disintegration of Paris and the beginning of the blitz, and after three years' absence from his homeland what he saw had an unreal, dreamlike quality to it. In contrast to the broken London he had left behind, where war was a constant presence, New York was intact and all but oblivious to events across the Atlantic. The frantic rush of people in the streets and inside the towering buildings seemed purposeless. After the blacked-out nights of Britain, the brilliant glare of the city's lights was shocking; the scream of a police siren could wake him in a cold sweat with his stomach tightening in knots.

Returning home to Minnesota for a visit, he found his father grayer, more worried about the federal deficit than anything else. The conversations turned on school and children, relatives and the weather, the cost of living, and he sat silent, unable to participate in this trivia, his mind filled with memories of the history he had witnessed. He was suffering the reentry problems that afflict soldiers and expatriates. During the years abroad they undergo a change, but so does their native land, and they discover that they and their countrymen are traveling different roads that no longer converge or coincide. A combination of his absence and what he had seen had created an unbridgeable chasm between himself and his family. Home was no longer home, he realized; "friends were no longer friends unless they thought as I did about the only things that mattered."

Severeid embarked on a lecture tour, assuming that the people who came to hear him wanted to be informed, but he learned that they really wanted to be entertained. During his travels he believed he discovered why Americans were so determined not to become involved in the war. It was the old Yankee fear of being taken for a sucker, of being gulled as they felt they had been in 1917.

Finally he went to Washington, the nation's command post, its "brain center," where the fate of the country would soon be decided, and where he was both troubled and puzzled by the spectacle of an enormously popular president who seemed incapable of acting until a majority of his countrymen had made up their minds. If Roosevelt was determined to take one agonizingly slow step at a time, taking the national pulse before he made a move, didn't he risk being too late to do any good? Should a president lead or follow the people? Considering the questions, Severeid decided that FDR probably understood better than anyone else in or out of government the exquisitely delicate mechanisms that make a democracy tick. On the one hand you had the sheer physical immensity of the country, the seemingly boundless spaces that promised security through their very remoteness from the rest of the world; then there were the tiny pockets of thought and culture and ethnic background, pockets of contrariness and doubt. Somewhere within all the conflicting emotions and loyalties and traditions lay a common thread that only the president could "touch and awaken." When it became essential for him to act the people would instinctively know that it was time to do so, and they would support him. But until that moment was at hand he would not take the ultimate step.

Severeid sat in the United States Senate while the debate over Lend-Lease was going on and marveled at the brilliance of Robert Taft's legal mind, which tore Roosevelt's bill apart, and marveled still more at the lack of imagination that failed to see the course of history. How could it be, he wondered, when America—not to mention the rest of the world—was moving steadily in a certain direction, that a strident minority could stand in the way and prevent the action that must be taken before it was too late? Too many of those who opposed America's entry into the war, among them his onetime liberal and populist friends, were applying the lessons of the First World War to the Second, missing the point entirely in assuming that "making war to save democracy would be the surest way of losing it." They perceived the struggle itself as the worst evil, ignoring what the consequences would be if the struggle was lost.

Without knowing of my existence, Mr. Severeid had read my mind, for that is where I was just then—my head alternately in the sand or the clouds, caught up in the notion that we should do everything we could to save Britain without going to war to do it, as if that were faintly possible now. In June of 1941 I returned to Pittsburgh after my sophomore year in college, to face a pending crisis. Tom Bray, Bobs's father, had been asked to come to Washington to work for the defense program, and the Brays were preparing to move. If I had considered the matter for other than selfish reasons (which I did not), I would have realized that he was an ideal choice to handle the allocations of steel for U.S. industry. His grandfather—the first Thomas J. Bray in the immediate family[1] to come to America—was from Wales, where generations of Brays had been iron and steel men, and he had designed and worked in mills in Ohio, West Virginia, and Pittsburgh. His Uncle Charlie Bray had been known as "one of Andy Carnegie's boys." His father, Thomas J. Bray, had started as an apprentice patternmaker, had become a draftsman and designer of mills, and liked to joke that without the factories he planned and built in Essen and Düsseldorf the Germans would hardly have dared start the Great War. In 1911, Tom's father became president of Republic Iron and Steel in Youngstown, and before he retired in 1928 he had transformed the company from near bankruptcy into one of the blue-chip independents. Poor eyesight kept Tom out of the First World War, and after starting work in his father's mills he had gone from Republic to Koppers to Carnegie-Illinois, where he was in charge of sales. Thanks to his heritage and experience, few Americans knew more about steel than Tom Bray, but he was not destined to go to Washington after all. He worked hard, he traveled constantly, every weekend he played seventy-two holes of golf, and by ignoring a persistent pain in his abdomen he brought on an early-morning trip to the hospital with what was diagnosed as a ruptured appendix. Peritonitis set in, and there was very little the doctors could do. A year earlier, scientists had discovered that a synthetic drug called sulfanilamide inhibited the action of a chemical in the body that was required by bacteria, but whether sulfanilamide—which was to become the miracle drug of World War II—was not yet generally available or whether it was unknown to physicians at the Sewickley hospital is beside the point. It was not used. For what seemed a lifetime, Bobs and I sat in a waiting room at the end of a hall, smoking, trying to reassure her mother and ourselves while her father raved deliriously until his agony was over. At the age of forty-four he was dead.

Within a couple of weeks I was on my way to the TAT Ranch east of Sheridan, Wyoming, where I had a job as a "hasher" that paid $50 and all I could eat for a summer's work. Hashers helped break horses to the saddle again after the winter's inactivity, washed dishes, cranked the ice-cream freezer, saddled and unsaddled horses, hauled garbage, took the dudes riding, met trains to and from the East, did just about every odd job imaginable. I was looking forward to the long rides in that incredibly clear air, fishing the mountain streams, working with cowboys and hashers I had

---

[1]They were all descended from Bishop Thomas J. Bray, who came to Maryland in the seventeenth century and was active in establishing free libraries for the Indians and blacks in the southern colonies.

met the year before. This summer, to make it ideal for me, Louise Bray had decided that she and Bobs should get away from the house and its memories in Sewickley, and they were coming to the ranch with a sister and her family.

The first leg of my trip was a night flight from Pittsburgh to Cleveland, where we had a long layover. It was just getting light when the Cleveland passengers began boarding the plane, and when a big man sat down in the seat next to me I turned to say hello and realized that it was Bob Feller, the Cleveland Indians' famous pitcher, who had thrown a no-hitter on opening day in 1940 and gone on to win 27 games that season, with an earned-run average of 2.61. He settled back in his seat at once and shut his eyes; I sat there awestruck, too stunned to speak. Should I tell him I was a pitcher at Yale? What would he think if I asked how he held the ball when he threw the fast one? I will never know; before I screwed up the courage to ask, we were landing in Chicago, and he got off the plane.

In a curious way, it was that experience more than almost any other that made me realize the war was going to include me. Feller's draft number had come up, he had decided to join the navy, and that very morning he was on his way to talk things over with the brass at the the Great Lakes Training Center in Chicago. (He finished out the 1941 season, winning twenty-five games.) It dawned on me then that if a man as important as Bob Feller was not going to be exempt, we were all going sooner or later, and that fall, when I returned to Yale and discovered that some of my friends had not come back to New Haven, I could see that it had started to happen. Some of them had been drafted, some had enlisted, and it hit home that the world we had known was changing.[2]

Whether the change was for better or worse was by no means clear to this college junior. I read the *New York Times* every day and *Time* every week and considered myself fairly knowledgeable about world affairs, but I was no particular fan of Mr. Roosevelt (for eight years his faults had been denounced at almost every meal in our home), and I often wondered just where he was taking us. I had listened attentively to Charles Lindbergh's talk at Yale the year before and agreed with his premise that America's strength and America's defenses were the most important pieces of business to attend to, and it was increasingly difficult to square that thesis with landing troops in Iceland, escorting convoys, and all the other bits of evidence that suggested we were going into this thing half-cocked, at the whim of the man in the White House. Everyone had seen and laughed at newsreel pictures of draftees in training with wooden rifles, trucks bearing signs with the word TANK, and all the rest of it, and as a member of a

[2]Even on a ranch in Banner, Wyoming, the long arm of the military was in evidence. As I packed to leave this place I loved, the sad talk among the cowboys was of how the army was buying up thousands of horses for cavalry mounts, and of how a small outfit like TAT would probably be forced to close.

household in which Roosevelt's promises and pronouncements were regarded with total skepticism, I had to ask myself if he knew what he was doing. My doubts were the doubts of many an American, and they were based on more than suspicion of Mr. Roosevelt. Take the implications of Lend-Lease.

At the time the administration won its battle for the program, Roosevelt promised a roomful of reporters that "when our production output is in full swing, the democracies of the world will be able to prove that dictatorships cannot win." He might better have put it the other way around: the real question before the house was whether production could get into full swing before the dictators won.

America's ability to furnish the mounting volume of supplies needed by the British, and now the Russians, was a long way from being achieved, with no guarantee in sight that the situation would improve. Unless the rate of arms production increased drastically we might become the arsenal of democracy too late to do any good, and the reluctance of business leaders to convert their operations to full-scale war production was traceable in some degree to the lack of a compelling incentive. The same was true of the American workers' inability to get fired up over making tanks for the British instead of, say, Chevrolet or Ford automobiles for Americans. The government in Washington was attempting through suasion to superimpose a wartime economy on a peacetime economy, and it just wasn't working. Whether it was going to work at any time in the future might well depend on Franklin Roosevelt's success in motivating the American people to go beyond business as usual. The cavalry, in other words, was not going to ride to the rescue of the wagon trains unless someone gave them a very good reason to do so, waved the flag, and shouted, "Charge!"

It is useful to remember that at this time the nation still had hundreds of idle plants, millions of idle workers, and the temptation was understandably strong to take up the slack by simply adding defense production to the normal output, at least until such time as a majority of Americans were back at work. It was a philosophy of business as usual, of guns *and* butter, of promising all things to everyone, but wars have a way of getting out of hand, of making more savage demands on an economy than anyone thinks possible, and this war was to be no exception.

From the day in 1937 when Mr. Roosevelt delivered his speech in Chicago about quarantining the aggressors (a measure that certainly carried the risk of war) until now, the public had been exposed to a good many words designed to camouflage what the government was really doing. Almost from the time the European war began, the Roosevelt administration had been doing one thing and calling it something quite different, so that even when active U.S. involvement in the conflict seemed inevitable, preparations for war were still called preparations for defense. The so-called defense industries (which not so long ago had been operated by "merchants of death") were turning out increasing quantities of smokeless powder, bullets, artillery shells, airplanes, ships, tanks—all weapons for use in war and presumably as useful on offense as defense. Yet Washington persisted in labeling them defensive. At the same time, massive buildups of armed forces were taking place—all for "defense," as if those young men were going to hang around the Atlantic beaches waiting for a German invasion to begin.

The American was awakening to what had to be done at some time in the onrushing future, and he heard a great deal of talk about democracy and freedom, totalitarianism and tyranny, and of how we had to defend the former and defend ourselves against the latter. We were going to do this by aiding the Allies, by putting an embargo on arms, by maintaining our neutrality, by lending or leasing weapons—but very little was said publicly by those in authority to suggest that if Hitler was going to be defeated the United States would have to be in it—*really* in it. As Arnold Whitridge had put it in his blast at America's undergraduates, "We shall have to do something besides hope for victory and sell secondhand ships to Great Britain strictly on a cash basis." Henry Stimson had recognized the incongruity when he said the United States could not permanently remain a toolmaker for other nations that did the fighting. Of all the cabinet members, the army secretary was the most outspoken advocate of involving the country in war, and he may have been the only one to sense the president's great fear. Certainly it was not publicly discussed at the time, and the evidence is fragmentary at best, but it seems evident that Roosevelt was reluctant to accept the argument—advanced by Stimson and Marshall, in particular—that Germany could be defeated only by a major Anglo-American assault on the European continent. (Churchill shared his reluctance. On February 9 he declared in a broadcast that Great Britain would not need American armies "this year, nor next year, nor any year that I can foresee.") Stimson's diary records his belief that the president "was afraid of any assumption . . . that we must invade Germany and crush Germany," a belief that must have been reinforced when FDR, late in September 1941, actually proposed reducing the size of the U.S. Army as a means of furnishing more equipment to the British and Russians.

Future invasions aside, it was clear that we were going to have to seize destiny in our hands and decide what it was we intended to fight *for*. If it turned out that we were to do battle with the Axis nations, the young men who were ordered to die for something bigger than themselves had to know what that something bigger was. In his State of the Union message in January of 1941, Mr. Roosevelt had struck out in that direction, offering his countrymen a vision of the New Jerusalem that would be theirs at the end of a long, dicey, and quite possibly very bloody road. For some time he had known he had to come up with something uplifting, even spiritual, if he was to stir the emotions of Americans, and he had hit upon the idea of the Four Freedoms—freedom of speech, freedom of worship, freedom from want, and freedom from fear.

Those Four Freedoms would appear again many times, three of them in the document signed and proclaimed by Messrs. Roosevelt and Churchill as the Atlantic Charter,[3] and all four in posters from the hand of the revered artist Norman Rockwell. Yet the struggle that was presumably coming entailed more than these noble visions suggested. No American had any idea of what might materialize in those dim corridors leading to the future, but if he believed the press handouts and speeches coming from Washington, he might assume that nothing at home was going to change. The forces of fascism would assuredly be vanquished one day, and in the process certain sacrifices might be required of the American people (though not many, it was to be hoped), but above all, the unique system we had perfected was not going to be altered. This notion was reflected, perversely, by the coal strike in April, by a wildcat strike at North American Aviation's Los Angeles plant in June (Roosevelt called out troops to take over the factory and drive off pickets), and by a glimpse of Detroit's latest models—some four million of them, each made of increasingly precious steel and other materials, dazzling the eye with more chrome than ever. Equally alarming was the soaring federal debt—$14 billion by summer—caused by piling the burden of defense spending upon a tax structure not geared to war. Yet the idea persisted: the American way of life would remain the American way of life, and that was that.

The trouble with such an assumption was that this war was more than another conflict over Europe's boundaries. Nazi barbarism was the farthest retreat from civilization the world had known, and if the struggle against it was to be won, even by so limited a method as sending all possible aid to Britain and Russia (which looked more unlikely all the time), surely America would have to change her tune, realizing that the end justifies the means. General Raymond Lee, the American military attaché for air in the London embassy, had given Harry Hopkins an appraisal of Britain's situation and of what might face America. ". . . should we find ourselves at war," he wrote, "I hope that it won't be a piecemeal affair. Total war requires throwing everything available at once, military, naval, air, economic, moral—including the kitchen stove, and following this up with everything else as soon as it can be got to working." If total war meant that the entire strength of the nation would be summoned to the cause, that mines and factories and laboratories, large companies and small, along with all available manpower, would be mobilized, then certainly in the summer of 1941 America was psychologically and philosophically unprepared for anything remotely resembling total war.

For example, if the need was for the greatest possible volume of output in a particular industry, that could require a pooling of machine tools—removing them from one company and handing them over to another; or it might necessitate sharing industrial ideas and techniques, or relocating

[3]To the dismay of many Americans, freedom of religion was not included in that proclamation—possibly in deference to our new ally, godless Russia.

workers, or assigning war work to one factory and civilian work to another. Now, these were revolutionary changes that struck at the heart of the system. Yet the assumption throughout the country was that business would continue as usual, and as yet no one had given much thought to the possibility that the prodigious effort that lay ahead might alter the role of women, might affect the status of black people, might break down America's class and racial barriers, might sweep up John L. Lewis's miners and Walter Reuther's autoworkers along with the executives of General Motors and the Morgan Bank in a whirlwind whose intensity and direction no man could predict, let alone comprehend. No one, in short, imagined that the whole fabric of American life might be ripped apart, or understood that in shouldering the gigantic task that had to be accomplished we might well lose some of the freedoms we thought we enjoyed.

One reason for this lack of understanding was that a genuine war economy demands all manner of controls—some of the same controls Hitler and Mussolini and Stalin employed—to ensure that certain vital materials are available to industry when they are needed (and possibly to that single wartime industry alone); that prices and wages are regulated; that the amount of meat or sugar or gasoline consumed by civilians is strictly and equitably curtailed through some system of rationing; that business is told what it can and cannot produce; and so on. The old system that set the rules by which capital and labor coexisted very likely might not survive if we became involved in this supreme undertaking, and Americans might find themselves with the type of society envisioned by an obscure Pittsburgh novelist, Thomas Bell, in a book about steelworkers called *Out of This Furnace.* Bell suggested that in the wake of the coming upheaval, what would count "wasn't where you were born or how you spelled your name or where your father had come from. It was the way you thought and felt about certain things. About freedom of speech and the importance of having one law—the same law—for rich and poor, for the people you liked and the people you didn't like." What he was implying was that even a mill hand should have the right to live as he pleased, that he might have a say in the uses to which wealth should be put, that human dignity and the value of human life meant more than corporate profits. If Bell was right, and if changes of that sort lay ahead, the United States was no more ready for them than it was for war in the summer of 1941.

———

The steelworker who rushed into the street in New Castle, Pennsylvania, to shout "Hallejulah!" upon hearing the news of war was echoing the frustrations of thousands of unemployed Americans. War meant jobs. Jobs meant money for the rent and the unpaid gas bill, money for new clothes for children wearing rags, money to buy milk, to repair the car and gas it up, to pay for license plates so you could drive again.

New Castle, in the heart of the Shenango Valley, midway between Pittsburgh and Lake Erie, had been made technologically obsolete and then abandoned by the industry that had once given it prosperity. In the 1890s the town had boasted one of the nation's first integrated steel mills, with a continuous flow from iron ore to finished product, and before the turn of the century its iron and steel works, which included the largest tinplate mills in the world, employed more than six thousand men. In 1898, every important steel company in town was bought by J. P. Morgan, who was said to have extracted a promise from each seller not to invest the proceeds in mills that would compete with the new steel trust Morgan was putting together with Andrew Carnegie. Whether or not the rumor was true was unimportant: the effect was the same, for Morgan's man, Judge Elbert H. Gary, who ran U.S. Steel, became the absentee owner of just about everything that mattered in New Castle, including the destinies of most of its working families.

The mill town had prospered during the Great War, but the peace and the changes that followed it brought only depression and misery. A 1927 survey sponsored by the Chamber of Commerce noted that "the Car Works, the Rubber Plant, the Baking Company, the Knitting Mill, the Brewery, and the Stove Works" had left town, and in 1931 the first of several severe body blows fell when U.S. Steel abandoned its Bessemer works, which cost the jobs of twelve hundred workers. (U.S. Steel had seen the writing on the wall if the hapless mill hands had not: between 1900 and 1935, Bessemer steel declined from 67 percent of all steel produced to 10 percent.) In 1939 came the crusher. In July of that year, U.S. Steel closed its Shenango tinplate works, the last of its New Castle properties, and three thousand more workers were out on the street. By then, U.S. Steel, along with Jones & Laughlin and other companies, had modernized some obsolete plants, built new ones, and replaced the hand-mill tinplate operations like those in New Castle with new strip mills.

In the old mills, hot and noisy and crowded with outmoded equipment and groups of workers who worked in relays at the furnaces, the iron was handled more than fifty times before it was finally turned into finished tinplate. In the strip mill, by contrast, a handful of workers, operating machinery by remote control, automatically released a huge chunk of iron from the furnace, rolled it into a thousand-foot coil, put it onto a conveyor, and transformed it into sheets to be fashioned into tin cans or automobiles. While the process produced tinplate for $15 a ton less than the hand mills, it also cut labor requirements by as much as 97 percent, throwing thousands of useful citizens and breadwinners onto the dole, dependent for their own and their families' survival on handouts from government and private relief agencies.

Between 1920 and 1939, New Castle's annual payroll had dropped by 57 percent, its employment by 64 percent, and when the 601 graduates of the high school class of 1939 set out in pursuit of a future to which they were presumably entitled, there was almost literally nothing for them to do in

ARCTIC OCEAN

Reykjavik
ICELAND

Tromsö

Narv

N

HITLER'S EUROPE

December 6, 1941

Namsos

Trondheim

Andalsne

NORWAY
1940

SWEDEN

ORKNEY
ISLANDS

Bergen

Oslo

Stockholm

Scapa Flow

SCOTLAND

Stavanger

North
Sea

N. IRELAND

DENMARK
1940

Copenhagen

Baltic Sea

IRELAND

ENGLAND

WALES

Birmingham

Coventry

London

NETHERLANDS
1940

Hamburg

EAS
PRUSS

Portsmouth

Dover

Amsterdam
Rotterdam

Berlin

ATLANTIC

English Channel

Dunkirk

Brussels

GERMANY

SUDETENLAND
1938

OCEAN

BELGIUM
1940

RHINELAND
1936

Prague

Paris

LUX
1940

CZECHOSLOVAKIA 193

Chartres

Munich

Tours

FRANCE
1940

Vienna

AUSTRIA
1938

Budap

Vichy

SWITZ.

Bordeaux

VICHY
FRANCE
1940

ITALY

Belgrad

YUGOSLAVI
1941

PORTUGAL

Marseilles

Toulon

Madrid

Rome

Lisbon

SPAIN

ALBA
1939

Naples

MEDITERRANEAN

SICILY

SEA

MOROCCO
1940

ALGERIA
1940

TUNISIA
1940

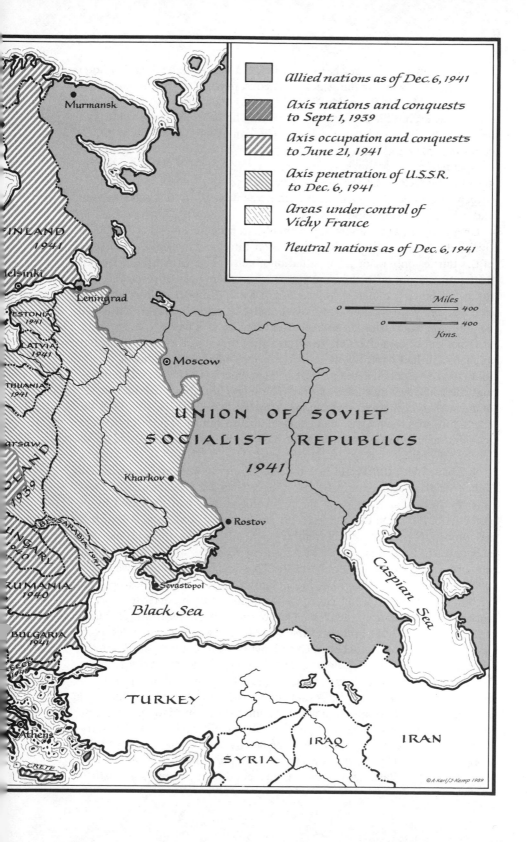

Murmansk

FINLAND 1941

Helsinki

Leningrad

ESTONIA 1941

LATVIA 1941

LITHUANIA 1941

Warsaw

POLAND 1939

HUNGARY 1940

RUMANIA 1940

BESSARABIA 1941

BULGARIA 1941

GREECE 1941

Athens

CRETE

⊚ **Moscow**

Kharkov ●

● **Rostov**

● **Sevastopol**

UNION OF SOVIET
SOCIALIST REPUBLICS
1941

Black Sea

Caspian Sea

TURKEY

SYRIA

IRAQ

IRAN

Allied nations as of Dec. 6, 1941

Axis nations and conquests to Sept. 1, 1939

Axis occupation and conquests to June 21, 1941

Axis penetration of U.S.S.R. to Dec. 6, 1941

Areas under control of Vichy France

Neutral nations as of Dec. 6, 1941

Miles
0 _____ 400
0 _____ 400
Kms.

©A.Karl/J.Kemp 1989

their hometown. Only one class officer found a job—as a bellhop in a hotel that had been struck by the American Federation of Labor. The president of the class, Merritt Reynolds, finally got part-time work as an usher in a movie theater, but the pay was so meager that he left to look elsewhere: and he was lucky; he got a chance to go to a Civilian Conservation Corps (CCC) camp in Arizona. As a school official put it, "The 1939 graduates are not competing for private jobs, there are none to compete for, but fighting to get into the CCC." Of the previous year's 554 high school graduates, 60 percent had joined the unemployed, 20 percent went on to another school, and 20 percent finally found work.

Unemployment and underemployment had been chronic in the iron and steel industries long before the Depression hit, and the economic disaster of the thirties only made a bad situation much worse. In April of 1930, for instance, one out of eight iron and steel workers was unemployed; the following January one in three was out of work. By 1933, 56 percent of all steelworkers were totally unemployed, and U.S. Steel declared that it had *no* full-time workers on its payroll. The industry as a whole was operating at 14 percent of capacity. One result was that the city of Pittsburgh, as late as 1940, still had 63,559 workers without jobs—an unemployment rate of more than 22 percent, as compared to 14.4 percent in the rest of the nation— and the cause was not hard to find. The heavy durable goods industries, along with housing and institutional construction projects, to which the city's mills sold their wares, had cut spending by almost 80 percent between 1929 and 1933, while expenditures for passenger cars and household goods fell by 62 percent during the same period.

Suddenly, with the impact of war-related orders, Pittsburgh's somnolent industrial plant began to stir. In 1940, the production of electrical machinery was up 26 percent over 1939; the following year it had increased by 80 percent. In the same two-year period, production of bituminous coal rose by almost 16 percent. By November 1941, $1.5 billion in contracts and subcontracts had been placed in Allegheny County, and the number of unemployment checks fell dramatically. That was fine, as far as it went. The difficulty was that production—in Pittsburgh or St. Louis or Seattle—had to be translated into a myriad of goods needed for the defense effort. A subchaser on order from the Dravo Corporation downriver from Pittsburgh was more than a steel hull and superstructure: it was diesel engines, compressors and blowers, deck guns and depth-charge racks, anchors and chain, propellers and steel shafts, compass and sonar gear, radio equipment, hundreds of valves and gauges, miles of electrical cable and fittings—which is to say an infinitude of parts and individual manufactured items, each made by a different supplier, each one having to be shipped to Dravo in time to be assembled into a seaworthy vessel capable of being manned by sixty-five men and officers to do battle with an enemy. And configurations of that magnitude were beyond the capacity of any single manufacturer to solve. It was a job for Washington, but despite a good deal of noise and bustle in the nation's capital, there was reason to wonder if anything would be accomplished in time to mean much to the British or Russians.

Much had been said about the need to produce the materials of war, but thus far little had been done to coordinate and meld the efforts of all those manufacturing establishments, large and small, across the country. The trouble was that no one individual or group yet had a grasp of the nation's ultimate requirements and of how to procure what was needed in an orderly fashion. A lot of patriotic folk out in the hinterlands knew that something needed to be done and had even taken it upon themselves to make a start. For instance, in Beaver County, Pennsylvania, midway between Pittsburgh and New Castle on the Ohio River, a committee had been formed in the autumn of 1940 representing all the groups in the community—business, labor, elected officials, religious leaders, and the like—and these people had sensibly calculated the county's manufacturing capacity, taken a census of its factories, machines, and labor force, and then tried to present this highly useful information to Washington.

Washington, unfortunately, was not ready to absorb data like these. No one knew quite what to do with the facts Beaver County had sent, and in the end the county's highly commendable effort came to nought. Behind that failure in communications between government and people was a tangled story of good intentions and half-starts that went back to the fall of 1938, when the financier Bernard Baruch returned from Europe and thought he had persuaded President Roosevelt to set up a Defense Coordination Board with Baruch as its chief. But nothing came of the plan; the president backed away, intimidated by the isolationist opposition.

A year passed, and in August 1939, President Roosevelt announced that he had appointed a number of prominent businessmen to a War Resources Board. The chairman was Edward R. Stettinius, Jr., the thirty-eight-year-old chairman of U.S. Steel, and the other worthies included Walter S. Gifford, chief of the American Telephone and Telegraph Company; General Robert E. Wood, of Sears, Roebuck; a partner in Lehman Brothers; a director of General Motors; the head of the Brookings Institute; and Karl Compton, an eminent physicist. It was a blue-chip group, but it quickly became apparent that the members had no idea what was expected of them, other than writing the usual report listing their recommendations. What they had to say, as might have been expected, was that defense production should be placed in the hands of the nation's industrialists, with the government requesting what was needed.

A good part of another year went by, and in June 1940, after allowing the War Resources Board to slip quietly into oblivion, Mr. Roosevelt named a National Defense Advisory Commission (NDAC)—with Stettinius, the fair-haired boy of steel (irreverently known to one and all as "Junior"), as adviser on strategic materials, plus a group of advisers on production, transportation, consumers, price stabilization, farmers, and unemployment. Very quickly, a new problem surfaced, one that was beyond the NDAC's ability to handle. The chief of the Army Air Corps, Major General Henry H. Arnold, had ordered 5,500 planes to be delivered by October, and he had money for 4,200 more, yet he had recently appeared before a committee of Congress to request additional funds. Rear Admiral John Towers had gone to the same committee with a similar story, and not illogically, congressmen asked both officers why the money already voted had not been contracted before they came back for more.

Hap Arnold's unhappy reply described the dilemma. "We have not placed the contracts [for 4,200 planes]," he said, "due to the fact that the industry feels that there are so many uncertainties, unknown quantities that they have to contend with." And what were those uncertainties? he was asked. Well, it had something to do with the Vinson-Trammell Act, which dealt with the limitation of profits; taxes were involved; so were labor problems.

The admiral put the case bluntly. "The reduction in profit has made it very difficult for the aircraft manufacturer to place subcontracts which work out about 5 percent net profit. It just does not interest the subcontractor." The gist of the testimony was that defense production was going nowhere until Congress put a reasonable excess-profits tax on *all* industry, instead of the current limitations on certain defense contracts, and unless the legislators also assured manufacturers that factories built specifically for defense work would not be subject to tax when the defense work came to a halt.

By now several things were becoming clear to Washington insiders. One was that there were no simple solutions to the defense production problem. Another was that the important-sounding boards named by the president might include titans of finance and industry, but the man in charge was indisputably Franklin D. Roosevelt. He definitely wanted no single "production czar" (which is what Bernard Baruch kept urging on him); *he* meant to be in charge of what was going on. And it was evident that the president had his reasons for placing these special agencies dealing with defense matters within the executive department's Office for Emergency Management. By keeping them out of the established federal departments, he could avoid congressional suspicion and opposition, since the implication was that they would be abolished when the emergency for which they had been set up had passed. An equally important reason was the president's belief that the regular departments of government were essentially incapable of handling the extraordinary demands of war; above all, they lacked talented personnel and the capacity to move quickly. Behind his groping for a solution to the question of how the nation's industrial strength could be harnessed and directed was the most important consideration of all. Roosevelt's budget director, Harold Smith, was to remark, "The president was the only one who really understood the meaning of the term *total war* and the necessity for it. The others believed you could fight a war with one hand and carry on domestic business pretty much as usual with the other."

It was a funny thing about Roosevelt, though: as plain as the need was to have a single, powerful individual take charge of the production effort, and as much as he was criticized for not doing so, he continued to keep authority centered in his own hands, even though he was far too busy to provide real impetus or leadership.

Once again, he resorted to an organizational solution, and in this he received some help from his secretary of war. Henry Stimson was alarmed by the lack of progress and realized that the NDAC was as ineffectual as the War Resources Board which had preceded it. Here was the president in December of 1940 proposing a vast program of Lend-Lease to supply the Allies while simultaneously arming the United States, relying on a mechanism for coordinating and managing it that was hopelessly ill-suited to the task. On December 18, Stimson and his newly named under secretary Robert Patterson, with Knox, and his under secretary James Forrestal, gathered in the Oval Room Study hoping to apply some pressure on the chief executive—pressure to appoint a strong, responsible head of the NDAC and to establish a clear chain of command. Stimson had in his pocket an outline of a plan, backed by cabinet members, the AFL, and the CIO, to reorganize the advisory commission and place full responsibility in a single head—William Knudsen, the production genius and, until lately, president of General Motors. When the discussion began, Stimson was agreeably surprised to see that Roosevelt was not following his usual practice of telling stories and joking, with his mind hopping about from one topic to another. He came directly to the point at issue.

In fact, he had thought matters through more comprehensively than his advisers had—even to the extent of considering the necessity of including controls to keep prices from getting out of hand when the war ended—and told them that he was naming a board headed by William Knudsen, with Sidney Hillman of the CIO as his number-two man, thus (he figured) mollifying business and labor, and thus (everyone else figured) creating an absolutely unworkable marriage of convenience, despite the presence on the board of Stimson and Knox to represent the government. On December 20, two days after the meeting, the Office of Production Management (OPM) was born.

It was worth noting that the presidential appointments to both the National Defense Advisory Commission and the Office of Production Management served notice that a truce was being declared between management and labor, and between the New Deal and the Republican Party. Whether this anointing of traditional foes and expecting them to pull side by side in harness was going to work or not remained to be seen, but what Roosevelt seemed to be saying was that we were all in this thing together, and the only way the defense effort was going to succeed was if everyone worked as a team, setting aside partisan politics and old scores. It was a brave notion, yet an important ingredient was still missing from the recipe—a real understanding by most of the president's appointees of what war was likely to demand. As Budget Director Smith had observed, the president was the only man who seemed to recognize the import of total war, and even he seemed reluctant to admit that you could not pile a massive defense effort on top of the normal peacetime economy, especially when the latter was only beginning to emerge from the worst hammering it had taken in the history of the republic. The requirements of total war went far beyond the summoning of leaders representing business, labor, and other entrenched interests to government service; they would mean the total mobilization of the entire country in an effort whose magnitude had never been conceived, much less seen, before.

═══

Autumn had come to America, and the weather turned freaky. New York State and New England were parched by drought; so was the rest of the East Coast as far south as South Carolina and Alabama. A hurricane roared across the Gulf of Mexico and smashed into east Texas, wiping out the rice crop and causing $25 million in property damage; floods raged in Arizona, tornadoes in Kansas, snow through Montana and Utah. Across the land, farmers were harvesting crops, the big horse-drawn combines were moving across the great plains, pickers were at work in the orchards of New England and the Northwest, in California's Imperial Valley, and in Maine's Aroostook County potato fields. In the heartland, attendance had never been higher at state fairs, and the farmers were better dressed and had more money to spend. In Dallas they were getting $100 a bale for cotton, but the worry now instead of prices was a potential shortage of help next year and a shortage of machinery parts right now. Factories in the industrial core of the nation were pouring out smoke, the surest sign that men were on the job once again. At the Douglas and Lockheed plants in California, Boeing in Seattle, United Aircraft in Hartford, Curtiss-Wright in Buffalo, back orders for planes were piling up, and hiring notices stayed posted. America was back at work and enjoying the feel of it.

Along with that, the public mood was different. Congressmen returning from vacation reported, almost to a man, that the folks at home were way out in front of them—isolationist districts were now middle-of-the-road, middle-of-the-roaders were now interventionist. One sure sign that change was in the making was that Everett McKinley Dirksen, darling of the *Chicago Tribune,* announced on the floor of the House his support for President Roosevelt's foreign policy: to oppose it, the Illinois representative told his stunned colleagues, "could only weaken the president's position, impair our prestige, and imperil the nation." Politically, it seemed, things were looking up for Mr. Roosevelt, but he had more than politics to consider.

Most troubling were the reports from five thousand miles to the east, where for the sixteenth time in two years Hitler's army was advancing on another nation's capital city. One disaster after another had overcome the

Russians; the Nazis were in the outskirts of Moscow and had encircled the country's second city, Leningrad, whose citizens were already beginning to starve, five thousand of them every day. No one, Russian or German, could possibly have guessed that before the war Hitler began was over, more than a million people would die in Leningrad alone, and perhaps a staggering 25 million throughout the USSR.

Just now, Russia's ability to go on fighting appeared to depend on an ability to keep open the supply line to Vladivostok and to keep the materials of war flowing. But U.S. aid to the Soviet Union and Britain was nowhere near what it should be, and in a radio speech on Labor Day, the president admitted it by saying that "unless we step up the total of our production and more greatly safeguard it on its journeys to the battlefields," we were going to give a lot of aid and comfort to the nation's enemies. So far the country had produced a lot of motion but not much output, and while some of the shortfall was attributable to the insatiable demands of America's clients, Britain and Russia, combined with those of the U.S. military, much of the fault lay within the federal bureaucracy.

Robert Wyman Horton thought he knew why. Horton was in charge of information at the Office for Emergency Management (OEM)—a sort of presidential holding company within the White House that was supposed to coordinate the defense activities of all government agencies except the War and Navy departments. From Horton's office came the news and background material concerning defense production which the public read or heard in the form of newspaper and magazine articles, speeches, and press conferences. A trim Vermonter with penetrating blue eyes who had been a newspaper reporter for most of his working life, first with the *Springfield Republican* and more recently as Washington correspondent for Scripps-Howard and Scripps's *New York World-Telegram,* Horton had arrived in Washington in the fading days of the Coolidge administration and had seen little since to increase his admiration for the city's bureaucrats. Yet here he was—one of them, in a manner of speaking, thanks to the maneuvering of Lowell Mellett, editor of the *Washington Daily News* and, in Horton's eyes, "the best editor I ever knew." Mellett did a lot of quiet, high-level recruiting for the president, and he had persuaded Horton to take the job at OEM. Because the information officer of that organization was *de facto* responsible for information concerning defense matters at all the other government departments except Army and Navy, and because the man in charge of it worked not for one of the government agencies but directly for the president, it was the most important assignment of its kind in the capital.

For some time now Horton had been observing the comings and goings of the dollar-a-year men from the top industries in America. On the whole, they were good fellows—patriotic and agreeable, the cream of the nation's business leaders—but most of them arrived in the capital with a double-bitted axe to grind, as a result of which the task of organizing the defense effort was going nowhere. On one side was their almost pathological hatred of Roosevelt. They believed that every move he made was aimed at socializing the country, that he was out to destroy big business, and that all his talk about the approach of war and what was going to happen if we didn't get cracking was so much political baloney, aimed at keeping himself in office.

On the other side, as Horton put it, "they brought their business with them" instead of leaving it behind, and with it a determination to protect and gain whatever corporate advantage they could out of the Washington assignment. Not only that: they argued over the size of their offices, they complained when someone else had a two-pen set on his desk and theirs was a single. Finally someone had the bright idea of putting them into the Federal Reserve building, where there were fireplaces in the offices, elegantly high ceilings, and oriental rugs, and where the dollar-a-year crowd felt more comfortable.

From Robert Horton's standpoint, nearly all of them had the wrong idea about public information. The fellows from industry were accustomed to working with their own public-relations consultants, they were mightily concerned about their personal and corporate image, and even when there was little enough credit to go around, they wanted to take as much of it as possible for themselves and their companies—all of which flew in the face of what Horton was trying to accomplish. In case anyone had any doubts about what that was, he spelled it out in a memorandum. The information office of the OEM, he announced, was going to tell the truth to the American public about progress or *lack* of progress in the defense program, on the theory that whatever happened in that program was the people's business. Information had nothing to do with politics or policy. It had to do with telling the truth. Period.

Typical of what was going on in those days was the experience of William Knudsen. The General Motors man was not your average dollar-a-year boy: Horton described him as one of the few who understood the mission all of them were charged with, and he was working like fury to accomplish it. But the Danish-born Knudsen was obliged to deal with the army's Quartermaster General's Office, and Horton said that meant dealing with what was the absolutely worst procurement office in the United States. At one point, the army was having difficulty obtaining the quality of armor plate it needed for tanks. Knudsen asked to see a sample of what they wanted; once he got his hands on a piece of steel or a component part he could often figure how to make it. But nothing happened. He asked again, and still no sample. Finally, someone discovered that the Quartermaster General's Office didn't want him to see it because he was a "foreigner" and might give away military secrets.

Another example of Washington-at-war but not really at war was the astonishing appearance of a study of all the press releases issued by Horton's office about the OPM. Someone had gone to considerable trouble and expense to count the number of times Knudsen's name and Hillman's name had been mentioned in those releases, in order to prove that the source— Horton, of course—was a New Dealer or socialist or worse who was playing up the role of the labor leader, Hillman, at the expense of the businessman, Knudsen. Horton was not surprised to learn that the National Association of Manufacturers was behind the study.

Looking back on those months, it strains belief that by autumn of 1941, after all the brave efforts to set a program in motion, defense production was still plagued with problems of obtaining or allocating raw materials, setting priorities, converting manufacturing plants from peacetime to wartime output, cutting down on civilian consumption, and just about everything else that was essential. For the failure to deliver enough arms to the British and Russians the government was blaming industry; industry was blaming the government; and in certain respects both sides were right.

Yet it is difficult at this remove not to fault the president himself for much of the failure. For reasons he never disclosed, he had been, and continued to be, dead set against putting a strong man at the head of the defense program. Perhaps he imagined that such a figure might be a rival; perhaps he feared that big business might take over the entire program and cartelize industry permanently. Neither in the election year of 1940 nor later did he dare risk losing the support of labor, for it would have been fatal to the production effort to have the unions restive under an industrialist at the helm. Whatever his concerns, they helped make a mess of the very thing at which America was supposedly so talented. What was wanted was someone capable of knocking heads together, insisting that the program begin to function properly—or else. But Roosevelt had neither the time nor the temperament for knocking heads, and the result was that the defense program continued to drift.

Walter Lippmann attributed this failing to FDR's penchant for "finagling"—a characteristic the president shared with the publisher Joseph Pulitzer. Being a blind man, Lippmann said, Pulitzer "lived on a yacht and tried to edit a paper in New York. He thought that the only way he could ever find out what was going on was to have two men in each job and have them quarrel. Then he'd hear the quarrel and make up his mind what ought to be done." Roosevelt employed the same method: putting two men in charge of production, they naturally quarreled, but the difference between the president and Pulitzer was that Roosevelt wouldn't change things when they went sour. Instead, he would "set up another office to do the same thing and then see what happened."

Here it was August 28, 1941, and the president was announcing yet one more organization, the Supply Priorities and Allocations Board (SPAB), which enlarged the membership of the Office of Production Management by a group that included Vice President Henry Wallace, Harry Hopkins, and Leon Henderson. Wallace was to serve as chairman, with Donald

Nelson of Sears, Roebuck as executive director. The new agency magnified the administrative snarls that already existed, yet in other respects it turned out to be an improvement, for whatever else might be said for the new team, all of them were deeply conscious of the need for immediate and drastic action, and as soon as they made it evident that we were going to have all-out war production and not war production as icing on the consumer-goods cake, things finally began to happen. Tough priorities and allocations were set, so that it gradually became clear how much of this item or that was to go for U.S. or foreign defense requirements, and how much—if any—for civilians. There was no question about the purpose and determination of these SPAB board members; the question at hand was whether the nation had time enough to carry out what they wanted to do. As Donald Nelson was to admit, "1941 will go down in history as the year we almost lost the war before we got into it."

Time was the enemy's ally. In all of 1939 the United States had produced a total of 2,500 aircraft. In November of that year, the Douglas Aircraft Company in California, bristling with orders for $80 million worth of planes, began hiring. Ten thousand were on the payroll by December, and more were added as the backlog of orders increased. Fuselages were coming off the assembly lines at a satisfactory rate, but engines were in short supply. Or if it was not engines, it was landing gear. Or aluminum. In the summer the government put on a drive for scrap aluminum, and a whopping seventy thousand tons of the metal—in the form mostly of used kitchen pots and pans—was gathered only to gather dust in collection depots until junk dealers picked it up, because (it was discovered too late) only the purest aluminum was suitable for aircraft.

Despite all the false starts and frustrations, however, signs of progress were evident. Tanks were starting to roll off Chrysler's assembly line. Working around the clock, the nation's shipyards were turning out one new merchant ship every day, and fourteen hundred of them were due for completion by 1942. (They would all be needed: not a week passed without reports that more U.S. ships had been sunk.) Naval vessels were coming down the ways on an average of one every three days. Three new battleships had been launched, two others commissioned, and in November alone the navy reported thirty-three ship launchings, fifty-two keels laid, and five new vessels joining the fleet. Each month saw an increase in aircraft production. In August, 1,854 planes were completed, and by the first of January, output was expected to exceed Germany's.

Even so, an awesome amount of catching up had to be done: we had to draw even before we could move ahead. And a more alarming fact was that production began faltering critically in the late autumn. Wrangling between bureaucrats and businessmen, between military chieftains and production bosses, was frequent and bitter; the agencies FDR had thrown together to run the show did not have the muscle to do it—only the power to plead or persuade. The fault again lodged in the White House doorway, and again it was a two-pronged problem: lack of leadership and lack of a plan.

Big Bill Knudsen, whom someone described as a Viking without the helmet, was never happier than when he had a blueprint in his hands, and in July he had gone to the president to discuss the military services' request for a threefold increase in munitions output and the need to devise a plan. Before any such buildup in war materials was allowed to happen, Knudsen said, we had to see if it made any sense. We had to determine whether such an increase was what is really needed, and if so, whether we had the industrial capacity and the other resources to make it feasible. The president was sufficiently impressed with the urgency and sensibility of the appeal that he called on Stimson, Knox, and Harry Hopkins to assess what was required "to defeat our potential enemies." He realized that the report he wanted meant that they would have to make certain assumptions as to the identity and capabilities of the nation's friends and foes, and in what areas of the world the United States military would be operating (which would make for interesting reading if it fell into the wrong hands). The object of the report, he went on, was to "explore the munitions and mechanical equipment of all types which in your opinion would be required to exceed by an appropriate amount that available to our potential enemies." In other words, decide who our potential enemies were likely to be; learn what total armaments in all categories they possessed; and then determine what the United States needed to produce to surpass them. Given the number of unknowns, it was as tall an order as ordinary mortals could receive.[4]

By early September, when no report had been forthcoming, the president was growing antsy, and he asked the two service secretaries to deliver the information by September 10; but understandably, the project was so complex that it was not finally completed for another two weeks, and even then it was less a report than a stack of documents. A purely military assessment of the world situation, its most important component was the Joint Army-Navy Board's latest statement of U.S. long-range strategic goals, based partly on earlier plans like Rainbow 5 and Plan Dog, and modified in the light of recent events and experience. It was not an optimistic paper, even though the study of which it was a part was called the Victory Program.

---

[4]The president might have been surprised to learn that one of his particular devils, Colonel Charles Lindbergh, who had Knudsen's same gift for mechanical and technological subjects, was thinking along remarkably similar lines, though for different reasons. The colonel believed that what was required "is an intelligent plan rather than great quantities of military equipment. It is not enough to simply build arms. We must have some idea of *how* and *where* we are going to use them. When we build planes, we must at the same time train the personnel to go with them, construct airports from which they are to be operated, etc., etc. In other words, it must be part of a balanced program if it is to be successful. . . . most of the people I talk to in the aviation industry say that their greatest problems lie in their relationship to the government."

According to the principal author, Major Albert Wedemeyer, who had studied at the War College in Berlin from 1936 to 1938 and was an authority on German military tactics and organization, Germany and her satellites could not be defeated by Great Britain and Russia without U.S. assistance. This meant that the United States would have to enter the war and employ some of its forces offensively in Europe or Africa or both. Nor could the British and Dutch stand off the Japanese in Southeast Asia without American help. These two assumptions meant that the United States, with its allies, must prepare to fight Germany and Japan simultaneously, and in keeping with earlier plans, the Joint Board recommended that the first objective must be "the complete military defeat of Germany." To implement this program, the nation would be obliged to support via arms deliveries the Allies' military operations against Germany, and follow that with "active participation in the war by the United States, while holding Japan in check pending future developments."

Analyzing the situation and concluding that U.S. and British strength was principally at sea and in the air, the Joint Board observed sagely that while naval and air power might prevent wars from being lost, they seldom, if ever, won them: "It should be recognized as an almost invariable rule that only land armies can finally win wars." So much for the hopes of Roosevelt and Churchill that victory could be won without an invasion of Europe.

The real shocker in the report was the size of the U.S. land army the military planners had in mind—eight million men, of whom five million would be required in Europe.

Once the long-range strategy was known, and once Donald Nelson had pried loose the army's and navy's estimates of requirements over the next two years, someone had to determine what it would take to turn estimates into reality, and that job fell to a team headed by Stacy May and Robert Nathan, who dwelt in a realm of research and statistics at OPM. They set out to transform what had always been thought of as a defense-*cum*-business-as-usual program into a blueprint for fighting a global war. This entailed translating raw materials into component parts and finished weapons, calculating the productive capacity of mills and the man-hours needed, determining the cost, and relating that to the nation's income. What they learned was that if U.S. production continued at its present levels—that is, at the rate necessary to accommodate civilian demands as well as the defense program—it would take another year for this country even to equal the combined output of Britain and Canada. Clearly, that course was out of the question. On the other hand, if the United States was to get serious about this and knuckle down to the program the military had to have, previous production levels would have to be at least doubled, and the final estimate of the funds required was as staggering as the projected size of the armed forces—at least $150 billion.

Then, the ultimate question: how much *could* the United States produce, if it went all-out? May and Nathan concluded that it was possible to produce war goods at the rate of $45 billion in 1942 and $65 billion the following year, which meant that "the entire program to date must be doubled and achieved by September 30, 1943, if the Victory Program objectives are to be fully achieved." There, in black and white, was the earliest date by which the United States could be ready for action.

Daunting as this realization was, the very existence of the Victory Program was a sign that America at last had owned up to where it was headed. As Donald Nelson observed, this blueprint "revolutionized our production and may well have been a decisive turning point." As things worked out, Nelson did not have time to read the massive study the day Stacy May delivered it to him. That was on December 4, 1941, and his thoughts were on an important dinner he was giving that evening in honor of Vice President Wallace, to which he had invited Bill Knudsen, Frank Knox, Stettinius, and a number of other important men in the defense program.

CHAPTER 49

———————— ◆ ————————

"The First Army ... is not in fact an army ..."

If Americans had a clear sense of purpose as 1941 began, they were not letting on. Franklin Roosevelt's third inaugural, which should have been a landmark of some sort, did not turn out to be the moving event a lot of people had expected. The day was sunny, cold with a biting wind, and the crowds lining the parade route had come, as they do every four years, to see one of the rare formal spectacles America puts on, to have a good time, glimpse the president, and go home knowing that they had witnessed history in the making. Despite three hours or so in the cold, they were jolly, wrapped in blankets with their feet in boxes or on newspapers, and one of the dignitaries riding in the procession thought to himself how curious it was that these people, coming from so many sections of the land, seemed so unaware that the nation faced a crisis.

When the president spoke at last—sunlight shining on his head and shoulders—his voice was strong and clear, but the crowd seemed to sense that he was not going to say anything new, perhaps because he had just delivered two important speeches on U.S. policy, and people milled around, talking, laughing, paying little attention to his words.

Organized labor began the year in a cantankerous mood and never let up—itching for more money now that those juicy defense contracts were being spread around. Not only did John L. Lewis and his United Mine

Workers give the president fits all year long, but strikes or walkouts—and sporadic violence—were a commonplace at major defense plants—Allis-Chalmers, Phelps-Dodge, International Harvester, Ford, and others.

It soon became apparent that the government would clamp down on certain strategic materials and equipment, and no one was greatly surprised to find oil-drilling and oil-refining machinery, nickel, tin, and such items restricted or preempted. But when Washington announced plans to ration rubber, reduce the production of automobiles, refrigerators, and washing machines by 50 percent, and require gas stations to close every night, the pinch began to be felt. That summer the Japanese freighter *Tatuta Maru* arrived in San Francisco, bringing what many believed to be the last shipment of silk from Japan. Since 81 percent of all the stockings sold in the United States were silk (only 18 percent were made of the new synthetic material nylon, which had emerged from Du Pont's laboratories in 1938), it looked as though women were going to be stuck with cotton mesh, rayon, or a combination of silk and lisle.

In Germany, the Nazis were getting even tougher on the Jews: in September, all Jews over six years of age were ordered to wear a large yellow Star of David with "Jude" in black lettering, and when the Roman Catholic dean of St. Helwig's Cathedral in Berlin had the temerity to pray for these persecuted people, he was taken into custody by the Gestapo. As a harbinger of things to come, Jacqueline Cochran flew a bomber across the Atlantic to Britain, the first woman to do so. In New York City, 62,000 air-raid wardens were enrolled in the civil defense program.

Wendell Willkie, back from his visit to Britain, was berating the Grand Old Party, endearing himself to none of them by calling on Republicans to "preach a positive doctrine" and seek a higher goal than "compromise and negation." Brooks Brothers was advertising officers' uniforms—"as in 1917–18 and other periods of American history . . . ready-made for prompt delivery"—at $52 for a suit of navy broadcloth, $58 for the army's olive drab. Andrew Mellon's gift to the nation, the National Gallery of Art, had just gone up in Washington; New York's Second Avenue El—one of the city's famed elevated railways—was coming down. Interstate passenger service was in good health, fortunately; if anyone doubted the nation's capacity to move people from one part of the country to another, he had only to look at the Pennsylvania Railroad ad in the August 11 issue of *Life* to see that the line was operating eighteen passenger trains daily between New York and Chicago, eight between Washington and St. Louis, and forty between New York and Washington.

Of all the improbable events in the news that spring, the most bizarre and baffling was the flight of Rudolf Hess to Scotland on May 10. Hess, the deputy Führer, Reichsminister without portfolio, member of the Ministerial Council for the Defense of the Reich, member of the Secret Cabinet Council for Germany, leader of the Nazi Party, the man who signed the infamous Nuremberg laws depriving Jews of their civil rights, and the fellow prison inmate to whom Hitler had dictated *Mein Kampf,* climbed into a fighter plane in southern Germany, took off, and when next seen, parachuted onto the estate of the Duke of Hamilton not far from Glasgow. (The number-three Nazi had met the titled Briton at the 1936 Olympic Games in Berlin and thought it probable that he had the king's ear.) He had come, he told the dumbfounded duke, on a "mission of humanity" to offer peace terms to England. Understandably perplexed, the duke telephoned his friend Winston Churchill, who was enjoying a Marx Brothers movie at a country estate that evening, and told him about his visitor. Churchill, thinking it as zany a story as the one he was watching on the screen, hung up, and then dispatched the head of the Foreign Office to Scotland to see what was afoot.

According to Hess's three-hour recitation to interrogators, the war between Britain and Germany was a terrible mistake ("suicidal for the white race," he called it), which could be rectified if they made peace, threw out the warmonger Churchill and his government, and joined hands to destroy the Bolsheviks. The Foreign Office man assessed the Nazi as a "simple, stupid" fellow whose astrologer had convinced him he could bring peace to the two warring nations. (The astrologer, it seems, had seen Hess in three of his dreams, piloting a plane to an unknown destination, and Hess took that to mean he should fly to Britain.) Unpersuaded, Hess's hosts took him to the Tower of London and locked him up,[1] and the world was left to wonder if there was more to the story than appeared on the surface (there was not), while the German press quickly announced that the emigrant (whose name Hitler ordered expunged from the records) lived in "a state of hallucination."

That was not the worst psychological blow the Nazis received. As nearly as one can pin it down, the idea originated with a Belgian refugee named Victor de Laveleye. In a shortwave broadcast from London he urged his countrymen to chalk the letter V (for *victoire*) on buildings and sidewalks as a pledge, a promise of ultimate deliverance. The Belgians took it up, and it spread to occupied Holland and France. Then a Colonel Britton, who spoke fluent French, German, Dutch, Polish, Czech, and Norwegian in addition to English, began pushing the idea regularly on BBC broadcasts to the continent, telling people to write the letter V everywhere, to tap it out in Morse code—three dots and a dash, dit-dit-dit-*da*—when they knocked on someone's door or summoned a waiter or blew an automobile horn. All over Europe people waved to each other with the first two fingers of their hand spread out; paid the bill in a restaurant and left behind on the table their knife and fork in a V; stopped clocks with the hands pointing to II and I. The BBC introduced programs with the first four notes of Beethoven's Fifth Symphony—the threatening three short bars and one

---

[1] When he died in 1987 in West Berlin's Spandau Prison, Rudolf Hess was ninety-three. He had spent his last forty-six years in jail.

long one. Whenever Winston Churchill appeared in public he gestured to cheering crowds with two stubby fingers giving the victory sign.

All Europe that was not with Hitler was against him, and in this simple symbol of hope and defiance, which did not depend on language, which could sweep unchallenged across every border, they had found the makings of organized resistance.[2]

In the U.S. Congress, two committees were busily burrowing into threats against their own government, real or imagined. The one making the louder noise and playing to the larger audience was the House Special Committee on Un-American Activities, referred to in newspapers as HUAC and headed by Representative Martin Dies of Texas. The driving force behind the committee may have been less un-Americanism than it was antiurbanism—an animus described by Dies as having "the support of nearly all small-town and rural congressmen" against "the men from the big cities which . . . are politically controlled by foreigners and transplanted Negroes." While these city slickers were suspected of having a sinister influence on various agencies of the government, the fear went beyond that. The nation had had periodic "Red scares" since 1919, and it was somewhat surprising to see Dies and his colleagues take off in that direction, since the committee had been funded by the House to investigate Nazi agents and fifth columnists. But Dies knew a live issue when he saw one, and ignored the Nazis, German-American Bund, Silver Shirts, and others of that ilk in favor of ferreting out Communists and New Dealers—two groups which he tended to equate.

The committee examined murals executed by painters in the Federal Art Project to analyze their social content; they watched performances by the Federal Theatre Project for evidence of subversion and concluded, in the words of committee member J. Parnell Thomas, that the FTP was not only "a branch of the communistic organization," but "one more link in the vast and unparalleled New Deal propaganda machine."

By the time the war in Europe began, thoughtful men like David Lilienthal realized that even the most rational citizens were fearful about how the outcome of the fighting might affect the United States. Regrettably, many people are *not* consistently rational, as Lilienthal knew, and in times of crisis their worst emotions—hatred, suspicion, envy—inevitably come to the surface. "That is the terrible thing that Germany has . . . inflicted on the world," he observed, "because you can spend a thousand years building a structure against the emergence of the underside of man, and it can be destroyed almost overnight." What we would soon see, he predicted, was "the dragon's teeth of hatred."

[2]In New York, which has never lacked for merchandisers, V for Victory pins promptly went on sale. Most of the better stores offered them in gold; at Tiffany's you could get a very nice one in diamonds.

Predictably, each Nazi victory magnified fears of fifth columnists and Quislings: one writer claimed that more than a million German agents were hiding here; tip-offs about spies and their activities poured in to the FBI; every minority group was suspect. Meanwhile, the Alien Registration Act of 1940, known as the Smith Act, required all aliens to register and be fingerprinted. Since the foreign-born were arriving in large numbers, that required a lot of fingerprinting and, it proved, a great many inquiries into political beliefs. As a result of the Smith Act—which made it a federal crime to belong to a "subversive" organization or engage in any "act or utterance" that might cause disaffection in the armed forces—Harry Bridges, leader of the West Coast Longshoremen's Union, was ordered deported "in the best interests of the United States," although the Australian had not been accused of any crime and no proof had been offered that he was a Communist, as claimed by the Department of Labor.[3] Meanwhile, they were locking up Communist Party members in Illinois and Oklahoma, and when Earl Browder, the head of the U.S. Communist Party, ran for president in 1940, he was obliged to do so from a prison cell.

While the Dies Committee gnawed at the fringes of American society in a tradition going back to seventeenth-century Salem—looking under the carpet for subversives, publishing names of suspects—one had to wonder if the mood its activities fostered had not been a factor in the deliberations of the Pulitzer Prize committee. The big novel of 1940 was Ernest Hemingway's *For Whom the Bell Tolls,* about the Spanish Civil War; the popular runner-up was Kenneth Roberts's *Oliver Wiswell,* the story of a young man in the American Revolution who regarded himself as a patriot because he remained loyal to his king. Neither book was chosen by the Pulitzer committee in 1941 as the best novel, and *The Saturday Review of Literature* did its best to explain why. Hemingway's novel, the magazine noted, "did not deal with an American subject; the text and treatment seemed a little stronger than previous subjects" ("stronger" presumably meaning that a sexual encounter between hero and heroine was described frankly). As for *Oliver Wiswell* (836 pages in hard cover, price $3), it was "too heavy on the debunking side . . . to become a harmonious addition to the many constructive and brighter-side works on the Pulitzer companion list in history." So the moral for novelists seemed to be: avoid foreign subjects, especially ideologically controversial topics and sex, write about America, keep it patriotic and "constructive." Brighten the corner where you are.

The Englishman Bertrand Russell was another victim of the public's intolerance of nonconformity. A mathematician and philosopher who had taught at Cambridge and UCLA, the third Earl Russell had accepted a post as chairman of the philosophy department at the College of the City of New

---

[3]Bridges was not in fact deported: at the hearing he was acquitted for lack of evidence; and despite repeated government efforts to send him from the country he finally became a U.S. citizen in 1945.

York. The appointment was thought to be a plum for the university and the city, until the Episcopal bishop of the diocese, the Right Reverend William Manning, took public exception to the philosopher's moral standards. Lord Russell was highly regarded for his clarity of expression, somewhat less so for his pacifist ideals, but his unusual views on marriage and morals were what stuck in the bishop's craw. Somehow—thanks to a rising tide of largely uninformed opinion, abetted by the Hearst newspapers, the American Legion, and sundry religious groups—a suit was filed in a New York court attacking Russell as "lecherous, salacious, libidinous, lustful, venereous, erotomaniac, aphrodisiac, atheistic, irreverent, untruthful, bereft of moral fiber." The judge revoked Russell's appointment, ruling that the Board of Higher Education was allowing a "Chair of Indecency" at CCNY, and the Englishman was obliged to accept a professorship at Harvard.

The other congressional committee that was making headlines in 1941 was headed by a plain, gray, bespectacled man from Missouri who got his political start as a small cog in a city machine and, by scrapping every step of the way, made it to the nation's capital as a United States senator. No one—least of all the Senate that funded it—expected Harry S Truman's committee to amount to much, but before the year was out it impressed the public as being quite possibly Congress's sole accomplishment.

Truman was a homespun Midwesterner—a farm boy who had come up the hard way. After commanding an artillery battery in the World War he went into the haberdashery business, became a protégé of Tom Pendergast, the notoriously corrupt Democratic boss of Kansas City, and was given a county judgeship, from which, through sheer determination, he managed to get himself elected to the Senate in 1934. He was seen as simple, humble, a "genial little man," as a woman meeting him for the first time described him. In Congress he voted consistently for New Deal legislation, in return for which he got nothing but the back of Roosevelt's hand (most painful of all, he received no federal patronage for his district), thanks to the Pendergast stigma. Fellow senators and representatives came to think highly of him—he was loyal, conscientious, an exceptionally hard worker who compiled an excellent record of accomplishment—but since he had been ignored by the president during his first term and had no personal financial resources, it was generally conceded that he had little chance to be reelected. (That was a common and continuing misconception concerning Harry Truman's political chances.) What he did have was an indomitable will to win and the temperament and driving energy to go with it, and win he did.

He had gained no defense contracts for Missouri from the army or navy, but he was disturbed to hear that money was being wasted in the construction of camps for soldiers, and took it upon himself to discover the truth. After a thirty-thousand-mile tour, during which he saw workers sleeping on the job and leaving valuable equipment unprotected and heard from workers, foremen, and contractors about the shocking waste of manpower, money, and material, he returned to Washington and proposed that the Senate appoint a committee to investigate the problems. "It won't do any good digging up dead horses after the war is over like last time," he said. "The thing to do is dig this stuff up now and correct it." Despite efforts of Republican senators to have him turn this investigation into something more political to embarrass Roosevelt, he made it clear that he had no axe to grind, he wasn't proposing a whitewash or a witchhunt: he wanted the facts, and his sole purpose was to expose any graft, inefficiency, or waste that existed in the defense program.

Starting in March with a piddling budget and four other junior senators (who had no seniority and therefore no power, their elder colleagues believed), the Truman Committee—or, more properly, the Senate Special Committee to Investigate the Defense Program—plunged into its task and immediately took on the sacred cows: it criticized the automobile industry for failing to convert to wartime production, criticized the army for ignoring small companies, criticized the Army Air Corps for not demanding higher output, blamed the dollar-a-year men for the lagging industrial effort, and by mid-August charged the army with the "needless waste" of $100 million in the construction of camps. Over the long haul, it was estimated that the Truman Committee saved the nation billions of dollars. At another level, because of the well-deserved acclamation for the committee, Mr. Roosevelt decided he should keep an eye on the junior senator from Missouri. He was an able fellow, after all, and his loyalty and capacity for work might be useful one day in another job.

———

Each generation produces a few characters who seem larger than life, capable of putting on a cameo performance whenever they appear onstage. One who was impossible to miss, whenever his turn came around, was John L. Lewis, striding into and out of the public eye with his bulldog jaws clenched, his black eyebrows beetling, looking for all the world like a stock-company villain in a role only he was capable of writing and performing. As he had threatened, Lewis resigned as president of the CIO after Roosevelt won the election, but not before making not one but two farewell appearances before that body's annual convention, inciting the 2,600 delegates to a howling, foot-stomping ovation that lasted for forty-three minutes before they would let him speak.

And when he spoke, it was classic Lewis. Someone said that the three great users of the English language of that generation were Winston S. Churchill, Edward R. Murrow, and John L. Lewis, and Lewis was pulling all the stops—purple passages, rolling phrases, quotations from poets and philosophers, even a paraphrase of the Gettysburg Address—until he came to the peroration with tears coursing down his cheeks. "Some great statesman once said that the heights are cold. I think that is true. The poet said, 'Who ascends to the mountain's top finds the loftiest peaks encased in mists and snow.' I think that is true." Then, reminding his audience that their departing leader was still "something of a man," and quoting from the twelfth-century scholar Gratian—"He shortly turns from the well who drinks his fill and the squeezed orange falls from the golden salver to the dung"—he who had ascended the mountain top stepped down and headed for his spiritual home, the United Mine Workers, the organization that was uniquely his own, which he had molded into the nation's biggest trade union.

The bituminous coal workers' contract was due to expire on March 31, 1941. As expected, Lewis presented a list of new demands, and just as predictably, the operators rejected them out of hand. President Roosevelt intervened and appealed to both sides; a federal mediator was appointed; Secretary of Labor Frances Perkins and production boss William Knudsen got into the act; the matter was turned over to the National Defense Mediation Board for arbitration. Everything was going according to the usual script, even to the settlement reached on July 5, when Lewis and the UMW won a major victory. But Big John wanted more.

By now it was apparent that Lewis was likely to cause a lot more trouble than the defense program could tolerate, and his popularity even within the labor movement was declining sharply. With Russia at war with Germany, pro-Communists and fellow travelers became intensely patriotic and turned on him. After fulminating against them and other foes, he moved suddenly and unexpectedly in a manner suggesting that he was out to even old scores with President Roosevelt.

The July contract settlement had been with the northern and southern Appalachian operators. That was followed by negotiations with the other coal producers, and by autumn all had accepted save the steel companies' captive mines. Headed by Myron Taylor of U.S. Steel, those owners dug in their heels over the question of the union shop: if they accepted it in their captive mines, they would get nothing but agitation until they allowed it in their mills, shipyards, and elsewhere. What they *were* willing to accept, it developed, was a settlement in which the government imposed a union shop on them in such a way that they would be able to renegotiate that issue in the future. Big Steel could see the writing on the wall: all but 5 percent of the employees in the captive mines were already union members. But Roosevelt flatly refused to be a party to any settlement in which the government required a union shop.

Negotiations went on; then Lewis ordered a walkout of the captive mine workers on September 15. Although the number of men involved was only a fraction of the total miners in the country, when you were dealing with John L. Lewis you never knew what step he might take next, and in this case the next step might be a nationwide strike. Unexpectedly, he volunteered a plan: he would reopen the mines for a month while the National Defense Mediation Board deliberated and tried to solve the dispute. The thirty days passed, the miners continued to dig, and when no decision was forthcoming from the NDMB, Lewis acted. He announced that the temporary agreement would end at midnight on October 25.

His opponents were stymied. The president would not order workers to join the union; the NDMB refused to rule on the issue; and when Mr. Roosevelt proposed that Myron Taylor and Lewis head a conference to resolve the issue, Taylor refused, thus handing the problem back to the White House. By this time what had surfaced as an argument involving a small fraction of the nation's coal miners had assumed the proportions of a national crisis.

Lewis knew the country could not stay out of the war much longer; he wanted his miners to obtain every possible benefit before that occurred and the government froze wages and bargaining rules at the prewar level, and he saw compromise now as abandoning the right to strike later. Roosevelt saw the dispute as an imminent threat to full-scale arms production, and since he regarded the union-shop issue as considerably less important than national security, he appealed to the UMW chief and his associates "as loyal citizens, to come to the aid of your country" and keep the mines operating.

To Lewis that was a low blow. At that moment, the mine closings were no threat; U.S. Steel had several weeks' supply of coal on hand, other companies had more, and Lewis was outraged that the president would question his patriotism and cast a simple union-management argument in that light. "This fight is only between a labor union and a ruthless corporation," he replied, suggesting that if the power of the state was to be used against him, an agent of labor, it should be used equally to restrain his adversary, "an agent of capital . . . a rich man named Morgan, who lives in New York." Two could play at innuendo.

Now it was Roosevelt's turn to be furious. He issued another appeal from "your government, through me" to the United Mine Workers, denounced in a radio broadcast the "dangerous minority of labor leaders" who were hamstringing production, and privately told a Morgan partner that Lewis was in "a psychopathic condition." His appeal to patriotism worked: an indignant public was behind him; Lewis was widely condemned in the press; congressmen called for his head; and one senator charged him with being a "traitor to American ideals." But as the pace of events accelerated, Lewis was strangely silent.

On October 29, the day after the captive mine workers struck, Lewis and Myron Taylor met for hours at a much-publicized meeting in Washington's Mayflower Hotel before adjourning to the White House, where it was announced that they had agreed to submit the issue to the NDMB (though neither party would agree in advance to be bound by the board's decision). The following morning Lewis called off the strike. Then, within a matter of hours, he stunned the nation by announcing a new strike deadline of November 15.

On November 10 the NDMB ruled against Lewis and the union shop by a vote of 9 to 2, and the two nay-sayers—the representatives of the CIO—

immediately resigned, effectively putting an end to the board. On Armistice Day, November 11, army intelligence agents were reportedly active in the coalfields and a military command post was set up in Pittsburgh. On November 14, Roosevelt summoned three industry leaders and Lewis and two other UMW men to the White House and ordered them to end the dispute. He wanted a full report on their action the following Monday, he said.

When Monday, November 17, arrived, two things had happened: the annual CIO convention was in session in Detroit, and the miners were on strike again. Big John, always a master of timing, knew that the CIO would back the walkout and that Roosevelt would not risk a confrontation with organized labor. By midweek, violence had erupted in the coalfields and thousands of other miners had abandoned the pits in sympathy with their fellow workers in the captive mines. That Saturday, Lewis had his revenge. The president capitulated and named a three-man arbitration board, consisting of U.S. Steel's Benjamin Fairless, John L. Lewis, and John Steelman of the U.S. Conciliation Service. Since Steelman was known to favor the union position, Lewis knew—as the president knew—that he had won. He agreed at once to "arbitration." The three men would consider the dispute and, it was supposed, come up with a recommendation in about two weeks—by the end of the first week in December.

———

President Roosevelt hated John L. Lewis and he hated Charles A. Lindbergh, and in both instances the feeling was reciprocated. Yet it is impossible to avoid the feeling that at times the president respected and secretly admired Lewis and could find ways to work with him, whereas he was contemptuous of Lindbergh, openly spiteful, determined that the aviation hero would pay in full measure for opposing the administration's foreign policy. It was not simply that Lindbergh was an isolationist. Behind the venom was a conviction FDR once revealed to Henry Morgenthau. "If I should die tomorrow," he told the Treasury secretary at lunch one day, "I want you to know this. I am absolutely convinced that Lindbergh is a Nazi."[4]

Nothing reveals more vividly the complex, contrary, stubborn, independent nature of Charles Lindbergh—who was certainly no Nazi—than the speech he delivered in Des Moines, Iowa, in the autumn of 1941. As every passing week brought the United States closer to war, Lindbergh made up his mind to name the groups he considered responsible for endangering the nation's future. For more than a year he had spoken of "powerful elements" that were trying to draw America into war, but he had never identified

———

[4]In this he was seconded by his waspish interior secretary, Harold Ickes, who was certain that Lindbergh consciously sought "ultimate power" for himself, and by one of his speech writers, Robert Sherwood, who was quoted as saying that Lindbergh was "a Nazi with a Nazi's Olympian contempt for all democratic processes."

them. Now that involvement in the conflict was "practically inevitable," he resolved to speak out, though he knew the uproar it would create. So the man who had not wanted to get involved in this business in the first place, who had done so because of a conscience that would not let him leave it alone, elected to lay everything on the line in his determination to keep the country out of war.

The America First Committee was eager for Lindbergh—its biggest drawing card and most popular speaker—to appear in the Iowa heartland, home of Henry Wallace and the widely read Cowles newspapers, the *Des Moines Register* and *Tribune,* which strongly supported Roosevelt's foreign policy. Lindbergh agreed to go, the meeting was set for September 11, and then chance intervened in the arrangements. President Roosevelt was to have given a speech several days earlier, but his mother died, and his address was postponed until September 11. Rather than change plans, the America First Committee decided on the unusual approach of broadcasting the president's talk to the audience, with the scheduled speakers to follow. Lindbergh didn't care for the arrangement, since the president "has the ability to arouse crowds [and] it gave us about as bad a setting as we could have had for our meeting,"⁵ but felt he had no choice but to go along with the committee's plan.

What the eight thousand Iowans in the Des Moines Coliseum heard was Roosevelt's rousing "shoot on sight" speech, which was a tough act for anyone to follow, and when the broadcast ended, the America First speakers filed onstage to be greeted by a mixture of boos and applause—the most unfriendly crowd Lindbergh had encountered. Nothing went right at first: hecklers shouted from the gallery and the loudspeaker wouldn't work. Then Janet Ayer Fairbank, the novelist, spoke, followed by Hanford MacNider, the Iowa businessman who had been head of the American Legion, and by the time Lindbergh began, promising to speak "with the utmost frankness" about who was responsible for trying to force the United States into the war, the audience was receptive and attentive.

Three important groups are "responsible for changing our national policy from one of neutrality and independence to one of entanglement in European affairs," he said. They are "the British, the Jewish, and the Roosevelt Administration." Behind these groups were less significant lobbies—capitalists, Anglophiles, intellectuals, and now the Communists; but they merely followed the lead of the three major war agitators. Although his most severe words were for the Roosevelt administration, and he spoke of his sympathy and understanding of the British, and especially of the Jews, what everyone in the audience and elsewhere in America heard was Lindbergh attacking the

⁵He qualified his characterization of Roosevelt's speaking ability by saying, "I refer to his national popularity and not to my own impression. From the standpoint of popular appeal, Roosevelt is possibly the greatest speaker of our time. Personally, I decided, after listening to two of his radio addresses in 1932 that I did not trust the man who gave them and that I did not want to see him President of the United States."

Jews for dragging us into the war with Hitler. So much was said and written then and later about this speech that it is worth seeing exactly what he did say on that subject. It consisted of three short paragraphs.

"It is not difficult to understand why Jewish people desire the overthrow of Nazi Germany. The persecution they suffered in Germany would be sufficient to make bitter enemies of any race. No person with a sense of the dignity of mankind can condone the persecution of the Jewish race in Germany. But no person of honesty and vision can look on their pro-war policy here today without seeing the dangers involved in such a policy, both for us and for them.

"Instead of agitating for war, the Jewish groups in this country should be opposing it in every possible way, for they will be among the first to feel its consequences. Tolerance is a virtue that depends upon peace and strength. History shows that it cannot survive war and devastation. A few farsighted Jewish people realize this, and stand opposed to intervention. But the majority still do not. Their greatest danger to this country lies in their large ownership and influence in our motion pictures, our press, our radio, and our government.

"I am not attacking either the Jewish or the British people. Both races I admire. But I am saying that the leaders of both the British and the Jewish races, for reasons which are understandable from their viewpoint as they are inadvisable from ours, for reasons which are not American, wish to involve us in the war. We cannot blame them for looking out for what they believe to be their own interests, but we also must look out for ours. We cannot allow the natural passions and prejudices of other peoples to lead our country to destruction."

When he named the three groups agitating for war, Lindbergh noted in his journal, "the entire audience seemed to stand and cheer . . . and whatever opposition existed was completely drowned out by our support." The next day he boarded the *Broadway Limited* for New York, and on Saturday, September 13, arrived in New York to find the *New York Times* bristling with attacks on his speech from across America, from Jewish and non-Jewish organizations, from Protestant and Catholic clergymen, politicians, and business leaders, and from a major spectrum of the press—excepting, of course, Father Coughlin's *Social Justice* and Gerald L. K. Smith's Committee of 1,000,000. Even supporters of America First were shocked. Norman Thomas, the Socialist and pacifist who respected Lindbergh and had shared an antiwar platform with him on a number of occasions, sympathized with the aviator, because he did not believe he was anti-Semitic. But he thought the speech "amazingly hurtful," and wrote to General Wood to say that it was "an enormous pity that our friend the Colonel will not take the advice on public relations which he would expect an amateur in aviation to take from an expert."

As right as Mr. Thomas was, this was more than a public-relations matter to Americans. Indeed, Lindbergh had known what sort of reaction to expect, and so had his wife, Anne, who was thrown into "black gloom" when she read the speech and begged him not to deliver it. She feared for the effect on him and the cause he was trying to promote; it was the one subject no one brought into the open in public, and to do so was "a match lit near a pile of excelsior," with the certainty that he would be accused of anti-Semitism and Jew-baiting, regardless of his intentions. Unable to talk him out of it, she had to respect his determination to speak the truth as he saw it while feeling a profound sense of grief over what he was doing. To a friend she wrote, "Isn't it strange, there is no hate in him, no hate at all, and yet he rouses it and spreads it." In the ongoing struggle between isolationists and interventionists, the Roosevelt administration was fair game, and so were the British, but Lindbergh's blind spot was not to understand—then or later—that the Jews were different. Even to name the Jews in this context, let alone to segregate them *en bloc* from the rest of American society as "other peoples," was to introduce an undercurrent of something entirely different into the great debate—an element that smacked of the horrors perpetrated inside Nazi Germany, no matter how carefully he tried to state his case.

"I'm just a stubborn Swede," Lindbergh once told a *New York Times* reporter, and he seemed eager to prove it in the wake of the speech. He could not understand General Wood's anxious concern about its effect. He could not comprehend why John Flynn, head of America First's New York chapter, who felt as Lindbergh did, called the speech "stupid" and "would rather see us get into the war than mention in public what the Jews are doing, no matter how tolerantly and moderately it is done." He did not welcome Herbert Hoover's advice that when you have been in politics long enough you learn not to say things just because they are true. Lindbergh's reaction was: "I am not a politician—and that is one of the reasons why I don't wish to be one. I would rather say what I believe when I want to say it than to measure every statement I make by its probable popularity."

A woman who worked for the Lindberghs once remarked that "he cannot tell a lie, even if he knows the truth is going to hurt. . . . He just has to tell the truth, and he expects other people to tell the truth to him." He was also a remarkably courageous man who was unafraid to face hatred and was willing to suffer extremes of obloquy for the sake of his principles. The trouble in Des Moines in September of 1941 was that what he had chosen to be candid about, for reasons both obvious and not so obvious just then, was the unmentionable subject, the topic the country did not choose to debate or even contemplate.[6] He had violated one of the sacred taboos, and

[6] Six weeks before the Lindbergh speech, the isolationists Gerald P. Nye and Bennett Champ Clark had demanded a Senate investigation of war propaganda in the movies, and Burton Wheeler appointed a subcommittee to do so. During the hearings, Wendell Willkie appeared as counsel for the motion-picture industry and charged that the hearings were anti-Semitic. (It was estimated that Jews controlled more than half of the industry.) Nye and his associates denied the accusation, but the hearings were adjourned and not reopened.

the public would not let him get away with it, no matter how rational an explanation he might have. Whatever this was going to mean for Charles Lindbergh, it was a political blunder from which America First never really recovered. A week after the speech, having deliberated long and hard over how to put the best face on it, the national committee issued a statement stating flatly that neither Colonel Lindbergh nor his fellow members were anti-Semitic. The committee deplored the injection of the race issue into the discussion of war and peace, claiming—rather astonishingly—that the interventionists had been the ones to do so, and went on to remind the public that America First had invited "men and women of every race, religion, and national origin to join this committee, provided only that they are patriotic citizens who put the interests of their country ahead of those of any other nation." But the damage was done.

On the heels of those two speeches on September 11—Roosevelt's and Lindbergh's—some of the heart seemed to go out of the America First movement. The president had struck a responsive chord with the "shoot on sight" message: the public was increasingly ready for tough talk, if not action. Yet it is not fair to lay the entire blame for a waning enthusiasm and energy at Lindbergh's door. Some of the committee's leaders were suffering from battle fatigue; they had been in this fight for a long while, after all, and they were struggling not only with the administration in Washington and a determined body of interventionists across the country, but with a tide of events no man or government could stem or control, and they were understandably worn out. Hanford MacNider stated his opinion that the committee had come to the end of the road. General Wood was of the same opinion, and suggested that the organization should either "adjourn" until the congressional elections of 1942, or disband. Lindbergh, Stuart, and others persuaded Wood not to quit, but although Lindbergh himself was determined to press on with the fight, he too found himself thinking about "building . . . a different type of life" in which he and Anne and the children would have a permanent home, perhaps in northern California or Oregon. He was "written out," he decided, believed he was speaking too much, and intended to withdraw gradually from the America First rallies. In October, three weeks after the Des Moines meeting, he spoke in Fort Wayne, Indiana. At the end of the month he appeared at a packed Madison Square Garden, where upwards of twenty thousand cheering people stood outside, unable to get seats, and was elated by what he called the most successful, enthusiastic meeting America First had ever held. Surely, he thought, there was "no better indication of how people feel about this war." Much encouraged, he planned to deliver at least one more speech before the end of the year—in Boston, on December 12, 1941.

General Marshall almost lost his army before it fought a battle, and the isolationists were largely to blame. The bleak tidings from the Balkans and the Middle East in the spring of 1941, instead of stiffening Washington's resolve to prepare for the worst, resulted in discouragement and near paralysis in Congress and a reluctance at the White House to initiate any changes that would arouse the noninterventionists. In this disturbing situation, Marshall faced the necessity of extending the service of draftees beyond a single year (a term due to expire in October), as well as continuing National Guard units in federal service beyond mid-September. At the time the bill was passed, critics of the draft had warned that the administration would renege on its commitment to send the boys home when their year was up, and since neither Roosevelt nor Congress was willing to take the heat on this inflammatory issue, that left it to the army.

Early in July, Marshall released his first report on the army's status since he had taken over as chief of staff two years before, describing the service's eightfold growth during that period, and he took advantage of the occasion to point out that now, just when the army was attaining a level of readiness where it might be counted on to defend the nation, it was going to collapse. Between 75 and 90 percent of the officers in regular army units were reservists whose term was about to end; in some divisions, as many as half the enlisted men would depart in October; and many vital support units would simply vanish. For weeks he and Secretary Stimson were on the Hill, lobbying senators and representatives, reminding them that the Selective Training and Service Act of 1940 allowed the twelve-month service provision to be extended if the national interest was imperiled. Surely, they asked one legislator after another, you will admit that we are threatened?

But Congress, sick of hearing complaints from inductees and their parents, lulled by the belief that the Germans were now tied down in Russia (though no one believed Russian resistance would last), and annoyed with the president for what they considered his lack of candor about the defense program, was not buying that argument. Marshall was told that not in forty years had there been such congressional fear of amending a bill; insiders were saying that a vote for it would be political suicide. Speaker Sam Rayburn believed the only way the army would get what it wanted was for the president to put the pressure on Democrats in the House, but Roosevelt was so sensitive to the violent attacks he was getting on this issue that he shied away from any involvement whatever. And Marshall, as he made the rounds of congressional offices, discovered to his amazement that the representatives seemed more willing to back the army if the arguments came from him, rather than the president. They needed facts and an expert's opinion, not political pressure, to pass on to constituents back home. What seemed to concern them most was those letters of complaint and abuse (many of which, Marshall managed to prove, were spurious, and came from relatively few citizens), and he reminded them that the business of soldiering means mud and heat and dust and biting insects, involves discomfort and inconvenience, missing meals, making long marches; but we have to treat these men as soldiers, he said.

For congressmen who were still on the fence he recalled how General Irvin McDowell had been forced to fight the disastrous First Battle of Bull Run prematurely because his troops' enlistments were about to expire. But Marshall's opponents were no less determined and resourceful than McDowell's. America First printed a million postcards, urging recipients to "write today to President Roosevelt that you are against our entry into the European War"; Senator Burton Wheeler had them mailed under his frank; and inevitably many of them turned up in disgruntled soldiers' hands. Before long the word OHIO began appearing on walls and fences near military camps across the country; it stood for "Over the Hill in October," and suggested to an already nervous Washington that the government might be faced with mass desertions if it insisted on extending the draft. Marshall, as might be supposed, was not sympathetic: "We cannot have a political club and call it an army," he snapped. Representative Wadsworth, who had cosponsored the original bill, despaired of his fellow Republicans—all but nineteen of whom were lined up against the extension—who were predicting riots, violence, and loss of the 1942 elections if this "outrage" was perpetrated. Joe Martin, the minority leader, gleefully held out hope that a vote against extension "might yet funnel the winds into our sails and blow us back again to the commanding position the Republican Party had enjoyed in the 1920s"; on the other side of the aisle the majority leader, John McCormack, counted forty-five Democrats opposed, with thirty-five more undecided. We are at peace, these dissenters were saying; we don't need to keep the draftees under arms. From Marshall, Wadsworth learned that the army was already chartering ships to bring national guardsmen back from the Philippines and Alaska in time to be discharged before the time limit ran out. The New York congressman was disgusted and troubled: we had approximately a million men in the draft, he noted, who had just begun to show some improvement and get used to their weapons, and to discharge them all and send them home "would leave us with an absolutely empty basket."

On August 7, the day President Roosevelt and his party, including General Marshall, arrived in Placentia Bay for the Atlantic Conference, the Senate took a vote. With only forty-five members in favor of extension and twenty-one unwilling to cast a vote, the measure squeaked through—but not on terms the administration had requested: the extension of service was for eighteen months, not for the duration of the emergency. On August 12, the day German tanks reached the shore of the Black Sea, a radioman aboard the *Augusta* received a message that the House of Representatives had passed the bill by a vote of 203 to 202. By a single vote, General George Marshall's army remained intact and was not disbanded.[7]

---

[7]As Mark Watson points out, the House bill was not identical to that passed by the Senate, but rather than return it to committee to have the differences resolved and risk resubmitting it to both chambers for another vote, House leaders begged the Senate to accept it without change—which was done.

What had been going on for the past half year and more was a novel and trying experience in a land that had never seen peacetime conscription. The business of screening and selecting from more than seventeen million registrants the 921,722 men who found themselves in the army by the spring of 1941 was nothing if not educational, for somewhat unexpectedly, the nation learned something about itself and about the human costs—especially to its youth—of a major economic depression. In order to keep the rejection rate low, the army's physical requirements were modest, to say the least: the conscript had to stand at least five feet tall and weigh a minimum of 105 pounds; he could not have flat feet, venereal disease, or a hernia; he must have twelve of his natural complement of thirty-two teeth ("six serviceable opposing posterior teeth" and the same number of anterior, was the requirement); he must have 20/40 vision or better. Even so, more than forty of every hundred selectees were rejected by the army as unfit for general military service—a grim reminder of the physical toll exacted by ignorance, apathy, malnutrition, vitamin and mineral deficiencies, and a shocking lack of proper medical and dental care during the Depression years. (Flat feet and dental defects led the disqualifying defects, hands down.) That was serious enough; almost as bad was the revelation that one man in five was illiterate.

In a pattern that was repeated all too often, an inductee would be examined by one of 6,443 local draft boards—composed of well-meaning, conscientious folk who volunteered for the task as a way to do something for their country—and would be told that he was fit for service and should say goodbye to his family and employer. Then, having burned his bridges, he would report to an army induction center only to be rejected for physical or mental reasons and be sent home. This experience was understandably unpopular with a lot of draftees, their employers, and the nation at large, and it was one of many indications that the entire defense effort was being bungled.

Those 921,722 citizen-soldiers randomly selected for service learned the realities and indignities of military life at its most basic, enduring the bullying of leather-lunged noncoms, endless hours of close-order drill on dust-choked parade grounds, calisthenics, weapons handling (when they had weapons), rifle practice, inspections without number, KP duty, night marches, the infinite boredom of barracks life; and soon enough the time came for the brass to see what stuff they were made of, and if they were capable of waging a war. The army was going on maneuvers in the summer of 1941, and it was to be the first such experience for the new draftees.

The purpose of war games, of course, is to simulate combat conditions, to train officers and troops to maneuver by day or night, to work on moving a regiment in the darkness so it can make a surprise attack at dawn, to practice ground-to-ground and ground-to-air communications with other units, to build pontoon bridges under the pressure of time, and so on—a primary objective also being to keep troops from getting confused or lost or killed.

Two years earlier—in August 1939, while Europe waited to see if Hitler would carry out his threat against Poland—vacationers driving through Connecticut, Massachusetts, Vermont, and upper New York State were shunted off highways to make way for long lines of army vehicles. America, they learned, was being invaded by a "Black" army which had landed on the Atlantic coast and was heading inland. Lying in wait was the "Blue" army, dug in along a line east of the Hudson from the Green Mountains to New York City, the Delaware Water Gap, and Philadelphia.

As a realistic training exercise, the 1939 maneuvers were a joke, and Major General Hugh A. Drum found it necessary to explain to newspapermen, "The First Army . . . is not in fact an army [but] a collection of individual units, lacking adequate army, corps, and divisional troops, partially equipped and woefully short in the manpower, weapons, and motors which experience has proved essential." Truth to tell, his army was at a mere 25 percent of its purported troop strength and in possession of a tiny fraction of its authorized weapons and vehicles. It had no airplanes whatever. Commenting on this farcical situation, General Robert Lee Bullard remarked bitterly that Rumania had more trained men in its army than the U.S. did, and that ten thousand real invaders could whip our "old-fashioned police force."

A year later the maneuvers were an improvement, but they revealed more about the nation's stinginess in equipping its military forces than anything else. These were the largest peacetime maneuvers ever held in the country, involving regulars, national guardsmen, and reserves, but what was painfully evident, in *Time* magazine's words, was that "the U.S. Army was grotesquely short of combat equipment." Between them, the invading and defending armies had only four real tanks; the others were trucks with TANK painted on the sides. Antitank guns were in fact lengths of drain pipe; substituting for antiaircraft guns, pie plates bearing the message ".50 caliber" were pasted onto obsolete Springfield rifles. Hundreds of trucks and other vehicles had to be rented by the day from civilian sources. Naturally enough, Americans who found themselves laughing at pictures of soldiers wearing World War I felt campaign hats charging across open fields with a wooden tripod labeled "6omm mortar" compared what they saw here with what they saw in newsreels of the superbly trained and equipped force that was overrunning France, and the contrast was sobering, to say the least. Yet in spite of the deficiencies evident to the public, the maneuvers proved of considerable benefit to the army. As the first corps-strength maneuvers to be held in the United States, they were closely observed by the chief of staff and the rest of the high command, who quickly spotted the outstanding combat infantry commanders. (Chief among them was Joseph W. Stilwell, recently returned from China, where he had observed at first hand the Japanese fighting machine, and who would see more front-line combat than any other American four-star general in World War II.) George Marshall began writing names in his "little black book" for future reference.

Hard at work, out of the public eye, was Lieutenant General Lesley McNair, chief of staff at general headquarters, whom George Marshall considered one of the best brains in the army. McNair had been working up a plan for building an army division from scratch, and then creating an army of two hundred or more divisions. He had a lanky aide, Mark Clark, who had served at Fort Lewis, Washington, for a couple of years and had made a name for himself by putting on night maneuvers, an amphibious movement, and other unorthodox exercises, and Fort Lewis had become something of a showcase, often visited by McNair, who gave Clark problems to work out with regular troops and National Guard units.

McNair's solution to the problem of creating new divisions began with ordering each of the existing divisions to establish cadres of regular army officers. From these cadres, McNair and Clark—with advice from George Marshall—selected three individuals they thought best qualified to run a division, a commander and two brigadiers, and those men, with their chief subordinates, were sent to Command and General Staff School at Fort Leavenworth, Kansas; regimental commanders and others went to special schools. As soon as the officers completed their courses, the draftees could be poured into the organization and the division was on its way—which meant, Clark said, that it would follow the day-by-day training program devised for it, based in part on lessons learned at Fort Lewis and elsewhere, and incorporating quite a few new techniques. This system of McNair's, which regularly cannibalized existing divisions for some of their best men (to the disgust of commanders), worked so well that it was eventually capable of producing three or four new divisions a month. For obvious reasons, McNair didn't want old-timers like Drum or Lear training the troops differently, and he sent Clark to inform Drum that he was expected to follow the new program. "Don't tell me how to train my troops," the major general informed the lieutenant colonel, and Clark reported to McNair that Drum "won't use our program." The solution to that proved to be simple: Drum soon perceived that no new divisions were being assigned to him, and "he got the message," said Clark.

Beginning in late May of 1941, the most ambitious maneuvers yet held in the United States got under way, involving half a million troops in four different armies, covering a four-month time span and a vast terrain from the West Coast to the Carolinas. Most of the old troubles and complaints persisted, new ones arose: army vehicles held up civilian traffic for miles; soldiers tramped through vegetable gardens and picked fruit in orchards; tanks obliterated pasture fences. The battle for Tennessee couldn't begin because someone had forgotten to bring safety pins for fastening colored ribbons to hats in order to identify the opposing armies; fortunately, a

Connecticut manufacturer saved the day by shipping eighty thousand pins. In Coffee County, Tennessee, a ninety-five-year-old Confederate veteran looked skeptically at a 37mm antitank weapon and declared, "These little cannons wouldn't hurt a flea. Why, in my war we had cannons three times that size." The town of Hope, Arkansas, offered the dirty, exhausted soldiers free baths, and storekeepers everywhere did a land-office business in watermelons, tobacco, candy, and soft drinks. Second Army discovered that using Piper Cub airplanes for scouting expanded its vision exponentially; piloting the planes were company salesmen, who gave officers a sales pitch whenever they took them up, and a recommendation went off to the War Department that light planes be used regularly for artillery spotting and reconnaissance.

The Tennessee and Arkansas maneuvers were preliminaries for the big event in Louisiana and Texas, and so were the critiques: reconnaissance was weak, the distribution of intelligence information too slow; communications were poor; discipline on the road and on the march was extremely lax (General Krueger criticized his men's "stupid disregard" of air attacks); and commanders universally neglected or ignored air-to-ground coordination. In a statement that revealed exactly where the Army Air Corps stood in those days, Major General Robert Richardson observed, "We must take the air into our confidence."

By September, some 400,000 men were slogging through sheets of rain and high winds in western Louisiana and eastern Texas, and now that the uncertainty of the draftees' future was settled, a new level of command was evident. Discipline was tighter, the training more intense and crisp, and while shortages of various weapons were everywhere apparent, this huge collection of men and equipment had the look of a real army. Eric Sevareid was one of the visiting correspondents who was routed out of bed at 3:00 A.M. in the steaming swamps for a hundred-mile drive, and he concluded that "half the art of handling a modern army in combat is the purely mathematical business of controlling traffic." Now that he had spent some time with these men, he no longer worried about the OHIO signs he had seen, no longer believed the draftees would desert; they were playing baseball, whistling at girls, griping, and they lacked the sullen, silent look of men whose spirit is broken. One incident told him all he needed to know about their morale. He encountered some paratroopers gathered in the darkness under a bridge, arguing heatedly with an umpire who said they had not wired the structure properly for blowing it up, and the sight reminded Sevareid of high school basketball players protesting a close decision— young men so upset they were slamming their caps on the ground, cursing, raging, with one angry sergeant in tears. He had seen French soldiers and knew they would not behave this way in a practice war, and while no one could tell for certain, it seemed to Sevareid that these young men in the Louisiana bayous had a competitiveness, a sense of team spirit and pride in their outfit, that would carry them a long way if it came to real combat.

During the grand finale—a clash between armies commanded by Lear and Krueger, involving the first complete armored corps in the U.S. Army, parachute troops, a thousand planes, and huge numbers of soldiers—two men who drew the particular attention of Marshall and McNair were a colonel named Dwight Eisenhower, who had done a brilliant job of planning, and the 2nd Armored Division's commander, Major General George Patton. When at last the maneuvers came to an end, it was time for the critique, conducted by Mark Clark for his boss, McNair, who was quite deaf. And after the critique came the laurels—announcement of the names of colonels who were being promoted to brigadier general. Clark read off the list and deliberately omitted Eisenhower's name. When he had finished, the men stood up to go, everyone talking at once, and Clark gaveled them to silence, saying, "I forgot one name—Dwight D. Eisenhower." And from somewhere in the room Ike's laugh was heard, very clearly, and the words, "I'll get you for this, you sonofabitch!"

Before calling it quits for the year, the army had scheduled one more exercise, involving First Army and IV Armored Corps in the Carolinas, as a test of tanks against antitank weapons. McNair was not pleased with the performance of officers or men—lack of discipline, a disregard of air threats, an inclination on the part of all units to travel on highways—but Marshall was encouraged; the exercises were an improvement over the Louisiana maneuvers. The time had come to sum it all up, and Secretary Stimson called together in his office his top staff, Marshall and his three deputies, plus McNair and Clark, to discuss the lessons of the 1941 exercises and to decide where to focus training efforts during the coming year. The war games had shown up a number of weaknesses, including inadequate training of small units, poor coordination between tactical air outfits and ground forces, and what Hap Arnold described as "awful" communications between ground and air. The horse cavalry, everyone agreed, was no longer of much value. But the final verdict on tank vs. antitank was not in yet; that question would require further study, although it was obvious that more medium tanks were needed. Before the meeting broke up, someone reported that the nation's ammunition factories were finally functioning efficiently, so with luck a larger supply of small-arms cartridges would be available during the coming winter.

The meeting adjourned and the nine men filed out of the secretary's office, their minds whirling with thoughts of all the work that must be done before the army would be ready for war. It was December 3, 1941.

———

None of those military men was aware of it yet, but if a shrewd, straight-talking Yankee with a no-nonsense point of view about the contributions science could and should make to the war effort had his way, the army stood a fair chance of getting some exotic weapons with which to replace its horse-mounted cavalry. Vannevar Bush had been a scientist and a teacher before becoming president of the Carnegie Institution in Washington, and, like many of his colleagues at the time of the "phony war," he was seriously troubled by America's lack of preparedness for a war that was going to be "a highly technical struggle, one in which techniques might indeed determine the outcome." He knew that the military was incapable of producing the sophisticated weaponry that would be needed—weaponry that was possible because of so many recent advances in science. He knew, moreover, that before anything of the sort could be accomplished, science would have to be organized.

The idea had been germinating for some time. While serving as chairman of the National Advisory Committee for Aeronautics (NACA), Bush had heard Charles Lindbergh speak admiringly of the way German science and technology had geared up for war, and he determined to mobilize this country's resources in the same manner—only better. That same NACA experience taught Bush how things worked in Washington, and since he had no personal pipeline to the highest levels of government, he arranged to be introduced to Harry Hopkins, as the best approach to President Roosevelt. They were unlikely colleagues, Bush and Hopkins, and as the former said, it was a minor miracle that they hit it off; but they had in common a quickness of mind, a salty, homespun way of putting things into perspective, and a talent for brevity. In fact, Bush had described his plan for enrolling American science in the war effort—which involved some very complex matters indeed—in four short paragraphs in the middle of a single sheet of paper.

Hopkins read it, agreed enthusiastically, and arranged an appointment for the scientist to see the president. When Bush arrived at the White House, he saw at once that Hopkins had already briefed Mr. Roosevelt, and inside ten minutes he was walking out of the Oval Study with what he wanted—a scribbled "OK—FDR" on the bottom of his memorandum proposing a National Defense Research Committee (NDRC). Bush and Hopkins then drafted a letter providing for close cooperation between the NDRC and the military, and on June 15, 1940—the day after Paris fell—Roosevelt signed it.

In short order, Bush acquired some funds, found office space, and assembled an exceptional group of associates. The last task cannot have been as simple as he made it sound, but he claimed afterward that the way in which the NDRC was manned was that "a need appeared, the man came, and formalities were worked out later." However it was done, he soon had with him James B. Conant, president of Harvard; Karl Compton, president of the Massachusetts Institute of Technology; Frank Jewett, president of the National Academy of Sciences; and Conway Coe, commissioner of patents. To keep the bureaucrats out of the scientists' hair and the scientists free of the restraints of business and government relations, budgets, contracts, patents, and other such details, he put those matters in a separate office reporting to him.

Bush was justifiably proud of his organization, and a year later, when the need clearly was for something more than a research organization, the NDRC became part of the Office of Scientific Research and Development (OSRD), which had its own funds and reported directly to the president.[8] (Before the war ended, he had reason to be grateful that he had done his work so thoroughly. The Germans, it was discovered, had failed utterly in the race for the atomic bomb for two reasons: first, as Bush said, "Hitler's insanity had eliminated their Jewish scientists," and second, the Nazis had "no genuine collaboration between scientists and military men." Thanks to Bush, the United States had both.)

As a despairing Leo Szilard had seen, what little progress was made in interesting the U.S. government in a nuclear program had all but come to a dead halt in the hands of the Advisory Committee on Uranium under Lyman Briggs. Unfortunately, Briggs was slow and methodical, the military men on the committee were in no hurry to make fools of themselves by endorsing a wild scheme, and the result was that two meetings were held in six months' time, with little to show for either. The beauty of Bush's new organization was that it could decide on its own hook what scientific skills were necessary and then undertake the research. In the fall of 1940, Bush recast the Committee on Uranium (though retaining Briggs as chairman on instructions from FDR). He dropped Commander Hoover and Colonel Adamson, since the NDRC was now the channel to the military, and added a number of such men as Merle Tuve, George Pegram, and Harold Urey to beef it up scientifically.

The United States possessed no developed reserves of uranium ore, and about the same time the NDRC got going, Alexander Sachs again appeared on the scene as a kind of *deus ex machina,* urging Lyman Briggs to communicate with the Union Minière du Haut Katanga, owner of the uranium mines in the Belgian Congo. Sachs suggested that the company ship a quantity of ore to America and, even if they retained title to it, pledge not to send it elsewhere without the agreement of the U.S. government. Fortunately, the director of Union Minière, Edgar Sengier, had been warned a year earlier by Sir Henry Tizard that uranium ore might play a vital role in the war to come, and in August 1940 Sengier instructed his people in Africa "to ship discreetly to New York, under some kind of name, an existing stock of rich ore." More than eleven hundred metric tons were loaded into two thousand steel drums during the fall of 1940, and by the time the Americans needed the stuff it was waiting for them in a Staten Island warehouse.

As matters stood in the spring of 1941, the uranium program had a working umbrella organization, it had some funds, it had uranium ore and a number of willing, able scientists, but it still lacked proof that enough of

[8]In the reorganization, Bush became head of OSRD and Conant took his place as director of NDRC.

the neutrons produced by fission would survive long enough to create and sustain a chain reaction. Bush could see that the program was likely to require enormous sums of money, but as yet he could not see any clear-cut results of a practicable nature to justify expenditures on such a level. And before anyone in the upper realms of government, not to mention Vannevar Bush, was going to get behind the program with the political and financial backing it needed, someone would have to demonstrate that what the physicists hoped to achieve was more than pie in the sky.

Bush invited the National Academy of Sciences to name a group of distinguished scientists to review U.S. progress to date, and by mid-May the committee, under the leadership of Arthur Holly Compton (Karl's brother), reached several important conclusions. One was that the existing Committee on Uranium cared more about generating power than it did about producing a weapon for war. Another was that an intensified effort must be made to produce a bomb of enormous explosive capacity.[9] Whether this could be done depended on a number of things—a successful chain reaction, for one, along with quantities of uranium or other fissionable material, and vast sums of money to construct factories which no one had yet designed. The report was a good one, but it was no answer to Bush's dilemma; as he and Conant perceived, it would be virtually impossible to obtain the funds required when they could not state with assurance that the expenditures would produce a weapon. Several engineers were added to the Compton committee, and in July a second report was forthcoming, endorsing the conclusions of the first, stressing again the need for a successful chain reaction, but again, to Bush's disappointment, failing to give him the engineering information he had hoped for—a prediction of the time, money, and difficulties to be faced, those data he must have before he could recommend a program. Once more, promising news came from across the Atlantic.

After the French physicists Hans Halban and Lew Kowarski escaped from Bordeaux in June 1940, they were installed at the Cavendish Laboratory in Cambridge with the cargo of heavy water Joliot had obtained from Norway, and they soon realized that all the top physicists in England were working on radar and had little time for anything else. (The saying among British physicists was that since most of them were working on war problems, pure physics was left to the refugees.) A research team at Oxford, led by another refugee, Franz Simon, who had won Germany's Iron Cross for bravery in the first World War and fled the Nazis in 1933 because he was Jewish,[10]

---

[9]Still another was the frightening idea that the radioactive products of fission should be developed as weapons. Although nothing came of this, it was still being discussed as late as 1943 by Fermi and Oppenheimer.

[10]In a land grateful for his contributions, he became Sir Francis Simon, Commander of the British Empire.

discovered in mid-December of 1940 the gas that offered the best prospects of separating U-235 from pure uranium by a gaseous diffusion method, described the type of factory needed to achieve this, and determined the amount of money needed to build and operate it, the amount of electricity required to power it, and the number of men to run it. That same month Halban and Kowarski proved that uranium oxide, using heavy water as a moderator, would produce a self-sustaining chain reaction. In the meantime, James Chadwick concluded that a reaction created by slow neutrons would produce an explosion little different from TNT, that it was necessary to create a chain reaction by *fast* neutrons, and that it might be better to use U-235 instead of natural uranium.

Otto Frisch had worked on this problem with Chadwick after fleeing Copenhagen, and one day in the late winter of 1940 he and Rudolf Peierls were talking in the laboratory when one of them raised the question of what the critical mass of U-235 might be. Peierls, of course, had previously calculated the critical mass of pure uranium, proving that the amount needed to produce a bomb was so huge that it could not possibly be carried on an airplane, but no one had given much thought to U-235, since it was supposed that the same principle would apply and since sizable quantities were not thought to be obtainable. When the two men did some calculations on an envelope and plugged these into the equation already devised by Peierls, they were staggered to find how small an amount would be required. As Peierls remarked, "our first calculation gave a critical mass of less than one pound."

The implications of their discovery were immense, at once making the technical problems appear manageable. There was no denying the difficulty of separating even a pound of U-235, but it was at least within the realm of possibility, and a bomb as small as their estimates suggested could certainly be carried in a plane. When Frisch and Peierls took the next step and calculated the force of the explosion that would be produced by U-235, the result was more than staggering—it was appalling.

As Szilard had learned from bitter experience, the foreigner—even one with valuable information in his possession—has a difficult time gaining access to those in authority in his adopted land, and Frisch and Peierls quickly learned the same lesson. Fortunately, an Australian physicist named Marcus L. E. Oliphant, who was working on radar, suggested they write to Sir Henry Tizard, chairman of the RAF's research program, and at last their vital message reached the ear of Professor George Thomson, chairman of the Maud Committee—the group in Britain charged with building a bomb. Even so, it was some time before their thesis was accepted.

The very idea of an atomic bomb was so novel and strange that few people in positions of power had any idea what a difference such a weapon might mean to the world. Even Winston Churchill, who was known for his receptivity to bizarre schemes, had difficulty with this one: after receiving the Thomson committee's report, he referred it to his military advisers with a lukewarm endorsement, saying, "Although personally I am quite content with the existing explosives, I feel we must not stand in the path of improvement. . . ." Another reason was that in Britain, as in the United States, a number of scientists considered the bomb project impracticable—a waste of time, energy, and money. Another group thought the undertaking possible and felt the bomb should be made, but could not agree on what should be done with it, when and if it became a reality. Perhaps a demonstration should be arranged to reveal its awesome power to the Germans, some said; perhaps the mere threat of it would be enough to end the war, said others. Even if the Germans managed to create a similar weapon, it was argued, that in itself might produce a standoff, as in the case of poison gas. Yet behind all the arguments against it remained the awful danger that the Nazis might get there first, and the belief that Hitler would not hesitate to use it.

The conclusions of Peierls and Frisch were reflected in the final report of the Maud Committee, signed by Thomson on July 15, 1941. "We entered the project with more skepticism than belief," the report read, but "we have now reached the conclusion that it will be possible to make an effective uranium bomb which would be equivalent as regards destructive effect to 1,800 tons of TNT." The paper estimated the size of the device, the amount of damage and the number of casualties it would cause under certain circumstances, and the probable amounts of money and materials and the number and types of personnel required to produce it, and outlined the problems still to be solved. In recommending a crash program for a U-235 bomb project, the committee assumed that a nuclear weapon might possibly be available in two years—perhaps in time to affect the outcome of the war, which meant that the uranium project was worth a major effort.

The Maud Committee's report, carried orally to Washington by a member of the National Defense Research Committee and mailed by Thomson on July 7, was exactly what Bush and Conant needed. For the first time, they could point to a reasonable expectation that something militarily useful would emerge from the uranium project. When George Thomson himself arrived in the States in October, he infected everyone he met with his optimism and enthusiasm, and a significant result was that Bush could now ask Arthur Compton and his group for specific technical information concerning the critical mass and destructive power of a U-235 bomb, plus tentative design data for a gaseous diffusion plant.

On October 9, 1941, Bush went to the White House to brief the president and vice president on what had been learned from the British, telling them that while this was by no means a guarantee of success, the signs were certainly favorable. He came away from the meeting with a clear understanding of what was to be done. Mr. Roosevelt endorsed a full exchange of information with the British, and two days later wrote Churchill suggesting just such a collaboration. Bush was to expedite work on the bomb in every way possible, short of having a plant actually constructed: when the time came for that, the president said, special plans might have to be devised, perhaps a joint effort with Canada—indicating that he was as concerned as ever about the twin bugaboos of isolationists and Congress. Finally, the utmost secrecy was to be observed: policy considerations were to be restricted to the chief executive and Vice President Wallace, Secretary of War Stimson, Chief of Staff Marshall, Conant, and Bush himself. What this amounted to was that Bush now had a green light to see if a bomb could be made and what it would cost. If his investigation should be positive enough to warrant production of a bomb, he was to return to the president for further approval. Meanwhile, he had a free hand to proceed.

On November 6, Compton's committee recommended an expanded program for the development of an atomic bomb, noting, "The possibility must be seriously considered that within a few years the use of bombs such as described here, or something similar using uranium fission, may determine military superiority." Then they stated flatly, "A fission bomb of superlatively destructive power will result from bringing quickly together a sufficient mass of element U-235. This seems to be as sure as any untried prediction based upon theory and experiment can be. . . ." Such fission bombs, they concluded, might be produced in significant quantities in three or four years. Forwarding this report to President Roosevelt on November 27, 1941, Bush observed that it was somewhat more conservative in its findings than the Maud study, partly because the committee included "some hardheaded engineers in addition to very distinguished physicists," who estimated that more time and a great deal more money than the British had foreseen would be needed for the job.

———

Ten days later, four scientists met in a sparse office at the Carnegie Institution in the capital. James B. Conant conducted the meeting in Bush's absence, and the three others, who had gathered to learn President Roosevelt's decision on the matter that interested them so profoundly, were Lyman Briggs, Arthur Compton, and Ernest Lawrence, the creator of a machine at California's Radiation Laboratory in Berkeley known as the cyclotron, for which he had been awarded a Nobel Prize in physics. Conant informed his colleagues that the president had accepted the Compton committee's recommendation, and that they were to proceed with an all-out effort to make an atomic bomb. For the time being they would use money made available by the Office of Emergency Management in the White House. They had six months for their development work, after which the president would decide whether the army should take over the task.

It was a Saturday, and after the meeting Lawrence took a taxi to the airport, eager to return to his laboratory and the calutron, his latest version of the cyclotron. Conant and Compton joined Bush for lunch at the Cosmos Club, where they talked about the decision and discussed the possibility of producing a quantity of the new element that had been identified by Glenn

Seaborg (which would become known as plutonium)—a step strongly recommended by Lawrence. By the time the lunch was over, they had agreed
to proceed simultaneously on four separate tracks to find the best way of
obtaining the explosive ingredient of the bomb: the gaseous diffusion, elec-
tromagnetic, and centrifuge methods, as means of obtaining U-235; and a
chemical extraction method for the new, as yet unnamed, element. That was
a lot of ground to cover in six months' time, and all of them were itching
to start.

The date was December 6, 1941, and Compton planned to take a train to
New York the following morning to talk matters over with the physicists
at Columbia.

PART IX

1941

PEARL HARBOR: DAY OF INFAMY

Secretary of State Cordell Hull escorts
Japan's Ambassador Kichisaburo Nomura (left)
and special envoy Saburo Kurusu to the
White House on November 17, 1941.

CHAPTER 50

———————◆———————

"...Japan is not prepared to fight a war with the United States."

T he two men had settled down to business in March, and for nine months—during the course of some forty or fifty meetings—they talked, doing little more than reiterate *ad nauseam* their own nation's policies. Usually they got together in the evening, in the informal, neutral setting of Cordell Hull's apartment at the Wardman Park Hotel, which was more conducive to a give-and-take exchange than the State Department (much as one sympathizes with Mrs. Hull for the countless cups of tea she must have served their visitor). The picture is an appealing one—two proud diplomats of disparate cultures and backgrounds, facing each other by lamplight in the gathering dusk, each doggedly explaining his nation's position in hopes that the other would understand at last and turn away from the calamity that was otherwise sure to come. It was obvious from the beginning that the two points of view were essentially irreconcilable, with the U.S. secretary of state lecturing Japan's Ambassador Kichisaburo Nomura like a Sunday-school teacher, moralizing about good and evil, the virtues of peace, and the wickedness of aggression; while his visitor solemnly repeated what he believed to be the nature of Tokyo's intentions.

To make matters more difficult, neither man could control or even gauge the determination of military expansionists in Tokyo, who were driven by several imperatives. The war in China, which was about to enter its fifth year, had cost Japan dearly in human lives, money, supplies, and equipment, not to mention anguish and frustration, and the worst of it was that the more territory the Japanese conquered the worse the drain on the economy at home, the more oil and steel and rice they needed. So the military greedily eyed the oil, tin, rubber, and foodstuffs of the Netherlands East Indies, Indochina, and Malaya, and in the final analysis the expansionists proved stronger and more determined than those who opposed them, which meant that whatever Hull and Nomura might have to say to each other was virtually pointless.

The setting for their conversations might allow for give-and-take, but the situation did not. The secretary took care to point out that they were not negotiating, merely holding exploratory discussions, but whatever one chose to call them, it was clear that from the U.S. point of view, they had a dual purpose. One was to implement the national policy of Europe first, while keeping the Japanese from moving too far, too fast in the Pacific, avoiding a crisis at all costs, to prevent them from crossing a line beyond which the Americans, the British, and the Dutch would have to employ military restraint, which those allies were not prepared to do. Caution meant time—time to build up military strength.

A broader goal was quite simply to keep the peace, to stop further Japanese encroachment on America's friends and allies in Asia and their sources of raw materials. Hull described his mission as "slowing Japan up . . . as much as we could by fighting a rear guard diplomatic action, without doing it so stringently as to drive her to get her supplies by making an attack on the Netherlands [East Indies]." It was a tricky tightrope act not to appease yet not to provoke, and Hull estimated his chances of success at no better than one in fifty or even one in a hundred, but he persisted stubbornly, driven by the nation's "imperative need [for] time to build up preparations for defense." Typically, he would ask Nomura if Japan expected the United States to sit idly by "while two or three nations [meaning Germany, Italy, and Japan] before our very eyes organized naval and military forces and went out and conquered the balance of the earth." At which the ambassador would bow and reply politely that his government was not bent on military conquest: as he had informed President Roosevelt at their first meeting, all Japan desired in China was "good will, economic cooperation, and defense against Communism"; but what troubled his country's leaders deeply was the pressure exerted on its economy by the discriminatory embargoes of American exports, notably oil and scrap iron. So the talks continued against the sweep of events half a world away, accomplishing nothing—a meaningless charade whose futility would one day be detailed in hundreds of printed pages.

The Hull-Nomura conversations came about as a result of the efforts of a couple of amateurs—two priests of the Catholic Foreign Mission Society at Maryknoll, New York, Bishop James Walsh and Father James Drought.

Early in November 1940 the two men paid a call on Lewis Strauss, an investment banker who advised the Maryknoll brethren, saying they planned to visit Japan, where they expected to meet with Foreign Minister Yosuke Matsuoka, in an effort to persuade him and others that Japan's present foreign policy would almost certainly lead to war with the United States. After hearing their story, Strauss wrote letters of introduction to some of his Japanese friends in the business community, and two months later the enterprising clergymen were home again, armed with messages of friendship from numerous business leaders and, more important, an unofficial document they had been led to believe came from Prince Fumimaro Konoye, the premier, addressed to President Roosevelt. While the letter was indeed from Konoye, the contents proved less important than the implicit message that the prime minister had substantial support within his cabinet for improved relations with Washington. Konoye himself, along with the emperor and the court, had never been enthusiastic about the Tripartite Pact, and it was now becoming clear that there was a rift between those who feared that the alliance would lead to war with the United States and those, led by the military and the foreign minister, to whose plans the German alliance was critical. When Hull and Roosevelt had a chance to digest the tidings brought by Walsh and Drought, they decided to do nothing until they heard from the newly appointed Japanese ambassador, Admiral Kichisaburo Nomura, who was due to arrive shortly.

Tokyo's emissary to Washington was a stolid, humorless man of great integrity. Sixty-three years old, he was unusually large for a Japanese (a six-footer who weighed two hundred pounds), and, except for a stint as foreign minister, this was to be his first real experience as a diplomat. He was a career man in the navy, and had had a tour as naval attaché in Washington during the First World War, when he made the acquaintance of Under Secretary of the Navy Franklin Roosevelt and many U.S. officers, who remembered him fondly as a man of goodwill and a friend to America. Since that time he had lost his right eye in Shanghai in 1932, when a Korean patriot tossed a bomb into the grandstand where he was sitting, and it was said that he brought five glass eyes with him when he was prevailed upon to come to Washington as ambassador. Nomura had not wanted or welcomed the assignment, but had been urged to take it by fellow naval officers who thought he might succeed in averting a breach in relations and a war they were not sanguine about winning. "I am old man. I am enjoy my retire life in Japan," *Time* quoted him as saying, but duty called and he perceived his role as "a fire extinguisher" to put out the flames that threatened to envelop the two countries. In February he arrived on his crucial diplomatic mission.

Unhappily for all concerned, Nomura had difficulty conversing with the secretary of state (as Hull put it, "He spoke a certain—sometimes an uncertain—amount of English") and covered up his lack of understanding with a good deal of mirthless chuckling and bowing. Nor was Hull the only source of his confusion: he did not always comprehend or agree with the instructions he received from Tokyo, and his tendency to improvise was exasperating to the Foreign Office and, in the long run, detrimental to the negotiations.

Hull and Nomura were both men of goodwill, each with his faults, to be sure, but genuinely interested in avoiding war. Indeed, as Nomura remarked to Yuzuru Sanematsu, the naval attaché in the embassy, who was a longtime friend, "If I didn't think there was a chance of a settlement, I would not have come to Washington." The reason their discussions went exactly nowhere was not their own doing: they were cast in the role of public performers, while behind the scenes forces were at work that were all but unstoppable by the best of intentions.

Hull was patient, precise, as old-fashioned as his pince-nez with the black ribbon, an unbending man of conviction who refused to budge from his position. That stance, stated as concisely as possible, was that the war in China must be settled peacefully, with "mutual respect of sovereignties and territories"; the neutrality of the Philippines must be guaranteed; Southeast Asia must be politically stabilized; and economic activities and trade relations between the United States and Japan must be settled amicably.

Nomura, for all his desire to prevent a break between the two nations, was a cat's-paw, caught in the middle of a struggle between the army's extremists in Japan, on the one hand, and the moderates, on the other, and as if that were not enough to torpedo his mission, his efforts, unbeknownst to him, were being compromised daily by the Americans, who had broken Japan's diplomatic code and knew—often before Nomura did—the exact nature of his instructions from Tokyo.

———

Since the autumn of 1940, U.S. intelligence had been reading these diplomatic messages—not only the communications between Tokyo and Washington, but those between the Japanese government and its embassies all over the world, notably those in Berlin and Rome. It was an unparalleled asset for a nation to possess. Since the Foreign Ministry did not always level with Nomura, and since the military—not the Foreign Office—was really in the saddle, the messages did not always reveal Tokyo's intentions fully or accurately, but they certainly gave Washington an incalculable advantage, not unlike that enjoyed by the British because of Ultra. Curiously, the American Magic—as the general system of decrypting the top Japanese diplomatic, or Purple, code was called, shared a common ancestry with Ultra. In 1923, General Marlborough Churchill, who was then chief of U.S. Army intelligence, heard from the American military attaché in Berlin that he had witnessed a demonstration of a remarkable coding machine by its inventor, who was trying to peddle it to a number of governments. According to the prospectus, the device—which was to become known as Enigma—was capable of producing 22 billion different cipher combinations. Whether or not that was accurate, anything remotely comparable was heady stuff to anyone interested in encoding secret messages, but U.S. Army intelligence did not even take a further look, since it had no funds with which to buy. Three years later an article about the machine appeared in a German journal; the inventor had reassigned his patents to a Ukrainian engineer named von Kryha, General Churchill was again alerted, and arrangements were made for a representative of the Kryha Coding Machine Company to demonstrate the device to a U.S. cryptanalyst.

The man who met Kryha's salesman in New York in 1926 was William F. Friedman, one of the world's foremost authorities in this arcane field. Russian-born, he was brought to the United States as an infant, and the family settled in Pittsburgh, where he attended Central High School before going on to the Michigan Agricultural College and Cornell, to become a geneticist. His work in that field was noted by a wealthy textile merchant, George Fabyan, who had established a center on a five-hundred-acre estate in Geneva, Illinois, to pursue his interests in cryptology, in genetics, and in proving that Francis Bacon wrote Shakespeare's plays. At the Fabyan Laboratory, which was taken over by the government during World War I as a training school in military cryptography, Friedman met his wife-to-be, Elizebeth Smith, who was busy breaking enemy codes, and after the war they both went to work in Washington—she as a cryptanalyst for the army and then for the navy, he devising cryptosystems for the army before being appointed chief cryptanalyst for the Signal Corps.[1]

Presumably Friedman liked what the man from Kryha showed him, because the Signal Corps placed an order for the Enigma machine in February 1927, yet such was military penury in those days that it was not delivered for more than a year, because no money was available to pay shipping and import costs. Another obstacle proved to be the State Department: in 1929 that agency withdrew its support for the work in which Friedman and his colleagues were engaged because the then secretary, Henry L. Stimson, opposed it on principle. "Gentlemen," he is reported to have said, "do not read each other's mail." Fortunately, Friedman—who was now chief of the Signals Intelligence Service—and his staff of three junior cryptanalysts and two clerks survived the cut in funds, and by 1934 he had come a long way toward unraveling the secrets of the Kryha Enigma machine. When, toward the end of the decade, he discovered that the Japanese had purchased a much more recent model, he decided to focus his attention on their, rather than the German, cryptosystem. Happily for the United States, this brilliant, determined man, after a year and a half of superhuman effort which

---

[1]Between the wars, both Friedmans were called to other duties: she to break codes used by rumrunners during Prohibition and to crack a cipher employed by Chinese opium smugglers; he to testify before Congress about coded messages that came to light in the Teapot Dome scandal. William Friedman published a book about his craft, *Elements of Cryptanalysis,* and years later he and his wife collaborated on a work disputing the thesis of their patron, George Fabyan, that Bacon was the real author of the Shakespeare plays and sonnets.

cost him a nervous breakdown, persistent depression, and physical pain, had completely deciphered the text of a Japanese message for the first time in August 1940.

By 1941 the army and navy each had Magic machines for decrypting the Purple code in Washington; and there was a machine in Cavite in the Philippines, and with the British in London. Hawaii did not have one. The navy had a number of interception stations in this country, the Philippines, and elsewhere in the Pacific; the army had seven. In the Navy Department a staff of about three hundred under Commander Laurence Safford were handling Magic; they received the intercepts, deciphered them, and then turned them over to Lieutenant Commander Alwin Kramer's translation group—one officer, two yeomen, and six translators, three of whom were still in training. Kramer himself was fluent in Japanese, but a lot of his time was occupied evaluating the messages (many of which were routine or of no particular significance) and, after checking with his boss, Commander Arthur McCollum, distributing them to the navy's approved recipients— Secretary Knox, Stark, the chief of the War Plans Division, and the director of naval intelligence. A similar arrangement existed in the army, where the Signals Intelligence Service under Colonel Otis Sadtler and his assistant Lieutenant Colonel Rex Minckler decoded messages and turned them over to Colonel Rufus Bratton for translation and evaluation. Like Kramer, Bratton had lived and studied in Japan and was skilled in the language, and he too was responsible for getting the material to Secretary Stimson (who by 1941 was only too happy to be reading someone else's mail), Marshall, and the director of military intelligence. The only others on the distribution list were Secretary of State Hull and the president's military aide, who delivered the messages to Mr. Roosevelt. When the translated intercepts were ready, they were put in folders, and these in turn were placed inside locked pouches. Each pouch was carried by special messenger (usually Kramer or Bratton) to the recipient, who opened it with his key, signed for the contents, and frequently read them while the messenger waited, after which the messenger took them back to his office and destroyed them— retaining only the master copy for the file.

The American cryptanalysts' successes were achieved in the face of formidable obstacles. Just to obtain the intercepted message in a timely manner was difficult enough. A radio operator received it and sent it by airmail, train, or ship to Washington (the Pan American clippers left Honolulu once a week in good weather; in foul weather the message was routed by ship, and might not reach the mainland for two weeks). Then the key to the encoded message had to be found, based on the amount of radio traffic that was going on in that key, before it could be deciphered by one of the Magic machines. After that, it must be translated, and because of the shortage of expert translators, the army and navy had to divide the job between them— the army handling traffic that arrived on even days of the month, the navy taking odd days. Expertise was needed because Japanese is so difficult to translate into English; but messages also consisted of groups of phonetic syllables, some of which had several different meanings, and it took a good man like Kramer or Bratton to sense the correct nuance, the right shade of meaning that fit the context of the diplomatic dialogue. Understandably, the understaffed, hideously overworked communications people were under the worst kind of pressure as the negotiations continued, yet by some miracle they managed to turn many of the messages around and put them into a smooth translation within twenty-four hours of when they were intercepted—sometimes on the very day. Some took longer, of course, but it must be remembered that by November of 1941 the navy was receiving an average of twenty-six Magic messages a day.

It can be argued—and has been, for years—that the stringent limitation on the number of people entitled to see these Magic translations severely handicapped certain officers in sensitive, vulnerable positions, who should have had access to the material, and indeed, the obsession for security, which seems to have started with General Marshall, and which kept certain commanders in the dark, was to cost America dearly in December of 1941. Against this, the argument against their receiving them was the imperative need to keep secret the fact that we had broken the Japanese code. The British had the identical problem with Ultra, and their decision was essentially the same, for the value of Magic and Ultra lay in the enemy's ignorance that his code had been penetrated, so he would continue to use it for messages, while the Americans and British profited accordingly. On the debit side, in the case of the British it meant that Coventry received no warning; in our case, it meant that Ambassador Grew in Tokyo was often in the dark, and that Admiral Kimmel and General Short in Hawaii did not receive a good deal of information they clearly should have had.

Worse, it was discovered during the congressional hearings on the Pearl Harbor attack that Washington *thought* those with a need to know were receiving the information. Admiral Stark, for instance, believed that Admiral Kimmel was reading certain key messages from the Japanese when in fact he was not. And although others in Washington knew that Kimmel was not privy to the information, and naturally assumed that Stark also knew, the chief of naval operations was going on the assumption that the man in charge at Pearl Harbor had the facts he needed at his disposal. Worse yet, army officials in Washington believed that the navy people in Honolulu not only had access to this privileged information but were sharing it with the appropriate army officers in Hawaii. Wrong again. Nothing sent from the Navy Department in Washington to the navy in Hawaii was ever passed on to the army there unless the message explicitly ordered it to be done. And such explicit instructions were almost uniformly lacking. As the war would demonstrate to British and Americans alike, it was essential to get the information from Ultra or Magic to the commander in the field, so he could make use of it in fighting and winning battles, but at this point the United States was not in the war and the lesson remained to be learned.

The difficulty of communicating was hardly unique to Admiral Nomura, yet at the core of the matter was the complete intransigence of the two governments he and Hull represented. Neither Japan nor the United States had the least intention of yielding on certain issues, even at the risk of war with the other. More important than anything else, the Japanese had invested four years of blood and treasure in what they always called the "China incident," and would under no circumstances entertain the idea of pulling out, as Messrs. Roosevelt and Hull kept righteously urging them to do. What the Japanese people knew about the war in China was what their government decided they should know, but certain information was impossible to control or conceal. In the late thirties the public began to feel the pinch in terms of creature comforts: rice was rationed, then clothing, and other items were increasingly difficult to obtain. But these were incidental to the human cost of the war. There was a tradition of sending boys off with a celebration when they went into the army, which made each neighborhood keenly aware of how many of its own were being called up. And while the great victories were celebrated with parades (no defeats were announced), everyone knew that white boxes by the hundreds, boxes containing human ashes, were delivered regularly by special railway car to the interior, to the peasant families whose sons would not be coming home. The message was driven home on October 19, 1938, when Emperor Hirohito arrived at Yasukuni, a Shinto shrine not far from the War Ministry, for a ceremony enshrining more than ten thousand men lost thus far in China. The next day the *Japan Times*—the English-language mouthpiece of the army—commented editorially on what the thousands of bereaved widows and parents and children of the slain had felt the evening before, as the solemn rites were conducted in complete silence in the dark shrine. The dead, it said, "become deities to guard the Empire. They are no longer human. They have become pillars of the Empire . . . they retain no rank nor other distinction. Generals and privates are alike [and] are worshiped by the Emperor and the entire population." That mystic aura was not something to be cast aside lightly because the president of the United States thought Japan should get out of China, and to suppose that the Japanese would do so, or to decide that the Japanese question had to turn on the Chinese question, was a profound miscalculation by the Roosevelt administration.

Understandably, the press made much of America's racially exclusionary immigration policies, which were so insulting to the Japanese; nor did newspapers let readers forget that the U.S. presence in the Orient made it a party to the long history of Europe's exploitation of Asian countries—another instance of white discrimination. Rightly or wrongly, the Japanese had convinced themselves that U.S., British, and Dutch racists and imperialists were encircling them militarily and strangling them economically;

that Japan was being cut off from the precious raw materials essential to settle the China incident; and among the army leaders, in particular, a kind of panic had set in, a panic that could only be laid to rest by gaining access to those sources of absolutely vital supplies.

From all sides and from within, pressure was building on Japan in 1941. Worst of all were the extraordinary demands of war on its resources. The government was badgered insistently by Berlin to divert the attention of the United States from the Atlantic. The moderates in Tokyo, meanwhile, were being pushed by the military to reach a diplomatic accommodation with the United States before that moment in the rapidly approaching future when war would be the only answer left to Japan. So on the one hand you had these forces driving Nomura to bring the discussions to a successful and rapid conclusion, and on the other, the intractable Hull, cautious by nature, stalling for time to allow the U.S. military buildup to proceed as long as possible. And Hull, of course, was under pressures of his own from the president and the military to hold out, with the British urging him to take a firmer line in the talks—to yield not an inch to the Japanese. In the United States, most of the responsible press concurred with the tough line, and the public, seeing only the American side of the matter and not knowing that the administration's policy called for delay, was increasingly angry over what appeared to be Japanese obstructionism. And while the diplomats talked and talked, the pot was coming to a boil.

During the months of American preoccupation with the European war, the troubles in the Far East resembled a bad toothache, always there, a painful, nagging ailment that would not go away, no matter how anyone wished it gone. In point of fact, those troubles that insinuated themselves so demandingly on the Roosevelt administration were nothing new: the forces that finally made war in the Pacific inevitable had been festering for generations, and the dilemma that became acute by 1941 was a residue of centuries of white imperialism in Asia,[2] aggravated by Japan's nationalist ambitions, in which the character of the Japanese people was no small factor.

While the Japanese looked outward, beyond the mists and treacherous seas that separated them from the mainland's coveted space, a perceptive, reflective European was peering just as intently at them, seeking to discover the secrets of a land and a people that had attracted him since childhood, when he had first seen the prints of Harunobu and Hokusai. His name was Kurt Singer, and he was a German in his mid-forties who had arrived in Japan in 1931 to teach and to learn. He was a scholar—an economist, one

[2]As John Toland has written, the war the United States finally had to wage in Asia "was not only a struggle against an aggressive nation fighting for survival as a modern power but an ideological contest against an entire continent. Millions of Orientals saw Japan's battle as their own, as a confrontation of race and color; they also saw in Japan's victories their own liberation from Western domination."

man said, with the soul of a poet—and fortunately for his wish to know the Japanese, he was physically tiny, fitting unobtrusively, unlike most western-ers, into Japanese society. Traveling, teaching, reading, and musing in that milieu for nearly nine years (until the institutions at which he taught, pressured by the Nazi Teachers' Association in Japan, refused to renew his contract because he was a Jew), he distilled the experiences of those critical years into a book whose title employed three objects representing what he called the geometry of Japanese life. Handed down from ruler to ruler as tokens of authority, these were symbols of virtues the nation was expected to cultivate: the mirror, which enables one to see things as they are, good or bad; the sword, firm, sharp, and decisive; and the jewel, signifying gentleness and piety.

Singer came to understand that the unpredictability of nature in the Japanese archipelago, coupled with the possibilities of awesome earth-quakes, floods, and tidal waves, had taught the inhabitants to accept and deal with catastrophe as a condition of life. The Japanese became "mon-soon-minded," as it were, able to switch back and forth between extremes of violence and silent, patient obedience, in the way that their favored poetry is "a single exclamation, cry, image, question . . . surrounded by a sea of silence." He detected another quality in these people that he believed central to their aggressiveness—a peculiar sensitivity to "the smell of decay, however well screened," which prompted them to strike at an enemy who betrayed a lack of firmness. It had led them into conflict with the Russians and Chinese, toward both of whom the Japanese attitude was one of con-tempt—contempt for a lack of strength and moral fiber.

Nothing perplexed Kurt Singer more than the Japanese joy in self-aban-donment, the desire to disappear or to die, in battle or by their own hand, so as to return to "that maternal realm from which the individual emerges only to perish." He compared it to the famous *haiku* of the frog jumping into the temple pond with a single splashing sound, or the words of an eighth-century priest, who likened life to the white wake behind a boat that has rowed away at dawn. The episode of the three human bombs—the Japanese soldiers who deliberately blew themselves up with a land mine to penetrate the defensive line outside Shanghai in 1931—was incomprehensi-ble to the average American and entirely understandable to the average Japanese.

If the Japanese way of thinking was totally alien to the westerner, defying his whole sense of logic, the Japanese national character nevertheless had made the country the only Asian power with the vigor and determination to resist western imperialism. And of more importance to the direction history was to take in 1941, that character allowed it to contemplate warring simultaneously with China, the nations of the British Commonwealth, and the United States in a conflict that must be fought across the vast wastes of the Pacific Ocean, and against odds that could only be described as fantastic. In contrast to Germany, which began the war well prepared to win it, Japan in 1941 lacked the industrial plant and organization, the resources, and—despite years of preparation—the armed might required for an undertaking of such magnitude. Experienced though the army was, it was insufficiently mechanized and tactically unsophisticated; and as powerful as the navy was, it was not up to the demands of a sea war on a scale encompassing a third or more of the globe. Finally, it was also that Japanese character which made it just about impossible for Cordell Hull and other American negotiators to understand the men who were literally or figuratively across the table from them. Because of their passion to lead a life unseen by others, the Japanese erect what Singer called a wall of inscrutability and silence, and their language is admirably suited to this purpose, for it abounds in ambiguities, avoids precision, and is as often a device for withholding as for stating. (As the westerner who tries unsuccessfully to convey directions to a Tokyo taxi driver discovers, often the spoken word cannot be understood unless its ideogram is known, and stranger yet, the ideogram often cannot be correctly pronounced.)

As far as the outside world was concerned, the first significant manifestation of Japan's territorial ambitions came in 1931, with the takeover of Manchuria, and within a decade not the slightest doubt remained that war between the United States and Japan would come. The question was when, and a cardinal principle of the Roosevelt administration's policy was to put off that date as long as possible. There was no little irony in the fact that an American naval officer, Commodore Matthew Perry, had sailed into Tokyo Bay in 1853 and simultaneously opened Japan to the world and the eyes of Japan to the wonders of the industrial revolution. Feudal Japan took to modern times with a vengeance, in the process becoming an important industrial power that showered immense wealth and political influence on the great family monopolies—eight of which eventually controlled more than half of all Japanese trade and industry. Meanwhile the sons and grandsons of Japan's military aristocracy were building powerful forces that astonished the great powers by seizing much of Korea from China, demolishing the Russian czar's navy, and—with control of Port Arthur, Dairen, and the railroads constructed by Russia—moving into southern Manchuria, that primitive, bandit-infested land. In the eyes of many Japanese officers in the Kwantung Army, Manchuria was the equivalent of America's frontier—not exactly a land of milk and honey, but an acceptable solution to the accelerating problems of overcrowding and poverty in the home islands, a source of raw materials and food, a market for manufactured goods, and, above all, a buffer against the Russian enemy. Until 1931, what prevented the army from realizing this bold dream was the opposition of the government, most notably of the imperial court, which perceived the idea as naked aggression, since the coveted territory was nominally the property of China, under the loose control of a warlord named Chang Tso-lin.

Traditionally (and by law after 1936), the military exercised a profound influence on the governance of Japan. Thanks to a tangled web of controls, no man could become prime minister without the approval of the armed forces, and while in office, he toed the line or was out. Since it was a requirement that ministers of both army and navy be selected from the ranks of active senior officers, by refusing to name a minister, either service could prevent the formation of a cabinet that did not have its support. Conversely, by reassigning an incumbent minister to duty elsewhere, either branch of the armed forces could bring about the fall of a government. Another useful device available to the military was that if a premier had the audacity to name a minister of navy or war who was not acceptable, the service simply made him ineligible by removing his name from the active duty list. More significantly, the military high command was directly responsible to the emperor (who was the commander in chief) on matters of national defense, and direct access to the benevolent royal figure held in universal reverence as the father of them all naturally gave the chiefs of the armed forces a power not shared by any civilian. Through a mythical process too complex for western minds to follow, the empire was conceived as a large family, encouraging the idea that all Japanese were brothers and must look up to their ruler as a father.[3] Respect for the emperor was in one sense only skin-deep, however, for having been educated as a constitutional monarch and instructed not to interfere in the workings of government, he was a man whose opinion was neither sought nor valued. Isolated inside the palace grounds, insulated from his people, the man on the Chrysanthemum Throne was at the apex of what American journalist Frank Gibney described as a web of contracts and commitments binding the Japanese citizen "in all directions—upwards to parents, ancestors, higher authority, downwards to children, employees, and servants." Within the social contract, the noblest virtue was to observe loyally one's commitments, and as long as he remained within the web the Japanese knew peace; outside it, released from his tightly controlled society, he often reacted with cruelty and brutality.

The army was quick to recognize the value of encouraging emperor worship for its own use, and in doing so, brought an old Japanese custom up to date: again to quote Gibney, the idea was to "solidify power through the authority of the throne, but keep the emperor himself from wielding it."

---

[3]The extremes to which homage could be taken were often amusing. Agnes Niyekawa was attending school near where the emperor and his family stayed from time to time, and whenever the royal personages were due to arrive, their route from the railway station to their villa was covered with small pebbles, because they made such a pleasant sound when the carriage ran over them. When the royal family departed, the pebbles were swept up and collected for future use. Before the procession, Agnes and other students lined up and stood for long periods, waiting for the great moment; when the carriage approached, they made a deep bow and held it until the carriage was almost out of sight, with the result that they never saw the royal personages.

And by insulating the throne from civilian control, of course, the military ensured that they would be responsible to no one but themselves.

With deep roots in the conservative countryside, which furnished many of the younger officers after World War I, it was inevitable that the army should resist the new ideas sweeping Japan in the twenties—revolutionary ideas, it seemed, that threatened to alter the government, politics, the family, schools, the workplace, and social customs, infusing them with western notions. Japan was a nation that lived on trade, after all, and was highly vulnerable to economic conditions in other countries. So when the economic depression of the thirties settled like a pall over the islands, generating poverty and near starvation in many small towns and farming communities, increasing resentment among small farmers and laborers against the capitalists who controlled the government, it was just as inevitable that the middle-rank officers—often angry sons of poor farmers—should take matters into their own hands. Seeking an outlet for a population that was growing by one million a year, a source of raw materials, and a market for manufactured goods, officers of the Kwantung Army concocted an "incident" near Mukden in 1931, followed that with a full-scale conquest of Manchuria, and set up the puppet state of Manchukuo, to the dismay of their own government in Tokyo and the rest of the world. When the League of Nations tardily condemned Japanese aggression in Manchuria, Japan's delegate, Yosuke Matsuoka—from whom more would be heard later—stalked out of the assembly and his nation resigned from the League, the first major break in the shaky collective for peace that had been created at Versailles. (Within a few months Nazi Germany followed Japan.)

The thirties were years of plots and assassinations in Tokyo, and tensions between nationalist fanatics and moderates reached a climax in 1936, when officers of the 3rd Regiment of the Imperial Guards Division mutinied in an attempt to set up a military dictatorship. Three civilian leaders were assassinated, others barely escaped, but when the emperor and the navy stood fast against the rebels the insurrection collapsed, and its leaders were executed. Ironically, the rebellion succeeded after all: in the wake of the uprising, the army's hard-liners took over, purged the ranks of those who opposed them, and in short order took steps that clearly established Japan as a militaristic state. From 1937 on, the army ran the country pretty much as it pleased: the labor movement was crushed, the Communist Party was outlawed and its members went underground, big business was either compliant or discredited, and the politicians were kept on a short leash. National defense was the excuse given for a mobilization law passed in March 1938, which effectively put an end to civilian control of the government and placed the economy on a war footing.

As in other totalitarian states, the press was rigidly controlled. Publications could find themselves closed by the army, editors dismissed for violating regulations, the paper's supply of newsprint cut off, presses smashed by troops—all for failure to conform. Domei was the only wire service in the country; NHK, the Japanese Broadcasting Company, the only radio; and both were under the thumb of the army. Resentment of America was stirred up by press and radio, which repeatedly made the point that the United States was frustrating Japan's efforts to end the China incident, and with its embargoes was the chief obstacle to the nation's ambitions in South Asia. Foreign movies disappeared, the use of foreign words was discouraged, and in the schoolrooms children memorized the words in their first readers:

> *March on, march on,*
> *Soldiers, march on.*
> *The sun is red,*
> *The rising sun is red.*
> *The flag of the sun!*
> *Banzai! Banzai!*

Agnes Niyekawa was born in Tokyo in 1924, but she spent most of her first ten years abroad, since her father was in the foreign service, and his job took the family to Seattle, Batavia, and Vienna, where they lived for six years. When they returned to Japan, Agnes spoke no Japanese, only German, because of which she was at first teased mercilessly by her classmates, and finally ignored. The message was clear: if you're Japanese, you stay in Japan and behave as a Japanese should; those who leave the country are no longer Japanese. (There was even a proverb appropriate to these "misfits"—"The nail that sticks out gets pounded in.") In her grade-school classroom, she remembered, much emphasis was placed on Japan's trading role, its dependence on raw materials from various parts of the world—the Dutch East Indies, in particular, for the rubber and oil it imported so that it could export finished goods. Much was made, too, of the Greater East Asia Co-Prosperity Sphere, of western domination of China, and of how the same thing must not happen to Japan.

═══

Not the least significant aspect of the 1936 trouble was the way it revealed the conflicting attitudes of the army and navy, forcing a solution that was to have profound effects on foreign policy. The rivalry between the two services went much deeper in Japan than in other countries and had its origin in feudal clans—one of which was located in a maritime community and took over the navy, while a rival seized the dominant position in the army. Where the army was ultraconservative and insular, slow to modernize, the navy was broad-gauged, innovative, and quite knowledgeable about the world. The navy, in other words, had been beyond the horizon and knew at first hand the strength and resources of the United States. But the navy was also deeply divided, between the "treaty group," which wanted peace with other nations, and the "squadron group," made up of young Turks who were moving into the positions of power.

When the army began lobbying for huge budget increases, ostensibly to protect Manchukuo from China, on the south, and from Russia, to the north,[4] the navy, not to be outdone in a contest for appropriations, advocated that Japan turn its attention southward—to the great treasure houses of French Indochina, the Netherlands East Indies, and Malaya, where resources vital to the nation lay. Any advance in that direction necessitated expansion of the navy, of course; and as for the risks, they existed both north and south. As one admiral summarized the probable consequences, the southern advance would mean opposition from the United States and Great Britain; the northern advance would bring collision with Russia. As it turned out, both services got their wish: the army and navy would *both* expand—the army to a level suitable to resist the Soviet Union's forces in the Far East, the navy "to secure command of the Western Pacific against the U.S. Navy." The resulting arms package translated into ten new divisions for the army, a large increase in planes and pilot training, two more battleships, seven new aircraft carriers, and a score of destroyers. It also meant a certain clash with China or Russia or one or more western powers.

In short order, the conquest of Manchuria was followed by an undeclared war with China, which in turn confronted the western powers with a direct challenge to their prestige, influence, and economic advantage in East Asia. Japan had maintained a military presence in Peking since 1900, when an expeditionary force of European, U.S., and Japanese troops put down the so-called Boxer Rebellion. In 1937 a minor squabble between Japanese and Chinese soldiers—which may have been accidental or may have been provoked by Communists—rapidly got out of hand, produced the so-called Marco Polo Bridge incident, and turned into full-scale warfare. Waves of Japanese planes bombed and strafed roads and towns, infantry and tanks moved on the rail centers in the northeast and fanned out toward the Yellow River, and Chiang Kai-shek, the Chinese Nationalist leader, drew a line in the sand, saying, "China's sovereign rights cannot be sacrificed, even at the expense of war, and once war has begun there is no looking back." As indeed there was not. A Japanese general, newly arrived on the scene to take command, proclaimed that he had been sent to "chastise the outrageous Chinese," and the military leaders in Tokyo confidently promised Emperor Hirohito that the war on the mainland would be over in a month. Imperial Army troops occupied Peking and marched on the great port of Shanghai, and with the beginning of total war with China, Japan took the first step toward an eventual conflict with the United States and Great Britain. The promised month dragged on, and four years later the war was no nearer to an end, while the drain on Japan's manpower and resources continued relentlessly.

[4] In armed border clashes in 1938 and 1939 that were all but ignored by the world's press, the Japanese were badly mauled by the Russians, suffering more than fifty thousand casualties largely because the enemy was highly mechanized (which the Japanese were not).

China may have been a strange and distant land, fought over by hordes of strange yellow people, but it was clear where America's sympathies lay in this conflict. There were several reasons for this curious affinity, no one of them an entirely satisfactory answer. The heritage of the lucrative and exotic China trade was one, as was the long association of so many Christian missionaries and, through them, their churches in the States. Chiang Kai-shek was known to be fighting communism, a stance always regarded positively in America, and his nation was perceived to be a friendly, wounded giant, long an innocent victim of European imperialism, struggling now for survival against Japanese aggressors who were not only in the wrong but were guilty of appalling atrocities. The godfatherly attitude toward China was in some respects the same idealized perception that had made missionary Pearl Buck's novel *The Good Earth* a best-seller; but important as American public opinion was to the Nationalist Chinese, more significant was the way it was reflected in the Roosevelt administration's foreign policy, which was emphatically pro-China, anti-Japanese. The difficulty here was that we had an attitude, but not a program: since 1937 we had managed to give Chiang a mere $25 million in aid, and because we continued to permit the sale of petroleum and scrap iron to Japan, that nation's leaders got the misleading impression that we would acquiesce in their present and future expansion in the Far East.

The hostilities in China had a peculiarly faceless quality to Americans, not only because they were so remote from the United States and were fought by soldiers who chanced to have yellow skins, but because the reports of fighting between Japanese and Chinese, between factions of the Kuomintang (Chiang Kai-shek's Nationalists), Communists, and warlords, were too confusing for the average man or woman in this country to absorb. But America's compassion was aroused as city after city fell to the Japanese—Peking, Tientsin, Soochow, Shanghai, one more brutally than another, with the unparalleled butchery climaxing in December 1937 in the rape of Nanking, where unarmed civilians were "hunted like rabbits," beaten, bayoneted, and burned alive, where some twenty thousand men were marched out of town and massacred, where a like number of women were raped and murdered, where a quarter million people were slaughtered.[5] The horrifying spectacle lent meaning to the Japanese proverb "A man away from home has no neighbors," and the only sign that could be considered remotely encouraging in this grim picture was that Japan appeared to be conquering territory, but not the Chinese people.

If China was something of an enigma, Japan was positively unfathomable to the westerner—the very model of the Mysterious East. In the decade from 1930 through 1939 an average of only 7,300 American tourists a year

---

[5]During the sack of the city the U.S. gunboat *Panay*, anchored up the Yangtze River from the Nationalist capital as a symbolic protector of U.S. lives and property, and clearly marked as an American vessel, was "accidentally" dive-bombed and sunk.

visited Japan, suggesting how few had any personal contact with that land, and whatever thought the uninformed American gave to the Japanese was a blend of amusement, fear, and scorn. During the nine decades since Commodore Perry's fleet of black-hulled ships appeared off Japan, that nation had achieved great power status without anyone in the western world quite understanding how, since few westerners made a real effort to comprehend the Japanese. The prevailing impression was of a people right out of Gilbert and Sullivan, only recently emerged from feudalism, reluctant to capitalize on the latest technology—especially military. Unlike the big, expansive Americans, they were small, secretive, and withdrawn; unlike the ingenious, inventive American producers of fine goods, they were imitative, unable to turn out anything but cheap, shoddy merchandise. They read and wrote backward; they sat on the floor to eat (and ate raw fish); they behaved with exaggerated politeness on one occasion and were unpardonably rude on the next. The stereotype was in fact a caricature—of a little man with buck teeth, slant eyes, and horn-rimmed glasses, bowing low while hissing, "So solly." There was more, of course, but unfortunately these half-truths and old wives' tales, these simplistic, deluded notions about the Japanese, were not limited to the public; they were too tragically common among American political and military leaders, whose general idea of a possible war in the Pacific was that it would be a completely one-sided affair between superior U.S., British, and Dutch forces on the one hand against inferior men and equipment on the other, and that it would be over in no time at all. Another item in this strange broth of misconceptions was that American isolationism never extended to the Pacific; in fact, some of the most outspoken advocates of America First favored a strong, big-stick policy in the Pacific, an attitude that brought a large segment of the public into line behind Roosevelt's dealings with the Japanese, even though he was reluctant to put matters to the test. Japan's sinking of the *Panay* was an outrage (though we were easily satisfied with an apology and payment of reparations); what stuck in the craw was her pretentions to naval equality with the United States and Britain. In 1934 the Japanese announced their intention of withdrawing from the 1922 Washington treaty limiting the construction of battleships and aircraft carriers, and when at the London Naval Conference in 1935 the Americans and British turned down their bid for parity, the Japanese walked out and promptly announced a plan to embark on a huge naval construction program.

What very few Americans took into account was that when the fifth decade of the twentieth century began, the Land of the Rising Sun was a dynamic nation of 74 million people crowded into an area less than half the size of California, whose leaders had a compelling sense that it must grow and expand, or degenerate into a second-rate power. And they had no intention whatever of permitting the alternative to occur.

The wonder was that responsible, supposedly well-informed men in Washington had actually persuaded themselves that the United States was in any shape militarily to deny the western Pacific to Japan. Even more incredible was the underestimation of the Japanese by President Roosevelt and some of his top advisers. One reason for this was the difficulty America's military people had in taking the Japanese army seriously when it appeared incapable of winning the war against a China that was all but unarmed. Another was that men like Stanley Hornbeck, head of the State Department's Far East desk, whose opinion in these matters counted heavily with Secretary Hull and President Roosevelt (though not with Admiral Richardson, who knew Hornbeck as the *bête noire* behind the movement of the Pacific Fleet to Hawaii), were convinced that the risk of war was not as great as Tokyo made it seem, that the Japs were bluffing. "We should keep all the time in mind one big, outstanding fact," Hornbeck declared, "that Japan is not prepared to fight a war with the United States."[6] Perhaps not, but it was unfortunate that the president did not listen more attentively to the ambassador in Tokyo, his old schoolmate Joseph Grew, who warned repeatedly of the tempo of Japan's advance through Asia, urging Washington to "keep our powder dry and be ready—for anything." Nor were the warnings of old China hands like Brigadier General Joseph Stillwell heeded. Vinegar Joe first went to China in 1920 and had had a tour most recently as military attaché to the U.S. embassy in Peking. If any man could tell Washington about the probability of war with Japan and the risks therein, it was he, but Stillwell could see that Washington's eyes were fixed on Europe, with no comprehension of how events in the Far East—particularly Japanese aggression—would affect the United States. Brashly, almost casually, the administration placed embargoes on exports critically needed by Japan without examining what the consequences might be, while Roosevelt's idea of a show of naval strength (the notion of having American ships "popping up here and there and keep the Japs guessing" that so dismayed Admiral Richardson) took no account whatever of the caliber of the Japanese fleet and its air arm. And month after month, following the president's lead, Cordell Hull went on delivering his withering lectures to Ambassador Nomura as if America's forces in the Pacific were in a position to back up his words.

In 1936, when General Douglas MacArthur retired as chief of staff to become the well-paid field marshal of the Philippine Commonwealth, he promised to prepare the islands' defenses so thoroughly that in ten years' time an invasion would cost the Japanese half a million casualties. But MacArthur and the Philippines were not to have ten years' time, and by 1940, the security of the islands was still in the hands of 7,500 U.S. troops, most of them Filipinos, scandalously ill equipped on the ground, possessing only a handful of obsolete aircraft, while MacArthur's Philippine army remained largely in the planning stage. The U.S. Asiatic Fleet, under the

---

[6]Hornbeck had been raised in China and had a built-in antipathy to the Japanese, along with his objections in principle to their expansion program.

command of Admiral Thomas Hart, had a cruiser, thirteen destroyers, seventeen submarines, and a number of small craft with which to defend the Philippines and assist the Dutch and British in the South China Sea. In reality, that made it little more than a scouting force, and for reinforcements it had to rely on Admiral Kimmel's Pacific Fleet in Hawaii—5,587 miles away. Yet, as *Time,* echoing the mood in Washington, put it, the U.S. Navy's "timbers shivered with pleasure at the prospect of action . . . in the Pacific." Indeed, to read that weekly news magazine, as millions of Americans did, was to see Japan the way Washington imagined it—a nation in a near-desperate fix, pushed by Hitler toward war with the Russians, driven by the needs of its own army and navy toward Southeast Asia, but lacking the resources or the strength to overcome the powerful forces, U.S., British, and Dutch, that stood in its path. It was all very logical, but it took no account whatever of the determination, strength, and resourcefulness of the Japanese.

CHAPTER 51

"We are a democracy and a peaceful people."

From 1937 on, determined Japanese expansionists hammered insistently at the need to join hands with Germany against the common enemy—Russia—and against the common barriers to territorial expansion—Great Britain and France. Another group, comprising the imperial court, the navy's "treaty" advocates, and important leaders in the business community, was as strongly opposed. The Nazi-Soviet Pact in 1939 briefly cooled the ardor of those favoring a German accommodation, but the incredible success of Hitler's war machine in western Europe in 1940 opened new vistas to the Japanese jingoes—vistas of opportunities ripe for the plucking in Indochina, the Netherlands East Indies, Thailand, Burma, and the Malay Peninsula. With the potential of resistance by France, Holland, and Britain all but nonexistent, the lure of alliance with Hitler was strong, since Germany was now the only European deterrent to Japan's ambitions and represented an insurance policy against attack by Russia.

In mid-July 1940 the army precipitated the fall of the moderate cabinet, which was succeeded by a government led by Prince Fumimaro Konoye. While most members of the new cabinet had been involved in the Manchuria adventure, three were of particular importance to the army. Distantly related to the emperor, the prime minister was close to the royal family, popular with the public, and a weak, irresolute man who could be easily swayed. (His indecisiveness was notorious: "He would not have made captain in the navy," said one officer scornfully.) General Hideki Tojo, the minister of war, was a bald fifty-five-year-old nicknamed "the Razor," who had served with the army in Manchuria and was known as a rigid disciplinarian and dedicated army loyalist. Foreign Minister Yosuke Matsuoka was described by a German diplomat as having the shy, bewildered look of a child who has lost his parents at a county fair, but was in fact the opposite of what that image suggests: he was an outspoken advocate of expansion, tirelessly energetic and strong-willed, with a mercurial, nimble mind and a ceaseless tongue, for which he was known as "Mr. 50,000 Words." (Matsuoka's reputation was such that the navy minister once observed, "The Foreign Minister is insane, isn't he?" And when it was suggested to old Prince Saionji, Japan's most honored elder statesman and a close adviser to Hirohito, that Matsuoka might be mad, Saionji replied, "It will improve him if he becomes insane.") For his agility in saying one thing and doing another, Cordell Hull observed that he was "as crooked as a basket of fishhooks."

It was this cabinet, prodded by the army, that determined an audacious new course for Japan at the end of July 1940. The public announcement on August 1 was couched in bland, unwarlike phrases: "Japan's foreign policy, which aims ultimately at the construction of a new order in Greater East Asia, will be directed, first of all, toward the complete settlement of the China affair, and to the advancement of the national fortune by taking a farsighted view of the drastic changes in the international situation and by formulating both constructive and flexible measures to meet these changes." Behind those politic lines was an imperialist dream that saw a docile China incorporated into the "new order" under Japan's leadership; a Japanese nation fully mobilized and allied with Germany and Italy in order to capitalize on its "farsighted view," and prepared to move south toward Indochina and beyond while Europe was preoccupied with its own war.

In the face of Japan's resolve, the United States had little with which to resist beyond protests, sanctions (at the outset, on aviation-quality gasoline and high-grade scrap iron), and the thin hope that the British and Chinese could survive. "This whole darn thing is hanging in the balance," Hull told Morgenthau in September 1940. "If the British go down, then the Japs will probably spread out over all the Pacific just like wild men. If the British hold on, why we'll be able to restrain [Japan] and put on additional impediments to them and a loan to China." In Tokyo, Ambassador Joseph Grew was close to despair: despite his efforts to improve relations between the two countries, he recognized that Japan had become "one of the predatory powers . . . unashamedly and frankly opportunist," threatening to usurp American and British interests in the Pacific.

When the Tripartite Pact between Germany, Italy, and Japan was signed in Berlin on September 27, 1940, by Ribbentrop, Ciano, and Japan's Ambassador Kurusu, Hull tried to put a good face on the matter by saying it merely confirmed what everyone already knew, but in fact it came as a surprise and a shock, and Hull admitted to Roosevelt that it might well force the United States into the war. Wendell Willkie was under no illusions as to its significance. "Let us not delude ourselves," he said. "Berlin, Tokyo, and Rome are linked by the dangerous dream of world conquest. . . . We must abandon the hope of peace." Churchill, fearing for Southeast Asia, naturally importuned Roosevelt to send part of the U.S. Fleet to Singapore, if only to show the flag, and while nothing came of this, Washington did announce that the Pacific Fleet would remain in Hawaii instead of returning to the mainland (to Admiral Richardson's dismay) and that more aircraft would be sent to the Philippines, while the Asiatic Fleet would be beefed up with additional submarines.

It was not much, but it was all that could be spared; as Roosevelt admitted to Harold Ickes, "I simply have not got enough navy to go round." Meanwhile the only insurance the United States could buy in the Far East was obtainable by sending aid to China, in hopes of enabling Chiang Kai-shek to hang on. In the fall of 1940, when the generalissimo requested five hundred aircraft, volunteer pilots to fly them, and a sizable loan, among other items, the best that could be done was to divert one hundred pursuit planes from the British to help defend the Burma Road. Some months later, responding to State Department pleas for increased aid to China, FDR signed an executive order (which was not made public) authorizing pilots and ground crews from the Army Air Corps to resign and join Colonel Claire Chennault's American Volunteer Group—later known as the Flying Tigers—as civilian employees of the Nationalist government.

February 1941 brought fears of a showdown, when rumors hit Washington and London that Japan was planning an offensive, probably against the Netherlands East Indies or even the Malay Peninsula, quite possibly aimed at Singapore and coordinated with a German attack on Britain. Later it proved that the Japanese had nothing so ambitious in mind then, but what stopped them from making any move at the time was a stiff warning by Britain and the appearance of one by the United States. In London, Foreign Secretary Anthony Eden called in the Japanese ambassador and gave him the message right between the eyes: Great Britain had no aggressive intentions whatever, but it was not going to remain idle while Japan determined the destiny of the Far East. Furthermore, if British territories were attacked, they would be defended vigorously. In Tokyo, Eugene Dooman, counselor of the American embassy, called on Chuichi Ohashi, the vice minister for foreign affairs, to let him know where matters stood. Dooman was the son of missionary parents; he had been born in Osaka, had spent more than two decades in Japan, and spoke the language fluently, so there was no chance whatever that Ohashi could fail to understand him. It would be absurd, Dooman pointed out, to suppose that the American people, at the very time they were supporting Britain in her war with Hitler, would countenance any break in communications between Britain and her dominions or colonies. So if Japan were to menace those lines of communication or otherwise prejudice their safety, "she would have to expect to come into conflict with the United States." Furthermore, while the United States sought no war with Japan, it was idle to assume that relations between Japan and the United States could be stabilized as long as Japan remained a partner of Germany and Italy and continued the war in China. When Mr. Ohashi, "greatly agitated and distrait," asked, "Do you mean to say that if Japan were to attack Singapore there would be war with the United States?" Mr. Dooman quietly replied in impeccable diplomatic style, "The logic of the situation would inevitably raise that question."

The odd fact about this business was that Dooman was under no instructions from the State Department, although he clearly had Ambassador Grew's approval for the astonishingly tough line he took. Washington was waffling, taking "moral steps" and recommending that U.S. nationals in China, Malaya, and the Philippines leave the Far East, while the president called in Ambassador Nomura for a serious talk and suggested that any warlike incident could cause an "uprising of American sentiment," whatever that might mean.

—

Meanwhile, Moscow. The idea of negotiating a treaty between Germany, Italy, Japan, and their common enemy, Russia, seems to have been Ribbentrop's, but Yosuke Matsuoka had appropriated it as his own, and he was now a man with a vision and a mission. Spurred by a manic conviction that he possessed a formula for world peace, and armed with the grudging acquiescence of Japan's military leadership, he traveled to Berlin, where Hitler and his foreign minister Ribbentrop hinted vaguely at the possibility of German-Russian hostilities, urged that the Imperial Army attack Singapore, and pledged that Germany would stand beside Japan if such an attack should result in war with the United States. Matsuoka managed to avoid committing his country to military action in behalf of the Third Reich and left for Moscow, where on April 13 he signed a neutrality pact with an uncharacteristically joyful Stalin, who celebrated by giving him a bear hug. Returning in triumph to Tokyo, he found that he was less a hero with his peers than he felt he deserved to be (he had, after all, succeeded in neutralizing Russia while ensuring the support of Germany, which was no mean feat); but opposition to the Tripartite Pact remained strong, on grounds that it would lead to war with the United States, and those in favor of continued negotiations with Washington were still in the saddle—though just barely.

Throughout the summer, Nomura's talks continued, with Hull, with Hull's colleagues, and occasionally with President Roosevelt, plagued by delays, misunderstandings, and miscalculations, becoming ever more complicated and confused, with each side convinced at times that it had achieved a breakthrough, only to discover that the other was not talking about the same plan, that the position taken did not relate to the proposal on the table, or that their allies objected to the terms. The tale of misconceptions, double entendres, and faulty translations could have played as a farce had not the consequences been so tragic. Konoye and the moderates in Tokyo were anxious to continue negotiations in the hope of realizing certain objectives without resort to war; the army was increasingly skeptical of diplomatic success and itching for a final decision; while Matsuoka, a loose cannon in the middle of this uneasy truce, kept insisting on cooperation with the Axis allies and a move south even if that meant war with the United States.

What finally doomed the Washington talks was some sharp words spoken in Batavia, on the northwest coast of Java, where negotiations had been going on for months between the Dutch and a delegation from Tokyo. On June 10, 1941, the stubborn Dutch, who had little besides courage to back their stand, flatly rejected Japan's proposals to seize control of the Netherlands East Indies by including them in its Greater East Asia Co-Prosperity Sphere. The reaction in Tokyo was one of fury. The Japanese blamed the United States and Britain for this humiliating failure, the military seized the reins, and the decision was made to take over by diplomatic or military means the unoccupied portions of southern Indochina, from which the armed forces could flank British-held Singapore and move against the East Indies when all was ready. Meanwhile, everything would await certain developments in Europe, for the Japanese ambassador in Berlin had informed Tokyo that a German attack on the USSR was likely. Like just about everyone else, the government had heard rumors of impending trouble, but concluded that the signs of war in eastern Europe were camouflage for the long-expected invasion of England.

As the Nazi-Soviet Pact set off World War II, so the shattering of that cynical agreement led directly to active U.S. involvement. When news of Hitler's invasion of Russia reached Tokyo, Matsuoka was all for scrapping the neutrality agreement he had negotiated in the Kremlin only two months earlier and urged an assault on Soviet forces in Siberia. But the emperor was opposed, and so was General Tojo, knowing that the Imperial Army was no match for the Russians in men, tanks, and aircraft—and besides, it was felt, Germany would soon be victorious without Japan's intervention. So the decision to move south was made for Japan: a conjunction of circumstances made it irresistible.

The policy lines were set by a liaison conference on June 30, and on July 2, at a meeting of the Privy Council in the imperial presence, the die was cast.[1] Operations against Russia would be deferred, temporarily at

---

[1]Liaison conferences—informal, freewheeling exchanges between the prime minister, foreign minister, war and navy ministers, and chiefs of staff of the military services—were usually held at the prime minister's official residence. Their purpose was to coordinate military and governmental activities, and occasionally other cabinet ministers or authorities sat in when outside expertise was needed. Decisions reached at a liaison conference were formally (and automatically) approved at an imperial conference at the palace in the presence of the emperor, with

least,[2] but "in case the German-Soviet War should develop to our advantage, we will make use of our military strength [and] settle the Soviet question. . . ." Considering all the death and destruction that were to result from a very few words, it is remarkable that America's lot should have been relegated to the explanatory notes attached to the main decisions: "Various measures relating to French Indochina and Thailand will be taken," the notes read, "with the purpose of strengthening our advance into the southern regions. In carrying out the plans . . . our Empire will not be deterred by the possibility of being involved in a war with Great Britain and the United States."

During the weeks of tension and uncertainty leading up to this momentous acceptance of war with the United States and Britain, the foreign minister became *persona non grata* in his own country. The other members of Prince Konoye's cabinet deplored his outrageous behavior, his frequent indiscretions, his unwelcome advocacy of a Siberian campaign, and were incensed by his continuing unauthorized conversations with the German ambassador; so on July 16 the man who had led Japan out of the League of Nations and into the Tripartite Pact was cast aside. Konoye disposed of the matter neatly by having his entire cabinet resign on a day when Matsuoka was sick in bed. Two days later he formed a new cabinet with a new foreign minister, Admiral Teijiro Toyoda, who was known to be friendly toward the United States and Britain. The premier believed that the appointment of Toyoda would create a favorable reaction in Washington, but unfortunately for his hopes, the Americans knew through Magic intercepts that the Japanese were about to move against southern Indochina. One message had been unmistakably specific: "The cabinet shakeup was necessary to expedite matters in connection with national affairs and has no further significance. Japan's policy will not be changed and she will remain faithful to the principles of the Tripartite Pact."

Since France was in no position to resist Tokyo's bullying, it was unnecessary to employ force in southern Indochina: Japanese armed forces took over naval bases at Saigon and Camranh Bay and eight airfields, and on July 28 fifty thousand troops disembarked in Saigon in an action that directly menaced the Philippines, Malaya, the Netherlands East Indies, and China's tenuous lifeline to the outside world. (In an entirely unrelated but significant incident that could have produced the "uprising of American sentiment" about which President Roosevelt had warned Nomura, a Japanese plane

the president of the Privy Council in attendance to speak for His Majesty—who traditionally was silent throughout the proceedings. His only function was to affix his seal to the document recording the decision.

[2] From Richard Sorge, the head of their espionage network in Tokyo, the Russians learned of the Japanese decision and promptly withdrew some 200,000 troops and hundreds of tanks and planes from the Siberian to the western front. Even at that, the Russian Far East forces still outnumbered the Japanese, but the reinforcements arriving in the west were an important factor in stemming the German advance.

flew directly for the American embassy in Chungking and aimed a bomb at the U.S. gunboat *Tutuila* anchored nearby. The bomb missed by about eight yards, and although the ship suffered some damage, there were no casualties.)

Washington reacted immediately and firmly to the Indochina movement. American commanders in the Pacific were warned to take precautionary measures, and a press release announced the freezing of all Japanese assets in the United States; that was followed by an executive order requiring an export license before any goods could be shipped to Japan, a move hailed by the American public as an end to appeasement. An editorial in *PM* crowed, "For a time [Japan] may bluster and retaliate, but in the end it can only whimper and capitulate." In a Gallup poll taken early in September, 70 percent of the interviewees said the United States should "take steps to keep Japan from becoming more powerful even if this means risking a war."

For those who had worked unstintingly for peace it was a black day. Cordell Hull, sick as much from exhaustion as anything else, was recuperating at White Sulphur Springs, and the news that the Japanese had advanced into southern Indochina just when he thought relations might be taking a turn for the better was a bitter pill, but he was soon on the telephone to the State Department, casting about for some way to resolve the dilemma peacefully. Poor Nomura, seeing how strongly the American people backed harsh measures, seeing the situation slipping rapidly beyond his grasp, requested that a senior diplomat be sent from Tokyo to help him. "I deeply fear lest I should make a miscalculation at this moment," he cabled, "and, besides, there is a limit to my ability. . . . I am unable to perceive the delicate shades of the policy of the government, and am quite at a loss what to do."

In Tokyo, Foreign Minister Toyoda sent Joseph Grew a note saying that unless the United States modified its position, "Japan would be forced to take some countermeasures. . . . This would be much to be dreaded . . . for the maintenance of friendly relations between Japan and the United States and the peace of the Pacific." The recipient of that message, who had worked as hard for the peace of the Pacific as any man alive, was keenly aware that nine years of dedicated diplomacy might soon vanish without a trace, and sadly noted in his diary that the vicious circle of reprisals and counterreprisals had begun. "Unless radical surprises occur in the world," he continued, "it is difficult to see how the momentum of the down-grade movement can be arrested, or how far it will go. The obvious conclusion is eventual war."

Surprisingly, the warhawks and the moderates were still at odds in Tokyo, with the navy's chief of operations contending that Japan must abandon the Tripartite Pact to avoid "a most desperate war"; oil reserves on hand, he calculated, would supply no more than 75 percent of the navy's needs for two years of combat, and the nation's home-front consumption alone was running at 300,000 tons per month. The debate ended with a decision not to retreat from Indochina, but to revive the lagging discussions in Washington by urging President Roosevelt to meet with Premier Konoye.

By August the American attitude toward Japan had hardened perceptibly. Hull complained to Nomura at the way the Japanese government "constantly stimulated" the press against the United States; privately, the secretary had concluded from his study of intercepted cables that nothing would stop Japan now but force; as for further talks, he had decided that he would "not take for granted a single word they say," and just so Admiral Nomura knew exactly where things stood, he informed him that as long as Japan stuck to a policy of conquest by force, no room existed for negotiations. (Tokyo, it might be noted, was insisting just as stubbornly that its decisions were "irrevocable," and certainly no one in authority there was prepared to abandon the national goals that had been set.)

Stimson was elated by the secretary of state's change of heart; he too called it the end of appeasement, yet a measure of the army secretary's satisfaction seems to have arisen from a change in Washington's thinking regarding the Philippines. For two decades military planners had considered the islands indefensible; now, suddenly, they looked to be the key to Allied defense in the area. Douglas MacArthur had been recalled to active duty; the Philippine armed forces, inadequate though they were, were incorporated into United States service; and the War Department convinced itself that an adequate force of B-17 Flying Fortresses, operating out of the islands, could prevent the Japanese from moving large numbers of troops into the South China Sea. In this, as in everything else these days, time was everything: Stimson told Hull on October 6, 1941, that the army would need three months to put an effective military force into place.

———

In August, while President Roosevelt and Sumner Welles were off in the North Atlantic, conferring with the British, the secretaries of state, war, and navy had gathered for their weekly War Council in Washington, and Stimson summed up the discussion: ". . . Hull, with his analytical mind, is asking searching questions of the navy what they'll do next in case any of these issues that he has been handling brings up an impasse and the need for force." In other words, gentlemen, are we prepared to have someone call our bluff? For starters, what do we say if the Japanese move into Thailand and the British ask for help? What do we tell the Dutch if the threat comes in the East Indies? What if the Japanese try to prevent us from getting supplies to the Russians by way of Vladivostok? And what if the Germans move on Dakar—should we transfer more of the Pacific Fleet to the Atlantic?

If Navy Secretary Knox had ready answers to these searching questions, Stimson did not record them, and in the meantime Roosevelt had returned with another hot potato for Hull (who was still simmering over the president's choice of Welles to accompany him to the meeting with the British).

As the secretary of state soon learned, the Newfoundland conference was opening up a whole new set of problems in the Far East. Making good on his promise to Churchill to deliver a stiff warning to Japan, without which, the prime minister believed, "the prevention of war between Great Britain and Japan appeared to be hopeless," Roosevelt set Hull to work on a statement and, when it was ready, summoned Nomura to the White House on August 17. The president was in good humor after the historic meeting with the British, and his cordial welcome to the Japanese ambassador was in sharp contrast to the message he proceeded to read very carefully. It was a warning, all right—by no means as strong as the one Churchill himself advocated, that "any further encroachment in the Southwest Pacific would compel . . . countermeasures even if these should lead to war"—but, even in the watered-down version preferred by Hull, the meaning was unmistakable. The essence was that if the Japanese took any new steps to dominate neighboring countries by force or threat of force, America would immediately do whatever it considered necessary to safeguard "the legitimate rights and interests of the United States." Nomura got the message straight this time and advised Tokyo that the situation was grave: relations now "hang by a hair," he reported.

Ambassador Grew knew the Japanese as few Americans did and was deeply concerned lest "a national psychology of desperation develops into a determination to risk all." Fearing the same "monsoon-mindedness" Kurt Singer had described—the quick, unpredictable switch to violence—he warned Washington that the army might take "sudden and surprise action," and now that the chips were down he urged the president to agree to the meeting with Konoye as "an act of high statesmanship." Grew had met secretly with the premier and knew the man was in a desperate race with the military; his political future was on the line, and his only out was an agreement with the United States. Konoye was prepared to offer concessions, Grew assured Washington; furthermore, he had the emperor's support and, if he brought home an accord with the president, he could readily put down any opposition.

Here you had the ambassador on the scene taking the Japanese proposal at face value, urging his government to accept; halfway around the world, Hull—backed by Hornbeck, Stimson, and others who were privy to the Magic intercepts—believing it insincere and nothing but a ruse. And then there was Roosevelt, sorely tempted to grab at the offer, if only to find a temporary way around the present impasse. The problem the president faced, of course, which seems not to have troubled Grew, was that he actually stood to gain little or nothing by such a meeting. Under no circumstances would the military have permitted Konoye to make significant concessions. Conversely, if Roosevelt met with the Japanese premier and was lucky enough to prevail on most items on the agenda, which is what he would surely set out to do, Konoye's government was certain to fall even before he arrived in Tokyo. More important to Roosevelt, whether or not he had his way at the conference, the U.S. public and Congress would undoubtedly see any accommodation as another Munich, another unwelcome appeasement of aggression that was bound to fail. Beyond which, the two nations' positions had become so hardened and so little trust existed between them that any agreement was highly unlikely.

Even so, it was not in America's interests to push Japan to the wall, and Roosevelt was not trying to do that when he issued the executive order requiring an export license for shipment of goods to Japan. As he remarked to a group of visiting civilian defense workers, it was in America's interest to export oil to Japan to keep that country out of the Dutch East Indies. But in this he was at odds with his secretary of the interior and his secretary of the Treasury.

Morgenthau had been arguing for at least a year that it made no sense whatever to sell steel and scrap iron to Hitler's ally, Japan, at a time when the United States should be saving them for its own and Britain's needs. But the State Department persisted in allowing American business to supply Japan with up to 90 percent of her scrap and refused to place an embargo on these materials. The oil situation was worse, Morgenthau argued. Japan had to import 90 percent of its oil, and here we were, on the brink of war with that country, supplying more than half of those requirements! "The time to put pressure on Japan was before she went into Indochina and not after," the Treasury secretary observed. "Then maybe Japan would have stopped, looked, and listened."

Harold Ickes, whose cabinet position made him petroleum coordinator for national defense, was foursquare behind an oil embargo as the surest way to involve the United States in the war. After Hitler invaded Russia, he wrote the president, saying, "To embargo oil to Japan would be as popular a move in all parts of the country as you could make. There might develop from the embargoing . . . such a situation as would make it not only possible but easy to get into this war in an effective way." But Roosevelt was not about to buy that. Instead, Ickes complained, the president's idea was to slip a noose around Japan's neck and give it a jerk now and then. The interior secretary preferred to draw the noose tight and hold it there, and since he was no man to mince around on tiptoes, Ickes took it upon himself to forbid the shipment of oil to Japan without bothering to get presidential approval. The result was a first-class row with Roosevelt and an offer by a hurt, angry Ickes to resign, which the president turned aside by soft-soaping the secretary, telling him what "a grand job" he was doing. At the same time Roosevelt explained that the situation was extremely delicate, that "the Japs are having a real drag-down and knock-out fight among themselves," and cautioned Ickes against roiling the waters until it was clear how the fight turned out. It was during this exchange that he admitted that he had not enough navy to go around—and that "every little episode in the Pacific means fewer ships in the Atlantic."

Having rapped Ickes across the knuckles for taking action and then

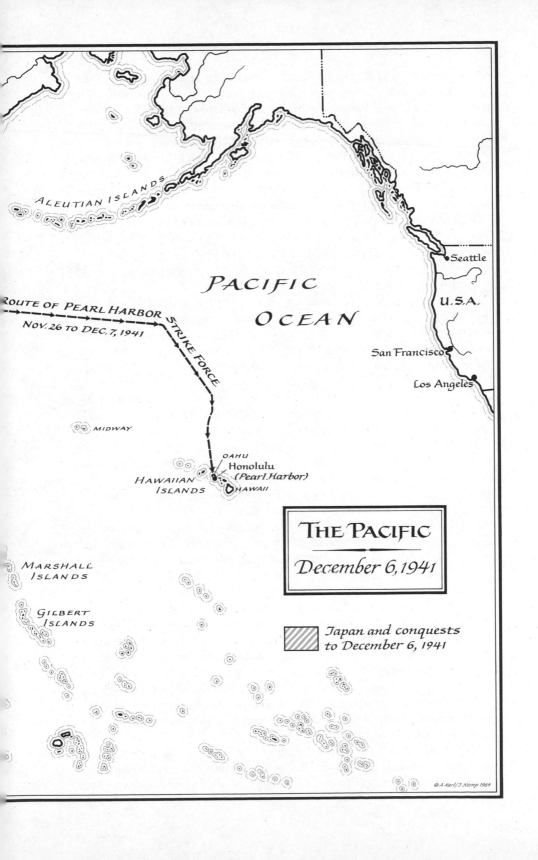

ALEUTIAN ISLANDS

PACIFIC

OCEAN

ROUTE OF PEARL HARBOR
NOV. 26 TO DEC. 7, 1941

STRIKE FORCE

Seattle

U.S.A.

San Francisco

Los Angeles

MIDWAY

OAHU
Honolulu
(Pearl Harbor)
HAWAIIAN
ISLANDS
HAWAII

MARSHALL
ISLANDS

GILBERT
ISLANDS

THE PACIFIC

December 6, 1941

Japan and conquests
to December 6, 1941

© A. Karl/J. Kemp 1989

patted him on the back, the president proceeded to make a hash of things by opting for ambiguity over precision. His idea was to keep petroleum policy loose, allowing himself flexibility, and to that end the White House announcement of the ruling on exports made no mention of oil. To Roosevelt, the meaning was all very clear, but to the subordinates who would carry out the order, and to the Japanese who would suffer the consequences, the impression was that all trade between the two countries—most particularly oil—was suspended. By failing to explain his intentions fully before he departed for the meeting with Churchill, the man in the White House unwittingly precipitated a crisis widely regarded as the event that led to war. (It can be argued, of course, that Japan's strike-south decision on July 2 persuaded FDR to take a tougher line, but certainly the embargo on oil made it plain to the Japanese that they were going to be defeated in their armchairs if they didn't make a move.)

Now, the Japanese were capable of doing without a lot of things, and could make adjustments or sacrifices to deal with shortages of certain materials, but the one commodity they simply had to have was oil—oil for industry and the armed forces. Forget their expansion plans: without oil, the long war in China must come to a humiliating end—an admission of defeat that was simply intolerable. So it is curious that the president, who understood that oil was absolutely vital to Japan, did not make it abundantly clear that his executive order should *not* shut off the flow. At any rate, he did not, and lacking guidance from Mr. Roosevelt, while he was at the Atlantic Conference, his subordinates took the action they assumed he wanted, thereby placing the Japanese in a position where they were all but forced to fight or abandon the dream of dominating East Asia. Although the president had perceived the executive order only as a means of applying leverage, it was applied so efficiently and effectively that no exports of any consequence reached Japan after August and no Japanese silk or other commodities were imported into the United States. Not until September did Mr. Roosevelt realize that a full embargo had been in effect, and by then he feared that a change in policy would be seen as a sign of weakness.

As the U.S. attitude stiffened during August, the Japanese army grew more insistent that negotiations must cease and preparations for war go forward. General Tojo was determined to have a final verdict by October 15: November, he reminded the cabinet, was the optimum time for landing operations; December was less satisfactory, though still within limits; January was impossible because of the monsoons. So, if the army was to move, the decision to do so must be made by mid-October at the latest, and the necessity to meet that target date produced a series of fateful conferences in the first week of September.

On the morning of the 5th, members of the liaison conference debated what was to be done if President Roosevelt did not respond affirmatively to the proposal for a meeting with Konoye, and after seven hours reached a conclusion, which read in part: "Our Empire, for the purpose of self-defense and self-preservation, will complete preparations for war, with the last ten days of October as a tentative deadline, resolved to go to war with the United States, Great Britain, and the Netherlands if necessary." Diplomatic efforts would go forward in the meantime, but should Japanese demands remain unmet by October 10, "we will immediately decide to commence hostilities against the United States, Britain, and the Netherlands."

When Prince Konoye showed a draft of this decision to Hirohito late in the afternoon, the emperor objected immediately: why, he asked, did preparations for war come first in the statement, and diplomatic negotiations second? He announced that he would discuss the matter with the chiefs of staff at the imperial conference the following day, but since that was an absolutely unprecedented step, Konoye suggested that His Majesty summon the two service chiefs to the palace that evening for an audience. When General Sugiyama and Admiral Nagano arrived, Hirohito repeated his concern that diplomatic efforts did not have priority, as they should; and reminded the officers that a policy setting a definite date for the commencement of hostilities could hardly be said to favor the prospects for peace.

During this exchange, the emperor turned to Sugiyama and asked how long a war with America would last, to which the general replied that operations in the South Pacific should be wound up in about three months. The emperor then reminded Sugiyama that when he was minister of war he had promised that the China incident would be over in one month and that it was now four years later and the war continued. Sugiyama in his embarrassment replied that the Chinese hinterland was very extensive. Indeed it was, the emperor responded, but compared to China, the Pacific Ocean was boundless. At that, the general hung his head, utterly at a loss for words.

Admiral Nagano stepped into the breach. Japan, he observed, could be compared to a patient suffering from a serious illness. If the doctors did not operate, the patient might suffer a long decline and ultimately die. On the other hand, an operation, though risky, might save the patient's life. He was certain that his colleague the general favored continued negotiations, but believed that in case of failure an operation would have to be performed.

At the end of this astonishing conversation, the emperor put a final question to the chastened officers and, by inference, to Konoye: did they favor giving precedence to diplomacy? Army, navy, and civilian leaders answered affirmatively, and the painful audience finally ended. It was an experience Admiral Nagano would not forget: "I have never seen the Emperor reprimand us in such a manner," he told a colleague, "his face turning red and raising his voice."

The following day, September 6, was miserable in Tokyo—dark clouds scudding across the sky, with rain driven on a cold wind out of the north. Inside the palace, the emperor's principal advisers assembled in the conference room knowing their duty was to make it official that Japan would go to war against the United States and Great Britain. The participants included the same men who had attended the previous day's liaison conference, plus the president of the Privy Council, Yoshimichi Hara, whose role was to represent His Majesty by asking questions the emperor might wish to ask, but did not. The emperor did nothing at these imperial conferences but listen—the fact of his presence making any decision binding—while the ordinary mortals, placed at right angles to him and opposite each other on both sides of long tables, sat rigidly with their hands on their knees, staring straight ahead, looking neither to right nor left during the proceedings, even when the time came for one of them to speak.

After hearing the members, one by one, present their views, which amounted to perfunctory endorsements of negotiations, followed by strong, unanimous recommendations that Japan prepare for war, Hara expressed his own and the emperor's concern that diplomacy was not being given adequate importance or weight, and requested the views of the military men. No one answered. Suddenly the silence was broken and the unthinkable occurred: the emperor's high-pitched voice demanded, "Why don't you speak?" The man who dared reply was the navy minister, Admiral Koshiro Oikawa, who stated that war preparations would begin, but that every effort would be made to negotiate. When nothing was heard from Sugiyama or Nagano, Hirohito spoke again, expressing regret that the supreme commanders had nothing to say. And at that he reached into a pocket, drew out a piece of paper, and proceeded to read a poem written by his grandfather, the Emperor Meiji:

> *That all the seas are brothers*
> *have I believed.*
> *Why stir waters in turbulence*
> *of enmity?*

He was accustomed to reread this poem often, he told his stunned listeners, to remind himself of the Emperor Meiji's dedication to peace. Later Konoye was to write, "Everyone was struck with awe, and there was silence throughout the hall." The military men were overcome, downcast with remorse, and elaborately apologetic for having caused the emperor displeasure, but essentially the decision had been made and everyone knew it. The conference approved the army's plan to "proceed with war preparations so that they can be completed approximately toward the end of October," at the same time the diplomats would attempt to achieve "Japan's minimum demands." Since those demands included the very items the United States had been rejecting since the talks began in March, the likelihood of acceptance was nil, war all but certain.

So Hull and Nomura continued talking as before, with each man increasingly pessimistic that diplomacy could save the situation in the Pacific. As Hull described those discouraging sessions, again and again he and the ambassador seemed "to come to a certain point and then start going around and around the same circle." Nomura was no less disheartened: sick of "this hypocritical existence, deceiving other people," he requested permission to return home.

Everywhere that autumn, the road to the future appeared to head downhill. On October 13 the new foreign minister, Shigenori Togo, cabled Nomura that the situation "is fast approaching a crisis," and three days later, with Prince Konoye's hopes for a meeting with President Roosevelt finally dashed, his government fell, after an obvious push from the military. He was replaced by the Razor—the tough, no-nonsense General Hideki Tojo—who was reported to be the only man capable of controlling the army. In Washington, Cordell Hull went on like a broken record as though nothing had happened, telling Nomura that until agreement on fundamental principles was reached, no particulars could be fruitfully discussed, while insisting that Japan pull out of China and Indochina and the Axis Pact. To Tokyo, that sounded like stonewalling, and every passing hour made the government more vehement in its demands for a speedy settlement. Word reached Washington of a statement by Japan's chief of naval intelligence that the fleet was "ready and itching for action," and Tojo was quoted as saying that the nation's policies were "immutable and irrevocable." Mid-October came and went, and while the Americans seemed intent on prolonging the negotiations, the Japanese had to make the final decision because of the drain on supplies and the waning weeks of good weather. To be patient any longer, Tojo warned his colleagues, "was tantamount to self-annihilation."

November brought a message from Winston Churchill to Franklin Roosevelt—an observation that the embargo appeared to be forcing Japan toward a decision for peace or war. If it should be the latter, the prime minister remarked, the British could take no independent action because of other commitments, but would stand behind the United States no matter what course it took. Japan, he speculated, "is more likely to drift into war than to plunge in." For Ambassador Grew, the clock was ticking louder and faster now: on November 3 he warned Washington that it would be dangerous to consider the Japanese preparations as mere sword-rattling; on the contrary, "action by Japan which might render unavoidable a conflict with the United States may come with dangerous and dramatic suddenness."

As indeed it might: on that same day, Admiral Osami Nagano, chief of naval operations, approved a plan for an ambitious operation on which Admiral Isoroku Yamamoto and a team of officers had been working since

January. The decision made clear, Churchill's contrary opinion not withstanding, that the Japanese had no intention of drifting into war. On November 5, at almost the same moment the British prime minister cabled Roosevelt, operational orders went out from Tokyo to military commands with the warning: "War with Netherlands, America, England inevitable; general operational preparations to be completed by early December." On November 7, the date for hostilities to begin was set for December 8, Tokyo time. That would be December 7 in the continental United States, and as far west as the international date line, beyond the Hawaiian Islands.

At last, Admiral Nomura was getting the help he wanted. A cable from the foreign ministry revealed that it would come, as he had hoped, in the person of his friend Saburo Kurusu, who would reach Washington in mid-November. Kurusu would explain to Nomura the exact situation in Tokyo, while assisting him to unravel "this bewildering maze," but the message contained a sinister note: "To make it sound good, we are telling the public that he is coming to help you quickly compose the unhappy relations between the two nations." Eager to keep the diplomatic waltz alive, the U.S. State Department arranged with Pan American Airways to delay the departure of its China Clipper from Hong Kong for two days so Kurusu could make the plane, and newspaper headlines in the United States traced the special envoy's progress across the Pacific to San Francisco, where he told the press in his best idiomatic American that he hoped to "break through the line and make a touchdown." Then he flew to Burbank to pick up a TWA flight to Chicago, New York, and finally to Washington, where he informed reporters he thought he had "a fighting chance" for success. On November 17, after a day's rest, he was presented to Hull and then to President Roosevelt.

Except for the unhappy fact that Hull and Sumner Welles took an instant dislike to him, Kurusu seemed a logical choice. As a young man he had been in the United States with the consular service and had met and married Alice Little of Chicago; he had friends here; he spoke fluent English. (With the benefit of hindsight, Welles wrote that those were the very assets that "would facilitate his mission of deceit"; Kurusu, he said, came to Washington "in the role of the goat tethered as bait for the tiger," and his "oily manner" and "naive protestations of sincerity and goodwill" were totally without conviction.) The catch was that even if Kurusu's mission had been completely without guile or subterfuge, no matter how skilled he was or how hard and sincerely he tried, from the time of the first working session he and Nomura had with Hull, they had been given exactly one week and a day in which to work out an agreement with the United States that would prevent a war. Tokyo had notified the two ambassadors that November 25 was the cutoff date for talking.

November 20—Thanksgiving Day—was no holiday for Cordell Hull. Nomura and Kurusu were ushered into his office and delivered what amounted to Japan's final offer. It was essentially a *modus vivendi*—a ninety-day truce calling for the United States to remove the freeze on exports and to supply the oil Japan required, while discontinuing aid to China. For its part, Japan would remove troops from southern Indochina (though not from the northern section of the country) and would "not . . . make armed advancement" into Southeast Asia or the South Pacific. The war in China would go on, obviously, and since no mention was made of Japan's abandoning its Axis partners, it had to be assumed that it would continue to be a member of the Tripartite Pact. All told, Secretary Hull observed, "The Japanese proposal of November 20 . . . was of so preposterous a character that no responsible American official could ever have dreamed of accepting it." That much was clear; far less so was what the United States could do next, for on November 22 an intercepted message from Tokyo revealed that the Japanese proposal was indeed a final ultimatum. Foreign Minister Togo extended the cutoff date for the negotiators from November 25 to the 29th, adding, "This time we mean it, that the deadline absolutely cannot be changed. After that, things are automatically going to happen."

If Cordell Hull thought that things were going hellward before, they were headed that way for certain now. Adolf Berle remarked, "We are getting close to ultimates." Until November 25 the secretary and his colleagues did their best to stave off the inevitable, even making their own last-ditch proposal for a ninety-day truce (which was vetoed by the British and Chinese). But Hull recognized that "the Japanese are in control of the whole situation, we are not . . ." and on the 25th, the last slim hopes for peace ebbed away. At a War Council that Tuesday, President Roosevelt raised the possibility that the Japanese might attack the following Monday; as Stimson reported his words, "the Japs are notorious for making an attack without warning, and the question was what we should do. The question was how we should maneuver them into the position of firing the first shot without allowing too much danger to ourselves." It must be remembered that Stimson was writing in his diary; even so, his words were ill-chosen. It was not that the administration *wanted* the Japanese to start shooting—everything that had been and was being done to prevent or delay that eventuality ran contrary to such an idea. The interesting point here is that the members of the War Council—Hull, Stimson, and Knox, meeting with Roosevelt— were certain beyond any reasonable doubt that the Japanese would strike at Thailand or Malaya, and should that occur, the question was how to arrange things so the United States could intervene without somehow seeming to be the aggressor or the instigator of hostilities. As these men knew better than most, a certain public sentiment existed for confronting Japan (perhaps in the air or on the sea; certainly not with American ground forces), but there was little enthusiasm for a war to defend Europe's imperial outposts in Southeast Asia. Later in the afternoon Stimson received a report that Japanese troop transports—some thirty to fifty ships, all told—

had been sighted moving south off Formosa, and the next day when he phoned to ask if the president had received the message, Roosevelt said he had not, and "fairly blew up—jumped into the air, so to speak," saying that this evidence of bad faith on the part of the Japanese, while they were negotiating for a truce, altered the situation completely.

Radiomen at the Navy Department were busy: on November 24 a message went off to Pacific commanders predicting an unfavorable outcome of the peace talks and suggesting the possibility of "a surprise aggressive movement in any direction including attack on Philippines or Guam." A measure of the importance attached to the signal was that addressees were instructed to "inform senior army officers their areas." Three days later a disgusted Hull described his lack of progress to Stimson, saying he was ready to wash his hands of the whole business and turn it over to the army and the navy. On the same day a message intended to put everyone on the alert was directed to the navy's Pacific commands: "This dispatch is to be considered a war warning. Negotiations with Japan . . . have ceased and aggressive move by Japan is expected within the next few days." Hostilities might take the form of an "amphibious expedition against either the Philippines, Thai or Kra peninsula or . . . Borneo."

In the interim—in the hours between the revelation that Japanese troop ships were heading south and the navy's war warning of November 27—Cordell Hull obtained President Roosevelt's approval and, without advising Stimson, Knox, or other friendly governments, submitted a new proposal to the two Japanese ambassadors. Known as the Ten-Point Plan, this astonishing document was essentially a restatement of America's toughest, most uncompromising demands on Japan—calling for abrogation of the Tripartite Pact, evacuation of their armed forces from China and Indochina, and abandonment of the Japanese puppet regime in Nanking. Since no one—least of all Hull—could have believed the Japanese would countenance anything like these terms, the only plausible explanation is that the secretary of state was again stalling for time, but the move threw Nomura and Kurusu into despair. They expressed themselves as "dumbfounded" when they studied the plan, and as they anticipated, Tojo read it at a liaison conference and pronounced it an ultimatum. What infuriated officials in Tokyo was their assumption (which happened to be incorrect) that Hull's demands that Japan quit China meant *all* of China—including Manchuria. Even moderate members of the government were stunned, believing the proposal demonstrated America's determination to go to war.

At the State Department, meanwhile, Stanley Hornbeck was advocating still more firmness. The Japanese, he predicted, might move into Siam or Yunnan, but he was betting five to one that the United States and Japan would not be at war by December 15, three to one against it by January 15, and even money that the two countries would not be at war by March 1. Sumner Welles, on the other hand, considered the odds against peace to be a thousand to one. By December 6 he raised them to a million to one.

On that Tuesday afternoon, when the prospects for peace looked so bleak in Washington, it was Wednesday morning, November 26, in the Kurile Islands. Dawn barely lightened the sky over Hitokappu Bay on the island of Etorofu, and visibility was just about nil because of the heavy cloud cover and swirling snow. The only indication that a fleet was getting under way was noise—the sounds of voices, running men, the rattle of anchor chains and the squeal of winches, the throb of engines as thirty ships came to life and weighed anchor. From the bridge of one ship to another, blinker lights flashed in the eerie half-light, as the huge gray shapes of battleships, cruisers, destroyers, submarines, tankers, and six aircraft carriers stood out to sea, bound for a destination three thousand miles and more to the east.

In Washington, everyone present at the War Council on Friday, November 28, had his eyes on the map. If those Japanese troop transports rounded Pointe de Camau, the southernmost tip of Indochina, and went on to land at Bangkok or farther west, on the Malay Peninsula, it would be the end of talking and the carefully calculated delays, and the beginning of something very different. Certainly if the Japanese reached the Isthmus of Kra, halfway down the peninsula, the British would have to fight, and so would the United States. It was agreed that before that took place, Japan must be warned of the consequences. The president would address a personal message to Emperor Hirohito,[3] reaffirming America's desire for peace and warning that war would surely result if Japan persisted with her present plans. At the same time, he would inform the American public of the imminent danger by means of a speech to Congress. That decision made, Hull, Stimson, and Knox were assigned to draft the two messages, and the president astonished them all by announcing that he was leaving for Warm Springs for a little vacation, but would return at once if they needed him.

It was the weekend of the Army-Navy football game, and Stimson and

[3] As a last-ditch effort to avoid war, a message to the emperor was doubtless an obvious idea, and in addition to those at the War Council, several other people seem to have had it at about the same time. On December 2, Bernard Baruch received a call from Raymond Moley, one of FDR's original brain trusters, urging him to see the American attorney who represented the Mitsui interests. The lawyer asked Baruch to help Kurusu get a message directly to President Roosevelt. Baruch talked to Pa Watson, and Watson conferred with Roosevelt, with the result that Baruch met Kurusu on December 3. Japan's special envoy said it was imperative that he see Roosevelt privately, that Hull was hostile and untrusting, and that the president must appeal directly to the emperor—going over the heads of the "warlords" in Tokyo who were "determined to shoot"—and offer to act as intermediary in the war between Japan and China. Without much confidence in the plan, Baruch dutifully delivered the message to Watson. Meanwhile, Kurusu seems also to have arranged for the message to reach Roosevelt by another route—through the second secretary at the embassy to a minister who was a friend of the president, who assured FDR that the suggestion truly came from Kurusu, who could not admit his role in it because of going outside channels and bypassing the government in Tokyo.

Knox headed to Philadelphia to see it, leaving Hull to hold the fort. Everyone was in a foul temper, with nerves frayed by the unrelenting pressure; as Hull complained to Berle, it seemed as though everybody was trying to run the nation's foreign policy, that they were coming at him "with knives and hatchets." He didn't like the idea of the president sending a message to Hirohito, didn't want him to speak to Congress, and worried that the "appeasers" had gotten to Roosevelt. Much less did he want the boss away from Washington, especially when he saw the *New York Times* of Sunday, November 30, which carried the story of an inflammatory speech Tojo had supposedly made the day before. All in all, it had been a full weekend for the secretary of state, and the next day he took to his bed, exhausted, leaving Sumner Welles to pursue the exasperating dialogue with the Japanese ambassadors.

Those gentlemen were understandably in a quandary. Deeply puzzled by Tojo's speech (it was openly belligerent, and Nomura and Kurusu went into a panic when they heard that it had prompted Roosevelt to leave Warm Springs and return to Washington),[4] they were equally bewildered by Tokyo's instructions that they should suddenly begin to procrastinate and string out the talks, when everything had been in such a rush. They awaited the government's reply to Hull's Ten-Point Plan, certain that "the United States government will take a bold step depending on how our reply is made." Nothing, they reported to Tokyo, would be worse than a response made solely to keep the negotiations going. More than mere words was needed, and Nomura must have drawn a deep breath as he wrote, "I would like to get a reply which gives a clearer impression of our peaceful intentions."

In Tokyo the cabinet assembled to explain to the "senior statesmen"—former prime ministers—why war was inevitable. Although a number of the senior statesmen disagreed with the government's arguments, they did not set policy. A ritual had been observed. Assurance was received from Berlin that Germany would join Japan immediately in the event of war, and when the emperor asked the navy minister and the chief of staff what the chances of success were, and received an optimistic reply, he told Premier Tojo to proceed with his plans. At a liaison conference the following day, Foreign Minister Togo asked Admiral Nagano what the zero hour was: "Otherwise," he added plaintively, "I can't carry on diplomacy." And Nagano, speaking in a whisper, replied, "The zero hour is December 8. There is still time, so you had better resort to the kind of diplomacy that will be helpful in winning the war."

[4]It was a curious business, that speech. In Tokyo, Ambassador Grew heard that "neither the prime minister nor any member of the cabinet had seen the text . . . in advance." No one could tell him who had written it. The address was read by proxy, which was not uncommon, but it was noted that "the substance and tone of the speech are different from all General Tojo's previous addresses." It was also apparent that it was made more provocative by a very bad translation.

When Togo suggested that they couldn't leave Nomura and Kurusu in the dark much longer, someone at the table replied, "Our diplomats will have to be sacrificed." It was essential to keep the United States preoccupied with negotiations, he added, so that Japan's plans would remain secret until the last moment.

On Monday, December 1, just after 2:00 P.M., the final ritual took place in the Imperial Palace. With the future of the empire in their hands, the participants were tense, weary from the long period of indecision, grim over the prospects of what might lie ahead. After reciting the long, fruitless course of U.S.-Japanese negotiations, Premier Tojo stated that Japan had no recourse except war against the United States, Great Britain, and the Netherlands "to secure its existence and self-defense." He emphasized that while the nation was eager for a speedy victory, it was prepared for a long war. At this moment, he concluded, "our Empire stands at the threshold of glory or oblivion." While his prime minister spoke, Hirohito sat silent on his dais; he "displayed no signs of uneasiness," one eyewitness wrote, but "seemed to be in an excellent mood, and we were filled with awe." When the proceedings ended he left the room without saying a word, while the others began signing the documents officially endorsing war.

When the papers were brought to him, Hirohito told the imperial chamberlain, Marquis Kido, that he had done what he could to prevent war and could do no more. His seal was affixed to the documents, legitimizing the decision.

——

At a time when the administration had just about all it could possibly do to cope with the situation in the Pacific, it was faced on December 4 with front-page stories in the president's least favorite newspaper, the *Chicago Tribune,* as well as the *Washington Times-Herald,* revealing details of the Victory Program, including plans for five field armies totaling 6.7 million men, a two-million-man air force, with another million in the navy, and attacking the "blueprint for total war on a scale unprecedented in at least two oceans and three continents." Under the headline "FDR'S WAR PLANS," the exposé by the *Tribune*'s Washington correspondent Chesly Manly announced that July 1, 1943, was "fixed as the date for the beginning of the final supreme effort by American land forces to defeat the mighty German army in Europe," ignoring the fact that military planners considered that the earliest date at which the armed forces might be ready for action.

Outraged isolationists on the Hill proclaimed that the nation had been betrayed, that the story proved what they had been saying all along. Stimson, furious, held a press conference next day and defended his department by asking, "What would you think of an American General Staff which in the present condition of the world did not investigate and study every conceivable type of emergency which may confront this country and every possible method of meeting that emergency?" Then, raging at the isolationists and the "infernal disloyalty we now have in America First and the McCormick family papers," he asked, "What do you think of the patriotism of a man or a newspaper which would take these confidential studies and make them public to the enemies of the country?" The attorney general gave his opinion that the newspapers had violated the Espionage Act, and members of the cabinet angrily recommended legal action, though no one quite knew who should be prosecuted. Who had leaked the story? The FBI was ordered to find the culprit,[5] but events were about to overtake the sensational story, and within three days it was no more than a footnote to history.

Friday, December 5, was another day when the news reaching Washington was unwelcome or worse. Mr. Roosevelt received a public opinion poll confirming what he already believed—that it would not be easy to sell the American people on aiding the British and Dutch in Southeast Asia even after it was known where the Japanese troops were landing. Only 51 percent of those interviewed thought the United States would go to war in the near future, while 27 percent said the country would not, and 22 percent had no opinion. Yet oddly enough, 69 percent of the respondents believed that America should take steps to keep Japan from growing more powerful—even if that meant war. This reflected what had been one of the most frustrating aspects of the past year for Roosevelt. As he told Harry Hopkins, all of Hull's negotiations with the Japanese were directed at protecting our rights in the Far East, without ever addressing the tough question of what we would do if Japan attacked the East Indies or Singapore. It was a real weakness of our policy, the president felt; he believed that an attack on the East Indies should result in our going to war with Japan, but he could never get Hull to agree, and without Hull, he had no hope of persuading Congress to go along with him—certainly not a Congress that had refused to appropriate funds to fortify the vulnerable island of Guam, a U.S. protectorate some 3,500 miles west of Hawaii, and that had barely agreed to arm American merchant ships that were being regularly attacked in the Atlantic.

As for the public's hard-liners who wanted to kick sand in Japan's face, it was possible that they had been taken in by what they read in such publications as *Time.* The magazine's December 8 issue (printed, obviously, before the Japanese reached Pearl Harbor) bristled with chest-thumping allusions to America and her friends. "Everything was ready," the lead article proclaimed. "From Rangoon to Honolulu, every man was at battle stations . . . [and] the U.S. position had the simple clarity of a stone wall. One nervous twitch of a Japanese trigger finger, one jump in any direction,

[5]Writing in the December 1987 issue of *American Heritage,* Thomas Fleming makes a case that the president himself may have arranged to leak the story, knowing that hostilities with Japan were imminent, and hoping to provoke Hitler into declaring war on the United States— which, of course, he did, thereby committing one of the major blunders of World War II.

one overt act, might be enough. A vast array of armies, of navies, of air fleets were stretched now in the position of track runners, in the tension of the moment of the starter's gun." Equally encouraging, Japan's war industry was "creaking," its shipbuilding "crippled for lack of steel," every gallon of aviation fuel burned up was irreplaceable, and with "economic strangulation" on the way, "the Dutch, the British, and U.S. possessions are more nearly impregnable."

That the magazine and the nation would shortly have to grapple with reality was evident from two reports: Japanese transports and warships had been seen in Camranh Bay in Indochina on December 5, Washington time; and on the following day British planes flying at the limit of their range from Malaya spotted three Japanese convoys—one of them with forty-six transports, a battleship, seven cruisers, and a number of destroyers—heading into the Gulf of Siam from Cambodia. With the monsoons blowing, weather prevented the pilots from determining if they were bound for Thailand or Malaya, and contact was lost for the next thirty hours. By the time they were sighted again, the convoys' destination was all too clear.

The British and Australians, alarmed by the reported troop movements, felt that they could postpone action no longer, and a message was drafted, warning Japan that force or the threat of force against Thailand would result in "appropriate measures" and if hostilities should unfortunately result, the responsibility would rest with Japan. Roosevelt, however, withheld approval of the note because he was determined to get a message of his own to the Japanese emperor. If he received no answer by Monday evening, December 8, he said, he would issue a warning the next day and the British and Australians should follow with theirs on Wednesday, December 10. That settled, the president and his advisers spent the remaining hours of Saturday afternoon, December 6, drafting a message to the man on the Chrysanthemum Throne. Recalling the long years of peace and friendship between the two nations, the president then listed the recent developments which "contain tragic possibilities" and observed that the people of the Philippines, the East Indies, Malaya, and Thailand could not "sit either indefinitely or permanently on a keg of dynamite." Together, he concluded, for the sake of humanity, Japan and America should dispel the dark clouds, "restore traditional amity and prevent further death and destruction in the world." He had just completed this when Mrs. Roosevelt stopped by his study with two guests—Judge Justine Polier and Paul Kellogg—who wanted to say hello. "Well, Justine," he remarked, "this son of man has just sent his final message to the Son of God."

That same Saturday, December 6, Hull, Adolf Berle, and others were working on the president's proposed message to Congress, which he intended to deliver on Monday or Tuesday. Berle left the State Department about 1:30, picked up his two daughters, and took them to a matinee performance of Sigmund Romberg's operetta The Student Prince. He was back at State by 7:00, and half an hour later someone from army intelligence phoned to say that they had decoded and translated the reply Japan was making to Hull's Ten-Point Plan. When he saw it, Berle realized that "it was not only a flat turn-down, but a coarse and gratuitous and insulting message as well." Nor was that all: an accompanying message instructed Nomura and Kurusu to keep Tokyo's response locked up until they received a signal to present it to Hull. "In other words," Berle concluded, "they were to hold up delivering the answer until certain military dispositions were completed." He worked awhile longer on the speech draft and went to bed about 1:00 A.M., feeling very uneasy, with waltz tunes from *The Student Prince* going round in his head like dirges from another time.

Washington was a capital where they rolled up the sidewalks at night, and the evening of Saturday, December 6, was no exception. The day had been balmy—warm for the season, and the only signs of late work in the government offices were in the State, War, and Navy departments. Frank Knox's annual report to the president had been issued this day, and it was a reassuring document, reflecting the secretary's opinion that the navy of which he was so proud was "second to none," a two-ocean force that was ready for any eventuality. After dusk the city was quiet, and by 8:30 the navy cryptographers had completed work on all thirteen parts of an incoming message from Tokyo (finishing it, in fact, before the code clerks at the Japanese embassy did), and Lieutenant Commander Alwin Kramer, knowing its importance, got on the phone to alert those who would receive copies that he had something they should see at once and that he would be delivering it shortly. After speaking to Knox about 9:00, Kramer left his office and was driven by his wife to the White House, where he handed the locked pouch containing the message to Commander Lester R. Schulz, the duty officer that night. Schulz found Mr. Roosevelt sitting in his second-floor study, talking quietly with Harry Hopkins, and while the commander waited, the president read the translated intercept without saying a word, while the restless Hopkins paced up and down, smoking. Then FDR handed the papers to Hopkins, and when he saw that he had finished reading, Roosevelt said flatly, "This means war."

Schulz recalled that the two men talked for five minutes or so about the disposition of Japanese forces, after which Hopkins remarked that since war was undoubtedly going to begin at the convenience of the Japanese it was too bad that we could not strike the first blow and prevent any sort of surprise.

"No," the president said, "we can't do that. We are a democracy and a peaceful people." Then, Schulz remembered, Mr. Roosevelt raised his voice and said, "But we have a good record." The impression Schulz retained was that whatever happened the president intended to stand on that record and not make the first move; no mention was made of when the Japanese might strike, or of sending further warnings to the Pacific. Roosevelt did say that he wanted to talk to Betty Stark, but when the White House operator who tried to reach the admiral reported that he was at the theater (he too was seeing *The Student Prince*), Schulz heard the president remark that he would call him later: he did not want to cause undue public alarm by having Stark paged at the theater.

In the course of their conversation, Roosevelt told Hopkins that he had just sent a telegram to Emperor Hirohito, but he could not know that his eloquent last-minute attempt, like so many other efforts to prevent war, would be plagued with more than its share of bad luck. Late in the evening of December 7, Tokyo time, Ambassador Grew received a triple-priority telegram from Hull alerting him that a message from the president to the emperor was on its way and should be communicated to Hirohito as quickly as possible. Alas for the last-ditch peace effort, the cable was not delivered to the embassy until 10:30 at night, although it had been received by the Japanese telegraph office at noon. When Eugene Dooman telephoned to arrange for Grew to see the foreign minister immediately, Togo's secretary balked at the prospect of disturbing his boss at such a late hour and asked if the ambassador's business couldn't wait until morning. Told that it could not, he made the appointment, and the American ambassador arrived at the foreign minister's residence at 12:15 A.M., requested an audience with the emperor, and then read the message aloud to Togo. He would study the document, Togo replied, and when Grew asked if that meant he could not see the emperor, the foreign minister said he would "present the matter to the Throne."

Grew bid him good night and was driven back to the embassy. It was then half an hour into Monday morning, December 8, in Tokyo.

CHAPTER 52

—◆—

"If you want the tiger's cubs, you must go into the tiger's lair."

Quentin Reynolds *looked* like a foreign correspondent—a rough-cut Richard Harding Davis—a tough, devil-may-care fellow in a trench coat who had seen just about everything and lived to tell the tale, and he had a way with people that made them open up when he was after a story. His friend Vincent Sheean remarked that a number of correspondents had been around longer than Reynolds during the London blitz, but few were better known or more popular. When Englishmen saw this jovial, warmhearted bear of a man on the street they asked for his autograph as though he were a movie star, and when he broadcast for the BBC "in a rumbling bass drawl which sounded ultra-American" the nation listened. Perhaps the English saw in him the promise of great efforts to be made in their behalf by the United States in the days to come; certainly his written and spoken tributes to their courage and perseverance, expressed so openly and enthusiastically, secretly pleased a people who knew that what they were doing deserved praise, but did not care to do the praising themselves.

It was natural enough that when Reynolds was back in the States for a visit in the middle of March 1941, talking to the editors at *Collier's,* President Roosevelt should want to see him, to hear his views on how things were going in Britain. Inevitably, their conversation turned to the Pacific and the Japanese.

"They hate us," said Roosevelt. "They come to me and they hiss between their teeth and they say: 'Mr. President, we are your friends. Japan wants nothing but friendship with America,' and then they hiss between their teeth again, and I know they're lying. Oh, they hate us," FDR went on, "and sooner or later they'll come after us."

And now it was December and time had run out, and the Japanese *were* coming after us. Although no one in the United States was aware of it, destiny was shortly to be made manifest in the form of a bold, unconventional idea, brilliantly conceived and superbly executed. Behind this idea was an able, determined Japanese admiral—a strategist who knew his enemy and what it would take to beat him. He was a gambler, and this was a gambler's idea, heaven knows—which was exactly why his conservative colleagues in the navy wanted no part of it and why the American military never gave the possibility a second thought.

For the idea to work, it had to be transformed into a complex plan, executed to perfection, and blessed with exceptional luck—all of which came to pass. The plan proved to be deficient in one extremely important detail, but apart from that original sin of omission the Japanese did everything right and got the luck they needed. The Americans did just about everything wrong, starting with their universal refusal to believe that such an attack was possible, and whatever luck they may have had going for them ran out very fast.

Admiral Isoroku Yamamoto, commander in chief of the Combined Fleet, was one of several high-ranking officers who had been summoned to Tokyo in September 1940 to decide what attitude the navy should adopt toward the Tripartite Pact with Germany and Italy, which was scheduled to be signed later in the month. The navy minister, Koshiro Oikawa, made the point that if the admirals opposed the treaty, the Konoye government would be forced to resign, and to avoid that he urged them to support it. Yamamoto had a question. He reminded Oikawa of his own recent service as vice minister, and said he recalled that some 80 percent of all strategic materials were imported from the United States, Great Britain, or areas under their control. Since an alliance with Hitler and Mussolini would surely mean the loss of those sources of supply, how did Japan propose to replace them? What Yamamoto received for his pains was an infuriatingly evasive reply which did nothing to change his view that the Axis Pact was a bad idea, and that war with England and America would be even worse.

During this visit to Tokyo he also went to see Fumimaro Konoye, the prime minister, who asked what he thought of the navy's prospects in the event of war with the United States. "If you insist on my going ahead," Yamamoto answered, "then I can promise to give them hell for a year or a year and a half, but can guarantee nothing as to what will happen after that." It might be too late to back out of the alliance with Germany and Italy, he added, but he urged the premier to do everything possible to avoid war with America.

Yamamoto, with Admirals Mitsumasa Yonai and Shigeyoshi Inoue, were the most prominent members of the so-called treaty group of navy brass opposed to war, and their reasons were those of thoughtful men who had seen much of the world, who knew the limitations of Japan's resources and the abundance of those in a nation like the United States. As a student at Harvard and an attaché in Washington, Yamamoto had acquired firsthand knowledge of America's immense natural resources, its scientific and technological superiority to Japan, and the potential of its mass-production system to build and replace weapons of war faster than any likely adversary. Yet while it might be absurd for Japan to contemplate war with America, Yamamoto was nothing if not patriotic, and as commander of the Combined Fleet he saw that the movement of the U.S. Fleet from California to Hawaii posed a potential threat to Japan's goals which neither he nor the nation could ignore.

Like other countries, the Japanese had contingency war plans—the most probable enemies being Russia, China, and the United States—and what had been prepared some years earlier by the general staff as a blueprint for dealing with America was by now an exercise in self-delusion. The theory went along these lines: Japan would launch an attack on the Philippines; when the U.S. Fleet sailed forth to the rescue of the islands, as it was bound to do, submarines would trail and attack it, crippling or destroying the armada piecemeal as it ranged farther and farther from its base, closer and closer to the assembled might of the Imperial Navy, poised for the kill. When the Americans came within favorable range, the Great All-Out Battle which was an article of faith with traditionalists[1] would ensue, and the U.S. Navy would vanish beneath the waves.

Yamamoto, who had lost two fingers of his left hand and carried scars on his lower body from more than a hundred fragments of a gun that exploded in the Battle of Tsushima, didn't buy the plan. The idea of letting the enemy come to him (assuming that was what the enemy chose to do) was anathema to a man who was fond of quoting the adage "If you want the tiger's cubs, you must go into the tiger's lair," and as a former commander of the 1st Carrier Division and a keen student of air power he believed he had the weapon to take into the lair.

During the Japanese navy's war games of 1940, at about the time the movement of the U.S. Fleet to Hawaii was first rumored, Yamamoto watched planes from the carriers track and "hit" the battleships again and again despite the warships' evasive tactics, and the sight convinced him that the only way to attack the U.S. Fleet at Pearl Harbor was from the air. Sometime that November he discussed his idea with Admiral Oikawa, and shortly after the beginning of the year—the Year of the Snake, as 1941 was

---

[1]The tradition of the decisive engagement was born after the turn of the century when Japan's greatest naval hero, Admiral Heihachiro Togo, defeated the Russians at Port Arthur in 1904 and destroyed their Baltic Fleet at the Battle of Tsushima the following year.

called in the Buddhist calendar cycle—he spelled it out in a long letter to the navy minister. No one in the service could have been more opposed to war with the United States and Britain just then, but since hostilities looked to be inevitable, he urged that Japan "devote itself seriously to war preparations."

The navy, he wrote, must "fiercely attack and destroy the U.S. main fleet at the outset . . . to decide the fate of the war on the very first day." Whether that fleet was in Pearl Harbor or offshore was beside the point: he would attack it from the air. To give himself adequate firepower while still achieving surprise, he wanted the entire 1st and 2nd Carrier Divisions and "all their air strength, risking themselves on a moonlight night or at dawn," supported by a destroyer squadron to rescue survivors of an enemy counterattack, with submarines attacking the enemy so as to blockade the entrance to Pearl Harbor, plus a number of tankers for refueling at sea. Simultaneously with this action, Japan would pursue its main objectives in the South China Sea, attacking the Philippines, the Dutch Indies, and Singapore. Then and later, to his subordinates and those in charge of the navy, Yamamoto repeated the thesis that lay at the heart of his plan: *if* war was inevitable, the only possible tactic was to annihilate America's naval strength at the first instant, for without the insurance against interference such an attack would give Japan, operations in the south would be impossible. Looked at another way, destruction of the U.S. Fleet in its supposedly impregnable Hawaiian base would give Japan a breathing spell—time enough, perhaps, to seize the territory and resources it wanted in Southeast Asia—and it was conceivable that America might be sufficiently discouraged by the catastrophe that it would negotiate a peace, giving Japan a free hand in the western Pacific.

Pearl Harbor, the great landlocked anchorage on the island of Oahu— two fifths of the distance between San Francisco and Tokyo—was first employed as a coaling station by the U.S. Navy in 1887, when the Hawaiian monarchy granted America certain rights. After annexation of the islands in 1900, the place was fortified and the waters deepened, and over the years the government poured enough money into improvements and maintenance that it was called "America's billion-dollar fist in the Pacific." The description was accurate enough, but the location of the base made it about as exposed as an expensive fist can be, and from 1931 on, one of the problems given to cadets in the Japanese naval academy was how to assault Pearl Harbor.

Curiously, while the daring plan to do exactly that was taking shape in his mind, Yamamoto was thinking about retirement. He was fifty-seven years old, it was customary for the command of the Combined Fleet to rotate frequently, and he had been in the job for two years. When he looked in the mirror he saw a prominent nose, full lips, and jutting chin, but he was also conscious of the old wounds, the short-cropped hair that was all gray, the belly that revealed too much good living and too little exercise.

These days he had the shape of a man whose center of gravity was pulling him down—no longer that of an agile forty-year-old who prided himself on the ability to do handstands on the prow of a moving launch. He had been in the navy for forty years, and along the way had fought in the Russo-Japanese war, done tours in the United States and Europe, attended the London Naval Conference, been vice minister of the navy. He had had the commands he wanted, and now he was half ready to call it quits. With luck, he wrote a friend, he would take it easy back home in the country, with no more demands on him than showing the local fellows how to play *shogi*. But it was not that easy. Writing to the commander of the Second Fleet, he suggested that the only way to avoid war might be for officers who shared similar views to request appointment to key posts where they might influence the ultimate decision. Should that fail, and should Japan go to war, "one would have to resign oneself to it as unavoidable and throw oneself wholeheartedly into the fight, yet I believe it should be delayed just as long as possible to allow Japan all available time to concentrate on preparing itself."

Perhaps if Yamamoto had pressed to leave the command of the Combined Fleet and be reassigned to the Navy Ministry, things might have turned out differently, but he did not. Instead, he threw himself wholeheartedly into the business at hand, and on January 7, 1941, submitted a nine-page document entitled "Views on Preparations for War" to Navy Minister Oikawa, outlining for the first time on paper his idea for an attack on Hawaii. It consisted of four sections, covering preparations for war, training, operational policy, and a "plan of operations to be followed at the outset of hostilities." Although he had written in red ink in the margin, "For the eyes of the minister alone; to be burned without showing it to anyone else," somehow it leaked. On January 27 the Peruvian envoy in Tokyo informed a friend in the U.S. embassy of a rumor that the Japanese planned a surprise attack on Pearl Harbor. The rumor was passed on to Ambassador Grew at once, and he cabled the State Department, advising that in the event of trouble with the United States, the Japanese "intend to make a surprise attack against Pearl Harbor with all their strength. . . ." The message was routed to the Office of Naval Intelligence, and ONI, unimpressed, informed Admiral Stark that "based on known data regarding the present disposition and employment of Japanese Naval and Army forces, no move against Pearl Harbor appears imminent or planned for the foreseeable future." In addition, the head of ONI's Far East Section advised Admiral Kimmel in Hawaii of Grew's telegram, noting, "The Division of Naval Intelligence places no credence in these rumors," and reassuring the commander in chief of the Pacific Fleet that no hostile action was anticipated.

The army dismissed the rumor in equally cavalier fashion, largely on grounds that "it was inconceivable that any source in the know would have communicated that to the [Peruvian] Ambassador." To give the Office of

Naval Intelligence its due, someone there did take the trouble to look further into the matter (as Ambassador Grew surely should have done), but when it was learned that the source of the rumor appeared to be the Peruvian envoy's cook, the incident was forgotten. With the benefit of hindsight, it seems clear that neither army nor navy took the report seriously for several reasons. As the army's chief of staff for intelligence put it, they knew it would be suicidal for the Japanese to make war against the United States, and it would be crazy to attack the fortresslike Hawaii and the powerful American fleet there, risking irreplaceable ships in hopes of achieving surprise and catching the defenders unprepared. It simply didn't make sense—unless, of course, the Japanese had found a way to accomplish the impossible.

———

By spring Yamamoto's idea had begun to sprout. To assess its feasibility, he turned to Takijiro Onishi, one of Japan's few genuine air admirals, who enlisted specialists from his staff, and called in Commander Minoru Genda of the 1st Carrier Division. Genda, who was known as "Madman Genda" at the naval staff college because of his radical aviation bias, was probably the best possible choice for the job of planning the details of the attack, and when he had seen Yamamoto's proposal he pronounced it difficult, but not impossible. He would begin work on it at once. Toward the end of April, Yamamoto sent a senior staff officer to Tokyo to outline the plan for the general staff.

Opposition to it was unanimous. It was too risky. Over and over, the top brass would repeat their fears: it was impossible to maintain secrecy or achieve complete surprise; there was no guarantee that the U.S. Fleet would be in port when the planes attacked; refueling at sea on such a scale was immensely difficult; the weather might prove disastrous; the strike force might be surprised itself, by a combination of naval vessels and land-based planes; bombing techniques were imperfect at best; nets across the harbor would prevent the use of torpedos. And so on. Worst of all, failure of a Pearl Harbor mission could put the vital southern operation at risk, depriving it of carriers, planes, and other support.

Three months later the same staff officer was sent on the same errand, with the same result, yet Yamamoto quietly went ahead with his preparations and the intensive training program he had begun for the mission he was determined to carry through.

Refining the plan alone took weeks. One obstacle Genda had to overcome was the conventional wisdom that carriers must be scattered, not only for their own safety, but because their traditional role was not to take the offensive but to provide air cover for the big battlewagons and heavy cruisers. Genda had another game in mind, however: he required the maximum concentration of aircraft over the target at the same time, and concluded that the only way to get all his planes in the air was to bunch the carriers themselves at the time the planes were launched. Like Yamamoto, Genda was offense-minded, having no use whatever for the Great Battle concept so admired by the general staff, and he even argued for making Pearl Harbor *the* major objective, in which the destruction of the U.S. Fleet would be followed up by occupation of Hawaii, forcing the Americans back onto the mainland. (Yamamoto for a time was intrigued with this same notion; knowing how hard it was to replace trained men, he speculated on the possibility of making a landing in order to round up every American naval officer in Hawaii. But an aerial attack on Oahu was difficult enough for the general staff to accept; invasion was out of the question.)

Genda's draft plan—most elements of which survived months of wrangling over details—consisted of three major objectives: to succeed, the attack must take the enemy completely by surprise; the first priority would be U.S. carriers—the real offensive weapon of the fleet; and as many American land-based planes as possible must be destroyed. Since the object was the annihilation of the U.S. Pacific Fleet, the stakes were high enough to justify certain risks. He wanted every available Japanese carrier to participate in the mission. Refueling at sea was essential, since a number of the ships involved had a limited cruising range. Because all types of bombing would be employed—torpedo, dive, and high-level—and because the Japanese lacked precision instruments comparable to the American Norden bombsight, the attack must be made by daylight, as early in the morning as practicable. Before he was through, Genda had thought of just about everything—except one conspicuously important item.

In his concentration on destroying the fleet and the air force, he and everyone else involved in the planning neglected to include as targets those mundane, unromantic adjuncts to every naval station, the "farms" of oil tanks, the machine shops and repair facilities, the dry docks, the submarine base on Quarry Point. Without them, Pearl Harbor had little reason to exist as a naval facility, for it was essentially a repair and refueling station in the central Pacific, extending the fleet's range two thousand miles beyond the U.S. West Coast. Every precious drop of oil—4.5 million barrels of it, which would have taken literally years to replace—had been transported across those miles and piped into surface storage tanks that enabled the fighting ships to remain at sea. A myriad of parts of every conceivable use, shape, and size were stored ashore, and the machine shops were equipped to make just about anything that could not be found in the warehouses. Yet none of these installations was on the list of targets, and the omission was to be the most expensive mistake the Japanese made.

Beginning in early May, final training for the mission—now known as Operation Z—began. In Kagoshima harbor, which was chosen because of its general resemblance to Pearl Harbor, the air unit from the carrier *Akagi* went to work first, under Lieutenant Commander Mitsuo Fuchida, who was put in charge of training all the flight crews. Fuchida was known as a hot pilot, aggressive, always ready for a fight; but he was a superb teacher, and that's what was wanted here. Recently he had concentrated on training pilots to make emergency carrier landings and takeoffs at night, and on increasing the accuracy of night bombing, and some of those skills—plus a great many more—would be called for in Operation Z.

Throughout the summer and fall the airmen worked at tactical problems continuously, flying up to twelve hours a day, experimenting with new techniques, testing and modifying weapons, devising new ones. Recognizing the ragged performance of high-level bombers, Genda put most of his faith in torpedo planes with their lethal weapon, but immediately he came up against a new problem. A torpedo loosed from the customary height of three hundred feet at relatively high speed plunged sixty feet or more into the water; but the water in Pearl Harbor was only thirty feet deep, which meant that the torpedo would plow into the mud at the bottom before it ever reached the target. So at Genda's insistence—although they knew nothing of the reason behind it, let alone their eventual mission—pilots began flying at dangerously low altitudes, practicing their runs over the buildings and smokestacks in the vicinity of the bay before dropping down as low as forty feet above the water to release their torpedoes. Eventually, the torpedoes themselves were modified by the addition of a wooden rudder that enabled them to run in shallower water. A new flight formation was devised for the horizontal bombers: instead of the usual nine-plane formation in the shape of an inverted V, a five-plane formation was found to produce more attack units, making it possible to deliver heavier fire against any given target. They discovered that if the pilot of a dive-bomber delayed releasing his bomb until he reached fifteen hundred feet (instead of the usual two thousand feet), accuracy increased substantially. They came up with a new, streamlined bomb for high-level use, which had greater penetration against a battleship's heavy armor plate. They worked the men in teams, building their confidence, efficiency, and *esprit de corps*. They incorporated into the plan a provision for a submarine attack, to ensure that any ships that might escape the aerial bombardment and put to sea would be sunk, and this led to the testing of midget two-man submarines with a capacity of two torpedoes, launched from a "mother" sub. During all this time, only a handful of senior officers were aware of the reasons for the specialized training; not until early September was the circle of insiders widened, when staff officers of the First Air Fleet were informed of their mission and instructed to undertake detailed studies of all the logistical problems that would face the task force—communications, weather predictions, navigation, refueling, the rate of fuel consumption, the best route to take, and all the rest of it. Finally, Yamamoto's concept was being converted to a battle plan.

At about the same time, in a suburb of Tokyo, the annual staff college conference was held, and here tabletop war games were conducted to determine how best to achieve Japan's goals in the southern operation. The actual size and grouping of forces, the naval and air fleet commanders, and rendezvous and landing sites had all been determined in advance, and for four intense days the simulated operational units converged on the Philippines, Borneo, and Malaya, moving on Singapore, isolating the Netherlands East Indies, cutting Britain's line of communications to Australia and New Zealand, while Formosa-based planes attacked MacArthur's air force in the Philippines, and aircraft out of Indochina flew sorties between the Gulf of Siam and the South China Sea.

At the Imperial Navy Staff College, one room was off limits to all but Admiral Yamamoto and a select group of some thirty officers, and here— once the games covering the immense southern theater had been played out—Operation Z got under way. Standing around a long table cluttered with charts and other papers, in a room dominated by maps, the men Yamamoto had chosen gathered to answer the two critical questions still troubling him: whether the secrecy of the operation—on which the element of surprise depended—could be maintained, and whether the attack itself was indeed feasible.

Before the simulated exercise could begin, the route the fleet would take to Hawaii had to be resolved. Vice Admiral Chuichi Nagumo, who would command the carrier strike force, called Kido Butai, wanted to avoid the potentially destructive storms of the northern route and head instead toward Wotje in the Marshall Islands, thence eastward and slightly northerly toward Oahu. Although it was longer by far than the northern route (more than eleven hundred miles), it offered the likelihood of relatively calm seas and sunny weather, plus the advantage of a Japanese-held anchorage for refueling. On balance, however, the northern route seemed a better bet. Leaving from a port somewhere near Hokkaido, the armada would sail due east, and when it was about a thousand miles north of Oahu, turn south and head for the target. This route had the advantage (crucial, as it turned out) of lying off the main shipping lanes between North America and Russia or Japan, and while it was exposed to the notorious weather patterns of the North Pacific, that very inclemency in autumn or early winter would enhance concealment of the large fleet. Furthermore, the Japanese had learned that American patrols were weakest north of Oahu. The northern route was the obvious one to take to achieve surprise, and the war games that followed proved the point conclusively. Nagumo complained in vain about the difficulties of maintaining formation and refueling in the towering seas and driving storms of the North Pacific. The northern route it would be, for only that way was there a chance of keeping the attack secret. Risks remained, to be sure, but if Operation Z dispensed with aerial reconnaissance and maintained strict radio silence, and if the submarines were forbidden to approach within three hundred miles of Hawaii lest they be spotted, the thing just might work. Meanwhile, first things first. It was decided that the initial step in concealing the movement was to keep secret the site at which the strike force would rendezvous before departing. If that leaked, the odds would lengthen unacceptably.

Observers from the general staff remained unconvinced. They argued that Yamamoto's plan still represented an "alarming risk" on its own, and might fatally jeopardize the crucial southern operation, especially if Nagumo's fleet suffered heavy damage, such as the loss of several carriers. The clincher, which could prove to be the most important question of them all, was this: what if the United States Fleet was not in or near Pearl Harbor at the time of the attack? What then?

⸺

The war games served their purpose, demonstrating at least that the Yamamoto plan was feasible, even though it carried substantial dangers and left dangling some unanswered questions.[2] But by now it was the end of September and time was closing in on the Japanese. As General Tojo had pointed out, December—before the monsoons began—was the last period of relatively decent weather for landing operations in the south; later than that, and the North Pacific route to Pearl Harbor could prove impossible, too. Equally serious was the continuing drain on the nation's oil supplies. Enough was available for no more than eighteen months of combat operations, and the consensus of the top command was that a further delay of six months would put an end to all their plans.

Just as he had set the controversy in motion, Yamamoto himself closed off the debate. In mid-October another series of tabletop maneuvers was held aboard his flagship, *Nagato,* at the end of which he announced his firm intention to go ahead with the attack, assuring his officers that the task force would get the carriers it wanted—six, not four, as the general staff kept insisting. Then, ever so reluctantly, the general staff suddenly changed its collective mind and caved in (apparently Yamamoto threatened to resign if he did not get his way on the carriers, and that was too much for the desk admirals to swallow). If Admiral Yamamoto had such confidence in his plan, it was said, he should have an opportunity to carry it out, and that ended the debate.

Early in November, following several days of maneuvers in which the full complement of aircraft took off from carriers in the darkness just before dawn, sought out targets in a simulated attack, and returned, Osami Nagano, chief of the naval general staff, issued orders in the emperor's name to "Chief Yamamoto of the Combined Fleet," saying, "In the interest of self-defense and survival, the Empire is due to open hostilities with the United States, Britain, and Holland in the first ten days of December.

[2]Astonishingly, according to his biographer Hiroyuki Agawa, Yamamoto held a secret meeting with Konoye on September 12, in the midst of the war games, at which the two discussed the proposed meeting between the premier and President Roosevelt. When Konoye asked what would happen if negotiations broke down, the admiral repeated his earlier surmise that Japan could last for a year and a half, and then expressed the hope once again that war with America could be avoided. He urged Konoye, "Don't treat the negotiations lightly, but approach them as though your life depended on the outcome."

Preparations are to be completed for the various operations involved. The commander in chief of the Combined Fleet is to carry out preparations for the operations under his command." In conformance with that order, Admiral Yamamoto issued one of his own, entitled "Combined Fleet Secret Operational Order No. 1," and on November 11 submarine crews were observed casting off their lines as the black-hulled boats slipped away, some bound southeast for Kwajalein in the Marshall Islands, where they would refuel before heading toward Oahu, others heading east—initially to keep a lookout for vessels north of Hawaii, and subsequently, after the air attack, to sink any ships that might escape. Yamamoto's plan was now a full-fledged operation. The attack on Pearl Harbor had begun.

On November 17, Yamamoto and his staff went aboard the carrier *Akagi,* where the admiral, looking grimmer than usual, addressed about a hundred officers on the flight deck, warning them against overconfidence, reminding them that they must be prepared for fierce resistance from a tough, resourceful foe. Then he took a few steps, gripped Mitsuo Fuchida's hand as he looked him straight in the eyes without saying a word, and headed for the wardroom, where the men drank a toast to the emperor and victory. The tentative date for the attack had been set for December 8, Tokyo time, when a full moon would facilitate takeoff from the flattops, and when it would be Sunday, December 7, in Hawaii. As the Japanese knew, it was customary for U.S. ships that had been at sea to return to port on Friday and depart again on Monday or Tuesday. Besides, Sunday was a holiday, when activity at the air and naval stations slowed to a crawl and everyone relaxed.

To Nagumo's dismay, the attack was to be canceled if negotiations with the United States proved successful—even if the mission had to be scrubbed at the last minute, in which event Kido Butai would return to a designated rendezvous and await instructions.[3] Every ship in the task force was now stripped for action: personal gear and all nonessentials had been taken ashore; food, ammunition, extra oil, gasoline, bombs, torpedoes, foul-weather gear, and antifreeze grease (to the surprise of unsuspecting crew members, who hadn't reckoned on cold weather) had been loaded aboard; and to ensure total radio silence, to prevent the enemy tracking the fleet by radio-direction-finder bearings, the operators' sending keys had even been removed. As Admiral Yamamoto watched from the quarterdeck of *Nagato,* the *Akagi* and several escort ships got under way; other vessels followed, one by one at different times, bound for the secret rendezvous in the black waters of Hitokappu Bay, a thousand miles to the north, where patrol boats

---

[3]Answering the argument of Nagumo and others that turning back would be destructive of morale and would not be practicable in any case, Yamamoto replied that any officer who didn't think he could obey an order to return to Japan could resign on the spot. No one took him up on it.

were already prohibiting fishermen from leaving port and officials had halted outgoing mail and telegrams from the tiny village.

—————

That all-important question of whether the U.S. Fleet would be at anchor in Pearl Harbor when the Japanese bombers arrived had troubled Admiral Yamamoto as much as any doubters on the general staff, and he had asked naval intelligence to collect as much data as possible on Hawaii, with special attention to the movement of those ships. The result was the assignment of a handsome twenty-nine-year-old reserve officer named Takeo Yoshikawa to his first job as a secret agent, with a salary of $150 a month and $100 a month expenses. He had had an excellent record at the naval academy and in his first posts before stomach trouble forced him to retire, but intelligence work appealed to him, he had worked in the British and American sections, and his encyclopedic knowledge of the U.S. Navy made him a natural for the task ahead.

On March 27, 1941 he arrived in Honolulu by ship, with a diplomatic passport, a new name—Tadashi Morimura—hair which he had allowed to grow long, and an insatiable curiosity about Pearl Harbor and whatever went on there. His cover was as a minor functionary, reporting directly to the consul general, Nagao Kita, but from the first he spent most of his time out of the office, gathering data by the simple and effective method of using his eyes and ears. A Japanese-style teahouse known as Shuncho-ro had a second-floor room and a telescope overlooking Pearl Harbor and the air base at Hickam Field. Around Pearl Harbor the hills and fields and highways provided excellent vantage points for observation, and Yoshikawa spent hours watching planes take off and land, counting them, noting their direction of flight and the time they returned, recording all of it meticulously on the charts he maintained in his room. Although he did not risk using binoculars for fear they would give him away, his mundane yet vastly important task required little more than good eyesight, ingenuity, and common sense. Tokyo wanted to know what U.S. ships were in Pearl Harbor, when they were there, where they were located, and how they were protected, and the way to find this out was to watch continuously, ask questions, and eventually acquire enough information about ships and airplanes to see if a particular pattern emerged. Before long it did. It soon became clear that Pearl Harbor was filled with warships on Saturdays and Sundays, and that most of them left port on Monday or Tuesday, remaining at sea until Friday—usually in the afternoon. (From this information, and from monitoring the radio traffic of ships and planes, Tokyo deduced that the normal fleet exercises were held in an area about forty-five minutes' flight from Pearl Harbor.) As for the aircraft that flew off on patrol, Yoshikawa noticed that almost none of them went north of Oahu, which led to the obvious conclusion that that side of the island was the least protected and presumably the most vulnerable.

The weeks passed and Tokyo's demands for precise information grew: as plans for Operation Z were refined and the deadline for departure approached, it was essential to establish at least two weeks in advance of the attack date whether Kimmel's ships would be in port that day, and to know what patrols the strike force might encounter in the vicinity of Oahu. Although neither Kita, the consul general, nor Yoshikawa, the busy spy, had been informed of the pending operation, or the reason the navy needed these data, they had begun to suspect, and their suspicions were surely confirmed by the secret request they received in the last week of September. Tokyo had divided the waters of Pearl Harbor into five areas, each carrying a letter designation from A to E. Using those letters, the consulate was to report on which vessels were at anchor, whether they were at wharves, buoys, or docks, and when two or more ships were tied up alongside each other.

That message was duly deciphered and translated in Washington (though not until October 9), and Colonel Bratton in G-2 immediately recognized it as something new and different—a kind of grid system for reporting what ships were in port and where they were located. Why? he wondered. Wasn't there something unusual here that should be run down? His boss, Brigadier General Sherman Miles, didn't think so: it struck him as more of the familiar Japanese curiosity about the navy's movements, or maybe it had something to do with when Kimmel's ships would head to sea, so Japanese subs could attack them. Bratton sent copies of the message to Secretary Stimson, General Marshall, and General Gerow, head of the War Plans Division, but no one expressed interest. Neither did the boys at ONI: intelligence assumed it was a new method of reducing the volume of radio traffic by using letters instead of descriptive phrases. Sure, it could be a clue to possible sabotage, but if anyone was on top of *that* problem, it was General Short. Bratton was told not to worry: in the event of an emergency, the fleet was not going to be hanging around Pearl—it would be at sea—so this was a big waste of time on the part of the Japanese consul.

Bratton's opposite number, Commander Kramer, was not greatly concerned, either. He passed the intercept along to Knox and Stark, to ONI, and to the White House, but he regarded it, as others had, as a Japanese device for simplifying communications by eliminating unnecessary verbiage. Anyway, he figured that Kimmel would deal with it, since the Pacific commander was receiving everything of this nature. Except that Kimmel was not.

What was increasingly evident about the top brass in Washington was that their thought processes had fallen into a pattern in which certain questions were excluded, or were not being asked. If the mind is locked in a certain direction—if, for instance, a man has decided that the Japanese will not or cannot attack Pearl Harbor, which is what everyone that mattered had concluded—then he will fit everything into that particular mindset. It was not that the idea of a surprise attack on Pearl Harbor had not occurred to the military—far from it. In 1936 the navy had organized its war games around the premise of a surprise attack on the base. The following year, one officer recalled, "we actually carried out a daylight attack, a dawn attack, on Pearl Harbor. . . . Carriers moved in at dawn and delivered a surprise attack on the army and navy installations. . . ." It was all sham, he went on, yet "it was in our minds all the time." Furthermore, the war plans under which Admiral Kimmel and General Short were to operate included the contingency of just such an attack by "Orange," as Japan was known.

Since the most likely and potentially destructive form of assault would probably come from carrier-launched aircraft, it was natural that two of the men in Oahu who had given special attention to the problem were the commander of the Hawaiian Air Force, Major General Frederick Martin (who reported to Short), and the man in charge of the navy's patrol aircraft, Rear Admiral Patrick Bellinger. Both were experienced, in some respects distinguished, pilots, and both were exceedingly worried about the capacity of their commands to perform adequately. Bellinger had even risked his neck by sounding off about the problems to Stark. He had come to Hawaii on October 30, 1940, he wrote, "impressed with the need for being ready today rather than tomorrow for any eventuality that might arise," and what he had discovered was that "we were operating on a shoestring and the more I looked the thinner the shoestring appeared to be." Early in March 1941, Admiral Kimmel told Bellinger to talk matters over with Martin and work out a plan for joint action, and less than a month later Kimmel and Short had in their hands a report that was as clear and alarming as a document could be. Summarizing the situation, Martin and Bellinger foresaw a "successful, sudden raid"—very likely "a dawn air attack . . . delivered as a complete surprise"—which could result in the inability of the fleet to engage in any offensive in the western Pacific for a long period. It appeared to them that Orange submarines and a fast raiding force might suddenly strike without a declaration of war, without U.S. intelligence detecting their approach, launching a surprise submarine attack on ships in the area and a surprise aerial bombardment of Oahu, "including ships and installations in Pearl Harbor."

After describing with uncanny accuracy the very carrier-based attack Admiral Yamamoto had planned, the Martin-Bellinger report recommended daily air patrols 360 degrees to seaward. Then they delivered the bad news to Kimmel and Short: desirable as these patrols might be, it was impossible to carry them out on a systematic, continuing basis with the limited personnel and aircraft at their disposal. On the heels of this unsettling report Admiral Kimmel received an unexpected message from ONI: examining what the Axis powers had done in the past, intelligence officers noticed that they frequently launched offensives on Saturdays, Sundays, or national holidays. That being the case, all naval districts were advised that appropriate watches and precautions should be in effect on weekends and holidays.

Just as the Martin-Bellinger report was a textbook study of how Orange might attack Oahu, a document produced by a colonel named William Farthing showed how such an assault might be thwarted by land-based planes. Farthing, a Texan who commanded the 5th Bombardment Group at Hickam Field, was called in by General Martin and instructed to prepare a report on "the air situation in Hawaii," which had been requested by the War Department. A month later Martin had what he wanted, and the Farthing study was sent to Washington on August 20, 1941. Briefly, the colonel proposed that the Hawaiian Air Force be beefed up in such a way that it could independently defend the island of Oahu, thereby providing "the Navy complete freedom of action." The key to his plan was to be found in three opening provisos: a complete, 360-degree search around the Hawaiian area during daylight hours—the same procedure Martin and Bellinger had recommended; an attack force of bombers on call, to hit any objective revealed by the search; and "if the objective is a carrier, to hit it the day before it could steam to a position offshore of Oahu where it could launch its planes for an attack." With astonishing foresight, Farthing predicted that Orange would avoid regular shipping lanes, would approach as close as possible under cover of darkness, and would attack in the early morning with the maximum number of aircraft—from six carriers.

Like Martin and Bellinger before him, Farthing was short on optimism. The sole reason for the existence of the military establishment on Oahu, he observed, was to defend the island as an outlying naval base, but if anyone believed that Hawaii was "the strongest outlying naval base in the world," capable of withstanding repeated attacks, he was seriously mistaken. "Plans based on such convictions are inherently weak and tend to create a false sense of security with the consequent unpreparedness for offensive action." And in case that did not lay the situation on the line for Washington, his recommendations should have. To defend the island properly would require 180 B-17 bombers and thirty-six long-range, torpedo-carrying, medium-range planes—"a small force when compared with the importance of this outpost."

These two on-site reports were as clear-eyed and solid as anyone could have asked in their analysis of the danger and the means of countering it. But both contained one insurmountable flaw: at no time during 1941 did the U.S. military possess the hardware or the manpower needed to carry out their advice. Quite justifiably, Colonel Farthing was asking for 180 B-17s. His request unfortunately came at a time when the total number of B-17s in existence, for use by the United States Army, Great Britain, the Philippines, and maybe even China, was 109.

—

Though Colonel Bratton had the uneasy sense that the Japanese device for locating U.S. ships in Pearl Harbor smelled fishy, he didn't connect the message with a move against Pearl Harbor. Perhaps Kimmel or Short, who were on the scene, might have done so—especially if they had seen it in the context of other messages between Honolulu and Tokyo (notably Kita's reply to this particular message, in which he was even more specific about how the location of vessels was to be indicated); but alas, neither Kimmel nor Short received those Magic intercepts or—in most instances—digests of them.

So Yoshikawa went right on spying openly on the great naval base and its dependencies; dressed in a bright aloha shirt, accompanied by one of his geisha friends from the teahouse or a girl from the office, he walked or rode buses and taxis all over the island, took a ride in a sightseeing plane from which the view of the Pearl Harbor anchorage and Hickam and Wheeler air bases was just about perfect, enabling him to note the direction of runways and the number of hangars, from which he estimated the number of aircraft at each field, and his priceless information kept flowing to Tokyo and to Yamamoto's staff, where it was all evaluated and digested and plugged into the final plans for the attack.

American officialdom was acutely aware that this sort of thing was going on and was all but helpless to prevent it. There was no censorship of the mails, no ban on photography or sightseeing, and when Congressman Martin Dies—who told reporters the Japanese spy system "would be a tremendous force to reckon with in the event of war"—proposed to unleash his House Un-American Activities Committee on the problem of espionage and subversion, he was invited to the White House for a quiet conversation with President Roosevelt, then with Cordell Hull. The secretary of state told him that negotiations with the Japanese were at such a delicate stage that an investigation might mean the end of the talks, and the United States, he added pointedly, was in no position to go to war in the Pacific. Somewhat surprisingly, considering his past record, Dies called off his plans, as did Senator Guy Gillette, who had been troubled by the same problem and was planning to look into the activities of Japanese consular officials in Hawaii and the West Coast, in particular. Hull talked the senator out of it by telling him how damaging such an investigation would be to U.S.-Japanese relations at this critical moment, saying, "Please, Senator, I appeal to you— don't rock the boat!" And the boat remained unrocked.

Informative as Yoshikawa's reports were, his youth and relative inexperience persuaded naval intelligence that they lacked authoritative detail, and on November 1, when the liner *Taiyo Maru,* ten days out of Yokohama, docked at Honolulu, two of the arrivals were Commander Toshihide Maejima, a submarine expert, and Lieutenant Commander Suguru Suzuki, a flier and intelligence officer, whose specialty was U.S. air power—particularly aircraft carriers. Neither man's name appeared on the passenger list (Maejima was on the rolls as ship's doctor, Suzuki as assistant purser), and neither had had a particularly restful journey. Since the *Taiyo Maru* had made a trial run over the very course to be followed by Admiral Nagumo's strike force, Maejima and Suzuki had spent much of the time, even after dark, at the ship's rail, scanning the horizon with binoculars for ships, checking and recording the weather, and—once the liner turned south toward Oahu—watching with special care for the first appearance of a U.S. patrol plane. They spotted one just two hundred miles from the island; and one hundred miles out they saw a number of planes in formation.

In port, neither man went ashore, but Nagao Kita visited them regularly. Yoshikawa was not permitted to come aboard lest he come under suspicion, but Kita brought him a questionnaire from Suzuki, consisting of more than a hundred questions, to which naval intelligence wanted complete and detailed answers, and as Yoshikawa diligently completed them, working to the verge of exhaustion, other members of the consulate staff boarded the *Taiyo Maru* daily, carrying newspapers wrapped around his voluminous reports. Just before the ship sailed for Yokohama on the afternoon of November 5, a messenger brought a diplomatic pouch containing Yoshikawa's final study and the best available maps of Oahu. By then, Maejima had satisfied his curiosity about the numerous problems that would face a Japanese submariner, one of which was the impossibility of seeing Kimmel's ships from outside the harbor; and Suzuki possessed information of every conceivable sort—photographs taken at ground level and from the air, figures on the thickness of armor plate on the battleships and of the concrete roof of hangars, Yoshikama's firsthand opinion (based on his own underwater observation) that no antisubmarine net was at the entrance to the harbor. Their chiefs would be pleased with what they carried home— most of it in their heads, in case they were searched; for they had noted the customs officials, FBI men, army intelligence, and counterintelligence personnel who came aboard the *Taiyo Maru* every day she was in port, carefully checking every passenger's luggage. No one, of course, examined the baggage of crew members.

On the return voyage the *Taiyo Maru* retraced the route Kido Butai would follow, and again the intelligence officers took careful notes on the weather, U.S. patrol planes, and other shipping (not a vessel was seen on either leg of the trip). Back in Japan, they reported to the general staff and naval intelligence, and their audience's relief was evident when Suzuki spoke of the weak air patrols north of Oahu, the presence of most capital ships in Pearl Harbor on the weekends, and the lack of activity evident at the military installations on Sunday, November 2; by and large, the picture sketched by the lieutenant commander was of a lazy, relaxed base under peacetime conditions, where many of the men slept late and many were on liberty, while those on duty appeared to be doing little more than killing time.

From Tokyo, Suzuki hurried off to Hitokappu Bay, arriving on November 22 in time to brief Nagumo, Genda, Fuchida, and others. Using large-scale models of Pearl Harbor and Oahu which Nagumo had aboard *Akagi,* Suzuki repeated what he had reported in Tokyo, with particular attention to the air strength evident[4]—including the PBY patrol planes, plus the army's two- and four-engine bombers and fighters, noting that the Americans seldom if ever put a lot of planes in the air over Oahu, and that patrols were generally excellent to the south and west, but inadequate to the north. All of this was more good news to Nagumo's staff, but Suzuki was unable to enlighten them on one key question: how many carriers were at Pearl Harbor? He saw none himself, he replied, but Yoshikawa had observed that three were attached to the fleet, and seemed to move in and out of the area the way other ships did. It was not the sort of news Nagumo wanted to hear; he was a worrier, and the thought of three U.S. carriers on the prowl was unsettling—not only because of the damage they could inflict on Kido Butai, but because of the decision that would have to be faced if his fleet encountered one or more of them: should the attack proceed as planned, or should his planes go after the American flattops?

It was late afternoon on November 25, dark in Hitokappu Bay, with a rough sea, when more than five hundred pilots crowded into the crew's quarters abroad *Akagi* to hear Nagumo outline the mission before their 0600 departure. For many this was the first indication of their destination, and as the admiral finished speaking and bid them "Good fight and good luck!" there was wild shouting and cheering, followed by a discussion by Genda and Fuchida, using the Pearl Harbor mock-up, of how the attack would be executed. Before the night was over, the fliers celebrated with a final *sake* party.

Nagumo had a mighty fleet under his command—thirty ships, including some of Japan's newest and best, spread out in a huge circle formation so that the distance from the van to the rear was about fifty miles—and as they steamed eastward, their passage unremarked by human eye, life went on about as usual in an unsuspecting world. The most violent earthquake recorded since 1755 struck Lisbon, Madeira, and the Azores, though without much damage. In India, five hundred members of the Congress Party were released from prison under a new government policy of leniency toward civil disobedience; even Jawaharlal Nehru, the man who had received the stiffest sentence, was allowed to go. In Cuba, President Fulgencio Batista requested that the legislature declare a state of emergency and place full governing powers in his hands. Other states of emergency were being declared because of those Japanese troop transports: in the Netherlands East Indies, for instance, and in Singapore, whose defenses had just been bolstered by the arrival of Britain's proud new battleship *Prince of Wales* and the battle cruiser *Repulse,* escorted by four destroyers. In Australia and

---

[4]In this single respect, the information Yoshikawa had given Suzuki was faulty; he considerably overestimated the number of American planes, reporting 455 army aircraft when in fact the Hawaiian Air Force had only half that many.

in Hong Kong, troops were on alert, and Rangoon was being reinforced. MacArthur's air force was reportedly standing by in Manila, where all leaves had been canceled; Corregidor, the rock fortress guarding Manila Bay, and the navy base at Cavite were blacked out.

In the United States, no sooner had John L. Lewis called off the captive coal mine strike than more than a million workers in nineteen railway unions threatened to walk out unless they received a wage increase of at least $1 a day. *Someone* was hard at work, apparently; the U.S. Navy announced the sort of news that had prompted Yamamoto's repeated warnings to the war party in Japan—thirty-three warships launched in November, keels laid for fifty-two more, while five new vessels had joined the fleet. President Roosevelt was at Warm Springs, relaxing in the swimming pool, chatting with the foundation's 116 polio victims, joking with his longtime secretary, Missy LeHand, who was recovering from acute neuritis, and enjoying a 4,300-calorie Thanksgiving dinner that had been twice postponed because of the Japanese crisis. An hour after he left the table, he was unexpectedly on board his special train, a grave look on his face, heading for Washington and a meeting with an overwrought Cordell Hull to discuss Premier Tojo's violent speech and what it might mean.

On the night of December 2, Nagumo's task force received a message reading, "Climb Mt. Niitake 1208."[5] This was the immediate result of the imperial conference where the final decision for war had been taken, and the curious phrase meant that hostilities would begin on December 8, Tokyo time. The strike force had just crossed the international date line, which put its calendars a day earlier than Tokyo's; it was then some nine hundred miles north and a little east of Midway, more than halfway to its destination.

━━━

On Thursday evening, December 4, twenty-four of Washington's high and mighty gathered in the North Lounge of the Carlton Hotel, because production boss Donald Nelson, who was throwing the party, realized that even though ships were sliding down the ways in increasing numbers, the nation's defense program was still a long way from being on track. It was his idea to get this crowd together in the interests of harmony. Ostensibly, it was a dinner in honor of Vice President Henry Wallace, and at the outset it was all sociability, the smoke from cigarettes and cigars floating to the high ceiling of the paneled room to hover over the cocktail talk and laughter. After they sat down to dinner, these two dozen pillars of government and industry, the talk continued amiably, but one man who was present remembered vividly the curious feeling of tension in the air, perhaps because of the incongruous mix of personalities. Nelson himself, Bill Knudsen,

[5]Mount Niitake on the island of Formosa was the highest peak in the Japanese empire—higher even than sacred Fuji.

Frank Knox, Ed Stettinius, and others were Republicans to a man. Most of them had been brought to the capital to help solve a critical production problem, but the problem had not been solved, there was a great deal of talk that they were somehow to blame for the failure, they didn't like the New Deal now any more than when they had first arrived in town, and besides, a certain amount of rivalry existed between them, which resulted in considerable jockeying for position and power. To top it off, the guest of honor was about as strange a bedfellow as any of them could possibly have imagined—a real wild-eyed liberal if ever there was one, and something of a nut, to boot. So it was not exactly a gemütlich group Donald Nelson had assembled. After the dessert plates had been removed and coffee, brandy, and cigars had been passed around the table, the speeches began, and very quickly it became evident that what had seemed like stress was all of that and more.

After Nelson and several guests had had their say, much of it dealing with the size of the production job, the ability of this very group to see it through, and the need for government and industry to pull together, the host called on the secretary of the navy, and Knox got to his feet, surveyed the faces before him in silence, and in a low, almost conspiratorial tone made insiders of them, saying that "within these four walls, I want you to know that our situation tonight is very serious—more serious, probably, than most of us realize. We are very close to war. War may begin in the Pacific at any moment. Literally, at any moment. It may even be beginning tonight, while we're sitting here, for all we know. We are that close to it."

Letting that sink in, his voice and manner changed, and he continued: "But I want you to know that no matter what happens, the United States Navy is ready! Every man is at his post, every ship is at its station. . . . Whatever happens, the navy is not going to be caught napping."

Amid the approving sounds from around the table he sat down, after which one of the other guests passed a note to Nelson, asking if he might say a few words. Nelson nodded approval and called on Robert Wyman Horton—the fellow in charge of information at the Office of Emergency Management who took such a dim view of the dollar-a-year men who were supposedly solving the nation's production problems. Now, Horton didn't care for Frank Knox any more than he did for some of the other businessmen who had been summoned to Washington. He had known him when Knox was publisher of the *Manchester* (New Hampshire) *Union-Leader,* and later, when he was hired by Hearst to put the chain's Boston paper back on its feet. Knox had the reputation of being an efficiency expert, and he had quickly made two moves aimed at improving the Boston paper's balance sheet: one was to remove the free sanitary napkins from the ladies' room; the other was to insist that before anyone on the paper received a new pencil he had to turn in the stub of the old one. Horton was puzzled as to why FDR had taken on Knox, because the publisher wasn't very bright and he hated the president; but Horton understood that Roosevelt badly needed some Republicans in his administration at this time in order to get business on his side. If he didn't accomplish that, he could be in very big trouble.

Yet dislike of Knox was not what prompted Horton to speak as he did. As he remarked later, "I just couldn't let him get away with the bullshit about how well prepared the navy was." Horton had seen otherwise with his own eyes, and he proceeded to give the group chapter and verse. He had gone over to the Navy Department the other day for a conference, he said. It was just before four o'clock in the afternoon, and he was "almost trampled underfoot in the lobby by captains and admirals, rushing out with golf bags over their shoulders. It seemed to me that the high-ranking people in the department were knocking off work rather early, if we're so close to a war."

Knox leaned toward Nelson, glared at him, and whispered, "Who *is* this son of a bitch?"

Undeterred, Horton continued. He had gone down Chesapeake Bay on a little outing on a Coast Guard patrol boat, and the chief in charge of the boat thought it might be fun to run into the Norfolk navy yard to see what they could see. They cruised all around the yard, right up to the British carrier *Illustrious,* which was in for repairs, saw everything they wanted to see, and not a soul stopped them or challenged their right to be there. On their way out through Hampton Roads they pulled in beside a dock to make a phone call, tied up alongside several minesweepers (again, no one challenged them or tried to find out if the boat really belonged to the Coast Guard), wandered around the pier looking unsuccessfully for a telephone, inquired of a sentry where the nearest phone was and were told that it was half a mile up the road. Sure, the chief with him was wearing a uniform, Horton said, but there are thirty places in Norfolk where you can walk in and buy a CPO's uniform. The guard "didn't know who we were, but he didn't ask for a pass and he didn't want to see any credentials. . . . We could have been spies, saboteurs, anything, but the navy . . . let us wander all over that base, after dark, for upwards of half an hour, without once bothering to find out who we were or what our business was. We could have blown the whole place to pieces, for all the obstacles the navy put in our way."

Then he looked over at Knox and said coldly, "Mister Secretary, I don't think your navy *is* ready."

CHAPTER 53

———◆———

"...the Japs are planning
some deviltry ..."

s much as Admiral Nagumo might be haunted by lack of knowledge
concerning the three American carriers, he could hardly have been
more distressed than Lieutenant Commander Edwin T. Layton, the
fleet intelligence officer at Pearl Harbor, whose responsibility it was to keep
tabs on Japan's naval forces for the admiral, and who had "lost" all the
carriers of the First and Second Japanese fleets—that is, the six carriers of
Divisions 1, 2, and 5, *Akagi, Kaga, Hiryu, Soryu, Shokaku,* and *Zuikaku.*

The U.S. Navy had three intelligence divisions in Hawaii—Layton's Fleet
Intelligence, Counter Espionage under Captain Irving Mayfield, and Combat Intelligence under Lieutenant Commander Joseph Rochefort, which
was the source of much of Layton's information. Rochefort was widely
regarded as one of the most experienced cryptanalysts in the navy, but since
it was his unit's business to determine the location of Japanese ships by
means of radio traffic analysis, he didn't have much time for intercepting
and decoding messages and sent most of what he received to Washington
for processing. At best, radio-traffic analysis was an inexact science, and on
November 1 it had been made even more difficult when the Japanese
changed their call signals. By the end of the month, Combat Intelligence
had partially unraveled the puzzle when suddenly the call signals were
changed again on December 1. This highly unusual departure from the

norm alerted Rochefort to the prospect that something big was in the offing, and his intelligence summary for that day suggested that this could be "an additional progressive step in preparing for active operations on a large scale."

The Americans had no way of knowing it at the time, but until October of 1941 their assessment of the Japanese navy's order of battle corresponded precisely with the facts, and what was more, they knew a good many details about Japan's move south toward the Philippines and Malaysia. All the units involved in that operation had been clearly identified by radio traffic, but since the carrier fleet had not been heard from in any traffic since November 16, Rochefort and Layton understandably concluded that those ships were still in home waters. When in port, or close to home, Japanese naval vessels typically switched to low frequencies to prevent direction-finder stations and intercept stations from listening in on their traffic. That this was probably what had occurred was further supported by the total absence of radio signals *to* the carriers, and Layton's best guess was that they were being held in readiness in home waters until the Japanese saw what the United States planned to do about their move into Southeast Asia. Layton knew that two Japanese task forces were already heading south— one into the South China Sea, probably to strike at the Kra Isthmus or somewhere in the Gulf of Siam, the other moving toward a destination in the Netherlands East Indies—and the U.S. presence on their flank, in the Philippines, was bound to make them extremely uncomfortable. If the negotiations in Washington collapsed, and the U.S. Pacific Fleet suddenly steamed west from Hawaii, the Japanese would want its carriers ready to sail in a hurry. Given the information available to Layton and the fact that the missing carriers were neither transmitting nor receiving, it was as good a guess as a man could make.

Layton, who reported directly to Admiral Kimmel, was better informed than any other intelligence officer in Hawaii, army or navy, for he received data from the Office of Naval Intelligence in Washington, from the Federal Bureau of Investigation in Washington and Hawaii, from Rochefort and Mayfield, from British sources in the Far East, from U.S. naval attachés and Foreign Service officers, and from a number of local sources he considered reliable, and what he knew as of December 6, 1941, was enough to put together what he called the "framework of an intelligence picture." He thought of a problem like this as a jigsaw puzzle: first you find the border and put together the framework, which gives you the scope of the picture; then you fit pieces together to form part of the pattern, or all of it, if possible.

What he had was quite an array of facts on which to make a presumption. The Japanese had changed their call signs on November 1 and December 1. The numerous reports of Japanese troop ships and naval escorts heading south had been confirmed by radio traffic. On November 24, the U.S. chief of naval operations had warned that Mr. Hull's chances of success in the negotiations looked "very doubtful" and suggested the possibility of "a surprise aggressive movement in any direction including attack on Philippines or Guam." On November 27, Stark sent out the "war warning." On November 28, the CNO sent Kimmel a copy of the army's war warning, which had prompted General Short's command to go to Alert Condition No. 1. On December 3, Washington reported that Japanese diplomatic and consular posts had been ordered to destroy most of their codes and ciphers and burn all sensitive documents—the classic sign that war is in the offing. On December 6, the FBI in Honolulu notified Layton that the consulate there had been burning papers for the last two days. And also on December 6, the commander in chief of the U.S. Asiatic Fleet reported sightings of Japanese ships in Camranh Bay. All of this added up to the likelihood of war within a matter of hours or days, at most, starting in Southeast Asia, perhaps in the Philippines, maybe even in Guam. But not a piece of Layton's puzzle suggested Hawaii. (Besides, Kimmel had already declared that such an attempt would be "national suicide" for the Japanese, and he and everyone else knew they would never attempt it.)

Layton was an intelligent man as well as an intelligence man, and he recognized how handicapped he was by the lack of political background information on which to make certain assumptions or informed estimates. What he had to guide him, by and large, was what he read in newspapers and magazines or what he heard from Kimmel, who carried on an active personal correspondence with Betty Stark, but since intelligence work is a great deal more than decoding messages or making educated guesses based on radio-direction-finder bearings, he had asked Commander A. H. McCollum, head of ONI's Far Eastern Division, to send him information based on decoded diplomatic messages—the stuff of the Magic intercepts. (Layton didn't know about Magic, but he had, on several occasions, received useful data based on what he assumed was deciphered material.) The request put McCollum on the spot, and he wrote back at some length, sympathetically for the most part, explaining that security made it impossible to broaden the circle of recipients of certain material, and telling Layton he would just have to rely on the Navy Department for "evaluated views of political situations." The conclusion of the letter was a classic example of the headquarters mind at work: "While you and the Fleet may be highly interested in politics," McCollum observed, "there is nothing you can do about it. Therefore, information of political significance, except as it affects immediate action by the Fleet, is merely of interest to you and not a matter of utility." Translated, this could mean that Layton and the commanding officer he served, whose intelligence needs he was expected to fill, were not supposed to speculate on U.S. or the enemy's political intentions, nor to hypothesize on the basis of what they knew about Japanese behavior or psychology. Washington would provide all they needed to know. But Washington, tragically, did not.

Americans of that generation were familiar with the legerdemain of Houdini and Thurston the Magician; they had watched W. C. Fields perform his incomparable version of the shell game; they knew that the hand is quicker than the eye, that misdirection is the secret of prestidigitation; so it is odd that no one in high places was on the lookout for the Japanese to pull a rabbit out of a hat. From the president on down, officials credited the Japanese with trickery and sneaky doings, but since everyone knew they were headed for Southeast Asia, that was where they were going—make no mistake about it. But they were also going somewhere else as well, and even when a few people caught on to what might be happening, no one listened, any more than they had heeded Ambassador Grew's warning about an attack on Pearl Harbor a year earlier. Once the official mind is locked in place, it is difficult to change.

Unfortunately, what information Washington provided Hawaii was often spotty, to say the least, and instructions were frequently ambiguous, vague, or left entirely too much to the discretion of the commander in the field. General Short, whose local intelligence resources were minimal (he had few of his own, and what he got from the navy was largely what the navy thought he should have—nothing too sensitive, and furnished on a most irregular basis), received only infrequent reports from Washington, and all too many of those on a level of the army's warning of November 27—a message more puzzling than illuminating. It began by stating the obvious: that Japan's future action was unpredictable. Then it declared that hostile action was possible at any moment. If hostilities could not be avoided, however, it was important that "Japan commit the first overt act." On the other hand, this policy "should not be construed as restricting you to a course of action that might jeopardize your defense." Short was to undertake reconnaissance and other measures considered necessary, but not in such a manner as to "alarm [the] civil population or disclose intent." He was to carry out the tasks assigned him in Rainbow 5, pertinent to Japan, and he was to limit dissemination of this warning to "minimum essential officers."

Since no one in Washington troubled to look into the matter, it is fair to repeat that the top military brass were both casual and negligent in assuming that the Hawaiian commands were kept well informed. Not only did Stark believe that Kimmel was seeing intercepts of the most important Japanese messages (which he was not), but Rear Admiral Richmond Kelly Turner, one of Stark's principal advisers, was under the totally erroneous impression that Kimmel had a Magic decoding machine, and that he and Short not only received but shared the identical sensitive information.

Although General Walter Short was unwittingly victimized by Washington and by his navy colleagues in Hawaii, both of whom were supposed to feed him information, he was also the victim of a personal obsession—fear of sabotage. Short's reading of the November 27 army warning message was that it was imperative to avoid war, that no international incident should be permitted to occur in Hawaii which Japan could regard as an overt act, and—since the message contained no specific mention of a coming attack—

that the sole possibility of "hostile action at any moment" was sabotage. So sabotage was what he prepared to combat. He never showed the warning to his field commanders, to see what they made of it or what they might suggest. His concerns focused almost exclusively on what he thought Japanese saboteurs might do, as a result of which he instructed his ordnance department to issue no ammunition to the troops and ordered that the shells for his mobile batteries be locked up several miles from the guns. Only when Major General Henry Burgin, the coast artillery commander, objected to being without ammunition did he give permission for shells for the fixed batteries to be near the weapons (provided they remained in boxes).

One of the many misunderstandings that led to so much tragedy was that the army and navy in Hawaii had different systems for going on alert and neither bothered to communicate that fact to the other. In the navy, No. 1 was full alert, No. 2 was less so, and No. 3 verged on the routine. The army's alert conditions were the exact opposite: No. 1 covered only sabotage, No. 2 was for an air attack, and No. 3 was a full alert. So, in the wake of the army warning of November 27, Kimmel and his staff were somewhat surprised to learn that the army had gone to a No. 1 alert condition, but assumed that Short's 25,000 well-trained troops would be ready for anything, when in fact they were concerned only with what enemy agents might attempt.

Short possessed a weapon that had been instrumental in saving the British from defeat at the hands of the Luftwaffe—radar. He also had something like a hundred lookout stations on high ground all over Oahu. But the general had a low opinion of radar; it was useless against sabotage, for one thing, and he viewed it more as a training tool than as something that could be put to practical use. Although he was later to admit that the task of the radar stations and the lookouts, the army's "sound detectors," and the communications network that connected them was to spot enemy ships or planes and report their presence immediately, he did not have the system in full operation at this time because the stations "were not alerted for aircraft attack or for attack by a landing force, or an all-out attack." In his positively stupefying rationale, the very eyes and ears that were supposed to warn of an enemy's approach were closed because no such approach was expected!

For his part, Kimmel concurred with Layton that the coming onslaught was aimed at Southeast Asia, so he made no change in the disposition of long-range air reconnaissance or patrols. Nor did he alter the predictable schedule of fleet movements which enabled agent Yoshikawa to state with assurance that most of the ships would be in port over the weekend. The admiral considered that the fleet was on a war footing, as it had been for some time, so there was no need for change in that regard, and he and his war plans officer agreed that there was no risk whatever of a surprise attack on Pearl Harbor. Consequently, he saw no reason to inform his air aide or Rear Admiral Bellinger, who was responsible for patrol aircraft, of the warnings contained in the November 24 and 27 messages. Nor did he notify General Short that the Japanese were destroying their codes.

Apart from specific failures, each commander had his own private vision of action on the day the alarm bell sounded. Husband Kimmel saw a fleet of mighty battlewagons and carriers, protected by destroyers, submarines, and an umbrella of aircraft, steaming out of the harbor and taking up formation to attack the Japanese. For Walter Short, action meant rounding up hordes of enemy saboteurs before they could destroy his precious caches of ammunition and weapons. What neither man reckoned on was the failure of the alarm bell to sound, or the possibility that Pearl Harbor might be the scene of action. That they were far from alone in this line of thinking is nowhere better illustrated than in a memorandum George Marshall wrote to the commander in chief of the U.S. armed forces.

Describing Oahu for President Roosevelt, the general noted that its fortification, its garrison, and its physical characteristics made it the strongest fortress in the world. Then he went on to describe how its defenders would deal with an attack, should anyone be so foolhardy as to attempt one:

With adequate air defense enemy carriers, naval escorts, and transports will begin to come under air attack at a distance of 750 miles. This attack will increase in intensity until within 200 miles of the objective the enemy will be subject to attack by all types of bombardment closely supported by our most modern pursuit.

There was a flaw somewhere in the scheme General Marshall outlined for the president, because on December 6, 1941, Admiral Nagumo's strike force had penetrated that invisible frontier 750 miles from Oahu and as yet not a U.S. ship or airplane had seen, much less attacked, it. At approximately the same hour Mr. Roosevelt finished writing his message to Emperor Hirohito, Nagumo's ships refueled for the last time, and the tankers, escorted by a destroyer, turned west toward Japan. A few hours later the admiral signaled his fleet to head south and increase speed. In the van were four destroyers; behind them in column the two battleships and the light cruiser; out on each flank a heavy cruiser; and behind this formidable shield of steel and firepower came two columns of aircraft carriers, three in each line, their hangar decks crowded with planes. Flanking them to port and starboard were most of the destroyers, with two more astern, trailed by three submarines. Two days earlier, the ocean had been so rough the ships rolled as much as 45 degrees to one side, but the fleet had been blessed with calm seas during the final refueling. That was by far the most hazardous moment of the whole voyage, since the maneuver had to be executed at a point that was within range of those B-17s in which General Marshall and Colonel Farthing put such faith, yet too distant from Oahu for the planes to take off from the carriers.

Not long after the refueling took place hundreds of miles north of him, agent Tasheo Yoshikawa checked the weather conditions in Honolulu and set out for Pearl Harbor, and when he returned to the consulate several hours later he had the information Tokyo needed so urgently. In addition to information on the movements of the fleet after December 4, he had been asked if any barrage balloons were in evidence in or around the harbor, and he replied that none were to be seen. Then he added gratuitously that the opportunity still existed "for a surprise attack." Whether he knew or only surmised what was afoot, Yoshikawa's astounding breach of security, even in an encrypted message, was the first such mention to appear in any traffic in or out of Tokyo, but regrettably his dispatch was not decoded by U.S. Army cryptanalysts until December 8.

One of the major difficulties in interpreting and utilizing the Magic intercepts was their sheer volume. So many existed that those deemed to be less important had to be set aside to await their turn. It was virtually impossible, moreover, to extract a single message and pin it down as the key to something hugely significant, or to link several pieces of information and detect a pattern. The historian Roberta Wohlstetter describes the problem as "noise"—a mass of signals, many of them utterly useless to those attempting to divine Japan's intentions, some of them ambiguous, some contradictory—and by December 6, the afternoon when President Roosevelt was drafting his message to Hirohito, the noise level was all but impenetrable. Yet curiously, on that very afternoon Japan's military intentions against the United States came closer to being revealed than at any other moment.

Dorothy Edgers was fairly new to Lieutenant Commander Alwin Kramer's cryptographic unit. She was a schoolteacher who had lived in Japan for more than thirty of her thirty-eight years, and her command of the Japanese language was such that she had been awarded a diploma accrediting her to teach it to Japanese people up to the high school level. McCollum, who had hired Mrs. Edgers, had been lucky to get her. Like most Saturdays, December 6 started off to be a slow day, with the staff leaving about 12:30, and after glancing through the deciphered cables in her basket and deciding that one in particular seemed more interesting than the others, Mrs. Edgers began translating it. The message proved to be from Consul General Kita in Honolulu; it had been sent on December 3 to the Third Section, or military intelligence, in Tokyo; and it had to do with movements of certain types of ships in and out of Pearl Harbor and described how information about such activities would be communicated to Japanese vessels standing offshore. Some of it was reminiscent of the famous church-tower signals to Paul Revere: different combinations of lights were to be displayed in the windows of certain houses in Oahu and Maui. And in case the lights were not visible, the information would be provided in faked want ads on radio station KGMB, with a Chinese rug for sale meaning one type of ship movement, a situation-wanted ad from a beauty parlor another.

Strange doings indeed, and Mrs. Edgers thought it worth a further look by someone higher up the ladder. She showed the message to Chief Yeoman Harold Bryant, who was standing in for Kramer while the latter made his rounds, delivering translations of intercepts. Bryant agreed that it was interesting and unusual, but since he didn't want the responsibility of telling her to work overtime on it, he suggested she let it go until Monday.

But Mrs. Edger's curiosity was piqued, and she decided to work without authorization, figuring that Kramer ought to know about this material. By now all the others except Bryant had gone home, and she continued to work in the almost empty office until she had completed her translation. Before leaving, she handed it to the chief, who said he would see that Kramer saw it as soon as he returned. The normal procedure was for Bryant to edit messages, especially those of obvious importance, put them into the form used by the unit, and deliver them to Kramer, who further edited the translation before they went to recipients. At a time when it was clear to just about everybody in the United States that the Japanese were moving toward war—quite likely with us—it was hardly surprising that Mrs. Edgers should find sinister Tokyo's keen interest in the U.S. naval base at Pearl Harbor and the bizarre methods by which the consulate in Honolulu was to report on American ships. Kramer didn't see matters quite as she did, however, and may have been annoyed that she had stayed on past quitting time to work on the message. In the event, he did not work on Kita's cable to Tokyo until December 8, 9, and 10, by which time he was all too unhappily aware of its significance. On Saturday afternoon, however, Kramer had something more pressing on his mind: the first thirteen parts of Japan's reply to Hull's proposal began to come in at 3:00 P.M., shortly after he returned to the office, and whatever he might have done with Mrs. Edgers' rough translation was forgotten in his eagerness to translate this important document.

━━━

While Nagumo's strike force plunged through heavy swells at a speed of twenty-four knots, General and Mrs. Short and their friends Lieutenant Colonel Fielder and his wife (Fielder was Short's G-2) were leaving the Schofield Barracks officers' club after a charity dinner dance. On the way home, they passed Pearl Harbor, where all the lights were ablaze, and Short turned to Fielder and said, "What a target that would make!"

The man whose fleet lay at anchor there was nursing his only drink of the evening at a small dinner party at the Halekulani Hotel in Honolulu. Admiral Kimmel (whose wife had remained on the mainland when he moved to Hawaii) mentioned to Rear Admiral Milo Draemel that Nagao Kita had invited him to stop by the consulate for a glass of champagne. Draemel, who didn't trust the Japanese, urged Kimmel not to go, and Kimmel said he wouldn't. He left the party early, at about 9:30; he didn't keep late hours, and anyway, he had a golf game with Short the next morning.

At the same time Kimmel and Short were driving home, Tokyo dispatched part fourteen of its reply to Hull's proposals, and when Alwin Kramer reached his office at 7:30 on Sunday morning, the message awaited him. The final paragraph stated: "The Japanese Government regrets to have to notify hereby the American Government that in view of the attitude of the American Government it cannot but consider that it is impossible to reach an agreement through further negotiations." What President Roosevelt had said meant war the previous evening was not war, evidently—not a declaration, at any rate—but clearly negotiations were at an end. Commander McCollum delivered a copy of the message to Admiral Stark, and the two of them, with Admiral Theodore Wilkinson, the director of ONI, discussed the virulent tone, wondering how it could mean anything but hostilities. Wilkinson suggested that they might send another warning to Pearl Harbor, but after some discussion, Stark decided against it.

Roosevelt received the material at about 10:00, and his reaction was more temperate than it had been the night before. Secretaries Hull, Knox, and Stimson had the message at about the same time, and after they met to discuss it, Stimson noted in his diary that "Hull is very certain that the Japs are planning some deviltry and we are all wondering when the blow will strike."

While Colonel Bratton was reading through the entire fourteen-part message to see if he could figure out what it meant, an intercept of a one-sentence cable from Foreign Minister Togo to Nomura was handed to him: "Will the Ambassador please submit to the United States Government (if possible to the Secretary of State) our reply to the United States at 1:00 P.M. on the 7th, your time." As Bratton said later, this hit him right between the eyes—"immediately stunned" him into "frenzied activity," was the way he put it—because of the implication that something vitally important was about to occur. He could recall no previous message that specified a delivery time as this did; after all, no ambassador set the hour when Hull would see him—it was the other way around. Furthermore, diplomacy didn't happen on Sundays: it was not a working day.

Everything pointed to the possibility, then, of an early-morning attack on an American installation in the Pacific, probably the Philippines, as Bratton saw it, and he dropped everything, turned his office over to his assistant, and went off in search of someone senior enough to take action, to get a warning to field commanders in the Pacific. It never occurred to him that the Japanese might attack in Hawaii, he said later. "Nobody in ONI, nobody in G-2, knew that any major element of the fleet was in Pearl Harbor on Sunday morning the 7th of December. We all thought they had gone to sea . . . because that was part of the war plan, and they had been given a war warning."

Commander Kramer's reaction to the short message was similar to Bratton's. For two years, earlier in his career, he had served as navigator aboard a destroyer operating out of Pearl Harbor, and instinctively he drew a time circle to determine how the 1:00 deadline might tie in with the Japanese convoy off Indochina. As he did so, it crossed his mind that 1:00 in Washington would be 7:30 A.M. in Pearl Harbor[1]—the quietest time of the week aboard ship, when the crews would be piped to breakfast, when only the men standing watch would be topside, with most of the crew ashore on leave. Kramer left at once on his delivery route with this and other messages, and outside Stark's office discussed the curious 1:00 deadline with Commander McCollum, who agreed that it must be related to the Japanese move against Malaya and the Kra peninsula.

Meantime, Bratton found neither Marshall nor Gerow nor Miles in their offices, so at 9:00 he telephoned Marshall's quarters at Fort Myer, only to be told that the general had gone horseback riding. Bratton told the orderly to find General Marshall and tell him it was vitally important that he call Bratton immediately. But either Bratton failed to get across the urgency or the orderly was not about to go chasing off cross-country in search of a four-star general; whatever the reason, Marshall never got the message until he came in from riding about 10:00. He phoned Bratton, who apparently conveyed his state of agitation but not much else, and the general told him he would come to the War Department as soon as he showered and changed his clothes. When he reached the Munitions Building, Bratton gave him the fourteen-part message, and he began to read. (Marshall was the only high official to whom Bratton had not delivered the first thirteen parts the previous evening, so this whole thing was news to the chief of staff.[2]) The colonel, who had been joined by General Miles, tried to direct Marshall's attention to the final section, but the general waved him off irritably and went on reading the fat sheaf of papers as the minutes ticked away.

When he finished he asked Bratton, Miles, and Gerow, who had joined them, what significance they attached to the 1:00 delivery time. It could jibe with an early-morning attack somewhere in the Pacific, Bratton volunteered. Everyone agreed, and Marshall reached for a scratch pad and quickly wrote a message in longhand to the army's Pacific commands. Then he telephoned Betty Stark to ask if he wanted naval commands in the area included as addresses. The admiral replied that he thought they had had enough warnings lately, but phoned back a few minutes later and asked that the phrase "Inform Navy" be added to the message. Did Marshall want to use navy facilities to send the dispatch? Stark inquired; they were extremely rapid when the situation required. No, Marshall replied, it should move

---

[1]At that time, Pearl Harbor used a time uniquely its own. Since it lay halfway between two time zones, it operated on a clock five and a half hours different from Washington's, four and a half hours (minus a day) from Japan's.

[2]It is worth noting, as Marshall's biographer Forrest Pogue points out, that the thirteen parts had been read and discussed "by the President, the Secretaries of State, Army, Navy, the Chiefs of Army and Navy Intelligence, the Chiefs of Army and Navy War Plans Divisions, and the Chiefs of Naval Operations," none of whom thought it necessary to warn the Pearl Harbor or Philippine commands.

quickly by army channels, and at 11:50 A.M. he handed the piece of paper to Bratton. Gerow called after the colonel to say that if a priority had to be indicated, the Philippines should get the message first—that was the most likely point of attack.

In the signals room more minutes passed while Colonel Edward French, who was in charge there, and a clerk tried to decipher Marshall's handwriting; finally Bratton read it to them, and the clerk typed:

Japanese are presenting at one pm eastern standard time today what amounts to an ultimatum also they are under orders to destroy their code machine immediately. Just what significance the hour set may have we do not know but be on alert accordingly. Inform naval authorities of this communication. Marshall.

French assured Bratton that the communication would go out within half an hour, but he neglected to say that atmospheric conditions had prevented the signals section from getting through to Hawaii for the past hour or so and he would have to send the coded message by commercial telegraph— Western Union to San Francisco, and from there to Honolulu by RCA teletype. Apparently no one thought to use the scrambler telephone, so the warning to General Short—whose command was third on the priority list, after Manila and Panama—went out at 12:17 P.M. and was received by the RCA office in Honolulu at 7:33 A.M. local time. No priority was indicated, so the young Japanese messenger put it with other telegrams for Fort Shafter, cranked up his motorcycle, and rode off toward Short's headquarters.

———

The night was overcast, with only the occasional fleeting glimpse of the moon's light they had hoped to have, and a strong northeast breeze had the carriers listing at a 15-degree angle. A few minutes before 2:00 A.M. a radio message came in to the strike force, relaying the final, all-important facts about the situation in Pearl Harbor. On the evening of the 5th, the report stated, the battleship *Utah* (which was in fact used only for towing targets for gunnery practice now) and a seaplane tender had entered the harbor, bringing the total there to nine battleships, three light cruisers, three seaplane tenders, and seventeen destroyers, plus four light cruisers and two destroyers in the docks. All the heavy cruisers and—here Admiral Nagumo's heart sank—all the carriers were at sea.[3]

Some of the Japanese pilots had slept little or not at all and were up and dressed at 3:30, writing a last letter home, mentally rehearsing their assignments. Commander Fuchida, who would be leading the first attack wave,

[3]Luckily, the *Enterprise* had sailed for Wake Island on November 28; the *Lexington* and five cruisers had headed for Midway on December 5; and *Saratoga* was on the West Coast for repairs.

had turned in after 10:00 and was up at 5:00, refreshed and ready for the day for which they had planned and trained so long. He put on red underwear and a red shirt he had purchased for just this occasion: if he should be wounded, he didn't want his men to see the blood. Two hours later, after a ceremonial breakfast of red rice and bream, he and the others assembled in the ready room for a final briefing on the attack plan, with particular attention to the high-level and torpedo-bombing tactics to be followed. Nagumo and Genda wished them success, Fuchida called them to attention, and they went up on deck and climbed into the planes. Each man tied a traditional battle headband around his head, a *hachimaki* on which the word *hissho* was printed, meaning "certain victory."

Heavy seas delayed the takeoff by about twenty minutes, but at last the six carriers turned almost due east into the wind and increased speed to twenty-four knots. The pilots slammed shut their cockpit canopies, and at 6:00 A.M., following the order to take off, engines roared in the predawn darkness and one by one, the heavily loaded aircraft of the first attack group picked up speed along the carrier decks, all but one[4] struggling into the air after the heart-stopping moment when each seemed about to plunge into the waves off the bow—forty-three Zero fighters first, then forty-nine three-man high-level bombers with Fuchida's plane in the lead, followed by fifty-one dive-bombers and forty torpedo bombers. The moment they were airborne, plane handlers began wrestling aircraft of the second attack group onto elevators and onto the flight decks, and just after 7:00 A.M. they took off. By the time the sun was rising, some 350 aircraft were on their way to Pearl Harbor, 220 miles to the south.

Reconnaissance seaplanes catapulted from the heavy cruisers and battleships were already circling to patrol altitude, ready to warn Nagumo instantly of any approaching American ships or planes, and the admiral ordered a turn south, where he would take up a position about 180 miles north of Oahu and wait for his planes to return.

---

[4]The pilot of the plane that crashed into the sea was rescued by a destroyer. One other plane was unable to accompany the flight because of engine trouble.

CHAPTER 54

---◆---

"My God, it's war!"

For a little more than three years, America had been living on borrowed time, and on December 7, 1941, the loan was called.

The reckoning began at 3:42 A.M., Hawaii time—not at all as Admiral Yamamoto had planned it, but with the sighting of one of the midget submarines he had been so reluctant to use for fear they would be discovered and alert the Americans to the attack. *Condor,* a U.S. minesweeper, spotted it outside the entrance to Pearl Harbor, signaled to the destroyer *Ward,* which was patroling nearby, and the *Ward*'s captain, Lieutenant William Outerbridge—who was completing his first night on board his first command—immediately sounded General Quarters and started a search. An hour later when no contact had been made the search was abandoned and the crew secured from GQ. At 6:40 the helmsman saw a periscope near the supply ship *Antares,* which was towing a barge into the entrance channel, and as the *Ward* raced toward the sub it quickly became apparent that it was following the barge, using it as a screen to get into the harbor.

The officer of the deck hailed Outerbridge, who ran to the bridge pulling on a Japanese kimono; he sounded General Quarters again, and as soon as the crew was at battle stations commenced firing. One shot slammed into the conning tower, the *Ward* ran over the sub and dropped depth charges, and after radioing headquarters one message that he decided was ambiguous, Outerbridge sent off another at 6:53. As a description of the opening engagement in a brutal war that would not end for four years, it was admirably concise and specific: "Attacked, fired on, depth-bombed, and sunk submarine operating in defensive sea area."

Neither Outerbridge nor the *Ward* was through for the day—not by a long shot. A few minutes later, after observing a sampan inside the restricted area, the destroyer had begun escorting it toward Honolulu when the sonar operator picked up another underwater contact. The skipper ordered full speed ahead in that direction, dropped another load of depth charges, and had the satisfaction of seeing a big black bubble of oil rise to the surface in the ship's wake. Ten minutes after sending his first message, he radioed again to the Fourteenth Naval District headquarters, telling it to stand by for further word. It promised to be an exciting morning.[1]

For a destroyer to sink two submarines in less than half an hour was extraordinary; for the feat to be achieved by a lieutenant on his maiden patrol aboard his first command made it just about miraculous, and that's the way headquarters viewed it. After the first signal was decoded and typed, which took almost twenty minutes, the duty officer, Lieutenant Commander Harold Kaminski, tried unsuccessfully to reach Admiral Bloch's aide, then got through to Kimmel's chief of staff, Captain Earle, who found it hard to believe his ears but told Kaminski to make a couple more calls and have the dispatch verified while he phoned Admiral Bloch. Somehow, in the ensuing conversations, Outerbridge's message that he had *fired on* the sub (and had therefore actually seen it) was forgotten, and much time was lost trying to decide if this was merely one more of the many false contacts reported by destroyers in these anxious days; there was a great deal of telephoning back and forth, and by and by someone decided to call Kimmel at his home, up on the slope of Makalapa Crater, east of Pearl Harbor, about five minutes' drive from headquarters. That was at 7:40, and the admiral said he would come to the office as soon as he shaved and dressed.

———

Within minutes of the *Condor*'s sighting of the midget sub off Pearl Harbor, Commander Yuzuru Sanematsu arrived at the entrance to the Japanese embassy in Washington. He had some work to attend to and had come in at 9:00 to finish it; he wanted to be on time for a golf date in the early afternoon. To his astonishment and disgust, the iron gate was unlocked, milk bottles and the Sunday papers were still on the doorstep, and a sheaf of telegrams was stuffed into the mail slot at the front door. Obviously the staff had overslept after the previous night's farewell party for Hidenari

---

[1]None of the midget submarines employed in the attack had the slightest effect, and all five were lost. One was beached, two were sunk, and two were lost at sea.

Terasaki, so the assistant naval attaché, grumbling to himself about negligence and sloppy work, gathered up the telegrams, opened the door, and went inside.

Before he was posted to the United States, Sanematsu had served as a kind of flag secretary to Yamamoto, at a time when the admiral was under such vicious attacks by rightist, prowar factions that it was feared he would be murdered. Every mail brought threatening letters from such groups as the League for Carrying Through the Holy War, demands for his resignation, open suggestions of blackmail (there were several women other than his wife in Yamamoto's life), and accusations that navy commanders were cowards, and since Sanematsu and several colleagues acted as appointments secretaries, they had the awkward and often extremely risky task of screening visitors for potential assassins. Sanematsu's sleeping quarters were nearby, and he kept a sword beside his bed.

By comparison with that duty, his time in America had been immensely pleasant—the most carefree period of his life, he said later: the job was fairly easy, and he especially enjoyed the language courses he took at the University of Vermont and Princeton. During 1941, the bad times began. Whenever he went out in public in Washington, he could feel "the cold eyes of Americans" on him as relations between his country and the United States worsened. He knew little about Japan's plans, but he had read the telegrams from Yoshikawa to Tokyo and realized they were not ordinary messages; the government's intense interest in Pearl Harbor led him to assume it would be a target. He also reasoned that it would come as a surprise, following the pattern set by Admiral Togo in the Russian war, and that it would be made on Christmas, since the American military personnel would be celebrating for two days, and would be caught off guard. In fact, he had made a bet with a navy colleague that Christmas would be the date. Then he received orders to destroy his code books, and he knew he had lost the bet: war was imminent and would come before Christmas, after all.

As other members of the staff arrived, the embassy took on an atmosphere of frantic chaos. After Terasaki's farewell party, after the last *sake* toast had been downed, the weary code-room crew had resumed work on the first thirteen parts of Tokyo's long reply to Hull's message, and after waiting in vain until dawn for the final section to arrive, went home, leaving only a single duty officer. At last the fourteenth part came in—delivered by commercial telegraph and marked VERY IMPORTANT in English, but by the time the duty man could collect his colleagues for the decoding, it was 10:00 in the morning, and Ambassador Nomura was having fits because of two "pilot" messages that had preceded this one, unnecessarily reminding him how delicate the situation was, instructing him to put the reply "in nicely drafted form," and then—worst of all—telling him that in preparing the message for Hull he was to be "absolutely sure not to use a typist or any other person. Be most extremely cautious in preserving secrecy." Here was Nomura suddenly confronted with the necessity of delivering a highly important, top-secret, exceptionally lengthy document to the American secretary of state, having to supply a clean, neat copy when the only official with a top security clearance who could type at all was the embassy secretary, Katsuzo Okumura.

At the time Sanematsu arrived, Okumura was at the typewriter, doing his uncertain best to complete the first thirteen parts, but his skills were modest, the results messy, and when he finished he realized he would have to do it over, this time with the assistance of an interpreter. After 10:00, while the code room worked on the fourteenth part, Okumura kept typing, making mistakes, he and his helper in a state of nerves because of that and some corrections received from Tokyo that necessitated even more retyping, and Nomura was in a lather, because he had just received the message that had so alarmed Colonel Bratton and Commander Kramer—the one ordering him to deliver all this to Secretary Hull at 1:00 P.M. The next two hours were a nightmare. The fourteenth section was not decoded until 12:30, but Okumura was still at his labors, trying to finish a clean copy of the first part, with the ambassador, properly attired for the vital 1:00 appointment, peering in the door, looking over the secretary's shoulder to see how the work was coming, all the while keeping an eye on the clock, urging the harassed Okumura to go faster. At last, recognizing the impossibility of meeting his deadline, Nomura called the State Department and requested an extension of time from Hull.

———

Eight thousand five hundred miles from Washington, Major General Lewis Brereton was the guest of honor at an elaborate party at the Manila Hotel. He had been named chief of the Far East Air Force, and although this evening's gala had been billed as "the best entertainment this side of Minsky's," Brereton could be forgiven if his mind occasionally wandered to the inadequacy of the forces with which he would have to meet the Japanese threat. Everybody on the scene was predicting that shooting might start somewhere in a matter of hours, and Brereton—whose entire strength consisted of 120 operational aircraft[2]—had ordered his chief of staff to put all airfields in the Philippines on combat alert. Fortunately, reinforcements were finally on the way. Twelve of the thirty B-17s due him were supposed to be en route from California, where they had been held up by weather and half a dozen other problems; unless something happened, they were scheduled to make their first landing at Hickam Field on Oahu shortly after dawn.

Brereton's boss was as anxious as he was for the Flying Fortresses to arrive. General Hap Arnold was convinced that if he could get enough of the big bombers to Manila, they would make an attack on the Philippines

[2]The number of planes on hand totaled 194—35 B-17s, 107 P-40s, and 52 P-35s—but of these only 30, 72, and 18, respectively, were operational on December 7.

all but impossible, and he had flown to California to talk things over with the crews of the 38th and 88th Reconnaissance Squadrons before they left for Hawaii. "War is imminent," he warned; they might run into trouble at any time.

"Then why don't we have machine guns?" asked Major Truman Landon, the group's leader. The problem was weight, obviously: they would need every gallon of gas they could carry on the long flight to Oahu and couldn't risk hauling ammunition as well, which was why each aircraft was manned only by a skeleton crew, with the machine guns packed in Cosmoline, the storage lubricant. The guns would have to be bore-sighted before they took off again for Clark Field in the Philippines, since it was beyond Hawaii where they could expect trouble. As a final piece of information, they were told before takeoff that Station KGMB in Honolulu would be on the air all night, playing music, and they could home in on that signal. Briefed and ready at last, six of them took off at 9:30 Saturday night; the others roared down the runway an hour later.[3]

———

Kahuku Point, the northernmost tip of Oahu Island, was the site of the army's Opana mobile radar station—one of five such units highly regarded for training purposes but not much else by General Walter Short—and on Sunday morning two privates, Joseph Lockard and George Elliott, were nearing the end of their 4:00-to-7:00 watch. At about five minutes to seven they had a call from the Fort Shafter Information Center, where contacts reported by the stations were logged and plotted, informing them that they could secure the set for the day. Since Elliott was new at the job, trying to learn how the thing worked, and Lockard was teaching him what he knew, the two decided to keep operating until the truck came to pick them up for breakfast.

The duty officer at the information center was also new to the work. Lieutenant Kermit Tyler had had this duty only once before and was here now because the major in charge thought it would be useful for pilots to learn about radar and its potential for intercepting aircraft. A few stations had called in to report contacts after 6:00 A.M., and by 6:45 a number of plots were clustered about 130 miles north of Oahu. Tyler had a look, made sure they were entered on the record, and by then it was 7:00, time for breakfast, and the end of the watch for the enlisted crew. Tyler himself had another hour to go.

Out at Opana at 7:03 A.M., Private Elliott was adjusting the controls with Lockard looking over his shoulder when suddenly a huge blip appeared on the oscilloscope—so big Lockard thought the set had gone on the blink again. As they watched, it became apparent that the blip was a very large formation of planes, 137 miles distant, 3 degrees east of north. Elliott phoned

[3]One bomber was forced to turn back during the night, leaving eleven to go on to Hawaii.

Shafter and reported the flight to Private Joseph McDonald, the telephone operator, who passed the news to Tyler; then, hearing the excitement and anxiety in Elliott's voice, McDonald asked the lieutenant to pick up the phone. Lockard took over from Elliott at the other end and told Tyler that the blips were getting bigger all the time—it was the largest sighting he had ever seen, and the planes were coming closer—by now they were ninety miles from the island. Since their primitive radar had no means of identifying aircraft, Tyler assumed first that the planes were from one of the navy's carriers; then he remembered hearing music playing on KGMB while he was on his way to the information center (and everyone knew that meant a flight of planes coming in from the West Coast), recalled that a number of B-17s were due from California, and told Lockard, "Don't worry about it." Then he hung up.

Lockard and Elliott were too interested to switch off the set. They watched intently as the planes came closer: at 7:25 they were sixty-two miles away; at 7:39, twenty miles; then they disappeared from the screen because they had entered the radar's "dead space" and were also cut off by the nearby mountains. By then the truck had arrived to take the men to breakfast, so they locked up the mobile unit, climbed into the truck, and drove off. It was 7:45.

═══

Death rode into Pearl Harbor wearing a red shirt. From his medium bomber, Mitsuo Fuchida looked down at a matted mass like white cotton five thousand feet below, and wondered if the cloud cover would break before they reached Oahu. They must be coming close now—it was after 7:00, and he had just picked up Station KGMB, playing Hawaiian music, and told his pilot to follow the signal; but now that they were so near he worried that they might overshoot the mark without sighting the target. Behind him, following the distinctive orange light on the tail of his plane, came the forty-eight other high-level bombers, each carrying a sixteen-hundred-pound armor-piercing bomb. Off to the right and below him were the Nakajima torpedo bombers; to the left and above, the two-seater Aichi dive-bombers, each with a five-hundred-pound bomb; and four or five thousand feet above were the Zero fighters, providing cover from attack. At 7:35 he picked up the report he had been waiting for: a reconnaissance plane catapulted from the heavy cruiser *Chikuma* two hours earlier was now soaring high above Pearl Harbor, and the pilot was relaying his observations. The enemy fleet was in the harbor, he said, and he could see the battleships, one heavy cruiser, and six light cruisers (though no carriers, to Fuchida's intense disappointment). Moments later he added weather conditions—moderate wind out of the east, some clouds over the mountains, but clear skies above the target—and having accomplished his mission undetected by the Americans below, he signed off and headed for Nagumo's fleet.

Just then the fliers could see breaks in the clouds, affording glimpses of the island's breathtaking beauty, purpled volcanic peaks skirted with white mist and clouds, lush green vegetation, ordered cane and pineapple fields, white surf, and around it all, the incredibly blue water of the Pacific. Fuchida realized that they were just over Kahuku Point at the northern tip of Oahu. If Privates Lockard and Elliott had chanced to look upward at the moment they were locking the door to their radar unit, they could have seen and heard the source of that giant blip they had tracked so faithfully for the past half hour. From this point the flight swung to the right, following the line of the coast in order to come in on Pearl Harbor from the west. Roughly halfway down that coastline was Waialua Bay, not far from where the dive-bombers and fighters would peel off, with the Zeros heading for Wheeler and Hickam fields to knock down any interceptors, the dive-bombers approaching Pearl Harbor from the northwest. Farther along, the torpedo bombers would begin a big, counterclockwise, fishhook swing that would take them below the entrance to Pearl Harbor before they doubled back over Hickam to hit Battleship Row on the southeast side of Ford Island. The last group of planes, Fuchida's high-level bombers, would make an even wider swing, following the entrance right into the harbor.

As the planes turned south and west to follow the coast, Fuchida could see that the sky over Pearl Harbor was clear; then the harbor itself, with a film of morning mist over it, became visible across the central Oahu plain. He focused his binoculars, saw the eight battleships, and reached for his Very pistol. The plan called for him to fire a single flare if they achieved surprise, two flares with a two-second interval between to indicate that the enemy had spotted them and was alert. In fact, the tactical plan depended on this initial signal, for if they had surprised the Americans the fighters would pull out of the formation and race ahead to establish control of the air, while the slow torpedo bombers would begin their long glide toward the targets. The idea, of course, was to let the latter loose their "fish" before the American ships were obscured by smoke from exploding bombs. Which meant that if all went according to plan, the dive-bombers and high-level bombers would attack after the torpedo planes had made their runs and were out of the way. If the enemy *had* been alerted, on the other hand, the torpedo bombers would wait until the Americans were busy with the other attacking planes before starting their run.

It had all been very carefully worked out, but it did not come off quite the way Genda and Fuchida had planned things, because human error intruded. At 7:40, knowing they had surprised the enemy, Commander Fuchida pulled open the canopy and fired a single flare. The torpedo bombers responded and started into their turn, but Fuchida decided that one of the fighter groups must not have seen the signal, because they were not moving into the planned formation. After waiting for another ten seconds, Fuchida fired a second flare, and while this one was seen by the fighter group leader and obeyed, Lieutenant Commander Takahashi, leading the dive-bombers, mistook it for a second flare meaning "no surprise," and took off on his alternate route toward Ford Island and Hickam Field. At the same time, Fuchida sent a message in Morse code to Kido Butai: "TO, TO, TO"—the first syllable of the Japanese word for "charge"—which was the prearranged signal indicating that the first wave of planes was attacking. Four minutes later, at 7:53 Hawaii time, he sent off the signal that everyone with a knowledge of Operation Z longed to hear: *"Tora! Tora! Tora!"* (the Japanese for "Tiger! Tiger! Tiger!")—which meant that they had caught the United States Pacific Fleet totally by surprise in its lair, exactly as Yamamoto had planned. At 7:55 the first Japanese bomb, made from scrap steel imported from America, exploded on Wheeler Field. It had traveled thirteen days by sea, plus two hours by air, across some three thousand formidable miles of Pacific Ocean, and had arrived exactly five minutes ahead of schedule.[4] Like all the other bombs that were to fall on Oahu on that bloody day, this one had been delivered by a first-class navy and what was probably the best-trained group of naval pilots in the world.

The man whose idea it was, who had been so confident that the attack was possible, sat at that moment in the operations room of his flagship, *Nagato,* in the harbor at Hashirajima. His eyes were shut and he seemed oblivious to the subdued talk of staff officers, the rustling of maps and papers, and the crackle of voices from the radio room across the passageway bringing news of the army's landings at Bataan in the Philippines and at Kota Bharu on the Malay Peninsula. Someone said, "It should begin any moment now," and as everyone's eyes went to the bulkhead clock, a radio-man hustled into the room to say that he had just heard the repeated "TO" signal. Admiral Yamamoto opened his eyes and asked the operator, "Did you get that message directly from the plane?" Yes, the man had. And now the reports from the attacking planes began to be heard—warships tor-pedoed—Hickam Field bombed and strafed—complete surprise; then un-coded messages from the Americans, jerky, frantic shorthand, and when Yamamoto heard one saying, "Jap—this is the real thing!" a small, fleeting grin crossed his face.

━━━

At 7:55 every morning, the duty crew of every ship in Pearl Harbor stood by for morning colors. Precisely at 8:00, when the jack was hoisted at the bow and the American flag at the stern, the sailors stood at attention, saluting, boatswain's pipes trilling, and on the big vessels the bands played "The Star-Spangled Banner." Seven battlewagons were moored in Battle-ship Row this morning, on the southeasterly face of Ford Island, tied up at bollards or mooring posts just offshore. At the northern end was *Nevada.* Behind her was *Arizona,* with the repair ship *Vestal* outboard; then *Tennes-*

[4]Despite this incredible performance, Admiral Yamamoto was disturbed that the attack had not begun precisely at 8:00 A.M., as ordered.

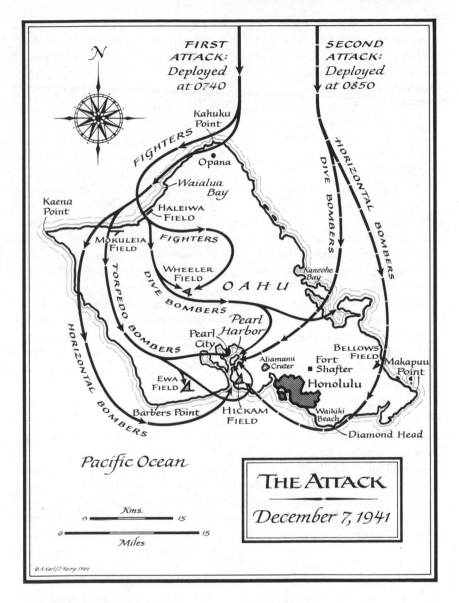

FIRST ATTACK: Deployed at 0740

SECOND ATTACK: Deployed at 0850

THE ATTACK
December 7, 1941

Pacific Ocean

Kms.
0   15
0   15
Miles

see, with *West Virginia* outboard; then *Maryland*, with the *Oklahoma* outboard. Aft of the *Oklahoma* was the tanker *Neosho*, and at the southern end of the row was *California*. On the *Nevada*, twenty-three bandsmen stood ready, holding their instruments and waiting for the leader's signal, when some of them noticed a number of planes in the sky—a lot of them, in fact—coming from several different directions. Some of the planes appeared to be diving toward the far end of Ford Island, where the navy PBYs were parked, and suddenly plumes of dust rose into the air, followed by the sound of explosions, and just as the band struck up the national anthem an airplane thundered in twenty or thirty feet above the water, dropped a torpedo, and opened up with a machine gun, missing everyone in the band and the Marine color guard but ripping the American flag on the fantail to shreds. The band leader was a man who had been at his job for a long time, and he knew that once you started playing "The Star-Spangled Banner" you didn't stop—and he didn't, nor did the musicians, not even when another plane flashed overhead, spraying bullets. When the last note died away, the bandsmen ran for cover.

Moments before, in the command center on Ford Island, Lieutenant Commander Logan Ramsey had a report that one of his PBYs had sunk a submarine a mile off the entrance to Pearl Harbor; the same incident had been reported by the destroyer *Ward;* and as he looked out the window, noticing the color guard marching out with the flag, he heard a plane dive overhead and turned to the duty officer and told him to get the pilot's number and report him. One of them glimpsed a band of red on the fuselage, saw something black fall from the plane, and heard the explosion. "Never mind," Ramsey snapped, "that's a Jap plane." Dashing across the hall to the radio room, he told the operators to send a message immediately in plain English: "Air Raid, Pearl Harbor. This is not a drill." That was at 7:58 A.M., and within minutes the same astounding message went out from CinC Pacific Fleet to CinC Atlantic Fleet, CinC Asiatic Fleet, and the chief of naval operations.

At Hickam Field, where the army bombers were based, a lot of brass were on hand and you could sense excitement in the air, because a flight of twelve B-17s from the coast was expected to land shortly. One of the officers waiting to see them was Colonel William Farthing, the base commandant, who had done his level best to get enough of those aircraft to give Hawaii an adequate long-range defense against attack. Out on the field, his own planes were lined up as close together as possible in order to comply with General Short's alert against possible sabotage. The planes were unarmed. Short's idea was that you got maximum protection against fifth columnists if you massed the planes in the open, where you could keep an eye on them, and stashed ammunition where enemy agents couldn't get at it. Half an hour's warning, he figured, would allow enough time to arm the planes and get them into the air. So at Hickam and at Wheeler, where all the new P-40 fighters were lined up in rows, they were prepared for saboteurs, but not for much of anything else.

Farthing and the other officers were in the control tower, watching for the B-17s to come in from the northeast, when a line of aircraft was seen approaching from another direction. Probably marines from Ewa Field, someone said, and the colonel commented that they were putting on a good show—very realistic maneuvers. He watched one of the planes flying slowly over Pearl Harbor and saw to his horror the red circle on the fuselage at the moment it dropped a torpedo. No sooner had that happened than all hell broke loose on Hickam, planes coming down on it from all directions, hangars and supply buildings and barracks exploding, wounded men screaming, incendiary bullets tearing into the parked aircraft, turning them into twisted wrecks of flame and smoke. It took just five minutes to reduce the field to total shambles.

Warren Johnson, who had been a telegrapher for the D&H Railroad in Vermont before signing up for the army in June, was with the 328th Signal Company at Hickam. Like everyone else there, he knew the B-17s were coming in, and when he heard planes approaching, he assumed that's what they were—either that or hotshot navy pilots, making strafing runs on the army field the way they often did on Sundays. Then he saw the insignia on the planes, heard the gunfire, and was suddenly conscious that machine-gun slugs were tearing into the dirt around him while on either side men were falling and he was not hit.

====

Admiral Kimmel was on the telephone, listening to the duty officer, Commander Murphy, report on the *Ward*'s activities, when someone interrupted at the other end. A pause, then Murphy repeated what he had just heard: "There's a message from the signal tower saying the Japanese are attacking Pearl Harbor and this is no drill." Kimmel ran outside and for several moments stood stock still, looking out across the harbor toward Ford Island, watching the planes with the rising sun on their fuselages and wings circle, make their bombing runs, climb, and return to strafe. On the lawn next door, Captain Earle's wife, who had dashed from her house at the same time, saw the admiral's stricken look, his face as white as his dress uniform. Theirs was an unparalleled vantage point from which to see the *Oklahoma* shudder as the first two torpedoes hit her, the *Arizona* all but disappear in a sheet of fire and smoke, and the admiral whose career had pointed toward the moment when he would stand on his quarterdeck leading his ships into battle stood instead on his front lawn helplessly watching that fleet's destruction. His car appeared at the door and Kimmel leaped in. He reached headquarters about 8:05 to find it the center of exploding bombs and machine-gun fire, with the ear-shattering, angry whine of planes overhead. All he could think of was what was happening to his ships—that, and how he could hit back at the Japanese. Down the hall, Lieutenant Commander Layton, whose premonitions were being so cruelly vindicated, was frantically looking through a sheaf of intelligence reports to see if he could find some clue to the whereabouts of the enemy fleet. With a member of his staff at his side, Kimmel was standing by the window, staring at the devastation, heartsick at the thought of the men who were lost and the ships destroyed, when a .50-caliber machine-gun bullet shattered the glass and hit him in the chest. Fortunately, it was spent and fell to the floor without hurting him. The admiral leaned over and picked the thing up, and as he held it in his hand, staring, said softly, "It would have been merciful had it killed me."

———

General Short heard bombs exploding and assumed at first that the navy was holding some sort of practice; several minutes later someone told him it was a real raid, and he immediately ordered Alert No. 3 and prepared, with his staff, to head for his emergency command headquarters under fifteen feet of rock in Aliamanu Crater, where he would direct the island's defense against landing parties. An intelligence officer who ran into him thought the general appeared confused; he refused to believe that any battleships had been sunk.

Without a minute's advance notice, this outpost of America's peacetime army and navy had been indoctrinated in the most abrupt and brutal manner to the realities of war. A good many of these officers and men had never heard a shot fired in anger. They had served as the volunteer guardians of a nation so paranoid about war that the officers were not permitted to wear uniforms in the capital city for fear of alarming the populace—most particularly the people's elected representatives—and at Pearl Harbor they were betrayed by a similar paranoia that prevented their leaders from seeing what might happen, kept them even from asking the right questions.

A congressman was to remark in the wake of this debacle, "We were in a state of preparedness instead of a state of alertness," and that was about the size of it. The bandsmen and storekeepers and yeomen, the signalmen and gunners, the pilots, mechanics, infantrymen, radar operators, average Americans not so far removed from the farms and villages of home—none of them had been warned to be ready for anything like this, yet under the worst imaginable circumstances they behaved as creditably as could ever be expected of men taken utterly by surprise. After the first shock they were dazed but not panicked, and they stood up to the attack with whatever came to hand—often enough, no more than defiance, that had them shaking their fists and cursing at the murderous planes. Men stood in the middle of airstrips in the face of the incoming fighters, futilely firing pistols and rifles at them because the antiaircraft ammunition had been hidden from saboteurs by their general, because their own fighter planes were neither fueled nor armed. On the *Oglala,* an old tub of a minesweeper that was hit by a torpedo, dive-bombed, and strafed, Admiral William Furlong, whose flagship this was, passed the order for all hands to abandon ship, but he and the gun crews remained aboard and kept firing at the enemy until the ship listed so badly that men on the machine guns were sliding off the deck. As the ship rolled over, Furlong and his gunners finally went over the side—manhandling their guns along with them so they could set them up on the pier and continue firing.

The repair ship *Vestal,* with a complement of some six hundred men under Commander Cassin Young, was tied up alongside the *Arizona.* The

Vestal had already been hit by two bombs and was afire when the battleship blew up; the vacuum created by the explosion put out the fires on the repair vessel, but the concussion blasted overboard nearly a hundred men, including the skipper. Debris of every description—huge chunks of metal, unexploded shells, parts of human bodies—crashed down on the deck, and finally someone gave the order to abandon ship. Before anyone went over the side an apparition appeared—a furious Commander Young, coated from head to foot with diesel oil from the water—demanding of the officer of the deck, "Where the hell do you think you're going?"

"We're abandoning ship," the man replied.

"You don't abandon ship on me," Young announced, and the crew returned to battle stations.

The cruiser *Phoenix* was moored a half mile from Battleship Row, and she was in apple-pie order, having been subjected to an inspection by Rear Admiral H. Fairfax Leary the day before (Leary wore white gloves, the better to detect dust). When the Japanese planes flashed by en route to Ford Island, the crew raced to battle stations and found that they had to hack the locks off ammunition boxes before they could load; then, before they could commence firing, they had to take down the awnings above the antiaircraft guns. To complete their frustration, all the fuzes on the shells were set at the required peacetime minimum, to prevent them from exploding until they were a safe distance from the ship—which was too far to damage the Japanese planes; as a final blow, many of the fuzes were defective, and those shells fell, unexploded, on shore.

At every military installation on Oahu on that bloody Sunday, acts of courage and dedication to duty were performed by ordinary men in uniform faced with what military men are taught to fear most—total surprise, delivered with overwhelming strength concentrated on a relatively small target. Take the case of two young officers from the *Oklahoma,* whose experience that day was neither more nor less unusual than that of hundreds of others. The *Oklahoma* had entered Pearl Harbor on Friday, after seventeen days at sea, and was moored alongside the *Maryland* at Berth F-5. Bill Ingram, a gunnery officer who had just made lieutenant (j.g.), told his buddy Fred Schweizer, a damage-control officer, that he would take the duty for him that weekend. Schweizer had been married in June and hadn't spent much time with his bride in the intervening months, so Ingram was standing his 4:00-to-8:00 watch on Sunday morning. When his relief arrived fifteen minutes early, he went to the wardroom, took off his pistol, sat down, and had just ordered poached eggs when he heard planes diving. Looking out the porthole, he saw one heading toward Ford Island as if it was going to crash. When he got up to get a better view of what was happening he saw another aircraft heading directly for the *Oklahoma,* and as it winged over, just missing the ship's mast, he noticed the red balls beneath the wings and thought, "These navy pilots are sure making it look realistic!" He was heading for the bridge when an explosion knocked him to the deck.

With a sinking feeling, he remembered that there was no ammunition near any of the 5-inch guns: because an admiral's inspection was scheduled, the skipper, Captain Howard Brody, who was a spit-and-polish man if ever there was one, had had the firing pins removed from each gun and taken to the gunner's locker to be shined, while the ammunition itself was hauled below so the magazines could be painted for inspection. Ingram went below decks to see what he could do about getting some ammunition topside, but by now the *Oklahoma* had been hit by two more torpedoes and had a 45-degree list. He was wearing a new pair of Wellington boots with soles so slippery he couldn't climb uphill along the sloping deck, but someone gave him a hand, and he made it onto the main deck. After the battleship was hulled by two more torpedoes the executive officer passed the order to abandon ship, telling the men to leave over the starboard side, climbing over it onto the bottom as the ship rolled over. No one knew it then, but at least thirty-two survivors were still trapped inside when a man on Ford Island watched her go—"slowly and stately . . . as if she were tired and wanted to rest." Just eight minutes after the first torpedo struck, Ingram stripped down to his shorts and slid into the water.

Forward of the *Oklahoma* the tanker *Neosho* was discharging aviation gas into tanks on Ford Island, and it occurred to Ingram that all hell was going to blow if she was hit; but somehow the tanker got underway and made it unscathed to the submarine base. Aft of *Oklahoma* was the *Arizona,* and while Ingram was in the water there was a sudden, searing flash and a colossal explosion, with a huge fireball rocketing so high into the air the concussion shook Fuchida's bomber thousands of feet overhead. More than a thousand men were killed when the *Arizona* blew up; oil and gas on the water started burning, and Ingram thought he was being strafed until he realized that the objects falling around him were unburned powder grains from the battleship's magazine. He made it to the *Maryland,* found a line that wasn't slippery with oil, and climbed aboard. Some of the crewmen were crouched under the overhang to avoid the gunfire, so he organized a gun crew and a work party to carry ammunition, and they began firing at the incoming planes.

Thanks to Ingram's generosity, Ensign Fred Schweizer and his wife were asleep in their apartment Sunday morning when the phone rang. The officer who had been his best man was on the line, telling him the island was under attack. "Who the hell could attack us?" Schweizer asked. "Turn on the radio," his friend said, and hung up in order to call someone else. All personnel were being ordered to report to their battle stations immediately, and as Schweizer dressed he could hear the sound of gunfire and see smoke off toward Pearl Harbor. Another officer arrived to pick him up, and as he kissed his wife goodbye, her eyes filled with tears when he said they couldn't wait for breakfast; telling her to stay with a friend whose father was the captain of a cruiser, he raced out the door. On the way to Pearl the traffic was jammed, roadblocks were being thrown up by national guardsmen and police, and the going was maddeningly slow. The closer they got to the harbor the more smoke they saw, great billowing oily black clouds of it, with planes flying in crazy patterns, shooting as they came. Schweizer jumped in a whaleboat that was ferrying men to their ships, and as they cleared the dock he could see the *Oklahoma* burning; the whole harbor seemed to be afire from the flaming oil on the water, and everywhere there were bodies—some dead, some still alive, crying for help. Before they reached the *Oklahoma* she had rolled over and was bottom side up, so Schweizer climbed aboard the *Maryland,* and found himself in charge of a gun crew. He had seen his own ship roll over and die, but his adopted battleship, though bottled up by the stricken *Oklahoma,* was at least protected from torpedoes even though it took hits from two bombs.

Sometime after 3:00 in the afternoon, a launch came by to pick men up to take them to Ford Island, and when Schweizer stepped aboard a familiar voice said, "Where the hell have you been? I've been fighting this war all by myself." It was Bill Ingram, who until now had been too busy to notice that he had lost all the fillings in his teeth and that both of his eardrums had burst during the battle. As they reached the beach, Ingram, Schweizer, and others began pulling survivors out of the water, some so badly burned that the skin came off their arms when they were grabbed. On shore, rumors were rampant: armed men were running around saying they hoped the Japs would come back so they could have another crack at them; some of the officers were organizing parties to repel invaders; the dead and wounded were everywhere; the entire area was devastated; and after Ingram left for the officers' club to try to find some clothes, Schweizer was assigned to an all-night watch—waiting for an invasion that never came.

That same slow-moving traffic that had frustrated Fred Schweizer and his friend had delayed the RCA messenger on his appointed rounds, with the result that General Marshall's warning to the commanding general in Hawaii—which reached Honolulu only twenty-two minutes before the attack—was not delivered to Fort Shafter until 11:45 A.M. Then it had to be decoded and given to Short's adjutant, with a copy sent off to Admiral Kimmel. Transmitted by the army message center in Washington at 12:00 noon, which was 6:30 A.M. Hawaii time (almost exactly when the first wave of Japanese planes took off from the carriers), it had taken eight and a half hours to reach its destination—eight and a half hours that saw the dawn of a new day and a new world for America, a world that would never be the same after those Japanese planes came barreling through Kole Kole Pass on the way to Pearl Harbor. As Walter Short read Marshall's observation about the diplomats' pending 1:00 deadline in Washington and saw the admonition to "be on the alert accordingly," he "about went through the roof," according to the aide who gave him the telegram. Kimmel reacted

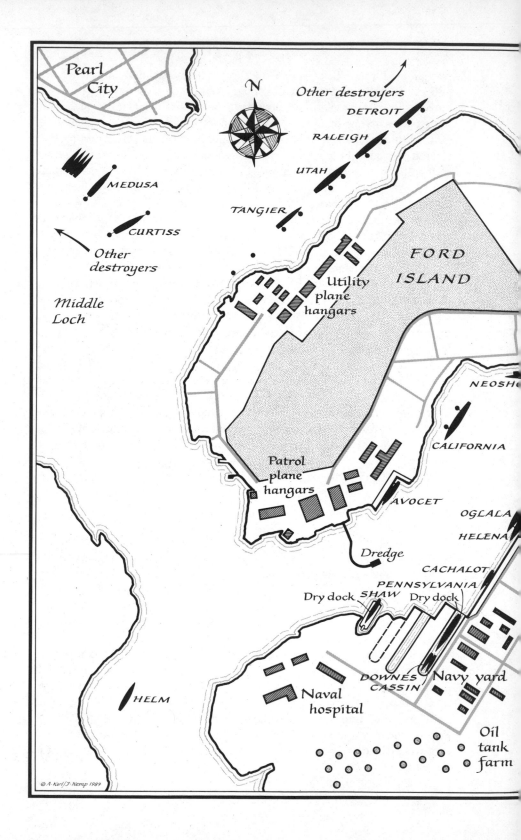

Pearl City

N

Other destroyers

DETROIT

RALEIGH

UTAH

MEDUSA

TANGIER

CURTISS

Other destroyers

Middle Loch

FORD ISLAND

Utility plane hangars

NEOSHO

CALIFORNIA

Patrol plane hangars

AVOCET

OGLALA

HELENA

CACHALOT

Dredge

PENNSYLVANIA

Dry dock SHAW Dry dock

HELM

DOWNES
CASSIN

Navy yard

Naval hospital

Oil tank farm

© A. Karl/J. Kemp 1989

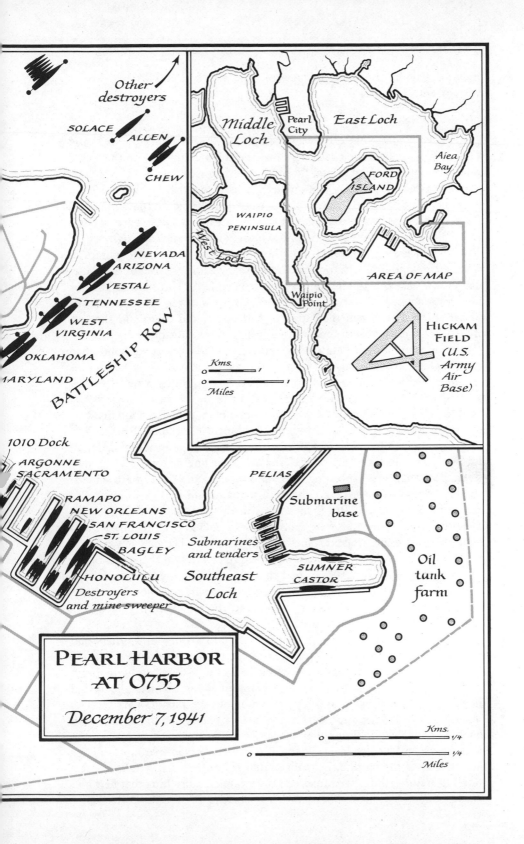

Other destroyers

SOLACE   ALLEN

CHEW

NEVADA
ARIZONA
VESTAL
TENNESSEE
WEST
VIRGINIA
OKLAHOMA
MARYLAND

BATTLESHIP ROW

Middle
Loch

Pearl
City

East Loch

Aiea
Bay

FORD
ISLAND

WAIPIO
PENINSULA

West Loch

Waipio
Point

AREA OF MAP

HICKAM
FIELD
(U.S.
Army
Air
Base)

Kms.

Miles

1010 Dock
ARGONNE
SACRAMENTO
RAMAPO
NEW ORLEANS
SAN FRANCISCO
ST. LOUIS
BAGLEY
HONOLULU
Destroyers
and mine sweeper

PELIAS

Submarine
base

Submarines
and tenders

SUMNER
CASTOR

Southeast
Loch

Oil
tank
farm

PEARL HARBOR
AT 0755

December 7, 1941

Kms.   1/4

Miles   1/4

the same way: he crumpled the piece of paper in a ball and fired it into the wastebasket.

═══

The attackers' initial objective was to eliminate American air defenses, and within a few minutes they had every major naval and air base on the island under fire. Fifteen minutes later the total air strength on Oahu—U.S. Army, Navy, and Marine Corps—had virtually ceased to exist. On Ford Island, all twenty-nine navy PBY patrol planes were demolished on the ground. At the Kaneohe base on the east coast, two separate attacks destroyed twenty-seven PBYs and crippled six others. All forty-nine planes at the marines' Ewa Field were out of action. Of the army's 126 late-model fighters at Wheeler Field, only forty-three would be salvageable. At Bellows Field— also on the east coast—the fighter squadron's planes had neither gas nor ammunition when the Japanese hit Pearl Harbor and weren't ready to take off for an hour. By then the Japanese had discovered them and the two planes that did manage to get off the ground were shot down.

Miraculously, two private planes, out for a Sunday-morning spin when the first wave struck, escaped. An attorney named Royal Vitousek and his seventeen-year-old son were idling along in their Aeronca when they saw the fighters approaching. Vitousek headed for the open ocean, hoping they wouldn't bother with him after sending a burst of machine-gun fire his way, and when he saw his opportunity, he hightailed it for John Rogers Airport—the civilian field east of Hickam. Landing, he found the place in an uproar. The Japanese had strafed the runway, but no one really comprehended what was happening; everyone thought the pilots were Americans and damned fools, practicing with live ammunition.

Another pilot named Jim Duncan was in the middle of a flying lesson, and he and his instructor were on a leisurely course over Kahuku Point when they heard gunfire and something hit the plane. Duncan saw tracers, heard bullets strike the fuselage, saw the big red circles on the wings of the planes as they flashed past, and had the presence of mind to dive toward the steep cliffs along the coast, figuring that they wouldn't follow him there. He was right, and he and his instructor and the Hui Lele Flying Club's bullet-riddled Aeronca made it back to John Rogers.

As ill luck would have it, the B-17s for which Farthing and others had waited so eagerly arrived at the height of the onslaught. Six of them, led by Major Landon, unarmed and low on fuel after a fourteen-hour flight, followed the KGMB music program to Honolulu and unwittingly started their descent into Hickam at the precise moment the Japanese arrived. As Landon made his turn into the runway, he saw planes coming at him with machine guns firing, glimpsed the Rising Sun on the aircraft, and at the same time heard a voice from the tower say, "You have three Japs on your tail." Closer to the ground, he realized that the antiaircraft guns were also shooting at him—those fired-up crews were going for anything that flew and never mind who they were—but somehow the major and the five pilots behind him managed to land in the chaos of Hickam. Two other B-17s made it to the Haleiwa airstrip, one landed on a golf course, one reached Wheeler and the eleventh was hit and destroyed while landing at Bellows air base, though most of the crew survived.

By some ghastly twist of fate, eighteen planes from the carrier *Enterprise*—which had run into heavy weather two hundred miles west of Oahu—had been ordered to land at Ford Island instead of returning to the ship, and shortly after 8:00 that morning they also arrived at the height of the attack, to be shot at by American antiaircraft guns or by Zeros. The Japanese knocked down four of them, the Americans one; another crash-landed on Kauai, and one pilot bailed out near Ewa Field. Somehow, the rest managed to land at Ford or Ewa, and, as soon as the attack was over, they were sent off to look for the Japanese carriers.

At 7:30 that evening six more planes off the *Enterprise*, which was still hunting for the Japanese fleet, requested permission to land on Ford Island and were told to turn on their landing lights and come in. The word was passed to hold fire, these are our planes—but one trigger-happy machine-gunner fired a burst, another followed, and despite the frantic efforts of officers to stop them, guns ringing Ford Island opened up on the American planes and shot down all but one.

Meanwhile, scores of sailors were frantically trying to rescue survivors trapped inside the *Oklahoma*. The men of America's peacetime navy, in which one hitch often led to another, and another, sometimes served on the same ship for twenty years or more. They counted not only their shipmates as buddies, but sailors from other ships in the fleet, whom they had known and shared liberties with and caroused with each time they came into port. So when men were in a desperate fix, as they were on the *Oklahoma,* the *Utah,* the *West Virginia,* [5] and other ships, all hands were prepared to pitch in, and welders and shipfitters worked around the clock with acetylene torches, losing all sense of time as they painstakingly opened the hulls, trying to follow the faint tapping from within that would lead them to survivors, hoping their torches would not use up all the oxygen inside and asphyxiate the men. On the *Oklahoma* the ordeal lasted until 5:30 on Monday afternoon, when the last of thirty-two living men was pulled from the fatally damaged ship thirty-six hours after she turned turtle in the mud.

The first wave of the Japanese attack had achieved the initial objective with deadly efficiency. All told, 188 American planes were destroyed and another 159 were damaged—many beyond repair. Meanwhile, the principal mission—the destruction of the U.S. Fleet—was equally successful, and at 8:50, just fifty-five minutes after the first wave appeared, the second flight swarmed across Oahu, some of them heading once again for Hickam and

---

[5] Three men, hopelessly caught inside the *West Virginia,* hung on to life until December 23, marking off each day on a steel bulkhead beside them.

the Ford Island fields, others for the crippled ships in the harbor. High up behind Diamond Head, Masayuki Tokioka had seen smoke rising from the direction of Pearl Harbor and went outside with his two young sons and a daughter. They looked up when five or six planes passed overhead, flying quite low, and one of the boys said, "Daddy, look at the airplane! It has a different sign on the wings!" Even then, Tokioka didn't believe these were Japanese planes: surely they must be U.S. planes on maneuvers, with the Rising Sun on the "enemy" to lend authenticity; as a member of the local civil defense organization he was soon asked to call others to let them know they had an emergency on their hands, but not until he saw two bombs drop did he finally credit what was happening.

Doris Obata was eleven years old and was attending 8:00 mass at St. Patrick's, in the Kaimuki suburb, when the priest announced that Pearl Harbor had been attacked and they should go home. One of the nuns was crying, and told some of the thoroughly baffled children that they would all meet in heaven. Running home, Doris could see black smoke billowing up from Pearl Harbor, twelve miles away, and all through the day the family listened to radio reports while her father and brother hung heavy curtains to black out the house before night. About 7:30 they heard a knock at the door. It was a soldier with a gun, who politely asked her father, who was with the *Nippu Jiji,* a bilingual paper, to come with him for interrogation and to bring a change of clothing. That was the last time they saw him until November 1945.[6]

Then and later, Barry Fox believed that the Japanese attacked the Kaneohe Naval Air Station first, that someone at the base notified Pearl Harbor, and was told to soak his head. No matter: as she remarked, Pearl Harbor was not one story but many, each person's his own. Hers began that day when she was awakened at 8:00 by the sound of machine-gun fire, which she put down to navy planes practicing on a target over the bay below their home. She went back to sleep until 8:30, when things began happening fast. From the living-room window overlooking Kaneohe Bay she saw that the entire peninsula where the air station was located was shrouded in smoke, and that six strange-looking aircraft circling overhead suddenly turned and "followed one another out of the circle like circus horses leaving the ring," flew low over their house, and disappeared to the southeast.

"My God," she thought, "it's war!" She ran to turn on the radio, but there was nothing—only a church service and a Japanese-language program, which she found reassuring. When her husband, Steve, joined her they concluded that the navy must be practicing laying down smokescreens.

[6]Along with thousands of other Japanese-Americans, Soichi Obata was caught up in one of the most disgraceful episodes in American history. Because of his newspaper position, he had been meeting cruise ships from Japan for many years, presenting tourists with the latest edition of the paper, and frequently entertaining visiting VIPs. Thanks to these activities, the FBI had had him on its enemy alien list since 1932, and on December 7 he was first taken for interrogation and then sent to California, where he was interned for four years.

Suddenly, their little white house, which was situated at the top of a hill, began to shake—once, then twice again, while the mountains around them roared with explosions, waking their six-year-old son and sixteen-year-old daughter, who asked, "What's all the noise?"

At 9:30, when the regular news broadcast was due, there was music instead; then a voice broke in, repeating the commands: "Keep off the streets! Do not use the telephone!" Orders followed for defense workers to report to various locations, then the voice of an announcer, who was obviously shaken ("That man is scared!" Steve said), yet they kept telling themselves and the children that these must be maneuvers. Not until 10:30, when they heard that twenty-five civilian doctors were summoned to the army's Tripler General Hospital, did they know for certain that it was war, and not until 11:30 did the radio tell them that the Japanese had attacked and martial law was in effect.

Alone on their hilltop they watched the smoke lift from the bay, disclosing a hangar still in flames and the skeletons of PBYs floating in the water. There was a strange loveliness to the green sea, the light blue sky, and the golden flames: they seemed so distant, so unconnected with dying men.

Steve, a retired doctor, got a call from the civil defense office, packed his bag, kissed his family goodbye, and walked down the lane, leaving Barry to wish that the children weren't there so she could cry and beat her fists against something hard. Off in the distance they could hear dull booming sounds, and she knew a sense of catastrophe: Where were *our* planes? she wondered. They tuned the radio to the mainland and from twenty-two hundred miles away learned what was happening on the other side of their mountain, but the news set them to worrying about friends elsewhere in the Pacific—at Wake, Cavite, Midway—and they turned the dial to Charlie McCarthy and Jack Benny. Hours later, after Barry and the children fixed up the kitchen for a blackout room (their white house was no military objective, but it sat on the crest of the hill like a tempting bull's-eye), she ate a snack, did some baking, and put food in the oven to keep warm for Steve. He returned with a sadness on his face that was "more than sadness. It was grief, despair, and pain, and horror," and when he saw the questions in her eyes he gestured toward the children and said, "When they're in bed. . . ."

But the children wanted no part of sleeping in their own rooms, and when at last they were bedded down in the living room, Steve told her, "It's unbelievable. From what I hear, we had thirteen planes left after this morning. They've wiped us out. They've knocked us flat. We've nothing left to fight with." The Japanese, he told her, were expected to invade on this side of the island, but he could not stay; he had to go back on duty at a first-aid station in Kaneohe. All he could do was leave some morphine for her and the children, embrace them all, and walk out into the darkness, saying in a husky voice, "You'd better lock the door."

Barry and the children played a game and sipped some cocoa, and after they were asleep she sat listening to rain fall, the refrigerator hum, the children breathing, and thought how tired she was and how difficult it would be to sleep. "The day that had gone so swiftly had rushed us through to dusk," she recalled, "and now the night was endless."

═══

In the second attack there were no torpedo planes, only high-level bombers, dive-bombers, and fighters; but this time the Americans had had a chance to draw breath, they were manning antiaircraft guns, they even had a few fighters in the air, and the assault was considerably more costly to the Japanese. Even so, the air bases were bombed and strafed repeatedly, with severe loss of life, and the wounded were brought in by the hundreds, overwhelming the medical personnel and facilities (mess-hall tables, with the breakfast dishes still on them, served as temporary cots). The planes were even shooting at vehicles on the roads leading to Pearl, paralyzing traffic; the *Nevada* was hit by seven or eight bombs while trying to get out of the Harbor, the *Pennsylvania* took a direct hit in dry dock, the bow of the destroyer *Shaw* was blown off by the explosion of a forward magazine, and the heavy cruiser *Honolulu* was damaged.

When it was over at last, Admiral Kimmel's mighty armada was all but demolished. Of his eight battleships—the core of the fleet—none remained whole, although six would eventually be repaired or salvaged. Ten other vessels were lost, sunk, or seriously damaged. Far worse was the human calamity. Casualties totaled 2,403 dead, missing, or fatally wounded (almost half the total number were lost on the *Arizona*) and 1,178 wounded.

At 9:45, less than two hours after the first bomb fell, the last plane of the second attack wave faded from sight to the north, and only Mitsuo Fuchida's plane remained on the scene, slipping in and out of the clouds over Oahu. The commander, who had trained those crews for their deadly task, circled overhead for almost another hour in order to report fully on the results of the attack, and at that moment, with his bird's-eye vision, he was probably the only man alive who could absorb all that had happened or comprehend the immensity of the thing. Surely no one on the ground was capable of doing so. Within minutes, the first wave of Japanese aircraft had simultaneously attacked Wheeler and Hickam airfields and virtually all the big ships in Pearl Harbor, with dive-bombers shrieking down on the targets, torpedo planes coming in at the level of the ships' masts, followed by high-level planes dropping strings of bombs, with the fighters swarming in from all directions like angry hornets, strafing planes and trucks and people on the ground—anything that moved. These flight crews had come three thousand miles for the killing, and they passed up no bets to make good on their mission. Along with all the dedication, the skill gained through superb training and rigorous practice, there was in each of them a kind of unholy rage—the rage of battle and vengeance and contempt for the enemy. The second wave, coming so quickly on the heels of the first, would have brought equal devastation had it not been that so much had already been done. Surveying what was visible beneath the pall of smoke, Fuchida could not be certain how many ships had actually been sunk; from his altitude it was impossible to tell whether some of them were still afloat or whether they had simply settled to the bottom of the shallow bay, but before leaving for the carrier *Akagi,* he made up his mind about one thing: they should make another attack and concentrate on the oil tanks and the repair facilities.

Despite Fuchida's urging, Admiral Nagumo had had enough. The operation had been successful beyond anyone's wildest expectations—an incredible victory at a cost of only twenty-nine planes and fifty-five men, with no damage whatever to any of his ships—and the admiral was not a man to push his luck. He had opposed Operation Z from the beginning as being too risky, but he had carried out his orders, and now he considered the mission accomplished. Yamamoto, who could have ordered him to return, was a commander who delegated authority, leaving decisions to the man on the scene, and his restraint when he learned that Nagumo was sailing for home is suggested by his remark to staff officers that even a burglar hesitates to go back for more. Yet he never forgot nor forgave Nagumo's original opposition to his plan, and believed he should have attacked again even though his orders did not call for it. All he said at this time was: "A man who wants to do a thing, will do it without being told. . . . I imagine Nagumo doesn't want to."

———

What the Japanese did not—could not—know was that their actions this day would ignite an equivalent level of rage and desire for vengeance in their victims, uniting them into one people as no other force could possibly have done. It was the only factor in the equation that Admiral Yamamoto had not foreseen. He had assumed the Americans would be so shattered and demoralized by the assault that they would give Japan what she wanted. And perhaps if Nagumo had made another attack as Yamamoto hoped he would do, utterly destroying what remained at Pearl Harbor—the tank farms and repair facilities, the dry docks, everything that would have made it impossible for the United States to mount any kind of offensive for a year or more to come—Yamamoto's hope for an uncontested conquest of Southeast Asia might have come true. As Admiral Chester Nimitz, who succeeded Kimmel on Christmas morning of 1941, said: "The several errors made by the Japanese on December 7, 1941, helped very materially to shorten the war." Had they returned and destroyed the dry docks and other repair facilities, the 4.5 million barrels of fuel oil in surface tanks, and the submarine base, the fleet would certainly have been forced back to the West Coast. But Nagumo was content with what had been achieved, and the Americans' great island base in the Pacific survived its wounds to fight as it had been intended to do from the beginning.

Stunned sailors at the Naval Air Station on Ford Island watch a fireball rise from the wreckage left by the Japanese attack. In Hawaii, 188 army and navy planes were destroyed, 159 damaged.

═══

After his morning meeting with Stimson and Hull, Secretary Frank Knox went back to his office, arriving there at 1:00 on Sunday afternoon, where he talked for about an hour with Betty Stark and Richmond Kelly Turner. As the two admirals were about to leave, the three men standing for a moment chatting with Knox's assistant, John Dillon, an officer came to the door. He had a dispatch from Commander in Chief, Pacific Fleet.

Knox read it, disbelief written all over the face of the man whose navy was not going to be caught napping.

"My God, this can't be true!" he exclaimed. "This must mean the Philippines!"

Stark looked over his shoulder at the message. "No, sir," he said. "This is Pearl."

CHAPTER 55

"... the worst day
in American history."

For most Americans, Sunday began quietly, with nothing to suggest that this was the last morning for almost four years when the nation would be at peace. It was cold and crisp, a glorious day across the eastern half of the country, as though Indian summer had been granted a stay of execution. The Roosevelts had company for the weekend—all old friends. The president's cousin Ellen Delano Adams and her husband, with their son and daughter-in-law, were there, as was Mrs. Charles Hamlin, known as Bertie, whom Franklin had met years before in Albany, at his Uncle Ted's inauguration as governor. The White House was silent when Bertie Hamlin awoke, and she dressed quietly, walked down the long hallway past the closed doors leading to the president's bedroom and study, went downstairs, and crossed Pennsylvania Avenue to St. John's Church on Lafayette Square, where the bells were pealing for morning worship. By the time she returned, a number of people were climbing the stairs from the East Entrance. The luncheon guests had arrived—some thirty-one of them, and a mixed bag they were, friends, relatives, minor officials, Army Medical Corps officers, prompting someone to observe that the First Lady's secretary was cleaning up around the edges of the invitation list.

Although they may have hoped to see the president, none of the guests much expected him to put in an appearance; he was understandably preoccupied with the tense situation in the Far East, and on top of that, Mrs. Roosevelt explained, his sinuses were acting up. He was having a relaxed lunch in his upstairs study with Harry Hopkins, who recalled that they were talking about "things far removed from war." Saturday, while the White House staff took half a day off for Christmas shopping, the president had worked late, and now, after finishing the lunch on his tray, he was enjoying the undemanding company of his old friend and his Scottie dog Fala, while he paid a little overdue attention to his stamp collection.

At the navy's communication station the clocks read 1348 when Chief Frank Ackerson was called to the Washington-Honolulu circuit to stand by for an urgent message. He read what it said and within two minutes Washington had acknowledged the Honolulu operator's message: "AIR RAID ON PEARL HARBOR THIS IS NOT A DRILL."

While the president and Hopkins talked, the telephone rang, and it was Frank Knox calling Roosevelt—a stunned, stricken secretary of the navy, reporting the staggering news from Pearl Harbor. Hopkins, hearing that Japanese planes were still attacking, reacted exactly as Knox had: there must be some mistake—surely Japan would not attack Hawaii. But the president thought the report was probably true. It was just the sort of surprise the Japanese *would* spring on us, he said—talking peace in the Pacific while plotting to overthrow it.

That morning the corridors in the Old State, War, and Navy Building had been deserted when Secretary Hull arrived at 10:15 for his meeting with Stimson and Knox. They discussed the draft of the president's message to Congress, on which Sumner Welles and Adolf Berle had worked most of Saturday, and afterward those two went at it again. By 2:00 they were ready to call it quits and go to the Mayflower Hotel for lunch, and were just leaving when Nomura and Kurusu arrived outside Hull's office with the fourteen-part cable which had caused the staff at the Japanese embassy so much grief. Secretary Hull was busy on the telephone: his visitors could not know it, but the president was calling to inform him of the report from Pearl Harbor, advising him to receive the ambassadors formally but under no circumstances to inform them of the attack. He was to accept the reply to his note "coolly and bow them out."

Hull let the agitated Japanese sit outside for fifteen minutes—a tense quarter of an hour that marked an end to innocence and the beginning of a new and different era in American history. When the two men were finally admitted to his office he greeted them coldly, kept them standing, and when Nomura handed him the note, explaining that he had been instructed to deliver it at 1:00, Hull asked why. Nomura said he did not know, but those were his instructions; the secretary retorted sharply that he was receiving the message at 2:00. Hull glanced perfunctorily through the document, and then, according to the subsequent State Department press release, said indignantly, "In all my conversations with you during the last nine months,

I have never uttered one word of untruth. This is borne out absolutely by the record.

"In all my fifty years of public service I have never seen a document that was more crowded with infamous falsehoods and distortions—infamous falsehoods and distortions on a scale so huge that I never imagined until today that any government on this planet was capable of uttering them."

If the Japanese wondered how a man could know so much about a document he had barely skimmed, they did not say, but Nomura was about to speak when Hull cut him short with a motion of his hand and gestured toward the door. The two ambassadors left without a word.

Thus the authorized version. But when Dean Acheson arrived at the department several hours later—having rushed in from his Maryland farm as soon as he heard the news on the radio—little groups of people stood in the corridor, talking in whispers, while the secretary, still in a towering rage, remained closeted with several intimates, and the word Acheson got from those who had overheard Mr. Hull ridding himself of the two Japanese was that he had done so in "native Tennesseean," calling them "scoundrels" and "piss-ants" in his fury.[1]

Henry Stimson was weary and he was feeling his seventy-four years. He had hoped to get away to his Long Island place for a rest, but the news that morning got progressively worse, convincing him that something bad was going to happen, so he stayed in Washington. He was eating lunch at Woodley, his handsome Southern Colonial home overlooking Rock Creek Park, when the president called and asked, in an excited voice, "Have you heard the news?"

"Well," the secretary of war replied, "I have heard the telegrams which have been coming in about the Japanese advances in the Gulf of Siam."

"Oh no," Roosevelt said, "I don't mean that. They have attacked Hawaii. They are now bombing Hawaii."

That was an excitement indeed, Stimson thought to himself, and as he prepared to leave for the White House it occurred to him that American forces in Hawaii might have won a major victory; the defense forces in the islands had been alerted, and were capable of inflicting severe damage on the attackers.

[1] As long as he lived, Kichisaburo Nomura maintained that he had had no advance knowledge of the Japanese attack on Pearl Harbor. In 1948 he told an interviewer from the New York Times that he was "the worst-informed ambassador in history," that both President Roosevelt and Secretary Hull knew more about Japanese intentions than he did, which may well have been true, thanks to Magic. He had supposed that Japan would march into Thailand, he said, and had not known the contents of the fourteen-part note until it was deciphered. What he was trying to tell Hull before he and Kurusu were summarily dismissed was that he assumed that diplomatic relations were to be broken off and that he and his staff would be returned to Tokyo while Ambassador Grew was sent home to the United States. "Mr. Hull's words were very strong," he admitted, "but not insulting. . . . Mr. Hull was very strong-minded and he had some very definite opinions."

At 2:28, Admiral Stark phoned the White House and informed the president that the first report was true, that the attack had caused some damage to the fleet and some loss of life—no one could yet say how much. Throughout the afternoon and evening the phone at the president's side continued to ring, each time bringing an even more distressing bulletin about the extent of the devastation. Roosevelt listened calmly to each report, usually without comment, and then returned to the business at hand.

About the time of Stark's first call, Mrs. Roosevelt was bidding goodbye to her departing luncheon guests when one of the ushers told her the news. The report was so stunning, she said, that there was complete quiet, and after she had seen her guests to the door she waited until Franklin was alone, hoping to slip into his study. It took only a quick glance to make her realize that he was concentrating on what had to be done and wouldn't talk of what had happened until the first strain was over, so she went back to work—work, at that moment, consisting of going through her mail and writing letters, with one ear cocked to the voices of people going in and out of the president's study, and finding the time and strength of character to concentrate on what she would say in her weekly radio broadcast that afternoon.

Roosevelt's first move, after Stark confirmed the report, was to summon Steve Early and dictate a statement for immediate release to the press, and at 2:30 Louise Hachmeister, who supervised the White House switchboard, called the three wire services, put them on a conference hookup, and asked, "All on? AP? UP? INS? Here's Mr. Early."

"This is Steve Early at the White House," the press secretary said. "At 7:55 A.M., Hawaiian time, the Japanese bombed Pearl Harbor. The attacks are continuing and . . . no, I don't know how many are dead." Almost instantaneously, alarm bells on teletype machines in every city across the country began to ring.

———

In London, Robert Trout was sitting in the BBC's Studio B-2, two stories underground. He had been stationed there since early November, temporarily replacing Ed Murrow, who had returned to the United States with Janet for some rest and recreation, and as he looked at the wall of the studio he found himself thinking that there was a huge bomb crater on the other side and that all that stood between him and the hole was a single course of bricks.

For these nightly broadcasts, CBS leased a transatlantic telephone line for ten minutes. Even though the transmission might last for only a fraction of that, ten minutes was the minimum rental, with the result that some of the time was used in preparing for the broadcast, testing voice levels, with engineers, announcers, and others in studios on opposite sides of the ocean conversing. Trout was waiting for his cue from Paul White to go on the air, while next to him, as always, sat a British censor: the procedure called for the censor to read the script the reporter had prepared in advance, approving it or asking him to delete or alter something, but both parties knew that the censor had his hand on the control by which he could cut off Trout if he extemporized and said something that was not permitted. The regulars like Murrow and Trout had a good working relationship with the censors, it was all very informal and friendly, and the censor actually served as a technician, by cutting Trout in and out.

Trout was wearing earphones, listening to the voices of a British engineer and an American in Riverhead, Long Island, discuss the transmission. He recognized other voices from the CBS studio in New York—John Charles Daly talking with someone, Major George Fielding Eliot speaking—none of it on the air, of course, just desultory conversation between people waiting for the broadcast to begin. Paul White loved to sit in front of the complex instrument panel, surrounded by gadgets, and he would either push a lever and tell Trout to start talking, or simply let his man in London listen to the broadcast and wait for the announcer to say, "And now we bring you Robert Trout in London—come in, Bob Trout." But tonight Trout realized that his cue was being delayed for some reason, and he didn't hear White's voice. He was also aware that the door to the studio in New York had opened, because he could hear the clatter of teletype machines in the hall outside, then a babble of voices, and someone saying, "Of course it means war . . . but why Pearl Harbor?" This is how he became aware of what had occurred.

Then White came on, to say he would have to tell Trout what they had just seen on the wire. "I already know," Trout told him. White didn't ask how he knew (he died before Trout ever had a chance to tell him); instead he said, "Okay, then, I'm cutting you in. Give us the reaction from London."

For a horrified moment, Trout couldn't believe his ears. He turned to the censor, who realized immediately the spot he was in, thought for a moment, and then nodded his approval—meaning that Trout could go ahead with the "reaction" as best he could.

"I have no idea what I said," Bob Trout recalled, "but somehow I put some words together and delivered a two-minute talk. Then I was off the air—though only for a while. I was on again any number of times that night."

A few minutes later Trout had a telephone call from Ambassador John G. Winant, who was visiting the British prime minister at Chequers, and was furious. Why hadn't Trout called the embassy to say we were at war before he began his broadcast? What did Winant think he should do, Trout wondered—call the American embassy and announce, "We are at war"? Until Winant asked the question, Trout hadn't realized that he had been the first person in Great Britain to learn that hostilities had begun between the United States and Japan.

Gil Winant had had a busy weekend. He was supposed to have gone to

Anthony Eden's country house on Friday evening to discuss the foreign secretary's forthcoming conversations with Stalin in Moscow (Eden was leaving for Russia on Sunday), but the news from the Far East intruded on the U.S. ambassador's plans. The most urgent piece of business was what he picked up from British intelligence—that two Japanese convoys had been sighted off Cambodia Point, moving westward toward the Kra Peninsula, and he cabled this news to the State Department. What with one thing and another, he didn't arrive at Eden's place until after midnight on Saturday, but his obliging host "found me some supper and we stayed up until the early hours of the morning discussing his mission." When Eden departed at 10:00, Winant left for Chequers, a hundred miles away, to see the prime minister, whom he found pacing back and forth outside the front door—the other guests having gone inside to lunch.

Churchill at once asked Winant if he thought war with Japan was imminent, and when the ambassador replied, "Yes," he stated with some vehemence, "If they declare war on you, we shall declare war on them within the hour."

After lunch most of the guests departed, leaving the prime minister to work and to rest, since he had been up most of the previous night, while Winant spent a quiet afternoon with Averell Harriman and his daughter. A few minutes before 9:00 they assembled in the dining room and found Churchill sitting alone, grim and silent; as soon as they took their places he called out to Sawyers, the butler, asking him to put the radio on the table so he could hear the news. Churchill switched on the little portable Harry Hopkins had sent after his visit, and as the sound of music faded away, it was replaced by a voice announcing that the Japanese had attacked the U.S. Fleet at Pearl Harbor. As the diners looked at each other incredulously, Sawyers came back into the room to assure them, "It's quite true. We heard it ourselves outside. The Japanese have attacked the Americans."

Churchill bounded to his feet and headed for the door, exclaiming, "We shall declare war on Japan."

Winant got up and hurried after him, saying, "Good God! You can't declare war on a radio announcement! Don't you think you'd better get confirmation first?"

Churchill walked through the hall to the office, which was manned twenty-four hours a day, and told them to put through a call to the White House.

"Mr. President, what's this about Japan?" Churchill asked when the connection was made.

"It's quite true. They have attacked us at Pearl Harbor," Roosevelt replied. "We are all in the same boat now."

After they talked briefly (no mention was made of the serious losses that had been suffered), the prime minister and his guests returned to the table and, as Churchill said, "tried to adjust our thoughts to the supreme world event which had occurred." To the man who represented England's last chance, the indomitable leader whose courage and conviction had rallied his countrymen when the nation seemed doomed, the news that America would be in the war—"up to the neck and in to the death"—was a gift from the gods. "So we had won after all!" he wrote later. He was confident now that "England would live; Britain would live; the Commonwealth of Nations and the Empire would live." After the long succession of defeats, the trials that were enough to scar men's souls—Dunkirk, the fall of France, the threat of invasion, the blitz, the U-boat war—he knew at last that there was "no more doubt about the end."

On December 2, in New York, some eleven hundred men and women had gathered at the Waldorf-Astoria in New York to honor the chief of the European staff of the Columbia Broadcasting System. After speeches in his praise by William Paley, Archibald MacLeish, master of ceremonies Elmer Davis, and William Shirer, after the reading of telegrams from the head of the BBC, Secretary of State Hull, Harry Hopkins, and Franklin Roosevelt, acknowledging the debt owed him by millions of Americans, the assembled guests rose to their feet with a roar of acclaim as Edward R. Murrow got up to speak. It was a tribute to a man who had brought the war as close to Americans as many of them hoped it would ever come, and for a moment he seemed stunned by the outpouring of affection and esteem, yet he of all people knew that the honor done him was also for the work of radio correspondents everywhere, who had come into their own since 1938.

It was fitting that the guests at the Waldorf and a national radio audience should hear Murrow define what lay behind Mr. Churchill's joy on the night of December 7. He and his colleagues had been trying to report a new kind of war, he told them, a war that is "twisting and tearing the social, political, and economic fabric of the world," and he asked his listeners to bear in mind that Britain was now in the third winter of that terrible conflict. With the blackout, a coal shortage, a monotonous diet, severe rationing of clothes, the absence of a host of consumer goods, the constant possibility of epidemics of disease, and over it all "the weight of that gun-powder sky," it was understandable that the British were bone-tired and that they were asking searching questions about America. By now they realized that Lend-Lease, vital as it was, would not win the war, that unless the United States came in at their side the best Britain could hope for would be stalemate, not victory.

Britons admitted that complacency had been their worst enemy; like the Americans, they had wanted only to be left alone; they understood America's reluctance to enter the war. But in the absence of evidence to the contrary they were wondering if the United States had the appetite for the greatness that was being thrust upon it, if its people realized that this world, or what might remain of it, was inevitably going to be run either from Berlin or from Washington. As Ed Murrow had put it to his audience of well-wishers just five days before the attack on Pearl Harbor, "No one who has lived and worked in London for the last three years can doubt that the important decision, perhaps the final decision, that will determine the course of human affairs will be made not in front of Moscow, not on the sands of Libya, but along the banks of the Potomac."

Murrow spoke about the durability of liberty in Britain, despite the bombings; about the people's resilience; especially about the broadening of democracy (the three great equalizers at work, he observed, were "an income tax of 50 cents on everybody's dollar, severe rationing of food and clothing, and a fairly equal distribution of bombs"); about the growing equality of women; about the decline of class-consciousness (it had been admitted, he said, that the boy capable of flying a Spitfire might be able to represent His Majesty's Government abroad after the war, even though he had not attended Eton or Harrow); and he assured his audience that the flame of courage was as high now as it had been at Dunkirk. Yet he kept returning to the questions the British asked, which, in the final analysis, came down to America's will to make the hard choices.

It was no longer a question of whether this nation wanted democracy to survive: that had been answered affirmatively. So it remained to be determined whether Britain must survive in order that democracy should endure. And if the answer to that was yes, then how far and how fast was the United States willing to move? Only the Americans could answer that, but if they did not do so soon, they would be forced to face up to another question an Englishman had put to him before he left London. "If Britain goes down or becomes too exhausted to care, will America not become the most hated nation on earth?" No decision would be without a price, Murrow said, but if the United States made a wrong decision in the present, "the future will take its inevitable revenge."

As much as anyone, Edward R. Murrow had taught his countrymen the bitter lesson of appeasement, and his graphic depiction of Britain's peril and need had been part of the process that saw them inch their way toward involvement. They were headed in that direction, certainly, but whether they would arrive before it was too late was the question—a matter that hinged ultimately on the amorphous ingredient known as the national will. Who can say where the truth lies when it comes to defining the national will, and who or what provides the impetus that transforms will into action? No poll will furnish the answer; nor can you hold a plebiscite on the issue of war or peace. The Constitution of the United States provides that Congress shall have the power to declare war, and to the extent that that body represents the voters of the country, a declaration of war may be said to express the national will. But Congress has not approached the ultimate question unless called upon to do so, and then only in response to challenges or threats too grievous to ignore. During the months prior to December 7,

1941, it cannot be said that the American people as a whole, or their representatives in the Capitol, were sufficiently convinced of the danger to the nation to warrant going to war, and had it not been for the attack on Pearl Harbor it is hard to see exactly what might have triggered such a decision, short of naval attacks by Germany too damaging or humiliating to disregard. The Atlantic war was heading for a showdown, to be sure; but as yet the cumulative damage had not been enough to light the fuse.

Whatever might have been, Ed Murrow was wrong in only one particular: the decision that was of such vital importance to the British was not made in front of Moscow, not on the sands of Libya, not even on the banks of the Potomac. It was not made by Americans, but for them, in Tokyo.

———

From New York, Ed and Janet Murrow had come to Washington, where they were to have dinner at the White House on Sunday evening, December 7. That afternoon Ed was playing golf at the Burning Tree club when a man rushed out of the clubhouse shouting that Pearl Harbor had just been bombed. Murrow went at once to the CBS office to confirm the report and phoned Paul White in New York. Earlier in the day, a friend had driven Janet to an army airfield near Washington so that she could see the planes awaiting shipment to England. She was amazed: the field was jammed with aircraft, and until then she had had no idea that Lend-Lease was producing aid on such a scale for Britain. In the afternoon she was with their hosts, listening to the New York Philharmonic, and when the program was interrupted with a bulletin about the attack, she assumed at once that their dinner engagement would be canceled. To her surprise, when she phoned the White House, Mrs. Roosevelt told her that they were still expected.

At 3:00 the president met with the War Council—Hull, Stimson, Knox—plus the two military chiefs, Marshall and Stark, and despite the gravity of the circumstances, Harry Hopkins remarked the absence of tension: these men for whom the imminence of war had been a constant presence reacted as Churchill did when he heard of the attack. They had concluded long since that the ultimate enemy was Hitler; they knew the Germans could never be defeated without force of arms; sooner or later, moreover, the United States was bound to be in the war, so it was an unexpected boon that "the crisis had come in a way which would unite all our people," as Stimson remarked.

Harry Hopkins saw things in an even more positive light: "Japan had given us an opportunity," he felt. Others looked on the day's bloody events not as opportunity but as unmitigated disaster, and Assistant Secretary of State Breckinridge Long expressed that point of view in the diary he kept for most of his life. "Sick at heart," he wrote. "I am so damned mad at the Navy for being asleep at the switch at Honolulu. It is the worst day in American history. They spent their lives in preparation for a supreme moment—and then were asleep when it came."

That state of mind was hardly unique to Long; it was the kind of reaction that was bound to surface publicly after the first shock wore off, and with the idea of controlling the damage promptly, Hopkins suggested to the president that he schedule two conferences that evening—one with the full cabinet, the other with legislative leaders. Roosevelt agreed on both counts, although the selection of congressional delegates presented a problem. Customarily, ranking members would be invited, but the president refused to have Hamilton Fish in the White House,[2] so the list was confined to a relative few—Vice President Henry Wallace; Speaker Sam Rayburn; Majority Leader John McCormack; Minority Leader Joe Martin; Democrats Tom Connally, Alben Barkley, and Sol Bloom; Republicans Charles McNary, Warren Austin, and Hiram Johnson (the isolationist, who was included by the president at the last minute). The cabinet was to meet at 8:30, the congressional delegation an hour later.

Grace Tully, one of the president's private secretaries, was resting at home that afternoon after the grueling demands of the past few weeks when the telephone rang. It was Louise Hachmeister, and, with a long list of people to call, she wasted no words: "The president wants you right away. There's a car on the way to pick you up. The Japs just bombed Pearl Harbor!" Twenty minutes later, Tully pulled into the White House driveway, which was swarming with extra police and Secret Service men, reporters, and military brass, and in the second-floor study she found Knox, Stimson, and Hopkins, who were joined a few moments later by Marshall and Hull, whose face looked as white as his hair. Since most of the news from Pearl Harbor was coming in to Admiral Stark at the Navy Department, it was her job to answer calls from him, take down the "fragmentary and shocking reports . . . by shorthand, type them up and relay them to the Boss." At first she used a telephone in the second-floor hall, but the noise and confusion were such that she moved into the president's bedroom; each time she put down the phone and rushed to the typewriter to transcribe her notes, a quartet of White House aides—General Watson, Admiral McIntire, Captain Beardall, and Marvin McIntyre—followed and crowded in behind her to peer over her shoulder as she typed. To all of them the news was shattering: each time Stark called she heard the shocked disbelief in his voice; the men around the president were first incredulous, then angry; and while "the Boss maintained greater outward calm than anybody else . . . there was rage in his very calmness. With each new message he shook his head grimly and he tightened the expression of his mouth."

After talking to Churchill, the president had a long conversation with General Marshall about the disposition of troops and the air force, and it was evident that Marshall was increasingly edgy, impatient to get back to the War Department, where he could be in touch with commanders in the

---

[2]He was Roosevelt's own congressman and a fellow Harvard man, but he had made a derogatory attack on the president's mother years before, and FDR neither forgot nor forgave.

field (he had already warned MacArthur to take every precaution). Roosevelt impressed on Hull the necessity of keeping all the South American republics informed; he ordered protection for the Japanese embassy and consulates, and had the Justice Department put Japanese citizens under surveillance;[3] Stimson and Knox were to see to the protection of U.S. arsenals, private munitions factories, and bridges (though under no circumstances was there to be a military guard at the White House). Then the discussion turned to Roosevelt's message to Congress, which he had already decided to deliver the following day. The president dug in his heels when Hull recommended a review of the entire history of relations with Japan; no, he said, it would be a short, precise message.

For an immensely energetic man whose infirmity bound him to a chair, all this activity was a relief and a release, a means of channeling that inner rage and putting it to work, and Eleanor Roosevelt could see that at that moment, "in spite of his anxiety Franklin was in a way more serene than he had appeared in a long time." Despite the confusion whirling around him, it occurred to some witnesses that the White House was the calmest place in town, with the president and his study the center of the hurricane's eye. Sumner Welles was close by during those hectic hours and thought that of all the times he had seen the president in action he had never had such reason to admire him. Sitting calmly at his desk, receiving a continuous flow of reports on a national disaster, "he demonstrated that ultimate capacity to dominate and to control a supreme emergency which is perhaps the rarest and most valuable characteristic of any statesman." With his talent for grasping the significance of each development, by the end of the evening he had personally handled every detail of the situation laid before him by his military advisers, he had written the text of a message to Congress, and he had overseen the text of the declaration of war to be submitted to that body. All the uncertainty of the recent past was over, and however daunting the future might be, it was calming to know what must be done.

The White House switchboard had an open circuit now to Governor Joseph Poindexter in Hawaii, who confirmed the news, or as much of it as he knew, and as he and the president spoke, the governor suddenly shouted into the phone and Roosevelt turned to the group in the room to say, "My God, there's another wave of Jap planes over Hawaii right this minute!"

Reports continued to come in to what was now the nation's command headquarters, and in the meantime those present were passing on to the

[3]Less than a week later, Adolf Berle reported, the State Department received definite word from Nomura's secretary that "Admiral Nomura and possibly Kurusu are planning to commit harakiri. . . . I do not blame them," he wrote; "it must be an unhappy fate to go down in history as having been the cover men for one of the greatest acts of international treachery in modern times." The upshot was that the two men were not permitted to have swords in their possession. As Berle saw matters, "they ought not to commit suicide here since it would probably be played up in Japan as murder and we want to get Grew back safe and sound. After they get back to Japan, they can do what they please."

others their fragmentary knowledge of events. Hull, still bitterly angry, repeated "in a tone as cold as ice" his remarks to the Japanese envoys, but as Grace Tully noted, "there was nothing cold or diplomatic in the words he used." Knox and Stimson were interrogated by the president on the situation in Hawaii, on why they believed this could have happened, on what might happen next, on what could be done to repair the damage, but as the bad news continued to pour in it became evident that the Pacific Fleet had been severely crippled, that the army and air units there were in no condition to fight off an invasion of Hawaii, and that the West Coast of the United States might even be an invasion target.

———

Meantime, bulletin by bulletin, a smattering of information at a time, the public at large was learning the news, struggling to comprehend and digest it and figure out how to react. Sunday afternoon still had a particular niche in the average American home; with morning church attendance behind them, the big midday dinner cooked, consumed, and cleaned up, members of the family could settle down to a few hours of quiet and rest—napping, listening to the radio, reading the Sunday paper, going for a leisurely walk. Professional football was beginning to make inroads into this domestic tranquillity, and at Washington's dingy Griffith Stadium, the crowd was watching the Redskins play their last game of the season against the Philadelphia Eagles when the first bulletin hit the press box. Nearby spectators heard the news from sportswriters, the word spread from seat to seat and section to section, and presently the loudspeaker announcer began paging high-ranking army and navy officers, telling them to get in touch with their offices immediately; this was interspersed with summons to editors and reporters, foreign ambassadors, and others, until individuals in every section of the grandstand seats were hurriedly leaving and running for their cars.

At the Polo Grounds in New York, no one expected the Brooklyn Dodgers to be leading the Eastern champion Giants, but that was exactly what was happening, and the radio audience was as intent on the play-by-play account as those in the stands were on the game they were watching. ". . . it's a long one down to the three-yard line," the announcer shouted; the ball was caught by Ward Cuff, who picked up a nice block by Leeman before he was hit hard around the twenty-seven-yard line—at which moment another voice broke in to say, "We interrupt this broadcast to bring this important bulletin from United Press: Flash! The White House announces Japanese attack on Pearl Harbor!" Predictably, the Mutual Broadcasting System was suddenly deluged with calls from furious fans, wanting to know what was happening in the game, and a New Jersey man who had been taken in by Orson Welles told the company's switchboard operator, "Ha! You got me on that Martian stunt; I had a hunch you'd try it again." Mutual put the Pearl Harbor story on the air immediately; astonishingly,

NBC and CBS decided not to interrupt scheduled music programs but waited until their 2:30 news broadcasts to announce the news.

At Fort Sam Houston in San Antonio, Texas, an army officer whose exceptional performance in the Louisiana maneuvers had won him a brigadier general's star was taking a nap after lunch, having told his aide that he was tired and didn't want to be awakened under any circumstances. Under these particular circumstances, however, the aide decided that disobedience was warranted, and he called General Eisenhower. From another room, Mamie heard her husband saying, "Yes? When? I'll be right down," and as he ran for the door, pulling on his uniform jacket, he told her he would be at headquarters and didn't know when he would be back.

Paul Tibbetts was flying a Douglas A-20 bomber from Fort Bragg to Savannah, Georgia, navigating by tuning in to a Savannah station and steering by radio compass. He was listening to a Glenn Miller recording and was about twenty miles from his destination when someone interrupted the music to announce the bombing of Pearl Harbor. For Tibbetts, that was the first news of the war whose end he would help to bring about less than four years later, piloting a B-29 Superfort called the *Enola Gay* over Hiroshima, Japan, carrying the first bomb to be produced as a result of the meeting held by James Conant in Washington the previous day.[4] Arthur Holly Compton, one of four men present at that meeting, had learned there that his mission into the unforeseeable future was to help create an atomic bomb, and now he was on a train bound for New York, to talk with physicists at Columbia. When the train stopped at Wilmington, Delaware, a boarding passenger told him that the Japanese had just attacked Pearl Harbor.

In Manhattan, the author Marcia Davenport was at one end of the apartment when she heard her husband, Russell, shout for her in a high, tense voice. He was listening to the New York Philharmonic broadcast, and when she ran into the room an announcer was talking about the attack on the U.S. Fleet. Neither of them quite believed what they were hearing; they stared at each other, wondering if it might be a hoax of some kind, while repeating, "Japan? *Japan?*" A few hours later the Lewis Douglases, who lived on the same floor, and several other friends they had invited for a pick-up supper sat talking, stupefied by the news, not knowing what to do, half expecting that Hitler might have planned an attack on the East Coast to coincide with Pearl Harbor, when suddenly they heard the wail of an air-raid siren. They all stopped talking and looked around the table at one another. What now? Was this real? Marcia Davenport turned on the radio and switched off the lights, and they waited in the dark until a voice finally

[4] By some extraordinary turn of fate and timing, a few minutes after the atomic bomb dropped from the *Enola Gay*, Mitsuo Fuchida flew into the area. This was the same Mitsuo Fuchida who had led the Japanese planes from their carriers to Pearl Harbor on December 7, 1941, bringing war to America, and as he flew past Hiroshima he wondered what had caused the curious mushroom-shaped cloud he saw rising above the city. So the man who was present at the beginning was there at the end, as well.

informed them that the sirens were being tested on account of the day's events.

The man the Davenports had tried so hard to get elected in 1940 was contemplating a trip to Australia on Sunday, December 7. That autumn the Australian government had invited Wendell Willkie to visit the commonwealth, as he had Britain, and he had not yet decided whether to go. As chance would have it, President Roosevelt had written him on December 5, saying he hoped Willkie would accept the invitation in the interest of Australian-American relations and the Allied cause, suggesting that he could make the trip in any capacity he chose—official or otherwise. The letter reached Willkie after Pearl Harbor, and it was several days before he replied to the president, saying he would think further about the wisdom of making the trip. Apart from that, however, he wanted to add something that was very much on his mind. Friends of Mr. Roosevelt's were suggesting that he could be extremely useful to the president in the national emergency, and Willkie hoped they had not troubled the chief executive on that score. Noting the incredibly anxious and burdensome days that lay ahead for the president, he wrote: "What I am trying to say—honestly, but awkwardly I am afraid, because it is not easy—is this: If any such well-meant suggestions about me are brought to you, I beg you to disregard them. There is on your shoulders the heaviest responsibility any man can carry and I would not add to it in the slightest way. Even to volunteer a willingness to serve seems to me now only an imposition on your attention. Every American is willing to serve."

On Sunday afternoon, December 7, that letter was not yet written, but Wendell Willkie knew precisely what the mood of the country was: everyone was willing to serve. The question for most of them would be how—and how soon.

———

The first news bulletin had attracted a crowd to the Japanese embassy on Massachusetts Avenue, and as they stood watching, smoke began to rise from the rear of the building, where the staff was burning diplomatic papers. Onlookers were tight-lipped and silent, and a woman who was there said their faces reminded her of a lynch mob she had once seen in Georgia.

In front of the president's house at 1600 Pennsylvania Avenue, another silent crowd had been collecting since the first announcement of the attack, and several hundred were on hand—some women and children, but mostly men with anger etched into their faces. These people were eager to do something and had no idea what shape action might take; mostly they had come here because they needed the reassurance of the White House, as if proximity to the embodiment of America's roots and her might would relieve their anxiety, their shock, and their horror, and even in the random comings and goings of high-level civilians and military men they found security of a sort, as if the very activity of important people could somehow set matters right.

At 3:05, Steve Early's secretary handed reporters a terse bulletin stating, "The attacks were delivered without warning and within an hour of a call by the Japanese Ambassador and their special envoy on Mr. Hull." Less than an hour later Early, seated in front of a sign acquired in happier days that read, "We Ain't Mad With Nobody," informed reporters that an army transport carrying lumber had been torpedoed thirteen hundred miles west of San Francisco. Distress signals had been picked up from another American cargo vessel seven hundred miles beyond the West Coast, prompting Early to comment that "their subs seem pretty well into our back yard." At 4:35 he held another press conference, this time to announce that the battleships *Oklahoma* and *West Virginia* were reported severely damaged, as was Hickam Field, where 104 were said to be dead, with more than three hundred wounded. Summoning reporters again at 6:50 P.M., Early asked if any Japanese newspapermen were present, and after being told there were none, he warned against relaying any unauthorized news to the Japanese, bringing home the realization that with war, censorship would soon be at hand.

———

Donald Nelson had never met Harold Ickes, and he was pleased and flattered to be invited for Sunday lunch at the interior secretary's farm. After dressing leisurely, he headed for Olney, Maryland, to join the Old Curmudgeon and his attractive red-haired wife, Jane, and he found himself in good company—including Hugo Black of the Supreme Court and Tom Connally from the Senate. A lot of the talk concerned the Ickeses' pigs and cattle and chickens, and Connally was full of amusing stories, which he told well. (Evidently, Nelson did not make much of a hit with his host. "He seemed energetic and forceful but lacking somewhat in background," Ickes noted in his diary. "Doubtless he has worked hard all of his life and has gotten ahead solely by his energy and ability.") Inevitably the conversation turned to the situation in the Far East, and Nelson said later that all agreed there would be no war with Japan in the foreseeable future. On the way home, listening to the radio in his car, he learned how wrong they had been.

Nelson drove instead to his office, where he found Robert Horton and Bruce Catton already working on a speech for him to deliver that evening. Someone at the agency arranged for time on one of the networks, and Nelson stood before a microphone and said about all there was for him to say—which was that the nation's resources would now be "mobilized with ruthless determination."

A few minutes before 5:00, President Roosevelt asked Grace Tully to come to his study, and she found him alone, with two or three neat piles of notes containing the information he had received in the last two hours before him on his desk. As she came in with her notebook, he was lighting a cigarette. He took a deep drag and said, "Sit down, Grace. I'm going before Congress tomorrow. I'd like to dictate my message. It will be short."

With that he took another long pull on the cigarette and began to speak in a calm tone as if he were dictating a letter, but she noticed that his diction was unusually incisive and slow, and that he specified each punctuation mark.

"Yesterday comma December 7 comma 1941 dash a day which will live in infamy dash the United States of America was suddenly and deliberately attacked by naval and air forces of the Empire of Japan period paragraph."

In less than five hundred words, spoken without hesitation or second thought, Roosevelt dictated the words intended to lay America's case before Congress and the world. The message had none of Churchill's soaring prose, no patriotic summons, no bugle calls to action—only a simple, direct recitation of the facts, as in the conclusion: "I ask that the Congress declare that since the unprovoked and dastardly attack by Japan on Sunday comma December 7 comma a state of war has existed between the United States and the Japanese Empire period end."

When Grace Tully had transcribed her notes, the president called Hull back to the White House to go over the draft. As he anticipated, the secretary of state had in hand a much longer message prepared by Sumner Welles, relating in explicit detail the long train of circumstances leading to war; again, Roosevelt was ready for him and would have none of it. He must have known that his wish in this grave instance was the wish of the whole American people, for he sensed that they wanted no oratory, no lawyer's brief, only the briefest summary of the facts, set forth by him in what might be described as controlled rage, so that the nation could get on with what needed to be done as quickly as possible. Except for a few minor changes of words, the only real addition he permitted was volunteered by Harry Hopkins, who suggested what appeared in the next-to-last sentence of the message: "With confidence in our armed forces—with the unbounding determination of our people—we will gain the inevitable triumph—so help us God."

Eleanor Roosevelt was carrying on gallantly downstairs, on the theory that her dinner guests had to eat somewhere and it might as well be here, but it was not a relaxed occasion for the visitors, who were acutely aware of the empty chair at the head of the table and the stream of worried-looking men scurrying through the hall to or from the study that was the focus of the nation's attention. Ed and Janet Murrow were with Mrs. Roosevelt, as were her young friends Joe Lash and Trude Pratt, and during dinner the president sent word that Murrow was to wait, that he wanted to see him.

After the meal, Janet departed to attend another party at which they were to have been the guests of honor, while Ed went upstairs to sit on a bench outside the president's study, and, while he waited to be summoned, observed the continuing procession of VIPs, overheard snatches of conversation as they passed, including a snarled rebuke to Frank Knox—"God-damit, sir, you ought not to be in charge of a rowboat, let alone the United States Navy!" Some years later, commenting on the charges that Roosevelt and his top advisers possessed advance knowledge of the attack on Pearl Harbor, Murrow recalled the opportunity he had had that night to observe those men off guard, and said, "If they were *not* surprised by the news from Pearl Harbor, then that group of elderly men were putting on a performance which would have excited the admiration of any experienced actor."

CHAPTER 56

———— ◆ ————

"That day ended isolationism . . ."

The affair in Pittsburgh that afternoon was billed in advance as "one of the biggest mass meetings ever staged here by the America First Committee," and the faithful began arriving early at Soldiers' and Sailors' Memorial Hall on Sunday, December 7, to hear Senator Gerald P. Nye of North Dakota and Mrs. Irene Castle McLaughlin, the widow and former dancing partner of Vernon Castle, who was killed in World War I. Given the rapid pace of events and the polarization of opinion in the country, something like what happened here was almost bound to take place, but it proved to be a demonstration of America First at its most inept, a sorry end to a protest movement that had begun with such high hopes and ideals.

As luck would have it, the audience was seated by 3:00, when the program was scheduled to begin, so these 2,500 Pittsburghers were innocently unaware of the catastrophe in Hawaii. In an anteroom offstage a reporter informed Nye that Pearl Harbor and Manila had supposedly been bombed; but lacking confirmation, and feeling that they should not hold up the meeting, the America First group decided that the show must go on. While Irene Castle McLaughlin was speaking, telling of the husband who was lost in the first war and the son she did not want killed in another, a couple walked in off the street and took seats in the audience. His name was

Enrique Urrutia, and although he was in civilian clothes he was a colonel in the United States Army; before leaving their house for an afternoon stroll he and his wife had heard the bulletin about Pearl Harbor, and on a whim had decided to drop in on the rally to see how the America First people would handle the situation.

Mrs. McLaughlin concluded her talk, and a former Pennsylvania state senator, Hale Sipe, then proceeded to denounce Joseph Stalin and Harry Hopkins as two of a kind and declare that the chief warmonger in the United States was Franklin D. Roosevelt. As the wild cheers from the crowd died, Colonel Urrutia rose from his seat and said, "Mr. Speaker, please, can I ask a question? I wonder if the audience knows that Japan has attacked us and that Pearl Harbor has been bombed by the Japanese." Unfortunately, the colonel was not in uniform, his English was heavily accented, and those on the stage and in the audience assumed he was the sort of heckler these meetings always attracted, so boos and jeers greeted his announcement, along with cries of "Get out, you don't belong here!" Urrutia, followed by his wife, was hustled from the hall by ushers.

Sipe continued his attack on the administration, collection baskets were passed, and it was almost 5:00 by the time Senator Nye got his chance to talk. Gerald the Giant-Killer was feisty, proud of his reputation as a stump speaker against Roosevelt and the policies that were taking the country into war, and he was not about to pass up an opportunity to harangue a crowd because of an unconfirmed report (though he had not troubled to check it out during the two hours he waited to speak). The unhappy result was that while hundreds of Americans were dying in Hawaii the senator from North Dakota set some sort of record for insensitivity by striking out at the administration for fighting Britain's war and at Britain for suffering fewer casualties than any of its allies, and lampooning the national debt and the destroyers-for-bases deal. He had been talking for half an hour when a local reporter walked onto the stage and handed him a note, stating that the Japanese had declared war on the United States.

Nye glanced at the piece of paper and with barely a pause completed his sentence: ". . . it is Naziism to do any thinking here in America." For another fifteen minutes he continued, interrupted only by cheers and shouts of "Impeach Roosevelt!" and at last he turned to the subject of the Far East and the administration's "studied effort to pick a war with Japan." At that point he stopped long enough to read what was written on the slip of paper before him. He seemed confused, one reporter noted, as if he had difficulty digesting it, before he spoke again: "I have the worst news that I have had in twenty years to report," he declared. "The Japanese Imperial Government at 4:00 P.M. announced a state of war between it and the United States and Britain." Then, incredibly, he proceeded to deliver the rest of his prepared speech, and when it was done and reporters gathered around to ask for comments on the Pearl Harbor disaster, he told them, "It sounds terribly fishy to me."

As the America First crowd filed from the hall to shiver in the waning sunlight, Pittsburgh was already beginning to adjust to the unfamiliar experience of being at war. Radio stations KDKA and WCAE were broadcasting details of proper air-raid conduct; Western Union traffic swelled by 30 percent with the exchange of telegrams between industrialists and defense agencies in Washington; Mayor Cornelius Scully proclaimed Pittsburgh's readiness for war and reminded listeners that he had always supported all-out aid to Britain; the local Foreign Policy Association received a telegram from Socialist Norman Thomas canceling his appearance in a debate on the subject "Should America Declare War on Germany?"; and people returning from Sunday-afternoon drives into the countryside noticed armed national guardsmen on the bridges across the Allegheny, Monongahela, and Ohio Rivers. The County Airport was abruptly closed to visitors, guards patrolled the field and hangars, and the boroughs of Sewickley, Ambridge, and Aliquippa sent out a call for men to stand watch over their municipal water systems.

Like most Americans, the leaders of the America First movement had paid little heed to the Far East and were as astonished as everyone else by the events of December 7, but fortunately the organization possessed voices more sensitive to reality than Gerald Nye. On Sunday evening the national office released a statement calling for its members to get behind the war effort until victory over Japan was won, and pledged to support the president as commander in chief. Chapters were urged to postpone all scheduled rallies and stop distributing noninterventionist literature, but the door was kept slightly ajar to continue opposition to the war in Europe.

As yet the diehards were not convinced that we were in a global conflict; they preferred to believe that it was an "isolationist Pacific war," as Freda Kirchwey wrote in *The Nation*. It would take a while, she supposed, for America to discover what Britain had painfully learned since the spring of 1940: that this war was "the penalty for our old sins against the democratic faith," and that what had brought it on was the appeasement of Japan, the unwitting encouragement of that country to believe that its ambitions could be realized without fighting. The trouble with buying off an aggressor, paying a little blackmail in the form of oil or wheat or scrap iron, was that it placed the ultimate decision in the hands of the enemy; he might overplay his hand and ask for more than he could collect, but as the Japanese had just demonstrated, he was the one who decided the time and place for the fighting to begin.

Then and later it was customary to sneer at the isolationists and pass them off as an aberration of the thirties, myopes who had failed to perceive reality. And certainly there was some truth in the accusation. Yet the charge fails to take into account that the isolationists' illusion was all of a piece with the ancient European dream of America as an innocent, uncorrupted land, untroubled by the Old World's wars, a new Eden where man might make a fresh start. "Liberty has still a continent to live on," Horace

Walpole had promised, and in what people had called the Great War—the one to make the world safe for democracy, which my father and his generation fought—Americans went off to Europe resolved to set matters right, singing ". . . we won't come back till it's over, over there." But there was no coming back to a sanctuary set apart by oceans, no holding off the world. One of the lessons of 1941, as of 1914, was that America, like it or not, was part of the whole. In the twentieth century no nation was an island.

———

Arthur Vandenberg was no appeaser, but he had struggled as hard as anyone against American involvement in the war, and a strong streak of vanity led him to preserve the printed record of his long battle with the administration. On that lazy Sunday afternoon he was pasting clippings into his scrapbook, bringing it up to date, and the smell of library paste and cigar smoke lay heavy in the room when the telephone rang at 4:00 bringing news of the Japanese attack. Immediately, he issued a statement to the press urging "victorious war with every resource at our command" and phoned Steve Early at the White House, asking him to tell Mr. Roosevelt that despite any differences they might have, he would support him without reservation in his reply to Japan. In later years he would write that "my convictions regarding international cooperation and collective security for peace took firm form on the afternoon of the Pearl Harbor attack. That day ended isolationism for any realist."[1] On December 8, before the Senate vote was taken, he made the only speech on the floor, determined to "swing the vast antiwar party in the country into unity with this unavoidable decision." As Walter Lippmann observed, the senator from Michigan had an endearing, almost spiritual quality that enabled him—unlike most people, who don't like to change their minds in public or retreat from a position until it is too late—to do so "with style and dash, and in a mood to shame the devils of his own weakness."

Charles and Anne Lindbergh were living on Martha's Vineyard, and when he heard the news he was working on the speech he planned to give in Boston a few days hence. In company with much of official Washington, he had expected an attack on the Philippines. "But Pearl Harbor! How did the Japs get close enough, and where is our navy?" he wondered. He appreciated the possibility of attacking Hawaii with carrier-based planes, but didn't see how they dared risk it—"unless our navy is asleep—or in the Atlantic." After telephoning Bob Stuart to suggest that the Boston meeting be canceled, he talked to General Wood, who remarked sourly of the president, "Well, he got us in through the back door."[2]

[1] Another factor in his conversion from isolationism was the influence of his nephew, Hoyt S. Vandenberg, who later became chief of staff of the U.S. Air Force. The younger man used to argue vehemently with his uncle, trying to make him see that the oceans were not "moats" any longer and that the airplane would be the dominant factor in any future war.

[2] Less than a week after the attack on Pearl Harbor the America First Committee announced

Lindbergh pondered how he could serve the country, now that it was at war. "I *must* take some part in it," he wrote, "whatever that may be."[3] To win, he knew, would require us to attack in Asia, in Europe, all over the world, and that meant raising and equipping an army of many millions, far more than America presently possessed. Enormous change lay ahead, but as he saw it, "Periods of great change bring advantages to some nations and disadvantages to others." It was a time to adjust our outlook and act accordingly.

Another man whose outlook would require some adjustment was John L. Lewis, whose triumph over the steel industry on the issue of the closed shop was proclaimed this very day. After three months of turmoil that had seen the collapse of the National Defense Mediation Board, several strikes, and considerable anguish on the parts of President Roosevelt, the Congress, and the general public, Lewis had his way. But the victory was a hollow one, thanks to the timing of the announcement: in those newspapers that carried the story, it was not much more than a filler, lost in the tale of infinitely more deadly strikes in the Pacific.

———

By evening, people were standing five and six deep on the sidewalk beyond the tall iron fence around the White House grounds, peering at the lighted windows in hopes of spotting movement inside, watching intently the arrival of each automobile to see if they could identify passengers, and by the time Harold Ickes appeared for the cabinet meeting the moon was up, misty and indistinct. He noticed especially how quiet and serious the crowds were, and decided their presence was an example of the human instinct to get close to the scene of action even if they could see or hear nothing. Some cabinet officers had been trying all afternoon to get back to Washington, and Ickes was pleased to see that everyone had made it. Frank Walker and Frances Perkins had flown from New York in a special plane; so had Henry Morgenthau. The Treasury secretary, exhausted by weeks of work on problems created by the preparations for war—taxes, finance, and inflation in particular—and despondent over the war reports from Europe and Asia, was planning to take a vacation in Arizona, and on Sunday the 7th had

---

that it would disband the organization. "Our principles were right," read the somewhat smug announcement. "Had they been followed, war could have been avoided." But, the statement continued, "We are at war" and the nation's only goal should be victory.

[3]In mid-January, Lindbergh met with Stimson, Lovett, and Arnold in hopes that he might be usefully employed in the Army Air Forces (as the Air Corps had been renamed a few months earlier), but Stimson immediately set the tone for that and later discussions by saying he would be extremely hesitant to put Lindbergh in any position of command because of the views he had expressed about the war. Lindbergh said he continued to believe that it was a mistake for the United States to get into the war, but now that we were there, he stood behind his country and wanted to help in any way he could. The talks went nowhere, and the upshot was that the aviator said he would try to make a contribution in the aircraft industry. In the spring he went to work as an adviser in Henry Ford's Willow Run plant.

lunch with his family at a New York restaurant before departing for Tucson. As he left the restaurant, his chauffeur gave him the news of Pearl Harbor and the Secret Service informed him that the president had been trying to reach him for two hours, so he drove to the airport and flew to the capital.

Promptly at 8:30 the full cabinet met, with the members forming a ring completely around the president's desk, and Ickes noticed at once how solemn Roosevelt was: no wisecracks or jokes this evening, not even a smile, and the calmness he had displayed earlier in the afternoon was largely gone, replaced by tension and signs of enormous fatigue. He began by telling them that this was probably the gravest crisis to confront a cabinet since 1861; then he filled them in on everything he had heard from Hawaii, making clear that what they had on their hands was the worst naval defeat in American history. Not only that: Guam had probably been captured and it was likely that Wake was gone, while the Japanese were advancing on Manila, Singapore, Hong Kong, and other locations in the Malay states. For all anyone knew, a night attack might be taking place in Hawaii at that very moment. Even though they had heard some of this news before they arrived, the detailed catalogue of catastrophe shocked the cabinet members—that, and the manner in which Roosevelt described the disaster. Frances Perkins said he actually had "physical difficulty in getting out the words that put him on record as knowing that the navy was caught unawares." It was obvious to her that he was "having a dreadful time just accepting the idea." Yet she knew him well, and she detected an evasive look, revealing the wave of relief he was reluctant to acknowledge—relief that the long period of tension, of not knowing what the Japanese would do and when they would do it, was over. The men in Tokyo, after all, had taken the decision for war or peace from the president's hands.

Throughout the meeting, according to Ickes, Hull behaved more than ever like a Christian martyr—indignant that he was the one to have been duped by the Japanese diplomats while their army and navy were plotting against us, since it was obvious that the expedition against Pearl Harbor had been in the works for months. Despite FDR's obvious annoyance, moreover, Hull was still plumping for a long presidential message to Congress, but when Roosevelt read his own draft aloud, all but the secretary of state agreed that he had struck exactly the right note.

Shortly after 9:30 the congressional leaders were ushered into the study, and the cabinet members moved back to let them have the chairs surrounding the president's desk. The president reviewed the situation with them in much the same words he had used with the cabinet, informing them that "The casualties, I am sorry to say, were extremely heavy," and that "we have lost the majority of the battleships there"; but when asked what he would recommend on the Hill the next day he evaded the question on grounds that much might happen between now and then and he didn't want to commit himself yet. Two important factors were involved here: no one knew whether Japan had actually declared war on the United States; and although the president fully expected Germany and Italy to join their Axis partner, that was not certain, either. But behind Roosevelt's reluctance to tip his hand was the notorious inability of congressmen to keep secrets. If he told them what was going to be in his message, the minute they left his study the news would be out—more than twelve hours before he intended it to be made public.

Following his summary of the attack, there was dead silence until the man most visibly outraged said what most others were thinking. Tom Connally of Texas, chairman of the Senate Foreign Relations Committee, asked, "How did it happen that our warships were caught like tame ducks in Pearl Harbor? I am amazed at the attack by Japan, but I am still more astounded at what happened to our navy. They were all asleep!" he exploded. "Where were our patrols? They knew these negotiations were going on." Knox was obviously deeply embarrassed by these and other questions, but made no attempt to reply. Unhappily, neither he nor anyone else present could answer, and shortly after 10:30 the meeting broke up and the congressmen and all the cabinet members except Hull filed out of the study. Ickes paused to speak to Hiram Johnson, whom he had not seen for two years or more, and was astonished at how the senator had failed. It seemed the supreme irony that this old, sick, ghostly reminder of the isolationist impulse that had dominated American politics for so long should be a mourner at the funeral of the movement he had done so much to foster, destroyed in the work of a moment half a world from home. Quietly, assuring Ickes that he would respect the confidence of his reply, Johnson asked, "Will the president ask for more than a declaration of war against Japan?"

Probably not, the secretary replied: he was sure that would be all FDR would request unless Germany and Italy declared war in the meantime. As they left, Ickes knew in his bones that the old isolationist would vote for war.

Now Sumner Welles came into the study with his draft of a war message. Roosevelt didn't like it now any more than he had when Hull described it, but the secretary of state was nothing if not stubborn, and continued to press for what Harry Hopkins called a "long-winded dissertation on the history of Japanese relations." After marveling at the president's patience, Hopkins decided that the only reason he gave the impression he would consider it seriously was to get rid of the State Department men.

Finally, Hull and Welles left, at 12:30 it was Ed Murrow's turn, and the president ordered beer and sandwiches. Joining them in the study was Colonel William Donovan, who was then engaged in setting up an intelligence organization that would be known as the Office of Strategic Services (OSS). Mr. Roosevelt, dead tired, his face ashen, asked Murrow a few questions about the bombing of London and the morale of the British, and then informed his visitors in detail about the losses at Pearl Harbor—the loss of life, how ships had been sunk at their moorings and planes destroyed on the airstrips, and as he said that he pounded his fist on the table and groaned—"On the ground, by God, on the ground!" For a reporter on this night of nights, it was the chance of a lifetime, since the details he gave them—with no indication that what he said should be off the record— would not be made public for hours, and in some cases for months. The president mentioned that he had talked with Churchill, who told him of attacks on British bases, and he asked Donovan if he thought this might be part of an overall Axis plan. The latter had no evidence to offer, but said it was certainly a reasonable assumption. Then Roosevelt asked a rather curious question, hinting once again at the isolationists' powerful influence on his thinking and his intense concern about public unity: did they believe the nation would now support a declaration of war? Both men assured him that it would.

As Murrow was taking his leave after more than half an hour's conversation, the president inquired, "Did this surprise you?"

"Yes, Mr. President," he replied.

"Maybe you think it didn't surprise us!" Roosevelt added.

On the way to his hotel Murrow stopped in at the CBS office and found Eric Sevareid. "It's pretty bad," he said, but Sevareid already knew. He had been working at the White House for hours that evening, collaring visitors as they emerged from the front door; after questioning them, he would rush back to the pressroom, where CBS had an open microphone, and ad lib on the basis of what he had learned.

"What did you think when you saw that crowd of people staring through the White House fence?" Murrow asked.

Sevareid replied, "They reminded me of the crowds around the Quai d'Orsay a couple of years ago."

"That's what I was thinking," Murrow said; "the same look on their faces that they had in Downing Street."

In the early hours of the morning Murrow returned to the hotel and for hours paced the floor, smoking continuously, debating whether or not he could reveal the information he had heard from the president. "The biggest story of my life," he kept telling Janet, "and I can't make up my mind whether it's my duty to tell it, or forget it." In the end, he decided it had been told him in confidence and he should not report what Roosevelt had said.[4]

[4]In later years, he told his son Casey and others that he would write the story of that evening one day and that it was important enough to pay Casey's way through college. Inevitably, this gave rise to speculation that the president had divulged something indicating that the attack came as no surprise to him, but on examination, that thesis does not hold up. In a broadcast in 1945, Murrow stated that when the president told him that he and others at the White House were surprised, "I believed him." One of Murrow's biographers, Alexander Kendrick, assumed that what he decided to keep secret was the details about Pearl Harbor; these were given him in confidence, and even though he was not bound by an off-the-record restriction, his conscience obliged him to say nothing, but to wait for the information to be made public by

Katherine Marshall was in bed, suffering from four broken ribs, and ever since hearing the news about Pearl Harbor on the radio she had longed to talk to her husband. When he didn't return by 7:00 she dressed and sat on the porch to wait for him. Long afterward the general arrived, and when he came in his face was grim and gray. He said nothing—only that he was tired and was going to bed. She tried to think of something she could do or say that might help, but she knew he wanted to be alone, so she walked past his door and went to her room.

The telephone awakened Ambassador Joseph Grew in Tokyo at 7:00 A.M. on December 8. It seemed only moments ago that he had delivered the president's message to the emperor to Foreign Minister Togo, but the call was urgent, requesting that he come as quickly as possible to see the minister, and without taking time even to shave, he threw on some clothes. When he arrived at 7:30 he found Togo grim, formal, and—as always—imperturbable. The Japanese official made a brief statement and then slapped down on the table the thirteen-page memorandum which Nomura had delivered to Hull. Togo had seen the emperor at 3:00 A.M. and this document constituted Hirohito's reply to Roosevelt, he said. Then he made a pretty little speech thanking Grew for his cooperation during the long negotiations and walked downstairs to see him to the door. Not a word was spoken about Pearl Harbor. Indeed, not until after he had shaved and breakfasted did Grew learn that the two countries were at war, and this was not confirmed until late morning, when a functionary appeared at the embassy and, hands trembling, read the official announcement.

Shortly thereafter, the embassy gates were closed and the ambassador was told that no one could enter or leave, that no cipher messages could be sent, and that all telegrams must be submitted to the Foreign Office for approval. The British ambassador and several others from the diplomatic colony managed to get past the police outside the gates and bid farewell to the Americans, and they were followed by a group of extremely polite Japanese, who apologized profusely before confiscating all the shortwave radios in the embassy. None of the Americans knew, of course, how long it would be before they might be exchanged for Japan's diplomats in Washington, and about sixty members of the staff assembled for cocktails that evening, livened by a few brave speeches. Arrangements were made for those who lived outside the compound to move into the embassy, sharing apartments, bunking down on mattresses on the floor.

the government. Eric Sevareid believed that "had anything happened that truly persuaded Ed that Roosevelt expected the attack, Ed would have at least talked about it in later years if not weeks or months," adding that there was speculation in Washington for weeks that Pearl Harbor was one of several possible targets of a Japanese attack. A Korean expatriate friend of Sevareid's urged him to believe that Pearl Harbor would be hit: he said he could not obtain an audience with anyone important in the State Department to tell them how he knew this.

Reflecting on the way Tokyo had borrowed *Blitzkrieg* tactics from its ally in Berlin, Grew concluded, "If the Japanese had confined themselves to the Far East and had attacked only the Philippines, there would have been pacifists and isolationists at home who would have said that we have no business in the Far East anyway, but once they attacked Hawaii it was certain that the American people would rise up in a solid unit of fury." The task ahead would not be easy, he knew, but Japan's defeat was absolutely certain, and he permitted himself a smile of satisfaction as he recalled how he had warned Washington to be ready for a step of "dangerous and dramatic suddenness"—precisely what had occurred.

Grew might be right that victory over Japan was certain, but what good was that if Britain and Russia should fall, if Hitler should triumph in Europe? Despite pressure from Stimson, in particular, who argued that Germany had pushed Japan to attack,[5] President Roosevelt resisted the temptation to declare war on Germany and Italy, hoping that Hitler would relieve him of the necessity to act. He detected "a lingering distinction in some quarters of the public between war with Japan and war with Germany," he told the British ambassador, and although Berlin was ominously silent, he decided to wait it out to see if the Führer would resolve his dilemma.

Hitler had his hands full. Winter had closed in on Russia, and his dream of conquering that nation in a single summer campaign ended as the days grew shorter and brutal cold and blizzards descended on the land. On December 6, to the utter surprise of the German high command, the Russians seized the initiative when the temperature was 35 degrees below zero, launched a major assault with one hundred fresh divisions, and threw back the Wehrmacht within twelve miles of the center of Moscow; simultaneously, Rommel's Afrika Korps began to retreat in the desert, and Hitler assumed control of all military operations. Curiously, despite the many warning signs from the Far East, the Japanese attack took him by surprise. In the spring he had urged his allies in Tokyo to move against Singapore, telling Matsuoka that one of the benefits would be to deter the United States from entering the war; but he had not contemplated hostilities between Japan and America. As Ribbentrop perceived, the Japanese attack "brought about what we had wanted to avoid at all costs, war between Germany and America," but Hitler himself was jubilant. Rejoicing in the news—"The turning point!" he proclaimed when he heard it—he dismissed the advice of those around him and made another monumental miscalculation: he would declare war on the United States.

Knowing virtually nothing about the United States, viewing it merely as a decadent bourgeois democracy incapable of waging or sustaining a

[5]On the contrary, the Japanese were so confident that they made their decision before they were certain Germany would join them, and not until noon on December 8 did Tokyo request the German government to declare war on the United States.

prolonged war, he disastrously underestimated its strength (an opinion bolstered by the apparent ease of the Japanese triumph), and despite the lack of the most elementary preparations (one of his headquarters officers admitted, "we have never even considered a war against the United States") and the certainty of U.S. intervention in the European war, he left his Wolf's Lair bunker on the evening of December 8, returned to Berlin, and began to prepare a speech to the Reichstag. On December 11, after denouncing Roosevelt as "the main culprit of this war" and a creature of the Jews, he announced to deafening applause that he had arranged for the American chargé d'affaires to be handed his passport. Now the fire he had ignited with the invasion of Poland on September 1, 1939, would rage around the world.[6]

―――

As Woody Guthrie told it, he had "walked out west," strolling from town to town playing his guitar and singing for tips in the boweries of forty-two states, and early in December he was on Los Angeles' Skid Row with a guitar-playing buddy named Cisco Kid. The way the two guitar players worked was to walk inside one of the numerous joints, ask the regular musicians if they wanted to take a break, take their place on the platform when they did, and ask the customers what they'd like to hear. If things went right, they might make 30 or 40 cents in tips at each place; but this particular night was a bad one for singing from one joint to the next—the rain had chased a lot of the regular customers home, and those who were left were mostly men in uniform, all of them talking about Japan and something going on at Pearl Harbor.

"It's worse than we figured," they heard someone say. A loudmouth in civilian clothes who had had too much to drink stood up and boasted that he'd "beat the livin' hell outa ever' goddam Jap in this town!" A few minutes later they heard the sound of glass shattering on the sidewalk outside, people running and yelling, and when they went out they saw the loudmouth with about ten friends, saying he was going to beat up all the Japs in L.A. Inside the Imperial Bar, next door, where the plate-glass window was smashed, several Japanese men and women were picking up the pieces,

---

[6]Although it is not within the province of this book, it is interesting to speculate on what might have happened if the Japanese had been content to expand in Asia without attacking the United States, or if Hitler had not made the fatal error—perhaps the single most important decision of World War II—of declaring war on the United States after Pearl Harbor.

Had the Japanese not attacked Hawaii, it seems unlikely that this country would have gone to war to salvage the outposts of European empire in the Pacific. On the other hand, had Hitler not acted so precipitately in the wake of Japan's strike at Pearl Harbor, America might have turned away from the European conflict in order to concentrate exclusively on Japan. In that case, Hitler might have dealt separately with Russia and Britain, without risking major U.S. intervention, with less chance that American arms would reach either of his foes in great quantity, and—just possibly—with an entirely different outcome in Europe.

and the civilian toughs began shouting, "Jap rats! Spies! Git 'em! Kill 'em!" as they moved across the street and headed toward the Imperial.

Cisco climbed up on a vegetable cart and tried to calm the mob, saying, "These little Japanese farmers, these Japanese people that run the old cafés and gin joints, they can't help it because they happen to be Japanese." But the toughs yelled back, calling him a coward and fifth columnist, and kept coming. A few others—some of them women, one holding a gallon wine jug at the ready—joined Guthrie and Cisco, and just as some railroad workers rolled by on a train, breaking the advance of the mob for a moment, Guthrie reached for his guitar and started to sing:

> We will fight together
> We shall not be moved
> We will fight together
> We shall not be moved
> Just like a tree
> That's planted by the water
> We
> Shall not
> Be moved.

"Everybody sing!" Cisco shouted, grabbing his guitar.

As the train went on by and slowly disappeared from sight, everyone in their group was singing. The bunch of toughs made a run at them, cursing, but by now sailors and soldiers had joined in on the song, locking arms with truck drivers and ranch hands and bartenders from nearby saloons; the rain poured down harder and harder, everyone sang louder and louder, a number of the toughs began to drift away, and though four or five of them approached within a few feet and waved their fists in the faces of the singers lining the curb, nobody touched anyone. At the moan of a siren and the arrival of a police wagon carrying fifteen or twenty cops with enough guns and clubs to win a war, the rioters suddenly vanished. When they heard the singing, the police shook their heads and waved their flashlights around, as if they were looking for something. One of them checked his address book and remarked to another, "The chief said this was where the riot was."

"Sing with us, officer?" asked Cisco.

"How does it go?" the cop asked.

"Listen." And they sang it again while the police stood around smiling, swinging their clubs, humming and listening.

Then they piled into their vehicle and headed off, but just before the taillights vanished around a corner, Guthrie could hear their voices:

> Just like a treeee
> Planted by th' waterrr

We
Shall not
Be
Mooooved!

———

Sunday, December 7, 1941, was my mother's and father's twenty-first wedding anniversary, and I had called them that morning from New York to wish them many more of the same. They were going to church, as they nearly always did, confident that the Reverend Hugh Thompson Kerr would reinforce their Presbyterianism in the most amiable manner imaginable. I was never sure how much they liked the idea of my spending a lot of time in New York City; after all, if you were paying someone's tuition at Yale, you probably thought he should stick to his studies there. But I was pretty well caught up on my work and had come to New York for several days, planning to stay through the weekend. Before leaving New Haven my classmate Dick Drain and I had written one of our occasional, purportedly humorous "Brothers Grim" columns for the *Yale Daily News,* and had turned in what both of us recognized as a piece of fluff for the Saturday, December 6, issue—a hasty, last-minute effort before Christmas vacation— in which, by pure coincidence, we imagined ourselves during the approaching "reading period" in Honolulu, taking in the sun and fun on Waikiki Beach.

I had been spending more and more time in New York that fall. Louise Bray had leased an apartment and Bobs was commuting to Sarah Lawrence as a day student; happily, the apartment had a spare closet-size bedroom where I was welcome to stay; and I had begun work on my senior thesis, which was to be a history of *The New Yorker,* and was doing much of the research at the magazine's office on West Forty-third Street. That Sunday morning we had a late breakfast and sat around reading the paper. After lunch Bobs and I went out for a long walk and sometime before 3:00 we were strolling down Madison Avenue, several blocks from her mother's apartment. Suddenly it was very cold, with the sun low in the sky, sinking behind the tall buildings, and I turned up my coat collar against the sharp wind. We passed a soda fountain, decided to have a hot chocolate, and while we sat at the counter the news came over the radio.

As in millions of other homes that night, we talked the hours away, for the first time contemplating a future in which the two of us might be separated for long periods, though we could not admit to the unspoken fear beneath the surface—the possibility that I might go off to war and not come back. Whatever else we may have thought about during that troubled evening, it never occurred to us that what lay ahead would prove to be the great divide for our generation—not only a chasm that would swallow up some of our closest friends, but the demarcation line against which we would measure time and change ever afterward, as the Civil War and the First World War marked them off for our great-grandfathers' and fathers' generations.

———

It was only two and a half weeks until Christmas, and a carol service was in progress in Dwight Hall, on Yale's freshman campus. A mixed group of students and faculty families raised their voices in the old Advent hymn, joyously singing out, "Gloria in excelsis Deo!" at the same time the announcer at the Polo Grounds in New York interrupted the Giants-Dodgers football game with the news that Pearl Harbor had been bombed.

All over the Yale campus, students were preparing for Monday classes when the word came, and it sent them rushing from their rooms, spilling out into the streets of New Haven, until two entire blocks on Elm Street were filled with undergraduates, churning about, moving without a destination, a mass of nervous energy seeking release in shouting, singing "Over There," yelling "On to Tokyo!" Long after dark they were on the march up Hillhouse Avenue to President Seymour's house, to serenade with "The Star-Spangled Banner" the aloof, dignified man who had been a delegate to the peace conference in Versailles only twenty-two years before. Seymour was sick in bed and had to dress, and while the students milled around waiting for him to appear, the secretary of the university led them in singing "Bright College Years," which nearly everyone regarded mistakenly as the alma mater, and which almost no one realized was set to the tune of Germany's World War I anthem "Die Wacht am Rhein." Its sentimental words were as much a product of another generation as the man to whom they were sung, but they had a particular poignancy at this moment, coming from a little band of America's youth, their hundreds of uplifted faces illuminated by the soft light from the president's house:

> Bright college years, with pleasure rife,
> The shortest, gladdest years of life;
> How swiftly are ye gliding by!
> Oh, why doth time so swiftly fly? . . .

At last the president appeared to address the "Men of Yale," recalling similar gatherings in 1898 and 1917, reminding them of the university's tradition of loyalty and service to the nation, telling them how proud he was that they were ready to serve. Seymour was not exactly a spellbinder, but the undergraduates listened politely enough, rewarded him with a chorus of "For He's a Jolly Good Fellow," and set off toward the center of town, shouting the rallying cry of so many football weekends—"On to the Taft!" The magic of the moment was gone, and Charles Seymour watched as the darkness swallowed them up.

The management of the Taft Hotel was resigned to occasional outpourings of enthusiasm by Yale students, but neither they nor their paying guests were prepared for the small army that swarmed through the lobby, past and over chairs, couches, and potted plants, a bobbing, weaving, boisterous snake dance that made its way noisily up the stairs, through the corridors to the top floor and down and out again onto the streets. For most students and the "townies" who had joined them, it seemed like good clean fun, but windows were broken, potted plants overturned, the hotel lobby was a mess, and beneath the fun ran an undercurrent of potentially destructive force, a mix of exhilaration and anger that reflected the shock of the day's news— that, and a kind of relief that the uncertainties of the past months had been resolved at last. Fortunately for everyone concerned, the police appeared in force, the students ran out of steam, and after a brief mass sit-down on the trolley tracks to demonstrate their independence, they broke up into little groups of two or three and slowly faded away in the night.

They could have no idea of the hardships and suffering that lay ahead, or the thin margin that would separate their country and its allies from defeat at times. As they strode through the cobbled streets of New Haven on that December evening, bursting with the force of youth and defiance, laughing, cheering, some with tears in their eyes, they could hardly imagine that they were seeing certain friends in the crowd for the last time, or know that the only future vestige of those names or faces would be the dimming memory of lost comrades forever young, glowing and strong, walking arm in arm through a college town on the night the Japanese bombed Pearl Harbor.

All that was for the future; for now, everything was lost in joyful exuberance and a surge of patriotism, the likes of which might not be seen again on that campus or another. During those borrowed years before the unsought war came to America, these students had favored America's entry into the war, or they had opposed it, or they had not known exactly where they stood, but the differences that had seemed so important didn't really matter any longer. What needed to be done now seemed very clear.

ACKNOWLEDGMENTS

On March 25, 1977, I interviewed General Mark W. Clark at his home in Charleston, South Carolina, and my notes on our conversation begin this way:

"On the day before I saw him, General Clark had been 3½ hours on the operating table for removal of a malignant tumor on his temple. Although he was obviously uncomfortable and in pain, his answers were clear and carefully thought out. He waved off my apology for imposing on him so soon after the operation, saying that he had agreed to an interview, I had traveled a long way to see him, and he had no intention of disappointing me."

My questions to Clark had to do, mainly, with the maneuvers of 1939, 1940, and 1941, and I had sought him out because he was close to General George Marshall and was one of the bright young men of that day, in the forefront of a group of officers who knew that the U.S. Army had to have mobility, above all, and who revolutionized the training of the soldiers who would fight World War II.

Not many of my sources were obliged to be as stoic as General Clark, but almost without exception they were equally cooperative and generous in providing the information I wanted. When I began this project, I was forced to sandwich the research in between books I was writing for American Heritage Publishing Company. Then I interrupted it almost entirely for a dozen years while editing a magazine William Blair and I launched in 1974—*Blair & Ketchum's Country Journal.* I mention this passage of time because a number of the individuals whose names appear below, who granted me interviews or helped in other ways, are no longer alive. I regret that they cannot see the book to which they contributed so willingly.

Over the course of eighteen years I gathered material for what has become *The Borrowed Years,* and during that long period I interviewed or corresponded with hundreds of individuals—prominent and not so prominent—whose intimate involvement with events between 1938 and 1941 lent fresh insights to the story. Each one has contributed in some way to this account, but I want to single out a few whose recollections or explanations furnished evidence which no amount of conventional research could have produced. They include:

Professor Eugene Wigner, Nobel laureate in physics, who made a long automobile journey in 1939 with Leo Szilard and persuaded Albert Einstein to write to President Roosevelt, warning him of the potential destructive power of nuclear energy.

Mrs. Alexander Sachs, widow of the man who delivered the Einstein letter.

People with close ties to the America First movement—among them Mrs. Anne Morrow Lindbergh, whose husband was the key spokesman for the organization; Senator William Benton; Kingman Brewster; and Robert Douglas Stuart, Jr., the group's founder.

Three men who facilitated Wendell Willkie's meteoric rise to political prominence: Oren Root, who had the idea for the Willkie Clubs; Samuel Pryor, one of

Willkie's close advisers; and John B. Hollister, who traveled on the candidate's campaign train.

Two individuals with important connections to the Roosevelt administration: James A. Farley and Judge Samuel Rosenman.

William Dunn, Robert Trout, and William S. Paley, whose intimate knowledge of CBS during the years before the United States became involved in the war was extremely helpful.

Particular thanks go to Mrs. Edward R. Murrow for permitting me to quote her diaries, which vividly record the awful time in London during the blitz, and for sharing her memories of dinner at the White House on the evening of December 7, 1941. Eric Sevareid told me about the visit her husband paid him on that same night, after his talk with President Roosevelt.

Hellmut Lewin journeyed to Havana in 1939 to meet his fiancée, who, with some nine hundred other Jewish refugees from the Nazi terror, was arriving on the ship *St. Louis.* He described what it was like to learn that Cuban—and later American— officials refused to let them land, forcing the ship's captain to turn back and head for Germany.

Robert Wyman Horton, who warned Secretary of the Navy Frank Knox on December 4, 1941, that his navy was not prepared for war.

Yuzuru Sanematsu, naval attaché in the Japanese embassy in Washington on December 7, 1941, to whom I am indebted for valuable information and for his hospitality in Tokyo. Mrs. Doris Obata Kumpel, whose story appears here, guided me to other Japanese-Americans and to Japanese who had much to say about their country at the time of the Pearl Harbor attack.

Frederick O. Schweizer and W. T. Ingram, former navy officers, whose experiences at Pearl Harbor I have related here.

My father, George Ketchum, on whose remarkable memory I relied, especially for details about the Republican convention of 1940 and the Willkie campaign.

═══

This book is an attempt to re-create selectively what was once the present, and as such, it is based almost entirely on contemporary evidence. I like to think of those sources—whether they were individuals I interviewed or whether they committed their recollections to paper—as "witnesses" to this three-year episode in America's recent past. I have tried to tell the story through their eyes: the eyes of people who were there, who participated in the events, or who saw them happen.

As that statement implies, my narrative owes much to reports by journalists and to others who recorded their observations, for it was a time when people still kept diaries and journals, when letters and memoranda were the common currency of communication.

Diaries, journals, government documents, contemporary periodicals, and books all figured largely in my research. I had some generous assistance from other historians—notably Bruce Catton, Richard Collier, Walter Lord, Forrest C. Pogue, John Toland, and Barbara Tuchman. But when you have been thinking about a subject for as many years as this one was going round in my head, much information that comes your way is acquired serendipitously, and that was certainly the case with *The Borrowed Years.* In no way could the select bibliography include all the conversations with friends and chance acquaintances, snippets of background material from newspapers and magazines, snatches of documentary films and recordings that came to my attention.

The planned research took me to various parts of the United States, including Hawaii, to Europe and Japan, and during the years I ran up a long list of indebtedness. The notes that follow indicate the manner in which certain individuals assisted me, but omit the less specific yet nonetheless important ways in which others helped.

One of the joys of writing history is that so many doors are thrown open to the serious inquirer. In the course of my research I have benefitted immeasurably from the generosity of individuals and institutions, and what follows is at best inadequate thanks for the many favors I have received.

Dr. Roger Sutton read the manuscript for Part IV, about the beginnings of the uranium project, and I am grateful for his extremely helpful comments. I also appreciate the kindness of Dr. Spencer Weart in reading and commenting on this material. It is important to say that while I have benefitted substantially from the comments and suggestions of these and many others—some of whom read portions of the manuscript—the final interpretations are my own, and in no way should those who assisted me be held accountable for the final result.

Every searcher into the past has a particular obligation to libraries whose resources are so freely offered, and I want to thank the staffs of those institutions whose facilities I have used. They include Sarah McFarland, head of the Reference Department at the Sawyer Library at Williams College; Rodney Armstrong, Director, and Jill Ericson, Reference Librarian, of the Boston Athenaeum; Dr. Spencer Weart, Manager, and Jean Hrichus, Librarian/Archivist, of the Center for the History of Physics, and Thomas A. Lowe, Assistant Librarian of the Niels Bohr Library—both facilities located at the American Institute of Physics in New York City; Sandra Rosenstock, Archivist, and Joanne Rudof, Manager, the Video Archive for Holocaust Testimonies at Yale University; Dr. William Emerson, Director, and Mrs. Elizabeth Denier and John Ferris, Archivists, at the Franklin D. Roosevelt Library; Judith Ann Schiff, Chief Research Archivist, Manuscripts and Archives, at the Sterling Memorial Library at Yale University; Robert Saudek and Mary Ahern at the Museum of Broadcasting in New York City; Dr. Ronald Grele at the Oral History Collection of Columbia University; the libraries at the Yale Club of New York and the Century Association; the Bennington College Library; the Mark Skinner Library in Manchester, Vermont; the Dorset Village Public Library in Dorset, Vermont; and the staff at the remarkable Northshire Bookstore in Manchester Center, Vermont, who have been a source of information and help. For assistance in obtaining photographs, I am indebted to Laurie Winfrey, of Carousel Research.

In addition to those named above, for assistance of all kinds and for favors large and small, I wish to thank Isao Ashiba, Lady Margaret Barry, Mrs. Susan Berger, Ami and Alice Berkowitz, William S. Blair, Darby Bradley, Charles W. Bray, Frederick Buechner, Tom Burnside, Lieutenant General Marshall Carter, Richard Dale Drain, Marjorie Dyer, Mrs. Thomas N. Fairbanks, Castle W. Freeman, Jr., A. Bartlett Giamatti, Walter Hard, Jr., James B. Harris, John L. Hawkes, Ralph Hetzel, Professor Gerald Horton, Mrs. David Humphreys, Oliver Jensen, Warren Johnson, Alvin Josephy, Yoshihisa Kajitani, Carlton G. Ketchum, David S. Ketchum, Thomas Bray Ketchum, Philip Kunhardt, Robert Lescher, Mrs. Reeve Lindbergh, Ray Lochner, John F. Loughran, Gideon de Margitay, Mike Marler,

Dr. Sarah Moskovitz, George M. Mott, Casey Murrow, Tomio Muto, Dr. Agnes Niyekawa, Mercedes Padro, Professor George Wilson Pierson, Colonel Russell Reeder, David Richardson, Ty Takichi Shigematsu, Tetsuo Shinjo, Professor William A. Shurcliff, Anne-Marie Soullière, John K. Tabor, Fumio Tamamuro, Tadao Tamaru, Mary Testa, John M. Thornton, Masayuki Tokioka, Arthur B. Tourtellot, Mrs. Evelyn Trotzky, William Warren, Mrs. Alec Webb, Bryan Wilkins, Mary Elizabeth Wise, and Julie Yannatta.

Two decades ago Evan Thomas, then an editor at Harper & Row, suggested that I consider writing a book about America in the years between the Munich Pact and Pearl Harbor. He proposed that I call it *The Borrowed Years*. That it has taken far longer to complete than either of us imagined does not diminish my gratitude for his part in the plot.

Samuel Vaughan has had this project under his editorial eye for more years than he may care to remember, and he has my thanks for patience as well as the incisive criticism and counsel he has provided so unfailingly.

Carl Brandt has been a source of wisdom, support, and cheerful encouragement during the occasional dark moment, and for these and other favors I am indebted to him.

To Mary Talbot, who typed portions of the manuscript and assisted in numerous other ways, my debt is large. The manuscript and I both profited from the sharp eye and incisive comments of the copy editor, Edward Johnson.

A writer who works at home is keenly aware of his obligation to family and friends who sympathize with his lonely occupation and make it possible for him to pursue it, uninterrupted and in relative peace. To Pauline Dunbar, Robert Matteson, Millie Ann Mickens, and Daniel O'Leary, my special thanks for their valued help.

My wife, Barbara Bray Ketchum, has been my companion through all this—the past that is my story, and the present. She shared in the memories and the search for information, cast a critical eye on the manuscript, offered comments that were always frank and perceptive, and was a source of boundless encouragement and support. For this and more, and especially for that dance we had at Betty Herr's house, she has my deepest gratitude.

NOTES

The following notes indicate the principal sources of assertions or quotations, so that the general reader interested in learning more will know which ones I found helpful. Most of the significant elements in this account are covered in the notes, but I have not provided citations for all the periodicals I perused for background information on the period. Works cited are identified more fully in the Bibliography.

Newspapers and magazines of the period are alive with illuminating information, and for international news reports I relied chiefly on the *New York Times*. For other contemporaneous reporting and comment I turned frequently to the weekly news magazines—*Time, Newsweek,* and *Life*—and to informed comment in such periodicals as *The New Yorker, Scribner's, Harper's, Atlantic Monthly, The New Republic, The Nation, Fortune,* and *The Saturday Review*.

Although broadcast journalism was in its infancy at the time, the U.S. public was fortunate to have Edward R. Murrow, Eric Sevareid, William L. Shirer, Raymond Gram Swing, Elmer Davis, and others bring them the news as it occurred.

PART I

CHAPTER I

Three Pittsburgh newspapers then published—the morning *Post-Gazette* and the evening *Press* and *Sun-Telegraph*—were very useful for events in my hometown.

Most of the details concerning events in the United States and abroad during the period from September 12 to September 22, 1938, come from the *New York Times*.

It is difficult to translate wages and prices of that day into terms of the present, since many commodities or services have increased at different rates; but I settled on the Consumer Price Index as the best available tool, and the figures given—$1 in 1988 equals $8.30 half a century earlier—are from the Bureau of Labor Statistics, Consumer Pricing Division.

Marcia Davenport's observation about life in the thirties is from *Too Strong for Fantasy,* a book that was helpful in many respects, especially for her personal observations about the period.

Here and later I have referred often to Arthur Schlesinger's splendid three-volume *The Age of Roosevelt* for revealing insights into the early Depression years and personalities intimately associated with the New Deal. The quotation from President Roosevelt about the campaign is from Vol. 1, p. 430. James MacGregor Burns's two volumes on Roosevelt—*Roosevelt: The Lion and the Fox,* covering the period to 1940, and *Roosevelt: The Soldier of Freedom,* dealing with the war years—focus on political aspects of the presidency, and were especially helpful for the period after 1936, when the third Schlesinger volume ends. Endlessly informative, wonderfully readable, the Schlesinger and Burns books are all but indispensable companions for understanding those troubled years.

The information on wages is from the two-volume *Historical Statistics of the United States: Colonial Times to 1970.*

The Rosenmans, pp. 372–73, discuss the public reaction to the president's "quarantine" speech, noting that opinion against it was almost unanimous and, to FDR, "shockingly surprising." This, with the silent treatment he received from his cabinet and Democrats in Congress, made him realize that he had made "a major mistake in timing." Their comments and those of Bruce Catton (pp. 14 *et seq.*) are interesting for their analysis of the problems Roosevelt faced in attempting to lead a public that had no wish to be led in this particular direction.

The quotation from the Muncie businessman is from Lynd and Merrell, p. 256.

CHAPTER 2

Descriptions of Pittsburgh from eighteenth- and nineteenth-century European travelers are from Lorant, pp. 52, 55, and 78. This oversize volume is of particular interest for the wealth of contemporary illustrations of the city and its people. Somewhat unevenly written by nine different authors, it is nonetheless a good general work on an unusually interesting city.

John Steinbeck observed that he knew of "no other decade in history when so much happened in so many directions," and there is almost no end to published material on the thirties. For general information on the Depression, McElvaine's scholarly and readable *The Great Depression* is excellent. A wealth of anecdotal material may be found in several collections of contemporary writings, including Paul M. Angle's *The Uneasy World,* with its many first-person acounts of events; Studs Terkel's interviews of Depression victims, *Hard Times;* and the Federal Writers' Project interviews collected by Ann Banks in *First-Person America.* In addition, I enjoyed Jellison's entertaining and highly selective *Tomatoes Were Cheaper* and Robert Bendiner's equally personal *Just Around the Corner,* both of which convey so much of the flavor of the times.

The quotation from Nora Mellon about her husband is from *Pittsburgher* magazine, Vol. 1, No. 1 (June 1977), p. 23. H. L. Mencken's uncharitable remarks about Pittsburgh are from Lorant, pp. 327–28. My sister, Mrs. Charles Whitehouse, was present that evening at the Pittsburgh Golf Club when the young lady from Virginia inquired about the Bessemers.

I am indebted to William Warren, then a graduate student at the University of Pittsburgh, for introducing me to several sources of information that were invaluable for my discussion of Pittsburgh's industry and workers, particularly the volumes by Horace Davis and Francis Courares. Although I could make only limited use of it, I found Courares's analysis of what he calls "the Craftsmen's Empire" extremely perceptive. Other sources used in this section were Stricker's article on the "prosperity" of labor in the twenties when, as he puts it, "even in the best of times, economic insecurity clouded the hopes of working-class families"; Tarr's study of transportation in Pittsburgh, especially on the impact of the automobile; Schroeder's material on the major steel companies; and 1940 housing census data on Allegheny County and Pittsburgh.

It would be difficult to find more engaging chroniclers of the great American industrial fortunes than Lucius Beebe, Stewart Holbrook, and Frederick Lewis Allen. Allen's *The Lords of Creation* was useful in this context, and his *The Big Change* and *Since Yesterday* are delightful commentaries on the period generally. The description of Pittsburgh millionaires is from Holbrook, p. 154, as is that of the Peacock mansion. McElvaine has interesting material on Andrew Mellon, his wealth, and his accomplishments as secretary of the Treasury. The doggerel about the Pittsburgh banker is from Jellison, p. 65.

CHAPTER 3

Here again, McElvaine's study of the Depression was helpful. The quotation from Will Rogers's broadcast is from my *Will Rogers: His Life and Times,* p. 299; and the tale of Peggy Terry appears in Terkel, pp. 62–69. McElvaine, p. 172, quotes the Oklahoman's letter to Eleanor Roosevelt.

Cyrus Sulzberger wrote a series of articles about the destitute for the *Pittsburgh Press,* and I have referred to his *A Long Row of Candles.* Other material on Pittsburgh at this time was drawn from the pages of the *Press,* March 10 and 24, October 29, and November 3, 1935. The item about the four men who were lashed in the Delaware jail comes from the issue of March 10; the abolition of the cat-o'-nine-tails was reported in the Delaware *State News* of July 6, 1972.

Allen, in *Since Yesterday,* p. 47, cites statistics on vagrancy in Kansas City, and Sevareid's description of riding the rails comes from his reminiscences of youth, p. 41.

The material on George Ketchum and the advertising agency he founded comes from three sources. At the urging of his children and grandchildren, who had heard him tell vastly entertaining and often implausible (because times had changed so much) stories of his early years, my father wrote a book covering his life until the time he launched the business. That was enough, he said; Chauncey Morley had written a history of the agency, so he had no need to elaborate further. The second source, then, is Morley's account (annotated by my father) of Ketchum, MacLeod & Grove from its beginnings in 1919 to 1960, when Morley retired. The third source is a less conventional one—my father's income tax returns, every one of which he kept from the time he first filed one until the year of his death.

The numbers on a tax return are supposed to be just that—figures reflecting a year's income and deductible expenses—yet they have a way of revealing the unexpected. An increase in personal exemptions tells us that a child was born, lightening the taxpayer's load to the government (though increasing expenses in other respects). A change of residence may suggest (if one knows the relative status of old and new addresses) that the path is upward, with a higher standard of living.

From George Ketchum's returns I deduce that 1926 was the first year he owned an automobile. I happen to remember that first car—a used black Packard four-door sedan with a burled-walnut dashboard, a cigarette lighter on a cord that reached to the backseat, and a luggage rack at the rear that held a trunk containing three fitted black suitcases.

From these returns I followed the family's changes of residence, the ups and downs in my father's income, his painful losses on the sale of securities, his interest payments and bad debts (one for $60 in 1932, with the notation "numerous attempts to collect, ending in debtor's refusal to pay: has since left city and present address unknown"), and his charitable contributions. Through all those years, fat and lean, he never failed to give generously to his church, his university, the community chest, and a host of other causes. Even in 1933 and 1934, two of the worst years for his business, his contributions were more than 1 percent of his salary.

The tax form itself underwent marked changes: from two pages prior to 1923, to four pages through 1941, and from then on to become ever longer and more complicated. From 1919 to 1923 the tax rate was 4 percent of taxable income, followed by four years of varying rates. In 1927 it settled down to 1½ percent on the first $4,000 and 3 percent on the next $4,000, with a top rate of 5 percent thereafter and a credit of 25 percent on earned net income. O, happy bygone days!

CHAPTER 4

William L. Shirer's *Berlin Diary* covers the period from January 1934 to December 1940. For almost that entire time he was based in Berlin, reporting on Hitler's Germany from a unique vantage point and with a practiced, perceptive eye. His splendid book *The Rise and Fall of the Third Reich,* published twenty years after he left Germany, is notable for its historical perspective, but for my purposes, discussing events prior to and including the Munich Pact, the diary entries had more feeling of immediacy.

Another man who saw the Nazis and Berlin from a different perspective, during the course of two incredibly trying years, was Nevile Henderson, the British ambassador. When Anthony Eden, then Stanley Baldwin's foreign minister, summoned Henderson to the Berlin post in January 1937, Henderson was the ambassador to Argentina and had lived abroad for a third of a century. Indeed, the last year in which he had spent as much as six months in England was 1905, and his immediate reaction to news of his assignment to Berlin, as he noted in *Failure of a Mission,* was a sense of his own inadequacy for what was then the most difficult and important of all foreign service posts, and a feeling that he had been "specially selected by Providence . . . to [help] preserve the peace of the world." There were those in England who thought him the wrong man in the wrong place, another of the Chamberlain appeasement crowd, a gullible man who was taken in by the Nazis, but for the historian, Henderson affords some unparalleled glimpses behind the scenes at the time of the Munich crisis.

Many of my descriptions of Nuremberg, Berlin, and Vienna owe much to Shirer and Henderson.

Another eyewitness to the events described here was William L. Strang, a veteran of Britain's diplomatic service since 1919, who accompanied the prime minister on his trips to Hitler's aerie and left a richly informative, vivid account of what he saw and heard. Back in London was another tireless diarist, Alexander Cadogan, permanent under secretary of the foreign office, whose detailed, often pungent comments on people and events provide a rare insight into British officialdom and illuminate the workings of the cabinet and the foreign office at an extraordinary hour in that nation's history.

Additional material is to be found in *Documents on German Foreign Policy, 1918–1945.* The first two books in Series D are particularly useful: Vol. 1, *From Neurath to Ribbentrop (September 1937–September 1938),* and Vol. 2, *Germany and*

Czechoslovakia (1937–1938). I have also referred to the third volume of *Nazi Conspiracy and Aggression.*

Larry William Fuchser's study of Chamberlain and appeasement is excellent. Unfortunately, the custodians of the Chamberlain papers refused him permission to quote directly from documents, which meant that paraphrases were necessary; even so, insights gained from the Englishman's private thoughts, many from the letters he wrote weekly to his spinster sisters during his entire public life, are revealing indeed.

In this chapter and elsewhere I have drawn on Erik Barnouw's study of broadcasting; the excerpt from Murrow's broadcast about Austria appears on p. 78. More on Murrow and his activities during this period is available in Sperber's thorough study.

Here and there I have quoted from Walter Lippmann's memoir in the Columbia Oral History Collection—that trove of private, taped interviews with individuals in just about every field of endeavor in the United States, which is an invaluable tool in the writing of twentieth-century American history. Inspired by Allan Nevins, the collection flourished under the directorship of Louis M. Starr. Mr. Chamberlain's remark to Mrs. Lippmann is from the Lippmann material.

The comment on Chamberlain's snub of Roosevelt is the first of many citations from that essential companion to these years, Winston Churchill—this particular one from *The Gathering Storm,* pp. 254–55. It is difficult to imagine studying this period without access to those majestic and incomparable volumes written by the man who saw and recorded history while shaping it and who was, among other things, his own best biographer.

The description of the Anglo-French meeting comes from another active participant in the events described here, Anthony Eden, and is from *The Reckoning,* p. 18.

Churchill's *The Gathering Storm,* pp. 196–97, is the source of the comment by Lothian.

CHAPTER 5

My description of the Nuremberg rally is based upon Henderson and the memoirs of Albert Speer, Hitler's personal architect, who became the dictator of Germany's wartime economy, and then spent twenty years in Spandau Prison, where he secretly wrote the voluminous memoirs.

Alfred Duff Cooper could not abide Ambassador Henderson's unwillingness to stand up to Hitler, and the remark quoted is typical. Cooper himself was regarded by many as a lightweight in the cabinet, but he had the courage of his convictions at the time of Munich and resigned from his Admiralty post because of his disagreement with Chamberlain's policies. Hugh Greene's comment on Henderson is from a BBC interview, published in *The Listener,* April 24, 1969.

The material on H. V. Kaltenborn and the marathon broadcasts about the Munich crisis comes from a variety of sources. Kaltenborn himself wrote extensively of them in *I Broadcast the Crisis,* and I have also used "The Reminiscences of H. V. Kaltenborn" (1950) in the Columbia Oral History Collection. I was fortunate to have an interview with Robert Trout on one of his trips to New York, and he spoke at length of Kaltenborn, CBS, Studio Nine, and his own experiences at the time of Munich. Thanks to Alvin Josephy, I got in touch with William Dunn, whose office was next door to Paul White's (where Kaltenborn had a cot set up for his use, and where his wife, Olga, brought him sandwiches during the long ordeal). Dunn's comments on the people and what was happening in CBS's New York headquarters were most illuminating. Asked if the men in the newsroom felt frustrated about the apathy of Americans toward events in Europe, he replied, "Their feelings didn't extend much beyond the technical problems of getting those broadcasts from Europe." They were only worried about the problem of getting the programs to work out successfully on the air. Arthur Bernon Tourtellot and William Paley read the material for this chapter, and their helpful remarks are reflected in the final version. Barnouw was another source of information on this subject, and I found the biographies of Edward R. Murrow by Sperber and Alexander Kendrick useful, as was an article about Murrow in *Scribner's,* December 1938.

CHAPTER 6

Duff Cooper's observations on Hitler's speech are from his memoirs, p. 228. Most news items in this chapter are taken from the *New York Times,* September 16 to 20, 1938.

A book that is essential to an understanding of domestic politics and goings-on inside the Roosevelt White House is Robert Sherwood's remarkable *Roosevelt and Hopkins.* When Hopkins died, his widow asked Sherwood—who had been one of the president's speech writers—to write the book her husband had been planning, and in the Hopkinses' house he found some forty file cabinets filled with papers, plus a great many more in a warehouse. To this he added material from dozens of interviews with people who had known Hopkins, and the result is an immensely readable and informative study of two powerful men whose mutual trust and collaborative efforts produced far-reaching results.

Most of the quotations from the Kaltenborn broadcasts are from Kaltenborn's book or the *New York Times.*

John Toland cites a private collection as the source of Chamberlain's letter to his sisters, which appears in Toland's biography of Hitler, pp. 462–63.

Cadogan, *passim,* comments on Chamberlain's thinking at this time and the motives behind his trip to Germany. For this and later journeys by the prime minister, Strang's observations are valuable, and Leonard Mosley reports some of the remarks by Horace Wilson and Chamberlain. The gaffe nearly committed by Halifax was recorded in an article on Munich in the *Observer* of October 6, 1968.

Harold Nicolson, whose *Diaries and Letters* for this period are a mine of information on the atmosphere in London and in the government, was a forthright critic of the Chamberlain policy, and his conversations with Anthony Eden and other opposition figures are of much interest.

Duff Cooper's arguments against appeasement appear on pp. 230 and 246 of his memoirs.

Joseph Lash records the conversations between the president and Ambassador Lindsay and the failed attempt to bolster Chamberlain's resolve in his *Roosevelt and Churchill,* pp. 25–27. Based largely on the correspondence between the American president and Britain's wartime prime minister, it is as much a study of these two men as a record of their endlessly interesting association.

CHAPTER 7

The major source for my account of the hurricane of 1938 was the *New York Times,* from September 18 to September 25, and I have also drawn on Joe McCarthy's book. Katherine Marshall's recollections are in *Together,* pp. 31–35, and the general's story is in Pogue, vol. I, pp. 315–19. Marcia Davenport relates her own experience in *Too Strong for Fantasy,* pp. 250–52.

CHAPTER 8

Once again, sources for the denouement of the Munich story are those cited for earlier chapters—especially Kaltenborn, Cadogan, Henderson, Shirer's two books, Nicolson, Strang, Duff Cooper, Fuchser, and the *New York Times*—with several additions.

The comments of William Bullitt, quoted occasionally in this book, are those of a sometime friend and confidant of Roosevelt who was at this time the U.S. ambassador in Paris, and was carrying on a personal correspondence with the man in the White House, often to the distress of the secretary of state, who was his nominal boss.

My description of the meeting in Godesberg is drawn principally from Henderson, Shirer, and Strang. Nicolson's account of Chamberlain's dramatic moment in the House of Commons is excellent; the several mentions of Queen Mary and her appearance there are drawn from Edwards, pp. 427–30. Fuchser, p. 159, mentions John F. Kennedy's presence, and the *Observer* article on Munich, previously cited, contains an account of the reaction in the diplomatic gallery. Davenport and Murphy, p. 324, report Jan Masaryk's comment to Chamberlain and Halifax.

The Munich meeting is described fully by Kaltenborn, and I have used other sources noted above, supplemented by Kennan.

The excerpt from Winston Churchill's speech of October 5, 1938, is from *Blood, Sweat, and Tears,* p. 66.

Fuchser, pp. 161–67, describes the private meeting between Chamberlain and Hitler and the agreement that resulted. Strang's eyewitness account is excellent.

CHAPTER 9

Leo Szilard's letter appears in the Weart and Szilard book, p. 48.

Bernard Baruch describes his trips to Europe and his conversations with President Roosevelt in *The Public Years,* pp. 271–76.

Bullitt's meeting with Roosevelt and the president's resolve to increase U.S. aircraft production are mentioned in Bullitt, p. 302, and Pogue, Vol. I, pp. 321–22.

Accounts of the Welles broadcast are numerous. One of the more perceptive in terms of its psychological impact is "The Night the Martians Came," by Charles Jackson. This is one of many original pieces in Isabel Leighton's sprightly collection describing the period 1919 to 1941, which she called *The Aspirin Age.* A "Profile" of Orson Welles by Russell Maloney appeared in the October 8, 1938, issue of *The New Yorker,* before the actor-director-producer contemplated putting on a dramatization of the Wells work; at the time, he had other prospects in mind, including *Danton's Death, The Duchess of Malfi,* and *Liliom.* Other useful sources are Allen's *Since Yesterday,* pp. 261–63; Daniels, pp. 302–3; Bendiner, pp. 245–47; and Koch's

The Panic Broadcast, which includes the radio play as presented. Robert Saudek told me of his own experience, and Arthur Tourtellot, who was until his death a special assistant to William Paley, gave me Paley's story about the man who sent the $2 bill.

PART II

CHAPTER 10

The best source of information about Charles Lindbergh during this period is his own remarkable wartime journals, a candid, day-by-day account of his activities and his thoughts about people, places, governments, and ideas—the product of a serious, inquiring mind.

Cole's volume on Lindbergh includes a good summary of his journeys through Europe investigating the air arms of many nations, and is a useful supplement to Lindbergh's own writings.

I am greatly indebted to Anne Morrow Lindbergh for reading and commenting on what I wrote about her husband. Her own published diaries and letters afford revealing glimpses into the lives of a very private couple during a time which began happily for them and became increasingly troubled as her husband's involvement in politics grew. Reeve Lindbergh was extremely helpful, lending me hard-to-find books and arranging a most enjoyable meeting with her mother.

The *New York Times* of August 27, 1974, carried a detailed obituary of Lindbergh; another source of information is Roger Butterfield's "Lindbergh" in the August 11, 1941, issue of *Life.*

General Raymond Lee's journal, with his incisive comments about London in this crucial time, expresses the views of a sympathetic and sensitive onlooker about the country in which he was an official guest. His remark about Kennedy appears on p. 241, and is only one of many private expressions reflecting his dismay at the ambassador's unfortunate aptitude for defeatism.

The Lindberghs described their visits to Germany in their journals: she in *The Flower and the Nettle,* pp. xxi and 437; he in *Wartime Journals,* p. 102. More is to be found in Shirer's *Berlin Diary,* p. 63, and Cole's *Lindbergh,* pp. 31–36. Leonard Mosley discusses Göring's attitude toward the Jews in his biography. Bullitt's amusing description of Göring is on p. 123 of his correspondence with President Roosevelt.

CHAPTER 11

A number of books describe the plight of European refugees, particularly the Jews, and I found Morse's *While Six Million Died* and Wyman's *Paper Walls* most useful for my purposes (Wyman's later volume, *The Abandonment of the Jews,* focuses on a period later than the one covered here). *Paper Walls,* p. 89, has Hitler's statement regarding the Jews; it also tells of Herschel Grynszpan and the reaction to the pogrom.

The excerpt from Dorothy Thompson's broadcast is from Sanders, pp. 230–32.

Hugh Greene was interviewed on the BBC, and his comments were reported in *The Listener,* April 24, 1969.

Alsop and Kintner, pp. 24–25, discuss FDR's actions in the immediate wake of Kristallnacht, and both Morse, pp. 109–24, and Lash, in his *Eleanor and Franklin,* p. 576, describe the efforts of Mrs. Roosevelt and Justine Polier to admit Jewish children to the United States.

Laura Fermi's *Illustrious Immigrants,* pp. 25–27, provides material on the refugee problem and the quotation from Martin Dies; statistics on the U.S. quotas are in Morse, pp. 109–24 and 191, and Lash, *Eleanor and Franklin,* p. 576. Morse, pp. 205 *et seq.,* discusses the distressing House hearings on the Wagner-Rogers bill.

The saga of the *St. Louis* is described variously, notably in the *New York Times* in its issues from June 1 through June 27, 1939, although little appeared in the paper until Cuba refused to admit the refugees. Two editorials on the subject were printed, but curiously, neither mentioned the refusal of the United States government to accept the passengers—only the inhumanity of Germany and Cuba. At the Video Archive for Holocaust Testimonies at Yale, I had the welcome assistance of Sandra Rosenstock, Archivist, and Joanne Rudof, Manager, in locating material, and thanks to their courtesy was able to view the film *Flight from Destiny.* Narrated by the historian Peter Gay, this collection of interviews with survivors of the voyage of the *St. Louis* is a poignant document indeed. To ensure the privacy of the interviewees, I have used none of their names in this book.

Thanks to Dr. Sarah Moskovitz at California State University in Northridge and Susan Berger of Hollywood, California, I reached Evelyn Trotsky of Bangor, Maine, and through her her father, Hellmut Lewin, who graciously told me the story of the bride he planned to meet when the *St. Louis* docked in Havana. Ami and Alice Berkowitz of Schenectady were unusually generous in suggesting sources of information on the subject of the ship, and sent me a copy of "Reflections on the Holocaust," which I found helpful in many ways. Morse includes the story of the *St. Louis* on pp. 219–33, and Lookstein discusses the reaction of Americans generally and of American Jews in particular to the plight of the passengers.

CHAPTER 12

Schlesinger's *The Politics of Upheaval* is a rich source of information on Father Charles Coughlin and Gerald L. K. Smith. Additional material may be found in Jellison, Adler, and "The Radio Priest," an interview with Coughlin by Robert S. Gallagher published in the October 1972 issue of *American Heritage.* Mencken's classic description of Smith is in the Schlesinger book, p. 65, and the quotations from Coughlin and Smith are from the same source, pp. 627, 629, and 630. The *New York Times* obituaries on both men are informative: Coughlin on October 28, 1979, and Smith on April 17, 1976.

Robert Sherwood, pp. 127–33, discusses isolationism and the various racial and religious groups that were particularly virulent on the subject, suggesting that this was a deeply perplexing problem to the White House. Selig Adler's examination of the isolationist impulse in America (see especially pp. 239–73) deals with the roots of that powerful theme in the nation's history, antiwar sentiment in the country in the twenties and thirties, and Roosevelt's efforts to mollify progressives in Congress who wanted nothing to do with foreign involvement. He traces the development of neutrality legislation and points out that the isolationist urge was often stronger among congressmen than among their constituents.

Robert Divine's concise and thoughtful study takes up the question of U.S. reluctance to assume a leadership role until it was almost too late, and points out how this nation's neutrality legislation misled Hitler into thinking America was indifferent to Europe's fate. It is a thoroughly enjoyable, challenging book, most helpful for the probing questions he raises.

Charles Lindbergh tells of driving his father around the state during election campaigns in a charming memoir about his boyhood, given to me by Reeve Lindbergh. Charles Sr. never shared his son's enthusiasm for mechanics or aviation, and on one occasion, after he went up in a plane with him and was safely back on the ground, spoke his mind to his law partner: "I don't like this flying business. See if you can't get the boy to come into our office, study law, and join the firm."

Will Rogers's remarks on European attitudes toward the United States appear in Jellison, pp. 145–46.

Dallek, pp. 153 et seq., reviews the Panay affair in some detail, pointing out that the U.S. reaction caused Roosevelt to realize that it had "raised American peace sentiment to new heights." Professor Dallek's book is by far the best analysis of President Roosevelt's foreign policy. Further information on the Panay episode and the Ingersoll mission to London appears in Watson, pp. 92–93; Abbazia, pp. 3–5; and Toland's The Rising Sun, pp. 55–56.

Material on the Ludlow amendment may be found in issues of the New York Times between December 20, 1937, and January 10, 1938, and Time magazine, December 27, 1937, and January 3, 1938.

CHAPTER 13

For material on the irresistible group of mavericks in the Senate—Borah, Wheeler, Johnson, and Nye—and their role, Schlesinger's The Politics of Upheaval makes delightful reading and is unusually informative. Jonathan Daniels's book on this period provides interesting background material on public attitudes as well as characterizations of these men. Current Biography for 1940 has articles on Borah and Wheeler; the volume for 1941 has Johnson and Nye.

Biographies and articles of all kinds exist in abundance on Joseph Kennedy and his career, but for my purposes the most useful publication was Michael Beschloss's fine study, Kennedy and Roosevelt: The Uneasy Alliance. He deals specifically with a theme that is at the heart of my own book—the struggle between an important isolationist, who was Roosevelt's ambassador in London, and the president over the then supreme question of American involvement in the European conflict. Kennedy's earlier career is also ably covered in Russell.

CHAPTER 14

The most authoritative biography of John L. Lewis is that of Dubofsky and Van Tine, who deal in detail with his life and times, and the transformation of trade unionism and its leadership in twentieth-century America. Contrary to what his public personality might suggest, Lewis was a remarkably private person, secretive in many ways, who preferred to conduct his affairs face to face or on the telephone and left behind few personal letters and almost no family correspondence. These two authors suggest that Saul Alinsky's biography "must be read with extreme caution," noting that Lewis himself considered it "inaccurate and misleading." On the other hand, Alinsky knew the labor movement, he knew Lewis personally, and while he disagreed with him violently on occasion, his book is well worth reading for its lively anecdotal and background material.

Good descriptions of Lewis and the labor upheaval during this period also appear in many general works, among them Bendiner, Manchester, Schlesinger's *The Coming of the New Deal,* and McElvaine.

Much of my information on the convention at Pittsburgh's Islam Grotto comes from the *Pittsburgh Press,* November 14–18, 1938. The excerpt from Lewis's 1937 speech in New York is from Dubofsky and Van Tine, p. 331.

Alinsky, pp. 90–96, describes the sit-down strikes of 1937—"the year of attack," he calls it—and I have relied on that source, pp. 155–56, and Dubofsky and Van Tine, pp. 314–17, for facts about the Memorial Day Massacre in South Chicago. The most vivid account of that tragedy is Howard Fast's "An Occurrence at Republic Steel," written for Isabel Leighton's *The Aspirin Age.* From that source, p. 398, comes the information concerning Paramount News's refusal to distribute films of the episode.

Lewis's 1937 Labor Day speech is quoted in Alinsky, p. 160; and Dubofsky and Van Tine discuss faltering CIO enrollment and the growing schism in the labor movement. The excerpt from Lewis's 1939 Labor Day speech is from Dubofsky and Van Tine, pp. 332–34.

In the writing of this section I benefitted greatly from conversations with Ralph Hetzel of Encino, California, who worked closely with John L. Lewis for some years as executive secretary at the CIO's national headquarters. Mr. Hetzel read and commented on my manuscript and gave me a number of important suggestions. William Warren was also helpful with suggestions for sources of information and with comments on the manuscript.

CHAPTER 15

As might be expected, the royal visit was extensively covered in the U.S. press, and I have relied on the *New York Times* for May 15 to June 11, 1939.

Eleanor Roosevelt's *This I Remember,* pp. 183–98, contains a full account by one of the principal participants, and even includes an appendix with complete instructions from the State Department on protocol to be observed during the visit.

Cantelon's article in *American Heritage* is a lively, entertaining view of the event, especially on the amusing and often caustic comments of congressmen and senators.

Beschloss makes the point, pp. 187–88, that Ambassador Kennedy was miffed at being treated like a messenger boy in the negotiations. Edwards, especially pp. 408 and 432–35, writes interestingly of the royal family and the king's personality.

In addition to accounts in the *New York Times* and Cantelon, Katherine Marshall reports on the receptions in Washington in *Together,* pp. 50–51. Former sergeant Blonigan's attitude toward royalty was quoted in the *Times* of June 11, 1939, and the following day's issue includes the king's remark to the two Scottish women. The story of the martinis is from Cantelon.

As noted, Eleanor Roosevelt wrote fully about the visit, and her description of the Hyde Park stay—and the poignant picture of the young couple's departure—is excellent.

Lash's *Roosevelt and Churchill,* pp. 202–3 and 63–64, quotes the king's notes on his conversations with the president, notably the latter's remarks on the subject of naval bases and U-boats. Stevenson, pp. 65–67, states that British intelligence had ceased giving certain secret information to Chamberlain.

CHAPTER 16

As with the royal tour, so in spades with the 1939 World's Fair—the newspaper and magazine coverage, especially in New York, was both copious and continuous—and the facts and figures in this section and the description of exhibits are based largely on daily coverage in the *New York Times* during 1939, plus numerous articles in *Time, Newsweek* (see especially the May 1 and May 8, 1939, issues for statistics), *Harper's, The New Yorker, Business Week* ("What Shows Pulled at the Fair?" in the November 4, 1939, issue), and *Scientific American* throughout this year.

A delightful account of the Fair's genesis, written by John Bainbridge and St. Clair McKelway, appeared in the April 14, 1941, *New Yorker.*

Walter Lippmann's comments appeared first in his column in the *Herald Tribune* and were reprinted in the July 1939 issue of *Current History.* Charles Lindbergh's remark is from his *Wartime Journals,* p. 398; and E. L. Doctorow's difficulty in finding the time capsule was reported in the *New York Times* of November 11, 1985.

I am much obliged to Alvin Josephy for his story of the hapless couple stuck on the parachute jump.

A story in the October 23, 1939, issue of *Time* has a summary of the Fair's financial plight after the first season of operation, and Joseph Shadgen's unhappiness is recorded in Bainbridge and McKelway's *New Yorker* article.

PART III

CHAPTER 17

Lash mentions Roosevelt's worries about the possible movement of the British fleet to Singapore in his *Roosevelt and Churchill,* p. 32, where he also discusses the response of cabinet members to the president's message to Hitler and Mussolini. (Dallek, p. 186, is the source of the remark by Henry Wallace.) Shirer comments on Hitler's speech and the reaction of the Reichstag in *Berlin Diary,* pp. 165–67, and at greater length in *The Rise and Fall of the Third Reich,* pp. 471–75, where he includes excerpts from the speech.

The messages from Bullitt to Hull appear in the volume of his letters, pp. 338–39, and the reactions by Nye and Borah are from Daniels, p. 313, and Sherwood, p. 116.

For the story of the Douglas plane crash and the controversy that resulted, I relied on daily reports in the *New York Times,* January 24 to 31, 1939; and the *Los Angeles Times,* January 24 to February 1. I am indebted to Julie Yannatta of Santa Monica, California, for assistance in locating accounts in the Los Angeles paper. *Time,* in its issue of February 6, 1939, also deals with the story. Further information appears in Alsop and Kintner, pp. 29–31; and Watson, pp. 133–34 and 301–2, discusses the matter from the U.S. military's point of view. Blum, pp. 70–78, describes Morgenthau's involvement, the role of Monnet, and the brouhaha in Congress.

Several sources are worth consulting for the efforts of Roosevelt and Hull to break the isolationist bloc and repeal the arms embargo, ending with the night meeting at the White House. Alsop and Kintner, pp. 40–46, describe it from the vantage of reporters who were on the scene; and Judge Rosenman, who was also closely involved, speaks of the frustrations encountered by the president during this time, pp. 376–78. Dallek's analysis, pp. 185–92, is good (Hull's story about the sheep appears on p. 189); and Adler, pp. 270–73, is useful.

CHAPTER 18

For the background of the Nazi-Soviet Pact and events just prior to the outbreak of war, several sources are noteworthy. Wheeler-Bennett's study of Munich, pp. 385–86 and 407–21, notes Hitler's analysis of French and British intentions and his estimate of whether those countries would go to war over Poland, Stalin's judgment concerning the Nazis' plans, and the negotiations leading to the pact. Toland's biography of Hitler has considerable detail about how and why the treaty came about, as does Mosley's study of Europe in the prewar years, *On Borrowed Time*, which describes the Polish background and characterizes Beck. Churchill's *The Gathering Storm*, pp. 362 *et seq.*, provides a dissident's view of British policy; while Cadogan's comment, pp. 166–67, that officials in London were all too aware of their military weakness is that of a knowledgeable insider.

Charles Bohlen treats at length, pp. 56–87, with what the U.S. embassy in Moscow knew of the situation, and is the source of my information about Johnny Herwarth and his activities. Hitler's reaction when he learned that Stalin had agreed to meet with Ribbentrop is credited by Mosley to Dr. Friedrich Gaus of the German Foreign Ministry. Toland's biography of Hitler, p. 555, tells how Hitler examined Hoffmann's photographs of Stalin.

Reaction in the United States was reported in *Time*'s issue of September 4, 1939, which is also the source of quotations from William Allen White, Browder, Kuhn, and Broun. Malcolm Cowley's recollections, especially pp. 1–3 and 14, describe his own feelings and those of Arthur Koestler—whose *Scum of the Earth* he quotes—upon learning the news. Laura Fermi's *Illustrious Immigrants*, p. 53, quotes Koestler's *Arrow in the Blue: An Autobiography*, regarding the fate of friends during those terrible days.

William L. Shirer's observations about the Nazi-Soviet Pact and his own activities as war approached come from his *Berlin Diary*, pp. 180–92. Count Galeazzo Ciano recorded his experience with Ribbentrop in his diaries, pp. 582–83.

Adolf Berle's opinion of Roosevelt's messages to Hitler appears on p. 243 of his diaries; the description of London and the quotation from Nicolson concerning Chamberlain are in Edwards, pp. 430–32.

CHAPTER 19

Sir Nevile Henderson's observations of Berlin during the final days of peace in 1939, pp. 258–308, make for fascinating, if depressing, reading. Written during and shortly after his tour in Berlin, the book reveals a man in over his depth, who seems even with the advantage of hindsight not to realize how he was taken in by Germany's dictator. John Toland's *Hitler* is also informative concerning the events of August.

The U.S. scene is described in lively detail in *Time*'s issue of August 21, 1939.

Information on Dorothy Thompson is available in biographies by Sheean and Sanders—the former by a fellow journalist in Europe, who regarded her as a close friend. The Sanders book is based largely upon Thompson's papers and numerous interviews with former friends and associates. Thompson's description of Hitler and her expulsion from Germany are mentioned by Sanders, pp. 167–68, and the exchange of letters with Nicolson appears on p. 272.

The excerpt from Edward R. Murrow's broadcast is from Bliss's *In Search of Light,* a collection covering more than two decades of his career. Unfortunately for my purposes, less than fifty pages are devoted to the period 1938 to 1941, but the selection is excellent, and makes clear why Murrow's extraordinary association with England was so important to that country and the information he conveyed so convincing to Americans.

The efforts of U.S. citizens to leave Europe are described in the September 4, 1939, issue of *Time,* and that and the following week's edition include information on the activity of various American officials. Bruce Baldwin's experience is mentioned in the twenty-fifth-reunion book of Princeton's class of 1939, Redpath's *'39 in '64,* p. xi.

Kendrick's biography is instructive on the attitudes and activities of Murrow, Shirer, and other CBS correspondents.

The quotation from Anne Morrow Lindbergh is from her book *War Within and Without,* p. 44. Kennedy's remark concerning Chamberlain is from Mosley, *On Borrowed Time,* p. 427; the message to Lipski from his government is on p. 430. Toland, *Hitler,* pp. 566–67, mentions Hitler's outburst and directive to Keitel, and Kendrick reports Kaltenborn's misplaced optimism. Hitler's announcement to the Reichstag was reported in the *New York Times* the following day.

Alsop and Kintner's *American White Paper* appeared not long after these events occurred and bears an immediacy lacking in many later accounts. Alsop was a remote cousin of both Franklin and Eleanor Roosevelt, who "offered me occasional hospitality and showed me much kindness during my early years as a reporter in Washington," so his perception of what went on inside the White House was more intimate than that of many other newspapermen. The description of Roosevelt receiving Bullitt's call appears on pp. 1–2; the events of a later hour come from pp. 59–62.

Watson, p. 156, and Pogue, Vol. 2, p. 2, recount General Marshall's actions. The excerpt from *The New Yorker*'s "Notes and Comment" comes from the issue of September 9, 1939.

CHAPTER 20

Nicolson's diaries, especially for September 1 to 3, are valuable for the mood in the House of Commons during these critical hours.

Fuchser, pp. 186–87, deals with the delayed declaration of war, noting that France's stalling made it appear that Chamberlain was leading Britain into another Munich. The revolt of his cabinet and the rising opposition in the House convinced Chamberlain to act—independently of France, if necessary.

Spears's two volumes, filled with a mixture of perceptive personal observations, military expertise, and an intimate knowledge of France and its people, are an important source on events from the summer of 1939 through the fall of France. Like Nicolson, Spears was seated in the House on September 1 to 3, and the description of Greenwood and his speech, in Vol. I, pp. 13–21, is eloquent. Colville, p. 40, is the source of the note about Greenwood's fondness for alcohol.

Chamberlain's lament to his parliamentary colleagues appears in Fuchser, p. 187; Joseph Kennedy's frantic call to the White House is recorded in Beschloss, p. 190.

Nicolson's observations about the first day of war appear on pp. 420–22. Lash, *Roosevelt and Churchill,* p. 61, quotes Churchill on how he prepared for a stay in the bomb shelter.

The story of Queen Mary and her descent on the hapless Duke and Duchess of Beaufort is related in Edwards, pp. 435–36. News of Finland's decision to cancel the Olympic Games is in *Time,* September 11, 1939; and Admiral Yamamoto's apprehension is described in the biography by Agawa, p. 13.

Lash's *Roosevelt and Churchill* is the authority for the beginnings of the Roosevelt-Churchill correspondence. Arthur Schlesinger's review of *The Supreme Partnership* in the October 1984 *Atlantic* is also pertinent. Baldwin (see pp. 21–22 and 453) was the correspondent who—to his lasting regret—took his editor's advice not to bother with Churchill during that gentleman's days in the political wilderness.

A number of sources treat the phenomenon of the *Blitzkrieg,* among them Benoist-Méchin, Cooper, and Deighton. Benoist-Méchin's chapter, pp. 43–57, on German preparations for war are interesting, and he emphasizes the role Guderian played in focusing attention on the use of armor. Cooper's extensive study of the German army deals in Chapter II with the strategic revolution that occurred in the Wehrmacht between wars. Deighton traces the renaissance of the German army after World War I, the origins of new tactical ideas, and how they were put into practice. The section entitled "Blitzkrieg: Weapons and Methods," pp. 99–176, is particularly valuable, and the foreword by General Walther Nehring, who knew Guderian well, is interesting.

Guderian's characterization of the tank as "a life-saving weapon" is in Sulzberger's *American Heritage Picture History of World War II,* p. 69; and the soldier's diary excerpt is taken from Wernick's *World War II: Blitzkrieg,* p. 32.

Lilienthal describes his family's reaction to the first war news in Vol. I, pp. 121–23. Excerpts from FDR's radio talk to the American people appear in Sherwood, p. 125; and reactions to the speech and the news from Europe are in the *New York Times* for this period and *Time,* September 4 and September 11, 1939.

Cole's book on Lindbergh, pp. 66–67, follows his activities upon his return from Europe, but the best source is Lindbergh's own *Wartime Journals,* from which I have quoted a number of excerpts between the time of his meeting with Arnold and the delivery of his first radio speech. Larrabee, pp. 224–27, discusses the effect of Lindbergh's warnings on General Arnold; Baxter, p. 14, mentions Bush's response.

Excerpts from the aviator's speech appear in Anne Morrow Lindbergh's *War Within and Without,* pp. 57–59, along with her own thoughts about the talk.

The quotation about the way Lindbergh "evokes a fervor" appears in Roger Butterfield's article "Lindbergh," in the August 11, 1941, issue of *Life.* Cole, p. 74, mentions the comments from Hoover and Arnold.

CHAPTER 21

The quotation from Molotov's note is the first of many citations in this chapter from the first volume of Cordell Hull's *Memoirs.* This is from p. 685.

A good source on the invasion of Poland and the suffering in Warsaw is Irving, pp. 15–28, which is extremely informative on all aspects of the land war in Europe. Another general work well worth consulting is Wernick's *World War II: Blitzkrieg.*

Material on Hull's early years may be found in Vol. 1, Chapter 1 of his *Memoirs.* Other sources include Schlesinger, *The Coming of the New Deal,* pp. 188–92; Burns, *Roosevelt: The Lion and the Fox,* pp. 148, 177, and 383; and Evins's article. Hull, Vol. 1, p. 684, mentions the precautions taken to avoid suggesting that repeal might aid Britain and France.

Robert Sherwood discusses the isolationists, pp. 127–32. These people were never far from the thoughts of Roosevelt and his White House aides, and Sherwood draws a fine picture of them. More material is in Adler, pp. 265–68. Tinkham is nicely characterized by Lindbergh, pp. 264–65, and by Daniels, 541 and footnote. Childs, *I Write from Washington,* especially pp. 163 *et seq.,* provides an interesting picture of the U.S. capital in those stormy days.

Many insights into Senator Vandenberg's thinking may be found in the edition of his papers. An egotist, Vandenberg was also a thoughtful man, and his record of his activities provides a good look into the mind of a serious opponent of intervention.

Both Dallek, p. 202, and Burns, *Roosevelt: The Lion and the Fox,* p. 396, mention the Tweedsmuir-Roosevelt exchange, and the president's comments to reporters are in Sherwood, p. 134. Dallek discusses the Neutrality Acts of 1935, 1936, 1937, and 1939 in considerable detail, and covers the attempt to repeal the arms embargo, pp. 187–205. Divine offers an excellent summary of Roosevelt's efforts to act as European peacemaker during this period.

Hull's victory claim appears in Vol. 1, p. 697, and his suggestion of a "combat zone" on p. 682. Vandenberg's comments are from his diary entry for October 27, 1939. The remark that the combat zones would aid the Germans is from Dallek, p. 212.

CHAPTER 22

In *The Gathering Storm,* Winston Churchill relates how HMS *Courageous* and *Royal Oak* were sunk by the Germans.

Contemporary accounts of the *City of Flint* saga appeared in *Time,* September 25 and November 6, 1939, and February 5, 1940. The note describing Captain Gainard's problems aboard the *Algic* is based on a story in *Time,* September 20, 1937.

The inter-American conference is covered in Dallek, pp. 205–6, and Welles, pp. 210–13. Sumner Welles was, of course, intimately involved in that meeting, both as a planner and as a leading participant.

Full reports on the *Graf Spee* incident are in *Newsweek* for December 25, 1939, and January 1, 1940, and in *Time* and *Life* for the same dates. The battle is also mentioned in Sulzberger's *American Heritage Picture History of World War II,* pp. 182 and 188, and in Baldwin, pp. 65–67.

Tom Wicker, writing in the *New York Times Book Review* for May 25, 1986, pictured the meeting fifty years earlier between Margaret Mitchell and H. L. Latham of Macmillan and traced the extraordinary history of *Gone With the Wind.* A story about the Atlanta premiere appeared in the December 25, 1939, issue of *Life.*

CHAPTER 23

Arthur Miller's comments on his undergraduate days were published in *Holiday* magazine's December 1953 issue in an article on the University of Michigan.

While many aspects of the Yale campus in the autumn of 1939 are based on personal recollection, I have been greatly assisted by friends and university officials. Among the latter, Professor George Pierson answered a number of my questions, and thanks to his encyclopedic knowledge of the institution and his remarkable *A Yale Book of Numbers*, I was able to locate most of what I needed. Judith Ann Schiff, chief research archivist at the university library, helped by responding to questions and sending me material. Anne-Marie Soullière obligingly supplied important facts and directed me to other sources of information.

Two close friends and Yale classmates, John K. Tabor and John M. Thornton, responded to appeals for information with characteristic generosity, taking time from busy schedules to write long and informative recollections.

Pierson's *A Yale Book of Numbers*, as suggested above, is an extremely useful tool, and material has been drawn from pp. 119 and 590, in particular. Other sources are the article on freshman year in Richardson's *A History of the Class of Nineteen Forty-three*, and Carroll's *Buildings and Grounds of Yale University*.

Bohlen, p. 91, alludes to the Moscow visits by foreign ministers of Estonia, Lithuania, and Latvia. Dallek, pp. 207–12, discusses Roosevelt's opinion of Kennedy as an appeaser, his efforts to prevent Finland from suffering the fate of the three small Baltic nations, and, pp. 216–20, his exchanges with diplomats in Europe at this time.

Liebling, in *Liebling Abroad*, p. 38, describes events in Paris during the phony war, and *World War II: Blitzkrieg* portrays life in the Siegfried and Maginot lines, noting the doubts that characterized French and British military relations. British bravado at this time is well treated in Moorhead's *Montgomery*, pp. 95–96.

PART IV

CHAPTER 24

Mrs. Alexander Sachs was an important source of information concerning her late husband, especially about his role in drafting the letter for Einstein and setting it before President Roosevelt. She graciously gave me a lengthy interview, sent me copies of the original letter drafted by Sachs and the final version signed by Einstein, and explained much about Sachs's activities and his relationship with Mr. Roosevelt.

A careful search by Mrs. Elizabeth Denier at the Roosevelt Library indicates that there is no record in the White House usher's diary that Sachs had an appointment on October 11, 1939. In his papers and elsewhere, Sachs makes the point of having a close, confidential relationship with the president, so it is probable that they had an off-the-record meeting that day. (The subject would have been reason enough for that.) Roosevelt's first recorded appointment was at 11:15 A.M., with one every fifteen minutes until 1:00, then lunch with Secretary Perkins, followed by appointments at

2:15, 3:00, 4:30, and 5:00 (the last with Frank Knox), and, in the evening, a birthday celebration for Mrs. Roosevelt. It is certainly possible that he may have seen Sachs before going to his office at 11:15, or Sachs might have slipped in during the afternoon. In any case, there is no record of the visit.

Geoffrey Hellman's "The Contemporaneous Memoranda of Dr. Sachs," published as "A Reporter at Large" in *The New Yorker* of December 1, 1945, is a good study of his subject, and covers the historic meeting with FDR and the aftermath—up to the time Sachs "faded happily and voluntarily out of the picture."

Sachs's own statement about his involvement appears in the Hearings before the Special Committee on Atomic Energy, United States Senate, Seventy-ninth Congress, First Session, November 27–30, and December 3, 1945, as "Statement of Dr. Alexander Sachs."

Added information is to be found in Clark's *Einstein,* Jungk, and Szilard's "Reminiscences" in Fleming and Bailyn.

Numerous accounts exist of the ferment in the physics community during the first four decades of the twentieth century, and I was greatly aided in locating appropriate material by members of the staff at the American Institute of Physics: Dr. Spencer R. Weart, Manager, and Jean Hrichus, Librarian/Archivist, of the Center for the History of Physics; and Thomas A. Lowe, Assistant Librarian of the Niels Bohr Library—to all of whom go my thanks for their courtesy and understanding. In addition, Dr. Weart kindly read the manuscript of this particular chapter.

For the layman with little more than a rudimentary knowledge of nuclear physics, edification is at hand in Clark's biography of Einstein and his *The Birth of the Bomb;* Kevles; Spencer Weart's *Scientists in Power;* and William Laurence's *Men and Atoms* and *Dawn over Zero.* Some useful articles are Jeremy Bernstein's two-part "Profile" of Isidor Rabi in *The New Yorker,* Otto Frisch's "How It All Began," and John Wheeler's "Mechanism of Fission."

Weart's excellent study provides much of the flavor of the European community of scholars, especially the French, and the intense rivalry that existed. The quotation from Oppenheimer about this period is from Jungk, pp. 8–9, as are the words of Nernst and Pascual Jordan. Laura Fermi's *The Story of Atomic Energy* is a straightforward account of those heady times.

Frisch tells how Enrico Fermi got off on the wrong track, and Laurence makes the point that neither Fermi nor Segré realized that they had split the atom. Weart explains that Hahn's dilemma was that of a scientist stepping uninvited into another discipline.

CHAPTER 25

Clark's *Einstein,* p. 164, recounts Lise Meitner's experience hearing Einstein read his first "invited paper," and Laurence, *Men and Atoms,* p. 19, quotes Meitner on Irène Joliot-Curie.

Otto Frisch's account of his fateful visit to his aunt is excellent, and both of Clark's books and Laurence's *Men and Atoms* elaborate on the story.

CHAPTER 26

Individual and institutional efforts in America to aid European scholars are well depicted by Laura Fermi in *Illustrious Immigrants,* especially pp. 28–77. Kendrick, p. 123, mentions the role played by Edward R. Murrow.

Material about Szilard appears in Hewlett and Anderson, in Laura Fermi's *Illustrious Immigrants* and *The Story of Atomic Energy,* and in Frisch's reminiscences, and Szilard tells his own tale lucidly and well in "Szilard Reminiscences" in Fleming and Bailyn and in "His Version of Facts" in Weart and Szilard.

Fermi wrote about aspects of his own work in "Physics at Columbia." More on the man and his career is related by Laurence, and by Laura Fermi in the two works cited here, and Norman Ramsey's superb memoir in the Columbia Oral History Collection is illuminating.

Wheeler's article discusses Niels Bohr's arrival in America and his stay at Princeton. The Washington conference is also described, and more details about it appear in Bush, p. 57; Weart and Szilard, p. 66; and Laurence, *Men and Atoms,* p. 101. Articles in *Time*'s issues of February 6 and March 13, 1939, are of interest. Weart's *Scientists in Power* notes Joliot's dismay upon learning the news and discusses the work of the French team.

Clark, *The Birth of the Bomb,* p. 666; Laurence, *Men and Atoms,* pp. 41 and 55; Hewlett and Anderson, p. 15; and Weart, *Scientists in Power,* p. 87, relate the early efforts of scientists, especially Fermi, to interest the U.S. government in nuclear research. Goudsmit discusses the goings-on in Germany that so alarmed scientists in Britain and the U.S.

CHAPTER 27

Szilard offers the best picture of his concerns about German physicists and his belief that secrecy must be observed by those in opposition to Hitler.

Bridgman's "Manifesto" appeared in the February 24, 1939, issue of *Science,* p. 179. News of the announcement was in the *New York Times* of the same date. William A. Shurcliff kindly shared with me his recollections of Professor Bridgman and told me of the survey of scientists' attitudes he conducted, the results of which were published in the *New York Times* of April 5, 1939, p. 9. Additional information on Bridgman is in the *Dictionary of Scientific Biography;* Professor Gerald Horton of the Harvard physics faculty, who worked with Bridgman and was one of the authors of that article, also shared with me a paper he wrote on Bridgman on the occasion of the latter's centenary.

The Peierls paper, which was to have profound implications for the development of an atomic bomb, is discussed in Clark's *The Birth of the Bomb,* p. 42, and Weart, p. 147.

I had the privilege of interviewing Professor Eugene Wigner of Princeton, and he discussed his conversations with Szilard, their expedition to Long Island to see Einstein, and what later occurred in Washington. Additional information on the Einstein episode may be found in Lapp's article, Szilard's reminiscences, Clark's *Einstein,* and Weart and Szilard.

Sachs's appearance on the scene is discussed by Szilard and Hewlett and Anderson. Weart and Szilard, p. 100, note Szilard's conclusion that Lindbergh was not the man they needed.

The quotation from *Discovery* appears in Clark's *Birth of the Bomb,* p. 25.

Sachs's meeting with the president is covered in Clark's *Einstein,* Hewlett and Anderson, and Lapp's article, and in Sachs's own testimony before the Senate committee.

CHAPTER 28

Much of the material in this chapter is drawn from Szilard, especially pp. 115–22. Further details about the first Advisory Commission meeting were given me by Professor Wigner, and may be found in Hewlett and Anderson and in Lapp.

PART V

CHAPTER 29

Full accounts of the Russo-Finnish war appeared in the *New York Times*, beginning December 1, 1939, and *Newsweek, Time,* and *Life* are also helpful. I found *Life*'s coverage in the December 11 and 25, and January 29, 1940, issues especially good; the photographs by Carl Mydans are more vivid than any words. David Bradley's descriptions of the Finnish countryside are splendid, and his conversations with Finns who fought in that war convey the feelings of those people sympathetically. Dallek, pp. 208–19, discusses the effect of the war in Washington, with Roosevelt's efforts to do something to aid the Finns.

An account of the service for Senator Borah appeared in *Time*'s issue of January 29, 1940.

Numerous characterizations of Sumner Welles occur in contemporary accounts, among them Sherwood, speaking of the animosity between Welles and Bullitt, pp. 135–36; Ickes, Vol. 3, *passim;* Bullitt, pp. 505–18; and Kennan, pp. 115–16. Additional material appears in Schlesinger's *Age of Roosevelt,* Vol. 1, p. 321; Burns's *Roosevelt: The Lion and the Fox,* pp. 371–73, 383, and 416; Dallek, p. 149; and Acheson's *Present at the Creation,* pp. 33–34. Welles's narrative of his trip is in *The Time for Decision.*

Churchill, *The Gathering Storm,* tells of Chamberlain's unfortunate speech, p. 584, and describes the German attack on the Scandinavian nations and Great Britain's frustrating efforts to retaliate on land and sea, pp. 583–657. An account of the then first lord of the Admiralty's report in the House of Commons is in Murrow, pp. 85–86. Baldwin, p. 93, quotes Leland Stowe's story in the *Chicago Daily News.* Lash, *Roosevelt and Churchill,* pp. 97–124, notes the president's anxiety over these events and his awareness that the Germans had added a new dimension to warfare.

CHAPTER 30

Even now, the sudden collapse of France and its elimination as one of the great powers is almost impossible to conceive. The course of action that brought it about is handled fully, day by day, in Benoist-Méchin's volume.

Sheean's *Between the Thunder and the Sun* and Spears discuss Reynaud's relationship with Madame de Portes.

The downfall of Chamberlain and his replacement by Churchill are described by the latter in *The Gathering Storm,* pp. 650–67, and is supplemented by Fuchser, pp. 191–93 and elsewhere. Murrow's broadcast about Lloyd George's speech is quoted in Sperber, p. 153.

As noted earlier, Winston Churchill was his own best biographer, and I have relied principally upon his own writings for information about him. The literature about him is immense, of course. William Manchester's superb volume covers the period from his birth in 1874 to the early 1930s, the beginning of his time out of office, in the "wilderness," before he became prime minister. Other sources include the works of men who worked closely with him in one way or another, among them Spears, Cadogan, Colville, Ismay, and Moran, his personal physician, and Harold Nicolson's "A Portrait of Winston Churchill" in *Life*. Murrow's broadcasts are helpful, as is Sheean's book. Additional material is in Davenport and Murphy; Lash's study of the U.S. president and the British prime minister; and *Time* magazine's cover story of January 2, 1950, featuring Churchill as the "Man of the Half-Century."

Bond, pp. 63 *et seq.,* discusses the Mechelin incident, which is also described in Wernick's *World War II: Blitzkrieg,* pp. 52–53.

Paris and its mood that spring are portrayed by Sheean, pp. 85–87, and Boothe, pp. 127–32.

CHAPTER 31

Although Church's offer of $1 million for Hitler attracted wide press attention, including the article in the *New York Times* of May 1, 1940, the Pittsburgh papers understandably dealt with the story at greater length, and coverage appears in the *Post-Gazette, Press,* and *Sun-Telegraph* from May 1 to May 5, with follow-up information into late June, by which time Dr. Church was advocating the execution of Hitler and Mussolini and ten years' "isolation" of the German and Italian people. An account of the episode by Jeffrey Zaslow appeared in *Pittsburgher* magazine in August 1979. Biographical material on Church is in two volumes of *The Story of Carnegie Tech* by Tarbell and Cleeton and in Harper's *Pittsburgh of Today*.

Clare Boothe Luce described her trip in *Europe in the Spring.* Apparently she hoped the book would advance her political ambitions, and it is interesting to note that it was published under her maiden (and stage) name and made no reference to her husband, as though she had traveled alone. Two of Henry Luce's biographers, John Kobler and W. A. Swanberg, state that he sailed from New York on April 13, 1940, to join his wife, after receiving her cable. He was with her in Brussels and on the trip to Paris, leaving her there when he returned to the United States.

Liebling's highly personal picture of Paris in the spring of 1940 conveys the flavor of the place and time. Another perceptive treatment of both is in Sheean.

Here again, Benoist-Méchin's volume was useful for its accounts of daily action at the front. The book also describes the fall of France and the establishment of the Vichy regime. The immediate prewar background, including Allied strategy and the problem of Belgian neutrality, is ably handled by Bond, who traces the campaign through the evacuation at Dunkirk. Spears's admirable volumes treat the campaign as he saw it, with excellent characterizations of the *dramatis personae,* especially the French.

Saint-Exupéry's sensitive view of the tragedy overwhelming his native land and his countrymen is in *Flight to Arras, passim.*

Churchill's *Their Finest Hour* cites the problems he faced when he assumed the office of prime minister, and describes his five trips to France during those hectic days before Britain's ally surrendered and before the decision was taken to evacuate the BEF.

CHAPTER 32

Between them, Richard Collier and Walter Lord had the good fortune to interview more than sixteen hundred eyewitnesses of the Dunkirk evacuation, and their fine accounts have the feeling of immediacy conveyed by people who participated in or saw history in the making. Both describe the harried retreat to the beaches as well as the evacuation itself, and many of the quotations from participants are from those volumes.

Nicolson's suicide pact with his wife is mentioned in Vol. 2 of his diaries and letters, pp. 88 and 90; from the same source, p. 100, comes the note about Queen Elizabeth's target practice. The queen's admirable comment is quoted by Sherwood, p. 147.

Spears, Benoist-Méchin, and Bond are excellent sources on the movements of opposing forces up to the time of Dunkirk, supplemented by Churchill's narrative in *Their Finest Hour* and by Ismay's memoirs. The best account of the famous "stop" order and what was going on inside Hitler's headquarters is in Warlimont, pp. 97–100. Here the author discusses the conflict between Hitler, Göring, Keitel, and Jodl, on the one hand, and Halder and Brauchitsch, in particular, on the other. Warlimont argues that Rundstedt's reason for halting the armored formations was to permit them to reorganize and that Hitler seized on this as an excuse. The Führer's Directive No. 13 of May 24 is reproduced in Trevor-Roper, pp. 27–30.

Lady Ismay's experience is related by her husband on p. 136 of his memoirs.

Richard Collier's story of Churchill dictating the speech to his secretary was based, as he kindly informed me, on an interview he had with Mary Shearburn. The text of Churchill's speech appears in *Blood, Sweat, and Tears,* p. 289.

CHAPTER 33

Vita Sackville-West's reaction to Churchill's speech is in Nicolson, Vol. 2, p. 93. Montgomery's appraisal of the new prime minister is quoted in Moorhead, p. 93; and Sevareid's comments on London are in *Not So Wild a Dream,* pp. 165 and 179.

Lash makes the point in his study of the American and British leaders, pp. 129–53, that without Churchill, Great Britain might have gone the way of France, and without Roosevelt, the United States might have followed a "fortress America" policy. The president, watching intently and anxiously from the sidelines in Washington, was quick to perceive the difference the new prime minister made in Britain's attitude and was equally quick to capitalize on it.

Time's issue of September 11, 1939, contains a good appraisal of Lothian at the time he arrived in Washington as ambassador. His speech in New Haven on June 19, 1940, was published in the *Yale Alumni Magazine.*

Barber, pp. 45–47, quotes Bullitt on inviting the pope to leave Rome, Mussolini's cynical remark to Badoglio, and Reynaud's message to Roosevelt. The excerpt from Mussolini's speech is from *Time,* June 17, 1940, as is the account of FDR's trip to Charlottesville.

CHAPTER 34

Trying to see and comprehend the fall of France through American eyes is immeasurably facilitated by the sensitive accounts of Eric Sevareid and A. J. Liebling. Sevareid, pp. 134–55, describes his personal trials in Paris and Bordeaux; Liebling's graphic description of his own adventures between those two cities is in "A Man Falling Downstairs," pp. 80–88 in *Liebling Abroad*. Superb writers, both reporters captured the horror and confusion of being a refugee in those harrowing days, while describing the collapsing leadership of a defeated nation.

Saint-Exupéry's agonizing picture of his homeland is in *Flight to Arras, passim.*

Dallek, pp. 222–30, discusses Reynaud's last-minute appeals to Roosevelt through Bullitt and Churchill. Hull's disgust with Bullitt is mentioned in Barber, pp. 51–54. Both Ismay and Sherwood note Churchill's refusal—at Dowding's prompting—to send any more fighters to France.

The entrance of German troops into Paris is described in the June 24, 1940, issue of *Time;* the surrender of the French in the Forest of Compiègne is covered the following week.

The saga of the heavy water and its last-minute shipment to England, thanks to the efforts of Halban, Kowarski, and "the Holy Trinity," is told by Weart, pp. 95–156. He also describes Joliot's activities following that episode.

The comments of Dowding and Cadogan are taken from Cadogan, p. 299. President Roosevelt's letter to Lewis Douglas is quoted in Lash's *Roosevelt and Churchill,* pp. 150–51.

PART VI

CHAPTER 35

Excerpts from Churchill's speech following the fall of France are taken from *Their Finest Hour,* pp. 225–26. Drew Middleton's observations appear in *The Sky Suspended,* pp. 6–12. The picture of de Gaulle's Bastille Day review is by Sevareid, p. 168.

Telford Taylor's study is valuable for its analysis of Hitler's problems in the summer of 1940, including the conflicting advice he was receiving from generals and admirals on the subject of invasion. Various issues of *Time* during July and August include descriptions of preparations under way in London and southern England against the coming attacks, as well as details of the plans to send children to the United States.

Much information on the evacuation of London's children is in Bailey's *America, Lost and Found,* in which he discusses his own departure and temporary adoption by an American family in Dayton, Ohio.

I am indebted to Lady Margaret Barry for information about her own voyage to America with thirteen children. She also shared with me her unpublished manuscript in which she describes this and other incidents in a rich and remarkable life.

J.F.C. Fuller discusses, pp. 83–89, Hitler's original goal of winning Britain's friendship, and the irony that that country was for a time his sole enemy, secure beyond the Strait of Dover. Although he cites Rundstedt's suggestion that Hitler never really wanted to invade England, he believes the reason for Germany's failure to conquer the British was its not realizing that a war of attrition and exhaustion—not direct assault—was the answer.

Hitler's changes of heart concerning the invasion are cited by Taylor, pp. 62–63, and the pertinent headquarters orders are in Trevor-Roper's study.

Radar was regarded by British scientists as far more important than nuclear research, and, of course, in terms of saving Britain, it was. Material on radar may be found in Bush; Clark's *The Birth of the Bomb;* Bernstein's *New Yorker* "Profile" of Isador Rabi, especially part 2; and Norman Ramsey's memoir in the Columbia Oral History Collection.

Information on Enigma and Ultra, how the British cracked the former by developing the latter, and how this affected battle strategy is in Buranelli and in Winterbotham's *The Ultra Secret.* Colville, p. 348, points out that it was not possible to decipher Luftwaffe signals within a short time of interception until May 1940, the time of Dunkirk. It took until the summer of 1941 to master German naval signals, and the British were unable to do much with the Wehrmacht's codes until 1942.

Mention is made of the July 11 arrival of weapons in Cadogan's diaries, p. 312.

That Hitler had at last made a decision in favor of Sea Lion is made clear by Trevor-Roper, pp. 34–37, and Winterbotham indicates on p. 41 how the British learned of German invasion plans. Reactions to the Führer's speech are noted in Taylor, pp. 60–61, and in the July 29, 1940, issue of *Time.*

Lash, *Roosevelt and Churchill,* p. 178, tells of Dieckhoff's memorandum on the subject of Roosevelt's speech.

CHAPTER 36

The literature on Franklin Delano Roosevelt is immense, but the indispensable companions for an overview of the man and his political career are, as noted above, Schlesinger's three volumes, Burns's two, and Sherwood's one. Geoffrey Ward's splendid *Before the Trumpet* covers FDR's family background, youth, and marriage. Eleanor Roosevelt's own volumes, particularly the autobiography, with its revealing glimpses into her husband's personality, are essential aids, as is Joseph Lash's sensitive study of Eleanor's relationship with Franklin. The Rosenmans' *Presidential Style* has a long chapter on Roosevelt, written from the perspective of one of his most influential advisers, who also edited his public papers and speeches. Other important writings by Roosevelt's close associates include works by Ickes, Lilienthal, and Perkins (in Martin's book) and Tugwell's perceptive *In Search of Roosevelt.*

The fourth volume of James Flexner's biography of Washington deals with the first president's views on a third term, and I have referred to my own *The World of George Washington.*

Marquis Childs's articles "They Hate Roosevelt" and "They Still Hate Roosevelt," published two years apart, are reminders of the phobic attitude many Americans had toward That Man in the White House. I am indebted to David S. Ketchum for recollections of his father's opinion of Mr. Roosevelt, which were no more complimentary than those of my own parents.

Roosevelt's first inaugural address is reprinted in my and Irwin Glusker's *Ameri-*

can Testament, as are several important pieces of legislation from the NRA years, and the president's "Four Freedoms" speech.

Hopkins's remarks on the subject of Roosevelt's receptivity to ideas, expressed after FDR's death, are in Sherwood, p. 881. William Allen White's comments on the president are in his autobiography, pp. 634–36 and 648–49. The Rosenmans discuss Roosevelt's awareness of the effectiveness of radio, pp. 333–35; and Lipstadt, pp. 4–5, mentions his avid consumption of newspapers. John Gunther is quoted by Jellison, p. 164.

Both Ward and Alsop provide insights into the mind and personality of the young Franklin Roosevelt, and these may be supplemented (with caution) by Alice Roosevelt Longworth's frequently acid remarks.

The Ickes exchange with Roosevelt is recorded by Dallek, p. vii, and Hopkins's remark about the president's jealousy is quoted by Walter Lippmann in his memoir in the Columbia Oral History Collection. Averell Harriman's statement appears in Grigg, p. 79. David Lilienthal's admiration for the Roosevelts' talent for greeting friends in a crowd, along with a fine description of Inauguration Day in 1941, are in the first volume of his journals, pp. 262–66.

Lash's *Roosevelt and Churchill,* pp. 34–45, covers the influence of Alfred Thayer Mahan on FDR; and Burns, *Roosevelt: The Lion and the Fox,* pp. 50–53 and 71–76, is particularly good on the young assistant secretary of the navy and Washington, D.C., during World War I. Eleanor Roosevelt's *Autobiography,* pp. 129–32, describes her husband's facility for winnowing the ideas of others when making decisions.

Ward, Eleanor Roosevelt, and Burns write informatively about Roosevelt's polio attack and its effects. The New York gubernatorial campaign is depicted in the Burns volume already cited, pp. 97–104, and two following chapters deal with Roosevelt's years in Albany and his nomination for the presidency in 1932.

Parmet and Hecht, pp. 27–34 and 175, are the source of Sara Roosevelt's comment about a third term, and the Roosevelt children's opposition to it, while the Burns book, pp. 409–11, and Sherwood, p. 171, mention FDR's comments about returning to private life. The latter source, p. 137, has an excellent discussion of why Roosevelt had to veil his intentions during 1939–40.

Hopkins's talk with his boss about potential successors is recorded by Sherwood, pp. 93–94, and Ickes's efforts to push for a third term are noted on p. 170.

I was fortunate to obtain comments and answers to a number of questions from Benjamin V. Cohen, James A. Farley, and Samuel I. Rosenman.

CHAPTER 37

Two sources of information about Wendell Willkie are of particular interest— Barnard's 1966 study, and that by Parmet and Hecht, which Oren Root and Samuel Pryor both considered the best book on the 1940 campaign. Roscoe Drummond's article on Willkie in Leighton's *The Aspirin Age* is written from the viewpoint of a reporter who traveled with his subject throughout the campaign and remained an admiring friend until Willkie's death. Marcia Davenport came to know Willkie through her husband; hers is a more limited view than those mentioned above.

I benefitted greatly from interviews and correspondence with a number of individuals who knew Willkie or participated in the GOP convention and campaign.

Foremost among them was my father, George Ketchum, who told me about that heady time in Philadelphia and wrote me a number of letters about the occasion. Oren Root granted me a long interview and answered numerous questions about his own important role before, during, and after the convention.

Barnard, p. 170, describes the excitement that had built up around Willkie. The observation about the candidate's instinct for public relations is from the Root interview.

Thomas Dewey's record in the primaries is detailed in Parmet and Hecht, pp. 76–81. Much of my information on Taft came from conversations with George and Carlton G. Ketchum, who knew the senator. Vandenberg's diary is valuable for his own views concerning his candidacy.

Material on Willkie's early life and his family is available in Barnard and in Drummond's article in Leighton's book. The former discusses in some detail the Commonwealth and Southern-TVA controversy, as do Parmet and Hecht. Barnard notes Willkie's assessment of his chances at winning the nomination and the independent nature of his ideas. The success of the Willkie clubs is reported in the June 24, 1940, issue of *Time*, which also describes the arrival of delegates in Philadelphia. Willkie's pledge that he would be unencumbered with obligations is quoted in Parmet and Hecht, p. 122.

CHAPTER 38

The story of the convention that participants remembered two and three decades later as the most gripping political moment of their lives is well documented in Barnard and in Parmet and Hecht. Daily papers and weekly news magazines covered the proceedings extensively, and issues of *Time* from June 24 through July are especially useful for a depiction of the scene in Philadelphia. The *New York Times* of June 28, 1940, includes all the balloting records.

In addition to those sources cited for Chapter 37, Howard A. DeWitt's "Miracle in Philadelphia" is of interest. He describes his article as a reappraisal, based on the thesis that the nomination, rather than a freak accident of amateurs outwitting professionals, was in fact "the result of a well-financed and smoothly organized public relations campaign."

The Stimson and Knox appointments and Republican reaction are from the *New York Times* of June 21–22 and *Time*, July 1, 1940. Ickes's comments are in Vol. 3 of his diaries, pp. 211–215. Lash quotes Mrs. Morgenthau's remark in *Roosevelt and Churchill*, p. 170.

An account of John L. Lewis's appearance before the Resolutions Committee is in *Time*, July 1; the labor leader's position on the draft is in Dubofsky and Van Tine, p. 348, and his support for Hoover is discussed on pp. 351–52.

Arthur Vandenberg's flirtations with Willkie and Taft are recorded in his diary.

As may be deduced, most of the information on the Pennsylvania delegation came from George, Carlton, and David Ketchum, all of whom were participants and keen, interested observers. Others who gave me valuable insights were Oren Root, Samuel Pryor, Jr., and John Hollister, who was working with Taft at the convention and later traveled on Willkie's campaign train.

CHAPTER 39

This chapter is based almost entirely on personal recollection. Some information on the history of Pittsburgh's debutante parties was included in "Whatever Happened to Pittsburgh Society?" in *Pittsburgher* magazine for June 1977. Particulars on the social seasons of 1940–41 appeared in the *Bulletin-Index* for November 21, 1940— that publication's "Special Debutante Issue."

PART VII

CHAPTER 40

The issues of *Time* for July 22 and 29, 1940, are filled with information about the presidential cruise, the preliminaries to the convention, and the convention itself. The Rosenmans, p. 356, and Parmet and Hecht, p. 194, describe the scene in the White House when the president and his aides listened to the broadcast from Chicago.

Harold Ickes's comments, Vol. 3, pp. 219–58, are lively, entertaining, and as biased as one might expect from a self-centered man who badly wanted to be on the ticket. Ickes has a good deal of material on Hopkins, whom he disliked intensely, but the best source of information on Roosevelt's agent in Chicago is Sherwood, especially pp. 2–3, 102–3, 173–79, and 203.

Senator Brandegee's remark about Harding, and information on the infamous smoke-filled room, are in Russell, pp. 214–16.

Tugwell's comment on Hull is in *In Search of Roosevelt,* p. 262; on p. 263 the deal Hopkins negotiated with the big-city bosses is discussed. Further information on events prior to and during the convention may be found in Burns, *Roosevelt: The Lion and the Fox,* pp. 409–30, and Parmet and Hecht, pp. 34–40. The latter give a detailed account of Farley's visit to Hyde Park, pp. 172–74, and discuss the Roosevelt family's opposition to a third term, pp. 175–76. Some of the material on James A. Farley's activities before and during the convention is from correspondence to the author.

A good description of Thomas D. Garry and his work with the public address system is in *Time,* July 29, 1940. Eleanor Roosevelt's account of her sudden trip to Chicago is in *This I Remember,* pp. 214–18.

CHAPTER 41

Robert Sherwood, who had a hand in writing it, quotes the president's acceptance speech on p. 185. Norman Thomas's remark is from Parmet and Hecht, p. 214.

Jones's study of Elmer Davis and his changing attitude toward U.S. intervention is valuable; in it he cites Davis's own article, "Broadcasting the Outbreak of War," in *Harper's* for November 1939.

W. L. White supplemented William Allen White's *Autobiography* with a chapter on the last two decades of his father's life, and he discusses the relationship between White and Roosevelt during this period.

The most complete account of the origins and subsequent development of White's Committee to Defend America by Aiding the Allies and the Century Group was published in the Sunday, September 22, 1940, edition of the *St. Louis Post-Dispatch*, which devoted three full pages to an article by Charles G. Ross. Members of both committees are identified; the Century group's original charter—a memorandum drawn up after the dinner meeting of July 25—is reprinted; and this information is accompanied by an article by the paper's Washington correspondent, Raymond P. Brandt, discussing presidential powers and the chronology of the destroyer deal. For assistance in obtaining this material I am obliged to Mike Marler of the *Post-Dispatch*.

Chadwin is instructive on the formation and subsequent activities of the White and Century committees; in an appendix he reprints "A Summons to Speak Out." Another good source is Lash's *Roosevelt and Churchill*, pp. 197–220. The advertisement written by Robert Sherwood appeared in *The New Yorker* for June 22, 1940, and in other publications.

Chadwin recounts Van Dusen's visit to the British ambassador, pp. 40–41. For a description of the clergyman, I am indebted to Frederick Buechner, who was one of Van Dusen's students.

General Pershing's radio address was reprinted in the *New York Times* on August 5, 1940, where Lindbergh's speech was reported. The comments by Senators Pepper and Lee, and the editorial cited, are in the next day's edition. Chadwin, pp. 90–91, has further details on the Pershing talk. The letter from Acheson and other attorneys was printed in the *New York Times* on August 11, 1940. Comments of Winston Churchill, Mussolini, and Raeder are in Lash.

CHAPTER 42

Eyewitness accounts of the Battle of Britain and the London blitz during 1940 are abundant, and I have relied especially on the diaries and personal recollections of Mrs. Edward R. Murrow; the published broadcasts of Edward R. Murrow and J. B. Priestley; books by Drew Middleton, Ben Robertson, Eric Sevareid, Vincent Sheean, and others, based on their own experiences and reports of events; and such contemporary reportage as the excellent weekly "Letter from London" by Mollie Panter-Downes in *The New Yorker*—all of which provided Americans with a vivid sense of what it was like to live on that embattled island. I would like to thank especially Mrs. Murrow, who gave me access to her diaries for this period and recalled in conversation the details of many events described here.

Two articles by Elmer Davis—a "letter" to the readers of *The Saturday Review of Literature* in the June 14, 1941, issue; and "Journey to England, 1941," in *Harper's* for August 1941—provide valuable background.

The quotation from Orson Welles is taken from a newsreel film clip made immediately following his famous broadcast.

An informative article about Edward R. Murrow's emergence as the leading commentator on Britain appeared in the December 1938 issue of *Scribner's* magazine. Murrow mentioned Lord Haw-Haw's messages from Germany in his broadcast of April 7, 1940. His description of bombs bursting in London is on pp. 179–80 of Bliss's collection of his broadcasts. Eric Sevareid, p. 170, tells of the narrow escape he, Murrow, and Larry LeSueur had.

Tributes to Murrow by Archibald MacLeish and William Paley, along with

Murrow's own remarks, were published by the Columbia Broadcasting System under the title "In honor of a man and an ideal . . ."

Many statistics on the numbers of men and planes involved in aerial combat, and losses on both sides, come from exhibits at the Royal Air Force Museum in Hendon, England. Another authoritative source is Churchill's *Their Finest Hour,* pp. 338–39; the British prime minister's characterization of the Luftwaffe attacks appears on p. 341. Field Marshal Rundstedt is quoted by Middleton, p. 248.

Robertson, pp. 88–107, vividly depicts the fighting he observed over the Dover cliffs. For the German point of view on the battle and the likelihood of invasion, see Irving, pp. 134–59; Speer, p. 85; and Shirer's *The Nightmare Years,* pp. 567–72. Telford Taylor's study of this critical engagement between Britain and Germany is a fine general review. The author cites on p. 154 the August 21 OKW message that no attacks on London were to be made unless by Hitler's order.

Shirer's reports on the initial RAF bombings of the German capital are in *Berlin Diary,* pp. 484 *et seq.*

The description of the massive bombing of London on September 7, 1940, is drawn from Mrs. Edward R. Murrow's diaries and conversations with her, and from Murrow, pp. 157–60, Sheean, pp. 210 and 218–29; and Robertson, pp. 119–23. Robertson's eloquent portrayal of the damage to London may be supplemented by "Letter from London" during this period. Vera Brittain records her experience in *England's Hour,* pp. 147–54; Priestley's ruminations appear on pp. 23–27, 106, and 129 of his collected broadcasts.

Shirer mentions the invasion rumors in *Berlin Diary,* p. 504, and Anthony Bailey recounts, pp. 20–21, the trauma of his final night before sailing for America.

Winston Churchill speaks of his visit to the Group Operations Room in *Their Finest Hour,* pp. 333–37; his companion at the time, General Ismay, graphically supplements that account in his memoirs, pp. 180–83.

Admiral Raeder's notation for the War Diary is quoted by Collier in *Eagle Day,* p. 263; although lacking an index, this book provides a splendid account of the Battle of Britain, and is based on more than four hundred interviews with participants.

F. W. Winterbotham tells, pp. 57–60, how he got the deciphered message to the prime minister and the effect this had on Churchill and his staff.

CHAPTER 43

Arnold Whitridge's article was published in the August 1940 issue of *The Atlantic Monthly,* the reply by Brewster and Klaw in September.

Interviews with Kingman Brewster and Senator William Benton were extremely helpful in tracing the beginnings of the America First movement. At best, it was a haphazard organization, held together by the dedication of a handful of individuals, one of the most important of whom was Robert D. Stuart, Jr. Mr. Stuart kindly answered questions and directed me to former associates who could shed light on various phases of the operation. In addition to giving me insights into the formation of an America First group at Yale, Kingman Brewster lent me a copy of his incisive article "Pre-War Uncertainty." Senator Benton was particularly helpful in assessing the role of General Robert E. Wood and the inner workings of the headquarters organization.

As mentioned earlier, Cole's studies of America First and of the part played by

Charles Lindbergh against intervention are especially valuable. The choice of a name, the roster of original members, and the enunciation of the organization's principles are discussed on pp. 14–16 of his *America First.*

Brewster's remarks to the Senate Foreign Relations Committee were printed in the *Yale Daily News* of February 8, 1941. The same newspaper, on October 31, 1940, covered the Lindbergh speech and the Roosevelt visit to New Haven; Charles Lindbergh's *Wartime Journals,* p. 413, notes his delight at Yale's reaction to his speech.

Dallek discusses, pp. 248–50, the selective service issue and its potential effect on the election. Sherwood's remarks on the campaign appear on p. 200 of his *Roosevelt and Hopkins;* his judgment of Willkie's mistake is on p. 176.

A good picture of the Willkie campaign is in Marquis Childs's *I Write from Washington,* pp. 203 *et seq.;* Childs traveled on the candidate's train and was a good friend.

For a discussion of the Tripartite Pact and its possible effect on U.S. policy, see Lash, *Roosevelt and Churchill,* pp. 222–24, and Langer and Gleason, especially Chapters 1 and 2.

Dubofsky and Van Tine, pp. 356–60, recall John L. Lewis's endorsement of Willkie and the union leader's visit to the White House. Dorothy Thompson's announcement is quoted by Sanders, pp. 266–70.

Burns, *Roosevelt: The Lion and the Fox,* Parmet and Hecht, Barnard, and Lash's *Roosevelt and Churchill* are important sources for the last hectic month of the 1940 campaign.

The best study of Joseph Kennedy's curious relationship with FDR is Beschloss, who tells of the ambassador's departure from London, his visit to Washington, and his speech endorsing the president on pp. 195–221. He mentions the Bullitt-Kennedy contretemps, p. 203; further details are in Bullitt, p. 437; and Ickes, Vol. 3, p. 147.

Roosevelt's Madison Square Garden speech is discussed by Parmet and Hecht, pp. 260–61; Sherwood, pp. 189–90; and Barnard, pp. 256–57. The same authors also deal with the Boston address.

Parmet and Hecht describe Roosevelt's Cleveland speech and note Joseph Martin's estimate of Willkie's chances, pp. 268–69.

Figures on the public opinion polls are in Dallek, p. 250. Barnard, p. 264, and Parmet and Hecht, p. 1273, provide the election returns.

Robert Sherwood, who was present at Hyde Park on election night, describes the scene, pp. 199–200. Willkie's reaction is noted by Parmet and Hecht, pp. 271–72.

PART VIII

CHAPTER 44

The first two volumes of Forrest Pogue's biography are the best sources of material on George C. Marshall during the period covered here. I have also referred to *Together,* the recollections of Marshall's second wife, for personal details. A good portrait of the newly appointed chief of staff, written by A. J. Liebling, appeared as a "Profile" in *The New Yorker* of October 26, 1940, and another excellent source is Eric Larrabee's *Commander in Chief,* which contains chapters on Marshall, King, Arnold, and others.

Dean Acheson's appraisal of Marshall is quoted by Grigg, p. 66; Marquis Childs, p. 252, speaks of the general's temperament for a crisis; and Ambrose, p. 6, cites his remark to Eisenhower. Marshall's admission of his temper is from Pogue, Vol. 2, p. 14.

Here and elsewhere in discussing the military command situation in Washington prior to World War II, I have relied on the splendid study written by Mark S. Watson for the Historical Division of the Army.

Material on the Roosevelt-Marshall relationship may be found in Larrabee, p. 109; Pogue, Vol. 1, pp. 324–25; Lash, *Roosevelt and Churchill,* p. 184; and Acheson, p. 165.

Ickes's comment on Woodring is in his Vol. 3, p. 120. Pogue, Vol. 1, pp. 317–19 and 326, notes the tension between Woodring and Johnson and the difficulties thus created for the chief of staff. Baruch, p. 277, describes how Johnson learned of Stimson's appointment.

Colonel Russell Reeder was characteristically generous in guiding me to information about the prewar army, answering questions at length, furnishing useful articles, and suggesting others who could assist.

Life's article on the woefully ill-equipped army appeared in the issue of December 19, 1938. For other graphic pictures of that military force, see Barbara Tuchman's *Stillwell,* pp. 259 *et seq.;* and Watson, especially pp. 18–24 and 148–57.

Oulahan's article has a wealth of details on the State, War, and Navy Building.

CHAPTER 45

Lord Lothian's remarks about the U.S. dilemma are contained in a letter quoted in Abbazia, p. 83.

I have followed Morgenthau's account (in Blum, pp. 138–43) of Marshall's meeting with Roosevelt, Woodring, and Johnson, since he was present. Pogue, Vol. 2, pp. 31–32, and Larrabee, pp. 120–21, also discuss that meeting and its aftermath. Catton, p. 21, mentions the reporter (probably Catton himself) who asked questions at air corps headquarters about the 50,000-plane request.

An examination of the War Plans Division's deliberations and the several Rainbow plans may be found in Watson, pp. 89–113, supplemented by Pogue, Vol. 2, pp. 122–24, and Spector, pp. 44–66. Dallek, p. 233, quotes the comments by Edwin Wilson and Claude Bowers.

Bedell Smith's pessimistic remark is cited by Larrabee, p. 47.

This and subsequent sections owe much to the splendid study by Langer and Gleason of the many pertinent documents dealing with the period between Japan's signature of the Tripartite Pact and that nation's attack on Pearl Harbor. Of comparable importance is the monumental *At Dawn We Slept,* by Gordon W. Prange, focusing on the preparations and execution of the Japanese attack and the diplomatic maneuvering that accompanied the former. Admiral Richardson's failed efforts to move the Pacific fleet back to California are discussed by Langer and Gleason, pp. 41–42; Prange, pp. 37–44; Larrabee, p. 48; and Lash, *Roosevelt and Churchill,* pp. 225–26.

Churchill, in *Their Finest Hour,* p. 544, describes the British attack at Taranto.

Knox's message to Stimson, with copies to the Pacific commanders, is quoted by Prange, pp. 44–46.

The navy's undeclared hostilities in the Atlantic are well documented by Abbazia, who cites Admiral Stark's memorandum to Secretary Hull, pp. 279–80. Characterizations of Stark appear in that volume, p. 67, and in Prange, p. 41; Larrabee, p. 32; Pogue, Vol. 2, pp. 125–26; and Sherwood, p. 164. Stark's Plan Dog is widely discussed: by Abbazia, pp. 120–21; Sherwood, pp. 271–72; Prange, p. 40; and Lash, *Roosevelt and Churchill,* pp. 266–67.

The joint U.S.-British military discussions and Roosevelt's position with respect to them are considered by Watson, pp. 120 *et seq.;* and more material is in Burns's *Soldier of Freedom,* pp. 85–88, and Langer and Gleason, p. 285. Abbazia, p. 145, includes figures on the constitution of the Atlantic Fleet at the time; Watson, p. 175, notes General Marshall's changing estimates of his needs.

The New Yorker's "Notes and Comment" in the July 6, 1940, issue included a brief description of the original Plattsburg group and its revival twenty-five years later. Watson, p. 189, discusses the move to initiate a civilian draft. An account of the dinner appeared on the front page of the *New York Times* for May 23, 1940. Pogue, Vol. 2, pp. 56–58, gives General Marshall's reasons for not wishing to be seen as a sponsor of the legislation. Comments by Walter Lippmann appear in his memoir in the Columbia Oral History Collection.

Stimson, pp. 318–24, recalls his speech at Yale and his summons from Roosevelt. Congressman James Wadsworth's important role is related interestingly in his Columbia Oral History memoir. Marshall's unfortunate acquiescence to the one-year term of service is recounted in Pogue, Vol. 2, pp. 130–31.

CHAPTER 46

Churchill's *Their Finest Hour,* pp. 555–67, has an account of Britain's dilemma, Purvis's mission, and the effort to enlist increased American aid. Tonnage losses of British ships are in the Appendix, p. 714.

The *New York Times* of December 3 *et seq.* carried details about Roosevelt's cruise, and Dallek, pp. 252–59, ably summarizes the president's approach to Britain's problem and his decision to resort to Lend-Lease. Further background may be found in Blum, 202–6; Lash, *Roosevelt and Churchill,* pp. 263–65 (where attribution of the phrase "arsenal of democracy" to Monnet appears); Davis, pp. 44–51; Burns, *Roosevelt: The Soldier of Freedom,* pp. 27–29; and Langer and Gleason, p. 248.

FDR's fireside chats are described by Burns in *Roosevelt: The Lion and the Fox,* p. 205, and in two issues of *American Heritage*—August 1983, p. 76, and February 1988, p. 37.

Brinkley, p. 51, records Senator Taft's reaction to Lend-Lease; Wheeler's comment and Roosevelt's retort are in Sherwood, p. 229; and the *Chicago Tribune*'s attack is in Burns, *Soldier of Freedom,* p. 45.

Langer and Gleason, pp. 269–78; and Barnard, pp. 274–85, graphically portray the scene at the congressional hearings on the Lend-Lease bill. Beschloss, pp. 232 and 238, records Kennedy's position; and Sherwood, p. 264, quotes Robert Hutchins. Aspects of Willkie's dramatic appearance and his subsequent trip to the U.K. are in Sherwood, p. 2; Barnard, pp. 279–84; Burns, *Soldier of Freedom,* pp. 43–49; Davis, pp. 52–55; Drummond in Leighton's *Aspirin Age,* pp. 444 *et seq.;* and Nicolson, Vol. 2, p. 142. Sherwood suggests, p. 263, that Willkie's statement led many Britons to believe that the United States would intervene in the war by spring.

Vandenberg's attitude is expressed in his diary; Stimson's diary is quoted by Lash in *Roosevelt and Churchill,* p. 265.

CHAPTER 47

Burns's *Roosevelt: The Soldier of Freedom,* p. 236, records Harry Hopkins's remark to Edward R. Murrow; further details are from Janet Murrow's diary. Richard Collier, in *1941,* p. 1, quotes Hopkins to Churchill on the cottagers. The story about Hopkins at Chequers is in Lash, *Roosevelt and Churchill,* p. 282; and Churchill's physician, Lord Moran, repeated excerpts from the American's Glasgow talk on p. 6 of his diaries. Sherwood, of course, is essential reading when it comes to Hopkins's activities, and citations here are from pp. 241–49.

Heinrichs, pp. 313–24, has details on the strength of Germany's surface and undersea fleets. For a full discussion of President Roosevelt's problems in the Atlantic war and his efforts to activate naval patrols, see Abbazia, especially pp. 62–81. The same author describes the dreadful conditions faced by North Atlantic patrols, pp. 241–42 and 322–24.

Blum, p. 193, cites Knox's remark about the need for U.S. military assistance. The exchange between Stimson and FDR is in Langer and Gleason, p. 243; and Ickes, Vol. 3, p. 466, records his own desire for a declaration of war.

Hitler's speculation on the chances of Russian and U.S. intervention is in Langer and Gleason, p. 146.

Abbazia, pp. 134–45, has useful information on Admiral King, as does Larrabee, pp. 153–71. The admiral's frustration over the condition of his command is well covered by Heinrichs, pp. 317–19. From Larrabee, p. 40, comes Missy LeHand's insight into Roosevelt's state of mind.

Janet Murrow describes the Murrows' narrow escape from a bomb in her diary for April 16, 1941.

Accounts of the fall of Crete, with its consequences for the Battle of the Atlantic, are in Churchill, *The Grand Alliance,* pp. 301–4, and Heinrichs, p. 322; and both authors describe the *Bismarck* episode.

Larrabee, pp. 44–46, discusses the divisions within the Roosevelt cabinet at this time.

The landing of the marines in Iceland is related by Abbazia, pp. 201–2, and the same author, p. 214, quotes Hitler's threat to torpedo U.S. vessels.

Lilienthal, Vol. 1, p. 234, describes the party of royal exiles from Norway— information given him by a sorely tried Eleanor Roosevelt. The presidential "cruise" is recounted in numerous sources, among them Phillips, *The 1940s,* p. 199; Lash, *Roosevelt and Churchill,* pp. 393–94; and Sherwood, pp. 352–65. An excellent account of Hopkins's mission to Moscow, his return to the U.K., and his voyage with Churchill to meet Roosevelt is in Sherwood, pp. 319–50.

Cooper, pp. 258–59, quotes Jodl's optimism on the invasion of Russia. Stimson's prediction appears in Sherwood, pp. 303–5.

Full details on the conference may be found in Cadogan's diaries for this period; in Churchill, *Their Finest Hour;* and in Lash, *Roosevelt and Churchill,* pp. 391–401. Pogue, Vol. 2, p. 144, cites General Marshall's hardheaded analysis of what it would take to beat the Germans.

Grigg, pp. 14–18, has an admirable discussion of the differences between president and prime minister and questions the depth of their friendship.

Langer and Gleason, pp. 682–88, and Lash, *Roosevelt and Churchill,* pp. 396–402, deal with the writing of the Atlantic Charter; and Cadogan's diaries are revealing in connection with the British point of view.

The *Greer* episode, Roosevelt's speech, and the public reaction are covered by Abbazia, pp. 223–31, and Dallek, pp. 287–92. The sinking of the *Reuben James* is described by Abbazia, pp. 293–306.

Ickes, Vol. 3, p. 650, cites his puzzlement over FDR's inaction.

CHAPTER 48

Sevareid, pp. 184–98, recounts his dismay over American apathy toward the war in Europe.

For much of the material on the Bray family I relied on an unpublished memoir written by Charles W. Bray.

The quotation from Stimson's diary about Roosevelt's reluctance to accept the likelihood of a landing in Europe is in Langer and Gleason, p. 735.

General Lee's letter to Hopkins is quoted by Sherwood, p. 302.

Useful data on New Castle, Pennsylvania, and unemployment in its mills appeared in the Ruttenbergs' article in *Harper's.* Statistics on the economic plight of the steel industry during the Depression are in H. Davis, p. 93; and the effects of war-related orders on the mills' activity is fully documented in *Impact of the War on the Pittsburgh, Pennsylvania, Area, passim.* Catton, pp. 34–35, cites the efforts of Beaver County citizens to communicate their strengths to Washington.

The September 2, 1940, issue of *Time* reports the visit of General Arnold and the admiral to the Capitol, seeking funds, as well as the discussion of excess profits.

Sherwood, pp. 157–60, tells of Roosevelt's determination to have no "production czar," and the president's perception of total war. More on this may be found in Catton, *passim.*

The president's Labor Day speech is quoted by Dallek, p. 287. Issues of *Time* for September and October describe conditions in America in the autumn of 1941.

Bruce Catton's first, and little-known, book, *The Warlords of Washington,* dealt with his observations of the Washington scene after he left a newspaper job to work as information officer and speech writer for Donald Nelson, and his is the shrewd, telling view of a skilled reporter. In that book I first read about Robert Wyman Horton. Then I had the remarkable good fortune to track him down in his Vermont home and obtain his recollections of prewar Washington through interview and correspondence. I am greatly indebted to him for his valuable information and the candor that characterized our discussions.

Donald Nelson's comment about almost losing the war before we entered it appears in Millis, p. 131, and it is a common theme, as noted by Robert Horton, and by Burns in *Roosevelt: The Soldier of Freedom,* pp. 193–94.

Knudsen's frustration and the resulting Wedemeyer report are discussed by Langer and Gleason, pp. 738–40; Catton, pp. 42–49; and Sherwood, pp. 410–18. Additional information is to be found in Larrabee, pp. 121–24.

CHAPTER 49

One of the best descriptions of the inaugural ceremonies is in Lilienthal, Vol. 1, 262–66.

Churchill, *The Grand Alliance,* pp. 48–55, has the prime minister's version of the Hess flight, and details appeared in the *New York Times* beginning on May 10, 1941, and in that paper's obituary of Hess on August 18, 1987. *Time,* July 28, 1941, reported the origin and manifestations of the "V for Victory" campaign.

The work of the Dies committee is related by McElvaine, pp. 272–74. Lilienthal, Vol. 1, pp. 171–72, assesses the growing climate of fear and distrust, and Perrett, pp. 87–103, adds more on the subject.

A running commentary on the Bertrand Russell affair appeared in the *New York Times* and *Time.*

The Rosenmans offer a memorable portrait of Harry Truman in *Presidential Style,* and Perrett, *passim,* discusses the committee's work.

As noted, Dubofsky and Van Tine's volume is an excellent guide to the life and career of John L. Lewis. His farewell remarks to the CIO are quoted, pp. 366 and 370, and the 1941 fight for the union shop is recounted, pp. 390–404. Additional information is in Alinsky, pp. 238–47.

Lash, *Roosevelt and Churchill,* p. 141, notes Roosevelt's condemnation of Lindbergh. As stated, the best account of Lindbergh's activities is in his *Wartime Journals,* which I have followed for the period that includes the Des Moines, Fort Wayne, and Madison Square Garden speeches. Cole's books on America First and Lindbergh are especially useful on this critical stage of the isolationist movement. In the Lindbergh volume, pp. 140–52, he discusses the charges of anti-Semitism. I am grateful to Anne Morrow Lindbergh for her comments on this subject. She has more to say in *War Within and War Without,* pp. 220–29. Cole's *Lindbergh,* pp. 197–201, records the waning enthusiasm within the ranks of America First, and Charles Lindbergh's intention to speak at no more rallies.

General Marshall's worries about extension of the draft are handled in Pogue, Vol. 2, pp. 146–54, and another valuable reference is Watson, pp. 218–31. Representative Wadsworth's memoir in the Columbia Oral History Collection affords additional insights, as do Walter Lippmann's notes in the same collection.

Much of my information on the draftees' physical condition comes from *Selective Service in Peacetime* (Hershey's report), pp. 213–14, supplemented by *Time*'s issue of October 23, 1941.

An interview with General Mark Clark was exceedingly helpful in connection with my account of peacetime maneuvers in this country. Clark was intimately involved, and offered information and opinions difficult to come by in any other way.

The comments of Generals Drum and Bullard appeared in *Newsweek,* August 21 and 28, 1939. *Time*'s issue of September 2, 1940, reported that year's war games.

Benjamin Franklin Cooling described the Tennessee and Arkansas maneuvers, and Eric Sevareid, pp. 203–4, offers a vivid picture of the men in the ranks. Watson, pp. 237–40, and Pogue, Vol. 2, pp. 162–65, deal with the Carolina maneuvers and evaluation of the war games.

Tuchman, pp. 261–96, discusses the changeover to the streamlined "triangular" division, and writes informatively of the maneuvers of 1939, 1940, and 1941, with emphasis on the impressive performance of General Joseph Stillwell.

Vannevar Bush is his own best witness to his determination to enroll the scientific community in the war effort. His observation on the reasons for Germany's failure are on p. 115.

Material on the Belgian Congo's supply of uranium ore is in Clark's *Birth of the Bomb,* p. 190. The same author has much on the work of Frisch and Peierls, pp. 50–51, and on Churchill's lukewarm endorsement of the Thomson report, p. 151.

The possibility of utilizing radioactive products of fission as weapons is asserted by Hewlett and Anderson, p. 37, and is the subject of an article in *Technology Review* for May/June 1985.

Baxter's history of the Office of Scientific Research and Development, pp. 423–28; and Hewlett and Anderson, pp. 40–44, describe U.S.-British exchanges of information on the nuclear project, and the findings of the Compton Commission.

The meeting at which Conant informed his fellow scientists of the president's decision is described by Nuel Pharr Davis, pp. 116–18; and by Kenneth Davis, pp. 78–87.

PART IX

CHAPTER 50

A number of excellent sources cover the background of the U.S.-Japanese conflict, that period of increasing tensions and diminishing options which ended on December 7, 1941. Among those emphasizing the diplomatic aspects of the situation are Robert A. Divine's brief and cogent volume; the book by Herbert Feis, whose long service in the State Department facilitated access to official documents and many participants; Langer and Gleason's classic study; Cordell Hull's memoirs; and Joseph Grew's account of his years in the Tokyo embassy at this critical period. Frank Gibney and Kurt Singer provide sensitive, penetrating glimpses of the Japanese people and their leaders, with special focus on the customs and historical background of the nation. Works by Walter Millis, Gordon W. Prange, Ronald W. Spector, and John Toland have much on political and military overtones, as well as diplomatic maneuvering.

I was aided immeasurably by conversations with the following individuals, to whom I am greatly indebted: Isao Ashiba, James B. Harris, Yoshihisa Kajitani, Doris Obata Kumpel, Tomio Muto, Agnes Niyekawa, Yuzuru Sanematsu, Ty Takichi Shigematsu, Tetsuo Shinjo, Fumio Tamamura, Tadao Tamaru, and Masayuki Tokioka.

Feis concludes, pp. 171–74, that the Hull-Nomura talks never really had a chance.

The curious story of the Maryknoll priests' efforts at mediating the crisis is told by Strauss, pp. 121–25; Langer and Gleason, pp. 314–15; and Feis, p. 174.

Time's story on Nomura appeared on September 22, 1941.

Thanks to Walter Lord and Isao Ashiba, I was privileged to meet Yuzuru Sanematsu, who, with his wife, welcomed my wife and me to their home on the outskirts of Tokyo. Since he was a naval attaché in Japan's Washington embassy, and a friend of numerous high-ranking navy officers, his testimony on certain aspects of this period was invaluable.

Numerous histories tell of Magic and its employment in decrypting the Japanese diplomatic code. Feis, Brown, Wohlstetter, Prange, Lewin—all are helpful. Brown relates the story of the Friedmans; Wohlstetter and Prange evaluate the role of key army and navy personnel. Wohlstetter, pp. 181–86, and Lewin, pp. 67–68, discuss the problem of distribution—that is, who had access to the information derived from Magic, and the dangers inherent in letting too many in on the secret.

I had the happy opportunity to talk with Dr. Agnes Niyekawa of the University of Hawaii about her experiences before the war, and how the war in China affected life in Japan.

Gibney's excellent study, p. 141, is the source of the Japan *Times* quotation concerning the war dead.

Toland, p. xiv, remarks on the ideological and racist aspects of the war in Asia.

To John F. Loughran, whose many years in Japan have given him a rare perspective on the people of that nation, I am indebted for acquainting me with Kurt Singer's remarkable volume. Its special value lies in the insights into Japanese traditions and their influence on the attitudes of the country in the prewar years.

In my interview with Dr. Niyekawa, she recalled the royal family's visit and the children's obligatory attendance.

Gibney, p. 139, quotes the doggerel recited by schoolchildren and tells, p. 121, the origins of the feud that separated army and navy officers. The discussion of the Japanese navy owes much to my conversation with Yuzuru Sanematsu, whose career was spent in that service.

Toland, p. 67, mentions the huge casualties suffered by the Japanese at Russia's hands in the late thirties.

Spector, pp. 42–43, spells out the levels of expansion achieved by both army and navy. The beginnings of Japan's undeclared war with China are depicted by Toland and Divine; Langer and Gleason, and Divine, discuss U.S. loans to China and trade policy—especially the sale of scrap iron and oil—with Japan.

Figures on American tourism in Japan during the thirties were provided by Mary Testa of the Japan Tourist Association in New York City. The number of visitors ranged from a low of 4,310 in 1932 (the effect of the Depression, presumably) to a high of 10,077 in 1937. After 1937 the numbers declined sharply, reflecting uneasiness over world conditions.

Langer and Gleason, pp. 321–22, cite Stanley Hornbeck's certainty that the Japanese were incapable of fighting the United States. Grew is quoted in Millis, p. 25; and Tuchman, p. 261, depicts Stillwell's attitude.

Time, November 24, 1941, lists the strength of the U.S. Asiatic Fleet and describes the mood in the Navy Department in Washington. A summary of Japanese armed strength appears in Spector, pp. 45 *et seq.*

CHAPTER 51

The twists and turns of American and Japanese policy are traced by Langer and Gleason's *The Undeclared War,* the indispensable guide to the period before U.S. entry into the war. Also valuable, even though it covers a much broader canvas, is

Robert Dallek's splendid account of Roosevelt's foreign policy. As in the previous section, Toland and Prange are important adjuncts.

Information about the controversial Matsuoka is available in Collier, Feis, Spector, and Toland.

The announcement of Japan's new policy is from Langer and Gleason, p. 5. The same source, pp. 18–49, has much to say concerning Japanese ambitions and U.S. and British fears. Willkie's comment is in Barnard, p. 319, and Roosevelt's remark to Ickes is in the latter's diaries, Vol. 3, p. 567.

Eden's warning to the Japanese ambassador is noted in Langer and Gleason, pp. 322–23; Dooman's tough talk to Ohashi is in the same source, pp. 325–26.

Prange deals with Matsuoka's mission to Berlin and Moscow. Langer and Gleason note the complex negotiations involving Japan, Germany, and the USSR, and Matsuoka's ouster. In the same volume, p. 656, is Nomura's appeal for assistance, and Toyoda's note to Grew, p. 654. Grew's diary notation is quoted by Feis, p. 248.

The hardening of Hull's attitude toward Japan is noted by Toland, p. 103, and by Langer and Gleason, pp. 659–62. Stimson, pp. 388–89, describes his own views. Roosevelt's warning to Nomura and the latter's report to Tokyo are covered by Prange, p. 191, and Langer and Gleason, p. 698.

Dallek, p. 274, records FDR's comments to defense workers.

The deliberations on an oil embargo and the negative effect of U.S. diplomacy on Japan are discussed by Dallek, pp. 274–75.

Langer and Gleason, Prange, and Toland are informative on meetings of the liaison conference; conversations between Konoye, the service chiefs, and the emperor; and the subsequent imperial conference.

The difficulty of translating Japanese poetry into English is suggested by the differing versions of Emperor Meiji's lines as they appear in Toland, p. 113; Gibney, p. 144; and Prange, p. 211. Through the good offices of Isao Ashiba, two authorities on Japanese poetry provided me with the translation used here.

The remarks of Hull and Nomura, expressing their discouragement, are quoted in Langer and Gleason, pp. 836 and 848; the same source, pp. 727–29, records Togo's cable to Nomura.

For communications between Roosevelt and Churchill during November and the Japanese decision to begin hostilities on December 8, 1941 (Tokyo time), I have relied on Langer and Gleason, pp. 837–54.

Kurusu's travels to the United States were chronicled in *Time,* November 24, 1941. Sumner Welles's tart commentary on the Japanese diplomat is on p. 295 of his book.

The rapidly deteriorating situation and the messages emanating from both capitals are well documented in Langer and Gleason and in Prange. The latter, p. 396, reports Stimson's conversation with FDR on Japanese troop transports.

Toland, p. 166, stresses that officials in Tokyo were sure that Hull's demands were for Japan to quit all of China, including Manchuria.

Kurusu's failed efforts to communicate directly with Roosevelt are reported by Baruch, pp. 288–91, and Prange, pp. 451–52.

Toland, p. 207, is the authority for saying Tojo's speech was made to seem even worse by a poor translation, and he discusses in detail, pp. 205–9, the crucial last-minute meetings in Tokyo that ended with Hirohito affixing his seal to documents approving war with the United States. Also see Prange and Langer and Gleason.

Pogue, Vol. 2, pp. 160–61, quotes Stimson's outrage at the stories in the *Chicago Tribune* and *Washington Times-Herald*.

Roosevelt's candid talk to Hopkins about the weakness of the Far Eastern policy under Hull is reported by Sherwood, pp. 428–29.

Grew, p. 489, has excerpts of Roosevelt's letter to Hirohito.

Berle, p. 382, records his own activities on December 6.

Much of the data in this and subsequent sections concerning the work of navy and army cryptographers come from the *Report of the Joint Committee on the Investigation of the Pearl Harbor Attack*. The material here is from Part 8, pp. 3900–3901. Toland, p. 223, describes Commander Kramer making his rounds.

Grew records his receipt of the telegram for Hirohito and his efforts to deliver it on pp. 486–87.

CHAPTER 52

Although I have already mentioned the importance of Prange as a source for this part, this chapter relies especially heavily for background upon that work. During the course of thirty-seven years of research on the story of Pearl Harbor, Gordon W. Prange interviewed hundreds of Japanese intimately involved in the planning and execution of the attack, and through interviews with Americans involved in one way or another, plus exhaustive research into archives, personal papers, and official reports, produced a work that is unlikely to be supplanted. Regrettably, he did not live to see his book in print. Although no more than one fourth of John Toland's *The Rising Sun: The Decline and Fall of the Japanese Empire* deals with the prelude to the attack and the operation itself, it is an invaluable companion, well documented and extremely readable.

Quentin Reynolds recalled his conversation with President Roosevelt in *Only the Stars Are Neutral*, p. 170.

Agawa's biography of Yamamoto, available in an English translation, provides an interesting portrait of the admiral, which was supplemented by Yuzuru Sanematsu's recollections of his friend and superior officer. Agawa quotes Yamamoto's promise to give the Americans hell for a year and half—but no longer—on p. 232, and his "Views on Preparations for War" on pp. 219–20.

The rumor of a surprise attack, cabled to the State Department by Ambassador Grew, is noted by Agawa, Toland, and Prange.

Prange offers an excellent description of the initial planning and the painstaking preparations that went into Operation Z; both he and Agawa discuss the reluctance at headquarters to go along with Yamamoto's daring plan.

Figures on the quantity of oil at Pearl Harbor are from Ewing, p. 11.

Agawa, Prange, and Toland provide valuable information on the training of pilots—in particular, the work of Fuchida and the techniques he stressed—which was such an essential part of the operation. The simulated attack and talks at the Imperial Navy Staff College are described by Prange, pp. 215–33. All three sources recount the last-minute preparations for departure.

The story of Yoshikawa's undercover assignment in Hawaii is related by Toland and Prange.

Collier, p. 210, mentions the U.S. Navy's assumption in the mid-thirties of a possible surprise attack on Hawaii, and Lewin, p. 68, describes the 1937 exercises. Wohlstetter, p. 68, notes that such a contingency was part of Plan Orange.

The Martin-Bellinger report is quoted in Prange, pp. 91–96; details of Farthing's study appear in the same volume, pp. 185–88.

Catton, pp. 3–12, relates the story of Nelson's dinner at the Carlton Hotel; I obtained further details from Catton himself and from Robert Wyman Horton, who proved to have the unscheduled star turn of the evening.

CHAPTER 53

Many of Franklin Roosevelt's critics were led to believe that the Japanese assault on Pearl Harbor had been provoked by the president—if, indeed, he had not conspired to bring it about—because the United States had ample evidence that such an operation was in the making. The best and most convincing study of the U.S. intelligence failure is Roberta Wohlstetter's book, based on thirty-nine volumes of congressional hearings, plus memoirs and diaries of American and Japanese involved. Her objective view of the surprise attack—which has profound implications for the nuclear age—indicates clearly that while U.S. officialdom awaited the blow that was certain to fall in Southeast Asia, it occurred to no one at the top command level that the Japanese might *also* strike at Pearl Harbor. The failure was the failure to ask the right questions, plus a refusal to believe the Japanese capable of such an action. Other useful sources on this aspect are Farago, Lewin, and Prange.

Wohlstetter, pp. 28–46, discusses the intelligence organization at Pearl Harbor, the signals it received, and what it deduced—especially about the movements of Japanese carriers. The same author quotes, pp. 167–68, the army's warning message to Short; her discussion of army and navy alert conditions is on p. 47. Lewin, pp. 65–66, is another source.

Short's opinion of the "sound detectors" is in Prange, p. 626.

Marshall's aide-mémoire to Roosevelt on the subject of Oahu is quoted by Wohlstetter, p. 69.

As noted earlier, Prange and Agawa describe in detail the movements of the Japanese fleet toward Hawaii.

For Dorothy Edgers's suspicions and her efforts to warn higher authority, see *Report of the Joint Committee on the Investigation of the Pearl Harbor Attack,* Part 9, pp. 4167–74; Part 12, pp. 267–68; Part 35, p. 321; and Part 36, pp. 303–4. Commander Kramer's relevant testimony is in Part 8, pp. 3893–910. Farago, pp. 325–28, and Toland, pp. 220–21, have additional information on this topic.

Short's remark to Fielder is in Prange, p. 481; the same source, pp. 485–95, has part fourteen of Tokyo's reply to Hull, and the reaction to it in Washington. Commander Kramer's interpretation of the message is in *Report of the Joint Committee,* Part 8, pp. 3909–10.

The launching of planes from Nagumo's task force is described by Lord, Fuchida, Prange, and Agawa.

CHAPTER 54

The exhaustive investigations into the Pearl Harbor disaster may be said to have begun on the night of December 7, 1941, when Secretary of the Navy Frank Knox decided to ask Roosevelt for permission to visit Oahu and learn for himself how the Japanese had caught the U.S. armed forces so unprepared. Shortly after Knox reported back to the president (leaving the latter noticeably dispirited), Roosevelt appointed Supreme Court Associate Justice Owen J. Roberts to head a commission to investigate responsibility for what had happened. The Roberts Commission was followed by an inquiry conducted by Admiral Thomas Hart, inquiries by a naval court and an army board, three lesser probes, and a full-dress congressional investigation. Much of this material has been sifted by Prange, Wohlstetter, and others.

Walter Lord, John Toland, and Gordon Prange, in particular, conducted searching interviews with the leading and the lesser participants in an effort to document the course of events on the chaotic 7th of December, 1941.

For my own purposes, I have had the generous assistance of many people, beginning with Walter Lord, who put me in touch with Doris Obata Kumpel and Isao Ashiba, both of whom directed me in turn to others who helped. And so it went—one interested individual suggesting someone else willing to assist. John Toland recommended that I see James B. Harris; George Mott put me in touch with Fred Schweizer and others; Fred Schweizer urged me to talk to Bill Ingram. This section, then, is a blend of many elements, the stories of dozens of people whose lives were affected in one way or another.

R. H. Brady of CinCPac kindly gave my wife and me an instructive tour of the base at Pearl Harbor, pointing out the various landmarks important to an understanding of what happened there in 1941. Mrs. Thomas N. Fairbanks provided information on the 1941 radar network on Oahu.

The fate of the midget submarines is chronicled by Stone.

Walter Lord relates the story of Lieutenant Outerbridge and the *Ward*.

Many details concerning activities at the Japanese embassy in Washington were provided by Yuzuru Sanematsu. Toland has additional information.

Nomura's instructions are noted by Prange, p. 466; Okumura's difficulties are mentioned in the same volume, pp. 489–90.

Watson is the source for the number of planes in Brereton's Far East command. The flight of the B-17s from California to Hawaii is described by Millis, pp. 328–29; Lord, pp. 105–6; and Prange, pp. 476–81.

The quotation from Tyler is from Lord, p. 45.

Prange interviewed both Genda and Fuchida for their version of the attack, and Fuchida also told his story in *Midway*. Yamamoto's anxious hours are described by Agawa, pp. 258–59.

Lord has an account of the *Nevada*'s band and Ramsey's order to send the message about the attack. He and Prange describe the scene at Hickam Field, Kimmel's view of the attack, and Short's reaction. Warren Johnson gave me his recollection in an interview.

The congressman was Hamilton Fish of New York, quoted by Prange, p. 729.

One of the most valuable accounts of the early stages of the attack was by Rear Admiral William F. Furlong, commander of the Pacific Fleet's minesweepers, who had the wit to dictate what he saw from his flagship, *Oglala,* just three hours after the first bomb exploded. His report is reprinted in Angle, pp. 67 *et seq.*

Prange, p. 514, quotes Commander Young, and the plight of the *Phoenix* crew is mentioned by Lewin, p. 79.

Through correspondence and conversations with Fred Schweizer and William Ingram I obtained their stories, and to both men I am deeply indebted.

The escape of the private planes is related by Lord, pp. 82–83.

Masayuki Tokioka told me about the experience he and his children had near Diamond Head. From Doris Obata Kumpel I learned the trials of her own family.

Barry Fox's recollections of the attack were published in the January 1943 issue of *Harper's*.

Agawa, p. 265, quotes Yamamoto on Nagumo's failure to follow up on the attack. Knox's reaction to the message from Pearl Harbor is in Prange, p. 527.

CHAPTER 55

How they got the news in Washington and elsewhere is recorded in diaries and memoirs, and by reporters on the scene at the time. Sherwood, as usual, is an important source of information about goings-on in the White House; Eleanor Roosevelt describes the scene in *This I Remember;* Lash's *Eleanor and Franklin* is helpful; the Franklin D. Roosevelt Library at Hyde Park has Mrs. Roosevelt's daily schedule of activities; and Brinkley offers interesting sidelights. Interviews with Mrs. Edward R. Murrow and Robert Trout were extremely valuable in this connection. Among the many reporters who recorded their observations were Jonathan Daniels in "Pearl Harbor Sunday: The End of an Era" (in Leighton) and Forrest Davis and Ernest K. Lindley.

Adolf Berle, Sherwood, Phillips, and Prange tell of Hull's activities and his instructions from Roosevelt on how to deal with the Japanese diplomats. Dean Acheson, p. 63, describes the scene in the corridors of the State Department. Pogue and Stimson record the reactions of General Marshall and the secretary of war. Nomura's recollections appeared in the *New York Times* of February 22, 1948.

Robert Trout told me how he happened to be the first person in the U.K. to learn the news of Pearl Harbor.

Churchill's *Their Finest Hour,* pp. 604–5, and Winant have slightly different versions of their evening together, and I have relied mainly on the former, thinking it more likely that he, not Winant, put through the call to the White House from Chequers.

Sperber, p. 204, describes the dinner for Edward R. Murrow at the Waldorf-Astoria; the remarks of the guest of honor were reprinted in MacLeish, Paley, and Murrow's "In honor of a man . . .". The Murrows' experiences in Washington on December 7 were reported to me by Mrs. Edward R. Murrow, and Sperber, pp. 205–6, has additional details.

Hopkins's notion that Japan had given the United States an opportunity is cited by Sherwood, p. 431. The same author describes the White House conference on the night of December 7. Breckinridge Long, (in Israel, pp. 227–28), records his own reactions.

A valuable insider's view of events at the White House that afternoon and evening is from Grace Tully, whose story is reprinted in Angle, pp. 72–74. Eleanor Roosevelt, in *This I Remember,* and Welles have more to add.

The scene at Griffith Stadium was described in *Newsweek,* December 15, 1941. The American Heritage record "Historic Voices and Music from World War II" has the broadcast from the Polo Grounds, and Manchester, pp. 256–57, reports the reaction of Mutual listeners and Dwight Eisenhower's response to the news. Ferrell, p. 39, offers further details about Eisenhower. *The New Republic,* December 15, 1941, contains interesting anecdotes about the way prominent Americans received the news.

How Paul Tibbetts learned of the attack is in Brinkley, p. 87, and Wyden, p. 47. Marcia Davenport, pp. 285–87, recalls how she and her husband heard about it.

Mitsuo Fuchida's flight over Hiroshima shortly after it was bombed is noted by Davis, p. 87, and was confirmed by Isao Ashiba.

Drummond, pp. 469–70, quotes Willkie's letter to FDR. Steve Early's bulletin is reported in *Newsweek,* December 15, 1941.

Ickes, Vol. 3, p. 661, mentions Donald Nelson's presence at lunch, and Brinkley, p. 87, states that Nelson heard the news on his car radio.

Tully, in Angle, p. 75, and Burns, *Roosevelt: The Soldier of Freedom,* pp. 165–67, tell how Roosevelt dictated his message to Congress and rejected a State Department draft.

Mrs. Edward R. Murrow informed me of what her husband gleaned while waiting to see the president.

CHAPTER 56

Here again, a multitude of sources chronicle the reactions of Americans to the news from Pearl Harbor. The *Pittsburgh Press* and the *Sun-Telegraph* for December 8, 1941, describe the America First meeting at Soldiers' and Sailors' Memorial Hall, and *Time,* December 15, quotes Nye's remarks to reporters. The *Bulletin-Index* for December 18 recounts the security measures taken in and around Pittsburgh.

Cole's *America First,* pp. 193–94, notes the action taken at the organization's headquarters, and the *Pittsburgh Press* of December 12 quotes the decision to disband.

Freda Kirchwey's essay appeared in *The Nation,* December 22.

Senator Vandenberg's reaction is from his diaries; Lindbergh's response to the news and his later efforts to serve the country are in his *Wartime Journals,* pp. 560–66 and 579–84. Lardner, in Leighton, p. 212, has more.

The scene outside and inside the White House is well depicted in Burns, *Roosevelt: The Soldier of Freedom,* pp. 164–65; Ickes, Vol. 3, pp. 661–66; and Sherwood, p. 433. Morgenthau's departure from New York is noted in Blum, p. 393. Dallek, p. 311, quotes Frances Perkins.

Sperber, p. 207; Kendrick, p. 240; and the Burns book just cited, p. 165, have details on Murrow's conversation with the president, and Eric Sevareid's recollection of Murrow's visit to the CBS office, mentioned in his book, was supplemented in a letter to me. Mrs. Edward R. Murrow described to me her husband's state of mind, and Casey Murrow recalled his father's statement that the story would pay for his college education.

Katherine Marshall's story is in *Together,* p. 99.

Joseph Grew, pp. 493–97, related his own experience.

FDR's vital decision to see if Hitler made the next move is noted by Dallek, p. 312. Abbazia, p. 365, states that the Japanese attack was a surprise to the Führer, and Irving, pp. 352–54, quotes Hitler's reaction and discusses his speech to the Reichstag.

Woody Guthrie, pp. 340 *et seq.,* recounts his experience in Los Angeles.

The Yale *Daily News* and the *New Haven Evening Register* of December 8, 1941, describe the activity on the Yale campus. Polly Buck, pp. 1–2, offers further details.

BIBLIOGRAPHY

ABBAZIA, PATRICK. *Mr. Roosevelt's Navy: The Private War of the U.S. Atlantic Fleet, 1939–1942.* Annapolis, Md.: Naval Institute Press, 1975.

ACHESON, DEAN. *Present at the Creation.* New York: Signet, 1970.

ADLER, SELIG. *The Isolationist Impulse: Its Twentieth-Century Reaction.* New York: Abelard-Schuman, 1957.

AGAWA, HIROYUKI. *The Reluctant Admiral: Yamamoto and the Imperial Navy.* Translated by John Bester. New York: Kodansha International, 1979.

ALINSKY, SAUL. *John L. Lewis: An Unauthorized Biography.* New York: Vintage, 1970.

ALLEN, FREDERICK LEWIS. *The Lords of Creation.* New York: Harper, 1935.

———. *The Big Change: America Transforms Itself: 1900–1950.* New York: Harper, 1952.

———. *Since Yesterday.* New York: Bantam, 1961.

ALSOP, JOSEPH. *FDR, 1882–1945: A Centenary Remembrance.* New York: Viking, 1982.

———, and ROBERT KINTNER. *American White Paper: The Story of American Diplomacy and the Second World War.* New York: Simon & Schuster, 1940.

AMBROSE, STEPHEN E. *The Supreme Commander: The War Years of General Dwight D. Eisenhower.* Garden City, N.Y.: Doubleday, 1970.

ANGLE, PAUL M., ed. *The Uneasy World: Selections from "The American Reader."* New York: Fawcett, 1968.

AVON, EARL OF [ANTHONY EDEN]. *The Reckoning.* Boston: Houghton Mifflin, 1965.

BAILEY, ANTHONY. *America, Lost and Found.* New York: Random House, 1980.

BAINBRIDGE, JOHN, and ST. CLAIR MCKELWAY. "That Was the New York World's Fair: Mr. McAneny and the Little Girl from Jackson Heights." *New Yorker,* April 19, 1941.

BALDWIN, HANSON W. *The Crucial Years: 1939–1941.* New York: Harper, 1976.

BANKS, ANN, ed. *First-Person America.* New York: Knopf, 1980.

BARBER, NOEL. *The Week France Fell.* New York: Stein & Day, 1976.

BARNARD, ELLSWORTH. *Wendell Willkie: Fighter for Freedom.* Marquette: Northern Michigan University Press, 1966.

BARNOUW, ERIK. *A History of Broadcasting in the United States.* Vol. 2, *The Golden Web, 1933 to 1953.* New York: Oxford University Press, 1968.

BARUCH, BERNARD M. *Baruch: The Public Years.* New York: Holt, Rinehart & Winston, 1960.

BAXTER, JAMES PHINNEY, 3RD. *Scientists Against Time.* Boston: Little, Brown/ Atlantic Monthly Press, 1946.

BEEBE, LUCIUS. *The Big Spenders.* Garden City, N.Y.: Doubleday, 1966.

BELL, THOMAS. *Out of This Furnace.* Pittsburgh, Pa.: University of Pittsburgh Press, 1976.

BENDINER, ROBERT. *Just Around the Corner.* New York: Dutton, 1968.

BENOIST-MÉCHIN, JACQUES. *Sixty Days That Shook the West: The Fall of France: 1940.* Edited with a Preface by Cyril Falls. New York: Putnam's, 1963.

BERLE, BEATRICE BISHOP, and TRAVIS BEAL JACOBS, eds. *Navigating the Rapids, 1918–1971: From the Papers of Adolf A. Berle.* New York: Harcourt Brace Jovanovich, 1973.

BERNSTEIN, BARTON J. "Oppenheimer and the Radioactive-Poison Plan." *Technology Review,* May/June 1985.

BERNSTEIN, JEREMY. "Physicist" [Isidor Isaac Rabi]. *New Yorker,* October 13, 20, 1975.

BESCHLOSS, MICHAEL R. *Kennedy and Roosevelt: The Uneasy Alliance.* New York: Norton, 1980.

BLISS, EDWARD JR., ed. *In Search of Light: The Broadcasts of Edward R. Murrow 1938–1961.* New York: Knopf, 1967.

BLUM, JOHN MORTON. *From the Morgenthau Diaries.* Vol. 2, *Years of Urgency: 1938–1941.* Boston: Houghton Mifflin, 1965.

BOHLEN, CHARLES E. *Witness to History, 1929–1969.* New York: Norton, 1973.

BOND, BRIAN. *France and Belgium, 1939–1940.* Cranbury, N.J.: Associated University Presses, 1979.

BOOTHE, CLARE. *Europe in the Spring.* New York: Knopf, 1940.

BRADLEY, DAVID. *Lion Among Roses: A Memoir of Finland.* New York: Holt, Rinehart & Winston, 1965.

BREWSTER, KINGMAN, JR. "Pre-War Uncertainty." In *Seventy-Five: A Study of a Generation in Transition.* New Haven, Conn.: Yale Daily News, 1953.

BRIDGMAN, P.W. " 'Manifesto' by a Physicist." *Science,* February 24, 1939.

BRINKLEY, DAVID. *Washington Goes to War.* New York: Knopf, 1988.

BRITTAIN, VERA. *England's Hour.* New York: Macmillan, 1941.

BROWN, ANTHONY CAVE, and CHARLES B. MACDONALD, eds. *The Secret History of the Atomic Bomb.* New York: Delta, 1977.

BUCK, POLLY STONE. *We Minded the Store: Yale Life and Letters During World War II.* New Haven, Conn.: privately printed, 1975.

BULLITT, ORVILLE H., ed. *For the President: Personal and Secret Correspondence Between Franklin D. Roosevelt and William C. Bullitt.* Boston: Houghton Mifflin, 1972.

BULLOCK, ALAN. *Hitler: A Study in Tyranny.* New York: Harper, 1952.

BURANELLI, VINCENT, and NAN BURANELLI. *Spy/Counterspy: An Encyclopedia of Espionage.* New York: McGraw-Hill, 1982.

BURNS, JAMES MACGREGOR. *Roosevelt: The Lion and the Fox.* New York: Harcourt, Brace & World, 1956.

———. *Roosevelt: The Soldier of Freedom.* New York: Harcourt Brace Jovanovich, 1970.

BURTNESS, PAUL S., and WARREN U. OBER, eds. *The Puzzle of Pearl Harbor.* Evanston, Ill.: Row, Peterson, 1962.

BUSH, VANNEVAR. *Pieces of the Action.* New York: Morrow, 1970.

CADOGAN, ALEXANDER. *The Diaries of Sir Alexander Cadogan, 1938–1945.* Ed. David Dilkes. New York: Putnam's, 1972.

CANTELON, PHILIP L. "Greetin's, Cousin George." *American Heritage,* December 1967.

CANTRIL, HADLEY, ed. director. *Public Opinion: 1935–1946.* Prepared by Mildred Strunk. Princeton, N.J.: Princeton University Press, 1951.

CARROLL, RICHARD C., ed. *Buildings and Grounds of Yale University.* 3rd ed. New Haven, Conn.: Yale University, 1979.

CATTON, BRUCE. *The War Lords of Washington.* New York: Greenwood Press, 1969.

CHADWIN, MARK LINCOLN. *The Warhawks: American Interventionists Before Pearl Harbor.* New York: Norton, 1970.

CHAMBERS, CLARKE A., ed. *The New Deal at Home and Abroad, 1929–1945.* New York: Free Press, 1965.

CHILDS, MARQUIS. "They Hate Roosevelt." *Harper's Monthly Magazine,* Vol. 172 (May 1936).

––––––. "They Still Hate Roosevelt." *New Republic,* September 14, 1938.

––––––. *I Write from Washington.* New York: Harper, 1942.

CHURCHILL, WINSTON S. *Step by Step: 1936–1939.* New York: Putnam's, 1939.

––––––. *Blood, Sweat, and Tears.* New York: Putnam's, 1941.

––––––. *The Unrelenting Struggle.* Boston: Little, Brown, 1942.

––––––. *The Second World War.* Vol. 1, *The Gathering Storm.* Vol. 2, *Their Finest Hour.* Vol. 3, *The Grand Alliance.* Boston: Houghton Mifflin, 1948, 1949, 1950.

CIANO, GALEAZZO. *The Ciano Diaries, 1938–1943.* Ed. Hugh Gibson. Garden City, N.Y.: Doubleday, 1946.

CLARK, RONALD W. *The Birth of the Bomb.* New York: Horizon, 1961.

––––––. *Einstein: The Life and Times.* New York: Avon, 1972.

CLEETON, GLEN U. *The Story of Carnegie Tech,* Vol. 2. Pittsburgh: Carnegie Press, 1965

CLEEVE, BRIAN. *1938: A World Vanishing.* London: Buchan & Enright, 1982.

COLE, WAYNE S. *America First: The Battle Against Intervention, 1940–1941.* Madison: University of Wisconsin Press, 1953.

––––––. *Charles A. Lindbergh and the Battle Against American Intervention in World War II.* New York: Harcourt Brace Jovanovich, 1974.

COLLIER, RICHARD. *The Sands of Dunkirk.* New York: Dell, 1961.

––––––. *Eagle Day: The Battle of Britain, August 6–September 15, 1940.* New York: Dutton, 1966.

––––––. *1941: Armageddon.* New York: Penguin, 1982.

––––––. *The Road to Pearl Harbor: 1941.* New York: Bonanza, 1984.

COLLINS, COLONEL JOHN M. "Depression Army." *Army,* January 1972.

COLVILLE, JOHN. *The Fringes of Power: Downing Street Diaries 1939–1955.* Vol. 1, *September 1939–September 1941.* London: Sceptre, 1986.

COOLING, B. FRANKLIN, III. "The Tennessee Maneuvers, June 1941." *Tennessee Historical Quarterly,* June 1965.

––––––. "The Arkansas Maneuvers, 1941." *Arkansas Historical Quarterly,* Vol. 26, No. 2 (Summer 1967).

COOPER, ALFRED DUFF. *Old Men Forget.* New York: Dutton, 1954.

COOPER, MATTHEW. *The German Army, 1933–1945: Its Political and Military Failure.* New York: Stein & Day, 1978.

COURARES, FRANCIS G. *The Remaking of Pittsburgh: Class and Culture in an*

Industrializing City, 1877–1919. Albany: State University of New York Press, 1984.

COWLEY, MALCOLM. "A Time of Resignations." *Yale Review,* Vol. 74, No. 1 (Autumn 1984).

CURIE, EVE, PHILIPPE BARRES, and RAOUL DE ROUSSY DE SALES, eds. *They Speak for a Nation.* Garden City, N.Y.: Doubleday, Doran, 1941.

DALLEK, ROBERT. *Franklin D. Roosevelt and American Foreign Policy, 1932–1945.* New York: Oxford University Press, 1981.

DANIELS, JONATHAN. *The Time Between the Wars: Armistice to Pearl Harbor.* Garden City, N.Y.: Doubleday, 1966.

DAVENPORT, JOHN, and CHARLES J. V. MURPHY. *The Lives of Winston Churchill: A Close Up.* New York: Scribner's, 1945.

DAVENPORT, MARCIA. *Too Strong for Fantasy.* New York: Scribner's, 1967.

DAVIS, ELMER. "Letter." *The Saturday Review of Literature,* June 14, 1941.

———. "Journey to England, 1941." *Harper's,* August 1941.

DAVIS, FORREST, and ERNEST K. LINDLEY. *How War Came.* New York: Simon & Schuster, 1942.

DAVIS, HORACE B. *The Condition of Labor in the Iron and Steel Industry.* New York: International Publishers, 1933.

DAVIS, KENNETH S. *Experience of War: The United States in World War II.* Garden City, N.Y.: Doubleday, 1965.

DAVIS, NUEL PHARR. *Lawrence and Oppenheimer.* New York: Simon & Schuster, 1968.

DEAKIN, F.W. *The Brutal Friendship.* New York: Harper & Row, 1962.

DEIGHTON, LEN. *Blitzkrieg: From the Rise of Hitler to the Fall of Dunkirk.* New York: Knopf, 1980.

DEWITT, HOWARD A. "Miracle in Philadelphia." *The Western Pennsylvania Historical Magazine,* Vol. 55, No. 4 (October 1972)

DIVINE, ROBERT A. *The Reluctant Belligerent: American Entry into World War II.* New York: Knopf, 1987.

Documents on German Foreign Policy, 1918–1945. Series D (1937–1945). Vol. 1, *From Neurath to Ribbentrop (September 1937–September 1938).* Vol. 2, *Germany and Czechoslovakia (1937–1938).* Washington, D.C.: U.S. Government Printing Office, 1949.

DUBOFSKY, MELVYN, and WARREN VAN TINE. *John L. Lewis: A Biography.* New York: Quadrangle/New York Times, 1977.

DYSON, FREEMAN. "Reflections: Disturbing the Universe." *New Yorker,* August 6, 13, 20, 1979.

EDEN, ANTHONY. See Avon, Earl of.

EDWARDS, ANNE. *Matriarch: Queen Mary and the House of Windsor.* New York: Morrow, 1984.

EISENHOWER, DWIGHT D. *Crusade in Europe.* Garden City, N.Y.: Doubleday, 1948.

EVINS, JOE L. "The Cordell Hull Birthplace and Memorial." *Tennessee Historical Society Quarterly,* Vol. 31, No. 2 (Summer 1972).

EWING, WILLIAM H. *Reflections on Pearl Harbor.* Fredericksburg, Texas: Admiral Nimitz Foundation, 1985.

FARAGO, LADISLAS. *The Broken Seal: "Operation Magic" and the Secret Road to Pearl Harbor.* New York: Bantam, 1968.

FEIS, HERBERT. *The Road to Pearl Harbor: The Coming of the War Between the United States and Japan.* Princeton, N.J.: Princeton University Press, 1950.

FERMI, ENRICO. "Physics at Columbia University: The Genesis of the Nuclear Energy Project." *Physics Today,* November 1955.

FERMI, LAURA. *Atoms in the Family.* Chicago: University of Chicago Press, 1954.

————. *The Story of Atomic Energy.* New York: Random House, 1961.

————. *Illustrious Immigrants: The Intellectual Migration from Europe, 1930–1941.* Chicago: University of Chicago Press, 1968.

FERRELL, ROBERT H., ed. *The Eisenhower Diaries.* New York: Norton, 1981.

FILLER, LOUIS, ed. *The Anxious Years.* New York: Putnam's, 1963.

FISCHER, LOUIS. *Men and Politics: Europe Between the Two World Wars.* New York: Harper & Row, 1966.

FLEMING, DONALD, and BERNARD BAILYN. *The Intellectual Migration: Europe and America, 1930–1960.* Cambridge, Mass.: Belknap Press/Harvard University Press, 1969.

FLEMING, PETER. *Operation Sea Lion.* London: Pan Books, 1975.

FLEMING, THOMAS. "The Big Leak." *American Heritage,* Vol. 38, No. 8 (December 1987).

FOX, BARRY. "That Day of Pearl Harbor." *Harper's,* Vol. 186, No. 1112 (January 1943).

FRISCH, OTTO R. "How It All Began." *Physics Today,* November 1967.

FUCHIDA, MITSUO, and MASATAKE OKUMIYA. *Midway: The Battle That Doomed Japan.* Annapolis, Md.: U.S. Naval Institute, 1955.

FUCHSER, LARRY WILLIAM. *Neville Chamberlain and Appeasement: A Study in the Politics of History.* New York: Norton, 1982.

FULLER, MAJOR-GENERAL J.F.C. *The Second World War, 1939–45: A Strategical and Tactical History.* New York: Duell, Sloan & Pearce, 1949.

GALBRAITH, JOHN KENNETH. *A Life in Our Times.* Boston: Houghton Mifflin, 1981.

GIBNEY, FRANK. *Five Gentlemen of Japan: The Portrait of a Nation's Character.* New York: Farrar, Straus & Young, 1953.

GOUDSMIT, SAMUEL ABRAHAM. *Alsos.* New York: Henry Schuman, 1947.

GRAFF, ROBERT D., and ROBERT EMMETT GINNA, eds. *FDR.* New York: Harper & Row, 1962.

GREW, JOSEPH C. *Ten Years in Japan.* New York: Simon & Schuster, 1944.

GRIGG, JOHN. *1943: The Victory That Never Was.* New York: Hill & Wang, 1980.

GRUNFELD, FREDERIC V. *The Hitler File.* New York: Random House, 1974.

GUTHRIE, WOODY. *Bound for Glory.* New York: Dutton, 1943.

HARPER, FRANK C. *Pittsburgh of Today: Its Resources and People,* Vol. 4. New York: The American Historical Society, 1931.

HEINRICHS, WALDO. "President Franklin D. Roosevelt's Intervention in the Battle of the Atlantic, 1941." *Diplomatic History,* Vol. 10.

HELLMAN, GEOFFREY T. "The Contemporaneous Memoranda of Dr. Sachs." *New Yorker,* December 1, 1945.

HENDERSON, SIR NEVILE. *Failure of a Mission: Berlin 1937–1939.* New York: Putnam's, 1940.

HEWLETT, RICHARD G., and OSCAR E. ANDERSON, JR. *The New World, 1939–1946.* State College, Pa.: Pennsylvania State University Press, 1962.

HINSLEY, F.H. *Hitler's Strategy.* Cambridge: Cambridge University Press, 1951.

Historical Statistics of the United States, Colonial Times to 1957. U.S. Bureau of the Census. Washington, D.C.: U.S. Government Printing Office, 1960.

HITLER, ADOLF. *Mein Kampf.* New York: Stackpole, 1939.

HOLBROOK, STEWART H. *The Age of the Moguls.* Garden City, N.Y.: Doubleday, 1953.

HUGHES, H. STUART. *The Sea Change: The Migration of Social Thought, 1930–1965.* New York: McGraw-Hill, 1977.

HULL, CORDELL. *The Memoirs of Cordell Hull.* New York: Macmillan, 1948.

HYMAN, SIDNEY. *The Lives of William Benton.* Chicago: University of Chicago Press, 1969.

ICKES, HAROLD L. *The Secret Diary of Harold L. Ickes.* Vol. 1, *The First Thousand Days, 1933–1936.* Vol. 3, *The Lowering Clouds, 1939–1941.* New York: Simon & Schuster, 1953, 1954.

Impact of the War on the Pittsburgh, Pennsylvania, Area. U.S. Dept. of Labor, Bureau of Labor Statistics, Industrial Area Study No. 1. Washington, D.C.: January 1943.

IRVING, DAVID. *Hitler's War.* New York: Viking, 1977.

ISMAY, HASTINGS. *The Memoirs of General Lord Ismay.* New York: Viking, 1960.

ISRAEL, FRED L., ed. *The War Diary of Breckinridge Long: Selections from the Years 1939–1944.* Lincoln: University of Nebraska Press, 1966.

JELLISON, CHARLES A. *Tomatoes Were Cheaper: Tales from the Thirties.* Syracuse, N.Y.: Syracuse University Press, 1977.

JONES, ALFRED HAWORTH. "The Making of an Interventionist on the Air: Elmer Davis and CBS News, 1939–1941." *Pacific Historical Review,* Vol. 42, No. 1 (February 1973), pp. 74–93.

JUNGK, ROBERT. *Brighter Than a Thousand Suns.* Translated by James Cleugh. New York: Harcourt Brace Jovanovich, 1958.

KALTENBORN, H. V. *I Broadcast the Crisis.* New York: Random House, 1938.

KARIG, WALTER, with EARL BURTON and STEPHEN L. FREELAND. *Battle Report: The Atlantic War.* New York: Farrar & Rinehart, 1946.

KEE, ROBERT. *The World We Left Behind: A Chronicle of the Year 1939.* London: Sphere Books, 1985.

KEEGAN, JOHN, ed. *Who Was Who in World War II.* New York: T. Y. Crowell, 1978.

KENDRICK, ALEXANDER. *Prime Time: The Life of Edward R. Murrow.* Boston: Little, Brown, 1969.

KENNAN, GEORGE F. *Memoirs: 1925–1950.* Boston: Atlantic Monthly Press, 1967.

——. *From Prague After Munich: Diplomatic Papers, 1938–1940.* Princeton, N.J.: Princeton University Press, 1968.

KETCHUM, RICHARD M. *Will Rogers: His Life and Times.* New York: American Heritage, 1973.

——, ed., with IRWIN GLUSKER. *American Testament: Fifty Great Documents of American History.* With introductory notes by Robert A. Divine. New York: American Heritage, 1971.

KEVLES, DANIEL J. *The Physicists.* New York: Vintage, 1979.

KNICKERBOCKER, H.R. *Is Tomorrow Hitler's?* New York: Reynal & Hitchcock, 1941.

KOCH, HOWARD. *The Panic Broadcast.* New York: Avon, 1970.

KROCK, ARTHUR. *In the Nation: 1932–1966.* New York: Paperback Library, 1969.

LAMONT, LANSING. *Day of Trinity.* New York: Atheneum, 1965.

LANG, DANIEL. *Early Tales of the Atomic Age.* Garden City, N.Y.: Doubleday, 1948.

LANGER, WILLIAM L., and S. EVERETT GLEASON. *The Undeclared War, 1940–1941.* Published for the Council on Foreign Relations. New York: Harper, 1953.

LAPP, RALPH E. "The Einstein Letter That Started It All." *New York Times Magazine,* August 2, 1964.

LARRABEE, ERIC. *Commander in Chief: Franklin Delano Roosevelt, His Lieutenants, and Their War.* New York: Harper & Row, 1987.

LASH, JOSEPH P. *Eleanor and Franklin: The Story of Their Relationship, Based on Eleanor Roosevelt's Private Papers.* New York: Norton, 1971.

———. *Roosevelt and Churchill, 1939–1941: The Partnership That Saved the West.* New York: Norton, 1976.

LAURENCE, WILLIAM L. *Dawn over Zero: The Story of the Atomic Bomb.* New York: Knopf, 1946.

———. *Men and Atoms: The Discovery, the Uses, and the Future of Atomic Energy.* New York: Simon & Schuster, 1959.

LEIGHTON, ISABEL, ed. *The Aspirin Age, 1919–1941.* New York: Simon & Schuster, 1949.

LEUTZE, JAMES, ed. *The London Journal of General Raymond E. Lee, 1940–1941.* Boston: Little, Brown, 1971.

LEWIN, RONALD. *The American Magic: Codes, Ciphers, and the Defeat of Japan.* Harmondsworth, England: Penguin, 1983.

LIDDELL HART, B.H. *The Other Side of the Hill.* London: Pan Books, 1978.

LIEBLING, A.J. "Chief of Staff" [General George Marshall]. *New Yorker,* October 26, 1940.

———. *Liebling Abroad.* Introduction by Raymond Sokolov. Wideview Books, 1981.

LILIENTHAL, DAVID. *The Journals of David E. Lilienthal.* Vol. 1, *The TVA Years, 1939–1945.* New York: Harper & Row, 1964.

LINDBERGH, ANNE MORROW. *The Wave of the Future: A Confession of Faith.* New York: Harcourt Brace, 1940.

———. *Hour of Gold, Hour of Lead: Diaries and Letters, 1929–1932.* New York: Harcourt Brace Jovanovich, 1973.

———. *The Flower and the Nettle: Diaries and Letters 1936–1939.* New York: Harcourt Brace Jovanovich, 1976.

———. *War Within and Without: Diaries and Letters 1939–1944.* New York: Harcourt Brace Jovanovich, 1980.

LINDBERGH, CHARLES L. *The Wartime Journals of Charles A. Lindbergh.* New York: Harcourt Brace Jovanovich, 1970.

———. *Boyhood on the Upper Mississippi: A Reminiscent Letter.* St. Paul: Minnesota Historical Society, 1972.

———. *Autobiography of Values.* New York: Harcourt Brace Jovanovich, 1978.

LIPPMANN, WALTER. "A Day at the World's Fair." *Current History,* July 1939.

LIPSTADT, DEBORAH E. *Beyond Belief: The American Press and the Coming of the Holocaust, 1933–1945.* New York: Free Press, 1986.

LOOKSTEIN, HASKEL. *Were We Our Brothers' Keepers? The Public Response of American Jews to the Holocaust, 1938–1944.* New York: Vintage, 1988.

LORANT, STEFAN. *Pittsburgh: The Story of an American City.* Garden City, N.Y.: Doubleday, 1964.

LORD, WALTER. *Day of Infamy.* New York: Bantam, 1958.

———. *The Miracle of Dunkirk.* New York: Penguin, 1984.

LYND, ROBERT S., and HELEN MERRELL. *Middletown in Transition.* New York: Harcourt, Brace & World, 1937.

MACLEISH, ARCHIBALD, WILLIAM S. PALEY, and EDWARD R. MURROW. "In honor of a man and an ideal . . ." Three Talks on Freedom, December 2, 1941. New York: Columbia Broadcasting System, n.d.

MANCHESTER, WILLIAM. *The Glory and the Dream: A Narrative History of America, 1932–1972.* New York: Bantam, 1980.

———. *The Last Lion: Winston Spencer Churchill. Visions of Glory: 1874–1932.* New York: Dell, 1984.

MARSHALL, KATHERINE TUPPER. *Together: Annals of an Army Wife.* New York: Tupper & Love, 1946.

MARTIENSSEN, ANTHONY. *Hitler and His Admirals.* London: Secker & Warburg, 1948.

MARTIN, GEORGE. *Madam Secretary: Frances Perkins.* Boston: Houghton Mifflin, 1976.

MCCARTHY, JOE. *Hurricane!* New York: American Heritage, 1969.

MCELVAINE, ROBERT S. *The Great Depression: America, 1929–1941.* New York: Times Books, 1984.

MCPHEE, JOHN. *The Curve of Binding Energy.* New York: Farrar, Straus & Giroux, 1974.

METZ, ROBERT. *CBS: Reflections in a Bloodshot Eye.* New York: Signet, 1976.

MIDDLETON, DREW. *The Sky Suspended.* New York: Longmans, Green, 1960.

MILLIS, WALTER. *This Is Pearl! The United States and Japan—1941.* New York: Morrow, 1947.

MOOREHEAD, ALAN. *Montgomery.* London: New English Library, 1974.

MORAN, LORD. *Churchill: Taken from the Diaries of Lord Moran. The Struggle for Survival, 1940–1965.* Boston: Houghton Mifflin, 1966.

MORSE, ARTHUR D. *While Six Million Died: A Chronicle of American Apathy.* New York: Ace, 1968.

MOSLEY, LEONARD. *On Borrowed Time: How World War II Began.* New York: Random House, 1969.

———. *The Reich Marshal: A Biography of Hermann Goering.* Garden City, N.Y.: Doubleday, 1974.

———. *Lindbergh: A Biography.* Garden City, N.Y.: Doubleday, 1976.

———. *Marshall: Hero for Our Times.* New York: Hearst Books, 1982.

MURROW, EDWARD R. *This Is London.* New York: Simon & Schuster, 1941.

Nazi Conspiracy and Aggression, Vol. 3. Office of United States Chief Counsel for Prosecution of Axis Criminality. Washington, D.C.: U.S. Government Printing Office, 1946.

NICOLSON, HAROLD. "A Portrait of Winston Churchill." *Life,* March 15, 1948.

———. *Harold Nicolson: Diaries and Letters.* Vol. 1, *1930–1939.* Vol. 2, *The War Years, 1939–1945.* Ed. Nigel Nicolson. New York: Atheneum, 1966, 1967.

OPPENHEIMER, ROBERT. "Niels Bohr and Atomic Weapons." *New York Review,* December 17, 1964.

OULAHAN, RICHARD. "Capital's Doughty Dowager Becomes a New Cinderella." *Smithsonian,* March 1986.

PANTER-DOWNS, MOLLIE. "Letter from London." *New Yorker,* with appropriate date.

PARMET, HERBERT S., and MARIE B. HECHT. *Never Again: A President Runs for a Third Term.* New York: Macmillan, 1968.

PARTON, JAMES. *"Air Force Spoken Here": General Ira Eaker and the Command of the Air.* Bethesda, Md.: Adler & Adler, 1986.

PERRETT, GEOFFREY. *Days of Sadness, Years of Triumph: The American People 1939–1945.* New York: Coward, McCann & Geoghegan, 1973.

PHILLIPS, CABELL. *From the Crash to the Blitz, 1929–1939.* New York: Macmillan, 1975.

———. *The 1940s: Decade of Triumph and Trouble.* New York: Macmillan, 1975.

PIERSON, GEORGE WILSON. *A Yale Book of Numbers: Historical Statistics of the College and University, 1701–1976.* New Haven, Conn.: Yale University, 1973.

POGUE, FORREST C. *George C. Marshall.* Vol. 1, *Education of a General, 1880–1939.* Vol. 2, *Ordeal and Hope, 1939–1942.* New York: Viking, 1963, 1966.

PRANGE, GORDON W., in collaboration with DONALD M. GOLDSTEIN and KATHERINE V. DILLON. *At Dawn We Slept: The Untold Story of Pearl Harbor.* New York: McGraw-Hill, 1981.

PRIESTLEY, J.B.: *All England Listened.* New York: Chilmark Press, 1967.

RADIO & TV CULTURE RESEARCH INSTITUTE. *50 Years of Japanese Broadcasting.* Tokyo: Nippon Hoso Kyokai, 1977.

REDPATH, FREDERICK L., ed. *'39 in '64: Princeton University Class of 1939 25th Year Book.* Caldwell, N.J.: Progress Publishing, 1964.

Report of the Joint Committee on the Investigation of the Pearl Harbor Attack. 39 vols. U.S. Congress, Washington, D.C.: 1946.

REYNOLDS, QUENTIN. *Only the Stars Are Neutral.* New York: Random House, 1942.

RICHARDSON, HENRY SMITH, JR., ed. *A History of the Class of Nineteen Forty-three.* New Haven, Conn.: Yale University, 1943.

ROBERTSON, BEN. *I Saw England.* New York: Knopf, 1941.

ROOSEVELT, ELEANOR. *This I Remember.* New York: Harper, 1949.

———. *The Autobiography of Eleanor Roosevelt.* New York: Harper, 1961.

ROSENMAN, SAMUEL, and DOROTHY ROSENMAN. *Presidential Style: Some Giants and a Pygmy in the White House.* New York: Harper & Row, 1976.

RUSSELL, FRANCIS. *The President Makers: From Mark Hanna to Joseph P. Kennedy.* Boston: Little, Brown, 1976.

RUSSETT, BRUCE M. *No Clear and Present Danger.* New York: Harper Torchbooks, 1972.

RUTTENBERG, HAROLD J., and STANLEY RUTTENBERG. "War and the Steel Ghost Towns." *Harper's,* January 1940.

SACHS, ALEXANDER. Statement in Hearings before the Special Committee on Atomic Energy, United States Senate, 79th Congress, 1st session, November

27, 28, 29, 30, 1945, and December 3, 1945. Washington, D.C.: U.S. Government Printing Office, 1945.

SAINT-EXUPÉRY, ANTOINE DE. *Flight to Arras.* Translated by Lewis Galantière. New York: Reynal & Hitchcock, 1942.

SANDERS, MARION K. *Dorothy Thompson: A Legend in Her Time.* Boston: Houghton Mifflin, 1973.

SAYLE, MURRAY. "Showa: God into Man" [Emperor Hirohito]. *Far Eastern Economic Review,* Vol. 135, No. 1 (January 1, 1987), pp. 26–37.

SCHLESINGER, ARTHUR M., JR. *The Age of Roosevelt.* Vol. 1, *The Crisis of the Old Order, 1919–1933.* Vol. 2, *The Coming of the New Deal.* Vol. 3, *The Politics of Upheaval.* Boston: Houghton Mifflin, 1957, 1958, 1960.

————. *The Cycles of American History.* London: Andre Deutsch, 1987.

SCHROEDER, GERTRUDE A. "The Growth of Major Steel Companies, 1900–1950." *The Johns Hopkins University Studies in Historical and Political Science,* Vol. 70, No. 2. Baltimore, Md.: Johns Hopkins Press, 1952.

Selective Service in Peacetime. First Report of the Director of Selective Service, 1940–41. Washington, D.C.: U.S. Government Printing Office, 1942.

SEVAREID, ERIC. *Not So Wild a Dream.* New York: Atheneum, 1979.

SHAYON, ROBERT LEWIS. *Historic Voices and Music from World War II.* An American Heritage Record. New York: American Heritage, n.d.

SHEEAN, VINCENT. *Between the Thunder and the Sun.* New York: Random House, 1943.

————. *Dorothy and Red.* Boston: Houghton Mifflin, 1963.

SHERWOOD, ROBERT E. *Roosevelt and Hopkins: An Intimate History.* New York: Harper, 1948.

SHIRER, WILLIAM L. *Berlin Diary: 1934–1941.* New York: Knopf, 1941.

————. *The Rise and Fall of the Third Reich.* New York: Simon & Schuster, 1960.

————. *20th Century Journey.* Vol. 2, *The Nightmare Years, 1930–1940.* Boston: Little, Brown, 1984.

SHUR, IRENE G., FRANKLIN H. LITTELL, and MARVIN E. WOLFGANG, eds. "Reflections on the Holocaust." *Annals of the American Academy of Political and Social Science.* Philadelphia: 1980.

SINGER, KURT. *Mirror, Sword and Jewel: The Geometry of Japanese Life.* Edited with an Introduction by Richard Storry. Tokyo and New York: Kodansha, 1985.

SLACKMAN, MICHAEL, ed. *Pearl Harbor in Perspective.* Honolulu: Arizona Memorial Museum Association, 1986.

SMITH, HOWARD K. *Last Train from Berlin.* New York: Knopf, 1942.

SNOW, C.P. "How the Bomb Was Born." *Discover,* August 1981.

SPEARS, EDWARD. *Assignment to Catastrophe.* Vol. 1, *Prelude to Dunkirk, July 1939–May 1940.* Vol. 2, *The Fall of France, June 1940.* New York: A.A. Wyn, 1955.

SPECTOR, RONALD H. *Eagle Against the Sun.* New York: Vintage, 1985.

SPEER, ALBERT. *Inside the Third Reich.* Translated by Richard and Clara Winston. New York: Macmillan, 1970.

SPERBER, A.M. *Murrow: His Life and Times.* New York: Freundlich, 1986.

STAVE, BRUCE M. *The New Deal and the Last Hurrah: Pittsburgh Machine Politics.* Pittsburgh: University of Pittsburgh Press, 1970.

STEEL, RONALD. *Walter Lippmann and the American Century.* New York: Vintage, 1981.

STEVENSON, WILLIAM. *A Man Called Intrepid: The Secret War.* New York: Harcourt Brace Jovanovich, 1976.

STIMSON, HENRY L., and MCGEORGE BUNDY. *On Active Service in Peace and War.* New York: Harper, 1947.

STONE, SCOTT C.S. "Pearl Harbor: The Way It Was—December 7, 1941." *Island Heritage,* Honolulu, Hawaii, 1986.

STRANG, LORD. *Home and Abroad.* London: Andre Deutsch, 1956.

STRAUSS, LEWIS. *Men and Decisions.* Garden City, N.Y.: Doubleday, 1962.

STRICKER, FRANK. "Affluence for Whom?—Another Look at Prosperity and the Working Classes in the 1920s." *Labor History,* Winter 1983.

SULZBERGER, C.L. *The American Heritage Picture History of World War II.* New York: American Heritage, 1966.

———. *A Long Row of Candles: Memoirs and Diaries, 1934–1954.* New York: Macmillan, 1969.

SZILARD, LEO. "Reminiscences." Edited by Gertrud Weiss Szilard and Kathleen R. Winsor. In Donald Fleming and Bernard Bailyn, *The Intellectual Migration: Europe and America, 1930–1960.* Cambridge, Mass.: Belknap Press/Harvard University Press, 1969.

TARBELL, ARTHUR WILSON. *The Story of Carnegie Tech.* Pittsburgh: Carnegie Institute of Technology, 1937.

TARR, JOEL A. *Transportation Innovation and Changing Spatial Patterns in Pittsburgh, 1850–1934.* Chicago: Public Works Historical Society, 1978.

TAYLOR, A.J.P. *The Origins of the Second World War.* New York: Fawcett, 1963.

TAYLOR, TELFORD. *The Breaking Wave: The Second World War in the Summer of 1940.* New York: Simon & Schuster, 1967.

TEAGUE, MICHAEL. *Mrs. L: Conversations with Alice Roosevelt Longworth.* Garden City, N.Y.: Doubleday, 1981.

TERKEL, STUDS. *Hard Times.* New York: Avon, 1971.

THOMAS, HUGH. *The Spanish Civil War.* New York: Harper, 1961.

TOLAND, JOHN. *But Not in Shame: The Six Months After Pearl Harbor.* New York: Signet, 1962.

———. *The Rising Sun: The Decline and Fall of the Japanese Empire, 1936–1945.* New York: Bantam, 1971.

———. *Adolf Hitler.* Garden City, N.Y.: Doubleday, 1976.

TREVOR-ROPER, H.R., ed. *Blitzkrieg to Defeat: Hitler's War Directives, 1939–1945.* New York: Holt, Rinehart & Winston, 1965.

TUCHMAN, BARBARA W. *Stilwell and the American Experience in China, 1911–45.* New York: Macmillan, 1970.

TUGWELL, REXFORD. *In Search of Roosevelt.* Cambridge, Mass.: Harvard University Press, 1972.

TUTTLE, WILLIAM M., JR. "Aid to the Allies Short-of-War versus American Intervention, 1940: A Reappraisal of William Allen White's Leadership." *Journal of American History,* 1970, pp. 840–58.

VANDENBERG, ARTHUR H. *The Private Papers of Senator Vandenberg.* Ed. Arthur H. Vandenberg, Jr. Boston: Houghton Mifflin, 1952.

VASSILTCHIKOV, MARIE. *The Berlin Diaries 1940–1945 of Marie "Missie" Vassiltchikov.* London: Methuen, 1987.

WARD, GEOFFREY C. *Before the Trumpet: Young Franklin Roosevelt, 1882–1905.* New York: Perennial Library, 1986.

WARLIMONT, WALTER. *Inside Hitler's Headquarters, 1939–45.* New York: Praeger, 1964.

WATSON, MARK SKINNER. *Chief of Staff: Prewar Plans and Preparations. United States Army in World War II.* Historical Division, Department of the Army. Washington, D.C.: 1950.

WEART, SPENCER. *Scientists in Power.* Cambridge, Mass.: Harvard University Press, 1979.

WEART, SPENCER, and GERTRUD WEISS SZILARD, eds. *Leo Szilard, His Version of Facts.* Cambridge, Mass.: MIT Press, 1978.

WELLES, SUMNER. *The Time for Decision.* New York: Harper, 1944.

WERNICK, ROBERT. *World War II: Blitzkrieg.* New York: Time, Inc., 1976.

WHALEN, R.J. "A Portrait of the Founder" [Joseph P. Kennedy], *Fortune,* January 1963.

WHEELER, JOHN. "Mechanism of Fission." *Physics Today,* November 1967.

WHEELER-BENNETT, JOHN W. *Munich: Prologue to Tragedy.* London: Macmillan, 1948.

WHITE, WILLIAM ALLEN. *The Autobiography of William Allen White.* New York: Macmillan, 1946.

WICKER, TOM. "Why, Miss Scarlett, How Well You've Aged." *New York Times Book Review,* May 25, 1986.

WILSON, MITCHELL. *Passion to Know: The World's Scientists.* Garden City, N.Y.: Doubleday, 1972.

WINANT, JOHN G. *A Letter from Grosvenor Square: An Account of a Stewardship.* London: Hodder & Stoughton, 1947.

WINKS, ROBIN W. *Cloak & Gown: Scholars in the Secret War, 1939–1961.* New York: Morrow, 1987.

WINTERBOTHAM, F.W. *The Ultra Secret.* New York: Harper & Row, 1974.

———. *The Nazi Connection.* New York: Harper & Row, 1978.

WOHLSTETTER, ROBERTA. *Pearl Harbor: Warning and Decision.* Stanford: Stanford University Press, 1967.

WYDEN, PETER. *Day One: Before Hiroshima and After.* New York: Warner, 1985.

WYMAN, DAVID S. *The Abandonment of the Jews: America and the Holocaust, 1941–1945.* New York: Pantheon, 1984.

———. *Paper Walls: America and the Refugee Crisis, 1938–1941.* New York: Pantheon, 1985.

INDEX

RICHARD M. KETCHUM is the author of a number of books of American history, including *The Winter Soldiers, Decisive Day, Faces from the Past,* and biographies of George Washington and Will Rogers.

As director of book publishing activities at American Heritage Publishing Company, he edited many of that firm's volumes, including *The American Heritage Picture History of the Civil War,* which received a special Pulitzer Prize citation.

He was the cofounder and editor of *Blair & Ketchum's Country Journal,* a monthly magazine about country living.

Born in Pittsburgh, Pennsylvania, he graduated from Yale University and commanded a subchaser in the South Atlantic during World War II.

He and his wife have a working sheep farm in Vermont and are active conservationists.